COMPLETE CompTIA® A+ Guide to PCs

SIXTH EDITION

CHERYL A. SCHMIDT
Florida State College at Jacksonville

Pearson
800 East 96th Street
Indianapolis, Indiana 46240 USA

Complete CompTIA® A+ Guide to PCs, Sixth Edition

ISBN-13: 978-0-7897-4976-5
ISBN-10: 0-7897-4976-9

Library of Congress Cataloging-in-Publication data is on file.

Printed in the United States of America

First Printing: February 2013

Trademarks

All terms mentioned in this book that are known to be trademarks or service marks have been appropriately capitalized. Pearson IT Certification cannot attest to the accuracy of this information. Use of a term in this book should not be regarded as affecting the validity of any trademark or service mark.

Warning and Disclaimer

Every effort has been made to make this book as complete and as accurate as possible, but no warranty or fitness is implied. The information provided is on an "as is" basis. The author and the publisher shall have neither liability nor responsibility to any person or entity with respect to any loss or damages arising from the information contained in this book.

Bulk Sales

Pearson IT Certification offers excellent discounts on this book when ordered in quantity for bulk purchases or special sales. For more information, please contact

U.S. Corporate and Government Sales

1-800-382-3419

corpsales@pearsontechgroup.com

For sales outside the United States, please contact

International Sales

international@pearsoned.com

Associate Publisher
Dave Dusthimer

Executive Editor
Mary Beth Ray

Development Editor
Andrew Cupp

Managing Editor
Sandra Schroeder

Senior Project Editor
Tonya Simpson

Copy Editor
Kitty Wilson

Indexer
Heather McNeill

Proofreader
Sheri Replin

Technical Editors
Chris Crayton
Jeff McDowell

Publishing Coordinator
Vanessa Evans

Interior Designer
Studio Galou

Cover Designer
Alan Clements

Compositor
Studio Galou

Art Production
Justin Ache
Katherine Martin
Marc Durrence
Amanda McIntosh
KC Frick

Photographers
Raina DeVoid
George Nichols

Contents at a Glance

Contents

About the Author

Cheryl Schmidt is a professor of Network Engineering Technology at Florida State College at Jacksonville. Prior to joining the faculty ranks, she oversaw the LAN and PC support for the college and other organizations. She started her career as an electronics technician in the U.S. Navy. She teaches computer repair and various networking topics, including CCNA, CCNP, VoIP, QoS, and wireless technologies. She has published other works with Pearson, including *IP Telephony Using CallManager Express* and *Routing and Switching in the Enterprise Lab Guide*.

Cheryl has won awards for teaching and technology, including Outstanding Faculty of the Year, Innovative Teacher of the Year, and Cisco Networking Academy Stand Out Instructor. She has presented at U.S. and international conferences. Cheryl keeps busy maintaining her technical certifications and teaching, but also loves to travel, hike, do all types of puzzles, and read.

Dedication

A Note to Instructors

I was a teacher long before I had the title professor. Sharing what I know has always been as natural as walking to me, but sitting still to write what I know is not as natural, so composing this text has always been one of my greatest challenges. Thank you so much for choosing this text. I thank you for sharing your knowledge and experience with your students. Your dedication to education is what makes the student experience so valuable.

A Note to Students

Writing a textbook is really different from teaching class. I have said for years that my students are like my children, except that I don't have to pay to send them through college. I am happy to claim any of you who have this text. I wish that I could be in each classroom with you as you start your IT career. How exciting!

Another thing that I tell my students is that I am not an expert. Computer repair is an ever-changing field and I have been in it since PCs started being used. You have to be excited about the never-ending changes to be good in this field. You can never stop learning or you will not be very good any more. I offer one important piece of advice:

> Consistent, high-quality service boils down to two equally important things: caring and competence.
>
> —Chip R. Bell and Ron Zemke

I dedicate this book to you. I can help you with the competence piece, but you are going to have to work on the caring part. Do not ever forget that there are people behind those machines that you love to repair. Taking care of people is as important as taking care of the computers.

Acknowledgments

I am so thankful for the support of my family during the production of this book. My husband Karl and daughters Raina and Karalina were such a source of inspiration and encouragement. Thanks to my colleagues, adjuncts, and students at my college who offered numerous valuable suggestions for improvement and testing the new material. I am especially grateful for the help and edits provided by Kathy A. Himle from Salt Lake Community College.

Many thanks are also due the folks at Pearson. The professionalism and support given during this edition was stellar. Thank you so much Pearson team and especially Drew Cupp, Mary Beth Ray, and two of the toughest technical reviewers I have had since my first and second editions, Chris Crayton and Jeff McDowell. You two kept me up late at night trying to figure out a way to make things better. I thank you so much for your conscientious efforts.

Finally, thank you to the students who have taken the time to share their recommendations for improvement. You are the reason I write this book each time. Please send me any ideas and comments you may have. I love hearing from you and of your successes. I may be reached at cheryl.schmidt@fscj.edu.

We Want to Hear from You!

As the reader of this book, *you* are our most important critic and commentator. We value your opinion and want to know what we're doing right, what we could do better, what areas you'd like to see us publish in, and any other words of wisdom you're willing to pass our way.

We welcome your comments. You can email or write to let us know what you did or didn't like about this book—as well as what we can do to make our books better.

Please note that we cannot help you with technical problems related to the topic of this book.

When you write, please be sure to include this book's title and author as well as your name and email address. We will carefully review your comments and share them with the author and editors who worked on the book.

Email: feedback@pearsonitcertification.com

Mail: Dave Dusthimer
Associate Publisher
Pearson IT Certification
800 East 96th Street
Indianapolis, IN 46240 USA

Reader Services

Visit our website and register this book at www.pearsonitcertification/register for convenient access to any updates, downloads, or errata that might be available for this book.

It Pays to Get Certified

In a digital world, digital literacy is an essential survival skill.

Certification proves you have the knowledge and skill to solve business problems in virtually any business environment. Certifications are highly-valued credentials that qualify you for jobs, increased compensation and promotion.

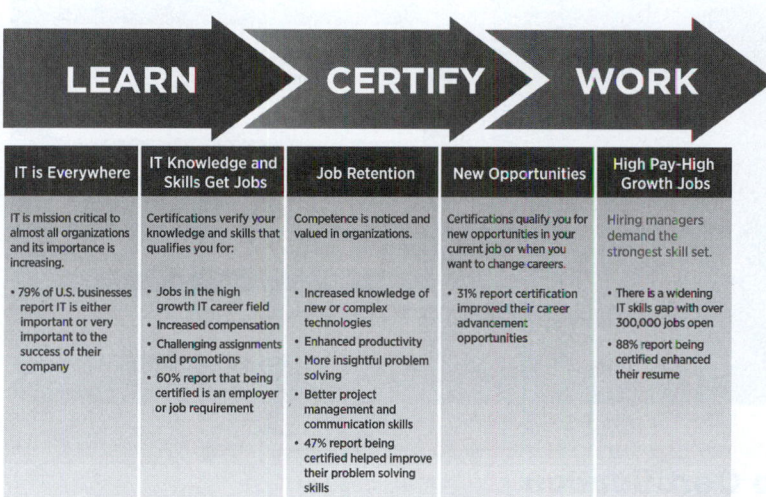

IT is Everywhere	IT Knowledge and Skills Get Jobs	Job Retention	New Opportunities	High Pay-High Growth Jobs
IT is mission critical to almost all organizations and its importance is increasing.	Certifications verify your knowledge and skills that qualifies you for:	Competence is noticed and valued in organizations.	Certifications qualify you for new opportunities in your current job or when you want to change careers.	Hiring managers demand the strongest skill set.
• 79% of U.S. businesses report IT is either important or very important to the success of their company	• Jobs in the high growth IT career field • Increased compensation • Challenging assignments and promotions • 60% report that being certified is an employer or job requirement	• Increased knowledge of new or complex technologies • Enhanced productivity • More insightful problem solving • Better project management and communication skills • 47% report being certified helped improve their problem solving skills	• 31% report certification improved their career advancement opportunities	• There is a widening IT skills gap with over 300,000 jobs open • 88% report being certified enhanced their resume

Certification Advances Your Career

- The CompTIA A+ credential—provides foundation-level knowledge and skills necessary for a career in PC repair and support.
- Starting Salary—CompTIA A+ Certified individuals can earn as much as $65,000 per year.
- Career Pathway—CompTIA A+ is a building block for other CompTIA certifications such as Network+, Security+ and vendor specific technologies.
- More than 850,000—Individuals worldwide are CompTIA A+ certified.
- Mandated/Recommended by organizations worldwide—Such as Cisco and HP and Ricoh, the U.S. State Department, and U.S. government contractors such as EDS, General Dynamics, and Northrop Grumman.

Some of the primary benefits individuals report from becoming A+ certified are:

- More efficient troubleshooting
- Improved career advancement
- More insightful problem solving

CompTIA Career Pathway

CompTIA offers a number of credentials that form a foundation for your career in technology and allows you to pursue specific areas of concentration. Depending on the path you choose to take, CompTIA certifications help you build upon your skills and knowledge, supporting learning throughout your entire career.

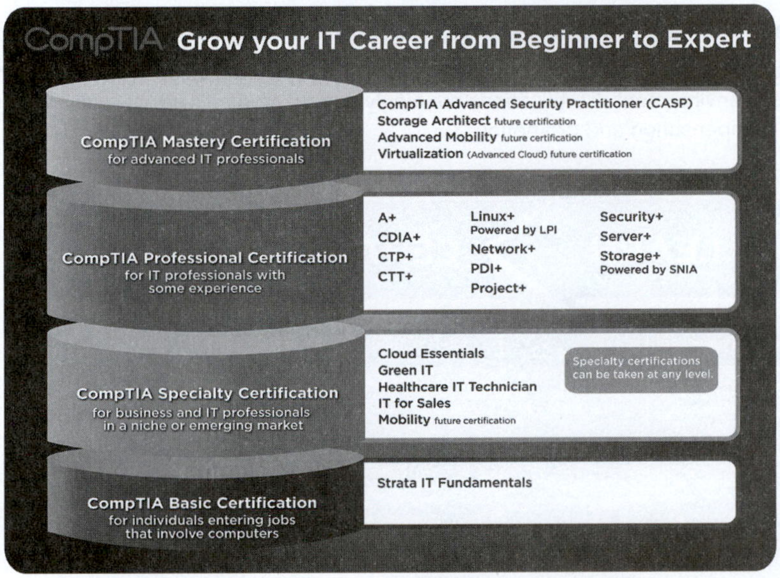

Steps to Certification

Steps to Getting Certified and Staying Certified	
Review Exam Objectives	Review the certification objectives to make sure you know what is covered in the exam. http://www.comptia.org/certifications/testprep/examobjectives.aspx
Practice for the Exam	After you have studied for the certification, take a free assessment and sample test to get an idea what type of questions might be on the exam. http://www.comptia.org/certifications/testprep/practicetests.aspx
Purchase an Exam Voucher	Purchase your exam voucher on the CompTIA Marketplace, which is located at: www.comptiastore.com.
Take the Test!	Select a certification exam provider and schedule a time to take your exam. You can find exam providers at the following link: http://www.comptia.org/certifications/testprep/testingcenters.aspx

Join the Professional Community

Join IT Pro Community
http://itpro.comptia.org

The free IT Pro online community provides valuable content to students and professionals.

Career IT Job Resources

- Where to start in IT
- Career Assessments
- Salary Trends
- US Job Board

Forums on Networking, Security, Computing and Cutting Edge Technologies

Access to blogs written by Industry Experts

Current information on Cutting Edge Technologies

Access to various industry resource links and articles related to IT and IT careers

Content Seal of Quality

This courseware bears the seal of **CompTIA Approved Quality Content**. This seal signifies this content covers 100% of the exam objectives and implements important instructional design principles. CompTIA recommends multiple learning tools to help increase coverage of the learning objectives.

Why CompTIA?

- **Global Recognition**—CompTIA is recognized globally as the leading IT non-profit trade association and has enormous credibility. Plus, CompTIA's certifications are vendor-neutral and offer proof of foundational knowledge that translates across technologies.
- **Valued by Hiring Managers**—Hiring managers value CompTIA certification because it is vendor- and technology-independent validation of your technical skills.
- **Recommended or Required by Government and Businesses**—Many government organizations and corporations either recommend or require technical staff to be CompTIA certified. (For example, Dell, Sharp, Ricoh, the U.S. Department of Defense, and many more.)
- **Three CompTIA Certifications ranked in the top 10**—In a study by DICE of 17,000 technology professionals, certifications helped command higher salaries at all experience levels.

How to obtain more information

Visit CompTIA online: www.comptia.org to learn more about getting CompTIA certified.

Contact CompTIA: Call 866-835-8020 ext. 5 or email questions@comptia.org

Connect with us :

Introduction

Complete CompTIA A+ Guide to PCs, Sixth Edition, is intended for one or more courses geared toward CompTIA A+ Certification and Computer Repair. It covers all the material needed for the CompTIA A+ 220-801 and 220-802 exams. The book is written so that it is easy to read and understand, with concepts presented in building-block fashion. The book focuses on hardware, software, mobile devices, virtualization, basic networking, and security.

Some of the best features of the book include the coverage of difficult subjects in a step-by-step manner, carefully developed graphics that illustrate concepts, photographs that demonstrate various technologies, reinforcement questions, critical thinking skills, soft skills, and hands-on exercises at the end of each chapter. Also, this book is written by a teacher who understands the value of a textbook from someone who has been in IT their entire career.

What's New in the Sixth Edition?

This update has been revised to include coverage of mobile devices such as smartphones and tablets, virtualization, and design. This edition differs from the Fifth Edition Update book in the following ways:

- Conformity with the latest CompTIA A+ Exam requirements, including the CompTIA A+ 220-801 exam, as well as the CompTIA A+ 220-802 exam.
- A new chapter on computer design was added after the hardware chapters. The chapter includes design activities with various scenarios.
- Mobile devices and virtualization technologies have been added to relevant hardware and software chapters. Labs have also been included.
- Chapters 1 through 10 focus on hardware and design. Chapters 11 and 12 are the operating system chapters. Chapter 13 and 14 cover Internet/networking concepts. Chapter 15 handles security concepts.
- The Internet Connectivity chapter was moved after the Windows chapters and before the Introduction to Networking chapter. The chapter was revamped to be a better introduction to Internet technologies, before the book dives into the details of supporting devices that connect to a wired or wireless network.
- Chapters 1 through 3 were reorganized to better flow through the basic concepts.
- The book has always been filled with graphics and photos, but even more have been added to target those naturally drawn to the IT field.
- The number of questions at the end of each chapter was reduced, but more questions are available in the test bank available from the Pearson Instructor Resource Center.

Organization of the Text

The text is organized to allow thorough coverage of all topics and also to be a flexible teaching tool. It is not necessary to cover all the chapters, nor do the chapters have to be covered in order.

- Chapter 1 covers beginning terminology and computer part and port identification. Chapter 1 does not have a specific soft skills section as do the other chapters. Instead, it focuses on common technician qualities that are explored in greater detail in the soft skills sections of later chapters.
- Chapter 2 details components, features, and concepts related to motherboards, including processors, cache, expansion slots, and chipsets. Active listening skills are described in the soft skills section in this chapter.

- Chapter 3 deals with system configuration basics. BIOS options, UEFI BIOS, and system resources are key topics. The soft skills section covers how one thing at a time should be done when replacing components.
- Chapter 4 steps the student through how to disassemble and reassemble a computer. Laptop disassembly is also covered. Tools, ESD, EMI, and preventive maintenance are discussed. Subsequent chapters also include preventive maintenance topics. Basic electronics and computer power concepts are also included in this chapter. Written communication tips are provided for the soft skills training.
- Chapter 5 covers troubleshooting skills and error codes. Good communication skills are stressed in the soft skills section.
- Chapter 6 covers memory installation, preparation, and troubleshooting. The importance of teamwork is emphasized as the soft skill.
- Chapter 7 deals with storage devices including the floppy drive and IDE PATA/SATA and SCSI (parallel and SAS) hard drive installation, preparation, and troubleshooting. SSDs are also covered. Phone communication skills is the target area for soft skills in this chapter.
- Chapter 8 covers multimedia devices, including optical drives, sound cards, cameras, scanners, and speakers. The chapter ends with a section on having a positive, proactive attitude.
- Chapter 9 deals with peripheral devices, including printers and video output devices. A discussion of work ethics finishes the chapter.
- Chapter 10 is the new computer design chapter. Not only are the specialized computers and components needed within those types of systems covered, but computer subsystem design is also included. The soft skills section targets recommendations for dealing with irate customers.
- Chapter 11 introduces operating systems, including Windows, Android, and iOS. The chapter also includes common desktop or home icons, how to manage files and folders, the registry, and how to function from a command prompt. The soft skills section includes tips on how to stay current in this fast-paced field.
- Chapter 12 covers Windows XP, Vista, and 7. Details include how to install, configure, and troubleshoot the environment. Avoiding burnout is the soft skill discussed in this chapter.
- Chapter 13 handles Internet connectivity. Analog and digital modems, cable modems, DSL modems, and mobile connectivity including wireless, WiMax, and broadband cellular are all discussed. Internet browser configuration is covered along with the soft skill of mentoring.
- Chapter 14 introduces networking. Basic concepts, terminology, and exercises make this chapter a favorite. An introduction to subnetting has been added. The focus of the soft skills section is being proactive instead of reactive.
- Chapter 15 describes computer, mobile device, and network security. The exercises include file and folder security, event monitoring, and local policy creation. The soft skills section is on building customer trust.

Features of This Book

The following key features of the book are designed to enable a better learning experience.

Chapter Objectives:

In this chapter you will learn:

- To recognize and identify important motherboard parts
- To explain the basics of how a processor works
- What issues to consider when upgrading or replacing the motherboard or processor
- How to add cards to computers and mobile devices
- The differences between PCI, PCI-X, AGP, and PCIe adapters and slots
- About motherboard technologies such as HyperTransport, Hyper-Threading, and multi-core
- The benefits of active listening

CompTIA Exam Objectives:

What CompTIA A+ exam objectives are covered in this chapter?

- ✓ 801-1.2 Differentiate between motherboard components, their purposes, and properties.
- ✓ 801-1.6 Differentiate among various CPU types and features and select the appropriate cooling method.
- ✓ 801-3.1 Install and configure laptop hardware and components.
- ✓ 801-5.3 Given a scenario, demonstrate proper communication and professionalism.
- ✓ 802-1.9 Explain the basics of client-side virtualization.
- ✓ 802-4.2 Given a scenario, troubleshoot common problems related to motherboards, RAM, CPU, and power with appropriate tools.

OBJECTIVES Each chapter begins with BOTH chapter objectives and the CompTIA A+ exam objectives

GRAPHICS AND PHOTOGRAPHS Many more have been added to better illustrate the concepts

ter and remove the computer
pen expansion slot. Some adapters
ptions include 16- and 32-bit PCI

Tech Tip

Enable SATA port

Many manufacturers require that you enable the motherboard port through the system BIOS before any device connected to the port is recognized.

TECH TIPS The chapters are filled with Tech Tips that highlight technical issues and certification exam topics

RAM is divided into two major types: **DRAM** (dynamic RAM) and **SRAM** (static RAM). DRAM is less expensive but slower than SRAM. With DRAM, the 1s and 0s inside the chip must be refreshed. Over time, the charge, which represents information inside a DRAM chip, leaks out. The information, stored in 1s and 0s, is periodically rewritten to the memory chip through the **refreshing** process. The refreshing is accomplished inside the DRAM while other

KEY TERMS IN CONTEXT As you read the chapter, terms that appear in blue are considered key terms and are defined in the glossary

Key Terms

access time..................216
cache memory..............203
CL rating......................216
CompactFlash..............226
DDR.............................205
DDR2...........................205
DDR3...........................205
DDR3L.........................205
DIMM..........................203
double-sided memory...208
DRAM..........................203
dual-channel................212
dual-voltage memory...217
ECC.............................209
flash memory...............226
fully buffered memory..208
microSD.......................226
miniSD.........................226
non-parity....................208
PAE.............................223
pages...........................221
parity...........................208
Performance utility......223
RAM.............................202
RDRAM........................205
refresh (process)...........203
registered memory.......207
quadruple-channel.......215
SD...............................226
SDRAM.........................205
SIMM...........................203
single-sided memory....208
SO-DIMM.....................207
SPD.............................208
SRAM...........................203
swap file......................221
triple-channel..............215
unbuffered memory......208
USB flash drive............227
virtual machine............224
virtual memory.............221
Windows Memory Diagnostics Tool..........225
xD...............................226

KEY TERMS LIST At the end of the chapter, all key terms are listed with page references to which to refer for context

Soft Skills—Active Listening

Active listening is participating in a conversation where you focus on what the customer is saying—in other words, listening more than talking. For a technician, active listening has the following benefits:

- Allows you to gather data and symptoms quickly
- Allows you to build customer rapport
- Improves your understanding of the problem
- Allows you to solve the problem more quickly because you understand the problem better
- Provides mutual understanding between you and the customer
- Provides a means of having a positive, engaged conversation rather than having a negative, confrontational encounter
- Focuses on the customer rather than the technician
- Provides an environment where the customer might be more forthcoming with information related to the problem

Frequently, when a technician arrives onsite or contacts a customer who has a technical problem, the technician is (1) rushed; (2) thinking of other things, including the problems that need to be solved; (3) assuming that he or she knows exactly what the problem is, even though the user has not finished explaining the problem; or (4) more interested in the technical problem than in the customer and the issues. Active listening changes the focus from the technician's problems to the customer's problems.

A common but ineffective service call involves a technician doing most of the talking and questioning, using technical jargon and acronyms and a flat or condescending tone. The customer, who feels vulnerable, experiences a heightened anxiety level. Active listening changes this scenario by helping you build a professional relationship with your customers. The following list outlines some measures that help you implement active listening.

Have a positive, engaged professional attitude when talking and listening to customers:

- Leave your prejudices behind; be polite and aware of other cultures and customs; be open-minded and nonjudgmental.
- Have a warm and caring attitude.
- Do not fold your arms in front of your chest because doing so distances you from the problem and the customer.

SOFT SKILLS **Technology is not the only thing you must learn and practice; each chapter offers advice, activities, and examples of how to be a good tech, an ethical tech, a good work mate, a good communicator, and so on**

Chapter Summary 229

6 Memory

Chapter Summary

- Memory on a motherboard is SDRAM, a type of RAM that is cheaper and slower than SRAM, the type of memory inside the CPU and processor housing.
- A DDR module fits in a DDR slot. A DDR2 module requires a DDR2 slot; a DDR3 module requires a DDR3 slot.
- RIMMs use RDRAM and were developed by Rambus, Inc. C-RIMMs are inserted into empty memory slots.
- Unbuffered memory is the memory normally installed in computers.
- ECC is used for error checking and is commonly found in high-end computers and servers. An older method of error checking was called parity.
- The CL rating or the timing sequence first number shows how fast the processor can access data in sequential memory locations. The lower the first number, the faster the access.
- SPD is a technology used so the memory module can communicate specifications to the BIOS.

CHAPTER SUMMARY **Recap the key concepts of the chapter, and use this for review to ensure you've mastered the chapter's learning objectives**

Review Questions

1. Which expansion slot would most likely be used to add an internal adapter to a new laptop? [ExpressCard/34 | ExpressCard/54 | mini PCIe | PC Card | USB port | PCI-X | mini PCI]
2. Which expansion slot would be *best* for a video card in a desktop computer? [PCI-X | PCIe | PCI | ExpressCard/54 | AGP]
3. A motherboard has a PCIe x16 expansion slot. Which PCIe adapter(s) will fit in this slot? (Select any that apply.) [x1 | x2 | x4 | x8 | x16 | x32]
4. Match the capacity to the description.

____ bit	a.	8 bits
____ kilobyte	b.	a 1 or a 0
____ megabyte	c.	approximately 1,000 bytes
____ byte	d.	approximately 1 million bytes
____ gigabyte	e.	approximately 1 trillion bytes
____ terabyte	f.	approximately 1 billion bytes

5. What is the front side bus?
   a. the internal data bus that connects the processor core to the L1 cache
   b. the internal data bus that connects the processor core to the L2 cache
   c. the external data bus that connects the processor to the motherboard components
   d. the external data bus that connects the processor to the L2 cache
6. A customer wants to upgrade the L2 cache. What will this definitely require?
   a. a motherboard purchase

REVIEW QUESTIONS Hundreds of review questions, including true/false, multiple choice, matching, fill-in-the-blank, and open-ended questions, assess your knowledge of the learning

Lab 1.3 Identification of Video Ports

Objective: To identify various video ports correctly

Procedure: Identify each video port in Figure 1.55.

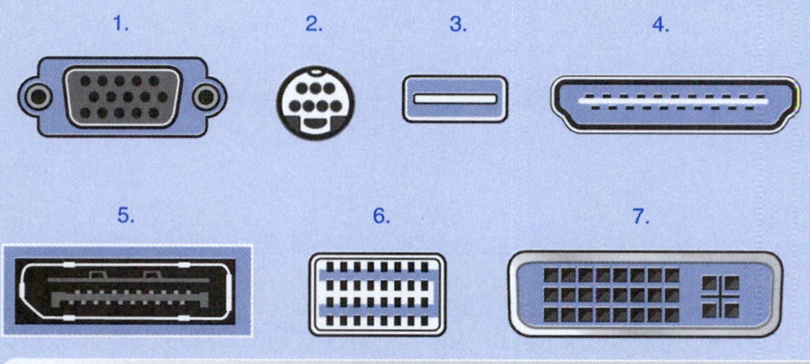

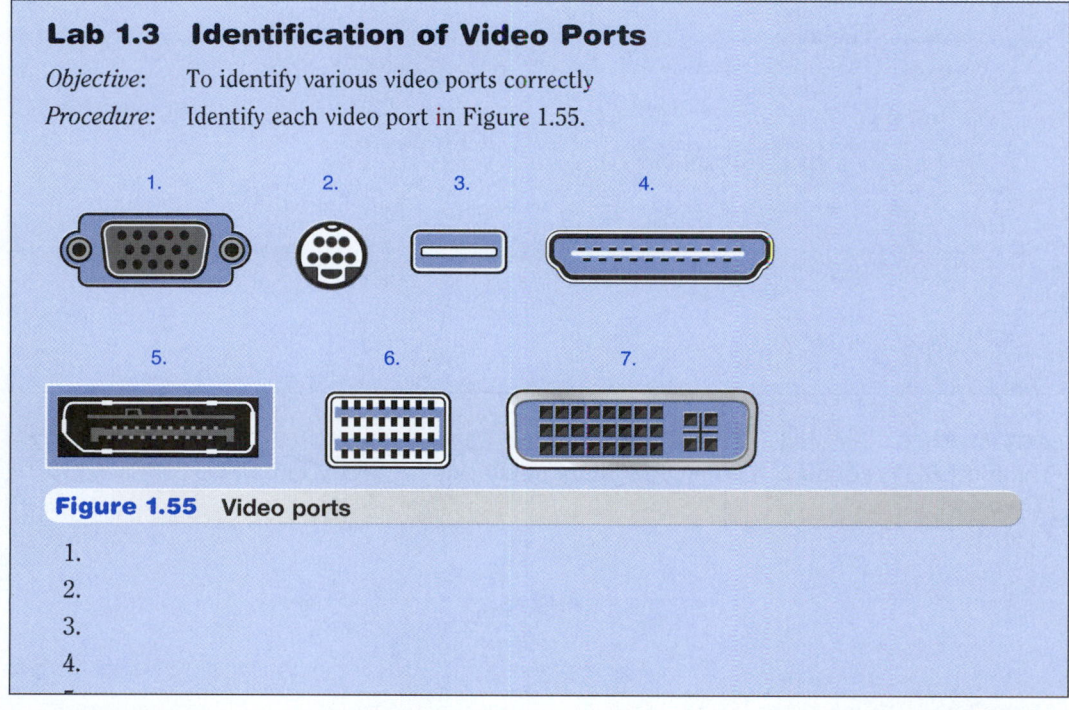

Figure 1.55 Video ports

1.
2.
3.
4.

LAB EXERCISES More than 125 labs enable you to link theory to practical experience

Activities 43

Activities

1 Introduction to Computer Repair

Internet Discovery

Objective: To obtain specific information from the Internet regarding a computer or its associated parts

Parts: Computer with Internet access

Procedure: Obtain technical information about a computer. Answer the following questions based on the information. More documents may need to be obtained in order to answer the questions.

Questions:

1. What ports are available on the front of the computer?
2. What ports are available on the back of the computer?
3. How many drive bays are available to install devices such as hard drives, optical drives, tape drives, and so on?
4. Were the photos in the documentation clear enough to differentiate between the different ports? If not, explain what is wrong.
5. List three safety precautions or procedures the documentation offers.

Soft Skills

Objective: To enhance and fine-tune a future technician's ability to listen, communicate in both written and oral forms, and support people who use computers in a professional manner

Procedure:

1. In a team environment, list three qualities that are important in a computer technician. Create scenarios that demonstrate these qualities. Share these findings in a clear and concise way with the class.
2. In a team environment, list three qualities that are not good practices for computer technicians. Create scenarios that demonstrate these qualities. Share these findings in a clear and concise way with the class.

Critical Thinking Skills

Objective: To analyze and evaluate information as well as apply learned information to new or different situations

Procedure:

1. Find an advertisement for a computer in a local computer flyer, in a newspaper, in a magazine, in a book, or on the Internet. List which components you know in one column and the components you do not know in the other column. Select one component you do not know and research that component. Write the new information and share with at least one other person.

ACTIVITIES **Extensive practice with Internet Discovery, Soft Skills, and Critical Thinking Skills round out your technical knowledge so that you can be prepared for IT work**

A+ Certification Exam Tips

- ✓ Review Table 6.2 right before the exam(s) in case you are asked to identify the memory type or DDR*x* name.
- ✓ Review Table 6.6, especially the Windows 7 and 32-bit Windows memory limitations.
- ✓ Know how to calculate what memory is needed for an upgrade or a new install.
- ✓ Be able to identify memory slots on a motherboard.
- ✓ Know how to populate memory when dual- or triple-channeling is being implemented.
- ✓ Be able to describe the difference between unbuffered and ECC memory.
- ✓ Know that memory chips are especially susceptible to ESD and how to prevent ESD damage when installing or removing memory.
- ✓ Review the troubleshooting symptoms and tips for the 220-802 exam.
- ✓ Keep in mind that the following professionalism skills are part of the 220-801 exam: (1) maintain a positive attitude and (2) be on time (or, if late, contact the customer). You should not forget to review the professionalism skills.

EXAM TIPS **Read through these tips on the CompTIA A+ exams so you aren't caught off guard when you sit for the exam**

CompTIA A+ Exam Objectives

Tables I-1 and I-2 summarize where you can find all the CompTIA A+ exam objectives covered in the book.

Table I-1 **CompTIA A+ 220-801 exam objectives**

Objective	Chapters
220-801	
1.0 PC Hardware	
1.1 Configure and apply BIOS settings.	3, 7, 8, 15
1.2 Differentiate between motherboard components, their purposes, and properties.	1, 2, 3, 4, 6, 14
1.3 Compare and contrast RAM types and features.	6
1.4 Install and configure expansion cards.	3, 8, 9, 13
1.5 Install and configure storage devices and use appropriate media.	1, 6, 7, 8
1.6 Differentiate among various CPU types and features and select the appropriate cooling method.	2
1.7 Compare and contrast various connection interfaces and explain their purpose.	1, 13, 14
1.8 Install an appropriate power supply based on a given scenario	4
1.9 Evaluate and select appropriate components for a custom configuration, to meet customer specifications or needs.	10
1.10 Given a scenario, evaluate types and features of display devices.	1, 9
1.11 Identify connector types and associated cables.	1, 7, 9, 13
1.12 Install and configure various peripheral devices.	1, 8, 9

Objective	Chapters
220-801	
2.0 Networking	
2.1 Identify types of network cables and connectors.	14
2.2 Categorize characteristics of connectors and cabling.	14
2.3 Explain properties and characteristics of TCP/IP.	14
2.4 Explain common TCP and UDP ports, protocols, and their purpose.	14
2.5 Compare and contrast wireless networking standards and encryption types.	14, 15
2.6 Install, configure, and deploy a SOHO wireless/wired router using appropriate settings.	14, 15
2.7 Compare and contrast Internet connection types and features.	13, 14
2.8 Identify various types of networks.	14
2.9 Compare and contrast network devices their functions and features.	13, 14, 15
2.10 Given a scenario, use appropriate networking tools.	14
3.0 Laptops	
3.1 Install and configure laptop hardware and components.	1, 2, 4, 6, 7, 8, 9, 14
3.2 Compare and contrast the components within the display of a laptop.	9, 14
3.3 Compare and contrast laptop features.	1, 8, 14, 15
4.0 Printers	
4.1 Explain the differences between the various printer types and summarize the associated imaging process.	9
4.2 Given a scenario, install, and configure printers.	3, 9, 14
4.3 Given a scenario, perform printer maintenance.	9
5.0 Operational Procedures	
5.1 Given a scenario, use appropriate safety procedures.	4, 14
5.2 Explain environmental impacts and the purpose of environmental controls.	4, 10
5.3 Given a scenario, demonstrate proper communication and professionalism.	1, 2, 4, 5, 7, 10, 15
5.4 Explain the fundamentals of dealing with prohibited content/activity.	15

Table I-2 CompTIA A+ 220-802 Exam Objectives

Objective	Chapters
220-802	
1.0 Operating Systems	
1.1 Compare and contrast the features and requirements of various Microsoft operating systems.	6, 11, 12, 15
1.2 Given a scenario, install and configure the operating system using the most appropriate method.	7, 11, 12, 14
1.3 Given a scenario, use appropriate command line tools.	11, 12, 14
1.4 Given a scenario, use appropriate operating system features and tools.	4, 6, 7, 8, 11, 12, 14, 15
1.5 Given a scenario, use Control Panel utilities (the items are organized by "classic view/large icons" in Windows).	4, 6, 8, 11, 12, 14, 15
1.6 Setup and configure Windows networking on a client/desktop.	13, 14, 15
1.7 Perform preventive maintenance procedures using appropriate tools.	7, 11, 12
1.8 Explain the differences among basic OS security settings.	14, 15
1.9 Explain the basics of client-side virtualization.	2, 11, 12, 14, 15
2.0 Security	
2.1 Apply and use common prevention methods.	12, 15
2.2 Compare and contrast common security threats.	12, 15
2.3 Implement security best practices to secure a workstation.	15
2.4 Given a scenario, use the appropriate data destruction/disposal method.	7, 15
2.5 Given a scenario, secure a SOHO wireless network.	15
2.6 Given a scenario, secure a SOHO wired network.	15
3.0 Mobile Devices	
3.1 Explain the basic features of mobile operating systems.	6, 11
3.2 Establish basic network connectivity and configure email.	1, 14
3.3 Compare and contrast methods for securing mobile devices.	15
3.4 Compare and contrast hardware differences in regards to tablets and laptops.	1
3.5 Execute and configure mobile device synchronization.	14
4.0 Troubleshooting	
4.1 Given a scenario, explain the troubleshooting theory.	5
4.2 Given a scenario, troubleshoot common problems related to motherboards, RAM, CPU, and power with appropriate tools.	2, 4, 5, 6, 14

Objective	Chapters
220-802	
4.3 Given a scenario, troubleshoot hard drives and RAID arrays with appropriate tools.	7
4.4 Given a scenario, troubleshoot common video and display issues.	9
4.5 Given a scenario, troubleshoot wired and wireless networks with appropriate tools.	13, 14
4.6 Given a scenario, troubleshoot operating system problems with appropriate tools.	6, 7, 11, 12
4.7 Given a scenario, troubleshoot common security issues with appropriate tools and best practices.	12, 15
4.8 Given a scenario, troubleshoot, and repair common laptop issues while adhering to the appropriate procedures.	1, 4, 9, 14
4.9 Given a scenario, troubleshoot printers with appropriate tools	9

Summary of Exam Domains by Chapter

Schmidt Table of Contents	220-801 Domains	220-802 Domains
Chapter 1: Introduction to Computer Repair	1, 5	3, 4
Chapter 2: On the Motherboard	1, 3, 5	1, 4
Chapter 3: System Configuration	1, 4	
Chapter 4: Disassembly and Power	1, 3, 5	1, 4
Chapter 5: Logical Troubleshooting	5	4
Chapter 6: Memory	1, 3	1, 3, 4
Chapter 7: Storage Devices	1, 3, 5	1, 2, 4
Chapter 8: Multimedia Devices	1, 3	1
Chapter 9: Other Peripherals	1, 3, 4	4
Chapter 10: Computing Design	1, 5	
Chapter 11: Basic Windows Operating Systems		1, 3, 4
Chapter 12: Windows XP, Vista, and 7		1, 2, 4
Chapter 13: Internet Connectivity	1, 2	1
Chapter 14: Introduction to Networking	1, 2, 3, 4, 5	1, 3, 4
Chapter 15: Computer and Network Security	1, 2, 3, 5	1, 2, 3, 4

chapter 1

Introduction to Computer Repair

Chapter Objectives:

In this chapter you will learn:

- Good qualities a technician should have
- What connects to different ports of a computer
- Important computer parts
- Basic computer terms

CompTIA Exam Objectives:

What CompTIA A+ exam objectives are covered in this chapter?

- ✓ 801-1.2 Differentiate between motherboard components, their purposes and properties.
- ✓ 801-1.5 Install and configure storage devices and use appropriate media.
- ✓ 801-1.7 Compare and contrast various connection interfaces and explain their purpose.
- ✓ 801-1.10 Given a scenario, evaluate types and features of display devices.
- ✓ 801-1.11 Identify connector types and associated cables.
- ✓ 801-1.12 Install and configure various peripheral devices.
- ✓ 801-3.1 Install and configure laptop hardware and components.
- ✓ 801-3.3 Compare and contrast laptop features.
- ✓ 801-5.3 Given a scenario, demonstrate proper communication and professionalism.
- ✓ 802-3.2 Establish basic network connectivity and configure email.
- ✓ 802-3.4 Compare and contrast hardware differences in regards to tablets and laptops.
- ✓ 802-4.8 Given a scenario, troubleshoot and repair common laptop issues while adhering to the appropriate procedures.

Overview

A computer technician must be a jack-of-all-trades: a software expert in various operating systems and applications; a hardware expert in everything ranging from processors to the latest laser printers; a communicator extraordinaire to handle the occasional irate, irrational, or computer-illiterate customer; a good listener to elicit computer symptoms from customers (and from the computer); an empathetic counselor to make customers feel good about their computers and confident in the technician's skills; and, finally, a master juggler of time and priorities. These traits do not come overnight, and not all of them can be taught—but a technician can constantly develop and fine-tune each of them.

This book covers computer support basics—the knowledge to get you started in the technology support industry. Standards related to computer repair are important, and technicians must recognize old and current standards and stay abreast of emerging ones.

There is no substitute for experience, and there is no substitute for knowing the basics of how individual computer parts work. The basics help you understand other emerging technologies as well as proprietary devices. Once a technician has a job in the industry, hands-on time will increase his or her depth of knowledge and experience. The classroom is the place to learn the ropes—the basics.

The best quality a technician can possess is logic. A good technician narrows a problem to a general area, subdivides the problem into possible culprits, and eliminates the possibilities one-by-one efficiently and logically. A technician is like a detective, constantly looking for clues, using common sense and deductive reasoning, gathering information from the computer and the computer user, and finally solving the mystery. Detective work is integral to a technician's job; therefore, throughout this book, **Tech Tips** provide important technical tips.

Tech Tip

What are Tech Tips?

Each chapter contains these technical tips to help you work smart in the real world of PC repair.

This book can help you achieve technical competence, but you should never forget the computer users. Many technicians like to work with things—computers, networks, printers, and so on—more than with people. This text cannot teach you to care about the people who use technology. You must remember that communication is as important as your technical skills.

Repairing computers is rewarding, but it can be frustrating if you do not understand the basics. With good reasoning ability and a good foundation in computer repair, no problem goes unsolved. Remember that if every repair were simple, then no one would need technicians.

CompTIA A+ Certification

An industry-standard certification called A+ is important for technicians, especially new technicians. This certification does not guarantee you a job, but the certification helps you get interviews and proves to companies that you have a higher level of understanding of computers and basic networking. The A+ certification consists of two exams: CompTIA A+ 220-801 and 220-802. You must pass both exams to achieve A+ certification. CompTIA provides official certification objectives for each exam. This book covers all the exam objectives for both exams.

Safety Note

Safety is covered in each chapter, especially in Chapter 4, but no book on computer repair can begin without stating that both the technician and the computer can be harmed by poor safety habits. To protect yourself and the computer, make sure to power off the computer and remove the power cord when disassembling, installing, or removing hardware, or doing preventive maintenance (cleaning). Never take an older CRT monitor or power supply apart unless you have been specifically trained on these components. The **MSDS** (material safety data sheet) is required to be made available to staff. The MSDS lists safety information such as handling, first aid, storage procedures, and disposal for any potentially harmful substances or materials, including those used with computer cleaning and repair.

Technicians have to be able to lift computers, servers, printers, monitors, and other devices. A common requirement in job advertisements or explained during interviews is in regard to lifting. Technical jobs frequently specify a maximum lifting requirement of 40 to 50 pounds. Use proper safety precautions, such as those shown in Figure 1.1. The type of equipment you need and things that you can do to prevent harm to the computer are covered more explicitly in Chapter 4, on power and disassembly.

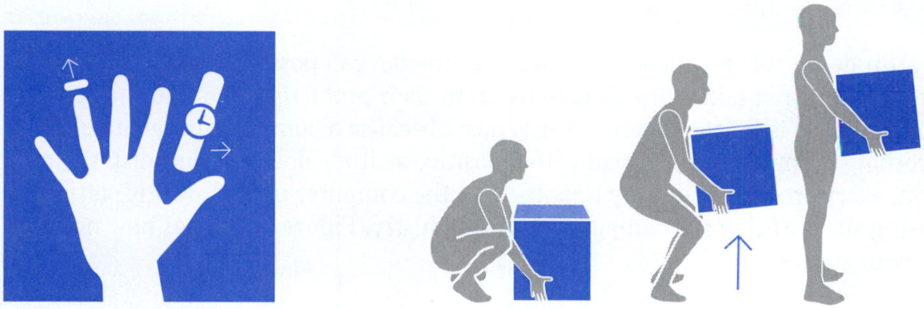

Remove jewelry before working inside of a computer
• Bend at the knees
• Use your legs to lift
• Use lifting aids when possible
• Ask for assistance when possible

Figure 1.1 Safety tips

Technician Qualities

Three of the most important qualities that a technician can have are active listening skills, a good attitude, and an appropriate level of "tech speak." Active listening means that you truly listen to what a person (especially one who is having a problem) is saying. Having active listening skills involves good eye contact, nodding your head every now and then to show that you are following the conversation, taking notes on important details, and avoiding distractions such as incoming cell phone calls or other activities. Clarify customer statements by asking pertinent questions and avoid interrupting the customer. Allow customers to complete their sentences. Many technicians jump into a problem the moment they hear the first symptom described by the user. Listen to the entire problem. Do not act superior because you know terms and things that they do not. Ask open-ended questions—questions that allow the user to expand on the answer rather than answer with a single word, such as *yes* or *no*. Figure 1.2 illustrates this point.

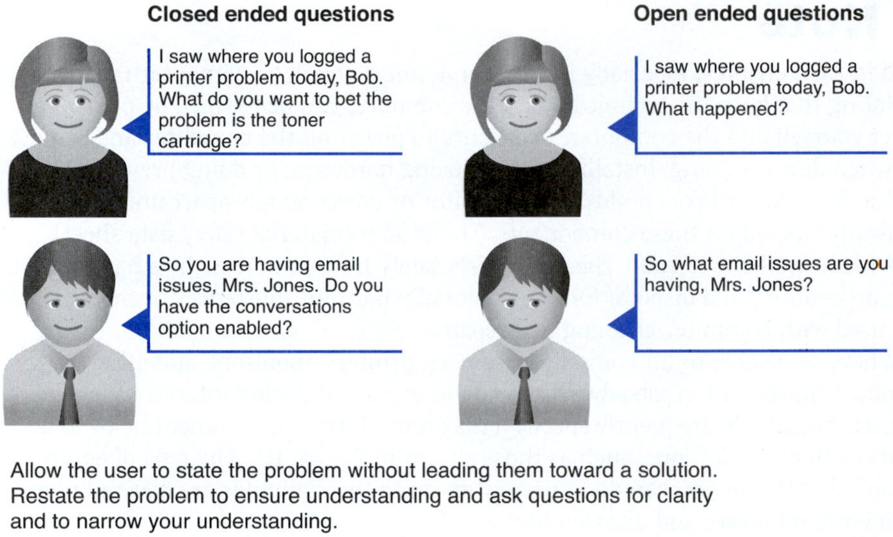

Allow the user to state the problem without leading them toward a solution. Restate the problem to ensure understanding and ask questions for clarity and to narrow your understanding.

Figure 1.2 Asking technical questions

A positive attitude is probably the best quality a technician can possess. Many technicians treat customers abruptly, not taking the time to listen to their problems or to find the best solutions. A good attitude is helpful when a user is upset because a computer or an attached device is not working properly. A technician with a positive attitude does not diminish the customer's problem; every problem is equally important to the computer user. A positive attitude is critical for being successful in the computer service industry. Figure 1.3 shows how negative attitudes affect your success.

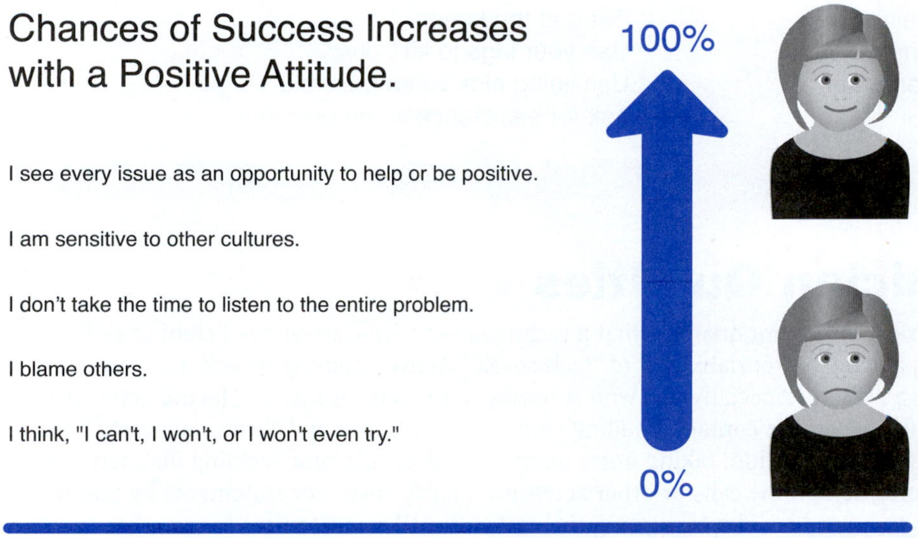

Chances of Success Increases with a Positive Attitude.
100%
I see every issue as an opportunity to help or be positive.
I am sensitive to other cultures.
I don't take the time to listen to the entire problem.
I blame others.
I think, "I can't, I won't, or I won't even try."
0%

Figure 1.3 Have a positive attitude

A technician must be familiar with and thoroughly understand computer terminology to (1) speak intelligently to other technical support staff in clear, concise, and direct statements; (2) explain the problem to the user; and (3) be proficient in the field. The field changes so quickly that technicians must constantly update their skills.

Unfortunately, some computer technicians use the technical language of the trade when speaking with people who are not attuned to the lingo. Using too many technical terms around end users serves only to confuse and irritate them. A technician should avoid using slang, jargon, acronyms, and abbreviations. In addition to knowing and using the correct terminology, a technician must use it appropriately and explain computer terms with simple, everyday language and examples. This book explains computer terminology in easy-to-understand terms and provides analogies that can be used when dealing with customers.

Basic Computer Parts

Computer systems include hardware, software, and firmware. **Hardware** is something you can touch and feel—the physical computer and the parts inside the computer are examples of hardware. The monitor, keyboard, and mouse are hardware components. **Software** interacts with the hardware. Windows, Linux, OS X, Microsoft Office, Solitaire, Google Chrome, Adobe Acrobat Reader, and WordPerfect are examples of software.

Without software that allows the hardware to accomplish something, a computer is nothing more than a doorstop. Every computer needs an important piece of software called an **operating system**, which coordinates the interaction between hardware and software applications. The operating system also handles the interaction between a user and the computer. Examples of operating systems include Windows XP, Windows Vista, Windows 7, Windows 8, OS X, and various types of Unix, such as Red Hat and Mandrake.

A **device driver** is a special piece of software designed to enable a hardware component. The device driver enables the operating system to recognize, control, and use the hardware component. Device drivers are hardware and operating system specific. For example, a printer requires a specific device driver when connected to a computer loaded with Windows XP. The same printer will most likely require a different device driver when using Windows 7. Each piece of installed hardware requires a device driver for the operating system being used. Figure 1.4 shows how hardware and software must work together.

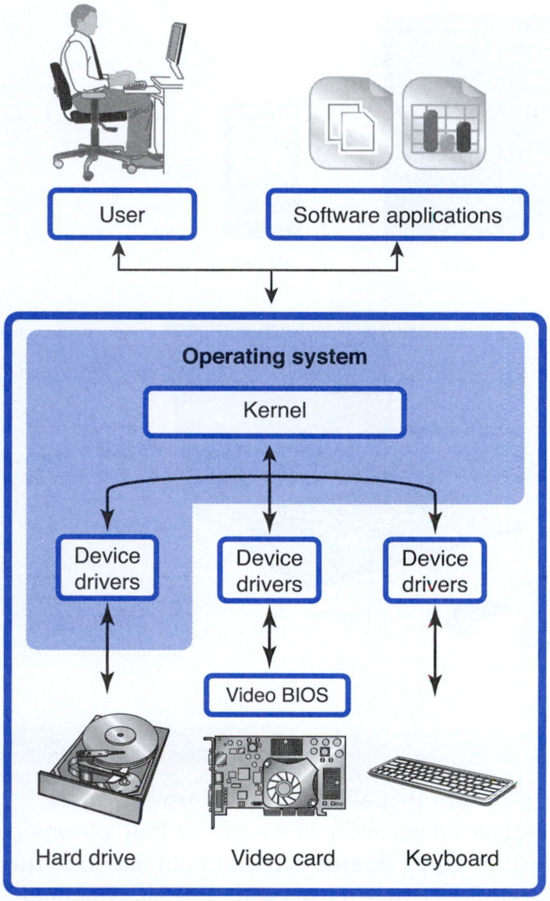

Figure 1.4 Hardware and software

Notice in Figure 1.4 the operating system kernel. The kernel is the central part of an operating system. The kernel is the connection between hardware and the applications being used.

Software applications are normally loaded onto the hard drive. When a user selects an application, the operating system controls the loading of the application. The operating system also controls any hardware devices (such as the mouse, keyboard, monitor through the video adapter, and printer) used with the application.

Firmware combines hardware and software into important chips inside the computer. It is called firmware because it is a chip, which is hardware, and it has software built into the chip. An example of firmware is the **BIOS** (basic input/output system) chip. BIOS chips always have software inside them. The BIOS has startup software that must be present for a computer to operate. This startup software locates and loads the operating system. The BIOS also contains software instructions for communication with input/output devices, as well as important hardware parameters that determine to some extent what hardware can be installed. For example, the system BIOS has the ability to allow other BIOS chips that are located on adapters (such as the video card) to load software that is loaded in the card's BIOS.

The simplest place to start to learn about computer technical support is with the devices themselves. Computer devices come in many shapes and sizes. The **PC**, or personal computer, comes in desktop models and mobile models, such as a laptops, ultrabooks, and netbooks. The old term **Internet appliance** was used for any device used to access the Internet. Of course, this is quite common today, as computers, laptops, smartphones, e-readers, tablets, and so on can all access the Internet. Figure 1.5 shows some of the computing devices technical staff are expected to support.

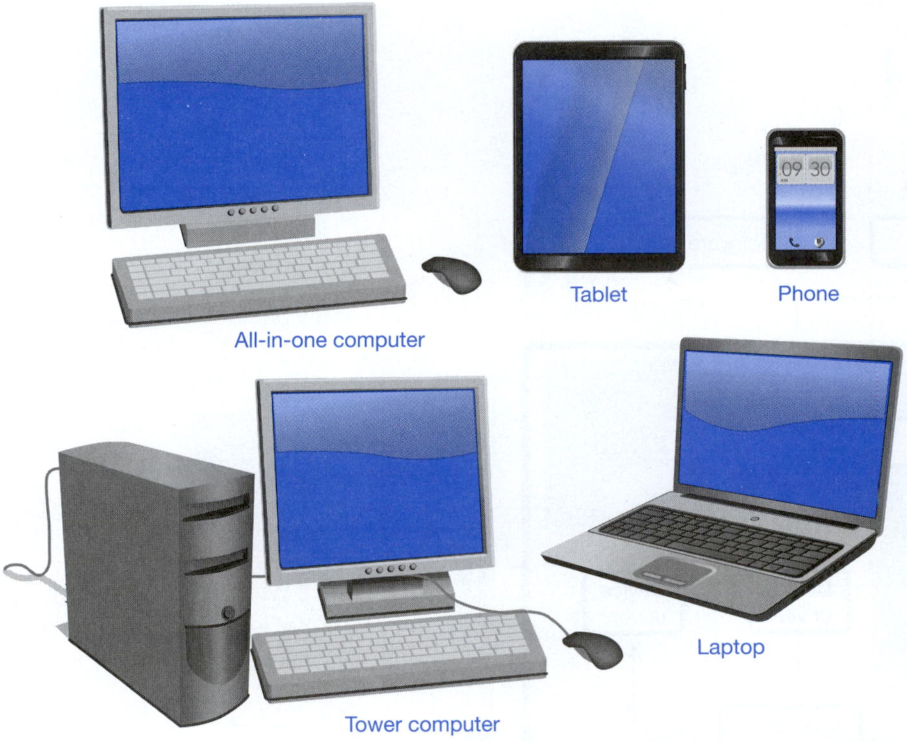

Figure 1.5 Computing devices

A PC typically consists of a case (chassis), a keyboard that allows users to provide input into the computer, a monitor that outputs or displays information, and a mouse that allows data input or is used to select menus and options. An **input device** is used to put data into the computer. A microphone, keyboard, mouse, or your finger (when used with a tablet or phone) are great examples. Also, biometric devices can be input devices. Common biometric devices are a finger swipe reader and an integrated camera that can be used for facial recognition to gain access to a device.

An **output device** such as a monitor accepts data from the computer. Some devices can be both input and output devices, such as a printer or a touch screen. In the case of a printer, data is sent from your computer to the printer, and the printer can send data (information), such as an out-of-ink message, back to the computer. Figure 1.6 lists common input and output devices.

Input devices

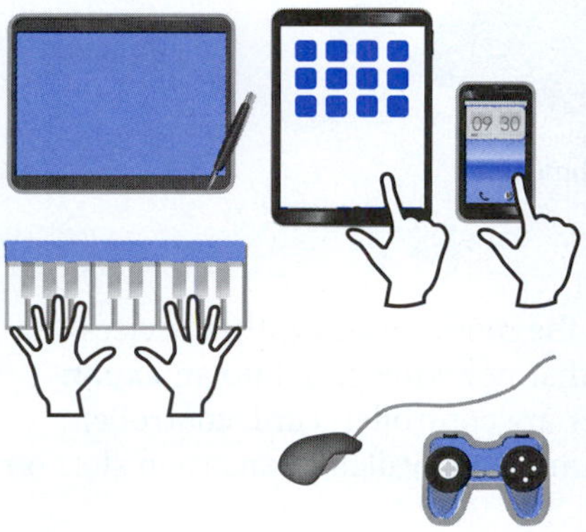

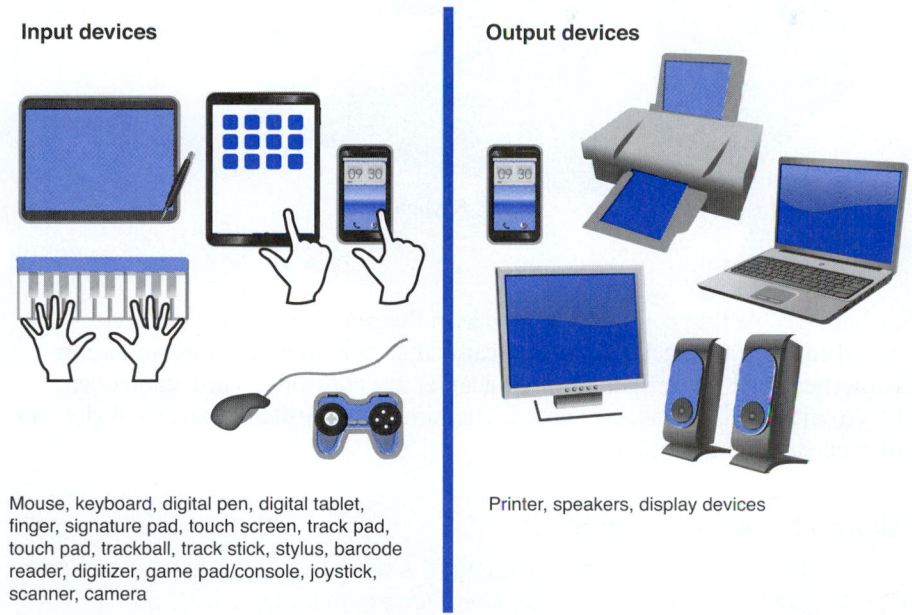

Mouse, keyboard, digital pen, digital tablet, finger, signature pad, touch screen, track pad, touch pad, trackball, track stick, stylus, barcode reader, digitizer, game pad/console, joystick, scanner, camera

Output devices

Printer, speakers, display devices

Figure 1.6 Input and output devices

A device that can be both an input device and an output device is a **KVM switch**. KVM stands for keyboard, video, mouse, and a KVM switch allows connectivity of multiple devices so they can be shared between computers. For example, one keyboard, one mouse, and one display could connect to a KVM switch. A KVM switch has cables that allow it to connect or output to two or more computers.

Once the computer cover or side is opened or removed, the parts inside can be identified. The easiest part to identify is the **power supply**, which is the metal box normally located in a back corner of the case. A power cord goes from the power supply to a wall outlet or surge strip. One purpose of the power supply is to convert the AC voltage that comes out of the outlet to DC voltage. The power supply distributes this DC voltage using power cables that connect to the various internal computer parts. A fan located inside the power supply keeps the computer cool, which avoids damage to the components.

A personal computer usually has a device to store software applications and files. Two examples of storage devices are the floppy drive and the hard drive. A slot in the front of many older computers easily identified the floppy drive. The **floppy drive** allows data storage to floppy disks (sometimes called diskettes, or disks) that can be used in other computers. Floppy disks store less information than hard drives. They are also obsolete, for the most part. The **hard drive**, sometimes called hard disk, is a rectangular box normally inside the computer's case that is sealed to keep out dust and dirt. An **optical drive** holds discs (CDs, DVDs, or BDs) that have data, music, video, or software applications on them. Mobile devices such as tablets and smartphones don't have storage devices such as this.

The **motherboard** is the main circuit board located inside a PC and contains the most electronics. It is normally located on the bottom of a desktop or laptop computer and mounted on the side of a tower computer. Other names for the motherboard include mainboard, planar, or systemboard. The motherboard is the largest electronic circuit board in the computer. The keyboard frequently connects directly to the back of the motherboard, although some computers have a keyboard connection in the front of the case. Figure 1.7 shows the major components of a tower computer.

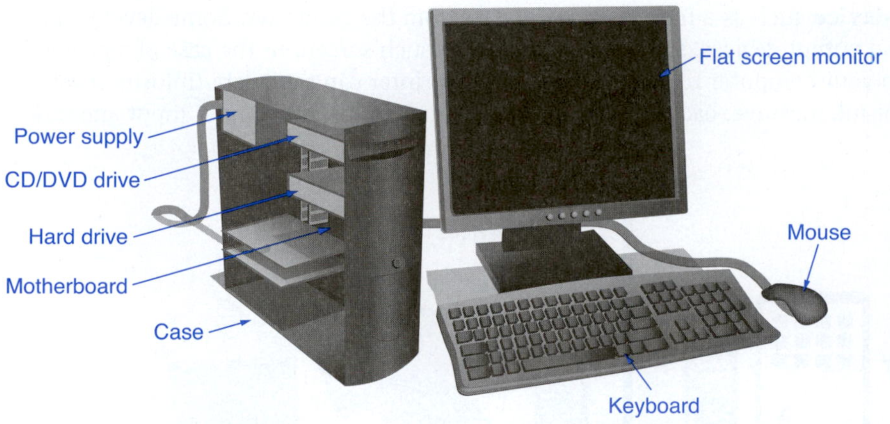

Figure 1.7 Tower computer

A device may have a cable that connects the device to the motherboard. Other devices require an adapter. **Adapters** are electronic circuit cards that normally plug into an **expansion slot** on the motherboard. Other names for an adapter are controller, card, controller card, circuit card, circuit board, and adapter board. The number of available expansion slots on the motherboard depends on the manufacturer.

Tech Tip

How to identify an adapter's function

Tracing the cable(s) attached to an adapter or looking at a device connected to an adapter can usually help with identifying an adapter's function. For example, typically a monitor has a cable going between it and a video adapter or motherboard.

The following are the generic steps for installing adapters:

1. Always follow the manufacturer's installation directions. Use an antistatic wrist strap when handling adapters. ESD (electrostatic discharge) can damage electronic parts. (See Chapter 4, "Disassembly and Power," for more details on ESD.)
2. Be sure the computer is powered off and unplugged.
3. Remove any brackets from the case or plastic covers from the rear of the computer that may prevent adapter installation. Install the adapter in a free expansion slot and reattach any securing hardware.
4. Attach any internal device cables that connect to the adapter, as well as any cables that go to an external port on the adapter, if necessary.
5. Attach any internal or external devices to the opposite ends of the cable, if necessary.
6. Power on any external devices connected to the adapter, if applicable.
7. Reattach the computer power cord and power on the computer.
8. Load any application software or device drivers needed for the devices attached to the adapter.
9. Test the device(s) connected to the adapter.

An adapter may control multiple devices, such as the microphone and speakers. An alternative to an adapter plugging directly into the motherboard is the use of a riser board. A **riser board** plugs into the motherboard and has its own expansion slots. Adapters can plug into these expansion slots instead of directly into the motherboard. Riser boards are used with rack-mounted servers and low-profile desktop computer models. The riser card is commonly inserted into a motherboard slot or attached using screws. Figure 1.8 shows how to install a riser board.

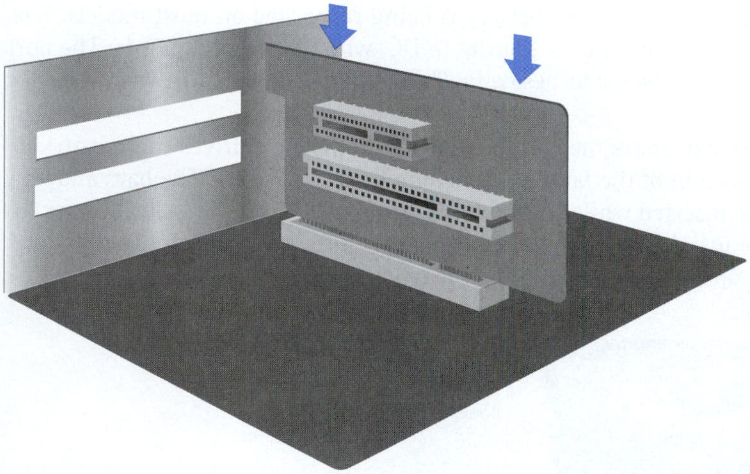

Figure 1.8 Installing a riser board

A laptop has similar parts to a tower or desktop computer, but they are smaller. Portable computers (laptops) normally use a battery as their power source, but they can have an AC connection. Laptop batteries are normally modules that have one or two release latches that are used to remove the module. Figure 1.9 shows common laptop parts.

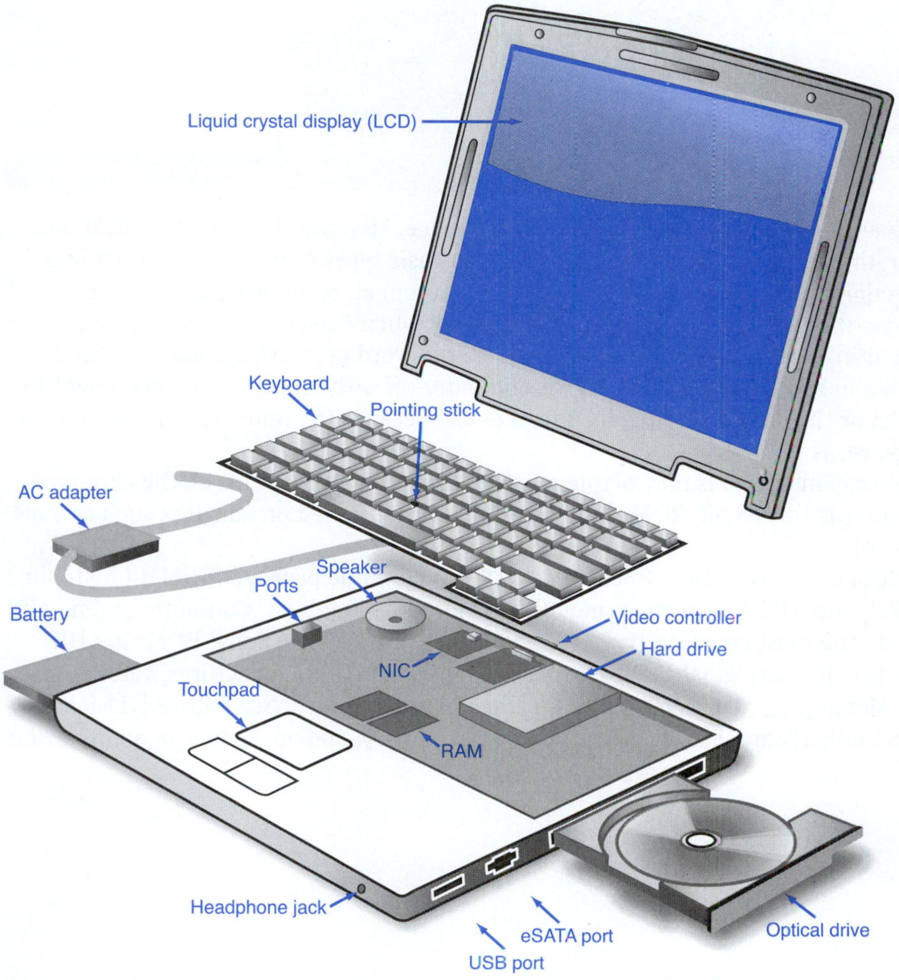

Figure 1.9 Laptop parts

When a laptop has an AC adapter attached, the battery is being recharged on most models. The laptop AC adapter converts the AC from the wall outlet to DC, which the laptop needs. The port sometimes has a DC voltage symbol below or beside it. This symbol is a solid line with a dashed line below it (⎓).

A laptop sometimes has one or more media bays to install removable drives such as an optical drive. A latch on the bottom of the laptop normally releases the drive. The bays allow hot swapping (a device can be inserted while the laptop is powered on), but it is always safer to shut down a computer before installing a device unless you are sure it is hot swappable. Figure 1.10 shows an example of an optical drive that requires case disassembly to remove the drive.

Figure 1.10 Integrated optical drive

Memory is an important part of any computing device. Memory chips hold applications, part of the operating system, and user documents. Two basic types of memory are RAM and ROM. **RAM** (random access memory) is the most common in all computing devices and is volatile memory—that is, the data inside the chips is lost when power is removed. When a user types a document in a word processing program, both the word processing application and the document are in RAM. If the user turns the computer off without saving the document to removable media or the hard drive, the document is lost because the information does not stay in RAM when power is removed.

ROM (read-only memory) is nonvolatile memory because data stays inside the chip even when the computer is turned off. ROM chips are sometimes installed on adapters such as a network or video card.

RAM and ROM chips come in different styles: DIP (dual inline package), DIMM (dual inline memory module), and RIMM (a memory module developed by Rambus). Computer and mobile device DIMMs are the most common type of RAM found in computers. Some ROMs are DIP chips. They are usually distinguishable by a sticker that shows the manufacturer, version, and date produced. Memory chips are covered in great detail in Chapter 6. See Figure 1.11 for an illustration of a motherboard, various expansion slots, memory, and an adapter in an expansion slot.

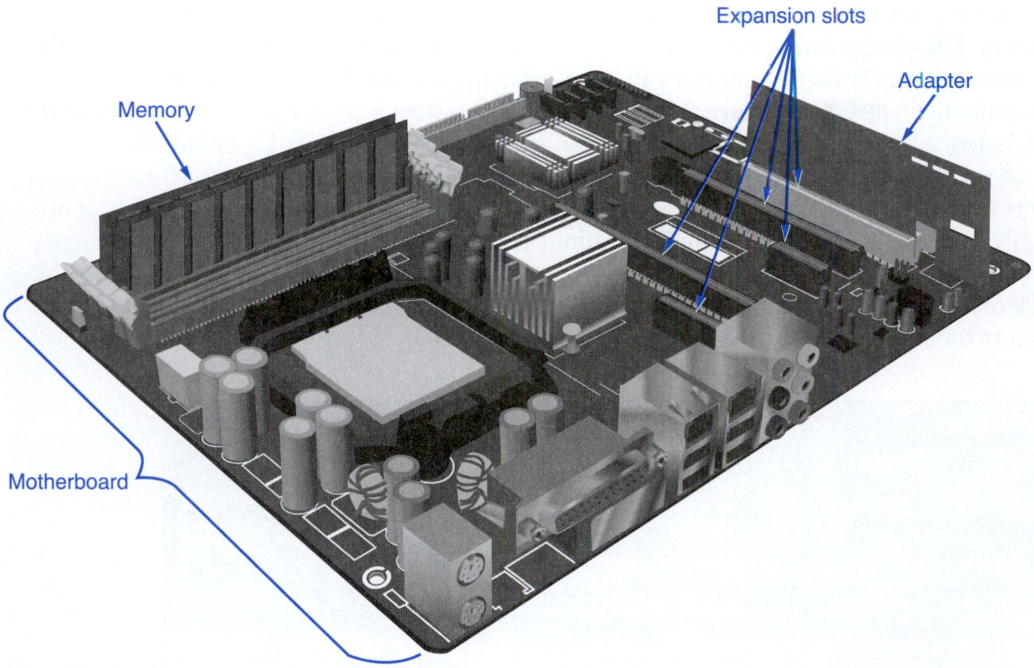

Figure 1.11 Motherboard with expansion slots and an adapter

Tablets and smartphones frequently have no field-serviceable parts (parts that can be replaced by a technician) and are typically not upgradable except for memory. Mobile devices and laptops do have RAM. Sometimes this RAM is not upgradable in mobile devices such as tablets and smartphones. However, storage is sometimes available using flash memory. **Flash memory** is very common with USB-based thumb drives used with PCs and laptops and is nonvolatile—that is, data is not lost when power is removed. Flash memory cards for mobile devices include CompactFlash and various types of **SD** (Secure Digital) cards: SD, miniSD, microSD, and **xD** (extreme digital). Figure 1.12 shows a photo of two of these memory cards.

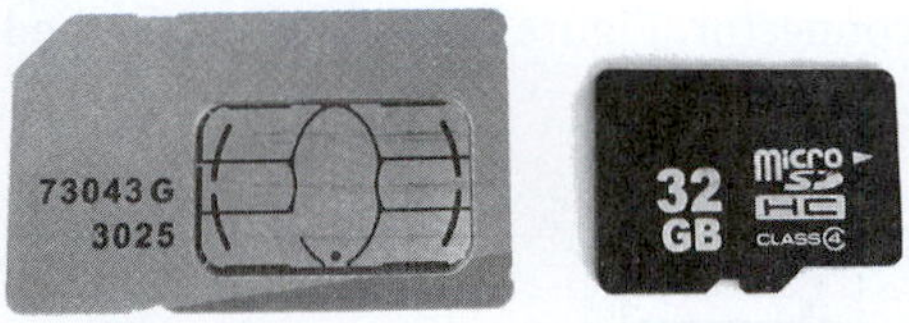

Figure 1.12 Mobile device flash memory storage

External Connectivity

A **port** is a connector on a motherboard or on a separate adapter that allows a device to connect to a computer. Sometimes a motherboard has ports built directly into the motherboard. Motherboards that have ports built into them are called **integrated motherboards**. A technician must be able to identify these ports readily to ensure that (1) the correct cable plugs into each port and (2) the technician can troubleshoot problems in the right area.

Many port connections are either male or female. Male ports have metal pins that protrude from the connector. A male port requires a cable with a female connector. Female ports have holes in the connector into which the male cable pins are inserted.

Some connectors on integrated motherboards are either D-shell connectors or DIN connectors. A **D-shell connector** has more pins or holes on top than on the bottom, so a cable connected to the D-shell connector can be inserted in only one direction and cannot be accidentally flipped upside down. Many documents represent a D-shell connector by using the letters DB, a hyphen, and the number of pins—for example, DB-9, DB-15, or DB-25.

A **mini-DIN connector** is round with small holes and is normally keyed. When a connector is **keyed**, the cable can only be inserted one way. Keyboard and mouse connectors, commonly called PS/2 ports, are examples of mini-DIN connectors. Today, a keyboard and mouse can also be connected to USB ports (as discussed later in the chapter). Figure 1.13 shows the back of a computer with an integrated motherboard. You can see a DIN and two D-shell connectors on the motherboard.

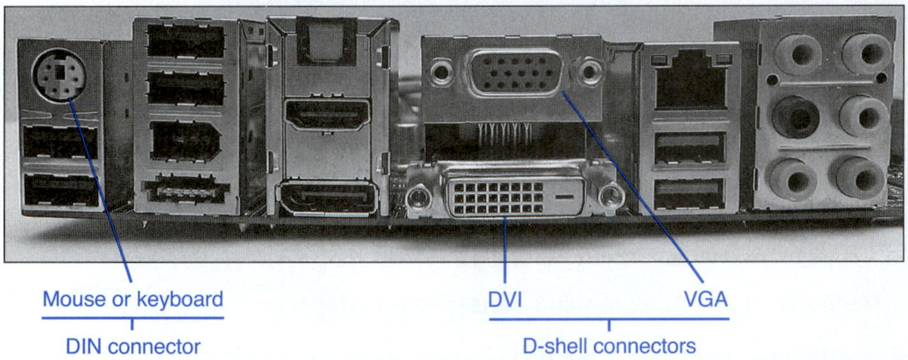

Figure 1.13 Mini-DIN and D-shell connectors

Mouse and Keyboard Ports

Mouse and **keyboard ports** have traditionally been 6-pin mini-DIN ports that are sometimes called PS/2 ports. Otherwise, USB ports are used for mouse/keyboard connectivity. Many manufacturers color code the PS/2 mouse port as green and the PS/2 keyboard port as purple and/or put a small diagram of a keyboard or a mouse by each connector. Figure 1.14 shows mouse and keyboard connectivity options.

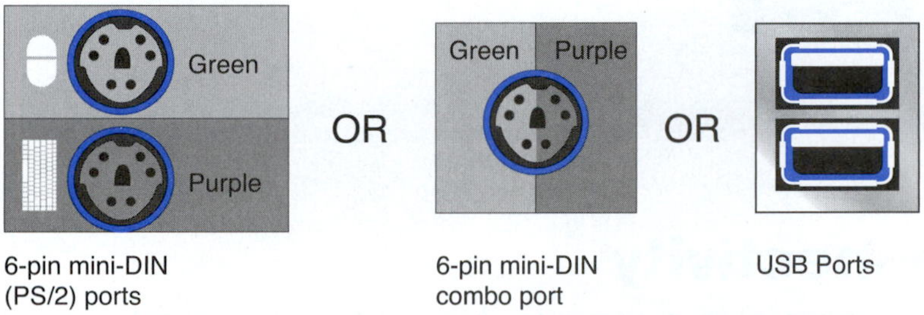

Figure 1.14 Mouse and keyboard ports

Mice and Keyboards

There are two basic types of mice—mechanical and optical. A **mechanical mouse** uses a rubber ball inserted into the bottom of the mouse. The rubber ball turns small metal, rubber, or plastic rollers mounted on the sides. The rollers relay the mouse movement to the computer. On the other hand, an **optical mouse** has optical sensors that detect the direction in which the mouse ball moves. It uses reflections from LEDs from almost any surface to detect the mouse location. Figure 1.15 shows a photo of mechanical and optical mice.

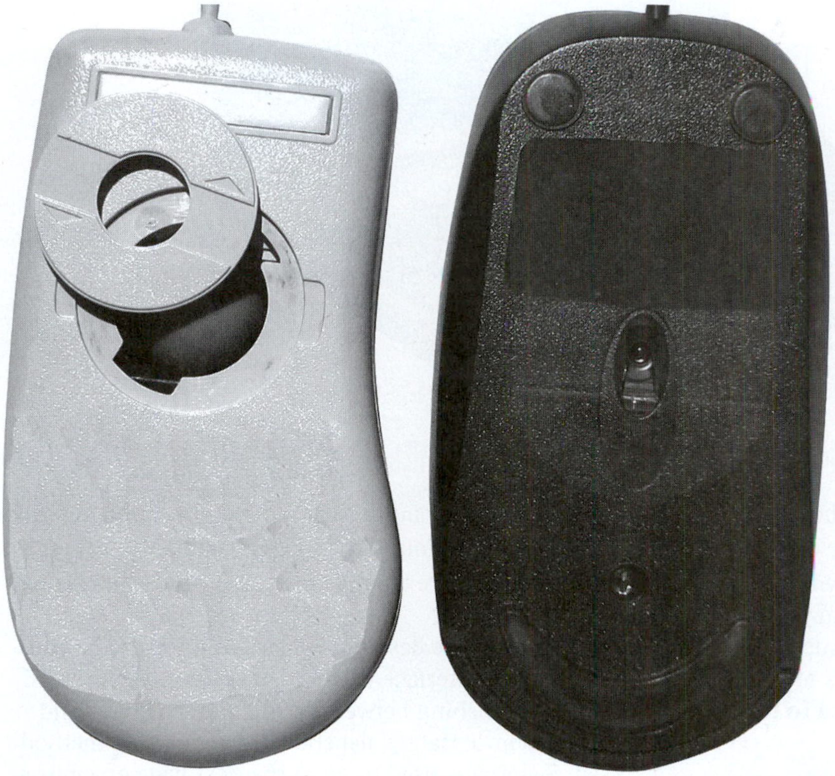

Figure 1.15 **Mechanical and optical mice**

Keyboards are input devices that connect to the keyboard port. There are two main types of keyboards: mechanical and capacitive. Mechanical keyboards are the cheapest and most common type. They use a switch that closes when a key is depressed. When the switch gets dirty, it sticks. Mechanical keyboards require more cleaning and are more error-prone than their capacitive counterparts. A capacitive keyboard is more reliable and more expensive than a mechanical keyboard because of the electronics involved in the design.

Tech Tip

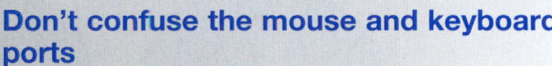

Don't confuse the mouse and keyboard ports

On motherboards that have two PS/2 ports, the mouse and keyboard ports are not interchangeable, even if they use the same pin configuration.

Laptops and netbooks usually have integrated keyboards as well as a variety of mouse replacement devices, such as trackpoint, touchpad, and/or one or two buttons used for clicking and right-clicking. You should always remove the battery and AC power cord before removing a laptop keyboard or any other internal laptop part. To remove a laptop keyboard, you commonly remove screws from the top or bottom of the laptop and slide or lift the keyboard out of the case. Always refer to the manufacturer's documentation before removing or replacing a laptop keyboard. Figure 1.16 shows the laptop keyboard removal process.

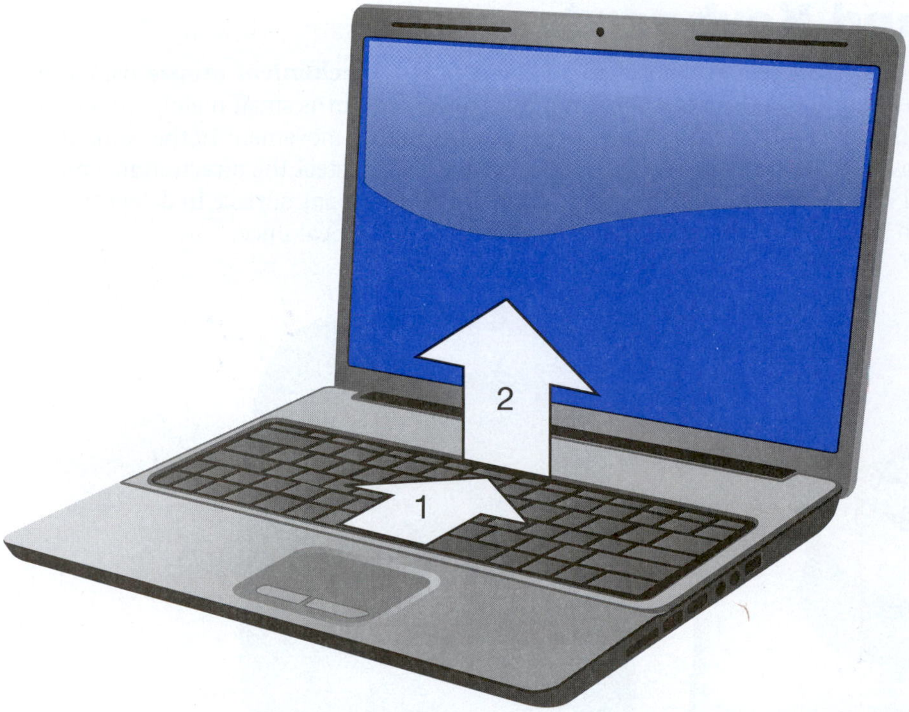

Figure 1.16 Laptop keyboard removal

Laptops and netbooks sometimes have the ability to have a backlight on the keyboard. This backlight is normally controlled through a key combination of the Fn key and an Fx key such as the one shown here: . Keyboard backlights are a handy feature for those who travel or take notes in a dimly lit room.

Mobile devices, such as smartphones as well as some desktop displays, use touch and **multitouch** technologies to allow a finger or a stylus to interface with the operating system. HTC Corporation's **TouchFlo** technology allows distinguishing between a finger and a stylus and responds appropriately, depending on the input method used. Swiping is used to go to the next page of applications or go to the next photo. Multitouch technology is simply the ability to accept multiple touches, such as when two fingers or a finger and a knuckle are used. Figure 1.17 shows a couple multitouch techniques.

Tech Tip

Laptop has a ghost cursor

When a laptop cursor moves randomly or moves within a sentence, adjust the pointer or touchpad sensitivity using the appropriate control panel.

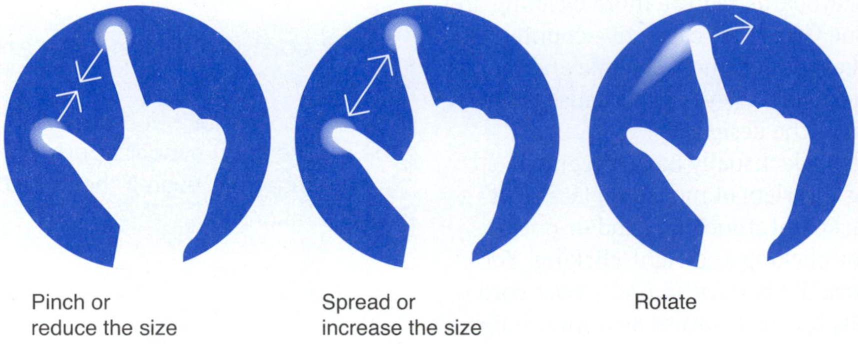

Figure 1.17 Multitouch techniques

Replacing the touchpad or mouse-like devices on mobile devices requires a little more work and disassembly than a keyboard. Sometimes internal drives, RAM, wireless network cards, and the motherboard must be removed before you can access the screws that hold the touchpad in place. These touchpads are also sensitive and may need to be adjusted through the Windows environment. For example, on the Toshiba NB255 netbook, the Synaptics touchpad settings in Windows 7 are accessed through the Hardware and Sound Control Panel applet. Locate the *Mouse* option under the *Devices and Printers* section, as shown in Figure 1.18.

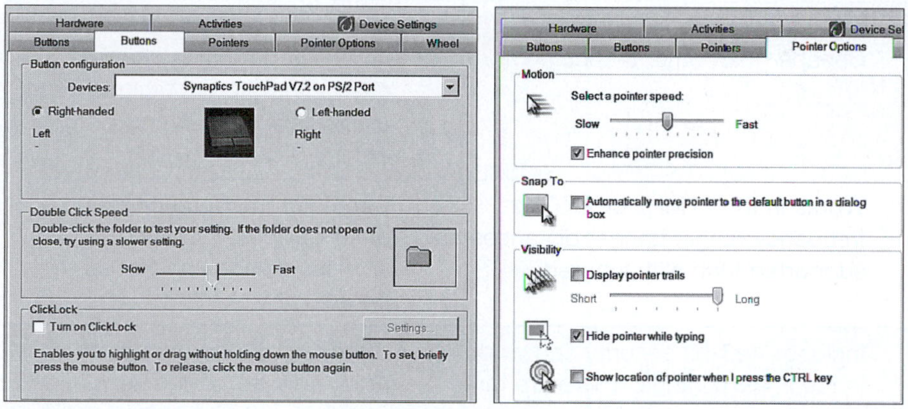

Figure 1.18 Toshiba netbook Synaptics touchpad settings

Wireless Input Devices

Many input devices, such as keyboards, mice, and headphones, have wireless connectivity. Technologies used to connect without a cord include infrared, radio, and Bluetooth. Many computing devices, especially smartphones and other mobile devices, have cordless connectivity integrated into the device; otherwise, a transceiver is connected to a USB port to allow connectivity to the computing device. Figure 1.19 shows a wireless presenter used with a computing device and a projector.

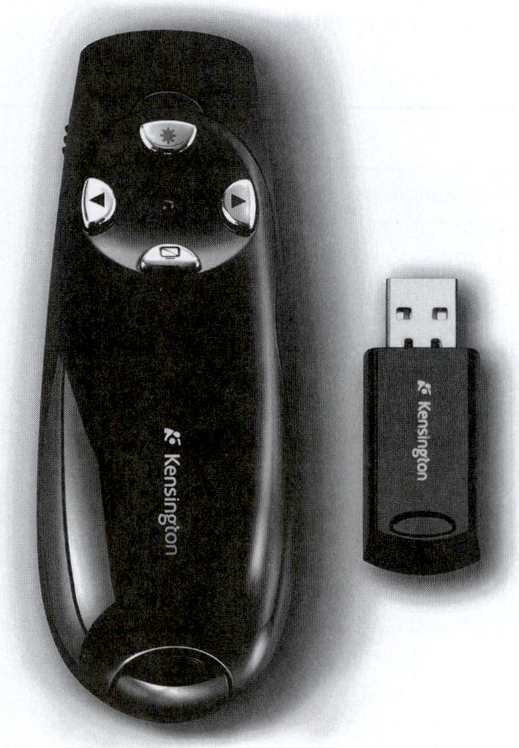

Figure 1.19 Wireless presenter

Table 1.1 summarizes the various wireless technologies used with input devices.

Table 1.1 Wireless input technologies

Technology	Description	Troubleshooting
Infrared	Used for very short distances. Cheaper than other technologies.	Check line of sight; check if device or battery is charged; ensure that no bright light, such as sunlight, is interfering with communication.
Radio	Works in the 27MHz or 2.4GHz frequency range. Longer distances are supported than with infrared.	Check for interference from other devices, including wireless devices on the same frequency.
Bluetooth	Includes 128-bit security and works in the 2.4GHz range. There are three classes of devices, with ranges up to 19.6 feet (6 meters), 72.1 feet (22 meters), and 328 feet (100 meters). Up to eight devices can be connected in a master–slave relationship, with only one device being the master.	Check for interference from other devices, including wireless devices on the same frequency. Also look for Windows, Apple iOS, or Android configuration issues.

Windows Vista and 7 support Bluetooth better than XP does. If Windows XP does not recognize a Bluetooth adapter, XP may provide generic software support. Laptops frequently use a function (Fn) key along with a key that has the Bluetooth symbol ( )to activate Bluetooth. Bluetooth is very popular on mobile devices using Apple iOS or the Android operating system. Table 1.2 shows basic configuration for the various operating systems.

Table 1.2 Bluetooth installation steps

Windows	Apple iOS	Android
Ensure that the device is powered and configured for pairing. Ensure that Bluetooth is enabled. On the Windows device, select *Hardware and Sound* Control Panel link > *Add a Bluetooth Device* > select the device and click *Next*. Note that if the device is a Bluetooth printer, use the Add a Printer Hardware and Sound Control Panel link. You may have to enter a passkey (PIN). Verify connectivity.	Ensure that the device is powered and configured for pairing. On the Apple device, select *Settings* > *General* > *Bluetooth* > ON. In the Devices field, you should see the name of the device. Select the device and select *Pair*. You may have to enter a passkey (PIN). Verify connectivity.	Ensure that the device is powered and configured for pairing. On the Android-based device, select *Settings* > *Wireless and network* > *Bluetooth settings*. Ensure that Bluetooth is enabled and select *Scan devices*. Select the device once it appears and then select *Accept*. You may have to enter a passkey (PIN). Verify connectivity.

If a Bluetooth device is not working in Windows, try the following:

- Select the Bluetooth icon (ʙ) in the systray on the taskbar and select *Show Bluetooth Devices*. If the device is not listed there, select *Add a device* and try to add it.
- Ensure that the device is charged, powered on, and in the appropriate mode to pair with another Bluetooth device, such as the computing device.
- Ensure that other 2.4GHz devices, such as wireless networks, automatic lighting and remote controls, cell phones, portable phones, and microwave ovens, are not interfering with the device.
- Remove unused USB devices.
- If passkeys (PINs) are used, ensure that the keys match.
- If a Bluetooth transceiver is used, move the transceiver to another USB port.
- Remove all other Bluetooth devices to aid in troubleshooting the problematic device.
- Use the *System and Security* Control Panel link > *Administrative Tools* > *Computer Management* tool. Select *Services and Applications* in the list to the left > *Services* in the right panel > locate and double-click *Bluetooth Support Service*. Ensure that the service is set to automatic or manual and is started.
- Ensure that Device Manager shows no issues with the Bluetooth transceiver driver (under the *Bluetooth Radios* section) or the Bluetooth device (sometimes shown under the *Other devices* category). Sometimes, the Bluetooth driver for the host computer must be updated for newer devices.

Figure 1.20 shows an issue with the Bluetooth device on a Windows 7–based laptop.

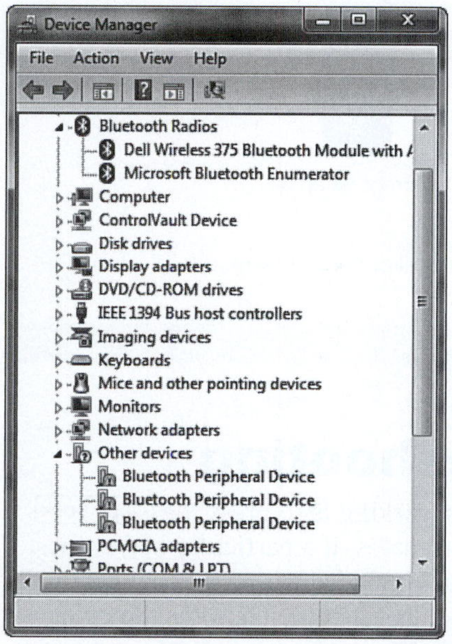

Figure 1.20 Windows 7 Bluetooth issue

You can use similar tricks with Apple iOS and Android devices: (1) Ensure that the device is powered, (2) ensure that Bluetooth is enabled, and (3) ensure that no other wireless networks/devices are nearby (move to another location to see). A common method used with Bluetooth devices is to restart the pairing mode on the Bluetooth device or rescan for a device from the iOS/Android computing device.

Mouse and Keyboard Preventive Maintenance

Mouse-cleaning kits are available in computer stores, but normal household supplies also work. Use the following procedures to clean an optical mouse:

- Wipe the bottom with a damp, lint-free cloth.
- Use compressed air to clean the optical sensors.

A mechanical mouse is harder to clean. Use the following procedures to clean a mechanical mouse:

- Remove the retainer ring or access cover and then remove the mouse ball. Clean with a mild detergent, mild soap, or alcohol. Rinse and dry completely.
- Use a cotton swab or lint-free cloth with alcohol to clean the mouse's inside rollers.
- Use a fingernail, a small screwdriver, or an unfolded paper clip to scrape rubber rollers.
- Unwrap and remove any roller obstructions.
- Replace the retainer ring or access cover.

Keyboards also need periodic cleaning, especially because most are mechanical. Figure 1.21 shows keyboard-cleaning techniques.

Figure 1.21 Keyboard cleaning techniques

Keyboard/Mouse Troubleshooting

One of the easiest ways to determine whether a keyboard is working is to press the Caps Lock or Num Lock key and watch to see if the keyboard light illuminates. If a particular key is not working properly, remove the key cap. The chip-removal tool included with a PC tool kit is great for this. A tweaker (small, flat-tipped) screwdriver also does a good job. After removing the key cap, use compressed air around the sticky or malfunctioning key.

If coffee or another liquid spills into the keyboard, all is not lost. Many people have cleaned their PC keyboard by soaking it in a bathtub or a flat pan of water. Distilled or boiled water cooled to room temperature works best. Afterward, the keyboard can be disassembled and/or scrubbed with lint-free swabs or cloths. You can also replace mobile keyboards/pointing devices or use external ones.

PC keyboards and mice are normally considered throw-away technology. The customer's cost to pay a technician to keep cleaning a keyboard over and over again would pay for many new capacitive keyboards. Keep this in mind when troubleshooting such inexpensive devices.

Video Port

A video port is used to connect a monitor. Video output can be the older method of analog (varying levels, such as seen with an audio signal) or the newer output method of digital (1s and 0s). Since the computer uses all digital signals, sending 1s and 0s is more efficient than having to convert the 1s and 0s to an analog signal. CRT (cathode ray tube) monitors were the big bulky ones that looked like old TV sets, and they accepted analog output from computers. Flat panel monitors, tabletop displays, mobile tablets, and laptop displays all accept digital signals. Figure 1.22 shows an older CRT compared to a flat panel monitor.

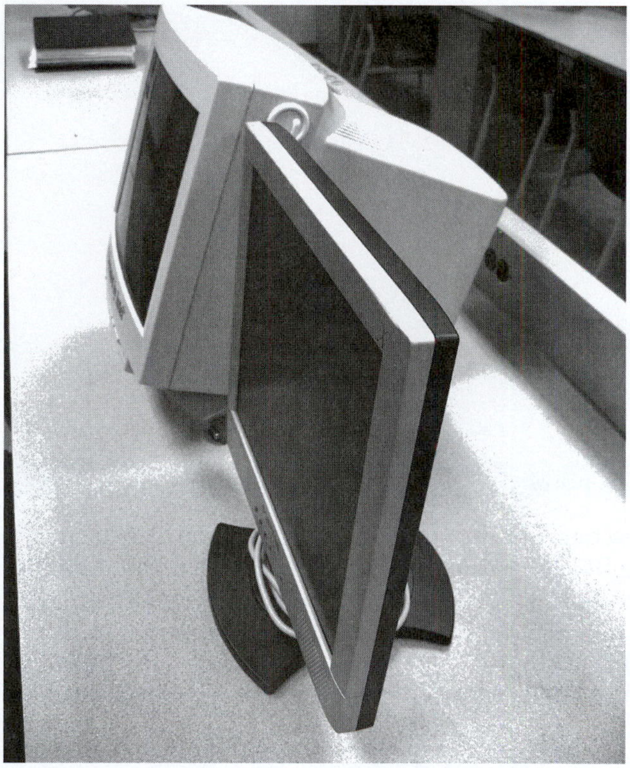

Figure 1.22 CRT and flat panel monitors

The **VGA port** was designed for analog output. A mini-VGA port is also available on some mobile devices. A newer port is a **DVI port** (Digital Visual Interface), and it has three rows of square holes. DVI ports are used to connect flat panel digital displays. Some flat panel monitors can also use the older VGA port. Some video adapters also allow you to connect a video device (such as a television) that has an **S-Video port**. Figure 1.23 shows a video adapter with all three ports. The top port is for S-Video, the center port is the DVI connector, and the bottom port is a VGA port.

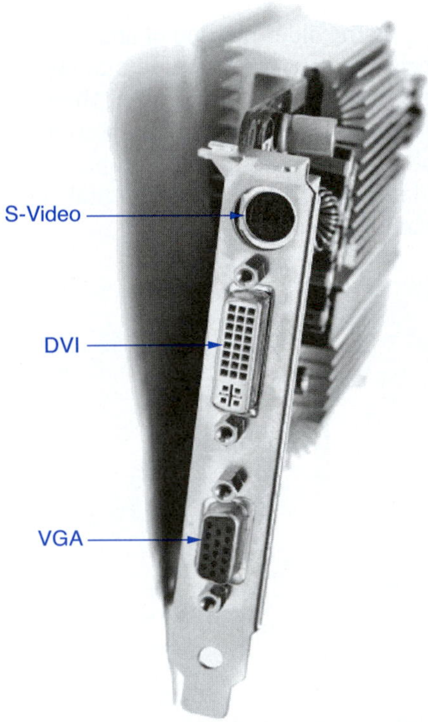

Figure 1.23 S-Video, DVI, and VGA ports

There are several types of DVI connectors, and the one used depends on the type of monitor attached. Two terms used with these DVI connectors are single link and dual link. A **single link** connection allows video resolutions up to 1920×1080. With a **dual link** connection, more pins are available to send more signals, thus allowing higher resolutions. The two major types of connectors are DVI-D and DVI-I. **DVI-D** is used for digital video connectivity only. **DVI-I** can be used for both digital and analog monitors and is the most common. A less common type is **DVI-A**, which is not shown in Figure 1.24 with the other DVI connector types.

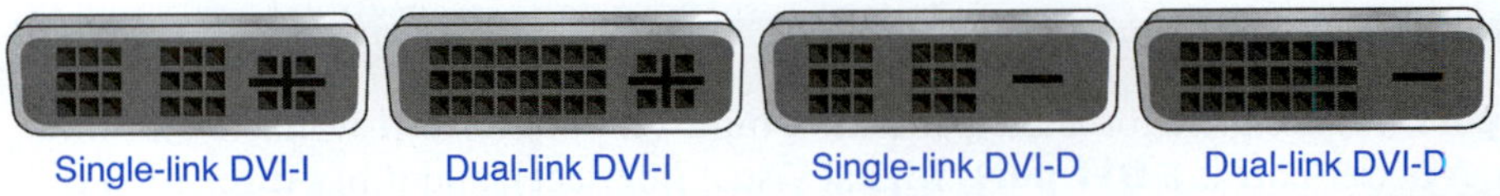

Figure 1.24 DVI connectors

Tech Tip

Match a monitor to the DVI port type

Be careful when installing a monitor. Ensure that the video port matches the DVI connection type for the monitor. Converters can be purchased to adapt to a monitor with a VGA port.

An upgrade to DVI is **HDMI** (High-Definition Multimedia Interface), which is a digital interface that can carry audio and video over the same cable. HDMI is found on cable TV boxes, televisions, video adapters, laptops, desktops, and tablets. MiniHDMI or microHDMI connectors are used with such devices as cameras, tablets, and smartphones. Table 1.3 describes the different HDMI ports.

Table 1.3 HDMI ports

HDMI connector type	Description
A	19-pin port found on a TV or PC that can have a Category 1 (standard) or Category 2 (high-speed) cable attached
B	29-pin port used with very high-resolution displays
C	19-pin mini port (2.42mm × 10.42mm) found on mobile devices
D	19-pin micro port (2.8mm × 6.4mm) found on mobile devices

Figure 1.25 shows an XFX video card that has an S-Video connector on the far left, an RCA jack, an HDMI connector, and a dual-link DVI-I connector.

Figure 1.25 Video ports, including an HDMI connector

An RCA jack is used for connections such as to a scanner or camera. Sometimes three RCA jacks are used for composite video, as shown on the top row of projector ports in Figure 1.26. The yellow connection is for video, and the red and white connections are for audio. Higher-quality connections are red, green, and blue RCA jacks for RGB/component video (see Chapter 9). Notice in Figure 1.26 that the projector has similar connections to PCs. Cables that convert between the different ports are available.

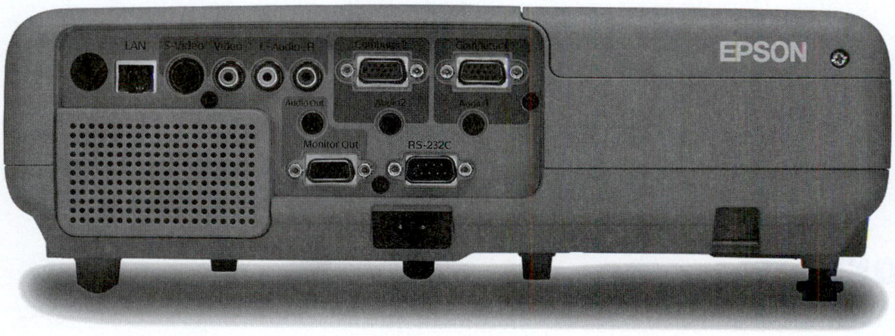

Figure 1.26 Projector ports

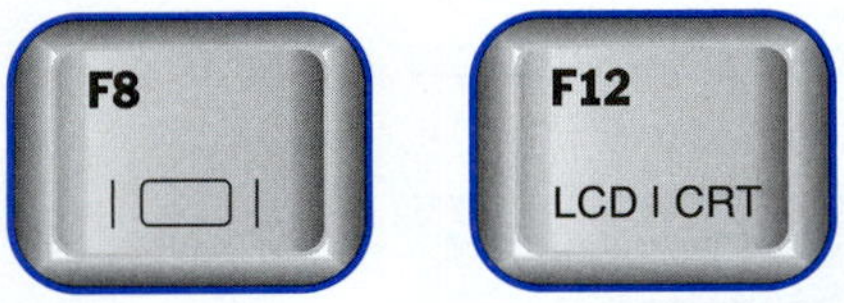

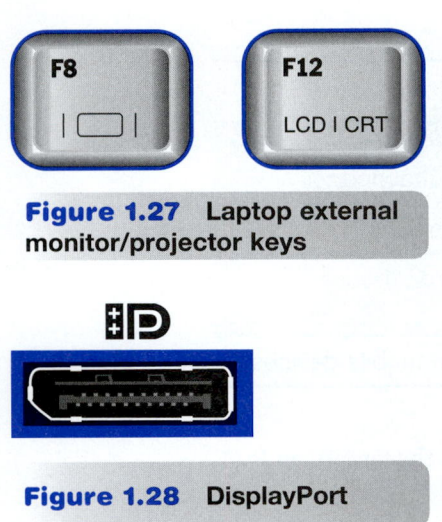

Figure 1.27 Laptop external monitor/projector keys

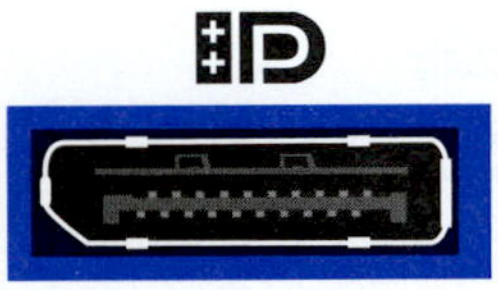

Figure 1.28 DisplayPort

Laptops and netbooks have external video ports. To send data out these ports, you have to hold down the Fn key and press a specific function key, such as F8 or F12, depending on the computer manufacturer. Figure 1.27 shows common symbols you might see on a keyboard.

When an HDMI, miniHDMI, or microHDMI connector is on an Android-based device, you connect the correct cable between the Android device and a video output device, such as a monitor or TV. Then, you launch an application such as your photo gallery. Tap the *HDMI Play* control icon. Some applications require no interaction for the HDMI output to work. Note that you might have to use the *Settings > HDMI* option to adjust the resolution. Note that some applications do not support HDMI output from a smartphone.

For Apple iOS devices, you can purchase an Apple Digital AV adapter. This cable is like a Y cable, and the end of the Y attaches to the Apple device. A power connector can connect to one of the Y prongs and an HDMI cable can attach to the other Y prong. TV standards up to 1080p are supported.

Another port that can send and receive audio and video signals is the **DisplayPort** developed by VESA (Video Electronics Standards Association). The port is designed to primarily output to display devices and can have a passive converter to be used to convert to a single-link DVI or HDMI port. A mini DisplayPort is also available on mobile devices. You use an active converter to convert to dual-link DVI. Figure 1.28 shows the DisplayPort. An exercise at the end of the chapter provides port identification practice with the variety of display ports you might see.

An updated port that uses some of the DisplayPort technology is the **Thunderbolt port**. The Thunderbolt interface was developed by Intel, with support from Apple. The port used on Apple computers is the same connector as the mini DisplayPort. Figure 1.29 shows a Thunderbolt port and cable.

Figure 1.29 Thunderbolt

USB Port

USB stands for Universal Serial Bus. A **USB port** allows up to 127 connected devices to transmit at speeds up to 5Gbps (5 billion bits per second). Devices that can connect to a USB port include printers, scanners, mice, keyboards, joysticks, optical drives, tape drives, game pads, cameras, modems, speakers, telephones, video phones, data gloves, and digitizers. Additional ports can sometimes be found on the front of a PC case or on the side of a mobile device. Figure 1.30 shows USB ports.

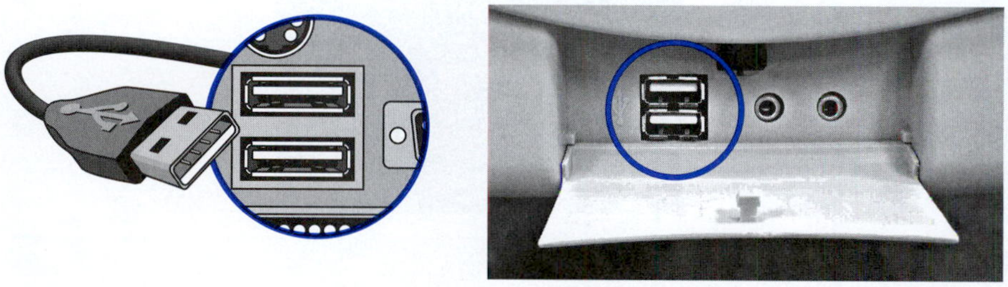

Figure 1.30 USB ports

USB ports and devices come in three versions—1.0/1.1, 2.0 (Hi-Speed), and 3.0 (SuperSpeed). USB 1.0 operates at speeds of 1.5Mbps and 12Mbps; version 2.0 operates at speeds up to 480Mbps. Version 3.0 transmits data up to 5Gbps. The 3.0 USB port, which still accepts older devices, is colored blue.

USB 3.0 is backward compatible with the older versions, which means that the cables from any 1.0/2.0 device work with a 3.0 port. To achieve USB 3.0 speeds, however, a 3.0 device, 3.0 port, and 3.0 cable must be used. The version 1 and 2 cables used 4 wires. Version 3 cables use 9 wires. Figure 1.31 shows the different version and speed symbols. Note that the port is not required to be labeled, and sometimes looking at the technical specifications for the computer or motherboard is the only way to determine port speed.

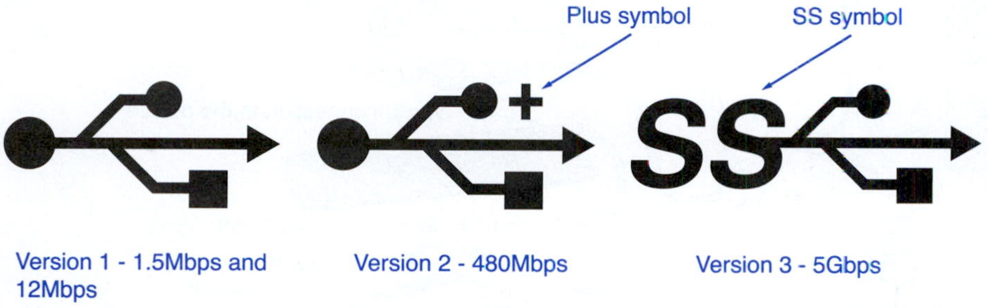

Figure 1.31 USB versions, speeds, and symbols

Each USB standard has a maximum cable length:

- Version 1.0/1.1: 9.8 feet, or 3 meters
- Version 2.0: 16.4 feet, or 5 meters
- Version 3.0: 9.8 feet, or 3 meters

USB cables can be longer than these specifications, but the standards are provided to ensure that devices function properly.

USB ports are known as upstream ports and downstream ports. An **upstream port** is used to connect to a computer or another hub. A USB device connects to a **downstream port**. Downstream ports are commonly known as Type A and Type B. A standard USB cable has a Type A male connector on one end and a Type B male connector on the other end. The port on the computer is a Type A port. The Type A connector inserts into the Type A port. The Type B connector attaches to the Type B port on the USB device. Figure 1.32 shows Type A and Type B connectors. There are also mini versions of these connectors. See Figures 1.36 and 1.46, later in this chapter.

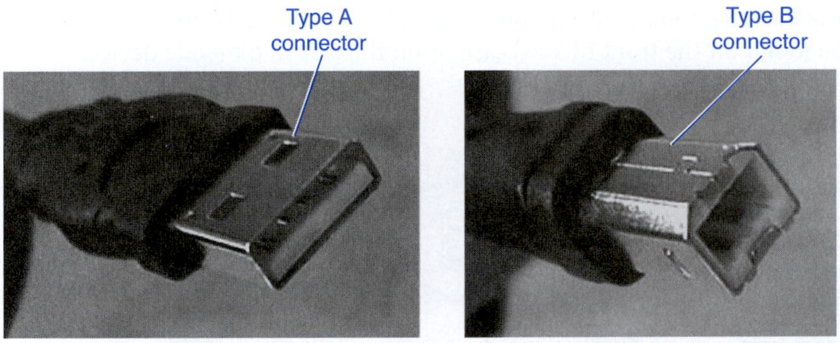

Figure 1.32 USB Type A and Type B connectors

A USB port can have more than one device attached to the port through the use of a USB hub. Many hubs can operate in two power modes—self-powered and bus-powered—and a hub may have a switch control that must be set to the appropriate mode. A **self-powered hub** has an external power supply attached. A **bus-powered hub** has no external power supply connected to the hub. Once all USB devices attached to a hub are tested, the hub's power supply can be removed and the devices retested. If all attached devices work properly, the hub power supply can be left disconnected. Figure 1.33 shows USB hub connectivity, and Figure 1.34 shows USB cabling rules.

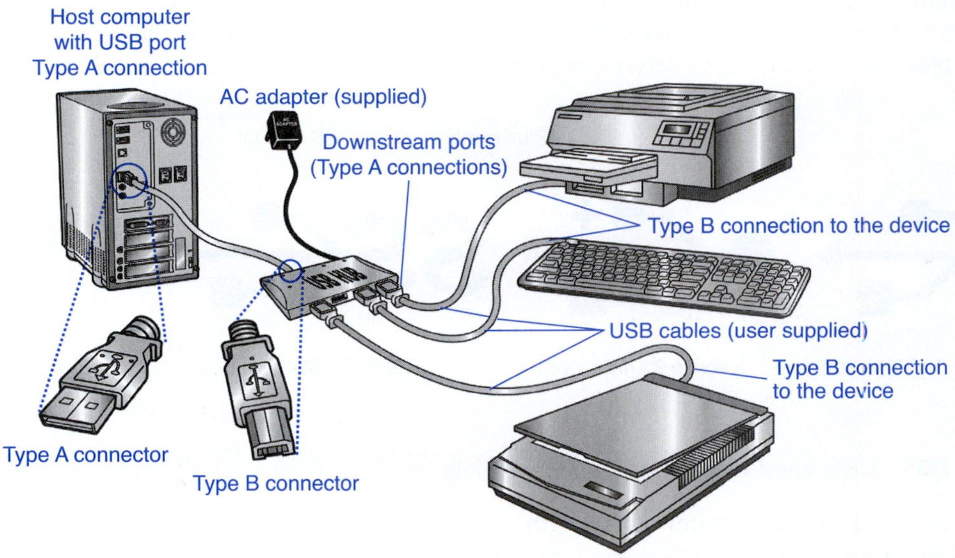

Figure 1.33 USB hub connectivity

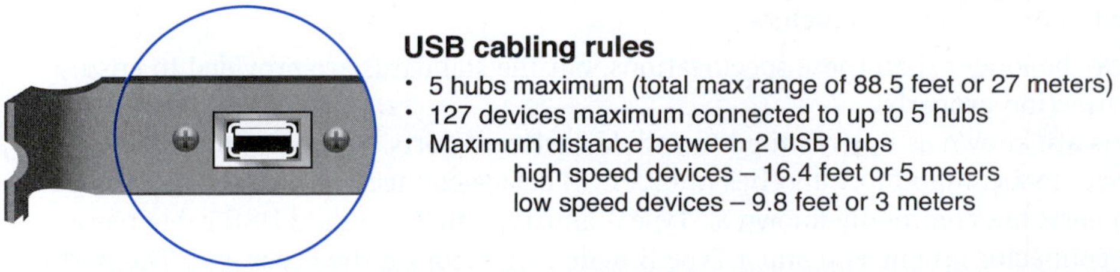
USB cabling rules
• 5 hubs maximum (total max range of 88.5 feet or 27 meters)
• 127 devices maximum connected to up to 5 hubs
• Maximum distance between 2 USB hubs
high speed devices – 16.4 feet or 5 meters
low speed devices – 9.8 feet or 3 meters

Figure 1.34 USB cabling rules

USB ports have always been able to provide power to unpowered devices such as flash drives. A **charging USB port** is a port designed to be able to provide power to run and charge attached devices. Note that not all USB devices can be charged this way. A **sleep-and-charge USB port** is one in which the port still provides power to the device (power to charge the device) even when the computer is powered off. See the computing device's specifications to see if a USB ports supports this feature.

To install a USB device, perform the following steps:

- Power on the computer.
- Optionally, install the USB device's software. Note that some manufacturers require that software and/or device drivers are installed before the USB device is attached.
- Optionally, power on the device. Not all USB devices have external power adapters or a power button because they receive power from the USB bus.
- Locate a USB port on the rear or front of the computer or on a USB hub. Plug the USB device into a free port. The operating system normally detects the USB device and loads the device driver. You may have to browse to the driver.

Converters are available to convert a USB port to a different type of connector (or vice versa), such as serial, parallel, PS/2 mouse/keyboard, or mini-DIN. Figure 1.35 shows a converter that inserts into a PS/2 mini-DIN connector and allows a USB mouse or keyboard to be connected if the device supports USB.

Tech Tip

Safely remove USB devices

To remove a USB device, do not simply unplug it from the port. Instead, click on the *Safely Remove Hardware* icon from the notification area. Select the USB device to remove. The operating system prompts when it is safe to unplug the device.

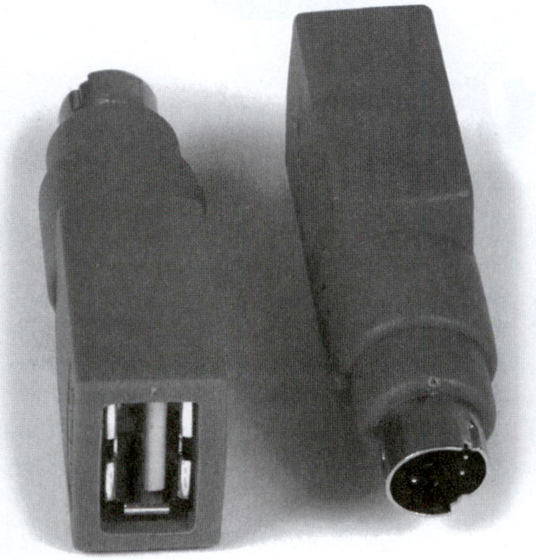

Figure 1.35 **Mini-DIN to USB converter**

A smaller USB port used on small devices such as USB hubs, PDAs, digital cameras, and phones is known as a mini-USB port. There are several types of smaller USB ports: mini-A, mini-AB, micro-B, and micro-AB. The mini-/micro-AB ports accept either a mini-/micro-A or a mini-/micro-B cable end. Figure 1.36 shows the standard Type A USB port found on a PC and the mini-B and micro-B ports found on mobile devices. The micro-USB ports are now a standard interface for smartphones.

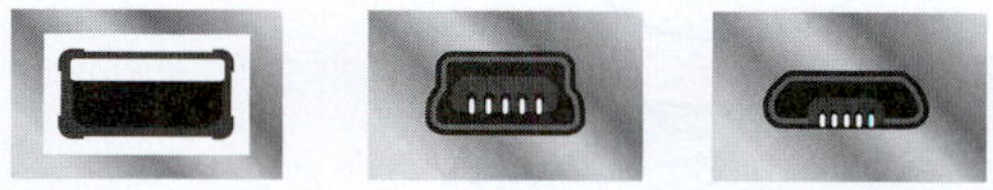

Figure 1.36 **USB Type A, mini, and micro ports**

USB has expanded into other fields. **USB OTG** (on-the-go) is a supplement to the USB 2.0 specification. Normally with USB, a device that does not have too much intelligence built into it attaches to a host—specifically, a PC. USB on-the-go allows a USB device, such as an audio player or a mobile phone, to have the capability of being the host device. This allows two USB devices to communicate without the use of a PC or a hub. The supplement allows a USB OTG device to still attach to a PC because USB OTG is backward compatible with the USB 2.0 standard.

Certified W-USB (wireless USB) supports high-speed, secure wireless connectivity between a USB device and a PC, at speeds comparable to Hi-Speed USB. Certified Wireless USB is not a networking technology; it is just another way that you can connect your favorite USB devices to a host. You just don't have to plug a cable into a USB port. Wireless USB supports speeds of 480Mbps at a range up to 3 meters (~10 feet) or 110Mbps up to 10 meters (~30 feet). Wireless USB uses ultra-wideband low-power radio over a range of 3.1 to 10.5GHz. Figure 1.37 shows the various USB logos that might befound on devices.

Figure 1.37 USB logos

Installing Extra USB Ports

Many motherboards support adding two or more USB ports by using a cable that attaches to motherboard pins otherwise known as a USB header. The ports mount in an expansion slot space but do not take an expansion slot. Even if the motherboard has such pins, the ports and cable assembly might have to be purchased separately. Figure 1.38 shows sample USB ports that attach to a motherboard.

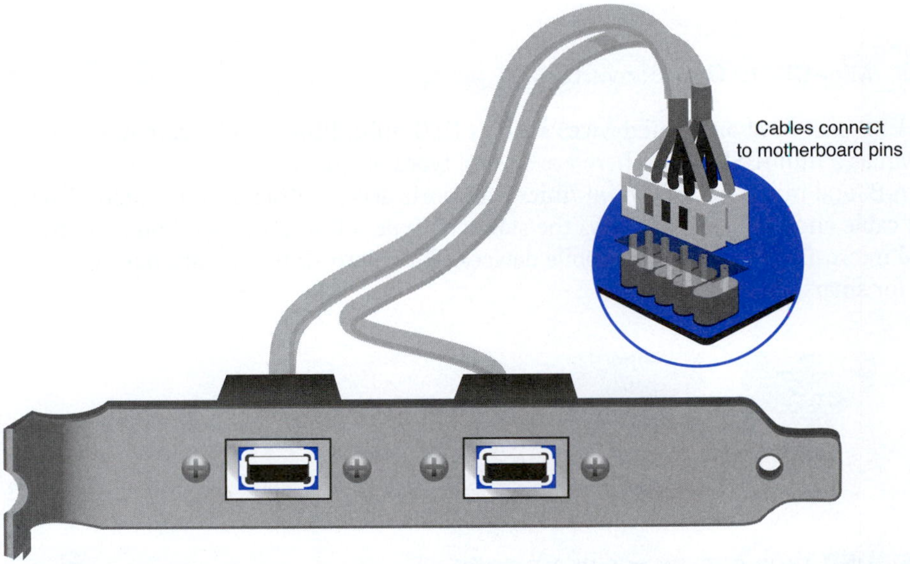

Figure 1.38 Installing extra USB ports

Keep in mind that if a motherboard doesn't have any pins, you can add more USB ports by purchasing a PCI or PCIe USB adapter with multiple ports. The adapter might not have the capability of providing power unless the adapter supports having a power cable from the power supply attached to the card.

For laptops that do not have a USB 3.0 port, you can use an eSATA port for an external device or add an Express-to-USB card if the laptop has an ExpressCard slot. Note that these USB ports on an ExpressCard might not be able to provide the power that a normal integrated USB port could provide.

USB Troubleshooting

To troubleshoot USB device problems, check the obvious first: the cabling and power. Verify whether any USB device that plugs into a USB hub works. If no devices work, swap the hub. If some work and some do not, attach an external power source to the hub, change its configuration, if necessary, and retest the devices. Restart the computer and retest the USB device.

USB 3.0 ports can provide 900mA (4.5W) of power—more power than the previous USB versions (500mA/2.5W). Note that a 3.0 port can go into low-power mode when the port isn't being used. You can verify how much power a USB device is using by examining the device in Windows Device Manager, following these steps:

1. Open *Device Manager*, using the following operating system–dependent control panel.
   Windows XP: *Performance and Maintenance* Control Panel
   Windows Vista: *System and Maintenance* Control Panel
   Windows 7: *System and Security* Control Panel
2. Locate and select *Device Manager*.
3. Expand the *Universal Serial Bus Hub Controllers* section.
4. Right-click on each *Generic USB Hub* option and select *Properties*.
5. Access the *Power* tab.
6. Locate the USB device and note how much power is being requested of the USB port/hub.

Figure 1.39 shows a bus-powered four-port USB hub that has two devices attached—a digital camera and a flash drive. The flash drive is using 100mA of power, and the camera is using 500mA.

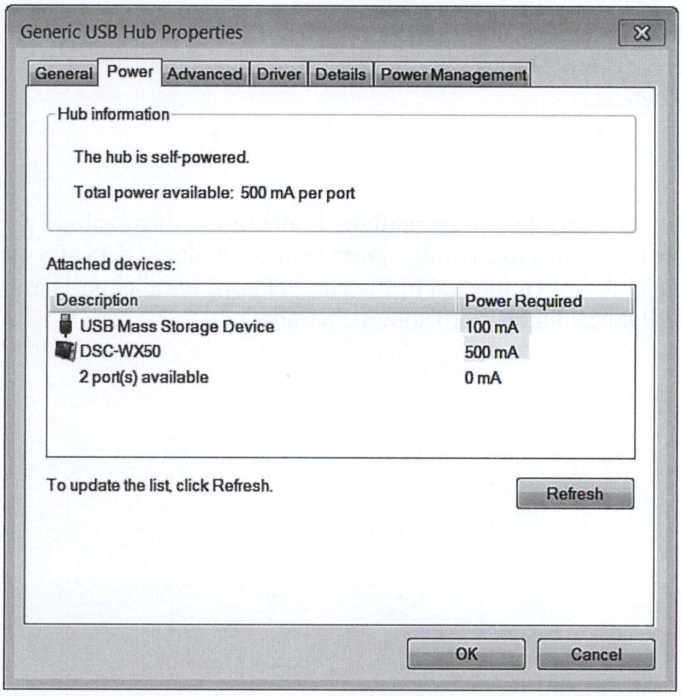

Figure 1.39 USB hub power requirements

A USB device could be drawing more power than is allowed. If this is the case, the computer can disable the port. The only way to re-enable the port is to restart the computer. If a device is using less than 50mA of power, the USB port never becomes active. Try plugging the USB device into a different USB port or verifying the device works on another computer.

A USB device requires a driver that may be loaded automatically. An incorrect or outdated driver could be loaded and causing problems. The following list can also help when troubleshooting USB devices:

- Use Device Manager to ensure that a hub is functioning properly.
- Ensure that the BIOS firmware is up-to-date.
- Use Device Manager to ensure that no USB device has an IRQ assigned and shared with another non-USB device.
- USB devices sometimes do not work in safe mode and require hardware support configured through the BIOS.
- Sometimes a USB device stops working on a hub that has an external power source. In such a case, remove the hub's external power source and retest.
- If a self-powered USB hub gets its power disconnected, the hub becomes a bus-powered hub and outputs only lower power on each port. Reattach the power cord or remove the hub and reattach.
- If a newly attached USB device reports that it is attached but does not work properly, upgrade the driver.
- Do not connect USB devices to a computer that is in standby mode or sleep mode. Doing so may prevent the computer from coming out of standby mode.
- For intermittent USB device problems, disable power management to see if this is causing the problem.
- Test a device connected to a USB hub by connecting it directly to a USB port that has nothing else attached. The problem could be caused by other USB devices or a USB hub.
- Remove the USB device's driver and reinstall. Sometimes you must reboot the computer to give the new drivers priority over the general-purpose drivers.
- If a USB device is running slowly, try attaching it to a different port that has fewer devices connected to the same port.

Verify that the USB port is enabled in BIOS if integrated into the motherboard or attached to the motherboard through an adapter cable. Always refer to the USB device manufacturer's website for specific troubleshooting details.

Parallel Ports

Parallel ports were used to connect older printers to computers. Some motherboards have a small picture of a printer etched over the connector. Parallel ports transfer 8 bits of data at a time to the printer or any other parallel device connected to the parallel port. Parallel ports are obsolete, having been replaced by USB ports. Figure 1.40 shows a parallel port.

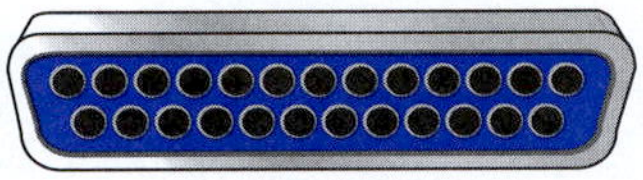

Figure 1.40 A parallel port

Serial Ports

A **serial port** (also known as a COM port, an RS-232 port, or an asynchronous [async] port) can be a 9-pin male D-shell connector or a 25-pin male D-shell connector (on old computers). Serial ports are used for external analog modems, printers, and some networking equipment. Serial ports, like parallel ports, are obsolete, having been replaced by USB ports.

Figure 1.41 shows two types of serial port markings. Figure 1.42 shows a USB-to-serial port converter you can use if a serial port is needed and only USB ports are available. You can purchase converters to convert almost any other type of port to a USB port.

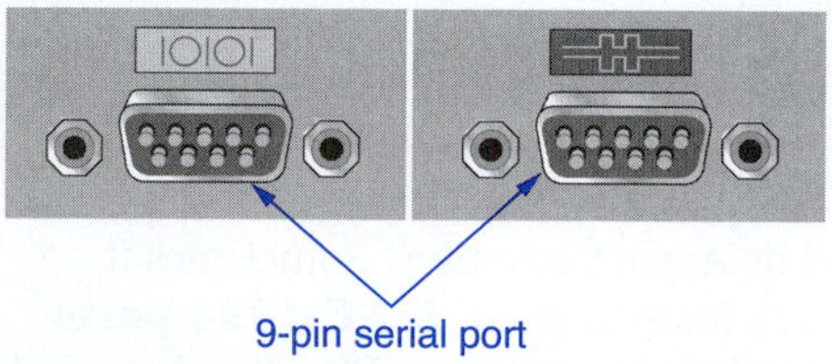

Figure 1.41 Serial port markings

Figure 1.42 USB-to-serial port converter

Audio Ports

A **sound card** converts digital computer signals to sound and sound to digital computer signals. A sound card is sometimes called an audio card and can be integrated into the motherboard or be on an adapter that contains several ports. The most common ports include a port for a microphone, MP3 player, or other audio device. One or more ports for speakers, a headphone port, and **S/PDIF** (Sony/Philips Digital Interface) in/out ports are used to connect to various devices, such as digital audio tape players/recorders, DVD players/recorders, and external disc players/recorders. There are two main types of S/PDIF connectors: an RCA jack used to connect a coaxial cable and a fiber-optic port for a TOSLINK cable connection. Sound cards are popular because people want better sound quality than what is available integrated into a motherboard. See Figure 1.43 for an illustration of a sound card.

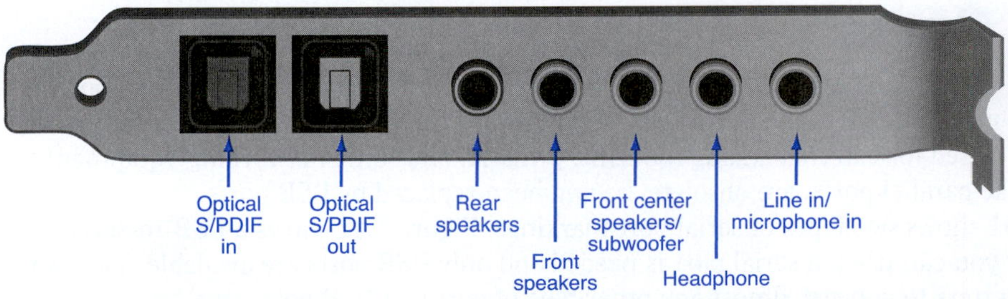

Figure 1.43 Sound card ports

IEEE 1394 Ports

The IEEE 1394 standard is a serial technology developed by Apple Computer. Sometimes it is known as FireWire (Apple), i.Link (Sony), or Lynx (Texas Instruments). **IEEE 1394 ports** have been more predominant on Apple computers but are also seen on some PCs. Windows and Apple operating systems support the IEEE 1394 standard. Many digital products have an integrated IEEE 1394 port for connecting to a computer. IEEE 1394 devices include camcorders, cameras, printers, storage devices, video conferencing cameras, optical players and drives, tape drives, film readers, speakers, and scanners.

IEEE 1394 has two data transfer modes—asynchronous and isochronous. The asynchronous mode focuses on ensuring that data is delivered reliably. Isochronous transfers allow guaranteed bandwidth (which is needed for audio/video transfers) but does not provide for error correction or retransmission.

Speeds supported are 100, 200, 400, 800, 1200, 1600, and 3200Mbps. IEEE 1394 devices commonly include the speed as part of their description or name; for example, a FireWire 800 device transfers at speeds up to 800Mbps. With FireWire, as many as 63 devices (using cable lengths up to 14 feet) can be connected (daisy chained). The IEEE 1394 standard supports hot swapping, plug-and-play, and powering of low-power devices.

An IEEE 1394 cable has 4, 6, or 9 pins. A 4-pin cable/connector does not provide power, so the device must have its own power source. The 6- and 9-pin connectors do provide power. A 6-pin connector is used on desktop computers and can provide power to the attached IEEE 1394 device. A 9-pin connector is used to connect to 800Mbps devices that are also known as IEEE 1394b devices. Figure 1.44 shows an IEEE 1394 port found on PCs, a mini port found on mobile devices, and a 9-pin port found on 800Mbps IEEE 1394 devices. Figure 1.45 shows three IEEE 1394 ports on an adapter.

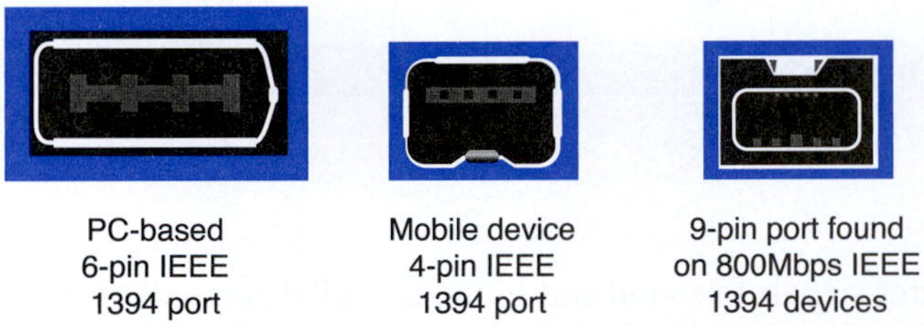

Figure 1.44 FireWire ports

Figure 1.45 IEEE 1394 adapter ports

An IEEE 1394 device can connect to a port built into the motherboard, an IEEE 1394 port on an adapter, another IEEE 1394 device, or a hub. A motherboard might have pins to connect additional IEEE 1394 ports. IEEE 1394 does not require a PC to operate; two IEEE 1394 devices can communicate via a cable. The IEEE 1394 bus is actually a peer-to-peer standard, meaning that a computer is not needed. Two IEEE 1394–compliant devices can be connected (for example, a hard drive and a digital camera), and data transfer can occur across the bus.

IEEE 1394c devices transmit at 800Mbps, but instead of using a 9-pin connector, they have an RJ-45 connector, like an Ethernet port (shown later in this chapter, in the "Network Ports" section). The IEEE 1394d standard uses a fiber connection. Table 1.4 provides a summary of the different IEEE 1394 standards.

Table 1.4 IEEE 1394 standards

Standard	Other names	Description	Cable
IEEE 1394	S100, S200, S400, and FireWire 400	Speeds of 100, 200, or 400Mbps half-duplex (one transmission direction at a time); 6-pin connector (later named the Alpha connector)*	~15 feet (4.5 meters) on a single cable; up to 60 feet (18 meters) with extra cables and a repeater
IEEE 1394a	S100, S200, S400, and FireWire 400	Added a 4-pin nonpowered connector	See IEEE 1394
IEEE 1394b	S800, S1600, S3200, and FireWire 800	Speeds up to 3200Mbps; added a 9-pin (Beta) connector and CAT5e or better UTP (unshielded twisted pair) cable*	~15 feet (4.5 meters) on a single cable; 330 feet (100 meters) with CAT5e or better or optical cable
IEEE 1394c	S800T	Up to 800Mbps over CAT5e or better UTP cable*	See IEEE 1394b
IEEE 1394d	N/A	Added support for single-mode fiber	N/A

*See Chapter 14 for more information on half-duplex and CAT UTP cabling.

Figure 1.46 shows various USB and IEEE 1394 connectors. The two leftmost connectors are mini-B and standard A USB connectors. The three connectors on the right are 6-, 4-, and 9-pin IEEE 1394 cables.

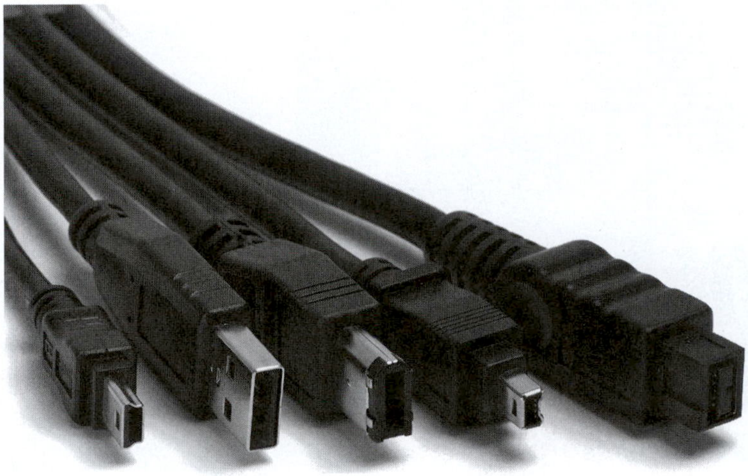

Figure 1.46 USB and IEEE 1394 cables

When connecting a FireWire device, always follow the manufacturer's instructions. Attach the device to an available port on the motherboard or an adapter, another IEEE 1394 device, or an IEEE 1394 hub port. The following are generic steps for installing a FireWire adapter:

1. Power off the computer and remove the AC power cord.
2. Remove the computer case so you can access the computer interior.
3. Locate an available expansion slot and optionally remove the slot cover and retaining screw. Not all computer cases have this now.
4. Firmly insert the FireWire adapter into the expansion slot.
5. Reinsert the retaining screw, if necessary.
6. Replace the computer cover and reattach the power cord.
7. Power on the computer. The operating system normally detects the newly installed hardware.
8. Insert the driver disc that ships with the adapter and browse to the location of the driver. Follow the prompts for installing the driver. Note that Windows normally detects the correct driver for the FireWire adapter, but the computer may have to be rebooted to recognize the adapter.

IEEE 1394 Troubleshooting

Use Device Manager to verify the correct installation for an IEEE 1394 device or port. To verify installation in Windows, open *Device Manager* and double-click the *1394 Bus Controller* option to verify that an IEEE 1394 host controller is present.

Tech Tip

What if IEEE 1394 is not working properly?

If a question mark appears by the IEEE 1394 host controller in Device Manager, remove or delete the driver and reinstall it. You may need to download a newer driver from the adapter manufacturer's website. If this does not work, change the adapter to a different expansion slot. If a red or yellow symbol appears by the FireWire controller, check the cabling, ensure that the device is not disabled, replace the driver, and check for a system resource conflict (see Chapter 3).

Like USB hubs, FireWire hubs can be self-powered or bus powered. A slide switch may be used to select the appropriate power mode. Most FireWire hub manufacturers recommend powering the hub only during installation. Once installed, test the FireWire devices, remove the hub power, and retest the devices. If all devices operate properly, leave the FireWire hub power adapter disconnected. With a cable that has a 6-pin connector at each end, connect the hub to the computer's FireWire port. Attach FireWire devices to the hub as needed.

Tech Tip

What if I don't have the right IEEE 1394 cable?

FireWire devices can have three types of connectors— 4-, 6-, and 9-pin connectors. A 4-pin cable does not provide for voltage over the IEEE 1394 bus. Placing a 6-pin connection on a FireWire 800 cable reduces connection speeds to a maximum of 400Mbps. Converters can be purchased to convert 4- to 6-pin or 6- to 9-pin connectors.

eSATA Ports

SATA (serial AT attachment) is used for connecting storage devices such as hard drives or optical drives. A 7-pin nonpowered **eSATA** (external SATA) **port** is used to connect external storage devices to computers at a maximum of approximately 6.6 feet or 2 meters. An eSATA port is commonly found on laptops to provide additional storage. If the internal hard drive has crashed, an external drive connected to an eSATA or USB port could be used to boot and troubleshoot the system.

A variation of the eSATA port is the **eSATAp port**, which is also known as eSATA/USB or power over eSATA. This variation can accept eSATA or USB cables and provides power when necessary. Figure 1.47 shows a standard eSATA port and an eSATAp (eSATA/USB combination) port.

eSATA port   eSATAp port

Figure 1.47 eSATA ports

Network Ports

Network ports are used to connect a computer to other computers, including a network server. The most common type of network port is an **Ethernet port**. A network cable inserts into the Ethernet port to connect the computing device to the wired network. A network port or an adapter that has a network port is commonly called a **NIC** (network interface card/controller).

Ethernet adapters commonly contain an **RJ-45** port that looks like an **RJ-11** phone jack, but the RJ-45 connector has 8 conductors instead of 4. UTP (unshielded twisted pair) cable connects to the RJ-45 port so the computing device can be connected to a wired network. AnRJ-45 Ethernet port can also be found on external storage devices. A storage device could be cabled to the wired network in the same fashion as the PC. Figure 1.48 shows an Ethernet NIC with an RJ-45 port.

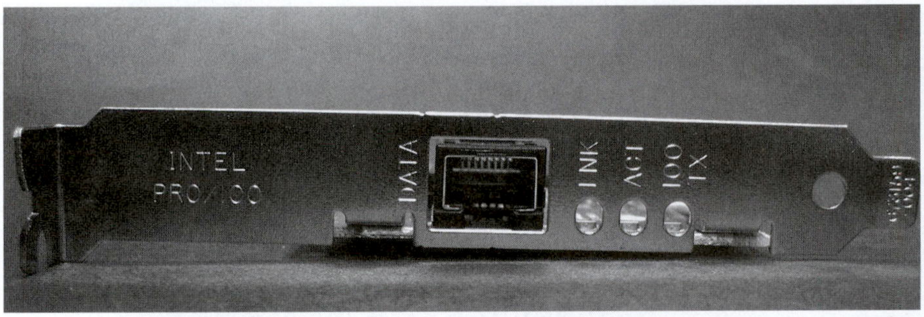

Figure 1.48 An RJ-45 Ethernet port

Modem Ports

A **modem** connects a computer to a phone line. A modem can be internal or external. An internal modem is an adapter that has one or two RJ-11 connectors. An external modem is a separate device that sits outside the computer and connects to a 9-pin serial port or a USB port. The external modem can also have one or two RJ-11 connectors. The RJ-11 connectors look like typical phone jacks. With two RJ-11 connectors, one can be used for a telephone and the other has a cable that connects to the wall jack. The RJ-11 connector labeled *Line* is for the connection to the wall jack. The RJ-11 connector labeled *Phone* is for the connection to the phone. An internal modem with only one RJ-11 connector connects to the wall jack. Figure 1.49 shows an internal modem with two ports.

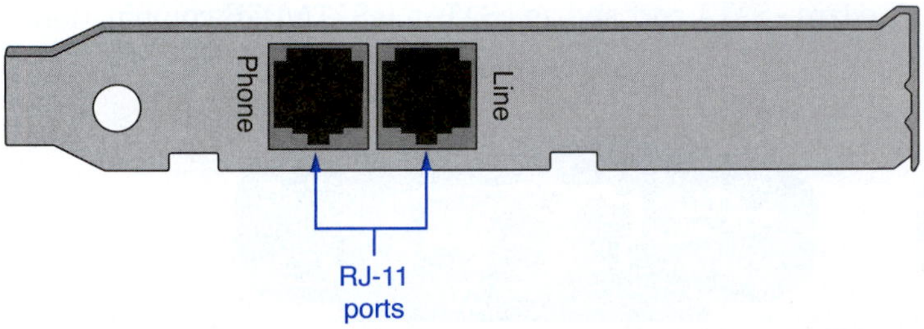

Figure 1.49 An internal modem with two ports

Pros and Cons of Integrated Motherboards

An integrated motherboard provides expandability because ports are built in and do not require separate adapters. If a motherboard includes the USB, network, sound, keyboard, mouse, and video ports, there is more space available for other adapters. The number of available expansion slots in a system depends on the motherboard manufacturer. Figure 1.50 shows integrated motherboard ports.

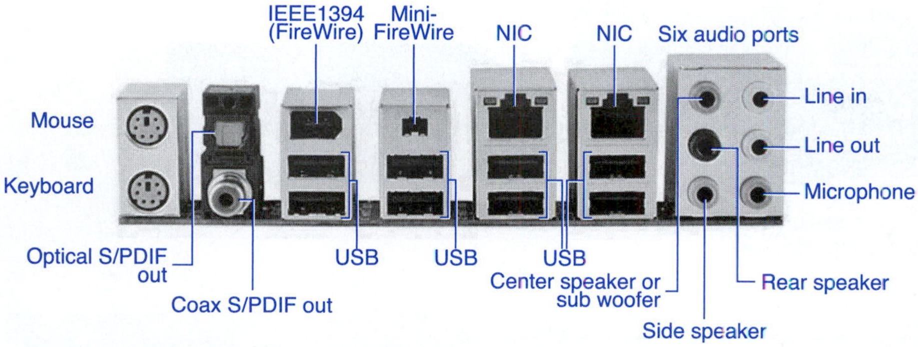

Figure 1.50 Integrated motherboard ports

Ports built into a motherboard are faster than those on an expansion board. All adapters in expansion slots run slower than the motherboard components. Computers with integrated motherboards are easier to set up because you do not have to install an adapter or configure the ports. Normally, systems with integrated motherboards are easier to troubleshoot because the components are on one board. The drawback is that when one port goes bad, you have to add an adapter that has the same type of port as the one that went bad. Furthermore, ports found on an adapter might be of higher quality or have more capabilities than an integrated port. See Figure 1.51.

Integrated port	Advantages to ports on an adapter
VGA DVI HDMI	• RAM that is not shared with motherboard RAM • Video GPU • Supports higher resolutions • Support for dual monitors
Sound	• Higher quality sound • Sound features such as surround sound and 3D sound • More input/output ports
NIC	• Faster connection • Could have fiber instead of copper

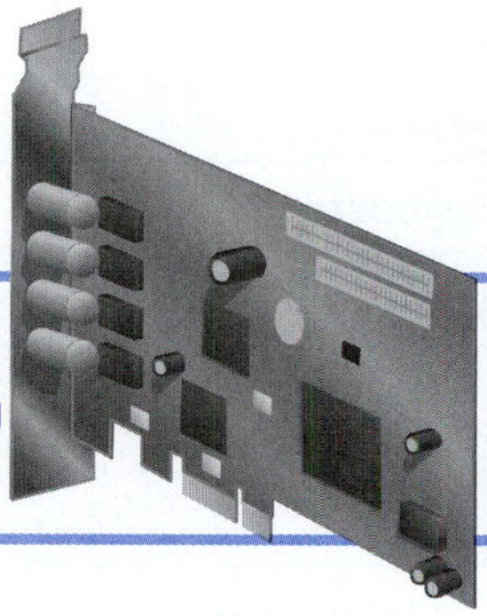

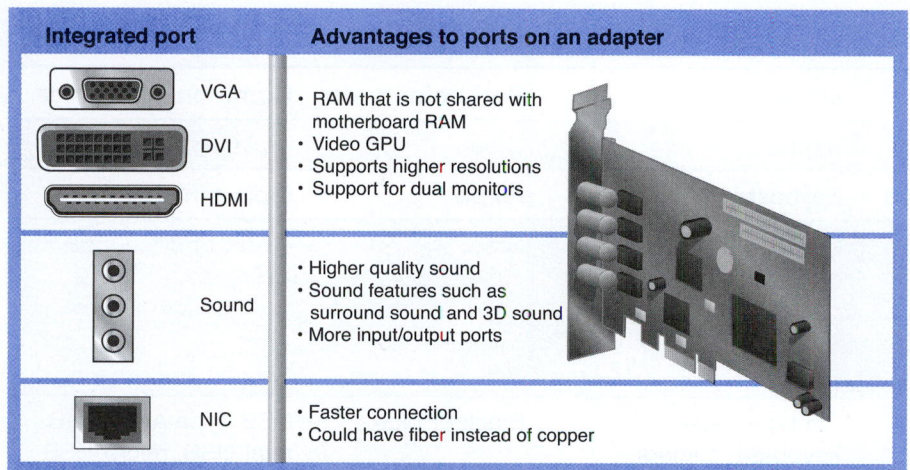

Figure 1.51 Advantages of adapters

Docking Stations and Port Replicators

Docking stations and port replicators add connectivity and expansion capability to laptop computers. A **docking station** allows a laptop computer to be more like a desktop system. A docking station can have connections for a full-size monitor, printer, keyboard, mouse, and printer. In addition, a docking station can have expansion slots or cards and storage bays.

To install a laptop into a docking station, close the laptop and slide the laptop into the docking station. Optionally (depending on the model), secure the laptop with locking tabs. Figure 1.52 shows a docking station and the ports that can be found on a docking station.

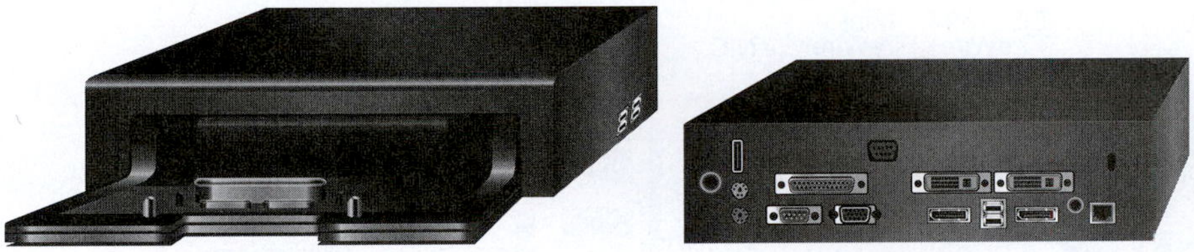

Figure 1.52 A laptop docking station and ports

The **port replicator** is similar to a docking station but does not normally include expansion slots or drive storage bays. A port replicator attaches to a laptop and allows more devices to be connected, such as an external monitor, keyboard, mouse, joystick, and printer. To use a port replicator, normally the external devices are connected first. Align the laptop connector with the port replication connector. Attach the port replicator to the laptop. Today, most laptops come with many integrated ports; therefore, docking stations and port replicators are not as popular. Also, port replicators and docking stations are normally proprietary, which means that if you have a particular brand of laptop, you must use the same brand docking station or port replicator.

Being able to identify ports quickly and accurately is a critical skill in computer repair. Table 1.5 lists the most common computer ports.

Table 1.5 Common computing device ports

Port	Usage	Port color code	Common connector
PS/2 mouse	Mouse	Green	6-pin mini-DIN
PS/2 keyboard	Keyboard	Purple	6-pin mini-DIN
IEEE 1394	Camcorder, video recorder, camera, printer, optical drive, scanner, speaker, hard drive	Gray	4-, 6-, or 9-pin IEEE 1394
USB	Printer, mouse, keyboard, camera, scanner, digitizer, external hard drive, optical drive	Black or blue	USB Type A , Type B, mini-USB, micro-USB
Parallel	Printer, tape backup	Burgundy (dark pink)	25-pin female D-shell
Serial	External modem, digitizer	Teal or turquoise	9-pin male D-shell
Video	Analog monitor (VGA or higher)	Blue	3-row 15-pin female D-shell or mini-VGA port
Video	DVI digital or analog monitor	White	3-row 18- or 24-pin female DVI , mini-DVI, or micro-DVI
Video	HDMI digital audio and video monitor	N/A	19 or 29-pin HDMI, mini-HDMI, or micro-HDMI

Port	Usage	Port color code	Common connector
Video	DisplayPort digital audio and video monitor	N/A	20-pin DisplayPort or mini-DisplayPort
Video	RGB/component video analog video output	Red, green, and blue	RCA jack
S-Video	Composite video device	Yellow	7-pin mini-DIN
Audio	Analog audio input	Light pink	1/8-inch (3.5mm) jack
Audio	Analog line level audio input	Light blue	1/8-inch (3.5mm) jack
Audio	Analog line level audio output from main stereo signal	Lime green	1/8-inch (3.5mm) jack
Audio	Analog line level audio for right-to-left speaker	Brown	1/8-inch (3.5mm) jack
S/PDIF	Audio input/output	Orange	RCA jack (coax) or TOSLINK (fiber)
Game port/ MIDI	Joystick or MIDI device	Gold	15-pin female D-shell
Ethernet	UTP network	N/A	8-conductor RJ-45
Modem	Internal modem or phone	N/A	4-conductor RJ-11
eSATA	External storage devices	N/A	7-pin eSATA port
eSATAp	External devices	N/A	Combination eSATA/ USB port

Chapter Summary

- Computer technicians should actively listen, have a positive attitude, refrain from using technical acronyms and terminology when speaking with nontechnical people, and be culturally sensitive.
- Easily identify important computer parts installed in a computer and as standalone parts: case, keyboard, mouse, motherboard, monitor, power supply, hard drive, optical drive, adapter, riser board, and memory.
- Easily identify various ports to determine what device attaches to them: VGA, DVI, HDMI, DisplayPort, USB, IEEE 1394, 3.5mm sound jack, PS/2, RJ-45, eSATA, parallel, serial, and RJ-11.
- The most popular method for adding functionality to desktops, laptops, and tablets is to use a USB port.
- USB 3.0 ports will accept 3.0 and older devices and provide more power. You can add additional ports by connecting a USB module to motherboard pins. This module takes an expansion space (but not a slot). A PCI/PCIe adapter can also be installed to provide additional ports. Cabling from the power supply to the adapter might be required to provide power to the new USB ports.
- Up to five USB hubs can be daisy-chained to one port. Upstream ports connect to the computer or another USB port. Devices connect to downstream ports.
- USB hubs can be self-powered or bus powered.
- IEEE 1394 devices do not have to have a computer port and can be cabled to each other; otherwise, an IEEE 1394 device can be cabled to a port or a hub.
- USB and IEEE 1394 troubleshooting issues commonly relate to power, drivers, or system resources.

Key Terms

Review Questions

1. Match the part to the description.

____ motherboard	a. converts AC to DC
____ RAM	b. holds the most data
____ optical drive	c. has the most electronics
____ hard drive	d. fits in an expansion slot
____ adapter	e. contents disappear when power is off
____ power supply	f. holds a disc

2. Match the port to the description.

____ DVI	a. Ethernet
____ VGA	b. TOSLINK
____ PS/2	c. up to 127 devices
____ USB	d. mouse/keyboard
____ NIC	e. CRT
____ S/PDIF	f. flat panel monitor

3. What is a visual indication that a cable is USB version 2.0?
4. What is another name for IEEE 1394?
5. How is an eSATAp port different from an eSATA port?
6. When considering VGA, HDMI, RGB/component, DVI, and DisplayPort, which video port can output both digital audio and video signals and is the most technologically advanced?
7. What is the most common DVI port?
8. Which has the faster transfer time when connected externally to a computer, USB 3.0, or FireWire 800?
9. What are the two ports most commonly used to attach a keyboard?
10. What type of memory is commonly found on a motherboard?
11. [T | F] When lifting a heavy computer, you should squat, bend at the knees, and use your legs to lift.
12. What should you remove before working inside a computer? [tie | necklace | shoes | ring]
13. Is the following question open ended or closed? You say your computer has been running slow since Monday. What applications have you installed this week? [open ended | closed ended]
14. List one example of having a positive attitude.
15. Which of the following devices are commonly output devices? Select all that apply. [digital piano | speakers | display | stylus | track stick | barcode reader | printer]

16. How can you control a laptop keyboard backlight?
17. How is a multitouch display different from a normal mobile display?

18. In which of the following situations would Bluetooth most likely be used?
    a. to connect to a corporate wireless network
    b. to attach a keyboard to a PC
    c. to connect a PC to a phone line
    d. to connect a flash drive to a camera
19. List one advantage of having an adapter rather than an integrated motherboard port.

20. Rewrite the following conversation into an open-ended question.
    Technician: Good morning. I have a service log that states you are getting an error message whenever you access a PDF file. Have you done your Acrobat updates lately?

Exercises

Lab 1.1 Identifying Tower Computer Parts

Objective: To identify various computer parts correctly

Procedure: Identify each computer part in Figure 1.53.

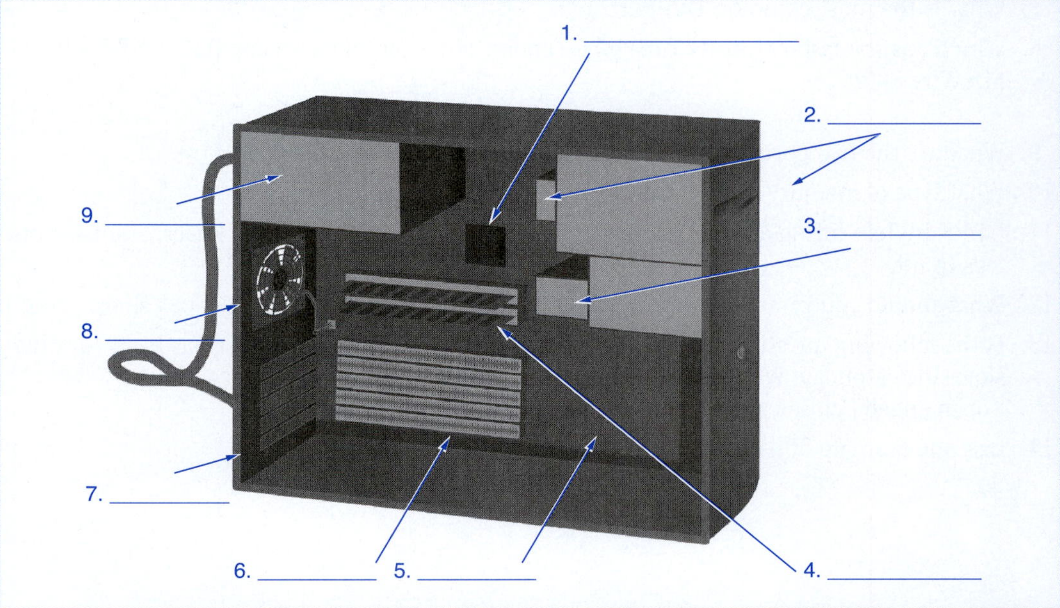

Figure 1.53 Tower computer parts

1.
2.
3.
4.
5.
6.
7.
8.
9.

Lab 1.2 Identification of Computer Ports

Objective: To identify various computer ports correctly

Procedure: Identify each computer port in Figure 1.54.

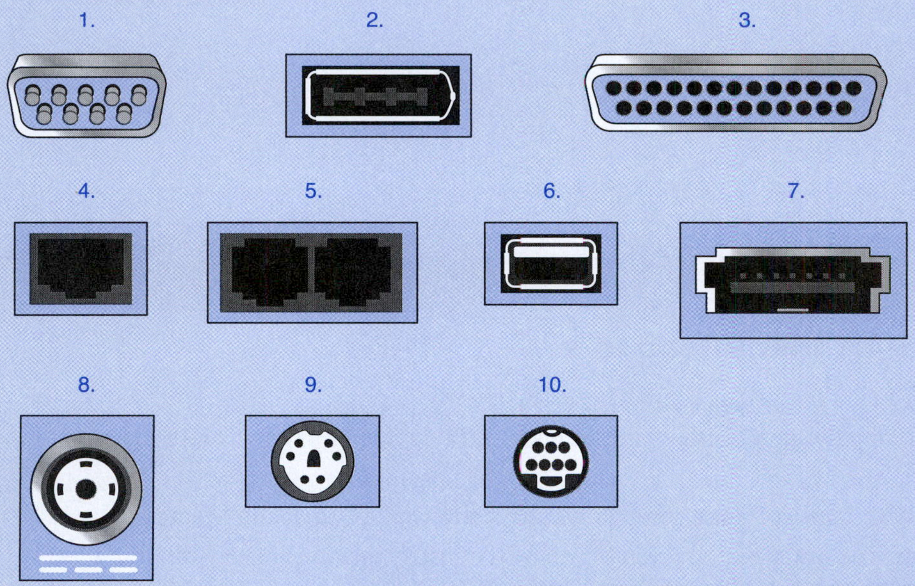

Figure 1.54 Computer ports

1.
2.
3.
4.
5.
6.
7.
8.
9.
10.

Lab 1.3 Identification of Video Ports

Objective: To identify various video ports correctly

Procedure: Identify each video port in Figure 1.55.

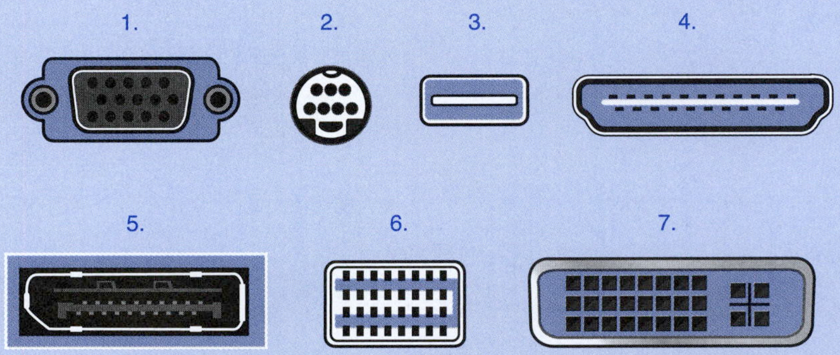

Figure 1.55 Video ports

1.
2.
3.
4.
5.
6.
7.

Lab 1.4 Port Identification

Objective: To identify various computer ports correctly

Parts: Computer ports, either built into a specific computer or as separate adapters

Procedure:

1. Contact your instructor for a computer on which to work or to obtain adapters.
2. Identify the computer port(s) given to you by the instructor. In Table 1.6, fill in the connector type, number of pins, and port type.

Table 1.6 Connector identification

Connector type (D-shell, DIN, etc.)	Number of pins	Port purpose (video, USB, NIC, etc.)
1. ______	______	______
2. ______	______	______
3. ______	______	______
4. ______	______	______
5. ______	______	______
6. ______	______	______
7. ______	______	______
8. ______	______	______
9. ______	______	______
10. ______	______	______

Activities

Internet Discovery

Objective: To obtain specific information from the Internet regarding a computer or its associated parts

Parts: Computer with Internet access

Procedure: Obtain technical information about a computer. Answer the following questions based on the information. More documents may need to be obtained in order to answer the questions.

Questions:

1. What ports are available on the front of the computer?
2. What ports are available on the back of the computer?
3. How many drive bays are available to install devices such as hard drives, optical drives, tape drives, and so on?
4. Were the photos in the documentation clear enough to differentiate between the different ports? If not, explain what is wrong.
5. List three safety precautions or procedures the documentation offers.

Soft Skills

Objective: To enhance and fine-tune a future technician's ability to listen, communicate in both written and oral forms, and support people who use computers in a professional manner

Procedure:

1. In a team environment, list three qualities that are important in a computer technician. Create scenarios that demonstrate these qualities. Share these findings in a clear and concise way with the class.

2. In a team environment, list three qualities that are not good practices for computer technicians. Create scenarios that demonstrate these qualities. Share these findings in a clear and concise way with the class.

Critical Thinking Skills

Objective: To analyze and evaluate information as well as apply learned information to new or different situations

Procedure:

1. Find an advertisement for a computer in a local computer flyer, in a newspaper, in a magazine, in a book, or on the Internet. List which components you know in one column and the components you do not know in the other column. Select one component you do not know and research that component. Write the new information and share with at least one other person.

2. Why do you think that computer components are considered "throw-away" technology? List your reasoning. In groups of three or four, share your thoughts. Nominate a spokesperson to share your group reaction in two sentences or less.

3. Provide five tips that might help someone identify the different computer ports. If possible, each person in the class should state a tip without duplicating someone else's tip.

A+ Certification Exam Tips

- ✓ Get a good night's rest the night before the exam.
- ✓ Ensure that you are knowledgeable and proficient with the terms and technologies listed in the official CompTIA A+ exam objectives.
- ✓ Ensure that you can identify the basic parts of the computer and explain the purpose of each one. Ensure that you know the following parts: hard drive, optical drive, power supply, motherboard, RAM, laptop AC adapter, and laptop video controller.
- ✓ Know what port(s) a specific device can use. Particular ports to know include HDMI, VGA, DVI, DisplayPort, USB, IEEE 1394, eSATA, eSATAp, PS/2, RJ-45, RJ-11, and Ethernet. (On 3×5 cards, write the names of ports you have a hard time remembering. Put a picture of the port on one side and the term on the other. Take the cards with you wherever you go the week before the exam and practice with them.)
- ✓ The following communication and professionalism skills are part of the 220-801 exam: (1) use proper language; (2) maintain a positive attitude; (3) listen and do not interrupt the customer; and (4) be culturally sensitive.

chapter 2

On the Motherboard

Chapter Objectives:

In this chapter you will learn:

- To recognize and identify important motherboard parts
- To explain the basics of how a processor works
- What issues to consider when upgrading or replacing the motherboard or processor
- How to add cards to computers and mobile devices
- The differences between PCI, PCI-X, AGP, and PCIe adapters and slots
- About motherboard technologies such as HyperTransport, Hyper-Threading, and multi-core
- The benefits of active listening

CompTIA Exam Objectives:

What CompTIA A+ exam objectives are covered in this chapter?

- ✓ 801-1.2 Differentiate between motherboard components, their purposes, and properties.
- ✓ 801-1.6 Differentiate among various CPU types and features and select the appropriate cooling method.
- ✓ 801-3.1 Install and configure laptop hardware and components.
- ✓ 801-5.3 Given a scenario, demonstrate proper communication and professionalism.
- ✓ 802-1.9 Explain the basics of client-side virtualization.
- ✓ 802-4.2 Given a scenario, troubleshoot common problems related to motherboards, RAM, CPU, and power with appropriate tools.

Processor Overview

At the heart of every computer is a special motherboard chip called the **processor**, which determines, to a great extent, the power of the computer. The processor is also called the CPU (central processing unit) or microprocessor. The processor executes instructions, performs calculations, and coordinates input/output operations. Each motherboard has electronic chips that work with the CPU and are designed to exact specifications. Whether these other electronic components can keep up with the processor depends on the individual component's specifications. The major processor manufacturers today are Intel, Motorola, VIA, Samsung, NVIDIA, Qualcomm, and AMD (Advanced Micro Devices, Inc.). Intel and AMD are the predominant manufacturers for desktop and laptop processors, and the other manufacturers target the mobile/smartphone markets.

Processor Basics

All processors use 1s and 0s. One 1 or one 0 is a **bit**. Eight bits grouped together are a **byte**. To a processor, the letter A looks like 01000001. Each character on a keyboard appears as 1 byte or 8 bits to the processor. Approximately 1,000 bytes is a **kilobyte** (kB). (1kB is 1,024 bytes to be exact, but the computer industry rounds off the number to the nearest thousand for ease of calculation.) Ten kilobytes is shown as 10K or 10kB. Approximately 1 million bytes is a **megabyte** (MB), but a true megabyte is 1,048,576 bytes. 540 megabytes is shown as 540MB, or 540M. Approximately 1 billion bytes (1,073,741,824 bytes) is a **gigabyte** and is shown as 1GB or 1G.

When information needs to be expressed exactly, binary prefixes are used. For example, when describing a value of 2^{10} (1,024), instead of saying that it is 1 kilobyte, which people tend to think of as approximately 1,000 bytes, the term kibibyte (KiB) is used. When describing a value of 2^{20}, or 1,048,576, the term mebibyte (MiB) is used. Table 2.1 shows the terms used with computer storage capacity and binary prefixes when exact measurements are needed.

Table 2.1 Storage terms and binary prefixes

Term	Abbreviation	Description
Kilobyte/kibibyte	kB/KiB	~1 thousand bytes/2^{10} bytes
Megabyte/mebibyte	MB/MiB	~1 million bytes/2^{20} bytes
Gigabyte/gibibyte	GB/GiB	~1 billion bytes/2^{30} bytes
Terabyte/tebibyte	TB/TiB	~1 trillion bytes/2^{40} bytes
Petabyte/pibibyte	PB/PiB	~1,000 trillion bytes/2^{50} bytes
Exabyte/exbibyte	EB/EiB	~1 quintillion bytes/2^{60} bytes
Zetabyte/zebibyte	ZB/ZiB	~1,000 exabytes/2^{70} bytes
Yottabyte/yobibyte	YB/YiB	~1 million exabytes/2^{80} bytes

Processors come in a variety of speeds, measured in **gigahertz** (GHz). Hertz is a measurement of cycles per second. One hertz equals one cycle per second. One gigahertz is 1 billion cycles per second, or 1GHz. The original PC CPU, the 8088 microprocessor, ran at 4.77MHz. Today's processors run at speeds over 3GHz.

The number of bits processed at one time is the processor's register size (word size). Intel's 8086 processor's register size was 16 bits, or 2 bytes. Today's CPUs have register sizes of 64 or 128 bits.

The 1s and 0s must travel from one place to another inside the processor, as well as outside to other chips. To move the 1s and 0s around, electronic lines called a **bus** are used. The electronic lines inside the CPU are known as the **internal data bus** or system bus. In the 8086 the internal data bus comprises 16 separate lines, with each line carrying one 1 or one 0. The word size and the number of lines for the internal data bus are equal. The 8086, for example, had a 16-bit word size, and 16 lines carried 16 bits on the internal data bus. In today's processors, 64 or 128 internal data bus lines operate concurrently.

For a CPU to communicate with devices in the outside world, such as a printer, the 1s and 0s travel on the **external data bus**. The external data bus connects the processor to adapters, the keyboard, the mouse, the hard drive, and other devices. An external data bus is also known as an external data path. You can see the external data lines by looking between the expansion slots on the motherboard. Some solder lines between the expansion slots are used to send data out along the external data bus to the expansion slots. Today's processors have 64- and 128-bit external data paths. Figure 2.1 shows the internal and external data buses.

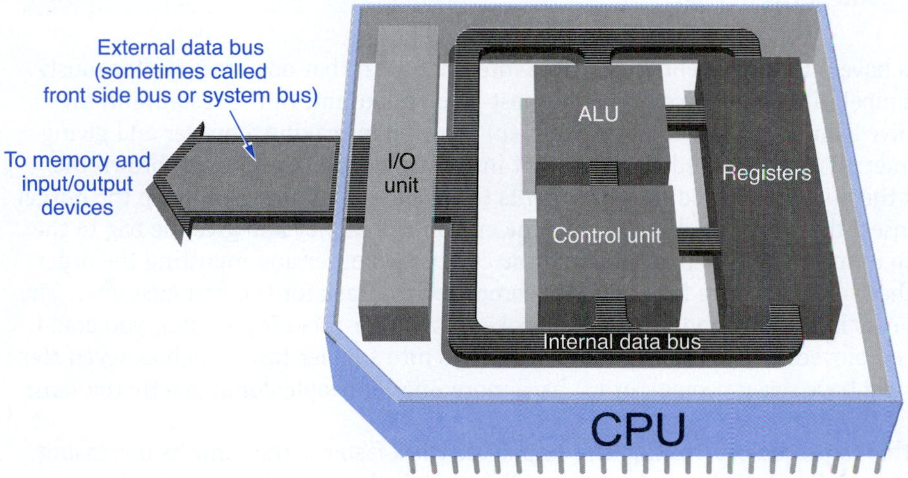

Figure 2.1 Internal and external data buses

A processor has a special component called the ALU (arithmetic logic unit), which does all the calculations and comparison logic that the computer needs. Figure 2.1 shows the basic concept of how the ALU connects to the registers, control unit, and internal bus. The control unit coordinates activities inside the processor. The I/O unit manages data entering and leaving the processor. The registers within the CPU are a very high-speed storage area for 1s and 0s before the bits are processed.

To make sense of all of this, take a look at a letter typed on a computer that starts out *Dear Mom*. To the computer, each letter of the alphabet is a different combination of eight 1s and 0s. For example, the letter *D* is 01000100, and the letter *e* is 01000101. Figure 2.2 demonstrates that the size of the bus greatly increases performance on a computer similar to the way that increasing the number of lanes of highway decreases congestion.

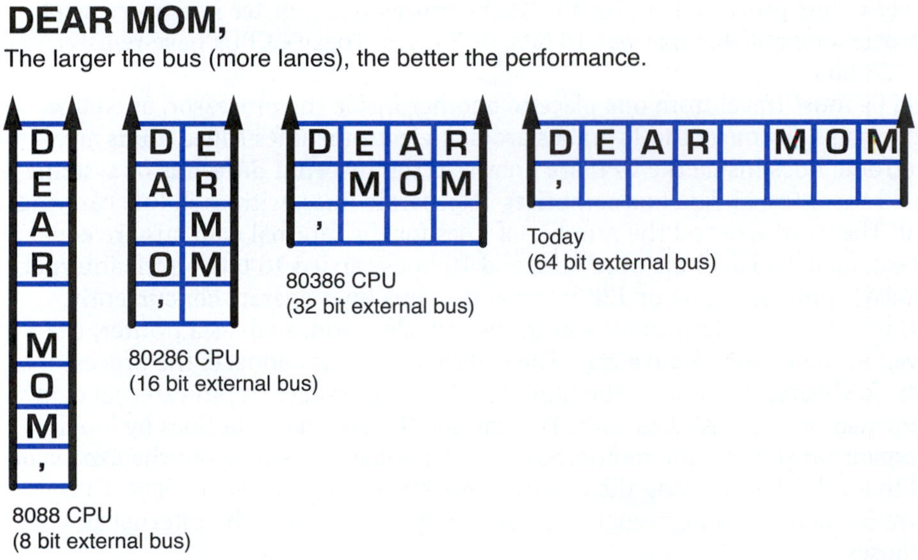

Figure 2.2 Bus performance

Processors have multiple pipelines (separate internal buses) that operate simultaneously. To understand pipelining, take the example of a fast-food restaurant. In the restaurant, say that there are five steps (and one employee per step) involved in making a burger and giving it to the customer: (1) Take the order and input it into the computer system; (2) brown the buns and cook the burgers; (3) add the condiments to the bun and burger; (4) wrap the burger add fries and insert them into the bag; (5) take the customer's money and give the bag to the customer. Keep in mind that the person taking the customer's order and inputting the order can serve another customer once he or she has completed this task for the first customer. The same is true for each person along the line. To make this burger process go faster, you could: (1) Make your employees work faster; (2) break the tasks into smaller tasks (such as seven steps instead of five and have seven people); or (3) have more lines of people doing exactly the same process tasks.

To relate this to processors, making the employees work faster is the same as increasing the CPU clock speed. Breaking the tasks into smaller tasks is the same as changing the structure of the CPU pipeline. Instead of performing the standard 5 tasks, the CPU might perform 6, 7, 14, 20, or even more steps. This allows each step to be acted upon more quickly, the task to be smaller, and production to be faster. Having more lines of people doing the same complete process is like having multiple pipelines.

A 32- or 64-bit CPU can have separate paths, each of which handles 32 or 64 bits. For example, if a processor has two pipelines, the Dear Mom letter can be in one pipeline, while a photo upload using a different application can be in the other pipeline.

A processor might have 12 pipelines for integers and 17 pipelines for floating-point numbers. (A floating-point number is a number that can include a decimal point.) Other processors contain anywhere from 20- to 31-stage pipelines. Debate continues about whether a longer pipeline improves performance.

Intel Processors

Traditionally, Intel has rated its processors by GHz and people have compared processors based on speed alone. Now, Intel arranges its products by family numbers. Within a family of processors, you can compare attributes such as speed and the amount of cache memory and other technologies. Table 2.2 shows Intel's processor families. Figure 2.3 shows an Intel ultrathin processor and a small form factor chipset used with mobile devices.

Table 2.2 **Intel processor families**

Processor family*	Comments
Core i7 Extreme	Multi-core with cache memory shared between cores. Used for desktop and mobile devices designed for gaming and virtualization.
Core i7	Multi-core with cache memory shared between cores and on-board memory controller. Good for virtualization, graphic/multimedia design and creation, and gaming.
Core i5	Midrange dual- and quad-core processor. Used for video, photos, email, and Internet access.
Core i3	Low-end desktop and mobile processor used for common tasks such as word processing and Internet access.
Pentium/Mobile	Single- or dual-core desktop/laptop processor for general computing.
Celeron/Mobile	Entry-level desktop or mobile device processor for general computing.
Centrino	Laptop processor for general computing that has extended battery life.
Atom	Mobile Internet device processor.

* Intel is constantly upgrading processors. For more information, visit www.intel.com.

Figure 2.3 **Intel ultrathin processor and chipset**

AMD Processors

AMD is Intel's largest rival in computer processors. Anyone buying a processor should research all models and vendors. Table 2.3 lists the AMD processor families. Figure 2.4 shows the AMD Opteron processor; the 64 indicates that it supports a 64-bit operating system and applications.

Table 2.3 **AMD processor families**

Processor family	Comments
FX	Multi-core (4-, 6-, or 8-core) high-performance desktop processor.
Fusion	Single- or multi-core mobile device processor that comes in three series (A, C, and E, with A being the highest performance). Combines the CPU with a **GPU** (graphics processor unit) to make an **APU** (accelerated processing unit). A GPU is a processor for video.
Phenom	Multi-core (3, 4, or 6 cores in a single package) high-end desktop for HD support, megamedia creation and editing, gaming, and virtualization. Supports 32- and 64-bit computing, 3DNow!, SSE, SSE2, SSE3, SSE4a, HyperTransport, and Direct Connect technologies.*

Processor family	Comments
Athlon/Mobile	Single- or multi-core (2-, 3-, or 4-core) desktop/mobile processor for productivity, photos, and music.
Sempron/Mobile	Lower-cost desktop/notebook processor for basic productivity, email, and web browsing.
Turion	Single- or dual-core notebook processor.

*These technologies are covered later in this chapter.

Figure 2.4 AMD Opteron processor

Speeding Up Processor Operations Overview

You can determine the speed of a processor by looking at the model number on the chip, but processors frequently have fans or heat sinks attached to them for cooling, which makes it difficult to see the writing on the chip. A processor commonly does not use its maximum speed in order to save power or stay cool.

Tech Tip

Locating your processor speed

An easy way to tell processor speed with Windows XP is to open *Windows Explorer* > right-click *My Computer* > *Properties*. In Vista/7, right-click the *Start* button > *Explore* > right-click *Computer* > *Properties*.

We have already taken a look at how increasing the CPU pipeline can, to some extent, improve processor operations, but other technologies also exist. We will start by defining some of the terms that relate to this area and associating those terms with concepts and the various technologies used. Table 2.4 list some terms related to speed.

Table 2.4 Motherboard speed terms

Term	Explanation
clock or **clock speed**	The speed of the processor's internal clock, measured in gigahertz.
bus speed	The speed at which data is delivered when a particular bus on the motherboard is being used.
FSB (front side bus)	The speed between the CPU and some of the motherboard components. This is what most people would term the motherboard speed. Sometimes the speed is listed in megatransfers per second, or MT/s. With MT/s, not only is the speed of the FSB considered but how many processor transfers occur each clock cycle. A 266 MHz FSB that can do four transfers per second could list as 1064MT/s. The FSB is being upgraded with technologies such as AMD's HyperTransport and Intel's QPI (QuickPath Interconnect) and DMI (Direct Media Interface).
back side bus	The speed between the CPU and the L2 cache located outside the main CPU but on the same chip.
PCI bus speed	The speed at which data is delivered when the PCI bus is being used. The PCI bus is the main bus used on the motherboard. Common speeds for the PCI bus are 33 and 66MHz, allowing bandwidths up to 533MBps.
PCIe bus speed	The speed at which data is delivered when the PCIe bus is being used. This bus is used for PCI Express cards.
AGP bus speed	The speed at which data is delivered when the AGP bus is being used. The AGP bus is an older standard used for video cards.
CPU speed	The speed at which the CPU operates. Some motherboards have a BIOS option to change the speed. Other motherboards either use motherboard jumpers or cannot be changed.
CPU throttling	Reducing the clock frequency to slow the CPU in order to reduce power consumption and heat. This is especially useful in mobile devices.

Cache

An important concept related to processor speed is keeping data flowing into the processor. Registers are a type of high-speed memory storage inside the processor. They are used to temporarily hold calculations, data, or instructions. The data or instruction the CPU needs to operate on is usually found in one of three places: the cache, the motherboard memory (main memory), or the hard drive.

Cache memory is a very fast type of memory designed to increase the speed of processor operations. When cache memory is integrated as part of the processor, it is called **L1 cache**. Included in the processor packaging, but not part of the CPU, is **L2 cache**, which some refer to as on-die cache. Finally, a third level of memory is found when using higher-end computer processors; it is called **L3 cache** and can be located in the CPU housing or on the motherboard. CPU efficiency is increased when data continuously flows into the CPU. Cache provides the fastest access. If the information is not in cache, the processor looks for the data in motherboard RAM. If the information is not there, it is retrieved from the hard drive and placed into the motherboard memory or the cache. Hard drive access is the slowest of the three.

An analogy best explains this. Consider a glass of cold lemonade, a pitcher of lemonade, and a can of frozen lemonade concentrate. If you were thirsty, you would drink from the glass because it is the fastest and most easily accessible. If the glass were empty, you would pour lemonade from the pitcher to refill the glass. If the pitcher were empty, you would go to the freezer to get the frozen concentrate to make more. Figure 2.5 shows this concept.

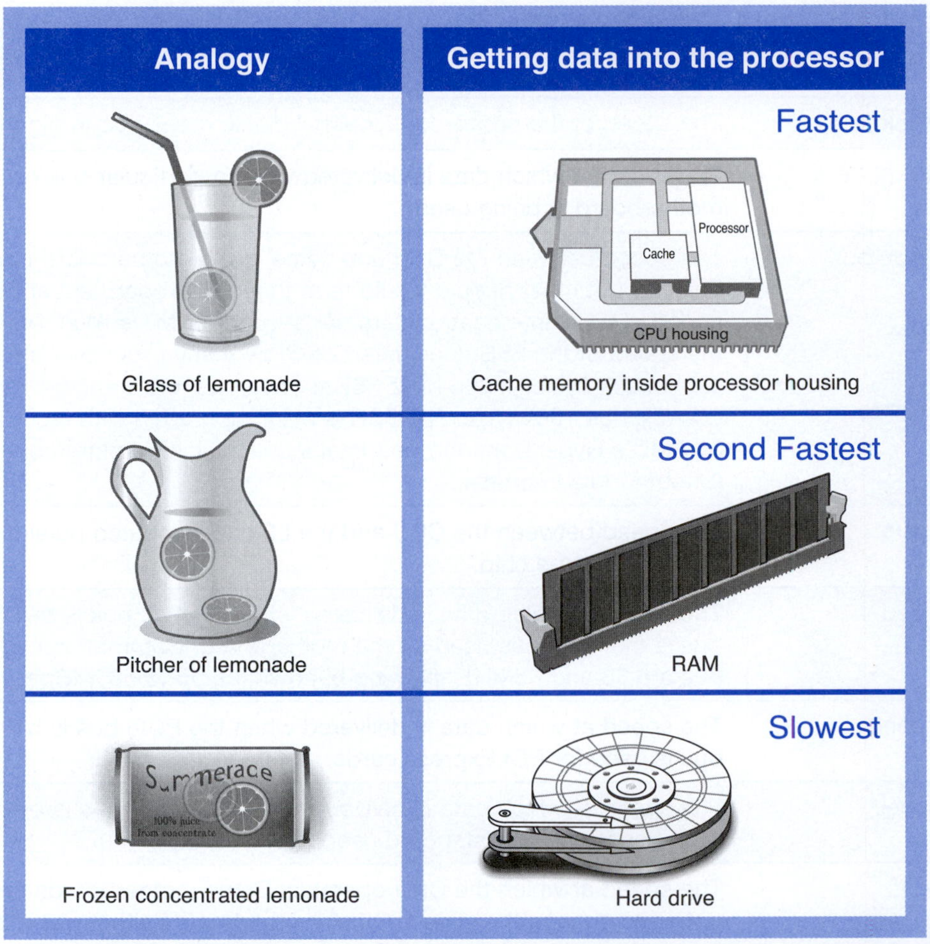

Figure 2.5 CPU data sources

Usually, the more cache memory a system has, the better that system performs, but this is not always true. System performance also depends on the efficiency of the cache controller (the chip that manages the cache memory), the system design, the amount of available hard drive space, and the speed of the processor. When determining memory requirements, you must consider the operating system used, applications used, and hardware installed. The Windows XP operating system takes a lot less memory than Windows 7. High-end games and desktop publishing take more RAM than word processing. Free hard drive space and video memory are often as important as RAM in improving a computer's performance. Memory is only one piece of the puzzle. All of the computer's parts must work together to provide good system performance. Figure 2.6 shows this hierarchy of data access for the CPU.

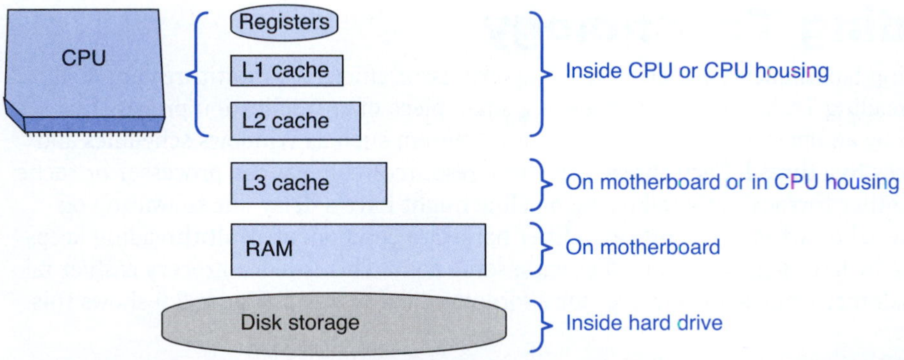

Figure 2.6 Data access hierarchy

Clocking

The motherboard generates a clock signal that is used to control the transfer of 1s and 0s to and from the processor. A clock signal can be illustrated as a sine wave. One clock cycle is from one point on the sine wave to the next point that is located on the same point on the sine wave later in time, as shown in Figure 2.7.

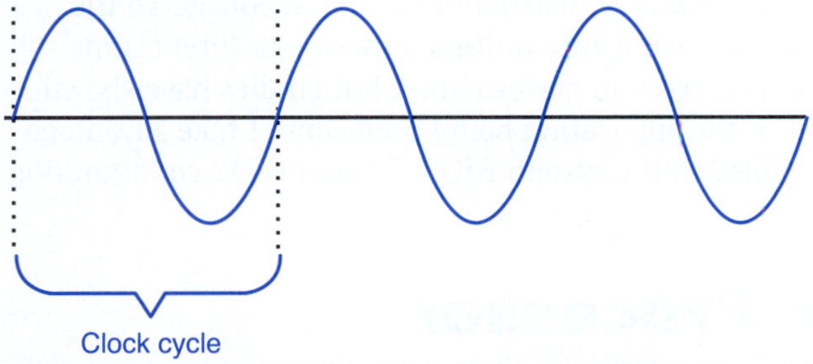

Figure 2.7 Clock cycle

In older computers, data was sent to the CPU only once during a clock cycle. Then, newer memory technologies evolved that allow data to be sent twice during every clock cycle. Today, data is sent four times during a single clock cycle, as shown in Figure 2.8.

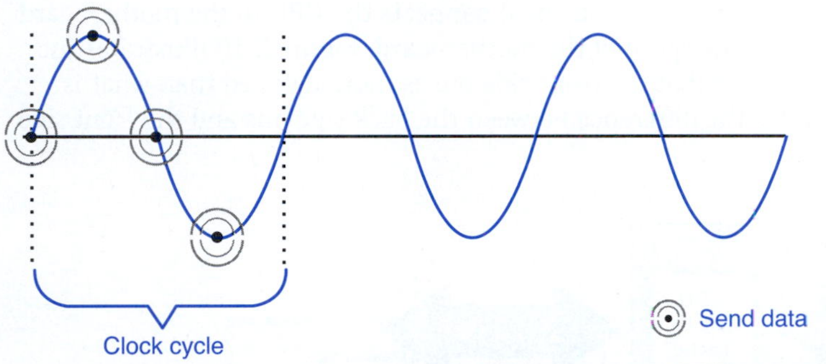

Figure 2.8 Clock cycle that clocks data four times per cycle

Threading Technology

Several threading techniques are used to speed up processor efficiency: multithreading and HT (Hyper-Threading Technology). A **thread** is a small piece of an application process that can be handled by an operating system. An operating system such as Windows schedules and assigns resources to a thread. Each thread can share resources (such as the processor or cache memory) with other threads. A thread in the pipeline might have a delay due to waiting on data to be retrieved or access to a port or another hardware component. Multithreading keeps the line moving by letting another thread execute some code. This is like a grocery cashier taking another customer while someone goes for a forgotten loaf of bread. Figure 2.9 shows this concept.

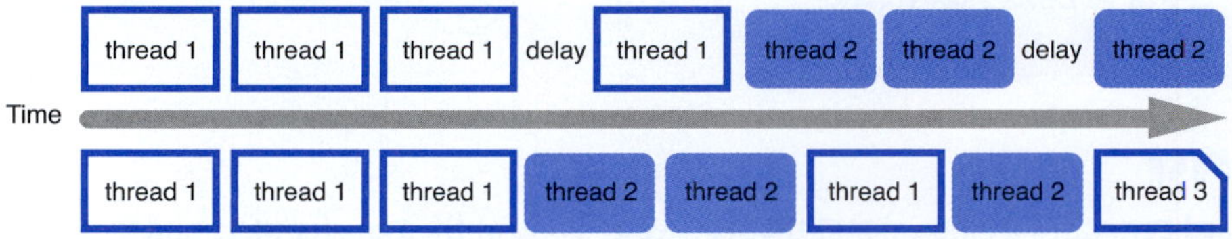

Figure 2.9 Multithreading

Intel's HTT (Hyper-Threading Technology, HT Technology, or simply shortened to **HT**) allows a single processor to handle two separate sets of instructions simultaneously. To the operating system, HT makes the system appear as if it has multiple processors. Intel claims that the system can have up to a 30 percent increase in performance, but studies have shown that the increase is application dependent. If the application being used cannot take advantage of the multithreading, then HT can be disabled in the system BIOS. System BIOS configuration is covered in Chapter 3.

Connecting to the Processor

We have considered various ways to speed up processor operations, including having more stages in the processor, increasing the speed of the clock, and sending more data in the same amount of time. Accessing L2 cache and motherboard components was a bottleneck in older systems because the CPU used the same bus to communicate with RAM and other motherboard components as it did with L2 and motherboard cache. The solution is DIB (dual independent bus). With DIB, two buses are used: a back side bus and a front side bus. The back side bus connects the CPU to the L2 cache. The FSB (front side bus) connects the CPU to the motherboard components. The FSB is considered the speed of the motherboard. Figure 2.10 illustrates the concept of a front side bus. Remember that the front side bus is more detailed than what is shown; the figure simply illustrates the difference between the back side bus and the front side bus.

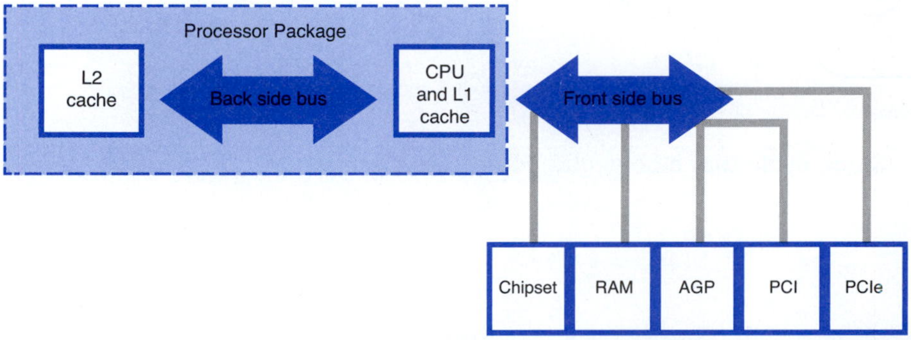

Figure 2.10 Front side bus

Many people think that the higher the CPU speed, the faster the computer. This is seldom true. Several factors contribute to computer speed. One factor is bus speed. Bus speed describes how fast the CPU can communicate with motherboard components, such as memory, the chipset, or the PCI/PCIe bus. The first Pentium CPUs ran at the same speed as the bus (60MHz); in time, CPUs got faster and buses stayed the same. Advances in technology have not reached the rest of the motherboard components (and it would cost too much to try to have them keep pace).

Intel and AMD have technologies to replace the front side bus in some parts. AMD's solution is Direct Connect. Direct Connect allows each of the processor cores to connect directly to memory, to the other motherboard components such as the expansion slots, and to other processor cores, using a high-speed bus called **HyperTransport**. Figure 2.12, later in this chapter, shows HyperTransport connectivity. Intel has QPI (QuickPath Interconnect) and DMI (Direct Media Interface), which are full-duplex (that is, traffic can flow in both directions simultaneously) point-to-point connections between the processor and one or more motherboard components. This type of connectivity is shown later in the chapter, in Figure 2.39.

Motherboard speed in recent times has been confusing. A multiplier is a number that, when multiplied by the front side bus speed, determines the CPU speed. Other names for the multiplier include CPU clock ratio, stepping value, bus frequency multiple, and bus frequency ratio. If the motherboard is using a 300MHz base clock frequency and the CPU multiplier is set to 9, then the speed of the CPU is 2.7GHz. Multipliers can be shown in .5 increments as well. The available multiplier and the bus speed are determined by the motherboard manufacturer.

Knowing the CPU speed is no longer an issue unless you are upgrading a computer to a faster processor or configuring the motherboard. Many motherboards accept processors with different speeds. The processor settings are static (cannot be changed) or can be configured through system BIOS, which is covered in more detail in Chapter 3.

Another bottleneck for computer performance is video. Computer users who want better video performance buy a separate video adapter that contains a GPU. Both Intel and AMD have integrated a GPU within the CPU on some of their processor models. An external video card with a GPU is not required, and graphical data is processed quickly, with reduced power consumption.

Tech Tip

Settings for CPU installations

When installing a processor, two BIOS settings can be important: CPU bus frequency and bus frequency multiple. The CPU bus frequency setting allows the motherboard to run at a specific speed. This speed is the external rate at which data travels *outside* the processor. The bus frequency multiple enables the motherboard to recognize the *internal* processor speed.

Multi-Core Processors

In the past, when two processors were installed, software had to be specifically written to support having multiple processors. That is no longer true. A **dual-core** processor combines two CPUs in a single unit. A tri-core processor has three processors in a single unit. Both Intel and AMD have **quad-core** CPU technologies, which is either two dual-core CPUs installed on the same motherboard, two dual-core CPUs installed in a single socket, or today's model of all four cores installed in one unit. Now there are **hexa-core** (six cores) and **octa-core** (eight cores) processors, as well. IT professionals in the field find it easiest to just say *multi-core* to describe the multiple cores contained in the same processor housing.

Single-core processors and early dual-core processors accessed memory through a memory controller, as shown in Figure 2.11. Today, the processor cores have their own memory controller built into the processor. Figure 2.12 shows how an AMD quad-core processor has an integrated controller and interfaces with the rest of the motherboard using a high-speed bus called HyperTransport. HyperTransport is a feature of AMD's Direct Connect architecture. With Direct Connect, there are no front side buses. Instead, the memory controller and input/output functions directly connect to the CPU.

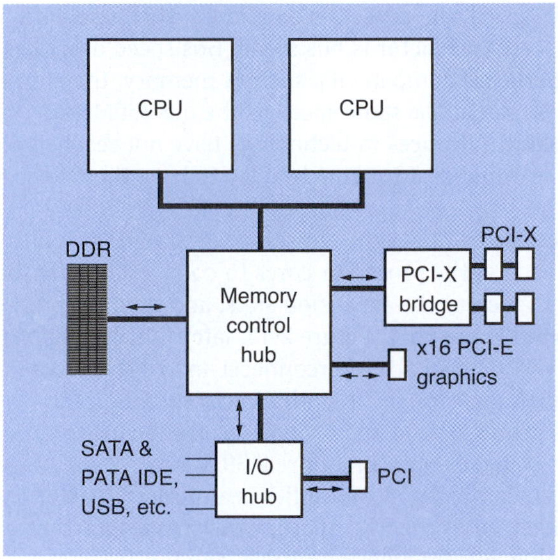

Figure 2.11 Older method of processors interfacing with memory

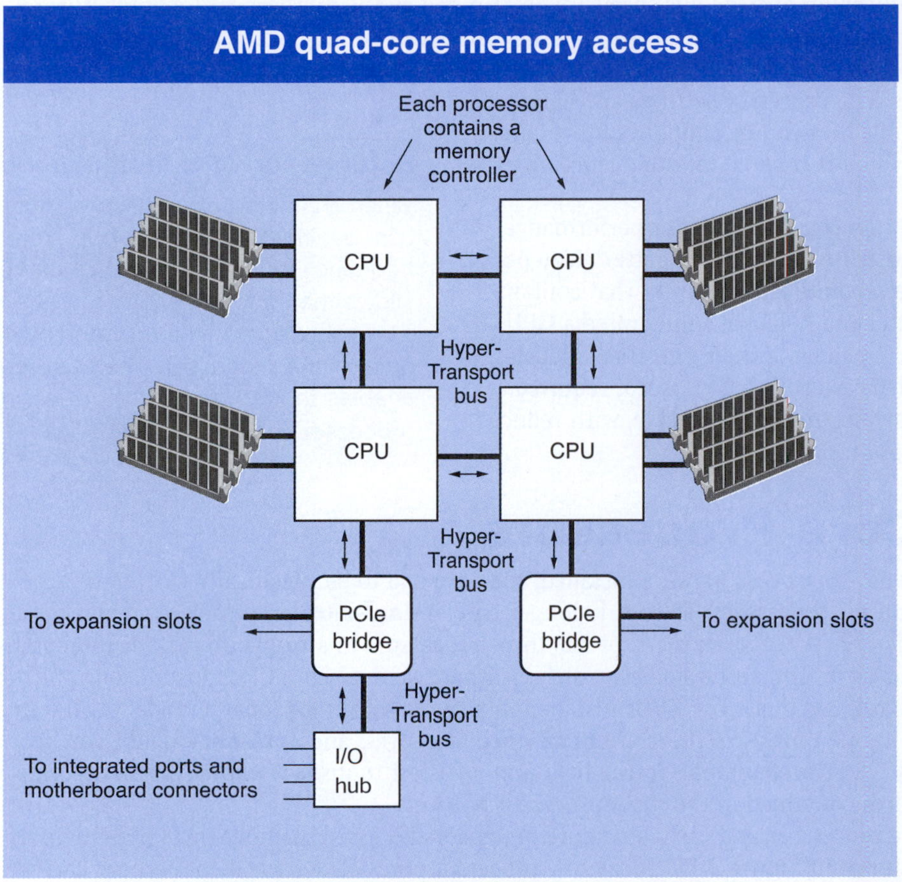

Figure 2.12 AMD quad-core memory access

In the past, dual processors were most beneficial in servers and gaming PCs, where software was written for and could take advantage of two-processor technology. Today, multi-core processors are useful to anyone. All applications can take advantage of the multi-core technology as well as the background processes that are associated with the operating system and applications. This improves operations when multitasking or when running powerful applications that require many instructions to be executed, such as drawing applications and games.

One advantage of having multiple processor cores is that home and business computers can take advantage of virtualization. **Virtualization** is having one or two virtual machines on the same computer. Virtualization software such as VMware Workstation or Microsoft Hyper-V allows one computer to act as if it were two or more computers. The computer could have two or more operating systems installed through the use of the virtualization software. Each operating system would have no knowledge of the other operating system. Windows 7 has Virtual PC, which allows an application to run within a virtual environment as if an older operating system were installed. The concept of virtualization is of interest to businesses so that legacy software can be put on a newer machine but kept separate from the main operating system or another virtualized machine on the same computer. Reduced costs and physical space are benefits of virtualization. Home computer users can install multiple operating systems in separate VMs (virtual machines) within the same physical box, with each VM being seen as a separate computer.

If the host computer had eight processor cores, these cores could all be allocated to each virtual machine. The cores could also be allocated evenly or unevenly between the VMs. Figure 2.13 illustrates this concept.

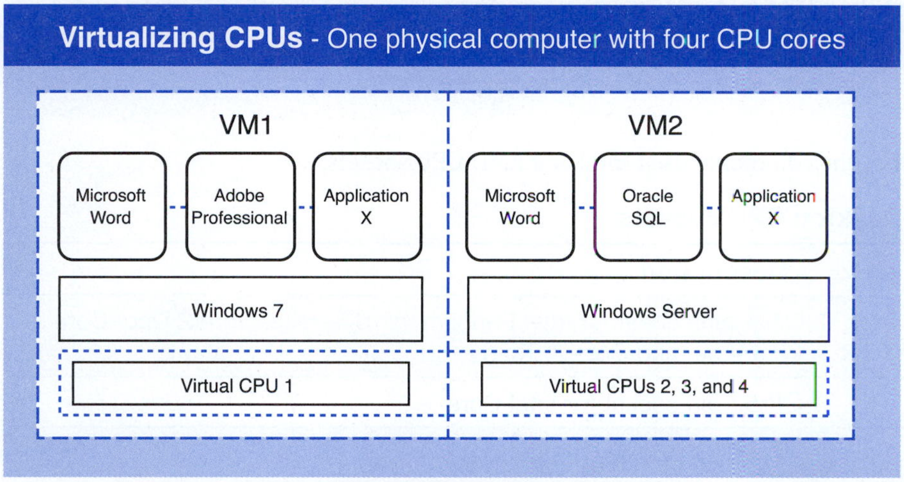

Figure 2.13 The concept of virtualization

Selecting a motherboard and processor is important when in a virtual environment. Not all processors were designed for virtualization. Refer to the virtualization software documentation to determine if the CPU being used is allowed to be used in a virtual environment. Another issue regarding processors and virtualization is licensing. For virtualization software that must be purchased (that is, is not freeware), the software manufacturer can charge on a per-processor or per-socket license basis or a per-core basis. If a CPU has four cores, then pricing might play into what virtualization software is purchased.

Sockets and Slots

A processor inserts into a socket or slot, depending on the model. Most processors today insert into a socket. There are different types of sockets: PGA (pin grid array), which has even rows of holes around a square socket; SPGA (staggered pin array), which has staggered holes so more pins can be inserted; PPGA (plastic pin grid array); µPGA (micro pin grid array); FCBGA (flip chip ball grid array); and LGA (land grid array) are all used with either AMD and/or Intel processors. Figure 2.14 shows an LGA775 socket.

Processor sockets are also called **ZIF** (zero insertion force) **sockets**; they come in different sizes. A processor socket accepts one or more specific processor models. The socket has a small lever to the side that, when lifted, brings the processor slightly up and out of the socket holes. When installing a processor, the CPU is aligned over the holes and the lever is depressed to bring the processor pins into the slot with equal force on all the pins. In Figure 2.14, notice the lever beside the socket.

Figure 2.14 An LGA socket

Tech Tip

Buying the right CPU

If you buy a motherboard and processor separately, it is important to ensure that the motherboard CPU socket is the correct type for the processor.

Table 2.5 lists the commonly used Intel and AMD CPU sockets.

Table 2.5 Desktop CPU sockets

Socket	Description
LGA 775	775-pin socket for Intel Pentium 4s, Celerons, Core 2 Duo, Core 2 Extreme, and Core 2 Quads
LGA 1150	1150-pin socket for Intel Core
LGA 1155	1155-pin socket for Intel Core
LGA 1156	1156-pin socket for Intel Core
LGA 1366	1366-pin socket for Intel Core i7, Xeon, and Celeron
LGA 2011	2011-pin socket for Intel Core i7 and Xeon
Socket 940	940-pin socket for Opteron and Athlon 64FX
Socket AM2	940-pin socket for AMD Athlon, Athlon X2, and Sempron
Socket AM2+	940-pin socket for AMD Athlon X2, Phenom X3, and Phenom X4
Socket AM3	940-pin socket for Phenom II X3 and Phenom II X4
Socket AM3+	942-pin socket for FX
Socket C32	1207-pin socket for Opteron
Socket F	1207-pin socket for Opteron
Socket FM1	905-pin socket for A-series Fusion
Socket FM2	Socket for Fusion

Processor Cooling

Keeping the CPU cool is very important. Both Intel and AMD have technologies that reduce processor energy consumption (and heat) by turning off unused parts of the processor or slowing down the processor when it starts to overheat. But these measures alone are not enough. Today's systems use fans and heat sinks. A heat sink looks like metal bars or fins protruding from the processor. The largest chip or cartridge on or inserted into the motherboard with a fan or a heat sink attached is easily recognized as the processor. Some systems have multiple fans to keep the CPU cool. Figure 2.15 shows a fan and a heat sink.

Figure 2.15 A CPU fan and heat sink

CPU fans frequently have a 3- or 4-pin cable that attaches to the motherboard. The motherboard might have a 3- or 4-pin connector. A 3-pin fan can be attached to a 4-pin motherboard connector, and a 4-pin fan cable can be connected to a 3-pin motherboard connector, as shown in Figure 2.16. Note that when a 3-pin cable attaches to 4-pin connector, the fan is always on and cannot be controlled, like a 4-pin cable to 4-pin connector can.

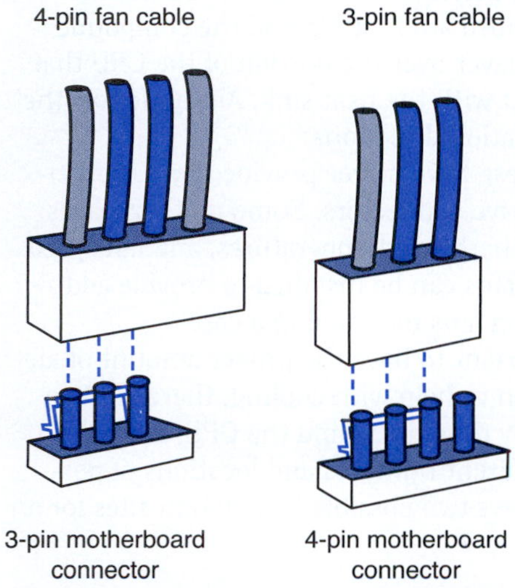

Figure 2.16 CPU fan connectivity

Additional motherboard components can also have heat sinks attached. These are normally the chipset and/or the I/O (input/output) controller chips. Figure 2.17 shows a motherboard with these cooling elements.

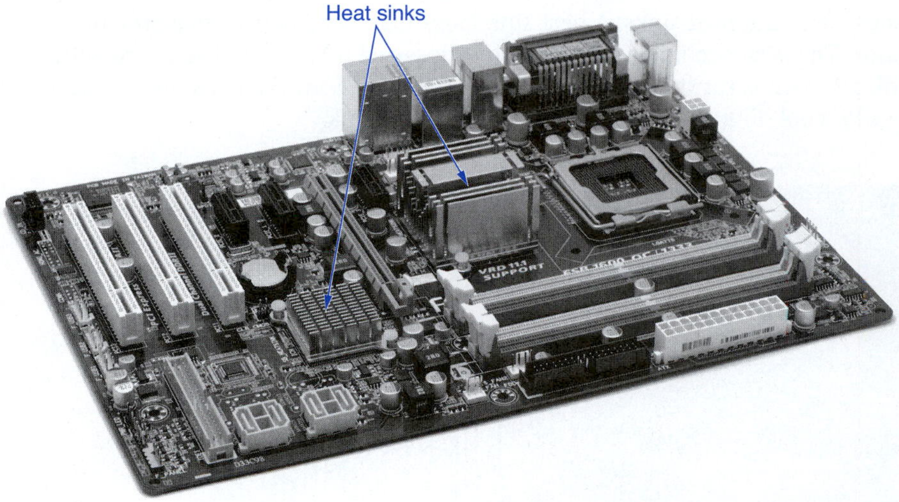

Figure 2.17 Motherboard heat sinks

Heat sinks and fans attach to the processor using different methods. The most common methods are screws, thermal compound, and clips. Clips can use retaining screws, pressure release (where you press down on them, and they release), or a retaining slot. Small screwdrivers can be used to release the clips that attach using the retaining slot. Clips for fans or heat sinks can be difficult to install. The type of heat sink and/or fan installed must fit the processor and case.

Tech Tip

When thermal paste acts like glue

Over time, thermal paste can act like glue, making the processor hard to separate from the heat sink. You can use a thermal paste cleaner, acetone, or denatured alcohol to separate the two parts. Do not pry!

When installing a heat sink, a thermal pad or thermal paste/compound may be used. A thermal pad provides uniform heat dispersion for the CPU. Thermal paste, compound, or grease is a substance applied to the top of the processor before a heat sink is attached. The thermal paste further reduces heat generated by the processor. If thermal paste is used, you should apply the prescribed amount. Spread the compound evenly in a fine layer over the portion of the CPU that comes in contact with the heat sink. Always follow the heat sink installation directions.

Some heat sinks are known as active heat sinks. These have power provided by a motherboard connection or through one of the power supply drive connectors. Some motherboards come with sensors that monitor CPU temperatures, motherboard temperatures, and fan speed. The BIOS can be used to configure the CPU. Additional fans can be installed to provide additional cooling for the PC. Figure 2.18 shows extra cooling fans mounted in a case.

Because heat sinks generate a lot of heat, it is important to have the proper amount of airflow in the right direction. If you install an additional fan to help with cooling, there are two likely places for fan placement: (1) near the power supply directly behind the CPU, and (2) on the lower-front part of the case. Different cases have different numbers and locations of possible mounting spots for the case fan(s). Figure 2.19 shows two possible installation sites for an additional fan.

Figure 2.18 Computer case auxiliary fans

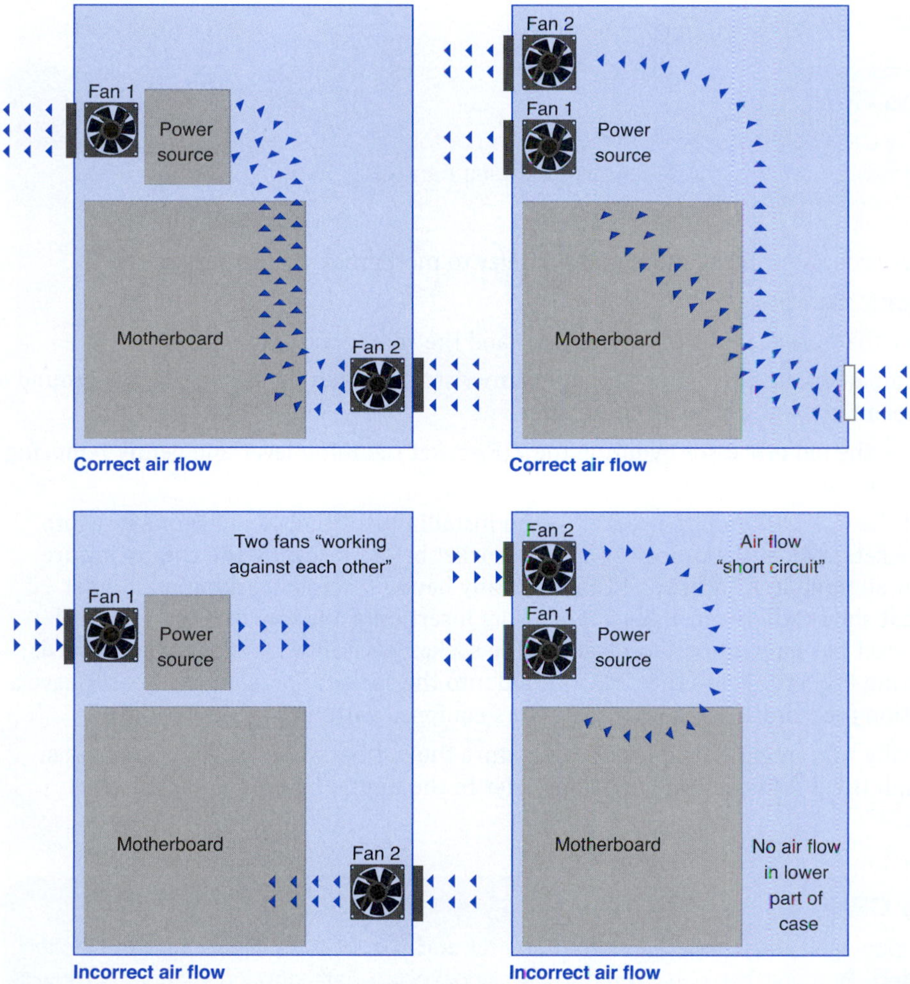

Figure 2.19 Placement of auxiliary fans

An alternative to a fan or heat sink for CPU cooling is a **liquid cooling system**. With a liquid cooling system, liquid is circulated through the system, including through a heat sink that is mounted on the CPU. Heat from the processor is transferred to the cooler liquid. The now-hot liquid is transported to the back of the system, converted to heat, and released outside the case.

Tech Tip

Air flow and ventilation

Air flow should be through the computer and over the motherboard to provide cooling for the motherboard components.

Liquid cooling allows higher clock speeds and is quieter than using a fan. However, some liquid cooling systems are difficult to install and require space within the case. Some liquid systems require the liquid to be periodically refilled. The good part about a liquid cooling system is that the CPU temperature remains constant, no matter how much usage the CPU is experiencing. This is not the case with heat sinks and fans. A similar but expensive cooling technology is phase-change cooling (also known as vapor cooling). Phase-change cooling uses a technique similar to a refrigerator: A gas is converted to a liquid that is converted back to gas.

Installing Processors

Processors are sold with installation instructions. Also, motherboard manuals (documentation) include the steps to upgrade or install the CPU. The following are the general steps for installing a processor:

Tech Tip

Handling the CPU

Always hold the CPU by the edges to avoid bending or touching the pins underneath. Do not lay the CPU down on a flat surface because the pins can easily bend.

Parts: Proper processor for the motherboard (refer to motherboard documentation)
Antistatic materials

1. Ensure that power to the computer is off and the computer is unplugged.
2. Place an antistatic wrist strap around your wrist and attach the other end to a ground or unpainted metal part of the computer.
3. Remove the old processor by lifting the ZIF socket retaining lever and gently removing the processor.
4. Insert the new CPU into the socket. When installing a CPU, it fits only one way into the socket. Look at the processor and the socket before inserting the chip to ensure proper alignment. A socket and CPU normally have a triangle marking or circular dot that shows where pin 1 goes. Processors insert only one way into the socket. If the socket has a retention lever, raising the socket lever allows a CPU to be inserted. Lowering the lever keeps the CPU inserted into the socket. Some motherboards have a retention mechanism used with processors equipped with mounted heat sinks.
5. Normally, you might be required to configure the motherboard by using jumpers or through BIOS software configuration. Refer to the motherboard manual for exact steps.

Tech Tip

Cooling the CPU

Do not apply power to the computer until the CPU and the heat sink, fan, and/or cooling unit are installed. Running the CPU without installing appropriate cooling mechanisms will overheat the CPU and destroy or weaken it.

Figure 2.20 shows a CPU being installed. Notice how the ZIF socket lever is raised.

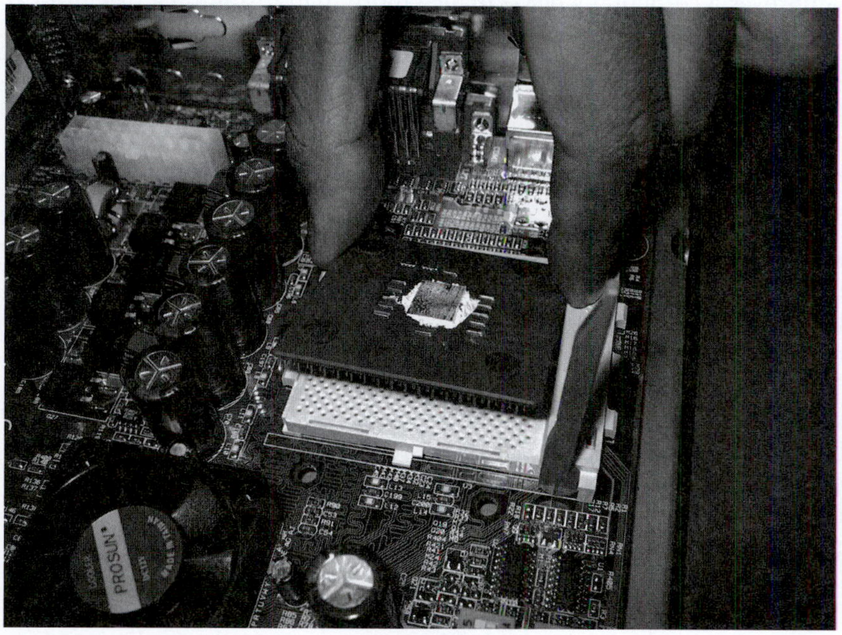

Figure 2.20 Installing a CPU

Two common questions asked of technicians are "Can a computer be upgraded to a higher or faster processor?" and "Should a computer be upgraded to a higher or faster processor?" Whether or not a computer can be upgraded to a higher or faster processor depends on the capability of the motherboard. When a customer asks if a processor should be upgraded, the technician should ask, "What operating system and applications are you using?" The newer the operating system, the more advanced a processor should be. Some games and applications that must perform calculations, as well as graphic-oriented applications, require a faster, more advanced processor.

When installing multiple processors, some motherboards require that the same processor model be used in each slot. This is not always true with newer motherboards. Refer to the motherboard documentation. The motherboard's documentation is very important when considering a CPU upgrade. Read the documentation to determine whether the motherboard can accept a faster processor.

Tech Tip

Upgrading your CPU

Do not upgrade a processor unless the documentation or manufacturer states that the motherboard supports a newer or faster processor.

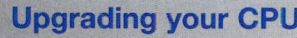

When upgrading a CPU on an older or newer system, an important consideration is CPU voltage. Different CPUs require different voltage levels. Inserting a CPU into a socket that has a lower or higher voltage supplied to it will damage the new CPU. A VRM (voltage regulator module) is integrated into the motherboard and can provide the appropriate voltage. The CPU can communicate to the VRM the voltage level desired, and the VRM can provide it. Running a processor at lower speeds and lower voltages can save on power consumption, especially on a mobile platform.

Throttle management is the ability to control the CPU speed by slowing it when it is not being used heavily or is hot. Usually this feature is controlled by a system BIOS setting and the Windows *Power Options* Control Panel. Some users may not want to use CPU throttling so that performance is at a maximum. Others, such as laptop users, may want to conserve power whenever possible to extend the time the laptop can be used on battery power.

Upgrading components other than the processor can also increase speed in a computer. Installing more memory, a faster hard drive, or a motherboard with a faster front side bus sometimes improves a computer's performance more than installing a new processor. All devices and electronic components must work together, transferring the 1s and 0s efficiently. The processor is only one piece of the puzzle. Many people do not realize that upgrading one computer component does not always make a computer faster or better.

Mobile Device Motherboards/CPUs

Mobile device motherboards are similar to desktop motherboards: A mobile device motherboard holds the majority of the electronics, contains a processor, has memory, and supports having ports attached. However, the processor on a mobile device is normally not as powerful as a desktop model, has less memory that may not be upgradeable, and has fewer ports. However, some powerful laptops have more power, upgradability, and ports than some low-end desktop models.

Laptop processors are not normally upgraded, but they do sometimes have to be replaced. Always refer to the laptop documentation for motherboard removal procedures. Always power the laptop off. Always remove the laptop battery. Use proper grounding procedures (further discussed in Chapter 4).

At a minimum, screws from the underside of the laptop have to be removed. Sometimes, hard drives, drives that insert on the side of the laptop, and memory must be removed before you can remove the motherboard. Figure 2.21 shows the underside of a laptop and how you might have to remove screws to get these parts out before you can remove the motherboard.

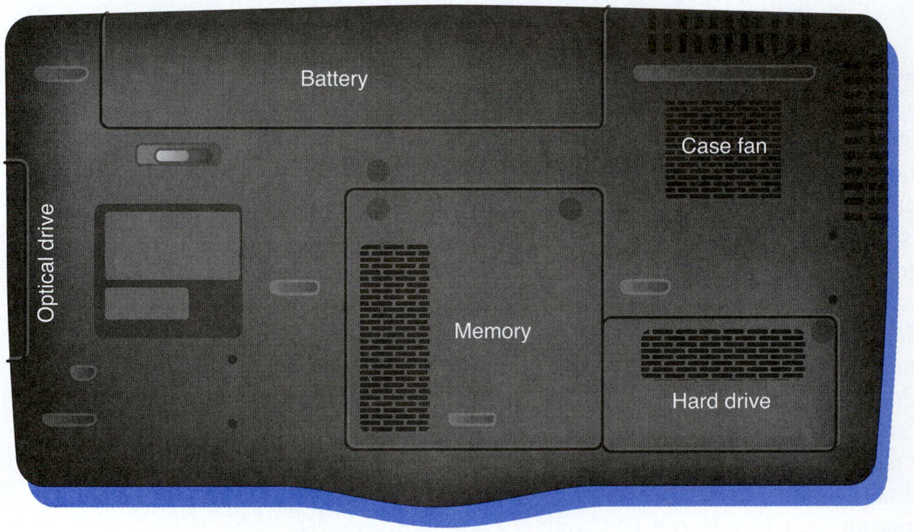

Figure 2.21 Laptop underside

Laptops and computers sometimes must have their processors replaced. Many mobile device processors have a heat sink and/or fan assembly attached. Furthermore, the processor ZIF socket must be loosened before you lift the processor from the socket, as shown in Figure 2.22.

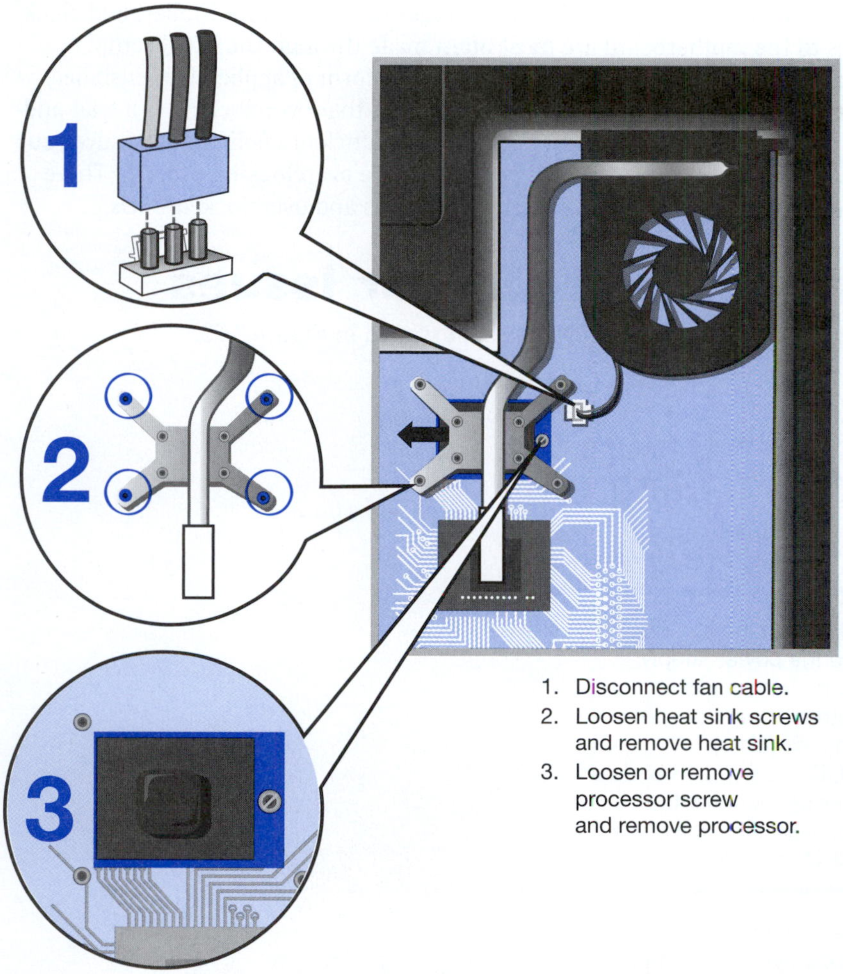

1
2
3
1. Disconnect fan cable.
2. Loosen heat sink screws and remove heat sink.
3. Loosen or remove processor screw and remove processor.

Figure 2.22 Laptop CPU removal

Overclocking Processors

Overclocking is changing the front side bus speed and/or multiplier to boost CPU and system speed. Before describing the overclocking steps, we must discuss the following related issues:

- Because the CPU is normally covered with a heat sink and/or fan, you cannot easily tell the CPU speed.
- CPU speed ratings are conservative.
- The CPU, motherboard, memory, and other components can be damaged by overclocking.
- Applications may crash, the operating system may not boot, and/or the system may hang when overclocking.
- The warranty is void on most CPUs if you overclock.
- When you increase the speed of the CPU, the processor's heat increases. Extra cooling, using fans and larger heat sinks, is essential.
- Devices may not react well to overclocking.
- The memory chips may need to be upgraded to be able to keep up with the faster CPU.
- You need to know how to reset the system BIOS in case the computer will not boot properly after you make changes.

Many motherboard manufacturers do not allow changes to the CPU, multiplier, and clock settings. The changes to the motherboard are most often made through the BIOS setup. However, CPU manufacturers may provide tuning tools in the form of applications installed on the computer for overclocking configuration. Keep in mind that overclocking is a trial-and-error situation. The primary problem with overclocking is insufficient cooling. Make sure you purchase a larger heat sink and/or extra fans before starting the overclocking process. There are websites geared toward documenting specific motherboards and overclocked CPUs.

Troubleshooting Processor Issues

Processor issues can appear in different ways, as illustrated in Figure 2.23.

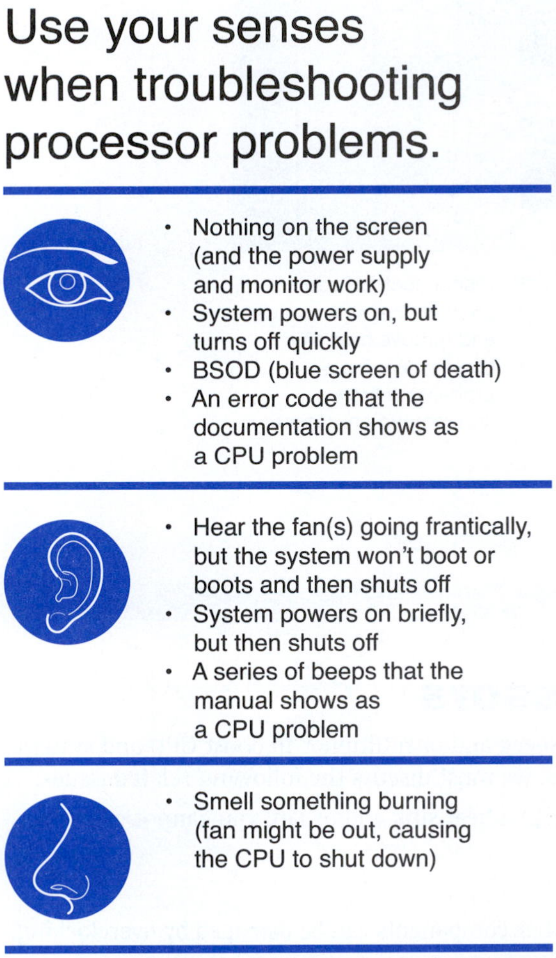
Use your senses when troubleshooting processor problems.
• Nothing on the screen (and the power supply and monitor work)
• System powers on, but turns off quickly
• BSOD (blue screen of death)
• An error code that the documentation shows as a CPU problem
• Hear the fan(s) going frantically, but the system won't boot or boots and then shuts off
• System powers on briefly, but then shuts off
• A series of beeps that the manual shows as a CPU problem
• Smell something burning (fan might be out, causing the CPU to shut down)

Figure 2.23 Detecting processor problems

The following measures can help you solve CPU issues:

- The number-one issue related to processor problems is heat. Ensure that the fans work. Ensure that you have enough circulation/cooling. Vacuum any dust from the motherboard/CPU. Cool the room more.
- Some system BIOS screens show the CPU temperature. (This is covered in more detail in Chapter 3.)
- Research any visual codes or audio beeps on the motherboard, using the computer manufacturer's website.

Processor issues and determining whether an issue is a CPU or motherboard problem are some of the hardest things to troubleshoot. When your video port doesn't work, you can insert a friend's video card to determine the problem. Diagnosing processor and motherboard issues isn't so simple. If you have power to the system (that is, the power supply has power coming out of it), the hard drive works (try it in a different computer), and the monitor works (try it on a different computer), then the motherboard and/or the CPU are prime suspects.

Expansion Slots

If a computer is to be useful, the CPU must communicate with the outside world, including other motherboard components and adapters plugged into the motherboard. An expansion slot is used to add an adapter to the motherboard, and it has rules that control how many bits can be transferred at a time to the adapter, what signals are sent over the adapter's gold connectors, and how the adapter is configured. Figure 2.24 shows expansion slots on a motherboard.

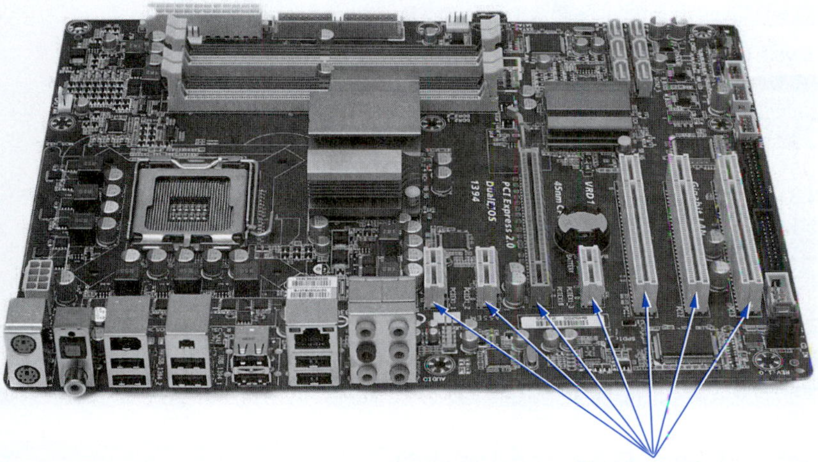

Figure 2.24 Motherboard expansion slots

Expansion slots used in PCs are usually some form of PCI (Peripheral Component Interconnect), AGP (Accelerated Graphics Port), or PCIe (PCI Express). Other types of expansion slots that have been included with older PCs are ISA (Industry Standard Architecture), EISA (Extended Industry Standard Architecture), MCA (Micro Channel Architecture), and VL-bus (sometimes called VESA [video electronics standards association] bus). A technician must be able to distinguish among adapters and expansion slots and be able to identify the adapters/devices that use an expansion slot. A technician must also realize the abilities and limitations of each type of expansion slot when installing upgrades, replacing parts, and making recommendations.

PCI (Peripheral Component Interconnect)

A previously popular expansion slot is **PCI** (Peripheral Component Interconnect). PCI comes in four varieties: 32-bit 33MHz, 32-bit 66MHz, 64-bit 33MHz, and 64-bit 66MHz. Figure 2.25 shows the most common type of PCI expansion slot. Figure 2.26 shows the various types of PCI slots that you might see.

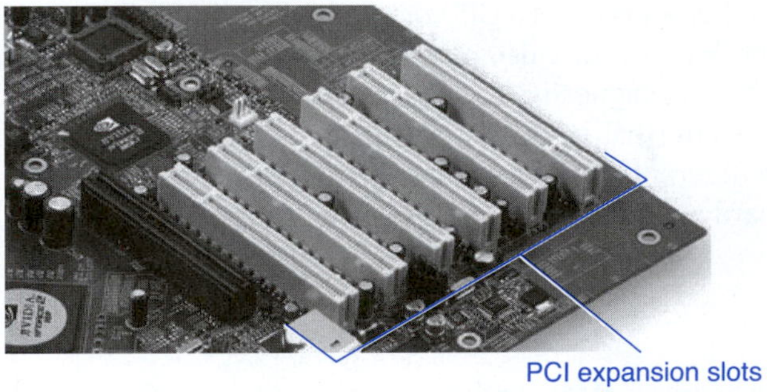

Figure 2.25 PCI expansion slots

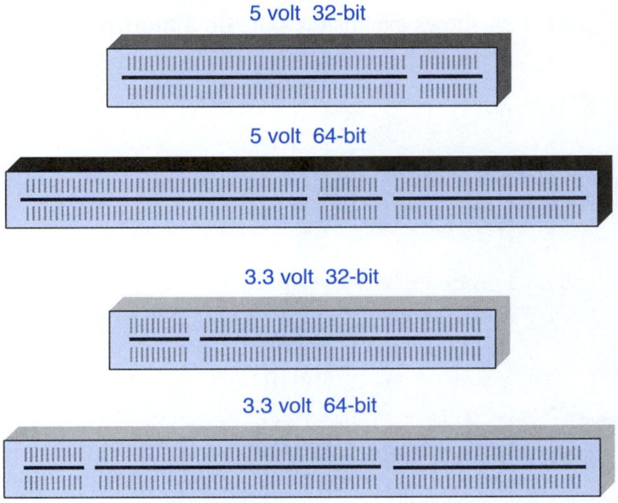

Figure 2.26 3.3-volt and 5-volt PCI expansion slots

An upgrade to the PCI bus called **PCI-X** can operate at 66, 133, 266, 533, and 1066MHz. PCI-X allows faster speeds and is backward compatible with the previous versions of the bus. A chip called the PCI bridge controls the PCI devices and PCI bus. With the PCI-X bus, a separate bridge controller chip is added. Figure 2.27 shows how the PCI-X bus integrates into the system board. Notice how a chip called the **north bridge** connects the CPU to RAM, the AGP expansion slot that might hold a video adapter, and the PCI bus.

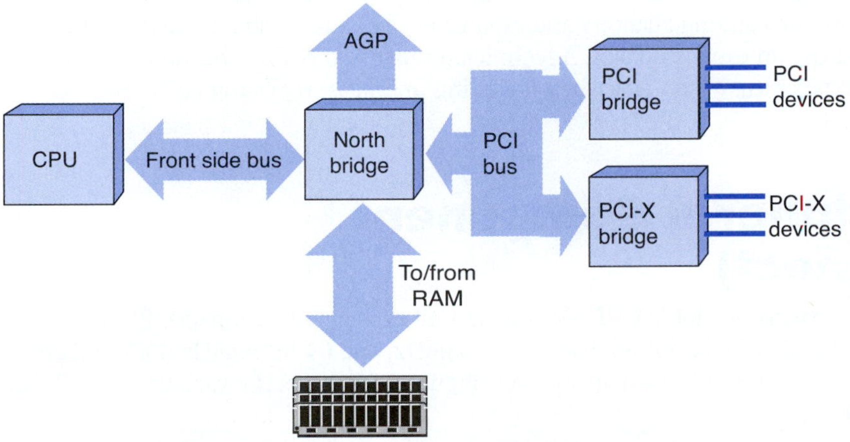

Figure 2.27 PCI-X block diagram

PCI-X adapters are most often found in network servers or high-end gaming workstations to control video or network adapters (such as Gigabit Ethernet). Today's motherboards have a limited number of PCI or PCI-X expansion slots because of a newer standard called PCI Express (PCIe), which is covered later in this chapter.

Tech Tip

PCI cards in PCI-X slots

Remember that older PCI cards can fit in a PCI-X expansion slot, but a PCI-X adapter requires a PCI-X expansion slot.

AGP (Accelerated Graphics Port)

AGP (Accelerated Graphics Port) is a bus interface for graphics adapters developed from the PCI bus. Intel provided the majority of the development for AGP, and the specification was originally designed around the Pentium II processor. AGP speeds up 3-D graphics, 3-D acceleration, and full-motion playback.

With AGP, the processor on the video adapter can directly access RAM on the graphics card or, when even more RAM is needed, access the memory on the motherboard. This helps with video-intensive applications, such as 3-D graphics, which are resource intensive and use a lot of memory. Software developers can produce better and faster 3-D graphics by using AGP technology. The best performance is achieved when applications use the RAM on the AGP adapter. Previous video adapters were limited by the bottleneck caused by going through an adapter and a bus shared with other devices. With AGP, the video subsystem is isolated from the rest of the computer. The different versions of AGP are known as 1x, 2x, 4x, and 8x. Table 2.6 summarizes the differences between the AGP versions.

Table 2.6 AGP versions

AGP Version	Bus speed	Transfer rate	Data path	Connector voltage
1x	66MHz	266MBps	32 bits	3.3V
2x	133MHz	512MBps	32 bits	3.3V
4x	266MHz	>1GBps	32 bits	1.5V
8x	533MHz	>2GBps	32 bits	1.5V

Figure 2.28 shows an illustration of an AGP slot compared with PCI and ISA expansion slots. ISA is the oldest expansion slot and one you still might see when troubleshooting older systems. ISA allows 16-bit transfers to the expansion slots and operates at a maximum of 10MHz. All of these expansion slots have been replaced by PCIe (covered next). Figure 2.29 shows various expansion slots.

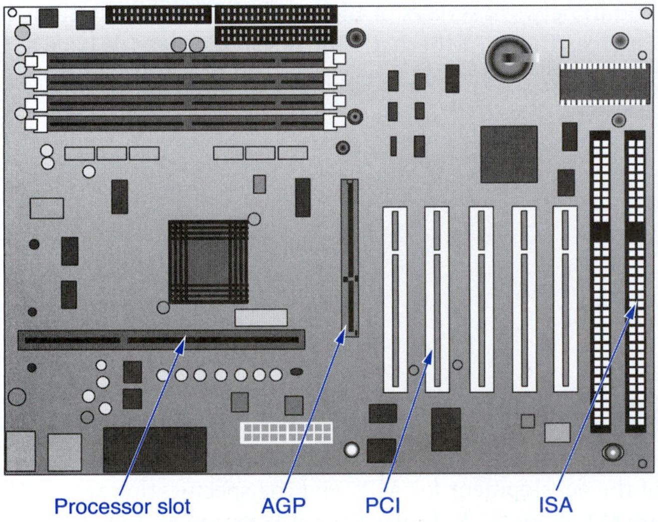

Figure 2.28 AGP and other expansion slots

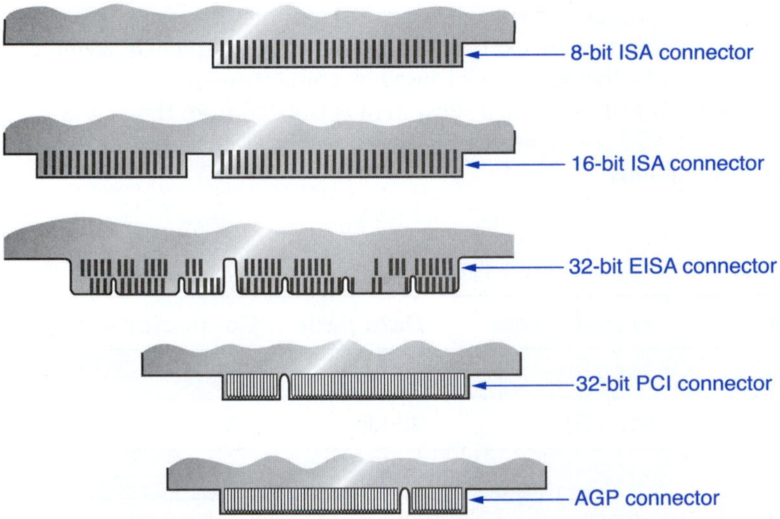

Figure 2.29 A comparison of older expansion slots

PCIe (Peripheral Component Interconnect Express)

PCI, PCI-X, and AGP have been replaced with **PCIe** (PCI Express), which is also seen as PCI-E. PCIe outperforms all other types of PCI expansion slots. Table 2.7 shows the different PCIe versions.

Table 2.7 PCIe versions

PCIe version	Speed (per lane per direction)
1.0	2.5GT/s (gigatransfers per second) or 250MBps
2.0	5GT/s or 500MBps
3.0	8GT/s or 1GBps
4.0	16GT/s or 2GBps

The older PCI standard is half-duplex bidirectional, which means that data is sent to and from the PCI or PCI-X card using only one direction at a time. PCIe sends data full-duplex bidirectionally; in other words, it can send and receive at the same time. Figure 2.30 shows this concept.

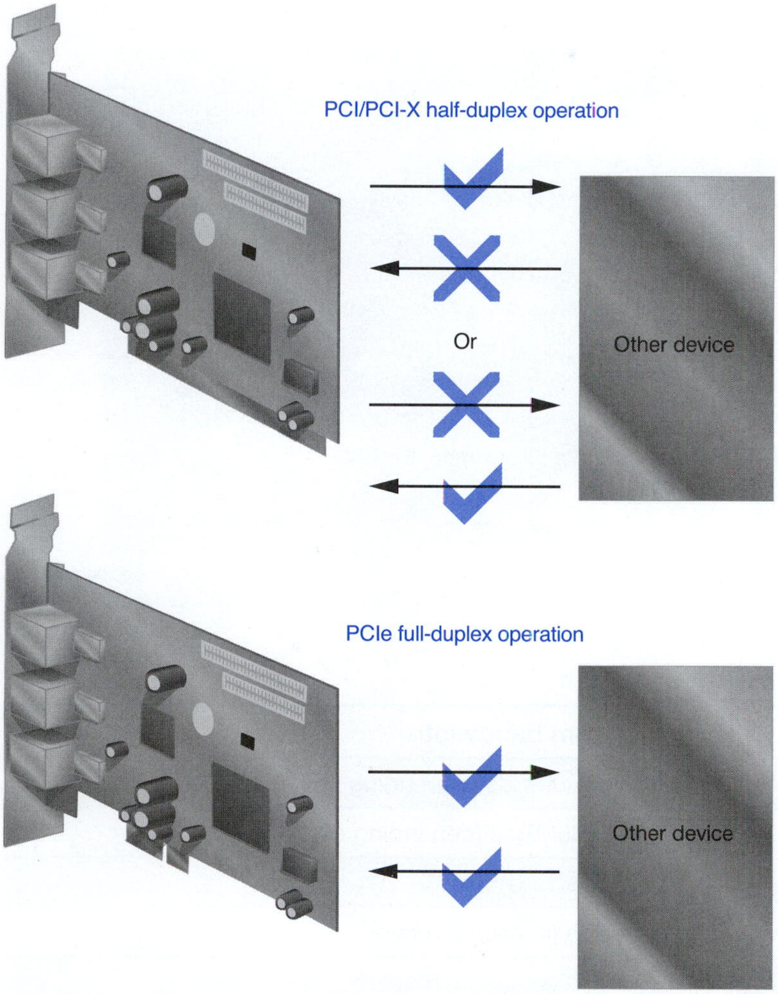

Figure 2.30 A comparison of PCI/PCI-X and PCIe transfers

The older PCI standards, including PCI-X, use a parallel bus where data is sent with multiple 1s and 0s simultaneously. PCIe is a serial bus, and data is sent one bit at a time. Table 2.8 shows a comparison of the PCI, PCI-X, AGP, and PCIe buses. Another difference between PCI and PCIe is that PCIe slots come in different versions, depending on the maximum number of lanes that can be assigned to the card inserted into the slot. For example, an x1 slot can have only one transfer lane used by the x1 card inserted into the slot; x2, x4, x8, x16, x32 slots are also available. An x16 slot accepts up to 16 lanes, but fewer lanes can be assigned. Figure 2.31 shows the concepts of PCIe lanes. Notice how one lane has two unidirectional communication channels. Also note how only seven lanes are used. PCIe has the ability to use a reduced number of lanes if one lane has a failure or a performance issue.

Tech Tip

PCI cards in PCIe slots

Older PCI, PCI-X, and AGP adapters will not work in any type of PCIe slots.

Tech Tip

Beware of the PCIe fine print

Some motherboard manufacturers offer a larger slot size (such as x8), but the slot runs at a slower speed (x1, for example). This keeps cost down. The manual would show such a slot as x8 (x1 mode) in the PCIe slot description.

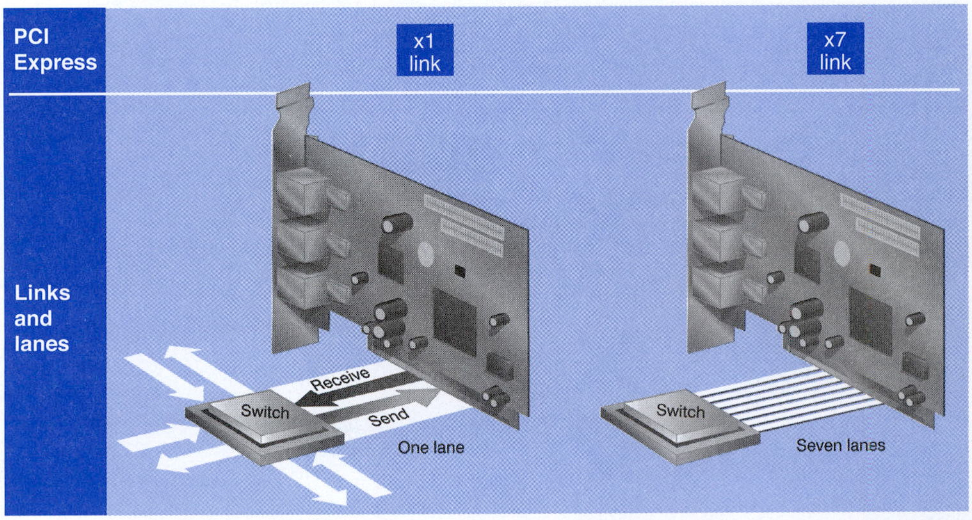

Figure 2.31 PCIe lanes

Table 2.8 Comparing bus bandwidth

Bus	Maximum bandwidth
PCI	133 or 266MBps (depending on bus speed)
PCI-X	266–4,266MBps (depending on bus speed)
AGP 2x	533MBps
PCIe x1	250MBps (in each direction)
PCIe x2	500MBps (in each direction)
PCIe x4	1,000MBps (in each direction)
PCIe x8	2,000MBps (in each direction)
PCIe x16	4,000MBps (in each direction)
PCIe x32	8,000MBps (in each direction)

A PCIe x1 adapter can fit in an x1 or higher slot. A larger card, such as a PCIe x16, cannot fit in a lower-numbered (x8, x4, x2, or x1) slot. Figure 2.32 shows this concept.

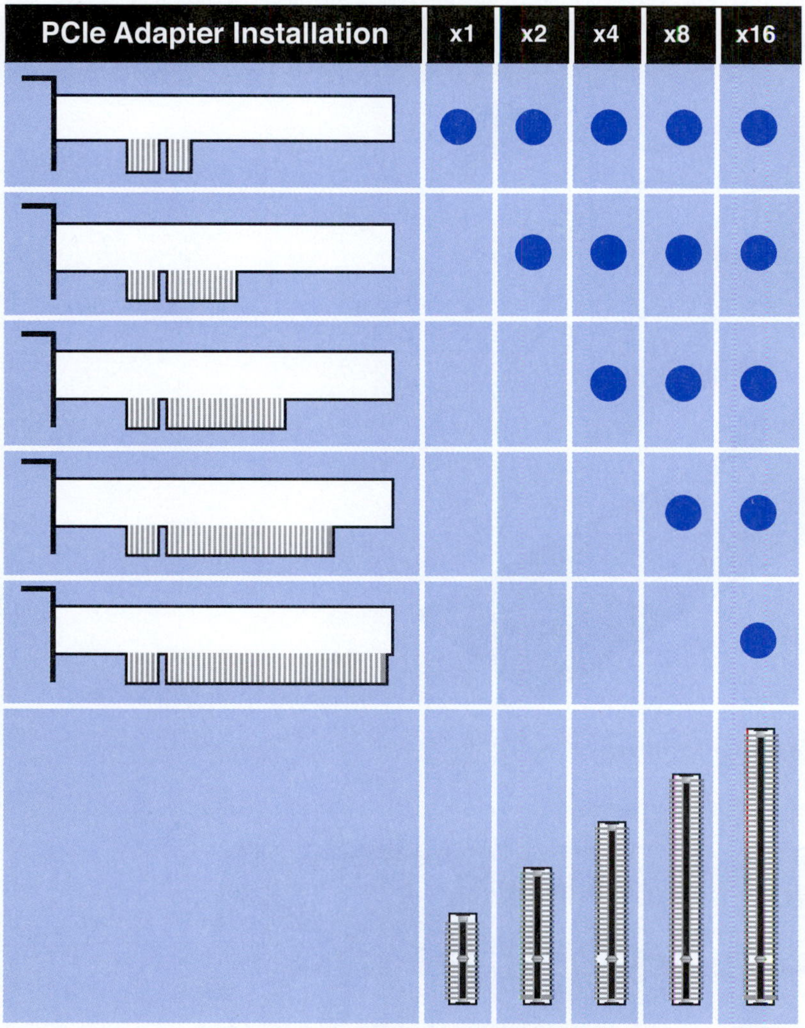

Figure 2.32 Correct slots for PCIe cards

Removing an adapter is normally just a matter of removing a retaining screw or plate and lifting the adapter out of the slot. Some AGP and PCIe expansion slots have retention levers. You move the retention lever to the side in order to lift the adapter from the expansion slot. Figure 2.33 shows an example of the PCIe adapter removal process. Figure 2.34 shows a motherboard with two x1 PCIe, one x16 PCIe, and four PCI expansion slots. Notice that the PCIe x16 slot has a retention lever.

Tech Tip

Removing PCIe adapters

If a PCIe adapter has a release lever, you must use the lever, or you may damage the board (and possibly the motherboard).

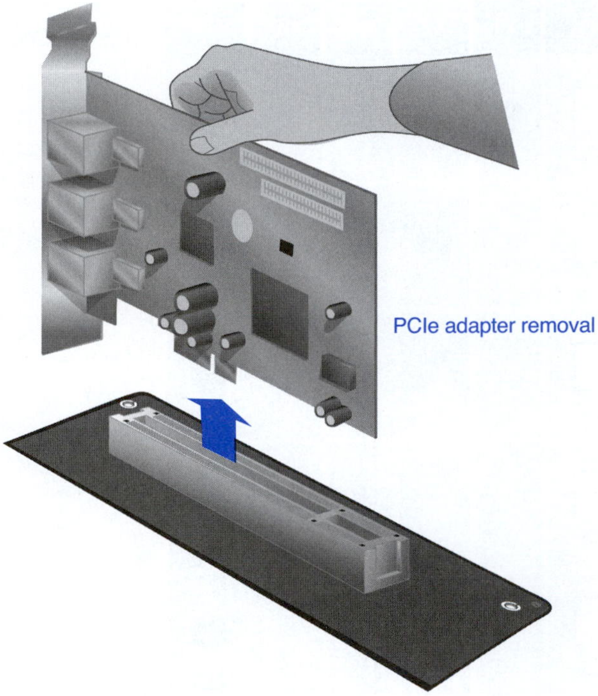

Figure 2.33 PCIe adapter removal

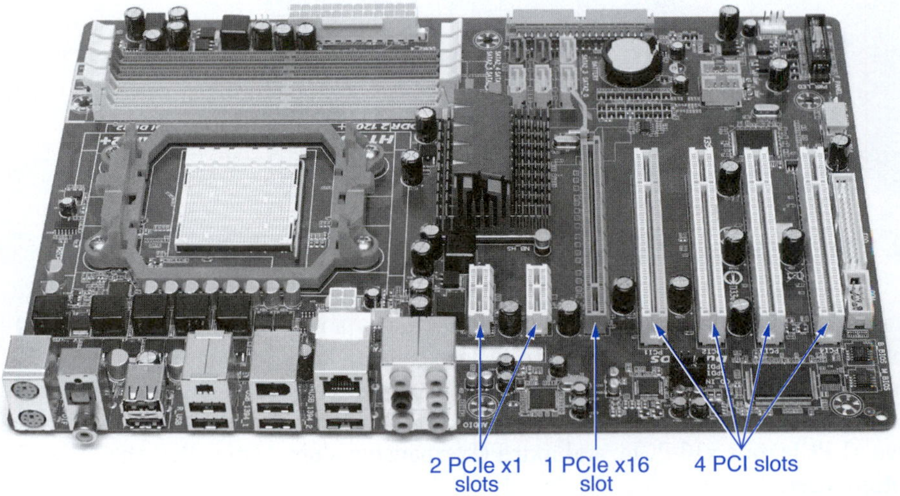

Figure 2.34 Motherboard with PCIe and PCI slots

Laptop Expansion

The **mini PCI** 32-bit 33MHz standard was developed to allow PCI upgrades and interface cards to be added to laptops, docking stations, and printers. Regular PCI cards are too large and require too much power for these technologies. Mini PCI cards allow SCSI, USB, IEEE 1394, wireless network, network, sound, modem, and other types of device or memory connectivity.

Mini PCI cards have three form factors—Type I, II, and III. Type I and II cards use 100-pin connectors, while Type IIIs use a larger 124-pin card. Manufacturers now use the 52-pin **mini PCIe** cards. To install a mini PCI or a PCIe adapter, you may have to disassemble the laptop or remove a screw from the bottom, as shown previously in Figure 2.21. Or you may have to lift a lid to access the expansion slot, as shown in Figure 2.35.

Figure 2.35 Mini PCI adapter installed in a laptop

An alternative to a mini PCI/PCIe internal adapter is a **PC Card** architecture. PC Cards (previously known as **PCMCIA**, or Personal Computer Memory Card International Association, cards) are small credit card–size adapters that you can use to upgrade a laptop by inserting them into a slot on the side of the laptop. The original standard was a 16-bit local bus standard, later upgraded to **CardBus**, which allows 32-bit transfers at speeds up to 33MHz (133Mbps). PC Cards come in three sizes: Type I, II, and III. PC Cards were replaced by ExpressCards.

Tech Tip

PCMCIA Association dissolved

All ExpressCard standards are now managed by the USB Implementer forum.

ExpressCard technology is the latest high-performance expansion standard for mobile computers. ExpressCard modules give users the ability to add a wide variety of plug-and-play applications to their computers, including memory, wired and wireless communications, multimedia, security, and networking. The ExpressCard standard supports PCIe, e-SATA, IEEE 1394 (FireWire), or USB 3.0 connectivity through the ExpressCard slot. Most PC Cards/ExpressCards support hot swapping. **Hot swapping** allows a card to be inserted into a slot when the laptop is powered on. PC Cards do not fit in ExpressCard slots. There are two types of ExpressCard: ExpressCard/34 and ExpressCard/54. The 34 means it is 34mm wide, and the 54 means it is 54mm wide (in an L-type card). Figure 2.36 shows the PC Card and the two ExpressCard form factors.

Tech Tip

Converters for PC Cards and ExpressCards

An adapter is available to connect a PC Card to an ExpressCard/34 or /54 slot.

Figure 2.36 PC Card compared to ExpressCards

Tech Tip

Universal slot is better

A laptop with a universal slot can accept either an ExpressCard/34 or an ExpressCard/54; however, an ExpressCard/34 slot accepts only ExpressCard/34 modules.

PCI, PCI-X, AGP, and PCIe are important for connectivity in both workstation and portable computers. Traditional PCI connectivity will need to be supported for several more years in new machines for backward compatibility and in computers already in use. PCIe is the current bus for internal and external device connectivity.

More Motherboard Connectors

Some connectors that are always a mystery to new technicians are AMR, CNR, and ACR. Intel developed AMR and CNR. **AMR** (Audio/Modem Riser) is a connector on a motherboard that manufacturers use to offer a different version of the same motherboard. The motherboard manufacturer installs an adapter into the AMR slot, and the adapter can perform both sound card and modem duties, without taking up one of the expansion slots. The cost is also lower to the manufacturer. The AMR connector is normally located beside or between the other motherboard expansion slots.

A **CNR** (Communications Network Riser) allows integration of network card functions with sound and modem. CNR shares space with a traditional expansion slot, such as PCI or PCIe, and it too is located beside or between the other expansion slots. Figure 2.37 shows a CNR expansion slot.

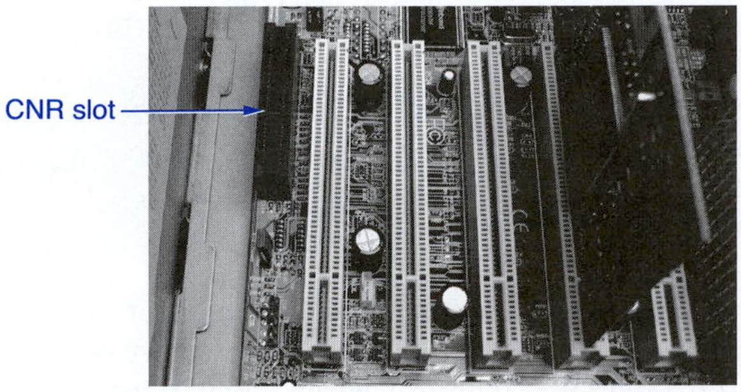

Figure 2.37 CNR slot

ACR (Advanced Communications Riser) was developed by a group of companies including AMD, VIA Technologies, Motorola, and 3Com. ACR not only supports audio, modem, and networking but also DSL modems. The ACR connector is a 120-pin PCI connector that has been reversed (turned around).

Chipsets

The principal chips on the motherboard that work in conjunction with the processor are known as a **chipset**. These allow certain features on the computer. For example, chipsets control the maximum amount of motherboard memory, the type of RAM chips, the motherboard's capacity for two or more CPUs, and whether the motherboard supports the latest version of PCIe. Common chipset manufacturers include Intel, VIA Technologies, ATI technologies (now owned by AMD), Silicon Integrated Systems (SiS), AMD, and NVIDIA Corporation.

Tech Tip

Know your chipset

A technician must keep informed about chipsets on the market; customers often ask for recommendations about motherboard upgrades and new computer purchases. A technician should at least know where to find the information.

Usually, a chipset goes with a particular processor and determines which memory chips a motherboard can have. Chipsets determine a lot about what a motherboard can allow or support. The chipset coordinates traffic to and from motherboard components and the CPU. When buying a motherboard, pick a proper processor and a good chipset. Figure 2.38 shows the Intel 975X chipset.

Finding your chipset

Tech Tip

To locate the chipset, which may be one or two chips, look in the motherboard documentation for a diagram that shows the location. If it's not shown, look in the documentation for the chipset manufacturer and then visually inspect the motherboard to locate the chip(s).

Notice in Figure 2.38 the **MCH** (memory controller hub). This important chip, sometimes called the north bridge, connects directly to an older Intel CPU. On a motherboard that has a newer AMD or Intel CPU, the MCH would be incorporated into the CPU. Also notice the iCH7R chip. The **ICH** (I/O controller hub), also known as the **south bridge**, is a chip that controls what features, ports, and interfaces the motherboard supports.

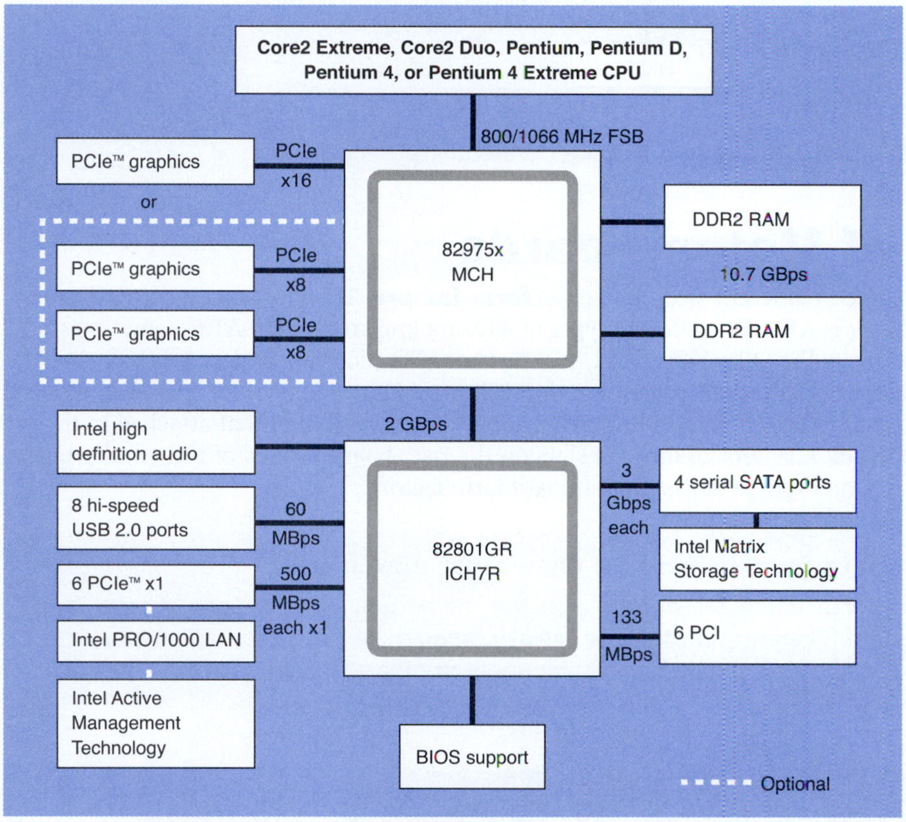

Figure 2.38 The Intel 975X chipset

Figure 2.39 shows the Z277 chipset, which connects to one of Intel's Core processors that has an integrated GPU. Notice how the processor handles things that were previously handled by the MCH part of a chipset.

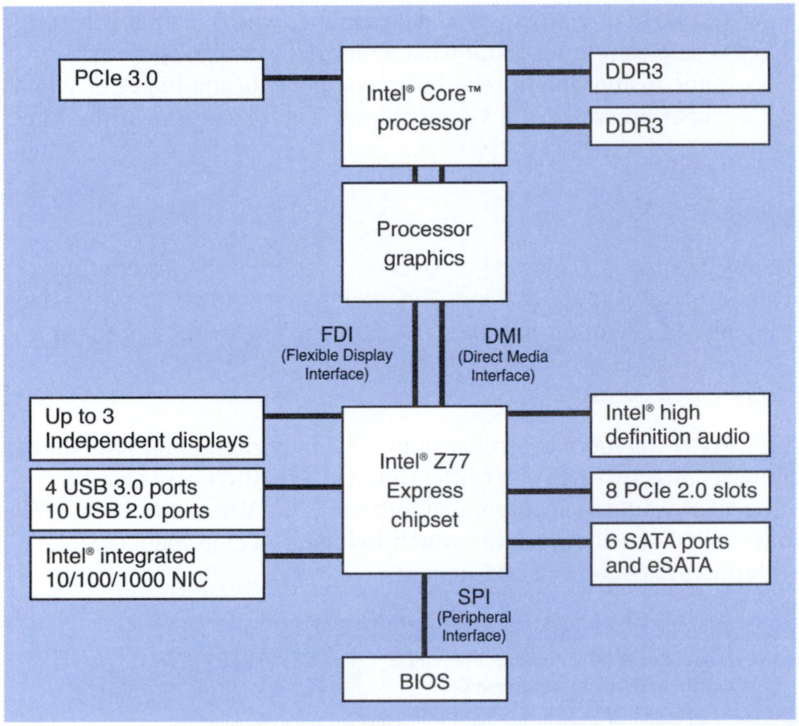

Figure 2.39 Intel Z77 Express chipset connectivity

Types of Motherboards

Motherboards come in different sizes, known as **form factors**. The most common motherboard form factor is ATX. The different types of ATX are known as microATX (sometimes shown as µATX), miniATX, FlexATX, EATX, WATX, nanoATX, picoATX, and mobileATX. A smaller form factor is ITX, which comes in a miniITX, nanoITX, and picoITX sizes. Some motherboards, such as the NLX and LPX form factors, had a riser board that attached to the smaller motherboard. Adapters go into the slots on the riser board instead of into motherboard slots. Figure 2.40 shows some of the motherboard form factors.

Tech Tip

The motherboard form factor and case must match

The case used for a computer must match the motherboard form factor. Some cases can accommodate different form factors, but you should always check. When building a computer or replacing a motherboard, it is important to obtain the correct form factor.

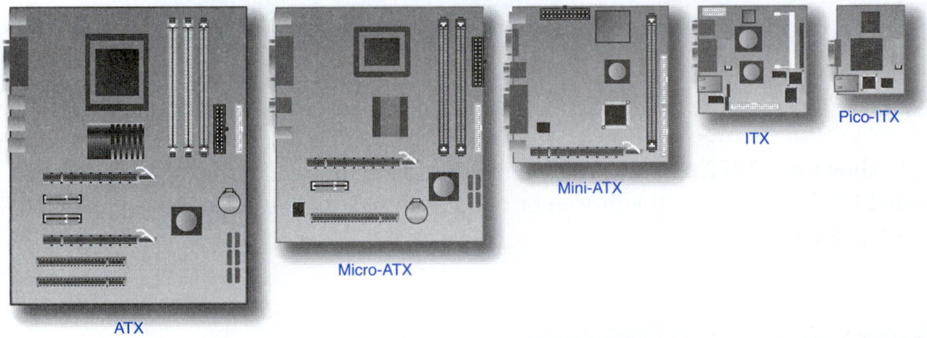

Figure 2.40 Motherboard form factors

The BTX form factor was intended to replace ATX. But further development of the BTX standard was canceled in favor of propriety form factors. Within the BTX family of form factors are the smaller versions called microBTX (sometimes shown as μBTX), nanoBTX, and picoBTX. The WTX (for Workstation Technology Extended) is an older form factor that is larger than ATX or BTX and was used with high-end workstations, such as those with multiple processors and more drives.

Figure 2.41 shows many of the motherboard components labeled. A technician should stay current on motherboard technologies.

Tech Tip

Go green with a motherboard or CPU

When upgrading or replacing a motherboard and/or processor, consider going green. Select a board that is lead free and uses a lower amount of power (wattage), one that uses a smaller form factor (such as microATX), one that has integrated video, or one that has all these features.

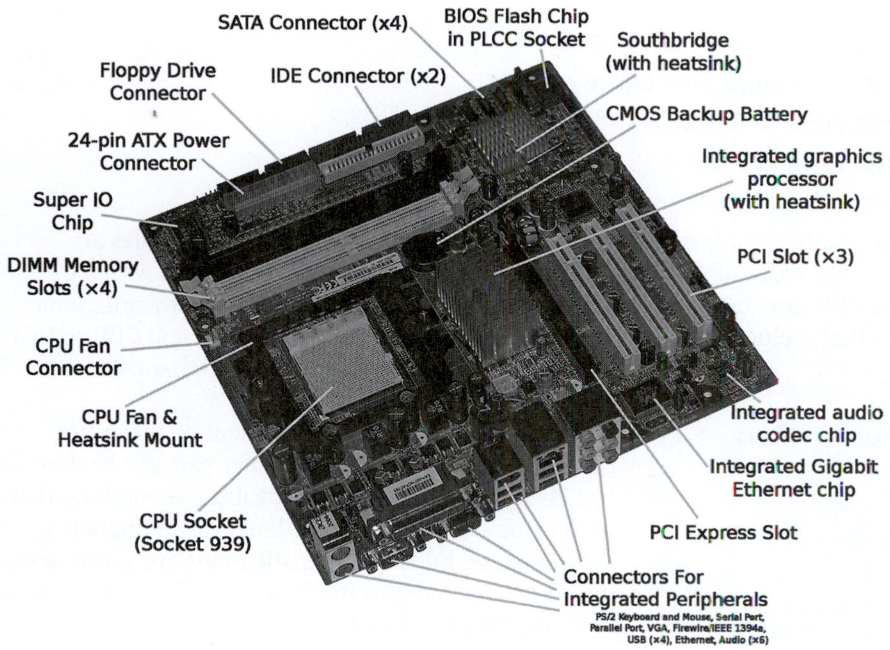

Figure 2.41 Motherboard components

Manufacturers sometimes design a case so that it requires a proprietary motherboard. With such a design, a replacement motherboard must be purchased from the original manufacturer and is usually more expensive than a generic option.

Upgrading and Replacing Motherboards

When upgrading a motherboard or processor, you must consider several issues. The following list guides you through making the decision (or helping a customer make the decision) of whether to upgrade a motherboard:

- Why is the computer being upgraded? For example, does the computer need more memory? Are more expansion slots needed? Does the computer need a bigger/faster CPU to run certain operating systems or applications? Is more space wanted in the computer area? Sometimes upgrading the motherboard does not help unless the other computer components are upgraded. The most expensive and fastest motherboard/CPU will not run applications well unless it has the proper amount of memory. Hard drives are another issue. If software access is slow, the solution might not be a new motherboard but a faster and larger hard drive or more RAM.

- Which type (ISA, PCI, AGP, or PCIe) and how many adapters are needed from the old motherboard? Does the new motherboard have the required expansion slots?
- What type of chipsets does the new motherboard support? What features, if any, would this bring to the new motherboard?
- Will the new motherboard fit in the current computer case, or is a new one required?
- If upgrading the CPU, will the motherboard support the new type of CPU?
- Does the motherboard allow for future CPU upgrades?
- How much memory (RAM) does the motherboard allow? What memory chips are required on the new motherboard? Will the old memory chips work in the new motherboard or with the new CPU?

Before replacing a motherboard, it is important to do all the following:

- Remove the CPU and CPU fan.
- Remove adapters from expansion slots.
- Remove memory chips from expansion slots.
- Disconnect power connectors.
- Disconnect ribbon cables.
- Disconnect external devices such as mouse, keyboard, and monitor.

Replacement motherboards do not normally come with RAM, so the old modules are removed from the bad/older motherboard. A motherboard usually does not come with a CPU. Make note of the CPU orientation before removing it from the bad/older motherboard. Some retailers sell kits that include the computer case, power supply, motherboard, and CPU so that the components match, function together correctly, and are physically compatible.

When upgrading any component or the entire computer, remember that the older part can be donated to a charity or educational institution. Something that one person considers outdated may be an upgrade to someone else. Educational institutions are always seeking components to use in classrooms. Many stores have recycling programs for computer parts.

Tech Tip

Use good antistatic measures when installing a motherboard

When replacing a motherboard or removing it from the case, place the motherboard on a nonconductive surface such as an antistatic mat or the antistatic bag that comes with the motherboard.

Motherboard Troubleshooting

Common symptoms of motherboard issues are similar to CPU problems: The system does not display anything, an error code appears, one or more beeps occur, the system locks, the system reboots, a Windows BSOD (blue screen of death) appears, or one or more of the ports, expansion slots, or memory modules fails.

Motherboard problems and power problems are probably the most difficult things to troubleshoot. Because various components are located on the motherboard, many things can cause errors. **POST** (power-on self-test) is one of the most beneficial aids for troubleshooting a motherboard. The meaning of any codes that appear on the screen should be researched. If multiple POST error codes appear, you should troubleshoot them in the order they are presented. The following list helps with motherboard troubleshooting:

- Is the motherboard receiving power? Check the power supply to see if the fan is turning. If the CPU or motherboard has a fan, see if it is turning. Check voltages going from the power supply to the motherboard. See Chapter 4 for directions.
- Check the BIOS settings (covered in Chapter 3) for accuracy.

- Check for overheating. Power down the computer and allow the computer to cool. Power on the computer with the cover off.
- Reseat the CPU, adapters, and memory chips.
- Remove unnecessary adapters and devices and boot the computer.
- Plug the computer into a different power outlet and circuit, if possible.
- Check if the motherboard is shorting out on the frame.
- Check the CMOS battery.
- With a motherboards that has diagnostic LEDs, check the output for any error code. Refer to the motherboard documentation or online documentation for the problem and possible solution.

Tech Tip

These concepts relate to Apple computers, too

Even though this book focuses on PCs, concepts related to CPU, motherboards, expansion slots, cache, and chipsets also apply to Apple computers. Apple computers and PCs have similar CPU and memory requirements.

Soft Skills—Active Listening

Active listening is participating in a conversation where you focus on what the customer is saying—in other words, listening more than talking. For a technician, active listening has the following benefits:

- Allows you to gather data and symptoms quickly
- Allows you to build customer rapport
- Improves your understanding of the problem
- Allows you to solve the problem more quickly because you understand the problem better
- Provides mutual understanding between you and the customer
- Provides a means of having a positive, engaged conversation rather than having a negative, confrontational encounter
- Focuses on the customer rather than the technician
- Provides an environment where the customer might be more forthcoming with information related to the problem

Frequently, when a technician arrives onsite or contacts a customer who has a technical problem, the technician is (1) rushed; (2) thinking of other things, including the problems that need to be solved; (3) assuming that he or she knows exactly what the problem is, even though the user has not finished explaining the problem; or (4) more interested in the technical problem than in the customer and the issues. Active listening changes the focus from the technician's problems to the customer's problems.

A common but ineffective service call involves a technician doing most of the talking and questioning, using technical jargon and acronyms and a flat or condescending tone. The customer, who feels vulnerable, experiences a heightened anxiety level. Active listening changes this scenario by helping you build a professional relationship with your customers. The following list outlines some measures that help you implement active listening.

Have a positive, engaged professional attitude when talking and listening to customers:

- Leave your prejudices behind; be polite and aware of other cultures and customs; be open-minded and nonjudgmental.
- Have a warm and caring attitude.
- Do not fold your arms in front of your chest because doing so distances you from the problem and the customer.

- Do not blame others or talk badly about other technicians.
- Do not act as if the problem is not your responsibility.

Focus on what the customer is saying:

- Turn off or ignore electronic devices.
- Maintain eye contact; don't let your mind wander.
- Allow the customer to finish explaining the problem; do not interrupt; avoid arguing with the customer or being defensive.
- Stop all irrelevant behaviors and activities.
- Mentally review what the customer is saying.
- Refrain from talking to co-workers unnecessarily while interacting with customers.
- Avoid personal interruptions or distractions.

Participate in the conversation in a limited, but active manner:

- Maintain a professional demeanor (suspend negative emotions); do not minimize or diminish the customer's problem.
- Acknowledge that you are listening by occasionally nodding and making comments, such as "I see."
- Use positive body language such as leaning slightly forward or taking notes.
- Observe the customer's behavior to determine when it is appropriate to ask questions.

Briefly talk with the customer:

- Speak with a positive tone; use a tone that is empathetic and genuine, not condescending.
- Restate or summarize points made by the customer.
- Ask nonthreatening, probing questions related to the customer's statements or questions.
- Do not jump between topics.
- Do not use technical jargon.
- Clarify the meaning of the customer's situation.
- Identify clues to help solve the problem and reduce your troubleshooting time by listening carefully to what the customer says.
- Follow up with the person at a later date to ensure that the problem is solved and to verify satisfaction.
- Offer different repair option or replacement options, if possible.

Chapter Summary

- Important motherboard parts include the following: processor, RAM slots/RAM, expansion slots (PCI, PCI-X, PCIe, and AGP), and cooling devices.
- Processors can be multi-core and contain very fast cache memory: L1 cache inside the processor and L2 cache outside the processor but inside the chip. Processors can also support L3 cache.
- Processors use HyperThreading to make efficient use of processor time.
- Processors must be kept cool with fans and/or heat sinks. A thermal paste is applied between a heat sink and a processor.
- The clock speed refers to the processor's internal clock. This is not the same as the FSB or bus speed.
- CPU throttling slows down the processor to prevent overheating.
- PCI/PCI-X is a 32- and 64-bit parallel bus. The AGP expansion slot has a dedicated path for video to the processor. PCI, PCI-X, and AGP have been replaced with the point-to-point serial PCIe bus.
- PCIe slots have a specific number of bidirectional lanes that are the maximum a card can use. A PCIe adapter can fit in a slot of the same number of lanes or a higher number of lanes.
- A chipset is one or more chips that coordinate communication between the processor and the rest of the motherboard. A chipset could have an MCH (north bridge) to coordinate between the CPU and some expansion slots as well as memory. The chipset could also have a ICH (south bridge) to coordinate between the CPU and the rest of the motherboard expansion slots and ports. The chipset dictates the maximum number and type of slots and ports on a motherboard. AMD and Intel have created technologies to address the slowness of the FSB: HyperTransport, QPI, and DMI.
- Laptops use mini PCI/PCIe slots for adapters and can use ExpressCards if the laptops have a slot in the side for these type of cards.
- When replacing a motherboard, ensure that the CPU socket and number/types of expansion slots are appropriate. When replacing a laptop motherboard, additional components may have to be removed.
- When replacing or upgrading the CPU, ensure that the motherboard supports the processor and that the heating device is attached before powering on the computer. When replacing a laptop CPU, a screw may have to be loosened before you can remove the old processor.
- When replacing a CPU, ensure that the heat sink or fan is attached before powering on the computer.
- Active listening is an important skill for a technician. Don't be distracted by people or technology, take notes, make good eye contact, and ask directed questions when appropriate.

Key Terms

ACR 76
active listening 81
AGP 69
AMR 76
APU 49
back side bus 51
bit 46
bus 47
bus speed 51
byte 46
cache memory 51
CardBus 75
chipset 76
clock 51
clock speed 51
CNR 76
CPU speed 51
CPU throttling 51
dual-core 55
ExpressCard 75
external data bus 47
form factor 78
FSB 51
gigabyte 46
gigahertz 46
GPU 49
hexa-core 55
hot swapping 75
HT 54
HyperTransport 55
ICH 77
internal data bus 47
kilobyte 46
L1 cache 51
L2 cache 51
L3 cache 51
liquid cooling system 62
MCH 77
megabyte 46
mini PCI 74
mini PCIe 74
north bridge 68
octa-core 55
overclocking 65
PC Card 75
PCI 67
PCIe 70
PCI-X 68
PCMCIA 75
POST 80
processor 46
quad-core 55
south bridge 77
thread 54
throttle management 63
virtualization 57
ZIF socket 57

Review Questions

1. Which expansion slot would most likely be used to add an internal adapter to a new laptop? [ExpressCard/34 | ExpressCard/54 | mini PCIe | PC Card | USB port | PCI-X | mini PCI]
2. Which expansion slot would be *best* for a video card in a desktop computer? [PCI-X | PCIe | PCI | ExpressCard/54 | AGP]
3. A motherboard has a PCIe x16 expansion slot. Which PCIe adapter(s) will fit in this slot? (Select any that apply.) [x1 | x2 | x4 | x8 | x16 | x32]
4. Match the capacity to the description.

____ bit	a.	8 bits
____ kilobyte	b.	a 1 or a 0
____ megabyte	c.	approximately 1,000 bytes
____ byte	d.	approximately 1 million bytes
____ gigabyte	e.	approximately 1 trillion bytes
____ terabyte	f.	approximately 1 billion bytes

5. What is the front side bus?
   a. the internal data bus that connects the processor core to the L1 cache
   b. the internal data bus that connects the processor core to the L2 cache
   c. the external data bus that connects the processor to the motherboard components
   d. the external data bus that connects the processor to the L2 cache
6. A customer wants to upgrade the L2 cache. What will this definitely require?
   a. a motherboard purchase
   b. a CPU purchase
   c. a ROM module purchase
   d. a RAM module purchase

7. Match the expansion slot to the definition.

____ ExpressCard	a. 32- or 64-bit parallel bus
____ AGP	b. used in laptops
____ PCI	c. just for video cards
____ PCIe	d. has varying number of lanes

8. What is the difference between Hyper-Threading and HyperTransport?

9. Which of the following would be a function of a chipset? (Select all that apply.)
   a. Process instructions obtained from RAM
   b. Set the maximum number of USB 3.0 ports allowed on a motherboard
   c. Coordinate between the CPU and motherboard components
   d. Temporarily hold documents and instructions
   e. Provide permanent storage
   f. Prioritize threads being queued for processing by the CPU
10. Which of the following statements is true regarding PCIe?
   a. A PCIe slot will not accept a PCI card.
   b. PCIe is a parallel bus technology.
   c. PCIe is a 32- or 64-bit bus technology.
   d. PCIe is being replaced by PCI-X.
11. [T | F] An x8 PCIe adapter will always transmit using eight lanes.
12. What is the significance of a motherboard specification that states the following: 1 PCIe x16 (x8 mode) slot?
   a. The slot accepts x8 or x16 cards.
   b. The slot can transmit traffic using 8 or 16 lanes.
   c. The slot can transmit in bursts of 8 or 16 bytes at a time.
   d. The slot accepts x16 cards but uses only 8 lanes.
13. What determines whether a motherboard can use a specific model of RAM, such as DDR2 or DDR3? [CPU | chipset | PCIe standard | processor speed]
14. A technician for a college is going to repair a problem in another building. A professor stops the technician to talk about her slow computer. The technician gives a little eye roll but stops and listens to the teacher. The teacher comments, "I can't get my email or even type my tests. The computer takes at least 20 minutes just to boot." As the technician looks around a little exasperated, he says "Uh huh." "I logged this problem over a week ago," continues the professor, "and no one has dropped by." "Uh huh," replies the technician again. "Do you know when you folks might get to that issue or have an idea about what might be the problem?" the professor asks. The technician looks at the professor and says, "It is probably a virus that has been going around. Jim was supposed to get to those. We will get to you as soon as we can." The technician's phone rings, and he walks away while talking on the phone.

List three active listening techniques and good customer support procedures that could improve this situation.

15. Explain how a technician might be culturally insensitive.

16. What is overclocking?

17. [T | F] When installing a CPU, orient pin 1 to pin 1 on the socket and align the other pins. Lower the ZIF socket lever and lock. Power on the computer to ensure that the CPU works. Power down the computer and install the heat sink and/or fan.

18. What is applied between a processor and a heat sink to increase heat dissipation?

19. What component would be affected by the LGA 2011 specification? [RAM | chipset | processor | expansion slot]

20. Where are mini PCIe cards normally installed?
    a. in tablet computers
    b. in smartphones
    c. on the bottom of a laptop
    d. in a slot adjacent to the processor

Exercises

Lab 2.1 ATX Motherboard Parts Identification Exercise

Objective: To identify various motherboard parts

Parts: None

Procedure: Using Figure 2.42, label each of the ATX motherboard parts.

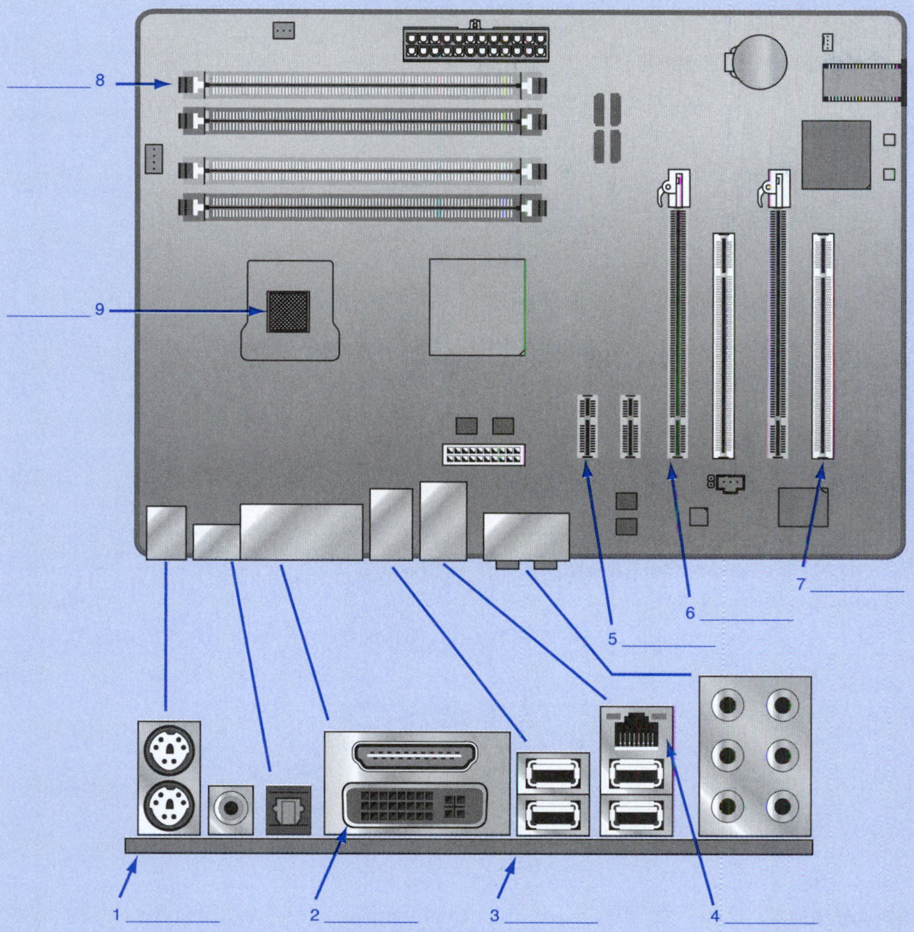

Figure 2.42 Motherboard parts

1.

2.

3.

4.

5.

6.

7.

8.

9.

Lab 2.2 Motherboard Analysis

Objective: To identify various motherboard parts

Parts: None

Procedure: Using the information you learned in this chapter and related to the specifications found in Figure 2.43, answer the questions that follow.

XYZ Motherboard Specifications

Form factor	ATX
Power connector	24-pin
CPU	
CPU socket type	LGA1155
CPUs supported	Celeron, Pentium, Core i3, i5, i7
Chipset	Intel Z77
Graphics	
Integrated GPU	Multi-VGA output support: HDMI/DVI/ RGB/DisplayPort ports
Memory	
Memory	4x240-pin
Memory standard	DDR3 2600(O.C.), 2400(O.C.), 2200(O.C.), 2133(O.C.), 1866(O.C.), 1800(O.C.), 1600, 1333
Maximum memory	32GB
Memory channel	Dual channel
Expansion slots	
PCIe 3.0/2.0 x16	2 (single x16 or dual x8)
PCIe 2.0 x16	1 (x4 mode)
PCIe 2.0 x1	2
PCI	2
Onboard LAN	
Max LAN speed	10/100/1000Mbps
Wireless LAN	WiFi 802.11 b/g/n
Rear ports	
PS/2	1 x PS/2 keyboard/mouse port
Video	D-sub + DVI
HDMI	1 x HDMI
DisplayPort	1 x DisplayPort
USB 1.1/2.0	2 x USB 2.0
USB 3.0	4 x USB 3.0
S/PDIF out	1 x optical
Audio	6 ports

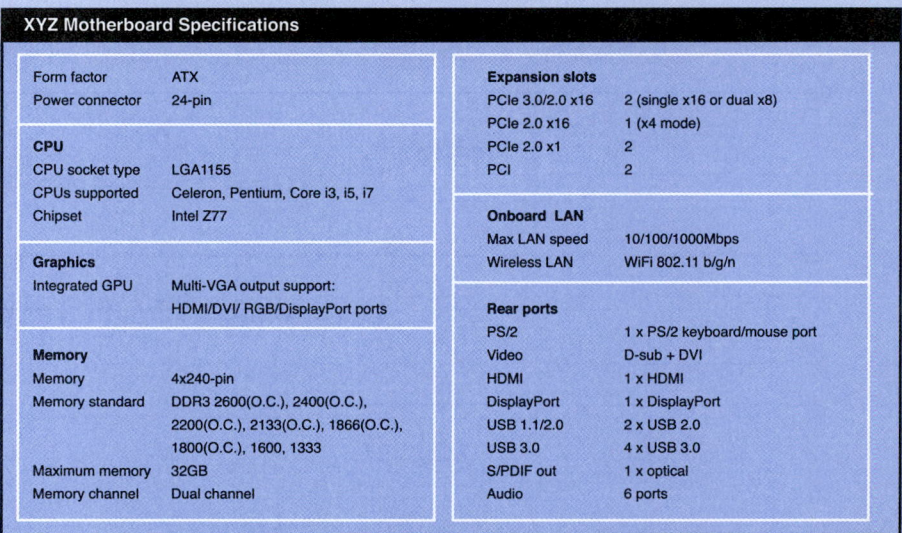

Figure 2.43 Motherboard advertisement

1. If someone you know were buying this motherboard, what type of case would you need to purchase?
2. What does LGA1155 tell you about this motherboard?
3. Does this motherboard come with a CPU installed?
   [Yes | No | Cannot tell from the information presented]
4. What motherboard component controls the maximum number of 3.0 USB ports this motherboard *could* have?
5. What processor(s) does this motherboard accept?
6. What do you think that the letters O.C. after some of the memory chips mean in relationship to this motherboard?
7. What is the most significant difference between a version 2.0 PCIe slot and a version 3.0 PCIe expansion slot?
8. What do you think the PCIe 3.0/2.0 x16 line that states "2 (single x16 or dual x8)" means?
   a. The adapter that goes into this slot can use a single lane that goes at x16 speeds or two lanes that go at x8 speeds.
   b. One single x16 adapter and/or one single x8 adapter can go into the expansion slots.
   c. One x16 adapter can go into one of the version 3.0 slots and achieve 3.0 speeds, OR two x16 adapters can be installed, but they can only transfer eight lanes at a time at 3.0 speeds.
   d. A single x16 adapter can be installed in one of the version 3.0 slots, or two x8 adapters can be installed in the two version 3.0 slots.
9. What can insert into the PS/2 port? (Select the best answer.)
   [mouse | keyboard | mouse or keyboard | display | external storage]
10. What type of video port is described as a D-sub in this documentation?
11. What is an advantage of having an integrated GPU in the CPU?

12. What is the most likely reason this motherboard manufacturer chose to include two PCI expansion slots?

Lab 2.3 Processor Speed, Processor Socket, and Ports

Objective: To identify various computer features such as the type of processor being used, processor socket, and additional expansion ports

Parts: Computer with Internet access

Procedure: Complete the following procedure and answer the accompanying questions.

1. Boot computer and determine the processor type and speed. Write down the processor type and speed.
2. Power off the computer. Open or remove the cover. Locate the processor. What type of processor socket is on the motherboard? If you are unsure, use the Internet as a resource. Write down the processor socket type.

   What model of processors can go into this type of socket?

   List the type of cooling that is used for the processor.
3. Look at the back of the computer, where the ports are located. List every port located on the computer and one device that could connect to the port.
4. Locate a picture of an IEEE 1394 port or connector on the Internet. Write down the URL for the site where you find this picture.
5. Using the Internet, locate one vendor that makes a motherboard that supports IEEE 1394 or has an integrated IEEE 1394 port. Write down the vendor's name and the URL where you find the information.

Activities

Internet Discovery

Objective: To obtain specific information on the Internet regarding a computer or its associated parts

Parts: Computer with Internet access

Procedure: Locate documentation on the Internet for a GIGABYTE GA-A75M-DS2 motherboard in order to answer Questions 1–12. Continue your Internet search in order to answer Questions 13 and 14.

Questions:

1. Does the motherboard support an Intel or AMD processor?
2. What chipset is used?
3. How many expansion slots are on the motherboard?
4. What form factor does this motherboard use?
5. What processors can be used on this motherboard?
6. Does the motherboard support having an integrated GPU in the CPU?
7. What type of CPU socket does the motherboard have?

8. How many and of what type of PCIe slots are there?
9. What type of memory does this motherboard accept?
10. Does this motherboard have an integrated IEEE 1394 port?
11. What is the maximum number and type of USB ports supported by this motherboard?
12. Write the URL where you found the motherboard information.
13. Find a vendor for a motherboard that uses the Intel X79 chipset. Document the model and vendor.
14. Find an Internet site that describes the dimensions of the extended ATX motherboard form factor. List the dimensions and the website.

Soft Skills

Objective: To enhance and fine-tune a future technician's ability to listen, communicate in both written and oral form, and support people who use computers in a professional manner

Activities:

1. On a piece of paper or an index card, list three ways you can practice active listening at school. Share this information with your group. Consolidate ideas and present five of the best ideas to the class.
2. In a team environment, determine two situations in which team members have experienced a situation in which a support person (a PC support person, sales clerk, checkout clerk, person being asked directions, and so on) could have provided better service if he or she had been actively listening. Share your findings with the class.
3. In teams of two, have one person tell a story and the other person practice active listening skills. The person telling the story should critique the listener. The pair should then exchange roles.

Critical Thinking Skills

Objective: To analyze and evaluate information and to apply learned information to new or different situations

Activities:

1. Find an advertisement for a computer in a local computer flyer, newspaper, magazine, or book or on the Internet. Determine all the information about the motherboard and ports that you can from the ad. Write down any information you do not understand. Research this information and share your findings with a classmate.
2. Your parents want to give you a new computer as a present. The one they are considering has a GPU integrated into the CPU. List at least one argument you might use for getting a different computer model.

3. Why do you think a motherboard has different buses that operate at different speeds?

A+ Certification Exam Tips

- ✓ Review the latest Intel and AMD processor slots the day of the exam. These are not ones that you might be dealing with on a daily basis.
- ✓ Review the specifications for the expansion slots, including how some of the diagrams look. Use the Internet to view motherboards to see if you can determine the type of expansion slot. The exam has graphics that are unlabeled. Do the same for other motherboard components, including the processor.
- ✓ Review the size and type of laptop PCI/PCIe adapters.
- ✓ Know that AGP was used only for a video adapter.
- ✓ Know the difference between the north bridge and the south bridge. Know the components that each bridge type connects to the CPU.

chapter 3

System Configuration

Chapter Objectives:

In this chapter you will learn:

- How to make configuration changes to a computer
- The importance of BIOS and UEFI BIOS
- How to replace a motherboard battery
- What system resources are and how to view/change them

CompTIA Exam Objectives:

What CompTIA A+ exam objectives are covered in this chapter?

- ✓ 801-1.1 Configure and apply BIOS settings.
- ✓ 801-1.2 Differentiate between motherboard components, their purposes, and properties.
- ✓ 801-1.4 Install and configure expansion cards.
- ✓ 802-1.4 Given a scenario, use appropriate operating system features and tools.
- ✓ 802-4.2 Given a scenario, troubleshoot common problems related to motherboards, RAM, CPU, and power with appropriate tools.

Configuration Overview

Installing and configuring the motherboard, the processor, RAM, or other devices can involve using the system BIOS Setup program, cabling certain motherboard pins, jumpering motherboard pins, setting switches, or using the operating system. The system **Setup** program allows you to configure the motherboard, power, and devices and enables you to set performance options.

Another configuration option involves motherboard pins. The motherboard contains pins that are used to connect cables such as those that go to the computer front panel. Look back to Figure 2.16 to see how the processor fan connects to pins on the motherboard.

Pins can also be covered by a **jumper** to enable or disable a particular feature, such as resetting all the system Setup settings. Figure 3.1 shows an enlarged jumper; the pins and jumper are much smaller in real life than the one shown. When a jumper is not in use, instead of putting it in a drawer, place the jumper over a single pin. This action does not enable anything, and it keeps the jumper safe and convenient for when it is needed later.

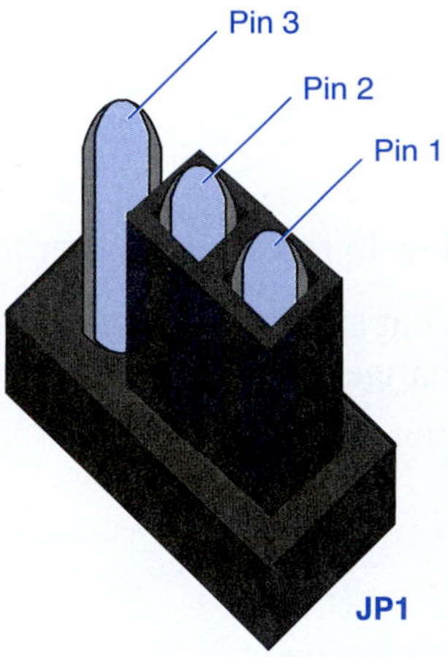

Figure 3.1 JP1 jumper block with pins 1 and 2 jumpered together

BIOS Overview

The BIOS (basic input/output system) is an important motherboard component that has the following functions:

- Holds and executes POST (power-on self-test)—a program that identifies, tests, and initializes basic hardware components
- Holds a basic routine called a bootstrap program that locates an operating system and allows it to load
- Holds Setup (also called BIOS setup, system Setup, and CMOS setup), which is a program that allows settings to be viewed and managed

The BIOS can also turn control over to an adapter's onboard BIOS so that it can initialize.

POST performs basic tests of individual hardware components, such as the motherboard, RAM modules, keyboard, optical drive, and hard drive. When a computer is turned on with the power switch, BIOS executes POST. An indication that POST is running is that the lights on the keyboard momentarily flash on and then off, or you will see the hard drive or optical drive light momentarily flash. Turning the computer on with the power switch is known as a cold boot. Users perform a cold boot every time they power on their computer. A technician performs a cold boot when he or she is troubleshooting a computer and needs POST to execute. BIOS can be configured to reduce the time and number of devices checked by POST.

You can restart a Windows XP computer with a warm boot by clicking the Start button > *Shut Down* > *Restart* > *OK*. You can also perform a warm boot by holding down the Ctrl key, the Alt key, and the Del key at the same time > *Task Manager* > *Shut Down* > *Restart* > *OK*. Warm booting causes any changes that have been made to take effect without putting as much strain on the computer as a cold boot does. In Windows Vista or 7, click on the Start button > right arrow adjacent to the lock button and select *Restart* or press Ctrl + Alt + Del, select the up arrow in bottom-right corner, and choose *Restart* from the menu.

When assembling, troubleshooting, or repairing a computer, a technician must go into a Setup program to configure the system. The Setup program is held in BIOS, and through the Setup program, you can see and possibly configure such things as how much RAM is in the computer, the type and number of drives installed, where the computer looks for its boot files, the current date and time, and so on. An error message is displayed if the information in the Setup program fails to match the hardware or if a specific device does not work properly.

There are two main ways to configure your system or an adapter: through the Setup program held in system BIOS and through the operating system. We examine the Setup program first.

Tech Tip

Using Setup to disable integrated ports and connectors

Motherboards include connectors for hard drives, optical drives, and so on. If any of these connectors fails, you can disable it through Setup and obtain a replacement adapter just as you would if an integrated port failed.

The Setup Program

Computers have Setup software built into the system BIOS chip on the motherboard that you can access with specific keystrokes determined by the BIOS manufacturer. During the boot process, most computers display a message stating which keystroke(s) will launch the Setup program. The message shown is usually in one of the four screen corners. See Figure 3.2. The keystroke can be one or more keys pressed during startup, such as the Esc, Ins, Del, F1, F2, or F10 keys. Another key combination is Ctrl + Alt + some other key.

Tech Tip

How to access setup

The key or keys used to access Setup is normally displayed briefly during the boot process. Otherwise, look in the motherboard documentation for the proper keystroke(s) to use.

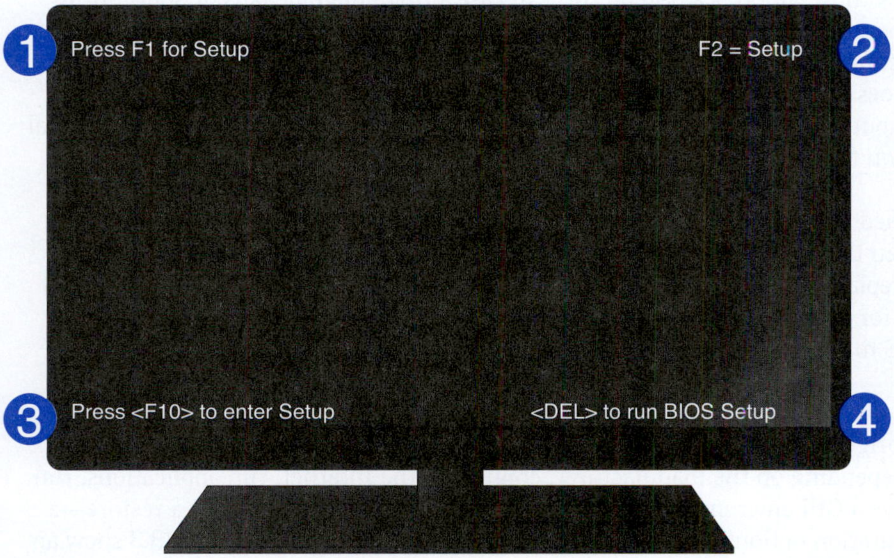

Figure 3.2 Setup keystrokes

Flash BIOS

Flash BIOS is the most common type of BIOS; it allows changing the BIOS without installing a new chip or chips. Common computer BIOS manufacturers include AMI (American Megatrends, Inc.), Phoenix, Byosoft (Nanjing Byosoft Co., Ltd), and Insyde Software. Many computer companies produce their own BIOS chips or subcontract with one of these companies to customize the BIOS.

The BIOS can be upgraded. The term used for this process is "flashing the BIOS." The following procedure is one example of flashing the BIOS:

1. After the system BIOS upgrade is downloaded from the Internet, execute the update.
2. Follow the directions on the screen or from the manufacturer.
3. Reboot the computer.

Tech Tip

How to remove BIOS write protection

Because the flash BIOS is frequently write protected, a motherboard jumper, switch, or BIOS setting may need to be changed to allow an update. Viruses can infect the flash BIOS, so you should keep the BIOS write protected until you need to update it. Refer to the computer or motherboard documentation to find the exact procedure for removing the write protection and updating the flash BIOS.

Another method some manufacturers support is downloading a program to a USB flash drive along with the BIOS update. The computer is booted from the USB drive to ensure that the BIOS update works. Those who overclock their processor prefer this option.

A computer may need a BIOS upgrade for a variety of reasons, including the following:

- To provide support for new or upgraded hardware
- To provide support for a higher-capacity hard drive
- For increased virus protection
- For optional password protection
- To solve problems with the current version

Some motherboards have a utility that allows recovery if a BIOS becomes corrupted or the BIOS update fails. Another option is a flash BIOS recovery jumper or switch used for BIOS recovery. A third option is a backup BIOS in case a BIOS upgrade fails or stalls during the upgrade process. Also, an alternative is having a portion of the BIOS that cannot be changed so that the computer can still boot, even if a BIOS update fails. If the motherboard manufacturer does not provide one of these alternatives, the motherboard will have to be replaced. A computer without an operational BIOS cannot boot. See the motherboard manual or documentation for specific BIOS details and the method that is being used to protect the BIOS.

UEFI (Unified Extensible Firmware Interface, and sometimes seen as simply EFI) is the interface between the operating system and firmware, which could be the traditional BIOS, or UEFI could replace the BIOS. The traditional BIOS has roots in the original PC; the BIOS always checked for certain things such as a keyboard before allowing the system to boot. A traditional BIOS made configuring kiosks and touchscreen technologies difficult. UEFI fixed these issues.

With UEFI, you can boot into the environment (which includes configuration parameters), but unlike the original BIOS environment, you can use your mouse and possibly do some of the following, depending on the manufacturer: connect to the Internet, run applications, run a virus scan, have a GUI environment, execute utilities, or perform a backup or a restore—a lot more configuration options and in a much easier-to-use environment. Figure 3.3 show an example of such an environment.

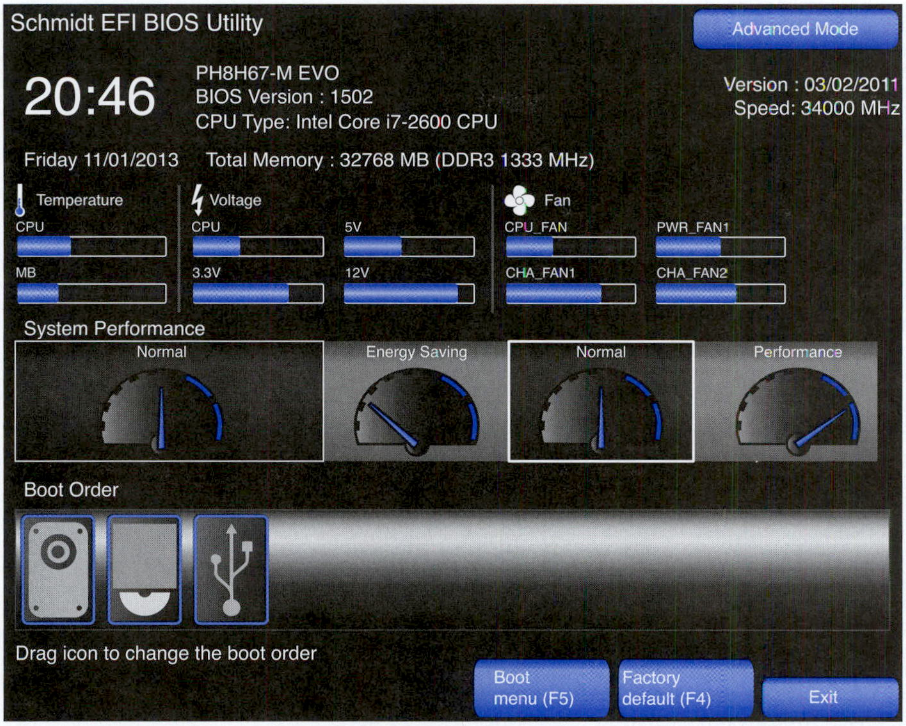

Figure 3.3 Sample UEFI main menu

Many manufacturers have moved to the UEFI type of BIOS for the following reasons:

- It is a graphical environment that provides mouse support.
- It enables you to have a virus-scanning utility that is not operating system dependent.
- It offers more BIOS software that is not just configuration screens.
- It offers optional Internet access for troubleshooting or download capabilities.
- It offers better system support for cooling, voltage levels, performance, and security.
- It provides support for increased hard drive capacities.

From the UEFI BIOS main menu, there might be icons you can use to access utilities or more advanced configurations. Figure 3.4 shows the type of menu options you might see if you clicked on the Advanced button from the main menu. Other manufacturers might have these category icons available from the main menu.

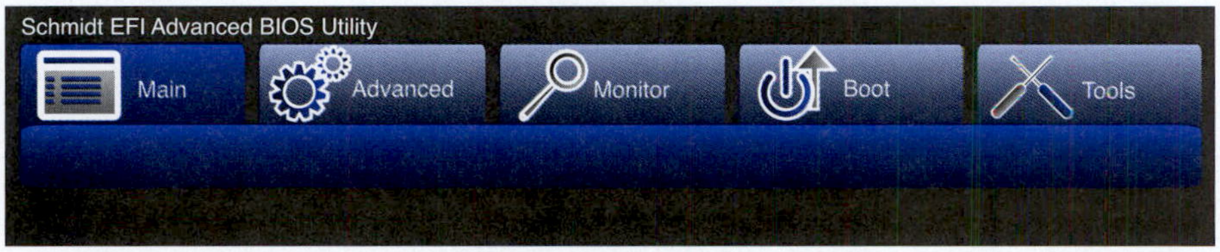

Figure 3.4 Sample UEFI advanced menu

3 System Configuration

Tech Tip

Using AC when flashing laptop BIOS

Attach AC power to a laptop when flashing the BIOS to avoid power loss during the BIOS update.

BIOS Configuration Settings

BIOS options vary according to manufacturer, but many options are similar. Table 3.1 shows some common BIOS settings and briefly explains each. Most Setup programs have help that can be accessed from within the Setup program to explain the purpose of each option.

Table 3.1 Common Setup options

Setup option	Description
System Information	Displays general information, such as the processor, processor speed, amount of RAM, type and number of hard drives and optical drives installed, BIOS manufacturer, and BIOS date.
General Optimization	Allows BIOS to boot faster by disabling features such as memory checking, booting to the network, and booting from removable drives.
Date/Time	Manually configures the system date and time.
Boot Sequence, Boot Drive Order, or Boot Menu	Prioritizes devices in the order the computer looks for an operating system.
CPU Configuration or Advanced CPU Settings	Contains settings such as CPU TM function, which affects CPU throttle management (slows the CPU when overheated); clock speed, which may not be changeable; PECI (Platform Environment Control Interface), which affects how the thermal sensors report the core temperature of your CPU; Max CPUID, which is used to be compatible with older operating systems; CPU Ratio control, which sets the CPU multipliers; and Vanderpool Technology, which is used with Intel virtualization.
Video Options	Allows configuration such as DVMT (dynamic video memory technology) to control video memory, aperture size (the amount of system RAM dedicated for the video adapter use), and which video controller is primary or secondary.
Onboard Device Configuration	Allows modification of devices built into the motherboard, such as audio, Bluetooth wireless, network, USB, or video ports.
Power on Password, Password Options, Supervisor Password, or User Password	Allows configuration of a password to enter the Setup program, to allow the computer to boot, or to distinguish between someone who can make minor changes such as boot options or date and time (user password) and someone who can view and change all Setup options (supervisor password).
Virus Protection	A small virus-scanning application located in BIOS. Some operating systems and software updates require disabling this option for the upgrade.
Numlock On/Off	Allows default setting (enabled or disabled) of the Num Lock key option after booting.
USB Configuration	Allows modification of parameters such as support for legacy devices, USB speed options, and the number of ports to enable.

Setup option	Description
HyperThreading	Allows enabling/disabling of Hyper-Threading technology.
Integrated Peripherals	Allows enabling/disabling and configuration of motherboard-controlled devices such as PATA/SATA ports and integrated ports including USB, audio, and network. Sets the amount of RAM dedicated for the AGP adapter's use. If the computer has an ample amount of RAM, increasing this setting can increase performance, especially in applications (such as games) that use high-definition graphics.
HD Audio Controller	Enables/disables a high-definition audio controller.
Advanced BIOS Options	Allows configuration of options such as CPU and memory frequencies, CPU, front side bus, north bridge, south bridge, chipset, and memory voltage levels.
IDE Configuration	Allows manual configuration of IDE devices such as PATA, hard drives, and optical drives.
SATA Configuration	Allows viewing Serial ATA values assigned by BIOS and changing some of the related options, as well as RAID configuration.
PCI/PnP Configuration	Allows viewing and changing PCI slot configuration, including IRQ and DMA assignments.
PCIe Configuration	Allows manual configuration of the PCIe version.
Virtualization Technology or Secure Virtual Machine Mode	Enable/disable virtualization so the virtualization software can access additional hardware capabilities.
ACPI (advanced configuration and power interface)	Determines what happens if power is lost, power options if a call comes into a modem, and power options when directed by a PCI or PCIe device or by mouse/keyboard action.
Hardware Monitor	Allows viewing CPU and motherboard temperature as well as the status of CPU, chassis, voltages, clock speeds, bus speeds, chassis intrusion, and power supply fans.
Execute Disable or No Execute	Can prevent executable code (viruses) from being executed from specific marked memory area.
Drive encryption	A secret key is used to encrypt the data on the hard drive. The computer will not boot without the correct password. The drive cannot be moved to another computer either unless the correct password is entered.
TPM (Trusted Platform Module)	Allows initialization and setting a password for the TPM motherboard chip that generates and stores cryptographic keys.
Lojack	Allows security settings to perform such tasks as locking the computer remotely, displaying an "if lost" message, data to be deleted if stolen, or the ability to locate the lost or stolen device.
Intrusion Detection/ Chassis Intrusion	Allows notification if the cover has been removed.

Tech Tip

Using default BIOS settings for a new system

When installing a new system, use the default BIOS settings until all components are tested.

Some motherboards have pins that, when jumpered together, remove the power-on password. Look at the computer or motherboard documentation for the exact procedure to remove the power-on password. Some motherboards distinguish between supervisor and user passwords. Another security option of some BIOS chips is whether a password is needed every time the computer boots or only when someone tries to enter the Setup program. The options available in Setup and Advanced Setup are machine dependent due to the different BIOS chips and the different chipsets installed on the motherboard. Always refer to the computer or motherboard documentation for the meaning of each option.

You must save your changes whenever you make configuration changes. Incorrectly saving the changes is a common mistake. The options available when exiting BIOS depend on the model of BIOS being used. Table 3.2 lists sample BIOS exit options.

Table 3.2 Sample configuration change options

Option	Description
Save & Exit Setup	A commonly used option that saves all changes and leaves the Setup program.
Exit Without Saving	Used when changes have been made in error or more research is needed.
Load Fail-Safe Defaults	Sets the default settings programmed by the manufacturer. Used when getting unpredictable results after changing an option.
Load Optimized Defaults	An option programmed by the manufacturer. It has more aggressive settings than the *Load Fail-Safe Defaults* option.

CMOS Memory

Settings changed in system BIOS are recorded and stored in **CMOS** (complementary metal-oxide semiconductor) found in the motherboard chipset (south bridge or I/O controller hub). CMOS is memory that requires a small amount of power, provided by a small coin-sized lithium battery when the system is powered off. The memory holds the settings configured through BIOS. Part of the BIOS software routine that runs after the computer is turned on checks CMOS for information about what components are supposed to be installed. These components are then tested.

Tech Tip

Incorrect Setup information causes POST errors

If you incorrectly input configuration information, POST error codes or error messages that would normally indicate a hardware problem appear.

The information inside CMOS memory can be kept there for several years, using a small coin-sized lithium battery. When the battery dies, all configuration information in CMOS is lost and must be re-entered or relearned after the battery is replaced.

Remember that POST runs whenever the computer cold boots, and it performs a hardware check on installed components. POST knows what hardware is *supposed* to be in the computer by obtaining the settings from CMOS. If the settings do not match, an error occurs.

When working on a computer with a POST error code, ensure that the user or another technician (1) has not changed the configuration through the Setup program or (2) removed or installed any hardware without changing the Setup program or updating the operating system. Correct system Setup information is crucial for proper PC operation.

Tech Tip

Don't clear CMOS after a BIOS update

Do not clear the CMOS immediately after upgrading the BIOS. Power down the system and then power it back on before clearing CMOS data.

Most motherboards allow clearing the settings saved in CMOS by a system BIOS setup option. However, if the saved setting is a forgotten password, then setting motherboard jumpers as shown in Figure 3.5 is usually an option. If all else fails, you can remove and replace the motherboard battery, but then all BIOS settings would be reset to the default settings.

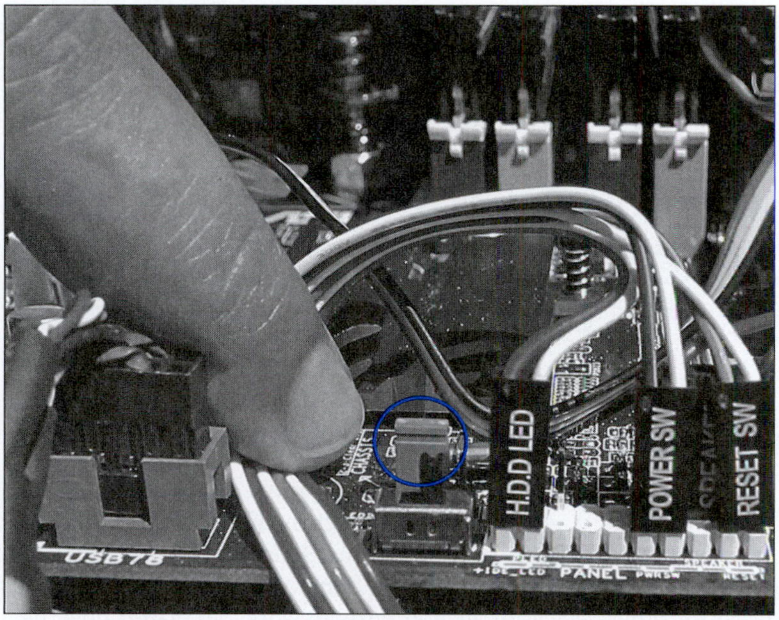

Figure 3.5 A CMOS password jumper

Motherboard Batteries

The most common battery used today is a CR2032 lithium battery, which is about the size of a nickel. Figure 3.6 shows a photo of a lithium battery installed on a motherboard. If you cannot find the motherboard battery, refer to the motherboard or computer documentation for the exact location.

Figure 3.6 Motherboard battery

Tech Tip

Battery replacement hints

Check the motherboard for any evidence of battery corrosion and verify that no battery acid has come in contact with the motherboard. If the motherboard is contaminated with battery acid, it will probably need to be replaced. A first indication that a battery is failing is the loss of the date or time on the computer.

No battery lasts forever. High temperatures and powering devices that use batteries on and off shorten a battery's life span. Computer motherboard batteries last three to eight years. Today, batteries last longer, and people replace their computers more frequently; therefore, replacing batteries is not the issue it once was.

Tech Tip

Using a battery recycling program

Many states have environmental regulations regarding battery disposal. Many companies also have battery recycling programs. The earth911.com website has information regarding recycling and disposing of batteries and computer components by zip code or city/state.

Other Configuration Parameters

Other possible parameters contained and set via the Setup program or operating system are IRQs (interrupt requests), I/O (input/output) addresses, DMA (direct memory access) channels, and memory addresses. These parameters are assigned to individual adapters and ports, such as disk controllers, and the USB, serial, parallel, and mouse ports. Sometimes these ports must be disabled through Setup in order for other devices or adapter ports to work. No matter how the parameters are assigned, collectively they are known as **system resources**. These are not the same system resources that we refer to when we discuss Windows operating systems. Let's take a look at three important system resources: IRQs, I/O addresses, and memory addresses.

IRQ (Interrupt Request)

Imagine being in a room of 20 students when 4 students want the teacher's attention. If all 4 students talk at once, the teacher is overloaded and unable to respond to the 4 individuals' needs. Instead, the teacher needs an orderly process of acknowledging each request, prioritizing the requests (which student is first), and then answering each question. The same thing happens when multiple devices want the attention of the CPU. For example, which device gets to go first if a key on the PS/2 keyboard is pressed and the PS/2 mouse is moved simultaneously? The answer lies in what interrupt request numbers are assigned to the keyboard and the mouse. Every device requests permission to do something by interrupting the processor (which is similar to a student raising his hand). The CPU has a priority system to handle such situations.

The processor prioritizes device requests through the use of IRQ. An **IRQ** (interrupt request) is a number assigned to an expansion adapter or port so orderly communication can occur between the device or port and the processor. For example, when a key is pressed and the mouse is moved simultaneously, the keyboard has the highest priority because of its IRQ number.

Older computers had 16 interrupts numbered 0 through 15. The chip that controls the interrupts is known as the interrupt controller chip. Today, computers have **APICs** (advanced programmable interrupt controllers) that support more interrupt outputs (24, for example) and provide more flexibility than a traditional system, which does not normally support more than one device to an interrupt. APICs allow sharing interrupts between devices. There are two common types of APICs: LAPIC (local APIC) and I/O APIC. LAPIC is normally integrated into each CPU and has its own timer, whereas the I/O APIC is used throughout any of the peripheral buses and is integrated into the chipset. The chipsets used today are backward compatible with the traditional interrupts used.

Interrupts for integrated ports and some devices can be set through a system's Setup program. Other adapter and device interrupts are set by using **Device Manager** in Windows or using various control panels. Figure 3.7 shows the various methods used to access Device Manager.

Tech Tip

How IRQs are assigned to multiple-device ports

Ports such as USB, SCSI, and IEEE 1394 (FireWire) that support multiple devices require only one interrupt per port. For example, a single USB port can support up to 127 devices but needs only one IRQ.

Run utility or command line	`devmgmt.msc`
Windows control panel	**XP:** Start button > Control Panel > System > Hardware tab > Device Manager > View menu option > Resources by Type **7:** Start button > Control Panel > System and Security > Device Manager > View Hardware and Devices > View menu option > Resources by Type
Windows Microsoft Management console	**XP:** Start button > Control Panel > Administrative Tools > Computer Management **7:** Start button > Control Panel > System and Security > Administrative Tools > Computer Management
Windows Explorer	**XP:** Right-click Start button > Explore > right-click My Computer > Properties > Hardware tab **7:** Right-click Start button > open Windows Explorer > right-click Computer > Properties

Figure 3.7 Accessing Device Manager

Figure 3.8 shows how IRQs appear in Device Manager > *View* > *Resources by type*. In Figure 3.7, notice that some interrupts have multiple entries. Multiple entries do not always indicate a resource conflict. They are allowed because PCI/PCIe devices may share IRQs. The next section goes into more detail on this issue.

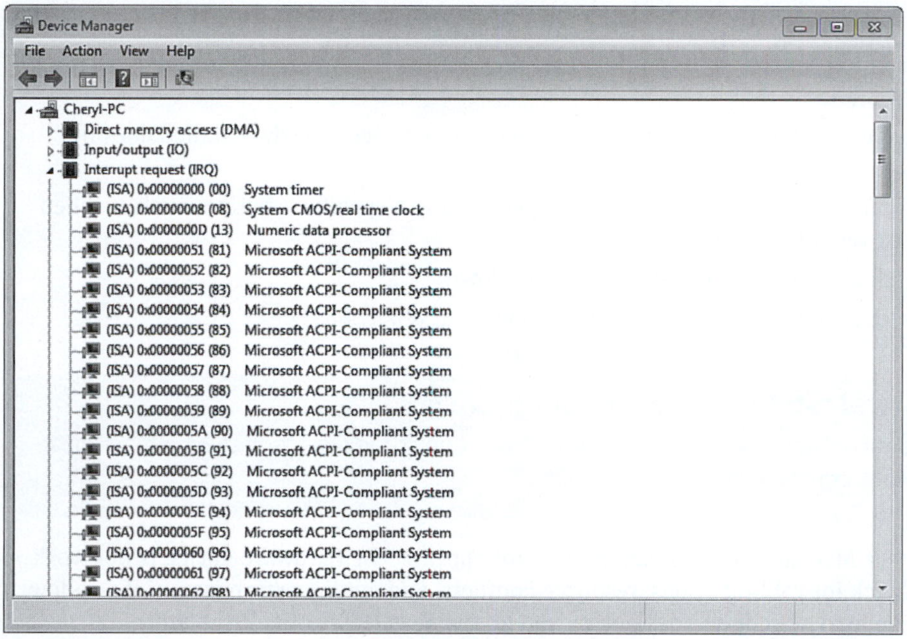

Figure 3.8 IRQs in Device Manager

Figure 3.9 shows an integrated network card's properties that cannot be changed through Device Manager; notice that the *Change Setting* button is grayed out. However, properties might be able to be modified through the system BIOS Setup program.

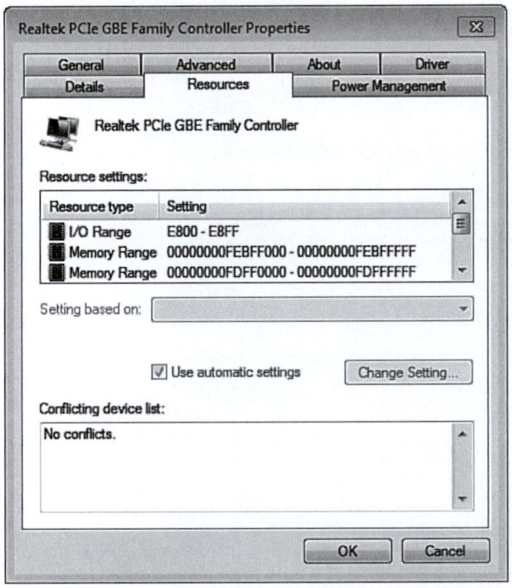

Figure 3.9 **Resources tab in Device Manager**

Tech Tip

Verifying resources with Device Manager

A little down arrow (Vista/7) or an X (XP) means disabled, and ! usually indicates a resource conflict or missing driver. An i indicates that the Use Automatic Settings feature is not being used for the device, and resources were manually configured.

Indications of a resource conflict (including IRQ, DMA, I/O address, and memory address conflicts) are as follows:

- The new device is installed and the new device or a device already installed does not work.
- The computer locks up or restarts when performing a specific function, such as when playing or recording audio.
- The computer hangs during startup or shutdown.
- A device does not work properly or fails to work at all.

Tech Tip

Use the General tab for troubleshooting

On the *General* tab of any adapter or port properties, check the *Device status* section for any error codes, including those for resource conflicts.

Within Device Manager, if an exclamation point appears, the hardware device is not working properly. Check for cabling issues, resource conflicts, and configuration issues. If a yellow question mark appears, Windows does not recognize the device. Try one of the following:

- See if there is a Windows update to check whether any new drivers are available. See Chapter 12 for more details on Windows updates.
- Manually update the driver. To do so, right-click the device in Device Manager > *Properties* > *Driver* tab > *Update Driver*. You could download this driver from the device manufacturer website or let Windows try to find the driver.

With any Device Manager issue, you can right-click the device and select *Properties*. On the General tab, notice if there are any error codes. Table 3.3 lists some Device Manager error codes and descriptions. You can review all these codes and more at Microsoft's TechNet website.

Table 3.3 Device Manager error codes

Error	Description
Code 1	The device does not have a device driver or is configured improperly.
Code 3	Either the device driver is corrupted or the system is running low on system resources.
Code 10	The device did not start. Try updating the device driver or researching the problem on the vendor website.
Code 12	A system resource conflict has occurred. Reboot the computer multiple times to see if the operating system can work out the conflict. Look for manually assigned (conflicting) resources.
Code 14	The device requires a system restart.
Code 18	The device driver needs to be reinstalled.
Code 19	Registry configuration information is corrupt or damaged. Uninstall the device and reinstall.
Code 22	The device is disabled.
Code 28	The drivers for the device are not installed.
Code 37	Windows cannot start the device driver. Reboot the computer.
Code 47	The device has been prepared for safe removal, but has not been removed from the computer.

PCI Interrupts

When a PC first boots, the operating system discovers what AGP, PCI, and PCIe adapters and devices are present and what system resources each one needs. The operating system allocates resources such as an interrupt to the adapter/device. If the adapter or device has a ROM or flash BIOS chip installed that contains software that initializes and/or controls the device, the software is allowed to execute during the boot process.

PCI/PCIe devices use interrupts called INTA, INTB, INTC, INTD, and so on. These interrupts are commonly referred to as PCI interrupts. Some motherboard documentation uses the numbers 1, 2, 3, and 4 to replace the letters A, B, C, and D. Devices that use these interrupts are allowed to share them as necessary.

PCI interrupts are normally assigned dynamically to the USB, PCI, PCIe, and SATA devices as the interrupts are needed. Table 3.4 shows an example of how a motherboard might make PCI IRQ assignments.

PCI interrupts can also be mapped to one of the traditional interrupts, usually IRQ 9, 10, 11, and 12. With so many devices installed in today's computers, this is solved with a technique called IRQ steering. IRQ steering allows multiple adapters to be mapped to the same traditional IRQ. PCI steering (another name for IRQ steering) allows multiple devices to share the same interrupt. Adapters should be able to share the same resources without conflicts. When IRQ steering is enabled and when an adapter needs an interrupt, the operating system finds an available interrupt (which may be currently used by another device that does not need it) and allows the requesting device to use it.

Tech Tip

When *not* to share a PCI IRQ

A technician should be able to verify the resources being used. If a device needs maximum performance, it should not share an IRQ with another device.

Table 3.4 Sample PCI interrupt assignments

	A	B	C	D	E	F	G	H
PCI slot 1						used		
PCI slot 2							shared	
PCI slot 3								shared
SATA		shared						
LAN		shared						
PCIe X16 1	shared							
PCIe X16 2	shared							
PCIe X1			shared					
USB controller 1							shared	
USB controller 2				shared				
USB controller 3			shared					
USB controller 4	shared							
USB controller 5		shared						
USB 2.0 controller 1							shared	
USB 2.0 controller 2		shared						
SATA controller 1		shared						
SATA controller 2				shared				

During the boot process, the system BIOS configures adapters. Windows examines the resources assigned by the BIOS and uses those resources when communicating with a piece of hardware.

Starting with PCI version 2.2 and continuing on with PCIe, an adapter can use a different type of interrupt method, called MSI or MSI-X. **MSI** (Message Signaled Interrupt) allows an interrupt to be delivered to the CPU using software and memory space. **MSI-X** supports more interrupts. This method was optional with PCI, but PCIe cards are required to support MSI and MSI-X.

Tech Tip

What to do when a conflict occurs in an older system

If you suspect a resource conflict with a card, move the card to another slot. PCI slot 1 in particular can cause resource conflicts with the AGP slot. If swapping slots does not work, you must make BIOS changes.

I/O (Input/Output) Addresses

An **I/O address**, otherwise known as an input/output address or port address, allows a device and a processor to exchange data. An I/O address is like a mailbox number; it must be unique, or the postal worker gets confused. The device places data (mail) in the box for the CPU to pick up. The processor delivers the data to the appropriate device through the same I/O address (mailbox number). I/O addresses are simply addresses for the processor to distinguish among the devices with which it communicates. Remember that you cannot deliver mail without an address.

Tech Tip

When is an I/O address needed?

Remember that every device must have a separate I/O address. Otherwise, the CPU cannot distinguish between installed devices.

I/O addresses are shown in hexadecimal format, from 0000 to FFFF. Some outputs are shown with eight positions, such as 00000000 to FFFFFFFF. Hexadecimal numbers are 0, 1, 2, 3, 4, 5, 6, 7, 8, and 9 just like the decimal numbers we use, but hexadecimal numbers also include the letters A, B, C, D, E, and F. Table 3.5 shows decimal numbers 0 through 15 and their hexadecimal and binary equivalents.

Table 3.5 Decimal, binary, and hexadecimal numbers

Decimal	Hexadecimal	Binary	Decimal	Hexadecimal	Binary
0	0	0000	8	8	1000
1	1	0001	9	9	1001
2	2	0010	10	A	1010
3	3	0011	11	B	1011
4	4	0100	12	C	1100
5	5	0101	13	D	1101
6	6	0110	14	E	1110
7	7	0111	15	F	1111

An example of an I/O address is 390h, where the lowercase h denotes hexadecimal. Table 3.6 uses this method and shows sample I/O addresses used in computers.

Table 3.6 Sample I/O addresses

I/O address	Device or port	I/O address	Device or port
0020-0021h	Programmable interrupt controller	00F0-00FFh	Numeric data processor
0040-0043h	System timers—clocks	03B0-03BBh	PCIe root port
0060h	Keyboard	0D00-FFFFh	PCI bus
0070h or 0071h	System CMOS/real-time clock	00C080-00C09Fh	USB host controller

Notice in Table 3.6 that the I/O address shown is a range of I/O addresses. Normally, devices need more than one hexadecimal address location. The number of extra addresses depends on the individual device and what business it does with the processor. In manuals or documentation for a device or an adapter, a technician might see just one I/O address listed. I/O addresses can be set for some devices and ports through the BIOS system Setup program, Device Manager, or various Windows control panels.

Tech Tip

What to do if only the starting hexadecimal number is shown

One problem for technicians is that some documentation and some Setup programs give only the starting hexadecimal I/O address and not the ending I/O address. The range of addresses the adapter uses can conflict with that of another adapter or device. Device Manager shows the full range.

Memory Addresses

The last important system resource is the memory address. A **memory address** is a unique address assigned to memory chips installed anywhere in the system. The memory address is used by the CPU when it accesses information inside the chip. Configuration problems can be caused by overlapping or conflicting memory addresses.

Tech Tip

An IEEE 1394 port uses the same system resources to access any devices attached to the same port

If one or more FireWire devices connect to a FireWire port (integrated or on an adapter), the devices use the same system resources that are assigned to the port.

Memory addresses are shown in hexadecimal. A sample memory address range would be A0000–BFFFFh. However, some documentation drops the last digit and does not include the full memory range that the memory chip takes. For example, memory on an adapter might be listed as C800h. In reality, this is C8000–C8FFFh. When you look at the memory address on the computer, the address may be shown with more hexadecimal places, as shown in Device Manager in Figure 3.10.

Some memory addresses are preset and cannot be changed. Others can be changed through Device Manager or various Windows control panels. Some BIOS chips allow the contents of memory chips to be copied into RAM. This is called ROM shadowing. Access from RAM is faster than from a ROM chip. Exercises at the end of the chapter help to identify IRQs, I/O addresses, and memory addresses for various devices and operating systems.

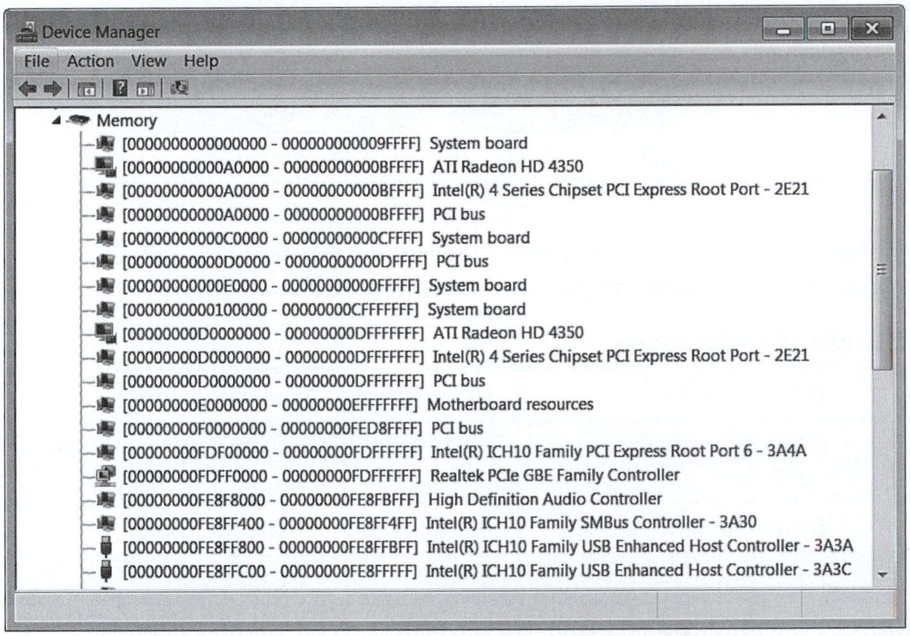

Figure 3.10 Memory addresses in Device Manager

Tech Tip

Changing system resources on integrated ports and devices connected to motherboard ports

System resources for integrated ports and motherboard connectors (hard drive, optical drive, USB, PS/2, and so on) are configurable through the BIOS Setup program.

Adapter Configuration

Configuration of adapters is easy if you follow the documentation and know how to obtain device drivers. Adapter documentation is frequently available through the Internet, as are many device drivers. Technicians must be familiar with using the Internet to download documentation, updated device drivers, and support files related to adapters and devices.

The system BIOS plays an important role as part of the startup routine. Not only does it check hardware for errors as part of POST, but also the BIOS detects installed adapters and, together with the operating system, determines what resources to assign to an adapter. This information is stored in a part of CMOS known as the **ESCD** (Extended System Configuration Data) area. Some system BIOS Setup routines allow resetting this information or manually configuring a resource such as an IRQ. Once information is configured in the ESCD area, the information stays there and does not have to be recomputed unless another device is added. After resources are allocated, the BIOS looks in the saved settings of CMOS to determine what device it should look to first for an operating system. This part of the BIOS routine is known as the bootstrap loader. If BIOS cannot locate an operating system in the first location specified in the saved settings, it tries the second device and continues on, looking to each device specified in the saved settings for an operating system. Keep in mind that once an operating system is found, the operating system loads.

PCI, AGP, and PCIe adapters, on the other hand, are the easiest adapters to configure because they support PnP. **PnP** (plug and play) allows automatic software configuration of an adapter. Once an adapter has been installed into an expansion slot, the technician normally does not have to worry about the adapter conflicting with other devices in the system. PCI, PCI-X, AGP, and PCIe adapters support PnP.

Normally, adapters do not have problems with system resource conflicts because the PCI/PCIe standards allow interrupt sharing. Also software interrupts can be used to avoid resource conflicts, especially with PCIe adapters. A PCI/PCIe card can be configured through the BIOS and system Setup software, as well as through software provided with the adapter.

Tech Tip

What to do if plug and play does not work

Plug and play (and sometimes a configuration utility supplied with a device) is used to configure system resources. Sometimes, a reboot is required for the changes to take effect. If the device does not work after the reboot, reboot the computer again (and possibly a third time) to allow the operating system to sort out the system resources. You can manually make changes if this does not work.

When you install an adapter in a Windows environment, the operating system detects the installation and adds the adapter's configuration information to the registry. The **registry** is a central database in Windows that holds hardware information and other data. All software applications access the registry for configuration information instead of going to the adapter. In a plug and play operating system, the system prompts for either the operating system discs or for software media from the adapter manufacturer.

Windows works in conjunction with the BIOS to configure adapters automatically. Windows attempts to make hardware installation easier by keeping track of the computer's configuration. When Windows boots, it compares the saved configuration with what is detected during initialization. When adding hardware, the system automatically detects it, or you can use the *Add/Remove Hardware* Control Panel (XP) or use *Devices and Printers* Control Panel link > *Add a device* (Vista/7).

Soft Skills—A Good Technician Quality: One Thing at a Time

The least effective type of computer technician is a "gun slinger." The term *gun slinger* brings to mind images of Wild West ruffians who had shooting matches with other gangsters in the town's main street. Gun slingers drew their guns frequently and with little provocation. They did not put much thought into their method or consider other possible resolutions. You must strive *not* to be this type of technician.

A gun slinger technician changes multiple things simultaneously. For example, if there is no display on the output, the technician might swap out the monitor, disable the onboard video port, add a new video adapter, power on the computer, and, when output appears, call the problem "solved." If a computer problem is repaired using such a technique, the technician never knows exactly what solved the problem.

A good technician, on the other hand, makes a list of symptoms (even if it is simply a mental list) followed by a list of things to try. Then the technician tries the possible solutions, starting with the simplest one (the one that costs the least amount of time to the computer user). The technician documents each step. After each approach that does not fix the problem, the technician puts the system back to the original configuration before attempting the next possible solution. This method keeps the technician focused on what has been tested, and if another technician takes over, the steps do not have to be repeated. Best of all, when one of the possible solutions fixes the problem, the exact solution is known.

Gun slinger technicians do not learn as fast as other technicians because they do not determine the real causes of problems. Each time they are presented with a problem similar to one they have seen in the past, gun slinger technicians use the same haphazard troubleshooting method. These technicians are actually dangerous to an organization because they are not good at documenting what they have done and determining exactly what fixes a particular problem.

Chapter Summary

- The system flash BIOS is used to enable/disable, configure, and troubleshoot motherboard components, expansion slots, and ports. When the computer is off, a motherboard battery holds saved settings in CMOS.
- An updated type of BIOS is UEFI BIOS, which allows the use of a mouse and a graphical environment. Security options, support for larger hard drives, antivirus software, and utilities may also be included.
- Each port and card uses system resources such as interrupts, I/O addresses, and memory addresses.
- PCIe cards can use traditional interrupts or software interrupts known as MSI or MSI-X.
- System resources can be viewed and changed using Device Manager. Specific Device Manager codes and messages help in troubleshooting conflicts.
- A good computer technician should methodically troubleshoot a problem by making only one change at a time and reverting the change if the change did not solve the problem. Furthermore, the technician documents the issue and its resolution for future problems.

Key Terms

Review Questions

1. When would a technician flash a BIOS?
   a. when the date and time start to be incorrect
   b. when a port or motherboard component does not perform at its maximum potential
   c. when the driver for a motherboard port is out of date
   d. when the motherboard has an upgrade such as a new processor, extra RAM, or an additional adapter installed into an expansion slot
2. What is the effect of setting an administrator password in BIOS?
   a. It prevents the computer from having multiple devices that can boot the system.
   b. It prevents the BIOS from being infected with a virus.
   c. It prevents a user from accessing the computer operating system.
   d. It prevents a user from changing system Setup settings.
3. What program is used to determine the driver version being used for a specific component? [BIOS | CMOS | Task Manager | Device Manager | system Setup]
4. List two symptoms of a device resource conflict.

5. Where would a CR2032 lithium battery most likely be used in a computing device?
   a. as a laptop battery
   b. inside the processor
   c. as a component on the motherboard
   d. within CMOS
6. What is the name of the Windows database where Windows configuration information is stored? [registry | BIOS | UEFI | Device Manager]
7. [T | F] If a power failure occurs during a BIOS update, the motherboard might have to be replaced.
8. What is the result of attaching a USB 2.0 device and a USB 3.0 device to a USB hub attached to a motherboard USB 3.0 port?
   a. The devices share system resources.
   b. The 3.0 device gets a higher-priority IRQ.
   c. If either of the devices is an externally powered device, that particular device gets a higher-priority IRQ. Otherwise, the two devices share an interrupt.
   d. The 3.0 device always has a higher-priority I/O address.
9. Which device properties tab has a *Device status* section that might contain helpful troubleshooting information or the status of the device?
   [General | Advanced | Driver | Details | Management]
10. A technician receives a complaint about a computer being slow to respond to typed keystrokes. The technician installs more memory and a new keyboard. The customer is happy. What, if anything, could have been done better?

11. What is another name for a PCIe software interrupt? [MSI | APIC | IRQ | PIRQ]

Consider the following BIOS configuration menu options for answering Questions 12 through 16:

Main Menu	Onboard Devices	Boot Device Priority
BIOS Information	PCIE Training	1st Boot Device
BIOS Version	LAN1 Controller	2nd Boot Device
Build Date	USB 1.1 Controller	3rd Boot Device
EC F/W Version	USB 2.0 Controller	4th Boot Device
CPU Information	USB 3.0 Controller	
Memory Information	Audio	
System Information	OnChip PATA Controller	
System Language	OnChip SATA Controller	
System Date	SATA	
System Time HDMI/DVI		

12. What menu item would you use to determine whether the system should be flashed?
    a. Main menu
    b. Onboard Devices
    c. Boot Device Priority
13. A computer is mounted inside a cabinet, and you want to know if an IEEE 1394 port is available. Which menu item would you use?
    a. Main menu
    b. Onboard Devices
    c. Boot Device Priority
14. [T | F] The system date and time must be configured through the system BIOS.
15. A technician keeps having to go to the BIOS main menu to configure date and time. What component is suspect? [CPU | BIOS | battery | chipset | CMOS]
16. A technician wants to boot from an eSATA external hard drive. Which submenu item is used? [OnChip SATA controller | SATA | PCIE training | 1st Boot Device]
17. A user cannot get a computer to boot. The technician replaces the motherboard and the hard drive. The system now works. What could the technician have done differently in this situation, if anything?

18. When would a technician use UEFI?
    a. when managing configuration through Device Manager
    b. when the date and/or time continues to be misconfigured
    c. when an adapter has just been installed
    d. when replacing a motherboard
19. A computer is being used in a medical office. For security reasons, the technician has been asked to reasonably ensure that no one attaches any external media. What would the technician probably do?
    a. Password protect the BIOS and disable unused ports.
    b. Swap out the motherboard for one that doesn't have extra ports.
    c. Assign user rights through user passwords on the computer.
    d. Encrypt the hard drive.
    e. Flash the chipset.
20. A technician for a small company set a BIOS password on every computer. The technician left the company, and the replacement technician needs to access the BIOS. What should the new technician do?

Exercises

Lab 3.1 Configuration Method Exercise and Review

Objective: To determine which configuration method a computer uses

Parts: A computer and Internet access

Procedure: Complete the following procedure and answer the accompanying questions.

1. Open the computer and look at the motherboard. Note that you may have to use the computer model number and the Internet to do research for parts of this lab or to answer some of the questions. Verify any information found on the Internet with what you see in the computer.
2. Document (write down) the location, name, and purpose of all motherboard jumpers.
3. Locate the motherboard battery and document the battery type.

   What is an advantage of having a battery that keeps CMOS information?

   How can you tell the purpose of the jumper(s)?

   What is one of the first indications of a failing battery?

   What is the keystroke(s) required to access the Setup program?

Lab 3.2 System Resource Configuration Through the Setup Program

Objective: To access the system resources through the Setup program

Parts: A computer

Procedure: Complete the following procedure and answer the accompanying questions.

1. Power on the computer.
2. Press the appropriate key(s) to enter the Setup program.
3. Go through the various menus or icons until you find an interrupt (IRQ) setting for a particular device or port. Write the device or port and the associated IRQ in the space below.

IRQ	Device or Port

   Why do different devices generally not have the same interrupt? So the processor can prioritize requests from devices that want attention at the same time.
4. Go through the various menus or icons until you find an I/O address setting for a particular device or port. Write the device or port in the space provided, along with the associated I/O address.

I/O Address	Device or Port

   Why must each device and port have a separate and unique I/O address?

   How do I/O addresses, interrupts, and memory addresses get assigned to an installed adapter?

   What is the best source for viewing interrupts, I/O addresses, and memory address that have been assigned?

5. Exit the Setup program.
6. Go to Device Manager and determine whether the information collected in Steps 3 and 4 is the same.

Instructor initials: ______________

Lab 3.3 Examining System Resources by Using Windows

Objective: To be able to view and access system resources by using Windows

Parts: A computer with Windows loaded

Procedure: Complete the following procedure and answer the accompanying questions.

1. Power on the computer and verify that Windows loads. Log on to the computer, using the user ID and password provided by the instructor or lab assistant.
2. Access the *Performance and Maintenance* Control Panel (XP), the *System and Maintenance* Control Panel (Vista), or the *System and Security* Control Panel (7).
3. Locate and access *Device Manager*.
4. Click the *View* menu option and select *Resources by type*.

   What four types of system resources are shown?

5. Click the plus sign (or arrow) by *IRQ* (interrupt request) or *Interrupt request* (IRQ).

   Are any interrupts in use by multiple PCI devices? If so, list one.
6. Click the help icon or *Help > Help Topics menu item*.
7. In Windows Vista/7, expand *Device Manager*. In all Windows versions, expand *Uninstalling and Reinstalling Devices*. Locate and select the *Remove a Driver Package from the Driver Store* option.

   Using the help function, determine how to find the name of the driver package in the driver store. Document your findings.

   Why would a technician need to know the name of a driver store?

8. Close the help window.

   What device, if any, is using IRQ8?

   Is this the standard IRQ for this device?

Instructor initials: ______________

9. Click the plus sign (or arrow) by *Input/output (I/O)*.

   What is the first I/O address range listed for the first occurrence of the Direct Memory Access controller?

10. Collapse the *Input/output* section. Click the plus sign (or arrow) by *DMA*.

    Are any DMA channels being used? If so, list them.

11. Click on any device listed in the IRQ section. Move your mouse slowly over the icons at the top until you locate the *Update Driver Software* icon. When the mouse is moved slowly enough, a description of the icon appears.

    What does the *Update Driver* icon look like?

12. Move your mouse slowly over the icons at the top until you locate the *Uninstall* icon. *Do not click this icon*. The Disable icon can be used to troubleshoot problem devices.

    In what situation do you think a technician would use this option?

13. Ensure that you still have a device selected in the IRQ section. Click the *Action* menu item and select *Properties*. The *Properties* window opens. Many devices have a *Troubleshooter* button located on the *General* tab.
14. Click the *Resources* tab. The resources tab shows what system resources a particular device is using.

    What resources are being used?

    What message displays in the *Conflicting device list* section?

    Is the *Use automatic settings* checkbox enabled?

Instructor initials: _____________

15. Click the *Cancel* button to return to Device Manager. Close Device Manager.

Lab 3.4 Device Drivers

Objective: To become familiar with finding driver, driver information, and current driver version.

Parts: A computer with Windows installed and access to Internet

Procedure: Use the Internet and a computer to answer the accompanying questions.

1. List three things fixed by the 7.12.8.1794 driver version for 64-bit Windows 7 for the ASUS PCI XONAR DG audio card.

2. What is the release date for the latest driver for a Creative Labs Sound Blaster Recon3D PCIe adapter on a 32-bit Windows 7 computer?

3. What are the device driver version and date for any USB Root Hub on the computer?

4. Locate a USB Enhanced Host Controller in Device Manager. Use the Driver tab and update the driver if possible. Record your results.

5. What is the latest driver revision for a StarTech PCIe 1000Mbps fiber network card that has the part number ST1000SPEX?

Activities

Internet Discovery

Objective: To obtain specific information on the Internet regarding a computer or its associated parts

Parts: Computer with Internet access

Procedure: Use the Internet to answer the following questions. Assume that the customer owns a Gateway NE56R12U notebook computer in answering Questions 1 and 2.

Questions:

1. A customer owns a Gateway NE56R12U laptop. Determine the procedure for accessing the computer's Setup program. Write the key(s) to press and the URL where you find this information.

2. How many (if any) PC Card/ExpressCard slots does this notebook have, and what type of slots are they? If this notebook does not have such slots, how does the manufacturer recommend that you upgrade this computer? Write the answer and the URL where you find the information.

3. Another customer owns a Tyan S7025 motherboard. How many and what type of PCIe slots does this motherboard have? Write the answer and the URL where you find the information.

4. On the same Tyan S7025 motherboard, what motherboard jumper is used to clear CMOS? Write the answer and the URL where you find the information.

5. On the same Tyan S7025 motherboard, what BIOS menu option is used to configure the I/O address and IRQ for the first serial port? Write the answer and the URL where you find the answer.

Soft Skills

Objective: To enhance and fine tune a future technician's ability to listen, communicate in both written and oral form, and support people who use computers in a professional manner

Activities:

1. In teams, come up with a troubleshooting scenario that involves a computer technician who uses gun slinging techniques and the same scenario involving a technician who is methodical. Explain what each technician type does and how they solve the problem. Also, detail how they treat the customer differently. Determine ways of how a gun slinger technician might be harmful to a computer repair business.
2. After exploring the BIOS options, turn to a fellow student, pretend he or she is a customer over the phone, and walk the student through accessing Setup. Explain the purposes of at least five of the options. Reverse roles and cover five other options. Be sure to act like a typical computer user when playing the customer role.
3. Brainstorm a troubleshooting scenario in which you fix the problem that involves accessing the Setup program and/or an adapter. Document the problem using a word processing application. Create an invoice using either a word processing or spreadsheet application. Share your documents with others in the class.

Critical Thinking Skills

Objective: To analyze and evaluate information as well as apply learned information to new or different situations

Activities:

1. Why do you think so few computers today have very few PCI adapters or slots?
2. Compare and contrast a post office with IRQs, I/O addresses, and memory addresses shown in Device Manager. For example, how might something that happens in a post office relate to an IRQ in a PC (or I/O address or memory address)?
3. Your parents want to buy a new computer, and they are doing research. They ask you to explain whether they should buy a PCIe or an AGP video adapter. Explain to them (either verbally or in writing) the differences between them and your recommendation.

A+ Certification Exam Tips

✓ A lot of questions from both exams can come from this chapter, especially in the troubleshooting areas. Review the troubleshooting bullets. Research issues on the Internet and read people's postings. Their stories and frustration (and successes) will stick in your mind and help you with the test.

✓ Go to at least one computer and go through the BIOS menus. Review what types of things can be configured through BIOS.

✓ Review the difference between a BIOS and a UEFI BIOS.

✓ Review different sections of Device Manager. Device Manager is a critical tool for troubleshooting computer issues. Know how to determine what driver is installed. Practice finding drivers on Internet sites.

✓ Know what issues look like in Device Manager. Trying to get Windows or BIOS to show an error within Device Manager on a machine that works properly is difficult, so use a search engine such as Google Images and type `Device Manager conflicts` as your search string. The resulting images are examples of Device Manager conflicts.

chapter 4

Disassembly and Power

Chapter Objectives:

In this chapter you will learn:

- How to prevent static electricity, RFI, and EMI from harming or interfering with a computer
- The tools needed to work on computers
- How to take apart a computer and put it back together
- How to perform basic voltage and continuity checks
- How to upgrade or replace a power supply
- Different power-saving techniques
- What type of power devices can be used to protect computers
- Tips for good written communication

CompTIA Exam Objectives:

What CompTIA A+ exam objectives are covered in this chapter?

- ✓ 801-1.2 Differentiate between motherboard components, their purposes, and properties.
- ✓ 801-1.8 Install an appropriate power supply based on a given scenario.
- ✓ 801-3.1 Install and configure laptop hardware and components.
- ✓ 801-5.1 Given a scenario, use appropriate safety procedures.
- ✓ 801-5.2 Explain environmental impacts and the purpose of environmental controls.
- ✓ 801-5.3 Given a scenario, demonstrate proper communication and professionalism.
- ✓ 802-1.4 Given a scenario, use appropriate operating system features and tools.
- ✓ 802-1.5 Given a scenario, use Control Panel utilities.
- ✓ 802-4.2 Given a scenario, troubleshoot common problems related to motherboards, RAM, CPU, and power with appropriate tools.
- ✓ 802-4.8 Given a scenario, troubleshoot, and repair common laptop issues while adhering to the appropriate procedures.

Disassembly Overview

It is seldom necessary to completely disassemble a computer. However, when a technician is first learning about PCs, disassembly can be both informative and fun. Technicians might disassemble parts of a computer to perform preventive cleaning or to troubleshoot a problem. It may also be appropriate to disassemble a computer when it has a problem of undetermined cause. Sometimes, the only way to diagnose a problem is to disassemble the computer outside the case or remove components one by one. Disassembling a computer outside the case may help with grounding problems. A **grounding** problem occurs when the motherboard or adapter is not properly installed and a trace (a metal line on the motherboard or adapter) touches the computer frame, causing the adapter and possibly other components to stop working. Don't forget to remove jewelry and use proper lifting techniques, as described in Figure 1.1 (see Chapter 1) before disassembling a computer.

Electrostatic Discharge (ESD)

You must take many precautions when disassembling a computer. The electronic circuits located on the motherboard and adapters are subject to ESD. **ESD** (electrostatic discharge) is a difference of potential between two items that causes static electricity. Static electricity can damage electronic equipment without the technician's knowledge. The average person requires a static discharge of 3,000 volts before he or she feels it. An electronic component can be damaged with as little as 30 volts. Some electronic components may not be damaged the first time static electricity occurs. However, the effects of static electricity can be cumulative, weakening or eventually destroying a component. An ESD event is not recoverable—nothing can be done about the damage it induces. Electronic chips and memory modules are most susceptible to ESD strikes.

Atmospheric conditions affect static electricity. When humidity is low, the potential for ESD is greater than at any other time; however, too much humidity is bad for electronics. Keep humidity between 45 and 55 percent to reduce the threat of ESD.

A technician can prevent ESD by using a variety of methods. The most common tactic is to use an **antistatic wrist strap**. One end encircles the technician's wrist. At the other end, an alligator clip attaches to the computer. The clip attaches to a grounding post or a metal part such as the power supply. The electronic symbol for ground follows:

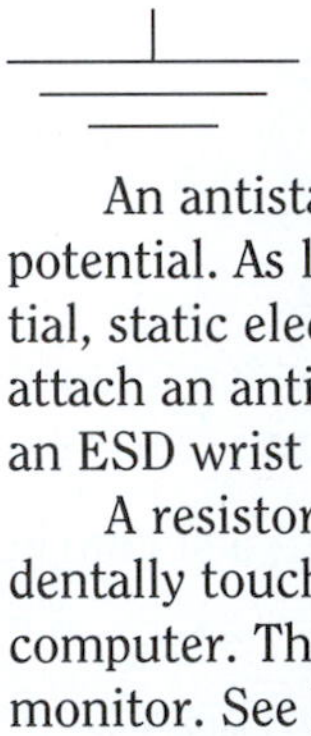

An antistatic wrist strap allows the technician and the computer to be at the same voltage potential. As long as the technician and the computer or electronic part are at the same potential, static electricity does not occur. An exercise at the end of the chapter demonstrates how to attach an antistatic wrist strap and how to perform maintenance on it. Technicians should use an ESD wrist strap whenever possible.

A resistor inside an antistatic wrist strap protects the technician in case something accidentally touches the ground to which the strap attaches while he or she is working inside a computer. This resistor cannot protect the technician against the possible voltages inside a monitor. See Figure 4.1 for an illustration of an antistatic wrist strap. Figure 4.2 shows a good location for attaching an antistatic wrist strap.

Tech Tip

When *not* to wear an antistatic wrist strap

Technicians should not wear an ESD wrist strap when working inside a CRT monitor because of the high voltages there.

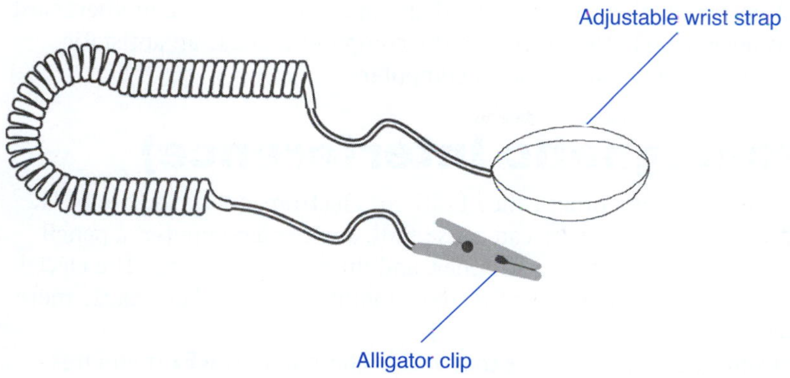

Figure 4.1 Antistatic wrist strap

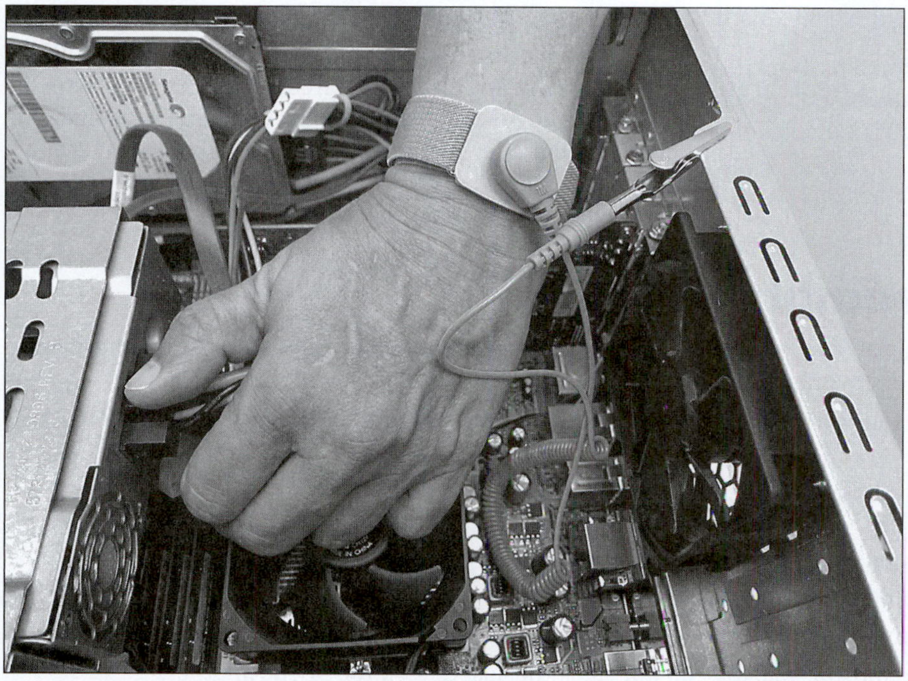

Figure 4.2 Attaching an antistatic wrist strap

Antistatic bags are good for storing spare adapters and motherboards when the parts are not in use. However, antistatic bags lose their effectiveness after a few years. Antistatic mats are available to place underneath a computer being repaired; such a mat may have a snap for connecting the antistatic wrist strap. Antistatic heel straps are also available.

If an antistatic wrist strap is not available, you can still reduce the chance of ESD damage. After removing the computer case, stay attached to an unpainted metal computer part. One such part is the power supply. If you are right-handed, place your bare left arm on the power supply. Remove the computer parts one by one, always keeping your left elbow (or some other bare part of your arm) connected to the power supply. If you are left-handed, place your right arm on the power supply. By placing your elbow on the power supply, both hands are free to remove computer parts. This method is an effective way of keeping the technician and the computer at the same voltage potential, thus reducing the chance of ESD damage. It is not as safe as using an antistatic wrist strap. Also, removing the power cable from the back of the computer is a good idea. A power supply provides a small amount of power to the motherboard even when the computer is powered off. Always unplug the computer and use an antistatic wrist strap when removing or replacing parts inside a computer!

EMI (Electromagnetic Interference)

EMI (electromagnetic interference, sometimes called EMR, for electromagnetic radiation) is noise caused by electrical devices. Many devices can cause EMI, such as a computer, a pencil sharpener, a motor, a vacuum cleaner, an air conditioner, and fluorescent lighting. The electrical devices around the computer case, including a CRT-type monitor and speakers, cause more problems than the computer.

A specific type of electromagnetic interference that affects computers is **RFI** (radio frequency interference). RFI is simply those noises that occur in the radio frequency range. Anytime a computer has an intermittent problem, check the surrounding devices for the source of that problem. For example, if the computer goes down only when the pencil sharpener operates or when using the optical drive, EMI could be to blame. EMI problems are very hard to track to the source. Any electronic device including computers and printers can be a source of EMI/RFI. EMI/RFI can affect any electronic circuit. EMI can also come through power lines. Move the computer to a different wall outlet or to a totally different circuit to determine if the power outlet is the problem source. EMI can also affect files on a hard drive.

Tech Tip

Replace empty slot covers

To help with EMI and RFI problems, replace slot covers for expansion slots that are no longer being used. Slot covers also keep out dust and improve the air flow within the case.

Disassembly

Before a technician disassembles a computer, several steps should be performed or considered. The following disassembly tips are helpful:

- Do not remove the motherboard battery, or the configuration information in CMOS will be lost.
- Use proper grounding procedures to prevent ESD damage.
- Keep paper, a pen, a phone, and a digital camera nearby for note taking, diagramming, and photo taking. Even if you have taken apart computers for years, you might find something unique or different inside this one.
- Have ample flat and clean workspace.
- When removing adapters, do not stack the adapters on top of one another.
- If possible, place removed adapters inside a special ESD protective bag.
- Handle each adapter, motherboard, or processor on the side edges. Avoid touching the gold contacts on the bottom of adapters. Sweat, oil, and dirt cause problems.
- Remember that hard drives require careful handling. A very small jolt can cause damage to stored data.
- You can remove a power supply, but do not disassemble a CRT-style monitor or power supply without proper training and tools.
- Document screw and cable locations. Label them if possible.

Tools

No chapter on disassembly and reassembly is complete without mentioning tools. Tools can be divided into two categories: (1) those you should not leave the office without and (2) those that are nice to have in the office, at home, or in the car.

Many technicians do not go on a repair call with a full tool case. Ninety-five percent of all repairs are completed with the following basic tools:

- Small and medium flat-tipped screwdrivers
- #0, #1, and #2 Phillips screwdrivers
- 1/4- and 3/16-inch hex nut drivers
- Small diagonal cutters
- Needlenose pliers

Screwdrivers take care of most disassemblies and reassemblies. Sometimes manufacturers place tie wraps on new parts, new cables, or the cables inside the computer case. The diagonal cutters are great for removing the tie wraps without cutting cables or damaging parts. Needlenose pliers are good for straightening bent pins on cables or connectors, and doing a million other things. Small tweaker screwdrivers and needlenose pliers are indispensable.

Many technicians start with a basic $15 microcomputer repair kit and build from there. A bargain table 6-in-1 or 4-in-1 combination screwdriver that has two sizes of flat-tipped and two sizes of Phillips screwdrivers is a common tool among new technicians. A specialized Swiss army knife with screwdrivers is the favorite of some technicians. Other technicians prefer to carry an all-in-one tool in a pouch that connects to their belt.

Tech Tip

Do not use magnetized screwdrivers

Avoid using a magnetic screwdriver when working on a computer. It can cause permanent loss of data on hard drives or floppy disks. Magnetism can also induce currents into components and damage them. Sometimes, technicians are tempted to use a magnetic screwdriver when they drop a small part such as a screw into a hard-to-reach place, but avoid using a magnetic screwdriver.

Alternatives to the magnetic screwdriver include a screw pick-up tool and common sense. A screw pick-up tool is used in hard-to-reach places and sometimes under the motherboard. If a screw rolls under the motherboard and cannot be reached, tilt the computer so that the screw rolls out. Sometimes the case must be tilted in different directions until the screw becomes dislodged.

There are tools that no one thinks of as tools but that should be taken on a service call every time. They include a pen or pencil with which to take notes and fill out the repair slip and a bootable disc containing the technician's favorite repair utilities. Usually a technician has several bootable discs for different operating systems and utilities. Often a flashlight comes in handy because some rooms and offices are dimly lit. Finally, do not forget to bring a smile and a sense of humor.

Tools that are nice to have but not used daily include the following:

- Multimeter
- Screw pick-up tool
- Screwdriver extension tool
- Soldering iron, solder, and flux
- Screw-starter tool
- Medium-size diagonal cutters
- Metric nut drivers
- Cable-making tools
- Cable tester
- Loopback plug
- Punch down tool
- Toner probe
- Wire stripper
- Crimper

- AC circuit tester
- Right-angled, flat-tipped, and Phillips screwdrivers
- Hemostats
- Pliers
- Optical laser cleaning kit
- Nonstatic vacuum or toner vacuum
- Disposable gloves
- Small plastic scribe
- T8, 10, 15, 20, and 25 Torx (star) screwdriver

You could get some nice muscle tone from carrying all these nice-to-have but normally unnecessary tools. When starting out in computer repair, get the basics. As your career path and skill level grow, so will your tool kit. Getting to a job site and not having the right tool can be a real hassle. However, because there are no standards or limitations on what manufacturers can use in their product lines, it is impossible to always have the right tool on hand. However, always remember that no tool kit is complete without an antistatic wrist strap.

Opening the Case

Opening or removing the case is sometimes the hardest part of disassembly. Some manufacturers have tabs or covers over the retaining screws, and others have retention levers or tabs that have to be depressed before the cover slides open or away. For some computers you must press a tab on top of the computer downward while simultaneously pressing upward on a tab on the bottom of the computer. Once the tabs are pressed, the cover can be pried open. Sound like a two-person job? Sometimes it is.

Some cases have screws that loosen but do not have to be removed all the way to remove or open the case. For all computer screws, make diagrams and use an egg carton and label each section of the carton with where you got the screws. When possible, refer to the manufacturer's directions when opening a case.

Cables and Connectors

Internal cables commonly connect from a device to the motherboard, the power supply to a device, the motherboard to the front panel buttons or ports, and/or from a card that occupies an expansion space to the motherboard. Cables can be tricky. Inserting a cable backward into a device or adapter can damage the device, motherboard, or adapter. Most cables are keyed so the cable inserts into the connector only one way. However, some cables or connectors are *not* keyed.

Removing a cable for the first time requires some muscle. Many cables have a pull tab or plastic piece used to remove the cable from the connector and/or device. Use this if possible and do not yank on the cable. Some cables have connectors with locking tabs. Release the locking tab *before* disconnecting the cable; otherwise, damage can be done to the cable and/or connector.

Be careful with hard drive cables. Some of the narrow drive cables, such as the one shown in Figure 4.3, are not as sturdy and do not connect as firmly as some of the other computer cables. Also, with this particular cable type, it does not matter which cable end attaches to the device. A 90°-angled cable (see Figure 4.4) may attach to devices in a case that has a limited-space design and may have a release latch.

Figure 4.3 Both cable ends are the same

Figure 4.4 90°-angled cable with a latch

Each cable has a certain number of pins, and all cables have a **pin 1**. Pin 1 on a cable connects to pin 1 on a connector. In the event that the pin 1 is *not* easily identified, both ends of the cable should be labeled with either a 1 or 2 on one side or a higher number, such as 24, 25, 49, 50, and so on, on the other end. Pins 1 and 2 are always on the same end of a cable. If you find a higher number, pin 1 is on the opposite end. Also, the cable connector usually has an arrow etched into its molding showing the pin 1 connection. Figure 4.5 shows pin 1 on a ribbon cable.

Tech Tip

Pin 1 is the cable edge that is colored

Pin 1 on a ribbon cable is easily identified by the colored stripe that runs down the edge of the cable.

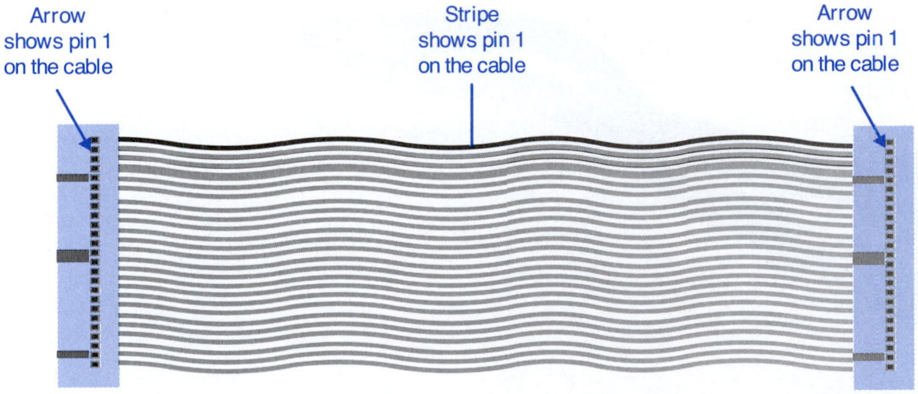

Figure 4.5 Pin 1 on a ribbon cable

Tech Tip

Snug connections

When connecting cables to a motherboard or internal components, ensure that each cable is connected tightly, evenly, and securely.

Just as every cable has a pin 1, all connectors on devices, adapters, or motherboards have a pin 1. Pin 1 on a cable inserts into pin 1 on a connector. Cables are normally keyed so that they insert only one way. Some manufacturers stencil a 1 or a 2 by the connector on the motherboard or adapter; however, on a black connector, it's difficult to see the small number. Numbers on adapters are easier to distinguish. When the number 2 is etched beside the adapter's connector, connect the cable's pin 1 to this side. Remember that pins 1 and 2 are always on the same side, whether on a connector or on a cable. Some technicians use a permanent marker to label a cable's function. Figure 4.6 shows an example of a stenciled marking beside an adapter's connector. Figure 4.6 illustrates the number 2 etched onto the adapter, but other manufacturers stencil a higher number, such as 33, 34, 39, or 40, beside the opposite end of the connector.

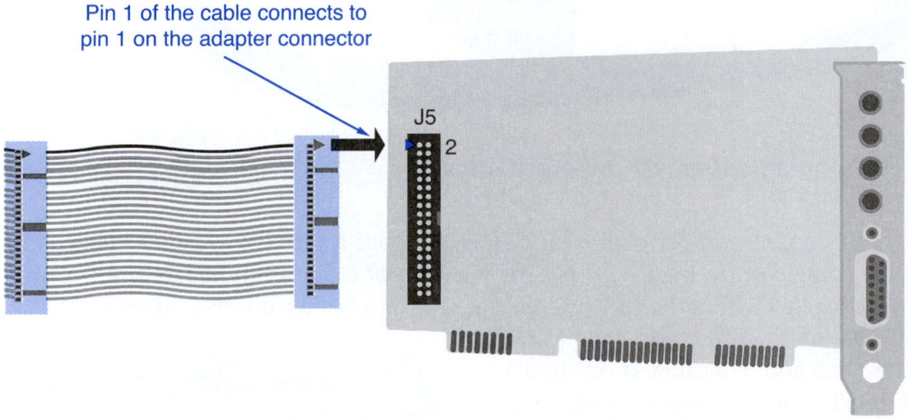

Figure 4.6 Pin 1 on an adapter

Motherboard connectors are usually notched so that the cable inserts only one way; however, not all cables are notched. Some motherboards have pin 1 (or the opposite pin) labeled. Always refer to the motherboard documentation for proper orientation of a cable into a motherboard connector. Figure 4.7 shows the motherboard connectors used for the thin cables shown in Figures 4.3 and 4.4. These connectors commonly have hard drives and optical drives attached. Figure 4.8 show three other motherboard connectors that are notched.

Figure 4.7 Motherboard connectors for narrow cables

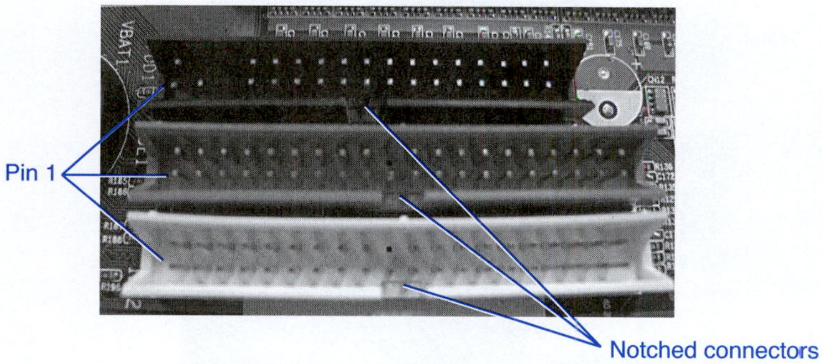

Figure 4.8 Three motherboard connectors

Some manufacturers do not put any markings on the cable connector; even so, there is a way to determine which way to connect the cable. Remove the adapter, motherboard, or device from the computer. Look where the connector solders or connects to the motherboard or adapter. Turn over the adapter. Notice the silver blobs, known as solder joints, on the back of the motherboard or adapter. Solder joints connect electronic components to the motherboard or adapter. The connector's solder joints are normally round, except for the solder joint for pin 1, which is square. Look for the square solder joint on the back of the connector. If the square solder joint is not apparent on the connector, look for other connectors or solder joints that are square. All chips and connectors mount onto a motherboard in the same direction—all pin 1s are normally oriented in the same direction. If one pin 1 is found, the other connectors orient in the same direction. Insert the cable so pin 1 matches the square solder joint of the connector. Figure 4.9 shows a square solder joint for a connector on the back of an adapter.

Tech Tip

Pin 1 is on the opposite end from the higher stenciled number

If a higher number, such as 39 or 40, is stenciled beside the connector, connect pin 1 and 2 of the cable *to the opposite end of that connector*.

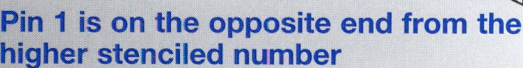

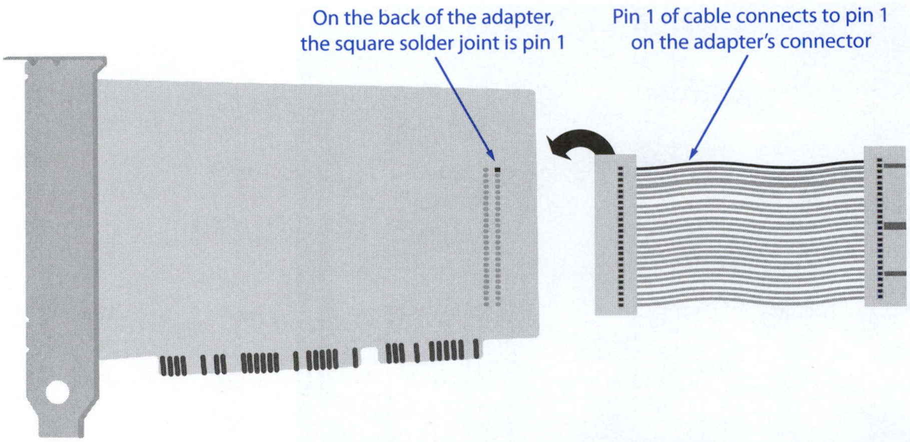

Figure 4.9 Pin 1 on a connector

Specific cables connect a motherboard to lights, ports, or buttons on the front panel. These include the power button, a reset button, USB ports, IEEE 1394 ports, a microphone port, a headphone port, speakers, fans, the hard drive usage light, and the power light, to name a few. Be very careful when removing and reinstalling these cables. Usually, each one of these has a connector that must attach to the appropriate motherboard pins. Be sure to check all ports and buttons once you have reconnected these cables. Refer to the motherboard documentation if your diagramming or notes are inaccurate or if you have no diagrams or notes. Figure 4.10 shows the motherboard pins and the connectors.

Figure 4.10 Motherboard front panel connectors

Storage Devices

Hard drives must be handled with care when disassembling a computer. Inside traditional hard drives are hard platters with tiny read/write heads located just millimeters above the platters. If dropped, the read/write heads can touch the platter, causing damage to the platter and/or the read/write heads. The platter is used to store data and applications. Today's mechanical hard drives have self-parking heads that pull the heads away to a safe area when the computer is powered off or in a power-saving mode. Always be careful neither to jolt nor to jar the hard drive when removing it from the computer. Even with self-parking heads, improper handling can cause damage to the hard drive.

A solid-state drive does not contain fragile heads. However, these drives are susceptible to ESD. Use proper antistatic handling procedures when removing/installing them. Store a solid-state drive in an antistatic bag when not in use. Avoid touching the drive with a metal tool.

Motherboards

Chapter 2 covered motherboard replacement extensively, and here we discuss issues related to building a computer from scratch or disassembling a computer: I/O shield, standoffs, and retaining clips. Some cases include a standard I/O panel shield that may need to be removed to install the I/O shield that comes with some motherboards. The **I/O shield** is a part what allows for optimum air flow and grounding for the motherboard ports. The I/O shield helps ensure the motherboard is installed correctly and properly aligned with the case. Figure 4.11 shows a motherboard I/O shield.

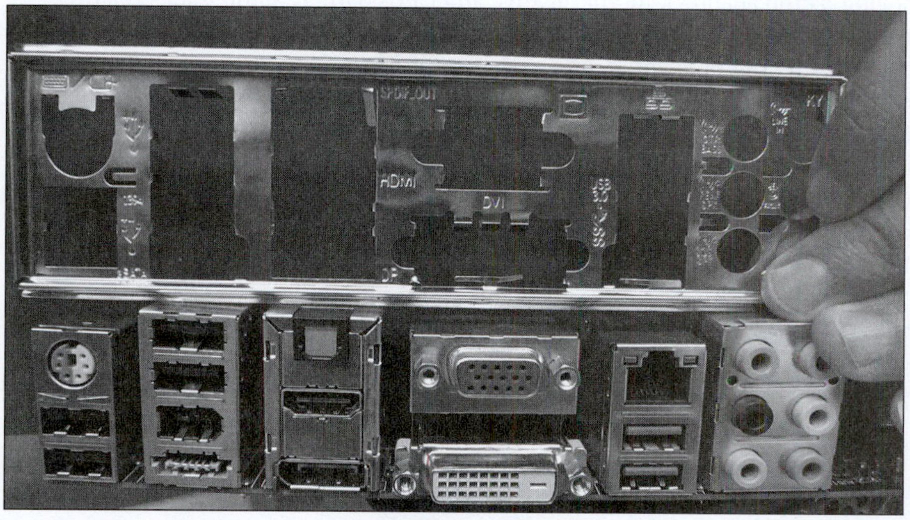

Figure 4.11 Motherboard I/O shield

Some computer cases have plastic or metal (commonly brass) **standoffs** that allow the motherboard to be screwed into the case without the motherboard solder joints touching and grounding to the computer case, causing the motherboard not to work. Some standoffs are plastic, and they slide into slots on the computer case. Do not remove these types of standoffs but just leave them attached and slide the motherboard out of the slots. The most common type of standoff is a metal standoff that screws into the case; this standoff has a threaded side that the motherboard sits on and a screw that attaches the motherboard to the standoff, as shown in Figure 4.12.

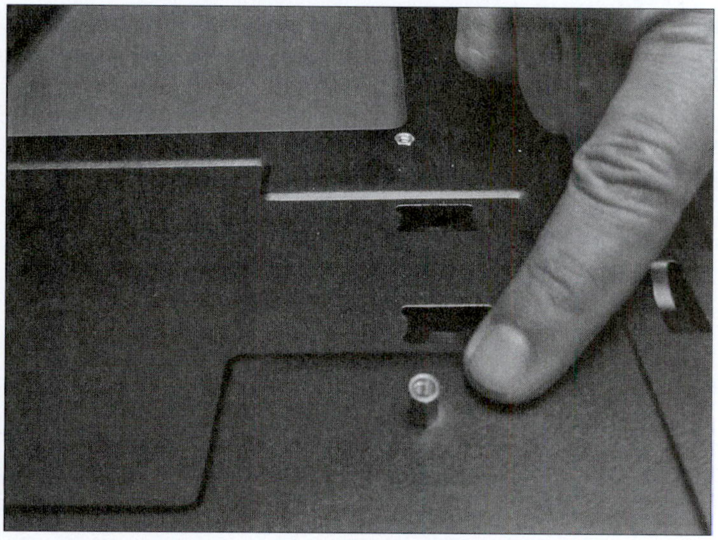

Figure 4.12 Motherboard standoff

Some motherboards not only have screws that attach them to the metal standoffs but one or more retaining clips. A retaining clip might need to be pressed down, lifted up, or bent upward in order to slide the motherboard out of the case. The case might contain one or more notches and require the motherboard to be slid in a particular direction (usually in the direction going away from the back I/O ports) before being lifted from the case.

Mobile Device Issues

Chapter 1 contains information on removing laptop keyboards, and Chapter 2 includes information on removing laptop adapters, motherboards, and CPUs. Other laptop issues relating to disassembling a laptop include memory, plastics, the DC power jack, and the speaker. Whenever taking anything out of a laptop, one of the major issues is tiny screws. Many manufacturers label the type of screen or location for ease of explaining disassembly. Always keep like screws together (in containers or an egg carton) and take notes. All the parts are manufacturer dependent, but the following explanation and graphics/photos should help with these portable devices.

Laptop memory and expansion cards are commonly located in a bottom compartment accessed by removing a screw. Figure 4.13 shows this on a netbook computer.

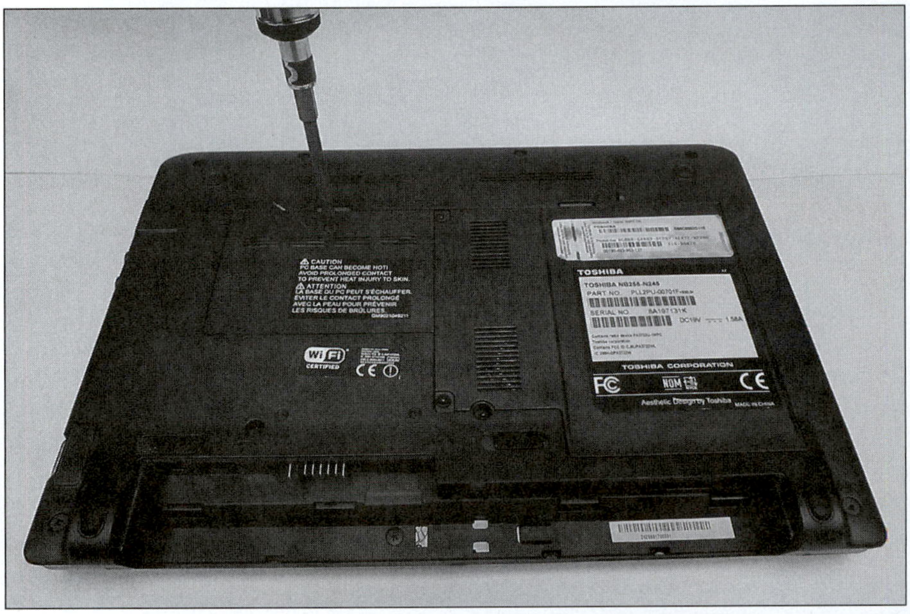

Figure 4.13 Netbook memory compartment

Some laptop and mobile device compartments require levering the compartment cover away from the case or removing plastic parts such as the cover that fits over a mobile computer keyboard. A plastic **scribe** is the best tool to use for this levering. Figure 4.14 shows a plastic scribe being used to lift the plastic part that is between the keyboard and the laptop screen.

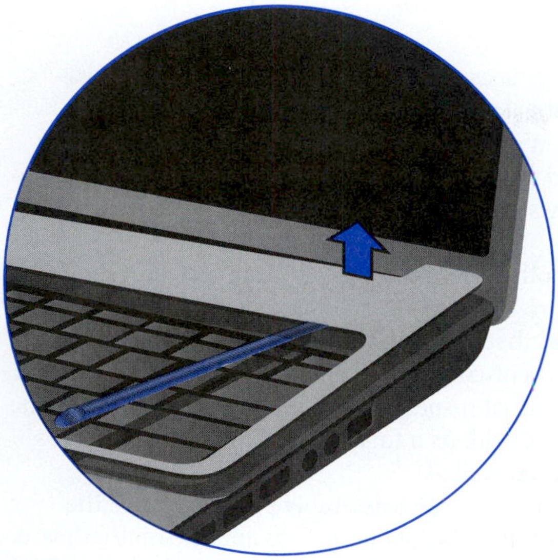

Figure 4.14 Scribe used to remove a laptop plastic piece

Laptop/netbook speakers commonly mount above or to the side of the keyboard. The keyboard usually has to be removed to reach the speakers. Sometimes, speaker cables run alongside the keyboard and must be pried out of the case. The DC power plug commonly has a similar cable, as shown in Figure 4.15.

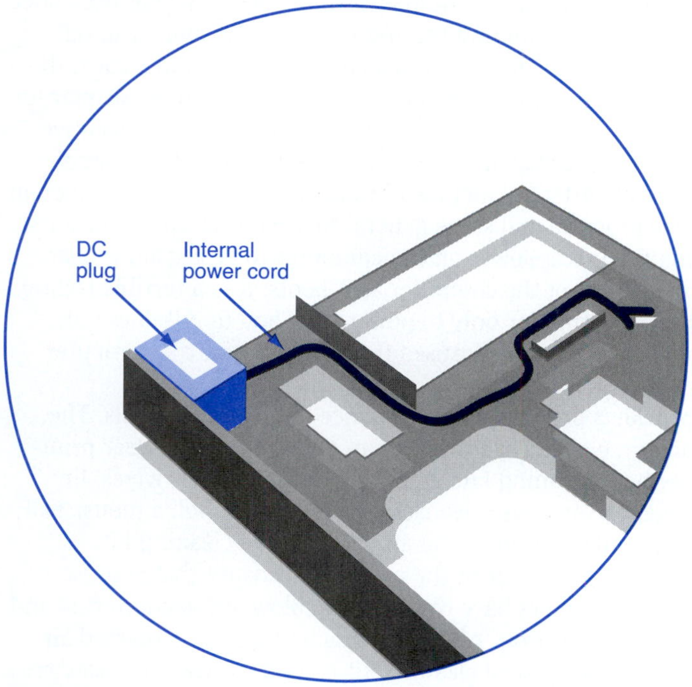

Figure 4.15 Laptop DC power plug cable

Reassembly

Reassembling a computer is easy if the technician is careful and properly diagrams the disassembly. Simple tasks such as inserting the optical drive in the correct drive bay become confusing after many parts have been removed. Writing down reminders takes less time than having to troubleshoot the computer because of poor reassembly. Reinsert all components into their proper place; be careful to replace all screws and parts. Install missing slot covers, if possible.

Three major reassembly components are motherboards, cables, and connectors. When reinstalling a motherboard, reverse the procedure used during disassembly. Ensure that the motherboard is securely seated into the case and that all retaining clips and/or screws are replaced. This procedure requires practice, but eventually a technician will be able to tell when a motherboard is seated into the case properly. Visual inspection can also help. Ensure that the ports extend fully from the case through the I/O shield. As a final step, ensure that the drives and cover are aligned properly when the case is reinstalled.

Cables and connectors are the most common source of reassembly problems once the motherboard is installed. Ensure that cables are fully attached to devices and the motherboard. Ensure that power cables are securely attached. Matching pin 1 on the cable to pin 1 on the motherboard connector is critical for older ribbon cables. Attaching the correct device to the correct cable can be difficult if proper notes were not taken.

Preventive Maintenance

Preventive maintenance includes certain procedures performed to prolong the life of a computer. Some computer companies sell maintenance contracts that include preventive maintenance programs. A computer in a normal working environment should be cleaned at least once a year. Typical preventive measures include vacuuming the computer/printer and cleaning the optical drive laser, keyboard keys, printers, and display screen. Be sure to power down the computer and remove the power cord for any computer, remove the battery and AC adapter for a laptop/netbook, and allow a laser printer to cool before accessing internal parts. Preventive exercises for many individual devices are described in their respective chapters. For example, the steps detailing how to clean CDs/DVDs/BDs are included in Chapter 8. This section gives an overview of a preventive maintenance program and some general tips about cleaning solvents.

When performing preventive maintenance, power on the computer to be certain it operates. Perform an audio and visual inspection of the computer as it boots. It is a terrible feeling to perform preventive maintenance on a computer only to power it on and find it does not work. You will wonder if the cleaning you performed caused the problem or if the computer had a problem before the preventive maintenance.

Repair companies frequently provide a preventive maintenance kit for service calls. The kit normally includes a portable vacuum cleaner, special vacuum cleaner bags for laser printers, a can of compressed air, a floppy head cleaning kit, urethane swabs, monitor wipes, lint-free cloths, general-purpose cloths, general-purpose cleanser, denatured alcohol, a mouse ball cleaning kit, an antistatic brush, gold contact cleaner, and an optical drive cleaning kit.

The vacuum is used to suck dirt from the inside of the computer. Ensure that you use nonmetallic attachments. Some vacuum cleaners have the ability to blow air. Vacuum first and then set the vacuum cleaner to blow to get dust out of hard-to-reach places. Compressed air can also be used in these situations. The floppy head cleaning kit is used to clean the read/write heads on the floppy drive. Monitor wipes are used on the front of the monitor screen. Monitor wipes with antistatic solution work best.

Urethane swabs are used to clean between the keys on a keyboard. If a key is sticking, remove the keyboard before spraying or using contact cleaner on it. Touchpads normally require no maintenance except being wiped with a dampened lint-free cloth to remove residual finger oil.

General-purpose cleanser is used to clean the outside of the case and to clean the desktop areas under and around the computer. Never spray or pour liquid on any computer part. Liquid cleaners are used with soft lint-free cloths or lint-free swabs.

Tech Tip

Be careful when cleaning LCD monitors and laptop displays

Use one of the following to clean LCD monitors and laptop displays: (1) wipes specifically designed for LCDs or (2) a soft lint-free cloth dampened with either water or a mixture of isopropyl alcohol and water. Never put liquid directly on the display and ensure that the display is dry before closing the laptop.

Denatured alcohol is used on rubber rollers, such as those found inside printers. An antistatic brush can be used to brush dirt away from hard-to-reach places. Gold contact cleaner is used to clean adapter contacts as well as contacts on laptop batteries and the contacts where the battery inserts. A useful CD/DVD/BD cleaning kit can include a lens cleaner that removes dust and debris from an optical lens; a disk cleaner that removes dust, dirt, fingerprints, and oils from the disk; and a scratch repair kit used to resurface, clean, and polish CDs, DVDs, and BDs.

Many cleaning solution companies provide MSDS (material safety data sheets) that contain information about a product, including its toxicity, storage, disposal, and health/safety concerns. Your state may also have specific disposal procedures for chemical solvents. Check with the company's safety coordinator for storage and disposal information.

Tech Tip

Know your state aerosol can disposal laws

Some states have special requirements for disposal of aerosol cans, especially those that are clogged and still contain some product.

To perform the preventive maintenance, power off the computer, remove the power cord, and vacuum the computer with a nonmetallic attachment. Do not start with compressed air or by blowing dust out of the computer because the dirt and dust will simply go into the air and eventually fall back into the computer and surrounding equipment. After vacuuming as much as possible, use compressed air to blow the dust out of hard-to-reach places, such as inside the power supply and under the motherboard. If you are performing maintenance on a notebook computer, remove as many modules as possible, such as the optical drive, battery, and hard drive, before vacuuming or using compressed air. Inform people in the immediate area that they might want to leave the area if they have allergies.

If you remove an adapter from an expansion slot, replace it into the same slot. If the computer battery is on a riser board, it is best to leave the riser board connected to the motherboard so the system does not lose its configuration information. The same steps covered in the disassembly section of this chapter hold true when you are performing preventive maintenance.

Tech Tip

Use a preventive maintenance call as a time for updates

A preventive maintenance call is a good time to check for operating system, BIOS, antivirus, and driver updates.

When you perform preventive maintenance, take inventory and document what is installed in the computer, such as the hard drive size, amount of RAM, available hard drive space, and so on. During the maintenance procedure, communicate with the user. Ask if the computer has been giving anyone trouble lately or if it has been performing adequately. Computer users like to know that you care about their computing needs. Also, users frequently ask questions such as whether sunlight or cold weather harms the computer. Always respond with answers the user can understand. Users appreciate it when you explain things in terms they comprehend and that make sense.

A preventive maintenance call is the perfect opportunity to check computers for viruses. Normally, first you clean the computer. Then, while the virus checker is running, you might clean external peripherals such as printers. Preventive maintenance measures help limit computer problems as well as provide a chance to interact with customers and help with a difficulty that may seem minuscule but could worsen. A preventive maintenance call is also a good time to take inventory of all hardware and software installed. In a preventive maintenance call, entry-level technicians can see the different computer types and begin learning the computer components.

Basic Electronics Overview

A technician needs to know a few basic electronic terms and concepts when testing components. The best place to start is with electricity. There are two types of electricity: AC and DC. The electricity provided by a wall outlet is **AC** (alternating current), and the type of electricity used by computer components is **DC** (direct current). Devices such as radios, TVs, and toasters use AC power. Low-voltage DC power is used for a computer's internal components and anything powered by batteries. A computer's power supply converts AC electricity from the wall outlet to DC for the internal components. Electricity involves electrons flowing through a conductor, similar to the way that water runs through a pipe. With AC, the electrons flow alternately in both directions. With DC, the electrons flow in one direction only.

Electronics Terms

Voltage, current, power, and resistance are terms commonly used in the computer industry. **Voltage**, which is a measure of the pressure pushing electrons through a circuit, is measured in **volts**. A power supply's output is measured in volts. Power supplies typically put out +3.3 volts, +5 volts, +12 volts, and –12 volts. You will commonly see these voltages shown in power supply documentation as +5V or +12V. Another designation is +5VSB. This is for the computer's **standby power**. This power is always provided, even when the computer is powered off. This supplied voltage is why you have to unplug a computer when working inside it.

The term *volts* is also used to describe voltage from a wall outlet. Wall outlet voltage is normally 120VAC (120 volts AC). Exercises at the end of the chapter explain how to take both AC and DC voltage readings. Figure 4.16 shows a photograph of a multimeter being used to take a DC voltage reading on the power connectors coming from a power supply. When the meter leads are inserted correctly, the voltage level shown is of the correct polarity.

Tech Tip

Polarity is important only when measuring DC voltage

When a technician measures the voltage coming out of a power supply, the black meter lead (which is negative) connects to the black wire from the power supply (which is ground). The red meter lead connects to either the +5 or +12 volt wires from the power supply.

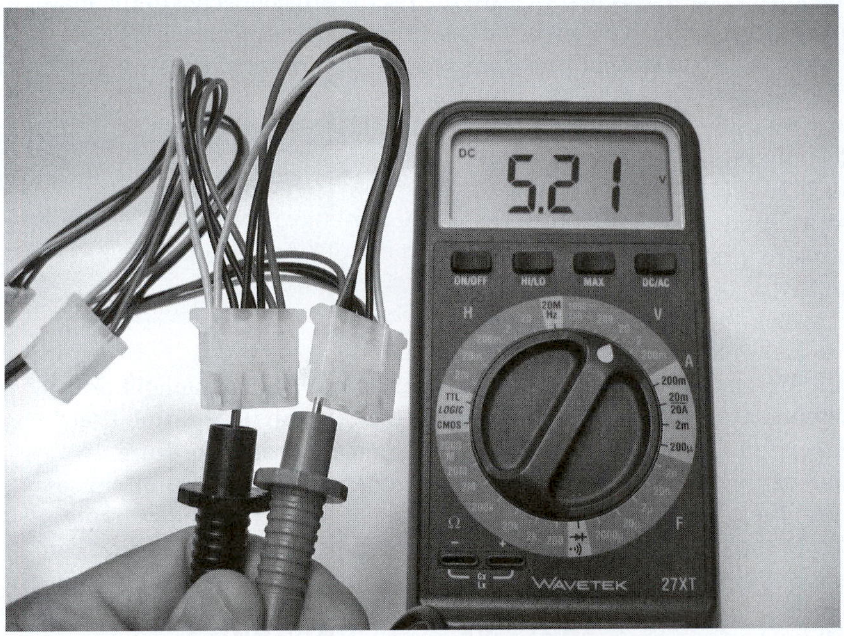

Figure 4.16 DC voltage reading

The reading on the meter could be the opposite of what it should be if the meter's leads are reversed. Since electrons flow from one area where there are many of them (negative polarity) to an area where there are few electrons (positive polarity), polarity shows which way an electric current will flow. Polarity is the condition of being positive or negative with respect to some reference point. Polarity is not important when measuring AC. Figure 4.17 shows rules to observe when working with meters.

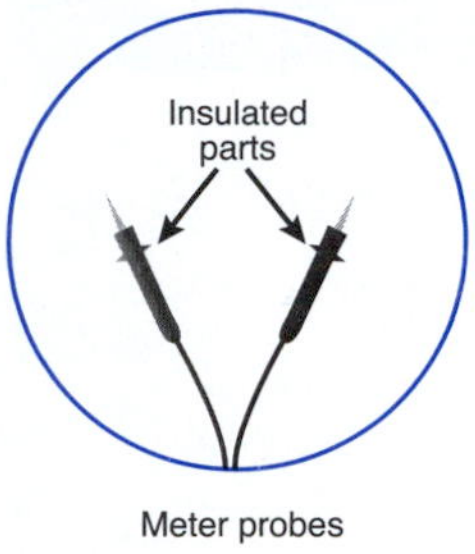

1. Select AC or DC on the meter (some meters automatically select AC or DC).

   VAC or ACV or ~ or $\tilde{V}$

   VDC or DCV or — or ⎓ or $\overline{V}$

2. Select the appropriate voltage range (0-10V, 0-100V, etc). The meter can be damaged if you measure a high voltage in a low range (but not the reverse). Use the highest range for unknown voltages.
3. Touch only the insulated parts of the meter probes.

Figure 4.17 Meter rules

Monitors and power supplies can have dangerous voltage levels. Monitors can have up to 35,000 volts going to the back of the CRT. Note that flat-panel displays and mobile device displays use low DC voltage and AC voltage, but not at the voltage levels of CRTs. 120 volts AC is present inside the power supply. Power supplies and monitors have capacitors inside them. A **capacitor** is a component that holds a charge even after the computer is turned off. Capacitors inside a monitor can hold a charge for several hours after the monitor has been powered off.

Current is measured in **amps** (amperes), which is the number of electrons going through a circuit every second. In the water pipe analogy, voltage is the amount of pressure applied to force the water through the pipe, and current is the amount of water flowing. Every device needs a certain amount of current to operate. A power supply is rated for the amount of total current (in amps) it can supply at each voltage level. For example, a power supply could be rated at 20 amps for the 5-volt level and 8 amps for the 12-volt level.

Tech Tip

Do not work inside a CRT monitor unless you have special training

Monitors require high-voltage meters and special precautions.

Power is measured in **watts**, which is a measurement of how much work is being done. It is determined by multiplying volts by amps. Power supplies are described as providing a maximum number of watts. This is the sum of all outputs: For example, 5 volts × 20 amps (100 watts) plus 12V 8 amps (96 watts) equals 196 watts. An exercise at the end of the chapter explains how current and power relate to a technician's job.

Tech Tip

Current is what kills people when an electrical shock is received

Voltage determines how much current flows through the body. A high-current and low-voltage situation is the most dangerous.

Resistance is measured in **ohms**, which is the amount of opposition to current in an electronic circuit. The resistance range on a meter can be used to check continuity or check whether a fuse is good. A **continuity** check is used to determine whether a wire has a break in it. A conductor (wire) in a cable or a good fuse will have very low resistance to electricity (close to zero ohms). A broken wire or a bad fuse will have a very high resistance (millions of ohms, sometimes shown as infinite ohms, or OL). For example, a cable is normally made up of several wires that go from one connector to another. If you measure the continuity from one end of a wire to the other, it should show no resistance. If the wire has a break in it, the meter shows infinite resistance. Figure 4.18 shows examples of a good wire reading and a broken wire reading.

Tech Tip

Always unplug a computer before working inside it

The power supply provides power to the motherboard, even if the computer is powered off. Leaving the power cord attached can cause damage when replacing components such as the processor or RAM.

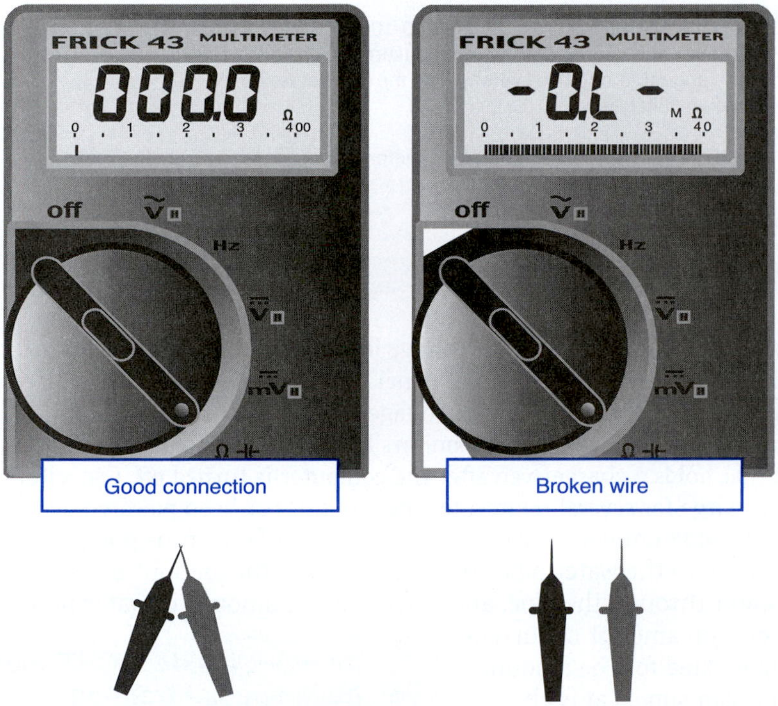

Figure 4.18 Sample resistance meter readings

Digital meters have different ways of displaying infinity. Always refer to the meter manual for this reading. When checking continuity, the meter is placed on the ohms setting, as shown in Figure 4.18. The ohms setting is usually illustrated by an omega symbol (Ω).

Tech Tip

Dealing with small connections and a meter

Some connectors have small pin connections. Use a thin meter probe or insert a thin wire, such as a paper clip, into the hole and touch the meter to the wire to take your reading.

Polarity is not important when performing a continuity check. Either meter lead (red or black) can be placed at either end of the wire. However, you do need a pin-out diagram (wiring list) for the cable before you can check continuity because pin 1 at one end could connect to a different pin number at the other end. An exercise at the end of the chapter steps through this process.

The same concept of continuity applies to fuses. A fuse has a tiny wire inside it that extends from end to end. The fuse is designed so that the wire melts (breaks) if too much current flows through it. The fuse keeps excessive current from damaging electronic circuits or starting a fire. A fuse is rated for a particular amount of current. For example, a 5-amp fuse protects a circuit if the amount of current exceeds 5 amps.

Tech Tip

Use the right fuse or lose

Never replace a fuse with one that has a higher amperage rating. You could destroy electronic circuits or cause a fire by allowing too much current to be passed by the fuse, defeating the fuse's purpose.

Take a fuse out of the circuit before testing it. A good fuse has a meter reading of 0 ohms (or close to that reading). A blown fuse shows a meter reading of infinite ohms. Refer to the section on resistance and Figure 4.18. An exercise at the end of this chapter demonstrates how to check a fuse.

A technician needs to be familiar with basic electronics terms and checks. Table 4.1 consolidates this information.

Table 4.1 Basic electronics terms

Term	Value	Usage
Voltage	Volts	Checking AC voltage on a wall outlet (typically 120VAC). Checking the DC output voltage from a power supply (typically +/– 12, +3.3, and +/– 5 VDC).
Current	Amps (amperes)	Each device needs a certain amount of current to operate. A power supply is rated for total current in amps for each voltage level (such as 24 amps for 5-volt power and 50 amps for 12-volt power).
Resistance	Ohms	Resistance is the amount of opposition to electric current. Resistance is used to check continuity on cables and fuses. A cable that shows little or no resistance has no breaks in it. A good fuse shows no resistance. If a cable has a break in it or if a fuse is bad, the resistance is infinite.
Wattage (power)	Watts	Watts is a measure of power and is derived by multiplying amps by volts. Power supply output is measured in watts. Also, A UPS (uninterruptible power supply) is rated in volt-amps. The size of UPS to purchase depends on how many devices will plug in to it.

Power Supply Overview

A power supply is an essential component within a computer; no internal computer device works without it. The power supply converts AC to DC, distributes lower-voltage DC power to components throughout the computer, and provides cooling through the use of a fan located inside the power supply. The AC voltage a power supply accepts is normally either 100 to 120 volts or 200 to 240 volts. Some dual-voltage power supplies can accept either. This type of power supply can have a selector switch on the back or can automatically detect the input voltage level. The power supply is sometimes a source of unusual problems. The effects of the problems can range from those not noticed by the user to those that shut down the system.

There are two basic types of power supplies: switching and linear. A computer uses a switching power supply. It provides efficient power to all the computer's internal components (and possibly to some external ones, such as USB devices). It also generates minimum heat, comes in small sizes, and is cheaper than linear power supplies. A switching power supply requires a load (something attached to it) in order to operate properly. With today's power supplies, a motherboard is usually a sufficient load, but a technician should always check the power supply specifications to be sure.

Tech Tip

Powering on a power supply without anything attached could damage the power supply

Do not power on a power supply without connecting to the motherboard and possibly a device such as an optical drive or hard drive. An ATX power supply usually requires a motherboard connection at a minimum.

Power Supply Form Factors

Just as motherboards come in different shapes and sizes, so do power supplies. Today's power supply form factors are ATX, ATX12V v1.x, ATX12V v2.x, and micro-ATX. Other form factors include LFX12V (low profile), SFX12V (small form factor), EPS12V (used with server motherboards and has an extra 8-pin connector), CFX12V (compact form factor), SFX12V (small form factor), TFX12V (thin form factor), WTX12V (workstation form factor for high-end workstations and select servers), and FlexATX (smaller systems that have no more than three expansion slots). Intel, AMD, and video card manufacturers certify specific power supplies that work with their processors and video cards. A computer manufacturer can also have a proprietary power supply form factor that is not compatible with different computer models or other vendors' machines. Laptop power supplies are commonly proprietary.

Tech Tip

The motherboard and power supply must be compatible

The motherboard form factor and the power supply form factor must fit in the case and work together. For optimum performance, research what connectors and form factors are supported by both components.

The ATX12V version 2 standard has a 24-pin motherboard connector instead of a 20-pin version 1 connector. This did away with the need for the extra 6-pin auxiliary connector. In addition, version 2 power supplies have a SATA power connector. Some 24-pin motherboard connectors accept the 20-pin power supply connector. Table 4.2 lists the possible ATX power supply connectors.

Table 4.2 ATX power supply connectors

Connector	Notes	Voltage(s)
24-pin	Main ATX power connector to the motherboard	+3.3, +5, +12, –12
20-pin	Main power connector to the motherboard	+3.3, +5, –5, +12, –12
15-pin	SATA connector	+3, +5, +12
8-pin	12V for CPU used with an ATX12V v1 power supply	+12
8-pin	PCIe video; connects to a PCIe video adapter. Note that some connectors are 6+2-pin meaning they accept either the 6- or 8-pin cable.	+12
6-pin	PCIe video; connects to PCIe video adapter	+12
6-pin	Sometimes labeled as AUX; connects to the motherboard if it has a connector	+3.3, +5
4-pin **Molex**	Connects to peripheral devices such as hard drives and CD/DVD drives	+5, +12
4-pin **Berg**	Connects to peripheral devices such as the floppy drive	+5, +12
4-pin	Sometimes labeled as AUX or 12V; connects to the motherboard for CPU	+12
3-pin	Used to monitor fan speed	N/A

Figure 4.19 shows a few ATX power supply connectors. Figure 4.20 shows more ATX power supply connectors.

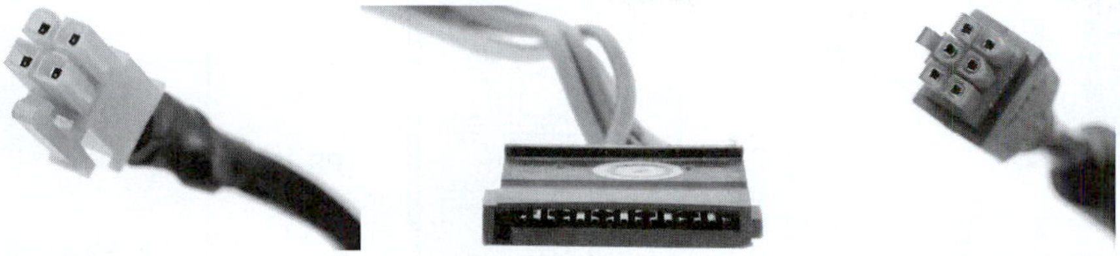

Figure 4.19 Common power supply connectors

Not all 24-pin motherboard connectors accept 20-pin power supply connectors

Tech Tip

You can purchase a 24-pin to 20-pin power adapter. The site http://www.formfactors.org provides information regarding power supply form factors.

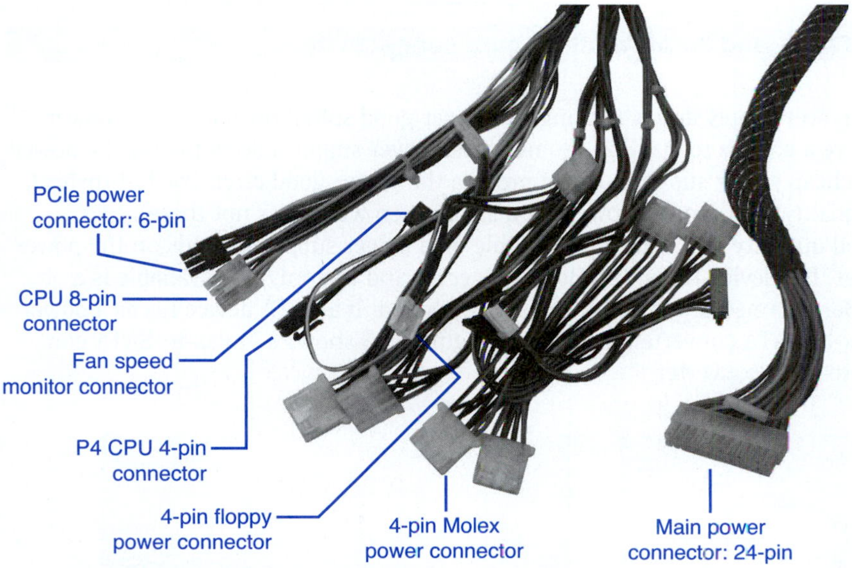

Figure 4.20 ATX power supply connectors

Figure 4.21 illustrates the compatibility between the ATX 20- and 24-pin motherboard connector standards. Notice in Figure 4.21 that the power cable is only one connector, notched so the cable inserts into the connector one way only. This is a much better design than older power supplies, where two connectors were used and could be reversed. Also, notice that a **power good signal** (labeled PWR_OK in Figure 4.21) goes to the motherboard. When the computer is turned on, part of POST is to allow the power supply to run a test on each of the voltage levels. The voltage levels must be correct before any other devices are tested and allowed to initialize. If the power is okay, a power good signal is sent to the motherboard. If the power good signal is not sent from the power supply, a timer chip on the motherboard resets the CPU. Once a power good signal is sent, the CPU begins executing software from the BIOS. Figure 4.21 also shows the +5vsb connection to provide standby power for features such as Wake on LAN or Wake on Ring (covered later in this chapter).

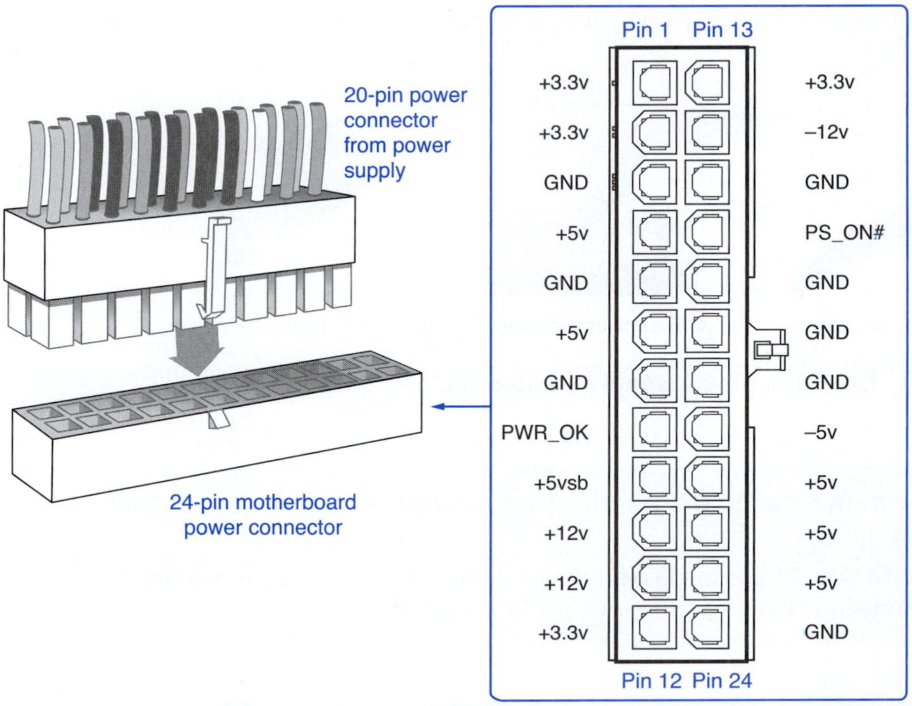

Figure 4.21 ATX 24- and 20-pin motherboard connectivity

A high-quality power supply delays sending the power good signal until all of the power supply's voltages have a chance to stabilize. Some cheap power supplies do not delay the power good signal. Other cheap power supplies do not provide the power good circuitry, but instead, tie 5 volts to the signal (which sends a power good signal even when it is not there).

The number and quantity of connectors available on a power supply depends on the power supply manufacturer. If a device requires a Berg connector and the only one available is a Molex, a Molex-to-Berg connector converter can be purchased. If a SATA device needs a power connection, a Molex-to-SATA converter is available. Figure 4.22 shows a Molex-to-SATA converter and a Molex-to-Berg converter.

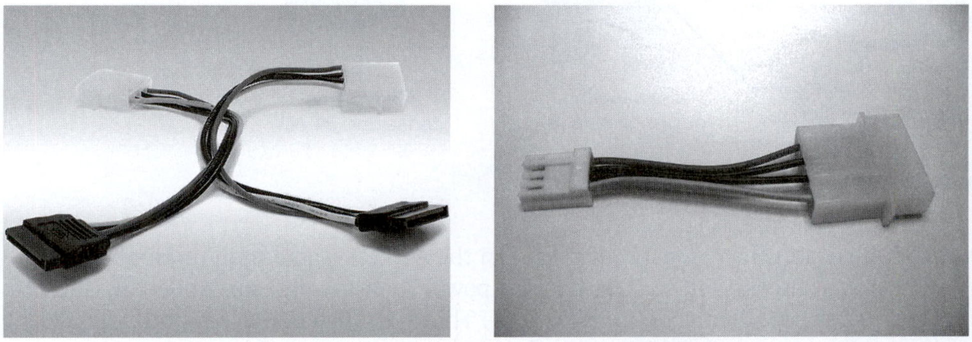

Figure 4.22 Molex-to-SATA and Molex-to-Berg converters

Power supply connectors can connect to any device; there is not a specific connector for the hard drive, the optical drive, and so on. If there are not enough connectors from the power supply for the number of devices installed in a computer, a Y power connector can be purchased at a computer or electronics store. The Y connector adapts a single Molex connector to two Molex connectors for two devices. Verify that the power supply can output enough power to handle the extra device being installed. Figure 4.23 shows a Y power connector.

Power converters and Y connectors are good to have in your tool kit

In case a service call involves adding a new device, having various power converters available as part of your tool kit is smart.

Tech Tip

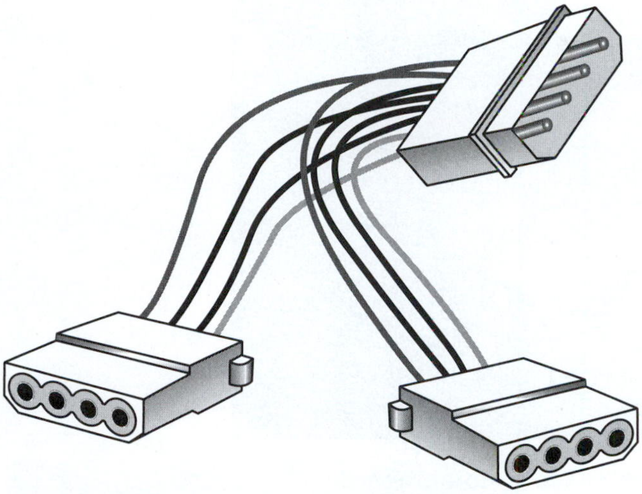

Figure 4.23 Y Molex connector

Purposes of a Power Supply

The power from a wall outlet is high-voltage AC. The type of power computers need is low-voltage DC. All computer parts (the electronic chips on the motherboard and adapters, the electronics on the drives, and the motors in the hard drive and optical drive) need DC power to operate. Power supplies in general come in two types: linear and switching. Computers use switching power supplies. The main functions of a power supply include the following:

- Convert AC to DC
- Provide DC voltage to the motherboard, adapters, and peripheral devices
- Provide cooling and facilitate air flow through the case

One purpose of a power supply is to convert AC to DC so the computer has proper power to run its components. An ATX power supply does not connect to the front panel switch as the old AT-style power supplies did. With the ATX power supply, a connection from the front panel switch to the motherboard simply provides a 5-volt signal that allows the motherboard to tell the power supply to turn on. This 5-volt signal allows ATX power supplies to support ACPI, which is covered later in the chapter, and also lets the motherboard and operating system control the power supply. Figures 4.24 and 4.25 show the front panel connections to the motherboard on two different computers.

On an ATX power supply that has an on/off switch, ensure that it is set to the *on* position

If an ATX power supply switch is present and in the off position, the motherboard and operating system cannot turn on the power supply. Some ATX power supplies do not have external on/off switches, and the computer can be powered down only via the operating system.

Tech Tip

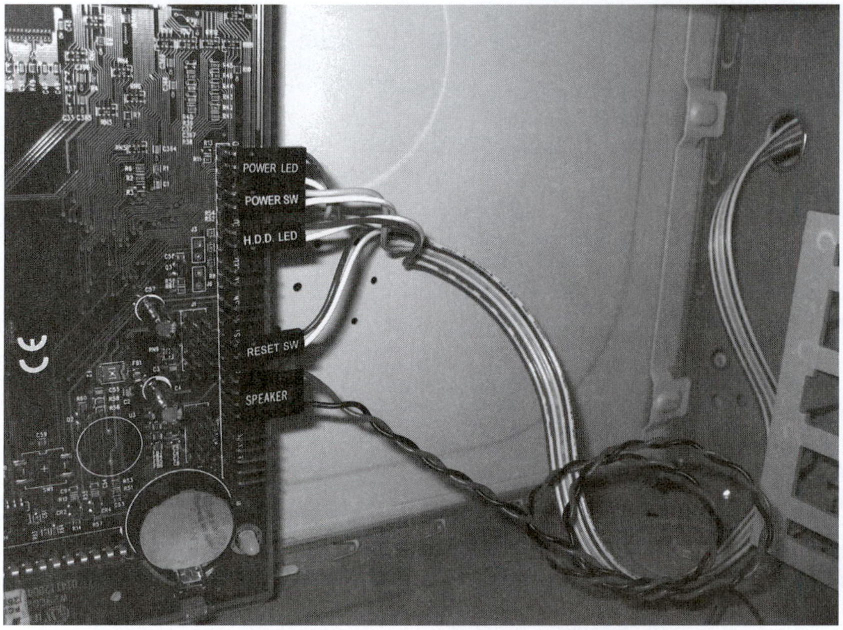

Figure 4.24 Front panel connections to a motherboard

Figure 4.25 Another view of front panel connections

Another purpose of a power supply is to distribute proper DC voltage to each component. Several cables with connectors come out of the power supply. With ATX motherboards, there is only a 20- or 24-pin connector used to connect power to the motherboard. The power connector inserts only one way into the motherboard connector. Figure 4.26 shows an ATX connector being inserted into a motherboard.

Figure 4.26 Installing an ATX power connector on a motherboard

Another purpose for a power supply is to provide cooling for the computer. The power supply's fan circulates air throughout the computer. Most computer cases have air vents on one side, on both sides, or in the rear of the computer. The ATX-style power supply blows air inside the case instead of out the back. This is known as reverse flow cooling. The air blows over the processor and memory to keep them cool. This type of power supply keeps the inside of the computer cleaner than older styles.

Don't block air vents

Whether a computer is a desktop model, a tower model, or a desktop model mounted in a stand on the floor, ensure that nothing blocks the air vents in the computer case. Do not place a laptop on a blanket or pillow, causing the vents to be blocked.

Tech Tip

Electronic components generate a great deal of heat but are designed to withstand fairly high temperatures. Auxiliary fans can be purchased to help cool the internal components of a computer. Some cases have an extra mount and cutout for an auxiliary fan. Some auxiliary fans mount in adapter slots or drive bays.

Be careful when installing an auxiliary fan

Place the fan so the outflow of air moves in the same direction as the flow of air generated by the power supply. If an auxiliary fan is installed inside a case in the wrong location, the auxiliary air flow could work against the power supply air flow, reducing the cooling effect. Figure 2.19 in Chapter 2 details how air flow can be aided with an auxiliary fan.

Tech Tip

Power Supply Voltages

Refer to Figure 4.21 and notice how +3.3, +5, –5, +12, and –12 volts are supplied to the motherboard. The motherboard and adapters use +3.3 and +5 volts. The –5 volts is seldom used. If the motherboard has integrated serial ports, they sometimes use +12V and –12V power. Hard drives and optical drives commonly use +5 and +12 volts. The +12 voltage is used to operate the device motors found in drives, the CPU, internal cooling fans, and the graphics card. Drives are now being made that use +5V motors. Chips use +5 volts and +3.3 volts. The +3.3 volts are also used for memory, AGP/PCI/PCIe adapters, and some laptop fans. The negative voltages are seldom used.

A technician must occasionally check voltages in a system. There are four basic checks for power supply situations: (1) wall outlet AC voltage, (2) DC voltages going to the motherboard, (3) DC voltages going to a device, and (4) ground or lack of voltage with an outlet tester. A **power supply tester** can be used to check DC power levels on the different power supply connectors.

Mobile Device Travel and Storage

When traveling with a laptop, remove all cards that insert into slots and store them in containers so that their contacts do not become dirty and cause intermittent problems. Remove all media discs such as CDs, DVDs, or BDs. Check that drive doors and devices are securely latched. Ensure that the mobile device is powered off or in hibernate mode (not in sleep/suspend or standby power mode, which is covered later in this chapter).

Carry the device in a padded case. If you have to place the device on an airport security conveyor belt, ensure that the device is not placed upside down, which could cause damage to the display. Never place objects on top of a mobile device or pick up a laptop by the edges of the display when the laptop is opened. When shipping a mobile device, place it in a properly padded box. The original shipping box is a safe container.

The United States has regulations about lithium batteries on airplanes. If battery contacts come in contact with metal or other batteries, the battery could short-circuit and cause a fire. For this reason, any lithium batteries are to be kept in original packaging. If original packaging is not available, place electrical tape over the battery terminals or place each battery in an individual bag. Spare lithium batteries are not allowed in checked baggage but can be taken in carry-on bags.

Like other electronic devices, laptops have heating issues. The following can help with laptop overheating:

- Locate air vents and keep them unblocked and clean. Do not place a laptop on your lap to work.
- In the BIOS settings, check the temperature settings for when fans turn on.
- Check the laptop manufacturer website or documentation for any fan/temperature monitoring gauges.
- Place a laptop on something that elevates it from the desk, such as drink coasters. In addition, pads, trays, and mats can be purchased with fans that are AC powered or USB powered.

Mobile Device Power

A portable computer (laptop/netbook/ultrabook/tablet) uses either an AC connection or a battery as its power source. On most models, when the mobile device connects to AC power, the battery normally recharges. Laptop batteries are usually modules with one or two release latches that are used to remove the module. Smartphone batteries either have a release latch or you slide part of the phone away and reveal the battery. Figure 4.27 shows a netbook computer with its battery module removed. Battery technologies have improved in the past few years, probably due to the development of more devices that need battery power, such as tablets, digital cameras, and portable CD, DVD, and BD players.

Tech Tip

Check input voltage selector

Some power supplies and laptops have input voltage selectors; others have the ability to accept input from 100 to 240 volts for use in various countries (dual voltage). Ensure that the power supply accepts or is set to the proper input voltage.

Figure 4.27 Netbook battery

NiCad (nickel cadmium) batteries originally used in laptops were replaced with lighter and more powerful NiMH (nickel-metal hydride) batteries. These batteries were replaced with **Li-ion** (lithium-ion) **batteries**, which are very light and can hold a charge longer than any other type. They are also more expensive. Mobile phones, tablets, portable media players, and digital cameras also use Li-ion batteries. These batteries lose their charge over time even if they are not being used. Use your laptop with battery-provided power. Ensure that a laptop that has an Li-ion battery is not plugged into an AC outlet all the time. Calibrate a laptop battery according to manufacturer instructions so the battery meter displays correctly.

Li-ion polymer batteries are similar to Li-ion batteries except that they are packed in pouched cells. This design allows for smaller batteries and a more efficient use of space, which is important in the portable computer and mobile devices industries. For environmentalists, the zinc-air battery is the one to watch. AER Energy Resources, Inc., has several patents on a battery that uses oxygen to generate electricity. Air is allowed to flow during battery discharge and is blocked when the battery is not in use. This battery holds a charge for extended periods of time. Another upcoming technology is fuel cells. Fuel cells used for a laptop can provide power for 5 to 10 hours.

Tech Tip

Do not power on after a temperature change

Computers are designed to work within a range of temperatures, but sudden change is not good for them. If a mobile device is in a car all night and the temperature drops, allow the device to return to room temperature before powering on. Avoid direct sunlight. Inside the computer case, it is usually 40°F hotter than outside.

Tech Tip

Do not fully discharge a Li-ion battery

Li-ion batteries do not suffer from the memory effect, as do some nickel-based batteries. Fully discharging a lithium battery, such as an Li-ion battery, is actually bad for it. However, most lithium batteries have a circuit to prevent the battery from being totally discharged.

Tech Tip

Keep Li-ion batteries cool

Li-ion batteries last longer if they are kept cool (not frozen). When you store an Li-ion battery, the battery should be only 40 percent charged and placed in a refrigerator to prolong its life.

Mobile devices rely on their batteries to provide the mobility. The following tips can help you get more time out of your batteries:

- Most people do not need a spare Li-ion battery. If you are not using an Li-ion battery constantly, it is best not to buy a spare. The longer the spare sits unused, the shorter the lifespan it will have.
- Buy the battery recommended by the laptop manufacturer.
- For a mobile device or smartphone, use an AC outlet rather than a USB port for faster charging.
- If using a USB port for charging a mobile device or smartphone, unplug all unused USB devices. Note that not all USB ports can provide a charge if the host device is in sleep mode.
- Do not use the optical player when running on battery power.
- Turn off the wireless adapter if a wireless network is not being used. For Windows-based devices, use the *Network and Internet* Control Panel. For smaller mobile devices, use flight mode to turn off both the wireless and the cellular (3G/4G) networks. Apple iOS devices can use *Settings* to access *Airplane Mode*. Android devices can use the *Settings* option to access *Flight mode* through the *Wireless and network* option.
- In the power options, configure the mobile device for hibernate rather than standby (covered later in the chapter).
- Save work only when necessary and turn off the autosave feature.
- Reduce the screen brightness. In Windows, use the *Display* Control Panel link found within the *Hardware and Sound* Control Panel. In Apple iOS, us the *Brightness & Wallpaper* setting; on an Android device, use the *Sound and display* option from the *Settings* application.
- Keep the hard drive defragmented especially before running on battery power.
- Avoid using external USB devices such as flash drives or external hard drives.
- Add more RAM to reduce swapping of information from the hard drive to RAM to CPU or to just be more efficient.
- Keep battery contacts clean with a dab of rubbing alcohol on a lint-free swab once a month.
- Use your mobile device until the battery is drained when possible and then recharge it. Constantly recharging the battery reduces the battery life. Most lithium batteries have a circuit that keeps the battery from being discharged completely.
- Avoid running multiple programs. To close an application on an iOS-based device, hold down on the icon from the home menu. On an Android-based device, use the *Applications > Manage Applications* option from the *Settings* application.
- Disable automatic updates. In Windows, use the *Windows Update* link from the *System and Security* Control Panel. On iOS or Android systems, disable push reports and application notifications that make sounds or vibrations from within the *Settings* option. Have the OS check less often for mail; use the *Mail, Contacts, Calendars* option to change the settings.
- Avoid temperature extremes.

All power supplies are not created equal

Tech Tip

A technician needs to replace a power supply with one that provides an equal or greater amount of power. Search the Internet for power supply reviews. A general rule of thumb is that if two power supplies are equal in wattage, the heavier one is better because it uses a bigger transformer, bigger heat sinks, and more quality components.

ACPI (Advanced Configuration and Power Interface)

Today's computer user needs to leave a computer on for extended periods of time in order to receive faxes, run computer maintenance tasks, automatically answer phone calls, and download software upgrades and patches. Network managers want control of computers so they can push out software upgrades, perform backups, download software upgrades and patches, and perform tests. Laptop users have always been plagued by power management problems, such as short battery life, inconsistent handling of screen blanking, and screen blanking in the middle of presentations. Such problems occurred because originally the BIOS controlled power. Power management has changed.

ACPI (Advanced Configuration and Power Interface) gives the BIOS and operating system control over various devices' power and modes of operation, as shown in Figure 4.28.

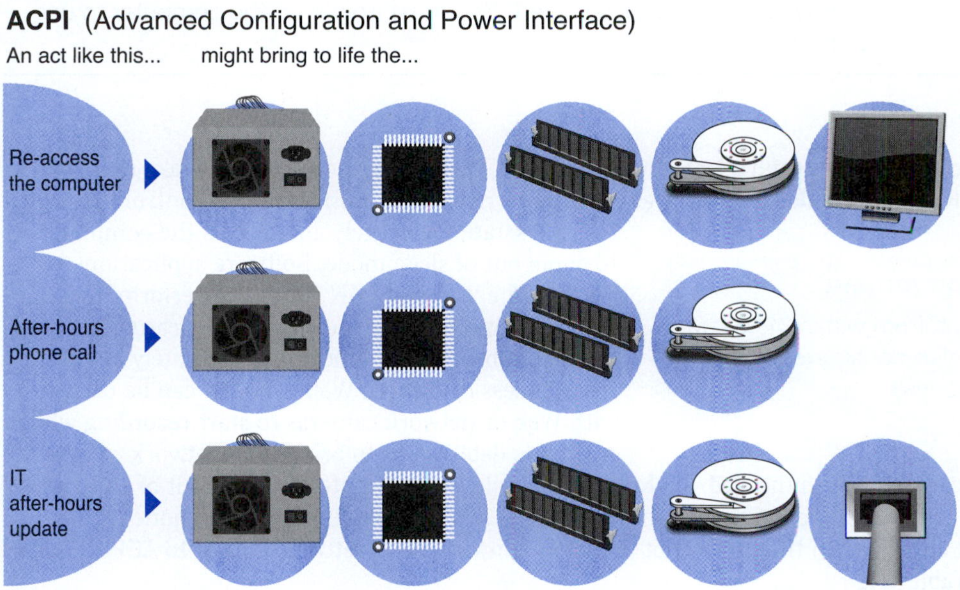

Figure 4.28 ACPI actions

With ACPI, the user can control how the power switch operates and when power to specific devices, such as the hard drive and monitor, is lowered. For example, the *Instant On/Off* BIOS setting can control how long the power switch is held in before the power supply turns on or off. Case temperatures, CPU temperatures, and CPU fans can be monitored. The power supply can be adjusted for power requirements. The CPU clock can be throttled or slowed down to keep the temperature lower and prolong the life of the CPU and reduce power requirements especially in portable devices when activity is low or nonexistent. ACPI has various operating states, as shown in Table 4.3.

Table 4.3 ACPI operating states

Global system state	Sleep state	Description
G0 Working	(S0)	The computer is fully functional. Software, such as the autosave function used with Microsoft products, can be optimized for performance or lower battery usage.
G1 Sleeping		Requires less power than the G0 state and has multiple sleeping states: S1, S2, S3, and S4.
	(S1)	CPU is still powered, and unused devices are powered down. RAM is still being refreshed. Hard disks are not running.
	(S2)	CPU is not powered. RAM is still being refreshed. System is restored instantly upon user intervention.
	(S3)	Power supply output is reduced. RAM is still being refreshed. Some info in RAM is restored to CPU and cache.
	(S4)	Lowest-power sleep mode and takes the longest to come up. Info in RAM is saved to hard disk. Some manufacturers call this the hibernate state.
G2	(S5)	Also called soft off. Power consumption is almost zero. Requires the operating system to reboot. No information is saved anywhere.
G3		Also called off, or mechanical off. This is the only state where the computer can be disassembled. You must power on the computer to use it again.

Two common BIOS and adapter features that take advantage of ACPI are Wake on LAN and Wake on Ring. The **Wake on LAN** feature allows a network administrator to control the power to a workstation remotely and directs the computer to come out of sleep mode. Software applications can also use the Wake on LAN feature to perform updates, upgrades, and maintenance tasks. The feature can also be used to bring up computers immediately before the business day starts. Wake on LAN can be used with Web or network cameras to start recording when motion is detected or to bring up a network printer so that it can be used when needed. **Wake on Ring** allows a computer to come out of sleep mode when the telephone line has an incoming call. This lets the computer receive phone calls, faxes, and emails when the user is not present. Common BIOS settings related to ACPI are listed in Table 4.4.

Tech Tip

Windows power management

Use the *Power Options* link from within the *System and Security* Control Panel to configure power from within the Windows environment.

Table 4.4 Common BIOS power settings

Setting	Description
Delay Prior to Thermal	Defines the number of minutes the system waits to shut down the system once an overheating situation occurs.
CPU Warning Temperatures	Specifies the CPU temperature at which a warning message is displayed on the screen.
ACPI Function	Enables or disables ACPI. This is the preferred method for disabling ACPI in the event of a problem.

Setting	Description
Soft-off	Specifies the length of time a user must press the power button to turn off the computer.
Deep S4/S5	Uses less power and only wakes from S4/S5 states with the power button or a RTC (real time clock) alarm, such as waking the computer to complete a task.
Power on by Ring, Resume by Ring, or Wakeup	Allows the computer to wake when an adapter or an external device supports Wake on Ring.
Resume by Alarm	Allows a date and time to be set when the system is awakened from Suspend mode. Commonly used to update the system during nonpeak periods.
Wake Up on LAN	Allows the computer to wake when a Wake on LAN signal is received across the network.
CPU THRM Throttling	Allows a reduction in CPU speed when the system reaches a specific temperature.
Power on Function	Specifies which key (or key combination) will activate the system's power.
Hot Key Power On	Defines what keystrokes will reactivate system power.
Doze Mode	When the system is in a reduced activity state, the CPU clock is throttled (slowed down). All other devices operate at full speed.
After Power Failure	Sets power mode after a power loss.

Windows 7 has three power plans available, and you can customize these power plans. You might want to customize a power plan when there is a problem with poor video quality when playing a movie. Use the *Change plan settings* link followed by the *Change advanced power settings* link to expand a section such as the *Multimedia settings* option. Table 4.5 shows the three main power plans you can just click and select.

Table 4.5 Windows 7 power plans

Power plan	Description
Balanced	The most common plan because it provides full power when you need it and saves power when the computer is not being used.
Power saver	Saves power by running the CPU more slowly and reducing screen brightness.
High performance	Select the *Show additional plans* link to see this option. This provides the maximum performance possible.

Sometimes, when a computer comes out of Sleep mode, not all devices respond, and the computer's power or reset button has to be pressed to reboot the computer. The following situations can cause this to happen:

- A screen saver conflicts with ACPI
- All adapters/devices are not ACPI compliant
- An adapter/device has an outdated driver
- The system BIOS or an installed adapter BIOS needs to be updated

Tech Tip

Power values for energy-efficient monitors

Always keep the screen saver timeout value shorter than the power saver timeout value, especially with green (energy-efficient) monitors!

To see if the screen saver causes a problem, use the *Display* Control Panel and set the screen saver option to *None*. Identifying a problem adapter, device, or driver will take Internet research. Check each adapter, device, and driver one by one. Use the *Power Options* Control Panel to change the power scheme. Also check all devices for a *Power Management* tab on the *Properties* dialog box. Changes can be made there.

Links on the left of the *Power Options* Control Panel provide access to advanced settings such as requiring a password to come out of sleep mode. The power options for a Windows 7 laptop are shown in Figure 4.29.

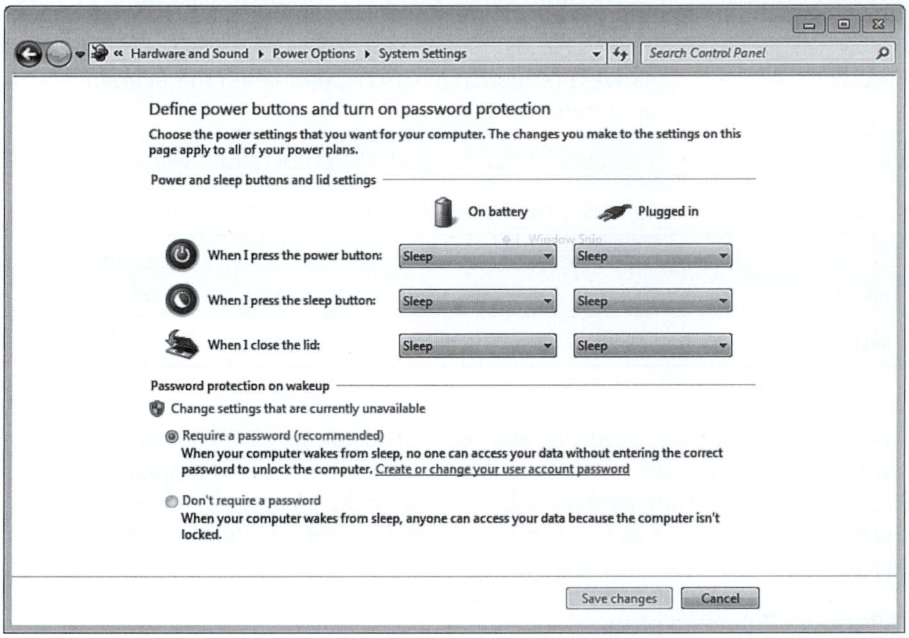

Figure 4.29 Windows 7 power settings

Other laptop *Power Options* Control Panel settings include the following links: *Require a password on wakeup, Choose what the power button does* (as shown in Figure 4.29), *Choose what closing the lid does, Create a power plan, Choose when to turn off the display,* and *Change when the computer sleeps*. Laptop power settings affect battery life. Users and technicians should adjust these settings to best fit how the laptop or mobile device is used.

In Windows Vista and 7, use the *Power Options* Control Panel to edit the power settings. Select the *Change advanced power settings* link to configure passwords, standby power behavior, and other power-related settings. If the computer does not go into the Sleep mode, check the following:

- Determine if ACPI is enabled in BIOS.
- Try disabling the antivirus program to see if it is causing the problem.
- Set the screen saver to *None* to see if it is causing the problem.
- Determine if all device drivers are ACPI compliant.
- Determine if power management is enabled through the operating system (use the *Power Options* Control Panel).
- Disconnect USB devices to see if they are causing problems.

Replacing or Upgrading a Power Supply

Power supplies are rated in watts. Today's typical computers have power supplies with ratings ranging from 250 to 500 watts, although powerful computers, such as network servers or higher-end gaming systems, can have power supplies rated 600 watts or higher. Each device inside a computer uses a certain amount of power, and the power supply must provide enough to run all the devices. The power each device or adapter requires is usually defined in the documentation for the device or adapter or on the manufacturer's website. The computer uses the wattage needed, not the total capacity of a power supply. The efficiency (more AC is converted to DC) is what changes the electricity bill.

Tech Tip

Watch the wattage

Many manufacturers overstate the wattage. The wattage advertised is *not* the wattage available at higher temperatures, such as when mounted inside a computer. Research a model before purchasing.

Some power supplies are listed as being dual or triple (or tri) rail. A **dual-rail power supply** has two +12V output lines. A triple-rail power supply simply has three +12V output lines for devices. Keep in mind that most manufacturers do not have two or more independent 12V sources; they all derive from the same 12V source but have independent output lines. Figure 4.30 shows how the +12V rails might be used.

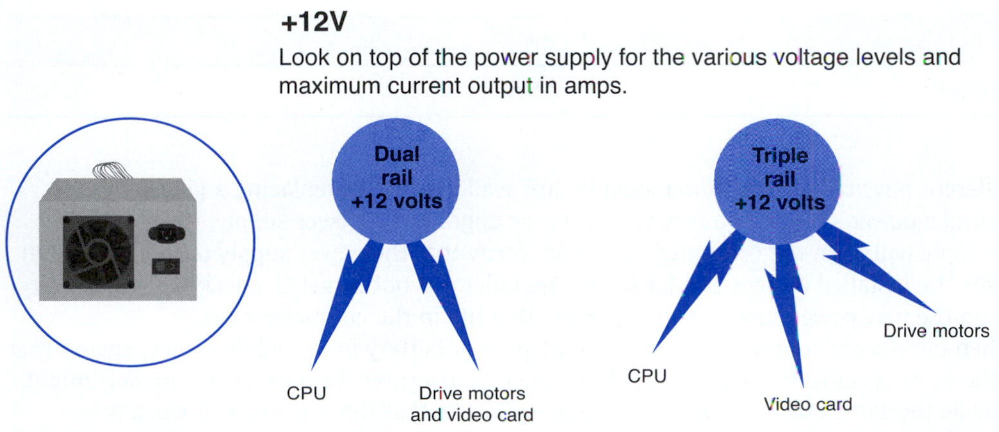

Figure 4.30 12V rails

Power supplies can be auto-switching or have a fixed input. An **auto-switching** power supply monitors the incoming voltage from the wall outlet and automatically switches itself accordingly. Auto-switching power supplies accept voltages from 100 to 240VAC at 50 to 60Hz. These power supplies are popular in mobile devices and are great for international travel. A power supply might also allow adjusting the input value by manually selecting the value through a voltage selector switch on the power supply. A fixed-input power supply is rated for a specific voltage and frequency for a country, such as 120VAC 60Hz for the United States.

Some people are interested in exactly how much power their system is consuming. Every device in a computer consumes power, and each device could use one or more different voltage levels (+5V, –5V, +12V, –12V, +3.3V). A power supply has a maximum amperage for each voltage level (for example, 30 amps at +5 volts and 41 amps at +12V). To determine the maximum power being used, in watts, multiply the amps and volts. If you add all the maximum power levels, the amount will be greater than the power supply's rating. This means that you cannot use the maximum power at every single voltage level (but since the –5V and –12V are not used very often, normally this is not a problem).

In order to determine the power being consumed, you must research every device to determine how much current it uses at a specific voltage level. Internet power calculators are available to help with this task. Table 4.6 lists sample computer components' power requirements.

Table 4.6 Sample computer component power requirements

Component	Power consumption
Motherboard (without processor)	5 to 150W
Processor	10 to 140W
Floppy drive	5W
PATA hard drive	3 to 30W
SATA hard drive	2 to 15W
Optical drive	10 to 30W
Non-video adapter	4 to 25W
AGP video adapter	20 to 50W
PCIe video card with one power connector	50-150W
PCIe video card with two power connectors	100-300W
Extra fan	3W
RAM stick	15W

Different physical sizes of power supplies are available. When replacing a power supply, purchasing a power supply for a new computer, or upgrading a power supply, verify that the power supply will fit in the computer case. Also, verify that the power supply produces enough power for the installed devices and for future upgrades. Do not forget to check that the on/off switch on the new power supply is in a location that fits in the computer case.

When purchasing a new power brick for a laptop or battery for a mobile device, ensure that it has the same specifications as the one from the manufacturer. Less expensive models might not provide the same quality as approved models. Ensure that the replacement has a power jack that does not wiggle when it is inserted into the device. Ensure that a laptop power brick has the appropriate DC voltage required by the laptop. Current (amperage) should be equal to or more than the original power brick.

Power management on both laptops and desktops is important. Most computer components are available as energy-efficient items. ENERGY STAR is a joint effort by the U.S. EPA (Environmental Protection Agency) and Department of Energy to provide device standards and ratings that easily identify products (including computer components) that are energy efficient. Many computers today are on more than they are off, and settings such as power options, CPU throttling, and some advanced BIOS settings affect power settings. A technician must be aware of all these options and be willing to offer advice such as turn the computer off when finished working on it; set the power management option to allow work to be performed at an affordable cost; disable options not being used, such as wireless capabilities when wired networking is functioning; be aware of monitor costs (CRT-type monitors take the most energy, followed by plasma displays and then LCD or flat-panel technology); and purchase energy-efficient parts and computers.

Symptoms of Power Supply Problems

The following is a list of symptoms of a power supply problem:

- The power light is off and/or the device won't turn on.
- The power supply fan does not turn when the computer is powered on.

- The computer sounds a continuous beep. (This could also be a bad motherboard or a stuck key on the keyboard.)
- When the computer powers on, it does not beep at all. (This could also be a bad motherboard.)
- When the computer powers on, it sounds repeating short beeps. (This could also be a bad motherboard.)
- During POST, a 02*X* or parity POST error code appears (where *X* is any number); one of the POST checks is a power good signal from the power supply; a 021, 022, . . . error message indicates that the power supply did not pass the POST test.
- The computer reboots or powers down without warning.
- The power supply fan is noisy.
- The power supply is too hot to touch.
- The computer emits a burning smell.
- The power supply fan spins, but there is no power to other devices.
- The monitor has power light, but nothing appears on the monitor, and no PC power light illuminates.

Solving Power Supply Problems

When you suspect that the power supply is causing a problem, swap the power supply, make the customer happy, and be on your way! Power problems are not usually difficult to detect or troubleshoot.

Tech Tip

Do not disassemble a power supply

Power supplies are not normally disassembled. Manufacturers often rivet them shut. Even when a power supply can be disassembled, you should not take it apart unless you have a background in electronics.

Do not overlook the most obvious power supply symptom. Start by checking the computer power light. If it is off, check the power supply's fan by placing your palm at the back of the computer. If the fan is turning, it means the wall outlet is providing power to the computer and you can assume that the wall outlet is functioning. Check the motherboard for LEDs and refer to the manual for their meaning. Test the power outlet with another device. Ensure that the power cord is inserted fully into the wall outlet and the computer. If you suspect that the wall outlet is faulty, use an **AC circuit tester** to verify that the wall outlet is wired properly.

On a mobile device that is running on battery power, check the battery charge icon through the operating system. Try using the device on AC power. If it works on AC power, try recharging the battery. If the battery does not recharge, replace it. Wiggle the AC power to see if the connection is loose. Remove the battery for a moment and then re-insert it (and attach AC power if battery power does not work). On a laptop, see if the power brick has a power light on it and whether it is lit. Try a different AC adapter from the same manufacturer because AC adapters are proprietary between laptop vendors.

If a mobile device or smartphone won't power on after recharging the battery, remove the battery for about a minute. Reinstall the battery and try powering on again. If the system will still not power on, try powering on with the power cable attached. If the system works with the power cable attached, the battery probably needs to be replaced.

The following troubleshooting questions can help you determine the location of a power problem:

- Did the power supply work before? If not, check the input voltage selector switch on the power supply and verify that it is on the proper setting.
- Is the power supply's fan turning? If yes, check voltages going to the motherboard. If they are good, maybe just the power supply fan is bad. If the power supply's fan is not turning, check the wall outlet for proper AC voltages.

- Is a surge strip used? If so, check to see if the surge strip is powered on, then try a different outlet in the surge strip, or replace the surge strip.
- Is the computer's power cord okay? Verify that the power cord plugs snugly into the outlet and into the back of the computer. Swap the power cord to verify that it is functioning.
- Is the front panel power button stuck?
- Are the voltages going to the motherboard at the proper levels? If they are low, something may be overloading the power supply. Disconnect the power cable to one device and recheck the voltages. Replace the power cable to the device. Remove the power cable from another device and recheck the motherboard voltages. Continue doing this until the power cord for each device has been disconnected and the motherboard voltages have been checked. A single device can short out the power supply and cause the system to malfunction. Replace any device that draws down the power supply's output voltage and draws too much current. If none of the devices is the cause of the problem, replace the power supply. If replacing the power supply does not solve the problem, replace the motherboard.

If a computer does not boot properly, but it does boot when you press Ctrl + Alt + Delete, the power good signal is likely the problem. Some motherboards are more sensitive to the power good signal than others. For example, say that a motherboard has been replaced and the system does not boot. At first glance, this may appear to be a bad replacement board, but the problem could be caused by a power supply failing to output a consistent power good signal.

Tech Tip

Check the power good (sometimes called power OK) signal

Check the power supply documentation to see if the power supply outputs a power good signal (rather than the normal +5 volts). Turn on the computer. Check the power good signal going into the motherboard power connector. Do this before replacing the motherboard. A power supply with a power good signal below +3V needs to be replaced.

Sometimes, none of these troubleshooting actions work. A grounding problem might be the issue. Build the computer outside the computer case, on an antistatic mat, if possible. Start with only the power supply, motherboard, and speaker connected. Even though it will normally produce a POST audio error, verify that the power supply fan will turn. Most power supplies issue a click before the audio POST beeps. Next, verify the voltages from the power supply. If the fan turns and the voltages are correct, power down the machine and add a video adapter and monitor to the system. If the machine does not work, put the video adapter in a different expansion slot and try again. If placing the video adapter in a different expansion slot does not work, swap out the video adapter.

If the video adapter works, continue adding devices one by one and checking the voltages. Just as any one device can cause the system not to operate properly, so can any one adapter. If one particular adapter causes the system to malfunction, try a different expansion slot before trying a different adapter.

If the expansion slot proves to be a problem, check the slot for foreign objects. If none are found but the problem still occurs, place a note on the expansion slot so that no one will use it.

Adverse Power Conditions

There are two adverse AC power conditions that can damage or adversely affect a computer: overvoltage and undervoltage. **Overvoltage** occurs when the output voltage from the wall outlet (the AC voltage) is over the rated amount. Normally, the output of a wall outlet is 110 to 130 volts AC. When the voltage rises above 130 volts, an overvoltage condition exists. The power supply takes the AC voltage and converts it to DC. An overvoltage condition is harmful to the components because too much DC voltage destroys electronic circuits. An overvoltage condition can be a surge or a spike.

When the voltage falls below 110 volts AC, an **undervoltage** condition exists. If the voltage is too low, a computer power supply cannot provide enough power to all the components. Under these conditions, the power supply draws too much current, causing it to overheat, weakening or damaging the components. An undervoltage condition is known as a brownout or sag. Table 4.7 explains these power terms.

Table 4.7 Adverse power conditions

Major type	Subtype	Explanation
Overvoltage	**spike**	A spike lasts 1 to 2 nanoseconds. A nanosecond is one-billionth of a second. A spike is harder to guard against than a surge because it has such short duration and high intensity.
	surge	A surge lasts longer (3 or more nanoseconds) than a spike. Also called transient voltage. Causes of surges include lightning, poorly regulated electricity, faulty wiring, and devices that turn on periodically, such as elevators, air conditioners, and refrigerators.
Undervoltage	**brownout**	In a brownout, power circuits become overloaded. Occasionally, an electric company intentionally causes a brownout to reduce the power drawn by customers during peak periods.
	sag	A sag occurs when the voltage from the wall outlet drops momentarily.
	blackout	A blackout is a total loss of power.

Electric companies offer surge protection for homes. Frequently, there are two choices. A basic package protects large appliances, such as refrigerators, air conditioners, washers, and dryers. It allows no more than 800 volts to enter the electrical system. A premium package protects more sensitive devices (TVs, stereos, and computers) and reduces the amount of voltage allowed to 323 volts or less. Some suppressors handle surges up to 20,000 volts. The exterior surge arrestor does not protect against voltage increases that originate inside the building, such as those caused by faulty wiring.

Adverse Power Protection

Power supplies have built-in protection against adverse power conditions. However, the best protection for a computer is to unplug it during a power outage or thunderstorm. Surge protectors and UPSs (uninterruptible power supplies) are commonly used to protect against adverse power conditions. A line conditioner can also be used. Each device has a specific purpose and guards against certain conditions. A technician must be familiar with each device in order to make recommendations for customers.

Surge Protectors

A **surge protector**, also known as a surge strip or surge suppressor, is commonly a multi-outlet strip that offers built-in protection against overvoltage. Surge protectors do not protect against undervoltage; they protect against voltage increases. Figure 4.31 shows a picture of a surge protector.

Figure 4.31 Surge protector

Most surge protectors have an electronic component called an **MOV** (metal oxide varistor), which protects the computer or device that plugs into one of the outlets on the surge strip. An MOV is positioned between the AC coming in and the outlet into which devices are plugged. When a surge occurs, the MOV prevents the extra voltage from passing to the outlets. An MOV, however, has some drawbacks. If a large surge occurs, the MOV will take the hit and be destroyed, which is better than damaging the computer. However, with small overvoltages, each small surge weakens the MOV. A weakened MOV might not give the proper protection to the computer in the event of a bigger surge. Also, there is no simple check for an MOV's condition. Some MOVs have indicator lamps attached, but they indicate only when the MOV has been destroyed, not when it is weakened. Still, having an indicator lamp is better than nothing at all. Some surge protectors also have replaceable fuses and/or indicator lamps for the fuse. A fuse works only once and then is destroyed during a surge in order to protect devices plugged into surge protector outlets.

Tech Tip

Do not create a trip hazard with a surge strip

When installing a surge protector, do not install it in such a manner that it causes a trip hazard because the cord lies in an area where people walk.

Several surge protector features deserve consideration. Table 4.8 outlines some of them.

Table 4.8 Surge protector features

Feature	Explanation
Clamping voltage	The level at which surge protector starts protecting the computer. The lower the value, the better the protection.
Clamping speed	How much time elapses before protection begins. The lower the value, the better the protection. Surge protectors cannot normally protect against power spikes (overvoltages of short duration) because of their rated clamping speed.

Feature	Explanation
Energy absorption/ dissipation	The greater the number of joules (a unit of energy) that can be dissipated, the more effective and durable a surge protector is. This feature is sometimes called energy absorption. A surge protector rating of 630 joules is more effective than a rating of 210 joules.
TVS (transient voltage suppressing) **rating**	This is also known as response time. The lower the rating the better. For example, a 330 TVS-rated surge protector is better than a 400 TVS-rated one.
UL rating	UL (Underwriters Laboratories) developed the **UL 1449 VPR** (voltage protection rating) standard to measure the maximum amount of voltage a surge protector will let through to the attached devices. The UL 497A standard is for phone line protection, and the UL 1283 standard is for EMI/RFI.

The federal government designates surge suppressor grades—A, B, and C. Suppressors are evaluated on a basis of 1,000 surges at a specific number of volts and amps. A Class A rating is the best and indicates tolerance up to 6,000 volts and 3,000 amps.

Which surge strip to buy?

When purchasing or recommending a surge protector, be sure it conforms to the UL 1449 standard and has an MOV status lamp. Also, check to see if the vendor offers to repair or replace the surge-protected equipment in the event that they are damaged during a surge.

Tech Tip

Surge protectors are not the best protection for a computer system because most provide very little protection against other adverse power conditions. Even the good ones protect only against overvoltage conditions. Those with the UL 1449 rating and an MOV status lamp are usually more expensive. Unfortunately, people tend to put their money into their computer parts, but not into the protection of those parts.

Line Conditioners

An alternative for computer protection is a line conditioner. **Line conditioners**, sometimes known as power conditioners, are more expensive than surge protectors, but they protect a computer from overvoltages, undervoltages, and adverse noise conditions over electrical lines. A line conditioner monitors AC electricity. If the voltage is too low, the line conditioner boosts voltage to the proper range. If the voltage level is too high, the line conditioner clamps down the voltage and sends the proper amount to the computer. Figure 4.32 shows a line conditioner.

Be careful not to plug too many devices into a line conditioner

A line conditioner is rated for a certain amount of current. Some devices, such as laser printers, can draw a great deal of current (up to 15 amps). Some line conditioners are not rated to handle these devices. Because laser printers draw so much current, if a computer and a laser printer are on the same electrical circuit, that circuit should be wired to a 20-amp circuit breaker. Most outlets in today's buildings are on 20-amp breakers.

Tech Tip

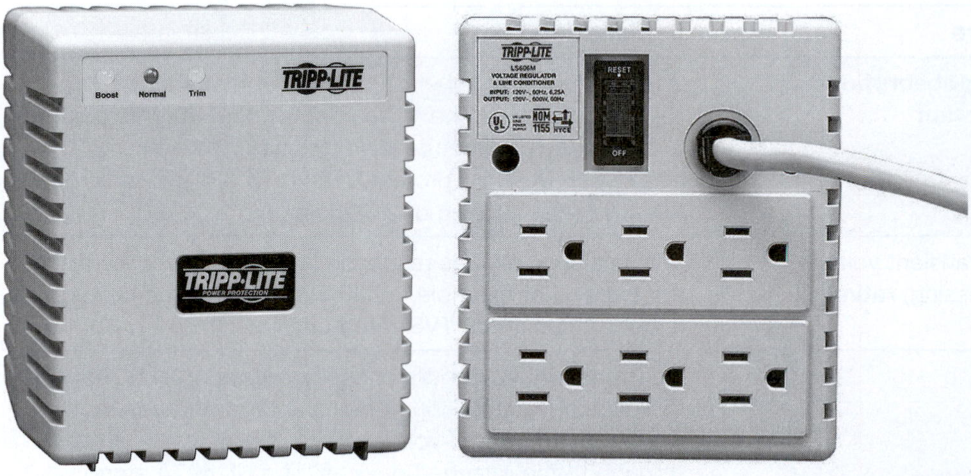

Figure 4.32 Line conditioner

Uninterruptible Power Supply (UPS)

A **UPS** (uninterruptible power supply), sometimes called an online (or true) UPS or a line interactive UPS, provides power to a computer or other device for a limited amount of time when there is a power outage. A UPS provides enough time to save work and safely shut down the computer. Some operating systems do not operate properly if power abruptly cuts off and the computer is not brought to a logical stopping place. A network server, the main computer for a network, is a great candidate for a UPS. Network operating systems are particularly susceptible to problems during a power outage. Some UPSs have a connection for a cable and special software that automatically maintains voltages to the computer, quits all applications, and powers off the computer. Some UPS units have USB and/or network connections as well.

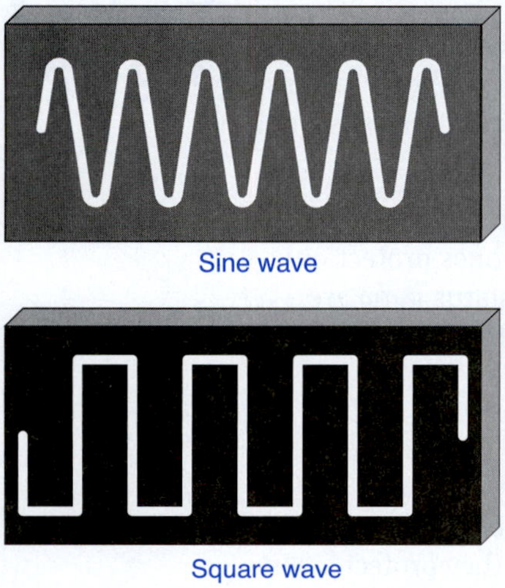

Figure 4.33 Sine wave and square wave

A UPS also provides power conditioning for the devices attached to it. The AC power is used to charge a battery inside the UPS. The battery inside the UPS supplies power to an inverter. The inverter makes AC for the computer. When AC power from the outlet fails, the battery inside the UPS continues to supply power to the computer. The battery inside the UPS outputs DC power, and the computer accepts (and expects) AC power. Therefore, the DC power from the battery must be converted to AC voltage. AC voltage looks like a sine wave when it is in its correct form, but cheaper UPSs produce a square wave (especially when power comes from the battery) that is not as effective. Some computer systems and peripherals do not work well on a 120VAC square wave, modified sine wave, or quasi-sine wave. Figure 4.33 illustrates a sine wave and a square wave.

A UPS can be the best protection against adverse power conditions because it protects against overvoltage and undervoltage conditions, and it provides power so a system can be shut down properly. When purchasing a UPS, be sure that (1) the amount of battery time is sufficient to protect all devices; (2) the amount of current the UPS produces is sufficient to protect all devices; and (3) the output waveform is a sine wave.

Tech Tip

Do not plug a laser printer into a UPS unless it has a rating less than 1400VA

Most UPSs cannot handle the very high current requirements of a laser printer.

To install a UPS, perform the following steps:

1. Connect the UPS to a wall outlet and power it on. When a UPS is first plugged in, the battery is not charged. See the UPS manufacturer's installation manual for the specific time it will take to charge.
2. Power off the UPS.
3. Attach device power cords, such as the PC, to the UPS. Ensure that the UPS is rated to supply power to the number and type of connected devices.
4. Power on the UPS.

A UPS has a battery inside that is similar to a car battery (except that the UPS battery is sealed). Because this battery contains acid, you should never drop a UPS or throw it in the trash. Research your state's requirements for recycling batteries. All batteries fail after some time, and most UPSs have replaceable batteries.

UPS troubleshooting is not difficult. In addition to following the manufacturer's recommendations for troubleshooting, try the following guidelines:

- If a UPS will not power on, check the on/off switch. Verify that the UPS is attached to an electrical outlet. Ensure that the outlet has power and that the circuit breaker for the outlet has not been tripped. Ensure that the battery is installed properly.
- Check whether the UPS unit has a self-test procedure and include a self-test button.
- With some UPS units, a beep indicates that a power interruption has occurred. This is a normal function.
- Some UPS units beep at a different rate when the battery is low. Others have a light indicator to indicate that it's time to recharge or replace the battery.
- If a UPS is overloaded—that is, has too many devices attached—the UPS may shut off, trip a circuit breaker, beep, or turn on a light indication for this problem.

Figure 4.34 shows the front of an American Power Conversion UPS. Notice the diagnostic lights on it.

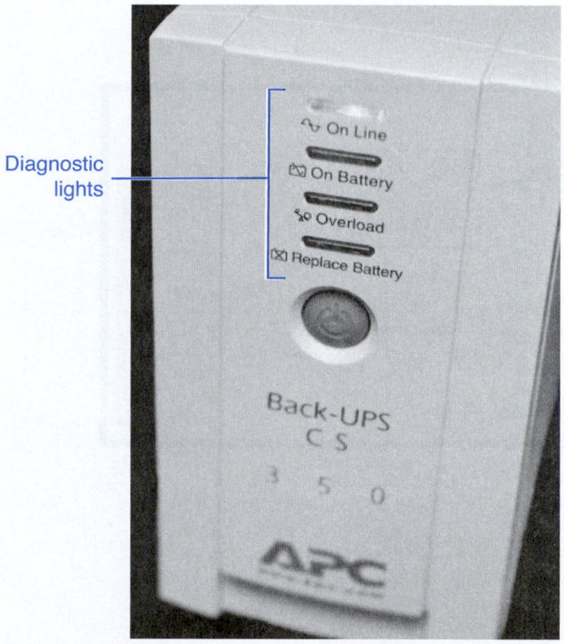

Figure 4.34 **Front of an American Power Conversion UPS**

Standby Power Supply (SPS)

A device similar to a UPS is an **SPS** (standby power supply). An SPS contains a battery like the UPS, but the battery provides power to the computer only when it loses AC power. It does not provide constant power, like the UPS. An SPS is not as effective as a UPS because the SPS must detect a power-out condition first and then switch over to the battery to supply power to the computer. As a result, SPS switching time is important. Any time under 5 milliseconds is fine for most systems. Figures 4.35 and 4.36 show the differences between how SPSs and UPSs work.

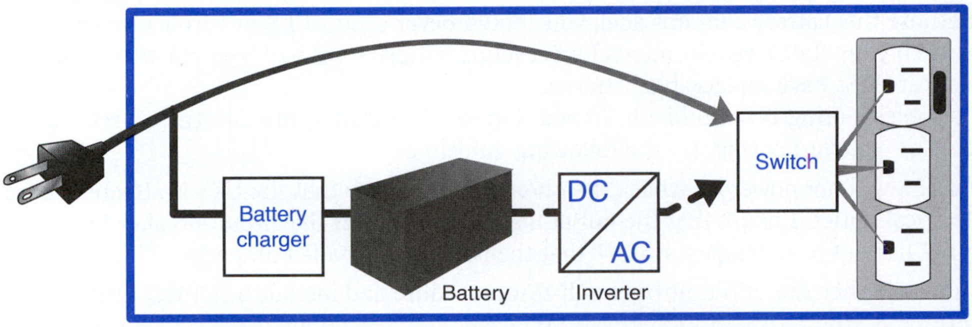

SPS/Line interactive UPS normal operation (solid line)

1. AC power is brought through the UPS.
2. The battery is charged simultaneously.
3. With some units, small over or undervoltages are evened out before sending through the UPS.

SPS/Line interactive UPS abnormal power operation (dashed line)

1. When high voltage or large undervoltage for some units and with loss of power is present in all units, DC power from the battery is sent to the inverter for as long as the battery lasts.
2. The DC power is converted to AC and provided to the attached devices.

Figure 4.35 SPS/line interactive UPS operation

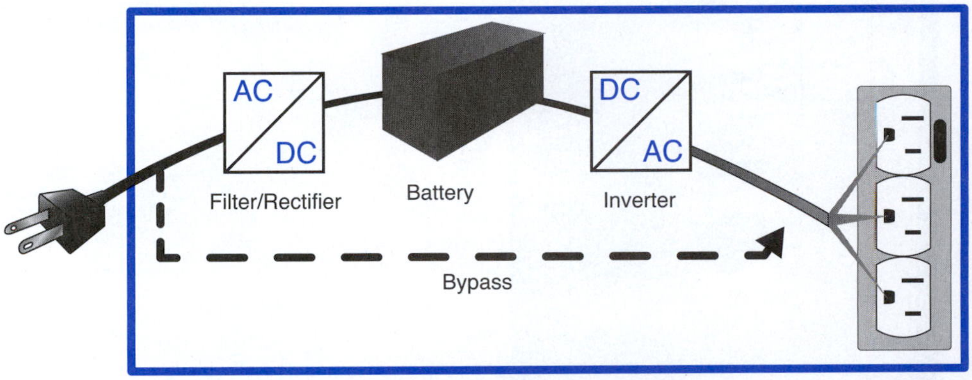

Online UPS normal operation (solid line)

1. AC power is brought into the UPS and cleaned up by the filter and converted to DC by the rectifier.
2. The battery is charged and outputs DC to the inverter.
3. The DC is converted to AC and provided to the attached devices.

Online UPS abnormal power operation (dashed line)

1. When the battery has died, the attached devices still receive power through the bypass circuit.

Figure 4.36 Online UPS operation

Phone Line Isolator

Just like AC power outlets, phone outlets can experience power fluctuations. A power surge can enter a computer through a modem, a device used to connect a computer to a phone line. Not only can a modem be damaged by a power surge on the phone line, but other electronics inside the computer, such as the motherboard, can be damaged. A **phone line isolator**, sometimes called a **modem isolator**, can be purchased at an electronics store. It provides protection against phone line surges. No computer connected to a phone line through a modem should be without one. Many surge protectors now come with a modem isolator built into the strip. Figure 4.31 shows an example of a surge strip that has modem protection integrated into the unit.

Power supplies and associated protection equipment are not exciting topics, but they are very important to a technician. Power problems can catch you unaware. Always keep power in your mind as a potential suspect when troubleshooting a computer.

Electrical Fires

No discussion of power is complete without a brief warning about fire. Electrical fires are uncommon in computers, but if one occurs, a technician must know what to do. If a fire occurs inside a computer or peripheral, unplug the equipment if possible, but do not put yourself in harm's way attempting to do this. Use a **Type C** or a **Type A-B-C fire extinguisher** to put out the fire. Type C fire extinguishers are made specifically for electrical (Type C) fires. Type A-B-C fire extinguishers can be used for Class A, Class B, and Class C fires. Class A fires involve paper, wood, cloth, or other normal combustibles. Class B fires involve flammable liquids and gases. It is also a good idea to have a dry chemical 20lb ABC fire extinguisher in homes for the electronics (including computers) located there. Home computer equipment should be listed on the home insurance policy. Figure 4.37 shows a Type A-B-C fire extinguisher.

Figure 4.37 Type A-B-C fire extinguisher

When a fire occurs, pull out the fire extinguisher pin. Aim the fire extinguisher nozzle at the base (bottom) of the fire. Squeeze the fire extinguisher's handle and move the nozzle back and forth in a slow sweeping motion. With electrical fires, the smoke is a breathing hazard. Burning plastics produce lethal toxic fumes. Always evacuate the people in the building and call the fire department.

Computer Disposal/Recycling

Computers and other electronic devices can contain materials such as beryllium, chromium, cadmium, lead, mercury, nickel, and zinc. The levels of these materials are increasing dramatically every year in landfills and can pose a threat to our environment. Plastics that are part of computers are hard to isolate and recycle. CRTs (cathode ray tubes) are found in older monitors and TVs and usually contain enough lead and mercury to be considered hazardous waste. However, the EPA has been successful in obtaining exclusions from the federal hazardous waste standards for unbroken CRTs, so they can be recycled more effectively.

Batteries contain acids that can burn or hurt body parts. Batteries can introduce lead and acid into the environment. Heavy metals can leach into the ground and water sources.

Every state and many cities have specific guidelines about how to dispose of electronics. These rules must be followed by technicians who replace broken computer equipment. For example, in Florida and New York, steps have been taken to increase CRT recycling; however, other states regulate all CRTs as hazardous waste and ban them from being sent to landfills. If you are unsure about how to get rid of any piece of broken electronic equipment, contact your direct supervisor for instructions.

The following list provides alternatives and suggestions for being environmentally conscious about discarding electronics:

- Donate equipment that is operational to schools and charities so that those who do not have access to technology can get some exposure. If the operating system is not transferred to another system, leave the operating system on it and provide proof of purchase along with documentation. Also, do not forget to erase all data stored on the computer before donating it.
- Recycle very outdated electronics. If the devices are so outdated that a school or charity does not want them, consider recycling them. Many companies accept old electronics and have determined ways to reuse some of their parts.
- Remove parts that do work and donate or recycle them.
- Buy electronics that are designed with saving resources in mind and are easy to upgrade, which extends their usefulness period; are energy efficient; contain fewer toxins; use recycled materials; and offer leasing or recycling programs.
- Check with the computer or component manufacturer to see if it has a recycling program. Most of them do.

Soft Skills—Written Communications Skills

When technicians are in school, they seldom think that the skills they should be learning involve writing. However, in the workplace, technicians use written communication skills when they document problems and use email. Advisory committees across the country say that in addition to having technical knowledge, it is important that technicians be able to communicate effectively both written and orally, be comfortable working in a team environment, and possess critical thinking skills (that is, solve problems even though they have not been taught the specific problem).

Regardless of the size of a company, documentation is normally required. The documentation may only be the number of hours spent on a job and a basic description of what was done, but most companies require a bit more. Documentation should be written so others can read and understand it. Keep in mind that if another technician must handle another problem from the same customer, it saves time and money to have good documentation. The following list includes complaints from managers who hire technicians. You can use this list to improve and avoid making the same mistakes:

- Avoids doing documentation in a timely manner
- Does not provide adequate or accurate information on what was performed or tried
- Has poor spelling, grammar, capitalization, and punctuation skills
- Writes in short, choppy sentences, using technical jargon
- Does not provide updates on the status of a problem

Email is a common means of communication for technicians. However, most technicians do not take the time to communicate effectively using email. The following is a list of guidelines for effective email communication:

- Do not use email when a meeting or a phone call is more appropriate.
- Include a short description of the email topic in the subject line.
- Do not write or respond to an email when you are angry.
- Send email only to the appropriate people.
- Stick to the point; do not digress.
- Use a spelling and grammar checker; if one is not included in the email client, write the email in a word processing application, check it, and then paste the document into the email.
- Use proper grammar, punctuation, and capitalization; do not write in all uppercase or all lowercase letters.
- Do not copy others unnecessarily.
- Write each email as if you were putting the message on a billboard; you never know how the content might be used or who might see it.

The number-one complaint about technical support staff is not their lack of technical skills but their lack of communication skills. Spend as much of your education practicing your communication skills as you do your technical skills.

Chapter Summary

- Wearing a wrist strap or staying in contact with unpainted metal keeps you and the computing device at the same electrical potential so you won't induce current into any part and weaken/damage it.
- EMI and RFI cause issues. Move the computer or the offending device and replace all slot covers/openings.
- When removing parts, have the right tools, lighting, antistatic items, and ample work space. Take notes. Don't use magnetized tools. Avoid jarring hard drives.
- Be careful installing an I/O shield and be aware of standoffs when dealing with the motherboard.
- Laptops and mobile devices frequently have compartments for memory and expansion card. These devices frequently have plastic parts that must be removed. A scribe helps with prying plastics and covers off. Laptop speakers and DC power plug frequently have cables that run along the back or sides of the device. Keep screws separated and take notes for any parts removal.
- Ribbon cables have a colored stripe indicating pin 1. Pin 1 of a cable must attach to pin 1 of a connector.
- Preventive maintenance procedures prolong the life of the computer. Vacuum before spraying compressed air.
- An MSDS describes disposal and storage procedures and contains information about toxicity and health concerns. Cities/states have specific disposal rules for chemicals, batteries, CRTs, electronics, and so on. Always know the disposal rules in the area where you work.
- AC power goes into the power supply or mobile device power brick. DC power is provided to all internal parts of the computing device. AC and DC voltage checks can be done and only with DC power does polarity matter. Use the highest meter setting possible with unknown voltage levels. Power is measured in watts.
- Continuity checks are done on cabling and a good wire shows close to 0 ohms.
- A power supply converts AC to DC, distributes DC throughout a unit, and provides cooling. The power supply must be the correct form factor and able to supply the current amount of wattage for a particular voltage level such as +5V or +12V. Multiple "rails" are commonly available for +12V since the CPU commonly needs its own connection. The number and type of connectors vary, but converters can be purchased.
- Li-ion batteries are used with mobile devices. If a device must be attached to AC power or a USB port to work, replace the battery with one of with the correct DC power jack, appropriate DC voltage level, and current (amperage) equal to or higher than the original power brick.
- Conserve mobile device power by adding more RAM, turning off wireless/Bluetooth, configuring power options, reducing screen brightness, and avoiding temperature extremes.
- You use ACPI to control power options through BIOS and the operating system. Wake on LAN and Wake on Ring are power features that allow a device to be powered up from a lowered power condition for a specific purpose.
- An AC circuit tester, multimeter, and power supply tester are tools used with power problems.
- Power issues include overvoltage conditions such as a surge or spike that can be helped with surge protectors, power conditioners, and UPSs. Power conditioners and UPSs help with undervoltage conditions such as a sag. A UPS is the only device that powers a computer when a blackout occurs.

- Ensure that a surge protector has a Class A rating and adheres to the UL 1449 standard.
- Ensure that a UPS outputs a sine wave from the battery and can output enough power for attached devices.
- Have a Type C or Type A-B-C fire extinguisher around in case of fire.
- In all communications and written documentation, be professional and effective. Use proper capitalization, grammar, punctuation, and spelling.

Key Terms

AC 134
AC circuit tester 153
ACPI 147
amp 135
antistatic wrist strap 120
auto-switching 151
Berg 138
blackout 155
brownout 155
capacitor 135
clamping speed 156
clamping voltage 156
continuity 135
current 135
DC 134
dual-rail power supply 151
EMI 122
energy absorption/dissipation 157
ESD 120
grounding 120
I/O shield 129
Li-ion battery 145
line conditioner 157
modem isolator 161
Molex 138
MOV 156
ohm 135
overvoltage 154
phone line isolator 161
pin 1 125
power 135
power good signal 139
power supply tester 144
preventive maintenance 132
resistance 135
RFI 122
sag 155
scribe 130
spike 155
SPS 160
standby power 134
standoff 129
surge 155
surge protector 155
TVS rating 157
Type A-B-C fire extinguisher 161
Type C fire extinguisher 161
UL 1449 VPR 157
undervoltage 154
UPS 158
volt 134
voltage 134
Wake on LAN 148
Wake on Ring 148
watt 135

Review Questions

1. What would happen if you removed the battery from the motherboard by accident?

2. List three tasks commonly performed during preventive maintenance.

3. Computers used in a grocery store warehouse for inventory control have a higher part failure rate than the other company computers. Which of the following is most likely to help in this situation?
   a. an antistatic wrist strap
   b. a preventive maintenance plan
   c. antistatic pads
   d. high wattage power supplies

4. Which of the following can prolong the life of a computer and conserve resources? (Select all that apply.)
   a. a preventive maintenance plan
   b. antistatic mats and pads
   c. upgraded power supply
   d. a power plan
   e. using a Li-ion battery as a replacement
   f. extra case fans
5. Which power component has a 20- or 24-pin connector?
   a. ATX power supply
   b. UPS
   c. line conditioner
   d. SPS
   e. surge protector
6. An optical drive randomly becomes unavailable, and after replacing the drive, the technician now suspects a power issue. What could help in this situation?
   a. a UPS
   b. a surge protector
   c. antistatic wipes
   d. a preventive maintenance plan
   e. a multimeter
7. Which unit would you recommend for the help desk people who sit at a computer for a 24/7 operation where help must be provided at all times?
   a. a UPS
   b. a surge protector
   c. an upgrade power supply
   d. a line conditioner
8. When disassembling a computer, which tool will help you remove the memory module?
   a. magnetic screwdriver
   b. needlenose pliers
   c. #1 or #2 Phillips screwdriver
   d. antistatic wrist strap
9. How would a technician normally access a memory module that needs to be replaced on a netbook? (Select the best answer.)
   a. by removing the DC power jack
   b. by removing a secured bottom compartment
   c. by removing the speaker
   d. by removing the display
10. Which part would be specialized when used with a laser printer?
    [surge strip | vacuum | multimeter | antistatic wrist strap]
11. Which two of the following would most likely cause a loud noise on a desktop computer? (Select two.) [motherboard | USB drive | power supply | case fan | memory | PCIe adapter]

12. A computer will not power on. Which of the following would be used to check the wall outlet? [power supply tester | UPS | multimeter | POST]
13. A computer will not power on. After checking the wall outlet and swapping the power cord, what would the technician use next?
    a. power supply tester
    b. UPS
    c. antistatic wrist strap
    d. magnetic screw driver
    e. nonmagnetic screw driver
14. Which of the following is affected by the power supply wattage rating?
    a. number of internal storage devices
    b. number of power supply connectors
    c. speed of the processor
    d. type of processor
    e. type of power supply connectors
15. Which of the following would help with computer heat?
    a. increased power supply wattage
    b. larger power supply form factor
    c. unplug unused power connectors
    d. install case fans
16. Lightning is prevalent in Jacksonville, Florida. What would you recommend for home owners who would like to keep working even when a storm is rolling through? [surge protector | phone line protector | UPS | line conditioner]
17. Consider the following email.

From: Cheryl a. Schmidt
To: Network Engineering Technology Faculty
Subj: [None]
We have little time to get the PMS done on the PCs and N/W gear. What software do you want?

Reword this email to illustrate good written communication skills.

18. List three recommendations for good technical written communication.

19. What type of fire extinguisher can be used on electronic equipment?

20. List three recommendations for saving power on a laptop.

Exercises

Lab 4.1 Performing Maintenance on an Antistatic Wrist Strap

Objective: To understand how to care for and properly use an antistatic wrist strap

Parts: Antistatic wrist strap
Computer chassis
Multimeter

Note: Electrostatic discharge (ESD) has great potential to harm the electronic components inside a computer. Given this fact, it is vitally important that you practice proper ESD precautions when working inside a computer case. One tool you can use to prevent ESD is an antistatic wrist strap. This tool channels any static electricity from your body to the computer's chassis, where it is dissipated safely.

Procedure: Complete the following procedure and answer the accompanying questions.

1. Examine the wrist strap for any obvious defects such as worn or broken straps, loose grounding lead attachments, dirt or grease buildup, and so on.
2. If necessary, remove any dirt or grease buildup from the wrist strap, paying close attention to the electrical contact points such as the wrist contact point, the ground lead attachment point, and the computer chassis attachment clip. Use denatured alcohol to clean these contact points.
3. If possible, use a multimeter to check continuity between the wrist contact point and the computer chassis attachment clip. A reading of zero ohms of resistance indicates a good electrical pathway.

   How many volts of static electricity does it take to harm a computer's electrical components?
4. Adjust the wrist strap so it fits snugly yet comfortably around your wrist. Ensure that the wrist contact is in direct contact with your skin, with no clothing, hair, etc., being in the way.
5. Attach the ground lead to the wrist strap and ensure it snaps securely into place.
6. Attach the computer chassis attachment clip to a clean metal attachment point on the computer chassis.
7. Any static electricity generated or attracted by your body will now be channeled through the antistatic wrist strap to the computer chassis, where it will be safely dissipated.

   How many volts will an ESD be before you will feel anything?

Should you use an antistatic wrist strap when working inside a monitor?

Instructor initials: ____________

Lab 4.2 Computer Disassembly/Reassembly

Objective: To disassemble and reassemble a computer correctly

Parts: A computer to disassemble

A tool kit

An antistatic wrist strap (if possible)

Note: Observe proper ESD handling procedures when disassembling and reassembling a computer.

Procedure: Complete the following procedure and answer the accompanying questions.

1. Gather the proper tools needed to disassemble the computer.
2. Clear as much workspace as possible around the computer.
3. Power on the computer.

   Why is it important to power on the computer before you begin?

External Cables

4. Turn *off* the computer and all peripherals. Remove the power cable from the wall outlet and then remove the power cord from the computer.
5. Note where the monitor cable plugs into the back of the computer. Disconnect the monitor including the power cord and move it to a safe place. Take appropriate notes.
6. Remove all external cables from the back of the computer. Take notes on the location of each cable. Move the peripheral devices to a safe place.

   Did the mouse cable connect to a PS/2 or USB port?

Computer Case Removal

7. If possible, remove the computer case. This is usually the hardest step in disassembly if the computer is one that has not been seen before. Diagram the screw locations. Keep the cover screws separate from other screws. An egg carton or a container with small compartments makes an excellent screw holder. Label each compartment and reuse the container. Otherwise, open the case as directed by the manufacturer.

Adapter Placement

8. Make notes or draw the placement of each adapter in the expansion slots.
9. On your notes, draw the internal cable connections *before* removing any adapters or cables from the computer. Make notes regarding how and where the cable connects to the adapter. Do not forget to include cables that connect to the motherboard or to the computer case.

   List some ways to determine the correct orientation for an adapter or cable.

Internal Cable Removal

10. Remove all internal cables. WARNING: Do not pull on a cable; use the pull tab, if available, or use the cable connector to pull out the cable. Some cables have connectors with locking tabs. Release the locking tabs *before* you disconnect the cable. Make appropriate notes regarding the cable connections. Some students find that labeling cables and the associated connectors makes reassembly easier, but good notes usually suffice.

Adapter Removal

11. Start with the left side of the computer (facing the front of the computer) and locate the leftmost adapter.
12. Write down any jumpers or switch settings for this adapter. This step may need to be performed after you remove the board from the computer if the settings are inaccessible.
13. If applicable, remove the screw or retaining bracket that holds the adapter to the case. Place the screw in a separate, secure location away from the other screws already removed. Make notes about where the screw goes or any other notes that will help you when reassembling the computer.
14. Remove the adapter from the computer.

    Why must you be careful not to touch the gold contacts at the bottom of each adapter?

15. Remove the remaining adapters in the system by repeating Steps 12–15. Take notes regarding screw locations, jumpers, switches, and so forth for each adapter.

Drives

16. Remove all power connections to drives, such as hard drives, floppy drives, CD/DVD/BD drives, and so on. Note the placement of each drive and each cable, as well as any reminders needed for reassembly.
17. Remove any screws holding the drives in place. Make notes about where the screws go. Keep these screws separate from any previously removed screws.
18. Remove all drives.

    Why must you be careful when handling a mechanical hard drive?

    What would you do differently when handling an SSD than a SATA hard drive?

Power Supply

19. Before doing this step, ensure that the power cord is removed from the wall outlet and the computer. Remove the connectors that connect the power supply to the motherboard.
20. Take very good notes here so you will be able to insert the connectors correctly when reassembling.
21. Remove the power supply.

    What is the purpose of the power supply?

Motherboard

22. Make note of any motherboard switches or jumpers and indicate whether the switch position is on or off.

    What is the importance of documenting switches and jumpers on the motherboard?

23. Remove any remaining connectors except those that connect a battery to the motherboard. Take appropriate notes.
24. Remove any screws that hold the motherboard to the case. Place these screws in a different location from the other screws removed from the system. Write any notes pertaining to the motherboard screws. Look for retaining clips or tabs that hold the motherboard into the case.
25. Remove the motherboard. Make notes pertaining to the motherboard removal. The computer case should be empty after you complete this step.

Instructor initials: ____________

Reassembly

26. Reassemble the computer by reversing the steps for disassembly. Pay particular attention to cable orientation when reinstalling cables. Before reconnecting a cable, ensure that the cable and the connectors are correctly oriented and aligned before pushing the cable firmly in place. Refer to your notes. The first step is to install the motherboard in the computer case and reconnect all motherboard connections and screws.
27. Install the power supply by attaching all screws that hold the power supply in the case. Reattach the power connectors to the motherboard. Refer to your notes.
28. Install all drives by attaching screws, cables, and power connectors. Refer to your notes. Attach any cables that connect the drive to the motherboard.
29. Install all adapters. Attach all cables from the adapter to the connecting device. Replace any retaining clips or screws that hold adapters in place. Refer to your previous notes and diagrams.
30. Connect any external connectors to the computer. Refer to previously made notes, when necessary.
31. Replace the computer cover. Ensure that slot covers are replaced and that the drives and the front cover are aligned properly. Ensure that all covers are installed properly.
32. Reinstall the computer power cable.
33. Once the computer is reassembled, power on all external peripherals and the computer. A chassis intrusion error message may appear. This is just an indication that the cover was removed.

    Did the computer power on with POST error codes? If so, recheck all diagrams, switches, and cabling. Also, check a similar computer model that still works to see if you made a diagramming error. A chapter on logical troubleshooting comes next in the book. However, at this point in the course, the most likely problem is with a cable connection or with an adapter not seated properly in its socket.

Instructor initials: ____________

Lab 4.3 Amps and Wattage

Objective: To determine the correct capacity and wattage of a power supply

Parts: Power supply

Internet access (as needed)

Procedure: Complete the following procedure and answer the accompanying questions.

1. Locate the documentation stenciled on the power supply, if possible.

   Can you determine from the documentation how many amps of current the power supply is rated for at 5 volts? If not, proceed to Optional Step 2.

2. Optional: Use the Internet to find the power supply's documentation on the manufacturer's website. Use the information you find to answer the remaining questions.

   How many amps is the power supply rated for at 5 volts?

   How many amps is the power supply rated for at 12 volts?

   How many +12V rails does the power supply have?

   What is the maximum rated output power of the power supply in watts?

Instructor initials: ______________

Lab 4.4 Continuity Check

Objective: To perform a continuity check on a cable and find any broken wires

Parts: Multimeter

Cable and pin-out diagram

Procedure: Complete the following procedure and answer the accompanying questions.

1. Obtain a meter, cable, and pin-out diagram from your instructor.
2. Set the meter to ohms.
3. Power on the meter.
4. Lay the cable horizontally in front of you. The connector on the left is referred to as Connector A. The connector on the right is referred to as Connector B.
5. Determine the number of pins on the cable connector. On a separate sheet of paper, write numbers vertically down the left side of the paper, similar to the numbering used in Lab 4.5. There should be a number for each connector pin. At the top of the numbers write Connector A as the heading. Create a corresponding set of identical numbers vertically on the right side of the paper.
6. Check the continuity of each wire. Document your findings by placing a check mark beside each pin number that has a good continuity check.

   What meter setting did you use to check continuity, and what meter symbol is used for this setting?

7. Power off the meter and return all supplies to the instructor.

Instructor initials: ______________

Lab 4.5 Pin-Out Diagramming

Objective: To draw a pin-out diagram using a working cable

Parts: Multimeter

Good cable

Procedure: Complete the following procedure and perform the accompanying activities.

1. Obtain a meter and a good cable from your instructor.
2. Set the meter to ohms.

Instructor initials: ____________

3. Power on the meter.
4. Lay the cable horizontally in front of you. The connector on the left is referred to as Connector A. The connector on the right is referred to as Connector B.
5. Touch one meter lead to Connector A's pin 1. Touch the other meter lead to every Connector B pin. Notice when the meter shows zero resistance, indicating a connection. Using the table that follows, draw a line from Connector A's pin 1 to any Connector B pins that show zero resistance. Add more pin numbers as needed to the table or use a separate piece of paper. Remember that all pins do not have to be used in the connector. There are no review questions; however, there is a connector table that contains connection lines. The lines will be cable dependent.

Connector A	Connector B
❒ 1	❒ 1
❒ 2	❒ 2
❒ 3	❒ 3
❒ 4	❒ 4
❒ 5	❒ 5
❒ 6	❒ 6
❒ 7	❒ 7
❒ 8	❒ 8
❒ 9	❒ 9
❒ 10	❒ 10
❒ 11	❒ 11
❒ 12	❒ 12
❒ 13	❒ 13
❒ 14	❒ 14
❒ 15	❒ 15
❒ 16	❒ 16
❒ 17	❒ 17
❒ 18	❒ 18
❒ 19	❒ 19
❒ 20	❒ 20

6. Power off the meter.

Instructor initials: ______________

7. Return all supplies to the instructor.

Lab 4.6 Fuse Check

Objective: To determine if a fuse is good

Parts: Multimeter
Fuse

Procedure: Complete the following procedure and answer the accompanying questions.

1. Obtain a meter and a fuse from your instructor.
2. Look at the fuse and determine its amp rating.

   What is the amperage rating of the fuse?

3. Set the meter to ohms.

Instructor initials: ______________

4. Power on the meter.
5. Connect one meter lead to one end of the fuse. Connect the other meter lead to the opposite end.
6. Look at the resistance reading on the meter.

   What is the resistance reading?

   Is the fuse good?

7. Power off the meter.

Instructor initials: ______________

8. Return all materials to the instructor.

Lab 4.7 Using a Multimeter

Objective: To check voltage and resistance levels using a multimeter

Parts: Multimeter
AA, AAA, C, D, or 9-volt battery
Extended paperclip or wire

Caution: Keep both hands on the behind the protective rings on the meter handles. See Figures 4.16 and 4.17.

Procedure: Complete the following procedure and perform the accompanying activities.

1. All voltage inside the computer is DC voltage (except for some parts inside the power supply, of course). Learning how to measure DC voltage is important for a technician. The best place to start is with a battery. Obtain a battery. Look carefully at the battery and determine where the positive end or connector is located (usually has a + (plus) symbol nearby) and where the negative end or connector is located.

   Why is it important to locate positive and negative on a battery?

2. Look carefully at the battery and determine the voltage rating. Document your findings.

   DC voltage**:**

3. Place the battery on a flat surface. If the battery is an AA, AAA, C, or D battery, place the battery so that the positive side (the side with a nodule) pointing toward your right side. If the battery is a 9-volt battery, place the battery so that the connectors are facing you and the positive connector (the smaller connector) is on your right side.

4. If the meter has leads that attach, attach the black meter lead to the appropriate port colored as a black port or has the COM labeling. Attach the red meter lead to the positive or port marked with a plus sign (+).
5. Turn on the meter. Set the meter so that it is measuring VDC (DC voltage). This may involve manually rotating a dial and/or pushing a button. Note that some meters can autodetect the setting, but most involve configuration.

   Document what you did to configure the meter for VDC.

   What indication, if any, did the meter show in the meter window that VDC is being measured?

6. Hold the meter leads so that the black lead is in your left hand and the right lead is in your right hand. Ensure your hands are behind the protective ring on the meter handle. Refer to Figure 4.16 if you are unsure.
7. Place the black meter lead to the negative side (left side or left connector). Also touch the red meter lead to the positive side (right side or right connector) of the battery. Make a note of the meter reading.

   DC volts:

   Based on your findings, is the battery good (usable in an electronic device)?

8. Now reverse the meter leads—place the black lead to the positive side and the red lead to the negative side. Record your findings.

   DC volts:

   What was different from the original meter reading?

9. Perform this voltage check on any other batteries given to you by the instructor or lab assistant.
10. Straighten a paperclip or obtain a wire. Place the paperclip or wire on a flat surface.
11. Change the meter so that it reads ohms. This is normally shown by the omega symbol (Ω).

    While having the meter leads up in the air (not touching each other), what does the meter display?
12. Touch the meter leads together to make a complete circuit or path.

    What does the meter display now?
13. Touch one meter lead to one end of the paperclip or wire, and touch the other meter lead to the opposite paperclip or wire end. Sometimes it is easier to just lay the meter lead on top of the wire close to the end.

    What is the meter reading?
14. Some meters have the ability to make a sound when a wire is good. This is frequently shown on your meter as a sound wave ( )))). If your meter has this ability, configure the meter and redo the test. You can see how much easier this would be than trying to hold your meter leads straight and watch the meter.

Instructor initials: ______________

15. Power off the meter. Disconnect the leads as necessary. Return all parts to the appropriate location.

Lab 4.8 Wall Outlet and Power Cord AC Voltage Check

Objective: To check the voltage from a wall outlet and through a power cord

Parts: Multimeter

Computer power cord

Caution: Exercise extreme caution when working with AC voltages!

Procedure: Complete the following procedure and perform the accompanying activities.

1. Set the multimeter to AC VOLTAGE (refer to the meter's manual if you are unsure about this setting). Important: Using a current or resistance setting could destroy the meter.
2. Power on the multimeter. Locate an AC power outlet. Refer to Figure 4.38 for the power connections.

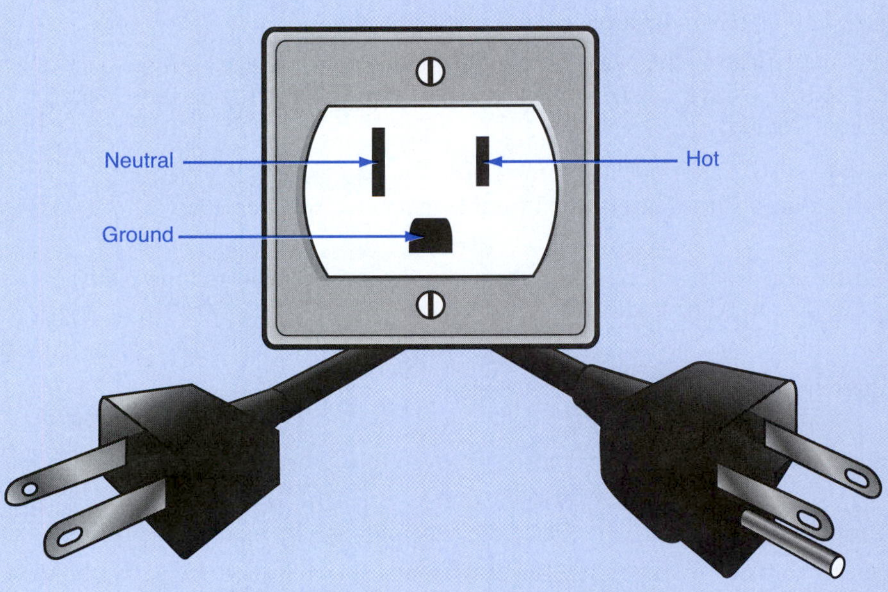

Figure 4.38 AC outlet

3. Insert the meter's black lead into the round (Ground) AC outlet plug.
4. Insert the meter's red lead into the smaller flat (Hot) AC outlet plug. The meter reading should be around 120 volts. Use Table 4.9 to record the reading.
5. Move the meter's red lead into the larger flat (Neutral) AC outlet plug. The meter reading should be 0 volts. Use Table 4.9 to record the reading.

Table 4.9 Wall outlet AC checks

Connections	Expected voltage	Actual voltage
GND to hot	120VAC	
GND to neutral	0VAC	
Hot to neutral	120VAC	

6. Remove both leads from the wall outlet.
7. Insert the meter's black lead into the smaller flat (hot) AC outlet plug.
8. Insert the meter's red lead into the larger flat (neutral) AC outlet plug. The meter reading should be around 120 volts. Use Table 4.9 to record the reading.
9. Plug the computer power cord into the AC wall outlet that was checked using Steps 3 through 8.
10. Verify the other end of the power cord is not plugged into the computer.
11. Perform the same checks you performed in Steps 3 through 8, except this time check the power cord end that plugs into the computer. Use Table 4.10 to record the reading.

Table 4.10 Power cord AC checks

Connections	Expected voltage	Actual voltage
GND to hot	120VAC	
GND to neutral	0VAC	
Hot to neutral	120VAC	

12. If the voltage through the power cord is correct, power off the meter. Notify the instructor of any incorrect voltages.

Instructor initials: ______________

Lab 4.9 Device DC Voltage Check

Objective: To check the power supply voltages sent to various devices

Parts: Multimeter
Computer

Procedure: Complete the following procedure and perform the accompanying activities.

1. Set the multimeter to DC VOLTAGE (refer to the meter's manual if unsure about the setting).
2. Power on the multimeter.
3. Power off the computer.
4. Remove the computer case.
5. Locate a Molex or Berg power connector. If one is not available, disconnect a power connector from a device.
6. Power on the computer.
7. Check the +5 volt DC output from the power supply by placing the meter's *black* lead in (if the connector is a Molex) or on (if the connector is a Berg) one of the grounds* (a black wire). Place the meter's *red* lead on the +5 volt wire (normally a red wire) in or on the connector. Consult Figure 4.39 for the layout of the Molex and Berg power supply connections. Figure 4.39 also contains a table with the acceptable voltage levels.

   *Use and check both ground connections (black wires going into the connector); do not check all the voltages using only one ground connection.

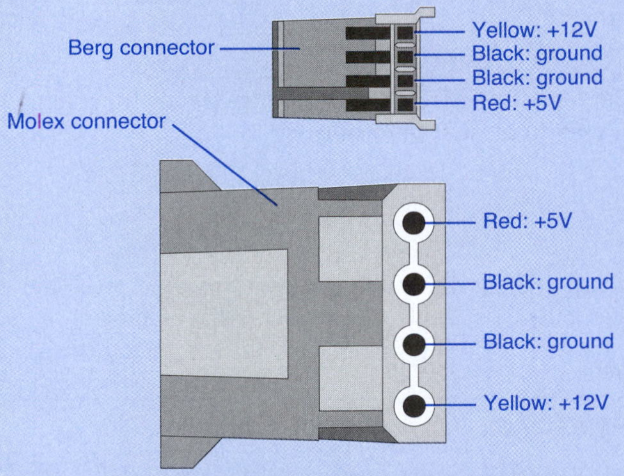

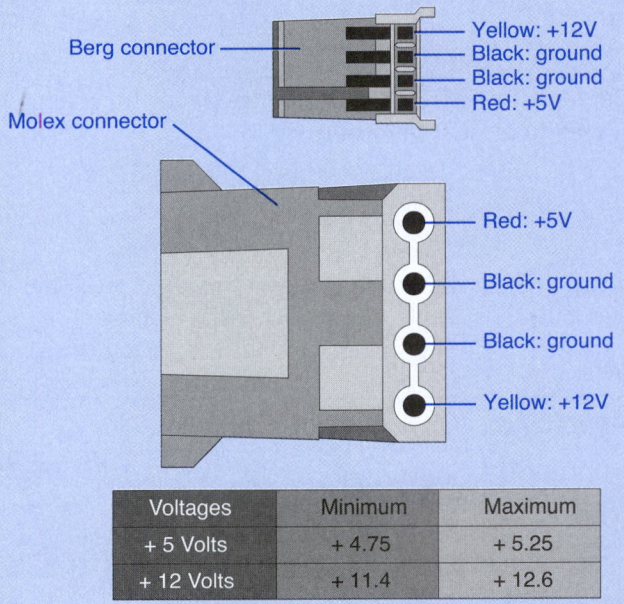

Voltages	Minimum	Maximum
+ 5 Volts	+ 4.75	+ 5.25
+ 12 Volts	+ 11.4	+ 12.6

Figure 4.39 **Molex and Berg power connectors**

Write the voltage level found for the +5 volt wire in Table 4.11.

Table 4.11 **+5 volt check**

Voltage being checked	Voltage found
+5 volts	

8. Check the +12 volt DC output by placing the meter's *black* lead in (if the connector is a Molex) or on (if the connector is a Berg) one of the grounds. Place the meter's *red* lead on the +12 volt wire in or on the connector. See Figure 4.39 for the layout of the Molex and Berg power supply connections. The figure also contains a table with acceptable voltage levels. Write the voltage level found for the +12 volt wire in Table 4.12.

Table 4.12 **+12 volt check**

Voltage being checked	Voltage found
+12 volts	

9. Notify the instructor of any voltages out of the acceptable range.
10. Power off the meter.

Instructor initials: ______________

11. Power off the computer.

Lab 4.10 Windows XP Power Options

Objective: To be able to control power options via BIOS and Windows XP

Parts: Computer with Windows XP loaded

Procedure: Complete the following procedure and answer the accompanying questions.

1. Power on the computer and ensure it boots properly before the exercise begins.
2. Reboot the computer and access BIOS Setup.

List the BIOS options related to power management.

Can ACPI be disabled via BIOS?

3. Exit the BIOS setup program without saving any settings. Boot to Windows XP.
4. From the *Start* button > access *Control Panel* > *Classic view* > and the *Power Options* Control Panel.

   On the *Power Schemes* tab, what is the current setting used?

   Using the *Power Schemes* drop-down menu, list the power schemes available.

   What is the current setting for the monitor power scheme?

   What is the current setting for the hard drive power scheme?

   What is the current setting for the system standby?

   What is the maximum amount of time the monitor can be on and then be shut off by the operating system?

5. Select the *Advanced* tab.

   Describe the power savings icon shown on this window.

   What options are available for the power button?

6. Select the *Hibernate* tab.

   How much disk space is required for hibernation?

7. Click *Cancel*.

Lab 4.11 Windows Vista/7 Power Options

Objective: To be able to control power options via BIOS and Windows Vista/7

Parts: Computer with Windows Vista or 7 loaded

Procedure:

1. Power on the computer and ensure it boots properly before the exercise begins.
2. Reboot the computer and access BIOS Setup.

   List the BIOS options related to power management.

   Can ACPI be disabled via BIOS?

3. Exit the BIOS Setup program without saving any settings. Boot to Windows Vista/7.
4. Access the current power settings by using the *Start* > *Control Panel* > *System and Maintenance* (Vista)/*System and Security* (7) > *Power Options*.

   What power plan is currently configured?

5. Select the *Create a power plan* link on the left. Type a unique name in the *Plan name* textbox. Click *Next*.

6. Use the *Turn off the display* drop-down menu to select a time. Use the *Put the computer to sleep* drop-down menu to select a time for the computer to go into reduced power mode. Note that on a laptop computer there will be two columns of choices: *On battery* and *Plugged in*.

   What global ACPI state do you think this would assign? Look back through the chapter to review.

7. Click the *Create* button. Notice that your new plan appears in the list of preferred plans. Also notice that the *Show additional plans* reveal arrow might be in the center of the window on the right if someone has hidden the additional plans. Click on *Show additional plans*, and other plans are revealed.
8. Click on the *Change plan settings* link under or beside the plan you just created. Select the *Change advanced power settings* link.

   List at least three devices for which you can have power controlled through this control panel.

9. Expand the USB settings, if possible, and the *USB selective suspend* setting.

   What is the current setting?

10. Expand the *Processor power management* setting, if possible.

    What is the minimum processor state?

    What is the maximum processor state?

11. Expand the *Multimedia* settings, if possible.

    What setting(s) is configured with this option?

12. Click the *Cancel* button to return to the Change settings window. Click the *Cancel* button again. Show the instructor or lab assistant your settings.

Instructor initials: __________

13. To delete a power plan you created (the default ones cannot be deleted), select the radio button for the original power plan. Refer to Step 4, if necessary. Under the plan you created, select the *Change settings for the plan* link. Select the *Delete this plan* link and click *OK*. The plan should be removed from the power options list. Show the instructor or lab assistant that the plan has been deleted.

Instructor initials: __________

Activities

Internet Discovery

Objective: To obtain specific information on the Internet regarding a computer or its associated parts

Parts: Computer with Internet access

Procedure: Complete the following procedure and answer the accompanying questions.

1. Locate an Internet site that provides tips for doing computer preventive maintenance.

   Write 10 of the tips and the URL where you found the information.

2. Locate an Internet site to buy a computer tool kit that contains non-magnetic screwdrivers.
   List the URL where you found the tool kit and at least three sizes of screwdrivers or bits provided.

3. Locate a surge protector for the whole house. Determine if it replaces the need for individual surge protectors.
   Write the name and part number as well as your findings.

4. A customer owns a Belkin 12-outlet surge protector with phone/Ethernet/coaxial protection and an extended cord.
   What is the warranty amount for this surge protector and at what URL did you find this information?

5. A customer has a Rosewill CAPSTONE-450 power supply.
   What is the power supply's maximum power output (in watts) and how many amps are provided for +3.3V, +5V, and +12V (combined amount for +12V)? Write the URL where you found this information as well.

6. A customer has an Enermax Liberty ELT500AWT power supply.
   Does this power supply comply with the ATXV12 version 2.2 or higher specification?

   How many PCIe connectors are provided?

   Does the power supply have any SATA power connectors? If so, how many?

   At what website did you find this information?

7. A customer owns a Toshiba Satellite R845-ST6N02 laptop.
   What type of battery provides power for the longest amount of time for this model? Write the URL where you found this information.

8. Your company has a Tripp Lite Smart 700 UPS.
   What are the part number and cost for a replacement battery? At what website did you find this information?

9. Locate an A-B-C fire extinguisher.
   Give the model, cost, and URL where you found this information.

Soft Skills

Objective: To enhance and fine-tune a future technician's ability to listen, communicate in both written and oral form, and support people who use computers in a professional manner

Activities:

1. Using the information gathered in Critical Thinking Skills Activity 1 or researching an appropriate replacement power supply for any computer, prepare a business proposal for the power supply as if you were offering it to a customer. Present your proposal to the class.

2. Work in teams to decide the best way to inform a customer about the differences between a line conditioner and a UPS. Present your description to the class as if you were talking to the customer. Each team member must contribute. Each classmate votes for the best team explanation.

Critical Thinking Skills

Objective: To analyze and evaluate information as well as apply learned information to new or different situations

Activities:

1. Locate a computer on the Internet that lists each device that is installed and the type of motherboard, integrated ports, and so on. Then locate a power supply calculator. Find a replacement power supply, based on the calculations performed. Write the details of what you looked for in the replacement power supply, the power supply, vendor, number and type of connectors, and cost.
2. For one of the computers in the classroom, locate an appropriate UPS that can provide power for 10 minutes. Write the details of your findings in a report.

A+ Certification Exam Tips

✓ Review the chapter summary. Quite a few questions are about preventive maintenance procedures. Don't forget that other chapters have preventive maintenance tips, too, including the chapters on storage devices, multimedia devices, and other peripherals chapters.

✓ Power down a computer, remove the power cord/power brick/battery, and allow a laser printer to cool before performing maintenance.

✓ Know what the +5 and +12 volts are used for in a computer.

✓ Review a couple of videos on laptop disassembly. Know where the common parts, including the following, are located on different vendors' products: memory, wireless antennas, mini PCI/PCIe adapters, DC power jack, and speakers.

✓ Know what tools are commonly used: flat-tip/Phillips screwdrivers, #0 Phillips screwdriver for laptop and mobile device screws, antistatic wrist strap (don't use in a CRT monitor or inside a power supply).

✓ Know all about static electricity, RFI, and EMI and how to prevent them.

✓ Know the purpose of various power protection devices: surge protector, line conditioner, SPS, UPS, and modem isolator.

✓ Know what type of fire extinguishers are used with electronic devices.

✓ Be able to identify all motherboard, PCIe adapter, and power supply power connectors.

✓ The following communication and professionalism skills are part of the 220-801 exam: Provide proper documentation on the services provided.

✓ Be familiar with all the power options that can be set on a desktop and a mobile device.

chapter 5

Logical Troubleshooting

Chapter Objectives:

In this chapter you will learn:

- How to perform basic troubleshooting procedures
- How BIOS controls the boot sequence and how that might help in troubleshooting
- The purpose of POST error codes
- The importance of good communication

CompTIA Exam Objectives:

What CompTIA A+ exam objectives are covered in this chapter?

- ✓ 801-5.3 Given a scenario, demonstrate proper communication and professionalism.
- ✓ 802-4.1 Given a scenario, explain the troubleshooting theory.
- ✓ 802-4.2 Given a scenario, troubleshoot common problems related to motherboards, RAM, CPU, and power with appropriate tools.

Troubleshooting Overview

When a computer does not work properly, technicians must exhibit one essential trait—the will to succeed. The main objective is to return the computer or peripheral to service as quickly and economically as possible. When a computer is down, a business loses revenue and productivity. Therefore, a technician must have a good attitude and a large amount of perseverance and drive to resolve the problem at hand quickly and efficiently, in a professional, helpful manner.

Technicians must also use all available resources. Resources can be documentation for a particular peripheral, motherboard, or computer; the Internet; your five senses; another technician; corporate documentation; textbooks; experience with similar problems; training materials; previous service history on a particular customer/computer; or an online database provided by a company or partner. Technicians can be stubborn, but they must always remember that time is money, and solving a problem quickly and with the least amount of downtime to the customer is a critical component of a computer support job.

Tech Tip

Back up data, if possible

Before any changes are made to a system, ensure that its data is backed up, if possible.

Solving a computer problem is easier if a technician uses reasoning and takes logical steps. Logical troubleshooting can be broken down into the following six simple steps:

1. Identify the problem.
2. Establish a theory of probable cause (question the obvious).
3. Test the theory to determine the cause.
4. Establish a plan of action to resolve the problem and implement the solution.
5. Verify full system functionality and, if applicable, implement preventive measures.
6. Document findings, actions, and outcomes.

Identify the Problem

Computer problems come in all shapes and sizes. Many problems relate to the people who operate computers—the users. Users may fail to choose the correct printer, sometimes push the wrong key for a specific function, or might issue an incorrect command.

Have the user demonstrate or re-create the problem. Because the user is often the problem, you can save a great deal of time by taking this step. Do not assume anything! A user may complain that "my hard drive does not work" when, in fact, there is no power to the computer. Often users repeat computer terms they have heard or read, but they do not use them correctly or in the right syntax. By asking a user to re-create a problem, a technician creates a chance to see the problem as the client sees it. Even during a phone consultation, the same rules apply. Whether diagnosing a problem on the phone or in person, be sure to follow these guidelines:

- Do not assume anything; ask the user to re-create the problem step-by-step.
- Ask the user if anything has been changed. Do not be threatening; otherwise, the user will not be forthright and honest. Use open-ended questions to get an idea of what is wrong. Use closed-ended questions to narrow the problem.
- Verify obvious things such as power to the monitor or speakers muted through the control panel.
- Do not assume that there is not a problem if the user cannot re-create it. Some problems occur intermittently.
- Back up data, if possible, before making changes.
- Use all your senses. Listen for noises such as from the power supply, case/CPU fans, or hard drive. Power off if you detect a burning smell.

Establish a Theory of Probable Cause

In order to establish a theory of probable cause (and do not forget to question the obvious), you have to have heard or seen the problem as explained by the user. A lot of times, you establish a theory based on analyzing the problem and determining whether the problem is hardware or software related (or both) by using your senses: Sight, hearing, and smell can reveal a great deal. Smell for burning components. Watch the computer boot, look for lights, listen for beeps, and take notes. Always question the obvious.

Frequently, a hardware problem is detected during the POST (power-on self-test) executed by the BIOS when the computer is first powered on. Knowing the steps taken during the boot process helps you troubleshoot:

1. The power supply sends a power good signal.
2. The CPU looks in BIOS for software.
3. The CPU executes POST from BIOS. Note that any errors are usually audio or motherboard LEDs or codes at this point.
4. System resources (I/O address, memory addresses, and interrupts) are retrieved from NVRAM (nonvolatile RAM or RAM that can be changed, but data is not lost when power is removed) and assigned to ports, devices, and adapters.
5. Video is initialized, and a cursor appears.
6. POST continues to check hardware and error messages and/or codes can now appear on the display.
7. Based on the boot order configuration in System Setup, the system checks for an operating system from the specified devices.
8. On the first device found that contains an operating, the operating system loads.

Note that the POST checks out the hardware in a sequential order, and if it finds an error, the BIOS issues a beep and/or displays a numeric error code. Make note of any error codes or beeps. The number or duration of beeps and the numeric error codes that appear are different for different computers. The secret is knowing the BIOS chip manufacturer. The computer or motherboard documentation sometimes contains a list of codes or beeps used for troubleshooting. A single beep is a common tone heard on a successful completion of POST because no hardware errors were detected. Table 5.1 lists the audio beeps heard on a computer with an AMI BIOS chip installed. Table 5.2 lists the POST error messages sometimes seen on computers.

Table 5.1 AMI BIOS audio beeps

Beeps	Description of problem
1, 2, or 3	Memory error
4, 5, 6, or 7	Motherboard component
8	Video issue

Table 5.2 Written BIOS POST error messages

Message	Description
BIOS ROM checksum error—System halted	The BIOS has a problem and needs to be replaced.
CMOS battery failed/error	Replace the motherboard battery.
CMOS checksum error—Defaults loaded	CMOS has detected a problem. Check the motherboard battery.

Message	Description
CMOS timer error	The system date/time has not been set. Check/replace the motherboard battery if this is not the first time this computer has been powered on.
Floppy disk(s) failed	The system has been configured to have a floppy disk installed and the drive has not responded. Check the drive connectivity and power. If no drive is installed, change the setting in BIOS Setup.
Hard disk install failure	The BIOS could not find or initialize the hard drive. Check the hard drive connectivity and power.
Intruder detection error	The computer chassis has been opened.
Keyboard error or no keyboard present	The keyboard could not be found. Check the cabling.
Keyboard is locked out—Unlock the key	Ensure that nothing rests on the keys during the POST.
Memory test fail	A RAM error occurred. Swap the memory modules.
Memory size decrease error	The amount of system RAM has decreased. Check to see if RAM has been stolen, needs reseating, or needs to be replaced.
Memory optimal error	The amount of memory in channel A is not equal to channel B. For optimal memory performance they should be equal. See Chapter 6 for more details.
Override enabled—Defaults loaded	The current settings in CMOS could not be loaded, and the BIOS defaults are used. Check the battery and CMOS settings.
Primary master hard disk fail	The PATA hard drive attached to the primary IDE connector and configured as master could not be detected. If a new installation, check the cabling, power, and master/slave/cable select settings. See Chapter 7 for more details.
Primary slave hard disk fail	The PATA hard drive attached to the primary IDE connector and configured as slave could not be detected. If a new installation, check the cabling, power, and master/slave/cable select settings. See Chapter 7 for more details.
Secondary master hard disk fail	The PATA hard drive attached to the secondary IDE connector and configured as master could not be detected. If a new installation, check the cabling, power, and master/slave/cable select settings. See Chapter 7 for more details.
Secondary slave hard disk fail	The PATA hard drive attached to the secondary IDE connector and configured as slave could not be detected. If a new installation, check the cabling, power, and master/slave/cable select settings. See Chapter 7 for more details.

A BIOS can be sold to various computer manufacturers, who are allowed to create their own error codes and messages. Look in the motherboard/computer manual or on the manufacturer's website for a list of exact error messages. Table 5.3 lists the audio beeps heard on a computer with a Phoenix BIOS chip installed.

Table 5.3 Phoenix audio beep codes

Beeps	Description
1-2-2-3	BIOS ROM (flash the BIOS/motherboard)
1-3-1-1	Memory refresh (RAM contacts/RAM)
1-3-1-3	8742 keyboard controller (keyboard/motherboard)
1-3-4-1	Memory address line error (RAM contacts/RAM/power supply/motherboard)
1-3-4-3	Memory error (RAM contacts/RAM/motherboard)
1-4-1-3	CPU bus clock frequency
2-2-3-1	Unexpected interrupt (adapter/motherboard)
2-4-2-3	Keyboard error
3-1-1-1	Onboard I/O port issue

In addition to hearing audio tones, or seeing numeric error codes or written messages, the motherboard might provide additional troubleshooting information. Some motherboards have a numeric display or colored indicators that display as part of the POST. The meaning of the visual clues can be found in the motherboard or computer manual.

POST error codes direct a technician to the correct general area only. Sometimes, multiple POST errors occur. If this is the case, start the troubleshooting process with the first error code detected.

Some technicians carry a **POST card** as part of their tool kit. A POST card is a PCI/PCIe adapter or USB-attached card that performs hardware diagnostics and displays the results as a series of codes on an LED display or LED lights. These are not as popular today as they once were because many BIOS manufacturers include powerful diagnostics as part of the System Setup program or diagnostics that can be executed from or downloaded from the computer manufacturer's website. Some motherboards have similar displays as the POST card built right on the motherboard, as shown in Figure 5.1.

Figure 5.1 Motherboard diagnostic display

When a numeric code appears or certain lights illuminate, you have to use the manual to determine the issue. Some motherboard LEDs are used in conjunction with depressible switches to test components. Figure 5.2 shows a motherboard LED, and Figure 5.3 shows some common uses of the motherboard LEDs.

Hardware errors might also occur. For example, the monitor might suddenly go black, the optical drive's access light might not go on when it attempts to access the optical disc, or the printer might repeatedly flash an error code. If you suspect a physical port problem, you can use a **loopback plug** to test the port. Loopback plugs are commonly used with the older ports, such as the parallel and serial ports. Today, RJ-45 loopback plugs are commonly used to test network port functionality.

Hardware errors are usually obvious because of POST error codes or errors that occur when accessing a particular device. Also, some peripherals, such as hard drives and printers, include diagnostics as part of the software that is loaded when the device is installed. These diagnostics are frequently accessed through the device's Properties window or from the Windows All Programs software list.

Figure 5.2 Motherboard LED

Examples of Motherboard Switches and LEDs

Switch	LED	Explanation
MemOK!	MemOK	Depress the MemOK switch to determine if the RAM modules are compatible. The MemOK LED illuminates if so.
EPU	EPU	Enable the EPU switch or enable through BIOS to allow the motherboard to moderate power consumption. When enabled, the EPU LED is lit.
	RAM	The RAM LED illuminates for a memory error.
	Power	The power LED commonly illuminates when power is applied, or if the computer is in either the sleep or soft off power mode.

Figure 5.3 Motherboard switch and LED usage

Software errors, on the other hand, occur when a computer user accesses a particular application or file or when the system boots. Sometimes, the problem can be resolved with a **warm boot**. Warm booting causes any changes that have been made to take effect without putting as much strain on the computer as a cold boot does. You can restart a Windows XP computer with a warm boot by clicking the *Start* button > *Shut Down* > *Restart* > *OK*. From the Windows Vista or 7 start button, click on the right arrow adjacent to the lock button or Shutdown and select *Restart*. In all Windows version, a warm boot can be performed through Task Manager by holding down the Ctrl key, the Alt key, and the Del key at the same time, selecting *Task Manager*, selecting the *Shut Down* option, selecting *Restart* from the drop-down menu, and clicking the *OK* button.

Tech Tip

Motherboard manual or website lists the latest error codes

Manufacturers constantly produce BIOS upgrades, and you can use the Internet to verify POST errors that occur and the recommended actions to take.

Files that affect the booting process, such as files in the Startup folder, are dependent on the operating system. If in doubt as to whether a problem is hardware or software related, use Windows Device Manager to test the hardware to eliminate that possibility. Every software program has problems (bugs). Software manufacturers offer a software **patch** or a **service release** that fixes known problems. Patches or service releases are usually available on the Internet from the software manufacturer. A **service pack** usually contains multiple patches and installs them at the same time rather than in multiple downloads.

Test the Theory to Determine Cause

Once you have a theory or suspect a general area, you need to determine the next steps needed to resolve the problem. If you go through the process for what you suspect and the problem is still unresolved, you might have to step back and reevaluate the problem. From there, you can establish a new theory or will need to escalate the problem to a more senior technician.

Divide the problem into logical areas and continue subdividing the problem until it is isolated. For example, if an error appears each time the computer user tries to write data to a CD, then the logical place to look is the optical drive system. The optical drive system includes the user's disc, the optical drive, electronics that tell the drive what to do, a cable that connects the drive to the controlling electronics, and the software program currently being used. Any of these may be the cause of the problem.

Ernie Friend, a technician of many years, advises students to divide a problem in half; then divide it in half again; then continue to divide until the problem is manageable. This way of thinking carries a technician a long way. Also, always keep in mind that you will beat the problem at hand! You are smarter than any problem!

Use Ernie's philosophy with the optical drive problem: Divide the problem in half and determine whether the problem is hardware or software related. To determine whether the software application is causing the problem, try accessing the disc from another application. If the second application works, then the problem is in the first application. If both applications have problems, the problem is most likely in the disc or in the drive hardware system. The next easiest thing to eliminate as a suspect is the CD. Try a different disc. If a different disc works, then the first disc was the problem. If neither disc accepts data, the problem is the optical drive, cable, or electronics. Swap parts one at a time until you locate the problem.

Tech Tip

Return original part if it does not fix the problem

Always reinstall the original part if the symptoms did not change. Then continue troubleshooting.

If a hardware problem is evident after a POST error or peripheral access/usage error occurs, consider the problem a subunit of the entire computer. For example, if a POST error occurs for the optical drive, the subunit is the optical drive subsystem. The subsystem consists of the drive, the cable, and the controlling circuits that may be on an adapter or the motherboard.

If a problem is software related, narrow it to a specific area. For example, determine whether the problem is related to printing, saving, or retrieving a file. This may give you a clue about what section of the application is having a problem or may even lead you back to considering other hardware components as the cause of the problem.

Tech Tip

Change or check the easy stuff first

When isolating a problem to a specific area, be practical; change or check the easy stuff first. Time is money—to the company or person whose computer is down and to the company that employs the technician.

When multiple things could cause a problem, make a list of possibilities and eliminate the potential problems one by one. If a monitor is down, swap the monitor with another before opening the computer and swapping the video adapter. Also, check with the computer user to see if anything about the computer has changed recently. For example, ask if anyone installed or removed something from the computer or if new software was loaded before or has been loaded since the problem started. If the problem is hardware related, you can use the Device Manager and Windows troubleshooting wizards to narrow it down to a subunit. Isolating a problem frequently requires part swapping, but try not to replace good parts. If a replacement part does not solve the problem, put the old part back in.

If you do not hear any unusual audio beeps or see any POST error codes and you suspect a software error, reboot the computer. Before Windows starts, press the F8 key to bring up the *Advanced Boot Options* menu. Select a menu option, such as *Repair your computer*, *Safe mode*, or *Last Known Good Configuration*.

Swapping a part, checking hardware settings, and referring to documentation are necessary steps in troubleshooting. Noting error or beep codes is just one element in the diagnostic routine. Determining what the problem is usually takes longer than fixing it. Software problems frequently involve reloading software applications and software drivers or getting software updates and patches from the appropriate vendor. The Internet is an excellent resource for these files and vendor recommendations. Hardware problem resolution simply involves swapping the damaged part. Sometimes, it is necessary to remove or disable unnecessary components and peripherals. This is especially true with notebook computers.

If swapping a part or reloading the software does not solve the problem, go back to logical troubleshooting. Step 2 reminds you to divide the problem into hardware and software related issues. Go back to that step if necessary.

Establish a Plan of Action and Implement the Solution

Every repair should involve a plan of action. Having a plan helps you through the problem resolution process. The plan of action should take you through resolving the problem and implementing the solution. Some repairs take multiple steps. You might have to apply a BIOS update before installing a new adapter. You might have to update the operating system or remove a virus before re-installing or upgrading an application. Having a plan instead of just doing things in a random order saves time, and time is money!

Verify Full System Functionality and Implement Preventive Measures

Never assume that a hardware component or the replaced software repairs a computer. The computer can have multiple problems, or one repair may not offer a complete solution. Verify full system functionality and have the user test the computer in normal conditions to prove that the problem is indeed solved. You may need to implement preventive measures such as cleaning the computer or device or installing a legal copy of antivirus software. Preventive measures also include cleaning up the hard drive and cleaning the optical drive laser lens. The chapters that follow describe preventive measures for common computing devices.

Figure 5.4 shows a simple troubleshooting flowchart; also keep in mind that each chapter has one or more troubleshooting sections to help with problems. In addition, the chapters toward the end of this book address problems related to operating systems.

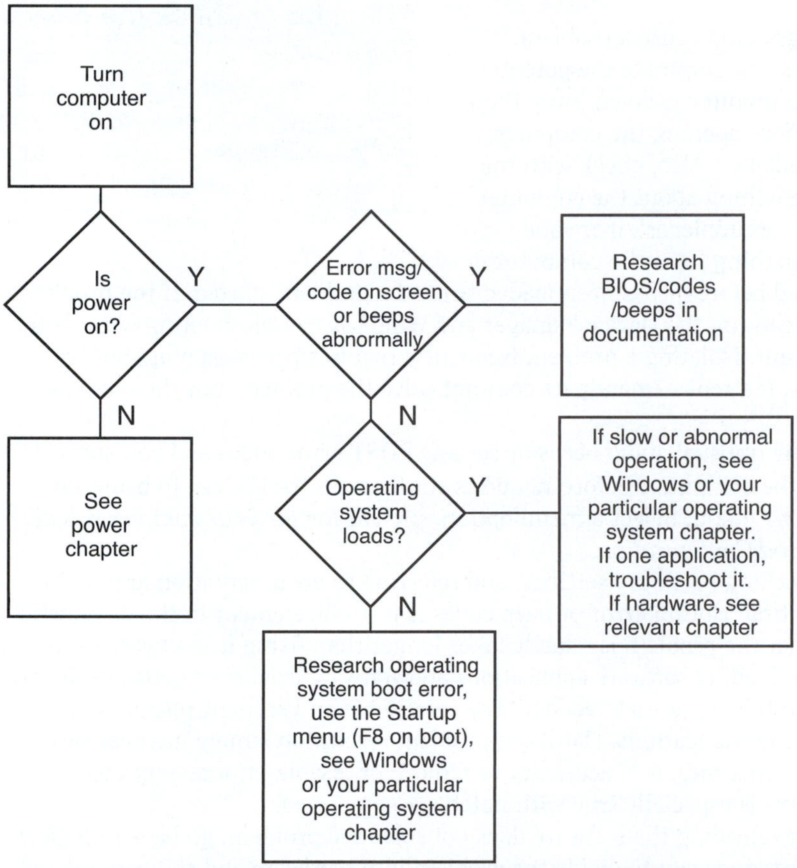

Figure 5.4 Basic troubleshooting flowchart

Soft Skills—Document Findings, Actions, and Outcomes and Provide Feedback

Many technicians feel that their work is done once a problem is solved, but it is not. Documenting the steps taken to resolve a problem in a clear, concise manner is important. A lot of times this documentation is put in a customer's record, or an invoice is generated as a result of the repair. Having easy-to-read and easy-to-understand documentation is important for nontechnical users who see this documentation as well as any follow-up repairs that you or another technician must do. One of the biggest complaints from employers is the inability of technical staff to articulate well in writing and verbally. By working on these soft skills, you can be a better asset to employers.

The best computer technicians are the ones who can repair problems, whom the users trust, and who explain problems in a way customers can understand. A repair is never finished until the user is informed. Technical training on new equipment or a procedure/process may be necessary. Realize that computer users are intelligent, even if they are not proficient in technical terminology. The following list can be used as a reminder for good customer support skills:

- Use clear, concise, direct statements when talking to customers.
- Be pleasant, patient, and professional.
- Listen to customers and allow them to complete their sentences. Do not interrupt.
- Ask questions when appropriate and when they are pertinent to the problem.
- Avoid using technical slang, jargon, or acronyms.
- Be culturally sensitive.
- Respect the customer's privacy and property. Think about how you would want to be treated if someone were working in your office on your computer. If you see something confidential, ask the customer to remove or put away the document/information.
- Do not become defensive or judgmental. If the customer is unprofessional to a point that you cannot do your job, excuse yourself and contact your supervisor. Under no circumstance should you lose your own professional demeanor.
- Maintain a positive attitude and do the best job that you can.
- Be on time. If you are going to be late, contact the customer and inform them.
- Offer repair/replacement options if possible.
- Provide written documentation applicable to the replaced purchased parts and services provided.
- Follow up at a later date to ensure that the solution was truly a total solution and to ensure customer satisfaction.

A good recommendation is to follow up with the customer one week after the repair to make sure the customer is satisfied and that the problem is solved. If the customer is unhappy, jump at the chance to make good on the repair. The best advertising is good referrals from satisfied customers. Keep in mind that the general rule of thumb is that if the customer is satisfied, he or she will tell 1 or 2 other people about the service. If the customer is dissatisfied, he or she will tell 10 other people about the problem.

Each computer repair is a different scenario because of the plethora of vendors, products, and standards in the marketplace. But this is one of the things that makes the job so interesting and challenging. Break down each problem into manageable tasks, isolate the specific issue, and use all available resources, including other technicians, documentation, and the Internet, to solve it. Keep a "can do" attitude with intermittent problems—the hardest type of problems there are to solve. Never forget to give feedback.

The remaining chapters are dedicated to specific devices or areas of the computer. Each device or area covered includes troubleshooting techniques you can use once you have narrowed down a problem. For example, if you find you have a memory problem, read Chapter 6 for details of operation and troubleshooting techniques.

Chapter Summary

- The six steps of troubleshooting are as follows: (1) Identify the problem, (2) establish a theory, (3) test the theory, (4) establish a plan of action, (5) verify full system functionality and, if applicable, implement preventive measures, and (6) document findings, actions, and outcomes as well as provide feedback.
- BIOS controls the boot process. Knowing the following steps can help with the troubleshooting process. The basic steps that the computer goes through to start up are as follows:
  1. Power good signal is sent from power supply.
  2. CPU looks in BIOS for software.
  3. The CPU executes the POST (only audio errors available at this point).
  4. Computer assigns system resources to ports, devices, and adapters.
  5. Computer initializes video—a cursor appears.
  6. POST continues checking hardware.
  7. Computer looks for an operating system from the BIOS-specified boot order devices.
  8. Computer loads the operating system or halts with an error.
- POST error codes are determined by the BIOS vendor and the company that makes the motherboard.
- POST codes can be audible beeps, numeric codes, or words.
- The BIOS can contain advanced diagnostics.
- The motherboard can contain diagnostic LEDs or a display.
- A POST card can be used to perform diagnostics.
- A loopback plug can be used in conjunction with diagnostics to check older ports or test network interface ports.
- Reinstall parts that do not solve the problem.
- Always document a problem as part of the troubleshooting process. Give users the appropriate documentation. Be professional in your oral and written communication. Provide feedback to the user.

Key Terms

Review Questions

1. Explain how a user, rather than the user's computer, might be the problem.

2. How can a technician determine whether a problem is hardware or software related?

3. The _____ chip executes POST. [BIOS | CMOS | CPU | RAM]

4. [T | F] The manufacturer of the RAM chip determines what error codes are shown during POST.
5. To troubleshoot an array of possible system startup problems, press the _____ key during the system startup process to bring up the Advanced Boot Options menu. [F1 | F2 | F8 | F12]
6. If a computer beeps once during POST, what is the problem?
   a. There is no problem
   b. CPU register test
   c. DRAM refresh
   d. Video initialization error
7. The _____ might have a numeric display mounted that shows an error code. [CPU | heatsink | POST | motherboard]
8. If a computer beeps once and then three times, then four times, then three more times during POST and the computer has a Phoenix BIOS, what is a possible suspect component? [keyboard | BIOS | memory | video]
9. A _____ is used to test a serial, parallel, or RJ-45 port. [multimeter | probe | torx | loopback plug]
10. An adapter that performs diagnostics and displays a code or LEDs is known as a _____. [POST card | probe | torx | DIGI card]
11. [T | F] When a technician is behind on time, it is okay to swap more than one part at a time.
12. Where can you find the latest information on POST error codes?
13. [T | F] During the *Test the theory* phase, you might be required to escalate the problem to a more experienced technician.
14. [T | F] After swapping a part in a computer and powering on, you can assume that the problem is solved.
15. What is the last and most important step in resolving a computer problem?
16. If a problem is hardware related, Windows Device Manager can be useful in getting the problem narrowed down to a subunit.
17. A computer problem is never solved until the user
18. You see a user's password taped to the side of the keyboard. What do you do?
    a. Call your boss.
    b. Ignore it.
    c. Use it later to access the user's data.
    d. Tell the user to change the password.
19. You spent more time than expected at a customer site. Now you are late for your next service call. What do you do?
    a. Call your boss and explain the situation.
    b. Call the next customer and explain that you are running late.
    c. Explain to the next customer the situation once you get there.
    d. Nothing. Get to the next customer site as soon as safely possible.

20. Place the six steps of troubleshooting in the order in which they occur.

____ First	a. Test the theory
____ Second	b. Establish a theory
____ Third	c. Document and provide feedback
____ Fourth	d. Identify the problem
____ Fifth	e. Verify system functionality
____ Sixth	f. Establish a plan of action

Exercises

Lab 5.1 Logical Troubleshooting

Objective: To solve a computer problem with logic

Parts: Computer

Procedure: Complete the following procedure and answer the accompanying questions.

1. In teams of two, one person leaves the room while the other person inserts a problem in the machine and powers it down.
2. The person who left the room powers on the computer with the problem and performs troubleshooting. Use the flowchart shown in Figure 5.5 and answer the questions that follow. Once the problem is solved, swap roles.

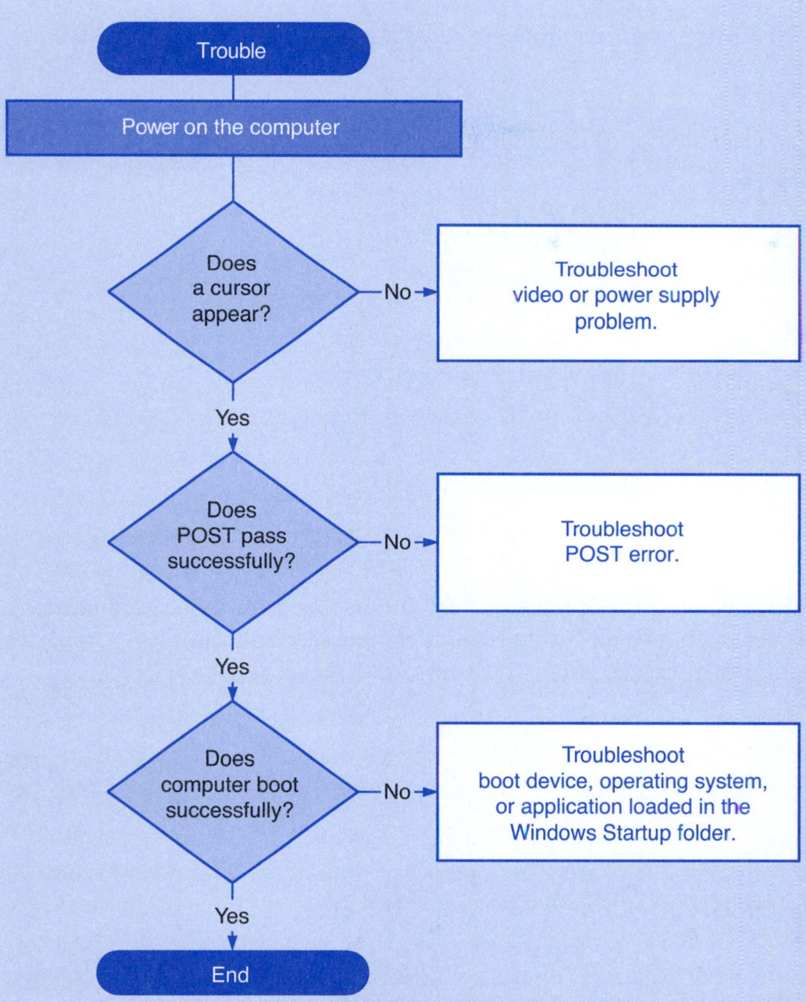

Figure 5.5 Troubleshooting flowchart

Do you hear any audio clues? If yes, list the symptoms.
Do any POST errors appear? If so, list them.
Are there any startup errors? If so, list them.
Are there any application-specific problems? If so, list them.
List any possible techniques to test. Test them one at a time. Document the solution.

Activities

Internet Discovery

Objective: To obtain specific information on the Internet regarding a computer or its associated parts

Parts: Computer with access to the Internet

Questions: Use the Internet to answer the following questions.

1. Locate a website that has a troubleshooting flowchart. Write three things the flowchart provides that you find helpful or confusing. Write the URL where the chart was found.

2. Locate one website that lists at least two BIOS vendors' error codes. Write the URL where this information was found.

3. A customer has a Toshiba Satellite 755D-S7360 laptop. What process does Toshiba recommend for flashing the BIOS?

4. On a Hewlett Packard Pavilion dv2500t notebook computer, this error message appears: "Non-System Disk error or Disk Error." Find three recommended solutions from Hewlett Packard and list them, along with the URL where this information was found.

5. An Apple iPad stops responding to touch after a period of time. What does Apple recommend for this, and at what URL did you find this information?

6. A customer has a Gateway E6610D PC that has a damaged power switch. Find and note the URL that details how to replace the switch.

Soft Skills

Objective: To enhance and fine-tune a future technician's ability to listen, communicate in both written and oral form, and support people who use computers in a professional manner.

Activities:

1. Perform Critical Thinking Skills Activity 1 before completing this activity. The two technicians who solved the problem must perform the following tasks:
   - Document the problem.
   - List everything that could have been the problem.
   - List procedures that were tried in the order performed.
   - Document the final solution.

The classmates who installed/created the problem must write a report detailing the following:

- Positive comments and suggestions for how the technicians communicated verbally
- Positive comments and suggestions for how the technicians communicated nonverbally
- Positive comments and suggestions for how the technicians acted professionally

2. Perform Critical Thinking Skills Activity 1 and Soft Skills Activity 1 before completing this activity. The four people on the team must present their written findings to the class and discuss their problem and solution. Other classmates evaluate the team on its presentation skills.

Critical Thinking Skills

Objective: To analyze and evaluate information as well as apply learned information to new or different situations.

Activities:

1. In teams of four, two people put a problem in the computer while the other two team members are out of the room. Once the two technicians return, one of the two students who installed the problem pretends to be a computer user with the problem. The two technicians act as a team to solve the problem. (See Soft Skills Activity 1 for the subsequent activity.)
2. Write a troubleshooting tip or procedure for any one computer item or step performed in class this term. Exchange your procedure with a classmate and critique each other's work by making comments and suggestions. Once your original paper is returned, rewrite it using suggestions you think are appropriate.
3. Write a plan of action for the following scenarios:
   - A computer powers up and works for about two hours and then shuts down and won't turn back on.
   - A flash drive won't work in a USB hub but works fine as a directly attached device.
   - The computer date and time continually needs to be reset.

4. Write the documentation used to generate an invoice for each of the three scenarios:
   - A computer powers up and works for about two hours and then shuts down and won't turn back on.
   - A flash drive won't work in a USB hub but works fine as a directly attached device.
   - The computer date and time continually needs to be reset.

A+ Certification Exam Tips

✓ Review the troubleshooting steps. Even though these steps are logical, when the steps are placed into written questions, they can become tricky. Try to think of the computer problems you solved during the chapter activities. Now relate those steps to the six troubleshooting steps. This will help you remember when you take the 220-802 exam. The six troubleshooting steps could be applied to specific troubleshooting scenarios.

✓ Review the boot process order and procedures. Knowing this list and the order in which things happen can help you with troubleshooting questions that may appear on the exams.

✓ If you know any technicians, ask them to tell you the problems they solved this week. Another idea is to get them to tell you a problem and you see if you can guess the top things that could cause that problem.

✓ Review the short customer support/soft skills section for the best practices in communication skills. The communication questions can sometimes have answers that are very similar. Use the review questions at the end of the chapter to help practice with those types of questions.

chapter 6

Memory

Chapter Objectives:

In this chapter you will learn:

- Different memory technologies
- How to plan for a memory installation or upgrade
- To install and remove memory chips
- How to optimize memory for Windows platforms
- Best practices for troubleshooting memory problems
- The benefits of teamwork

CompTIA Exam Objectives:

What CompTIA A+ exam objectives are covered in this chapter?

- ✓ 801-1.2 Differentiate between motherboard components, their purposes, and properties.
- ✓ 801-1.3 Compare and contrast RAM types and features.
- ✓ 801-1.5 Install and configure storage devices and use appropriate media.
- ✓ 801-3.1 Install and configure laptop hardware and components.
- ✓ 802-1.1 Compare and contrast the features and requirements of various Microsoft operating systems.
- ✓ 802-1.4 Given a scenario, use appropriate operating system features and tools.
- ✓ 802-1.5 Given a scenario, use Control Panel utilities.
- ✓ 802-3.1 Explain the basic features of mobile operating systems.
- ✓ 802-4.2 Given a scenario, troubleshoot common problems related to motherboards, RAM, CPU, and power with appropriate tools.
- ✓ 802-4.6 Given a scenario, troubleshoot operating system problems with appropriate tools.

Memory Overview

Computer systems need software to operate; without software, a computer is an expensive doorstop. For a computer to operate, the software must reside in computer memory. Upgrading memory is simple, but a technician must understand memory terminology, determine the optimum amount of memory for a system, install the memory, fine-tune it for the best performance, and troubleshoot and solve any memory problems.

The two main types of memory are **RAM** (random-access memory) and ROM (read-only memory), and the difference between them is shown in Figure 6.1.

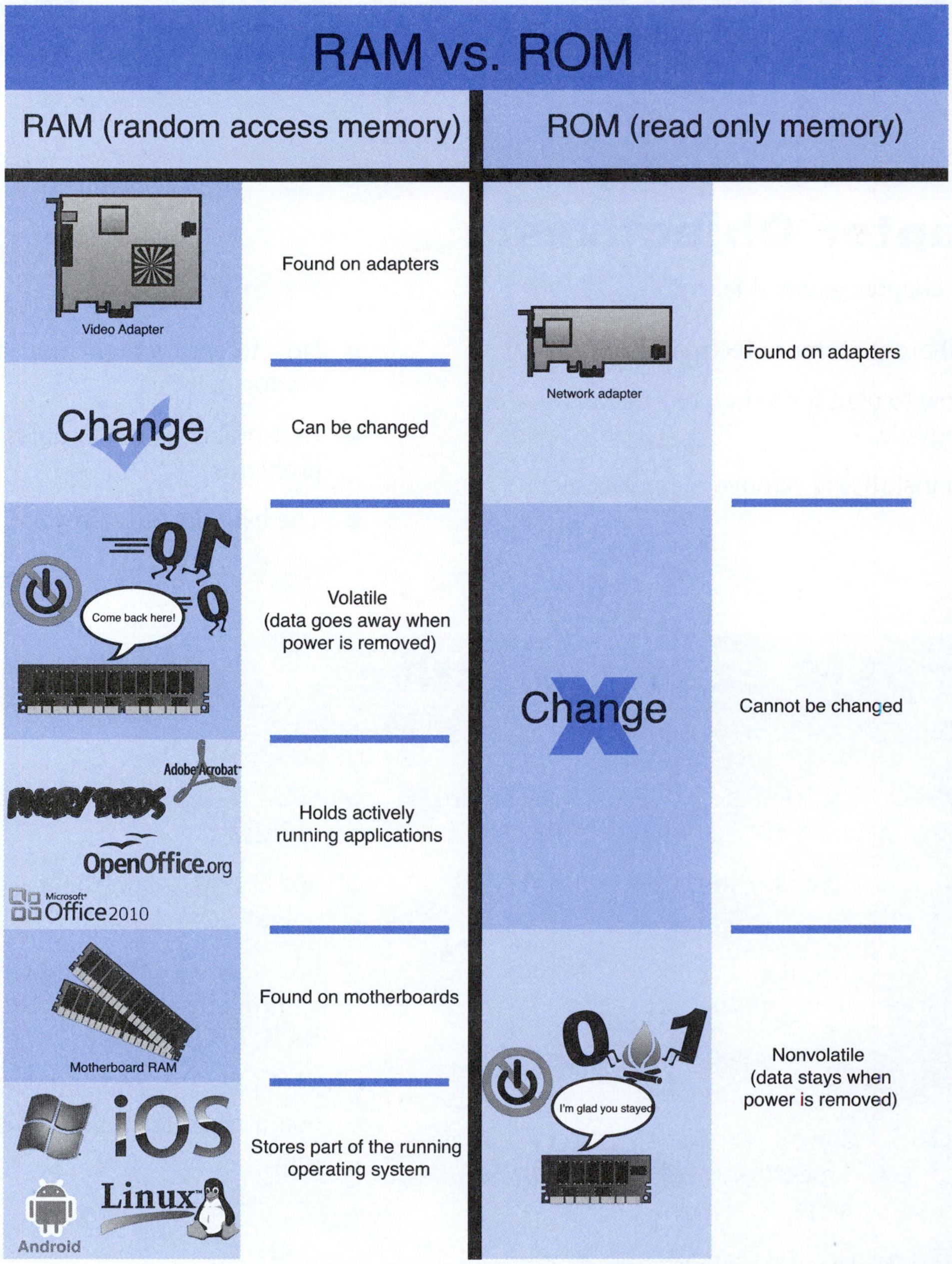

Figure 6.1 RAM versus ROM

RAM is divided into two major types: **DRAM** (dynamic RAM) and **SRAM** (static RAM). DRAM is less expensive but slower than SRAM. With DRAM, the 1s and 0s inside the chip must be refreshed. Over time, the charge, which represents information inside a DRAM chip, leaks out. The information, stored in 1s and 0s, is periodically rewritten to the memory chip through the **refreshing** process. The refreshing is accomplished inside the DRAM while other processing occurs. Refreshing is one reason DRAM chips are slower than SRAM.

Most memory on a motherboard is DRAM, but a small amount of SRAM can be found inside the processor inside the processor housing, and sometimes on the motherboard. SRAM is also known as **cache memory**. Cache memory holds the most frequently used data so the CPU does not return to the slower DRAM chips to obtain the data. For example, on a motherboard with a bus speed of 233MHz, accessing DRAM could take as long as 90 nanoseconds. (A nanosecond [ns] is one-billionth of a second.) Accessing the same information in cache could take as little as 23 nanoseconds.

Tech Tip

The CPU should never have to wait to receive an instruction

Using pipelined burst cache speeds up processing for software applications.

The CPU fetches a software instruction from memory, and then the processor sits idle. In a fast-food restaurant, this is the same as not allowing waiting customers to be served until the first customer has his or her food. Most restaurants serve the next customer while the food is being prepared and open more registers when lots of customers are waiting. With pipelining, the processor is allowed to obtain more software instructions without waiting for the first instruction to be executed. Opening more registers is similar to how manufacturers use processor models with more pipelines. Using cache memory and using pipelining are popular technologies used today.

The data or instruction that the processor needs is usually found in one of three places: cache, DRAM, or the hard drive. Cache gives the fastest access. If the information is not in cache, the processor looks for it in DRAM. If the information is not in DRAM, it is retrieved from the hard drive and placed into DRAM or the cache. Hard drive access is the slowest of the three. In a computer, it takes roughly a million times longer to access information from the hard drive than it does from DRAM or cache.

Tech Tip

Free hard drive space and video memory are often as important as RAM in improving a computer's performance

RAM is only one piece of the puzzle. All of a computer's parts must work together to provide good system performance.

When determining a computer's memory requirements, you must take into consideration the operating system used, applications used, and hardware installed. The Windows XP operating system takes a lot less memory than do Windows 7 and 8. High-end games and desktop publishing take more RAM than word processing.

Memory Physical Packaging

A DIP (dual in-line package) chip has a row of legs running down each side. The oldest motherboards use DIP chips for the DRAM. **SIMMs** (single in-line memory modules) came along next. Two types of SIMMs were used: 30-pin and 72-pin. The memory chip used today is a **DIMM** (dual in-line memory module), which has 168, 184, or 240 pins. Figure 6.2 shows the progression of memory packaging.

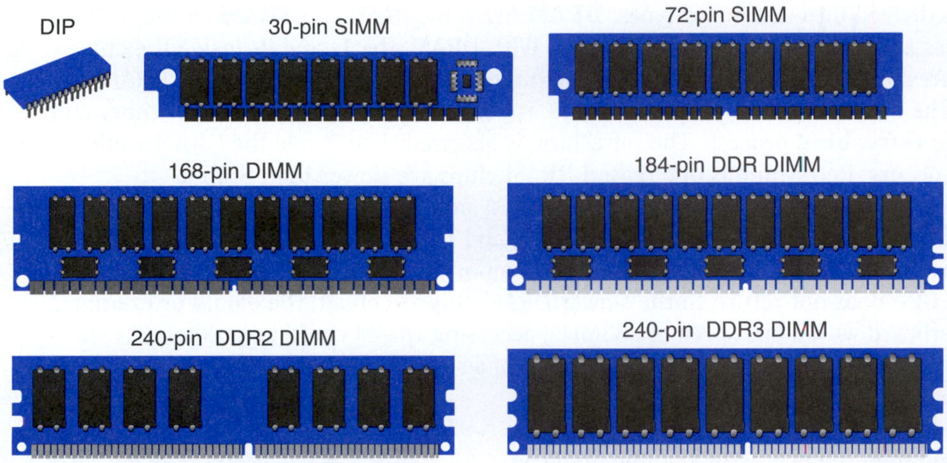

Figure 6.2 Memory chips/modules

Memory chips are also called memory sticks, or a technician might call one memory module a stick of memory or RAM. RIMMs are used in older Intel Pentium 4 computers. Figure 6.3 shows a RIMM. The RIMM has two notches in the center.

> **Tech Tip**
>
> **Use tin or gold memory modules**
>
> Memory module contacts are either tin or gold (although most are gold). If a computer is designed to accept tin memory modules and you install gold ones, over time a chemical reaction between the metals can damage the connector.

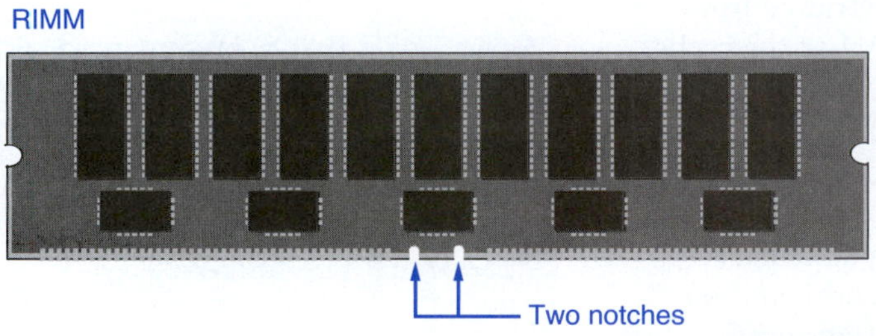

Figure 6.3 184-pin RIMM

Planning the Memory Installation

Now that you know a little about memory types, let us look at the practical side—how to go about planning a memory installation. Some key points to follow:

- Refer to the system or motherboard documentation to see what type of memory is supported.
- Determine what features are supported.
- Determine how much memory is needed.
- Determine how many of each memory module is needed.
- Research prices and purchase memory module(s).

Planning the Memory Installation—Memory Technologies

Technology has provided faster DRAM speeds without increasing the cost too greatly. These DRAM technologies include FPM (fast page mode) RAM, EDO (extended data out) RAM, BEDO (burst EDO) RAM, SDRAM (synchronous DRAM), DDR (double data rate) RAM, and RDRAM (Rambus DRAM). The motherboard must be designed to use one of these technologies, or the faster memory *will not* speed up the computer. Table 6.1 explains some of the memory technologies.

Table 6.1 Memory technologies

Technology	Explanation
FPM (fast page mode)	FPM, EDO, and burst EDO speed up DRAM on sequential accesses to the memory chip. For example, if you have a 50ns DRAM and a 50ns FPM memory module, both types take 50 ns to access the chip the first time. On the second try, the FPM SIMM is accessed in 40ns. Used with SIMMs.
EDO (extended data out)	See explanation for FPM. A 50ns EDO memory module would take 50ns to access the chip, but on the second access, only 25ns are needed. Used with 72-pin SIMMs and 168-pin DIMMs.
BEDO (burst EDO)	See explanation for FPM. A 50ns BEDO memory module would take 50ns to access the chip, but on the second access, only 15ns are needed. Used with SIMMs and 168-pin DIMMs.
SDRAM (synchronous DRAM)	Performs very fast burst memory access similar to BEDO. New memory addresses are placed on the address bus before the prior memory address retrieval and execution is complete. SDRAM synchronizes its operation with the CPU clock signal to speed up memory access. Used with DIMMs.
DDR (double data rate)	Sometimes called DDR SDRAM or DDR RAM and developed from SDRAM technology. DDR memory can send twice as much data as PC133 SDRAM because with DDR, data is transmitted on both sides of the clock signal (rising and falling edges instead of just rising edge).
DDR2	Sometimes called DDR2 RAM. DDR2 uses 240-pin DIMMs and is not compatible with DDR.
DDR3	The latest in DDR technology that is an upgrade from DDR2 (8 bit prefetch buffer compared to 4 bits with DDR2). The technology better supports multi-core processor-based systems and more efficient power utilization.
DDR3L	A DDR3 module that runs at a lower voltage (1.35V) than the 1.5V or higher DDR/DDR2/DDR3 modules. Less voltages means less heat and less power consumed.
RDRAM (Rambus DRAM)	Developed by Rambus, Inc., and packaged in 184-pin RIMMs (which is a trademark of Rambus, Inc.). Must be installed in pairs with dual- and quad-channel motherboards. When RIMMs are used, all memory slots must be filled, even if a slot is not needed because the memory banks are tied together. Put a C-RIMM (continuity RIMM), which is a blank module, in any empty (unfilled) slot.

Whether a motherboard supports faster memory chips is determined by the chipset, which performs most functions in conjunction with the processor. A chipset is one to five electronic chips on the motherboard. The chipset contains the circuitry to control the local bus, memory, DMA, interrupts, and cache memory. The motherboard manufacturer determines which chipset to use.

Tech Tip

Use the right type of memory chips

The chipset and motherboard design are very specific about what type, speed, and features the memory chips can have. Refer to the motherboard documentation.

Most people cannot tell the difference between DDR, DDR2, and DDR3 memory modules. Even though DDR uses 184 pins and DDR2/3 use 240 pins, they are the same physical size. DDR3 modules also have 240 pins but will not fit in a DDR2 slot. Figure 6.4 shows DDR2 and DDR3 DIMMs, and Table 6.2 lists many of the DIMM models.

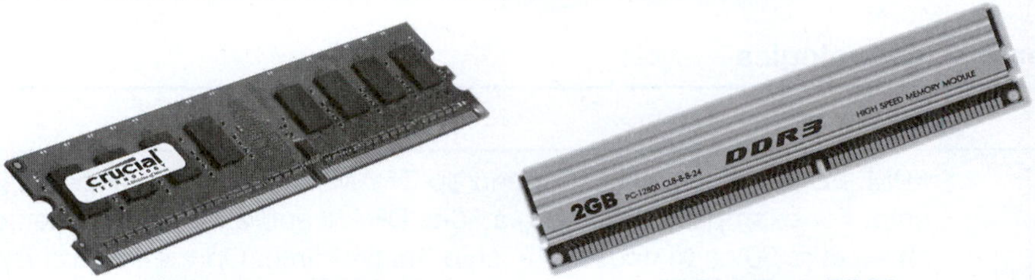

DDR2 240-pin DIMM

DDR3 240-pin DIMM

Figure 6.4 DDR2 and DDR3 DIMMs

Table 6.2 DIMMs

Memory type	Other name	Clock speed	Data rate (transfers per second)
PC2-4200	DDR2-533	266MHz	533M
PC2-5300	DDR2-667	333MHz	667M
PC2-6400	DDR2-800	400MHz	800M
PC2-8000	DDR2-1000	500MHz	1G
PC2-8500	DDR2-1066	533MHz	1.07G
PC2-9200	DDR2-1150	575MHz	1.15G
PC2-9600	DDR2-1200	600MHz	1.2G
PC3-6400	DDR3-800	400MHz	800M
PC3-8500	DDR3-1066	533MHz	1.06G
PC3-10600	DDR3-1333	666MHz	1.33G
PC3-12800	DDR3-1600	800MHz	1.6G
PC3-16000	DDR3-2000	1000MHz	2G
PC3-17000	DDR3-2133	1066MHz	2.13G

Because a DIMM can be shown with either the PC*x*- or DDR*x*- designation, which type you are buying can be confusing. A brief explanation might help. DDR2-800 is a type of DDR2 memory that can run on a 400Hz front side bus (the number after DDR2 divided in half). Another way of showing the same chip would be to use the designation PC2-6400, which is the theoretical bandwidth of the memory chip in MBps.

Mobile Device Memory

Laptop, netbook, and tablet computers are major parts of today's business environment. The memory chips used with laptops are different from the ones used in desktop or tower computers. Portables that use DIMMs use special types such as a **SO-DIMM** (small-outline DIMM). Older laptops used a 144- or 172-pin microDIMM. The portable computers that used RIMMs used SO-RIMMs (small-outline RIMMs). SO-DIMMs are the most popular, and they come in a 72-pin version for 32-bit transfers and 144-, 200-, or 204-pin versions for 64-bit transfers. Figure 6.5 shows the difference between DDR, DDR2, and DDR3 SO-DIMMs.

Even though a DDR SO-DIMM appears to have an identical notch as the DDR2 SO-DIMM, they are different by just a fraction and cannot fit in each other's slots. Figure 6.6 shows a photo of a SO-DIMM.

Many netbooks cannot be upgraded. Many laptops have only one memory slot, so when you upgrade, you must replace the module that is installed. Laptops can also be upgraded with PC Cards or ExpressCards, but this type of upgrade is not as fast as the memory installed on the motherboard. Some smartphones can be upgraded with Flash memory cards. Tablets can sometimes have additional flash memory cards as well. Refer to Figure 1.12 to see these.

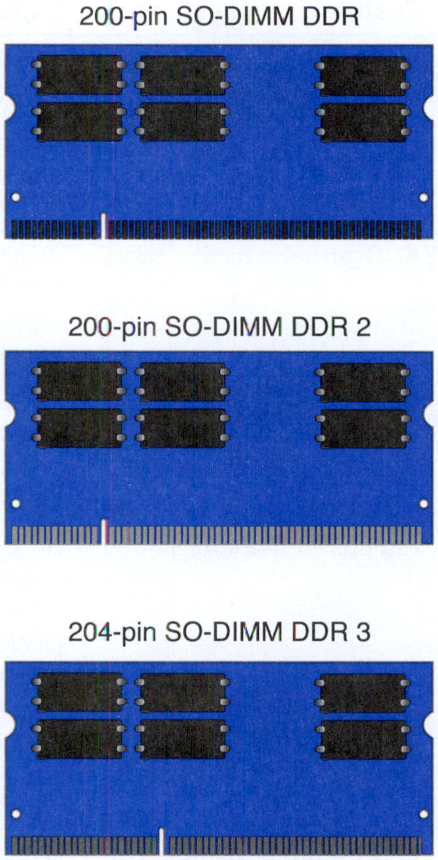

Figure 6.5 SO-DIMMs

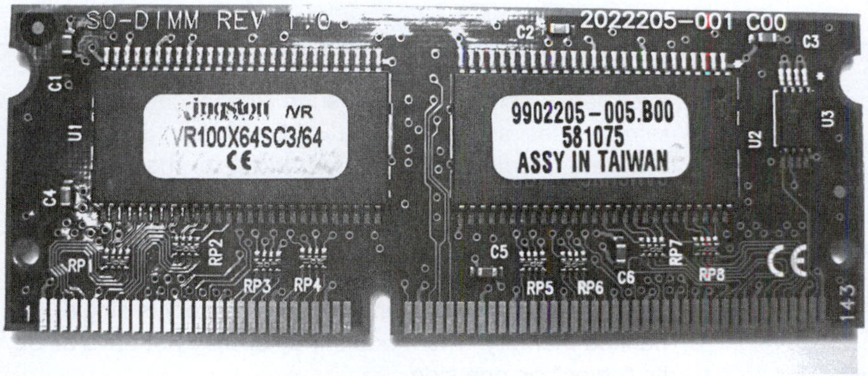

Figure 6.6 Photo of a SO-DIMM

Planning the Memory Installation—Memory Features

In addition to determining what type of memory chips are going to be used, you must determine what features the memory chip might have. The computer system or motherboard documentation is going to delineate what features are supported. Table 6.3 helps characterize memory features.

Table 6.3 Memory features

Feature	Explanation
parity	A method for checking the accuracy of data going into or out of memory chips.
non-parity	Chips that do not use any error checking. Most memory modules today are non-parity because the memory controller circuitry provides error correction.
ECC (error correcting code)	An alternative to parity checking that uses a mathematical algorithm to verify data accuracy. ECC can detect up to four-bit memory errors and correct one-bit memory errors. ECC is used in higher-end computers and network servers.
unbuffered memory	The opposite of registered memory, used in low- to medium-powered computers. Unbuffered memory is faster than registered or fully buffered memory.
registered memory	Registered memory modules have extra chips (registers) near the bottom of the chip that, unlike unbuffered DDR or DDR2 modules, delay all data transfers by one clock tick to ensure accuracy. They are used in servers and high-end computers and tend to be taller than unbuffered memory modules. If you install a registered memory module into a system that allows both registered and unbuffered memory, all installed memory must be registered modules.
fully buffered memory	A technology used in network servers and Apple computers. Requires a special memory controller. Fully buffered memory buffers the data pins from the channel and uses point-to-point serial signaling connections similar to PCIe. These chips are sometimes advertised as FBDIMMs.
SPD (serial presence detect)	Memory modules that have an extra EEPROM that holds information about the DIMM such as capacity, voltage, refresh rates, and so on. The BIOS can read and use this data to adjust motherboard timing for the best performance.
single-sided memory	A memory module that has one "bank" of memory and 64 bits are transferred out of the memory module to the CPU. A better term for single-sided memory is single-banked memory. The module may or may not have all of its "chips" on one side.
double-sided memory	A single memory module developed in a special way that it actually contains two memory modules in one container (two banks). If the motherboard slot has been designed to accept this type of memory module, data is still sent to the CPU 64 bits at a time. This is a way for having more banks of memory on the motherboard without requiring more memory slots. These modules normally have memory chips on both sides, but all modules with chips on both side are not double-sided memory.

Tech Tip

How parity works

If a system uses even parity and the data bits 10000001 go into memory, the ninth bit, or parity bit, is a 0 because an even number of bits (2) are 1s. The parity changes to a 1 only when the number of bits in the data is an odd number of 1s. If the system uses even parity and the data bits 10000011 go into memory, the parity bit is a 1. There are only three 1s in the data bits. The parity bit adjusts the 1s to an even number. When checking data for accuracy, the parity method detects if one bit is incorrect. However, if 2 bits are in error, parity does not catch the error.

Keep in mind that some motherboards may support both non-parity and ECC (error correcting code) or may require a certain feature such as SPD (serial presence detect). It is important that you research this *before* you look to purchase memory.

A memory module may use more than one of the categories listed in the two previous tables. For example, a DIMM could be a DDR3 module, be registered, and support ECC for error detection. Most registered memory also uses the ECC technology. Memory modules can support either ECC or non-ECC as well as be registered or unbuffered as the type of technology.

Memory technology is moving quite quickly today. Chipsets also change constantly. Technicians are continually challenged to keep up with the features and abilities of the technology so that they can make recommendations to their customers. Trade magazines and the Internet are excellent resources for updates. Never forget to check the motherboard's documentation when dealing with memory. Information is a technician's best friend.

Planning for Memory—The Amount of Memory to Install

When you want to improve the performance of a computer, adding memory is one of the easiest upgrades. The amount of memory you need depends on what operating system you are using, what applications you are using, how many applications you want to have open at the same time, the type of computer you are using, and the maximum amount allowed by your motherboard. But first, we should look into memory capacities.

Think of a memory chip like a giant spreadsheet where each cell holds one bit. If you had 64 million cells, then the chip would hold 64 million bits. If each cell held 8 bits, then the chip would hold 64 million bytes, or 64MB. Capacities for DIMMs are 256MB, 512MB, 1GB, 2GB, 4GB, 8GB, 16GB, and 32GB (and probably more before this book is revised).

Memory chips are sometimes shown with varying numbers. For example, a chip may be shown as 256M×64 and actually be a GB memory module. The 256M×64 is describing the memory chip in more detail—there are 256 million locations with 64 bits in each location. 256 million times 64 is the chips capacity in mega*bits*. Divide by 8 and you get the chips capacity in *megabytes*. When parity or ECC is used with DIMMs, you see the second number as *72*; for example, 256M×72 is still GB. Those extra 8 bits are used for error checking. Table 6.4 shows sample memory configurations. The module description might be like the ones you would see in memory advertisements.

Table 6.4 Memory capacities

Capacity in megabytes	Module description	Module locations (in millions)	Bits in each location	Capacity in megabits
256	32M×64	32	64	2,048
512	64M×64	64	64	4,096
1,024 (or 1GB)	128M×64	128	64	8,192
2,048 (or 2GB)	256M×64	256	64	16,384

Capacity in megabytes	Module description	Module locations (in millions)	Bits in each location	Capacity in megabits
2,048 (or 2GB)	256M×72	256	64 (8 parity/ ECC)	16,384
4,096 (or 4GB)	512M×64	512	64	32,768
4,096 (or 4GB)	512M×72	512	64 (8 parity/ ECC)	32,768
8,192 (or 8GB)	1024M×64	1024	64	65,536

The operating system you use determines to a great extent the starting point for the amount of memory to have. Generally, the older or less powerful your operating system is, the smaller amount of RAM you need. Table 6.5 is the *starting point* for calculating memory requirements. Remember that as you want to run more applications simultaneously and the higher the application function (such as gaming or photo/video/sound manipulation), the more memory you will need. Also note that the memory recommendations shown in Table 6.5 are not the minimum requirements listed by the operating system creators. Notice that Apple computers (OS X) have similar memory recommendations to PCs.

When upgrading memory, you need to know a couple of key pieces of information.

- How much memory you are starting with?
- How many motherboard RAM slots are currently being used and whether you have any slots free?
- What is the maximum amount of memory that your motherboard supports?

Table 6.5 Minimum operating system starting memory recommendations

Operating system	Minimum amount of RAM to start calculations
Windows XP Professional	512MB
Windows Vista/Windows 7	1GB
Windows 8	2GB
Mac OS X Mountain Lion	2GB
Linux	Depends on shell (some as little as 64MB)

Tech Tip

Windows may have memory limitations

Even if your motherboard allows more memory, your operating system has limitations. Upgrade your operating system if this is the case. Table 6.6 shows the Windows memory limits.

Table 6.6 Windows XP/Vista/7 memory limits

Operating system	32-bit version limit	64-bit version limit
XP Starter edition	512MB	N/A
XP (all other editions)	4GB	128GB
Vista/7 Starter edition	1GB (Vista)/2GB (7)	N/A

Operating system	32-bit version limit	64-bit version limit
Vista/7 Home Basic	4GB	8GB
Vista/7 Home Premium	4GB	16GB
Vista/7 Business/Professional/ Enterprise/Ultimate	4GB	128GB (Vista)/192GB (7)

To determine how much memory you have, access the *System Information* window (right-click *My Computer* or *Computer* > *Properties*) or from a command prompt type `MSINFO32` and press [Enter]. Scroll down to see the memory information. Figure 6.7 shows how a computer system currently has 8GB of RAM installed (8.00 GB Total Physical Memory).

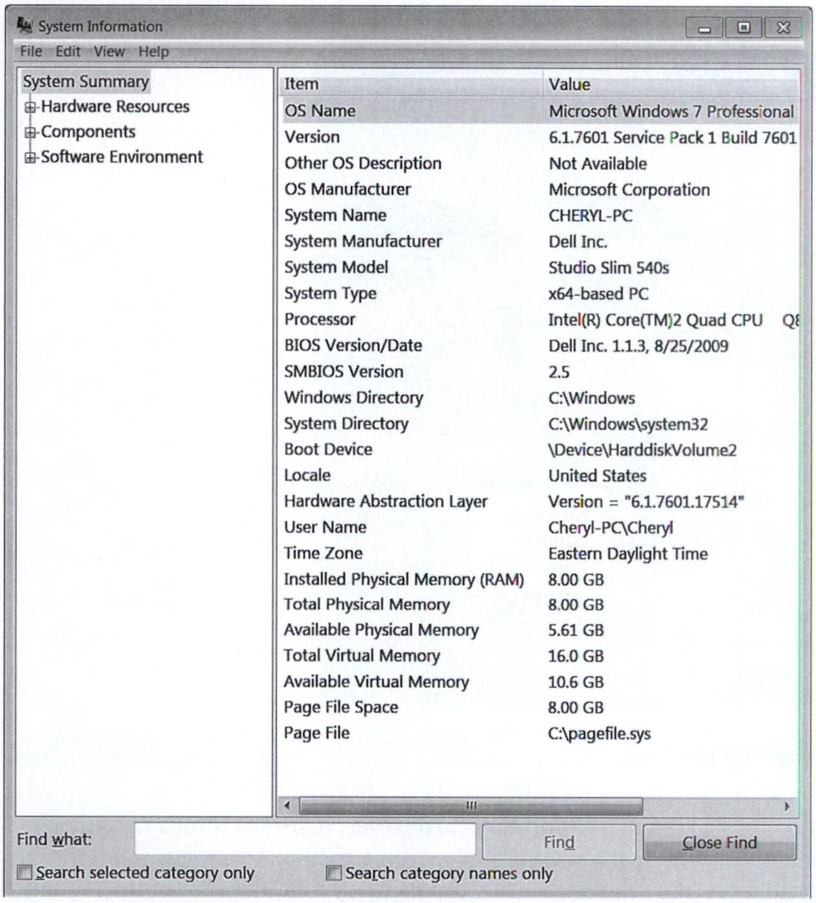

Figure 6.7 **System Information window**

To determine how many slots you are currently using and whether you have any free, you need to either (1) access the BIOS to see if the BIOS shows this information or (2) remove the computer cover and look on the motherboard to see which memory slots have installed modules and if there are any free slots. Some memory sites have a software program that determines the type of memory you are using and makes recommendations. However, because you want to be a proficient technician, you can determine this for yourself.

Tech Tip

Every motherboard has a maximum

Each motherboard supports a maximum amount of memory. You must check the computer or motherboard documentation to see how much this is. There is not a workaround for this limitation. If you want more memory than the motherboard allows, you must upgrade to a newer motherboard.

Planning for Memory—How Many of Each Memory Type?

A motherboard has a certain number of memory slots determined by the motherboard manufacturer. What type of memory module inserts into the slot and the features that the memory module can have are all determined by the motherboard manufacturer.

Most motherboards today support dual-channel memory. **Dual-channel** means that the motherboard memory controller chip handles processing of memory requests more efficiently by handling two memory paths simultaneously. For example, say that a motherboard has four memory slots. Traditionally, the memory controller chip, commonly called the MCH or memory controller hub, had one channel through which all data from the four slots traveled. With dual-channeling, the four slots are divided into two channels with each channel having two slots each. Figure 6.8 shows this concept.

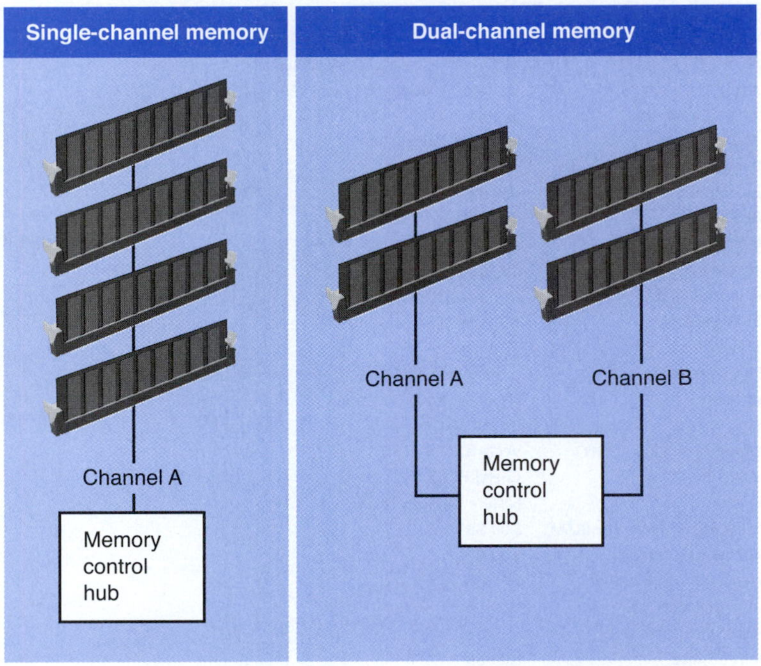

Figure 6.8 Dual-channel memory

Dual-channeling increases a system's performance. However, it speeds things up only if the memory modules match exactly—same memory type, same memory features, same speed, and same capacity. Note that on some motherboards, the memory modules on Channel A and Channel B do not have to be the same capacities, but the total capacity of the memory module in Channel A should match the total capacity of the memory modules installed in Channel B. Some motherboards require this. Figure 6.9 illustrates this concept.

Tech Tip

Dual-channel should use exact memory module pairs

Channel A and Channel B (sometimes labeled Channel 0 and Channel 1) should have matching memory modules. Buy a kit to ensure that the two modules are exactly the same.

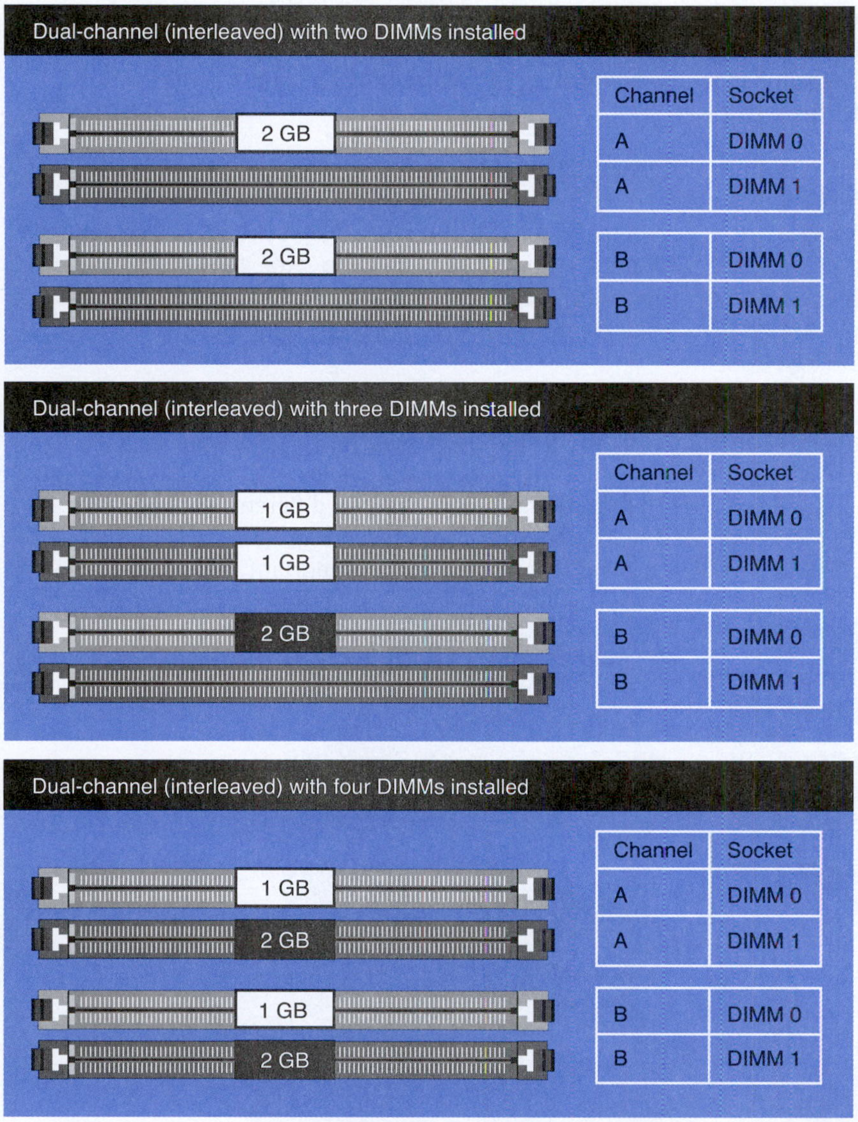

Figure 6.9 **The total capacity of the memory module installed in Channel A should match the total capacity in Channel B**

Notice in Figure 6.9 that in the first example, two identical memory modules are inserted. One memory module is in Channel A, and the other in Channel B. Motherboard manufacturers frequently require that the memory modules match in all respects—manufacturer, timing, and capacity—in order to support dual-channeling.

In the next example in Figure 6.9, three DIMMs are used. Some manufacturers support dual-channeling with three DIMMS, but you should always check the motherboard or system documentation to ensure that this is the case. Another example that is not shown in the figure is where an uneven amount of memory is installed in Channel A than in Channel B—for example, Channel A has 2GB, and Channel B has a 1GB memory module. Some motherboards can dual-channel for the first 1GB. Only if the motherboard supports this can dual-channeling be achieved this way.

In the last example shown in Figure 6.9, all four DIMMs are installed. Notice how the Channel A total capacity matches the Channel B total capacity (3GB in both channels, for a total of 6GB). When dual-channeling, buy memory modules in pairs from a single source. Memory vendors sell them this way.

Tech Tip

Beware of RAM over 4GB

Do not install over 4GB on a computer with a 32-bit operating system such as 32-bit Windows. The operating system will not be able to see anything over 4GB. As a matter of fact, even when a system has 4GB installed, the 32-bit operating system shows the installed amount as slightly less than 4GB because some of that memory space is used for devices attached to the PCI/PCIe bus.

To plan for the correct amount of memory, you must refer to the motherboard documentation, and each motherboard is different. An example helps with this concept. Figure 6.10 shows a motherboard layout with four memory slots that has different labeling than shown in Figure 6.9. Remember that motherboard manufacturers can label their motherboards any way they want. This is part of why the documentation is so important.

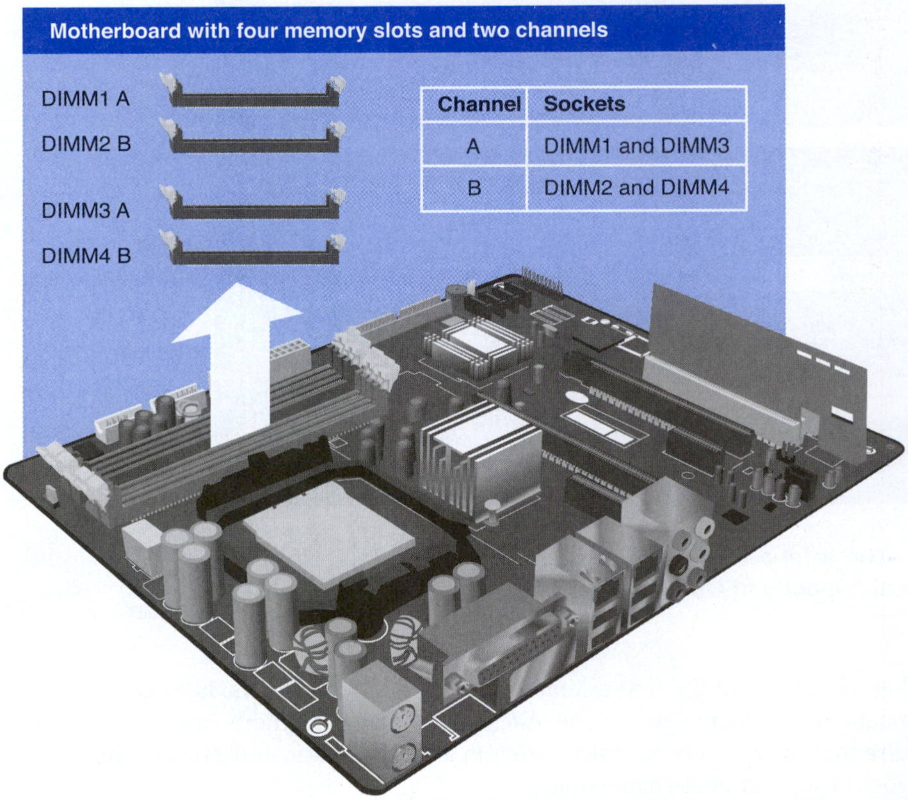

Figure 6.10 Motherboard with four memory slots and two channels

The motherboard in Figure 6.10 allows 512MB, 1GB, and 2GB unbuffered non-ECC DDR2-533 240-pin DIMMs, for a maximum of 8GB. Pretend the customer wants 2GB of RAM. What could you do? How many memory modules do you buy, and what capacities? Table 6.7 shows the possible solutions. The best solution is the second one because it has the largest-capacity chips taking advantage of dual-channeling, with slots left over for more upgrading.

Table 6.7 Possible solutions

Solution	Number and size of memory module(s) needed
1	Four 512MB DIMMs installed in DIMM1, DIMM2, DIMM3, and DIMM4 slots (dual-channeling)
2	Two 1GB DIMMs installed in DIMM1 and DIMM2 slots (dual-channeling)
3	Two 1GB DIMMs installed in DIMM1 and DIMM3 slots
4	One 2GB DIMM installed in DIMM1

Some newer motherboards and server motherboards support **triple-channel** memory, where three memory modules work together, or **quadruple-channel** memory, where four memory modules are accessed simultaneously. Figure 6.11 shows a motherboard that has six memory expansion slots and supports triple-channeling. Labs at the end of this chapter help you with these concepts.

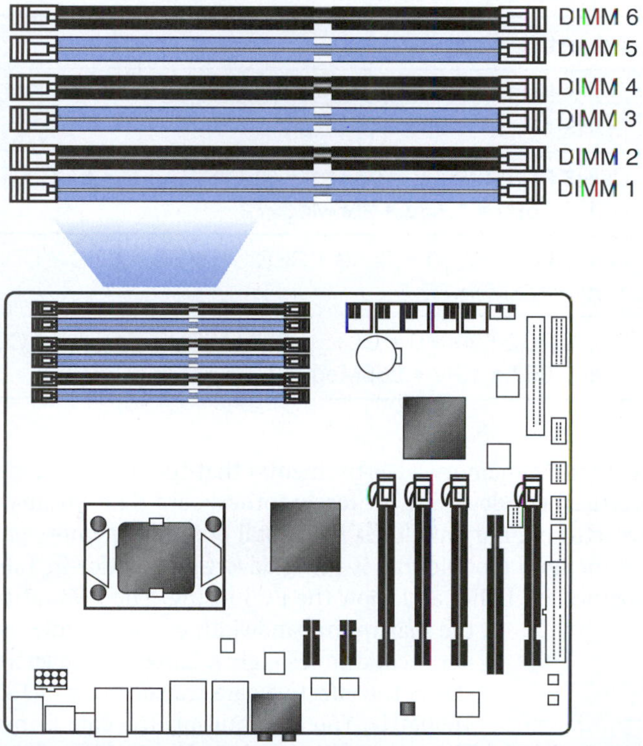

Dual-channel Configuration	DIMM 1	DIMM 2	DIMM 3	DIMM 4	DIMM 5	DIMM 6
Two modules	X		X			
Four modules	X	X	X	X		

Triple-channel Configuration	DIMM 1	DIMM 2	DIMM 3	DIMM 4	DIMM 5	DIMM 6
Three modules	X		X		X	
Six modules	X	X	X	X	X	X

Figure 6.11 Motherboard with six memory slots and three channels

Planning for Memory—Researching and Buying Memory

The researching and buying step of planning for a memory installation/upgrade is the step most likely to make your head spin. Different websites list memory differently. Some give you too much information and some too little. A few, such as Kingston Technology (http://www.kingston.com) and Crucial (http://www.crucial.com), specialize in memory and make it as painless as possible. Nevertheless, as a technician, you should be familiar with all aspects of memory and memory advertisements.

A confusing aspect of buying memory is memory speed. Memory speed can be represented as ns (nanoseconds), MHz, or the DDR PC rating. **Access time** describes how fast information goes into a memory chip or is removed from the chip and is measured in nanoseconds (ns). As for MHz or PC ratings, the higher the number is the faster the speed.

To understand memory, it is best to look at some examples. Table 6.8 shows sample memory advertisements.

Table 6.8 Sample DIMM advertisements

Memory module	Advertisement
2GB	DDR3 PC3-10600 • CL=9 • UNBUFFERED • NON-ECC • DDR3-1333 • 1.35V • 256Megx64
2GB	DDR3 PC3-12800E • CL=11 • REGISTERED • ECC • DDR3-1600 • 1.35V • 256Megx72
2GB kit (1GBx2)	DDR3 PC3-10600 • CL=9 • REGISTERED • ECC • DDR3-1333 • 1.5V • 128Megx72
2GB	DDR2 PC2-5300FB • CL=5 • FULLY BUFFERED • ECC • DDR2-667 • 1.8V • 256Megx72

Notice in Table 6.8 (as in most memory advertisements) that the memory capacity is shown first. The third advertisement down is a kit for a motherboard that has dual-channeling capabilities. It includes two 1GB memory modules, for a total of a 2GB memory gain. Also pay attention to the type of memory module that is being advertised. Notice in Table 6.8 that the first three memory modules are DDR3 and show the PC3 rating. The PC3 rating describes the maximum bandwidth of the module (transfers per second times eight). Later, the advertisement also shows the effective data transfer rate of 1333MHz or 1600MHz. You can multiply the data transfer rate by eight to see the bandwidth, which is sometimes the rounded number.

Tech Tip

Nanoseconds and the race track

The lower the number of nanoseconds, the faster the access time of the memory chips. Think of access time like a track race—the person with the lowest time wins the race and is considered to be the fastest. Chips with lower access times (lower amount of nanoseconds or CL rating) are faster than those with higher access times (larger numbers).

For example, look at the first module, which is a DDR3 1333MHz module. 1333 times eight equals 10664. You will see the PC3 rating as 10600. Some vendors add an E to the PC3 number to show an ECC module or a F or FB to the PC3 number to show that the module has the fully buffered feature.

Another listing in the memory advertisement shown in Table 6.8 is the **CL rating**. CL (column address strobe [CAS] latency), is the amount of time (clock cycles) that passes before the processor moves on to the next memory address. RAM is made up of cells where data is held. A cell is the intersection of a row and a column. Think of it as a spreadsheet application. The CAS signal picks which memory column to select, and a signal called RAS (row address strobe) picks which row to select. The intersection of the two is where the data is stored.

Motherboard manufacturers sometimes list a minimum CL or CAS latency value for memory modules. Motherboard documentation, memory magazine advertisements, and online memory retailers list the CL rating as a series of numbers, such as 3-1-1-1. The first number is the CL rating—a CL3, in this example. The 3-1-1-1 is more detailed in that for a 32-bit transfer, it takes three clock cycles to send the first byte (8 bits), but the next 3 bytes are sent using one clock cycle each. In other words, it takes six clock cycles to transfer the 32 bits. Note that DDR3 CL ratings are higher, such as 9-9-9-24 or 11-11-11-28.

Also notice in Table 6.8 that memory features are listed—fully buffered, unbuffered, and registered. Be sure that the type of memory for which you planned is the type you are researching to buy. The voltage level for the memory module is shown (these are standard values), as is the capacity. With the capacity, if you see the number 64 at the end, the module does not use parity. If you see 72, the memory module uses either parity or ECC. The majority of the time, the 72 is for an ECC memory module.

Tech Tip

Buy the fastest type of memory a motherboard allows

Buying memory that is faster than the motherboard allows does no good. This is like taking a race car on a one lane unpaved road: The car has the ability to go faster, but it is not feasible with the type of road being used. Sometimes you must buy faster memory because the older memory is not sold. This is all right, as long as it is the correct type, such as DDR2 or DDR3.

Tech Tip

The higher the CL rating, the slower the memory

A rating of CL9 waits nine clock cycles before moving to the next memory address. A rating of CL8 waits less time, or eight clock cycles before moving to the next memory address.

Laptop and netbook memory advertisements are very similar to desktop memory advertisements, as shown in Table 6.9.

Table 6.9 Sample SO-DIMM advertisements

Memory	Advertisement
2GB	204-pin SO-DIMM DDR3 1333 Unbuffered 1.35V CAS Latency 9
4GB	204-pin SO-DIMM DDR3 1333 Unbuffered 1.5V CAS Latency 10
8GB kit (2×4GB)	204-pin SO-DIMM DDR3 1600 Unbuffered 1.5V CAS Latency 9

Notice in Table 6.9 that the 2GB memory module runs at 1.35V and the others run at 1.5V. Some motherboards support **dual-voltage memory**, which means the motherboard supports the memory module that runs at the lower 1.35V level. 1.35V memory modules use less power and generate less heat. Note that all memory modules must be 1.35V modules to operate at 1.35 volts.

Tech Tip

Usually, you can mix CL memory modules

Most systems allow mixing of CL modules; for example, a motherboard could have a memory module rated for CL8 and a different memory module rated for CL9. However, when mixing memory modules, the system will run at the slower memory speed (CL9), which has more clock cycles to wait.

Installing Memory Overview

The following is the best method to determine which memory chips to install in each bank:

1. Determine which chip capacities can be used for the system. Look in the documentation included with the motherboard or the computer for this information.
2. Determine how much memory is needed. Ask users which operating system is installed and which applications they are using. Refer to documentation for each application to determine the amount of RAM recommended. Plan for growth.
3. Determine the capacity of the chips that go in each bank by drawing a diagram of the system, planning the memory population on paper, and referring to the documentation of the system or motherboard.

Depending on the type of motherboard, the number of banks available on the motherboard, whether the computer memory is being upgraded, and whether the memory is a new installation, some memory chips may need to be removed to put higher-capacity chips into the bank. Look at what is already installed in the system, refer to the documentation, and remove any existing modules, as necessary, to upgrade the memory.

Tech Tip

Memory safety reminder

Before installing a memory module, power off the computer, disconnect the power cord from the back of the computer, and use proper antistatic procedures. Memory modules are especially susceptible to ESD. If ESD damages a memory module, a problem may not appear immediately and could be intermittent and hard to diagnose.

Removing/Installing Memory

When removing a DIMM or a RIMM and using proper ESD-prevention techniques, push down on the DIMM retaining tabs that clasp over the DIMM. Be careful not to overextend the tabs when pushing on them. If a plastic tab breaks, the only solution is to replace the motherboard. The DIMM/RIMM lifts slightly out of the socket. Always ensure you are grounded to prevent ESD by using an antistatic wrist strap or maintaining contact with metal with a bare part of your arm. Lift the module out of the socket once it is released. Figure 6.12 shows how to remove a DIMM/RIMM.

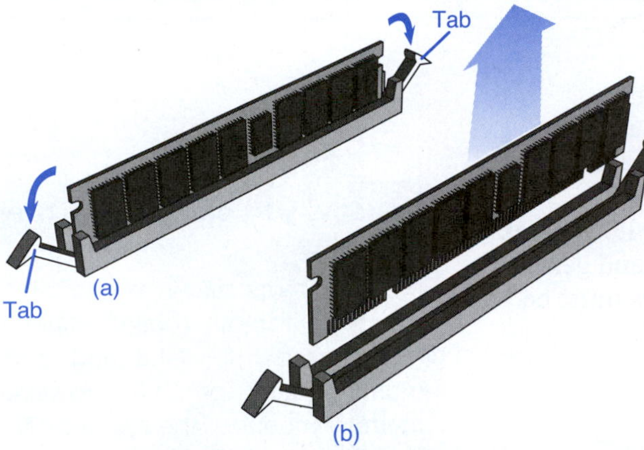

Figure 6.12 DIMM/RIMM removal

A DIMM/RIMM has one or more notches on the bottom where the gold or tin contacts are located. The DIMM inserts into the memory socket only one way. The DIMM memory socket has two tabs that align with the DIMM notches. Look at the DIMM and notice where the DIMM notches are located. Look at the DIMM socket and notice where the tabs in the socket are located. The DIMM will not insert into the memory socket unless it is oriented properly.

A DIMM/RIMM is inserted straight down into the socket, not at a tilt like the SIMM or a SO-DIMM. Make sure the side tabs are pulled out before you insert the DIMM and close the tabs over the DIMM once it is firmly inserted into the socket. If the DIMM/RIMM does not go into the slot easily, do not force it and check the notch or notches for correct alignment. However, once the DIMM is aligned correctly into the slot, push the DIMM firmly into the slot and the tabs should naturally close over the DIMM or on the sides of the DIMM. Figure 6.13 illustrates how to insert a DIMM or a RIMM. Figure 6.14 shows a close-up of how the tab needs to fit securely in the memory module notch.

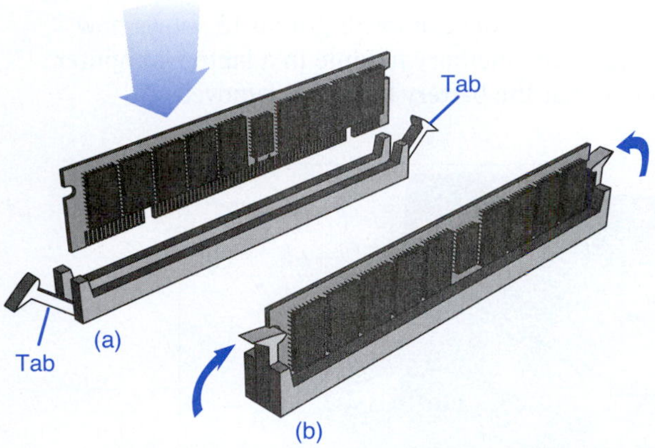

Figure 6.13 DIMM/RIMM installation

Figure 6.14 Secure DIMM tab

Today's motherboards automatically recognize new memory; however, some advanced BIOS options exist for tweaking memory performance. With some computers, the Setup program can be used to select parity, non-parity, or ECC options. Always refer to the motherboard or the computer system documentation.

Many laptops and netbooks have only one memory slot, so when you upgrade, you must remove the module that is installed. Always refer to the manufacturer's documentation when doing this. Always turn off the laptop and remove the battery pack before upgrading memory. When installing memory into a mobile device, refer to the documentation to see if a retaining screw on the bottom of the unit must be removed or if the keyboard must be removed in order to access the memory slots. Be sure the laptop memory notch fits into the key in the memory slot. Laptop memory is normally installed at a 45-degree angle into the slot. Press down on the module until it locks into the side clips. The trick to installing memory is to push firmly into the slot and then into the side clamps. Figure 6.15 shows how to access the memory module in a laptop computer. Notice that the battery has been removed.

Tech Tip

POST error codes are normal after a memory installation/upgrade

Some computers show a POST error message or automatically go into the Setup program. This is normal. The important thing to notice during POST is that the memory shown in BIOS should equal the amount of memory installed.

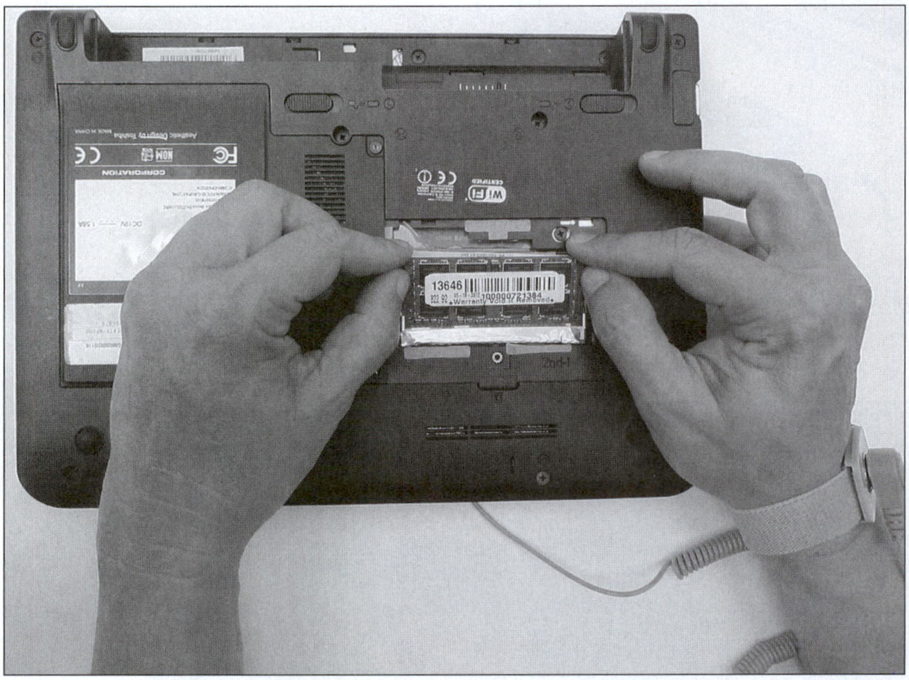

Figure 6.15 Accessing a laptop memory module

Adding More Cache/RAM

Most computers today have cache built into the processor. The motherboard manufacturer determines whether any cache can be installed. Check the documentation included with the motherboard or computer to determine the amount of cache (SRAM).

Adding more RAM can make a noticeable difference in computer performance (up to a point, of course). When a computer user is sitting in front of a computer waiting for a document to appear or waiting to go to a different location within a document, it might be time to install more RAM. If you have several opened applications on the taskbar, click one of them, and have to wait several seconds before it appears, it might be a good idea to upgrade your RAM.

Windows Disk Caching

Virtual memory is a method of using hard disk space as if it were RAM. Virtual memory allows the operating system to run larger applications and manage multiple applications that are loaded simultaneously. The amount of hard disk space used is dynamic—it increases or decreases as needed. If the system begins to page frequently and is constantly swapping data from RAM to the hard drive, the cache size automatically shrinks.

Tech Tip

Hard drive swap file tips

If multiple hard drives are available, a technician might want to move the swap file to a different drive. Always put the swap file on the fastest hard drive unless that hard drive lacks space. It is best to keep the swap file on a hard drive that does not contain the operating system. You can configure the computer to place the swap file on multiple hard drives. The amount of virtual memory is dynamically created by the operating system and does not normally need to be set manually. If manually set, the minimum amount should be equal to the amount of RAM installed.

A **swap file** is a block of hard drive space that applications use like RAM. Other names for the swap file include page file and paging file. Look back to Figure 6.7 and see in the System Information screen the data on Total Virtual Memory, Available Virtual Memory, and Page File Space. For optimum performance in any Windows operating system, set aside as much free hard disk space as possible to allow ample room for virtual memory and caching. Keep your hard drive cleaned of temporary files and outdated files/applications.

To adjust the virtual memory size in Windows XP, do the following:

1. Open the *System* Control Panel (select *Performance* and *Maintenance* if using Category view).
2. Click on the *Advanced* tab and locate the *Settings* button located in the Performance section.
3. Click on the *Advanced* tab and look for the *Change* button in the Virtual Memory section.
4. Change the size parameters and click on the *OK* button twice.

To adjust the virtual memory size in Windows Vista/7, do the following:

1. Open the *System and Security* Control Panel. Select the *System* link.
2. Select the *Performance Information and Tools* link at the left bottom and select *Advanced Tools*.
3. Select the *Adjust the appearance and performance of Windows* link. Select *Continue* if a UAC (User Account Control) dialog box appears.
4. Select the *Advanced* tab and click the *Change* button. Change the parameters and click the *OK* button twice.

32-bit Windows uses 32-bit demand-paged virtual memory, and each process gets 4GB of address space divided into two 2GB sections. One 2GB section is shared with the rest of the system while the other 2GB section is reserved for the one application. All the memory space is divided into 4KB blocks of memory called **pages**. The operating system allocates as much available RAM as possible to an application. Then the operating system swaps or pages the application to and from the temporary swap file as needed. The operating system determines the optimum setting for this swap file; however, the swap file size can be changed. Figure 6.16 illustrates how Windows uses virtual memory.

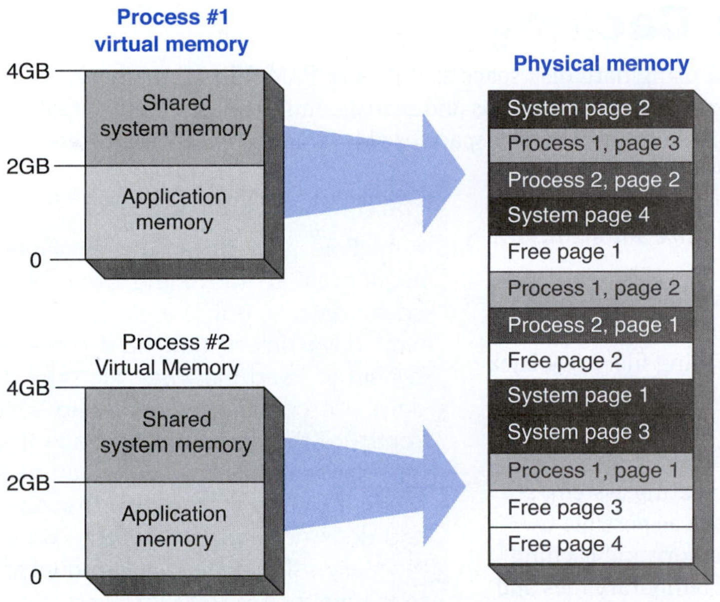

Figure 6.16 Windows virtual memory usage

In Figure 6.16, notice that each application has its own memory space. The Memory Pager maps the virtual memory addresses from the individual processes' address space to physical pages in the computer's memory chips. Figure 6.17 shows how all this relates to RAM and hard drive space.

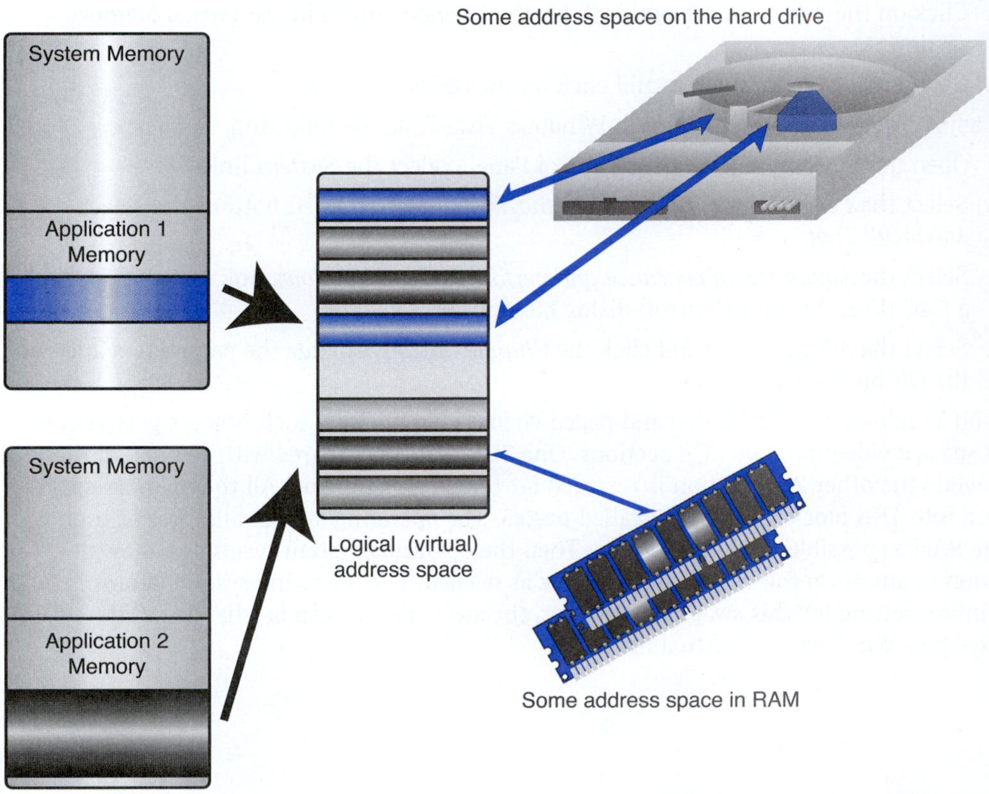

Figure 6.17 Virtual memory

32-bit Windows XP has a natural limitation of 4GB of physical memory. **PAE** (physical address extension) is provided by Intel for motherboards that support this feature and when 32-bit Windows operating systems are being used. PAE allows up to 64GB of physical memory to be used (if the motherboard supports it). You can view whether a system supports PAE by viewing the computer's properties through Windows Explorer. An exercise at the end of this chapter demonstrates this process.

Monitoring Memory Usage Under Windows

Windows has the **Performance utility** within Task Manager to monitor memory usage. To access Task Manager, press Ctrl+Alt+Del. Use the *Performance* tab, which has graphs that visually demonstrate the CPU and memory usage. Figure 6.18 shows the Task Manager *Performance* tab, and Table 6.10 lists the Task Manager *Performance* tab fields.

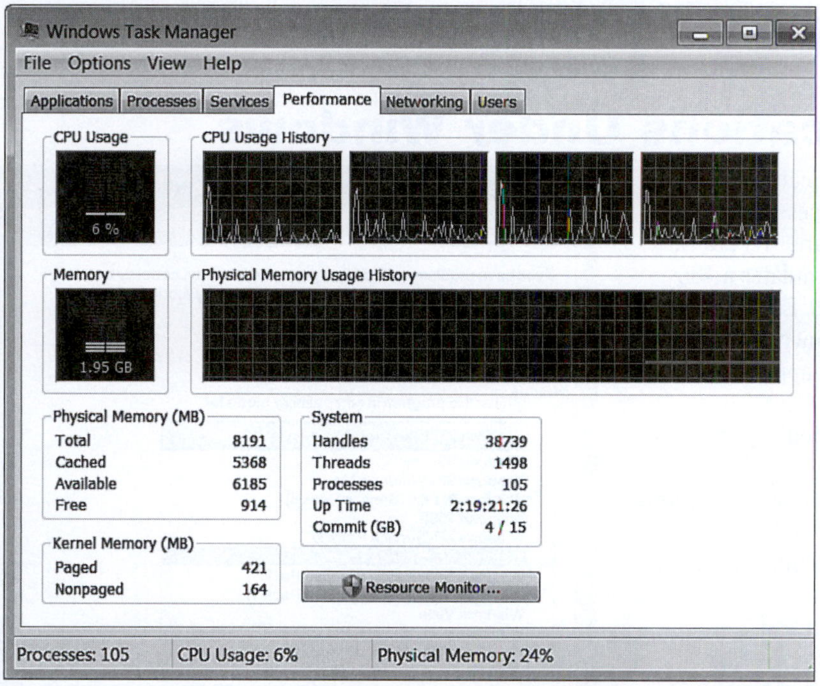

Figure 6.18 Windows Task Manager Performance tab

Table 6.10 Task Manager Performance tab fields

Field	Description
Total Physical Memory	The amount of RAM installed
Cached Physical Memory	Memory pages that could be written to disk and be made available
Available Physical Memory	The amount of memory (physical and paged) for application use
Free Physical Memory	The amount of available physical RAM
Paged Kernel Memory	Memory that can be used by applications as needed that can be copied to the paging file (which frees up RAM)

Field	Description
Nonpaged Kernel Memory	This memory is only available to the operating system and stays in RAM
Handles	The number of resources the operating system is currently dealing with
Threads	The number of objects contained within currently running processes that are executing program instructions
Processes	A running executable program, such as Notepad or a service that is currently running
Up Time	How long the system has been up
Commit	A snapshot of virtual memory requests—note that if the commit charge exceeds the total physical memory, the system is probably paging to the hard disk too much. Add more RAM.

Old Applications Under Windows

Each 8- or 16-bit application runs in an NT/2000/XP process called NT Virtual DOS Machine (NTVDM). The NTVDM process simulates a 486 computer running DOS. Each older application runs in its own address space. However, 16-bit applications share address space in the NT environment. Many dated applications do not operate in the NT/2000/XP environment because these applications frequently make direct calls to hardware, which NT, 2000, and XP do not allow.

For Windows Vista and 7, Microsoft states that some older software might not run properly and offers the Compatibility mode tool. Right-click the application icon from the *Start* menu and select *Properties*. Use the *Compatibility* tab to select the Windows version for which the application was written. Figure 6.19 shows this window. You can also configure virtual machines using virtualization software such as Microsoft's Virtual PC or VMware Workstation. A **virtual machine** allows you to reduce hardware costs by running multiple operating systems simultaneously on a single computer (without one interfering with the other). Virtualization used to be used only with servers, but many home computers and corporate desktops are virtualized today.

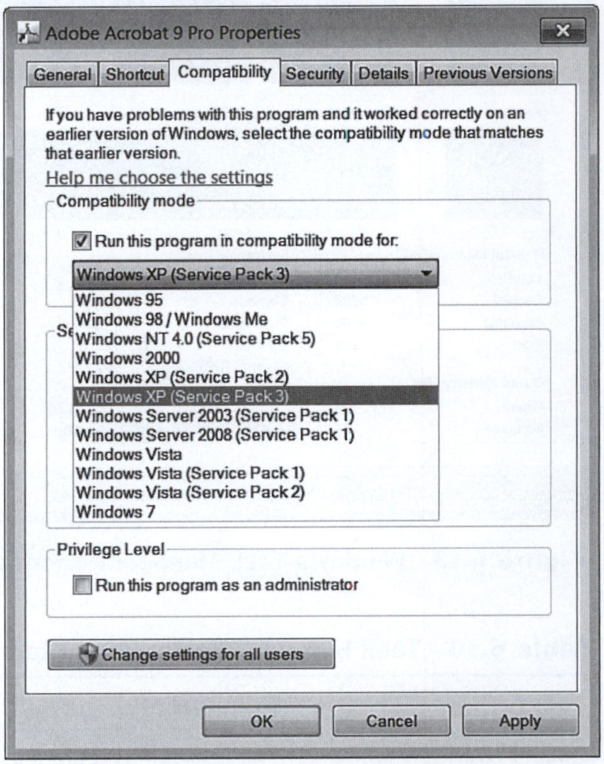

Figure 6.19 Compatibility tab

Troubleshooting Memory Problems

You can get "out of memory" errors, POST code errors, motherboard diagnostic lights or codes, system slowdowns, and application locking due to memory problems with any operating system. With any of these problems, no matter which operating system is being used, check the amount of available memory and free space on the hard drive. Sometimes you must close all applications, reboot the computer, and open only the application that was running when the out of memory error occurred because some applications do not release the memory space they hold. The following tips and troubleshooting steps help with memory management:

- Add more RAM. To see the amount of physical memory (RAM) currently installed, right-click the *My Computer* or *Computer* and select *Properties*.
- If you just installed new memory and an error appears, this is normal. Enter Setup because the BIOS knows something has changed.
- If you just installed new memory and the computer will not boot, check your installation by pushing harder on the memory module to ensure that it is fully seated into the slot. Check for loosened cables that you might have caused. Ensure that you are installing the right memory type. You might need to upgrade your BIOS so that your motherboard recognizes the increased amount of RAM.
- Use the Vista/7 **Windows Memory Diagnostics Tool**, using one of the following methods
  - Use the *System and Maintenance* (Vista) or *System and Security* (7) Control Panel > *Administrative Tools* > *Windows Memory Diagnostic Tool*.
  - Boot into the Advanced Boot Options menu (press F8 upon startup). Press Esc. Press Tab to move to the *Tools* section. Press Enter to use the *Windows Memory Diagnostics Tool* to thoroughly test your RAM.
  - Use the original Windows operating system disc to boot the computer. Enter the language requirements and then use the *Repair your computer* link. From the System Recovery Options window, select *Windows Memory Diagnostic Tool*.
  - Use the command `mdsched`.
- Delete files/applications that are no longer needed and close applications that are not being used. Empty the Recycle Bin.
- Adjust the size of the virtual memory.
- Do not put the swap file on multiple partitions that reside on the same hard drive. Use multiple hard drives, if necessary.
- Put the swap file on a hard disk partition that does not contain the operating system.
- Put the swap file on the fastest hard drive.
- Remove the desktop wallpaper scheme or use a plain one.
- Adjust your Temporary Internet Files setting. From Internet Explorer, click the *Tools* > *Internet Options* > *Settings* button. Adjust how much disk space is set aside for caching Web files.
- Defragment the hard drive. See Chapter 7 for steps.

If you receive a message that SPD device data is missing or inconclusive, your motherboard is looking for SPD data that it cannot receive from the memory module. If this is a new module, ensure that it supports SPD. If it is an older module, you need to replace one of your memory modules.

Tech Tip

Upgrading memory is one of the easiest ways to help with performance issues

Keep in mind that sometimes there is nothing to do but buy more RAM—but try the previously mentioned tips first.

POST usually detects a problem with a memory chip, and most BIOS chips show an error code or message. The motherboard might also contain diagnostic lights or a code. If either occurs turn off the computer, remove the cover, and press down on any memory modules and reboot. Another option is to clean the memory module slots with compressed air and reinstall the module.

The key to good memory chip troubleshooting is to divide and conquer. Narrow the problem to a suspected memory module and then swap banks, if possible. Keep in mind that most memory problems are not in the hardware but in the software applications and operating system.

Tech Tip

Adding more memory did not allow my application to load or run faster

Today's operating systems rely almost as much on hard drive space as they do on RAM because of multitasking (using multiple applications simultaneously). Lack of hard drive space is almost as bad as not having enough RAM.

Flash Memory

Flash memory is a type of nonvolatile, solid-state memory that holds data even when the computer power is off. PCs use flash memory as a replacement for the BIOS chip. Network devices, smartphones, and tablets use flash memory to store the operating system and instructions. Some tablets can use external flash media for storage. Digital cameras use flash memory to store pictures; scanners use flash memory to store images; printers use Flash memory to store fonts. Flash memory does not have to be refreshed like DRAM and it does not need constant power like SRAM.

Various flash memory technologies that are used for storage applications have really advanced in the past few years. These technologies include CompactFlash, Secure Digital cards, MultiMediaCards (MMCs), xD cards, and Flash drives. **CompactFlash** (CF) has two main standards: CompactFlash and CF+. CompactFlash is a small, 50-pin removable storage device that allows speeds up to 133MBps. The first CF device was introduced by the SanDisk Corporation. CF cards can store up to 137GB. The CF+ standard allows increased functionality with cards available for Ethernet, fax/modem/wireless, and barcode scanners.

Tech Tip

Don't format CF cards with Windows

If Windows is used to format a CF card, it will place a different file system on the card. Windows can be used to read files from the card or place files on the card, but best practice is to use the formatting option on the device instead of using Windows to format a CF card.

CF cards can be inserted directly into many devices, such as cameras, smartphones, network devices, and tablet PCs. A CF card uses flash memory, which does not require a battery to keep the data saved to it. A CF card can also be installed into a computer with a PC Card/ExpressCard adapter or a CF card reader.

The CF technology is also used in solid-state drives. Sometimes called microdrives, these devices fit in a Type II (5mm) CF card slot. The Type I (3.3mm) slot is a common one included in cameras. Solid state drives are covered in more detail in Chapter 7.

Other flash memory technologies include some of the following types of flash media cards: MMC, RS-MMC/MMC Mobile, MMCplus, **SD**, **miniSD**, **microSD**, SDHC, miniSDHC, microSDHC, SDXC, microSDXC, **xD**, and more since this book was published. Figure 6.20 shows how small this media can be. Some flash media cards require an adapter to be placed in a tablet or mobile device. Figure 6.20 shows such an adapter.

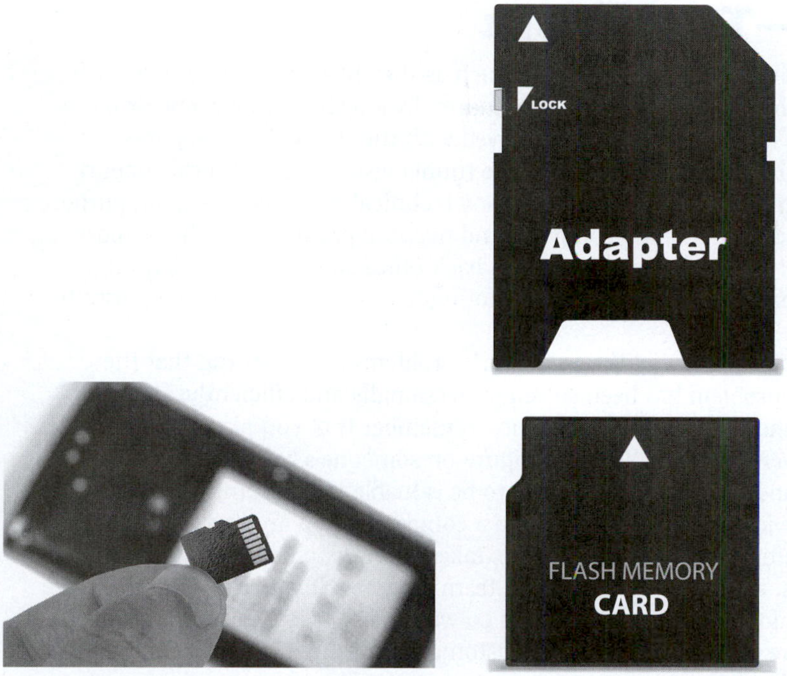

Figure 6.20 Flash memory media

When you install flash media into an Android tablet or phone, you can use the *Settings > Storage* option to view the internal memory capacity as well as any additional memory storage. For an iOS-based device, go to *Settings > General* to see the amount of memory installed.

USB flash drives (sometimes called thumb drives, memory bars, or memory sticks) allow storage up to 256GB, with higher capacities expected. These drives connect to a USB port and are normally recognized by the Windows operating system. A driver may be required for an older operating system. After attaching the drive to a USB port, a drive letter is assigned and Windows Explorer can be used to copy files to the drive.

Tech Tip

The number-one cause of flash drive failure is improper removal

When you are finished using a flash drive, double-click the *Remove Hardware* icon located in the system tray/notification area. The icon has a green arrow. You may have to click on the left arrow or up arrow to see this icon. Click *Safely Remove Hardware*. Select the appropriate flash drive and then click *Stop* and *OK*. When a message appears that you can safely remove the drive, pull the flash drive from the USB port.

Various models are available, including drives that fit on a neck chain, inside watches, and on a key ring. Security features that are available on flash drives include password protection to the drive and data encryption. Flash drives are a very good memory storage solution, and they are inexpensive and easy to use. Figure 6.21 shows a flash drive.

Figure 6.21 Flash memory thumb drive

Memory is one of the most critical components of a computer, and it is important for a technician to be well versed in the different memory technologies. Because memory is one of the most common upgrades, becoming proficient and knowledgeable about populating memory is important. Lab exercises follow that help prepare you for the workforce and installing/upgrading memory.

Soft Skills—Teamwork

Technicians tend not to like working in teams as much as they like working on their own. Much of a technician's job is done solely. However, normally a technician has one or more peers, a supervisor, and a network of partners involved with the job such as suppliers, subcontractors, and part-time help. It is easy to have tunnel vision in a technical support job and lose sight of the mission of the business. Many technical jobs have the main purpose of generating revenue—solving people's computer and network problems for the purpose of making money. Other technicians have more of a back-office support role—planning, installing, configuring, maintaining, and troubleshooting technologies the business uses to make money.

Technicians must focus on solving the customer's problems and ensuring that the customer feels his or her problem has been solved professionally and efficiently. However, you cannot lose sight of the business-first mentality; remember that you play a support role whether you generate revenue or not. You are a figure on someone's balance sheet, and you need to keep your skills and attitudes finely tuned to be valuable to the company. No matter how good you are at your job, you are still better to a company if you are part of a team than if you're on your own. Being the person who is late, takes off early, chats too much with customers, blames others, and so on is not being a team member. If you are going to be late for work or leave early, inform your supervisor and co-workers so they can take care of any issues that arise. If you are going to be late for a customer appointment, contact them and let them know you are running late.

Technicians need to be good team players and see themselves as a reflection of their company when on the job. Teamwork is part of the skill set that employers seek as much as they want you to have technical skills. Think of ways that you can practice teamwork even as a student, and refine those skills when you join the workforce!

Figure 6.22 Teamwork

Chapter Summary

- Memory on a motherboard is SDRAM, a type of RAM that is cheaper and slower than SRAM, the type of memory inside the CPU and processor housing.
- A DDR module fits in a DDR slot. A DDR2 module requires a DDR2 slot; a DDR3 module requires a DDR3 slot.
- RIMMs use RDRAM and were developed by Rambus, Inc. C-RIMMs are inserted into empty memory slots.
- Unbuffered memory is the memory normally installed in computers.
- ECC is used for error checking and is commonly found in high-end computers and servers. An older method of error checking was called parity.
- The CL rating or the timing sequence first number shows how fast the processor can access data in sequential memory locations. The lower the first number, the faster the access.
- SPD is a technology used so the memory module can communicate specifications to the BIOS.
- Double-sided memory is one module that acts like two modules (not that it has chips on both sides even though it most likely does). A motherboard must support using double-sided modules.
- Before installing memory, plan your strategy: read the manual to see the type of memory, determine the total amount of memory, determine if any memory is to be removed, determine the memory to purchase, and be mindful of getting the most out of your memory by implementing dual-, triple-, or even quadruple-channeling.
- When implementing dual-, triple-, or quadruple-channeling, buy matching memory modules.
- Any 32-bit operating system is limited to 4GB of memory.
- Particular versions of Windows have memory limitations. For example, Windows 7 Starter edition is limited to 2GB, but any of the other Windows 7 versions can go to 4GB for the 32-bit versions. 64-bit version limitations are as follows: XP is 128GB. Vista/7 Home Basic is 8GB. Vista/7 Home Premium is 16GB. Vista higher versions are limited to 128GB. Windows 7 higher versions are limited to 192GB.
- RAM is very susceptible to ESD events. Use proper antistatic handling procedures, including using an antistatic wrist strap.
- Before removing or installing memory, disconnect the power cord and remove the battery on a mobile device.
- Laptops and netbooks can sometimes be upgraded with SO-DIMMs. Tablets and smartphones can sometimes be upgraded and have additional storage using flash memory cards.
- Having as much RAM in the system as possible is an important performance factor. So is having free hard drive space because hard drive space is used as memory. This is called virtual memory, and the information stored temporarily on a hard drive is stored in an area known as a page file, paging file, or swap file. The swap file should be on the newest drive that has the most free storage.
- Use Task Manager to monitor memory performance.
- Use POST, motherboard LED/display output codes, BIOS diagnostics, and the Windows Memory Diagnostic Tool to diagnose memory problems.
- Flash media is used to provide memory or additional storage space for computing devices and includes USB flash drives, CF cards, and smaller cards, such as SD, microSD, miniSD, and xD.
- A technician is part of a business and should contribute to the team. A technician should professionally represent a company.

Key Terms

Review Questions

The following specifications for motherboard RAM are used for Questions 1–5:

Considering the features that are shown and the documentation provided, which memory features are needed for a desktop computer with the following specifications:

- Four 240-pin DDR3 SDRAM DIMM sockets arranged in two channels
- Support for DDR3 1600+MHz, DDR3 1333MHz, and DDR3 1066MHz DIMMs
- Support for non-ECC memory
- Support for up to 16GB of system memory

1. Of the given features, which one(s) would be applicable to this computer? (Select all that apply.) Note that all memory is unbuffered unless specified.

   [unbuffered | registered | 204-pin SO-DIMM | 240-pin DDR2 DIMM | 240-pin DDR3 DIMM | ECC]
2. Say that a computer has 4GB of memory. Write all combinations of memory population in the slots.
3. [T | F] The memory used in this system does not do error checking.
4. What does the statement "Four 240-pin DDR3 SDRAM DIMM sockets arranged in two channels" mean?

5. Would there be an issue if a motherboard contained 6GB of RAM and the computer had 32-bit Windows 7 installed? If so, detail the issue.

Consider the following memory advertisements for laptop memory used in Questions 6, 7, and 8:

a. 2GB (2×1GB) Dual channel kit DDR2 667MHz PC2-5300 desktop DIMM Compatible with PC2-5300 (667MHz), PC2-4200 (533MHz), and PC2-3200 (400MHz)
b. 2GB 200-pin DDR2 800MHz PC2-6400 SO-DIMM CL6 1.8V, 256Mx64, non-ECC
c. 2GB (1×2GB) 1333MHz DDR3 desktop unbuffered DIMM
d. 4GB (2×2GB) XMS2 PC2-6400 800MHz 240-pin dual channel DDR2 desktop memory Latency of 5-5-5-18
e. 4GB (2×2GB) 240-pin DDR2 PC2-6400 memory kit unbuffered non-ECC, 1.8V, CL6
f. 4GB (2GB×2) 204-pin PC3-8500 SO-DIMM DDR3-1066 memory kit, CL7, unbuffered, non-ECC, 1.5V, 256Mx64
g. 8GB (2×4GB) 1333MHz PC3-1066 204-pin SODIMM memory kit, 1333MHz unbuffered CL9
h. 8GB (2×4GB) 240-pin DDR3 1600MHz (PC3 12800) SDRAM, 1.5V, 9-9-9-24
i. 8GB (2×4GB) DDR3 dual channel kit 1600MHz CL9 non-ECC low latency 240-pin

6. In these advertisements, which memory module(s) can be accessed the fastest?

7. In these advertisements, which memory module(s) would work as an upgrade for the netbook given the following specifications:

   Configured with 1GB DDR2 (works at 667MHz, max 2GB), 1 main memory slot, which is occupied.

8. A customer wants to dual-channel 4GB of RAM on a desktop computer. The customer currently has 1GB of RAM in memory slot 1. Which memory module(s) would be best to buy, given the following documentation from the motherboard manual? (Memory module slots in order from closest to the CPU: 1, 3, 2, 4.)

   Do not install ECC memory modules.

   - If you remove your original memory modules from the computer during an upgrade, keep the old ones separate from any new modules you may have. If possible, do not pair an original module with a new module. Otherwise, the computer may not start properly.
   - The memory configurations are as follows:
   - A pair of matched modules in DIMM connectors 1 and 2
   - A pair of matched modules in DIMM connectors 1 and 2 and another pair in connectors 3 and 4.

   If you install mixed pairs of PC2-5300 (DDR2 667MHz) and PC2-6400 (DDR2 800MHz), the memory modules function at the speed of the slowest memory module installed.

9. What is the minimum number of memory modules to purchase in order to triple-channel (tri-channel)?
10. What type of memory feature will be needed if data accuracy is paramount for a new computer?
11. What is the minimum amount of RAM recommended to install 32-bit Windows 7?

    [512MB | 1GB | 2GB | 4GB]

12. What method is most effective for preventing an ESD event when installing RAM?
    a. placing the computer on an antistatic mat
    b. wearing an antistatic wrist strap
    c. staying in contact with an unpainted metal part of the computer
    d. wearing rubber-soled shoes and using the buddy system and have another technician standing by
13. What type of memory module is used in a laptop or netbook?
    [RIMM | DIMM | SIMM | SO-DIMM]
14. Which of the following is an example of DDR3 RAM?
    [PC100 | PC2100 | PC2-6400 | PC3-133 | PC3-6400]
15. List one easy way to tell how much RAM is installed in a computer.
16. [T | F] A DDR SO-DIMM can fit in a DDR2 SO-DIMM expansion slot.
17. List one way that a tablet computer's memory might be upgraded.
18. Give an example of how a technician might show teamwork while working on a help desk.
19. A system already has installed two 1333MHz memory modules when a technician adds two more modules that operate at 1600MHz. What will be the result of this action?
    a. The computer won't boot.
    b. The computer might freeze at times.
    c. The memory will operate at the 1333MHz speed.
    d. All memory will operate at the 1600MHz speed.
20. An Android tablet has a flash memory card added. How can a technician verify the system can see and use this memory?

Exercises

Lab 6.1 Configuring Memory on Paper, Part 1

Objective: To be able to determine the correct amount and type of memory to install on a motherboard

Parts: Internet access or access to magazines or ads that show memory prices

Procedure: Refer to Figure 6.23 to answer the questions. This motherboard supports 184-pin DDR SDRAM PC1600, PC2100, PC2700, and PC3200 modules. The capacities supported are 64MB through 1GB for a total of 3GB maximum.

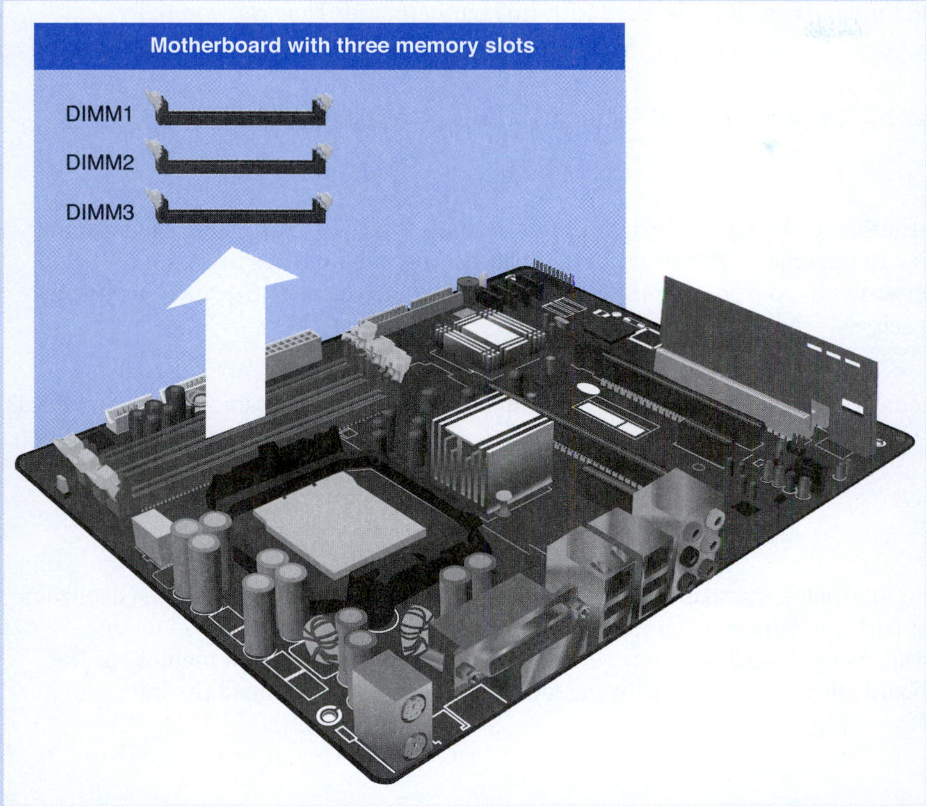

Figure 6.23 Motherboard with three memory slots

Questions:

1. What memory modules are needed if the customer wants 1.25GB of RAM? (What capacities and how many of each capacity?)

2. What memory slots will be used to install the memory based on the information provided?

3. Using the Internet, a magazine, or a list of memory modules, determine the exact part numbers and quantities of memory modules that you would buy. List them with the location of where you obtained the information.

4. Based on your research, did you change your mind about which memory modules you are buying if this was your own machine? Why or why not?

5. During your research of memory modules, did you come upon the words single-sided or double-sided? If so, in what context?

6. Can DDR2 memory modules be used with this motherboard? How can you tell?

7. Is the parity, non-parity, or ECC feature used? How can you tell?

8. This motherboard already has 256MB of RAM installed in the DIMM1 slot. The customer would like to upgrade to 768MB of RAM. What memory modules are needed if the customer wants to go from 256MB to 768MB of RAM? (What capacities and how many of each capacity?)

9. What memory slots will be used to install the memory based on the information provided?

10. Using the Internet, a magazine, or a list of motherboard and memory modules, determine the exact part numbers and quantities of memory modules that you would buy to replace this motherboard with a newer one and populate with as much memory as the motherboard allows. List them with the location of where you obtained the information.

Lab 6.2 Configuring Memory on Paper, Part 2

Objective: To be able to determine the correct amount and type of memory to install on a motherboard

Parts: Internet access or access to magazines or ads that show memory prices

Procedure: Refer to Figure 6.24 and Table 6.11 to answer the questions. This motherboard supports 533/667/800MHz memory DDR2 memory modules. The capacities supported are 1GB and 2GB for a total of 8GB maximum. It is not recommended to use a three DIMM configuration with this board. Memory channel speed is determined by the slowest DIMM populated in the system.

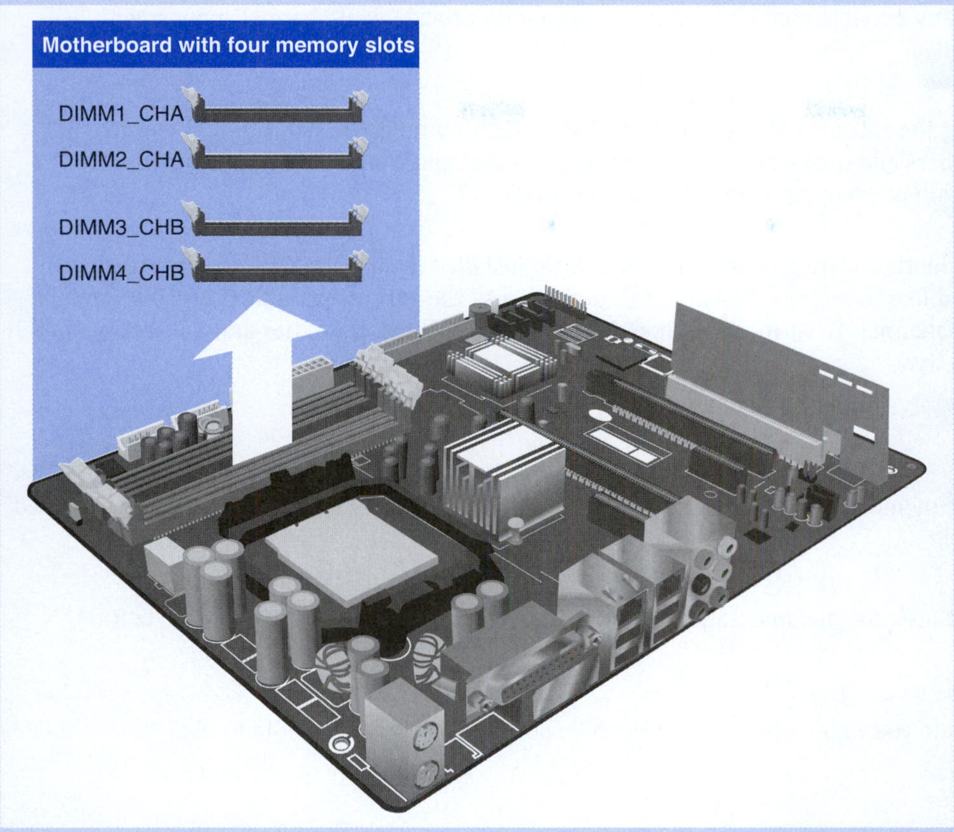

Figure 6.24 Motherboard with four memory slots and two channels

Table 6.11 Motherboard single-/dual-channel combinations

		Sockets			
Mode	**Scenario**	**DIMM1**	**DIMM2**	**DIMM3**	**DIMM4**
Single	1	Populated			
	2		Populated		
	3			Populated	
	4				Populated
Dual-channel	1	Populated		Populated	
	2		Populated		Populated
	3	Populated	Populated	Populated	Populated

Questions:

1. What memory modules are needed if the customer wants 3GB of RAM? (What capacities and how many of each capacity?)

2. Can any possible memory module combination provide dual-channel support with 3GB installed?

3. Using the Internet, a magazine, or a list of memory modules, determine the exact part numbers and quantities of memory modules that you would buy. List them with the location of where you obtained the information.

4. This motherboard already has 1GB of RAM installed in the DIMM1 slot. The customer would like to upgrade to 4GB total memory, use the existing module if possible, and use dual-channel. What memory modules are needed? (What capacities and how many of each capacity?)

5. What memory slots will be used to install the memory based on the information provided?

6. What does the documentation mean when referencing DDR2 533/667/800MHz RAM?

7. How do you know which one of the 533, 667, or 800 type of module to use?

8. Using the Internet, a magazine, or a provided list of memory modules, determine the exact part numbers and quantities of memory modules that you would buy. List them with the location of where you obtained the information.

Lab 6.3 Configuring Memory on Paper, Part 3

Objective: To be able to determine the correct amount and type of memory to install on a motherboard

Parts: Internet access or access to magazines or ads that show memory prices

Procedure: Refer to Figure 6.25 and Table 6.12 to answer the questions. This motherboard supports the following memory configurations:

Up to 2GB utilizing 256MB technology

- Up to 4GB utilizing 512MB or 1GB technology
- Up to 8GB utilizing 1GB technology
- The desktop board supports either single or dual-channel memory configurations. The board has four 240-pin DDR2 SDRAM DIMM connectors with gold-plated contacts. It provides support for unbuffered, non-registered single or double-sided DIMMs, non-ECC DDR2 533/667/800MHz memory, and Serial Presence Detect (SPD) memory only.

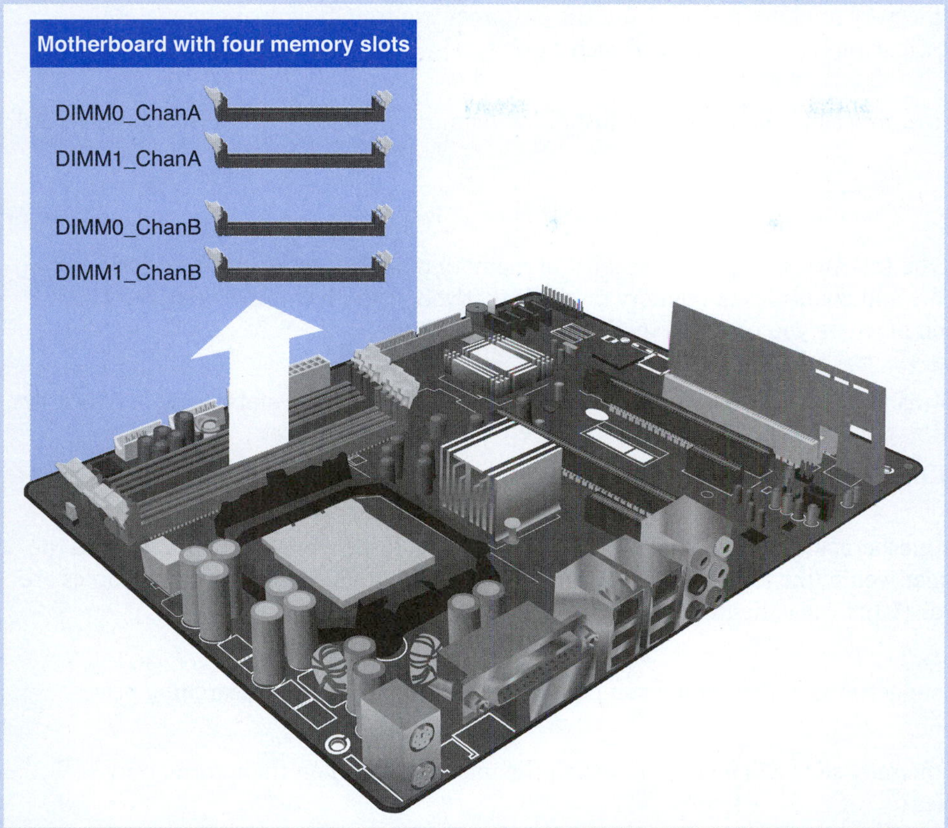

Figure 6.25 Motherboard with four memory slots and two channels

Table 6.12 Motherboard single-/dual-channel guidelines

Installed memory	Guidelines
2 DIMMs dual-channel	Install a matched pair of DIMMs equal in speed and size in DIMM0 of both Channel A and Channel B.
4 DIMMs dual-channel	Follow the directions for two DIMMs and add another matched pair of DIMMs in DIMM1 of both channels A and B.
3 DIMMs dual-channel	Install a matched pair of DIMMs equal in speed and size in DIMM0 and DIMM1 of Channel A. Install a DIMM equal in speed and total size of the DIMMs installed in Channel A in either DIMM0 or DIMM1 of Channel B.
Single channel	All other memory configurations result in single channel memory operation.

Questions:

1. How can this motherboard support 8GB of RAM with only four slots?

2. What memory features, if any, are used? (Select all that apply) [parity | non-parity | ECC | registered | fully buffered | unbuffered | SPD]

3. What memory modules are needed if the customer wants 3GB of dual-channel RAM? (What capacities and how many of each capacity?)

4. What memory slots will be used to install the memory based on the information provided?

5. Using the Internet, a magazine, or a list of memory modules, determine the exact part numbers and quantities of memory modules that you would buy. List them with the location of where you obtained the information.

6. Will it matter if the motherboard has tin contacts in the memory slots? Why or why not?

7. Can DDR memory modules be used with this motherboard? How can you tell?

8. If this motherboard already has 1GB of RAM installed in the DIMM0_ChanA slot and the customer would like to upgrade to 2GB of dual-channel RAM, what memory modules are needed? (What capacities and how many of each capacity?)

9. What suggestions, if any, would you make to the customer before researching prices?

10. What memory slots will be used to install the memory, based on the information provided?

    Using the Internet, a magazine, or a list of memory modules, determine the exact part numbers and quantities of memory modules that you would buy. List them with the location of where you obtained the information.

Lab 6.4 Configuring Memory on Paper, Part 4

Objective: To be able to determine the correct amount and type of memory to install on a motherboard

Parts: Internet access or access to magazines or ads that show memory prices

Procedure: Refer to Figure 6.26 to answer the questions. The motherboard supports the following memory configurations:

- 1GB, 2GB, 4GB unbuffered and non-ECC DDR3 DIMMs can be used in the DIMM slots (1, 2, 3, and 4) for a total of 32GB max using DDR3 1066/1333MHz modules.
- Recommended memory configurations are modules in DIMMs 1 and 3 or modules in DIMMs 1, 2, 3, and 4.
- Single- and dual-channel modes are supported.
- You may install different sizes in Channel A and B. The dual-channel configuration will be the total size of the lowest-sized channel. Any excess memory will operate in single-channel mode.
- >1.65V DIMMs are recommended.
- Use the same CAS latency and obtain from the same vendor if possible.
- The default memory operation frequency is dependent on SPD.

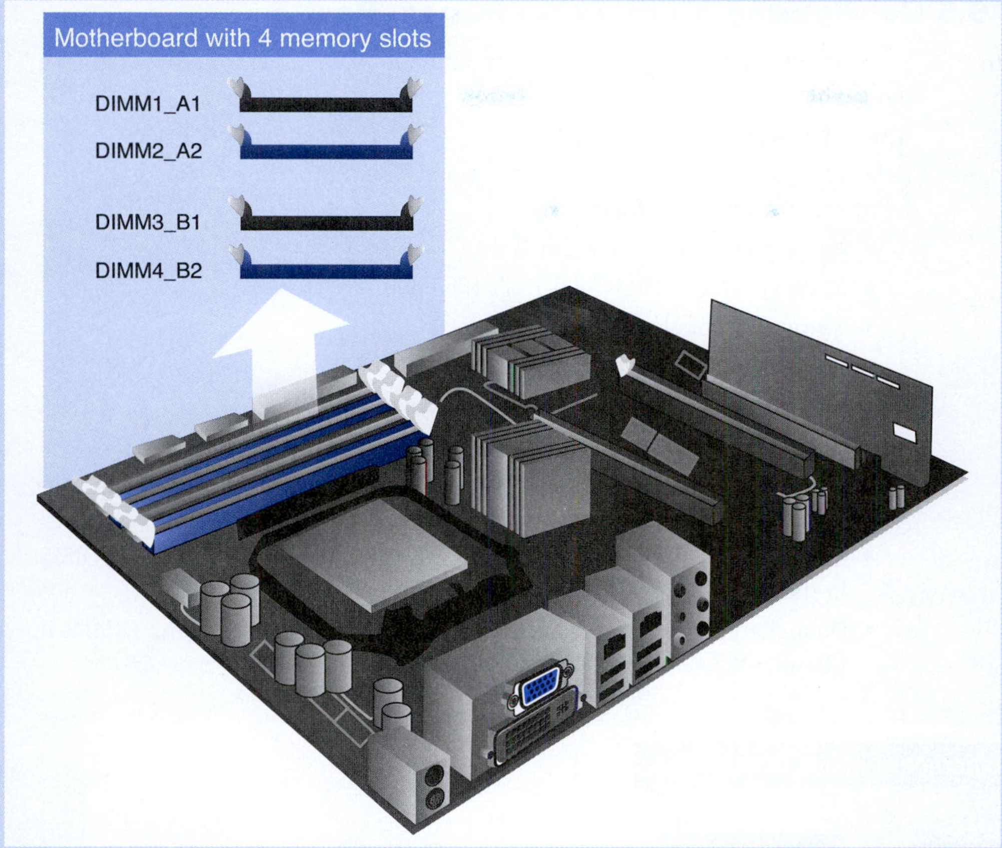

Figure 6.26 Second motherboard with four memory slots and two channels

Questions:

1. What memory features, if any, are used? (Select all that apply.)
   [parity | non-parity | ECC | registered | unbuffered | SPD]
2. The customer wants 4GB of RAM. What memory modules are needed? (What capacities and how many of each capacity?)
3. What memory slots will be used to install the memory suggested in Question 2?
4. Using the Internet, a magazine, or a list of memory modules provided by the instructor, determine the exact part numbers and quantities of memory modules that you would buy. List them with the location of where you obtained this information.
5. In what type of systems would ECC modules most likely be used?
   [student desktop | smartphones | tablets | servers | netbooks]
6. What is the purpose of ECC modules?
7. What is the purpose of SPD?

Lab 6.5 Configuring Memory on Paper, Part 5

Objective: To be able to determine the correct amount and type of memory to install on a motherboard

Parts: Internet access or access to magazines or ads that show memory prices

Procedure: Refer to Figure 6.27 to answer the questions. The motherboard supports the following memory configurations:

- Max memory supported: 16GB
- Memory types: DDR3-1600/1333/1066/800
- Memory channels: 3
- Number of DIMMs: 4
- ECC supported: Yes
- Connectors use gold-plated contacts
- Unbuffered, non-registered single- or double-sided SPD DIMMs with a voltage rating of 1.65V or less
- Optimal performance can be achieved by installing three matching DIMMs in the ChanA, ChanB, and ChanC memory slots.
- Dual-channel operation can be achieved by installing matching DIMMs in ChanB and ChanC or all four memory slots.

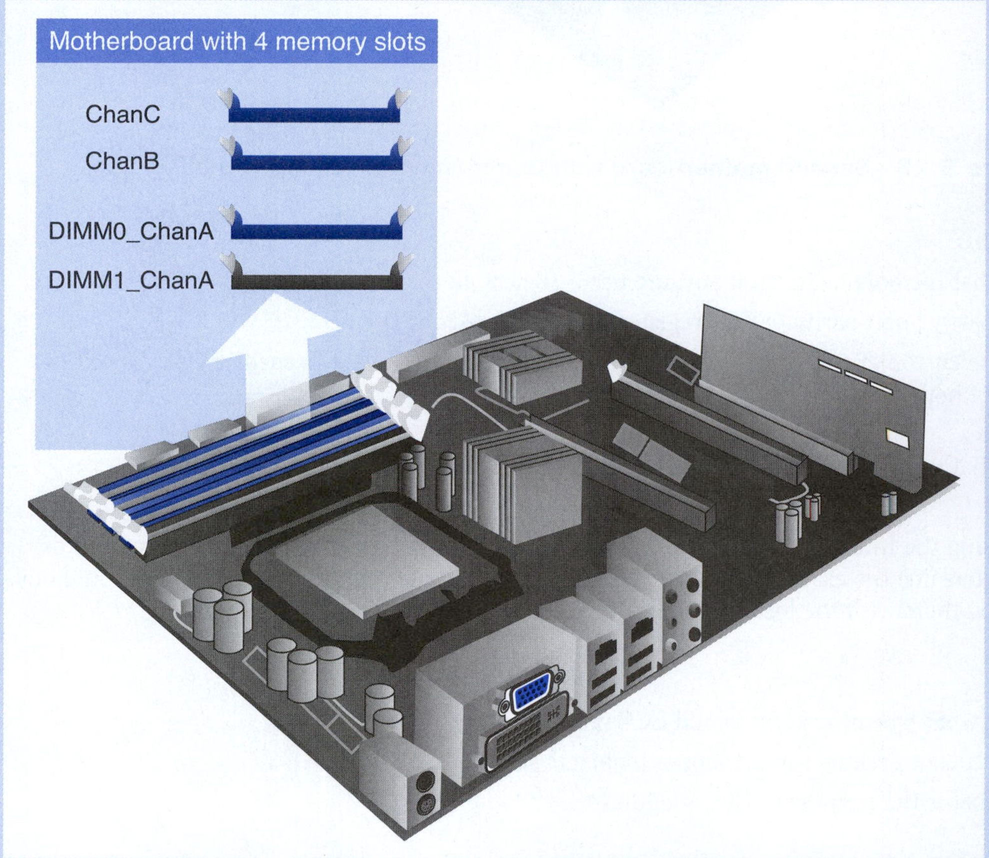

Figure 6.27 Triple-channel motherboard

Questions:

1. What memory features, if any, are used? (Select all that apply.)
   [parity | non-parity | ECC | registered | unbuffered | SPD]

2. The customer wants 8GB of RAM performing triple-channeling. Can this be done? Why or why not? [Yes | No]

3. What memory modules are needed to put 8GB of memory on the motherboard? (What capacities and how many of each capacity?) Justify your choice.

4. What memory slots will be used to install the memory suggested in Question 3?

5. Using the Internet, a magazine, or a list of memory modules provided by the instructor, determine the exact part numbers and quantities of memory modules that you would buy. List them with the location of where you obtained this information.

6. The user has 32-bit Windows 7 installed on this computer. Will there be any issues with the 8GB of RAM? If so what might those issues be?

7. List one method a technician could use to ensure the 8GB are recognized by the system.

Lab 6.6 Examining Memory Resources Using Windows XP

Objective: To be able to view memory resources currently being used by Windows XP

Parts: A computer with Windows XP installed

Procedure: Complete the following procedure and answer the accompanying questions.

1. Power on the computer and verify that XP loads. Log on to XP using the user ID and password provided by the instructor or lab assistant.
2. Access the *Administrative Tools* Control Panel. (For the *Category* view, click *Performance and Maintenance*.)
3. Double-click the *Computer Management* icon. Click *Device Manager* in the left panel to select it. Click the *View* menu option and select *Resources by type*.
4. In the right window, click the memory option plus sign to expand the option. The first entry is normally the system board.

   What memory addresses are used by the system board?
5. Right-click the first system board memory address shown. Select *Properties*.

   What tabs are shown in the window?
6. Click the *Resources* tab. All memory resources used by the motherboard are shown.

   List the memory ranges used by the motherboard and shown on the Resources tab.

   Can the motherboard memory resources be changed on the Resources tab?
7. Click the *Cancel* button. Right-click any of the memory addresses that have adapters shown in the right panel. Access the *Resources* tab.

   Can any of the memory resources be changed?
8. Close the *Computer Management* window.

Lab 6.7 Using the System Information Tool in Windows XP to View Memory

Objective: To be able to view memory resources currently being used by Windows XP

Parts: A computer with Windows XP installed

Procedure: Complete the following procedure and answer the accompanying questions.

1. Open Windows Explorer.
2. Right-click *My Computer* and select *Properties*. (An alternate way to do this is to type `msinfo32` from the Run utility and press Enter.)

   On the General tab at the bottom of the screen, how much physical RAM is installed?

3. If the machine supports PAE, under the line that shows the amount of physical memory the words *Physical Address Extension* are shown.

   Does this computer have the PAE installed?

4. Click *Cancel* to close the *System Properties* window.

Lab 6.8 Using Windows XP Task Manager to View Memory

Objective: To be able to use the *Task Manager* tool to view memory resources currently being used by Windows XP

Parts: A computer with Windows XP installed

Procedure: Complete the following procedure and answer the accompanying questions.

1. Press Ctrl+Alt+Del keys.
2. Click the *Performance* tab.

   What percentage of the CPU is being used?

   What is the significance of the number shown by *Threads*?

   Is the total amount of physical memory RAM, cache memory (virtual memory), or both?

   How much RAM is available?

   As a technician, what commit charge section is most important to you and why?

   How much memory is the operating system taking that no other applications can use?

   How can you tell how many applications and services are currently running?

3. Close the *Task Manager* window.

Lab 6.9 Examining Memory Resources Using Windows 7

Objective: To be able to view memory resources currently being used by Windows 7

Parts: A computer with Windows 7 installed and rights to use Device Manager

Procedure: Complete the following procedure and answer the accompanying questions.

1. Power on the computer and verify that Windows 7 loads. Log on to Windows 7 using the user ID and password provided by the instructor or lab assistant.

2. Access the *System and Security* Control Panel. Under the *System* section, select the *Device Manager* link.
3. Click the *View* menu option and select *Resources by type*. Click the *Memory* arrow to expand the option. The first entry is normally the system board.

   What memory addresses are used by the system board?

4. Right-click the first system board memory address shown. Select *Properties*.

   What tabs are shown in the window?

5. Select the *Resources* tab. All memory resources used by the motherboard are shown.

   List the memory ranges used by the motherboard and shown on the Resources tab.

   Can the motherboard memory resources be changed using the Resources tab options?

6. Click the *Cancel* button. Right-click any of the memory addresses for an adapter and access the *Resources* tab.

   Can any of the memory resources be changed?

7. Close the *Device Manager* window.

Lab 6.10 Using the System Information Tool in Windows 7 to View Memory

Objective: To be able to view memory resources currently being used by Windows 7

Parts: A computer with Windows 7 installed and rights to use the System Information Tool

Procedure: Complete the following procedure and answer the accompanying questions.

1. To access the System Information tool, click *Start* and select *Control Panel*.
2. Select the *System and Security* Control Panel. Select the *System* link.
3. On the bottom-left side, select the *Performance Information and Tools* link.
4. From the left panel, select the *Advanced tools* link.
5. Select the *View advanced system details in System Information* link. Note that an alternate way to do this is to run `msinfo32` from the *Search programs and files* textbox or enter `msinfo32` at a command prompt that has administrative privileges.

   How much physical RAM is installed?

   How much physical RAM is available?

   How much total virtual memory does the machine have?

   How much available virtual memory does the machine have?

   What is the location and size of the page file?

6. Click the *Close Find* button to close the System Information window.

Lab 6.11 Using Windows 7 Task Manager to View Memory

Objective: To be able to use the Task Manager tool to view memory resources currently being used by Windows 7

Parts: A computer with Windows 7 installed and rights to use Task Manager

Procedure: Complete the following procedure and answer the accompanying questions.

1. After logging on to a Windows 7 computer, press the Ctrl+Alt+Del keys and select the *Start Task Manager* link.

2. Access the *Performance* tab.
   What percentage of the CPU is being used?

   What is the significance of the number shown by *Threads*?

   Is the total amount of physical memory RAM, cache memory (virtual memory) or both?

   How much RAM is available?

3. Click the *Resource Monitor* button and select the *Overview* tab.
   What is the percentage of used physical memory?

4. Expand the *Memory* section.
   List three executable (.exe) files running in memory.

5. Open an application such as the Calculator accessory. Locate the application in the *Memory* section.
   How many kilobytes are shown for the application in the *Commit* column?

   How many kilobytes are shown for the application in the *Working Set* column?

   How many kilobytes are shown for the application in the *Shareable* column?

   How many kilobytes are shown for the application in the *Private* column?

6. Select the *Memory* tab.
   How much memory is reserved for hardware, if any?

7. Hold the mouse pointer over the colored bar portion of physical memory that represents the amount of memory "In Use." A description of this portion of the bar appears.
   What is the exact purpose of the "In Use" section?

8. Hold the mouse pointer over the colored bar that shows how the "Standby" portion of physical memory is being used.
   What is the exact purpose of the "Standby" section?

   Determine the exact purpose of the "Free" section. Document your findings.

9. Close the System Resource Monitor window and the application window you opened to learn about the System Resource Monitor. Close the Task Manager window.

Lab 6.12 Determining Memory Resources in an iOS-Based Device

Objective: To be able to use the Apple-iOS operating system to determine the amount of memory

Parts: An Apple iPhone or iPad

Procedure: Complete the following procedure and answer the accompanying questions.

1. Ensure that the Apple device is powered on.
2. Access the Home screen (by pressing the Home screen button [□]). Tap on the *Settings* option. Note that you may have to swipe your finger to access the *Settings* option if multiple pages of icons are present.
3. Tap the *General* option. Tap the *About* option. Locate the *Capacity* option, which shows is the total amount of memory installed.

   How much memory is available on the device?

4. Locate the *Available* option, which shows the amount of memory that is not being used.

   How much memory is free?

5. Return to the Home screen.

Lab 6.13 Determining Memory Resources in an Android-Based Device

Objective: To be able to use the Android operating system to determine the amount of memory

Parts: An Android-based device

Procedure: Complete the following procedure and answer the accompanying questions.

Note: The Android operating system is an open source operating system. Options vary from device to device, but most configuration options are very similar.

1. Ensure that the Android device is powered on.
2. Access the Home screen (by tapping the Home icon ⌂. Tap the *Settings* option. Note that you may have to swipe your finger to access the Settings option if multiple pages of icons are present.
3. Tap the *Storage* option. Locate the total amount of storage.

   How much memory is available on the device?

4. Locate how much memory is available (not being used).

   How much memory is free?

   How much memory is being used by applications?

   Does this device have external storage? If so, how could you tell?

5. Return to the Home screen.

Activities

Internet Discovery

Objective: To become familiar with researching memory chips, using the Internet

Parts: A computer with Internet access

Procedure: Use the Internet to complete the following procedure.

1. Power on the computer and start an Internet browser.
2. Using any search engine, locate two vendors that sell memory chips.
3. Create a table like the one below and fill in your findings for each of the memory sites.

	Site 1	Site 2
Internet URL		
Type of DIMM		
Largest-capacity DIMM		
Pros of website		
Cons of website		

Soft Skills

Objective: To enhance and fine-tune a future technician's ability to listen, communicate in both written form and oral form, and support people who use computers in a professional manner

Activities:

1. On your own, use the Internet to find a utility that tests soft skills or your personality. Compare your scores with others in the class. Make a list of how you might improve in specific weak areas. Present your findings to a group and share your group findings with another group.

2. Note that this activity requires two computers. In groups of two, have one person describe in great detail to the other person how to upgrade the computer's memory by removing memory from one computer and adding it to the other. The person doing the physical installation can do nothing unless the partner describes how to do it. Reverse roles for removing the memory and re-installing back in the original computer. At the end of the exercise, the two participants describe to the teacher what they experienced.

3. In small groups, find a video that describes how to do something on the computer. Critique the video for how the speaker might do a better job communicating to people who are not technicians. Share the video with the class along with your recommendations for doing it better. As an option, script a short presentation for how to do something. Tape/record it if possible and have the class critique each group's presentation.

Critical Thinking Skills

Objective: To analyze and evaluate information as well as apply learned information to new or different situations

Activities:

1. Refer to Figure 6.10 and Table 6.7 in this chapter. Compare and contrast Solution 2 with Solution 3 as it relates to dual-channeling. Write a list of your findings and share them with the class.

2. Using Figure 6.10 in the chapter again, list the repercussions of discovering that the motherboard supports both single-side and double-sided memory modules. What would the memory population look like for 8GB (the maximum) of RAM?

3. Download a motherboard manual from the Internet or use one provided in the classroom. Find the memory section and make a list of any terms or directions that are given that you do not understand. In groups of four or five, share your lists and come up with as many solutions as possible. Share your group list with the class. Write any unsolved questions on the board and bring the answers to those questions back in a week.

A+ Certification Exam Tips

- ✓ Review Table 6.2 right before the exam(s) in case you are asked to identify the memory type or DDR*x* name.
- ✓ Review Table 6.6, especially the Windows 7 and 32-bit Windows memory limitations.
- ✓ Know how to calculate what memory is needed for an upgrade or a new install.
- ✓ Be able to identify memory slots on a motherboard.
- ✓ Know how to populate memory when dual- or triple-channeling is being implemented.
- ✓ Be able to describe the difference between unbuffered and ECC memory.
- ✓ Know that memory chips are especially susceptible to ESD and how to prevent ESD damage when installing or removing memory.
- ✓ Review the troubleshooting symptoms and tips for the 220-802 exam.
- ✓ Keep in mind that the following professionalism skills are part of the 220-801 exam: (1) maintain a positive attitude and (2) be on time (or, if late, contact the customer). You should not forget to review the professionalism skills.

chapter 7

Storage Devices

Chapter Objectives:

In this chapter you will learn:

- How to install a floppy drive
- Basic hard drive terms
- About IDE, SCSI, PATA, SATA, parallel SCSI, SAS, and SSD technologies
- How to configure storage devices
- How to fix storage device problems
- How to keep the hard drive healthy
- Effective phone communication

CompTIA Exam Objectives:

What CompTIA A+ exam objectives are covered in this chapter?

- ✓ 801-1.1 Configure and apply BIOS settings.
- ✓ 801-1.5 Install and configure storage devices and use appropriate media.
- ✓ 801-1.7 Compare and contrast various connection interfaces and explain their purpose.
- ✓ 801-1.11 Identify connector types and associated cables.
- ✓ 801-3.1 Install and configure laptop hardware and components.
- ✓ 801-5.3 Given a scenario, demonstrate proper communication and professionalism.
- ✓ 802-1.2 Given a scenario, install and configure the operating system using the most appropriate method.
- ✓ 802-1.4 Given a scenario, use appropriate operating system features and tools.
- ✓ 802-1.7 Perform preventive maintenance procedures using appropriate tools.
- ✓ 802-2.4 Given a scenario, use the appropriate data destruction/disposal method.
- ✓ 802-4.3 Given a scenario, troubleshoot hard drives and RAID arrays with appropriate tools.
- ✓ 802-4.6 Given a scenario, troubleshoot operating system problems with appropriate tools.

Storage Devices Overview

Storage devices hold the data we are so fond of generating and keeping—photos, PDFs, documents, spreadsheets, movies, and whatever else we can think to save. This data is stored on optical media, flash media, magnetic media such as hard drives, and floppy disks, as shown in Figure 7.1.

Figure 7.1 Storage devices

Data can also be stored "in the cloud." This means that there are storage devices available through the Internet to store data. Some storage is provided by an Internet provider or as a service for a mobile device. Some companies, such as SugarSync, Inc., and DropBox, provide a limited amount of free storage, with the option to pay for more. Since mobile devices have limited or no storage capability, cloud storage is a viable, if not necessary, option. Figure 7.2 illustrates this concept, but keep in mind that "in the cloud" is just a ton of hard drives out there somewhere.

Figure 7.2 Cloud storage

Floppy Drive Overview

Floppy drives are seldom seen in a computer today, but a technician might see one. A floppy drive subsystem consists of three main parts: (1) the electronic circuits or the controller, (2) the 34-pin ribbon cable, and (3) the floppy drive (sometimes called the "a" drive). The electronic circuits give the floppy drive instructions: "Floppy drive, go to this location and read some data! The internal floppy drive ribbon cable connects the floppy drive to the electronic circuits. The floppy drive is the device that allows saving data to disk media. If a floppy drive is required today, it is typically connected to the computer using a USB port.

Troubleshooting and installing floppy drives involves these three main areas and the media. Media refers to the disks inserted in the floppy drive. Almost any floppy drives are 3.5-inch 1.44MB.

Floppy Media and Construction

The media inserted in a floppy drive is a **disk** or floppy disk. On one side, a disk has a sliding write-protect window that allows the disk to be written to or protected from any writing or changing of data that is occurring. If you close the window, data can be written to the disk. If the window is open, the disk is write-protected and data cannot be written on the disk.

Tech Tip

At the first sign of trouble on a floppy drive, clean the heads

Over time, the read/write heads become dirty. When a technician sees read/write errors occurring, the first step is to clean the read/write heads.

Floppy drives have two **read/write heads** that are responsible for placing the data, the 1s and 0s, onto the disk. The disk inserts between the two heads of the floppy drive. One read/write head mounts on the top, the other on the bottom.

Floppy Drive Installation or Replacement

Installation of floppy drives is simple after you ensure that you have the following:

- An available drive bay
- An available floppy power connection or a Molex-to-floppy power converter
- A motherboard floppy connector or an additional adapter
- A floppy cable

Figure 7.3 shows a motherboard floppy connector.

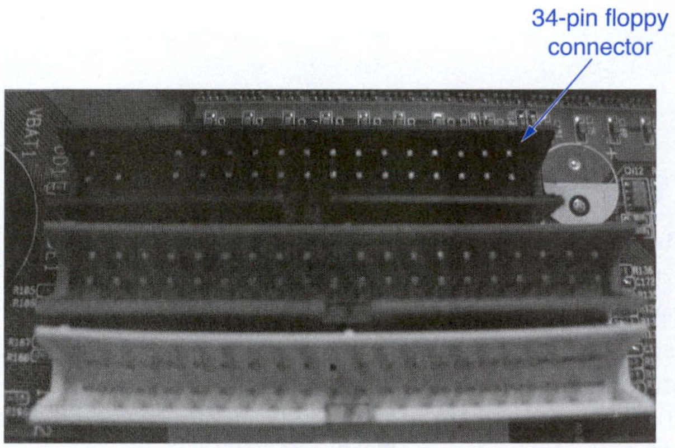

Figure 7.3 Floppy connector on a motherboard

The floppy cable is unique to the computer because of the twist at the end of the cable that attaches to the floppy drive. Figure 7.4 shows a floppy drive cable that attaches from the motherboard to the floppy drive. Keep in mind the end with the twist connects to the drive.

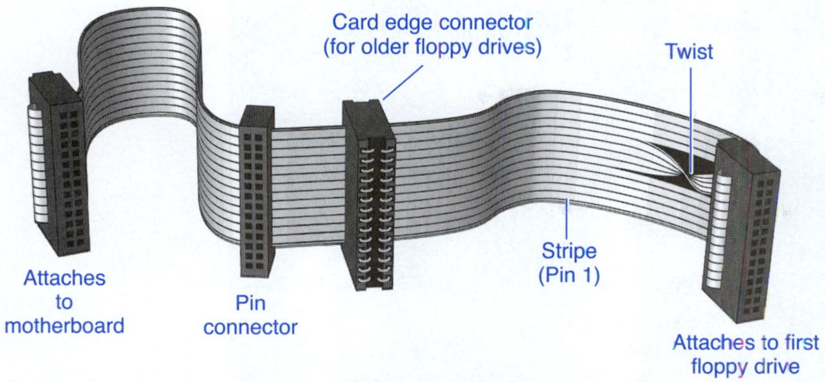

Figure 7.4 Floppy drive cable

Pin 1 on the cable needs to attach to pin 1 on the connector. Pin 1 on a cable is easy to find because of the colored stripe that is on one side of the cable. Pin 1 on an adapter or a motherboard is not always easy to locate. Some manufacturers put a small 1 or 2 by the end where the cable's pin 1 inserts. Other manufacturers put larger numbers at the opposite end. For example, if you see the number 33 or the number 34 on the motherboard where the floppy cable inserts, pin 1 and pin 2 are on the *opposite* end of the connector. Installation is nothing more than mounting the floppy drive to the computer case and connecting the cable between the drive and motherboard or adapter.

Tech Tip

Attach cable correctly or destroy devices and components

Devices, adapters, controlling circuits, and so on can be damaged if a cable plugs into the connector the wrong way. Some cables are keyed so they insert only one way into the connector. Most cables that connect to the floppy drive are keyed, but the other end of the cable that connects to the controlling circuits is sometimes not keyed.

Hard Drive Overview

Hard drives are some of the most popular devices for storing data. They store more data than floppy drives and move data faster than tape drives. Today's hard drive capacities extend into the terabytes. Hard drives are frequently upgraded in computers, so it is important for you to understand all the technical issues. These issues include knowing the parts of the hard drive subsystem, how the operating system and the BIOS work with a hard drive, how to configure a hard drive, and how to troubleshoot it. The hard drive subsystem can have up to three parts: (1) the hard drive, (2) a cable that attaches to an adapter or the motherboard, and (3) control circuits located on an adapter or the motherboard.

Hard Drive Geometry

Traditional mechanical hard drives are magnetic hard drives. These hard drives have multiple hard metal surfaces called platters. Each platter typically holds data on both sides and has two read/write heads, one for the top and one for the bottom. The read/write heads float on a cushion of air without touching the platter surface. Data is written by using electromagnetism. A charge is applied to the read/write head creating a magnetic field. The metal hard drive platter has magnetic particles that are affected by the read/write head's magnetic field allowing 1s and 0s to be "placed" or "induced" onto the drive, as shown in Figure 7.5.

Figure 7.5 Writing to a hard drive

The hard drive platters spin at different rotational rates called RPMs (revolutions per minute). Common ones are 5400, 7200, 10,000, and 15,000 rpm. The faster the rpm, the faster the transfer rate and generally, an increased cost.

If a read/write head touches the platter, a **head crash** occurs. This is sometimes called HDI (head-to-disk interference), and it can damage the platters or the read/write head, causing corrupt data. See Figure 7.6 for an illustration of a hard drive's actuator arms, heads, and platters. Figure 7.7 shows the inside of a hard drive. You can see the top read/write head and the platters. Keep in mind that you should not remove the cover from a hard drive because you could allow particles into the sealed drive area.

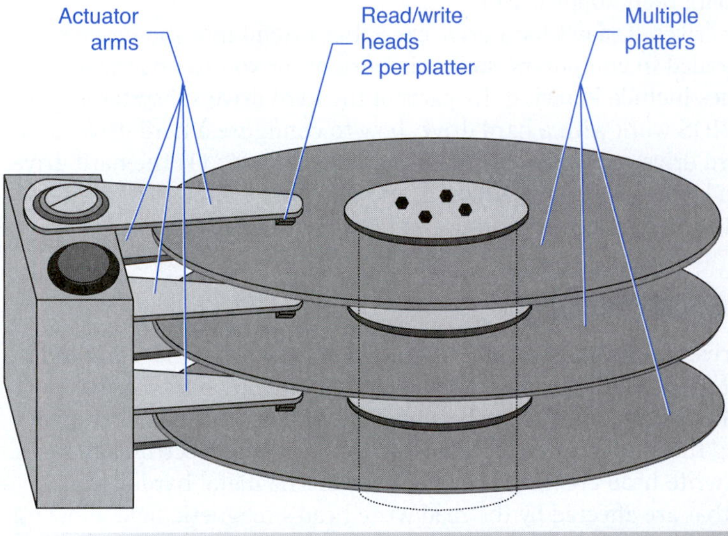

Figure 7.6 Hard drive geometry

Figure 7.7 Hard drive with cover removed

The hard drive surface is metallic and has concentric circles, each of which is called a track. Tracks are numbered starting with the outermost track, which is called track 0. One corresponding track on all surfaces of a hard drive is a cylinder. For example, cylinder 0 consists of all track 0s; all of the track 1s comprise cylinder 1, and so on. A track is a single circle on one platter. A cylinder is the same track on all platters. Figure 7.8 shows the difference between tracks and cylinders. Notice in Figure 7.8 that a concentric circle makes an individual track. A single track on all the surfaces makes an individual cylinder.

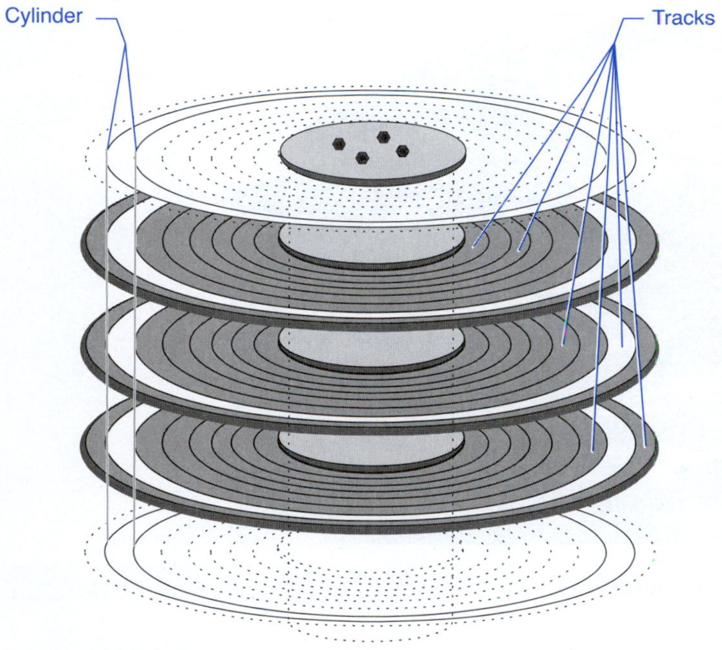

Figure 7.8 Cylinders versus tracks

Each track is separated into **sectors**, with the circle divided into smaller pieces. Normally, each sector stores 512 bytes, as shown in Figure 7.9.

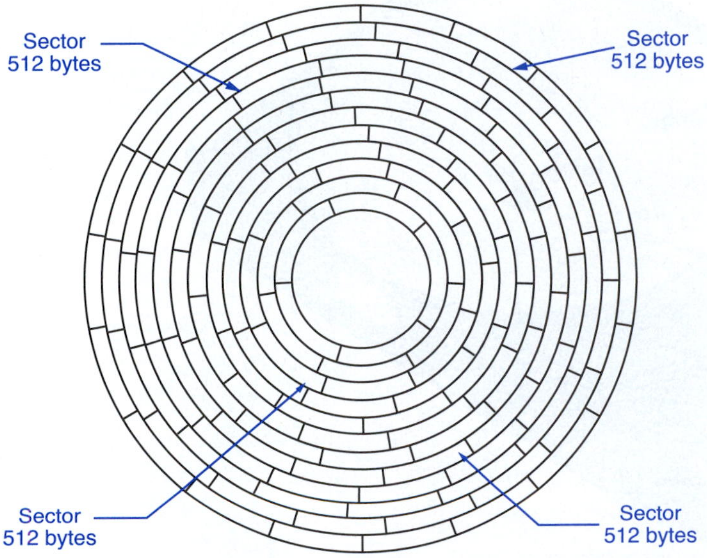

Figure 7.9 Hard drive sectors

Hard drives also come in different physical sizes (form factors). For desktop and small server models, 5.25-inch (not very popular) and 3.5–inch drives are available. The 2.5-inch form factor is designed for laptops and netbooks. A 1.8-inch form factor is available for use and can be found in SSDs, ultrabooks, and ultraportable devices such as MP3 players. Some PC Card/Express bus storage card/drives are available, but external hard drives are more popular. Figure 7.10 shows various hard drive sizes. Figure 7.11 shows a 2.5-inch hard drive installed in a netbook.

Figure 7.10 Hard drive form factors

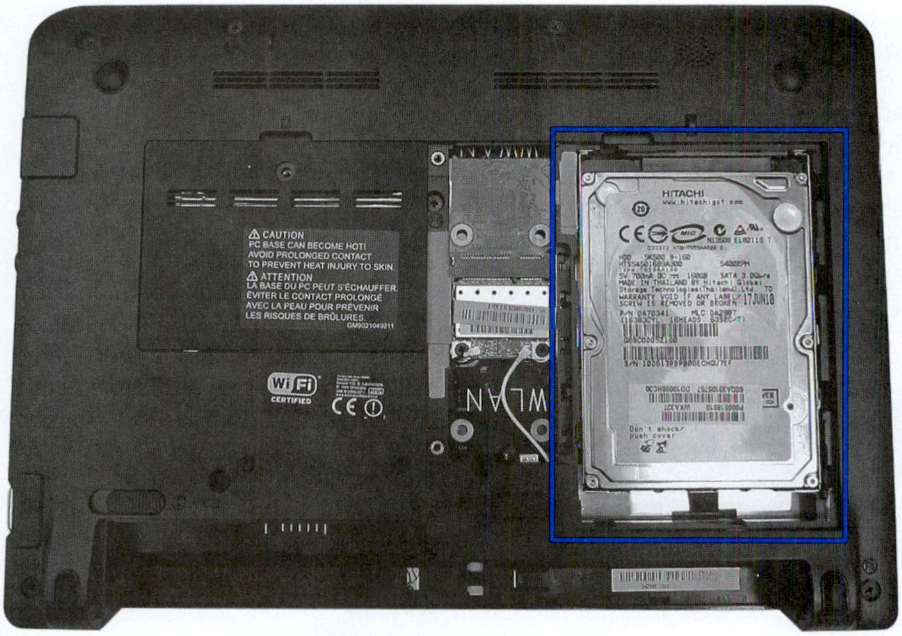

Figure 7.11 Installed 2.5-inch hard drive

A hard drive can also be placed inside an enclosure and attached externally using a USB, eSATA, eSATAp USB/SATA combo port, or IEEE 1394/FireWire. Figure 7.12 shows a 3.5-inch IDE PATA or SATA to USB or eSATA Sabrent enclosure that includes a cooling fan. Notice that the cooling fan has a filter that protects the fan from dust particles.

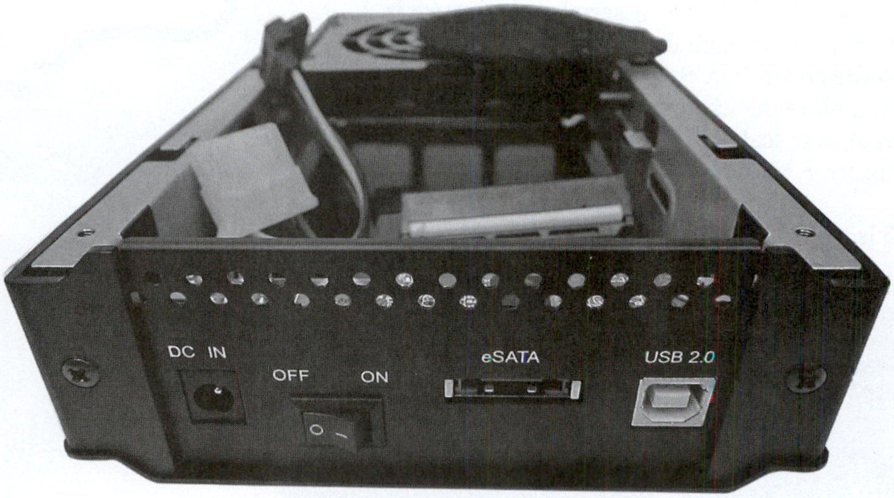

Figure 7.12 Sabrent external hard drive enclosure

Hard Drive Interfaces Overview

A hard drive system must have a set of rules to operate. These rules specify the number of heads on the drive, what commands the drive responds to, the cables used with the drive, the number of devices supported, the number of data bits transferred at one time, and so on. These rules make up a standard called an interface that governs communication with the hard drive. There are two major hard drive interfaces: **IDE** (integrated drive electronics), also known as the ATA (AT Attachment) or **EIDE** (Enhanced IDE) standard, and **SCSI** (Small Computer System Interface). IDE is the most common in home and office computers. SCSI is commonly found in network servers.

Both IDE and SCSI started out as parallel architectures. This means that multiple bits are sent over multiple paths. This architecture requires precise timing as transfer rates increase. Also with both types of devices, multiple devices can attach to the same bus. With parallel IDE or **PATA** (Parallel ATA), it was only two devices and with SCSI it was more, but the concept is the same. When multiple devices share the same bus, they have to wait their turn to access the bus and there are configuration issues with which to contend. Figure 7.13 shows the concept of parallel transfer.

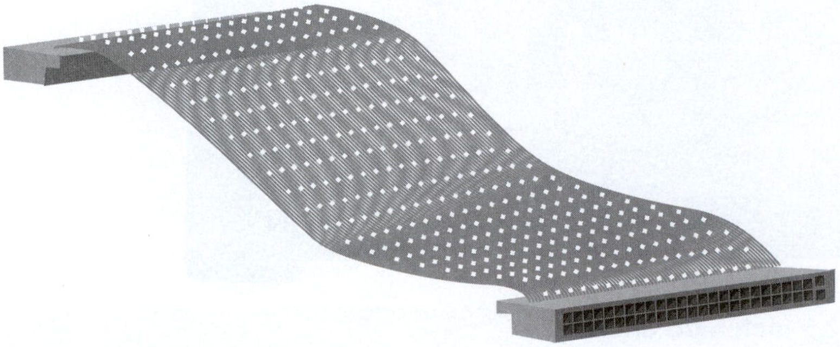

Figure 7.13 Parallel transfer

Today, the trend is toward serial architectures. Both the IDE and SCSI standards have a serial architecture available. The ATA serial device is known as a **SATA** (Serial ATA) device, and the serial SCSI serial device is known as a **SAS** (Serial Attached SCSI) device. A serial architecture is a point-to-point bus where each device has a single connection back to the controller. Bits are sent one at a time over a single link. More devices can attach to this type of architecture because it scales easier and configuration is much easier. Figure 7.14 illustrates the concept of serial data transfer.

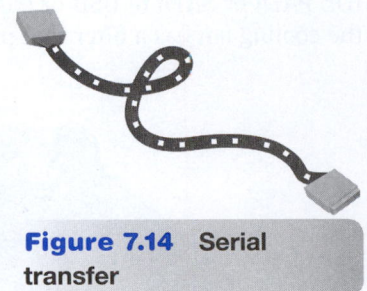

Figure 7.14 Serial transfer

Figure 7.15 is a photo of a PATA cable and a SATA data cable.

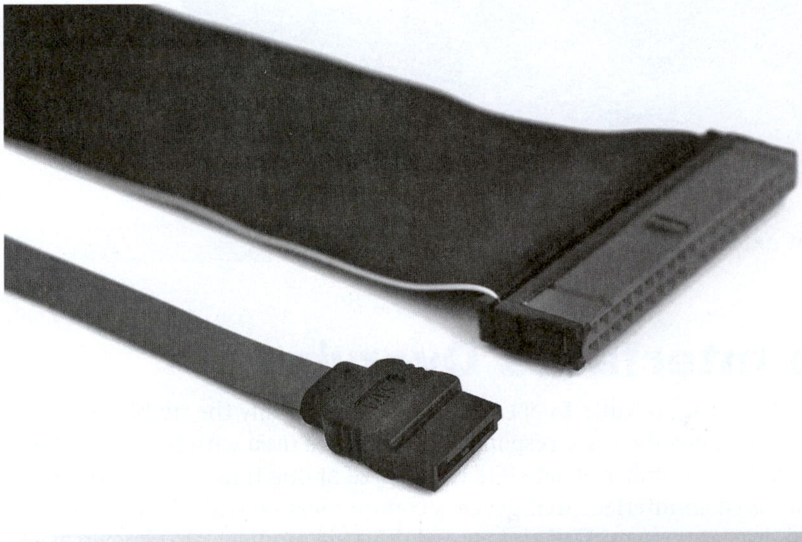

Figure 7.15 PATA and SATA data cables

IDE (Integrated Drive Electronics)

IDE (Integrated Drive Electronics) is not only for traditional mechanical hard drives but for other internal devices, such as tape, Zip, and optical drives. The original IDE standard was developed only for hard drives and is officially known as ATA (AT Attachment). Later, other devices were supported by the standard and the standard evolved to ATA/ATAPI (AT Attachment Packet Interface). ATAPI increased support of devices such as CD/DVD and tape drives. There are two types of ATA—PATA (Parallel ATA) and SATA (Serial ATA).

PATA is the older IDE/EIDE type, which uses a 40-pin cable that connects the hard drive to an adapter or the motherboard and transfers 16 bits of data at a time. Each cable normally has either two or three connectors. Many motherboards have both SATA and PATA IDE connectors. Figure 7.16 shows the difference between a PATA and a SATA motherboard connection.

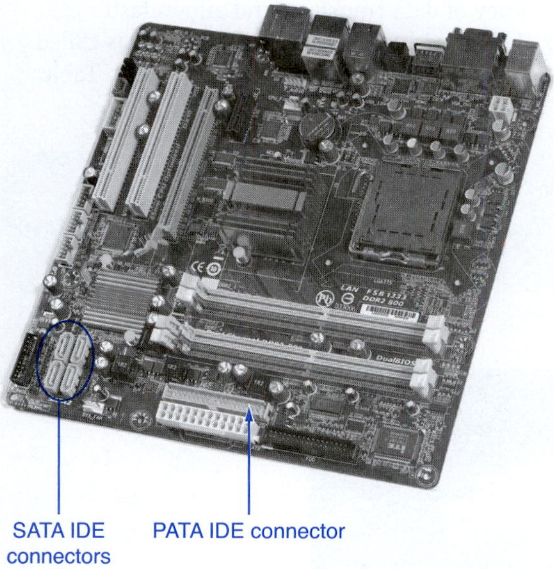

Figure 7.16 SATA and PATA motherboard connectors

A motherboard that has two IDE connectors can have up to four PATA devices, two per motherboard connection. Figure 7.17 shows a PATA IDE hard drive. Notice the 40-pin connector on the left and the power connector on the right.

Figure 7.17 PATA IDE hard drive

Tech Tip

If a PATA cable has two connectors and two devices are needed, buy another cable

One 40-pin motherboard PATA connector can support up to two PATA devices. However, some cables only have two connectors—one that connects to the motherboard and one that attaches to the PATA device. If a second device is added, a new cable must be purchased.

The original IDE interface supported up to two drives and is also known as the ATA-1 Standard (AT Attachment Standard). The ATA-5 standard (also known as Ultra ATA/66 or ATA/66) was important because the PATA cable changed. A 40-pin cable is used with this standard as with the other standards, but the cable is different—it has 80 conductors. The 40 extra conductors are ground lines, which are situated between the existing 40 wires. These ground lines reduce crosstalk, improves the accuracy of data transfers, and allows faster speed. Signals from one wire can interfere with the signals on an adjacent wire; this is called crosstalk. Figure 7.18 shows the older 40-pin cable and the newer 80-conductor cable. Table 7.1 shows the ATA standards.

Tech Tip

80-conductor PATA IDE cable is now required

The 80-conductor cable works with older PATA devices, but is required with any PATA drive today.

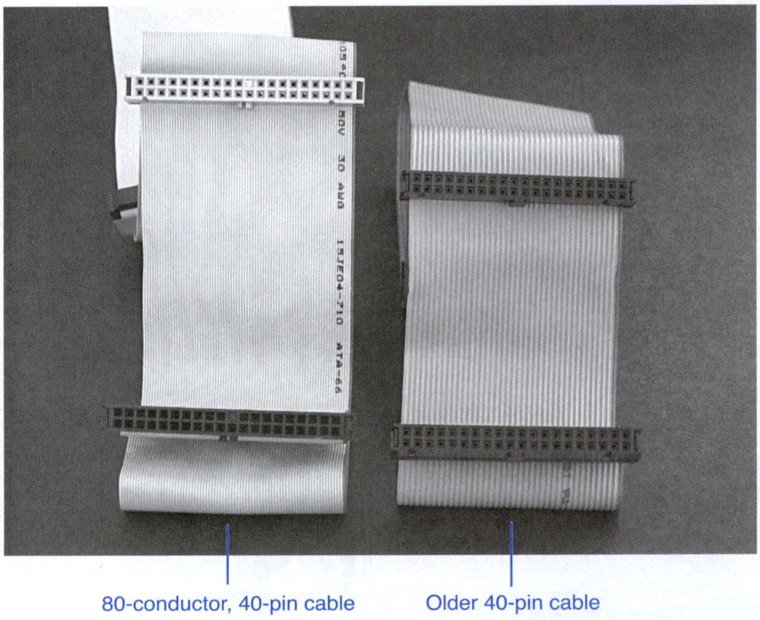

Figure 7.18 80- and 40-conductor cable

Table 7.1 IDE PATA standards

ATA standard	Speed (Mbps)	Cable	Notes
ATA-1	3.3	40-pin	IDE hard drives
ATA-2	8.3 and 16.6	40-pin	Supports other devices besides hard drives; sometimes called EIDE

ATA standard	Speed (Mbps)	Cable	Notes
ATA-3	8.3 and 16.6	40-pin	Includes SMART
ATA-4	33	40-pin	Also called Ultra DMA/33 or Ultra ATA/33
ATA-5	66	40-pin (80 conductor)	Also called Ultra DMA/66 or Ultra ATA/66
ATA-6	100	40-pin	Also called Ultra DMA/100 or (80 conductor) Ultra ATA/100
ATA-7	133	40-pin (80 conductor)	Also called Ultra DMA/133 or Ultra ATA/133

The newer ATA standard is SATA (Serial ATA). The original specification transfers data at 1.5Gbps (sometimes seen as 1.5Gb/s) and is called **SATA 1** or SATA I. The 3Gbps version is known as **SATA 2** or SATA II, and the latest release is **SATA 3** or SATA III running at a maximum of 6Gbps. These devices are commonly seen marked as SATA, SATA II, and SATA III.

SATA is a point-to-point interface, which means that (1) each device connects to the host through a dedicated link (unlike the traditional parallel IDE where two devices share the host link), and (2) each device has the entire interface bandwidth. SATA uses a smaller, 7-pin cable that is more like a network cable than the traditional IDE ribbon cable. SATA supports both internal and external devices. Figure 7.19 shows an internal SATA drive with the cable attached. The connector to the right of the cable is where the power connector attaches.

Figure 7.19 SATA hard drive and data cable

An internal SATA device uses a 15-pin SATA power connector rather than a Molex that the older hard drives used. A Molex to SATA cable converter can be purchased, but the connector can only provide 5 and 12 volts, not 3.3 volts. The good news is that most SATA drives do not use the 3.3V line. Figure 7.20 shows the older Molex power connector compared to the internal SATA power connector.

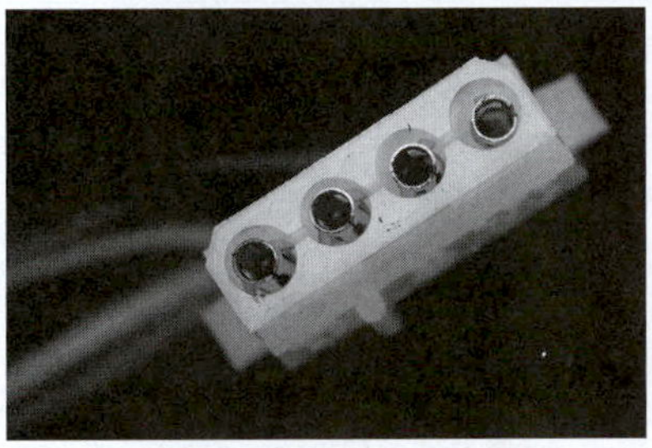

Molex power connector used with PATA devices

Internal SATA power connector

Figure 7.20 Hard drive power connectors

Internal SATA data cables are limited to a maximum of 3.3 feet (1 meter). The internal SATA data cable is more likely to be inadvertently unplugged or partially unplugged than the PATA cable. Special cables with locking mechanisms or in an L shape for hard to reach places or low profile form factor cases can be purchased. Figure 7.21 shows these 7-pin internal SATA device cables.

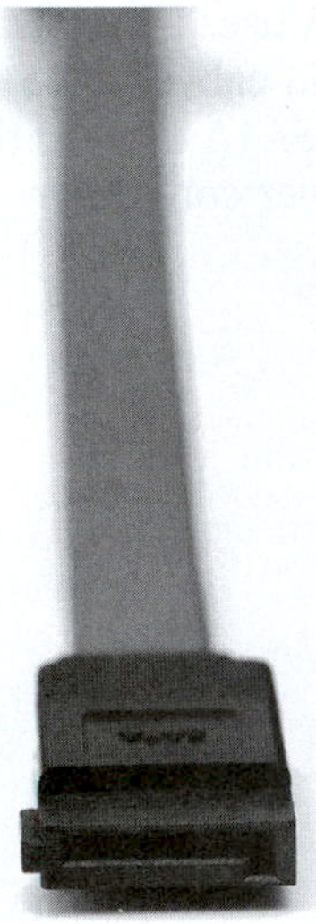

Standard

Locking

L-shaped

Figure 7.21 Internal SATA data cables

eSATA (External SATA) provides external device connectivity using the SATA standard. allows shielded cable lengths up to 6.56 feet (2 meters), with faster connections than USB 2.0 or most IEEE 1394 types. However, the standard eSATA connection does not provide power to external devices, but an eSATAp combo USB/eSATA port can provide power. Figure 7.22 shows an eSATA cable and eSATA port. An eSATA cable can be rated for 1.5, 3, or 6Gbps. eSATA cables are limited to 3.3 feet (1 meter) for 1.5Gbps devices and 6.56 feet (2 meters) for 3/6Gbps transfers. The eSATA connector may be integrated (especially in a laptop) as a combination USB/eSATA port.

eSATA 3.0Gbps cable

eSATA port

Figure 7.22 eSATA cable and port

Internal and external SATA devices are also found in laptops and netbooks. Tablets and smartphones do not normally contain drives, but use flash memory instead. Just a short time ago, internal SATA devices tended to be smaller in capacity in mobile devices than in desktop computers, but that is no longer true. Internal SATA devices can connect to the older PCI or the newer PCIe bus. External SATA devices are connected using the same methods as a desktop—eSATA or eSATAp. Refer to Figure 7.11 to see an internal hard drive in a netbook.

SSD (Solid State Drive)

SSDs (solid state drives) are storage devices that use nonvolatile flash memory technologies instead of hard drive technologies. SSDs connect to the computer through several types of interfaces: SATA, SAS, PCIe, USB, PATA, and SCSI. SSDs eliminate the number-one cause of hard drive failure: moving parts. SSDs typically use flash memory and can therefore be low heat producing, reliable, quiet, secure, long-lasting, and fast. SSDs are being installed in laptops and desktop models as internal and external units. SSDs are common in tablets and some mobile devices. They are also used in environments such as temperature extremes or where the drive might be jolted. SSDs can be used in conjunction with mechanical hard drive storage. SSDs are used in the following industries:

- Medical—CRT/MRI image storage, monitoring equipment, portable devices
- IT—Video surveillance, wireless base stations, security appliances
- Industrial—Robotic systems, test equipment, manufacturing devices
- Automotive—Diagnostics, store safety information, store travel statistics

Another difference between hard drives and SSDs is how data is actually written. Write amplification and wear leveling are two terms used with SSDs that technicians should understand. To write data, an SSD may have to do an erase operation, move data to another location, and then write the information to memory. Still, overall performance is increased. **Write amplification** is the minimum amount of memory storage space affected by a write request. For example, if there is 4KB of information to be written and the SSD has a 128KB erase block, 128KB must be erased before the 4KB of information can be written. Writing takes longer than reading with SSDs.

Wear leveling is a technique used to erase and write data using all of the memory blocks instead of the same memory blocks repeatedly. SSD manufacturers are using various technologies: (1) software to track usage and direct write operations, (2) a certain amount of reserved memory blocks to use when a memory block does fail, and (3) a combination of the two techniques.

Two types of technologies used with SSDs are SLC and MLC. **SLCs** (single-level memory cells) store 1 bit in each memory cell and last longer than MLCs, but they are more expensive. **MLCs** (multi-level memory cells) store more than 1 bit in each memory cell and are cheaper to manufacturer, but they have slower transfer speeds.

The main drawback to SSDs is cost. SSDs are expensive compared to hard drives. As with flash drives, each memory block of an SSD has a finite number of reads and writes. An SSD that writes data across the entire memory capacity will last longer. Some companies are including software with the drive that tracks or estimates end of life. Figure 7.23 shows the insides of an SSD.

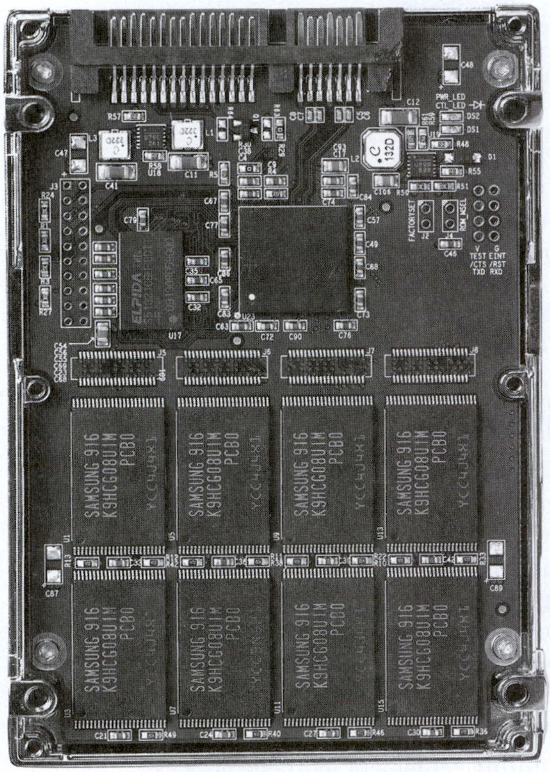

Figure 7.23 Solid state drive

SCSI (Small Computer System Interface)

SCSI (Small Computer System Interface) can control many different types of devices such as scanners, tape drives, hard drives, optical drives, printers, and disk array subsystems. SCSI comes in two types: parallel SCSI (usually referred to as simply SCSI) and SAS (serial attached SCSI), which is covered in the next section. The parallel SCSI standard allows connection of multiple internal and external devices to the same adapter. All devices that connect to the same parallel SCSI controller share a common data bus called the SCSI bus (or SCSI chain). Features such as increased speed and multiple device support cost more. Parallel SCSI is more expensive than PATA drives.

The SCSI host adapter (usually a separate card, but it can be built into the motherboard) connects the SCSI device to the motherboard and coordinates the activities of the other devices connected. Three basic standards of SCSI are called SCSI-1, SCSI-2, and SCSI-3. Figure 7.24 shows a SCSI hard drive, and Table 7.2 shows parallel SCSI standards.

Figure 7.24 SCSI hard drive

Table 7.2 SCSI standards

SCSI standard	SCSI term	Speed (MBps)
SCSI-1	Narrow	5
SCSI-2		
	Fast	10
	Wide	20
	Fast-Wide	20
SCSI-3	Ultra	20
	Ultra	40
	Ultra-Wide	40
	Ultra2-Wide	80
	Ultra3	160
	Ultra160	160
	Ultra160+	160
	Ultra320	320
	Ultra640	640

The latest SCSI devices that might be found in a PC are known as SAS (Serial Attached SCSI). SAS devices connect through a serial architecture which means they attach in a point-to-point bus. SAS devices are more expensive than SATA IDE devices because they target the enterprise environment where high reliability and high **MTBF** (mean time between failures—the average number of hours before a drive is likely to fail) is important. SAS drives come in two flavors—3 and 6Gbps. SAS devices are normally hard drives, but SAS could also be used for other devices such as tape drives. Figure 7.25 shows SAS drives that would insert into a network server.

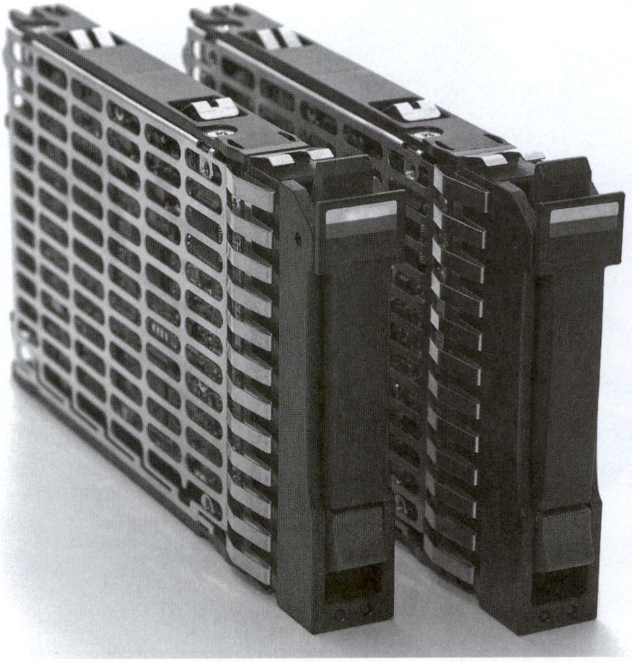

Figure 7.25 SAS drives

SCSI storage devices are more frequently found in a network environment. Other types of SCSI used with networking include FC (Fibre Channel), SSA (Serial Storage Architecture), and iSCSI.

Storage Device Configuration Overview

Drive configuration sometimes includes setting jumpers on the drive and sometimes on the associated adapter and ensuring proper termination. Termination is a method used to prevent signals from reflecting back up the cable. Each drive type has a normal configuration method. However, individual drive manufacturers may develop their own configuration steps. Always refer to the documentation included with the drive, adapter, or motherboard for configuration and installation information.

PATA Physical Installation

PATA IDE devices (including hard drives) are simpler to configure than parallel SCSI devices. The overall steps for installing a PATA device are as follows:

1. Keep the drive in the protective antistatic container until you are ready to install.
2. Use proper antistatic handling procedures when installing the drive and handle the drive by the edges; avoid touching the drive electronics and connectors.
3. Turn off and remove the power cord when installing the drive.

4. Determine how many devices will attach to the same cable and configure their jumpers accordingly.
5. Physically mount and secure the device in the computer and attach the proper cable.
6. Configure the BIOS, if necessary.
7. If a hard drive, prepare the drive for data as described later in the chapter.

Actually, these steps apply to SATA and SCSI as well except for configuring jumpers and for SATA, determining how many devices attach to the same cable because SATA is a point-to-point architecture and only one device attaches to the connector.

Older motherboards frequently had two PATA IDE connectors (although a few had three or four). The IDE connectors are known as the primary or primary IDE channel, secondary or secondary IDE channel, and if there are third or fourth connectors, they are known as the tertiary channel and quaternary channel respectively. Figure 7.26 shows a motherboard with four integrated IDE connectors.

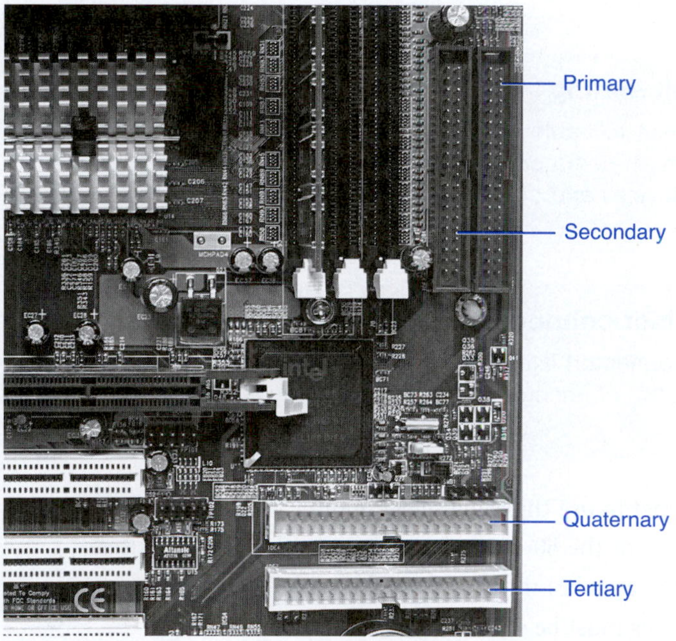

Figure 7.26 PATA motherboard connectors

Each channel (connector) can have a master and a slave device. To distinguish between the devices, use the channel name followed by the words **master** or **slave**. The two settings are simply used to distinguish between the two devices because only one of the two devices (master or slave) can transmit data when connected to the same IDE channel (cable). For example, if two hard drives are installed on the primary channel, they are called primary master and primary slave.

PATA IDE devices are normally configured using jumpers. The four options commonly found are single, master, slave, and cable select. The **single** IDE setting is used when only one device connects to the cable. The master IDE setting is used in conjunction with the slave setting and both are used when two IDE devices connect to the same cable. One device is set to the master setting while the other device uses the slave setting. The **cable select** IDE option replaces the master/slave setting. The device automatically configures itself to either the master setting or the slave setting depending on the specific cable connector to which the device attaches. To use the cable select option, a special 80-conductor, 40-pin cable is needed. This cable has pin 28 disabled. All 80-conductor (40-pin) cables that meet the ATA specifications automatically support cable select, and the connectors, are color-coded according to the specifications. Figure 7.27 shows the connections for an 80-conductor cable.

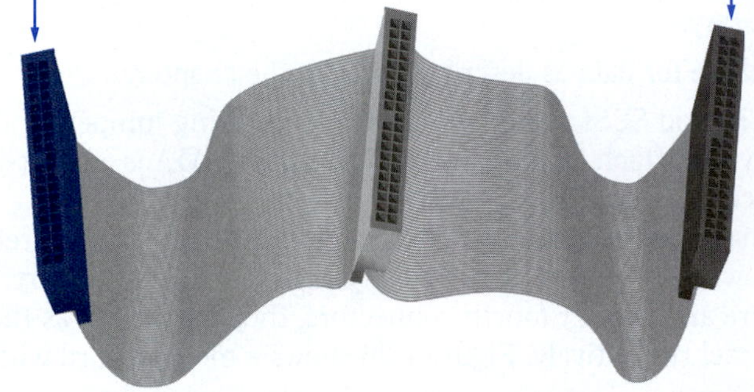

Figure 7.27 80-conductor PATA IDE cable connections

> **Tech Tip**
> **Check your PATA IDE default setting**
> Most PATA hard drives come preset to cable select, whereas most other PATA devices, such as tape drives and optical drives, come preset to any of the settings. It is always best to check the settings of installed devices and of any new devices being installed.

> **Tech Tip**
> **Determining which cable select connector to use**
> The master connector (the black connector) is at the end of the cable. The slave connector (the gray one) is in the middle of the connector, and the blue connector attaches to the motherboard.

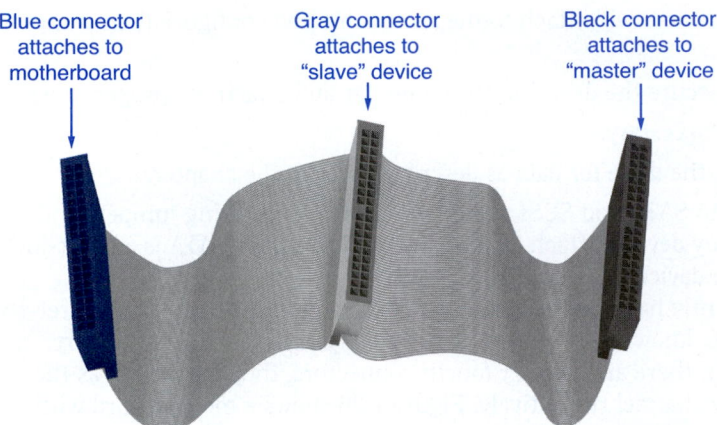

The following criteria must be met to use the cable select option:

- A special IDE cable select cable or the 80-conductor (40-pin) cable must be used.
- The host interface (controlling circuits) must support the cable select option.
- The one or two attached devices must be set to the cable select option.

> **Tech Tip**
> **Do not use the 40-conductor cable with the cable select option**
> Do not set to the cable select option unless the 80-conductor cable is installed. If two devices are set to the cable select option and a regular IDE cable is used, both devices are configured as master and will not work properly.

There are two methods of configuring PATA IDE devices: (1) configure one device as master and the other device as slave or (2) configure both devices to the cable select option. By doing this, the device that connects to the black connector becomes the "master" and the device that connects to the gray connector becomes the "slave." Whichever method is used, the following are recommendations:

- When two IDE devices connect to the same cable, the faster or larger capacity device should be configured as master. Hard drives are normally the fastest IDE devices.
- When only one device (the master) connects to an older 40-conductor IDE cable, connect the device to the end connector (the one farthest from the motherboard) for best performance. Some devices show errors when there is only one IDE device and it connects to the center cable connector.

- If there are two PATA IDE devices installed in the computer, a hard drive and an optical drive, install the hard drive on one IDE channel (primary) and the optical drive on the secondary IDE channel.
- Avoid putting a hard drive and an optical drive on the same channel. The optical device uses a more complicated command set than the hard drive and it can slow down the hard drive.
- If you have two optical drives and you transfer data frequently between the two, it is best to put them on separate channels. However, putting one of these devices with a hard drive is not a good idea either.
- For optimum performance, connect the hard drive that you boot from to the primary IDE motherboard connector and configure it as master.

Figure 7.28 illustrates how multiple PATA devices connect to the motherboard.

Watch out for PATA cable lengths

IDE devices connect to a 40-pin, 80-conductor ribbon cable. The maximum IDE cable length is 18 inches, which presents a problem with tower computers. Some companies sell 24- or 36-inch IDE cables. These do not meet specifications. If IDE problems or intermittent problems occur, replace the cable with one that meets specifications.

Tech Tip

Almost all PATA IDE devices ship with cable select option selected. Figure 7.29 shows an illustration of two PATA IDE hard drives configured with the cable select option.

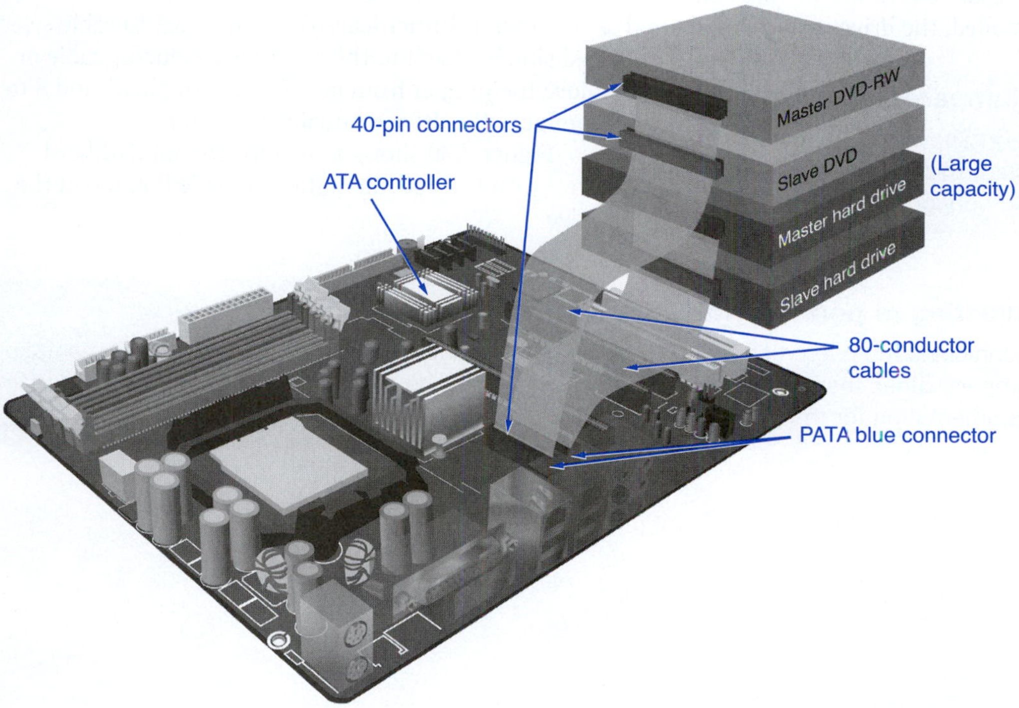

Figure 7.28 PATA device connectivity

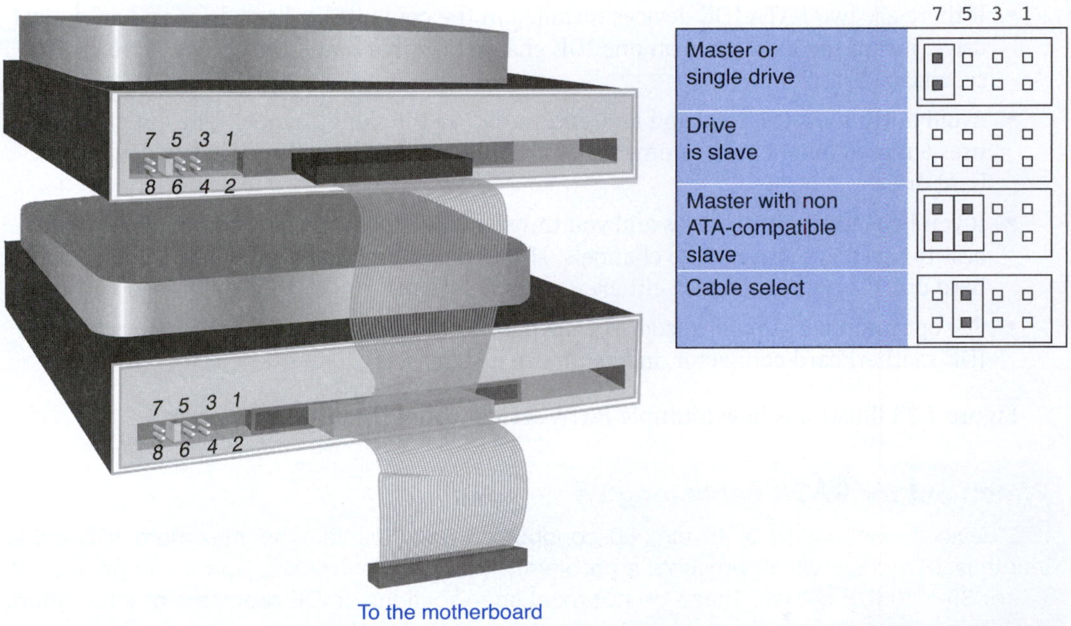

Figure 7.29 Two PATA devices configured with cable select

The table in Figure 7.29 shows several possible configurations. A similar table is found either on top of a hard drive or in the documentation included with the hard drive. The third alternative is to use the manufacturer's Internet site. If only one IDE hard drive is to be installed, the drive is to be configured as the master. Either leave the jumper set to cable select and simply attach to the black 80-conductor cable or move the jumper from pins 5 and 6 to pins 7 and 8 to configure the drive manually as master.

Figure 7.30 shows a Western Digital IDE hard drive with the documentation stenciled on top of the drive.

Tech Tip

Closed means jumpered or enabled

When documentation shows an option as closed, jumpered, or enabled, this means to put a jumper over the two pins to configure the option.

Tech Tip

Adjusting to poorly written documentation

Technicians must learn to adjust to poorly written and sometimes confusing documentation. Jumpers other than the master/slave jumpers may be present, but you must refer to the documentation for the proper settings.

Figure 7.30 Western Digital PATA hard drive

SATA Physical Installation

SATA drives are easy to install. Most internal drives require a special host adapter that supports one to four drives or an integrated motherboard connection. Each drive is seen as a point-to-point connection with the host controller.

SATA drives do not have any master/slave, cable select, or termination jumpers or settings. A serial 7-pin data connector attaches from the SATA controller to the internal SATA drive. A 15-pin cable connects power to the drive. The internal SATA power connector is not a Molex or Berg connector; it is a different type of connector. A cable converter can be obtained if a Molex connector is the only one available from the power supply. Figure 7.31 shows an internal SATA hard drive with associated cabling. Notice the Molex-to-internal SATA cable converter in the photo.

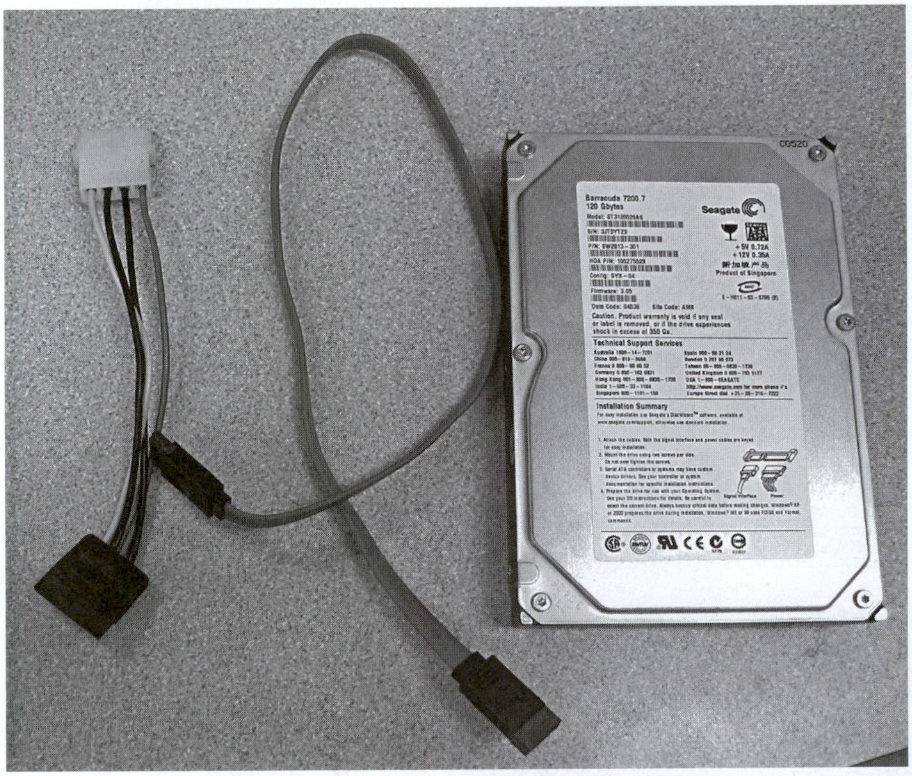

Figure 7.31 **SATA hard drive and cables**

There are also products available that allow a Serial ATA hard drive to connect to a standard IDE controller. Figure 7.32 shows how two SATA drives attach to a motherboard that has two SATA connectors.

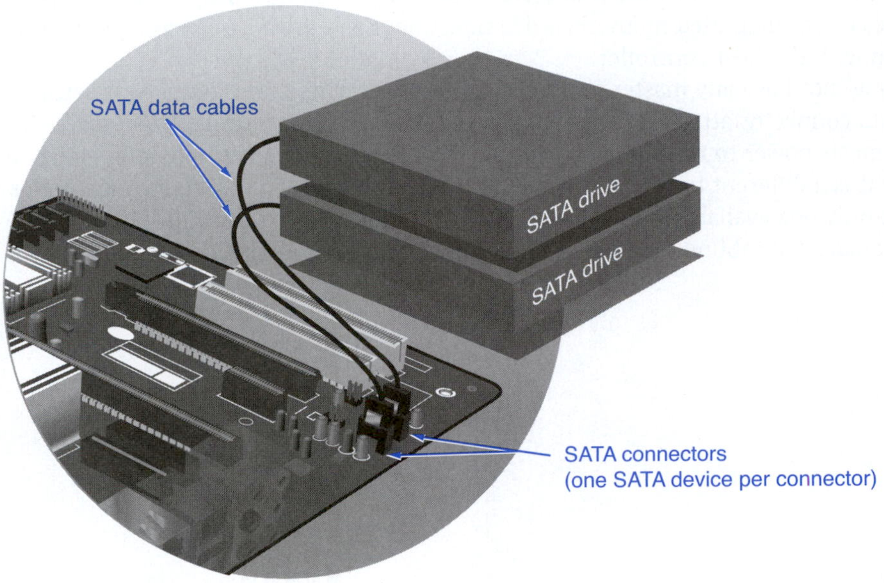

Figure 7.32 **SATA connectivity**

To install a SATA host adapter, power off the computer and remove the computer power cord. Remove the computer cover and locate an open expansion slot. Some adapters have jumpers for configurable options. Some common options include 16- and 32-bit PCI operations, adapter BIOS enabled/disabled, and Mode 0 enabled/ disabled. Some adapters may provide master/slave emulation options. Most adapters' default settings will work, but always refer to the adapter's documentation for details.

Tech Tip

Enable SATA port

Many manufacturers require that you enable the motherboard port through the system BIOS before any device connected to the port is recognized.

To install an internal SATA hard drive, power off the computer, and remove the computer's power cord. Physically mount the drive into a drive bay. Connect the SATA signal cable between the drive and the host controller. Connect the SATA power cord to the drive and an available Molex connector from the power supply. Figure 7.33 shows an installed SATA hard drive attached to a host adapter.

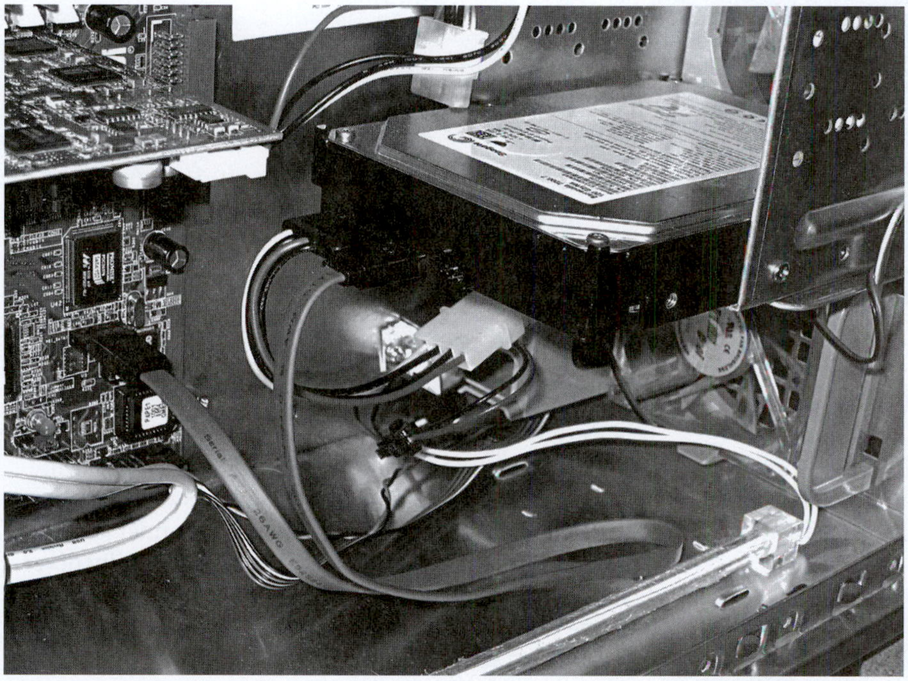

Figure 7.33 Installed SATA hard drive and adapter

An external (eSATA) drive normally has no jumpers, terminators, or switches to be configured. However, when installing a faster drive to a slower port—such as when installing a 3.0Gbps drive to a 1.5Gbps port—a jumper may need to be configured so the drive is compatible with the port. Always refer to the drive manufacturer's documentation when installing a drive. Attach the power cord to the drive, if applicable, and insert the other end of the power cord into a wall outlet. Attach one end of the eSATA cable to the drive. Plug the other end of the cable into an eSATA port on the computer. Note that some systems use the original SATA 1.5Gbps (sometimes called SATA 1) port, and the drive may be a 3.0Gbps (sometimes called SATA 2) drive. A cable converter may be necessary. Laptops sometimes have combination USB/SATA ports called eSATAp ports. eSATA ports are sometimes disabled in BIOS and sometimes require BIOS changes, updates, and/or device drivers. Figure 7.34 shows an external hard drive that supports IEEE 1394 (FireWire), eSATA, and USB as you can see from the ports on the back of the unit.

Figure 7.34 External hard drive

Before switching on eSATA drive power, ensure that the drive is positioned where it will stay during operation and that all data and power cords are attached securely. Switch on the drive power. The drive mounts. When a drive is mounted, a communications channel is opened between the drive and the operating system. Whenever the drive is to be disconnected, it is to be unmounted. Some drive manufacturers provide software for backing up data or configuring the drive in a RAID configuration. Use the Windows Disk Management tool to ensure that the drive is recognized. Both RAID and the Disk Management tool are covered later in this chapter.

Tech Tip

Unmounting an eSATA drive

To unmount an eSATA drive, click the *Safely Remove Hardware* icon in the systray/notification area. Select the appropriate drive letter. Remove the drive when prompted by the operating system.

SSD Physical Installation

For a desktop computer, an SSD can be internally mounted and connected to a SATA/PATA motherboard or an adapter port. An SSD can also attach as an external device to a SATA, USB, or FireWire port. An SSD can be mounted as a replacement part for a laptop hard drive. SSDs do not normally require special drivers. Always refer to the SSD mounting directions provided by the manufacturer. The following steps are generic ones:

1. If installing an SSD internally into a desktop computer, power off the computer and locate an empty drive bay, a power connector of the appropriate type (or buy a converter), and an available SATA/PATA port or free PATA connector on a PATA cable.

2. Attach mounting brackets to the SSD. Mounting brackets may have to be purchased separately, be provided with the drive, or be provided as spares that came with the computer.
3. Slide the SSD into the drive bay and secure it, if necessary.
4. Connect the data cable from the motherboard or adapter to the drive.
5. Attach a power cable to the SSD.
6. Re-install the computer cover and power on the computer.

Tech Tip

Beware of static electricity

SSDs are flash memory and are susceptible to static electricity. Use proper ESD handling procedures when installing an SSD.

If installing an SSD internally into a laptop, power off the computer, disconnect the AC adapter, and remove the battery. Remove the drive bay access cover and install the SSD. Reattach the access cover, battery, and AC adapter, if necessary. Power on the laptop. Figure 7.35 shows an internal SATA SSD.

Figure 7.35 Internal SSD

The BIOS should recognize an internally installed SSD. If it does not, go into the system BIOS setup and ensure that the connector to which the SSD attaches is enabled. Be especially careful with SATA ports and port numbering. Configure the system to automatically detect the new drive, save the settings, and reboot the system.

If installing an external SSD, attach the appropriate USB, SATA, or IEEE 1394 (FireWire) cable from the drive to the computer. Power on the SSD. The system should recognize the new drive.

Tech Tip

Use only one technology

If an external drive supports more than one technology, such as eSATA, FireWire, and USB, attach only one type of cable from the drive to the computer.

Parallel SCSI Configuration

Configure a parallel SCSI device by doing the following:

1. Setting the proper SCSI ID
2. Terminating both ends of the SCSI chain
3. Connecting the proper cable(s)

The parallel SCSI chain consists of several SCSI devices cabled together. The SCSI chain includes SCSI devices and a single controller, sometimes called a host adapter. The SCSI controller is usually a separate adapter, but it may be built into the motherboard. The SCSI chain includes internal SCSI devices that connect to the SCSI host adapter and any external SCSI devices that connect to an adapter's external port. Multiple SCSI chains can exist in a system, and a computer can contain up to four SCSI host adapters. A SCSI-1 host adapter supports up to seven internal or external devices. SCSI-2 or higher adapters support up to 15 internal or external devices.

SCSI ID Configuration and Termination

Each device on a SCSI chain, including the SCSI host adapter, is assigned a **SCSI ID**. (Some SCSI hard drive manufacturers refer to this setting as the drive select ID.) The SCSI ID allows each device to share the same SCSI bus, and it assigns a priority for each device. The SCSI interface allows a SCSI device to communicate directly with another SCSI device connected on the same SCSI chain. The higher the SCSI number, the higher the priority of the device on the SCSI chain. SCSI IDs are normally set using switches, jumpers, SCSI BIOS software, or manufacturer-provided software.

Standard SCSI devices (8-bit devices) recognize SCSI IDs 0 through 7. Wide SCSI devices (16-bit devices) recognize SCSI IDs 0 through 15. The SCSI ID priority values are as follows from highest priority value to lowest. Figure 7.36 shows the SCSI priority numbers, from highest to lowest.

Tech Tip

Power on all external SCSI devices *before* turning on the computer

The host adapter detects all SCSI devices along the SCSI chain during the boot process. However, if a SCSI device is not used frequently the device can be powered off. The rest of the SCSI devices operate even if a SCSI device is powered off. If two devices have the same SCSI ID, a SCSI ID conflict occurs and the devices will not work properly. Setting an improper SCSI ID (priority) setting results in slower SCSI device performance.

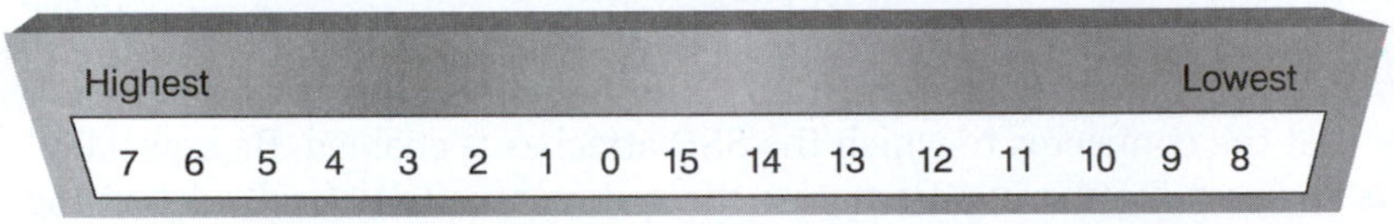

Figure 7.36 SCSI ID priority levels

The SCSI host adapter is normally preset to SCSI ID 7, the highest priority, and should not be changed. Slower devices such as scanners, optical drives, or video encoders should be assigned a higher SCSI ID such as 6 or 5 for a standard SCSI device and 15 or 14 for a Wide SCSI device, so they receive ample time to move data onto the SCSI bus. SCSI ID 0 is the default for most SCSI hard drives. A development that is helpful in setting SCSI IDs is SCAM (SCSI Configured AutoMatically).

Termination of SCSI devices is very important. Proper termination of SCSI devices keeps the signals from bouncing back up the cable and provides the proper electrical current level for the SCSI chain. The SCSI bus cannot operate properly without terminating both ends of the SCSI bus. Improper termination can make one, many, or all SCSI devices not work properly. Over time, improper termination can damage a SCSI adapter or a SCSI device. SCSI termination is performed in several ways: (1) by installing a SIPP (single inline pin package),

(2) by installing a jumper, (3) by setting a switch, (4) by installing a terminator plug, (5) by installing a pass through terminator, or (6) with software.

When setting or removing termination, refer to the documentation included with the adapter or device. If the terminator to an external SCSI device is not provided with the device, it must be purchased separately. Some internal SCSI cables do not have a terminator built into them.

Figure 7.37 shows a SCSI hard drive. The SCSI ID configuration is shown with the diagram on the bottom-right side.

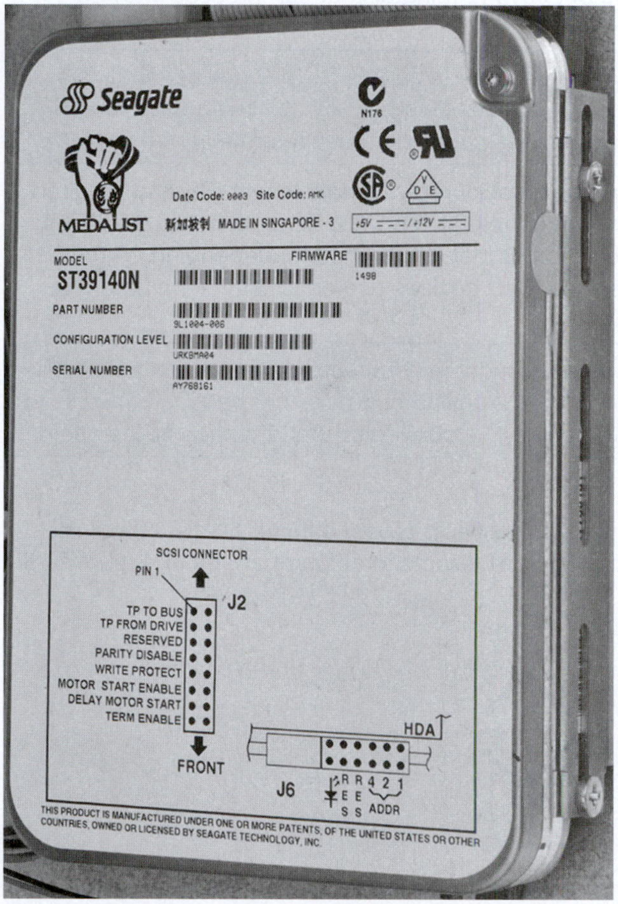

Figure 7.37 SCSI hard drive

There are several types of SCSI electrical signals and terminators. The three major categories are SE, HVD, and LVD. Table 7.3 explains them. The majority of terminators in use are either active or the FPT active terminator.

Table 7.3 SCSI electrical signals/terminator technologies

Technology/term	Explanation
SE (single-ended) terminator	Terminators used by most SCSI devices. It can use passive and active terminators. It has a maximum bus length of 9 feet (2.7 meters).
Passive terminator	Terminators used on SCSI-1 devices. They are not good for long cable distances because they are susceptible to noise interference.

Technology/term	Explanation
Active terminator	Terminators that can be used on SCSI-1, -2, and -3 devices. They allow for longer cable distances and provide the correct voltage for SCSI signals. This type must be used with Fast, Wide, or Fast-Wide SCSI devices. A passive and an active terminator can be used on the same chain. SCSI-3 requires active termination.
FPT (forced perfect termination)	A special type of active terminator that can be used with SE devices.
HVD (high-voltage differential)	A technology that was used in a few SCSI-2 devices that allowed a longer SCSI bus length. HVD devices must use HVD terminators (sometimes called differential terminators).
LVD (low-voltage differential)	A technology that is backward compatible with SE and required on all devices that adhere to the Ultra SCSI standard. LVD bus length can be up to 39 feet (11.88 meters) depending on the number of devices. LVD devices use either LVD terminators or LVD/SE terminators.
Pass-through terminator	A terminator used by most internal hard drives. It has an extra connector and allows a device that does not have terminators to be terminated through the connector that attaches to the cable.

Being able to distinguish among various SCSI devices is very difficult because there are many SCSI flavors. Special icons are placed on SCSI devices to differentiate them. Figure 7.38 shows these icons.

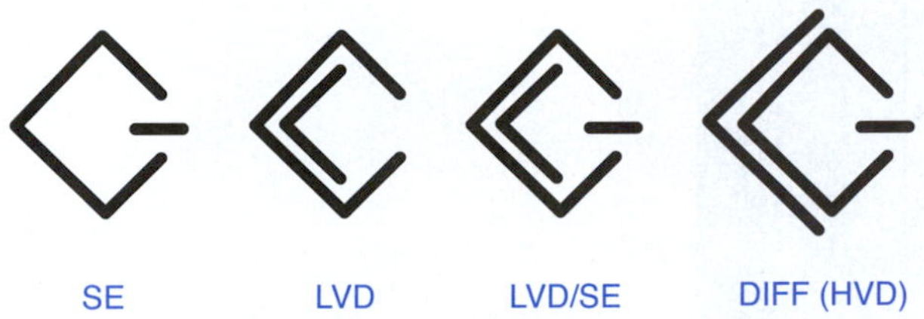

Figure 7.38 SCSI symbols

If only internal devices connect to a SCSI host adapter, terminate the adapter and the last internal device connected to the cable. Remove the termination from all other devices. When connecting only external devices to the SCSI host adapter or motherboard, terminate the adapter and the last external device. Remove the terminations from all other external devices.

Figure 7.39 shows SCSI IDs and termination for an internal and external device scenario. If both internal and external devices attach to the SCSI host adapter, the last internal device connected to the SCSI cable is terminated as well as the last external device. All other devices and the SCSI host adapter must have their terminators removed. The SCSI chain in Figure 7.39 consists of two internal SCSI devices (a CD drive and a hard drive) and two external SCSI devices (a tape drive and a scanner). The two ends of the SCSI chain that must be terminated are the CD drive and the scanner. All other devices are not terminated. Note that some SCSI adapters stay terminated even if they are in the middle of the chain or they treat the external chain as one SCSI bus and the internal chain as a separate SCSI bus. Refer to the documentation to see about these types of issues.

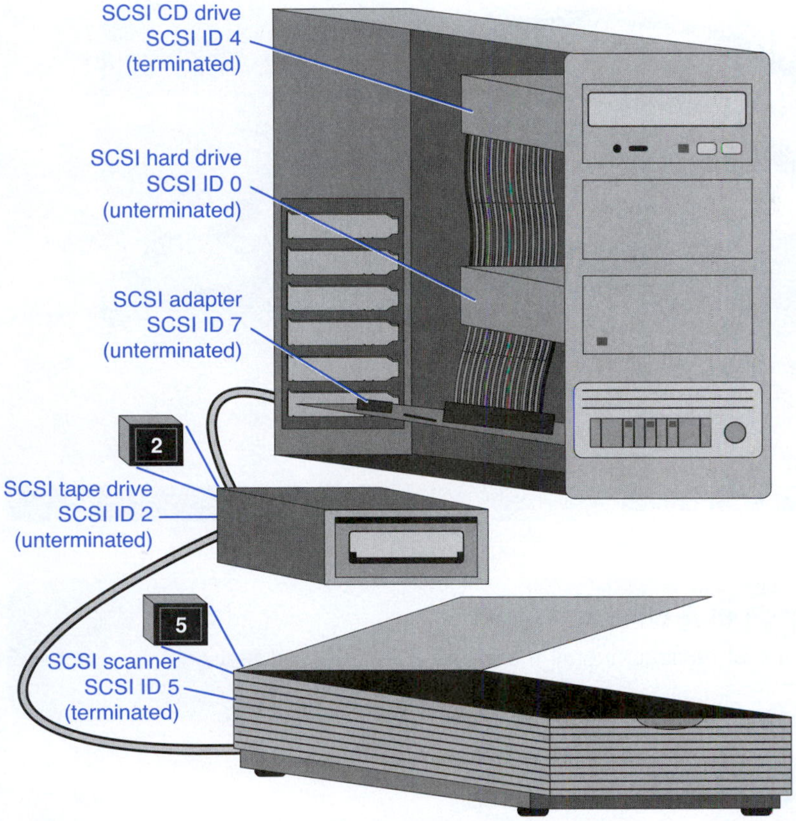

Figure 7.39 Internal and external SCSI devices—termination

A smart technician plans the configuration of a drive before installing the drive in the system. A good plan of attack is the best strategy to avoid problems during installation. Draw the configuration on a piece of paper to help get the installation straight in your mind. To help new technicians with different configurations, the exercises at the end of the chapter contain sample practice configurations.

Tech Tip

Use software that comes with the SCSI adapter for configuration

Newer SCSI cards have either a software utility that ships with the adapter or a software program built into the adapter's ROM chip that allows configuration through software.

SCSI Cables

Parallel SCSI cabling allows multiple devices to be connected to one SCSI host adapter and share the same SCSI bus; this is called daisy chaining. Daisy chaining is like connecting multiple Christmas light sets together. If multiple internal SCSI devices attach to the SCSI adapter, then use an internal SCSI cable with multiple connectors. Most internal SCSI-1 and SCSI-2 cables are 50-pin ribbon cables. Internal SCSI-3 cables are 68-pin ribbon cables.

To connect external SCSI-1 devices, a 50-pin Centronics to 50-pin Centronics cable is used. The SCSI-1 cable is also known as an A Cable. The SCSI-2 standard has a 50-pin D-shell connector that connects to the SCSI host adapter and a Centronics connector that connects to the external device. For 16-bit SCSI devices, a second 68-pin cable, called the B Cable, must be used in addition to the A Cable. SCSI-3 has a 68-pin cable called the P Cable. Figure 7.40 illustrates some SCSI cables.

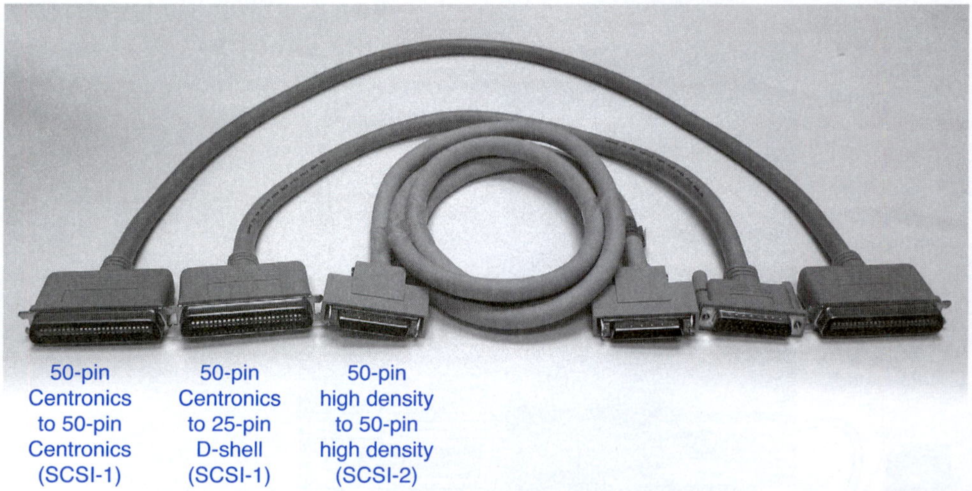

Figure 7.40 External SCSI cables

Tech Tip

Install one SCSI device at a time and test

When installing multiple SCSI devices, install them one at a time and test each one before installing the next one.

SAS Installation

SAS drives are probably the easiest drives of all to install. They normally install into a server, but some business computers and home computers that need a reliable hard drive that lasts longer than the other types will pay the additional money for a SAS drive. SAS drives normally do not require data or power cables to be attached. They get power through the SAS host connection in the computer. That is why drives are normally mounted in hard drive slots or bays on servers. Most home and business computers don't have SAS host interfaces. A cable can be bought and the maximum length is 13.1 feet (4 meters). Also, the drive might have to be installed into a SAS tray or carrier before you can slide into the computer. Figure 7.41 shows a server that has two bays for SAS drives.

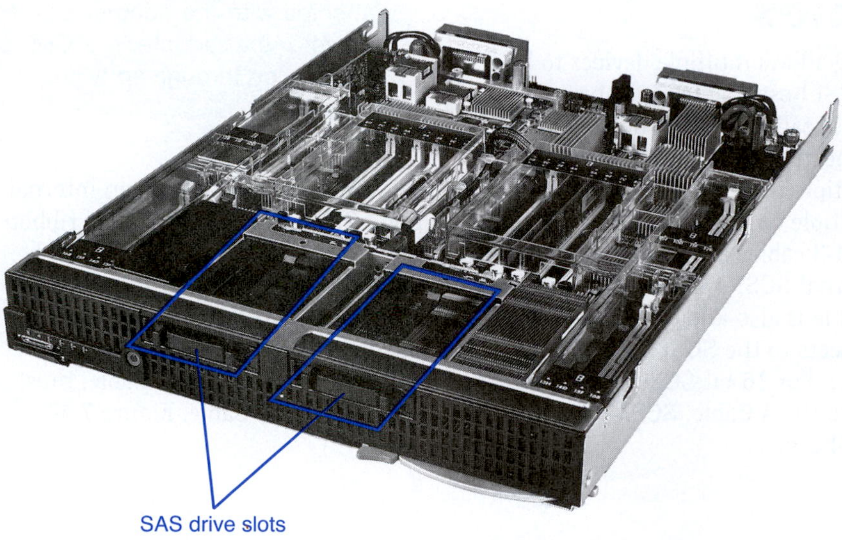

Figure 7.41 Server with SAS drive bays

An interesting point about SAS is that some SAS connectors can accept SATA 3 devices. However, the reverse is not true—you cannot attach a SAS device to a SATA connector.

Mobile Device Storage

Laptops traditionally had a PATA or SATA hard drive installed, but today they have an SSD instead of or in addition to these hard drive types. Other mobile devices such as ultrabooks and netbooks use SSDs as well. A mini PCI or PCIe adapter can be used to connect the drive to the system, or the drive can be directly attached to the motherboard. Additional storage can be provided by devices that connect to USB, eSATA, eSATAp, or IEEE 1394 ports. PC Cards or ExpressCard hard drives can also be used to provide storage expansion. For external drives, attach the drive to external power if necessary. Some USB devices use external power, some are powered and connect to one USB port, while still others require two USB ports. Some manufacturers may require you to install software before attaching the drive. Once installed, use Device Manager to ensure the drive is recognized by the operating system. If the drive is a FireWire device, the drive may appear under the IEEE 1394 Devices section of Device Manager.

Two methods are used with hard drives installed in portable computers: proprietary or removable. With a proprietary installation, the hard drive is installed in a location where it cannot be changed, configured, or moved very easily. Proprietary cables and connectors are used. With removable hard drives, the laptop has a hard drive bay that allows installation/removal through a single connector that provides power as well as data signaling. Otherwise, the drive could have separate data and power connectors. Figure 7.42 shows an internal SATA hard drive that is used in a portable computer.

Figure 7.42 Laptop internal hard drive

Tech Tip

What to do if you want more storage space for a laptop

Laptops do not normally allow a second hard drive. However, you can add an additional hard drive to the USB, eSATA, combo eSATAp, or IEEE 1394 (FireWire) port.

System BIOS Configuration for Hard Drives

A hard drive is configured through the system BIOS Setup program. Setup is accessed through keystrokes during the boot process. In today's computers, the setting is Auto, and the BIOS automatically detects the hard drive type. The drive type information is saved in CMOS.

Hard drives are normally configured using the Auto-Detect feature included with BIOS. The Auto-Detect feature automatically determines the drive type for the system. For SCSI hard drive installations, sometimes the BIOS setting is type 0 or None. Once the system boots, the SCSI controller's BIOS initializes and the SCSI hard drive takes over and boots the system. Even though the drive type number is set to 0 or None, if this step is omitted, the hard drive will not operate.

Tech Tip

Configure BIOS according to the drive manufacturer's instructions

Drive manufacturers normally include documentation describing how to configure the drive in BIOS Setup. Also, they provide software for any system that does not recognize the drive.

Table 7.4 shows the most commonly used PATA/SATA hard drive settings. SATA drives can be set in different modes of operation: (1) legacy mode, which is used in a system that doesn't have SATA drivers natively, (2) **AHCI** (Advanced Host Controller Interface) mode, which, when enabled, allows SATA drives to be inserted/removed when power is on and use commands that allow the host circuits to communicate with attached devices to implement advanced SATA features, and (3) RAID mode. RAID is discussed later in this chapter. Note that the BIOS is also where you select the drive that you want to boot the system.

Table 7.4 **Common hard drive BIOS settings**

Hard drive type	BIOS setting
IDE PATA/SATA/SCSI/SAS	AUTO
SATA	SATA mode: IDE mode (no AHCI or RAID)
SATA	SATA mode: SATA or AHCI (AHCI enabled)
SATA	SATA mode: RAID (AHCI and RAID enabled)
Older parallel SCSI	TYPE 0

Hard Drive Preparation Overview

Once a hard drive is installed and configured properly and the hard drive type is entered into the Setup program, the drive must be prepared to accept data. The two steps of hard drive preparation are as follows:

1. Partition the drive.
2. High-level format the hard drive.

Tech Tip

Low-level formatting

There is such a thing as low-level formatting done at the hard drive factory. Some manufacturers provide software that allows you to low-level format the drive. This should only be done at the direction of the manufacturer.

Partitioning a hard drive allows a drive letter to be assigned to one or more parts of the hard drive. **High-level formatting** prepares the drive for use for a particular file system. This allows the drive to accept data from the operating system. For today's computers, a drive cannot be used until it has been partitioned and high-level formatted; thus, technicians must be very familiar with these steps.

Partitioning

The first step in preparing a hard drive for use is partitioning. Partitioning a hard drive divides the drive so the computer system sees the hard drive as more than one drive. DOS and Windows 9x have a software program called `FDISK` that partitions hard drives. That process has been replaced by the **Disk Management** program that is available after the operating system is installed, or by using the **`diskpart`** utility from the command line. Disk Management is normally used to partition additional hard drives and to manage all of them. The first hard drive in the system is normally partitioned as part of the Windows installation process. Additional partitions can be created using Disk Management once the operating system is installed.

Partitioning provides advantages such as the following:

- Dividing a hard drive into separate subunits that are then assigned drive letters, such as `C:` or `D:`, by the operating system
- Organizing the hard drive to separate multiple operating systems, applications, and data
- Providing data security by placing data in a different partition to allow ease of backup as well as protection
- Using the hard drive to its fullest capacity

The original purpose of partitioning was to allow for loading multiple operating systems. This is still a good reason today because placing each operating system in its own partition eliminates the crashes and headaches caused by multiple operating systems and multiple applications coexisting in the same partition. The type of partition and how big the partition can be depends on the file system being used. A **file system** defines how data is stored on a drive. The most common Windows file systems are FAT16, FAT32, exFAT, and NTFS. The file system that can be used depends on what operating system is installed, whether the device is an internal device or external, and whether files are to be shared. Table 7.5 lists file systems and explains a little about each one.

Tech Tip

How to determine what file system is being used

Right-click any drive in Windows Explorer and select *Properties*. The *General* tab shows the type of file system being used.

Table 7.5 File systems

File system type	Description
CDFS (Compact Disk File System)	A file system for optical media.
FAT	Also called FAT16. Used with all versions of Windows. 2GB partition limitation with old operating systems. 4GB partition limitation with all versions of Windows XP and higher.
FAT32	Used with all versions of Windows 9x and higher. Supports drives up to 2TB. Can recognize volumes greater than 32GB, but cannot create them that big.
exFAT	Commonly called FAT64. A file system made for removable media (such as flash drives and SD cards) that extends drive size support up to 64ZB in theory, but 512TB is the recommended max. Made for copying large files such as disk images and media files. Supported by Windows XP SP3, Vista, and 7. Use the `format /?` command to see if exFAT is available.
NTFS	Used with Windows XP, Vista, and 7. Supports drives up to 16EB (16 exabytes, which equals 16 billion gigabytes), but in practice is only 16TB (16 terabytes, which equals 16 thousand gigabytes). Supports file compression and file security. NTFS allows faster file access and uses hard drive space more efficiently. Supports individual file compression and has the best file security.

An even better reason for partitioning than loading multiple operating systems or separating the operating system from data is to partition the hard drive for more efficient use of space. The operating system sets aside one cluster as a minimum for every file. A **cluster** is the smallest amount of space reserved for one file and is made up of a specific number of sectors. Figure 7.43 illustrates the concept of a cluster. Keep in mind that the number of hard drive sectors per track varies. The outer tracks hold more information (have more sectors) than the inner tracks.

Tech Tip

How to convert partitions

Use the **CONVERT** program in Windows to convert a FAT16, FAT32, or exFAT partition to NTFS. Access a command prompt window. Type the following command:

```
CONVERT x: /FS:NTFS
```

where *x* is the drive letter of the partition being converted to NTFS.

Press Enter and then press Y (Yes) and press Enter. Close the command prompt window and restart the computer. You can add a `/V` switch to the end of the command for a more verbose operation mode. Any type of partition conversion requires free hard drive space. The amount depends on the size of the partition.

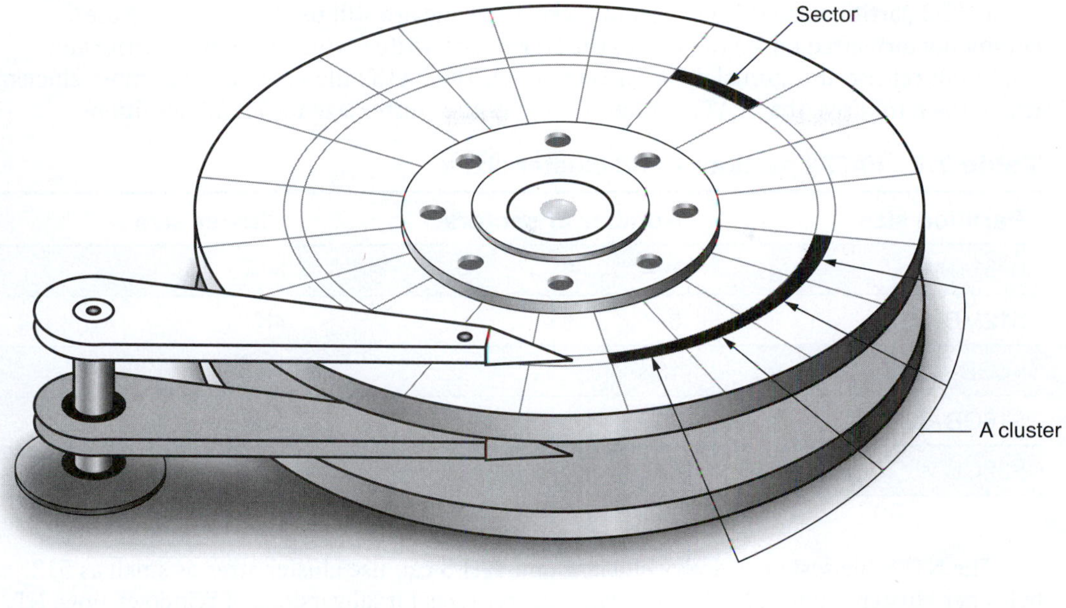

Figure 7.43 Cluster

Table 7.6 shows that partitioning large drives into one FAT partition wastes drive space. An efficiently partitioned hard drive allows more files to be saved because less of the hard drive is wasted.

Table 7.6 FAT16 partitions and cluster size

Partition size	Number of sectors	Cluster size
0–15MB	8	4K
16MB–127MB	4	2K
128MB–255MB	8	4K
256MB–511MB	16	8K
512MB–1GB	32	16K
>1GB–2GB	64	32K
>2GB–4GB	128	64K

Applications should be in a separate partition from data files. The following are some good reasons for partitioning the hard drive and separating data files from application files:

- Multiple partitions on the same hard drive divide the drive into smaller subunits, which makes it easier and faster to back up the data (which should be backed up more often than applications).
- The data is protected from operating system failures, unstable software applications, and any unusual software problems that occur between the application and the operating system.
- The data is in one location, which makes the files easier and faster to back up, organize, and locate.

FAT32 partitions have been around a long time and are still used. Flash drives are commonly formatted for FAT32 due to the NTFS "lazy write," which prolongs a write and might not release an external drive for some time. The FAT32 file system makes more efficient use of the hard drive than FAT16. Table 7.7 shows the cluster size for FAT32 partitions.

Table 7.7 FAT32 partitions and cluster sizes

Partition size	Number of sectors	Cluster size
0–511MB	N/A	N/A
512MB–8GB	8	4K
>8GB–16GB	16	8K
>16GB–32GB	32	16K
>32GB	64	32K

The NTFS file system is a very efficient one. NTFS can use cluster sizes as small as 512 bytes per cluster. Table 7.8 lists the default cluster sizes for all versions of Windows since NT, including Windows Vista and 7.

Table 7.8 NTFS partitions and cluster sizes

Partition size	Number of sectors	Cluster size
0–16TB	8	4KB
16TB–32TB	16	8KB
>32TB–64TB	32	16KB
>64TB–128TB	64	32KB
>128TB–256TB	128	64KB

The Windows Setup installation program can be used to create a partition, and the Disk Management tool or `diskpart` utility can be used when the operating system is installed. Use the Disk Management tool to partition and manage any drive that is installed after the first hard drive. The first hard drive is partitioned initially through the Windows installation process. Figure 7.44 shows a screen capture from Windows 7. Notice that the external drives and optical drives also display in the Disk Management window. The file system is shown for each drive too such as the exFAT file system on one of the attached flash drives (F:).

Tech Tip

Benefits of NTFS

NTFS supports disk quotas, which means that individual users can be limited on the amount of hard drive space. It can also automatically repair disk problems. For example, when a hard drive sector is going bad, the entire cluster is moved to another cluster.

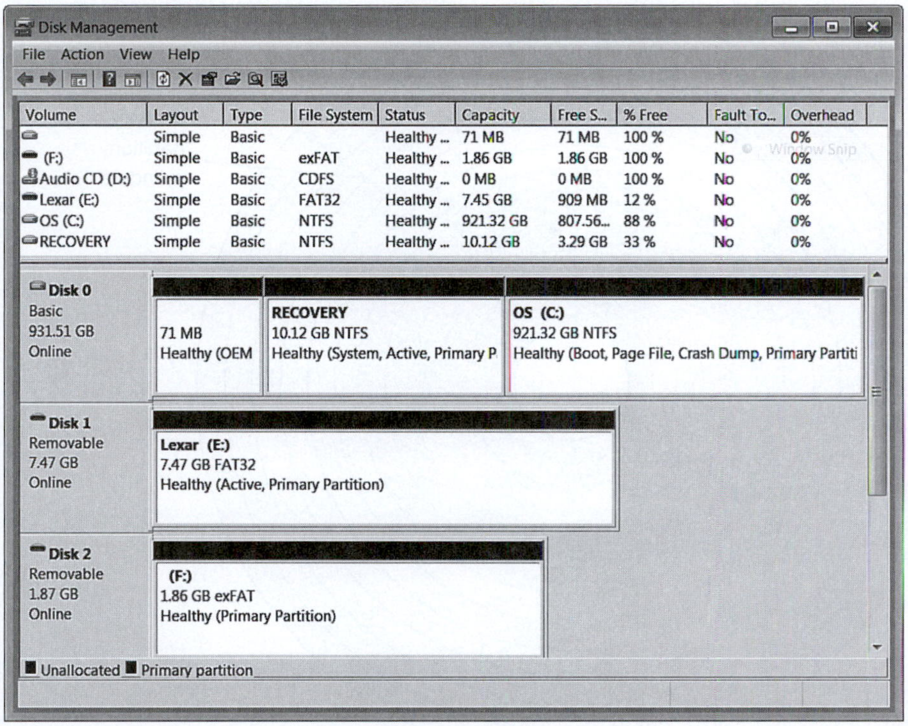

Figure 7.44 Windows 7 Disk Management tool

Partitions are defined as primary and extended. If there is only one hard drive installed in a system and the entire hard drive is one partition, it is the **primary partition**. The primary partition on the first detected hard drive is assigned the drive letter `C:`.

eSATAs might already be partitioned

Some eSATA drives are already partitioned and formatted. Others have software that runs when the drive is connected for the first time. All of them should allow repartitioning and reformatting.

Tech Tip

If the drive is divided so only part of the drive is the primary partition, the rest of the cylinders can be designated as the **extended partition**. An extended partition allows a drive to be further divided into **logical drives**. A logical drive is sometimes called a **volume**. A volume is assigned a drive letter and can include a logical drive as well as removable media such as a CD, diskette, DVD, BD, or flash drive. There can only be one extended partition per drive. A single hard drive can be divided into a maximum of four primary partitions. Remember that a partition is a contiguous section of storage space that functions as if it is a separate drive. See Figure 7.45 for an illustration of how one hard drive can be divided into partitions.

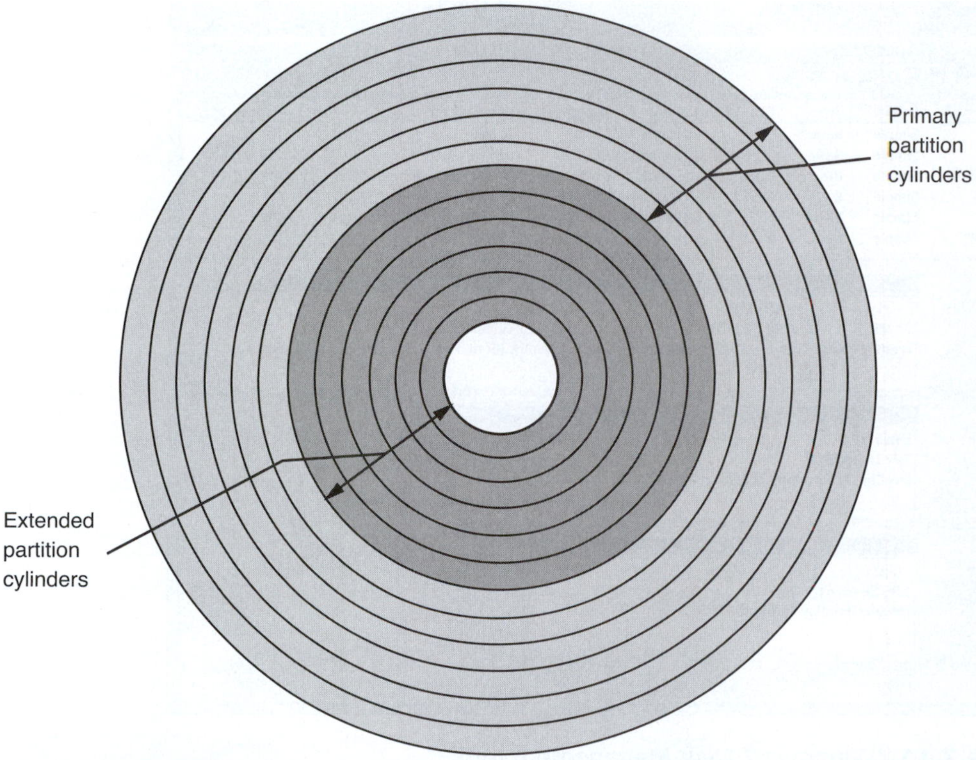

Figure 7.45 Hard drive partitioning

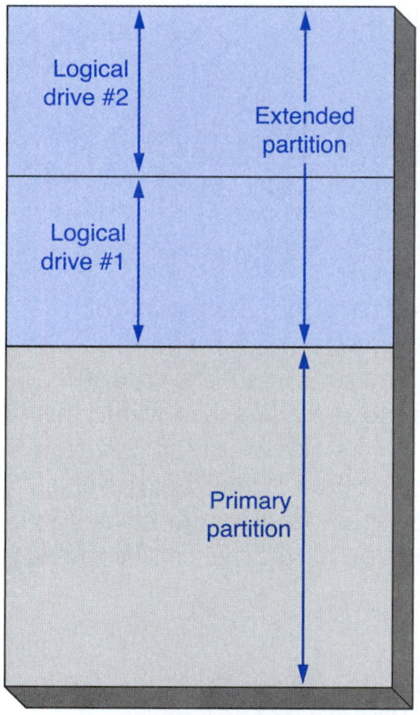

Figure 7.46 Two logical drives

The first hard drive in a computer system must have a primary partition, but it does not require an extended partition. If the drive has an extended partition, it can be further subdivided or split into logical drives that appear as separate hard drives to the computer system. Logical drives created in the extended partition are assigned drive letters such as `D:`, `E:`, or others. The only limit for logical drives is the number of drive letters. An extended partition can have a maximum of 23 logical drives with the drive letters `D:` through `Z:`. A second operating system can reside in a logical drive. Figure 7.46 shows an illustration of a hard drive divided into a primary partition and an extended partition further subdivided into two logical drives.

If two hard drives are installed in a computer, the first hard drive *must* have a primary partition. The second hard drive is not required to have a primary partition and may simply have a single extended partition. If the second hard drive does have a primary partition, it can have an extended partition, too.

When a hard drive is first installed and partitioned, the outermost track on the platter (cylinder 0, head 0, and physical sector 1) is reserved for the partition table. The partition table holds information about the types of partitions created and in what cylinders these partitions reside. The partition table is part of the **MBR** (master boot record) that contains a program that reads the partition table, looks for the primary partition marked as active, and goes to that partition to boot the system. Figure 7.47 shows the location of important parts of the hard drive that allows booting, partitions to be read, and files to be accessed.

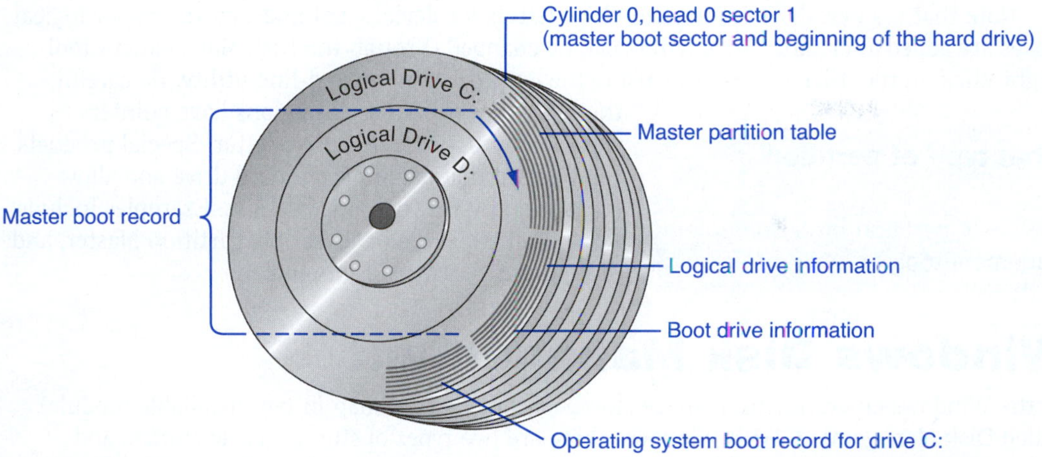

Figure 7.47 Hard drive structure

NTFS has two additional terms that you need to be aware of as a technician: system partition and boot partition. A Windows **system partition** is the partition on the hard drive that holds the hardware-specific files needed to load the operating system. A Windows **boot partition** is the partition on the hard drive that contains the operating system. The boot partition and the system partition can be on the same partition with Windows.

The **HPA** (Host Protected Area) is a hidden area of the hard drive used to hold a copy of the operating system; sometimes installed applications use the HPA when the operating system becomes so corrupted that a re-installation is necessary. Many manufacturers provide a BIOS setting or a keystroke that can be used when the system boots in order to access this area. The HPA is commonly found on the hard drive beyond the normal data storage locations; it reduces the amount of storage space available for data.

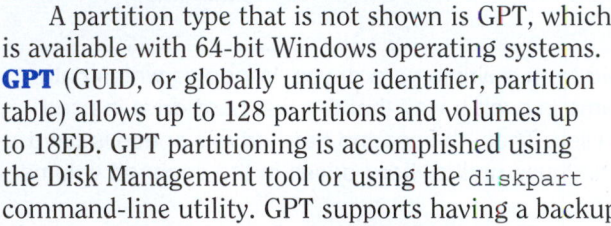

> **Tech Tip**
>
> **What happens when different types of partitions are deleted?**
>
> When a partition is deleted, all information in the partition is lost. A partition can be resized by deleting the partition and re-creating it, but the Disk Management program removes all information in the deleted partition. When logical drives in an extended partition are deleted, all data is lost. The other logical drives within the extended partition retain their information.

Look back to Figure 7.44, at the first partition on Disk 0, the hard disk. This is a OEM (original equipment manufacturer) partition. This partition is followed by a recovery partition and then the C: partition.

A partition type that is not shown is GPT, which is available with 64-bit Windows operating systems. **GPT** (GUID, or globally unique identifier, partition table) allows up to 128 partitions and volumes up to 18EB. GPT partitioning is accomplished using the Disk Management tool or using the `diskpart` command-line utility. GPT supports having a backup partition table in case the primary partition has become corrupted. A GPT disk can also have more than the MBR-based disk limit of four primary partitions.

> **Tech Tip**
>
> **You lose data when converting to GPT**
>
> MBR-based partitions can be converted to GPT and vice versa, but data is not preserved. This is more commonly seen with systems that have a UEFI BIOS. Back up data if you convert!

How Drive Letters Are Assigned

An operating system assigns drive letters to hard drives during the partitioning step. The order in which the partitions are assigned drive letters depends on three factors: (1) the number of hard drives, (2) the type of partitions on the hard drives (primary or extended), and (3) the operating system.

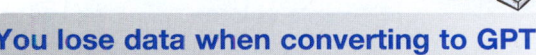

Note that if a new drive is installed, drive letters for devices, volumes, partitions, or logical drives are added afterward. Drive letters can be changed through the Disk Management tool (right-click on the drive letter) or by using the `diskpart` command-line utility. Be careful, though, because some applications have pointers to specific files on a specific drive letter. Special products can be used that partition the hard drive and allow repartitioning without any data loss. Examples include Acronis's Disk Director, EaseUS's Partition Master, and Avanquest's Partition Commander.

Tech Tip

Determining what type of partition you have

To determine the type of partition on a computer, use the Disk Management tool.

Windows Disk Management

In the Windows environment, manage storage devices with a snap-in (an installable module) called Disk Management. With Windows, there are two types of storage: basic storage and dynamic storage. The big difference between these two is that you can make partitions and resize changes with a dynamic drive, but cannot with a basic disk. Table 7.9 explains these and other associated terms.

Table 7.9 Logical disk management terms

Term	Description
Basic storage	One of the two types of storage. This is what has traditionally been known as a partition. It is the default method because it is used by all operating systems.
Basic disk	Any drive that has been partitioned and setup for writing files. A basic disk has primary partitions, extended partitions, and logical drives contained within the extended partitions.
Dynamic storage	The second type of storage; contrast with basic storage. Allows you to create primary partitions, logical drives, and dynamic volumes on removable storage devices. More powerful than basic storage. Uses a dynamic disk.
Dynamic disk	A disk made up of volumes. A volume can be the entire hard disk, parts of the hard disk combined into one unit, and other specific types of volumes, such as single, spanned, or striped volumes. Cannot be on a removable drive.
Simple volume	Disk space allocated from one hard drive. The space does not have to be contiguous.
Spanned volume	Disk space created from multiple hard drives. Windows writes data to a spanned volume in such a way that the first hard drive is used until the space is filled. Then, the second hard drive's space is used for writing. This continues until all hard drives in the spanned volume are utilized.
Striped volume	Data is written across 2 to 32 hard drives. It is different from a spanned volume in that each drive is used alternately. Another name for this is striping or RAID 0 (covered in the next section).
System volume	Holds the files needed to boot the operating system.
Boot volume	Holds the remaining operating system files. Can be the same volume as the system volume.
RAW volume	A volume that has never been high-level formatted and does not contain a file system.

Managing dynamic disks

Tech Tip

Use the Disk Management tool (found in the *Computer Management* console) to work with dynamic disks or to convert a basic disk to a dynamic one. Once accomplished, the conversion process cannot be reversed.

Figure 7.48 shows some of these concepts.

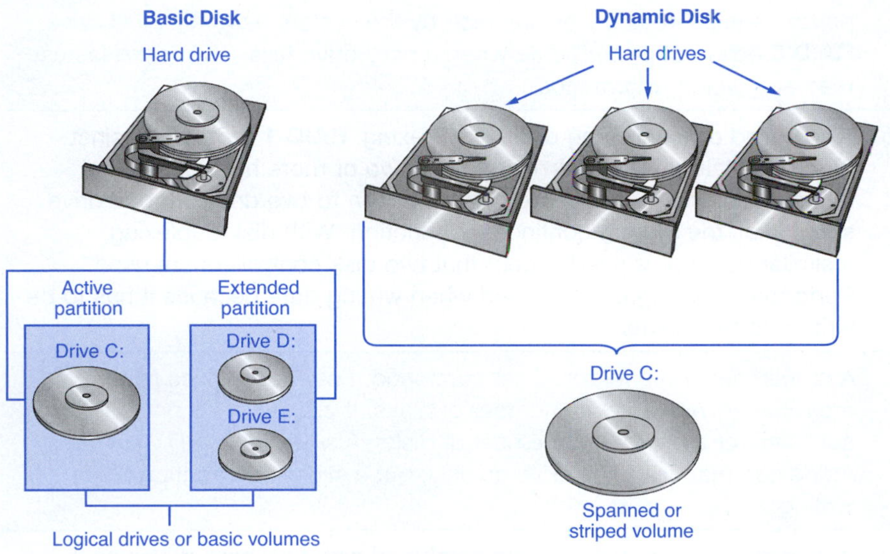

Figure 7.48 Disk management concepts

Fault Tolerance

RAID (redundant array of independent disks) allows reading from and writing to multiple hard drives for larger storage areas, better performance, and fault tolerance. Fault tolerance is the ability to continue functioning after a hardware or software failure. A RAID array can be implemented with hardware or software. Hardware RAID is configured through the BIOS. Generic hardware RAID steps are as follows:

1. Ensure that the motherboard ports that you want to use are enabled.
2. Ensure that you have RAID drivers for the hard drives used in the RAID.
3. Physically install and cable the hard drives.
4. Enter BIOS and enable RAID.
5. Configure the RAID in BIOS or through a special key sequence to enter the RAID BIOS configuration.
6. Install Windows on the RAID, using the Custom (Advanced) Installation option.

Software RAID is configured through Windows or through software provided by the RAID adapter manufacturer. If you want to be able to control the RAID through Windows and resize the volumes or make adjustments, then use a software RAID. A lab at the end of the chapter helps with this concept.

RAID comes in many different levels, but the ones implemented in the Windows environment are 0, 1, and 5. Windows XP supports simple, spanned, and striped volumes. Windows Vista Business and higher support simple, spanned and striped volumes. Windows 7 Professional and higher supports simple, spanned, striped, and mirrored volumes. Keep in mind that a spanned volume does not provide redundancy or fault tolerance like most of the RAID levels do. Some motherboards support "nested" RAID, which means RAID levels are combined. This method also increases the complexity of the hard drive setup. Table 7.10 explains these levels.

Table 7.10 RAID

RAID level	Description
0	Also called disk striping or disk striping without parity. Data is alternately written on two or more hard drives, which increases system performance. These drives are seen by the system as one logical drive. **RAID 0** does not protect data when a hard drive fails. This is the fastest read and write performance.
1	Also called disk mirroring or disk duplexing. **RAID 1** protects against hard drive failure. **Disk mirroring** uses two or more hard drives and one disk controller. The same data is written to two drives. If one drive should fail, the system continues to function. With disk duplexing, a similar concept is used except that two disk controllers are used. Performance is slightly degraded when writing data because it has to be written to two drives.
0+1	A striped set and a mirrored set combined. Four hard drives minimum are required with an even number of disks. It creates a second striped set to mirror a primary striped set of disks. Also called RAID 01. This mode can read from the drive quickly, but a slight degradation when writing.
1+0	A mirrored set and a striped set combined with four hard drives as a minimum. The difference between 1+0 and 0+1 is that 1+0 has a striped set from a set of mirrored drives. Also called RAID 10. This mode can read from the drive quickly, but a slight degradation when writing.
5	Also called disk striping with parity. **RAID 5** writes data to three or more hard drives. Included with the data is parity information. If a drive fails, the data can be rebuilt from the other two drives' information. This level can read and write data quickly.

Figure 7.49 shows the different types of RAID. With RAID 0, blocks of data (B1, B2, B3, etc.) are placed on alternating drives. With RAID 1, the same block of data is written to two drives. RAID 5 has one drive that contains parity information (P) for particular blocks of data such as B1 and B2.

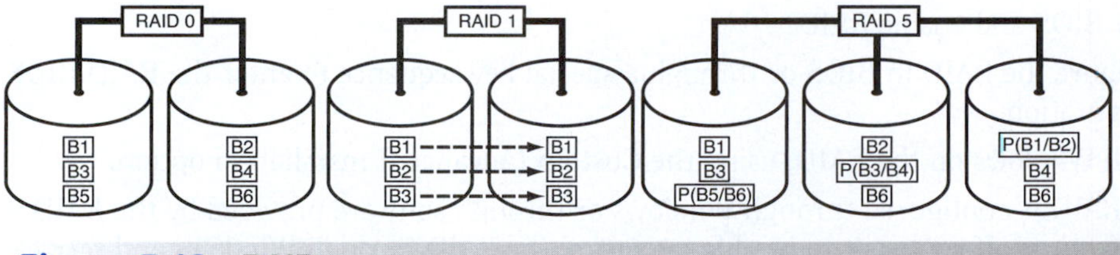

Figure 7.49 RAID concepts

RAID drives are often hot swappable—they can be removed or installed while power is applied to the computer. USB, SATA, and SAS all support hot swapping, but it is not required. Always refer to the drive and computer manual before hot swapping any hard drive.

RAID for a home or business computer used to require a separate RAID adapter and software to perform the RAID. Now many motherboards support RAID as well as the Windows XP, Vista, and 7 operating systems. Many times, you must configure the motherboard BIOS for RAID as part of your initial configuration. Table 7.11 shows some common RAID BIOS configuration parameters.

Table 7.11 RAID BIOS configuration settings

BIOS setting	Description
SATA mode: AHCI Mode	A mode that may mean that hot swapping is supported. A set of commands that can be used to increase storage performance.
SATA mode: RAID Mode or Discrete SATA Mode	Allows you to select a particular RAID level and the drives associated with the RAID.
SATA drives: Detected RAID Volume	Usually an information screen that shows the type of RAID configured, if any.
SATA drives: eSATA Controller Mode	Allows configuration of RAID through the eSATA port.
SATA drives: eSATA Port x Hot Plug Capability	Allows enabling or disabling hot swapping for eSATA ports.

High-Level Formatting

The second step in preparing a hard drive for use is high-level formatting. A high-level format must be performed on all primary partitions, logical drives located within extended partitions, and GPT partitions before data can be written to the hard drive. The high-level format sets up the file system so it can accept data.

NTFS allows support for multiple data streams and support for every character in the world. NTFS also automatically remaps bad clusters to other sections of the hard drive without any additional time or utility. During the installation process, Windows allows for a **quick format** (where you see the word "(quick)" after the option) or a full format (sometimes called a standard format). The **full format** scans for and marks bad sectors. This prevents the operating system from being installed on a sector that may cause operating system issues. The quick format simply prepares the drive for data and takes a lot less time than a full format. Use the full format if you suspect the drive has issues. Figure 7.50 shows the difference between how a FAT16 partition and an NTFS partition is set up when the high-level formatting is completed.

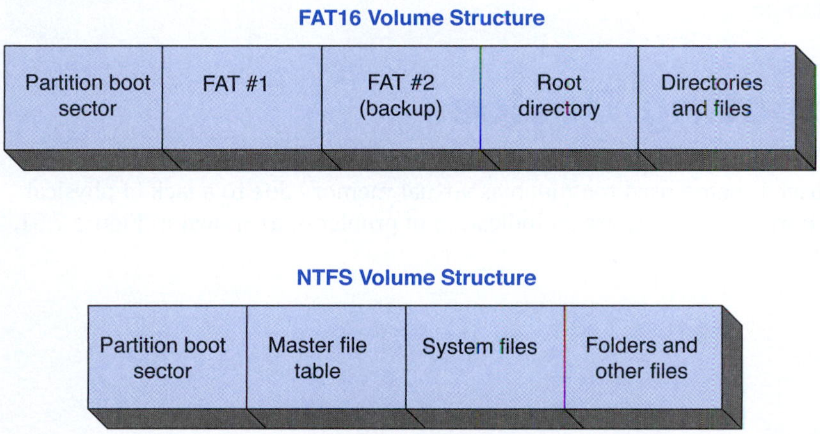

Figure 7.50 FAT16 and NTFS volume structures

The high-level format creates two **FATs** (file allocation tables): one primary and one secondary. The formatting process also creates the root directory that renumbers the sectors. The FAT keeps track of the hard disk's file locations. It is similar to a table of contents in a book as it lists where the files are located in the partition. Table 7.12 shows the differences between the file systems.

Table 7.12 Comparing file systems

Specification	FAT16	FAT32	NTFS	exFAT
Maximum file size	4GB	4GB	~16TB	~16EB
Maximum volume (partition) size	4GB (2GB, if shared with a really old computer)	32GB (max format)	2TB (or greater)	64ZB (512TB recommended)
Maximum files per volume	64KB	4MB	4GB	Not defined (but 2,796,202 per folder)

*Higher capacities—up to 16EB (exabytes)—are possible.

High-level formatting can be performed using the `FORMAT` command or by using Windows Disk Management tool. The area of the disk that contains information about the system files is the **DBR** (DOS boot record) and is located on the hard drive's cylinder 0, head 1, sector 1. The more common term for this today (since DOS is no longer a major operating system) is **boot sector** or volume boot record.

Additional drive partitions and drives installed after the first hard drive partition is created use the Windows Disk Management tool to apply high-level formatting to the drive. The first hard drive partition is normally high-level formatted as part of the operating system installation process. The exercises at the end of the chapter explain how to partition and high-level format a hard drive.

Tech Tip

How to change the cluster size

If you want to adjust the cluster size on a partition, you can do it during the high-level formatting step, using the `FORMAT` command. The syntax for the command is as follows:

```
FORMAT driveletter: /FS:NTFS /A:clustersize
```

where *`driveletter`* is the letter of the partition and *`clustersize`* is the size you want each cluster in the partition to be.

Troubleshooting Devices

Because many hard drives are mechanical devices, they make noises. Sometimes these noises are because the hard drive is being used too much as virtual memory due to a lack of physical RAM. Some noises are normal and some are an indication of problems, as shown in Figure 7.51.

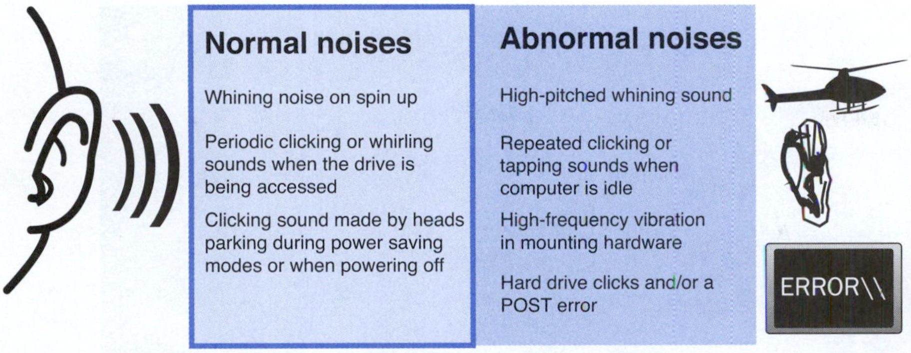
Normal noises
Whining noise on spin up
Periodic clicking or whirling sounds when the drive is being accessed
Clicking sound made by heads parking during power saving modes or when powering off
Abnormal noises
High-pitched whining sound
Repeated clicking or tapping sounds when computer is idle
High-frequency vibration in mounting hardware
Hard drive clicks and/or a POST error
ERROR\\

Figure 7.51 Hard drive noises

Most problems with new drive installation stem from improper configuration of jumpers on PATA drives or problems with cabling. The following tips assist with checking possible problems.

- Check the physical settings, if necessary (power cable, jumper settings, secure data cable, data cable pin 1 orientation, and device placement on data cable).
- Check the drive type setting in BIOS Setup and ensure that the ports are enabled (especially SATA ports).
- If after you have configured the drive, installed it, and powered it on, the BIOS shows the drive type as "None, Not installed," or displays all 0s in the drive parameters even though you set it to automatically detect the drive, then the BIOS is not able to detect it. Check BIOS SATA mode and BIOS version. Check all jumper settings, check cable connection(s), and check the power connection. If two PATA drives connect to the same cable, disconnect the slave drive. In Setup, reduce any advanced features to their lowest values or disable them. Increase the amount of time the computer takes to initialize the hard drive by going into Setup and modifying such features as hard drive boot delay or set the boot speed to the lowest value. This gives the hard drive more time to spin up and reach its appropriate RPM before data is read from it. Make sure the motherboard port is enabled.
- Has the drive been partitioned and one partition marked as the active partition? Has the drive been high-level formatted?
- Verify that the mounting screw to hold the drive in the case is not too tight. Loosen the screw and power up the computer. Figure 7.52 shows the mounting screws for a hard drive installed in a tower case.

What to do with a Stop 0x000000xx Kernel xxx error — **Tech Tip**

If your computer has a boot sector virus or data cannot be read from the paging file, run antivirus software for the potential virus. If there is a paging file error such as the one shown, search for the error code on the Internet.

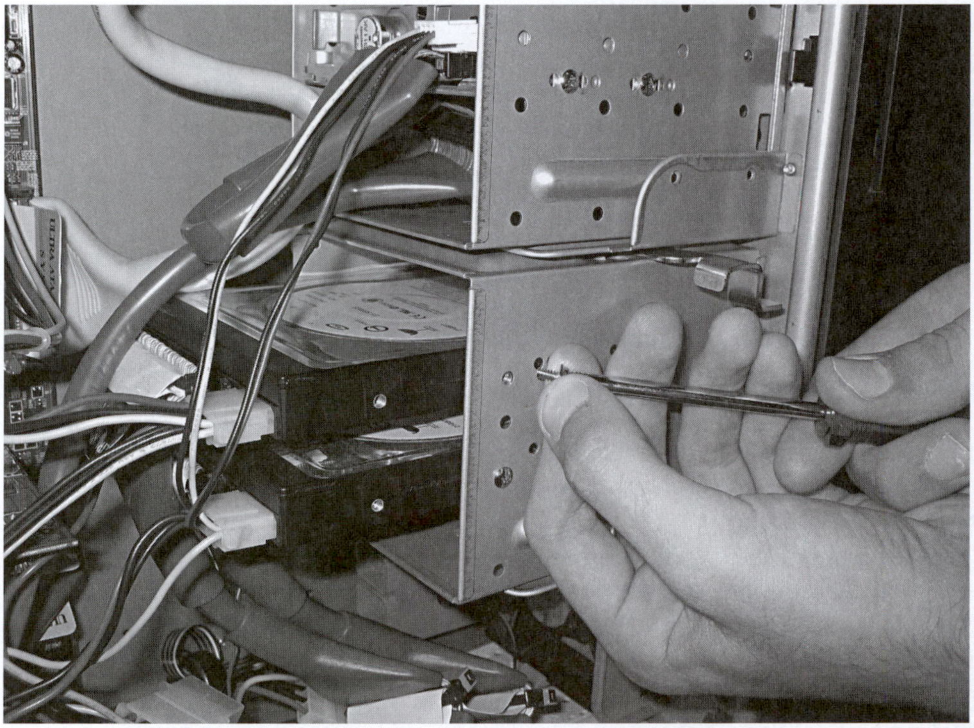

Figure 7.52 Hard drive mounting screws

- If during partitioning the "No fixed disks present" error appears, check the hard drive cabling, power connection, configuration jumpers, and BIOS configuration.
- If the hard drive does not format to full capacity, (a) your BIOS may not support the larger drive and/or the BIOS must be upgraded, or (b) you have selected a file system that does not support larger partitions, or you need an updated driver.
- If on initial boot after setting up a hard drive in BIOS Setup, you see the message "HDD Controller Failure, Press F1 to continue," the system is not partitioned or high-level formatted. Press the necessary key and boot from a disc and then partition and high-level format the hard drive. If the message continues, check the cabling and/or jumper configuration(s) on the hard drive.
- If during power-on the hard drive does not spin up or the hard drive spins down after a few seconds, check the power connector, the data cable, the drive recognized in BIOS, jumper settings, energy management jumpers or settings in Setup, and any software that came with the drive that enables power management. Disable power management in BIOS and/or the operating system. Try installing the drive in another system.
- If the system locks or you get a BSOD (blue screen of death), write down the code, if any, and try a warm boot (Ctrl+Alt+Del). If the drive is recognized after the warm boot, the Setup program may be running too fast for the drive to initialize. Refer to the hard drive documentation to see if the hard drive has a setting to help with this problem.

Tech Tip

"Disk boot failure" message

If you get a "Disk boot failure" message, use Disk Management to check that the primary partition is marked as active.

The following are generic guidelines for hard drives that have worked but are now having problems:

- Run a virus-checking program after booting from a virus-free boot disk. Many viruses are specifically designed to attack the hard drive. If you have to wipe the hard drive to ensure the virus is erased before reinstalling the operating system, applications, and data, ensure you do a full format and not a quick one as part of the operating system installation process.
- Has there been a recent cleaning of the computer or has someone recently removed the top from the computer? If so, check all cables and verify that they correctly connect pin 1 to pin 1 of the adapter or motherboard. Check the power connection to the hard drive.
- If the hard drive flashes quickly on boot up, the controller is trying to read the partition table in the master boot record. If this information is not found, various symptoms can be shown, such as the error messages "Invalid boot disk," "Inaccessible boot device," "Invalid partition table," "Error loading operating system," "Missing operating system," or "No operating system found." Use the `DISKPART` command from recovery console or Windows Recovery Environment (WinRE) to see if the hard drive partition table is okay. Try running `FDISK /MBR` from Recovery Console (XP), `bootrec /FixMbr` (Vista/7) or use a hard drive utility to repair the partition table.

Tech Tip

Does your hard drive stick?

Place a hand on top of the drive as you turn on the computer. Does the drive spin at all? If not, the problem is probably a "sticky" drive or a bad drive. A hard drive must spin at a certain rpm before the heads move over the surface of the hard drive. To check if the drive is sticking, remove the drive and try spinning the spindle motor by hand. Otherwise, remove the drive, hold the drive in your hand, and give a quick jerk with your wrist. Another trick that works is to remove the hard drive from the case, place the drive in a plastic bag, and put in the freezer for a couple of hours. Then, remove the drive and allow it to warm up to room temperature. Re-install the drive into the system and try it.

- Do you receive a message such as "Disk Boot Failure," "Non-System Disk," or "Disk Error"? These errors may indicate a boot record problem. The solution is to boot from a bootable disk or CD to see if drive `C:` is available. The operating system may have to be reloaded. Also, verify that the primary partition is marked as active.
- If you receive a message "Hard drive not found," "No boot device available," "Fixed disk error," or "Disk boot failure," the BIOS cannot find the hard drive. Check cabling.
- When Windows has startup problems, Recovery Console and the *Advanced Options* menu are used. Many times startup problems are due to a virus. Other utilities that help with MBR, boot sector, and system files are `FIXBOOT`, `FIXMBR`, System File Checker, and the *Advanced Boot Options* menu. To use `FIXBOOT`, type the `FIXBOOT x:` command, where `x:` is the drive letter of the volume that has the problem. To use `FIXMBR`, type `FIXMBR` from a command prompt. `FIXBOOT` is used in XP Recovery Console to rewrite the boot sector. Vista and 7 use `bootrec /Fixmbr` or `bootrec /Fixboot` from the Windows Recovery Environment (WinRE).

Tech Tip

Use System File Checker

You can run the System File Checker program from the command prompt by typing `sfc /scannow`. The System File Checker is also needed after removing some viruses.

- The following messages indicate problems with the master boot record or the system files: "Invalid partition table," "Error loading operating system," "Missing operating system," or "A disk read error has occurred." In Windows XP, an additional two messages could be "NTLDR is missing" or "NTLDR is corrupt."
- When Windows has startup problems due to incompatible hardware or software or a corrupted installation process, the *Advanced Boot Options* menu can help. This option can be selected by pressing the F8 key during the boot process.

- If an insufficient disk space error appears or performance is bad (slow response), delete unnecessary files, including .tmp files, from the hard drive, empty the Recycle Bin, and save files to an optical disk, a flash drive, or an external hard drive and remove the moved files from the hard drive. Use the Disk Cleanup and Defragmenter tool. Another option is to add another hard drive and move some (or all) data files to it.
- For eSATA drives, check the power cabling and data cabling. Ensure that the data cable is the correct type for the port and device being used. Partition and format the drive before data is written to it. Ensure that the port is enabled through BIOS. The BIOS may require an update, or a device driver may be required (especially if the drive is listed under "other devices" in Device Manager). BIOS incompatibilities are the most common issue with installations. Note that some operating systems report SATA drives as SCSI drives.
- If the computer reports that the hard drive may have a defective area or if you start getting read/write failure notices, right-click on the hard drive volume > *Properties* > *Tools* tab > *Check now*. The drive may need to be replaced soon.
- If drives fail frequently in a particular computer, check for heat problems, power fluctuations, vibrations, improper mounting screws or hardware that might cause vibrations, and environmental issues such as dust, heat, magnetic fields, smoke, and nearby motors. Consider an SSD if the computer is in a harsh environment.

Table 7.13 shows some of the normal and problem drive status messages seen in the Windows Disk Management tool. These status messages can help with drive management, troubleshooting, and recovery.

Table 7.13 Disk Management status states

Disk Management State	Description
Active	The bootable partition, usually on the first hard drive, is ready for use.
Dynamic	An alternative to the basic disk the dynamic disk has volumes instead of partitions. Types of volumes include simple volumes, volumes that span more than one drive, and RAID volumes.
Failed	The basic disk or dynamic volume cannot be started; the disk or volume could be damaged; the file system could be corrupted; or there may be a problem with the underlying physical disk (turned on, cabled correctly) or with an associated RAID drive. Right-click the disk and select *Reactivate disk*. Right-click the dynamic volume and select *Reactivate volume*.
Foreign	A dynamic disk from another computer has just been installed. Right-click the disk and select *Import Foreign Disks*.
Healthy	The drive is ready to be used.
Not Initialized	A basic disk is not ready to be used. Right-click the disk and select *Initialize Disk*.
Invalid	Operating system cannot access the dynamic disk. Convert the disk to a basic disk (by right-clicking the disk number and select *Convert to basic disk*).
Offline	Ensure that the physical disk is turned on and cabled correctly. Right-click it and select *Reactivate Disk* or *Activate*.

Disk Management State	Description
Online (errors)	Use the hard drive error checking tool: In Explorer, right-click the hard drive partition and then select *Properties*, the *Tools* tab, and *Check now* button.
Unallocated	Space on a hard drive has not been partitioned or put into a volume.
Unknown	A new drive has not been initialized properly. Right-click it and select *Initialize disk*. The volume boot sector may be corrupted or infected by a virus.
Unreadable	The drive has not had time to spin up. Restart the computer and rescan the disk (using the *Action* menu item).

RAID Issues

When you add a RAID to a computer, you increase the complexity of the disk management. When two hard drives are configured in a RAID, they are seen as one volume and managed as one volume. Multiply that by the different types of RAID and the number of hard drives involved in the RAID, and you have a real opportunity for some fun issues. The following issues can help you with RAID configurations:

- If you have done RAID through the BIOS, you cannot manage the RAID through Windows (it is grayed out and shows as no fault tolerance). If you want to manage the RAID through Windows, you will have to break the RAID in BIOS (remove the RAID) and then re-create the RAID in Windows. Backup your data before doing this.
- Sometimes as part of the RAID configuration, you need a driver disk for the Windows installation or RAID failure troubleshooting process. Follow the motherboard or RAID adapter manufacturer's directions on how to create this disk (usually a USB drive or optical disc even though the directions on the screen may say floppy disk).
- If Windows won't allow you or give you the option to do a RAID, check BIOS settings and ensure that AHCI has been enabled for the drives.
- If disk mirroring isn't an option in Windows Disk Management, check your Windows version. You must have a Windows Professional or higher edition to do the RAID.
- Windows 7 is already installed in a system. If you install a hardware RAID through BIOS and use the Windows 7 drive in the RAID, Windows will no longer boot and you see a BSOD (blue screen of death). If you want to keep the hardware RAID, re-install Windows 7. You may have to get drivers before doing this. If you want Windows 7 to boot again, remove the hardware RAID. You can also use the BSOD code shown to research the error.

Preventive Maintenance for Hard Drives

Keeping a computer system in a clean and cool operating environment extends the life of the hard drive. The most common hard drive failures are due to moving parts (heads and motors) and power fluctuations and/or failures. Performing preventive maintenance on the entire computer is good for all components found inside the computer, including the hard drive subsystem.

Windows has three great tools to use in hard drive preventive maintenance (see Figure 7.53): Error-checking (*Check now* button), Disk Cleanup, and Disk Defragmenter. From within Windows, you can use Check Disk (XP)/Error-checking/Check now (Vista/7) to locate **lost clusters**, which are clusters disassociated from data files. These clusters occupy disk space. These tools are also good for intermittent read/write errors. Locate the drive in Explorer, right-click the drive and select *Properties* > *Tool* tab > *Check now*. A program called **CHKDSK** can be executed from within the GUI or from Recovery Console or command prompt recovery environment to do the same thing from a prompt.

Figure 7.53 Disk maintenance

Windows also has a program called **Disk Cleanup** that removes temporary files, removes offline Internet files, empties the Recycle Bin, compresses unused files, removes unused programs, and prompts you before doing any of this. To access Disk Cleanup, follow these steps:

1. Click the *Start* button > *All Programs* > *Accessories* > *System Tools* > *Disk Cleanup*.
2. Select the drive letter and click *OK*.
3. On the Disk Cleanup tab, click in the checkboxes for the options desired and click *OK*.

Over time, as files are added to a hard drive, the files become fragmented, which means the clusters that make up the file are not adjacent to one another. Fragmentation slows down the hard drive in two ways: (1) the FAT has to keep track of scattered clusters and (2) the hard drive read/write head assembly must move to different locations on the drive's surface to access a single file. Figure 7.54 illustrates fragmentation of three files (F1, F2, and F3) and the results after defragmentation has been executed on the hard drive. **Defragmentation** is the process of placing files in contiguous sectors. Notice the results of the defragmentation process in Figure 7.54.

Tech Tip

Running Disk Cleanup from a command prompt

To run Disk Cleanup from a command prompt, type `cleanmgr` and then press [Enter].

How to defragment in Windows

Tech Tip

To access the defragmentation tool in Windows, open *Explorer*, locate a hard drive letter, right-click it, and select *Properties* > *Tools* tab > *Defragment Now* button.

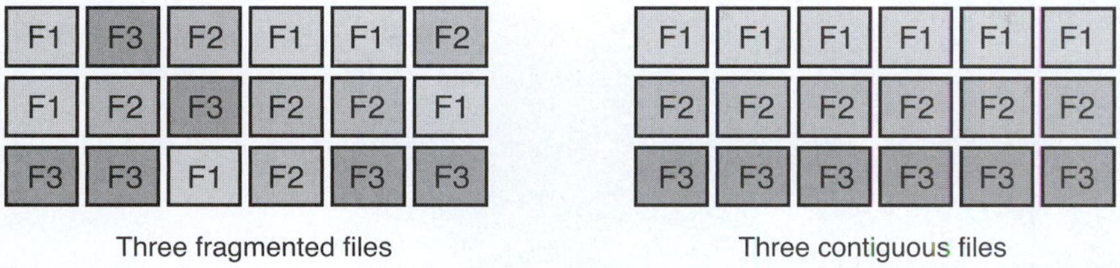

Figure 7.54 **Fragmented hard drive**

Windows includes a program that defragments the hard drive. This program places the file clusters in adjacent sectors. Use the Start button > *All Programs* > *Accessories* > *System Tools* > *Disk Defragmenter*. Defragmenting the hard drive makes for faster hard disk access. These measures also extend the life of the hard drive because the drive's mechanical movements are reduced.

Tech Tip

SSD defragmentation kills

Do not defragment an SSD as you would a magnetic hard drive. Defragmentation causes more reads and writes, which reduces the life span of the SSD.

You should periodically defragment files on a mechanical PATA or SATA hard drive. Users who delete files often and have large files that are constantly revised should especially make use of the defragmentation tool. You can use the Disk Defragmenter *Analyze* (XP)/ *Analyze disk* (Vista/7) to check whether a drive partition needs to be defragmented.

In Windows Vista/7, when the analysis is done, check the amount of fragmentation in the Last Run column. When the fragmentation is above 10 percent, defragment the hard drive. Note that Windows 7 automatically schedules your hard drive to be defragmented every Wednesday at 1 a.m. if the computer is powered on. Otherwise, defragmentation runs automatically the next time thereafter the computer is powered on. You can adjust this scheduled time through the Disk Defragmenter tool. By default, Windows 7 will not defragment an SSD drive automatically as doing so would reduce the lifetime of the drive.

Tech Tip

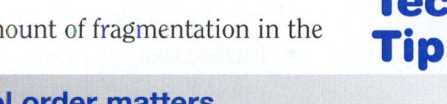

Tool order matters

Use the Error-checking (Check now) and Disk Cleanup tools before running the Disk Defragmenter tool.

Data Security

Another preventive maintenance procedure for a hard drive is performing a backup of the data and operating system. Most people do not realize that the most important part of any computer is the data that resides within it (see Figure 7.55). Data cannot be replaced as hardware can be. Traditionally, backups have been saved to magnetic tape—quarter-inch cartridge, LTO (linear tape-open) or DLT (digital linear tape) being the most common types—but CDs, DVDs, BDs, and external drives are viable alternatives today. Some people use optical discs to back up the data and periodically do a full backup to an external drive.

Figure 7.55 Keeping your data safe

The following tips help with protecting the operating system and data:

- Backups use the file archive bit. A **full backup** backs up all selected files and sets the archive bit to off. An **incremental backup** backs up all files that have changed since the last backup. The files selected are the ones that have the archive bit set to on. The backup software resets those archive bits to off. A **differential backup** backs up files that have changed since the last full backup (files that have the archive bit set to on), but the backup software does not reset the archive bit like the incremental backup does.
- Ensure that operating system and application service packs and updates are applied regularly.
- Install antivirus software and keep the virus definitions updated.
- Have an alternate boot source (optical disc, thumb drive, another hard drive, operating system discs, etc.).
- Use **BitLocker** drive encryption to protect an entire disk volume including the operating system, user files, swap files, and hibernation files. It is available on Vista/7 Enterprise and Ultimate, and Windows 8 Pro and Enterprise. BitLocker requires two NTFS disk partitions.
- Place operating system files and data files on separate hard drive partitions/volumes to make backups easier to manage.
- Do backups routinely. Have a routine maintenance plan that you recommend to users. Important data should be backed up daily or frequently, but routine data is usually handled by a monthly backup. The sensitivity and importance of the data determines how frequent backups are performed.
- **Drive wiping** and overwriting: If donating a computer or replacing a hard drive, the data on the drive needs to be removed once it has been transferred to the new drive or not needed any longer. Furthermore, the hard drive partitions need to be deleted and re-created. Some hard drive manufacturers have a utility that rewrites (sometimes called **overwrites**) the hard drive with all 1s or all 0s to prevent data remnants from being recovered. You can use the SDelete utility that can be downloaded from Microsoft (http://technet.microsoft.com/en-us/sysinternals/bb897443.aspx) or use the `format` and `cipher` commands. `Format` *`x`*`: /p:`*`n`* (where *`x:`* is the drive letter and *`n`* is the

number of passes) to format a disk volume with a zero in every sector. Then use the `cipher /w x:` command, where `x:` is the hard drive volume letter. The `cipher` command writes all unused sectors with 0s, then 1s, and then a random number. Because this command is performed on unused sectors, it is important to remember to use the format command first. A degaussing tool can also be used. Degaussing uses electromagnets to change the magnetic field of the platters.

- Some data is so sensitive that the company policy is to use an overwriting utility or the `format/cipher` commands and then open the drive and physically damage each platter with a drill, a screwdriver, or other implement to mar each platter and then destroying the pieces with a hammer.

Tech Tip

A second hard drive makes an excellent backup device

Hard drives are inexpensive and easy to install. Install a second one to back up your data.

Tech Tip

For critical data, keep backups in a different location

Offsite storage for critical data is important even for home users in case of disaster such as flooding, fire, or theft.

Windows comes with a backup utility, but many external hard drives come with their own software that is easier to use, has more features, and allows easy and selective data backup scheduling. No matter what method of backup you use, test your backup for restoration. Install to a different drive if necessary.

Probably the most asked question of those with hard drive failures or failing/failed sectors is regarding file recovery. Windows does not have file recovery software other than locating and repairing lost clusters. However, there are third-party file recovery utilities that can be used. Many times files cannot be recovered unless the file recovery utility was installed prior to the loss. There are companies that provide data recovery services.

Mobile devices sometimes have an additional password for their hard drive. That way, if the device is stolen, the hard drive cannot be inserted into another device and used without knowing the hard drive password. It is a password in addition to the power on password or Windows password. If this option is available, it is configured through the BIOS.

Tech Tip

Don't use the same hard drive as a backup device

Backing up data to a different partition on a hard drive is *not* a good idea. Even though there is some chance that your data might be saved, it is more likely the drive will fail. The drive is a physical device that may have moving parts—motor, heads, and so on. Mechanical failure is always a possibility.

Even though much data is stored locally for most users, many companies are favoring centralized storage even for individual users. This protects the company's interest, and it also ensures that backups are done on a regular and reliable basis. Another option in business is a thin-client environment in which no hard drives are included with the system. Storage is provided across the network. This reduces hardware and software costs and PC maintenance staffing costs, and it makes data security easier to manage.

Removable Drive Storage

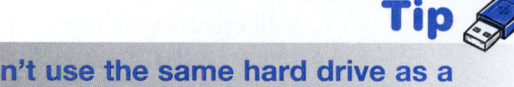

IDE and SCSI have been the two most common types of hard drives, but these interfaces have also been used for internal and external storage devices such as optical drives and tape drives. IDE PATA has traditionally only been used for internal devices, but now with SATA, external devices are available. SCSI has always supported internal and external devices. These external devices can also attach to the parallel port (not common today) or the USB port (a very popular option).

Tape drives can be attached using SCSI or IDE (SATA only) or can attach to parallel, USB, eSATA, or IEEE 1394 ports if they are external devices. Tape drives are installed using similar methods of like devices that use these ports. When tapes are used, the most common types of tapes used for backups are DAT (digital audio tape) and Traven. The most common type of removable storage is optical (CD/DVD/BD).

Tech Tip

Storing data in the cloud

Many folks, especially those who travel frequently, use data storage servers at their company or use the services of an Internet storage site. The services of such a site include backing up the data stored on their drives and having redundant hard drives in their servers. This is known as cloud storage or offsite storage.

Disk Caching/Virtual Memory

An easy way to speed up the hard drive is to create a **disk cache**. This puts data into RAM where it can be retrieved much faster than if the data is still on the hard drive. When data is read from the hard drive, the next requested data is frequently located in the adjacent clusters. Disk caching reads more data from the hard drive than requested. The data is placed in a reserved portion of RAM called the cache. Cache on a hard drive controller, sometimes called a data buffer, allows the read/write heads to read more than just one sector at a time. A hard drive can read up to an entire track of information and hold this data until needed without returning to the hard drive for each sector.

Both IDE and SCSI drives can contain 2MB to 128MB or more of RAM (cache memory). Because many drives are mechanical devices, they take time to reorder write data to the platters. With cache memory installed, information can be prefetched from the computer's system RAM and stored in the hard drive's cache memory. This frees up the system RAM for other tasks and improves the system and hard drive's performance.

A different way of using a hard drive is with virtual memory. Virtual memory is a method of using hard disk space as if it were RAM. The amount of RAM installed in a system is not normally enough to handle all of the operating system and the multiple applications that are opened and being used. Only the program and data of the application that is currently being used is what is in RAM. The rest of the open applications and data are stored in what is called a swap file or a page file on the hard drive. When you click over to a different application that is held in the swap/page file, data is moved from RAM into the swap file and the data you need to look at is moved into RAM for faster access and data manipulation.

Windows uses VMM (Virtual Memory Manager). The disk cache is dynamic—it increases or decreases the cache size as needed. If the system begins to page (constantly swapping data from RAM to the hard drive), the cache size automatically shrinks. In Windows, the virtual memory swap file (sometimes called the page file) is called `PAGEFILE.SYS`. To manually configure virtual memory in Windows 7, right-click *Computer* > *Properties* > in left pane, select *Advanced system settings* > *Advanced* tab > in the *Virtual memory* section, click *Change*. Then, to manually configure the settings, clear *Automatically manage paging file size for all drives* and adjust the settings as needed.

32-bit Windows versions use 32-bit demand-paged virtual memory, and each process gets 4GB of address space divided into two 2GB sections. One 2GB section is shared with the rest of the system while the other 2GB section is reserved for the one application. All the memory space is divided into 4KB blocks of memory called "pages." The operating system allocates as much available RAM as possible to an application. Then, the operating system swaps or pages the application to and from the temporary swap file as needed. The operating system determines the optimum setting for this swap file; however, the swap file size can be changed. Look back to Figure 6.17 in the Memory chapter (Chapter 6) to review this concept.

64-bit Windows can have 2 or 4GB for each 32-bit process. For 64-bit software, 7 or 8TB is the maximum. The operating system kernel gets 8TB maximum.

Tech Tip

Where should you keep a swap file?

If multiple hard drives are available, a technician might want to move the swap file to a different drive. Always put the swap file on the fastest hard drive, unless that hard drive lacks space. The swap file can reside on multiple hard drives. It is best to keep the swap file on a hard drive that does not contain the operating system.

Adding more physical RAM helps with caching

One of the most effective ways to speed up a computer is to reduce the amount of data that has to be swapped from the hard drive to RAM. This is done by increasing the amount of motherboard RAM.

Tech Tip

Soft Skills—Phone Skills

Technicians must frequently use the phone in the normal course of business. This includes speaking with customers who call in, those who you must call, and vendors and technical support staff. Many technicians' full-time job involves communication via the telephone.

Phone communication is different from in-person communication because on the phone you have only your words and voice intonation to convey concepts, professionalism, and technical assistance. When dealing with someone in person, you can use some of the following techniques that are not allowed during normal phone conversations:

- Gesture to emphasize points.
- Draw a graphic to illustrate a concept.
- Perform steps needed for troubleshooting faster because you can do them rather than step someone through them.
- Show empathy more easily with your body language, actions, and voice.

When dealing with someone on the phone, the following pointers can help. Some of the tips apply to everyday technical support as well:

- Identify yourself clearly and pleasantly.
- Avoid using a condescending tone.
- Be patient and speak slowly when giving directions.
- Use active listening skills (covered in Chapter 2); avoid doing other tasks when on a call with someone.
- Avoid using acronyms and technical jargon.
- Avoid being accusatory or threatening.
- If the customer is irate, try to calm him down and help him; however, if he continues to be belligerent, turn the call over to your supervisor.
- Escalate the problem if it is beyond your skill level; do not waste the customer's time.
- Do not leave people on hold for extended periods without checking back with them and updating them.
- Speak clearly and loud enough to be heard easily.
- Avoid having a headset microphone pulled away so it is hard to hear you; if you are asked to repeat something, speak louder or adjust the microphone or handset.
- Avoid eating, drinking, or chewing gum when on the phone.

Good interpersonal skills are even more important when on the phone than with face-to-face interactions. Before getting on the phone, take a deep breath and check your attitude. Every customer deserves your best game, no matter what type of day you have had or what type of customer you have previously spoken to.

The rest of this chapter is devoted to questions and exercises to help with storage concepts. Good luck with them!

Chapter Summary

- If you have to replace a floppy drive, attach the drive to the last connector (the one after the twist) but clean the heads first before replacing in case that is causing the problem.
- Hard drive form factors include 3.5-, 2.5-, and 1.8-inch drives. Hard drives come in different speeds: 5400, 7200, 10,000, and 15,000 rpm. The faster the rpm, the more money the drive normally cost, but the drive transfers data faster.
- Common drives today are PATA, SATA, and SSD for desktop and mobile computers. SCSI used to be used in servers and some desktops, but has evolved to SAS for servers.
- PATA drives are internal only, connect to a 40-pin ribbon cable that can have two devices per motherboard connector/cable. Multiple motherboard connectors can be present and are called primary, secondary, tertiary, and so on in BIOS.
- PATA drives are configured using jumpers. The devices on one cable must be configured as either master and slave or both as cable select. If cable select is used, the master device must connect to the end of the cable. An 80-conductor, 40-pin cable is used today. PATA drives use Molex power connectors.
- SATA drives can be internal or external and connect using a 9-pin 3.3 feet (1 meter) maximum internal connector, an external eSATA connector (3.3-foot [1-meter] maximum for 1.5Gbps devices and 6.56-foot [2-meter] maximum for 3 or 6Gbps devices), or an eSATAp combo eSATA/USB port. SATA 1 (I) drives operate at a maximum of 1.5Gbps, SATA 2 (II) drives at 3Gbps, and SATA 3 (III) drives at 6Gbps. SATA internal drives use a unique SATA power connector. A Molex to SATA converter can be purchased, but 3.3 volts is not supplied to the drive; most drives do not use the 3.3-volt line. External drives use an external power source unless plugged into an eSATAp combo port, which can provide power.
- SATA drives require no jumper, and only one device can connect to a SATA motherboard/adapter port.
- SSD drives have become more common in desktops, laptops, netbooks, and ultrabooks. They are often used in harsh environments, dirty environments, heavy movement environments, and harsh temperature environments. They are extremely fast, but expensive and connect using PATA, SATA, USB, eSATA, or IEEE 1394 (FireWire) connections.
- SSD drives erase data in blocks instead of by marking available clusters in the FAT with traditional drives. SSD drives should not be defragmented. SSD drives use various technologies to ensure functionality such as that all of the memory gets used evenly (wear leveling) and reserved spare memory blocks.
- Hard drives must be partitioned and high-level formatted before they can be used to store data.
- Partitioning separates the drive into smaller sections that can receive drive letters. The smaller the partition the smaller the cluster size. A cluster is the smallest space for a single file to reside. A cluster consists of four or more sectors. Each sector contains 512 bytes.
- Partitioning can be done through the Windows installation process or using the Disk Management tool.
- Several hard drive divisions are available using partitioning: primary, extended, and logical drives. Logical drives reside within the extended partition. Logical drives and primary partitions receive drive letters.

- An HPA or protected partition may be used for system recovery by computer manufacturers.
- Multiple drives can be configured in a hardware or software RAID implementation. Hardware RAID is done through using the BIOS or a RAID adapter. Software RAID is done using the Windows Disk Management tool.
- Spanning is supported in Windows Vista Ultimate and Windows 7 Professional and higher. Spanning is simply configuring more than one hard drive and making it appear to the operating system as one drive; data fills the first drive than the second drive.
- RAID 0 or disk striping does not provide fault tolerance, but does provide fast efficient use of two or more drives.
- RAID 1 is disk mirroring and this method does provide fault tolerance by having an exact copy of a drive in case one drive fails.
- RAID 5 is disk striping with parity where parity data is kept on one of the three minimum drives. This parity data can be used to rebuild one drive if one of three or more drives fail.
- File systems in use are FAT16, FAT32, exFAT, and NTFS. FAT32 and exFAT are used for external drives such as flash thumb drives. NTFS is used for internal drives and provides features such as better cluster management, security, compression, and encryption.
- If a drive or computer is to be donated or recycled, erase corporate and personal data from the drive. Delete all data, delete all partitions, use a drive wiping and overwriting utility. Physically destroy (shred, drill, and degauss or use electromagnetism) the platters if the drive contained extremely sensitive data.
- If a drive fails to be recognized as a new installation, check cabling and BIOS settings especially for a disabled SATA port.
- Normal mechanical drive noises include a clicking when going into sleep mode or being powered down due to self-parking heads.
- Abnormal drive noises include a couple of clicks with a POST beep and/or error, repeated clicking noises, high frequency vibration due to improper or poor mounting hardware, and high pitched whining sound.
- If a drive fails after operating for a while, check for a virus. See if the BIOS has a virus checker. Try a warm boot to see if the drive has not spun up to speed yet. Check cabling, especially on SATA. Review any recent changes. Use the Windows Advanced Boot Options menu, Windows Recovery Environment (Windows RE), System File Checker, and `fixboot`, `fixmbr`, `bootrec /Fixmbr`, and `bootrec /Fixboot` commands. Boot from an alternate source and check Disk Management for status messages related to the hard drive.
- Back up data onto a different drive. Keep critical data in an offsite location.
- Hard drive space is used as RAM. Ensure enough storage space is available for the operating system.
- When speaking on the phone to anyone, be clear in your statements, don't use technical jargon, keep your tone professional, and do not do other tasks, including eating or drinking.

Key Terms

Review Questions

Consider the following internal hard drive specifications in answering Questions 1–7:

- SATA 6Gbps transfer rate
- 1TB capacity
- Minimizes noise to levels near the threshold of human hearing
- 3.5-inch 7200 rpm
- 32MB buffer size

1. Which SATA version is being used?
   [1 | 2 | 3 | Cannot be determined from the information given]
2. What file system is best to be placed on this drive when you install it into the customer's computer?
3. Which drive preparation steps are *required* to be done if this drive was added as a new drive? (Select all that apply.) [defragmentation | low-level format | high-level format | error checking | RAID | virus checking | partitioning | striping | duplexing]
4. This drive is meant to be quiet. List two noises that the drive could make that would indicate issues to you.

5. Would a drive running at 5400 rpm run more efficiently or less efficiently than this drive?
   [more efficiently | less efficiently]

6. What is this drive's form factor? [6Gbps | 1TB | 3.5-inch | 7500rpm | 32MB]
7. How many other devices could be on the same cable that connects this device to the motherboard?

   [0 | 1 | 2 | 3 | cannot be determined]
8. If only two drives were available, which RAID levels could be used? (Select all that apply.)

   [0 | 1 | 5 | 10]
9. Of the RAID levels listed, which ones provide fault tolerance in case one drive fails?

   [0 | 1 | 5 | 10]
10. What is the difference between spanning and striping?
    a. Spanning is done in hardware, and striping is done in software.
    b. Spanning is done within RAID, and striping is done in Windows or through BIOS.
    c. Spanning takes two drives, and striping takes three drives.
    d. Spanning fills one drive before moving to the next drive, while striping alternates between the drives.
    e. Spanning is RAID 0, and striping is RAID 1.
11. A tile and carpet warehouse has several computers used in the inventory process. The computers in the warehouse area have a higher hard drive failure rate than those in the office area. Which solution will help this company?
    a. Replace the hard drives with SSDs.
    b. Place antistatic mats under the computers and on the floor where people stand or sit to use the computer.
    c. Install more powerful power supplies.
    d. Install additional CPU fans.
    e. Replace the drives with higher-RPM drives.
12. Which of the following would provide the fastest transfer rate for an internal hard drive?

    [PATA | SCSI | IEEE 1394 | SATA | USB]
13. Which of the following would provide the fastest transfer rate for an external hard drive?

    [PATA | SCSI | IEEE 1294 | eSATA | USB 2.0]
14. A user with an older laptop has just been given an internal SATA drive, but the laptop currently has an internal PATA drive. What would be the best solution for this user?
    a. Remove the internal drive and replace it with the new drive.
    b. Obtain a hard drive enclosure and attach the drive as an external device.
    c. Buy a PATA/eSATA converter and install the drive in the laptop.
    d. Buy a Molex to SATA converter and install the drive in the laptop.
15. What is a drawback of SSDs?

    [installation time | MTBF | maintenance requirements | cost | speed | reliability]
16. You are installing an older PATA optical drive. Which cable connector attaches to the motherboard? [gray | black | white | blue] Which cable connector attaches to the drive if it is the only device on the cable? [gray | black | white | blue]
17. What tool do most Windows 7 users use to check for lost clusters?

    [Error-checking (Check now) | `chkclust` | Disk Defragmenter | Disk Cleanup]
18. [T | F] By default, Windows 7 will automatically defragment all attached hard drives at 1 a.m. Wednesday or the next time that the computer is powered on after that time.
19. [T | F] If you have enough RAM installed, the hard drive will not be used as cache memory.

20. You are speaking to a customer on the phone who is very upset. The customer curses and starts yelling. What should you do?
    a. Hang up on the caller.
    b. Ask the caller if you can put them on hold while they calm down.
    c. Speak to the user using a calm, professional tone.
    d. Stay calm but raise your voice level a little to show the importance and professionalism of your technical question.

Exercises

Lab 7.1 Configuring a PATA IDE Hard Drive on Paper

Objective: To be able to configure a PATA IDE hard drive

Procedure: Refer to the following figures and answer the accompanying questions.

Questions:

See Figure 7.56 to answer Question 1.

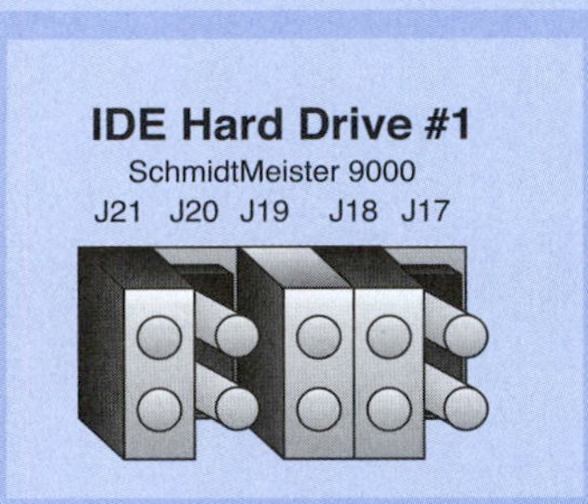

Jumper	Setting	Comments
J17	Cable Select	Open = disabled* Jumpered = enabled
J18	Master/Slave	Open = slave in a dual drive system Jumpered = master in a dual drive system Jumpered = master in a single drive system*
J19	Write Cache	Open = disabled Jumpered = enabled*
J20	Reserved	For factory use
J21	Spare	

* - Default setting

Figure 7.56 Lab 7.1 documentation

1. Using Figure 7.56, circle the jumpers to be enabled (set) to configure IDE Hard Drive #1 as if it is the only drive connected to an IDE port.

2. Now pretend that you have two hard drives that use the same jumpers as in Step 1. Using the following drawing, circle the jumpers to be enabled (set) to configure IDE Hard Drive #1 as the master drive connected to an IDE port. Keep in mind that IDE Hard Drive #2 shares the same cable with Hard Drive #1.

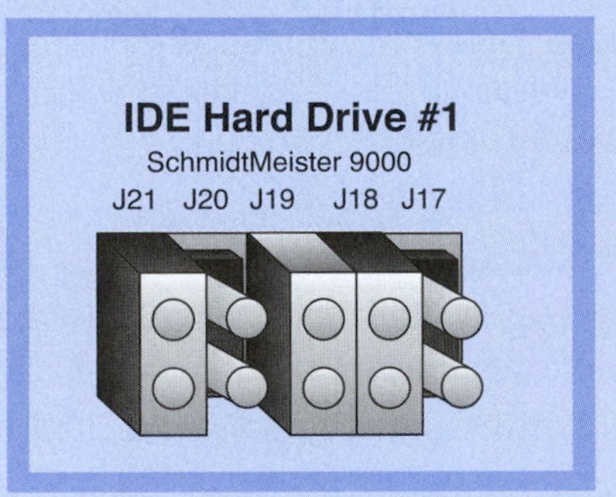

3. Using the following drawing, circle the jumpers to be enabled (set) to configure IDE Hard Drive #2 as the slave drive. Keep in mind that IDE Hard Drive #2 shares the same cable with Hard Drive #1.

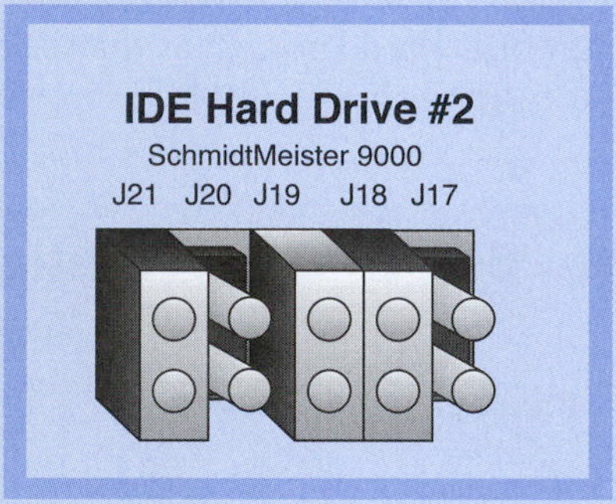

See Figure 7.57 to answer Questions 4 and 5.

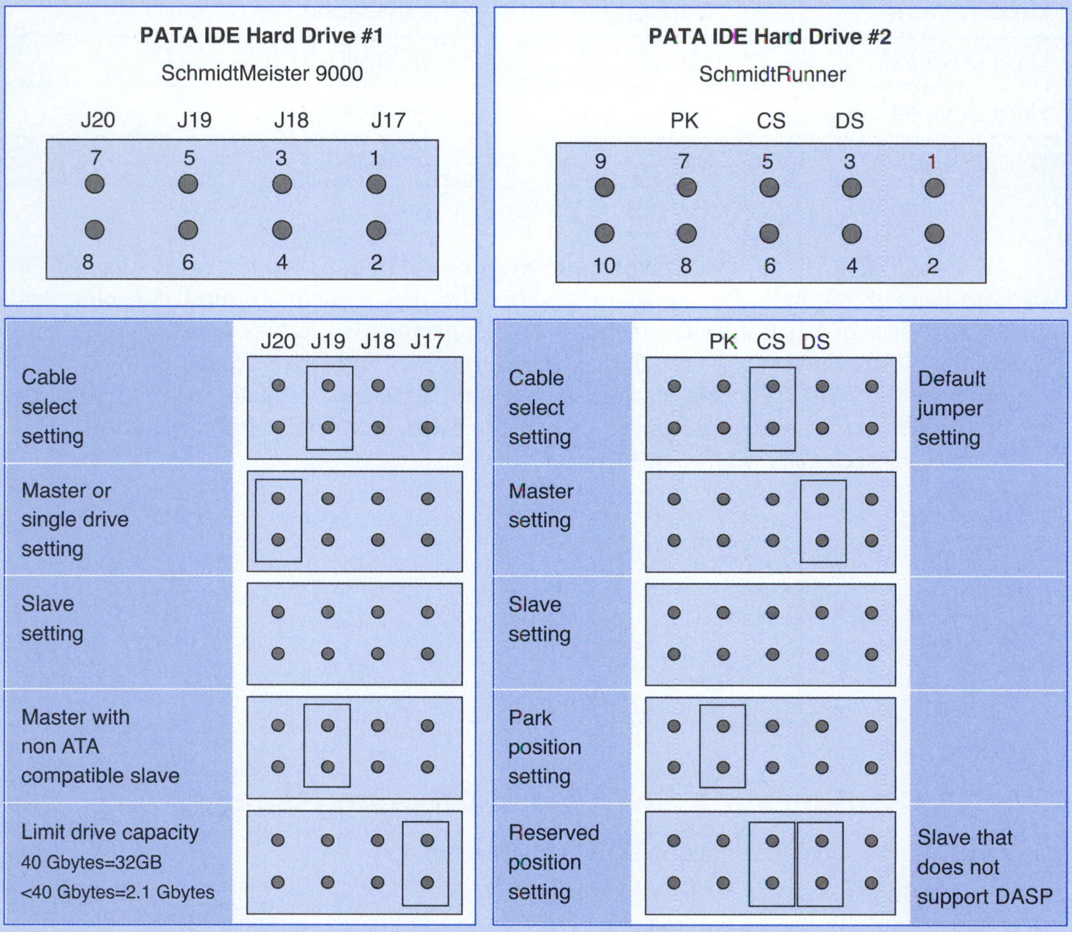

Figure 7.57 Lab 7.1 documentation

4. List the jumpers that will be enabled (set) to configure IDE Hard Drive #1 as the master drive connected to a PATA IDE port. Keep in mind that IDE Hard Drive #2 shares the same cable with Hard Drive #1.

5. List the jumpers that will be enabled (set) to configure IDE Hard Drive #2 as the slave drive. Keep in mind that IDE Hard Drive #2 shares the same cable with Hard Drive #1.

Lab 7.2 Configuring a PATA IDE Cable Select Configuration

Objective: To be able to configure a PATA IDE cable

Procedure: Refer to the following table and answer the accompanying question.

Question: The information in Table 7.14 relates to three PATA IDE devices being installed in a system.

Table 7.14 Three PATA IDE devices

Device name	Capacity	Cache
Hard Drive #1	750GB	8MB
Hard Drive #2	1TB	16MB
DVD/CD-RW drive	N/A	2MB

1. All of the PATA IDE devices support cable select configuration. The system is supplied with two IDE motherboard connectors and two IDE 80-conductor 40-pin IDE cables. On a blank piece of paper, draw the motherboard connectors, IDE cables, and IDE cable connectors. Write the name of each device (Hard Drive #1, Hard Drive #2, and DVD/CD-RW drive) by the PATA IDE cable connector to which it attaches. Designate the motherboard connections as Primary or Secondary. Designate the IDE devices as primary master, primary slave, secondary master, or secondary slave.

Lab 7.3 Configuring a SATA Hard Drive on Paper

Objective: To be able to configure SATA hard drive jumpers

Parts: Internet access is needed for one question

Procedure: Refer to the following figures and answer the accompanying questions

Questions:

See Figure 7.58 to answer Questions 1–3.

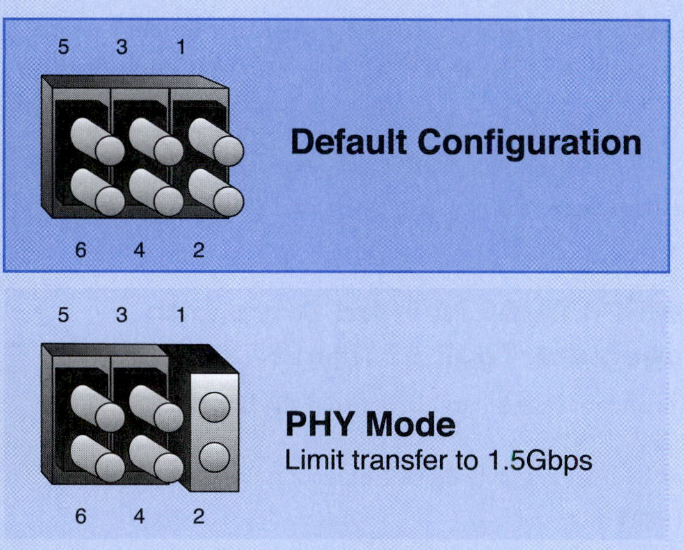

Figure 7.58 Lab 7.2 documentation

1. Considering the information provided, when would you change the jumpers on this drive?

2. Considering the information provided, what version of SATA does this drive use natively? [SATA 1 | SATA 2 | SATA 3]
3. If this hard drive was to be installed in a desktop model, what form factor would this drive most likely be?

See Figure 7.59 to answer Question 4.

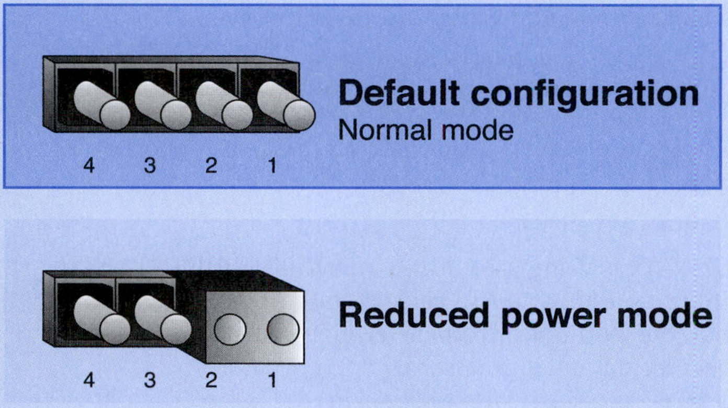

Figure 7.59 Lab 7.2 documentation

4. The information provided in Figure 7.59 is from a laptop computer used in a business environment. What do you think would be the effects of installing a jumper on pins 1 and 2 on this drive?

5. Use the Internet to determine and SATA jumper settings for a particular vendor's laptop replacement hard drive. Write the jumper settings and explanation for the jumpers. Write the URL where you found this information.

6. What is the form factor for the hard drive referenced in Question 5?

Lab 7.4 Installing an IDE PATA/SATA Hard Drive with Windows XP Disk Management Tool, `diskpart`, and `convert`

Objective: To be able to configure and manage a hard drive using the Windows XP's Disk Management tool

Parts: Windows XP computer with an available PATA connection or SATA port
IDE PATA/SATA hard drive

Procedure: Complete the following procedure and answer the accompanying questions.

Notes: Use proper antistatic and gentle handling procedures when dealing with hard drives. You must be a user who has administrator rights to configure hard drives. If two optical drives are installed, one can be replaced by the new hard drive to perform this lab.

1. Power on the computer and log in.
2. There are several ways to get to the window used to manage hard drives. Practice using the Windows Disk Management tool and the `diskpart` command-line tool. Through Windows Explorer, right-click *My Computer* and select *Manage*:
   a. Click the *Start* button, click *Run*, and type `compmgmt.msc`, and press Enter.
   b. Click the *Start* button, click the *Control Panel* (ensure that you are in Classic view), double-click the *Administrative Tools* Control Panel, and double-click the *Computer Management* icon.
3. In the console tree shown in the left pane, select the *Disk Management* option. The disks and volumes already installed in the computer display in a graphical manner on the right.
4. Right-click the drive partition labeled `C:` and select *Properties*.

   What type of file system is being used? [FAT16 | FAT32 | NTFS]

   What is the total capacity of the drive?

   What is the amount of free space?
5. Shut down the computer and remove the power cord.
6. Remove the computer cover. If PATA is being used, locate an available IDE PATA connector on the motherboard or an available PATA cable connector. If SATA is being used, locate a free SATA port on the motherboard and determine which port this is. Use the motherboard or system documentation, if necessary.
7. If a PATA is being installed, determine whether the other device on the same cable (if installed) uses cable select or master/slave jumpers by removing the drive and examining it. Handle the drive carefully.

   If a PATA drive is being installed, is there a second device on the same cable? If so does the device use the cable select, master, or slave jumper?

   If a SATA drive is being installed, what SATA port will be used for the new drive? Show the instructor.
8. If necessary, re-install the drive into the machine and reconnect the power and data cables. On the hard drive given to you by the instructor, if PATA is being used, configure

the drive to the appropriate setting of cable select, master, or slave. If SATA is being used, power on the computer, enter Setup, and ensure that the SATA port is enabled. Enable the port, if necessary.

9. Mount the IDE hard drive (the one given to you by the instructor) into the case.
10. Attach the IDE data cable and attach a power cable.
11. Re-install the power cord and power on the computer. The *Found New Hardware* balloon appears.
12. Using previously described procedures, open the *Computer Management* tool. Click the *Disk Management* option in the left window pane. Notice that the drive appears as a new disk in the Disk Management window. If it does not appear as a new disk, right-click the disk number (not the area where you partition the drive) and select *Activate*. If this Activate option does not appear, power down the computer and check all cabling and settings. Note that the drive you were given may have been partitioned already and assigned a drive letter. If the drive was already partitioned and a drive letter assigned, right-click the drive and select *Delete Partition* and *Yes*.

    Was the drive already assigned a drive letter and partitioned?

13. Right-click the new drive you just installed and select *New Partition*. The *New Partition* wizard appears. If the SATA drive is detected in BIOS but not in the Disk Management tool, the drive will have to be initialized. The top half of the window shows devices that Windows knows how to access. Locate the new drive in the lower half of the screen. Because the disk does not contain a valid Windows signature, right-click the appropriate disk number (Disk 1, Disk 2, etc.) and select *Initialize Disk*. After installing a drive, Windows must prepare the drive before it is partitioned. When you first start the Disk Management tool, a wizard might appear. If you cancel the wizard before the disk signature is written, the drive status is not initialized and must be initialized before partitioning can begin.

    What is the difference between a primary partition and an extended partition?

    What is the maximum number of primary partitions, as described on the screen?

14. Ensure that the *Primary Partition* radio button is selected and click *Next*.
15. Enter a partition size that is 32GB or smaller.

    What partition size did you choose?

16. Click *Next*.

    How many drive letter devices are there?

17. Select the drive letter you want assigned (normally you would want the next drive letter available) and click *Next*. You are asked if you want to format the partition.

    What file systems does XP allow you to select for Disk Management when you use this tool?

    Are there any file systems supported by XP that are not shown?

18. Select the *FAT32* option. Assign the volume label as a couple of letters from each of the lab partner's last names. Note that there is an 11 character maximum for FAT32 partitions and a 32 character maximum for NTFS partitions.
19. Select (enable) the *Perform a Quick Format* checkbox and click *Next*. Click the *Finish* button.

    How can you tell from the window whether a partition is FAT32 or NTFS?

20. Right-click in the unallocated drive space on the drive you just installed and select *New Partition*. The *New Partition* wizard appears. Click *Next*.
21. Select the *Extended Partition* radio button.

    According to the description information shown, what can an extended partition contain?

22. Click *Next*. The extended partition size needs to be the default amount shown (the rest of the drive). Click *Next*. Click *Finish*. The extended partition appears.
23. Right-click in the extended partition and select *New Logical Drive*. Click *Next*. The *Logical Drive* radio button is selected by default. Click *Next*.
24. The size for the logical drive needs to be one half the value currently shown on the screen.

    What amount of space did you choose for the logical drive size?

25. Click *Next*. Accept the drive letter default assignment and click *Next*.
26. Change the file system type to FAT32.
27. Make the volume label one of the partner's first name (up to 11 characters).
28. Select the *Perform a Quick Format* checkbox to enable. Click *Next* and click *Finish*.
29. Right-click the free space for the drive you installed. Using the same process, create an NTFS logical drive with the volume label as your first name and perform a quick format.

Instructor initials: ____________

30. You can change a FAT16 or FAT32 partition to the NTFS file system by using the `convert` command from a command prompt. Once it is changed, you cannot go back. Also, data is preserved (but should be backed up before the conversion, just in case).

    Using the Disk Management window, what disk number is the drive you just installed? [0 | 1]

    Write the drive letter of the FAT32 primary partition on the drive you just installed. This drive letter will be used in the coming steps.

    Write the volume label used for this partition. This label is case sensitive, so write carefully.

31. Click the *Start* button. Select *Run*. Type `cmd` and press Enter. A command prompt window appears.
32. Type **`convert /?`** to see a list of options. These options tell you what to type after the convert command.

    What option is used to run convert in verbose mode?

    What option is used to convert a volume to NTFS?

33. Type `convert x:` (where `x:` is the drive letter you wrote down in Step 30) `/fs:ntfs`. For example, if the drive letter you wrote down is d: type `convert d: /fs:ntfs`. Notice the space between the drive letter and the `/fs:ntfs`.

    `/fs:ntfs` is used to convert the existing file system (FAT16 or FAT32) to NTFS. You are prompted for the volume label for the drive. Enter the volume label you wrote down in Step 30 and press Enter. Don't forget that it is case sensitive. The partition is converted and can never be turned back into FAT32 unless the drive is reformatted.

34. Use the same process to convert the FAT32 logical drive to NTFS. Look up the volume label and the drive letter before starting.

Instructor initials: ____________

35. From the *Computer Management—Disk Management* window, right-click the last logical drive on the hard drive you just installed.

36. Select the *Delete logical drive* option. Click *Yes*.
37. Partitions can be created from the Disk Management window, but they can also be created using the `DISKPART` command utility. Click the *Start* button, click *Run*, type `cmd` and press Enter.
38. From the command prompt, type `diskpart` and press Enter.

    How does the prompt change?
39. Type `help` and press Enter. Use the help command to find out what commands are available.

    What command is used to make a new partition?

    What command can be used to give a drive partition a drive letter?
40. Type `create ?` and press Enter.

    What two options can be used with create?
41. Type `create partition ?` and press Enter.

    What type of partitions can be created?
42. Press the ⇧ key once. The same command appears. Backspace and replace the `?` with `logical` so the command reads `create partition logical`. Press Enter.

    What does the feedback say?

    What command do you think (based on help) would be used to select a drive?
43. Type `select disk x` (where *x* is the disk number you selected in the first question of Step 30). A prompt says the disk is selected.
44. Retype the `create partition logical` command or use your ⇧ and press it until that command appears and press Enter.
45. Look back at your *Disk Management* window and see how the part of the drive previously marked as free space is now a logical drive.
46. At the command prompt, type `detail disk` to see the logical drive you just created. Notice how it does not have a file system or a drive letter assigned.

    Based on the command output, what drive letters are currently used?
47. At the command prompt, type `assign` and press Enter.

    Look in the Disk Management window and see what drive letter was assigned. Write the drive letter.
48. At the command prompt, type `exit` to leave the `DISKPART` utility.
49. Type `help` at the command prompt to look for a command to help us high-level format the drive. The commands scroll by too fast, so type `help | more`. (The `|` keystroke is made by holding down the Shift key and pressing the key above the Enter key.) Press Enter. One page at a time is shown. Press the Spacebar once to see the next page of commands.
50. In the next command, you are going to have to fill in some of the blanks to perform the step correctly. The parameters are as follows:

    `x:` is the drive letter documented in Step 47.

    `/v:name` where `name` is the second partner's first name (up to 32 characters).

    `/fs:ntfs` is telling the system to use the NTFS file system. Other options could be `/fs:fat` or `/fs:fat32`, but we are using NTFS this time.

    `/q` does a quick format.

    Type the command `format x: /fs:ntfs /v:name /q` and press Enter. When asked to proceed, press Y and press Enter.
51. View the results in the Disk Management window. The last partition should be a logical drive that has a drive letter and is NTFS now.

7 Storage Devices

52. Using whatever method you would like, copy one file to each of the three partitions you have created. Call the instructor over to show the three files and the *Disk Management* window. Do not proceed unless you have these parameters done.

Instructor initials: ____________

53. Starting with the partition on the far right in the *Disk Management* window for the drive you just installed, right-click each partition and delete each partition. Call the instructor over when the drive shows as one block (black) of unpartitioned hard drive space.

Instructor initials: ____________

54. Shut down the computer. Remove the power cord. Remove the data cable from the hard drive you just installed. Remove the power cord from the hard drive you just installed. Remove the hard drive. If necessary, re-install the optical drive, data cable, and power cord. Re-install the computer cover and the power cord.
55. Boot the computer. Open *My Computer* by clicking the *Start* button, and locating the *My Computer* icon. Ensure the optical drive is recognized. If it is not, redo Step 54.
56. Show the instructor the optical drive in the My Computer window and give the hard drive to the instructor.

Instructor initials: ____________

Lab 7.5 Installing an IDE PATA/SATA Hard Drive with the Windows 7 Disk Management Tool, `diskpart`, and `convert`

Objective: To be able to configure and manage a hard drive using Windows 7 Disk Management console

Parts: Windows 7 computer with an available PATA connection on the motherboard, an available PATA cable connection, or motherboard SATA port

Procedure: Complete the following procedure and answer the accompanying questions.

Notes: Use proper antistatic and gentle handling procedures when dealing with hard drives.

You must be a user who has administrator rights to configure hard drives.

If two optical drives are installed, one can be replaced by the new hard drive to perform this lab.

1. Power on the computer and log in.
2. There are several ways to get to the window used to manage hard drives. Practice using both methods. (a) Click the *Start* button, type `compmgmt.msc` in the Search box and press Enter or (b) in Windows Explorer, right-click *Computer* and select *Manage*.
3. In the console tree shown in the left pane, select the *Disk Management* option. The disks and volumes already installed in the computer display in a graphical manner on the right.
4. Right-click the drive partition labeled `C:` and select *Properties*.

   What type of file system is being used? [FAT16 | FAT32 | exFAT | NTFS]

   What is the total capacity of the drive?

   What is the amount of free space?

5. Shut down the computer and remove the power cord.
6. Remove the computer cover. If PATA is being used, locate an available IDE PATA port on the motherboard or an available PATA cable connector. If SATA is being used, locate a free SATA port on the motherboard and determine which port this is by looking at motherboard labeling or by using documentation.

7. If PATA is being used, determine whether the other device on the same cable (if installed) uses cable select or master/slave jumpers by removing the drive and examining it. Handle the drive carefully.

   If a PATA drive is being installed, is there a second device on the same cable?

   If so, does the device use the cable select, master, or slave jumper? Show the instructor.

   If a SATA drive is being installed, what SATA port will be used for the new drive?

Instructor initials: __________

8. If necessary, re-install the PATA drive into the machine and reconnect the power and data cables. On the hard drive given to you by the instructor, if PATA is being used, configure the drive to the appropriate setting: cable select, master, or slave. If SATA is being used, power on the computer, enter Setup, and ensure that the SATA port is enabled. Enable the port if necessary.
9. Mount the hard drive (provided by the instructor or lab assistant).
10. Attach the data cable and attach a power cable.
11. Re-install the power cord and power on the cable.
12. Using previously described procedures, open the *Computer Management* console. Click the *Disk Management* option in the left pane. Note that the drive you were given may have been partitioned already and assigned a drive letter. If the drive was already partitioned and a drive letter assigned, right-click the drive, select *Delete Volume*, and click *Yes*. If the drive shows the status of Invalid, right-click the drive and select the *Convert to basic disk* option.

    Was the drive already partitioned?

    Was the drive already assigned a drive letter?

13. Right-click the new drive you just installed and select *New Simple volume*. The New Simple Volume Wizard appears. Click *Next*.

    What is the difference between a simple volume and a spanned volume?

    What is the minimum number of drives required to create a striped volume?

14. Enter a partition size that is less than 32GB and still leaves room on the hard drive.

    What partition size did you choose?

15. Select a drive letter (normally the next drive letter available and taking note of your options so you can answer the first question) and click *Next*.

    How many drive letters are available as an option?

    What file systems are supported when you use this tool?

    Are there any file systems supported by Windows 7 that are not shown? If so, what are they?

16. Select the *FAT32* option. Assign the volume label as a couple letters from each lab partners' last names. Note that there is an 11-character maximum for FAT32 partitions and a 32-character maximum for NTFS partitions. Select (enable) the *Perform a quick format* check box and click *Next*. Click the *Finish* button.

    How can you tell from the information in the window whether a partition is FAT32 or NTFS?

17. Right-click in the unallocated drive space on the drive you just installed and select *New Simple Volume*. The New Simple Volume Wizard appears. Click *Next*.
18. Click *Next*. Select a partition size less than 32GB, but still live some space on the drive. Click *Next*.

    What amount of space did you choose for the logical drive size?

19. Accept the drive letter default assignment and click *Next*.
20. Change the file system type to FAT32.
21. Make the volume label a unique name.

    Write the volume label chosen.

22. Select (enable) the *Perform a quick format* check box. Click *Next*, review the settings, and click *Finish*.
23. Right-click the free space for the drive you installed. Using the same process, create an NTFS simple volume (but still leave some space on the drive), add a unique volume label, and perform a quick format.

Instructor initials: ________________

24. You can change a FAT16 or FAT32 partition to the NTFS file system by using the `convert` command at a command prompt. Once a partition is changed, you cannot go back to a previous file system type. Also, data is preserved (but should be backed up before the conversion, just in case of problems).

    In the Disk Management console, what disk number is used for the newly installed drive? [0 | 1 | 2 | 3]

    Write the drive letter of the first FAT32 primary partition on the newly installed drive. Note that this drive letter will be used in the coming steps.

    Write the volume label used for the first FAT32 partition. This label is case sensitive, so write it carefully.

25. Click the *Start* button. Locate the *Command Prompt* menu option. Normally, it is located in Accessories. Right-click the *Command Prompt* menu option and select *Run as administrator*. Click *Yes*.
26. Type `convert /?` to see a list of options. These options tell you what to type as an option after the `convert` command.

    What option is used to run convert in verbose mode?

    What option is used to convert a volume to the NTFS file system?

27. Type `convert x: /fs:ntfs` (where `x:` is the drive letter you wrote in Step 24). For example, if the drive letter written in Step 24 is `d:`, type `convert d: /fs:ntfs`. Notice the space between the drive letter and `/fs:ntfs`. `/fs:ntfs` is used to convert the existing file system (FAT16 or FAT32) to NTFS. You are prompted for the volume label for the drive. Enter the volume label you documented in Step 24 and press Enter. Do not forget that the volume label is case sensitive. The partition is converted and can never be returned to a previous type of file system such as FAT32 unless the drive is reformatted.

28. Use the same process to convert the second FAT32 partition to NTFS. Look up the volume label and the drive letter before starting.

Instructor initials: ________________

29. In the *Computer Management—Disk Management* window, right-click the last partition on the newly installed hard drive.
30. Select the *Shrink Volume* option. Reduce the amount of hard drive space and click *Shrink*.

    What was the result in the Disk Management console?
31. Right-click the second partition on the newly installed drive. Select *Extend Volume*. A wizard appears. Click *Next*. Use the space available on the same drive and click *Next* and then *Finish*.

    What message appeared?

    According to the information in the dialog box, do you think changing this volume to a dynamic disk will matter?
32. Click *No* and return to the Disk Management console. Review the disks and determine the disk number and drive letter of the boot volume.

    Write the disk number of the boot volume. [0 | 1 | 2 | 3]

    Write the drive letter of the partition that holds the boot volume.
33. Right-click the second partition of the newly installed drive and select *Delete Volume*. Click *Yes*.
34. Partitions can be created from the Disk Management console, and they can also be created using the `diskpart` command utility. Return to the command prompt.
35. At the command prompt, type `diskpart` and press [Enter].

    How does the prompt change?
36. Type `help` and press [Enter]. Use the `help` command to determine what commands are available.

    What command is used to make a new volume?

    What command can be used to give a drive partition a drive letter?
37. Type `create ?` and press [Enter].

    What two options can be used with create?
38. Type `create partition ?` and press [Enter].

    What type of partitions can be created?
39. Press the up arrow (⇧) key once. The same command appears. Backspace and replace the question mark with the word `primary` so the command reads `create partition primary`. Press [Enter].

    What does the feedback say?

    What command do you think (based on Help) would be used to select a drive?

7 Storage Devices

40. Type `select disk x` (where *x* is the disk number documented in Step 24) and press [Enter]. A prompt says the disk is selected.
41. Retype the `create partition primary` command or press the [↑] key until that command appears and press [Enter].
42. Look back to the Disk Management console and notice that the part of the drive previously marked as free space is now a partition.
43. At the command prompt, type `detail disk` and press [Enter] to see the partition you just created.

    Based on the command output, what drive letters are currently used?

44. At the command prompt, type `assign` and press [Enter].

    Look in the Disk Management console window to determine what drive letter was assigned. Write the drive letter.

    What volume label, if any, was assigned?

45. At the command prompt, type `exit` and press [Enter] to leave the `diskpart` utility.
46. Type `help` at the command prompt and press [Enter] to look for a command to help with the high-level formatting of the drive. The commands scroll too quickly, so type `help | more` and press [Enter]. (The | keystroke is made by holding down the Shift key and pressing the key above the [Enter] key.) One page at a time is shown. Press the space bar once to see the next page of commands.
47. The next command requires filling in some parameters to perform this step correctly. The parameters are as follows:

    `x:`, the drive letter documented in Step 44.

    `/v:name` where `name` is a unique volume name with up to 32 characters.

    `/fs:ntfs`, which tells the system to use the NTFS file system. (Other options could be `/fs:fat`, `/fs:fat32`, or `/fs:exfat`, but this lab is using NTFS.)

    `/q` which does a quick format.

    Type the command `format x: /fs:ntfs /v:name /q` and press [Enter]. Note that if you get a message that the arguments are not valid, you did not exit the `diskpart` utility and did not do Steps 45 and 46. Go back and do them. When asked to proceed, press `Y` and press [Enter].
48. View the results in the Disk Management console. The last partition should be a partition that has a drive letter, a volume name assigned, and uses the NTFS file system.
49. Using whatever method you would like, copy one file to each of the three partitions you have created. Call the instructor over and show the instructor the three files and the Disk Management console. Do not proceed unless you have these parameters done.

Instructor initials: ______________

50. Close the command prompt window.
51. Starting with the partition on the far right in the Disk Management console for the newly installed drive, right-click each partition and delete each volume. Call the instructor over when the drive shows as one block (black) of unpartitioned hard drive space.

Instructor initials: ______________

52. Shut down the computer. Remove the power cord. Remove the data cable from the newly installed hard drive. Remove the power cord from the newly installed hard drive. Remove the hard drive. If necessary, re-install the optical drive, data cable, and power cord. Re-install the computer cover and power cord.

53. Boot the computer. Open Windows Explorer and select *Computer*. Ensure that the optical drive is recognized. If it is not, redo Step 52.
54. Show the instructor the optical drive in the Computer window and give the hard drive and any cable back to the instructor/lab assistant.

Instructor initials: ________________

Lab 7.6 Striping and Spanning Using Windows 7

Objective: To be able to configure and manage a striped volume or a spanned volume on a hard drive using the Windows 7 Disk Management console

Parts: Windows 7 computer

Motherboard or adapter that supports RAID 0

Two IDE PATA or SATA hard drives

Procedure: Complete the following procedure and answer the accompanying questions.

Notes: Use proper antistatic and gentle handling procedures when dealing with hard drives.

You must be a user who has administrator rights to configure hard drives.

This lab assumes that you can install and configure two or more SATA or PATA hard drives and have them recognizable in the Disk Management console. The optical drive may have to be disconnected if PATA RAID is being used and only one PATA motherboard is available when a SATA drive boots the computer. If SATA RAID is being used, the motherboard SATA ports may need to be enabled through BIOS. Depending on the RAID controller, you may need to access the RAID menu or BIOS to designate which two drives are participating in the RAID.

1. Optionally, install a RAID adapter. Cable the drives to SATA or PATA ports on the motherboard or on an adapter. Enable BIOS options as necessary.
2. Power on the computer and log in. Select the *Disk Management* option. The two newly installed hard drives should be visible in the Disk Management console. Initialize the drives, if necessary by right-clicking them and selecting *Initialize Disk*.

   What disk numbers are assigned to the newly installed hard drives?

3. In the Disk Management console, right-click in the unallocated space of the newly installed drive with the lowest numbered disk. Select *New Spanned Volume*. A wizard appears. Click *Next*.
4. Select the second drive number written as the answer in Step 2 in the Available: pane and click *Add* to move the drive to the Selected: pane. At least two drives should be listed in the Selected: pane. Click *Next*.
5. Select a drive letter to assign to the spanned volume. Click *Next*.
6. Select *NTFS* using the drop-down menu and add a volume label. Select (enable) the *Perform a quick format check box*. Click *Next*. Click *Finish*.
7. When a message appears to convert a basic disk to a dynamic disk, click *Yes*. Verify that the spanned volume appears.

   When using the Disk Management tool, how can you tell what two drives are a spanned volume?

8. Show the instructor the spanned volume.

Instructor initials: ________________

9. Use Windows Explorer to view the drive letters assigned and total capacity of each of the two drives.

   What drive letter was assigned to the spanned volume?

   What is the total capacity of the spanned volume?

   Which RAID level is spanning, if any?

10. In the Disk Management console, right-click in the newly created spanned volume space and select *Shrink Volume*. Select a smaller amount of space in the *Enter the amount of space to shrink in MB:* textbox.

    How does the Disk Management tool change?

11. Show the instructor the shrunken volume.

Instructor initials: ______________

12. In the Disk Management console, right-click in the spanned volume and select *Delete Volume*. When asked if you are sure, click *Yes*.
13. To create a striped volume from within the Disk Management console, right-click the lowest-numbered disk of the two newly installed drives and select *New Striped Volume*.
14. In the Available: pane, select the second newly installed disk and click the *Add* button to move the drive to the Selected: pane. Click *Next*.
15. Select a drive letter or leave the default. Click *Next*.
16. Leave the default system as NTFS and select (enable) the *Perform a quick format* check box. Click *Next*. Click *Finish*. Click *Yes*.

    How do the disks appear differently than the spanned volumes in the Disk Management console?

17. Open Windows Explorer.

    How many drive letters are assigned to a RAID 0 configuration?

18. Copy a file to the RAID 0 drive. Show the instructor the file and the Disk Management console.

Instructor initials: ______________

19. Right-click in the healthy volume space of either RAID 0 drive.

    Can a RAID 0 volume be shrunk?

20. Select the *Delete Volume* option. Click *Yes*. Show the instructor the unallocated space.

Instructor initials: ______________

21. Power down the computer, remove the power cord, and remove the two newly installed drives.
22. Power on the computer and, if necessary, return the BIOS settings to the original configuration. Ensure that the computer boots normally. Show the instructor that the computer boots normally.

Instructor initials: ______________

Lab 7.7 Windows XP Backup Tool

Objective: To be able to back up data using the Windows XP Backup tool

Parts: Windows XP computer

Procedure: Complete the following procedure and answer the accompanying questions.

Notes: You must be able to save data somewhere (floppy, USB drive, thumb flash drive, hard drive, and so on) in order to perform this exercise.

1. Power on the computer and log in.
2. Click the *Start* button > *All Programs* > *Accessories* > *System Tools* > *Backup*. Another way of accessing it is to directly go to the partition that contains the information to be backed up (such as `c:`), right-click the drive letter in Windows Explorer, select *Properties*, select the *Tools* tab, and click the *Backup now* button.
3. Click *Next* to skip the opening page. Select *Backup files and settings* and click *Next*. The page where you must decide what to backup appears. For most users, the *My documents and settings* option backs up their data and that is all that is needed. For this exercise, select the *Let me choose what to back up* radio button. Select *Next*.
4. In the Items to Back Up window, expand any documents so that a couple of files show in the right window. Select two or three files to be backed up. Click *Next*.
5. Select a place to store the backup by using the *Browse* button. If unsure, contact your instructor or lab assistant. Click *Next*.
6. Click the *Advanced* button.

   What type of backups are allowed?

   When you select one of the backup types, a description is shown in the window. Based on the description shown, what is the difference between an incremental and a differential backup?

7. Ensure *Normal* is selected and click *Back*. Click *Finish*.

   How much time did Windows take to back up the files?

8. Click the *Report* button when done.

   How many bytes were backed up?

9. Close the log window.

Instructor initials: ______________

10. Click the *Close* button.

Lab 7.8 Windows 7 Backup Tool

Objective:	To be able to use the Backup tool provided with Windows 7
Parts:	Windows 7 computer and administrator rights
	Flash drive with 1GB of free space (2GB drive is recommended)
Procedure:	Complete the following procedure and answer the accompanying questions.
Notes:	This lab does not back up the hard drive, but simply illustrates the concept of using the Backup tool.

1. Power on the computer and log on using a user ID and password that has administrator rights.
2. Use the Windows Help and Support tool to answer the following questions. Use the key terms `backup tool` to get started.

   Is shadow copies of shared folders a feature found in Windows 7? [Yes | No]

   What is the purpose of the shadow copies of shared folders?

   What command is used to create and manage system image backups for Windows 7–based computers?

   What are four Windows-based backup tools?

List one recommended location for storing a backup.

If a flash drive is to be used, what is the minimum amount of free space that must be available on that drive?

3. Copy at least one file to the Recycle bin.
4. Insert a flash drive. Ensure the drive is visible through Windows Explorer.
5. Using Windows Explorer, create a folder called Backup on the flash drive.
6. Locate the *System and Security* Control Panel and select the *Backup and Restore* link.
7. If a backup has not been performed before, you will need to select the *Set up backup* link. If a backup has been performed before, select the *Change settings* link.

   Notes: You may need to use the *Refresh* button to be able to see the flash drive. If the flash drive does not appear, ensure it is viewable through Windows AND has OVER 1GB of free space available. Select the appropriate drive letter. Click *Next*.

   Select the *Let me choose* radio button. Click *Next*. If the system is not set up to do the backup on demand, you may have to click the *Change schedule* link to modify it so the backup can be done now. Then, select the *$Recycle Bin* checkbox. Note that you may have to expand the *Computer* option as well as the *C:* drive in order to locate this checkbox. Click *Next*. Select the *Save settings and run backup* button.
8. While the backup is occurring, select the *View Details* button.

   Why do you think a technician would use this option?

   Were you surprised at the time it took to perform the backup?

Instructor initials: ______________

9. When the backup is complete, click the *Close* button, delete the backup from the flash drive, eject the flash drive and give to the instructor, if necessary, and close all windows.

Lab 7.9 Windows XP/Vista Hard Disk Tools

Objective: To be able to use the tools provided with Windows XP or Vista to manage the hard disk drive

Parts: A computer with Windows XP/Vista loaded and administrator rights/password

Procedure: Complete the following procedure and answer the accompanying questions.

Note: The defragmentation and Error-checking (*Check now*) process can take more than 60 minutes on larger hard drives.

1. Power on the computer and log on using a user ID and password provided by the instructor or lab assistant that has administrator rights.
2. Click the *Start* button, select *All Programs*, select *Accessories*, select *System Tools*, and click *Disk Cleanup*.
3. If on Vista, select the *My files only* link. The drive selection window appears. Using ▼, select a drive letter and click the *OK* button.
4. The *Disk Cleanup* window appears. Ensure that *only* the following checkboxes are checked (enabled) for lab purposes:

   Temporary Internet files

   Recycle Bin

   Web client/Publisher Temporary Files (XP)

   Temporary Files

   Compress Old Files (XP)

Click the *OK* button.

5. When prompted, if you are sure, click the *Yes* (XP) or *Delete Files* (Vista) button. Enter the administrator password, if necessary.

   List at least two related topics that are available from the Help and Support Center when getting help on the topic of disk cleanup.

Instructor initials: ______________

6. Click the *Start* button, select *All Programs*, select *Accessories*, select *System Tools*, and click *Disk Defragmenter*.
7. In XP, select a drive volume in the top portion of the window. In Vista, click on *Select volumes*. Select a particular drive to use. Vista users proceed to step 10 after answering the question for this step.

   What percentage of free space is shown for the drive?

   In Vista, select the How does Disk Defragmenter help? link. What does Vista help say about using the computer during defragmentation?

8. In XP, click the *Help* button (the button that looks like a piece of paper with a question mark on it). Click the *Best practices* hyperlink.

   Based on the XP help information shown, should hard drive volumes be analyzed before defragmenting them?

9. Close the XP *Help* window and click the *Analyze* button on XP computers. When finished answering the question for this step, click the *Close* button.

   Is defragmentation recommended?

10. In XP, click the *Defragment* button. In Vista, click the *Defragment now* button and the *OK* button.

    What would be the determining factor for you in recommending how often a particular computer user should make use of this tool?

    List one more recommendation that you would make to a user regarding this tool.

11. In XP, click the *View Report* button. In Vista, skip this step and the questions related to this step.

Instructor initials: ______________

   How many files are fragmented?

   List one file that did not defragment.

   What is the average file size?

12. Click on the *Close* button and close the *Disk Defragmenter* window.
13. Open Windows Explorer. Locate and right-click the hard drive (`c:`) and select *Properties*. Select the *Tools* tab and the *Check now* button. In Vista, if the User Account Control window appears, click *Continue*.

14. In the window that appears, select the *Scan for and attempt recovery of bad sectors* check box and ensure that the *automatically fix file system errors* check box is not checked (not enabled). Click *Start*.

    For Vista users, click the *View details* link to answer these questions:

    How many files were processed?

    How much space does the system take?

15. Call the instructor over when the utility is finished (before you click *OK*). Click *OK* again and close the utility window.

Instructor initials: ____________

Lab 7.10 Windows 7 Hard Disk Tools

Objective: To be able to use the tools provided with Windows 7 to manage the hard disk drive

Parts: Windows 7 computer and administrator rights

Procedure: Complete the following procedure and answer the accompanying questions.

Notes: The defragmentation and Error-checking (Check now) process can take more than 60 minutes on larger hard drives.

1. Power on the computer and log on using a user ID and password that has administrator rights.
2. Click the *Start* button, select *All Programs*, select *Accessories*, select *System Tools*, and click *Disk Cleanup*.
3. The Disk Cleanup window appears. Ensure that *only* the following checkboxes are checked (enabled) for lab purposes:

   Temporary Internet Files

   Recycle Bin

   Temporary Files

   Game Statistics Files (if available)

   Click the *OK* button.
4. When prompted if you are sure, click the *Delete Files* button.

   List at least two related topics that are available from the Help and Support Center when getting help on the topic of disk cleanup.

5. Using Windows Explorer, right-click on the hard disk drive letter to check for errors. Select *Properties*.
6. Click the *Tools* tab. In the Error-checking section, click the *Check now* button.
7. Any files and folders that have problems, you can either select *Automatically fix file system errors* or you can just have the check performed with a generated report at the end. A more thorough disk check can be done using the *Scan for and attempt recovery of bad sectors*. This disk check locates and attempts repair on physical hard disk sections and can take a very long time. The most comprehensive check is to check for both file errors and physical problems on the hard disk surface with the *Automatically fix file system errors and Scan for and attempt recovery of bad sectors*.

   For this exercise, just de-select (disable) the *Automatically fix file system errors*. Note that the Scan for and attempt recovery of bad sectors check box is automatically disabled (not checked). Click *Start*.

What message appeared when the scan was complete?

Instructor initials: ______________

8. Click the *Close* button.
9. Either return to the hard drive *Properties* window and select *Defragment now* or click the *Start* button, select *All Programs*, select *Accessories*, select *System Tools*, and click *Disk Defragmenter*.
10. Select a particular drive to use. Select the *Analyze disk* button.

    In the Windows Explorer Properties window General tab, what percentage of free space is shown for the drive?

    From the Disk Defragmenter window, select the Tell me more about Disk Defragmenter link. What does Windows 7 help say about using the computer during the defragmentation routine?
11. From the Disk Defragmenter window, click the *Defragment disk* button.

    What would be the determining factor for you in recommending how often a particular computer user should make use of this tool?

    List one more recommendation that you would make to a user regarding this tool.
12. If class time is an issue, click the *Stop Operation* button. Click the *Close* button. Close the hard drive *Properties* window.

Activities

Internet Discovery

Objective: To obtain specific information on the Internet regarding a computer or its associated parts

Parts: Computer with Internet access

Questions: Use the Internet to answer the following questions. Write the answers and the URL of the site where you found the information. Assume you have just purchased a Seagate Barracuda 3TB 7200 rpm 6Gbps hard drive in answering Questions 1–3.

1. What type of cables are needed for this drive? Do they come with the drive? Write the answer and the URL where you found this information.
2. How much cache does this drive have?
3. If the computer does not have an available Molex connector or SATA connector, what one recommendation could you make?

4. A customer has a Western Digital WD3200AAKB Caviar Blue PATA hard drive. What are the possible jumper settings for this drive? Write the answer and the URL where you found this information. [Single | Master | Slave | Cable Select | Dual (Master) | Dual (Slave) | Slave Present]
5. Based on the same drive as in Question 4 and information you learned in this chapter, if a customer had a drive already configured to cable select and wanted you to install the Western Digital drive, what setting must be set on the new drive? [Single | Master | Slave | Cable Select | Dual (Master) | Dual (Slave) | Slave Present]
6. Find an eSATA and an internal SATA hard drive that are equal or close to equal in capacity. What is the price difference between the two? Write the answer and the URL where you found this information.

Watch the laptop hard drive installation video at the following URL to answer Questions 8–10 (if this link does not work, find a video that shows a laptop hard drive installation):

http://www.youtube.com/watch?v=EHxZN_NSiRI

8. List one reason cited in the video for not opening a laptop case.
9. Besides unplugging the AC power plug, what other recommendation was given regarding power before installing the drive?
10. [T | F] Some laptops use a caddy to hold the drive. Western Digital drives can accept a caddy.

Soft Skills

Objective: To enhance and fine-tune a technician's ability to listen, communicate in both written and oral form, and support people who use computers in a professional manner

Activities:

1. In groups of two, pretend one of you has a hard drive problem. The other student pretends to help you on the phone. Share your phone conversation with two other groups. Select the best group and scenario.
2. With two other classmates, come up with 10 additional tips for good phone support that were not listed in the chapter. Share your ideas with the class.

3. As a team, plan the installation of three storage devices. Two of these devices are PATA and the other one is SATA. In addition there are two SCSI devices to attach to the same controller. In your plan, detail what things you will check for, how you obtain the documentation, and what obstacles could appear as part of the installation process. Share your plan with others.

Critical Thinking Skills

Objective: To analyze and evaluate information as well as apply learned information to new or different situations

Activities:

1. List three things that could cause a computer to lock up periodically. What could you do to fix, check, or verify these three things?

2. A customer wants to either upgrade or replace his hard drive. Go through the steps you would take from start to finish to accomplish this task.

3. You have a department of 20 workstations. Develop a backup plan for the department. Use the Internet to research other backup plans.

A+ Certification Exam Tips

- ✓ Know everything about how to configure PATA, SATA, and SSDs.
- ✓ Know the cable limitations for PATA and internal/external SATA.
- ✓ Know the purposes of the Error-checking (Check now), Disk Cleanup, and Defragmenter tools.
- ✓ Use a computer to review the disk tools and how to get to them.
- ✓ Review all the troubleshooting tips for the 220-802 exam.
- ✓ Be familiar with the following Disk Management concepts: drive status and what to do if the status is not in the healthy state, mounting, extending partitions, splitting partitions, assigning drive letters, adding drives, adding arrays.
- ✓ For the 220-802 exam, know what a normal hard drive sounds like and what sounds a hard drive in trouble makes.
- ✓ Install a couple of practice drives for the 220-802 exam and cable them up incorrectly or misconfigure the jumpers so you see the POST errors and symptoms.
- ✓ Be very familiar with the Disk Management tool and the messages seen there.
- ✓ Know common BIOS configurations required for PATA and SATA devices.
- ✓ Know how to configure a RAID.
- ✓ Know the difference between the various RAID levels.
- ✓ Know what to do to a drive that is being resold, repurposed, or has classified material stored on it.
- ✓ Know how to speak professionally.

chapter 8

Multimedia Devices

Chapter Objectives:

In this chapter you will learn:

- To compare optical drive and disc technologies
- To determine optical drive specifications and features from an advertisement or specification sheet
- To determine the best interfaces and ports used to connect optical drives
- How to install, configure, and troubleshoot optical drives, sound, scanners, and digital cameras
- How to use Windows to verify optical drive, audio ports, scanner, and digital camera installations
- How to provide support with a positive, proactive attitude

CompTIA Exam Objectives:

What CompTIA A+ exam objectives are covered in this chapter?

- ✓ 801-1.1 Configure and apply BIOS settings.
- ✓ 801-1.4 Install and configure expansion cards.
- ✓ 801-1.5 Install and configure storage devices and use appropriate media.
- ✓ 801-1.12 Install and configure various peripheral devices.
- ✓ 801-3.1 Install and configure laptop hardware and components.
- ✓ 801-3.3 Compare and contrast laptop features.
- ✓ 802-1.4 Given a scenario, use appropriate operating system features and tools.
- ✓ 802-1.5 Given a scenario, use Control Panel utilities.

Multimedia Overview

The term *multimedia* has different meanings for people because there are many types of multimedia devices. This chapter focuses on the most popular areas—optical drive technologies, sound cards, cameras, and speakers. These devices collectively allow you to create and output sound, music, video, movies. The chapter is not intended to be a buyer's guide for multimedia devices or an electronics "how it works" chapter; instead, it is a guide for technicians with an emphasis on installation and troubleshooting.

Optical Disk Drive Overview

CD (compact disc), **DVD** (digital versatile disc or digital video disc), and **Blu-ray** drives are collectively called **ODDs** (optical disk drives) because they use optical discs that are read from, written to, or both. Optical discs are great to use when creating or playing music CDs or movie DVDs, or for backing up data. CDs are the oldest technology, but this technology is still in use today in combination with DVD and **BD** (Blu-ray disk)technologies. Drives can be obtained that can handle CD, DVD, and BD media. Figure 8.1 shows a BenQ CD drive and its various front panel controls.

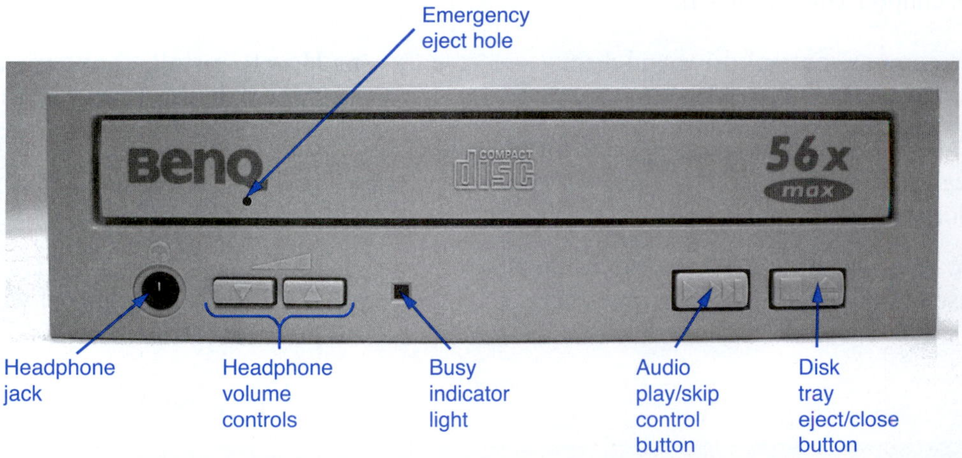

Figure 8.1 BenQ CD drive front panel controls

A CD has pits or indentations along the track. Flats, sometimes called lands, separate the pits. Reading information from a CD involves using a laser diode or similar device. The laser beam shines through the protective coating to an aluminum alloy layer, where data is stored. The laser beam reflects back through the optics to a photo diode detector that converts the reflected beam of light into 1s and 0s. The variation of light intensity reflected from the pits and lands is detected as a series of on/off signals that are then converted into binary code. CD and DVD drives use red laser technology, whereas Blu-ray drives use blue-violet laser technology. The blue-violet laser technology has a shorter wavelength, which means that smaller data pit sizes can be used to create higher disc capacities. This translates to more cost, too. Figure 8.2 shows an inside view of a CD drive. The newer technologies operate in a similar fashion.

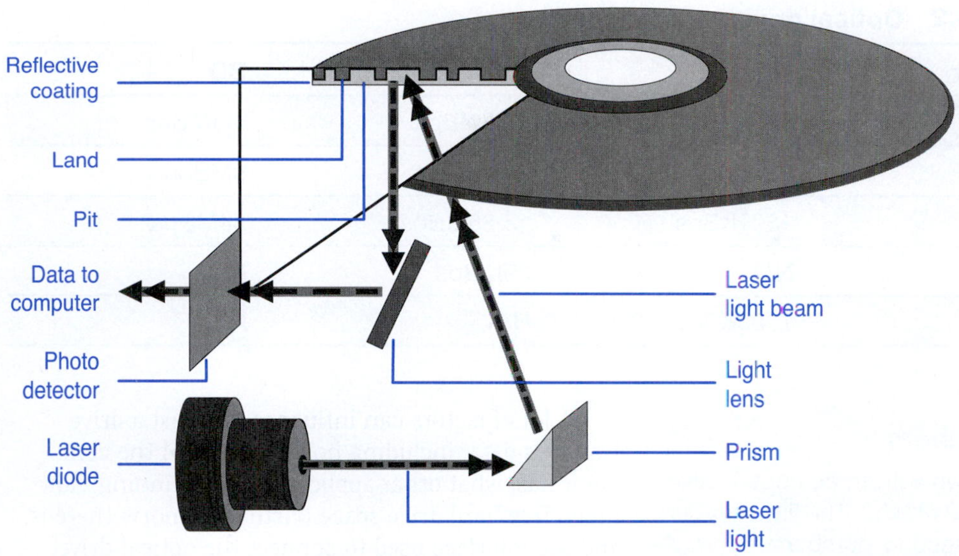

Figure 8.2 Inside a CD drive

Optical Drive Features

Optical drives that have an "R" designation can only read from a disk. Drives that have an "RW" or "RE" designation can perform both reads and writes. Drives with a "DL" designation use dual-layer technology where two physical layers are available on the same side of the disc. The laser shines through the first layer to get to the second layer. Table 8.1 lists common media used.

Table 8.1 Optical writeable media

Media type	Description
CD	650 or 700MB
DVD-5	4.7GB single-sided single layer
DVD-9	8.5GB single-sided dual layer
DVD-10	9.4GB double-sided single layer
DVD-18	17.1GB double-sided dual layer
BD	25GB single layer
BD DL	50GB dual layer
Mini BD	7.8GB single layer
Mini BD DL	15.6GB dual layer

Optical drives come in a variety of types, classified by the x factor: 1x (single-speed), 2x (double-speed), 32x, 48x, 52x, and higher. Optical drives do not operate at just a single speed, though; the speed varies depending on the type of media being read and whether writing is being done. Table 8.2 shows the generic transfer rates for the different x factors and types of optical drives.

Table 8.2 Optical drive transfer speeds

x factor	CD	DVD	BD
1x	150KBps	1.32MBps	4.5MBps
2x	300KBps	2.64MBps	9MBps
12x	1800KBps	15.85MBps	54MBps
22x	N/A	29MBps	N/A
52x	7800KBps	N/A	N/A

Tech Tip

How to read the numbers

ODDs are frequently shown with three consecutive factor numbers, such as 52x32x52. The first number is the write speed, the second number the read/write speed, and the third number is the maximum read speed used when reading a disc.

A lot of factors can influence how fast a drive transfers data, including how much RAM the computer has, what other applications are running, how much free hard drive space (virtual memory) there is, and the interface used to connect the optical drive; even how much RAM is on the video card can influence an ODD that has video content. Data is stored as one continuous spiral of data on optical discs. This concept is shown in Figure 8.3. Data is, of course, in 1s and 0s, and spaced a lot closer, but the idea of one continuous spiral is important for the write-once technologies. Pits on a DVD are half the size of a CD, and the tracks are closer together so more data can be stored.

Tech Tip

Keep the data coming

One problem with ODDs occurs when data is written to the disc. If the drive does not receive data in a steady stream, a buffer underrun error occurs, and the disc is ruined if it is an -R or +R disc. To avoid this problem, avoid performing other tasks when burning data to disc.

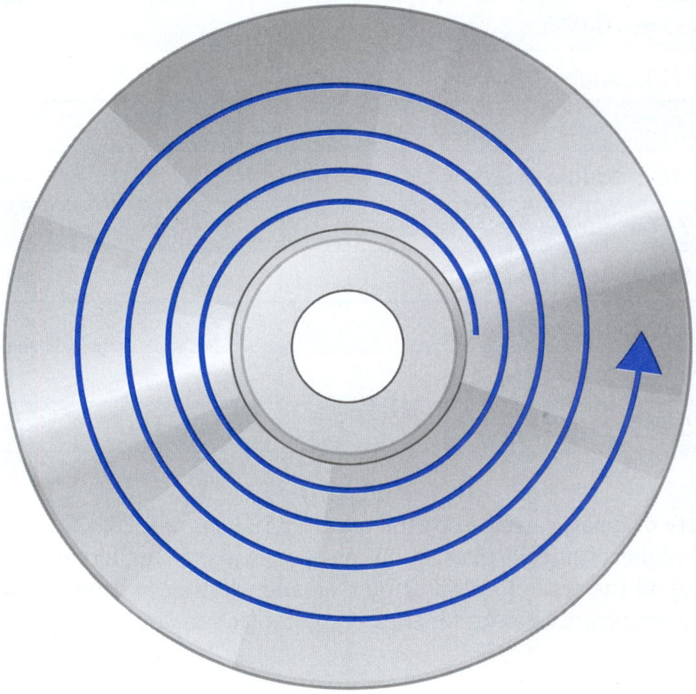

Figure 8.3 Optical disc

The steps for copying files to a disc using Windows Explorer in Windows 7 follow:

1. Insert an optical disc. From the window that appears, select *Burn files to disc using Windows Explorer*.
2. Name the optical disc and select the format type. Click *OK*.
3. Open Windows Explorer and select any file(s) you want to copy. Drag them to the optical disc drive in the left panel. Continue for any files that may be in other folders.
4. After selecting files, click the optical drive letter in the left panel. All files should list in the right panel.
5. Right-click the optical drive letter and select *Close session*.

Tech Tip

Some optical drives cannot read Blu-ray discs

Some optical drives cannot read Blu-ray discs because CD/DVD drives use a red laser, and Blu-ray drives use a blue-violet laser. Drives that have both lasers are available.

One way to reduce transfer time when writing data to the drive is by having buffer memory on the drive. When requesting data, the drive looks ahead on the disc for more data than requested and places the data in the buffer memory. **Buffer memory** holds the extra data in the drive and then constantly sends data to the processor instead of the processor waiting for the drive's slow access time. Buffer memory is not enough. Having little hard drive space or RAM can still slow down or abort the recording process.

One feature that you might use to compare if two drives have the same x factor is the random access time. The **random access time** is the amount of time the drive requires to find the appropriate place on the disc and retrieve information. Another important comparison point is MTBF (mean time between failures) which is the average number of hours before a device is likely to fail. A closely related term that you might see instead of MTBF is **MCBF** (mean cycles between failure) which is found by dividing the MTBF by the duration time of a cycle (operations per hour). The MCBF is actually a more accurate figure because not all drives are used the same amount of time per hour. Keep in mind that for any of these, the lower the number, the better the performance.

Both DVD and BD drives have **region codes**. The world is divided into six regions for the DVD drive and three regions for a BD drive. The drive must be set for the correct region code or else the DVDs made for that area do not work. When a disc is inserted, the decoder checks what region it is configured for (or in the case of software decoding, what region the drive is configured for) and then checks for the region code. If the two match, then the movie plays. Table 8.3 shows the region codes for DVD and Blu-ray drives.

Table 8.3 DVD/Blu-ray region codes

DVD region code	Geographic area	Blu-ray region code	Geographic area
1	U.S. and Canada	A	North/Central/South America, Southeast Asia, Taiwan, Hong Kong, Macau, and Korea
2	Europe, Near East, Japan, and South Africa	B	Europe, Africa, Southwest Asia, Australia, and New Zealand
3	Southeast Asia	C	Central/South remaining Asian countries, China, and Russia
4	Australia, Middle America, and South America		
5	Africa, Asia, and Eastern Europe		
6	China		

A nice feature to have in a drive is the ability to use the computer to label the disc such as Hewlett-Packard's LightScribe. The drive and disc must support this technology. Do not use the labels you can attach to the top of the disc. These can come off or not be put on properly and cause vibration and read issues. Write on the non-data side of the disc with a permanent marker as a last resort. Many drive features or capabilities can be determined by looking at the symbols on the front of the drive, as shown in Figure 8.4.

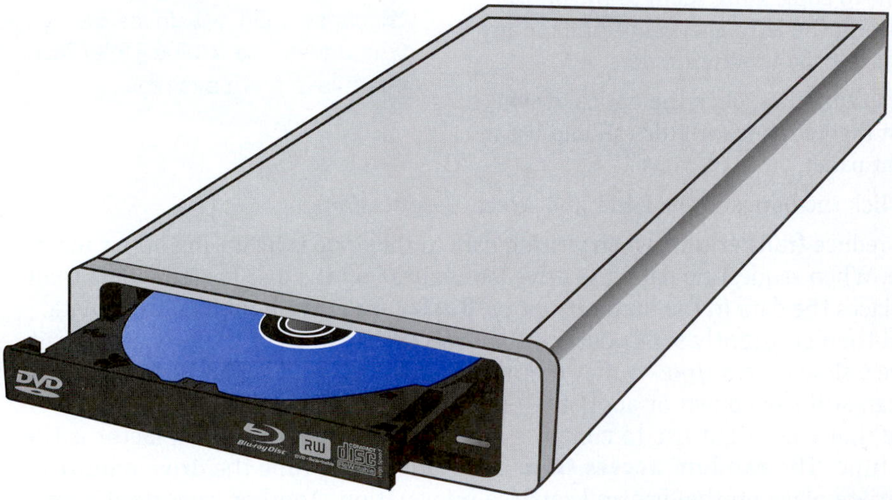

Figure 8.4 Optical drive symbols

Optical Drive Interfaces and Connections

An optical drive can be internally mounted and attached to a PATA or SATA interface, or the drive can be externally attached to a USB, IEEE 1394 (FireWire), eSATA, or eSATAp (combo SATA/USB) port. Figure 8.5 shows an external combo drive that can read CDs, DVDs, and Blu-ray discs.

Figure 8.5 External optical drive

In both desktop and portable computers, the SATA interface is the most common for internal devices and USB for external devices. Laptops and ultrabooks tend to have slot-loaded (like a car optical disc player) instead of the tray-loaded desktop models. Figure 8.6 shows a laptop with a slot-loaded drive.

Figure 8.6 Laptop slot-loaded optical drive

The following will help you decide what optical drive interface to recommend:

- Is the drive going to be internal or external? If it will be internal, open the case to see if a drive bay is available. Check for a PATA or SATA interface on the motherboard. If PATA is being used, remember that in desktop models, two devices can connect to a single motherboard connector; however, SATA requires one port for each device. Remember that internal devices tend to be cheaper than external.
- If the drive will be internal, check that a power connection is available. A Y connector or Molex to SATA power converter may have to be purchased.
- If the drive will be external, check what eSATA, eSATAp, USB, or IEEE 1394 ports are available. Some USB hard drives take two ports. Ensure the drive comes with cabling or purchase separately.
- Check with the customer about features they may like to have, such as buffer memory and writing labels.
- If the customer wants to upgrade the drive, find out why. Many times, slow access is due to other components in the computer, not the drive.

Optical Drive Installation

One thing to be concerned about with an optical drive is whether the drive is to be installed horizontally or vertically. Not all drives can be installed vertically, but most drives today can go either way.

The steps for installing an internal optical drive are almost identical to the steps for installing a hard drive:

1. Download the latest drivers before installation.
2. Install any necessary mounting brackets.
3. Ensure that a proper port/interface is available. Ensure that a power connector is available. Set the appropriate configuration jumpers if necessary. Refer to the drive documentation.
4. Turn off the power. Remove power cords. Remove the laptop battery.

5. Install the drive. The laptop keyboard may have to be removed to access the drive. Always refer to laptop instructions for replacing drives to ensure the warranty is not voided.
6. Attach the power and data cables.
7. Enter BIOS to check drive status. Ensure that the port is enabled. Ensure that the drive is recognized. Note that you may need to reboot the machine once to see this. If the drive is not recognized in BIOS (at least that there is a drive attached), recheck settings and cabling.
8. If necessary, install drivers and/or software as part of the installation process. See Figure 8.7. Get the drive functional by using the driver that came with the drive, if possible. Then upgrade the driver once the drive is recognized by the system.

Tech Tip

PATA connectivity

When connecting an optical drive to a PATA connector that already has a drive attached to one of the PATA cable connectors, you have to know the jumper settings on the already installed drive to correctly install the optical drive. The installed drive settings may have to be adjusted when a second device is added to the cable. The optical drive should be the slave device.

Figure 8.7 Installing software

For an external drive, download the latest drivers, ensure that you have the correct port, attach external power to the device as necessary before attaching to the port, attach the cable to the device, and attach the other end of the cable to the computer. Again, you may need a driver upgrade and/or to install some software as part of this process. Remember to check Device Manager to ensure that the device is recognized by the operating system.

Tech Tip

Always test the installation

Test the installation by using the device—play something or write to a disc that you bring along. Ensure that the customer tries the disc and is comfortable with the changes caused by the installation.

Troubleshooting Optical Drive Issues

Windows has troubleshooting tools in the Help and Support Center. Here's how you use them:

1. Click *Start* and select *Help and Support*.
2. Select the *Fixing a problem* help topic (XP)/*CDs and DVDs* (Vista)/or type `troubleshooting` in the Search textbox (Windows 7).
3. Select the *Games, Sound and Video Problems* link (XP)/an appropriate topic (Vista)/or *Open the Hardware and Devices troubleshooter* link (7).
4. In the XP right panel, use the *Games and Multimedia Troubleshooter* link. In Windows Vista and 7, proceed to reading the list provided in the troubleshooting window.

Tech Tip

Check the easy stuff first

Verify that the correct type of optical disc is in the drive, is inserted correctly (label side up), and is not dirty or damaged. Test the disc in another drive. Verify that the ODD has a drive letter. Check Device Manager for errors.

The following is a list of problems, along with possible solutions and recommendations:

Tech Tip

You can see video but can't hear or vice versa

Verify that the computer has the hardware and software requirements for DVD playback. Update the optical drive drivers.

- If a drive tray cannot be opened, make sure there is power attached. Use Windows Explorer to locate the drive, right-click the drive, and select *Eject*. Some drives have an emergency eject button or a hole you can insert a paperclip into to eject the disc. Refer to Figure 8.1 to see an example of the eject hole.
- If a drive is not recognized by the operating system, check cables, the power cord, and the configuration (master/slave, cable select, SATA speed, port enabled in BIOS).
- If a drive busy indicator flashes more slowly than normal, the disc or laser lens may be dirty. Refer to the manufacturer's recommendations for cleaning. See the next section, on preventive maintenance, for details on how to clean a disc.
- If the drive cannot read a disc, ensure that the drive supports the disc being used. Ensure the disc label is facing up. Ensure that the disc is clean and without scratches. Try the disc in another machine or try a different disc to see if the problem is with the drive or the disc.
- If a drive is not recognizes as a recordable device (*Properties* and the Recording tab is missing), an updated driver or registry edit is probably needed.
- If a DVD sound track works but video is missing or distorted, check the cabling. Verify the video drivers. Try changing the display resolution and the number of colors.
- If a message appears about an illegal DVD or BD region error or region code error, change the region if possible. Otherwise, you can't use the disc without a different drive that matches.
- If a drive reads only CDs and not DVDs or Blu-ray discs, update the driver.

- Some optical drive problems are resolved by using DirectX. **DirectX** allows people who write software to not have to write code to access specific hardware directly. DirectX translates generic hardware commands into special commands for the hardware, which speeds up development time for hardware manufacturers and software developers. DirectX may need to be re-installed or upgraded. Access the DirectX Diagnostic Tool in Windows by entering `dxdiag` in the Start/Run or Search dialog box.
- Check to see if there is a more recent driver for the drive.
- If a drive keeps opening the tray, check for a stuck eject button. Check for a virus. Remove the data cable (but leave the power cable attached) to see if it is the drive or a signal being sent to the drive to open.
- If you can hear sound from a DVD, but not a CD, get an updated optical drive driver.
- If you continue to have errors when writing to a disc, clean the laser lens or record at a lower speed. Avoid multitasking when writing.
- If you get a message stating that the DVD decoder is not installed, download a decoder from the DVD drive manufacturer or the computer manufacturer if the drive came with the computer. A **decoder** makes it possible for the disc images to be played/viewed through software on your computer.
- Not to worry if you get a message from an application that requires a disc in a specific drive letter, but because of adding drives, the optical disk drive letter has changed. You can change the drive letter using the Windows Disk Management tool. Right-click the drive in the left panel and select *Change Drive Letter and Paths*.
- Blu-ray requirements are much more stringent—ensure all your video drivers, DVD drivers, the display, and video cable are all compliant for playing Blu-ray discs.

Preventive Maintenance for ODDs and Discs

CDs and DVDs have a protective coating over the aluminum alloy–based data layer that helps protect the disc. Blu-ray has a requirement that the BD media be scratch resistant. They are less likely to need preventive maintenance. However, fingerprints, dust, and dirt can still negatively affect CD and DVD performance.

Tech Tip

Handle discs with care

Always handle a disc by the edges and keep the disc in a sleeve or case to aid in good performance. Never touch a disc's surface, and store discs in a cool location.

When reading information, the optical drive laser beam ignores the protective coating and shines through to the data layer. Even if the disc has dirt on the protective coating, the laser beam can still operate because the beam is directed at the data layer rather than the disc surface. However, if dust or dirt completely blocks the laser beam, the laser beam could be reflected or distorted, thus causing distortion or data corruption. Special cleaning discs, cloths, and kits are available for cleaning optical discs. A soft lint-free cloth and spit or glass cleaner works too. Figure 8.8 shows proper handling during the cleaning process.

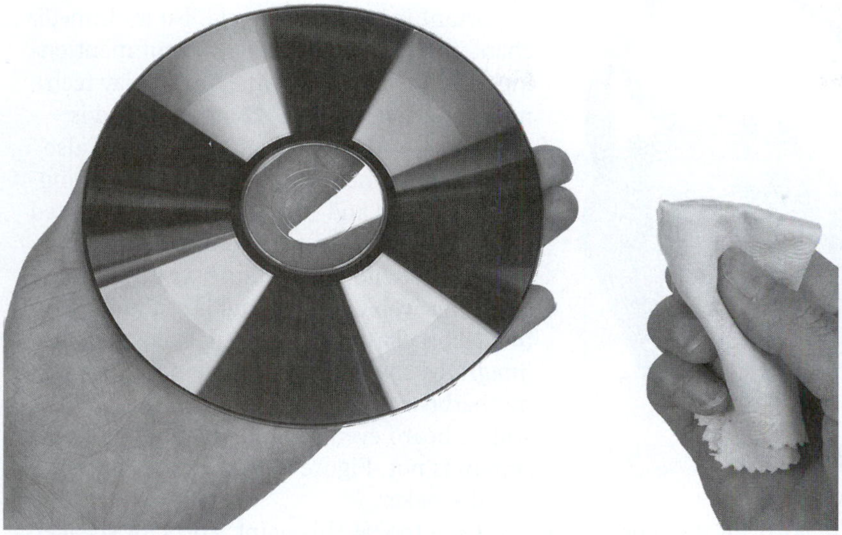

Figure 8.8 Disc cleaning

Mild abrasives or special disc repair kits can be used to repair scratched discs. Examples of mild abrasives include plastic, furniture, or brass polish. When applying the abrasive, do not rub in circles. Instead, use the same technique as cleaning: start from the innermost portion and rub outward. The abrasive can remove the scratch if it is not too deep. A wax such as furniture or car wax can be used to fill the scratch if it is not removed by the abrasive.

Tech Tip

Cleaning discs

When using a cleaning cloth, wipe the disc from the inside (near the center hole) to the outside of the disc (*not* in a circular motion) on the side of the disc that has data.

A special component of the optical drive, the **laser lens** (also known as the objective lens) is responsible for reading information from the disc. If the laser lens gets dust, dirt, or moisture on it, the drive may report data or read errors. Some drives have the lens encased in an airtight enclosure and others have a self-cleaning laser lens. If the drive does not have this feature, look for a laser lens cleaning kit. Also, the laser lens can be cleaned with an air blower like ones used on a camera lens. Cleaning the laser lens should be part of a preventive maintenance routine. Some drive manufacturers include a special plate to keep dust away from the internal components. In any case, keep the disc compartment closed to prevent dust and dirt from accumulating on the laser lens and other drive parts.

Tech Tip

No cable from the optical drive to the sound card

With Windows XP, if you enable CCDA (compact disc digital audio), you do not have to attach a cable from the optical drive to the sound card or motherboard. Sound is output via the optical drive data cable. *Access Device Manager*, locate and right-click the CD/DVD drive and select *Properties* tab, and enable the *Enable digital CD audio* checkbox. Sound is automatically handled this way in Vista/7.

Figure 8.9 Motherboard speaker

Video and sound technologies are very important in today's IT world. No multimedia chapter would be complete without mentioning sound and digital cameras. Display technologies are in the next chapter. Sound is important to the end user, but sound is also important to the technician, so before going into installing and configuring sound-related devices, don't forget that sometimes when these devices don't work such as when the computer won't boot, sound is still important to a technician. Motherboards have a small integrated speaker or one that attaches to motherboard pins that allows POST sounds to still be heard even if the more advanced sound system is not. Figure 8.9 shows the motherboard speaker.

A review of sound ports on the motherboard is good, too, at this point. Ports for speakers and headphones are typically 1/8-inch (3.5mm) connectors that accept TRS (tip ring sleeve) connectors. Figure 8.10 shows common motherboard sound ports.

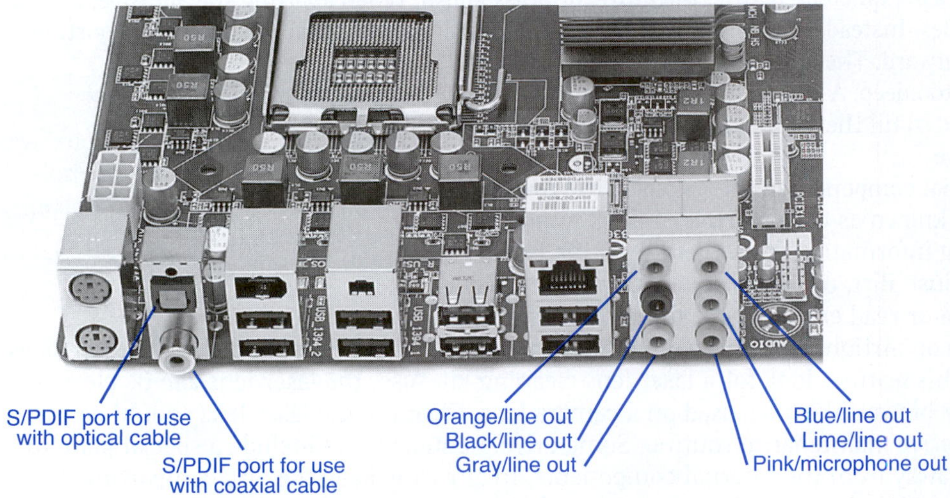

Figure 8.10 Motherboard audio ports

Notice in Figure 8.10 the connection for S/PDIF. S/PDIF are the newest type of sound ports. S/PDIF can be used to carry audio signals between audio devices and stereo components or the output of a DVD player in a PC to a home theater or some other external output device. S/PDIF ports can attach using a RCA jack attached to coaxial cable or a TOSLINK connector attached to a fiber-optic cable.

One connection that is not shown in Figure 8.10 is an older 15-pin female MIDI port. **MIDI** (musical instrument digital interface) is used to create synthesized music. Traditionally, a MIDI device such as a digital piano keyboard would connect using the MIDI interface and the traditional microphone or line out ports. MIDI instruments today typically have a USB connection. If not, a cable converter can be purchased.

Optical drives have the capability of producing sound, usually through a front headphone jack and through a connection to sound through the motherboard or an installed sound adapter. Audio discs can be played on these drives, but the sound does not sound as good through the drive's headphone jack as it does through a stereo system or speakers. Figure 8.11 shows typical sound card ports and the type of devices that might connect to these ports. Table 8.4 shows the colors that are normally found on sound ports.

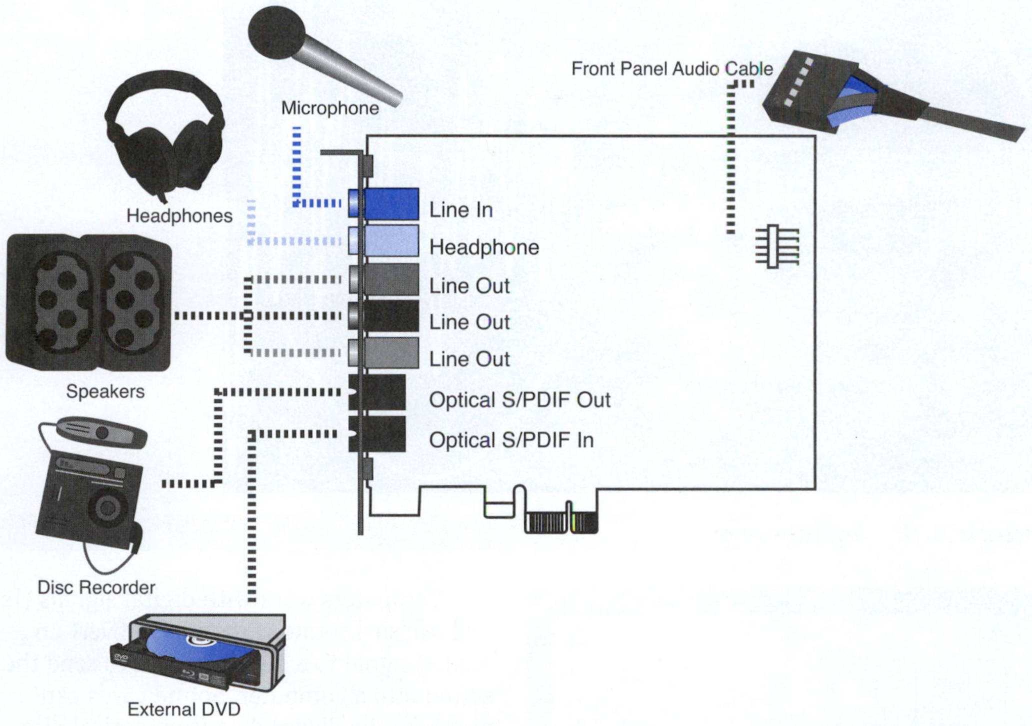

Figure 8.11 Sound card port connectivity

Table 8.4 Sound port colors

Color	Purpose
Orange/gold	Center speaker or subwoofer
Black	Rear speaker
Light blue	Line in
Lime green	Line out/front channel speakers
Pink	Microphone
Gray	Side speaker

Theory of Sound Card Operation

Sound cards have a variety of options that can include an input from a microphone, an output to a speaker, a MIDI interface, and the ability to generate music. Take the example of bringing sound into the computer through a microphone connected to a sound card. Sound waves are shown as an analog waveform, as shown in Figure 8.12.

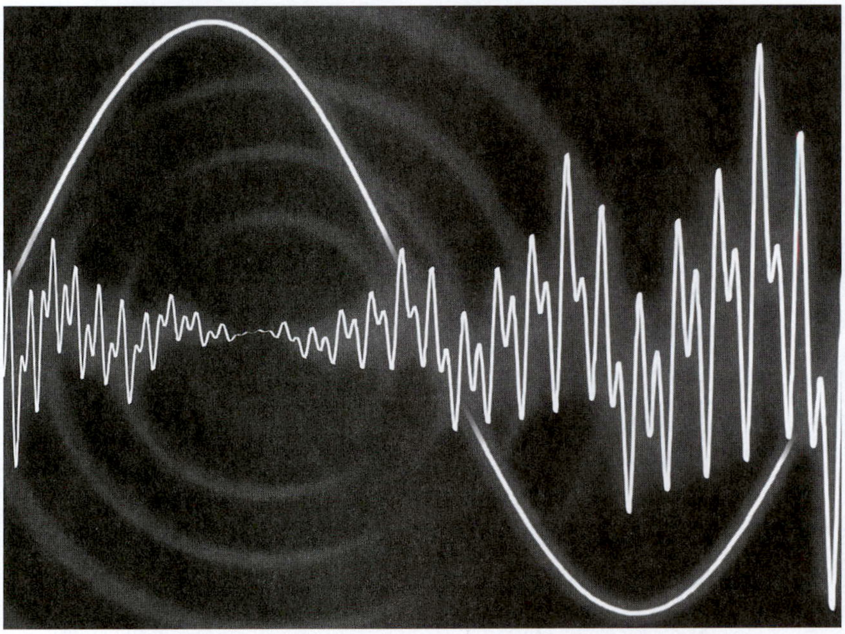

Figure 8.12 Sound waves

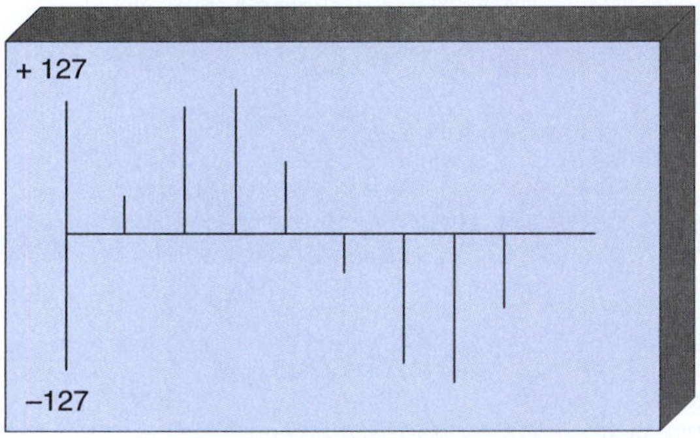

Figure 8.13 8-bit sampling

Computers work with digital signals (1s and 0s), so a sound card must convert an analog signal to a digital format to send the sound into a computer. Sound cards can also take the digital data from optical disc media and output the sound to the speakers. To convert an analog waveform to 1s and 0s, samples of the data are taken. The more samples taken, the truer the reproduction of the original signal.

The first sound cards made for the computer sampled the data using 8 bits. Eight 1s and 0s can give a total of 256 ($2^8 = 256$) different values. The analog waveform goes above and below a center value of 0. Because one of the 8 bits denotes negative or positive value, only 7 bits can represent sampled values. $2^7 = 128$. The values can be 0 through +127 or 0 through –127. (The total value range is between –127 and +127.) Figure 8.13 shows an example of sampling.

The more samples taken by a sound card, the closer the reproduction is to the original sound signal. The sound card **frequency response** is dependent on the sample rate. This is also known as the sample rate or sample frequency. For a good reproduction of sound, the sound wave is sampled at twice the range desired. For example, a person's hearing is in the 20Hz to 20KHz range. Twice that range is approximately 40,000 samples per second. The frequency response for a musical CD is 44,100 samples per second, a good quality sound reproduction for human ears. The first sound cards for computers used eight bits to sample the sound wave and had a frequency response of approximately 22,000 samples per second (22KHz). The sound produced from the original sound cards was better than the beeps and chirps previously heard from the computer. The sound was still grainy, better than an AM radio station but not as good as an FM radio station or a musical disc.

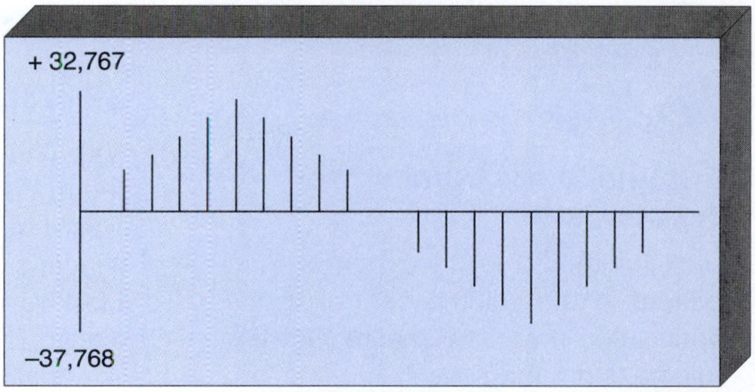

Figure 8.14 16-bit sampling

Next, 16-bit sound cards arrived for computers. The number of possible levels sampled with 16 bits is 65,536 (2^{16} = 65,536). When positive and negative levels are sampled, the range is –32,767 to +32,767. The frequency response with 16-bit sound cards is 44KHz, the same resolution as stereo audio CDs. 24-bit sampling results in a 96kHz sample rate that is sometimes called the audio resolution. The increase in the number of sampling levels and the frequency response allows sound cards to produce quality sound equal to audio discs. See Figure 8.14 for an example of 16-bit sampling. Keep in mind that when more samples are taken, the sound card provides a better frequency response.

DVDs require a 48KHz sampling rate for audio output. Therefore, sound card sampling rates should be a minimum of 48KHz for DVDs and 44.1KHz for CDs.

Installing Sound Cards

The steps involved in installing a sound card are similar to the steps involved in installing any other adapter. Refer to the manufacturer's instructions when installing devices and adapters.

1. Power off the computer, remove the computer case, and locate an empty expansion slot (making sure it is the appropriate type of slot).
2. Attach appropriate cables, such as the audio cable, from the optical drive to the adapter.
3. Attach external devices, such as speakers.
4. Power on the computer. Windows should detect that new hardware has been installed (if Windows does not, use the *Add Hardware* Control Panel in XP or the *Hardware and Sound > Add a device* link in Vista/7).
5. Load the appropriate device drivers for the sound card.

Once a sound card is installed, there are normally other programs and utilities from the sound card manufacturer that you can install as you would any other application.

Tech Tip

Safely remove USB devices

To remove a USB device, do not simply unplug it from the port. Instead, click the *Safely Remove Hardware* icon from the notification area. Select the USB device to remove. The operating system prompts when it is safe to unplug the device.

Tech Tip

Disable motherboard sound when installing an adapter

If you install a sound card into a computer that has sound built into the motherboard, you must disable the onboard sound before installing the new adapter.

Tech Tip

If sound is not coming from the computer

Look for the *Mute* checkbox or icon located in the volume control in the Notification area and ensure that the volume is not muted.

Sound Cards Using Windows

With Windows XP the *Sounds and Audio Devices* Control Panel and in Vista/7 the *Hardware and Sound* Control Panel link is used to change sound and adjust multimedia settings. All Windows operating systems allow controlling volume through a taskbar volume icon located in the lower-right portion of the screen. This icon can be used to mute or adjust sound.

Audio drivers are vastly improved in Windows XP and higher to accommodate multiple streams of real-time audio and allow a kernel-mode process to handle audio management. This means that the operating system can control all aspects and improve audio performance. Digital audio can be redirected to any available output including USB and IEEE 1394 (FireWire).

Windows also includes a set of APIs (Application Programming Interfaces), which are commands that developers use to communicate with the sound card. DirectX has specific APIs that have commands relating to audio. In DirectX, Microsoft adds such things as DirectSound3D that has more 3-D audio effect commands, supports hardware acceleration, and allows simulation of audio sounds in certain environments, such as a tunnel or underwater. It allows software and game developers to create realistic audio environments such as muffling effects and audio directional effects (that is, the direction a sound comes from).

You can tell whether a device has integrated sound or a sound adapter installed by inspecting the *Sound, video and game controller* category in Device Manager. The left side of Figure 8.15 shows a screen capture of Device Manager from a computer that has integrated sound on the motherboard. Note that integrated sound may be located in the *System devices* or *Other devices* categories.

Microphones are commonly used in conference calls and VoIP (voice over IP) calls. VoIP is a technology where phone calls are digitized and transmit using the data network rather than using a traditional corporate digital voice network or the PSTN (public switched telephone network—in other words, the traditional phone network). Microphones can be attached to a headset, a separate device, integrated into the computer display, or integrated into the device such as with mobile devices. To see your microphone settings on a Windows device, use the *Hardware and Sound* Control Panel, in the Sound section locate and select *Manage audio devices*, and click the *Recording* tab. Figure 8.16 shows a microphone that is built into a flat panel monitor. Once you select the microphone, you can use the *Properties* button to adjust the microphone settings.

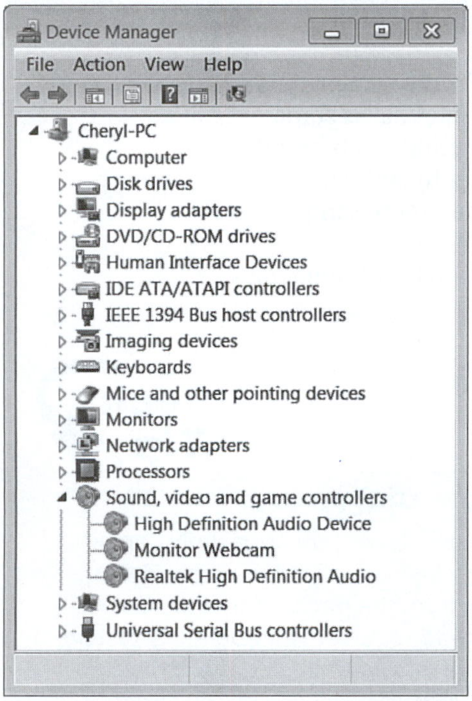

Figure 8.15 Integrated sound card in Device Manager

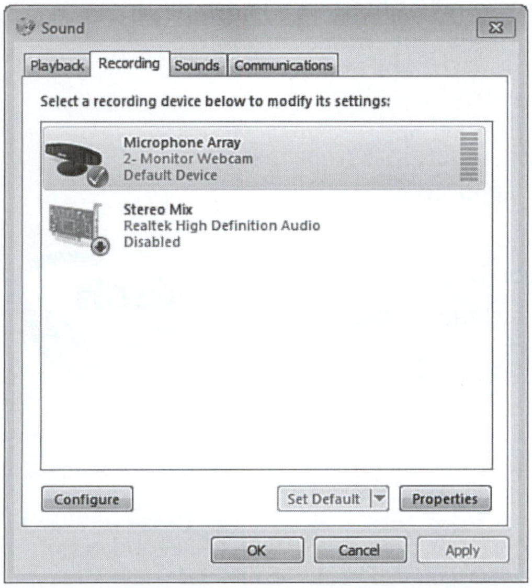

Figure 8.16 Integrated display microphone

Mobile Device Sound

Mobile devices are more limited in their sound options than are desktop computers. However, a portable device normally has an integrated microphone, a line out connector for headphones, and sound integrated into the motherboard. Sometimes the speakers must be replaced. Laptop, netbook, or ultrabook speakers tend to mount in the back corners of the device or extend along the internal sides. Figure 8.17 shows two different models of mobile device speakers.

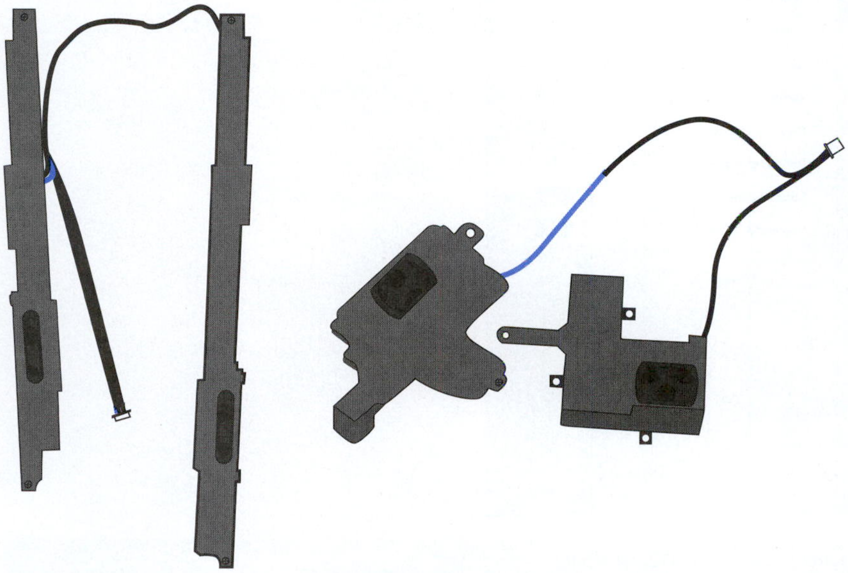

Figure 8.17 Laptop speaker connectivity

Another option for laptops and desktop computers is using a USB port or adding a USB sound card. USB sound devices work with both analog and digital signals. Insert the sound card into a USB port and have instant quality sound. Keep in mind that if the sound device is powered by the USB port, this shortens battery life.

Wireless sound connectivity is also an option. A PC or a laptop that has wireless network connectivity can have music stored on it. A wireless receiver allows music to be played anywhere within wireless network range.

Laptop devices normally can control sound with buttons above the keypad or by selecting a combination of keys such as Fn + F6. The icon on the F6 key (or whatever key is used) is normally an icon of a sound wave getting louder or softer (🔊) or an icon of an up or down arrow (▼).

For Android mobile devices, use the *Sound Setting* option to mute and modify the ringtone. Optionally, you can also select sounds to be played such as when the screen unlocks or when switching between screens. Android smartphones normally have microphones of course, but not all Android-based tablets do.

For Apple iOS devices, use the *General Settings* option. Then locate *Sounds*. The speaker volume and sounds heard for email, phone calls, reminders, keyboard clicks, and so on are set on this screen. Both Android and Apple iOS–based mobile devices have volume controls on the sides. Figure 8.18 shows the sound settings on an Apple iPad2.

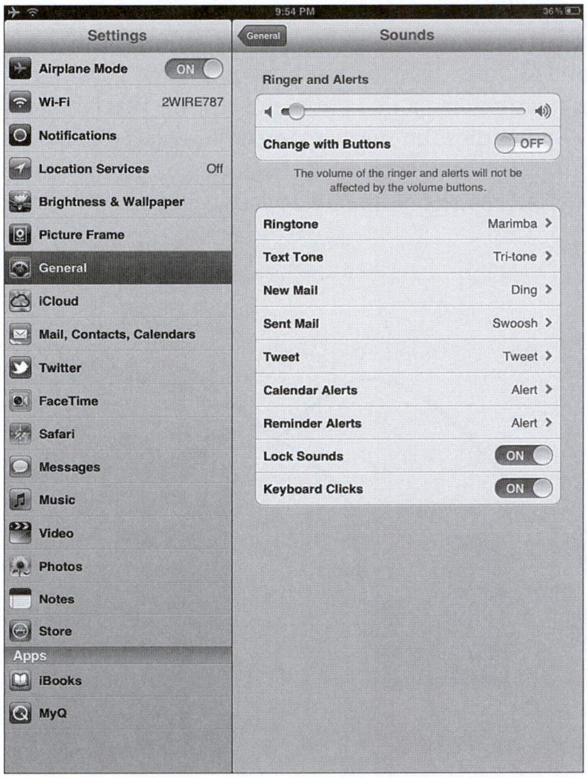

Figure 8.18 Apple iPad2 sound settings

Microphones in tablets normally do not have controls like netbooks, laptops, and PCs. Instead, the microphone is controlled through an application that supports a microphone, such as a notepad that allows you to add audio notes or record a lecture or an online conference application. Inside the application, there is normally a little icon of a microphone that you tap to be able to start recording. External microphones can be added using wireless Bluetooth connectivity or an external microphone for those tablets that have a jack. Smartphones, of course, have integrated microphones.

Speakers

Most people connect speakers to a sound card or integrated sound ports. The quality of sound is personal; sounds that are acceptable to one person are not always acceptable to someone else. Table 8.5 shows some features to look for in speakers.

Table 8.5 Speaker features

Feature	Description
Amplification	Increases the strength of the sound. Sound cards usually have built-in amplification to drive speakers. Amplification output is measured in watts and most sound cards provide up to four watts of amplification (which is not enough for a full-bodied sound). Many speakers have built-in amplifiers to boost the audio signal for a much fuller sound.
Power rating	How loud the volume can go without distorting the sound. This is expressed in watts per channel. Look for the RMS (root-mean-square) power rating. 10 to 15 watts per channel is an adequate rating for most computer users.

Feature	Description
Frequency response range	The range of frequency (sounds) that the speaker can reproduce. Humans can hear from 20Hz to 20KHz, and the range varies for each person. Therefore, whether a computer speaker is appropriate depends on the person listening to the speaker because speaker quality is subjective. Room acoustics and speaker placement also affect sound quality.
Shielding	Cancels out magnetic interference and keeps magnetic interference away from other devices. Speakers usually have a magnet inside them that can cause distortion to a device such as a monitor. These magnets can also cause damage to disks and other storage media. The best CD/DVD/BD drive and sound card combination can be downgraded by using inexpensive, poorly shielded speakers.

Most computers come with internal or external speakers. Sometimes the external speakers produce poor quality sound. Also, some of the external speakers are battery-powered, which might not be desired. Speakers with an external power source are best. One speaker commonly connects to the sound card port, and the other speaker is daisy-chained to the first speaker. Some speakers have an external volume control. Be mindful of this as it is another thing to check for when sound does not occur. Figure 8.19 shows computer speakers that are powered with an AC adapter.

Tech Tip

How to choose speakers

Listen to them without headphones, using an audio (non-software) CD, DVD, or BD.

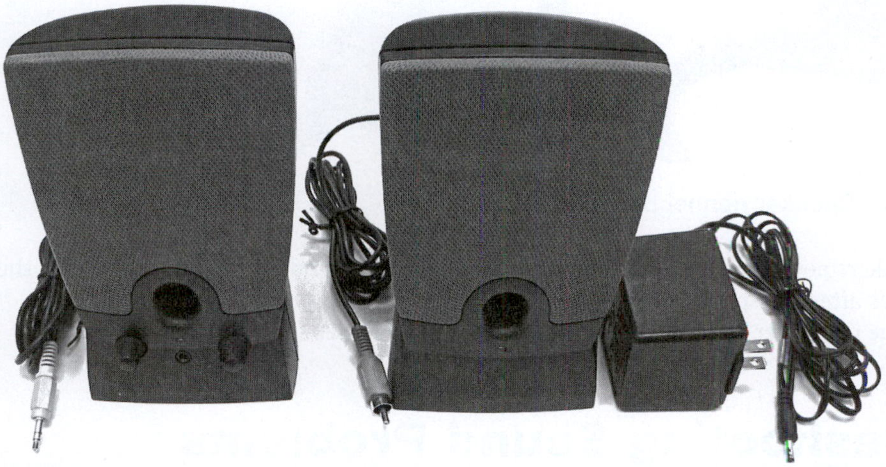

Figure 8.19 Front view of speakers

USB, IEEE 1394 (FireWire), and wireless solutions can also be used to provide connectivity for speakers. Digital audio is sent over the bus, and an external speaker converts the signal into sound. When audio is converted inside the computer, interference from internal electronic components and external sources (especially if an expansion slot does not have an adapter installed and the case has an opening) can cause audio interference. The drawback to USB is that it puts more work on the CPU. However, in today's multi-processor environment, this may not be an issue. The following is a list of extras to look for in speakers:

- An external volume control
- Headphone jacks

- Headphone and microphone pass-through connectors (so you do not have to dislodge the computer to reach the jacks)
- AC adapter
- Connectors for the speakers to connect to the sound card
- If the sound card is capable of 3D sound, a four- or six-speaker system is an enhancement

Two speakers are normally joined by a cable that may or may not be removable. Figure 8.20 shows how a cable that plugs into the right speaker would have the other end connected to the left speaker.

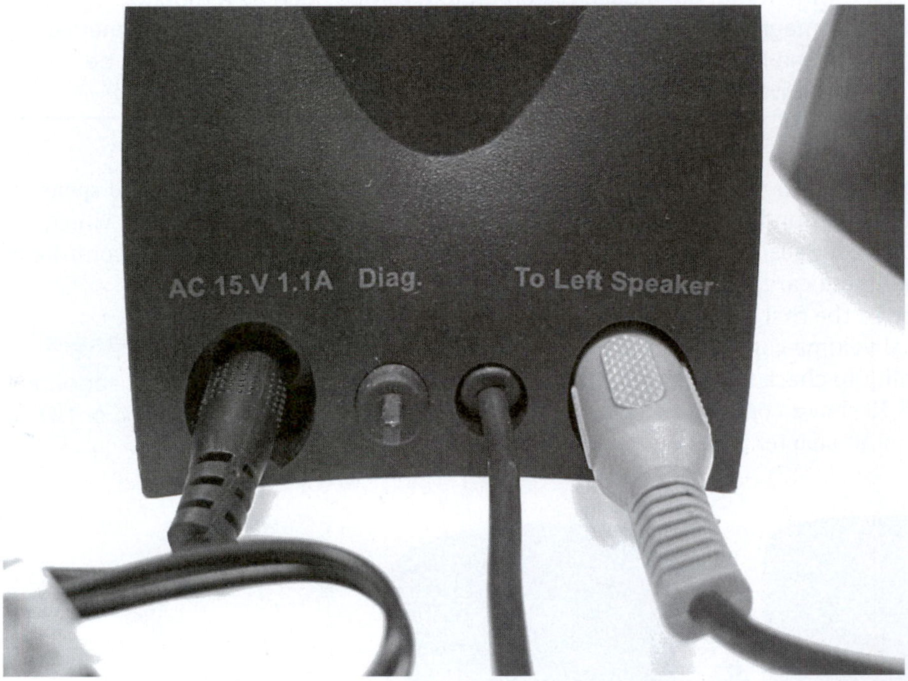

Figure 8.20 Speaker connections

When speakers power on, they sometimes emit a popping sound. This is normal, but if the sound continues after the speakers are powered on, the speaker is probably picking up interference from the computer or another device. Try moving the speakers farther away from the computer.

Troubleshooting Sound Problems

The following is a list of common sound problems and solutions:

- If a speaker is emitting unwanted sounds, make sure there are no empty adapter slots in the computer. Next, check the speaker wires for cuts, move the sound card to another expansion slot, and move the speakers farther away from the computer. Finally, move the computer away from the offending device or the offending device away from the computer. If the speakers produce a humming noise and are AC powered, move the speaker power cord to a different wall outlet. Plugging the speakers into the same circuit as the computer is best.
- If sound is a problem or if any solution directs you to update your sound driver, access *Device Manager* and expand the *Sound, video, and game controllers*, *System devices*, or *Other devices* option. Locate and right-click the integrated sound or the sound card and select *Properties*. Select the *Driver* tab and use the *Update driver* button.

- If the sound card is not working, check Device Manager to see if the sound card is listed twice. If there are two entries for the same sound card, remove both of them by clicking each entry and clicking the *Remove* button. Restart Windows, and the operating system should detect the adapter and either install a device driver or prompt for one. For best results, use the latest device driver from the sound card manufacturer or computer manufacturer in the case of integrated ports.

Tech Tip

Check the easy stuff first

1. Are speakers plugged into the correct port on the sound card?
2. Is the volume control muted? If so, take it off mute.
3. Is the volume control on the speakers turned up?
4. From within Windows, does the device appears to be playing the disc but no sound can be heard? In this case, the problem is definitely in the sound system.
5. Do the speakers have power?

- If you do not see a sound icon in the bottom-right corner of the screen, use the *Sounds and Audio Devices* (Windows XP) Control Panel to ensure that the sound card is listed. On the *Volume* tab, ensure that the *Place volume icon in the taskbar* checkbox is enabled. In Vista/7, open the *Appearance and Personalization* Control Panel. In the Taskbar and Start Menu section, select *Customize icons on the taskbar*. Select the *Notification area* tab and locate the Volume icon. Use the checkbox to display the icon in the Notification area.
- If audio is low no matter what disc or system sound is played, the speakers may not be amplified speakers or they may not be connected to the correct sound card port. Also, do not forget to check the computer sound settings through the icon on the taskbar or the *Sounds and Audio Devices* (XP) or *Hardware and Sound* (Vista/7) Control Panel. If a yellow question mark is there, right-click the sound card, select *Properties*, and check the Device status section to see the issue. Many issues require driver updates.
- If one disc does not output sound but other discs work fine, the disc may use a later version of DirectX than the one installed. Check the recommended DirectX version for the disc. Also, the disc may have a problem.
- If building a computer, install the sound card after installing the video card, hard drive, and optical drive, but before anything else. Some sound cards are inflexible about system resource changes.
- For headphone issues, ensure the cable attaches to the correct line out port. Determine if you want the speakers disabled. Normally, if you plug into the headphones line out port, the speakers cut off.
- For Android or iOS devices, check the volume control and whether the device is muted.
- On tablets or smartphones, check if any other applications might be using the microphone that are still running by using the Android *Settings* > *Apps* > *Running* tab. Select the application and select *Force stop*. For Apple iOS devices, push the home button twice to see running applications > tap the one you want to close.

If sound does not come out of the optical drive after the drivers and software load, try the following troubleshooting tips:

- Be sure an audio disc is inserted into the drive.
- If sound no longer comes out of the speakers, check the speaker cables.
- Check the proper installation of the audio cable.
- Ensure that the speakers or headphones connect to the drive or to the sound card or integrated sound port.
- If using speakers, check the insertion of the cable jack on the back of the sound card. Verify that the speakers have batteries installed or an AC adapter connected.
- If using headphones, verify that the headphones work on another device before using them to test the drive.

- Get updated drivers from the sound card manufacturer's website.
- If the monitor's image quality decreases after installing a sound card with speakers, move the speakers farther away from the monitor.

Scanners

A **scanner** is a popular input device that allows documents including text and pictures to be brought into the computer and displayed, printed, emailed, pressed to an optical disc, and so on. A scanner is commonly built into an MFD (multifunction device) such as a printer, scanner, and/or fax machine. These are also called AIOs, or all-in-one devices. The most common types of scanners are listed in Table 8.6.

Table 8.6 Types of scanners

Scanner type	Comments
Flatbed (sometimes called desktop scanner)	Can scan books, paper, photographs, and so on; takes up a great deal of desk space
Sheetfed	Enables a document to be fed through an automatic document feeder similar to a fax machine; good for scanning many documents simultaneously
Handheld	Slowly moves across the document; user must have patience and a steady hand; portable unit
Film	Scans picture film instead of picture prints
Barcode reader	Reads barcodes in checkout lanes and in retail establishments; handheld device

Figure 8.21 shows a handheld scanner.

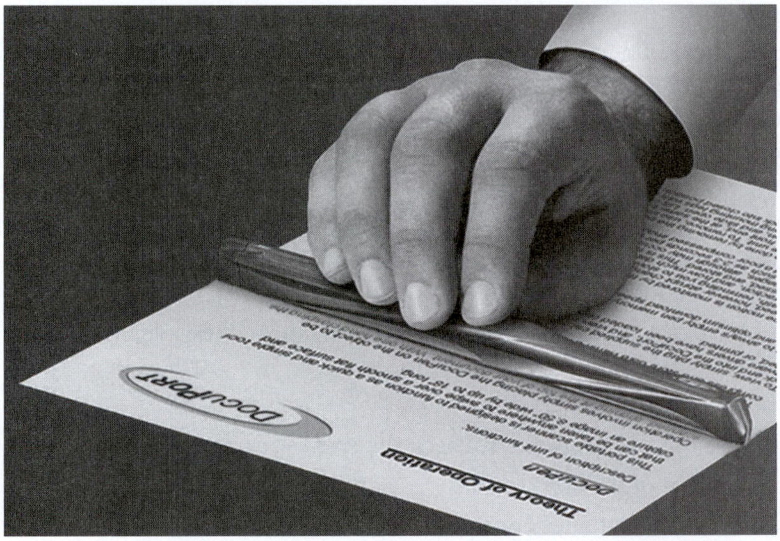

Figure 8.21 Handheld scanner

Scanners normally attach to a computer using one of the following ports:

- Parallel (though not very often today)
- USB
- IEEE 1394 (FireWire)
- RJ-45 Ethernet
- Wireless

USB is the most common connectivity option.

USB devices are easy to install, and USB hubs allow system-integrated USB ports to be turned into multiple USB ports. To install a USB scanner, always follow the manufacturer's directions. The following steps are generic:

1. Install software and drivers.
2. Unpackage and unlock or remove special packaging.
3. Connect the data or network cable as well as the power cable.
4. Power on the scanner. Some scanners have a calibration process that needs to be performed. There may be a special switch or pushbutton that locks/unlocks the scan head.
5. Configure options and default settings.
6. Scan a document to test it.
7. Ensure that the customer is trained and has all scanner documentation.

Figure 8.22 Flatbed scanner

Figure 8.22 shows a flatbed scanner. Notice the rails down the right side. These rails guide the scan head assembly (the part with the ribbon cable attached). Figure 8.23 outlines how a flatbed scanner works.

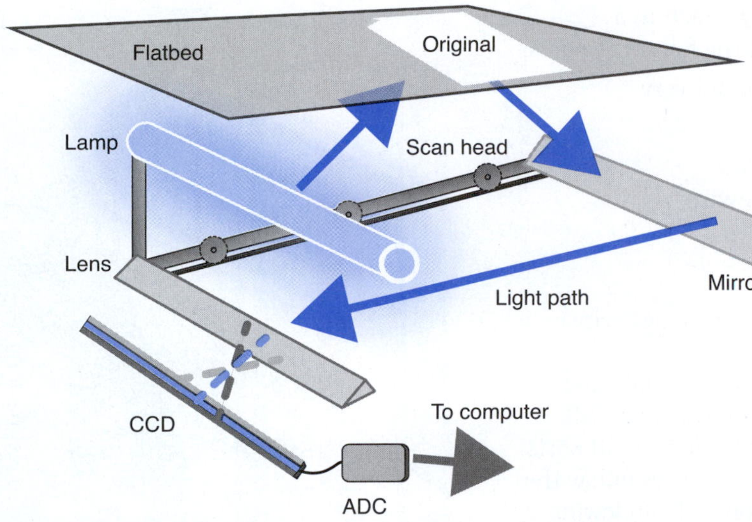

1. A document is placed on the scanner's glass plate. There is a lamp under the glass.

2. The lamp (fluorescent, CCFL [cold cathode fluorescent lamp], or Xenon) turns on. Light reflects from the document.

3. The scan head is used to capture the reflected light. It moves slowly down the document by way of a belt. The light reflects through a series of mirrors to the CCD (charge-coupled device) array.

4. The CCD array holds light sensitive diodes. The diodes convert light into varying voltage levels. The voltage levels are sent to an ADC (analog to digital converter).

5. The ADC converts the voltage levels to pixels. A pixel is a dot and is the smallest unit in a picture or document.

6. The pixels are sent through the scanner interface to the computer where the image is displayed.

Figure 8.23 How a flatbed scanner works

A scanned image can be saved in several formats. When scanning a document or graphic for web pages, select PNG, PDF, JPEG, or GIF format. The most common graphic file formats are listed in Table 8.7. There are many terms associated with scanning, and Table 8.8 lists the most common of them.

Table 8.7 Scanner file formats

File format	Comments
JPEG (Joint Photographic Experts Group)	Small file size; good for web pictures; not good for master copies; always compresses the file; file extension is .jpg
GIF (Graphic Interchange Format)	Limited to 256 colors; small in size; good for web pictures; file extension is .gif
TIFF (Tag Image File Format)	Good for master copies; large size; file extension is .tif
PNG (Portable Network Graphics)	Not supported by all applications or older applications; supports 24- and 48-bit color; file extension is .png
PDF (Portable Document Format)	Used for web-based forms and scanned words; file extension is .pdf

Table 8.8 Scanner terms

Scanner term	Comments
Resolution	Measured in dpi (dots per inch); determined by the number of sensors in the CCD array and by the precision of the stepper motor; common resolutions include 300, 600, 1200, 2400, 3200, 4800, 6400, and 9600
Bit depth	The number of bits used for color; the more bits, the more colors and color depth; common configurations are 24, 30, 36, and 48 bits
Interpolation	Software used by the scanner to achieve a greater resolution by filling in the pixels around the scanned pixels
OCR (Optical Character Recognition)	Software that processes printed or written text characters; not all scanners ship with OCR software
TWAIN	A driver that is used so that applications can access and acquire images directly from the scanner

Resolution is an important concept when scanning a document or photo. When scanning something, always think about whether the output is intended for the printer or the monitor. Setting the scanner's resolution to the maximum amount for every scan is not a good idea. Table 8.9 shows some sample resolutions for scanning.

Table 8.9 Scanner resolutions

Type of document	Use	Scanner color setting	Recommended resolution (dpi)
Any	Displaying on a monitor	Color, grayscale, or black and white	150
Text	Copying or emailing	Color, grayscale, or black and white	150
Black-and-white photo	Saving, using a website or email	Grayscale	75–300
Color photo	Copying, printing, or creating a document such as a photo or postcard	Color	300
	Using in a website or email	Color	75–150
	Saving	Color	75–300

A scanner's plate glass needs to be cleaned periodically. To test the cleaning, scan a full page without a document loaded onto the scanner. See if the results yield any smudges or streaks. Use these best practices:

- The best cleaning method is to put optical surface cleaning fluid on an antistatic cleaning cloth and then wipe the glass.
- Never spray cleaner directly on the glass.
- Do not use rough paper towels.
- A commercial glass cleaner or water can be used.

Tech Tip

Protect the scanner glass

Be careful with sharp objects such as staples around a scanner. A scratched or damaged glass surface results in permanent marks on scanned images.

- Always remove all cleaner residue from the glass.
- Do not press down on the glass.
- Do not use an abrasive or corrosive solvent.
- Keep the glass dust free.

Digital Cameras

Video recording capabilities can be built into a computer or a mobile device, an attachment to a computer, or a standalone digital camera or camcorder used for the purpose of taking photographs or recording movies. A digital camera resolution is measured in pixels. The resolution is the number of horizontal and vertical pixels the camera can use to display an image. Today, digital camera resolution technology has evolved into MPs (megapixels). A camera's photosensors determine how many pixels can be used. Common resolutions for integrated tablet cameras and smartphones is 1.2 to 5MP or more compared to 4 to 18MP found in digital cameras. (Of course, these numbers will be higher the moment this book goes to press.)

Tech Tip

Caring for a digital camera

Remove disposable (alkaline) batteries from a digital camera when it's not being used for an extended period so they do not leak battery fluids into the camera.

Some of cameras store the photographs or movies on flash media (mini-SD, microSD, xD, Compact Flash, etc.) or hard drives, usually in the JPEG file format, but some cameras can save in RAW or TIFF formats. Table 8.10 shows camera storage media, and Table 8.11 lists common file formats.

Table 8.10 Digital camera data storage

Storage type	Comments
Compact Flash (CF)	Introduced by SanDisk; uses flash memory; does not require a battery to store photos once power is removed; includes CF-I and CF-II
SmartMedia	Developed by Toshiba; smaller and lighter than CF; can purchase an adapter card with PC Card/ExpressBus ATA adapter for data transfers
Memory Stick	Created by Sony; small in size; can read/write with a standard floppy disk drive with the purchase of a Memory Stick reader; includes MS (memory stick), MSD (memory stick duo), M2 (memory stick micro)
Secure Digital	Size of a postage stamp; does not require power to retain data; uses flash memory technology; has the ability for cryptographic security; different types include SD, miniSD, microSD, and SDHC
PC Card/ExpressBus drives	Consumes more power than memory technology
MMC (multimedia card)	A type of flash memory used in many portable devices, including cameras; works in many devices that support SD cards and is less expensive; types include MMC, RS-MMC (reduced size MMC), MMCmicro, DV-MMC (dual voltage), MMCplus (faster), MMCmoblile, and MiCard (has two detachable parts—one side for USB and the other side for use with a card reader)

Table 8.11 Digital camera file formats

File type	Description
RAW	Outputs raw, unprocessed data; does something with the photos after being removed from the camera
JPEG	Most common type; saves more photos due to compression
TIFF	Larger file size (fewer photos) due to retaining image quality
WAV	Used for voice memos
MOV	Used for movie files

A memory card reader or multi-card reader is a popular device that many people attach externally or have integrated into a computer or mobile device. A reader has multiple slots that allow different memory media to be read. This device is called many names, and common ones include 15-in-1 reader, 8-in-1 reader, or 5-in-1 reader (depending on how many different slots or types of memory modules it accepts). The reader instantly recognizes inserted memory cards, which can be copied into the computer and manipulated. The media card slots are assigned drive letters that are accessible through Windows Explorer. Figure 8.24 shows one of these readers.

Tech Tip

No drive letter

If the media does not appear in Windows Explorer, the reader may have been temporarily uninstalled. Use the Safely Remove Hardware tool in the systray, unplug the cable from the port, and reinsert the cable to ensure the operating system recognizes the reader. If the card reader or ports are still not available or if they are integrated into the computer, restart the computer.

Figure 8.24 Memory card reader

Figure 8.25 Web cam

Another popular type of digital camera is a **web cam**, which is short for web camera—a digital camera that attaches to a PC for use in transmitting live video or recording video. Web cameras can also be found that attach to VoIP phones and activate when a phone session occurs for instant web conferencing. Some web cams have a small visor that can be flipped over the lens to prevent video when desired. Figure 8.25 illustrates a web cam. Web cams can also connect wirelessly to a PC or a laptop or can be integrated into the display or mobile device.

To access an integrated camera in a flat panel display, you normally use a control panel or software the comes with the camera, such as the Dell Webcam Control, shown in Figure 8.26, used with a camera integrated into a display. If you ever get a "Bandwidth exceeded" message when you have a camera being used, try lowering the camera resolution in whatever software is being used.

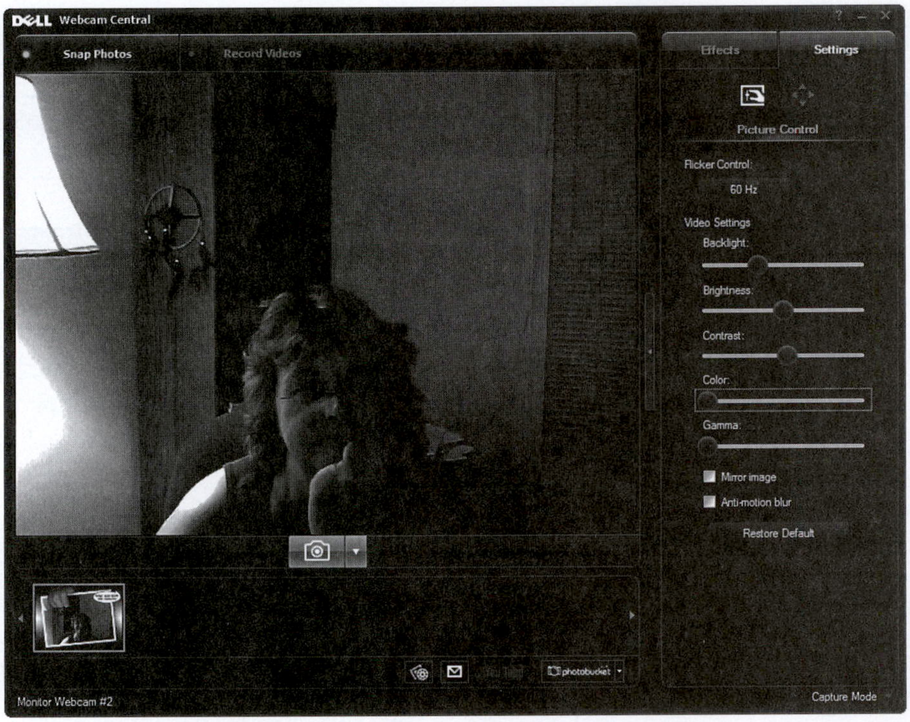

Figure 8.26 Dell Webcam Control software

To operate an integrated camera on an Apple iOS or Android device, use the *Camera* option from the home page. Use the *Photos* application (iOS) or *Gallery* application (Android) to see the saved images.

Regardless of what multimedia device is integrated or connects to a computer, all devices attach and install similarly. When installing a new device for a customer, don't forget to allow the customer to test the device while you are still there. Also, remember to leave all documentation related to the installation with the customer. They paid for the device and are entitled to the documentation.

Soft Skills—Attitude

A technician's attitude is one of his or her greatest assets. Some consider having a good attitude as simply being positive at work, but this is not the entire picture. A technician with a good attitude has the following traits:

- **Is proactive, not reactive.** A good technician actively looks for a solution rather than waiting for someone to instruct him or her.
- **Seeks solutions instead of providing excuses.** A positive person does not continually apologize or talk in a subservient tone. For example, a positive technician explains issues such as late deliveries in a professional, positive manner.
- **Accepts responsibility for actions taken.** If you forget something or take a misstep, then you should apologize and explain to the customer what happened. Truth goes a long way with customers. A positive technician does not constantly shift blame to other departments or technicians. Even if the other department or technician is responsible, the person with a positive attitude handles the customer and then talks to the other department or technician about the problem.
- **Deals with priority changes professionally.** In the IT field, computer and network problems arise that cause us to reprioritize tasks weekly, daily, and even hourly. These are normal occurrences and a person with a positive attitude understands this.

- **Cooperates and enjoys working with others.** A positive attitude is contagious, and others like being around it.
- **Maintains professionalism even when working with a coworker who is unethical, unprofessional, or uncooperative.** A technician with a good attitude does not let someone else's poor attitude be a negative influence.
- **Embraces problems as challenges to learn and develop skills.** Sometimes, after joining the IT field, a technician becomes complacent and does not seek new skills. The IT field requires that you constantly improve and refine your skills. See a tough problem as a challenge, not a burden. With such an attitude, problems will not frustrate you, but will serve as a catalyst for an advancement or makes you a better technician.

You should exhibit all these traits consistently to establish a positive mental attitude and make it part of your daily habits.

Chapter Summary

- Install ODDs using the same rules of configuration as for SATA and PATA hard drives.
- Use the appropriate media for the type of drive installed.
- Don't multitask when writing data to an optical disc.
- Optical drives and discs have region codes that must match.
- When purchasing an optical drive, features to look for include ample buffer memory and reduced random access times, MTBFs, and MCBFs.
- For stuck optical discs, use the *Eject* option from Windows Explorer or the emergency eject hole.
- Keep the laser lens clean.
- Wipe dirty discs in an inward-to-outward (not circular) motion.
- It's important to ensure that device and video drivers are up to date.
- DirectX (`dxdiag`) is used to troubleshoot multimedia issues.
- A decoder must be installed for video to play from a disc correctly.
- A motherboard normally has a small speaker used for POST codes when sound does not work properly.
- If a sound card is installed, disabled the motherboard sound ports.
- The higher the sampling rate, the better the audio quality.
- For sound issues, check muting, volume controls, cables, and device conflicts.
- Laptop speakers are commonly mounted on the side or back of the laptop case. The keyboard may have to be removed to replace the speakers.
- Microphones are used for VoIP and are tested/managed through the *Recording* tab of the Sound window.
- Scan documents at a resolution suited for the final output (print, web, display).
- Do not spray cleaner directly on the scanner glass, but do keep the glass clean.
- Digital cameras commonly have storage media that can be removed and attached directly to a PC using a memory card reader.
- Web cams can be integrated into a display or mobile device or an external unit that is used for conference calls or recording video.
- A technician should have a positive attitude, be proactive, and maintain professionalism when working with others.

Key Terms

Review Questions

Consider the following optical drive specifications as you answer Questions 1–7:

- SATA interface half-height internal BD-ROM
- Max. 4X BD-ROM/BD-RE SL and 4X BD-ROM/BD-R/BD-RE DL CAV reading
- Max. 8X DVD-ROM/+R/+RW/+RDL/-R/-RW/-RW DL CAV reading
- Max. 32X CD-ROM/R/RW CAV reading
- Random access times: BD—250ms; DVD—160ms; CD—150ms
- Buffer size 2MB
- System requirements for HD Blu-ray playback: Intel Pentium D 3.0+, 1GB+ of RAM, Windows XP SP2/Vista/7, HDCP capable display or TV for digital output.

1. Which SATA version is being used?
   [1 | 2 | 3 | Cannot be determined from the information given]
2. Can Blu-ray discs be created on this unit? How can you tell?
3. What is the maximum number of devices in addition to this drive on the same cable that connects to the motherboard?
   [none | 1 | 2 | cannot be determined from the information given]
4. What does the term *random access time* mean?
5. What is the purpose of buffer memory?
6. Can a DVD±RW disc be read in this drive? How can you tell?
7. What does BD-RE DL mean?
8. A technician has been troubleshooting a laptop power issue and now the speakers don't work. What should the technician do first?
   a. Replace the speakers.
   b. Re-install the original power supply.
   c. Check the speaker cabling.
   d. Replace the power supply with another one.
9. Select the non-sound port.
   [RJ-45 | S/PDIF | TOSLINK | RCA | 1/8-inch TRS]
10. Which optical media has the highest capacity? [DVD | CD | BD]
11. Which drive would have two lasers?
    a. a drive the could handle a 8.5GB single-sided dual-layer disc
    b. a drive the could handle a double-sided single-layer disc
    c. a drive that could handle a 25GB dual-layer disc
    d. a drive that could handle a DVD or a Blu-ray disc

12. A PCIe sound card is being installed. Which two steps are most likely going to be done by the technician? (Select two.)
    a. Upgrade the power supply.
    b. Install a driver.
    c. Flash the BIOS.
    d. Disable the integrated ports in BIOS.
    e. Configure jumpers on the adapter.
    f. Delete the integrated port drivers.
13. Which utility is best used to troubleshoot sound issues?
    [Disk Management | DirectX | BIOS diagnostics | Device Manager]
14. Which icon would be used on a laptop to turn down the volume?
    a. 
    b. 
    c. 
    d. 
15. A user has attempted a scanner installation to the computer's front USB ports because all the back ports were taken. However, the scanner will not function. What should the technician try next?
    a. Replace the scanner.
    b. Replace the USB port.
    c. Re-attach the USB cable that leads from the front panel to the motherboard.
    d. Add a version 2.0 or higher USB hub to the back USB port.
16. [T | F] Paper towels are okay to use to clean a scanner.
17. [T | F] Part of the installation process for a digital camera built into a tablet is to calibrate the camera.
18. Which multimedia device requires calibration as part of the installation process?
    [camera | sound card | scanner | optical disc drive]
19. Which item would more likely be used with a digital camera than with a scanner?
    [flash media | 1.8-inch hard drive | laser lens | optical cleaning cloth]
20. Which scenario is one that shows a positive attitude?
    a. A technician returns a borrowed disc to a team member after having the disc more than six months.
    b. A technician leaves documentation for a newly installed optical drive with the customer even though the customer treated the technician poorly during the installation.
    c. A technician eagerly helps reorganize a wiring closet for the company.
    d. A technician smiles when an angry customer is taking out her computer problems on the technician.

Exercises

Lab 8.1 Sound and Optical Drives in Windows XP

Objective: To be able to use the tools provided with Windows XP to manage sound devices and optical media drives

Parts: A computer with Windows XP loaded

Procedure: Complete the following procedure and answer the accompanying questions.

Note: Parts of this lab may be different due to the hardware installed and the version of XP installed.

1. Power on the computer and log on using the user ID and password provided by the instructor or lab assistant.
2. Click the *Start* button and click *Control Panel*. If in Category view, click *Sounds, Speech, and Audio Devices*. Open the *Sounds and Audio Devices* Control Panel.

   What are the five tabs shown in the *Properties* window?

   Is the *Place volume icon in the taskbar* checkbox enabled or disabled?
3. The *Volume* tab is used to control the default sound device. In the Device volume section, a slider bar controls sound volume. The *Mute* checkbox turns off sound completely. If the *Place volume icon in the taskbar* checkbox is unchecked, click in the checkbox and click the *Apply* button. A volume control icon appears in the task-bar. Click the *OK* button.
4. Double-click the volume control icon in the taskbar. The *Playback Control* window opens. This window is where sound might be muted if sound is not emitting from speakers. Close this window.
5. Right-click the volume control icon in the taskbar and select *Adjust Audio Properties*. The *Sound and Audio Devices Properties* window opens.
6. Return the *Place volume icon in the taskbar* checkbox to its original setting. Refer to Question 2. Click the *Apply* button.
7. Click the *Advanced* button in the Device volume section. The *Playback Control* window opens. This window is used to adjust sound volume for individual sound devices. Close the *Playback Control* window.
8. Click the *Speaker Volume* button. A checkbox at the bottom allows you to keep the left and right speaker controls the same as they are changed. Click the *Cancel* button.
9. Click the Speaker settings section's *Advanced* button. The *Advanced Audio Properties* window appears. This screen allows you to select the speaker type or to disable external speakers.
10. Click the *Performance* tab. Click the *Help* button (the question mark button) and point to the *Hardware acceleration* slider bar.

    Based on the information in the Help screen, what is the purpose of the Hardware acceleration slider bar?
11. The four settings for hardware acceleration are listed in Table 8.12.

Table 8.12 Hardware acceleration settings

Performance setting	Purpose
None	No acceleration; the computer operates in emulation mode
Basic	Only the required acceleration features are enabled
Standard	DirectSound is enabled
Full	DirectMusic and DirectShow are enabled

12. Click somewhere in the *Advanced Audio Properties* window to remove the *Help* window. Use *Help* to determine the purpose of the *Sample rate conversion quality* slider bar.

    Based on the information found in the *Help* screen, what is the purpose of the *Sample rate conversion quality* slider bar?

13. Close the *Help* screen, click the *Cancel* button, and click the *Sounds* tab.

    What is the current setting, if any, for the *Sound scheme*?

14. Click the *Sound scheme* down arrow and select *Windows Default*. In the Program events section, click the *Asterisk* option. Click the *Play* button (the right-arrow button located beside the *Browse* button).
15. Set the *Sound scheme* back to the original setting and click the *Apply* button. Refer to Step 13 if necessary.
16. Click the *Audio* tab, which allows you to specify audio devices such as the default playback device, recording device, and MIDI playback device used for different tasks.
17. Click the *Voice* tab, which has a similar purpose except it is for voice playback and recording devices.
18. Click the *Hardware* tab. This is an important tab for technicians. Devices are listed in the window. Select a CD or DVD drive and click the *Properties* button. Ensure the *Properties* window contains a *Driver* tab.

    What device was selected?

19. Click the *Driver* tab. The *Driver* tab can be used to upgrade a driver, list the current driver version, roll back to an older driver version, and uninstall the driver.

    What driver version is currently installed?

20. Click the *Cancel* button and click the *Troubleshoot* button. The *Help and Support Center* window appears.

    List one problem shown in the *Help and Support Center* window.

Instructor initials: ______________

21. Close the *Help and Support Center* window. Click the *Cancel* button. Double-click the *My Computer* desktop icon.

    What device letters are listed in the *Devices with Removable Storage* section?

22. Right-click the CD or DVD drive icon.
23. Click *Properties* and select the *AutoPlay* tab. Press ▼.

    List two devices shown in the drop-down menu.

24. Click the *Help* button and click somewhere in the *AutoPlay* window.

    Based on the information found in the Help window, what is the purpose of the *AutoPlay* tab?

    What actions can be performed on a music CD?

25. Click the *Sharing* tab, which allows others access to the CD over a network. Click the *Share this folder* radio button.
26. Click the *Permissions* button, which assigns specific network users and specific permission to the drive. This is particularly important for CD-RW drives. Click the *Cancel* button.

27. Click the *Caching* button.

    What are the three caching settings?

Instructor initials: ______________

28. Click the *Cancel* button. In the *Properties* window, click the *Cancel* button.

Lab 8.2 Sound and Optical Drives in Windows 7

Objective: To be able to use the tools provided with Windows 7 to manage sound devices and optical media drives

Parts: A computer with Windows 7 loaded and that has Internet access

Procedure: Complete the following procedure and answer the accompanying questions.

Note: Parts of this lab may be different due to the hardware installed and the version of Windows 7 installed.

1. Power on the computer and log into Windows 7.
2. Click the *Start* button and access the *Sound* Control Panel.

   What tabs are shown in the window?

   Answers will vary based on the sound card installed or integrated into the system, but a sample answer follows: playback, recording, sounds, and communications.

   What is the default playback device?

3. With the default playback device selected, click the *Configure* button.

   What audio channels are available?

4. Select the *Test* button. As directed, click the speaker.

   What was the result?

5. Click the *Cancel* button and ensure the *Playback* tab is selected. Click *Properties*. The Speakers Properties window opens.

   What jack information displays?

6. Click *Properties*.

   What is the device status?

7. Select the *Driver* tab.

   What is the driver version?

   What is the purpose of the *Roll Back Driver* button?

   Can the audio be disabled from this window?

8. Click the *Cancel* button. Select the *Levels* tab.

   What audio options are available?

9. Click the *Advanced* tab.

   How many bits are used for sampling?

   What is the frequency response?

10. Click *Cancel*. Select the *Recording* tab.

    Are any devices attached to the Line-In port?

11. Select the *Sounds* tab. In the Program window, select any task that has a speaker icon to the left of it. Click *Test*.

    Did sound emit? [Yes | No]

12. Select the *Sound Scheme* drop-down menu.

    What options are available?

    For what is the checkbox in this section used?

13. Click *Cancel*. Close the control panel window.
14. Open *Windows Explorer* and select *Computer* from the left panel. In the right-panel, right-click the optical drive. Notice the Eject option, which can be used to eject a stuck disc.
15. Point to the *Share with* option and select *Advanced Sharing*. The Sharing tab opens. This option allows you to share a disc with others.
16. If you closed the last window go back into the optical drive properties and select the *Hardware* tab. In the All disk drives: window, select the optical drive.

    What is the device status?

17. Select the *Properties* button. Select the *DVD region* tab if a DVD drive is installed.

    What is the DVD region code? Write *Not applicable* as your answer if a CD drive is installed.

18. Select the *Driver* tab.

    What version of the driver is installed?

    What is the date of the driver?

19. Use the Internet to determine whether a newer device driver is available. Show this driver to the instructor or lab assistant.

Instructor initials: ______________

20. In the device's properties window, click *Cancel*.
21. In the original optical drive properties window, select the *Customize* tab.

    What type of things can be customized from this tab?

22. Click the *Cancel* button. Close the Windows Explorer window.
23. Click the *Start* button and open *Help and Support*.

    Using Help and Support, determine the two formats used to burn a disc.

    According to the Help and Support, which disc burning format stores the files on the hard drive until it is time to burn the disc?

According to the Help and Support, how much hard disk space is needed to burn a CD when the type of format used stores the data on the drive until such a time it is going to be burned to disc?

24. Close the *Help and Support* window.

Lab 8.3 Optical Drive Installation Lab

Objective: To install, configure, and test an optical drive

Parts: A computer with Windows XP loaded.

An optical drive with accompanying cable and mounting equipment if necessary

Procedure: Complete the following procedure and answer the accompanying questions.

1. Obtain an optical drive designated by the instructor or student assistant.

   What type of drive is this?

   [CD-ROM | CD-R | CD-RW | DVD-R | DVD+R | DVD+RW | DVD-RW | DVD6RW | DVD-R DL | DVD+R DL | BD-R | BD-RE]

   List the drive manufacturer and model number.

   If possible, determine if a driver is available for Windows XP and list the website on which you located this information.

   What is the latest driver revision number or date of the latest revision?

   What type of interface does the optical drive use? [PATA IDE | SATA | SCSI | Parallel | USB | FireWire]

2. Power off the computer, remove the power cord, open the computer, if necessary, and determine whether a cable and interface are available to install the drive. If not, obtain them.
3. Configure the drive as necessary for the type of interface being used.

   What drive settings did you select?

4. If appropriate, install the drive into the computer and attach power.
5. If an external device is being installed, a device driver may need to be installed at this point. Always refer to the device installation instructions. Whether the drive is internal or external, attach the correct interface cable to the drive.
6. Power on the computer, load a device driver, if necessary, and ensure that the operating system recognizes the drive. Troubleshoot as necessary until the drive works.

   What tests did you perform to ensure the drive works?

7. Tell the instructor when the drive is successfully installed.

Instructor initials: ____________

8. Remove the drive and re-install the computer cover. Power on the computer and ensure no BIOS errors appear.

Instructor initials: ____________

Lab 8.4 DirectX Diagnostics in Windows XP

Objective: To be able to use the DirectX tool provided with Windows XP

Parts: A computer with Windows XP loaded and administrator rights

Procedure: Complete the following procedure and answer the accompanying questions.

1. Power on the computer and log on using the user ID and password provided by the instructor or lab assistant.

2. Click *Start*, *Run*, type **dxdiag**, and press Enter. The DirectX tool may ask you to agree to allow an Internet connection for an update.

   Once the tool is shown and the System tab is displayed, what DirectX version is running?

3. Click the *Next Page* button. The DirectX Files tab information displays.

   What notes, if any, display?

4. Click the *Display* tab.

   How much RAM is on the video adapter?

   Are any DirectX features enabled? If so, which ones?

5. If available, test DirectDraw by clicking the *Test DirectDraw* button. Click *Yes, OK,* and answer the questions that follow.
6. If available, test Direct3D by clicking the *Test Direct3D* button. Click *Yes, OK,* and answer the questions that follow.
7. Click the *Next Page* button.

   What acceleration setting, if any, is set?

8. If the *Test DirectSound* button is available, click it after attaching speakers and turning the volume up slightly.

   Could you tell the difference between the sounds?

9. Click the *Music* tab.

   What ports are available on this page?

10. Click the *Next Page* button.

    What input-related devices are there?

11. Click the *Network* tab. Select the *DirectPlay Voice Options* button. Click the *Run wizard* button. Follow the directions on the screen. When finished, click *Exit*.

Lab 8.5 DirectX Diagnostics in Windows 7

Objective: To be able to use the DirectX tool provided with Windows 7

Parts: A computer with Windows 7 loaded and with administrator rights and Internet access

Procedure: Complete the following procedure and answer the accompanying questions.

Note: This lab may vary due to the equipment installed and the Windows 7 version and service pack.

1. Power on the computer and log into Windows 7.
2. Click the *Start* button, in the *Search programs and files* textbox, type **dxdiag** and press Enter or select the `dxdiag` link. The DirectX tool may ask you to allow an Internet connection for an update.

   Once the tool is shown and the System tab is displayed, what DirectX version is running?

   How much RAM is installed in the computer?

   What is the size of the page file?

   How much of the page file is currently used?

3. Click the *Next Page* button. The next tab displays.
   What notes, if any, appear on the tab?

4. Ensure you are on the *Display* tab.
   How much RAM is on the video adapter?
   Are any DirectX features enabled? If so, which ones?
   Research the words RAM, video adapter, and DirectX on the Internet to help with this answer and give a brief description of the features.

5. Ensure a *Sound* tab is being used.
   What is the device type being used?
   What is WDM? If you do not know, research it on the Internet.

   What driver file is being used?
   What does WHQL logo mean? If you do not know, research this term on the Internet.

6. Click the *Input* tab.
   List any direct input devices displayed.

7. Expand any USB devices in the Input Related Devices section.
   List any USB devices that are considered to be input devices.

8. Expand any PS/2 devices in the Input Related Devices section.
   List any PS/2 devices that are considered to be input devices.

9. Close the DirectX Diagnostics window.

Lab 8.6 Installing a Sound Card and Speakers in Windows XP

Objective: To install and configure a sound card

Parts: A computer with Windows XP loaded and an available expansion slot
Sound card
Speakers
Optional audio disc

Procedure: Complete the following procedure and answer the accompanying questions.

Note: The available expansion slot and sound card should be the same type.

1. Power on the computer and log on using the user ID and password provided by the instructor or lab assistant.
2. Examine the sound port(s) available on the computer.

   How many ports that could be found on a sound card are integrated into the motherboard?

   For what is each port used?

3. Connect power to the speakers if necessary and attach speakers to the computer.
4. Access the *Sounds and Audio Devices* Control Panel. On the *Volume* tab, notice that there is a *Mute* checkbox. This checkbox being selected is a common reason for sound not coming out of speakers. Also notice that there is a *Place volume icon in the taskbar* checkbox. Enable this checkbox and click the *Apply* button. The sound icon appears in the systray (far right) portion of the taskbar.
5. Select the *Speaker volume* button.

   Can you adjust the left and right volume separately from this window?
6. Click the *Advanced* button located in the Speaker Settings section.

   What does the *Speakers* tab allow you to configure?

   On the *Performance* tab, what is the default setting for Hardware acceleration?

   On the *Performance* tab, what is the default setting for the Sample rate conversion quality?
7. Click the *Cancel* button. Select the *Sounds* tab. Locate and click the *Exit Windows sound* in the *Program events* window. Any sound that has the sound icon to the left of it can be played as a test of the speakers. Click the *Play* button, ▶, which is located beside the *Browse* button.

   Can you hear the sound? If not, troubleshoot as necessary. Do not proceed until you hear sound.
8. Click the *Audio* tab.

   What is the default sound playback device?
9. Click the *Hardware* tab. Locate and select the *Intel 82802BA/BAM AC'97 Audio Controller* or whatever audio controller is installed. Click the *Troubleshoot* button. The sound troubleshooter opens.

   What is the first statement listed in the possible problems?

10. Close the *Sound Troubleshooter* window. Click the *Cancel* button in the *Sounds and Audio Devices Properties* window.
11. Access *Device Manager*. Expand the *Sound, video and game controllers* section. Right-click the integrated audio controller. Select *Properties* and click the *Resources* tab.

    What I/O address ranges are used by the integrated sound card?

    What interrupt is used?
12. Click the *Cancel* button to leave this window.
13. Reboot the computer and access the BIOS Setup program. Locate and disable the integrated sound ports. Save the settings.

    What key did you press to enter the Setup program?
14. Power off the computer and remove the power cord.

15. Access the computer expansion slots and remove any slot covers or retention bars if necessary.
16. Install the sound adapter and ensure it fits snugly into the expansion slot. Re-install any retention bar as necessary.
17. Re-install the power cord to the computer and power on the computer. The *Found New Hardware* balloon should appear. You may be prompted for a device driver and to restart the computer in order to use the new PCI/PCIe adapter.
18. Attach the speakers to the newly installed sound card.
19. Using the process previously described, play a Windows sound or an audio CD using the newly installed adapter.
20. Access *Device Manager*. Expand the *Sound, video and game controllers* section. Right-click the newly installed sound card option and select *Properties*. Click the *Resources* tab.

    What I/O address does the adapter use?

    What interrupt does the sound card use?
21. Click the *General* tab.

    What location is the card located in according to the information displayed?

    What is the device status according to the information displayed?
22. Power down the computer and remove the power cord.

Instructor initials: ______________

23. Unplug the speakers from the sound card. Remove the sound adapter and re-attach any slot covers.
24. Re-install any covers necessary to access the expansion slots and the power cord. Power on the computer and enter the Setup program.
25. Through BIOS Setup, re-enable the integrated sound ports. Save the settings.
26. Re-attach the speakers to the integrated sound and test them. Troubleshoot as necessary.

Lab 8.7 Installing a Sound Card and Speakers in Windows 7

Objective: To install and configure a sound card

Parts: A computer with Windows 7 loaded and an available expansion slot

Sound card with drivers or Internet access

Optional audio disc

1. Before powering on the computer, determine the current audio capabilities.

   How many sound ports are integrated into the motherboard?

   Draw each port and list the purpose of the port. If you do not know, use the Internet to research the computer model.
2. Connect power to the speakers and attach to the computer if necessary.
3. Power on the computer and log in to Windows 7.

   Access the *Hardware and Sound* Control Panel. Select the *Sound* link.

   On the Playback tab, how many playback devices are listed?
4. Right-click the Speakers that are enabled and select *Properties*.

   What name is currently assigned the output device?

5. Click in the General tab textbox and change the name to something more meaningful.

   List the name assigned.

   What output jacks are available for this output device?

   What controller is controlling the speakers?

6. Click the speaker controller *Properties* button.

   What driver version is installed?

7. Close the Properties window. Back in the Speakers Properties window, select the *Levels* tab.

   What settings can you control on this tab?

   The tabs that are available vary depending on what speakers are installed. What other tabs are available for the speakers on your computer?

8. Select the *Advanced* tab. Test the quality of the sound output using the *Test* button. Troubleshoot the system if necessary if sound does not emit.

   How many bits are used in converting analog sounds into digital audio?

9. Select the *Default Format* drop down menu. Notice how this is the window where you allow applications to control or change the speaker settings.

   List two other available formats if possible.

10. Click *Cancel* twice to close the Speaker Properties windows.
11. Power on the computer and enter the BIOS Setup program.

    What key did you use to enter Setup?

12. Locate and disable the integrated sound ports. Save the settings and exit BIOS Setup.
13. Log in to Windows 7.

    What main category did you use to access the sound port configuration?

14. Using whatever method you would like ensure that sound does not emit from the speakers any more.

    What method did you use?

15. Shut down the computer and remove the power cord.
16. Access the computer expansion slots and remove any slot covers or retention bars if necessary.
17. Install the sound adapter into an empty expansion slot and ensure it fits snugly into the slot. Re-install any retention bar as necessary.
18. Re-attach the power cord and power on the computer. The computer should detect that a new device has been installed. You may be prompted for a device driver and to restart the computer in order to use the new adapter. If you don't have a device driver, go to a computer that has Internet access and download the appropriate driver for the sound card you installed. Note that you may have to power down the computer and look at the sound card (and possibly remove it) in order to get the appropriate model required to download the correct driver.
19. Attach the speakers to the appropriate ports on the newly installed sound card.
20. Using any method you desire including previously demonstrated methods or by playing an audio disc, test the new sound cad.

21. Access *Device Manager* and expand the *Sound, video and game controllers* section.
22. Right-click the newly installed sound card and select *Properties*.

    What I/O address does the adapter use?

    What is the device status?

Instructor initials: ______________

23. Power down the computer and remove the power cord.
24. Unplug the speakers from the sound card. Remove the sound card and re-attach any slot covers.
25. Power on the computer and re-access BIOS Setup.
26. Re-enable the integrated sound ports and save the settings.
27. Re-attach the speakers.
28. Re-attach the power cord. Boot the computer and log in to Windows again. Test the speakers.
29. Return all parts to the proper location.

Lab 8.8 Installing a USB Scanner

Objective: To be able to install a USB scanner and driver on a Windows-based computer

Parts: USB scanner, USB cable, scanner driver, scanner software/utilities, computer with Windows loaded

Procedure: The procedures outlined below are guidelines. Refer to the scanner's installation instructions for exact procedures.

Installing the Scanner Driver

1. Insert the scanner driver media into the drive. Sometimes you must also select what type of interface connection is going to be used. If this is the case, select *USB*. The software installer sometimes includes additional software programs that can be used to control the scanner and to manipulate scanned images. Many drivers require the computer to be restarted once the installation process is complete.

Connecting the Scanner

2. Some scanners ship with a carriage safety lock. If this is the case, remove the safety lock.
3. With the computer powered on, connect one end of the USB cable to the scanner's USB port and attach the other end to a USB computer port or a USB hub port.
4. If necessary, attach the power cable to the scanner. Attach the other power cable end to an electrical outlet.
5. Power on the scanner.
6. Optionally, if the scanner has a calibrate routine, execute the calibration.

Using the Scanner

7. If the scanner software program(s) did not install during driver installation, install the scanner software programs now.
8. Insert a document to be scanned.
9. Access the scanner software program through the *Start* button and scan the document.

Instructor initials: ______________

Lab 8.9 Changing the Drive Letter of an Optical Drive Using the Disk Management and `diskpart` Utility

Objective: To reassign the optical drive letter

Parts: Windows computer with administrator rights

Procedure: Complete the following procedure and answer the accompanying questions.

1. Using Windows Explorer, determine the current optical drive letter.

   What drive letter is being used by the ODD drive?

2. From the Start button menu in the Search program and files textbox, type **`Disk Management`** and press Enter.
3. Locate the optical drive in the bottom half of the Disk Management window.
4. Right-click the drive in the left side of the panel where the drive letter is located and select *Change Drive Letter and Paths*.
5. Select *Change* and use the *Assign the following drive letter:* drop down menu to select a different drive letter.

   What drive letter did you choose?

6. Click *OK* and *Yes* to the notification that some programs might not work properly.
7. At a command prompt, type **`diskpart`** and press Enter. Type **`list volume`** and press Enter. Look down the Type column for an optical drive. and locate the drive to be changed. Ensure that the drive letter in the Ltr column is the same drive letter written down in Step 5.

   Write the volume number that is listed in the same row as the optical drive.

8. At a command prompt, type **`select volume x`** (where ***x*** is the number you wrote in Step 7). A message appears, stating that the volume is selected. If the message does not appear, recheck your steps, starting from the beginning of the lab.
9. Type **`assign letter=x`** (where ***x*** is the newly assigned drive letter). A message appears, stating that the drive letter assignment was successful. If this message does not appear, redo the exercise.
10. Use Explorer to verify the reassignment, refreshing the screen if necessary,. Show the instructor or lab assistant your reassigned drive letter.

Instructor initials: ____________

11. In the `diskpart` utility or the Disk Management window, return the drive to the original drive letter. Refer to the answer to the question in Step 1 if you do not remember the original drive letter. Use Windows Explorer to show the instructor or lab assistant that the drive letter has been reassigned.

Instructor initials: ____________

Activities

Internet Discovery

Objective: To obtain specific information on the Internet regarding a computer or its associated parts

Parts: Computer with access to the Internet

Questions: Use the Internet to answer the following questions.

1. Find a website that sells internal optical drives.

   List the cost of one drive and the website URL.

2. What is the cost of a disc that works in a DVD+/-RW drive?

   List the cost and website URL.

3. Find the driver version for a Sound Blaster Recond3D PCIe adapter that is going in a 64-bit Windows 7 computer.

   Document the driver version and URL where you found this information.

4. An HP G4050 Scanjet scanner attaches to a Windows Vista computer. When the scanning software is accessed, the error "The computer cannot communicate with the scanning device" appears.

   List the six recommended steps.

5. The president of a company has just bought a Canon EOS Rebel T4i digital camera.

   What type of memory media does this camera accept? Write the answer and URL where you found the answer.

6. A customer has a Plextor PX880SA DVD+/RW drive.

   How much buffer memory does the drive contain and what interface(s) does it support? Write the answers and URL.

Soft Skills

Objective: To enhance and fine-tune a technician's ability to listen, communicate in both written and oral form, and support people who use computers in a professional manner

Activities:

1. List some tips on how to determine whether a computer has an optical drive installed, as if you were stepping through it over the phone with a customer who is not a technician. Practice with a classmate, using your instructions.

2. The class is divided into groups of five. Each group makes a list of three categories that relate to multimedia devices. The five groups share their lists and determine which group works on which category. In 30 minutes, each team comes up with five answers with the corresponding questions for their category. The answers are rated from 100 to 500 with 100 being the easiest question. The teams play *Jeopardy!*, with the rule that no team may choose its own category.

Critical Thinking Skills

Objective: To analyze and evaluate information, and apply information to new or different situations

Activities:

1. For this activity, you need an advertisement of an optical drive, including the technical specifications. Make a list of all terms related to the drive that you do not know. Using books, the Internet, or other resources, research these terms and define them.
2. Form teams of two. Several multimedia devices are needed. The devices are numbered. Each team selects a number and installs, configures, and tests the associated device. Each team documents its installation and shares its experience (including lessons learned) with the rest of the class.

A+ Certification Exam Tips

- ✓ Review the disc media types and capacities before the exam.
- ✓ Ensure that you know how to install and configure an optical drive, a sound card, and a scanner.
- ✓ Know common sound issues and the easy fixes for them.
- ✓ Maintaining a positive attitude is the professionalism and communication skill that is part of the 220-801 exam.
- ✓ Review the troubleshooting tips in each of the multimedia sections for help on the 220-802 exam.

chapter 9

Other Peripherals

Chapter Objectives:

In this chapter you will learn:

- To identify the components of the video subsystem
- The various display types including laptop displays
- Basic display terminology
- To install a video card
- Basic video troubleshooting techniques
- How each type of printer operates
- The steps required to install a printer
- Preventive printer maintenance
- How to control printers from Windows and make printer adjustments
- To solve common printer problems
- Techniques for ethical and professional behavior

CompTIA Exam Objectives:

What CompTIA A+ exam objectives are covered in this chapter?

- ✓ 801-1.4 Install and configure expansion cards.
- ✓ 801-1.10 Given a scenario, evaluate types and features of display devices.
- ✓ 801-1.11 Identify connector types and associated cables.
- ✓ 801-1.12 Install and configure various peripheral devices.
- ✓ 801-3.1 Install and configure laptop hardware and components.
- ✓ 801-3.2 Compare and contrast the components within the display of a laptop.
- ✓ 801-4.1 Explain the differences between the various printer types and summarize the associated imaging process.
- ✓ 801-4.2 Given a scenario, install and configure printers.
- ✓ 801-4.3 Given a scenario, perform printer maintenance.
- ✓ 802-4.4 Given a scenario, troubleshoot common video and display issues.
- ✓ 802-4.8 Given a scenario, troubleshoot and repair common laptop issues while adhering to the appropriate procedures.
- ✓ 802-4.9 Given a scenario, troubleshoot printers with appropriate tools.

Chapter Overview

Even though the book has covered many peripherals so far, such as hard drives, optical drives, mice, keyboards, and other USB/IEEE 1394 devices, other peripherals that have unique characteristics and technologies are still to be explored. Two of these technologies are video and printing. Each has associated terminology, concepts, and installation/troubleshooting tips. Let's explore video first.

Video Overview

Video quality is very important to computer users. A display is one of the most expensive computer components. Users usually derive the most gratification from their display, although sound quality is now becoming as important. Technicians must look at video as a subsystem that consists of the display, the electronic circuits that send the display instructions, and the cable that connects them. The electronic video circuits can be on a separate video adapter or built into the motherboard. Figure 9.1 illustrates a computer video subsystem.

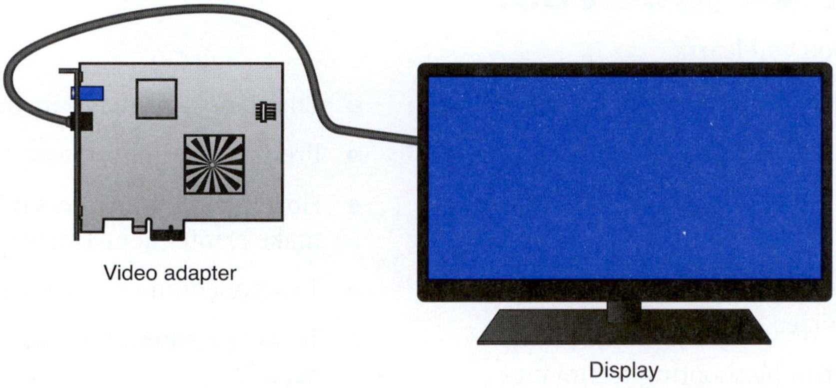

Figure 9.1 Video subsytem

Types of Video Output Devices

Video output devices such as monitors, projectors, and even TVs are commonly used with desktop and laptop computers. Monitors can be classified several ways—color or non-color, analog or digital signals used to produce colors, and the type of video adapter used. The easiest way to classify video output is by the way in which the output is created—the technology. Table 9.1 lists some of the most popular display output technologies.

Other technologies used in video output include LCoS, SED, and FED. LCoS (liquid crystal on silicon) is similar to DLP (Digital Light Processing) except that it uses liquid crystals instead of mirrors for higher resolutions. SED (surface-conduction electron-emitter display) and FED (field-emission display) technologies are similar: both use electron emitters to energize color phosphor dots to produce an image. The electron emitter used is what makes them different.

Table 9.1 Video output technology

Technology	Description
CRT (cathode ray tube)	Older bulky monitors. A CRT monitor has three color beams (red, green, and blue) directed at a phosphorous dot on the back of the monitor tube. The result is a single image on the screen called a **pixel**, or picture element. Figure 9.2 shows how a dot triad makes a pixel. Dot pitch is the distance between like-colored phosphorous dots on adjacent dot triads. The lower the dot pitch, the sharper the image.
LCD (liquid crystal display)	Technology is used in laptops, flat panel monitors, TVs, tablets, smartphones, and projectors. Two glass substrates have a thin layer of liquid crystal between them. One glass substrate is the color filter, with three main colors—red, green, and blue—that allow millions of colors to be displayed. The other glass substrate is the TFT (thin film transistor) array, which has the technology to direct the liquid crystal to block the light. A **backlight** (that can be a fluorescent lamp or LED technology) extends behind the combined glass assembly, and the light is always on. This is why an LCD monitor appears to sometimes glow even when it's off and why crystals are needed to block some of the light to create the intensities of light. Liquid crystals are sensitive to temperature changes. Laptop displays may appear distorted in cold or hot temperatures due to the liquid crystals. Figure 9.3 shows the inside parts of an LCD monitor.
LED (light-emitting diode)	A low-power, low-heat, long lasting electronic device used in many technologies—calculators, home, business, and auto lighting, fiber optics, and displays. LED displays still use liquid crystals; the displays just use an LED backlight instead of **CCFL** (cold cathode fluorescent lamp). LED displays have better color accuracy and are thinner than the LCDs that use CCFLs.
OLED (organic LED)	Does not require a backlight like LCDs but has a film of organic compounds placed in rows and columns that can emit light. Is light weight and has a fast response time, low power usage, and a wide viewing angle.
DLP (Digital Light Processing)	A Texas Instrument technology used in projectors and rear projection TVs. DLP has an array of mounted miniature mirrors, one of which is smaller than the width of a human hair and represents one or more pixels. The mirrors are used to create a light or dark pixel on a projection surface by being repositioned to different angles to reflect light. A color wheel or LEDs are used for the primary colors red, green, and blue. Figure 9.4 illustrates the concepts of DLP technology.
plasma	Displays that work similarly to LCDs except that they have plasma gas in little chambers. When electricity is applied inside the chambers, excited electrons hit red, green, and blue phosphorous dots that glow. Many believe that plasma displays require less energy than CRTs. This is not necessarily true. However, LCDs do take less energy than CRTs.

Tech Tip

Recycle CRTs

CRTs contain toxic substances that can cause health risks to humans if CRTs are disposed of improperly. Consider donating a CRT or using a website such as http://www.epa.gov/osw/conserve/materials/ecycling/donate.htm instead of throwing it away.

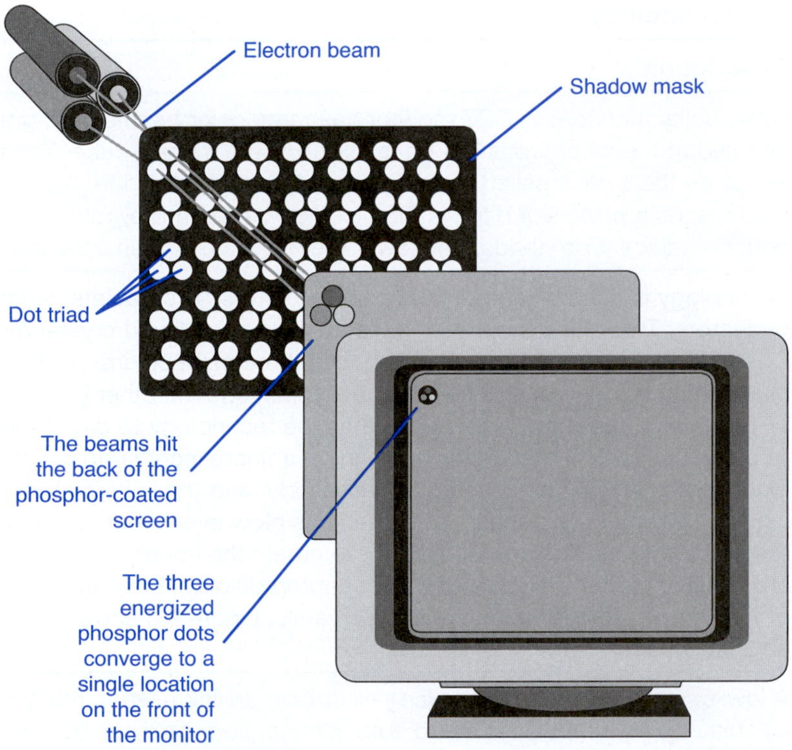

Figure 9.2 CRT pixel creation

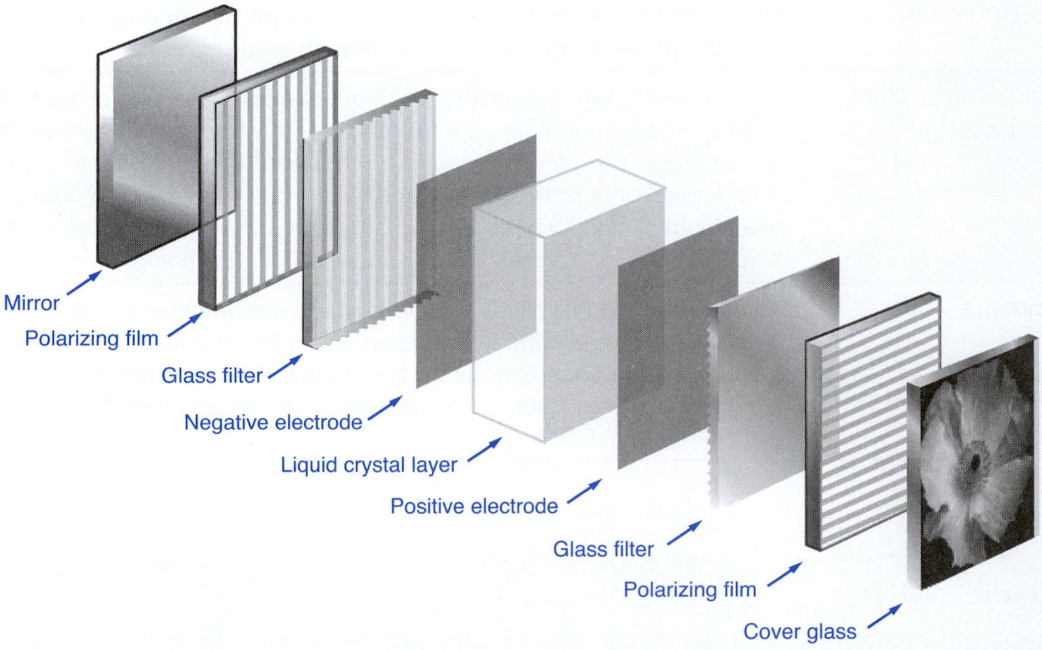

Figure 9.3 LCD technology

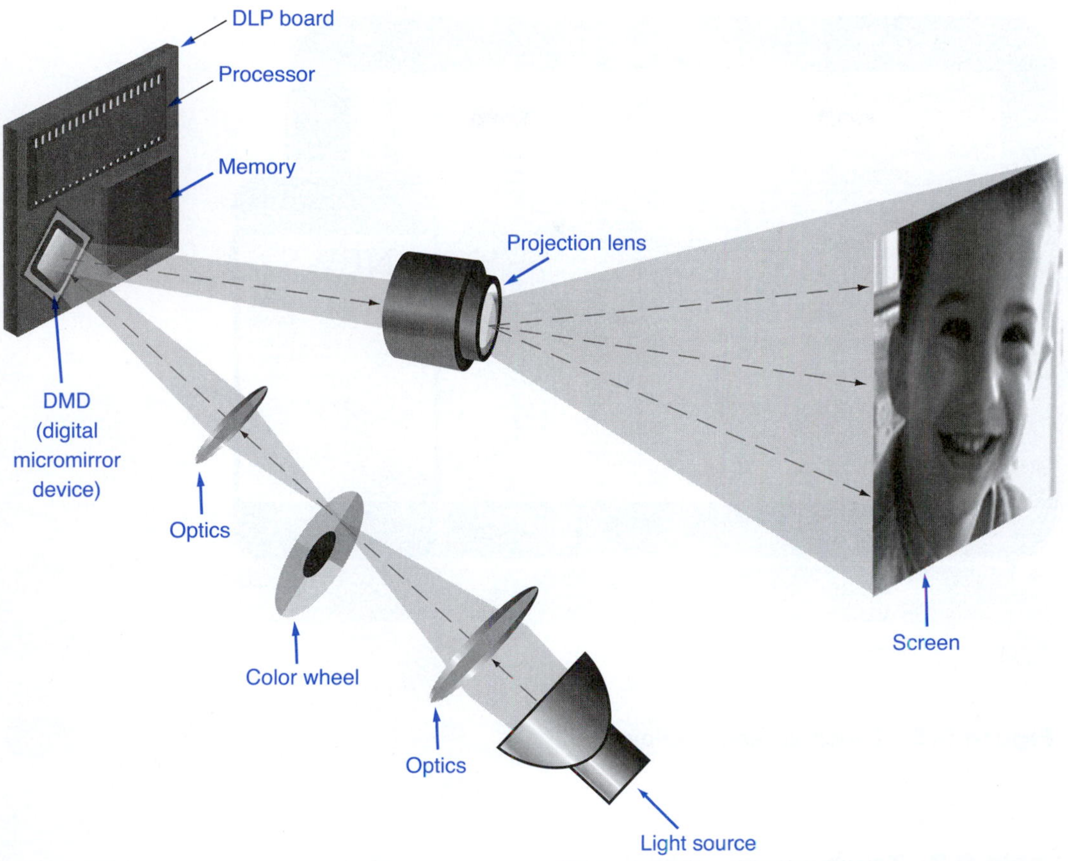

Figure 9.4 DLP technology

Touch screen displays are used with PCs, tablets, and smartphones. They respond to contact on the screen rather than keyboard or mouse input. They are both an input and output device and are used in situations where information is to be controlled and in public areas such as kiosks in airports, malls, and entrance areas of schools or businesses. Touch screen monitors normally attach to a USB, IEEE 1394, VGA, DVI, or HDMI port, a combination of these ports, or wirelessly. Special drivers and software are used to control the monitor.

There are several technologies used to manufacture a touch screen display. The two most common ones are resistive and capacitive. Resistive touch screens have a flexible membrane stretched over the face of the display. The membrane contains a special metal oxide coating and has spacers that are used to locate the touched spot on the screen. Resistive touch screens are good in manufacturing or medical areas where the personnel wear gloves. A stylus can also be used with these types of displays.

Capacitive touch screens are more durable than resistive screens. They respond to a touch or multiple touches on the display and easily detect contact. Most touch screens are the capacitive type. Some mobile devices allow you to calibrate the screen or lock the screen orientation using the *Settings* option. The screen orientations of mobile devices have been greatly enhanced due to accelerometers and gyroscopes. An **accelerometer** detects the screen orientation and adapts what is shown on the screen based on that orientation. A **gyroscope** measures and maintains that orientation. These technologies allow you to turn an iPad horizontally to better see a picture in a wide format. Figure 9.5 shows two touch screen devices. Table 9.2 lists some of the different technologies used with touch screen displays.

Figure 9.5 Touch screen displays

Table 9.2 Touch screen technologies

Technology type	Description
Four-wire resistive	1.7- to 24-inch displays with high resolution. Has a short life span (1 to 2 million touches) and low brightness. Accepts input from finger, gloved hand, or stylus.
Five-wire resistive	10.4- to 24-inch displays with resolution up to 1024×1024. Has a longer life span (30 to 35 million touches) than four-wire resistive and low brightness. Accepts input from finger, gloved hand, or stylus.
Capacitive	12- to 24-inch displays with resolution up to 1024×1024. Has a longer life span than any of the resistive types (100 million touches) and high brightness. Accepts finger input.
Surface wave	10.4- to 30-inch displays with high resolutions. Lasts a long time (50 million touches) and has high brightness. Accepts input from finger, gloved hand, or soft stylus. Tends to have the longest warranties.
Infrared	10.4- to 42-inch displays with high resolutions, long term reliability (more than 100 million touches), and high brightness. Accepts input from finger, gloved hand, and stylus.

Video Terminology and Theory

Video has unique terminology associated with it. It is important for a technician to be familiar with video terminology. Let's start with an important term—resolution. A monitor's **resolution** is the maximum number of pixels on the monitor. Two numbers separated by an × (meaning *by*) describe a monitor's resolution, such as 1024×768 (1024 "by" 768). The first number, 1024, is the number of pixels that fit horizontally across the screen. The second number, 768, describes the number of pixels that fit vertically on the screen. The possible monitor resolutions depend on the monitor and the video adapter. Table 9.3 lists important video features with which technicians need to be familiar.

The monitor **refresh rate** is for a specific resolution. If the electron beam has to handle more pixels, it will naturally take longer. Video card capabilities are the main factor in determining what refresh rate the monitor uses, provided the monitor can perform it.

To set the refresh rate for the display on an XP computer, use the *Display* Control Panel. Select the *Settings* tab > *Advanced* button > *Adapter* tab > click the *Refresh rate* down arrow to see a listing of possible settings. The Optimal setting is the default. If you select another setting, click the *Apply* button and a warning message normally appears. Click the *OK* button and the monitor changes. A dialog box asks if you want to keep this setting. Selecting *No* will reset to the default. If the mouse does not work or the mouse pointer does not appear on this screen, just press [Enter], and the *No* selection will be accepted.

Tech Tip

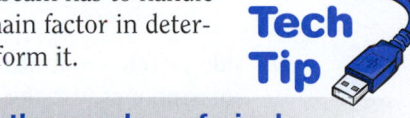

Determining the number of pixels

To determine the number of pixels a display has, look at the resolution, such as 1920×1200. Multiply the horizontal pixel number (the first number—1,920 in this example) by the vertical number of pixels (the second number shown, or 1,200 in this example). The result is the total number of pixels, which in this example is 2,304,000 (approximately 2.3 million pixels).

Table 9.3 Video features

Feature	Description
Refresh rate	In CRTs, the maximum times a screen is scanned or redrawn in one second. Measured in hertz (Hz). An electron beam continuously sweeps left to right, scanning every row of pixels.
Horizontal scanning frequency	The speed that the beam traverses the screen to refresh the pixels. The rate for one line to be drawn. Determined by the video adapter and ranges from 35 to 90kHz.
Vertical scan rate	The number of times the electron beam draws from the top-left corner to the bottom-right corner and back again to the top left. A slow rate can cause a monitor to appear to flicker.
Multi-scan monitor	A monitor that can lock onto different vertical and horizontal scanning frequencies. Also called multi-synch or multiple-frequency.
Interlacing	A monitor that scans only the odd-numbered pixel rows. Then the electron beam returns and scans the even-numbered pixel rows. Causes a flickering on the screen.
Degauss	In CRT monitors, removal of a magnetic field that can build up around the monitor, causing distortion on the display. The method used to degauss depends on the manufacturer, but common methods include (1) power cycling the monitor; (2) using a degauss button located on the front of the monitor; and (3) accessing the monitor menu, using a front panel button, and locating the degauss option (which may be an omega symbol Ω).

To set the resolution in Vista/7, access the *Personalization* Control Panel link > *Display* link. Use the *Adjust Resolution* and the *Colors* options to customize the display. To adjust the refresh rate, click the *Advanced Settings* button in the Screen Resolution window > *Monitor* tab > use the *Screen refresh rate* drop-down menu to customize.

Tech Tip

The higher the resolution, the smaller a pixel appears on the screen

Selecting a higher resolution will make the icons in Windows appear smaller. Use the *Display* Control Panel to adjust icon size.

On tablets and smartphone displays, the resolution cannot be changed, but the multitasking gestures and screen rotation can be customized. On an iPad, use the *General Settings* option to set whether one finger touch is used or if multitasking gestures (more than one finger to control the screen) is used. Use the *Use Side Switch to:* option to select the purpose of the iPad side switch—to mute sound or to lock the screen so it doesn't rotate. On Android tablets or smartphones, use the *Sound and display* option to select such options as the font size, default orientation mode, adjust brightness, screen timeout values, and power mode, as well as to enable/disable output to a TV (and the mode used).

Displays sometimes have a button that allows a menu to be accessed or have several buttons used to adjust the image quality. Common buttons include the following:

- Power—Powers the monitor on and off
- Input—Available when both analog and digital (VGA, DVI, HDMI, or DisplayPort) input connectors are on the monitor and used to select between the options
- Auto adjust—Automatically refines the monitor settings, based on the incoming video signal
- Brightness—Controls the intensity of the image or the luminance of the backlight on an LCD
- Contrast—Adjusts the degree of difference between light and dark
- Position—Moves or adjusts the viewing area by using horizontal and vertical controls
- Reset—Resets the monitor to default settings

Many flat panel displays are controlled through the *Display* control panel or custom software.

LCD (Liquid Crystal Display)

LCD is a video technology used with mobile devices and flat screen displays that are powered by a low-voltage DC power source. They are more reliable and have a longer life span than CRT monitors. The liquid crystals used in these displays are sensitive to temperature changes. That is why they might appear distorted in cold or hot temperatures.

There are two basic types of LCD: passive matrix and active matrix. The difference between the two lies in how the screen image is created. To see a video on how an LCD works, go to http://www.youtube.com and search for "Engineer Guy LCD monitor teardown."

The cheaper of the two, passive matrix, is made up of rows and columns of conductors. Each pixel is located at the intersection of a row and a column. (This is a similar concept to a cell in a spreadsheet.) Current on the grid determines whether a pixel is turned on or off. Each pixel has three cells in a color monitor: one for red, one for green, and one for blue. Another name for passive matrix is STN (supertwist nematic), which is a technology that twists light rays to improve the display's contrast. Passive matrix displays are not as bright as active matrix displays.

Active matrix displays have a transistor for each pixel. The number of transistors depends on the maximum resolution. A 1280×800 resolution requires 1,024,000 transistors (1280×800 and more are added for color). This technology provides a brighter display (more luminance). Active matrix monitors take more power than passive matrix, but both of them require less power than CRT-based displays. Another name for active matrix monitors is TFT (thin film transistor). TFT displays use three transistors per pixel (one for each color). Table 9.4 lists some common terms and explanations used with LCD/LED displays, and Table 9.5 has some of today's LCD technologies.

Table 9.4 Display characteristics

Characteristic	Description
Viewable size	The diagonal length of the LCD screen surface. Sometimes called VIS (viewable image size).
Native resolution	The optimum setting for an LCD, shown as the number of pixels that go across the screen followed by the number of pixels that go up and down the screen. Examples include 1024×768 and 1280×800.
Response time or synchronization rate	The time it takes to draw one screen (lower is faster and better) so you don't see blur when there is action on the screen.
Pixel response rate	How fast a pixel can change colors in milliseconds (lower number is faster).
Viewing angle	At certain angles, the display becomes hard to read. The viewing angle is the maximum angle that you can still see the image on the screen properly. Some displays have different viewing angles for horizontal and vertical perspectives.
Aspect ratio	A ratio of monitor width to height. Common monitor aspect ratios are 4:3 or 5:4, but newer widescreen formats, such as 16:9 or 16:10, are becoming more prevalent.
Contrast ratio	The difference in light intensity between the brightest white and darkest black, but measured in different ways by manufacturers. A higher-contrast ratio such as 800:1 is better than 500:1.
Portrait/landscape mode	Physical turning of a monitor so that the edge of the monitor that is on the left is turned to become the top or bottom of the monitor. Not all monitors have this capability.
Luminance or brightness	How much light a monitor can produce, expressed in cd/m2 (candelas per square meter) or nits. An example of a computer display is 50 to 500 nits. (200 to 250 is acceptable for most users, but 500 is better if video clips or movies are used.)
Lumen	A measure of light output or brightness—how much visible light is coming out of equipment such as lamps, lighting equipment or projectors. This measure is important when comparing products for a room that has lots of exposure to sunlight, for example.
Dead pixel	The number of pixels that do not light up on an LCD screen due to defective transistors. LCD panels with dead pixels can still be used and are common. Dead pixels can be (and usually are) present on LCDs—even new ones. Research the LCD manufacturing standard from a particular vendor for dead pixels before purchasing an LCD.

Table 9.5 LCD technologies

Technology type	Description
TN (twisted nematic)	The majority of displays use this technology. It is the cheapest to make and fastest to display.
VA (vertical alignment)	Better viewing angles, color, and brightness, but the response time is not too good.
IPS (in-plane switching)	A Hitachi technology that tends to be pricey and can have a slow response time, but these have really good color and viewing angles.
PLS (plane to line switching)	A Samsung technology that has brighter and clearer images, improved viewing angle, and low production costs.

LCDs do not have multiple frequency settings, as CRTs do, nor do they flicker (no beam tracing across and down the screen). The number of pixels on a screen is fixed. Manufacturers use image scalers to change resolution. Pixelation is the effect caused by sending a different resolution out to the display than the display design specifications. The LCD monitor must rely on interpolation or scaling of the output rather than having things displayed in the native resolution (the optimum choice).

Tech Tip

Set the flat panel resolution to the native resolution

You can change the resolution through the *Display* (XP) or *Personalization* (Vista/7) Control Panel, but it is best if left to the resolution for which it was designed. Otherwise, the output will not be as sharp as it can be. Use the *Display* (XP/Vista/7) Control Panel to change the font size if the icons are too small.

LCDs are found in the desktop and mobile device markets. The desktop monitors that use this technology are called flat panel displays. With flat panel displays, the viewing area is the same as the display measurements (so no trick advertisements). Popular sizes include 14-, 15-, 17-, 18-, 21-, and 23-inch monitors.

Laptops use LCDs and have a video cable that connects the LCD to the motherboard. Either a CCFL or LED backlight bulb is used on many models so images on the screen can be seen. The CCFL type connects to an inverter. The inverter converts low DC voltage to high AC voltage for the backlight bulb. Screens larger than 15.4 inches may need two CCFL backlight bulbs. An LCD with an LED backlight does not need an inverter. An OLED display doesn't need an inverter or a backlight. Figure 9.6 shows a laptop with a CCFL backlight.

Tech Tip

Liquid crystals are poisonous

Be careful with cracked LCDs. If liquid crystals (which are not liquid) get on you, wash with soap and water and seek medical attention.

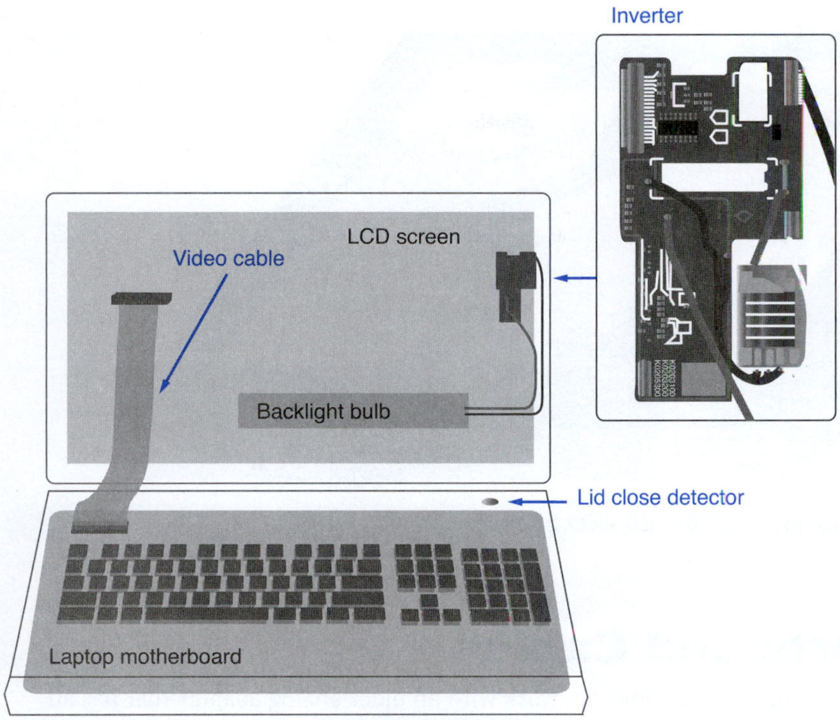

Figure 9.6 Laptop video connectivity

The lid close detector can be a physical switch or a magnetic switch located close to the back edge of the keyboard portion of a laptop. The laptop can be configured through power management configuration to go into hibernation, sleep, or standby mode when the laptop is closed.

Tech Tip

Is it worth fixing a laptop display?

Laptop displays can be expensive to repair, but if the inverter or backlight is the faulty part, the repair cost is negligible.

The laptop display may need to be replaced as part of a repair. When removing a laptop display, always refer to the directions from the computer manufacturer. The following are generic:

1. Use proper antistatic precautions and remove the screws that hold the screen bezel in place.
2. Gently pry the plastic bezel that protects the screen edge from the case.
3. Remove the screen retaining screws.
4. Gently lift the screen from the case. Be very careful with the connectors. Flip the screen so the back of the screen is visible.
5. Notice the cable that runs up the back of the display. Gently disconnect the cable at the top of the display and the cable that connects to the motherboard. Some are cables you squeeze to release, others have pull tabs or you gently pull from the socket. Figure 9.7 shows the back side of an LCD that uses an LED backlight. Look back to Figure 9.6 to see the display connections for an LCD display that uses a CCFL backlight.

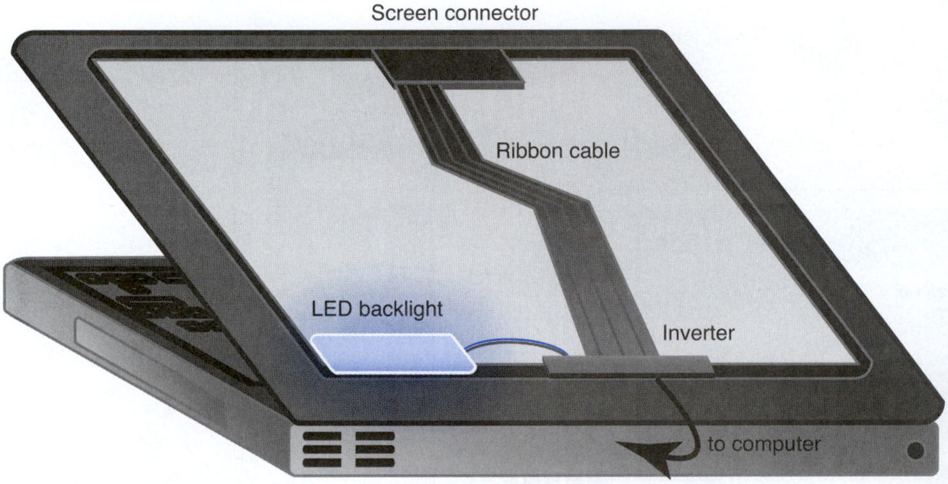

Figure 9.7 Removing a LCD with LED backlight

Video Ports and Cables

Flat panel monitors are digital, but some can work with an older analog adapter that has an analog port, such as an AGP port. This is not a good idea because the digital signal output from flat panel monitors must be converted to analog. The issue of colors with the old monitors is no longer relevant since today's flat panel monitors use transistors to control colors. Some monitors and TVs also provide USB connectivity. Some LCDs have a USB cable from the computer to the monitor. Many monitors act as a USB hub and provide multiple USB ports.

With the flat panel monitors, you need an AGP or PCIe adapter that has a DVI (digital video/visual interface) or HDMI (high-definition multimedia interface) port. This would be a good time to review the video ports covered in Chapter 1. Figure 9.8 shows an adapter with three common video ports (from left to right): HDMI, VGA, and DVI.

Figure 9.8 Video adapter with HDMI, VGA, and DVI ports

Use a digital adapter for a flat panel monitor

Tech Tip

Using an analog adapter is not recommended for connecting a flat panel display unless the flat panel display accepts analog input. The computer uses digital signals. The digital signals get converted to analog at the video adapter, it is sent to the monitor as analog, and then the monitor has to convert it back to digital for the display output.

With VGA ports, the analog video signals are sent using a VGA cable. The VGA standards did not specify a cable length maximum, but with higher resolutions, a higher quality cable is required. DVI, which uses digital video signals, is a similar situation. The standard does not specify cable lengths, but you sometimes have to install a DVI repeater (booster) for longer distances used with higher resolutions. Note that older DVI ports were not designed to output to some of the newer display formats (no matter what cable you use). With DisplayPorts and HDMI ports, cabling standards do exist, as shown in Figure 9.9.

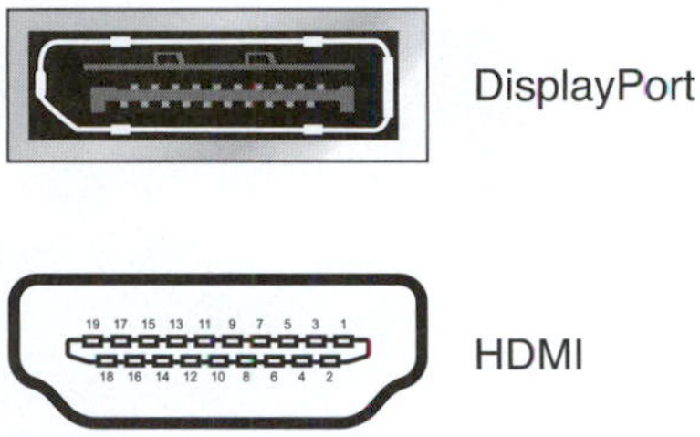

Connector type	Cabling
DisplayPort v 1.0 DisplayPort v 1.1/2	2 meters (~6 feet) max Longer distances with fiber
HDMI	Type A/Category 1 (standard) 720p/1080i Type B/Category 2 (high speed) 1080p resolutions up to 2560x1600 Type C (mini-connector) Type D (micro-connector) Maximum of 10 meters (~32 feet) with quality/high speed cabling

Figure 9.9 DisplayPort and HDMI cabling

A new type of port you might see on a PCIe card or on an Apple computer is a **Thunderbolt** port. A Thunderbolt port looks like a mini-DisplayPort, but it has a lightning bolt beside it. The Thunderbolt port can provide power to up to seven daisy-chained devices (up to 10.5W). The maximum length of a Thunderbolt cable is 10 feet (about 3 meters). Figure 9.10 shows the port.

DVI must match the monitor DVI connection type

Tech Tip

Be careful when installing a video subsystem. Ensure that the video card installed matches the DVI connection type for the monitor. Converters can be purchased to adapt to VGA.

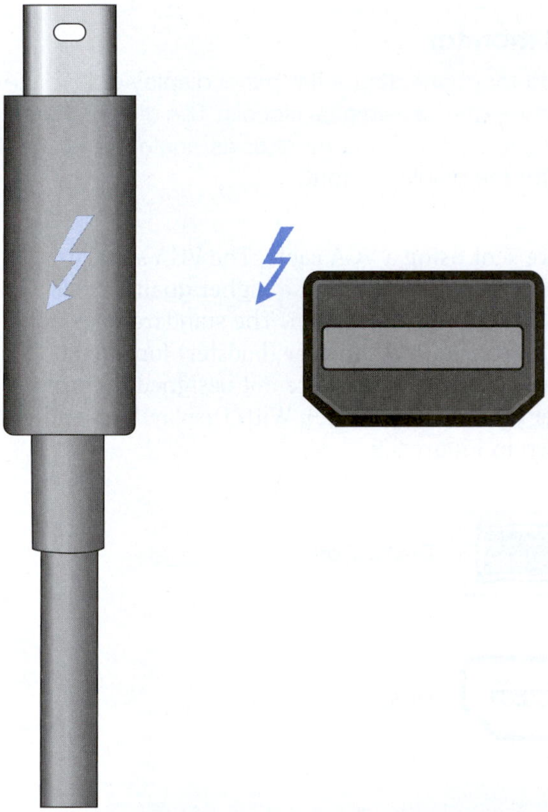

Figure 9.10 Thunderbolt connectivity

Tech Tip

Converting DVI to HDMI

A DVI-to-HDMI cable can be used to connect a PC with a DVI port to a device such as a home theater system or flat screen TV that has an HDMI port.

Multiple Displays

A popular business and home display option is to have two displays connected to the same computer. Another option would be to have a laptop with an external monitor attached, and both the laptop display and the external monitor display are active. To have two monitors connected to a single computer, you have several methods of configuration:

- Use the two video ports on the motherboard (not common).
- Use the integrated motherboard port and buy a video card with one video port. (This is the cheapest solution, but the motherboard might disable the integrated video port automatically.)
- Buy a video card that has two video ports (best option).
- Buy two video cards. (Usually the motherboard has one expansion slot for a video card, and that means using an older and slower technology expansion slot for the second video card.)

Once Windows recognizes the second monitor (two monitors appear in Device Manager), in Windows XP, use the *Appearance and Themes* > *Display* Control Panel > *Settings* tab > click *Identify* so that a large number appears on each monitor. Click the monitor icons and drag them on the screen to arrange the display. In Windows 7 use the *Appearance and Personalization* Control Panel > select the *Adjust screen resolution* link > locate the *Multiple displays* drop down menu to see the desktop options. Note that if the *Multiple displays* option is not shown, Windows does not recognize the second monitor. Troubleshoot hardware connectivity, monitor input mode if the monitor has multiple input ports, and verify system BIOS options. An exercise at the end of this chapter demonstrates this. Figure 9.11 shows an adapter with two DVI connectors that could be used for this purpose. Notice how the card also has an S-video port for a connection to a TV or other video output.

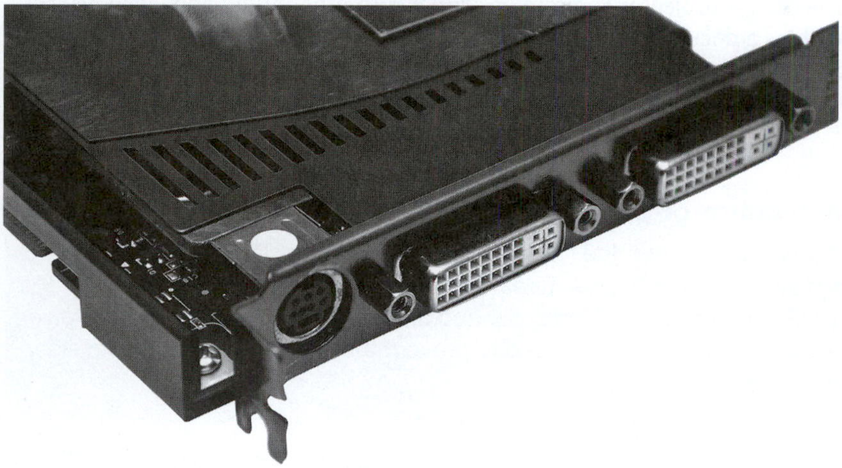

Figure 9.11 Dual-display connectivity

Another variation that some network administrators, technicians, other people, or businesses want is the ability to use the same monitor (and sometimes mouse and keyboard) for two or more different computers. This is best done through a KVM (keyboard, video, mouse) switch, which allows at least one mouse, one keyboard, and one video output to be used by two or more computers. Figure 9.12 shows a KVM switch.

Many people would rather use software to do this function and remotely access the desktop of another computer. Windows calls this built-in software feature Remote Desktop. Remote Desktop is covered in Chapter 12, and a lab at the end of that chapter demonstrates how to use the Remote Desktop utility.

Tech Tip

Dual-monitor modes of operation

You can have the same information shown in two monitors, extend your desktop across two monitors, or choose what items are on each desktop.

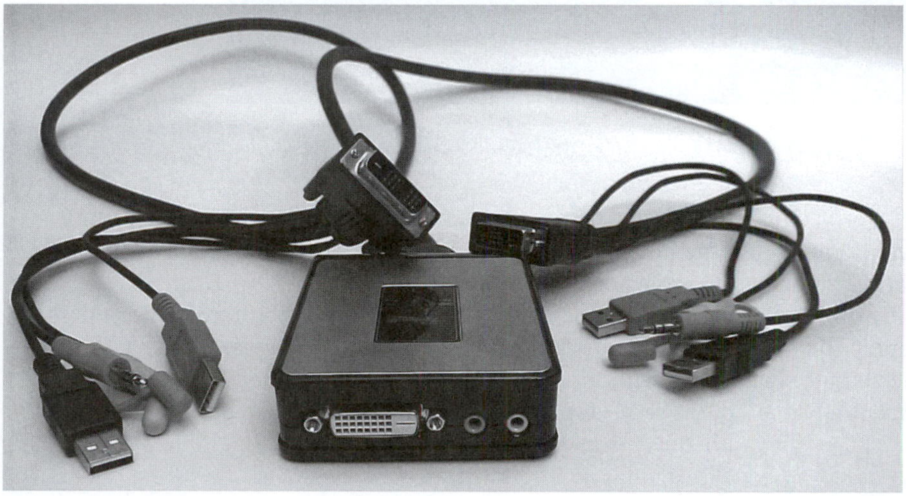

Figure 9.12 KVM switch

Projectors

Monitors, cameras, TVs, and web cams are not the only peripherals that connect to computer video ports. Projectors are becoming common devices, and technicians must be familiar with them. A projector allows what is being displayed on a computer to be projected onto a larger screen. A projector has similar connections to those described for video cards. Cables that convert between the different formats are available. Figure 9.13 shows some of the connectors available on a projector. A projector sometimes connects to other audio and video devices besides computers, such as a document camera, speakers, optical disc players, and smart boards. The VGA in and out ports are two of the most common ports seen on a projector for connecting video. S-video is also quite common. The newer projectors have DVI, DisplayPort, and HDMI ports.

Tech Tip

Using an external monitor or projector with a laptop

For most laptops, you can hold down the Fn key and press a specific function key to (1) use only the LCD display; (2) use only an external monitor or projector that attaches to the external video port; or (3) use both the LCD display and an external video device. The *Power Options* Control Panel might also need to be used to prevent the laptop from going into sleep mode during a presentation.

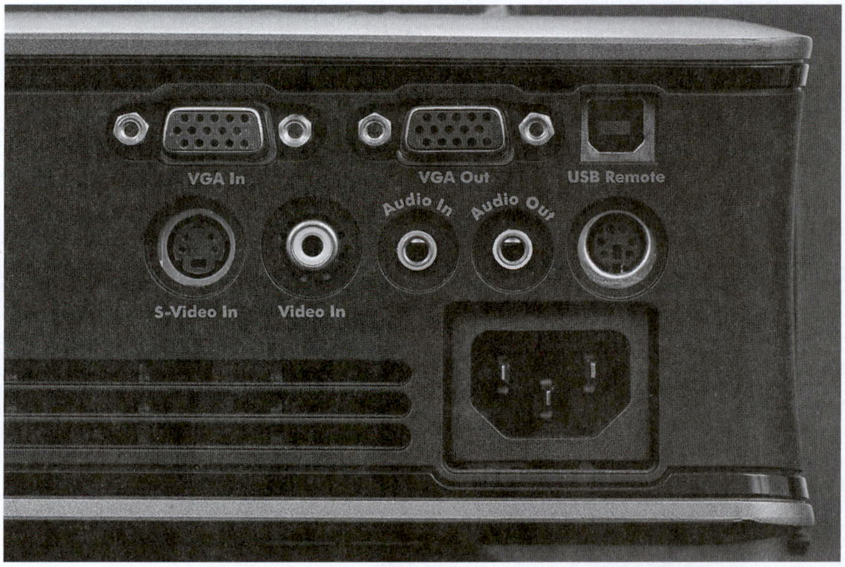

Figure 9.13 Projector ports

To connect a projector to a PC and a monitor, you need a video distribution (sharing) device or two video ports from the PC. A laptop frequently has a video port available for connecting an external monitor or a projector.

The specific numbered function key depends on the laptop manufacturer. Most vendors put a small graphic that looks like a monitor on the function key or the words CRT/LCD. Table 9.6 shows some commonly used configurations. Figure 9.14 shows the common laptop keys used when connecting a laptop to a projector and using the external video port.

Table 9.6 Laptop external monitor/projector keystrokes

Vendor	Keystrokes used
Acer, Asus, and Toshiba	Fn + F5
Compaq	Fn + F4
Dell	Fn + F8
HP	Fn + F4 or Fn + F5
Lenovo and Sony	Fn + F7

Figure 9. 14 Laptop external monitor/projector keys

Figure 9.15 shows a projector that has a lot of ports. As with video cards, you expect to see VGA, DVI, or HDMI ports, but ports that are often seen on TVs, gaming consoles, optical disk players or stereos are also available on projectors. **Composite video** is normally a yellow port (like the one labeled Video in Figure 9.15). The audio RCA ports are normally red and white. **Component/RGB video** analog ports are normally colored red, green and blue and have the symbols YPrPb above them. (Y is for the luminescence, or brightness, and Pr and Pb are for the color difference signals.) An RJ-45 connector connects the projector to an Ethernet network. Many projectors also have wireless network capabilities.

Treat your projector well. Do not immediately unplug the power to a projector after a presentation; instead, allow the projector to cool down first. You can turn off the projector, but the fan still runs on some models to quickly cool the projector. Keep the filter clean to extend the life of the projector bulb.

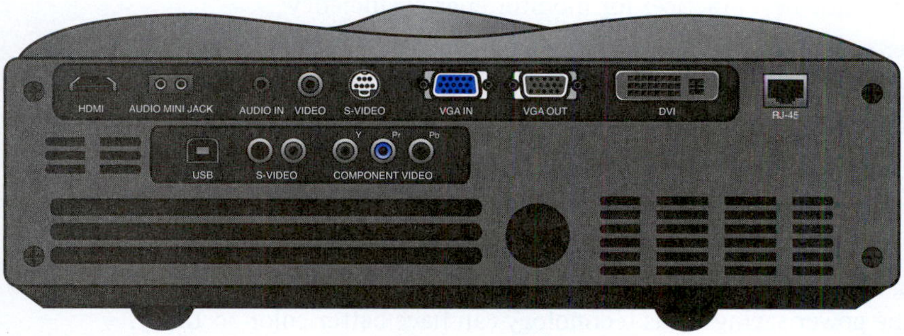

Figure 9. 15 Projector ports

Monitor Preventive Maintenance

It is simple to perform preventive maintenance on a monitor. Static builds up on the face of a monitor, and the screen attracts dust and dirt the way a television does. Antistatic cleaning wipes are available at computer and office supply stores. Some monitors also have a button on the front that, when pushed, removes static electricity from the front of the monitor.

A CRT monitor can also be cleaned with a soft dampened cloth and mild household detergent, glass cleaner, or isopropyl alcohol. Do not allow any liquid to get near the edge of a CRT. The liquid can seep inside the monitor case and cause damage. If using a CRT cleaning spray or glass cleaner, spray the cleaner on the cloth, not on the monitor. If the monitor has a nonglare screen or any type of special coating, see the manufacturer's instructions for cleaning it.

Tech Tip

Unless specifically trained, don't remove a CRT case

A CRT monitor holds 20,000 or more volts (depending on the monitor size and components). Voltage can still be present after the power is turned off. Most technicians who work on monitors have special training in working on high-voltage equipment.

LCDs can be cleaned with wipes specifically designed for LCDs. Also, a soft cloth dampened with water or a mixture of isopropyl alcohol and water can be used to wipe an LCD. Do not use glass cleaner to clean LCDs, and never apply liquid directly to a monitor of any type. On a laptop, ensure that the display is dry before closing the laptop lid. Mobile device screens can be wiped with a soft cloth. Do not use any type of liquid on a touch screen.

Monitor Energy Efficiency

A monitor's life span is normally 30,000 to 60,000 hours. The heat generated inside a monitor can reduce the life span of the monitor's components. Three things contribute to display power utilization:

- Size—The larger the screen, the more power used.
- Technology—LCDs require less power than plasma displays. LCDs that use LEDs for backlighting require less power than displays that use CCFLs. OLED monitors use even less power.
- Settings—Settings include brightness (brighter settings require more power) and power saver modes.

Some monitors have energy-conservation capabilities. These green monitors have software that reduces the power, leaving only enough to allow the monitor to be reactivated to a usable state quickly. The Environmental Protection Agency (EPA) produced ENERGY STAR guidelines to which many monitor manufacturers adhere. According to ENERGY STAR, displays that meet their criteria (http://www.energystar.gov) are 20 percent more efficient than other displays.

The following are some best practices for monitor energy efficiency:

- Use the power switch to turn off a monitor when you are finished using it for the day.
- Use the Windows *Power Options* Control Panel to enable Sleep mode for a monitor after a period of inactivity.
- On a laptop, adjust the contrast or brightness level to a lower one to prolong the life of the backlight.
- On a laptop, turn off Windows Aero to conserve power and battery life.
- When buying a new laptop, consider one that uses an LED backlight instead of CCFL. In addition to the power savings, this technology can have better color accuracy.

To modify the power-saving features, use the *Display* (XP)/*Power Options* (Vista/7) Control Panel. In XP, click the *Screen Saver* tab and click the *Settings* button to display the *Power Management Properties* window. In Vista/7, select the *Change plan settings* link.

Tech Tip

Energy-efficiency monitor settings

Use energy-efficiency BIOS settings, energy-efficiency software, or Windows energy-efficiency settings only if the connected monitor supports them. A non-green monitor can be damaged if you enable these settings. Check a monitor's documentation to determine whether it supports energy-efficiency modes.

Privacy

In the past, when monitors did not have fast refresh rates, screen savers were very important. A screen saver changes the image on the monitor constantly to keep any particular image from burning into the screen. With old monitors, if an image stayed on the screen for an extended period of time, an imprint of the image was left on the screen permanently. Today's monitors have high enough refresh rates so that screen savers are not necessary, but now they are an entertainment art form. LCDs use a different technology than CRTs and have never needed screen savers.

Screen savers can provide password protection that may be important to some users. With the password screen saver enabled, a user can leave his or her work area, and no one can access the computer without the screen saver password.

In Windows XP, to enable the screen saver, use the *Display* Control Panel. In Vista/7, use the *Personalization* Control Panel along with the *Display settings* link. Click the *Screen Saver* tab and click the *Screen Saver* down arrow to display an options list. The *Blank Screen* option takes the least amount of memory and does not use CPU time. Another resource saver is to remove the display's wallpaper option (also found through the *Display* Control Panel).

As a display option, antiglare filters can be used. An antiglare filter helps in certain lighting environments and when outside light affects the display. Antiglare filters are also available for mobile devices and smartphones.

Another display add-on is a privacy screen. A **privacy filter**, also known as a privacy screen, distorts the display output for anyone except for the person looking directly at the screen. This is good for managers and people who have confidential business matters on their screen when someone might walk up to or by the desk.

Video Adapters

Using millions of colors, motion, sound, and video combined, a computer's video subsystem has made dramatic technological advances. The video adapter controls most of the display output. Video adapters use the PCI, AGP, or PCIe interface. The bus connects the video card to the processor. The processor accepts data in 16-, 32-, or 64-bit chunks depending on the processor and the bus interface. One of the challenges of interfacing video is finding a good video adapter that uses a high-performance system architecture such as PCIe.

On the motherboard, the processor and the chipset are responsible for how quickly data travels to and from the video adapter. Such things as upgrading the chipset (motherboard), the processor, or the video adapter to a faster interface, speed up video transfer to the monitor. However, special features on the video adapter can also speed up video transfer.

Some video adapters have their own processor called the **GPU** (graphics processing unit). Other names include video processor, video coprocessor, or video accelerator). The GPU assists in video communication between the video adapter and the system processor. GPUs are also found in gaming systems, smartphones, tablets, and laptops. Figure 9.16 shows a video adapter with a video processor. The processor has a fan installed on top of the GPU. GPUs commonly have fans and/or heat sinks attached. Look back to Figure 9.8 to see a different view of the GPU.

AGP video cards sometimes required extra power and could use a Molex power connector. PCIe cards may require either a 6- or 8-pin connector from the power supply. The 6-pin cable can provide an additional 75 watts of power, while the 8-pin cable can provide an additional 150 watts. A PCIe video card could require multiple power cables as well.

Figure 9.16 Video adapter with GPU

Some video processors are 64- or 128-bit processors. Many users (and technicians) have a hard time understanding how a 128-bit video processor works in a 32-bit or 64-bit expansion slot. The 64 or 128 bits refers to the number of bits the video adapter's accelerator chip accepts at one time. The 64-bit (or higher) video processor controls many video functions on the video adapter otherwise handled by the motherboard processor. Anytime information is processed on the adapter rather than the motherboard processor, performance is faster. When signals pass to the motherboard processor through an expansion slot, performance slows. Most video cards today contain a GPU because video is one of the biggest bottlenecks in a computer system.

Specialized Video Cards

A specialized use of video is with TV tuner cards and video capture cards. A **TV tuner card** allows TV signals to be brought into the computer and output to the monitor. Some TV tuner cards have the ability to record video. Figure 9.17 shows a photo of a TV tuner card. Notice how the card connectors are different. The two protruding connectors allow a coaxial cable connection.

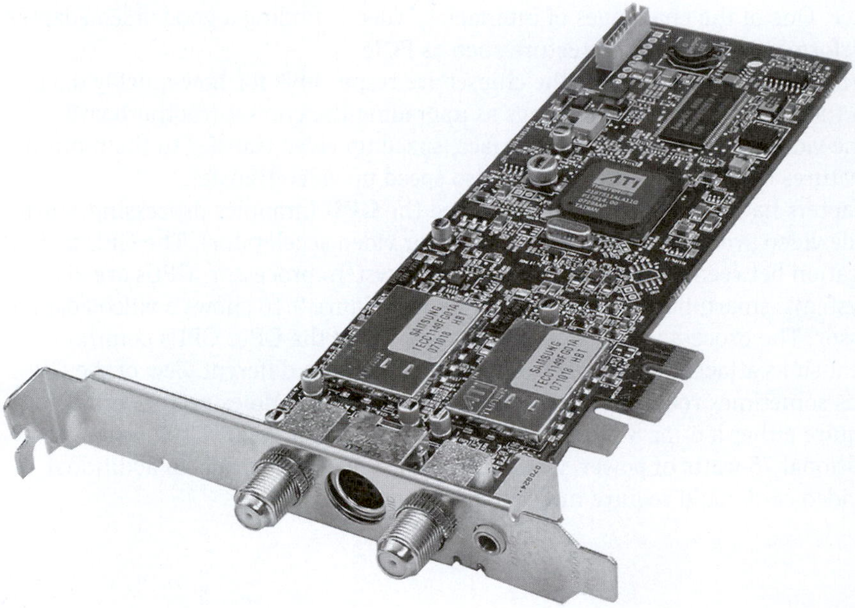

Figure 9.17 TV tuner adapter

A **video capture card** usually has specialized software that allows video to be captured from a camera, tape, VCR, game console, TV channel, optical media, recorder, or live audio and video and manipulated into a presentation, an archived file, or a saved document or streamed onto the Internet. Not all video capture cards support audio. Video surveillance systems sometimes use video capture cards.

Another specialized use of video is SLI (scalable link interface) from NVIDIA. SLI links two or more PCIe video cards to share processing on graphics-intensive operations. AMD's CrossFire and CrossFireX performs similarly by allowing multiple GPUs to be used cooperatively in the same computer. Note that the system chipset must be compatible with SLI or CrossFire technologies and you will probably need a power connector from the power supply for each video card.

Video Memory

One of the most important functions of a video processor is to transfer data to and from a video adapter's memory. Memory chips on the video adapter can be regular DRAM chips (including DDR2 and DDR3).

Tech Tip

How much video memory?

The amount of video adapter memory determines the number of colors available at a specific resolution.

The objective is to get data in and out of the video card memory chips as quickly as possible for a reasonable cost. The adapter must handle a large amount of data due to the increasing number of pixels and colors displayed. Ample, fast memory on a video card allows higher resolutions and more colors to appear on the screen, without the screen appearing to flicker.

All parts of the video subsystem must work together to get a clear picture on the screen. A very expensive video adapter with 16 trillion megabytes of memory connected to a monitor with a poor dot pitch will display a distorted picture on the screen. An expensive monitor connected to a PCI video adapter with only 256KB of memory will not provide the fastest refresh rates, and the monitor will appear to flicker as a result. The adapter needs to contain enough memory to sustain the number of colors at the specific resolution at which the user must work. A technician cannot perform magic on poorly matched video components. The only solution is to upgrade the weak link.

Memory on a video card stores screen information as a snapshot of what appears on the screen. The video adapter manufacturer determines the maximum amount of video memory. Some manufacturers make video adapters that are not upgradable. Check the adapter's documentation before making a purchase or recommendation.

To determine the amount of video memory an adapter needs, multiply the total number of pixels (the resolution) by the number of bits needed to produce a specific number of colors. Different combinations of 16 1s and 0s create 65,536 (64K) possible combinations as 2^{16} = 65,536. For example, take a system that needs 65,536 colors at the resolution 1024×768. To determine the minimum video memory necessary, multiply 16 (the number of bits needed for 64K of colors) by 1024 by 768 (the resolution). The result, 12,582,912, is the number of bits needed to handle the combination of 64K colors at 1024×768. Divide the bits by 8 for the number of *bytes* needed. This is the minimum amount of memory needed on the video card: 12,582,912 . 8 = 1,572,864, or 1.5MB. The user needs more video memory if more colors, a higher resolution, or video motion is desired.

Table 9.7 lists the number of bits required for different color options.

Table 9.7 Bits required for colors

Number of bits	Number of colors
4	16
8	256
16	65,536 (65K)
24	16,777, 216 (16M)

Some video cards offer 32-bit color. The extra bits are used for color control and special effects, such as animation and game effects. Determining the amount of video memory may have seemed confusing; an exercise at the end of this chapter provides practice for configuring different scenarios. Table 9.8 lists the minimum amounts of video memory needed for specific configurations.

Table 9.8 Minimum video memory requirement examples

Total video memory needed (shared and on card)	Color depth	Resolution
1MB	16-bit (65,536 colors)	640×480
2MB	24-bit (16 million colors)	800×600
2MB	16-bit (65,536 colors)	1024×768
4MB	24-bit (16 million colors)	1024×768
6MB	32-bit (true color)	1400×1050
6MB	24-bit (16 million colors)	1600×1200
8MB	32-bit (true color)	1600×1200

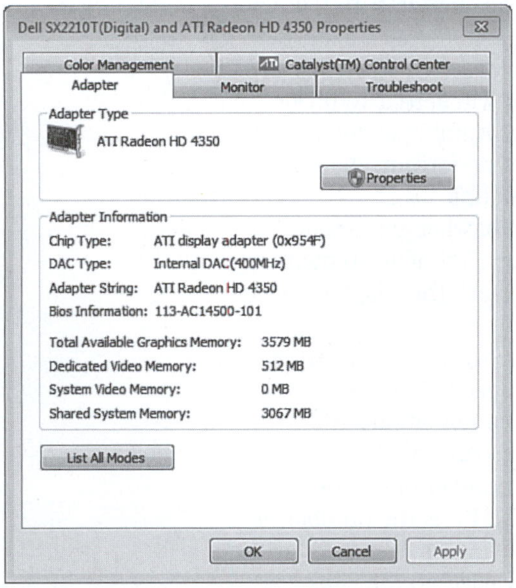

Figure 9.18 Shared system memory for video

If 2-D or 3-D graphics are being used, the calculations shown in Table 9.8 can be used as a starting point, but more memory is needed. For 2-D graphics, multiply the answer by 16 more bits. For 3-D graphics, multiply the final number by 48 bits. Then divide by 8 to find out how many bytes.

Video RAM is RAM that is used for video exclusively. When this RAM is not enough, motherboard RAM is used. When motherboard RAM is being used in addition to video card RAM, the amount of motherboard RAM being used is known as **shared system memory**, or shared video memory. You see this when you examine the video display properties. Some systems allow customization through system BIOS or a special control panel provided by the video adapter manufacturer. Common system BIOS options to control shared system memory include AGP Aperture Size and Onboard Video Memory Size. Figure 9.18 shows a video card that has 512MB of RAM installed on the video card (Dedicated Video Memory). The Shared System Memory amount is how much motherboard RAM is allowed to be used by the video card (and the operating system and the applications).

Tech Tip

Checking how much video memory you have

Use the Windows XP *Display* Control Panel > *Properties* > *Settings* tab > *Advanced* button > *Adapter* tab. For Vista/7, use the *Personalization* Control Panel > *Display* link > *Change display settings* link > *Advanced settings* > *Adapter* tab.

Installing a Video Adapter

The first step in installing a video adapter is to do your homework:

1. Make sure you have the correct interface type and an available motherboard slot. PCIe and AGP are the most common.
2. Gather tools, if needed. If a tool is needed, it will be a screwdriver to remove the slot-retaining bracket and to re-insert the screw that holds the adapter.
3. Download the latest drivers for the video adapter.
4. Make sure the adapter has a driver for the operating system you are using.
5. Ensure that the power supply can supply enough power when the adapter is added. Some high-end video adapters require a PCIe 6- or 8-pin or AGP Molex power connector. Some PCIe cards can use a power cable adapter that converts two Molex power connectors to the PCIe power connector. Other video cards can receive adequate power (up to 75 watts) through the PCIe expansion slot.

Tech Tip

Installing a new video adapter

When you install a new video adapter, if it does not work, disable the onboard video port by accessing system BIOS Setup.

Before installing the adapter, power off the computer and unplug it. For best results and to prevent component damage, use an antistatic wrist strap. Access the motherboard by removing a side panel or removing the computer's cover. Remove any previously installed video adapters (if performing an upgrade) by removing the screw. Use both hands and lift the board upward; you may need to rock the board slightly from side to side to remove it. If no video adapters are installed, remove the retaining screw and remove the expansion slot cover. Place the retaining screw to the side.

Sometimes with a tower computer, it is best to lay the computer on its side to insert the video adapter properly. Line up the video adapter's metal connectors with the interface slot. Push the adapter into the expansion slot. Make sure the adapter is flush with the expansion slot. Figure 9.19 shows a video adapter being installed in a tower. Notice that the technician is observing proper ESD procedures. Also notice that a cable from the motherboard S/PDIF out connector attaches to this video card for audio output. Make sure sections of the adapter's gold connectors are not showing and that the card is not skewed. Re-install the retaining screw, if necessary. Connect the monitor to the external video connector. Power on the monitor and computer.

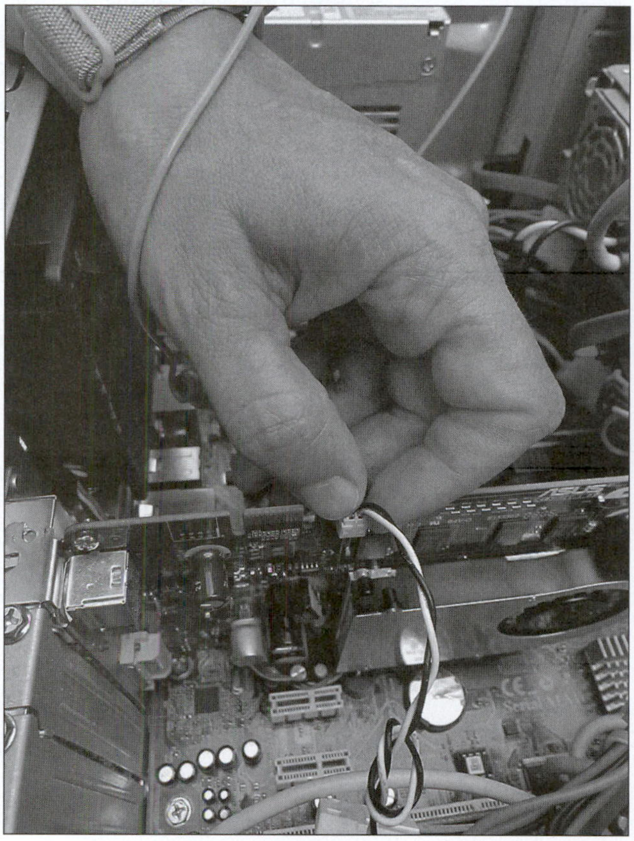

Figure 9.19 Video adapter installation

A video adapter usually has a set of drivers or software to enable the adapter to work to its full potential. Individual software drivers from the manufacturer provide system compatibility and performance boosts. The Internet provides a wonderful way for technicians to obtain current video drivers from adapter manufacturers. Be sure to use the proper video driver for the operating system. Always follow the adapter manufacturer's instructions for installing drivers.

Troubleshooting Video

As with other troubleshooting, when troubleshooting a video problem, check simple solutions first. Do not assume anything! Verify that the monitor's power light is on. If it is not, check the power cable connectors, surge strip, and wall outlet. Verify that the brightness and contrast settings have not been changed. Laptop users can use the appropriate Fn key and appropriate keystroke to adjust brightness/contrast. Check or disable power-saving features while you're troubleshooting. Double-check the monitor cable connected to the video port. Ask the user if any new or upgraded software or hardware has recently been installed, including an operating system automatic update.

Tech Tip

Laptop display troubleshooting

To troubleshoot a laptop display, connect an external monitor to the video port. Use the Fn key and appropriate keystroke to enable the external monitor port. If the external monitor works, the video circuits are fine. The laptop display has an issue. A dim or black display is commonly the DC-to-AC inverter or the backlight.

In the video subsystem, if a piece of hardware is defective, then it is the monitor, adapter, motherboard port, or cable. If replacement is necessary, always do the easiest solution first. Replace the monitor with one that is working.

Many video problems involve a software driver or improperly configured settings problem. Anything wrong on the display can be a result of a bad video driver, an incompatible driver, an incorrect driver, or an incompatible system BIOS version. The best way to be sure is to download the exact driver for the monitor and the display adapter/port from the Internet or obtain it from the manufacturer. Some troubleshooting tips related to video follow. Remember, these are only suggestions. Research and contact, if necessary, the monitor, motherboard, or video adapter manufacturer for specific instructions on troubleshooting its equipment.

Common video problems include the following:

- Bent or broken video pins cause color shifts and/or image distortion. Carefully examine the monitor's cable ends. The cable may appear to correctly plug into the connector even when the pins are bent and do not fit properly into the connector. If you find one or more bent pins, carefully use needle-nose pliers to gently straighten the pins.
- If you suspect a video driver problem, boot to Safe Mode, which uses a standard (generic) VGA driver to see if the problem is resolved and to determine whether it is a software driver problem.
- If the CRT screen appears distorted around the edges of the monitor or the color appears distorted, check for any other equipment, such as other monitors, speakers, magnets, and fluorescent lighting, that might cause interference with the monitor. Move the monitor from its current location to see if the situation improves or if the problem goes away.
- Another possible problem with color distortion is CRT magnetization from an outside source. Degaussing circuits neutralize a magnetic field. Some monitors have degaussing controls built into them, so try letting a monitor's internal degaussing circuits fix the problem. Turn on the monitor and computer for one minute. Then turn off the monitor. Leave the monitor off for 30 minutes. Then turn the monitor on again for 1 minute, followed by turning it off and leaving it off for 30 minutes. Continue to do this for several cycles.
- Do not use a degausser on an LCD monitor. On LCD monitors, use the vendor-provided software to make adjustments for distortion.
- If a screen has intermittent problems or poor quality, lower the refresh rate or update the video driver.
- Set a laptop to the native resolution (the resolution for which the LCD was made).
- If a cursor appears momentarily before the computer boots and then nothing is displayed or a distorted display appears, check for a video driver problem.

- A laptop may start normally, but its screen may not display the Windows startup screen. Sometimes a faint image seems to be evident or no image is displayed, but you can hear the hard drive. The inverter most likely needs to be replaced. This is a commonly replaced component in an LCD.
- If a laptop sometimes flickers or the display appears and then disappears if you move the laptop lid, this is usually a result of a bad or poorly connected video cable. Horizontal or vertical stripes on the screen are also signs of this problem.
- If you change the resolution or number of colors and the output is distorted, change the settings back to the original settings, if possible, reboot to Safe Mode or use the Last Known Good Configuration boot option, and reduce the resolution or number of colors.

Tech Tip

What to do if a laptop display goes black, red, dim, or pink

Most likely this is because the backlight bulb is faulty. Otherwise, the problem is the DC-to-AC inverter. Connect an external monitor to the laptop external video port. If the external monitor works, most likely the backlight bulb is the culprit.

Tech Tip

Laptop display is black

Check the laptop close switch that is located in the main part of the laptop, close to the back and near to where the display attaches to the laptop. Check the power management settings, which can be configured to go into hibernate, sleep, or standby if the laptop is closed. Also check the video cable from the motherboard to the display.

- Monitor flickering is normally caused by an incorrect refresh rate setting, which can be changed: Windows 7 *Display* Control Panel > *Change display settings* > *Advanced settings* > *Adapter* tab. It can also be caused by proximity to other video devices, speakers, refrigerators, and fluorescent lighting. In such a situation, move the monitor or offending device.
- Windows is not supposed to hang during the boot process because of video driver incompatibility. Instead, the operating system loads a default video driver. If video is a problem while working in Windows, boot to Safe Mode or use the Last Known Good Configuration boot option and then load the correct driver. You could also use the driver rollback option if a new driver has just been installed.
- If a BSOD (blue screen of death) appears, try rebooting the computer. You can also boot to Safe Mode and reload a video driver from there.
- Check the monitor settings to verify that the monitor detection is accurate. In Windows XP, use the *Display* Control Panel's *Settings* tab. In Vista/7, use the *Personalization* or *Display* Control Panel > *Display settings* > *Settings* tab.
- If nothing outputs after you have installed a video adapter, check the following: card inserted fully into the slot, connectors not properly attached, adapter not supported by the motherboard, auxiliary power not attached to adapter, insufficient power from the power supply, and improper driver installed.
- Any monitor that won't come out of power saver mode might need one of the following done: (1) update the video driver, (2) flash the system BIOS, (3) check the BIOS power settings to ensure that ACPI is enabled so Windows settings can be used, or (4) determine whether the problem is being caused by the monitor or the port. Connect a different monitor. If the video port is built into the motherboard, disable it through BIOS and insert a video card; otherwise, replace the video adapter to see if the port/adapter is causing the problem. Most likely it is a driver/Windows/BIOS ACPI setting problem.

Tech Tip

Monitor disposal rules

Many states have specific disposal procedures that must be followed for monitor disposal.

- If video performance appears to be slow, adjust the monitor to a lower resolution or a lower number of colors (or both). See the exercise at the end of this chapter for step-by-step instructions. Check the video adapter driver to determine whether it matches the installed adapter or whether it is generic. Obtain the specific adapter's latest driver from the Internet.
- If the computer is on for a while, but then the display has issues, check for overheating in the computer or on the video adapter. Check for adequate power output from the power supply.
- An **artifact** is something that appears on your screen that should not appear, such as green dotted or vertical lines, colored lines on one side of the screen, tiny glitters, or an unusual pattern. If the display shows an artifact, check for an overheating GPU, insufficient air flow, and a problematic video driver. An integrated video chip may also be going bad.
- On a smartphone display that has issues such as ghost cursors, flickering display, dim display, or no display, check power levels, cursor, brightness, and screen timeout settings, and remove the screen protector during troubleshooting. Turn off the phone and turn it back on again. If the phone has been exposed to liquid, power off the phone, remove the battery, and allow the phone to thoroughly dry.
- On a mobile device, if an error code appears or the screen display is not easily read, power off the device and power on the device again. If that doesn't fix the problem, power off the device, remove the battery, if possible, reinsert the battery, and power on again.

Printers Overview

Printers are a difficult subject to cover because many different models exist (of course, that can be said about any peripheral); but the principles are the same for different categories of printers. The best way to begin is to look at what printers have in common. All printers have three subsystems: (1) the paper transport subsystem, (2) the marking subsystem, and (3) the print engine subsystem. Table 9.9 describes these subsystems.

Table 9.9 Printer subsystems

Subsystem	Description
Paper transport	Subsystem that pulls, pushes, or rolls paper through the printer. This can be done using a belt, tractor feed, or rollers. Some printers can even have a duplexer, which is an attachment option that allows printing on both sides of the paper.
Marking	Parts responsible for placing the image on the paper (also called the marking engine). This includes ribbons, ink (print) cartridges, toner cartridges, any moving part that is inside one of these, and anything else needed to print the image.
Print engine	The brains of the operation. It accepts data and commands from the computer and translates these commands into motion. It also redirects feedback to the computer.

Keep the three printer subsystems in mind when setting up a printer and troubleshooting it. Knowing how a specific type of printer places an image on the paper also helps when troubleshooting the printer.

Printer Ports

Printers connect to parallel (IEEE 1284), serial, infrared, IEEE 1394 (FireWire), Ethernet, or USB ports. They can also connect through a wireless network or using wireless USB. Most printers attach to a PC by using the wired USB port. With USB printers, the USB host controller (built into the motherboard or on an adapter) powers up and queries all USB devices about what type of data transfer they want to perform. Printers use bulk transfer on the USB, which means data is sent in 64-byte sections. The USB host controller also assigns to each USB a device so that the host controller can track them. Even though a USB port can provide power to smaller devices, a USB printer normally has its own power source.

USB is a good solution for printers because it is fast, and there are usually several ports available—or a hub can be added to provide more ports. USB uses only one interrupt for the devices connected to the bus.

Networked Printers

Many home users and almost all businesses use networked printers (printers that can be used by more than one computer). Printers can be networked using the following methods:

- A printer that is connected to a computer can be shared or made available to other computers through the Windows operating system. The other computers must be networked in some way.
- A printer can have a network card integrated into it or installed that allows it to participate as a network device. This includes wireless networks.
- A printer can attach to a device called an external **print server** (similar to attaching a printer to a computer), and the print server attaches to the network.

A networked printer can reduce costs. Laser printers can be expensive—especially ones that produce high-speed, high-volume, high-quality color output. Buying one printer and allowing users to access it from their individual desktops can be cost-effective. It also reduces the amount of office or home space needed. Network printing is a viable alternative to using a computer's USB port.

A print server connects to a network and allows any computer that is also connected to a network to print to it if the networks are the same or connected to one another. Some print servers can handle both wired and wireless connections. In this case, the print server attaches to a network switch, and a network wireless router or wireless access point attaches to the same switch. Any PCs (wired or wireless) can print to the printer that attaches to the print server. Figure 9.20 illustrates this concept.

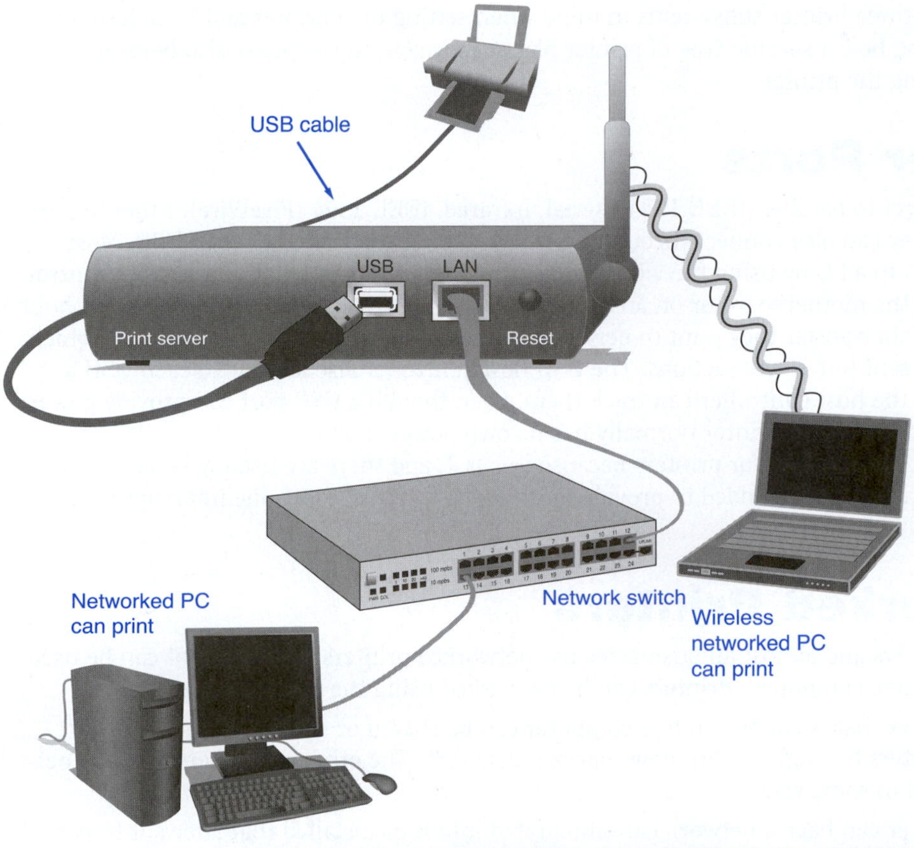

Figure 9.20 Wireless and wired print server connectivity

Wireless Printers

A PC can connect wirelessly to a printer using different methods: (1) The print server to which the printer connects can have wireless capabilities, and wireless PCs can connect to the printer through the print server (as previously described and illustrated); (2) the printer can have a wireless NIC (network interface card) installed or attached via a USB port; or (3) the printer can have integrated Bluetooth capabilities or a Bluetooth adapter attached via a USB port. Printers with wireless capabilities are common, but the wireless adapter may have to be purchased separately. Refer to Chapters 14 and 15 for more information on wireless networking theory and issues related to installing wireless devices.

Categories of Printers

Printers can be categorized according to how they put an image on paper. Printer categories are impact (otherwise known as dot matrix), inkjet, laser, and thermal. There are more types, but these make up the majority of printers used in the workplace and home. Computer users normally choose a printer based on the type of printing they need to do. Table 9.10 describes the four major printer categories.

Each of the four basic printer types is discussed in greater detail in the following sections. The theory of operation for each printer type mainly concerns the marking subsystem.

Table 9.10 Printer categories

Type of printer	Description
Impact	Also known as a dot matrix printer. Good for text printing of multiple copies and can produce limited graphics. Uses ribbons, which keeps costs down. The only printer that can do multiple-part forms and supports the 132-column paper needed by some industries.
Inkjet	Much quieter, weighs less, and produces higher-quality graphics than dot matrix. Uses a print cartridge, sometimes called an ink cartridge, that holds the ink used to produce the text and graphics; the cartridge costs $10 to $60 and can print 100 to 200 pages, depending on the manufacturer, the size of the cartridge, what is printed, and the print quality settings. Color can be done by dot matrix printers, but inkjet printers are best for color printing.
Laser	Produces the highest-quality output at the fastest rate. Cartridges can cost $20 to $350. Common in the corporate network environment where users share peripherals. Used for graphic design and computer-generated art where high-quality printing is a necessity. Some can produce color output, but at a much higher cost. Some even have stapling capabilities.
Thermal	Uses special paper that is sensitive to heat. An image is created where the heat is applied. Commonly used as ticket printers or receipt printers in retail outlets and gas stations.

Impact Printers

Impact printers are frequently called dot matrix printers because of the way they create an image on paper. Such a printer has a **printhead** that holds tiny wires called **printwires**. Figure 9.21 shows an Oki Data Americas, Inc., printhead. The printwires are shown on the front of the printhead. The printwires can get out of alignment and produce misformed characters.

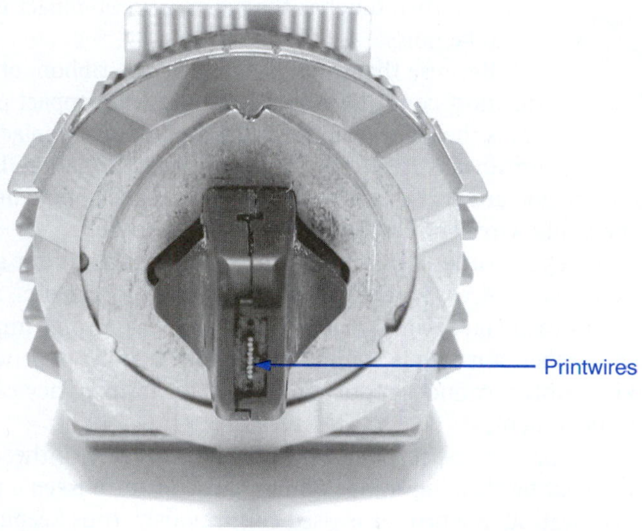

Figure 9.21 Impact printer printhead

The wires individually strike a ribbon hard enough to create a dot on the paper. The dots collectively form letters or images. The speed at which the printhead can place characters on a page is its **cps** (characters per second) rating. The number of printwires in the printhead determines the quality of printing; the more printwires, the better the print quality. The most common printwires are 9, 18, and 24. The 24-pin printers can print NLQ (near letter quality) output.

Each printwire connects to a solenoid coil. When current flows to the printwire, a magnetic field causes the wire to move away from the printhead and out a tiny hole. The printwire impacts a ribbon, creating a dot on the paper. Figure 9.22 shows an impact printer printhead. To show the individual printwires, the casing that covers the printwires has been removed from the illustration.

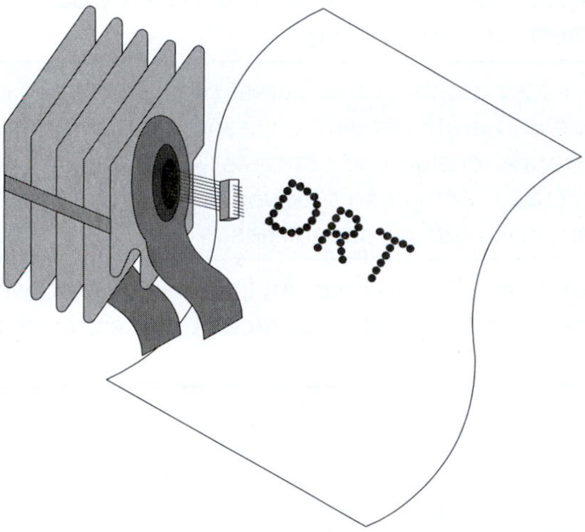

Figure 9.22 **Impact printhead operation**

Each wire connects to a spring that pulls the printwire back inside the printhead. The images created are nothing more than a series of dots on the page. Dot matrix printers are also called impact printers because the printwire springs out of the printhead. The act of the printwire coming out of the printhead is called pin firing. The impact of the printer physically striking the ribbon, which in turn touches the paper, causes impact printers to be noisy.

> **Tech Tip**
>
> **One direction is not a problem**
>
> Most impact printers print bidirectionally. When the printhead gets too hot, the printer prints only in the left-to-right direction. This is normal.

Because the printwire impacts the ribbon, one of the most common points of failure with impact printers is the printhead. It can be expensive to replace printheads frequently in a high-usage situation; however, refurbished printheads work fine and are available at a reduced price. The companies that refurbish them usually replace the faulty wires and test the printhead thoroughly.

Impact printers are the workhorses of printers. One advantage of an impact printer is that it can print multiple-part forms such as invoices, purchase orders, shipping documents, and wide forms. Multiple-part forms print easily on an impact printer because the printer impacts the paper so hard. The maximum number of multiple copies each printer handles depends on the printer model. Laser and inkjet printers cannot produce multiple-part forms. They can only make multiple copies of the same document.

Do not stack things on top of any printer, especially an impact printer. The printhead gets hot, and you should not add to the heat by stacking things on top of the printer. Keep a printer in a cool environment to avoid overheating. If a printer is used continuously, thus keeping the printhead hot, consider purchasing a second printer to handle the workload.

Inkjet Printers

Inkjet printers are much quieter than impact printers. An inkjet printer also has a printhead, but the inkjet's printhead does not have metal pins that fire out from the printhead. Instead, the inkjet's printhead has many tiny nozzles that squirt ink onto the paper. Each nozzle is smaller than a strand of human hair. Figure 9.23 shows a photo of an inkjet print cartridge. Notice the three rows of nozzles on the cartridge on the left.

Figure 9.23 Inkjet print cartridge

One great thing about some inkjet printers is that the printhead includes the nozzles and the reservoir for ink. When the ink runs out, you replace the entire printhead. The inkjet printer printhead is known as the print, or ink, cartridge. An ink cartridge has up to 6,000 nozzles instead of the 9-, 18-, or 24-pin configuration of the impact printer. This is one reason why the inkjet quality is preferable to an impact printer. Replacing the printhead, one of the most frequently used parts, keeps repair costs low but consumable costs are high. Two alternatives are for the manufacturers to use (1) a combination of a disposable printhead that is replaced as needed and a disposable ink tank, or (2) a replaceable printhead similar to the impact printer.

Inkjet printers, also called bubble jet or thermal printers, use thermal (heat) technology to place the ink on the paper. Each print nozzle attaches to a small ink chamber that attaches to a larger ink reservoir. A small amount of ink inside the chamber heats to a boiling temperature. Once the ink boils, a vapor bubble forms. As the bubble gets hotter, it expands and goes out through the print cartridge's nozzle onto the paper. The size of the ink droplet is approximately two ten-thousandths (.0002) of an inch, smaller than the width of a human hair. As the small ink chamber cools down, suction occurs. The suction pulls more ink into the ink chamber for the production of the next ink droplet.

An alternative for producing the ink dots is to use piezo-electric technology, which uses pressure, not heat, to eject the ink onto the paper. Some companies use this technology to obtain high resolutions. **DPI** is the number of dots per inch a printer outputs. The higher the dpi, the better the quality of inkjet or laser printer output. Figure 9.24 shows the basic principle of how an inkjet printer works.

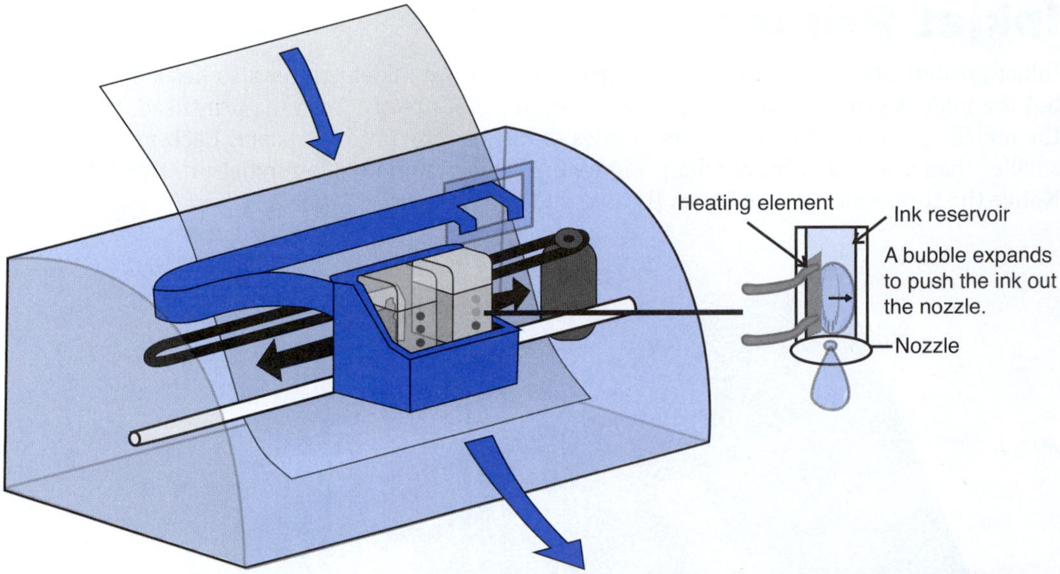

Figure 9.24 How an inkjet printer works

Most inkjet printers have different modes of printing. The draft mode uses the least amount of ink, and the NLQ (near letter quality) mode uses the most ink. The quality produced by an inkjet printer is equal to or sometimes higher than that of a laser printer, and inkjet printers print in color, whereas many laser printers print only in monochrome (black and white).

Tech Tip

Be aware of optimized dpi

Many inkjet printers now show their dpi as *optimized* dpi. Optimized dpi does not describe how many drops of liquid are in an inch but in a specific grid.

Color inkjet printers usually have a black cartridge for text printing and a separate color cartridge or separate cartridges for colored ink. Buying an inkjet printer that uses a single cartridge for all colors is cheaper on the initial printer purchase but more expensive in the long run. The black ink usually runs out much more quickly than the colored ink. Users should buy an inkjet model with separate cartridges for black ink and colored ink.

There are some alternatives to inkjet technology. Table 9.11 outlines four of them.

Table 9.11 Other printer technologies

Type of printer	Description
Solid ink	Sometimes called phase change or hot melt printers; uses colored wax sticks to create vivid color output. The wax stick is melted and sprayed through tiny nozzles onto the paper. The wax is smoothed and pressed as the paper is sent through rollers. The sticks can be installed one at a time as needed. The wax does not melt or bleed onto hands, clothing, or internal printer parts. It can print more colors, is faster, has fewer mechanical parts, and is cheaper than color laser printers but is more expensive than normal inkjet printers.
Dye sublimation	Also known as dye diffusion thermal transfer printers; uses four film ribbons that contain color dyes. The ribbons are heated and applied to the paper. The quality is high, but the printers are expensive.

Type of printer	Description
Thermal wax transfer	Uses wax-based inks like the solid ink printer, but prints in lower resolutions.
Large format inkjet	A wide printer to print large-scale media such as CAD drawings, posters, and artwork.

Inkjet printers are perfect for small businesses, home computer users, and individual computer office work. Some models of inkjet printers include faxing, scanning, copying, and printing capabilities. For higher output, a laser printer is more appropriate. A drawback to using ink is that sometimes the ink smears. Ink manufacturers vary greatly in how they respond to this problem. If the paper gets wet, some inkjet output becomes messy. The ink also smears if you touch the printed page before the ink dries. The ink can also soak into the paper and bleed down the paper. Using good-quality paper and ink in the ink cartridge helps with this particular problem. Some manufacturers have a printer operation mode that slows down the printing to give the ink time to dry or a heating process to prevent smudges. See this chapter's section on printer supplies for more information on choosing the correct paper for different printers.

Laser Printers

The term *laser* stands for light amplification by stimulated emission of radiation. A laser printer uses a process similar to a copy machine's electrophotographic process. Before describing how a laser printer works, identifying the major parts inside the printer helps to understand how it works. Figure 9.25 shows a side view of a laser printer with a toner cartridge installed.

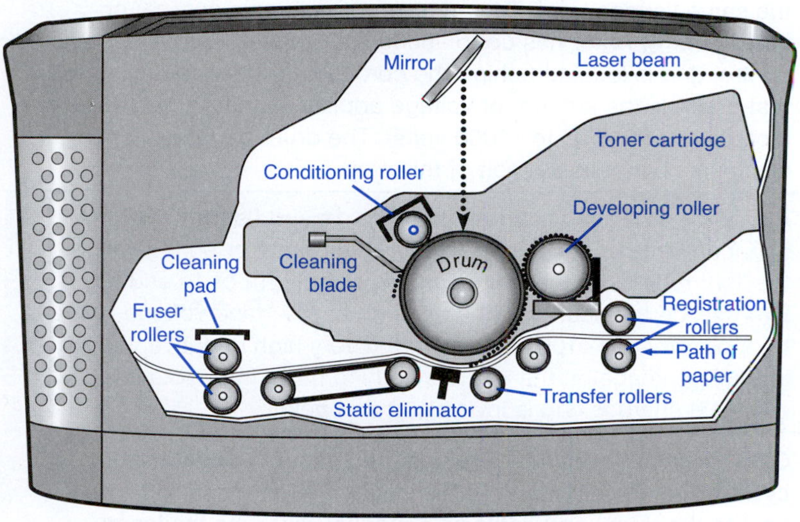

Figure 9.25 **Laser printer parts**

The computer sends 1s and 0s out the port and down the cable to the printer. Because data gets written to a laser drum by placing "dots" close together—similarly to how an inkjet printer squirts dots close together—the data must be prepared before the seven steps of getting the data onto the paper begin. The processing is the preparatory step, where the data is rasterized or converted into dots. Data transmits either through an array of LEDs or through a laser beam. The light beam strikes the photosensitive drum located inside the toner cartridge. Laser toner particles are attracted to the drum. The paper feeds through and the toner transfers to the paper. The toner is then fused or melted onto the paper. Table 9.12 summarizes the seven step laser printing process.

A **fuser cleaning pad** located above the top **fusing roller** lightly coats the roller with silicon oil to prevent the paper from sticking to the roller, which is often coated with Teflon. The cleaning pad also removes any residual toner from the roller. The cleaning pad is usually replaced when the toner cartridge is replaced. Figure 9.26 shows a fuser cleaning pad being removed.

Tech Tip

Laser printers *do* make weird noises

A laser printer frequently makes an unusual noise that is a result of the fusing rollers turning when the printer is not in use. If the rollers didn't turn like this, they would have an indentation on one side. Users not familiar with laser printers sometimes complain about this noise, but it is a normal function of a laser printer.

Table 9.12 Laser printing process steps

Step	Description
Processing	Also known as raster image processing. Gets the data ready to print. The laser printer converts the data from the printer language such as HPPCL (Hewlett-Packard Printer Control Language), Adobe PostScript, or Microsoft OpenXPS (Open XML Paper Specification) into a bitmap image. The laser printed page is made up of very closely spaced dots. Each row of dots is a scan line. The processing step gets the data ready to "write" a scan line.
Charging	Also known as conditioning. Gets the drum ready for use. Before any information goes onto the drum, the entire drum must have the same voltage level. The primary corona (main corona) or **conditioning roller** has up to –6000VDC applied to it. A primary control grid is located behind the corona wire or conditioning roller that controls the amount of voltage applied to the drum's surface (approximately –600 to –1000 volts). The drum gets a uniform electrical charge as a result of this step.
Exposing	Also known as the writing phase. Puts 1s and 0s on the drum surface. Whether the printer uses a laser beam or an LED array, the light reflects to the drum surface in the form of 1s and 0s. Every place the beam touches, the drum's surface voltage reduces to approximately –100 volts (from the very high negative voltage level). The image on the drum is nothing more than dots of electrical charges and is invisible at this point.
Developing	Gets toner on the drum (develops the image). A **developing cylinder** (or developing roller) is inside the toner cartridge (right next to the drum) and contains a magnet that runs the length of the cylinder. When the cylinder rotates, toner is attracted to the cylinder because the toner has iron particles in it. The toner receives a negative electrostatic charge. The magnetic charge is a voltage level between –200 and –500 volts. The magnetized toner particles are attracted to the places on the drum where the light beam strikes. A **density control blade** controls the amount of toner allowed through to the drum. The image is no longer transparent on the drum. The image is black on the drum surface.

Step	Description
Transferring	Transfers an image to paper. A **transfer corona** (roller or pad) is located at the bottom of the printer. It places a positive charge on the back of the paper. The positive charge is strong enough to attract the negatively charged toner particles from the drum. The particles leave the drum and go onto the paper. At this point, the image is on the paper, but the particles are held only by their magnetic charge.
Fusing	Melts the toner onto the paper. Heat and pressure make the image permanent on the paper. The paper, with the toner particles clinging to it, immediately passes through fusing rollers or a belt that apply pressure to the toner. The top roller applies intense heat (350°F) to the toner and paper that literally squeezes and melts the toner into the paper fibers.
Cleaning	Wipes off any toner left on the drum. Some books list this as the first step, but the order does not matter because the process is a continuous cycle. During the cleaning stage a wiper blade or brush clears the photosensitive drum of any excess toner. Then an **erase lamp** neutralizes any charges left on the drum so the next printed page begins with a clean drum.

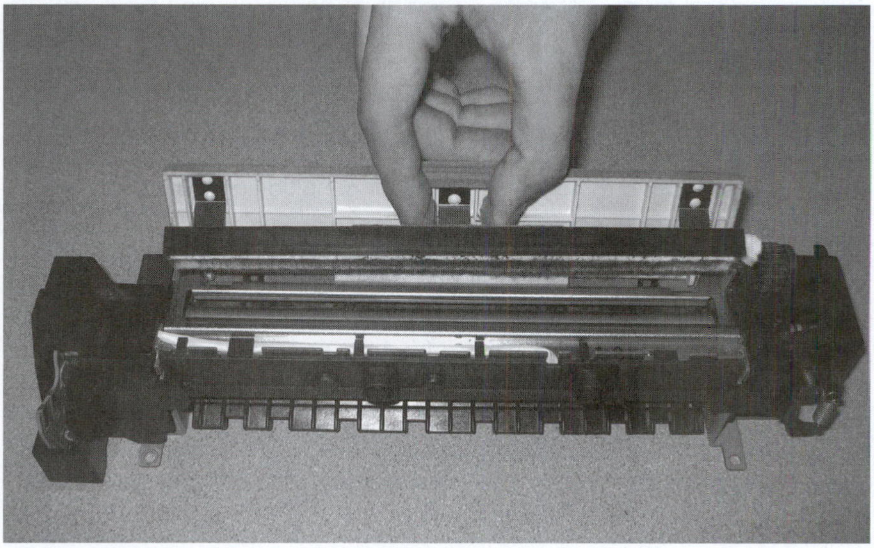

Figure 9.26 Fuser cleaning pad

Every laser printer that uses the seven-phase process is known as a write-black laser printer. These laser printers produce a black dot everyplace the beam touches the drum. Most laser printers use write-black technology. Write-white laser printers reverse the process, and the toner attracts everywhere the light beam does *not* touch the drum surface. Write-black printers print finer details, but write-white laser printers can produce darker shades of black areas.

To help with this flood of data about laser printers, Table 9.13 lists the major parts of a printer and briefly describes the purpose of each part.

Table 9.13 Laser printer parts

Part	Purpose
AC power supply	The main power supply for the printer
Cleaning blade	Wipes away excess toner from the drum before printing the next page
Cleaning pad	Applies oil to the fusing roller to prevent sticking; also removes excess toner during the fusing stage
Conditioning roller	Used instead of a primary corona wire to apply a uniform negative charge to the drum's surface
Control panel assembly	The user interface on the printer
Density control blade	Controls the amount of toner allowed on the drum (usually user adjustable)
Developing cylinder	Rotates to magnetize the toner particles before they go on the drum (also called the developing roller)
Drum (photo-sensitive)	Accepts light beams (data) from LEDs or a laser; can be permanently damaged if exposed to light; humidity can adversely affect it
Duplexing assembly	A laser printer option that allows two-sided printing
ECP (electronic control package)	The main board for a printer that usually holds most of the electronic circuitry, the CPU, and RAM
Erase lamp	Neutralizes any residual charges on the drum before printing the next page
Fuser (fusing) assembly	Holds the fusing roller, conditioning pad, pressure roller, and heating unit
Fusing rollers	Applies pressure and heat to fuse the toner into the paper
High voltage power supply	Provides a charge to the primary corona or conditioning roller, which in turn puts a charge on the drum
Main motor	Provides the power to drive several smaller motors that drive the gears, rollers, and drum
Pickup (feed) rollers	Rollers used along the paper path to feed the paper through the laser printer
Primary corona (main corona)	Applies a uniform negative charge to the drum's surface
Separation (separate) pad	A bar or pad in a laser printer that can have a rubber or cork surface that rubs against the paper as it is picked up
Scanner unit	Includes a laser or an LED array that is used to write the 1s and 0s onto the drum surface
Toner	Powder made of plastic resin particles and organic compounds bonded to iron oxide
Toner cartridge (EP cartridge)	Holds the conditioning roller, cleaning blade, drum, developing cylinder, and toner; always remove before shipping a laser printer
Transfer corona wire (transfer roller or belt)	Applies a positive charge on the back of the paper to pull the toner from the drum onto the paper

Figure 9.27 shows a laser printer toner cartridge, and Figure 9.28 shows the parts inside the cartridge.

Figure 9.27 Laser printer toner cartridge

Figure 9.28 Inside a laser printer cartridge

Be careful working inside laser printers

Be very careful when working inside a laser printer. There are high voltages in various parts as well as high temperatures in the fusing area. Turn off the printer and let it cool down before servicing it. Remove power from the printer when possible.

Tech Tip

Tech Tip

A word about spilled toner

Toner melts when warmed; small toner spills outside the printer can be wiped using a cold, damp cloth. Toner spills in the printer require a special type of vacuum with special bags. Toner on clothing can normally be removed by washing in cold water. Do not put the clothing in a dryer if the toner has not yet been removed. The toner will melt into the clothing making the toner impossible to remove.

Thermal Printers

Thermal printers are used in a lot of retail establishments and at kiosks, gas pumps, trade shows, and basically anywhere someone needs a little printer to print a small document such as a receipt. IT staff commonly have to service thermal printers. A thermal printer uses special paper that is sensitive to heat. A printhead has closely spaced heating elements that appear as closely spaced dots on the heat sensitive paper. A **feed assembly** is used to move the thermal paper through the printer. Figure 9.29 shows examples of thermal printers.

Figure 9.29 Thermal printers

Paper

The type of paper used in a printer can affect its performance and cause problems. Impact printers are the most forgiving because a mechanism physically impacts the paper. On the other hand, inkjet printers spray ink onto the paper, so the quality of paper determines how well the ink adheres. If the paper absorbs too much of the ink, the printout appears faded. For a laser printer, how well the paper heats and absorbs the toner also affects the printed output. Paper is a big factor in the quality of how long the ink lasts and the quality of print produced.

Erasable-bond paper does not work well in laser printers because the paper does not allow the toner to fuse properly. Paper is rated in pounds (abbreviated lb) and shown as 20lb or 20#. A higher number indicates heavier, thicker paper. Many types of paper are available for inkjet and laser printers: transparency paper for overhead projectors, high-gloss paper, water-resistant inkjet paper, fabric paper, greeting cards, labels, recycled paper, and so on. Recycled paper may cause printer jams and can produce lower print quality.

The highest-quality paper available does not work well if the surrounding area has too much humidity. Humidity is paper's worst enemy. Humidity causes paper to stick together and reduces the paper's strength, which causes feed problems. Paper affected by humidity is sometimes noticeable because of the lumpy look it gives the paper. If you detect damaged paper, discard and recycle it immediately. For best printing results, keep paper stored in a non-humid storage area and fan the paper before you insert it into the printer's bin.

Paper options also relate to printers. Some impact printers allow you to remove the normal paper feeder and attach a tractor-feed option that allows continuous paper to be fed through the printer. Figure 9.30 shows how the paper with holes on both sides feeds through the impact printer. Both impact and inkjet printers have special feeders or you move a slide bar to feed envelopes or unusual sized paper through. Laser printers sometimes ship with additional trays and must be configured for this option. Any printer that has non-standard paper installed, must be configured for that paper size using the *Printers and Faxes* (XP), *Printers* (Vista), or *Devices and Printers* (7) Control Panel. Laser printers normally allow manual feeding and have a front cover that allows paper, labels, transparencies, and other unusual sizes and types of paper to be used.

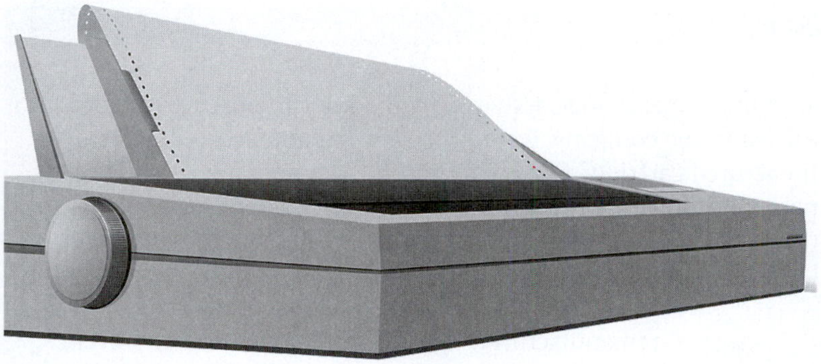

Figure 9.30 Tractor-fed paper

How to control printer trays and manual feed options

Tech Tip

In Windows, the *Paper* tab on the printer *Properties* tab is commonly used to configure where you want the printer to look for paper to be used. Most printers also allow the default order in which the printer looks for paper to be configured through either the manufacturer-provider software or the printer *Properties* window.

Refilling Cartridges, Re-inking Ribbons, and Recycling Cartridges

Much controversy exists about re-inking impact printer ribbons, refilling inkjet cartridges, and buying remanufactured laser cartridges. Many people who are concerned about the environment recycle their cartridges. Even if a company or an individual user decides not to purchase remanufactured products, some send their empty cartridges to companies that do the remanufacturing. Refilling ink cartridges significantly lowers printing costs.

If you refill ink cartridges, you should add new ink before an old cartridge runs completely dry. Also, be sure the refill ink emulates the manufacturer's ink. Some ink refill companies use inferior ink that, over time, has a corrosive effect on the cartridge housing. A leaky cartridge or one that bursts, causing ink to get into the printer, is trouble. Figure 9.31 shows an inkjet refill kit.

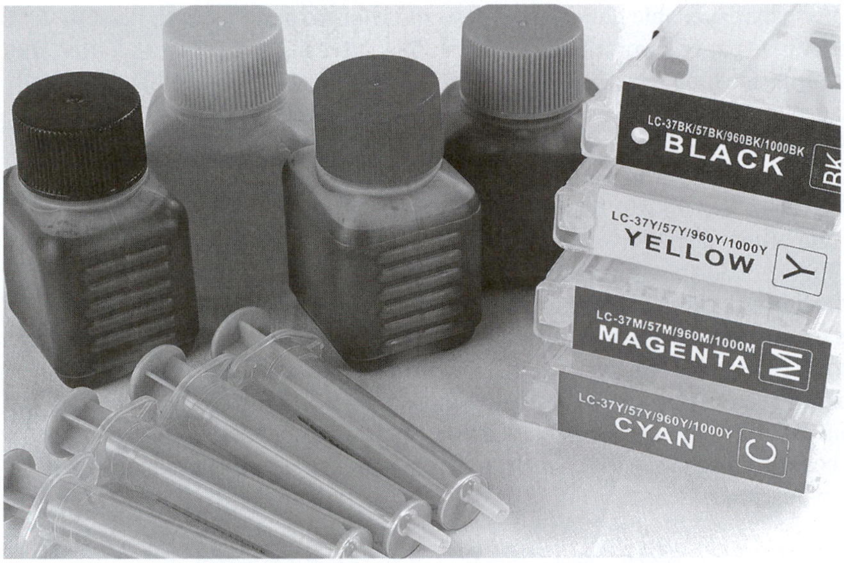

Figure 9.31 Inkjet refill kit

Some ink refill companies have an exchange system. The old ink cartridges are placed into a sealed plastic bag and returned to the company, where they are remanufactured. In return, the company ships a remanufactured cartridge filled with ink. If the empty ink cartridge sent to the company does not meet the company's standards criteria, the cartridge is thrown away.

Tech Tip

Beware of toner cartridges

Toner powder is harmful if inhaled. Wear a mask when refilling. Also, wear gloves when replacing or refilling a toner cartridge to prevent toner from entering your skin pores.

When it comes to laser cartridge remanufacturing, the most important components are the drum and the wiper blade that cleans the drum. Many laser cartridge remanufacturers use the same parts over and over again. A quality refill company will disassemble the cartridge and inspect each part. When the drum and wiper blade are worn, they are replaced with new parts. Some states have disposal requirements for inkjet and laser printer cartridges.

Re-inking an impact printer ribbon is not a good idea. It can cause a mess, and the ink is sometimes an inferior quality that causes deterioration of the printhead over time. Because impact printer ribbons are so inexpensive, you should just replace them.

Printer Installation

A printer is one of the easiest devices to install. Refer to the printer documentation for exact installation and configuration specifics (see Figure 9.32). The following steps explain how to install a printer that attaches to a USB port:

1. Take the printer out of its box and remove the shipping materials. The number-one reason new printers do not work properly is failure to properly remove all the shipping safeguards.

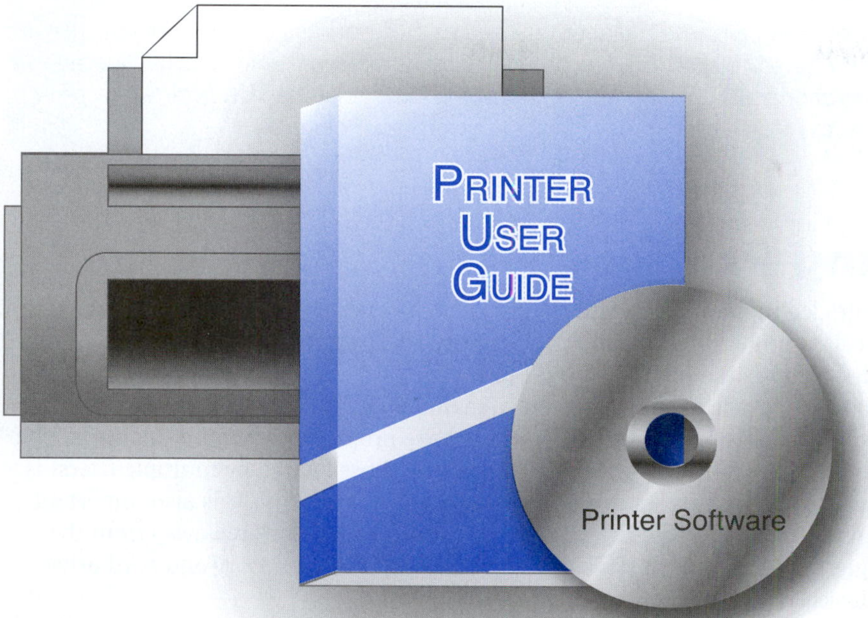

Figure 9.32 Printer installation, using software and a manual

2. Connect the power cord from the printer to the wall outlet, surge protector, or UPS outlet. Note that most UPS units are not rated high enough for a laser printer to be connected to them.
3. Load paper and the ribbon/ink/cartridge into the printer, according to the manufacturer's instructions.
4. Turn on the printer and verify that the power light is on.
5. Install the print driver by following the manufacturer's instructions for the particular operating system being used.
6. Attach the USB cable to the printer and to the computer. Note that this cable might not be provided with the printer.
7. Configure options and default settings.
8. Perform a test print to verify communication between the computer and printer. Most inkjet printers have a calibration process that must be performed before normal printing. This calibration procedure is also performed when an ink cartridge is replaced.
9. Train the user on printer operation and leave all printer documentation with the customer.

> **Tech Tip**
>
> **Educate the user on printer functionality and print cartridges**
>
> As part of the installation process, ask the user to print something and show him or her any unique features. Inform the user that the cartridge that comes with the printer does not last long and to order a new one as soon as possible.

If a printer connects wirelessly using Bluetooth or an 802.11 wireless network, see Chapter 1 for Bluetooth connectivity and Chapters 14 and 15 for 802.11 wireless connectivity.

Tech Tip

For a successful printer installation

The keys to a successful printer installation are to read the printer documentation, use a good cable, load the latest printer drivers (from the manufacturer), and test its operation. Many hours of frustration for the computer user and the technician can be avoided by doing the research before the installation rather than after a problem occurs.

Upgrading Printers

Printers can be upgraded in many ways, and the options available are vendor and printer dependent. The most common upgrades include memory and tray/paper feed options. The most commonly upgraded printers are inkjet and laser printers.

The most common upgrade for laser printers is memory. Many laser printer manufacturers use DIMMs and SO-DIMMs now, but some printers have proprietary memory modules. The amount of memory storage available for printers (especially those shared by multiple users) is very important because printing errors can occur with too little memory. It is also important to have some means of storage so that the documents can be sent and stored away from the computer that requested the print job. This frees up the computer's memory and hard drive space to do other tasks.

Tech Tip

Printer memory upgrades

Many memory technologies are available for printers, but the common ones are RAM modules, flash memory, and proprietary memory modules. These technologies are installed in the same manner as on a computer. Hard drives can also be attached to some printers for additional storage.

Paper storage trays and feeders are another common upgrade. Laser printers frequently come with various paper storage tray options. When multiple people share a printer, a small-capacity paper tray can be a nuisance. Inkjet printers often have different paper feed options related to photograph printing. Paper designed for printing photographs is available in various sizes. Special paper feed options can be purchased that are mounted onto a printer for rolls or different sizes of paper. With the increased popularity of digital photography, these printer options are quite popular.

Printer Preventive Maintenance

Impact printers usually require cleaning more often than any other type of printer because they are frequently used for continuously fed paper or multiform paper and are often installed in industrial environments. Paper chafe, dust, and dirt cause an insulating layer of heat to form on the printer components, which causes them to fail faster. It is important to vacuum impact printers more often than other printers.

Inkjet printers require little preventive maintenance. Keep the interior and exterior clean of dust and particles. Use a soft brush or nonmetallic vacuum nozzle to remove dust. Do not use any type of lubricants on the print cartridge bar. Use the printer's software or maintenance procedure for aligning the print cartridge each time it is replaced. Some printers have a "clean" maintenance procedure that can be done through the software that ships with the printer. Some of these processes do not clean the printhead well even when using this procedure, and the printheads tend to clog during usage. Remove the printhead and clean with a lint-free cloth or with a dampened cotton swab. Allow the cartridge to dry thoroughly and reinstall.

Laser printers, on the other hand, do require some periodic maintenance. The list that follows can help:

- Be careful about using compressed air to clean a laser printer that has loose toner in it. The compressed air could push the toner into hard-to-reach places or into parts that heat up, causing the parts to fail. Be sure to vacuum up laser printer toner before using compressed air inside a laser printer.
- If a transfer corona is used, clean it when replacing the toner cartridge. Some printers include a small cleaning brush for this purpose. Some toner cartridges include a cotton swab. The transfer corona wire is normally in the bottom of the printer, protected by monofilament wires. Be extremely careful not to break the wires or the transfer corona.
- Ozone is a gas produced by laser printers that use a corona wire. Some printers have an ozone filter that removes the ozone gas as well as any toner and paper dust particles. The ozone filter needs to be replaced after a specific number of usage hours. Check the printer documentation for the filter replacement schedule. If you forget to replace the ozone filter, people in the immediate vicinity may develop headaches, sore eyes, dry throat, nausea, irritability, and depression. Most home and small office laser printers do not have ozone filters. When using these printers, the surrounding area must be well ventilated.
- The fuser cleaning pad (sometimes known as the fuser wand) sits above the top fusing roller and is normally replaced at the same time as the toner cartridge. However, the cleaning pad sometimes becomes dirty before it is time to replace the cartridge. In this case, remove the cleaning pad. Hold the pad over a trash can. Use the shaft of a small flat-tipped screwdriver to rub along the felt pad. Replace the cleaning pad and wipe the screwdriver with a cloth.
- The fusing roller sometimes has particles cling to it. When the assembly cools, *gently* scrape the particles from the roller. A small amount of alcohol on a soft, lint-free cloth can help with stubborn spots.
- If the laser printer uses a laser beam to write data to the photosensitive drum, the laser beam does not directly touch the drum. Instead, at least one mirror is used to redirect the laser beam onto the drum's surface. The mirror(s) need to be cleaned periodically with a lint-free cloth.

Tech Tip

Laser printer preventive maintenance is important

If any toner appears inside a laser printer, do *not* use a normal vacuum cleaner to get it out. The toner particles seep through the vacuum cleaner bag and into the vacuum's motor (where the particles melt). Also, the toner can become electrically charged and ignite a fire. Special HEPA (high-efficiency particulate air) vacuum bags are available for some computer and/or laser printer vacuum cleaners.

Thermal printer preventive maintenance involves cleaning the heating element and removing debris from the printer. Isopropyl alcohol or premoistened thermal cleaning swabs can be used to clean the thermal printhead and rollers. Compressed air can be used, too. Allow the thermal printer and laser printer to cool before performing preventive maintenance.

For some printers, preventive maintenance kits are available for purchase. Quality printer replacement parts and preventive maintenance kits are important to a technician. If a printer must be sent out for repair, warranty work, or for some other reason, make sure to remove the toner cartridge, platen knobs, and power cords before packing the printer in a box. Check with the receiving company to see if you should send the toner cartridge separately.

Tech Tip

What if you just performed maintenance on a printer, and now the printing looks bad?

After performing preventive maintenance on a printer, the pages may appear smudged or slightly dirty. Run a few print jobs through the printer to allow the dust to settle (so to speak). Never perform any maintenance on any computer part or peripheral without testing the results.

Printers in the Windows Environment

The operating system plays a big part in controlling a printer. When working in a Windows environment, there are three essential areas for a technician to know (besides knowing how to print): (1) configuration utilities, (2) managing the print driver, and (3) printer settings. Sometimes these areas overlap.

To print in Windows, use one of the following methods:

- Open the file in the appropriate application. Click the *File* menu item and click the *Print* option.
- Drag the file to print to the printer's icon in the *Printers* folder.
- Create a shortcut icon on the desktop for a specific printer and drag the file to this icon.
- Right-click the filename and select the *Print* option.
- From within the application, press the Ctrl+P keys to bring up the *Print* window.
- From within an application, click the printer icon located under the menu bar.

If multiple print jobs are in the printer queue, you can reorder them by right-clicking on a document and selecting *Properties*. On the *General* tab, change the priority. A lower number, such as 1, indicates a lower priority than a higher number such as 3.

You can use the *Printers and Faxes* (XP)/*Printers* (Vista)/*Devices and Printers* (7) Control Panel to add a printer, remove a printer, temporarily halt a print job (pause the printer), and define or change printer settings, such as resolution, paper type, and paper orientation. The Windows Add Printer wizard steps you through the installation process. This utility starts automatically when Windows detects a newly connected printer. Once the wizard starts, you must select whether the printer is a local printer (used by only one computer) or a network printer. If the local printer option is selected, you will have to install a print driver. From the *Add a network, wireless or Bluetooth printer* link, you can add a networked printer. See Chapter 14 for more information on configuring network devices. See Chapter 1 for more information on Bluetooth configuration. For best performance, always use the latest driver from the printer manufacturer for the operating system installed.

Tech Tip

Using the printer icon in the notification area

When a print job occurs, Windows normally shows an icon of a printer in the notification area (the right side of the task bar). When the print job is still accessible, you can double-click the printer icon, click the document, and pause or cancel the print job by using the *Documents* menu option.

A **default printer** is the printer that applications use without any configuration changes. Even if you reply *No* to this prompt, you can change a printer to the default printer at a later date. Right-clicking a specific printer icon also gives you access to the *Printer Properties* window. Through this window, several tabs are available, depending on the printer model. Common tabs include *General*, *Sharing*, *Ports*, and *Advanced*. Figure 9.33 shows the *Printer Properties* window. Notice that the *General* tab has a *Print Test Page* button that can be used to test connectivity between the computer and the printer, and the test can be used to ensure that the print driver is working.

Tech Tip

Setting a printer as the default printer

Use the *Printers and Faxes* (XP), *Printers* (Vista), or *Devices and Printers* (7) *Control Panel* > right-click the appropriate printer > *Set As Default*. The default printer has a check mark next to the printer icon.

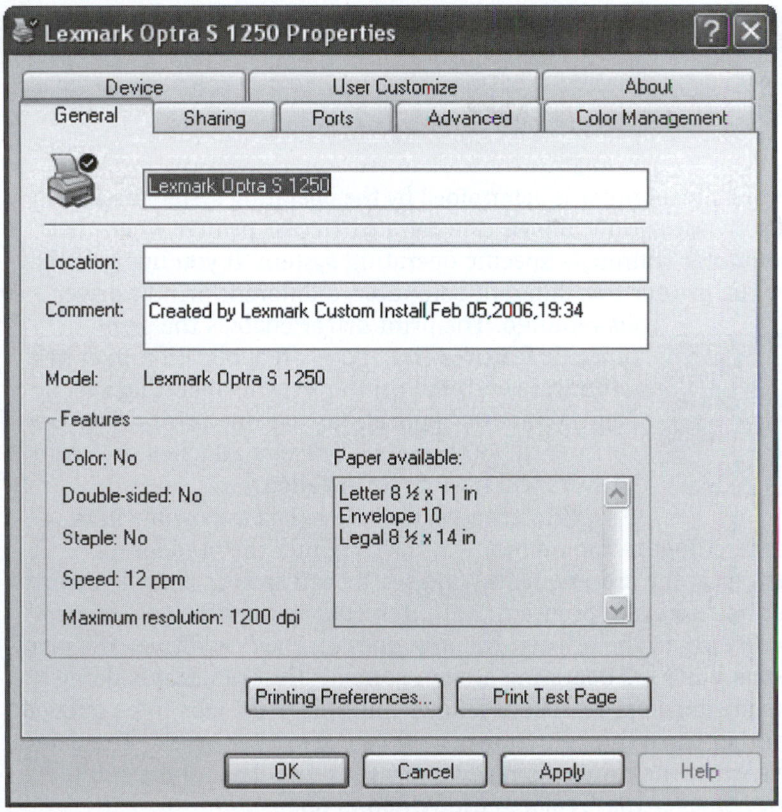

Figure 9.33 **Printer Properties window**

You can use Windows Device Manager to examine system resources and check for problems:

- To access Device Manager in XP, open the *System* Control Panel > *Hardware* tab > *Device Manager* button.
- In Vista/7, access the *System* Control Panel > *Device Manager*.

A printer's *Properties* option contains useful tools and settings. Table 9.14 lists the common printer *Properties* window tabs and their general purposes.

Table 9.14 **Printer *Properties* tabs overview**

Tab	Description
General	Displays the printer name and has a button for printing a test page
Sharing	Shares the printer over a network
Ports	Sets the LPT port number or displays the current port
Advanced	Allows setting of resolution, graphics intensity (darkness), graphics mode, spooling (transmission delay), and defaults
Paper	Selects different paper trays, paper size, and two-sided printing on some models
Fonts	Displays and installs printer fonts
Device Options	Adjusts print density and quality, displays amount of RAM installed in the printer, and adjusts printer memory tracking

> **Tech Tip**
>
> **Printer Properties *General* tab has a Print Test Page button**
>
> The *General* tab is normally where you find a button that allows communication between the PC and the printer to be tested with a test page.

How an application outputs to a printer is determined by the operating system used. A **print driver** is a piece of software specifically written for a particular printer when that printer is attached to a computer running a specific operating system. If you upgrade the operating system or move the printer to a different computer, a different printer driver is required. The print driver enables the printer's specific features and allows an application to communicate with the printer via the operating system. Windows applications use one print driver per printer. If you have two printers attached, two print drivers will have to be installed.

> **Tech Tip**
>
> **Use the latest print driver**
>
> For best results and performance, use the driver provided by the manufacturer designed for the operating system being used.

Printers accept as much data as possible from a computer, process that data, output it, communicate to the computer the need for more data, accept more data, and repeat the process. With Windows, a print spooler is used. A **print spooler**, or print manager, is a software program that intercepts an application's request to print. Instead of going directly to the printer, the data goes on the hard drive. The print spooler service built into the Windows operating system controls the data that is going from the hard drive to the printer. A print spooler allows multiple print jobs to be queued on the hard drive so that other work can be performed while the printer prints. The data is sent from the hard drive when the printer is ready to accept more data. Some printers come with their own print manager that replaces the Windows one.

If you right-click a printer and select *Properties* (or sometimes the window is under *Printer properties*), you can control the print spooler from the *Advanced* tab, as shown in Figure 9.34.

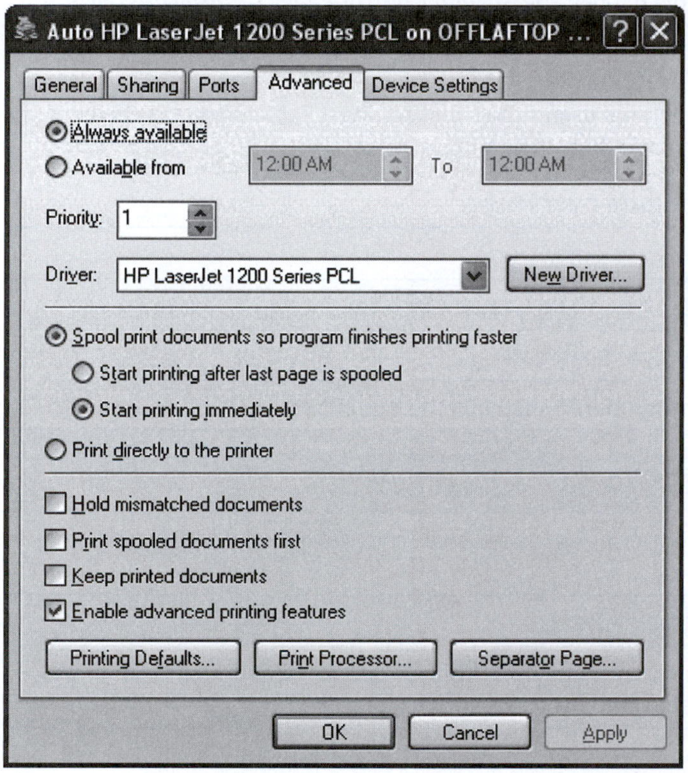

Figure 9.34 Spool settings

A print spooler runs as a service in Windows. The print spooler service relies on another service called the RPC (Remote Procedure Call) service and optionally the HTTP service in order to operate. To verify whether the services are running, type `services.msc` at a command prompt, in the *Run* textbox, or in the *Search programs and files* textbox on the *Start* button menu. In the resulting screen, you can see that the Print Spooler and Remote Procedure Call (RPC) services have a status of Started, as shown in Figure 9.35.

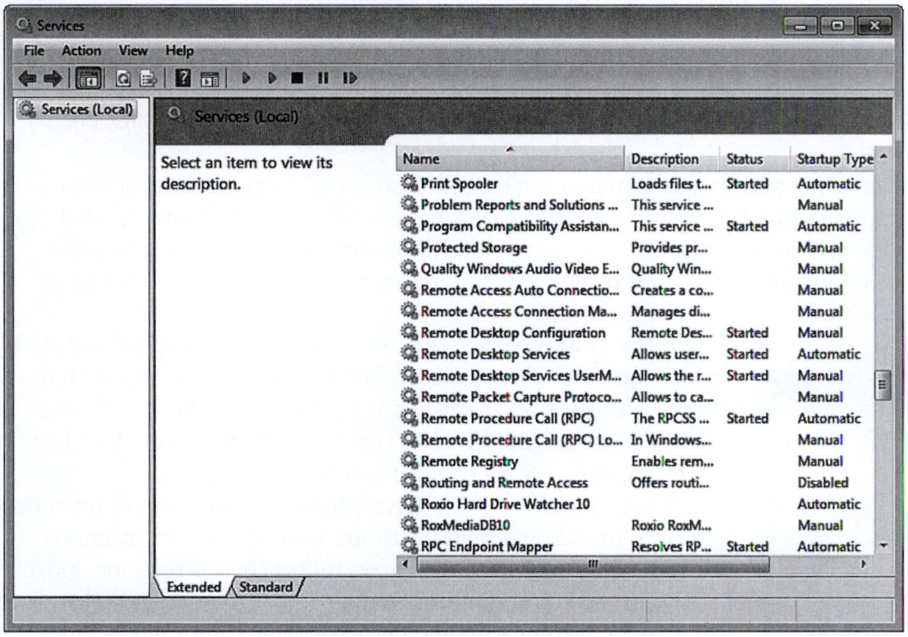

Figure 9.35 Print Spooler service

When not to use spooling

If you have less than 300MB of hard drive space, turn off spooling. Note that if a printer is shared, spooling must be enabled.

Tech Tip

Windows Printer Troubleshooting

The most common printing test is a test page from an application or from a specific printer's *Properties* or *Printer Properties* window, using the *General* tab. Remember that Windows uses a single print driver for all applications. Check the status lights on the front of the printer for any abnormal indications. Windows has a Troubleshooter tool. Access Windows XP's Troubleshooter tool by clicking *Start* > *Help and Support* > *Troubleshooter* in the *Search* window. You may have to click the *Full-text search* matches to see the *List of troubleshooters* option. Scroll down in the right pane to see and click *Printing*. For Vista/7, click the *Start* button > *Control Panel* > type `troubleshooting` in the search box > *Troubleshooting* > locate *Hardware and Sound* > *Use a printer*.

If the Troubleshooter tool does not help, run a self-test on your printer by following the manufacturer's directions. If the self-test works, the printer is usually fine, and the problem lies in the cable, port, software driver, or printer settings.

Tech Tip

Try printing from Notepad

If a printer self-test works, try printing from Notepad. Restart the computer and click the *Start* button. Click *Programs* or *All Programs* and then click *Accessories*. Click the *Notepad* option. Type a few characters and then *Print*. If the file prints, your problem may be a print problem that affects only one application, or the printer does not have enough memory for complex output, such as high-end graphics.

Free hard drive space is important for print spooling. Insufficient free space can cause print jobs to have problems. Even if there appears to be enough hard drive space to spool a printing job, the printer may still need more RAM installed to print a large or complex document.

A print spooler and/or associated services, such as RPC and HTTP, can cause problems and can be stopped or paused. Locate the specific PrintSpooler, RPC, or HTTP service used by the printer (open services by typing `services.msc`). Right-click on the service and select *Properties*. From the window that appears, you can start, stop, pause, or resume a service, as shown in Figure 9.36.

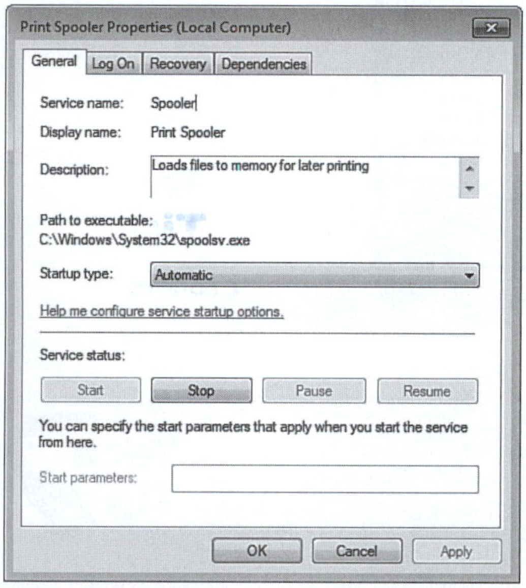

Figure 9.36 Managing the Print Spooler service

If the printer works, then the printer, port, and printer cable are all operational, and the problem is in the operating system. To see if the printer driver is the problem, use the *Add Printer Wizard* to install the Generic/Text Only printer driver. See Lab 9.1 at the end of this chapter for more information.

If you reload a printer driver, the old printer driver must be removed first. Some manufacturers have specific instructions for removing their drivers. Always follow their directions. Most of them say to do something similar to the following: Right-click the specific printer icon and click the *Delete* option. Click the *Yes* button when prompted if all the associated printer files are to be deleted. To re-install the printer, use the Add Printer wizard. Refer to Lab 9.1 at the end of this chapter, if necessary.

The print queue sometimes causes problems. A single document will be in the queue and not print for some reason. Depending on what rights the user has, sometimes a technician must clear the print queue. The following methods can be used:

- Open the *Printers and Faxes* (XP)/*Printers* (Vista)/*Devices and Printers* (7) Control Panel. Locate the printer icon, right-click, and select *Open*. Right-click the first document (the one that is causing the problem) and select *Cancel*. To cancel all print jobs, you can select *Cancel all documents* from the *Printer* menu option.
- If the print job has already gone to the printer and is no longer stored on the hard drive, you may not be able to use the first method. In this case, use the *Printer* menu or *Cancel* button to cancel the print job.
- Turn the printer off and back on again.

Note that if you get an access denied message, it means you must be logged on as an administrator to control the print queue.

General Printer Troubleshooting

The printing hardware subsystem consists of the printer, cable, and communications port. If something is wrong with the hardware, the problem is normally in one of these three areas. Always check the connections and the power between the areas. The printer has the highest failure rate of the three because it is a mechanical device with motors, plastic gears, and moving parts. If an error code or message appears on the front panel, refer to the manual or online documentation. Printers normally have a self-test routine. Refer to the printer's documentation to determine how to run the test. If a printer's self-test operates properly, the printer is operational. In this case, a remaining print problem has to do with the port, cable, or software.

> **Tech Tip**
>
> **The paper gets stuck**
>
> If a printer is having trouble feeding paper, you should look to see how far the paper went along the paper path before it jammed or could not go any farther. Many paper-feeding problems are due to poor paper quality or the inefficiency of the rubber rollers that move the paper along the paper path. Rubber rollers are normally found in the paper transport system on all printer types, and over time, the rollers become slick from use and do not work properly.

If a printer gives a "paper out" message, but paper is installed in the printer, then check the paper sensor. Sometimes this sensor is an optical sensor, and sometimes it is a plastic piece that flips out. Take the paper out and reinsert it. Ensure that there is no blockage and that the sensor is not sticking (not flipping out properly). Dust and debris can cause both blockage and sensor sticking.

Some printers have upgradable firmware. Just as a computer's flash BIOS can be upgraded, printers may need a firmware upgrade to correct specific problems. Printer firmware updates can normally be obtained from the printer manufacturer's website.

Another problem could be that the printer is not configured for the correct port. Check that the printer is configured for the proper port. Refer to the printer's documentation for specifics on how to configure the printer for a specific port.

> **Tech Tip**
>
> **What to do with slick printer rollers**
>
> Special cleaners such as Rubber Rejuvenator are available for rubber printer rollers that have a hard time picking up paper and sending it through the printer. Some printers have a special cleaning page for cleaning the rollers. Refer to the printer's manual for exact procedures. If a cleaner is unavailable, scrub the rollers with a wire brush or sandpaper to roughen them up a bit, which will enable them to pick up the paper better. If you do not have a wire brush or sandpaper, use the sharp edge of a paper clip to roughen up the rubber part of the roller so it can grip the paper. Vacuum up all debris before using the printer.

Connect a working printer to the port, install the proper print driver and verify the port works. If the printer uses the USB port, consult the following list of troubleshooting options:

- If the computer stops responding and the USB device is suspect, power the computer off and then back on again.
- The BIOS settings may have to be enabled for USB devices. Different BIOS manufacturers list the USB settings differently. The USB settings may be located under the heading *Enabling onboard USB* or within the PCI section. If you install a USB host adapter and the motherboard also supports USB ports, you may have to disable the motherboard ports through BIOS.
- Use Device Manager to check whether USB is listed. Look at the *Universal Serial Bus controllers* section. If USB is not listed, check the BIOS settings or update BIOS. If the USB device is listed, ensure that there are no resource conflicts.
- If there is a USB hub connected to the USB port, disconnect the hub and connect the USB printer directly to the USB port to see if the problem is the hub.
- With the computer's power on, disconnect the USB printer and reconnect it. Go into Device Manager and ensure that there is only one listing for the USB printer.

- Some USB devices have device drivers. Check the Internet for updated drivers.
- Disconnect the USB printer while the computer is powered on. Power down the computer. Then power on the computer. Insert the USB printer cable into the USB port. The system should automatically detect and install the printer.
- Verify that the USB device works by plugging it into another USB port or another computer's USB port.
- Check that the proper USB cable is being used. Remember that cables are not normally faulty, but they can be overtightened and undertightened. If you see garbled characters, check the cable and then the print driver.

A USB cable can be rated as SuperSpeed, Hi-Speed, or Low-Speed. The SuperSpeed and Hi-Speed cables have more shielding and can support higher speeds. If a SuperSpeed or Hi-Speed USB device attaches to a Low-Speed cable, the device operates at the lower speed. Make sure you have the proper USB cable for a printer that attaches to a USB port.

On the software side, troubleshooting involves narrowing down the problem to the print driver. Because Windows uses one print driver for all applications, check the printing from within several software packages. Use a simple text program such as Notepad to see if simple text will print. Printers need memory to print multiple pages of complex graphics. If a printer prints a couple pages and then stops, or if it prints half a page, ejects the paper, and then prints the other half of the page and ejects the paper, the printer's memory needs to be upgraded. If printing does not occur in all the software packages tested, the problem is most likely the software driver. See the earlier section for specific Windows printer troubleshooting tips.

Tech Tip

The paper could be the culprit

If a printer has trouble feeding paper, ensure that you're using the correct type of paper. One vendor says that 80 percent of all paper jams are due to inferior paper quality, poor paper condition such as damage due to humidity, or an operator-related problem such as the wrong paper size selected in the software program.

Impact Printer Troubleshooting

When technicians state that a printhead is not firing, this means that one or more of the printwires are not coming out of the printhead to impact the ribbon. A printhead that is not firing is evidenced by one or more white lines appearing where the printed dots should be. On a printed page, the white line appears horizontally in the middle of a line. The most likely problem is the printhead. However, be aware that the problem could be a bad driver transistor on the main circuit board or a loose cable that attaches to the printhead. But because the printhead is a mechanical part, it is the most suspect.

If the print is light and then dark, the printer ribbon may not be advancing properly. One of the shafts that insert into each end of the ribbon may not be turning, or the set of gears under the shaft may not mesh properly. Also, there is a motor that handles ribbon movement, and this motor may need replacement. A faulty ribbon can also cause the carriage to seize up. Remove the ribbon and power up the printer. If the carriage moves when the ribbon is removed, but it will not move when the ribbon is installed, replace the ribbon. Some printers have belts that move the printhead across the page. A worn, loose, or slipping belt can cause erratic printing.

If the printer prints continuously on the same line, be sure the setting for tractor-fed paper or friction-fed paper is correct. Or, the motor that controls paper movement may need replacement. If the printer moves the paper up a small bit after printing, the model may have the Auto Tear Off feature enabled. The Auto Tear Off feature is used with perforated forms needed in many businesses. See the printer's documentation to disable this feature.

Tech Tip

Light printing can be caused by several things

Adjust the printhead gap to place the printhead closer to the ribbon or replace the ribbon. Also, the platen could be misaligned with the bottom paper-feed rollers.

Inkjet Printer Troubleshooting

Inkjet printers frequently have a built-in printhead cleaning routine. Access the routine through the printer's buttons or through software. Most manufacturers recommend cleaning the inkjet cartridge only when there is a problem such as lines or dots missing from the printed output. Otherwise, cleaning the inkjet cartridge with this method wastes ink and shortens the print cartridge's life span.

Usually, inkjet manufacturers include an alignment program to align the dots more precisely. Use the alignment program when vertical lines or characters do not align properly. If the colors do not appear correctly, run the printer manufacturer-provided color calibration routine. Refer to the printer's documentation for troubleshooting programs, such as the printhead cleaning, calibration, and alignment routines.

Laser Printer Troubleshooting

Laser printers have more mechanical and electronic circuitry than the other printer types, which means there are more things that can go wrong. The following list contains some common symptoms and possible solutions:

- If black streaks appear on the paper or the print is not sharp, check the fuser cleaning pad for toner particles and use a small screwdriver to scrape off the excess particles before re-installing.
- If output appears darker in some spots than others, remove the toner cartridge. Gently rock the toner cartridge back and forth to redistribute the toner. If this does not fix the problem, turn down the toner density by using the *Printers* Control Panel or software provided by the printer manufacturer. Also, the paper could be too smooth.
- If printing appears light, adjust the darkness setting on the printer or through the printer's operating system settings. The toner cartridge could be low. Damp paper could also cause this symptom. Use fresh paper of the proper weight and finish. If the print appears consistently dark, adjust the darkness setting.
- If a horizontal line appears periodically throughout the printout, the problem is one of the rollers. Check all the rollers to see if one is dirty or gouged and needs to be replaced. The rollers in a laser printer are not all the same size; the distance between the lines is the circumference of the roller. This allows you to easily tell which rollers are definitely not the problem and which ones are likely candidates.
- When white vertical line(s) appear, the corona wires may have paper bits or something else stuck on them. It may also mean that something is caught in the developer unit (located in the cartridge). Replace the cartridge to see if this is the problem.
- If the opposite side of the printed page has smudges or appears dirty, the fuser could be faulty, the wrong type of paper could be being used, or the toner may be leaking.
- If creases appear in the paper or if you frequently get printer jams, check the paper path for labels or other debris.

Many laser printer problems involve the toner cartridge, which is a good thing because the cartridge is a part people normally have on hand. Various symptoms can occur because of the toner cartridge: ghost images, smearing, horizontal streaking, vertical streaking, faded printing, one vertical black line, one horizontal black line, a white streak on one side, a wavy image, and so on. One of the easiest things to do is to remove the toner cartridge, hold the cartridge in front of you with both hands, and rock the cartridge away from you and then back toward you. Re-insert the cartridge into the printer and test the printer.

Sometimes, the primary corona wire or the conditioning roller inside the toner cartridge needs to be cleaned. Clean the corona wires with the provided brush or with a cotton swab. Dampen the cotton swab with alcohol, if necessary. Clean the conditioning roller with a lint-free cloth, and dampen the cloth with alcohol, if necessary.

To prove whether a problem is in the toner cartridge or elsewhere in the printer, send any output to the printer. When the printer is through with the writing stage and before the toner fuses to the paper, open the laser printer cover and remove the paper. (Determining exactly when to open the cover may take several attempts.) If the paper is error-free, the problem is most likely in the transfer corona (or transfer roller) or fusing assembly.

Tech Tip

What if a printer needs more memory?

Alternatives to adding memory are to send fewer pages of the print job at a time, reduce the printer resolution, reduce the size of the graphics, or standardize the fonts (by not using as many font types, styles, or font sizes). Also ensure that there is ample free hard drive space.

Another common problem occurs when the laser printer does not have enough memory. One symptom of this is that when printing, the printer blinks as if it is accepting data. Then the printer quits blinking, and nothing appears or the printer prints only half the page. This could also be caused by insufficient hard drive space when spooling is enabled. Some printers give an error code if there is not enough memory.

Experience is the best teacher when it comes to printers. If you work on a couple impact models, a couple inkjet printers, and a couple laser printer models, you will see the majority of problems. Each type of printer has very few circuit boards to replace. Normally, the problems are in the moving parts or are software related.

Soft Skills—Work Ethics

Ethics is a set of morals by which you live or work. Employers want employees who possess a high ethical standards. This means they want people who are honest, trustworthy, and dependable. IT technicians are exposed to many personal things—passwords, private data, and visited Internet sites, just to name a few. Employers do not want to worry about their technicians taking things that belong to others, looking at data that does not relate to the computer problem at hand, and taking or giving away things from the office.

The best ruling factor in ethics is to always be professional. For example, if you are in a situation where someone asks you to give them another person's password, ask yourself whether divulging the information is professional. When opening a customer's documents and reading them, ask yourself whether you are being professional. If the answer is no, stop reading. If you are in a customer's office and accidentally see the person's password taped to a CD case, let him know that you have seen it, suggest that he not write down his passwords in a conspicuous place, and recommend that he change his passwords right away. One of the biggest assets an IT professional can have is his or her reputation. Being ethical at work goes a long way in establishing a good reputation.

Finally, every IT person can probably remember at least one instance when he or she was asked to do something unethical—charge for more time than was actually spent on a job, provide access to a room or an area where access is normally restricted, or grant privileges that others at the same level do not have. When put in such a situation, there are a few options: (1) Be polite and refuse, (2) adamantly refuse, or (3) report the person to a supervisor. Recommending what to do is difficult, but for most offenses, being polite and refusing is the best course of action and is the most professional. If a request is against corporate policy or could hurt others in the company, you need to report this to a company manager or security. Your own boss may be the best person to inform.

Chapter Summary

- Common video ports for monitors and computing devices include VGA, DVI, DisplayPort, and HDMI. Other types of video ports seen on adapters or projectors include Thunderbolt, S-video, component/RGB, and composite.
- CRT monitors are large and bulky. LCD monitors are thin.
- LCD monitors can use CCFL or LEDs for the backlight.
- Pixels on LCD monitors that do not illuminate are called dead pixels.
- LCD monitors are designed for a specific resolution, called the native resolution. The display should be configured for this resolution and not changed.
- With an LCD monitor, the viewable size is the true size of the display that can be seen.
- The aspect ratio is a monitor's ratio of width to height.
- The contrast ratio is a value that describes the difference in light intensity between the brightest white and the darkest black. The greater the difference between the two values, the more contrast the monitor can display.
- Use a specific key along with the Fn key to output a laptop display to an additional external display or for use instead of the internal display.
- Never apply liquid directly to a display.
- Video adapters commonly use AGP or PCIe slots and contain a GPU, fans/heat sinks for the GPU, and memory. Some motherboards/chipsets support installing two video adapters that work cooperatively. These adapters commonly require more power and a separate Molex (AGP) or 6-/8-pin (PCIe) power connector from the power supply.
- If you are not using the onboard video port for dual displays, disable the port in BIOS. Note that some adapters will not work when you disable the onboard port and that a BIOS may automatically disable the port.
- Video memory can be separate from motherboard RAM, can be shared system memory, or can be a combination of both. The amount of available memory affects the maximum resolution and the number and depth of colors that can be seen.
- A KVM switch can be used to allow multiple computers to use one display, mouse, and keyboard.
- A privacy screen can help protect information on a screen from those passing by the display.
- States commonly have rules about electronic device disposal.
- When a computer shows a blank screen, check power, power cables, and the surge protector/UPS. Try booting to Safe Mode.
- Four types of printers commonly seen in businesses are impact, inkjet, laser, and thermal printers. Laser and inkjet printers do high-quality printing. A laser printer's supplies cost more than other printers' supplies but last longer and work out to a lower cost per page.
- Printers can be shared using the operating system and a computer connected to a network. A printer can also have its own wired or wireless networking connectivity. With wired networking, the printer has a direct connection to the network. Wireless networking includes 802.11 and Bluetooth technologies. A hardware print server can be attached to a printer to allow sharing, too.
- Impact printers use printwires to impact a ribbon. Inkjet printers use pressure or heat to squirt ink dots onto paper. A laser printer works like a copying machine to produce output.
- The laser printer printing steps include processing and rasterizing the data followed by conditioning (charging), writing (exposing), developing, transferring, fusing, and cleaning.

- Impact printers can use normal-sized paper and fan-folded paper with pin holes that are fed by a tractor. Laser printers can have extra drawers for paper. A duplexing assembly option can be attached to allow a printer to print on both sides of the paper without intervention. Impact printers use special heat-sensitive paper.
- Print drivers must match the Windows version.
- A printer uses a print spooler or hard drive space that keeps data flowing to the printer in large print jobs. The print spooler can be stopped and started using the Services window (`services.msc`).
- A computer technician needs to show ethical work behavior around customers and peers.

Key Terms

accelerometer 383
artifact 404
aspect ratio 387
backlight 381
CCFL 381
charging 412
cleaning 413
component/RGB video 395
composite video 395
conditioning roller 412
contrast ratio 387
cps 408
CRT 381
default printer 422
density control blade 412
developing 412
developing cylinder 412
DLP 381
dpi 409
erase lamp 413
exposing 412
feed assembly 416
fuser cleaning pad 412
fusing 413
fusing roller 412
GPU 397
gyroscope 383
impact printer 407
inkjet printer 407
laser printer 407
LCD 381
LED 381
lumen 387
native resolution 387
OLED 381
pixel 381
plasma 381
print driver 424
print server 405
print spooler 424
printhead 407
printwire 407
privacy filter 397
processing 412
refresh rate 385
resolution 385
shared system memory 400
thermal printer 407
Thunderbolt 391
transfer corona 413
transferring 413
TV tuner card 398
video capture card 398
viewable size 387

Review Questions

Consider the following display as you answer Questions 1–6:

- 70,000:1 dynamic contrast ratio
- 16:9 widescreen offers distortion-free images at 1920×1080 (1080p) resolution. Made for multimedia and optimized for HD content
- 1 D-sub input (15 pin), 1 DVI input

1. What is the purpose of the contrast ratio?
    a. It is a ratio of a monitor's width to height.
    b. It allows a comparison of another monitor in regard to the difference in light intensity between the brightest white and the darkest black.
    c. It allows an expression of how much light the monitor can produce.
    d. The maximum angle that you can stand back and still view the screen and the images on the screen properly.

2. What value is the aspect ratio for this monitor?
   a. 70,000:1
   b. 16:9
   c. 1920×1080
   d. 1 D-sub input (15 pin), 1 DVI input
3. What is the purpose of the aspect ratio?
   a. It is a ratio of a monitor's width to height.
   b. It allows a comparison of another monitor in regards to the difference in light intensity between the brightest white and the darkest black.
   c. It allows an expression of how much light the monitor can produce.
   d. The maximum angle that you can stand back and still view the screen and the images on the screen properly.
4. What is the native resolution?
5. If someone changed the resolution on the monitor to 1680×1050, what would be the result when viewing the Windows desktop?

   [The icons would be smaller. | There would be no discernible difference. | The icons would be larger.]
6. Which video ports are on this monitor? (Select all that apply.)

   [DVI | HDMI | VGA | DisplayPort | S-video | composite | component]
7. A laptop display is not showing anything, but the technician can hear the hard drive working. The technician connects an external monitor and the monitor works. What should the technician try next?
   a. Replace the laptop display.
   b. Try connecting another external monitor.
   c. Replace the laptop display connector.
   d. Use the appropriate Fn key to retest the output to the display.
8. What is the purpose of a laptop inverter?
   a. to convert DC to AC for the CCFL backlight
   b. to attach the keypad to the keyboard
   c. to allow specific keys to be used as a numeric keypad when enabled
   d. to allow the display to be flipped backward
9. What video port supports transmission of both audio and video signals?

   [VGA | component | HDMI | DVI]
10. A technician installs a video card because the integrated video port does not work anymore. However, when the technician installs the card into the system, nothing outputs. What is the most likely problem?
    a. The monitor is bad.
    b. The cable is bad.
    c. The onboard port has not been disabled.
    d. The new video card is bad.

11. What method does a technician *normally* use to print a test page to prove that connectivity exists between the computer and the printer and to prove that the driver is working properly?
    a. Use a self-test button on the printer.
    b. Use Notepad and print.
    c. Use at least two applications and print.
    d. Use the Print Test Page button from the printer properties General tab.
12. Which type of printer would a glass blower who sells art at trade shows most likely use to print receipts? [impact | inkjet | thermal | laser]
13. What program is used to restart the print spooler in Windows?
    [Device Manager | Services | System Information | DirectX]
14. A Samsung laser printer is showing an error message on the screen that says that the paper is out, but the user shows you that there is plenty of paper in the bin. What should you do?
    a. Turn the printer off and back on again.
    b. Check the paper sensor for debris or dust.
    c. Use the reset sensor to reset the printer paper counter.
    d. Use the Print Test Page button from within Windows to verify connectivity.
15. Which type of printer would contain a fuser assembly?
    [impact | inkjet | laser | thermal]
16. [T | F] Use compressed air with a plastic nozzle to remove toner from a laser printer.
17. For what do you use a printer-duplexing assembly?
    a. two sided printing
    b. multiple paper trays
    c. wired and wireless network connectivity
    d. rasterization
18. What component could cause ghost images on laser printer output?
    [drum | fusing assembly | LED array/laser | pickup rollers | paper sensor]
19. A college president's administrative assistant calls to report that some pages of the board of trustees' 500-page document are printing only half a page. What is the problem, and what can the technician recommend to do to get the document printed?
    a. The print cartridge is defective. Replace the cartridge and reprint.
    b. The print cartridge has toner that is not evenly distributed. Remove the cartridge, gently shake it back and forth, reinstall the cartridge, and reprint.
    c. The printer does not have enough memory. Ask the user to print a smaller number of pages each time.
    d. The printer mainboard has issues. Use compressed air to remove dust and debris. Try to reprint. Order a replacement mainboard and use another printer if the printing fails again.
20. One of the technicians in your shop frequently swaps parts that do not fix the problem. The parts taken out of customer machines are taken to build private customer computers. This is an example of poor _____.
    [professionalism | work ethics | relations | troubleshooting skills]

Exercises

Lab 9.1 Exploring Video in Windows XP

Objective: To explore video properties using Windows XP

Parts: A computer with Windows XP installed

Procedure: Complete the following procedure and answer the accompanying questions.

1. Power on the computer and log on using the user ID and password provided by the instructor or lab assistant.
2. Click the *Start* button and click *Control Panel*.
3. If in Category View, click *Performance and Maintenance*. In both views, open *Administrative Tools* and double-click the *Computer Management* icon.
4. In the left window, click *Device Manager*. In the right window, expand the *Display Adapters* option.

   If the monitor flickers and redraws the screen incorrectly when a window is moved or resized, what three things are recommended?
5. Right-click a specific video adapter and select *Properties*.

   What bus does the video adapter use?

   Can the display adapter be disabled through the *General* tab? [Yes | No]
6. Click the *Driver* tab and click the *Driver Details* button.

   What video driver version is being used?

   List the driver files being used including the path.
7. Click the *OK* button.

   What three other things can be done through the *Driver* tab?
8. Click the *Resources* tab.

   List the memory addresses used by the video adapter.

   What IRQ does the video adapter use?
9. Click the *Cancel* button to return to Computer Management. Expand the *Monitors* option. Right-click a specific monitor and select *Properties*.

   What tabs are available in the monitor's *Properties* window?

   Can the monitor's refresh rate be changed with the monitor's *Properties* window? [Yes | No] If so, what tab is used? If not, what method is used to change the refresh rate?
10. Click the *Cancel* button. Close the *Computer Management* window.

Lab 9.2 Exploring Video in Windows 7

Objective: To explore video properties using Windows 7

Parts: A computer with Windows 7 installed

Procedure: Complete the following procedure and answer the accompanying questions.

1. Power on the computer and log into Windows 7.
2. Click the *Start* button and select *Control Panel*.

3. Open the *System and Security* Control Panel.
4. Access the *Device Manager* link located under the *System* category.

   Assuming that the monitor flickers and redraws the screen incorrectly when a window is moved or resized, what three things would you recommend based on what you learned in this chapter?

5. Right-click a specific video adapter and select *Properties*.

   What bus does the video adapter use?

   Can the adapter be disabled using the General tab? [Yes | No]
6. Click the *Driver* tab.

   What video driver version is being used?

   Can the display adapter be disabled using the *Driver* tab?
7. Click the *Driver Details* button.

   List at least two driver files being used, including the full path.

8. Click the *OK* button.

   List three other things that can be accomplished using the *Driver* tab.

9. Click the *Resources* tab.

   List at least two memory address ranges used by the video adapter.

   What IRQ does the video adapter use?

10. Click the *Cancel* button to return to Device Manager. Expand the *Monitors* category. Right-click a specific monitor and select *Properties*.

    What tabs are available in the *Properties* window?

    Can the monitor refresh rate be changed with the *Properties* window? [Yes | No] If so, what tab is used? If not, what method is used to change the refresh rate?

Instructor initials: _______________

11. Click the *Cancel* button. Close the *Device Manager* window. Close the *System* Control Panel window.

Lab 9.3 Configuring a Second Monitor Attached to the Same PC

Objective: To connect two monitors and configure XP/Vista

Parts: A computer with Windows XP/Vista loaded

Two video adapters with monitors attached *or* one video adapter that has two video ports with monitors attached

Note: One monitor should be installed, configured, and working before beginning this exercise.

Procedure: Complete the following procedure and answer the accompanying question.

1. Power on the computer and log on using the user ID and password provided by the instructor or lab assistant.
2. Enter *BIOS Setup* and verify whether an option exists to select the order video adapters initialize. Ensure the adapter that is currently installed initializes first. Save the settings.
3. Power off the computer, remove the power cord, and install the second video adapter, if necessary. Attach the second monitor to the video port on either the newly installed video adapter or the second video port on the original video adapter.
4. Power on the computer. If a new video adapter has been installed, Windows will prompt you for the appropriate driver. If this does not occur, manually add the adapter using the *Add Hardware* Control Panel.
5. Right-click an empty space on the desktop and select *Properties* (XP) or *Personalization* > *Display settings* link (Vista). Click the *Settings* tab. Two blue numbered boxes appear in the top section. If you arrange the boxes to be side by side, the monitor output will be spread across the two monitors from left to right. If you vertically arrange the boxes, the desktop will be shown on both screens from top to bottom. Windows supports up to 10 monitors in a single system.
6. Select the *Display* drop-down menu to select the individual monitor. Once selected, the resolution and quality can be adjusted. Ensure the *Extend my Windows desktop onto this monitor* checkbox is enabled. Click *Apply*. For some monitors, Windows may have to be restarted.

   List one instance where you think this technology would be useful.

Lab 9.4 Configuring a Second Monitor Attached to a Windows 7 PC

Objective: To connect two monitors and configure them using Windows 7

Parts: A computer with Windows 7 installed

Two video adapters with monitors attached *or* one video adapter with two video ports with monitors attached

Note: One monitor should be installed, configured, and working *before* beginning this exercise.

Procedure: Complete the following procedure and answer the accompanying questions.

1. Power on the computer and log into Windows 7.
2. Enter BIOS Setup and verify whether an option exists to select the order in which video adapters initialize (if two adapters are installed). Ensure that the currently installed adapter initializes first. Save the settings.

3. Power off the computer, remove the power cord, and install the second video adapter, if necessary. Attach the second monitor to the video port on either the newly installed video adapter or the second video port on the original video adapter.
4. Power on the computer. If a new video adapter has been installed, Windows will prompt you for the appropriate driver. If this does not occur, manually add the adapter, using the *Add Hardware* or *Hardware and Sound* Control Panel, or verify in Device Manager that Windows has installed a driver. Note that this function works best when the monitors use the same driver.
5. Access the *Display* Control Panel category found under *Hardware and Sound*. Select the *Change display settings* link. Two numbered boxes appear in the top section when the adapters are recognized by the operating system. (If two displays are not shown, redo Step 4.) If you arrange the boxes to be side by side, the monitor output will be spread across the two monitors from left to right. If you vertically arrange the boxes, the desktop will be shown on both screens from top to bottom. If necessary, you can drag the monitor icons so they are arranged in the same way as the monitors are located on the desk.
6. Use the *Identify* button to verify which monitor is the one designated with the number 1 and which monitor is designated with the number 2. The numbers appear on the monitors.

   Do two numbers appear? If not, redo Step 5.
7. Use the *Multiple displays* drop-down menu to select how the monitors are displayed: (1) *Extend your displays*—the most commonly used option, which spreads the desktop across the monitors. (2) *Duplicate your displays*—has the same image on both monitors. This is the default setting and is good when a laptop is being used to project or connect to a large external monitor. (3) *Show your desktop on only one monitor*—sometimes used on a laptop to keep the laptop screen blank while connecting to a large desktop monitor.

   What option did you choose?
8. Select the *Display* drop-down menu to select a particular monitor. Once this is selected, adjust the resolution and quality.
9. Click *Apply*. If needed, restart Windows.

Instructor initials: _______________

Lab 9.5 Determining the Amount of Video Memory

Objective: To determine how much memory should be installed on a video adapter, based on customer requirements

Parts: None

Questions: Answer the questions, using the situation given.

1. What is the minimum memory (512KB, 1MB, 2MB, 4MB, or 8MB) a video adapter needs if a user wants a 1024×768 resolution with 16 million colors available?
2. What is the minimum memory (512KB, 1MB, 2MB, 4MB, or 8MB) a video adapter needs if a user wants an 800×600 resolution with 65,536 colors available?
3. A video card has 128MB of memory and is a 32-bit color adapter. The user wants to display 16 million colors at a resolution of 1024×768 and plays games that have 3D graphics. Is the amount of installed memory on the video adapter adequate? Justify your answer.

4. A video card has 256MB of memory. The user complains that when watching video clips, the sound and video are sometimes choppy. Upon investigation, the technician determines that the total graphics memory is 1535MB, dedicated memory is 256MB, and shared system memory is 1279MB. What does this mean?

What would you recommend to this customer if you were the technician?

5. What is the minimum recommended memory for a video card purchased for a brand new system? Explain your answer.

Lab 9.6 Determining the Minimum Video Memory Installed

Objective: To understand how to calculate the amount of video memory based on the number of color bits and resolution settings

Parts: Windows XP/Vista computer

Procedure: Complete the following procedure and answer the accompanying questions.

1. Turn on the computer and verify that the operating system loads. Log in using the user ID and password provided by the instructor or lab assistant.
2. Right-click an empty Desktop space and select *Properties* > *Settings* tab (XP) or *Personalize* > *Display settings* link (Vista). The *Display Properties* window opens.
3. Answer the questions that follow. When finished, close any open windows.
4. Click the *Settings* tab.

Questions:

1. In the Colors section, what is the number of bits used for color?
2. How many colors can be displayed using the number found in Question 1?
3. What is the current resolution setting? (This number is listed as *x* by *x* pixels.)
4. Calculate the amount of memory required by multiplying the two numbers that make up the resolution. These numbers are your answer to Question 3. (For example, if the resolution is listed as 1024×768, the calculation would be 1024 × 768 = 786,432.)

   ____________ × ____________ = ____________

   horizontal bits　　vertical bits　　TOTAL 1
5. Take the result of Question 4 (TOTAL 1) and multiply by the number of color bits (the answer to Question 1). The result is the minimum amount of video memory installed *in bits*.

   ____________ × ____________ = ____________

   TOTAL 1　　color bits　　TOTAL 2
6. Take the result of Question 5 (TOTAL 2) and divide by eight to determine the minimum amount of video memory installed *in bytes*.

   ____________ ÷ ____________ = ____________

   TOTAL 2　　8　　video memory in bytes

Lab 9.7 Exploring Video Memory on a Windows 7 Computer

Objective: To understand how to calculate and view the amount of video memory

Parts: A computer with Windows 7 installed

Procedure: Complete the following procedure and answer the accompanying questions.

Note: This process depends on the video adapter manufacturer. You may need to modify the initial steps to find the details for the video memory.

1. Power on the computer and log into Windows 7.
2. The monitor properties and the video adapter properties are needed to answer the questions. A common way to access both is through Device Manager. Also, the *Display* Control Panel category can be used. You may need to select the *Advanced settings* link. Some video adapters have their own control panel.
3. Answer the questions that follow.
   a. How many bits are used for color? Note that if 30 bits are used, just use 24 bits as your calculation for this exercise. The extra bits are normally for color depth.

   b. How many colors can be displayed using the number found in the first question? Refer to the chapter if necessary.

   c. What is the current resolution? Note that this number is listed by *x* by *x* pixels.

   d. Calculate the amount of video memory required by multiplying the two numbers that make up the resolution. These numbers are the answers found in the second question. For example, if the resolution is listed as 1920×1080, the calculation would be 1920 × 1080 = 2,073,600. Write your total.

   ____________ × _____________ = _______________________

   Horizontal bits   Vertical bits   TOTAL 1

   e. Take the resulting total and multiply by the number of color bits (the total found in the first question.

   ____________________ × _____________ = ____________________

   TOTAL 1   No. of color bits   TOTAL 2

   f. Take the result of the previous step, TOTAL 2, and divide by eight to determine the minimum amount of video memory needed *in bytes*.

   _________________________÷ 8 = ____________________

   TOTAL 2 (video memory in bits)   TOTAL 3 (video memory in bytes)

   g. How much total available graphics memory is shown?

   h. Is any dedicated video memory used? If so, how much?

   i. Is any shared system memory used? If so, how much?
4. When finished, close any open windows.

Lab 9.8 Installing a Generic/Text Only Print Driver on a Windows XP Computer

Objective: To install a generic print driver on a Windows XP computer and examine printer properties

Parts: A computer with Windows XP installed

Notes: (1) A printer is not required to be attached to the computer for this lab to be executed; (2) in order to install a printer, you must log on as Administrator (or use a user ID that belongs to the Administrator's group) or a user ID that belongs to the Power Users' group (that has the specific permission to load/unload a device driver).

Procedure: Complete the following procedure and answer the accompanying questions.

1. Power on the computer and log on using the user ID and password provided by the instructor or lab assistant.

   Is a printer attached to the PC? If so, does it attach using the parallel port or the USB port?

2. Click the *Start* button > *Printers and Faxes* and the *Add a Printer* wizard appears > *Next* > disable (uncheck) the *Automatically detect and install my Plug and Play printer* radio button > *Next* > ensure the LPT1 port is chosen (no matter if a printer attaches to the PC already—you will not be printing from this print driver) > in the *Manufacturer* column, select *Generic* > in the *Printers* column, select *Generic/Text Only* > *Next* > in the *Printer name* textbox, type `Class Printer` > select *No* when asked if you want to use this printer as the default printer (unless there is no printer attached and the system forces you to select *Yes*) > *Next* > *Next* > *No* when you are asked *Do you want to print a test page* > *Finish*.

3. From the *Printers and Faxes* Control Panel, locate the *Class Printer*, right-click it, and select *Properties*.

   What tabs are available with the generic print driver?

   What button do you think would be useful to a technician when troubleshooting a printing problem?

4. Click the *Printing Preferences* button. Click the *Landscape* radio button.

   For what do you think this feature is used?

5. Select the *Paper/Quality* tab. Click the *Paper Source* drop-down menu.

   What options are available even with a generic print driver?

6. Select the *Advanced* button.

   List three paper size options.

7. Click *Cancel*; click *Cancel* again. Click the *Sharing* tab.

   What do you think is the purpose of the *Sharing* tab?

8. Click the *Ports* tab. Notice how LPT1 is checked. If you made a mistake during installation and selected the wrong port, you could change it here. Click the *USB* option and *Apply*.

9. Click the *Question Mark* button in the upper-right corner of the *Properties* window. Hold the mouse pointer over the *Enable printer spooling* option at the bottom of the *Ports* tab and click. A help window appears.

   What is the purpose of the *Enable printer pooling* based on the information shown in the help window?

10. Select the *Advanced* tab. Notice the spooling options in the middle of the window.

    What is the default print spooling option?

11. Select the *Printing Defaults* button. Through this option, you can select the default quality and orientation the printer uses to print. Users must change the settings if they want something other than this. Click *Cancel*. Click the *Separator Page* button.

    What is the purpose of a separator page?

12. Click *Cancel*. Click *OK*.
13. To rename the Class Printer driver, ensure that *Class Printer* is selected in the *Printers and Faxes* Control Panel. Select the *Rename this printer* link in the left panel. The *Class Printer* name highlights and is able to be renamed. Type `IT Group Printer`. Click in any blank space in the window.
14. To delete the IT Group Printer, ensure that IT Group Printer is selected in the *Printers and Faxes* Control Panel. Select the *Delete this printer* link in the left panel > *Yes*.

Lab 9.9 Installing a Local Printer on a Windows XP Computer

Objective: To install a local printer on a Windows XP computer

Parts: A computer with Windows XP installed and a printer physically attached to an LPT, COM, or USB port

Appropriate printer driver for XP

Notes: (1) Always refer to the printer installation guide for installing a new printer. Some printers have their own CD and installation wizard that installs the driver and software; (2) in order to install a printer, you must log on as an Administrator (or use a user ID that belongs to Administrators group) or a user ID that belongs to the Power Users group (that has the specific permission to load/unload a device driver).

Procedure: Complete the following procedure and answer the accompanying questions.

1. Power on the computer and log on using the user ID and password provided by the instructor or lab assistant.
2. Attach the printer cable to the correct computer port. Attach the power cord to the printer if necessary and insert the other end into a wall outlet. Power on the printer.
3. Windows normally detects a plug and play printer and may complete all the installation steps automatically.

   Did Windows XP automatically detect and install the printer? [Yes | No]

4. If the Found New Hardware wizard appears, select the *Install the software automatically (recommended)* option and click *Next*. Follow the installation instructions on the screen. Print a test document to ensure the printer works correctly.

   Did the printer print correctly? If not, follow the non-plug and play instructions. [Yes | No]

Lab 9.10 Exploring a Windows 7 Printer

Objective: To explore printer options available through Windows 7

Parts: A computer with Windows 7 installed and an installed printer

Procedure: Complete the following procedure and answer the accompanying questions.

Note: This process depends on the printer manufacturer. You may need to modify the initial steps to find the details for the specific printer.

1. Power on the computer and log into Windows 7.
2. Access the *Devices and Printers* Control Panel. Right-click on the installed printer and select *Printing Preferences*.

   What is the default print quality mode for this printer?

   Is this the most cost-efficient mode available? If not, what is?
3. Using various *Printer* Control Panel options, answer the following questions.
   a. List one instance in which a technician might use the *Pause Printing* option. If you do not know for sure, research the answer on the Internet.

   b. List the steps necessary to share this printer with other computers.

   c. When would a technician use the *Use Printer Offline* option? If you do not know for sure, research the answer on the Internet.

   d. List information that might be important for business documentation purposes.

   e. What information is provided for troubleshooting printing problems?

   f. To what port does the printer attach. Machine dependent
4. When finished, close any open windows.

Activities

Internet Discovery

Objective: To obtain specific information on the Internet regarding a computer or its associated parts

Parts: Computer with access to the Internet

Questions: Use the Internet to answer the following questions.

1. A customer has a home workstation. His teenager received the EA Need for Speed Most Wanted game as a present. The customer wants to buy a video card that will allow this game to run. Determine and document the minimum graphics card requirements. Then locate a video card to fulfill this need. Include the model and basic specifications of the card as part of your documentation.

2. What does Samsung state might happen to a 22-inch LED S22B310B monitor if a supersonic humidifier is used near this monitor? Write the answer and the URL where you found this information.

3. You have a suspect Toshiba Satellite P205 laptop display inverter. Find a replacement part. Write the cost and URL where you found the inverter.

4. Locate a website that has a video of how to replace a Toshiba Satellite display. Write the URL and a few sentences describing the helpfulness of the video and whether you would recommend this video to a student new to laptop upgrades. Use correct capitalization, punctuation, and grammar.

5. A customer has a broken USB inkjet printer that would cost more to repair than to replace. The customer is considering an Epson Artisan 730 all-in-one-printer as a replacement. The customer would also like to have wireless connectivity as a future connectivity option. Will this printer meet the customer's needs? Explain your answer and write the URL where the information was found.

6. What is the latest print driver version for a Cannon PIXMA MG3120 printer if the customer has 64-bit Windows 7 installed? Note that you just want to reload the printer driver. Write the version number and the URL where you found the information.

7. A customer has a Lexmark E460 laser printer connected to a computer that has just been upgraded to 32-bit Windows 7. Does Lexmark provide a Windows 7–capable printer driver for this printer? Write the answer and the URL where you found the solution.

8. How do you reset the HP LaserJet P2035 to factory default settings? Write the answer and list the URL where you found the answer.

Soft Skills

Objective: To enhance and fine-tune a technician's ability to listen, communicate in both written and oral form, and support people who use computers in a professional manner

Activities:

1. Access a monitor setup menu. Make a list of some of the settings that would be helpful to a computer user. Include in your list a description of the function. Document this in such a way that it could be given to users as a how-to guide.

2. Write a paragraph describing someone with a negative attitude, including explanations of how the person exhibited the negative traits. Then write a paragraph that details how the person with the negative attitude could have done things in a more positive way. Share your findings with an assigned group.

3. The class is divided into seven groups. Each group is assigned a laser printing process. The group has 20 minutes to research the process. At the end of 20 minutes, each team explains the process to the rest of the class.

4. Pretend you have a job as a computer technician. You just solved a printer problem. Using good written communication skills, document the problem as well as the solution in a professional format. Exchange your problem/solution with a classmate and critique each other's writings. Based on their suggestions and your own background, refine your documentation. Share your documentation with the rest of the class.

Critical Thinking Skills

Objective: To analyze and evaluate information as well as apply learned information to new or different situations

Activities:

1. A person wants to build a computer and needs help with the video system. Using materials or magazines provided by the instructor or Internet research, recommend the PC video system, keeping in mind that the customer has a motherboard with PCIe slots; uses word processing, spreadsheets, and web browsing; and has a budget of $500 for these components.
2. A person wants to build a computer and needs help with the video system. Using materials or magazines provided by the instructor or Internet research, recommend the PC video system, keeping in mind that the customer has a motherboard with an AGP slot, plays a lot of computer-based games, and does not have a particular budget for components.
3. Two networked PCs and a printer are needed for this activity. Connect a printer to a PC. Install the printer, configure the default settings to something different from the current settings, share the printer, and print from another PC that connects to the same network.
4. Interview a technician regarding a printing problem. List the steps that technician took and make notes about how he or she might have done the steps differently, based on what you have learned. Share the experience with the class.

A+ Certification Exam Tips

- ✓ Study the differences between CRT and LCD monitors.
- ✓ Know the difference between using CCFL or LEDs in an LCD monitor.
- ✓ Know how a laptop display connects to the rest of the laptop.
- ✓ Know that there is commonly a cable that connects from the inverter/backlight to the top of the laptop display.
- ✓ Be able to describe how to connect an external monitor to a laptop, and make adjustments for various combinations of laptop only, external monitor only, and laptop along with the external monitor. Also know how power options might need to be adjusted.
- ✓ Be able to configure monitor properties including resolution, refresh rate, native resolution, and power settings.
- ✓ Be able to describe the purpose of an accelerometer and gyroscope.
- ✓ Study the video slots, ports, and cables. Know the particulars.
- ✓ Know how impact (dot matrix), inkjet, laser, and thermal printers work.
- ✓ Be able to configure printer options, including paper trays.
- ✓ Know how to review and control the print driver and print spooler.
- ✓ Know the ports on a projector and how lumens influence where a projector might be used.
- ✓ Review all the troubleshooting sections before taking the CompTIA 220-802 exam.

chapter 10

Computer Design

Chapter Objectives:

In this chapter you will learn:

- To select computer components based on the customer's needs
- The components best suited for a particular computing environment
- How to design for specific computer subsystems, such as the video or storage subsystem

CompTIA Exam Objectives:

What CompTIA A+ exam objectives are covered in this chapter?

- ✓ 801-1.9 Evaluate and select appropriate components for a custom configuration, to meet customer specifications or needs.
- ✓ 801-5.2 Explain environmental impacts and the purpose of environmental controls.
- ✓ 801-5.3 Given a scenario, demonstrate proper communication and professionalism.

Design Overview

Why would employers want technicians to be able to design computers? If you needed a car repaired, wouldn't it be nice to have a person who could design cars to advise you? They would know the best engines, the most fuel-efficient body design, what parts might not work well with other parts, and so on. They would know a lot about all parts of the car. The same is true about those who can design computers: They know a lot about computer parts and how those parts interact with one another.

When you first learn about computers, you learn the language, or lingo. You learn terms like RAM and CPU. Later, when you hear such words, you form images in your mind. You do more than just recognize the words; you actually know what different parts look like. Then you can explain what a part does to someone else. You continue to grow in a particular area. Designing something is right up there with troubleshooting something well. It involves knowing what you are talking about.

Benjamin Bloom chaired a committee that created a classification of learning objectives that was named Bloom's Taxonomy. Look at Figure 10.1 to see how people normally progress through the learning process. Notice that creating is at the very top. Of course, employers want people who can design...that's the folks who know all the things that it takes to be able to design.

Figure 10.1 Bloom's Taxonomy

This chapter helps you learn how to select components within subsystems such as video or audio as well as for complete computer builds based on the type of customer and the customer's needs. Even if you are designing just a subset of a computer, such as the video subsystem or an optical drive subsystem, you must know how that subset interacts with other components that might need to be upgraded as well. Be sure to check out the exercises at the end of the chapter that help put all this together. Practice is one of the best teachers.

Computer System Design

Different types of computer users need different types of computer systems. Table 10.1 shows common types of computers that are needed for specific uses.

Table 10.1 Computer system configurations

Use	Special hardware components
Graphics/CAD/CAM	Very powerful and multiple cores in the processor (or multiple processors) Maximum system RAM Very precise high-end video card(s) with maximum video RAM and GPU Large display or dual displays Large-capacity hard drive(s) as well as an SSD Possible digital tablet and/or scanner Quality mouse
Gaming PC (for video-intensive games)	Very powerful and multiple cores in the processor (or multiple processors) Very high-end video cards (with maximum video RAM and GPU that can share resources) High amount of RAM Quality sound card and speakers High-end system cooling Large display or dual displays Quality mouse Possible gaming console Headphones with microphone Possible 3D glasses (if supported by the video card and monitor)
Audio/video editing PC	Multiple powerful multi-core processors (or multiple processors) Maximum system RAM Specialized video card with maximum video RAM and GPU Specialized sound card and speakers Very fast and large-capacity hard drive Dual displays Quality mouse Possible digital tablet Possible scanner
Virtualization PC	Multiple powerful processors (maximum CPU cores) that support virtualization Maximum RAM Multiple fast large-capacity hard drives and SSDs 1000Mbps (1Gbps) NIC Possible **NAS** (network-attached storage) for increased storage space that can be shared with other devices
On the road	Laptop, netbook, ultrabook, or tablet Good amount of RAM Possible projector Possible SSD (if jarring or dropping due to handling is a concern or if high speed is needed) Smartphone Possible thermal printer for sales-oriented tasks Possible portable speakers and headphones with noise cancellation

Use	Special hardware components
HTPC (home theater PC)	Computer with compact form factor case and motherboard with quiet fans and quiet power supply fan Surround-sound audio ports HDMI video output **AV hard drive** (audio/video hard drive [AVHD]) that is quiet **Media player** to stream entertainment, watch videos and view photos, or listen to music Possible wireless connectivity **DVR** (digital video recorder) to record TV shows, transfer data from a camcorder or camera, or store movies or media for playback TV tuner card or cable card to receive pay channels Large display with multiple HDMI, USB, component, composite, and so on audio/video ports and possible wireless connectivity May have a Linux-based operating system Optional gaming device
Home server (computer used to store data, function as a web server, function as a print server, be accessible from outside the home, control devices, and/or manage backups)	Medium to large case Multiple processors or multiple cores in the processor Lots of RAM Multiple hard drives in a RAID configuration 1000Mbps (1Gbps) NIC Server applications, including media streaming, file sharing, and print sharing Possible NAS Possible KVM switch
Industrial computer	Meets recommended hardware requirements based on applications installed Optional enclosure for wet, dry, or outdoor environments Optional enclosure for a laptop's external keyboard and mouse for unsecure or outdoor environments Optional LCD enclosure for harsh, outdoor, public, high-traffic, or industrial environments Optional privacy display screen Case with air filters that may be removable for cleaning
Thick client (the most common type of computer in the work environment)/standard user	Meets recommended requirements for running Windows and desktop applications Optional privacy display screen for work environments
Thin client (a computer that normally has a display, mouse, keyboard, and network connectivity; runs applications from a server)	Meets recommended requirements for running Windows and basic applications 100Mbps minimum/1Gbps preferred network connectivity Optional privacy display screen for work environments

When you are planning to design an entire computer system, looking at what the user will be doing with the computer is important. Keep in mind that there are many ways to go green and conserve energy in your computer design. The company requesting the design may require green specifications. Cases, motherboards, processors, power supplies, printers, displays, and other computing devices can be designed with energy conservation in mine. The **EPEAT rating system** was designed to work with the EPA in identifying products that have a green (and clean) design. **ENERGY STAR** is another program that has strict energy efficiency standards that a product must meet in order to be ENERGY STAR compliant. Products that earn the ENERGY STAR rating today have low total energy requirements, low power modes, and efficient power supplies.

You can also be conscientious of energy requirements when designing a subsystem. Many times the request for an upgrade will not be for the entire computer, but for a subsystem of the computer. In such a case, the best practice is to look at the subsystem as a unit. The following sections look at the computer subsystems.

Motherboard and Associated Component Design

The motherboard, chipset, and CPU are all directly related to one another and should be designed in conjunction with one another. Using a motherboard that has the Ivy Bridge chipset, for example, gives you up to four USB 3.0 ports, a built-in GPU, or a PCIe v3.0 video card expansion slot. You might consider the AMD 990FX chipset, but you won't get a PCIe v3.0 slot from it (unless there is an upgrade after this book goes to press). Some technicians choose a motherboard based on a specific chipset. Why? Because there might be issues with a specific chipset, but the customer might still need high-end video or USB version 3.0 ports. There might be only one chipset that gives you two PCIe v3.0 slots for bridging video cards or a high number of USB 3.0 ports. In any case, this is something to consider.

Choosing a processor involves selecting Intel or AMD, determining how many processors you want, and selecting a specific model. Throughout the years, both manufacturers tend to have had a low-end model for cheaper, less powerful computers, a midrange processor that gives pretty good bang for the buck (price), and very powerful processors. Don't forget CPU cooling, either. If you select one of the high-end CPUs, you must have appropriate cooling for it.

When comparing processors, you might also want to consider the nanotechnology used. Processor technology length is measured in **nanometers**. A nanometer is .000000001 in length (1×10^{-9}). Processors and chipsets created using the 22nm technology can have more transistors in the same amount of space as the processors/chipsets created using the 32nm or 45nm technology. Traditionally, the smaller the technology, the lower the heat produced. With heat lowered, some components can be made to go faster, but that is not always the case.

Memory ties into processor technology because the type of motherboard/chipset you have will dictate the type of memory supported, the maximum amount of memory the motherboard manufacturer might consider putting on the motherboard, and the maximum memory speed that can be used. Whenever a technician is upgrading or replacing a motherboard, compatibility with existing components or the new ones is a must.

The most important design consideration for memory is to take advantage of dual-, triple-, and quad-channeling when possible. Ensure that the DIMMs are purchased together and installed according to the recommendations set forth in the motherboard/computer manual. Encourage the end user to buy as much RAM as he or she can initially afford. This one area is one of the most influential considerations on the user computing experience. Beef up this subsystem component as much as possible. Figure 10.2 shows a replacement motherboard, with RAM and processor.

Figure 10.2 Motherboard components affected by design

When dealing with the motherboard, consider the following:

- Motherboard form factor
- Chipset
- Whether the CPU is included or needs to be purchased separately
- CPU size
- Motherboard socket size
- Nanotechnology used with the processor and/or chipset (22nm, 32nm, 45nm, etc.)
- CPU cooling
- RAM
- Number and type of I/O (input/output) ports
- Traditional BIOS or UEFI (replacement for traditional BIOS)

Power Supply and Case Design

When selecting a power supply, it is all about the size (form factor), total wattage for specific voltage levels, number of connectors, and power efficiency. One issue you must consider is how many connectors connect to the same cable. When you have several high-powered devices, you want to be able to connect them with separate power cables, if possible, instead of using two connectors along the same cable. Also, be careful with cables that do not have at least four wires. These are peripheral cables to power 12-volt fans and are normally labeled as fan connectors. Some power supplies have detachable cables that connect between a power supply connector and a device connector. You attach the number and type of cables you need. Buy additional cables of a specific type, as needed. Figure 10.3 shows detachable cables.

Figure 10.3 Detachable cables for some power supplies

When replacing, upgrading, or purchasing a power supply, consider the following:

- Enough power cables for video cards
- Number and type of power cables (SATA, Molex, PCIe, fan)
- Form factor
- Wattage for the 12-volt line
- Total wattage—use an online power-use calculator
- Quietness
- MTBF (mean time between failures)
- Overvoltage, overcurrent, undervoltage, and short-circuit protection
- Warranty

Keep in mind that the power supply and the case (and the motherboard, too) have to be the same form factor. Some cases accept multiple motherboard form factors. Cases may or may not include the fans that go with the cases. Most cases have at least two locations for fans—one at the front of the case and one at the rear. Fans tend to come in 40, 60, 80, 90, 92, 120, or 140mm sizes. Look for the following key features in a new case:

- Size (ATX, micro-ATX, BTX, ITX, mini-ITX, etc.), type (desktop or tower), and physical dimensions
- Number and type of front panel ports
- Number and placement of fans
- Cable management
- Number of expansion slots (need to match or come close to how many are on the motherboard)
- Number and type of accessible drive bays including internal or external
- Outside texture and design (metal, aluminum, plastic, acrylic, see-through)
- Ease of cover removal
- Method of securing expansion cards (screw, plastic tab, single plastic bar)
- Ability to lock case panels to deter entry

Table 10.2 lists recommendations for cases/power supplies for the different types of users.

Table 10.2 Power supply and case design

Use	Design considerations
Graphic/CAD/CAM, gaming PC, home server, audio/video editing computer, or virtualization computer	500W or higher power supply ATX mid- or full-sized tower Two or more case cooling fans
Home theater PC (HTPC) or media center or thin client	300W or higher power supply ATX mini- or micro-sized tower
Thick client or normal user	300W or higher power supply ATX mini-, micro-, or mid-sized tower

Figure 10.4 PC case with removable internal hard drive trays

Air filters can be cheaply purchased for intake openings (not exhaust) to filter dirt and dust. It is important that you know the direction air is flowing through a system before installing. Some cases come with removable air filters that can be cleaned thoroughly. Some power supplies have air filters installed. Air filters, external storage device enclosures, and special computer and laptop enclosures can help protect against airborne particles that can harm the computer or device.

Figure 10.4 shows a computer case that has removable drives for internal hard drives. Note that even though SATA drives are hot swappable (you can remove them while power is applied), your SATA controller (motherboard) must support this feature, the drive must support it, a SATA power connector must be used, and the drive cannot be in use or used to boot the operating system. For best results, power down the computer before removing an internal SATA drive just to be safe.

Storage Subsystem Design

The storage subsystem consists of magnetic or flash technologies for internal or external hard drives, flash storage (including SSDs), or optical drives. Some of these devices are shown in Figure 10.5.

Figure 10.5 Assorted storage devices

When adding, replacing, or building a storage subsystem, you must take into account the customer needs, how long the customer plans on storing the data, and how long the customer thinks the storage subsystem will be in use before being upgraded or replaced. Table 10.3 helps with the storage device options.

Table 10.3 Storage subsystem design considerations

Feature	Design considerations
Internal connectivity	PATA or SATA
Internal power	Molex or SATA power connector
Internal physical size	2.5, 3.5, or 5.25 inches and must have an available expansion slot in the case
External connectivity	USB, IEEE 1394 (FireWire), eSATA, eSATAp port A NIC may be required for cloud (Internet) storage May need a media reader for flash media
External power	Provided by the USB, IEEE 1394, or eSATAp port; otherwise, external power must be used
Storage technology	Magnetic (hard drive or optical drive; SATA1.5, 3, or 6Gbps (SATA1, SATA2, or SATA3) or flash memory (SSD, flash drives, and flash media)
Special storage considerations	RAID requires multiple drives NAS to share storage with other computers
Hard drive speed	5400, 5900, 7200, 10000, or 15000 RPM for magnetic drives Transfer rate for SSDs **IOPS** (input/output operations per second) for both magnetic drives and SSDs, which is a measurement that takes into account sequential reads/writes as well as random reads/writes.
Optical drive capability	Read-only or read/write

Feature	Design considerations
Optical drive technology	Red-violet and/or blue laser(s)
Drive buffers	Both hard and optical drives can have buffers that can increase data transfer rates
PATA considerations	PATA devices must be designed for balanced use of master and slave devices
External considerations	What other devices may share the port External cages/enclosures can be purchased to turn an internal device into an external device

Audio Subsystem Design

The audio design consists of the audio ports and speakers. When upgrading or building, let the customer listen to the speakers, if possible. Table 10.4 lists audio design considerations.

Table 10.4 Audio subsystem design considerations

Feature	Design considerations
Number of speakers	Two for a casual user or gamer Three to seven for a music, video, or gaming enthusiast A 5.1 surround sound system commonly has a center channel speaker, two front channel speakers for left/right audio, two rear channel speakers for left/right audio, and a subwoofer for low frequency (bass) sound effects. A 7.1 surround sound system has the same speakers as 5.1, with an additional two center channel speakers for left/right audio.
Microphone	Integrated into the display, headset, or external Headset is best for conference calls
2.0 or 2.1	A 2.0 audio subsystem has two channels (left and right), with the amplifier within one of the two speakers A 2.1 audio subsystem has two speakers and a subwoofer for the lower-frequency sounds
Port connectivity	3.5mm mini-plug, S/PDIF TOSLINK, S/PDIF fiber, or wireless
Sound card	PCI, PCIe, or integrated into the motherboard Number of type of ports need to match speaker connectivity
Cabling	Avoid trip hazards Shelving, wall plates, wall inserts, wall hangers Speaker location planning

Figure 10.6 shows the type of audio design you might see in a home theater.

Figure 10.6 Home theater audio placement

Display Subsystem Design

Displays are very important to the computing experience. With replacing, upgrading, and installing, display design specifications are important. Table 10.5 shows some design considerations for displays.

Table 10.5 Display subsystem design considerations

Feature	Design considerations
Size/aspect ratio	Physical location, space available, and cost are normally the dictating features
Number of displays	Two displays or a single widescreen display is popular in home and work environments
Type of display	Plasma, LCD with CCFL backlight, LCD with LED backlight (LED), or OLED Touch screen
Display conferencing features	Integrated microphone or webcam
Contrast ratio	Higher number is better (but not all vendors give true numbers)

Feature	Design considerations
Video adapter	Slot type Number and type of ports Number of cards and support for sharing of resources (SLI and CrossFire, for example) RAM GPU Power and cooling requirements Power connectivity requirements

Mobility Design

Today's computing environment has lots of mobile devices. Mobile devices are critical to a design solution. Mobile devices will most likely be in addition to more stationary devices, such as workstations, printers, and scanners. Laptops, netbooks, and ultrabooks frequently have external peripherals, and very few internal parts except for the memory and the SSD can be upgraded. Tablets and smartphones have few or no internal upgradable components. Table 10.6 compares desktop and laptop components. Table 10.7 compares different mobile devices. Keep in mind that these components are constantly being upgraded, and new processors and memory speeds, for example, may be available in different models.

Table 10.6 Desktop and laptop component comparison

Component	Desktop	Laptop
Processor	LGA 775, 1155, 1156, 1366, and 2011; Socket AM2, AM3, AM3+, FM1, and F	Mobile processors that are either surface mounted or socketed
Memory	DDR3 DIMMs 1066, 1333, 1600, 1866, 2200, 2400, 2600, 2666, or 2800	DDR3 SO-DIMMs 1066, 1333, 1600, 1866
Power supply	ATX, mini-ATX, micro-ATX, ITX, or proprietary	Proprietary
Network	10/100 or 10/100/1000Mbps port	10/100 or 10/100/1000Mbps port
802.11 wireless	May be installed	Normally included
Bluetooth wireless	May be installed	May be installed
Optical drive	PATA, SATA 3Gbps, or SATA 6Gbps CD/DVD RW and/or Blu-ray	SATA 1.5, 3, or 6Gbps CD/DVD RW and/or Blu-ray
Hard drive	Internal 2.5- or 3.5-inch SATA 3Gbps or 6Gbps running at 5400, 5900, or 7200 RPM or an SSD	Internal 2.5-inch SATA 1.5, 3, or 6Gbps running at 5400, 5900, or 7200 RPM or an SSD
Keyboard	Wired or wireless	Integrated
Mouse	Wired or wireless	Integrated touchpad/touchstick

Table 10.7 Mobile device design

Mobile device	Common features
Laptop	Requires higher-than-normal RAM and video, if used for gaming Normally has the most powerful processor, RAM, and storage capability of mobile devices Possible touch screen
Netbook	No optical drive Might not be able to upgrade RAM Low weight Low cost Possible touch screen
Tablet PC	Touch screen Android, Apple iOS, or Google Chrome, proprietary operating system Little, if any, port connectivity Integrated camera Integrated microphone
Smartphone	Android, Apple iOS, or proprietary operating system Upgradable flash media Touch screen Integrated camera Integrated microphone

If you can design computer subsystems or an entire computer, you know a lot about the pieces that go into a computer and how they interact. Practicing with different scenarios can help, and there are exercises at the end of the chapter to help you build this skill. You won't believe how much you will learn by looking at component specifications. Start reading computer component specifications when you shop to increase your knowledge.

Soft Skills—Dealing with Irate Customers

One of the most difficult tasks a technician faces is dealing with people who are angry, upset, or frustrated. This is a common issue for those who come to help or try to troubleshoot a problem over the phone. Dealing with irate customers is a skill that you can fine-tune. Listening to peer technicians tell how they have successfully (or unsuccessfully) dealt with a difficult customer can also help. Realize that not only do customers want their computer problems fixed, they sometimes just need to vent and be heard. Because a technician is the person with the knowledge for at least the start of the resolution and the technician is in front of or on the phone with the person who is not able to do something on the computer, the technician is the common scapegoat and must try to listen to the irritated customer.

Some key tips for dealing with difficult customers are shown in Figure 10.7.

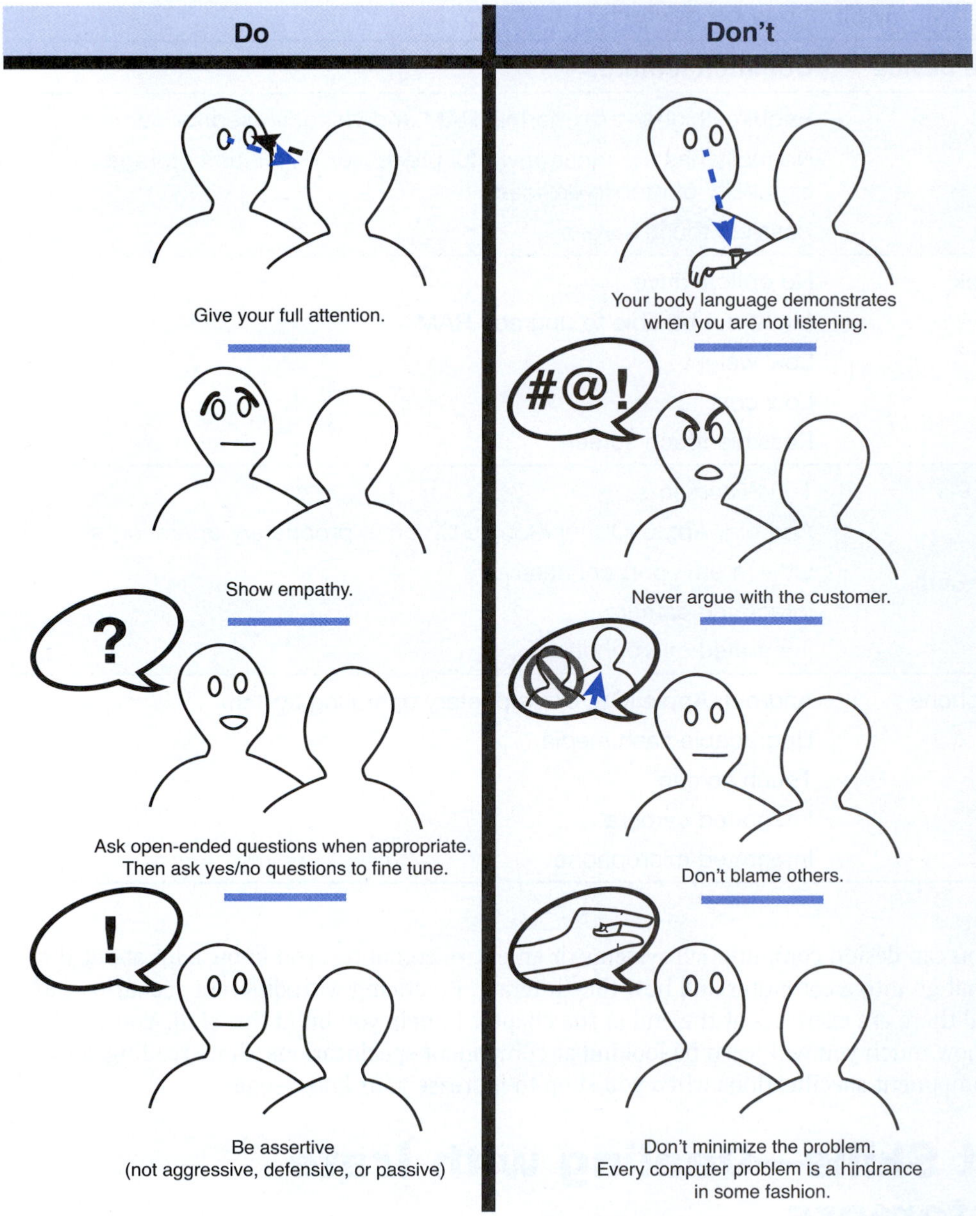

Do
Don't
Give your full attention.
Your body language demonstrates when you are not listening.
Show empathy.
#@!
Never argue with the customer.
?
Ask open-ended questions when appropriate. Then ask yes/no questions to fine tune.
Don't blame others.
!
Be assertive (not aggressive, defensive, or passive)
Don't minimize the problem. Every computer problem is a hindrance in some fashion.

Figure 10.7 Dealing with irate customers

The last suggestion in Figure 10.7 about being assertive is one that many people do not understand. Aggression involves dominating a conversation or situation by threatening, bullying, being sarcastic, or showing belittling behavior and/or actions. Some technicians consistently demonstrate aggressive behavior. This reflects poorly on the technician and the company that the technician represents. Passive behavior involves letting others dominate you and expressing yourself apologetically. Technicians who are passive frequently apologize while the customer is trying to explain the problem. Assertive behavior involves being respectful of another person but not allowing him or her to take advantage or dominate the situation. This is the middle ground you want to strive for when dealing with customers.

When dealing with an irate customer, you want to stay calm and maintain your professionalism. Once the customer has calmed down a bit, more information about the problem can be gleaned with less anger mixed into the conversation. Dealing with angry customers is just as much a part of a technician's job as it is with anyone else who works in a service industry. Consider customers' points of view and never forget that they are the ones who must use the devices that you repair.

Chapter Summary

- A graphic/CAD/CAM computer needs multiple powerful multi-core processors, maximum RAM, a high-end video card with maximum RAM and GPU, a large display/multiple displays, a large-capacity hard drive(s), SSD, and a good input device(s).
- A gaming PC needs a multi-core processor, a large amount of RAM, a sound card and speakers, additional system cooling, a large display and/or multiple displays, and good input/output devices.
- An audio/video editing PC needs multiple powerful multi-core processors, maximum RAM, a good video card with maximum RAM and GPU, a sound card, a fast and large-capacity hard drive, dual displays, and a good input device(s).
- A virtualization computer needs multiple powerful multi-core processors, maximum RAM, multiple fast hard drives, an SSD, and a 1Gbps NIC.
- A mobile computer is commonly a laptop with lots of RAM and an SSD, mobile tablet, smartphone, and possible devices such as a projector, thermal printer, portable speakers, or headphones with noise cancellation.
- An HTPC has a small form factor with quiet internal devices, a surround sound card, a TV tuner or cable card, and HDMI video output.
- A home server has a medium to large case, multiple powerful multi-core processors, lots of RAM, RAID, server applications such as media streaming, file sharing, print sharing, and a 1Gbps NIC.
- Processors and chipsets are created using a specific nanotechnology. Common technologies used are 22, 32, and 45nm. The smaller the number, the less space for the same number of transistors.
- When designing a motherboard, the CPU size and motherboard CPU socket must match.
- The power supply, motherboard, and case form factors must match.
- Power supplies must have the correct amount of wattage, wattage for a specific power level, and an appropriate number/type of power cables.
- Air filters and enclosures can help in environments where airborne particles are a concern.
- When designing for internal devices, use PATA or SATA and have the correct power connector. Ensure that an internal connector is available.
- When designing for external connectivity, ensure that a USB, eSATA, eSATAp, or IEEE 1394 port is available; ensure that enough power is provided to power the device through the port or use an external power supply; and ensure that not too many devices share the same cable, which can affect performance.
- For audio, ensure that the correct number and type of input/output ports are available.
- For common usage, the 2.0 two channel audio subsystem is used. A 2.1 audio subsystem adds a subwoofer as a third output device for lower frequencies.
- Display design should include physical space consideration, type of display, features that might be integrated into the display such as a microphone or camera, a video port, and memory/GPU/additional power requirements.
- Mobile designs include all the same major components as a desktop system plus 802.11 and Bluetooth wireless capabilities as well as integrated input devices such as a keyboard and touchpad.

Key Terms

Review Questions

1. What technology would allow someone to store data from multiple computers and possibly access the data by using the Internet? [HTPC | nanometer | DVR | NAS]
2. Which technology is most likely to be used in a home theater configuration? [KVM switch | nanometer | DVR | RAID]
3. List three design recommendations for a home server.
4. List one advantage of using detachable cables on a power supply.
5. Which of the following would most likely be a design consideration for a gaming PC rather than a computer used for virtualization?
   a. high amount of RAM
   b. NAS
   c. multiple fast, large-capacity hard drives
   d. additional system cooling
6. In what computer design environment would an air filter most likely be required? [industrial | gaming | home theater | virtualization | mobile | home server]
7. In which computer design environment would an external SATA drive most likely be required? [industrial | gaming | home theater | virtualization | mobile | home server]

8–10. Group the following computer components into three design subsystems. In other words, group the components that need to be considered together when designing a subsection of a computer. Each group must include at least two components. All components are used.

power supply	CPU	chipset
video card	case	CPU cooling
motherboard	display	RAM

Group 1 components: ______________________________

Group 2 components: ______________________________

Group 3 components: ______________________________

11. A motherboard advertisement lists UEFI as one of the motherboard features. What is UEFI?
    a. a port
    b. a BIOS replacement
    c. an internal interface
    d. a type of storage device
12. Which three design environments would have the largest display needs? (Select three.)
    [CAD | industrial | gaming | home theater | virtualization | thick client | home server]
13. In what design environment would a privacy display screen most likely be used?
    [CAD | industrial | gaming | home theater | virtualization | thick client | home server]
14. When designing, with what computer component would you consider the nanometer measurement?
    [hard drive | motherboard | display | CPU | power supply | air filter]
15. Which two components could have an ITX form factor? (Select two.)
    [hard drive | motherboard | display | CPU | power supply | air filter]
16. What is the minimum power supply wattage that would be suitable for an HTPC?
    [200 | 300 | 400 | 500]
17. [T | F] The SATA interface can support hot swapping.
18. What are common physical sizes of internal storage devices? (Select all that apply.)
    [1.25 inches | 2.5 inches | 3.5 inches | 5 inches | 5.25 inches | 6 inches]
19. Which computer design environment would have the most need for a laptop enclosure?
    [industrial | gaming | home theater | virtualization | mobile | home server]
20. [T | F] When dealing with an irate customer, it is best to listen to the customer vent.

Exercises

Lab 10.1 Computer System Design

Objective: To be able to recommend a complete system based on the customer's needs or placement of the system

Parts: Internet access

Procedure: Use the Internet to research specific computers, based on the given scenario.

1. A home-bound elderly person has just had the hard drive fail that was installed in a really old computer. The person has decided to replace the computer rather than fix the broken one. The elderly person uses the computer to shop for family members, check email, play basic computer card games with others online, and view pictures on CDs or DVDs sent by family members. Internet access is through a DSL modem that connects to the USB port and still works. Find a suitable computer on the Internet. The customer would like to keep the cost around $700, including installation, if possible. Write the computer model, basic description, cost, and cost of installation.

2. A graphic artist would like a second computer as a mobile solution and would like your assistance finding a suitable laptop. The graphic artist does mostly video graphics creation but would like to be able to work some when traveling. Find three possible solutions. Provide the computer model, basic description, and costs of the three laptops.

3. A sports complex wants to have a kiosk with a touch screen and that holds a computer that runs specialized software. The software allows folks to search for events and get detailed walking directions to the events and/or a specific sports field. No network connectivity is required. Locate a computer with an HDMI output for connectivity with the touch screen for this outdoor kiosk located in a year-round sports complex. List the model number, basic description, and your fee for installing this system.

4. A purchasing department is going to a thin-client environment. Select one desktop thin-client computer model and one mobile thin-client model from different manufacturers that can be used in the 10-person department. The models need to support dual displays. Detail any model numbers, basic parts descriptions, and costs.

5. A small company is expanding and is hiring an administrative assistant for the sales manager. Select a computer, monitor, keyboard, and an inkjet all-in-one printer for this assistant, who will be using Microsoft Office–type applications. The boss has put a $1,200 limit (not counting shipping) on the entire purchase. Provide a detailed list, description, and costs of parts chosen.

6. Select a CAD/CAM manufacturing design computer that uses 64-bit AutoCAD Mechanical 2013 software. Research the AutoCAD Mechanical application's video requirements. Provide a detailed list, description, and cost of parts chosen including the video card and display. Price is no object. (Note that AutoCAD Mechanical requires a 1280×1024 display with true color.)

Lab 10.2 Design Components

Objective: To be able to recognize the unique components for a specific computer design scenario

Procedure: Using the list of components, identify which components would be used in the scenarios given. Note that any one component can be used multiple times.

Components

A. Multiple powerful processors
B. Maximum RAM
C. Lots of RAM
D. Multiple large capacity hard drives
E. Large capacity hard drive
F. RAID
G. Sound card and speakers
H. Powerful video card and RAM on the card
I. Multiple displays
J. Large display
K. DVR
L. TV tuner or cable card
M. 1000Mbps NIC
N. Computer enclosure
O. KVM switch

Scenario 1

Identify the unique components from the provided list for a computer used for audio and video editing.

Scenario 2

You need to build a computer to test out the Chrome operating system along with your current Windows operating system. You have decided to do this in a virtual environment. Identify the unique components that would be in the computer.

Scenario 3

A customer wants a computer in the den where the TV and surround sound components are located. Identify the unique components that would be in this computer.

Scenario 4

A tire shop would like to have a computer in the lobby where information about the latest and upcoming sales are displayed. The owner is concerned about theft. What unique component would be needed for this situation?

Scenario 5

A computer programmer works from home but likes to work from several types of computers—a mobile tablet, laptop, and desktop—and to be able to work on any mobile device when traveling. The programmer has decided to create a server to store and access everything from anyplace. The programmer does not want to have to buy another keyboard, mouse, or display for the server but wants to share these components connected to the desktop computer with the server. What unique components would be part of this system?

Lab 10.3 Subsystem Design Components

Objective: To be able to design a subsystem of a computer, based on design requirements

Parts: Internet access

Procedure: Use the Internet to research specific computers, based on the given scenario.

Scenario 1

You have just ascertained that a customer's older ATX Pentium 4 motherboard in a home computer is bad. The customer wants a motherboard upgrade or replacement. The existing motherboard has a PCI sound card and VGA port that the user would like to continue using. The RAM on the existing motherboard has 512MB of DDR2 memory. The hard drive and optical drive use PATA for connectivity, and the customer would like to continue using these devices and the current operating system. The customer does light computer work but likes listening to broadcasts and music on the computer. Locate suitable replacement upgraded component(s). The budget is $250, including labor. Detail the item, item description, and cost.

Scenario 2

A customer has been given a micro-ATX motherboard, an Intel Core i5 quad-core processor, and RAM. The customer has two 3.5-inch SATA drives and one 5.25-inch optical drive from other computers. The customer would like assistance getting a case and a power supply to handle all these devices. The customer does not have a lot of room but wants a tower case that provides good air flow through the computer. The customer has a budget of $200 for this. Locate a power supply and case for the customer. Detail the items, item descriptions, and costs.

Scenario 3

A retired naval officer has just gotten into classical music and now wants surround sound in his office. Select an appropriate sound subsystem. The budget is $200. The office system has both PCI and PCIe expansion slots available. List the components, a description of each component, and the cost.

Scenario 4

A college graduate has started her own website design business. She wants a video card that supports two 18- to 20-inch displays. Recommend a video subsystem for her. The budget is $500 maximum. List the components, a description of each component, and the costs.

Scenario 5

Locate a motherboard, power supply, RAM, CPU, and mid-sized case that are compatible with one another for an administrative assistant. The budget is $600. List the components, a description of the components (ensure that you list the type of RAM the motherboard supports), and the costs.

Activities

Internet Discovery

Objective: To become familiar with researching computer items used in designing systems or subsystems

Parts: Internet access

Procedure: Use the Internet to answer the following questions. Write the answers and the URL of the site where you found the information.

1. Locate the Bloom's Taxonomy chart that has been modified by Andrew Churches to include verbs for the digital age. Write at least five verbs that Andrew Churches recommends as being relative to the top level of the taxonomy—the creating level—and the URL where you found the chart.

2. Locate minimum requirements for either a student computer or a staff computer at a particular school. Write the requirements, school name, and the URL where you found this information.

3. What are the minimum recommended video standards for use when playing Diablo III on a PC? Write the answer and the URL where you found this information.

4. What are the minimum processor, RAM, and display resolution requirements for a client who wants to run AutoCAD LT 2012 software? Write the answer and the URL where you found the information.

5. Find a monitor that supports the minimum display resolution found in Question 4. List the monitor manufacturer, model number, and URL where you found the information.

   True color just means 24-bit color, and it is determined by the video card (and the amount of memory available to the video card). Even though the display resolution requirements say 1024×768, the AutoCAD folks don't expect that to be the resolution you use—just the minimum requirements. Any large display with good ratings will do. Note that most CAD folks would have at least two, if not three, of these monitors.

6. Find a website that shows at least three recommendations for dealing with irate customers. Write three recommendations and the URL where you found this information.

Soft Skills

1. Interview or email someone who works in your school to determine the school's minimum hardware requirements for its new computers. Document your findings.
2. In teams of two, find a video that shows how to deal with an irate customer. Document at least three observations from the video and the URL.
3. In teams of two, three, or four, design a computer for a specific purpose. State the purpose and provide all the models, descriptions, and costs. Compete with other teams for the best design.

Critical Thinking Skills

1. Refer to Table 10.1, which provides recommendations for hardware components. Find at least one type of computer configuration for which you disagree with the special hardware components; if you agree with them all, then think of one that should be added. List the component and the reason for your disagreement or addition.
2. Locate an image that shows Bloom's Taxonomy map, as modified by Andrew Churches. Explain why designing (in the creating stage) is a higher-level skill than the evaluating stage, which includes experimenting, judging, monitoring, and testing.
3. Do you think most technicians are good at designing? Explain your opinion.

A+ Certification Exam Tips

- ✓ Review Table 10.1, which describes the different computer uses and recommended components. The specific types of custom configurations on the exam include the following computer types: (1) graphic/CAD/CAM design, (2) audio/video editing, (3) virtualization, (4) gaming, (5) home theater, (6) standard thick client, (7) thin client, and (8) home server.
- ✓ Be able to explain the purpose of specific components, such as enclosures and air filters, and how they are used as environmental controls.
- ✓ The exam has very specific criteria for proper communication and professionalism. A specific part of this section is dealing with a difficult customer or situation. Remember to avoid arguing with the customer and/or being defensive. Do not minimize the customer's problem. Avoid being judgmental. Clarify customer statements by asking open-ended questions (which allows the customer to freely explain the situation) to narrow the scope of the problem and by restating the issue or question to verify your understanding.

chapter 11

Basic Operating Systems

Chapter Objectives:

In this chapter you will learn:

- To identify and use common desktop and home screen icons
- To manipulate files and folders in Windows and on mobile devices
- How to modify the Start menu and home screen on mobile devices
- How to create a system image in case of emergencies
- About the Windows registry
- How to work from a command prompt
- Techniques to stay current in field

CompTIA Exam Objectives:

What CompTIA A+ exam objectives are covered in this chapter?

- ✓ 802-1.1 Compare and contrast the features and requirements of various Microsoft operating systems.
- ✓ 802-1.2 Given a scenario, install, and configure the operating system using the most appropriate method.
- ✓ 802-1.3 Given a scenario, use appropriate command line tools.
- ✓ 802-1.4 Given a scenario, use appropriate operating system features and tools.
- ✓ 802-1.5 Given a scenario, use Control Panel utilities.
- ✓ 802-1.7 Perform preventive maintenance procedures using appropriate tools.
- ✓ 802-1.9 Explain the basics of client-side virtualization.
- ✓ 802-3.1 Explain the basic features of mobile operating systems.
- ✓ 802-4.6 Given a scenario, troubleshoot operating system problems with appropriate tools.

Basic Operating Systems Overview

Computers require software to operate. An **operating system**, sometimes called an OS, is software that coordinates the interaction between hardware and any software applications, as well as the interaction between a user and the computer. Examples of operating systems include Apple's Mac OS X and iOS; Windows XP, Vista, 7, and 8; and the different types of Unix/Linux, such as Sun Solaris, Red Hat, SUSE, Google Chrome OS, and Android. One advantage of Linux-based open source operating systems such as Android is that the code that makes up the operating system is open to view and improve upon or change. This sometimes allows for more community-driven features that are not as easily changed in closed source or proprietary software such as Windows or OS X.

An operating system can be a GUI (graphical user interface) or a command-based interface, or it can contain both, which is the most common. An operating system contains commands and functions that both the user and the computer understand. An example of this is **Windows Explorer**, sometimes called simply Explorer, which is an application used to manage files and folders, as shown in Figure 11.1.

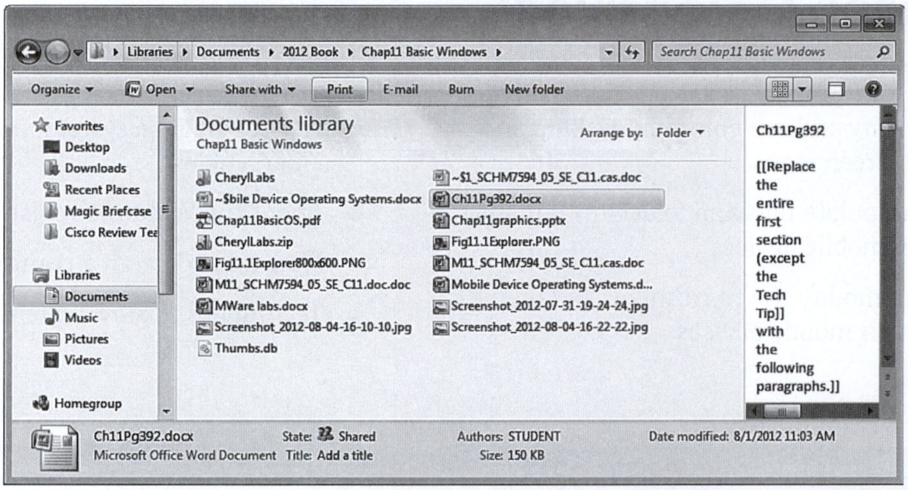

Figure 11.1 Windows Explorer

A **file** is an electronic container that holds computer code or data. Another way of looking at a file is to think of it as either a box of bits or an electronic piece of paper with information on it. In Figure 11.1, Ch11Pg392.docx is an example of a file. A folder holds files and can also contain other folders. In Figure 11.1, CherylLabs is a folder. With Windows Explorer, you can create, copy, or move files or folders. The operating system is also responsible for handling file and disk management and that is why the Windows Explorer tool is part of the standard Windows operating system.

Another GUI environment is also available with a smartphone or a tablet. In this GUI environment, a finger, multiple fingers, or a stylus is your input device to interact with the operating system. Figure 11.2 shows an Apple iPad home screen.

Figure 11.2 Apple iPad home screen

An alternate environment used by technicians when there is trouble is the command prompt environment. From a command prompt, you can type commands that are specific to the operating system. For example, say that you type the word `hop` at a command prompt. The word "hop" is not a command that the computer understands (has been programmed to understand), so an error message appears because the computer does not know what to do. However, if you type `dir` at a command prompt, the computer recognizes the command and displays a directory—a listing of files. Figure 11.3 shows a command prompt environment.

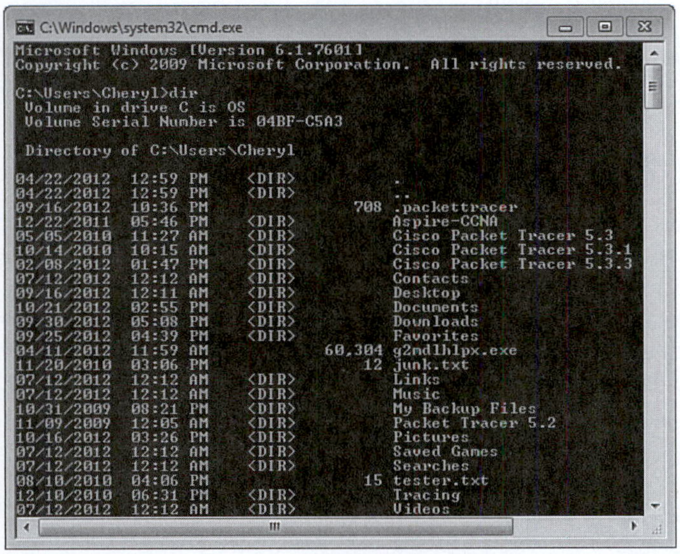

Figure 11.3 Windows command prompt

A technician must be familiar with the GUI environment and must be able to function from a command prompt when the only possibility is to execute a fix by typing a command at a command prompt. Not only must a technician be very familiar with the tools and environments, but he or she must know multiple operating systems. This makes for a challenging and ever-changing environment. Figure 11.4 shows how an operating system is the coordinator of all hardware and software. The operating system is the core, or software, that computer device needs in order to function.

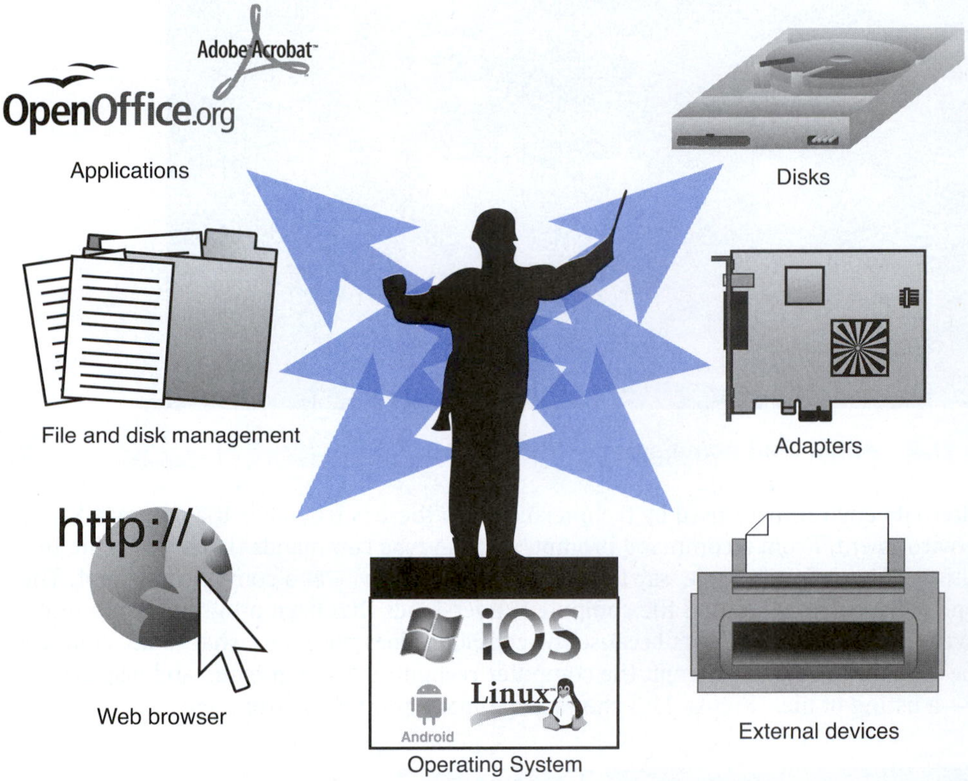

Figure 11.4 The operating system coordinates everything

Basic Windows Usage Overview

When a Windows-based operating system first boots, there may be a logon screen. A user ID and password is entered as part of the operating system installation process. Once in the Windows environment, the desktop appears. The **desktop** is the area on the screen of a GUI environment where all work is performed. It is the interface between the computer user and computer files, applications, operating system, and installed hardware. The desktop contains **icons**, which are pictures that provide access to various devices, files, and applications on the computer. The desktop can be customized so that the most commonly accessed applications or files are easily accessible. Figure 11.5 shows the major components of the desktop.

Tech Tip

Accessing the XP Administrator account

The Windows XP welcome screen does not contain the local Administrator account icon on the welcome screen. To get to that account, press Ctrl+Alt+Del twice and log in with the Administrator account user ID and password.

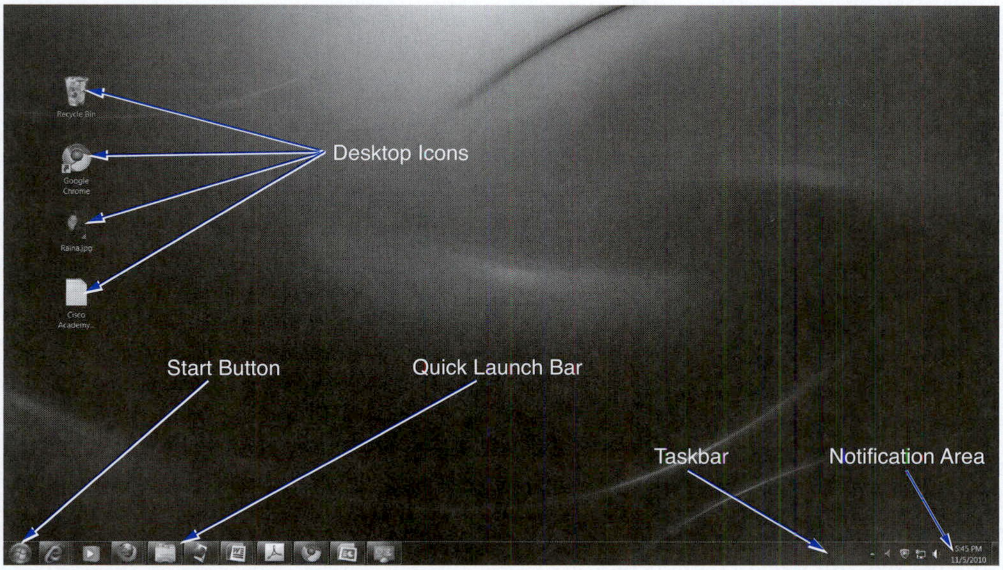

Figure 11.5 Windows desktop

Tech Tip

Copying and moving

When you are copying a file or folder, use the *Copy* and *Paste* functions from the *Edit* Explorer menu option. When you are moving a file or folder, use the *Cut* and Paste functions.

The Google Chrome icon shown in Figure 11.5 is a desktop icon called a shortcut. A **shortcut** represents a **path** (a location on a drive) to a file, folder, or program. It is a link (pointer) to where the file or application resides on a disk. When a shortcut icon is double-clicked, Windows knows where to find the specific file the icon represents by the associated path. Users and technicians frequently place shortcuts on the desktop and it is important to know how to create or troubleshoot them.

By default, the Windows XP/Vista/7 desktop displays the Recycle Bin icon only. However, some people like to have the some Windows icons displayed. Common desktop icons are listed in Table 11.1.

Table 11.1 Common Windows desktop icons

Icon	Purpose
My Documents/ Documents	Used to access a folder located on the hard drive that is the default storage location for files
My Computer/Computer	Used to access hardware, software, and files
My Network Places/ Network	Used to access network resources, such as computers, printers, scanners, fax machines, and files
Recycle Bin	Holds files and folders that have been deleted
Internet Explorer	Starts the Internet Explorer application, which is used to access the Internet

To discover the path to the original file used to create a shortcut, right-click the shortcut icon and select *Properties*. Click the *Shortcut* tab and look in the *Target* textbox for the path to the original file. The *Find Target* (XP) or *Open File Location* (Vista/7) button can be used to locate the original file.

Tech Tip

How to delete a file permanently

If you hold down the Shift key when deleting a file, the file is permanently deleted and does not go into the Recycle Bin.

An important desktop icon is the Recycle Bin, which is used to hold files and folders that the user deletes. When a file or folder is deleted, it is not really gone. Instead, it goes into the Recycle Bin, which is actually just a folder on the hard drive. The deleted file or folder can be removed from the Recycle Bin just as a piece of trash can be removed from a real trash can. Deleted files and folders in the Recycle Bin use hard drive space.

The contents of the Recycle Bin take up hard drive space. To change how much space is reserved for the Recycle Bin or the drive on which the deleted files in the Recycle Bin are stored, right-click on the *Recycle Bin* and select *Properties*. Labs at the end of the chapter illustrate how to copy, move, and delete files and folders (Labs 11.5 and 11.13) and how to empty the Recycle Bin (Labs 11.1 and 11.2).

Tech Tip

Keeping the desktop organized

Sometimes the desktop is cluttered with icons the user puts on it. To organize the desktop nicely, right-click an empty desktop space, point to the *Arrange icons* (XP) or *View > Auto arrange icons* (Vista/7).

One way to modify the desktop is to change the wallpaper scheme. A wallpaper scheme is a background picture, pattern, or color. Other changes to the desktop include altering the color scheme that is used in displaying folders, and enabling a screen saver which is the picture, color, or pattern that displays when the computer is inactive. Labs 11.1 and 11.2 at the end of the chapter explain how to change these settings.

Whenever anything is double-clicked in Windows, a window appears. Windows are a normal part of the desktop as are the taskbar, Start button, and Quick Launch bar. The **taskbar** is the bar that commonly runs across the bottom of the screen. The taskbar holds buttons that represent applications or files currently loaded into the computer memory. The taskbar also holds icons that allow access to system utilities such as a clock for the date and time and a speaker symbol for access to volume control. Figure 11.5 shows the taskbar.

The **Start button** by default is located in the desktop's lower-left corner on the taskbar and is used to launch applications and utilities, search for files and other computers, obtain help, and add/remove hardware and software. Figure 11.6 shows the Windows XP Start button menu.

Tech Tip

What to do if the Start button is not on the desktop

If the Start button does not appear on the desktop, hold down the Ctrl key and press the Esc key. Another way to bring up the Start menu is by pressing the ⊞ (Windows key) on the keyboard.

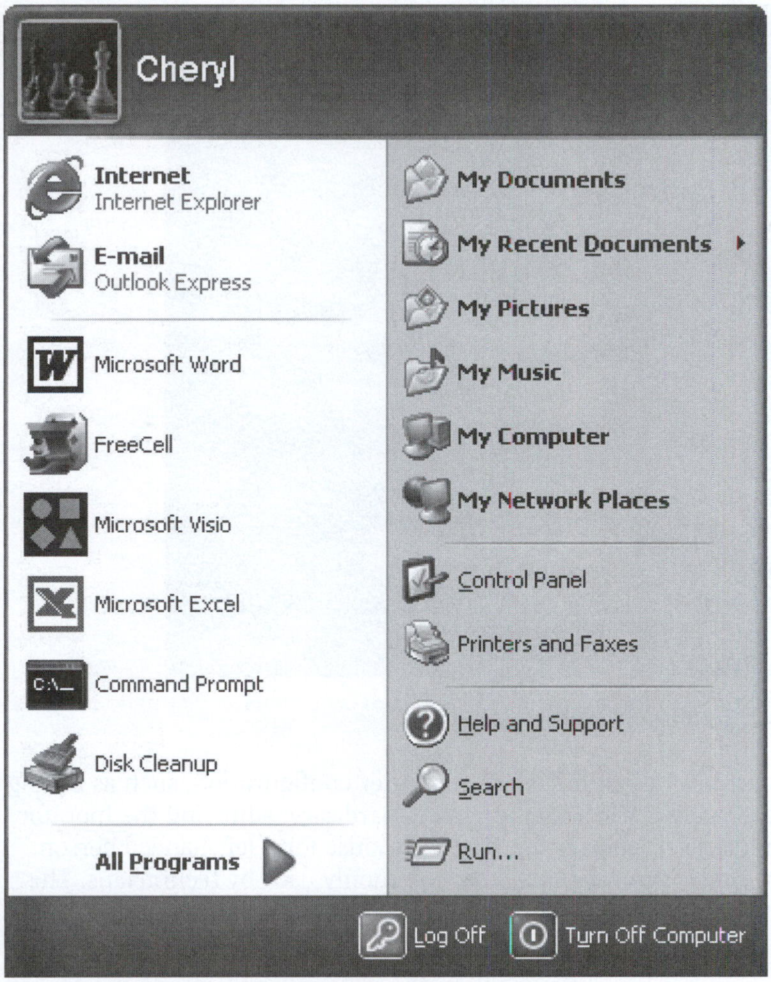

Figure 11.6 Windows XP Start button menu

Need hard drive space? Empty the Recycle Bin

A technician must remember that some users do not empty the Recycle Bin. Emptying the Recycle Bin frees up space on the hard drive.

Tech Tip

The *Shut Down*, *Turn Off Computer*, and *Restart* options on the Start button menu are used to shut off and restart the computer. The *Standby*, *Hibernate*, and *Sleep* options are available on computers that support power-saving features and are commonly used with laptops, ultrabooks, and netbooks.

In Windows Vista and 7, the *Switch User*, *Log Off*, *Lock*, *Restart*, *Sleep*, and *Shut down* options are available from a right arrow on the Start button, as shown in Figure 11.7. Notice the exclamation mark inside the shield beside the word Shut down in Figure 11.7. This shows that Windows updates are ready to be installed and will be installed before the computer is shut down.

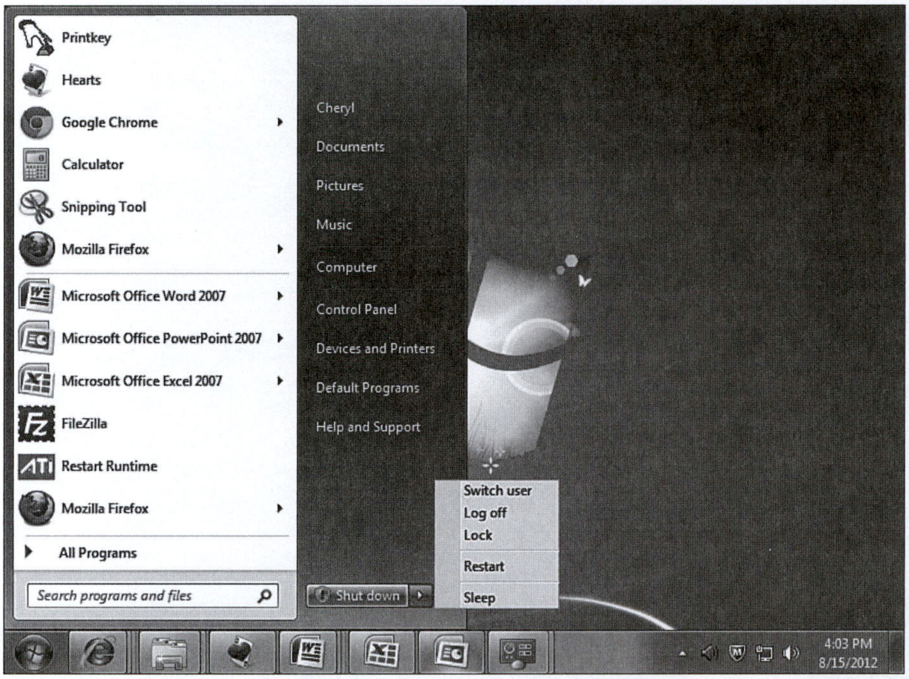

Figure 11.7 Windows 7 Shut down options

The **Control Panel** Start button option allows computer configuration, such as adding software, removing software, adding hardware, removing hardware, adjusting the monitor settings, configuring a screen saver, and configuring the mouse for a left-handed person. Control Panel is one of the Start menu options most commonly used by technicians. The Control Panels can be viewed in classic view or category view. Classic view is the older Windows style. Labs 11.1 and 11.2 at the end of the chapter demonstrate the use of control panels.

The taskbar has three main areas (see Figure 11.8 and 11.1): (1) the Start button on the far left, (2) icons for commonly used applications or open applications, and (3) the notification area on the far right. The two closest icons to the right of the Start button in Figure 11.8 (Internet Explorer and Windows Explorer) are "pinned" to the taskbar—that is, they are always on the taskbar. The other icons shown in Figure 11.8 (Hearts, Microsoft Word, Microsoft Excel, SugarSync File Manager, Mozilla Firefox web browser, and Windows Control Panel) are open applications.

Figure 11.8 Windows 7 taskbar

On the far right of the taskbar is the **notification area** or systray (XP), where information about an application or a tool can be found. In Figure 11.8, the icons from left to right are McAfee Security (where you could quickly double-click to see the security status of the system or cause an immediate virus scan), a network icon (where a technician could quickly ascertain whether or not Internet access was available), Windows speaker control (to quickly mute or adjust sound volume), and the date and time. Other icons are available by clicking on the up arrow to the left of the McAfee Security icon. Notice the space to the far right immediately after the date/time. Click on this area to instantly show the desktop area. Click on the area again and whatever window you were working within reappears. The *Show Desktop* option is also available by simply right-clicking an empty space on the taskbar. Labs 11.1, 11.2, 11.4, and 11.5 demonstrate how to use and control the Windows desktop environment.

Technicians frequently interact with the Windows operating system through a dialog box. A dialog box is used within the operating system and with Windows applications to allow configuration and operating system preferences. The most common features found in a dialog box are a checkbox, a textbox, tabs, a drop-down menu, a Close button, an OK button, a Cancel button, and an Apply button. Figure 11.9 shows a sample dialog box.

Tech Tip

How to modify the buttons shown on the taskbar

Launch the application. Locate the application icon on the taskbar. Right-click and select *Pin this program to taskbar.*

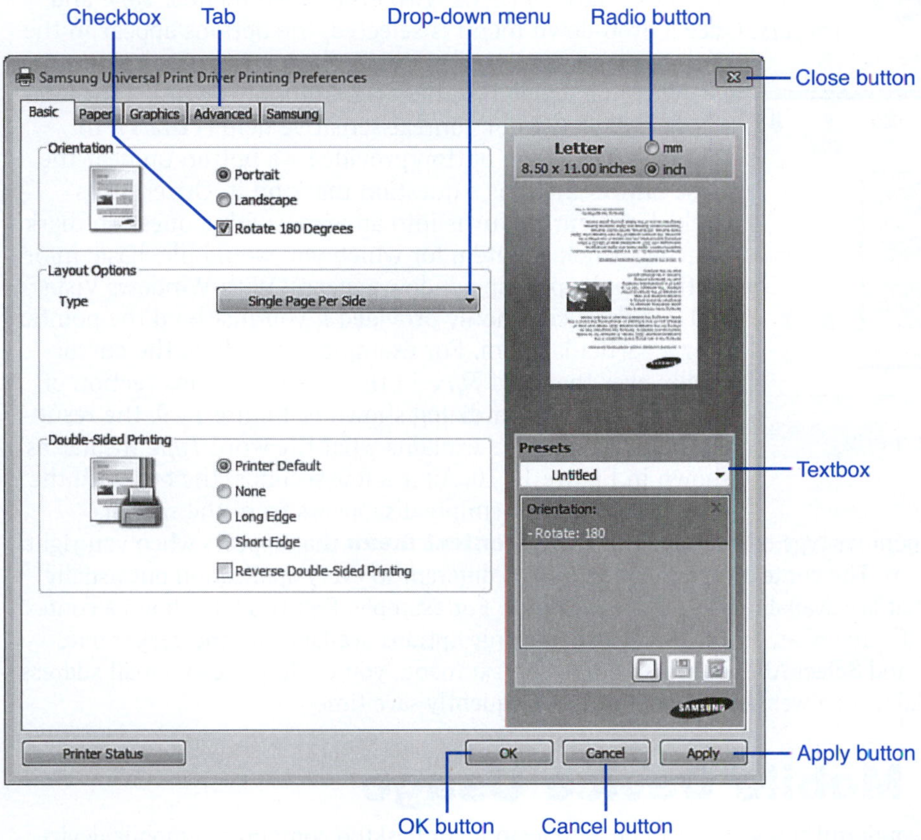

Figure 11.9 Samsung printer dialog box components

A textbox is an area where you can type a specific parameter. When the inside of a textbox is clicked, a vertical line appears or the entire default word (like *Untitled* in Figure 11.9) would be highlighted. Any typed text is placed to the right of the insertion point, or you can just type to replace the highlighted word. Textboxes sometimes have up and down arrows that can be used to select an option or allow a user to type in a new parameter.

Tabs frequently appear across the top of a dialog box. Each tab holds a group of related options. Click once on the tab to bring that particular major section to the window's forefront. The tabs shown in Figure 11.9 are Basic, Paper, Graphics, Advanced, and Samsung.

The **Close button**, which is indicated by an X, is used to close the dialog box window. When the Close button is used, changes made inside the dialog box are not applied. When the **OK button** is clicked, all options selected or changed within the dialog box are applied. When the **Cancel button** is clicked, anything changed within the dialog box is not applied—the options are left in their original state. The **Apply button** is used to make changes immediately (before clicking the OK button).

Tech Tip

Click *OK* or *Apply* to make it work

To apply a change, inexperienced technicians often make the mistake of clicking the *Close* button (the button with an X on it) instead of the OK or Apply button. When the Close button is used, changes in the dialog box are not saved or applied.

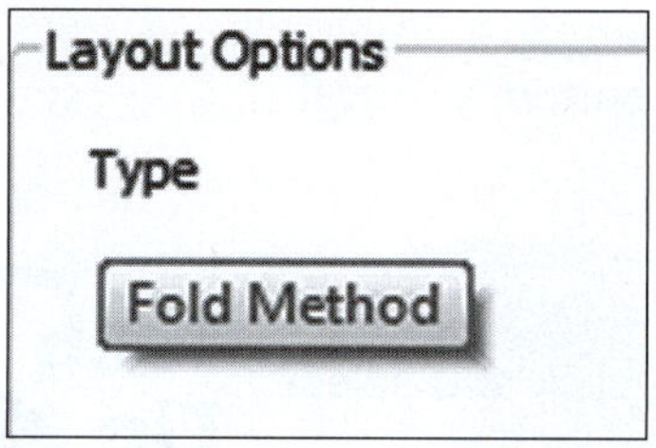

Figure 11.10 Dialog help

When checked, a checkbox option is enabled (turned on). Clicking inside a checkbox option places a check mark inside the checkbox, such as the one for Mirror margins, shown in Figure 11.9. A similar dialog box option is a radio button. A **radio button** is a circle that, when enabled, has a solid dot inside it. If a radio button that already has a dot in it is clicked, the dot disappears, and the option is disabled. In Figure 11.9, the *Portrait* radio button is enabled and the *Landscape* radio button is disabled.

Drop-down menus are presented when you click a down arrow to see the options. Figure 11.9 has two drop-down menus: *Type* and *Presets*. Once a drop-down menu is selected, the options appear in the drop-down menu.

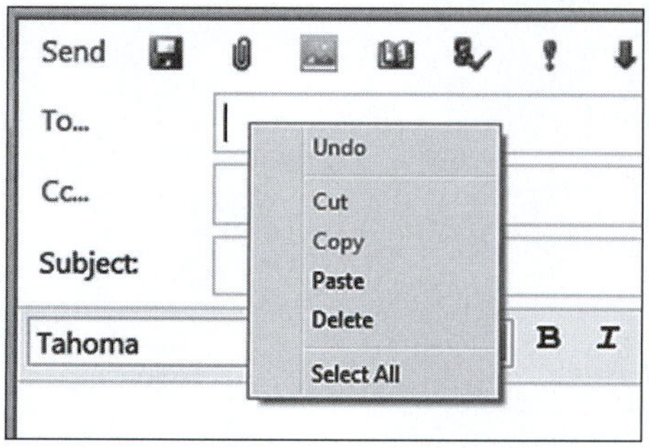

Figure 11.11 Context menu

Within a dialog box, help is commonly provided through a help button (XP) or context-sensitive help (Vista/7). In Windows XP, a help button provided—a button up near the close button that has a question mark on it. Once this is clicked, the cursor turns into an arrow with a question mark attached. Click any item for which you would like basic information, and a pop-up window appears. With Windows Vista and 7, help is commonly provided if you just hold the pointer over a particular item. For example, if you hold the cursor briefly over the word *Type* in the Layout Options section of the Samsung printer dialog shown in Figure 11.9, the resulting help that appears explains what the word *Type* means, as shown in Figure 11.10. After a few seconds, the box with the words *Fold Method* simply disappears from the screen.

Another popular type of interaction is with a **context menu** that appears when you right-click on an item. The context menu that appears is different in every application but usually has options that are available from the main menu. For example, Figure 11.11 shows a context menu for the To line of an email. Notice that the only options available are the darker ones—Paste, Delete, and Select All. So, by using this context menu, you could paste an email address you just copied from a website. Context menus frequently save time.

Basic Mobile Device Usage

With all the wonderful things you can do with a laptop or desktop computer, a mobile device or smartphone can do a variety of tasks that those devices can do, in addition to providing you the ability to do the tasks while on the go. Additional mobile applications have been created as a result. For example, when you go shopping, not only can you have your shopping list with you, but you can use your camera as a barcode scanner and scan a grocery item and see if any online coupons match that item. Such an application would not normally be found on a desktop computer. The mobility factor made someone think of creating the application—or *app*, as it is commonly known. Two of the most popular mobile operating systems are iOS and Android.

Apple iOS is found only on Apple devices. Android was created by Google and is open source. The starting place for any mobile device running either iOS or Android is the **home screen**. The home screen is where application icons are found. Multiple screens can extend the space for the home screen. You can use your finger to swipe to an additional page of icons. To access the home screen, tap (Apple's term) or touch (Google's term) the home button or the home icon which looks something like a house. Figure 11.12 shows an ASUS tablet home page that uses Android as the operating system. Note that the notification area for a smartphone is usually provided by pulling down a menu from the top of the screen.

Figure 11.12 ASUS tablet home screen

Notice in Figure 11.12 how the **system bar** extends across the bottom of the screen. The back button on the far left is used to return to the previous page. If the keyboard screen is open, the back button will close the keyboard. The home button is used to return to the main home page, but keep in mind that other home pages may be available to the left or right. An Apple iPad or iPhone has a physical home button (not a tap) beside the screen. On an iPad, pushing the home button beside the display removes the keyboard.

The third icon from the left on the system bar is the recent apps button. The recent apps button shows thumbnail views of recently used applications. If you touch a thumbnail, the application opens full screen. In the far right corner is the mobile **notification area** that contains icons such as the battery life, wireless signal strength, time, or external media connectivity. Note that on a smartphone, the notification area is commonly a swipe from the top of the display.

When interacting with a mobile operating system, some common terms are used to control the applications and icons. These terms are described in Table 11.2. As you can tell from this list of terms, some interaction requires multitouch. Not all screens support this feature. Refer to Figure 1.17 to see multitouch techniques.

Table 11.2 Mobile operating system interaction

Term	Description
Touch or tap	Press an icon or area. Used to open an application.
Double tap	Press an icon or area twice. Used to enlarge an area of a screen or an item such as a picture.
Long touch or touch and hold	Press and hold on an icon or area. Used to move an icon from one home screen to a different home screen or to unlock a tablet
Swipe or flick	Press and move to the left or right or up and down. Used to move from one home screen to another or to open the notification area on a smartphone.

Term	Description
Scroll	Press and move up or down. Used to quickly go through a list of files or pictures.
Pinch or pinch close	Using two fingers spread apart, bring the fingers closer together. Used to zoom out from an object or area.
Spread or pinch open	Using two fingers close together, move the fingers apart. Used to zoom in on an object or area such as when you want to be able to see a closer view of a map or to read words.

If the tablet or smartphone goes to sleep, press the power button and optionally enter a pattern, PIN, or passcode. On an Android device if a lock icon displays, press and drag the lock icon to the unlock icon or center of the display. Pressing the home button also awakens an iPad. Slide the *slide to unlock* bar to the right and optionally enter the passcode. Figure 11.13 shows the Apple iPad lock.

Figure 11.13 Apple iPad lock screen

Applications, commonly called *apps*, for mobile devices come with the device, can be downloaded free of charge, or can be purchased through the App Store (Apple iOS devices) or Google Play (Android devices). As a result of the mobility features, new apps are being developed constantly, and applications that might not be of much use with a desktop computer are very handy on mobile devices. Table 11.3 shows common mobile apps.

Table 11.3 Common mobile apps

Android apps	iOS apps
Gmail	Mail
Google Play/Android Market	App Store

Android apps	iOS apps
Google Maps	Maps
Gallery	Photos
MyLibrary	iBooks
Browser	Safari
Play Music	iTunes
Clock	Calendar

One commonly used application is GPS. With **GPS** (Global Positioning System), satellites send location information to a receiver on a mobile device. Most mobile devices have GPS capability. Mobile apps provide directions for how to get to a store or where another person is located, as well as showing how far you have walked.

Some people disable the GPS capability until they want to use it because of geo-tracking. **Geo-tracking** is the ability to track where you are located or, more accurately, where your phone is located. Many applications and social media rely on such data to "publish" your current location or the location of friends you have selected. Vendors have pay plans that include the ability to track family members. Companies are using geo-tracking to locate lost and stolen mobile devices. Figure 11.14 shows the concept of geo-tracking.

Figure 11.14 Geo-tracking in action

Gaming on smartphones and tablets has been enhanced through the use of accelerometers and gyroscopes. An accelerometer detects the device orientation and adapts what is shown on the screen, based on the device orientation. This is how you can hold a tablet in portrait mode and then move it to a horizontal position to show a landscape picture better. A gyroscope measures or maintains orientation. Apple's iPhone4 was the first smartphone to include both gyroscope and accelerometer technologies.

Managing Windows Files and Folders

Technicians often create, delete, and move files and folders. You need to be able to do these tasks quickly and without error. It is important to remember to think about what file and folder you want to work with, where the files and folders are located now, and where you want the files or folders to be eventually.

Each drive in a computer is represented by a drive letter followed by a colon. For example, the floppy drive is represented by A:, and the first hard drive partition is represented by C:. The optical drive, flash drive, and any external drive is each represented by a drive letter followed by a colon. Discs or drives hold files. A file is kept on some type of media, such as a floppy disk, flash drive, hard drive, tape, or optical disc. Each file is given a name, called a filename. An example of a filename is WIN7CHAP.DOCX.

Files are usually kept in folders to organize them. In older operating systems, a folder was called a directory, and you still see this term today. A folder within a folder is called a subfolder or subdirectory. Windows 7 has automatic groupings, with each one called a **library** for saving files. The Windows 7 libraries include the following: Documents, Music, Pictures, and Videos. By default, applications save files in one of these libraries. You can also create additional libraries as needed.

Every file and folder is given a name and an extension. An **extension** is added to the filename, and the extension can be three or more characters long. The filename and the extension are separated by a period. An example of a filename with an extension is BOOK.DOCX, where BOOK is the name of the file and DOCX is the extension.

In older operating systems, the maximum number of characters in a filename was eight, and the extension could only be three characters. For this reason, older filenames are called short filenames or 8.3 filenames. Filenames in modern Windows versions can be up to 255 characters long and are sometimes referred to as long filenames. An example of a long filename is WINDOWS 7 CHAPTER.DOCX.

Normally with Windows, the application automatically adds an extension to the end of the filename. In most views, Windows does not automatically show the extensions. To view the extensions in XP Windows Explorer, perform the following steps: *Tools* > *Folder Options* > *View* tab > uncheck the *Hide file extensions for known file types* checkbox > *OK*. In Vista/7, select the *Organize* drop-down menu > *Folder and search options* > *View* tab > uncheck the *Hide extensions for known file types* checkbox > *OK*.

Tech Tip

Characters you cannot use in filenames and folder names

Folders and filenames can have all characters, numbers, letters, and spaces *except* the following: / (forward slash), " (quotation mark), \ (backslash), | (vertical bar), ? (question mark), : (colon), and * (asterisk).

When Windows recognizes an extension, the operating system associates the extension with a particular application. Filename extensions can tell you a lot about a file, such as what application created the file or what its purpose is. Table 11.4 lists the most common file extensions and their purpose or what application creates the extension.

Table 11.4 Common file extensions

Extension	Purpose or application	Extension	Purpose or application
AI	Adobe Illustrator or Corel Trace	JPG or JPEG	Joint Photographic Experts Group file format—graphics file
AAX	Audible enhanced audio file	MPG or MPEG	Movie clip file
BAT	Used to execute commands from one file and is commonly known as a batch file	ONE	Microsoft OneNote file
BMP	Bitmap file	PCX	Microsoft Paintbrush
CAB	Cabinet file—a compressed file that holds operating system or application files	PDF	Adobe Acrobat—portable document format
COM	Command file—an executable file that opens an application or tool	PNG	Microsoft Paint or Snipping Tool graphics file format
DLL	Dynamic Link Library file—contains executable code that can be used by more than one application and is called upon from other code already running	PPT or PPTX	Microsoft PowerPoint
DOC or DOCX	Microsoft Word	RTF	Rich text format
DRV	Device driver—a piece of software that enables an operating system to recognize a hardware device	TIF or TIFF	Tag image file format
EPS	Encapsulated postscript file	TXT	Text file
EXE	Executable file—a file that opens an application	VXD	Virtual device driver
GIF	Graphics interchange file	WPS	Microsoft Works text file format
HLP	Windows-based help file	WRI	Microsoft WordPad
INF	Information or setup file	XLS or XLSX	Microsoft Excel
INI	Initialization file—Used in older Windows environments	ZIP	Compressed file

A topic closely related to the search feature and finding specific files is indexing. **Indexing** is the process used in Windows to quickly search common locations for files and folders, including all libraries, the Start button menu, and Internet Explorer browsing history. To modify what locations get indexed, use the *Start Search* textbox (Vista) or *Search programs and files* (7) > type `indexing` > select *Indexing Options* from the resulting list. Use the *Modify* or *Advanced* buttons to change the settings. If you don't want a file to be indexed and easily found, you can right-click on the filename, select *Properties* > *Advanced* button > disable (uncheck) the *Allow this file to have contents indexed in addition to file properties* option.

When you save a file in a Windows application, the application automatically saves the file to a specific folder or library. This is known as the default folder or default library. With many applications, this folder is the *My Documents* (XP) or *Documents* (Vista/7) folder. In documentation, installation instructions, and when writing the exact location of a file, the full path is used. A file's path is like a road map to the file and includes the drive letter plus all folders and subfolders as well as the filename and extension. For example, if the `Chap1.docx` file is in the *Documents* folder on the first Windows XP hard drive partition, the full path is `C:\Documents\Chap1.docx`. The first part is the drive letter where the document is stored. The `C:` represents the first hard drive partition. The name of the document is always at the very end of the path. In the example given, `Chap1.docx` is the name of the file. Everything in between the drive letter and the filename is the name of one or more folders where the `Chap1.docx` file is located. The folder in this example is the *Documents* folder.

If the `Chap1.docx` file is located in a subfolder called *Computer Book* that is located in the folder called *Documents* (sometimes called the parent folder), then the full path is `C:\Documents\Computer Book\Chap1.docx`. Notice that backslashes are always used to separate the folder names as well as the drive letter from the first folder name. Figure 11.15 shows how the `Windows XP tables.vsd` long filename looks in graphical form using Windows Explorer. The full path for this file would be as follows:

`D:\Documents and Settings\Cheryl\My Documents\A+ Textbook\Windows XP tables.vsd`

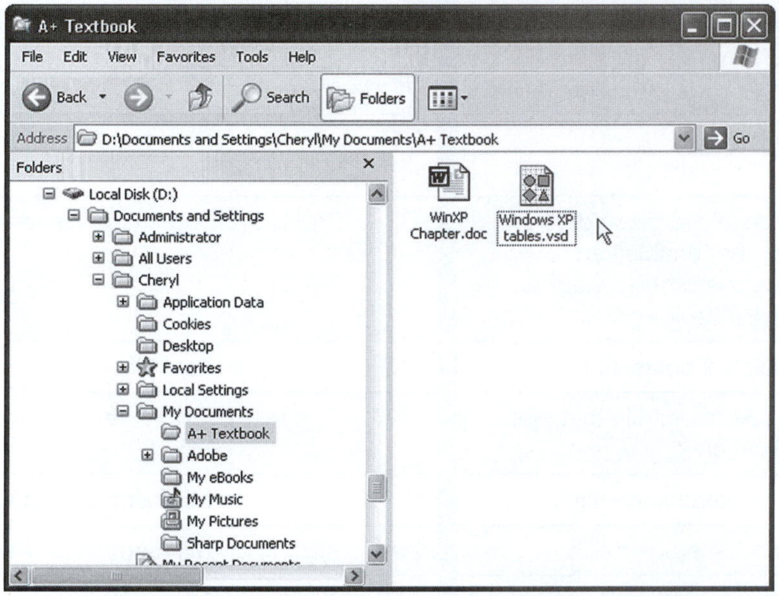

Figure 11.15 Long filename in Windows XP Explorer

Tech Tip

Removable media files are permanently deleted

When deleting a file or folder from a floppy disk, an optical disc, a memory card, an MP3 player, a digital camera, a remote computer, or a flash drive, the file or folder is permanently deleted. It does not go into the Recycle Bin, as is the case when a file is deleted from a hard drive.

In Windows Vista/7, the full path does not show automatically. In Vista/7, from Windows Explorer, click anywhere to the right of the words in the address bar. The full path shows and is highlighted, as shown in Figure 11.16.

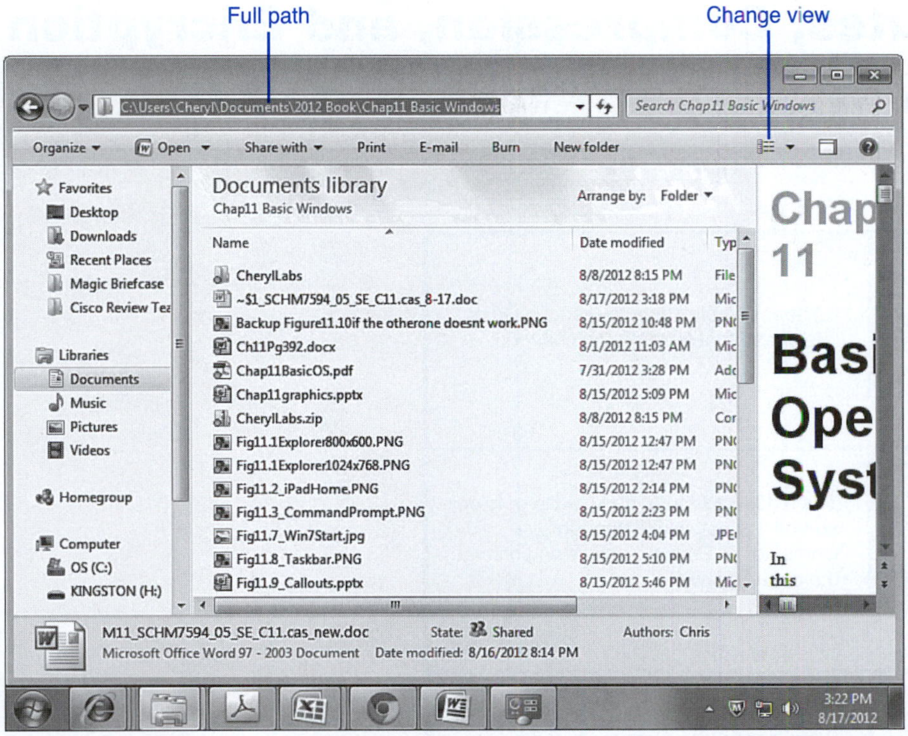

Figure 11.16 Full path in Windows 7 Explorer

To change what information is displayed or how the information is displayed in Windows Explorer, use the *View* menu option in XP or the *Change view > More options* down arrow in Vista/7, as shown in the upper-right corner of Figure 11.16. Table 11.5 explains these options.

Table 11.5 Windows Explorer display options

Explanation	Windows XP option	Windows Vista/7 option
File/folder name shown	List	List
File/folder shown with size, extension, and modification date	Details	Details
Small graphics with the file or folder name shown under the icon	Icons	Small Icons
Reduced size icons with file/folder contents shown	Thumbnails	Content
Multiple columns of file/folder icons with name, application, and size shown	Tiles	Tiles
Varying size file/folder icons	N/A	Medium Icons, Large Icons, Extra Large Icons

Attributes, Compression, and Encryption

My Computer (XP), *Computer* (Vista/7), and *Explorer* can be used for setting attributes for a file or folder. The file and folder attributes are read-only, hidden, archive, and system, as shown in Figure 11.17.

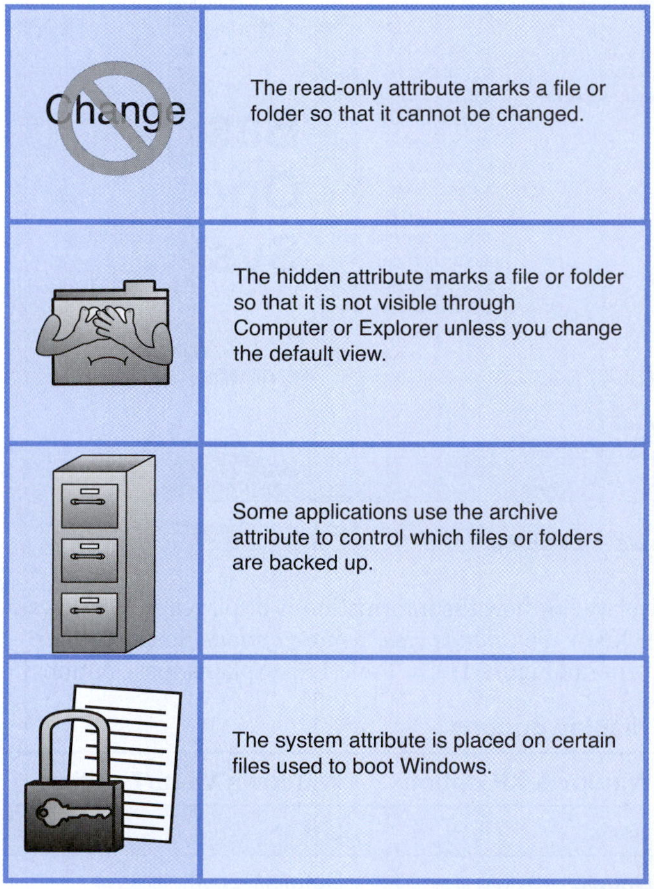

Change
The read-only attribute marks a file or folder so that it cannot be changed.
The hidden attribute marks a file or folder so that it is not visible through Computer or Explorer unless you change the default view.
Some applications use the archive attribute to control which files or folders are backed up.
The system attribute is placed on certain files used to boot Windows.

Figure 11.17 **Windows file/folder attributes**

Tech Tip

How to change a file or folder's attributes

To change a file or folder's attributes, right-click the filename or folder name > *Properties* > click attribute checkboxes to enable them. (If the file is not a system file, the system attribute is unavailable.) Click *Apply*.

All Windows-based applications can read from and write to compressed files. The operating system decompresses the file, the file is available to the application, and the operating system re-compresses the file when the file is saved. As for the archive attribute, Windows files and folders have the archive attribute set by default. This is sometimes referred to as having the archive bit set. Backup software frequently has three options that use this archive attribute/bit:

- Full—A full backup is a backup of all files on a particular hard drive partition (a particular drive letter). Some software allows the option of doing a full backup while clearing the archive attribute from a file. This is used with an incremental backup.

- Incremental—An incremental backup makes a backup of files that have changed since the last full backup. If a full backup clears the archive bit, if a file is copied or modified, the copied file or the modified file (not the original) has the archive bit set. The incremental backup copies files that have the archive bit set (and clears the archive bit for that particular file so that another incremental backup can be done at a later time).
- Differential—A differential backup backs up files that have changed since the last full backup like the incremental backup does. The difference is that the differential backup does not reset the archive bit.

Lab 11.15 at the end of the chapter demonstrates the concept of backups.

If a hard drive is partitioned for the NTFS file system, files and folders can be compressed or encrypted. Figure 11.18 provides more information on these concepts.

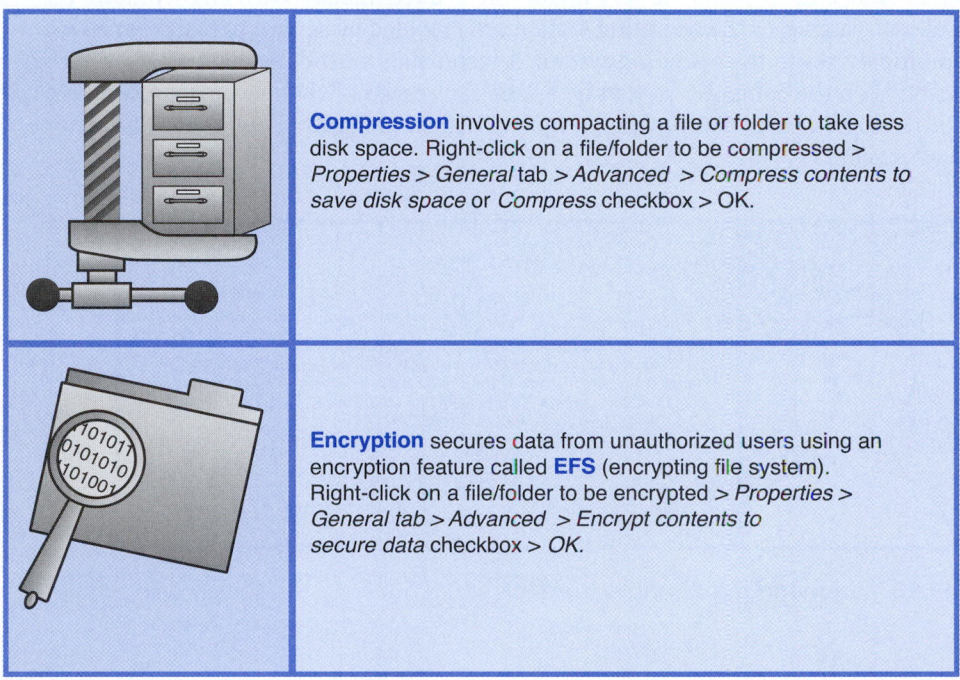

	**Compression** involves compacting a file or folder to take less disk space. Right-click on a file/folder to be compressed > *Properties* > *General* tab > *Advanced* > *Compress contents to save disk space* or *Compress* checkbox > OK.
	**Encryption** secures data from unauthorized users using an encryption feature called **EFS** (encrypting file system). Right-click on a file/folder to be encrypted > *Properties* > *General tab* > *Advanced* > *Encrypt contents to secure data* checkbox > *OK.*

Figure 11.18 Windows compression and encryption

Compression causes your computer to slow down

Tech Tip

When compression is enabled, the computer's performance can degrade because when a compressed file is opened, the file must be uncompressed, and then it must be recompressed in order to be saved or closed. Degradation can also occur if a compressed file is transferred across a network because the file must be uncompressed before it is transferred.

What happens when a compressed file is moved or copied?

Tech Tip

Moving or copying a compressed file or folder can alter the compression. When moving a compressed file or folder, the file or folder remains compressed. When copying a compressed file or folder, it is only compressed if the destination folder (where you are moving it to) is already compressed. When adding a file to an encrypted folder, the file is automatically encrypted.

Compressed files, system files, and read-only files cannot be encrypted. Windows Vista/7 Starter, Home Basic, and Home Premium versions do not fully support encryption, but the other Windows Vista/7 versions do. In the older versions, the `cipher` command can be used at the command prompt to decrypt files, modify an encrypted file, and copy an encrypted file to the computer. The older Windows version cannot encrypt. When a file or folder is encrypted with EFS, only authorized users can view or change the file. Administrators designated as recovery agents have the ability to recover encrypted files when necessary. Labs 11.8 and 11.14 at the end of the chapter demonstrate how to manipulate file attributes, compression, and encryption.

Determining the Windows Version

The version of an operating system is very important to a technician. With any Windows version, upgrades or patches to the operating system are provided by service packs. A **service pack** has multiple fixes to the operating system. A technician must determine what operating system version is on the computer so that he or she can research whether or not a service pack is needed or research a particular problem. Figure 11.19 shows quite a few ways to determine the Windows version.

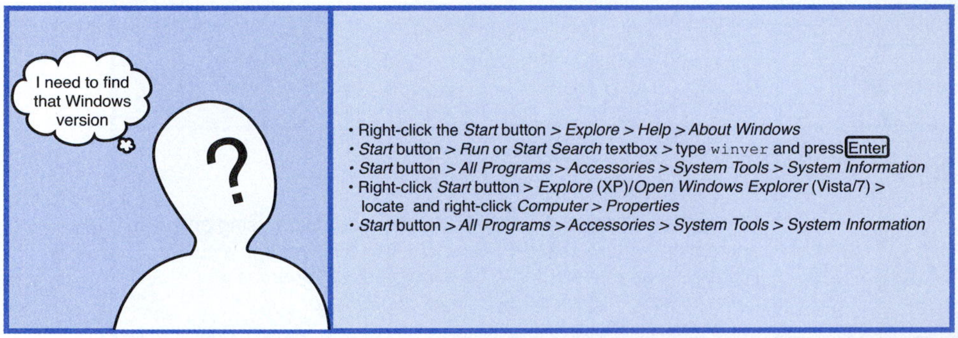

Figure 11.19 Locating the Windows version

Windows Registry

Every software and hardware configuration is stored in a database called the **registry**. The registry contains such things as folder and file property settings, port configuration, application preferences, and user profiles. A **user profile** contains specific configuration settings such as the specific applications to which the user has access, desktop settings, and the user's network configuration for each person who has an account on the computer. The profile is different for each person who has an account on the computer. The registry loads into RAM (memory) during the boot process. Once in memory, the registry is updated continuously by changes made to software, hardware, and user preferences.

The registry is divided into five subtrees. Subtrees are also sometimes called branches or hives. The five standard subtrees are as follows: `Hkey_Local_Machine`, `Hkey_Users`, `Hkey_Current_User`, `Hkey_Current_Config`, and `Hkey_Classes_Root`. Each of these subtrees has keys and subkeys that contain values related to hardware and software settings. Table 11.6 lists the five subtrees and their functions. The registry can contain other subtrees that are user defined or system defined, depending on what hardware or software is installed on the computer.

Table 11.6 Windows registry subtrees

Registry subtree	Subtree function
`Hkey_Local_Machine`	Holds global hardware configuration. Included in the branch is a list of hardware components installed in the computer, the software drivers that handle each component, and the settings for each device. This information is not user specific.
`Hkey_Users`	Keeps track of individual users and their preferences.
`Hkey_Current_User`	Holds a specific user's configuration, such as software settings, how the desktop appears, and what folders the user has created.
`Hkey_Current_Config`	Holds information about the hardware profile that is used when the computer first boots.
`Hkey_Classes_Root`	Holds file associations and file links. The information held here is what allows the correct application to start when you double-click a filename in Explorer or My Computer/Computer (provided that the file extension is registered).

Editing the Windows Registry

Most changes to Windows are done through the various control panels, but sometimes the only way to make a change is to edit the registry directly. Lab 11.9 at the end of the chapter illustrates this procedure. Depending on the Windows operating system being used, one or two registry editors are available: `regedit` and `regedt32`. Figure 11.20 shows the Windows 7 `regedit` utility.

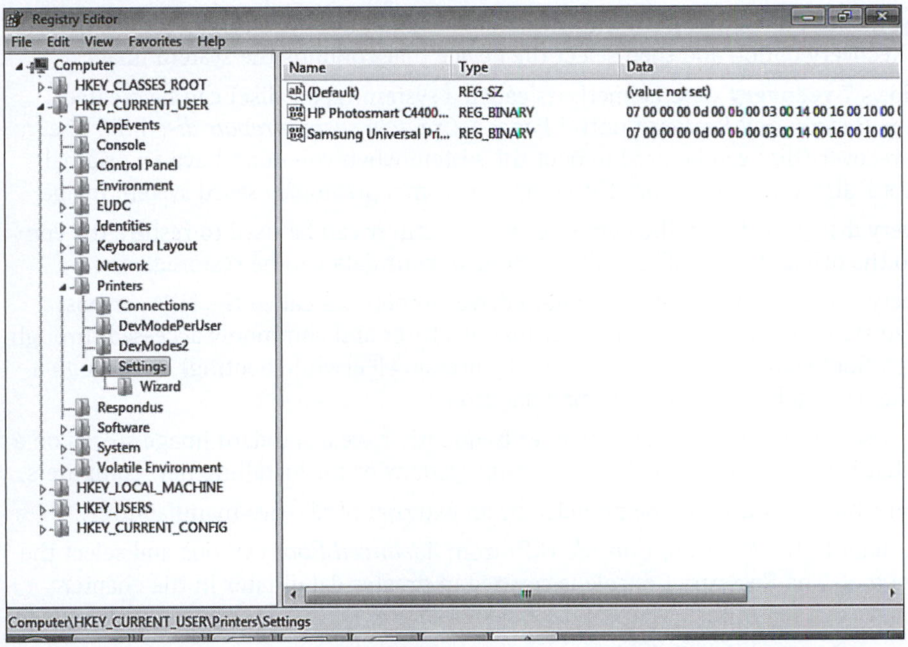

Figure 11.20 `REGEDIT` **in Windows 7**

Notice in Figure 11.20 that subtrees appear in the left window, such as `Hkey_Classes_Root` and `Hkey_Current_User`. If you click the arrow (Vista/7) or plus symbol (XP) beside a subtree, more subkeys appear. After several layers, when you click a folder in the left window, values appear in the right window. These values are the ones you must sometimes change to fix a problem. Labs 11.1, 11.2, and 11.9 at the end of the chapter demonstrate how to modify the registry.

Tech Tip

Make a backup of the registry before you change it

Before making changes to the registry, you should make a backup of it. This way, if the changes do not work properly, the changes can be easily reversed.

For 64-bit versions of Windows, the registry is divided into 32- and 64-bit keys. The 32-bit keys are kept in a subfolder called *Wow6432Node*, located within the *Hkey_Local_Machine* key (*Software* folder). On some machines, the vendor may have a subfolder under Software; it is this vendor subfolder that contains the *Wow6432Node* folder. Just do a search for *Wow6432Node* to find it.

Recovering the Windows OS

When a computer starts performing badly and the operating system tools do not seem to help, you may need to replace the operating system. A virus could also cause extensive damage, resulting in the need for an operating system recovery. How this process is done depends on what measures have been taken (or not been taken, in some cases) and the type of environment where the computer is located (home or work). The list that follows describes some of the common methods used to recover an operating system:

- A Windows 7 **system image** can be created using the *Backup and Restore* Control Panel > *Create a system image* link. The system image contains the operating system and all user files that can be saved to one of three locations:
  - Optical discs
  - Hard drive (Do not store on the same hard drive as the operating system.)
  - Network location (Keep in mind that you have to be able to get to the network location to get the image. This might be difficult if the computer is not working. You could burn the image from another computer that works.)

  When you boot the system from the Windows 7 original disc, you can select the System Image Recovery option and then select the device that contains the system image.
- A Windows 7 **recovery disc** (sometimes called a system repair disc) can be created using the *Backup and Restore* Control Panel > *Create a system repair disc* link. The system recovery disc can be used to boot the system when you don't have an original Windows 7 disc and then restore the computer from a previously saved system image.
- A recovery disc provided by the computer manufacturer can be used to restore the computer to the original "as sold" condition. None of your data will be restored.
- A recovery partition or section of the hard drive (sometimes called the HPA, or host protected area) created by the computer manufacturer and commonly accessed through Advanced Boot Options (which you access by pressing F8 while booting) or through a keystroke defined by the computer manufacturer.
- You can use imaging software. Companies frequently have a standard image stored on a server that is used to replace failing operating systems or for installing new computers.
- Backup/restore software may be provided by an external hard drive manufacturer.
- You can boot to the *Recovery Console* (XP) from *Advanced Boot Options* and select the recovery tool. The Recovery Console is covered in greater detail later in the chapter.

- You can use original operating system discs or image. This method is a risky one because the original discs or image do not contain the latest service packs. Download service packs and copy the service pack to an optical disc *before* re-installing the operating system. Research the service pack requirements before installing. Ensure the computer is disconnected from any network before re-installing the operating system and service packs! Do not connect to the network until the service packs have been installed, or virus infection may result.
- You can to *Safe Mode* (XP, Vista, or 7) or *Recovery Console*(XP) from *Advanced Boot Options* (F8 while booting) and use the *System Restore* tool to restore the operating system to a time when it worked.

Recovering a Mobile OS

When any mobile device will not boot, attach the power cord and allow it to charge for a while before retrying the boot. If the device still won't boot, remove the battery for a minute, re-install the battery, re-attach the power cord, and allow the device to charge for a while before retrying the boot. If the device still won't boot, remove any external devices, including SD memory cards, and repeat the steps just described.

> **Tech Tip**
>
> **Bad software installation**
>
> If you have recently installed software that might be causing a device not to boot, you need to boot the device in Safe Mode. How to get into this mode varies from one mobile device vendor to another. Common techniques include holding the Menu icon, volume up, or volume down buttons while powering on the device.

Apple provides iCloud for backing up data and storing it in a remote location (in the cloud). Common items that might be backed up include contacts, photos, configuration settings, mail, calendar, and app data. An Android device uses the Google Gmail account to access the Google Play store and previously backed up data and settings, including any downloaded content, contacts, email, and calendar information. There are free apps and apps that charge for cloud storage, but the Apple- or Google-provided storage is best for smart device configuration settings.

If an Apple iPhone iOS becomes corrupt, connect the iPhone to the computer using a USB cable. Open iTunes if the application does not launch automatically. Select the iPhone from the devices that appear on the left. From the summary page, click *Restore*. Do not unplug the iPhone during this process.

For an Android phone, check with the phone manufacturer for OS recovery procedures. For other backed-up data, you can use a wireless network, the cellular network, or a USB connection. To transfer files, connect an Android device to a computer using a USB cable. Access *Settings > Wireless & Networks > More > Tethering & portable hotspot* to enable USB tethering.

Most mobile devices allow you to do a hard factory reset. Do this procedure only as a last resort because all data (except for data stored on an SD memory card) will be erased. Like the Safe Mode, this process is different for each mobile device, so check the Internet for the specific mobile device model.

Virtualization Basics

Have you ever seen a TV service that allows you to watch multiple different sports channels at once in smaller windows, or a service that allows you to watch a smaller screen of a different channel in the corner of a larger window? That is like virtualization in the computer world. **Virtualization** of a PC involves a computer that has a virtual application like a VMware Workstation or Oracle VirtualBox, or Microsoft Virtual PC that has other instances of one or more operating systems. Virtualization would allow someone to run multiple operating systems on the same computer without affecting each other, share hardware like CPU, RAM, USB ports, NIC, and hard drive space, and provide a test environment or an operational environment for software that might not be compatible on a specific platform. Figure 11.21 shows the concept of virtualization, and Table 11.7 has some terms commonly used with virtualization.

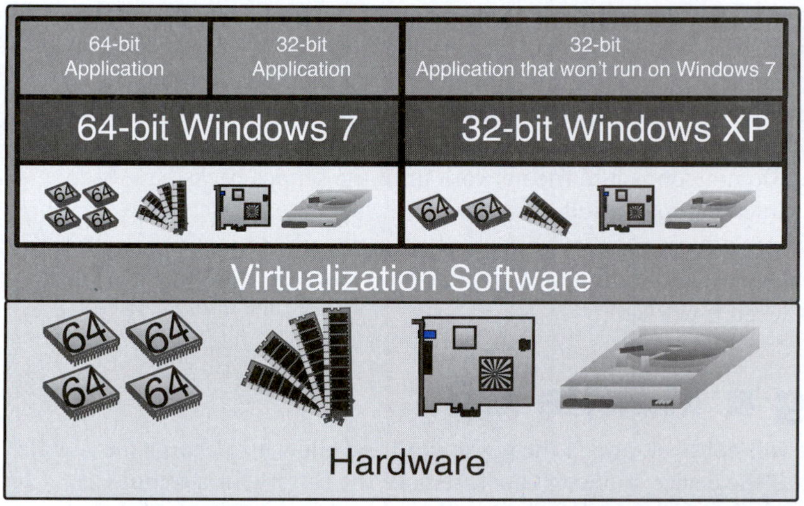

Figure 11.21 PC virtualization

Table 11.7 Virtualization terms

Term	Description
Host machine	The real computer
Virtual machine	Also called a VM; a separate operating system from the host computer that has specifically chosen hardware components
Hypervisor	Also called virtual machine monitor or virtual machine manager; the software that is used to create the virtual machine and allocate resources to the virtual machine
Snapshot	Similar concept as restore point; a copy or backup of the VM at a particular point in time; the snapshot can be used to revert the VM to that point in time

Notice in Figure 11.21 that there are fewer CPUs and less RAM in the VM (virtual machine) on the right than CPUs virtually "installed" in the left VM. Within one virtual environment, you should not (and, in some instances, cannot) "install" more hardware than is on the host machine (the real machine), even though some virtual software allows you to do so. For example, say that the virtual machine on the left in Figure 11.21 is assigned the full amount of RAM that is on the host machine, 4GB. The virtual machine on the right is assigned 2GB. The total is 6GB, but the host machine has only 4GB. This is allowed and common in the virtual environment. Some virtualization software (but not all) allows you to select 6GB for the virtual machine on the left, but doing so causes degradation in the virtual environment.

Working with VMs makes restoring an operating system (or a VM that holds an operating system) much easier than using the restoration methods previously described. Technicians today are expected to know the basics of working within a virtual environment. Chapter 12 provides more information on installing and configuring VMs.

Recovery Console/WinRE

Recovery Console is used when Windows XP does not boot and other startup options do not solve the problem. **WinRE** (Windows Recovery Environment) is used for the same purpose in Windows Vista and 7. Recovery Console is a command prompt only environment. WinRE has a list of recovery options including a command prompt only environment.

Recovery Console allows access to hard drive volumes without starting the GUI (graphical user interface). In other words, Recovery Console allows you access to a command prompt from which you use commands to start and stop services, repair and access hard drive volumes, replace corrupt files, and perform a manual recovery.

Recovery Console is not loaded onto a system by default, but it can be installed from the XP CD and then loaded through the boot menu or executed from the XP CD. Normally technicians run Recovery Console from the original XP CD when there is a problem.

> **Tech Tip**
>
> **Recovery Console requires the Administrator password**
>
> You must have the Administrator password to access the full potential of Recovery Console. Without it, many options are not available and the system will not be able to be repaired.

To run Recovery Console from the XP CD, use the XP CD and press R at the Welcome to Setup screen to select the repair the installation option. Press the number that corresponds to the partition where XP is loaded. An Administrator password prompt appears. Type the Administrator password and press Enter. A command prompt appears.

The drive letters available at the Recovery Console command prompt might not be the same ones you used in the GUI environment. Use the `map` command to see the drive letters (and the volumes that do not have drive letters).

Recovery Console has four default limitations of which a technician should be aware:

- By default, no text editor is available in Recovery Console.
- Files cannot be copied to removable media such as floppy disks or flash drives while in Recovery Console; write access is disabled.
- The Administrator password cannot be changed from Recovery Console.
- Some folders, such as Program Files and Documents and Settings, are inaccessible from the Recovery Console prompt.

The WinRE environment in Windows Vista and 7 provides access to tools to troubleshoot the operating system when the tools within the operating system cannot be accessed or don't work properly. The tools are available through a special recovery partition accessed through Advanced Boot Options (F8 while booting) or from the original Windows installation disc. Select *Repair your computer*, and use the *System Recovery Options*. System Recovery Options are covered in detail in Chapter 12.

Command Prompt Overview

Quite a few computer problems are software-related, and many hardware installations have software programs that allow the hardware to work. Running diagnostic software is something a technician also performs from time to time. Even with the advent of newer and more powerful operating systems, a technician still must enter basic commands into the computer while troubleshooting. Being able to function from a command prompt is a skill that a technician still must use sometimes. When an operating system does not work, the technician must be able to input commands from a prompt.

> **Tech Tip**
>
> **Run Device Manager from a prompt**
>
> From a command prompt or from the *Search text* textbox (Vista)/*Search programs and files* (7), type `mmc devmgmt.msc` to start Device Manager. Note that you can access the Microsoft Management Console and still get to Device Manager by simply typing `mmc`.

An operating system has two types of commands—internal and external. Internal commands are not visible, no matter what view you choose in Windows Explorer; however, after you enter the commands, they execute. Internal commands are built into the operating system and execute much faster than external commands. Two examples of internal commands are `dir` and `copy`. Use the `dir` command to view a list of files and directories. Use the `copy` command to make a duplicate file or folder.

External commands can be seen when viewing files through Windows Explorer. External commands execute slower than internal commands because the external commands must retrieve data from a disk or hard drive. For example, you can do a search through Windows Explorer using the *Search* option from the Start button (XP), *Search text* textbox (Vista), or *Search programs and files* textbox (7), to find the `attrib.exe` command, but you cannot use the same technique and find the `copy` command. Both commands work from a command prompt, but `attrib.exe` is an external command and `copy` is an internal command. The `attrib` command is used to set an attribute such as read-only or hidden on a file or folder manually.

There are several ways to access a command prompt when the computer is functional:

- *Start* > *Run* (XP), *Start* > *Search programs and files* textbox in Vista/7 > type `cmd` and press Enter.
- *Start* > *Run* (XP) or *Start programs and files* textbox in Vista/7 > type `command` and press Enter; note that when this option is used, the keyboard arrow keys do not bring up previously used commands as the `cmd` command does.
- *Start* > *All Programs* > *Accessories* > *Command Prompt* (XP, Vista, and Windows 7).

Command Prompt Basics

Drive letters are assigned to hardware devices when a computer boots. For example, the first floppy drive gets the drive letter `A:`. The colon is part of the device drive letter. The first hard drive in a system gets the drive letter `C:`. The devices detected by the operating system can use drive letters `A:` through `Z:`.

Tech Tip

Maximum number of files in the root directory

A FAT (also called FAT16)-formatted partition or flash drive can hold a maximum of 512 files or directories. A drive will send an "out of space" error message if there are more than 512 files in the root directory even if the drive has gigabytes of available space. Creating directories helps to organize files and keep the root directory uncluttered.

All communication using typed commands begins at the **command prompt**, or simply a prompt. A command prompt might look like `A:\>` or `C:\>` or `C:\Windows>`. Commands are typed using a keyboard. Capitalization does not matter when using a command prompt, but commands *must* be typed in a specific format and in a specific order. Practicing commands from a command prompt is the best way to become proficient at using them.

Files can be organized like chapters in a book; however, on a computer, these file groupings are called a folder (GUI environment) or a **directory** (command prompt environment). The starting point for all directories is the **root directory**. From the root directory, other directories can be made. The root directory is limited as to how many files it can hold.

It is easier to see some of the file structure concepts from within Windows XP Explorer than in Windows 7 Explorer. Figure 11.22 shows that the root directory of the C: drive contains folders such as Binaries, Config.Msi, Dell, and Documents and Settings.

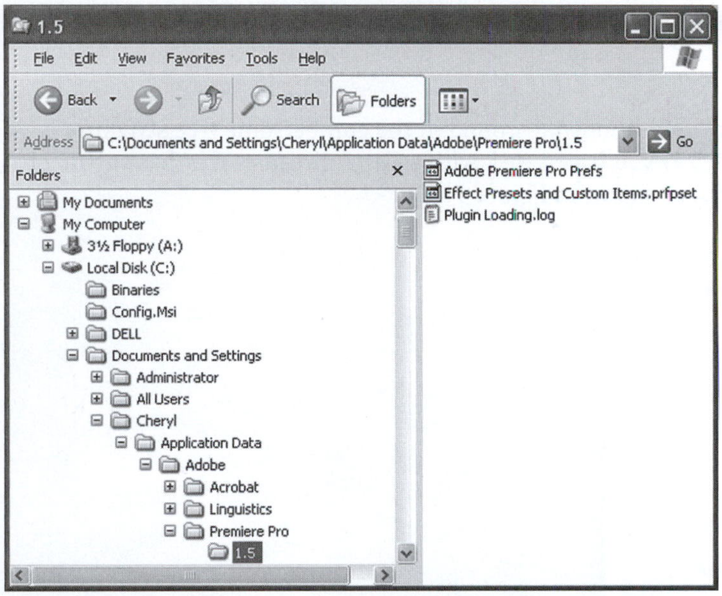

Figure 11.22 Sample file structure

When the + sign beside the *Documents and Settings* folder is clicked, the folders within the folder, such as the folders *Administrator, All Users,* and *Cheryl,* are displayed. Within the *Cheryl* folder, there is a folder within called *Application Data*. When you expand the *Application Data* folder, one folder called *Adobe* exists. When the *Adobe* folder is expanded, three folders are shown: *Acrobat, Linguistics,* and *Premier Pro*. Within the *Premier Pro* folder is another folder called *1.5*. When you click the *1.5* folder, the contents of the folder displays on the right—*Adobe Premiere Pro Prefs, Effect Presets and Custom Items.prfpset,* and *Plugin Loading.log*. The path to the *Plugin Loading.log* file is shown at the top of the window. You would have to add the name of the file to the end of the path that is shown for the complete path:

```
C:\Documents and Settings\Cheryl\Application Data\Adobe\Premiere Pro\1.5\Plugin
Loading.log
```

Every folder along the path is shown, starting with the root directory of `c:` (`c:\`). The path tells you exactly how to reach the file.

An infinite number of files can exist under each directory. Each filename within a directory must be unique, but other directories can contain the same file. For example, let us assume that the *Cheryl.txt* file exists in the *Windows* directory. A different *Cheryl.txt* file (or the same one) can exist in the *Lotus* or *Utility* directory (or all three directories for that matter). It could also be the exact same file called *Cheryl.txt* that exists in all three folders. However, a second *Cheryl.txt* file cannot exist in the same folder (directory).

Files are kept in directories (folders) or in the root directory. A **subdirectory** can be created beneath another directory. For example, if a directory (folder) has the name *Book,* below the directory can be subdirectories titled *Chap1, Chap2, Chap3,* and so on. In Figure 11.22, the three folders under the *Adobe* folder would be considered subdirectories.

Moving Around from a Command Prompt

The most frequently used command for moving around in the cumbersome tree structure is `cd` (change directory). For example, say you have a disk with a *Test1* directory that has subdirectories called *Sub1*, *Sub2*, and *Sub3*, as shown in Figure 11.23.

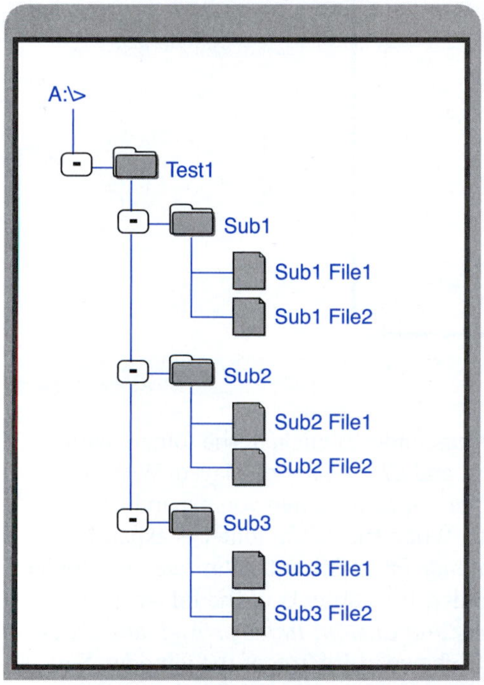

Figure 11.23 Sample tree structure

Assume that the prompt is at `A:\>`. To move to the *Sub2* subdirectory (subfolder), type the command `cd Test1\Sub2`. The prompt changes to `A:\Test1\Sub2>`. Another command that works is `cd A:\Test1\Sub2`.

To move to a subdirectory that is on the same level as the *Sub2* directory (such as *Sub1* or *Sub3*), several commands are possible. One way is to type `cd..` to move back one level and then type `cd Sub1`. Notice that there is not a backslash (\) between `cd` and `Sub1`. You omit the backslash only when moving one level down the tree structure shown in the figure. From the `A:\Test1>` prompt, you can type `cd Sub1`, `cd\Test1\Sub1`, or `cd A:\Test1\Sub1` to get to the *Sub1* subfolder. However, if the prompt shows you are at the root directory (`A:\>`), either `A:\Test1\Sub1` or `cd Test1\Sub1` must be used. The other commands given do not operate properly because of the current location within the tree structure. Practice is the best way to master moving around from a prompt. Labs 11.12, 11.13, 11.14, and 11.15 at the end of the chapter help with this concept.

The `TYPE` Command

A useful command is the `type` command, which is used to display text (.txt) or batch (.bat) files on the screen. Many times *Readme.txt* files are included with software applications and utilities. The `Type` command allows viewing these files; however, most of the time, these files occupy more than one screen. So, using the `| more` parameter after the `type` command permits viewing the file one screen at a time. After viewing each screen, the [Spacebar] is pressed. For example, `type readme.txt | more` allows viewing the text file one page at a time.

Copying Files

The **copy** command is used to make a duplicate of a file. The copy command is an internal command meaning it cannot be found as an executable file on the hard drive or Windows disc. The operating system can always find an internal command no matter where in the directory structure the command is located. The command allows you to copy a file to a different disk, copy a file from one directory to another, copy a group of files using wildcards, or rename a file as it is being copied. A **wildcard** replaces one or more characters. ? and * are examples of wildcards, where ? represents a single character and * represents any number of characters.

The copy command has three parts, separated by spaces:

- The command itself (copy or xcopy)
- The source (the file being copied)
- The destination (where the file is being copied to)

In technical documentation, this would be shown as `copy source target`.

The destination is optional if the file copies into the current directory. For example, if working from the `E:\>` command prompt and copying a file called *Document.txt* from the hard drive's root directory, then the command could be `copy C:\Document.txt`. The destination is omitted because the file automatically copies to the current drive and directory (which is `E:\`). The same function can be accomplished by typing `copy C:\Document.txt E:\`, which has all three parts—the `copy` command, the *source* (a file called *Document.txt* located on the hard drive or `C:\Document.txt`), and the destination (the root directory of E or `E:\`).

The command requires all three parts if the destination is *not* the current drive and directory. For example, take the situation of being at the `C:\>` command prompt. To copy the `format.com` command from the hard drive to a disk located in the `E:` drive, type the following command:

```
copy C:\Windows\System32\format.com  E:\
```

Note that the `copy` command is first. Then the source, the location, and name of the file being copied—`C:\Windows\System32\format.com`—is next. Last is the destination, `E:\`, or the root directory of the flash drive where the file is to be placed. If the current directory is the `C:\Windows\System32` hard drive directory, then the source path does not have to be typed. Instead, the command would look like the following:

```
C:\Windows\System32> copy format.com E:\
```

The backslash (\) after the `E:` is not necessary if the flash drive does not have directories (folders). The `copy` command does not need the entire path in front of the command because `copy` is an internal command.

> **Tech Tip**
>
> **Use the complete path if you are unsure about what command to use**
>
> New technicians commonly make mistakes in specifying a command's path. If you are a beginner, the safest way is to type the complete path of the command, source, and destination locations.

Before using any command, consider the following questions:

- What command do you want to issue?
- Where is the command located in the directory structure?
- Where in the directory structure are you currently working?
- If you are copying a file or moving a file, in what directory does the file need to be placed?

The ATTRIB Command

The `attrib` command sets, removes, or shows the attribute of a file or a directory. Attributes change how a file or directory is displayed on the screen or what can be done with the file or directory. Possible attributes are read-only, archive, system, and hidden:

- The read-only attribute protects files so they cannot be accidentally changed or deleted.
- The archive attribute marks files that have changed since they were last backed up by a backup program.
- The system attribute designates a file as a system file; files with this attribute do not show in directory listings.
- The hidden attribute allows file hiding and even directory hiding.

Set each attribute using the `+x` switch, where `x` is `r` for read-only, `-a` for archive, `h` for hidden, or `s` for system. Remove each attribute using the `-r`, `-s`, `-h`, or `-a` switch with the `attrib` command. One command can set more than one attribute on files or directories. For example, to make the *Cheryl.txt* file hidden and read-only, type `attrib +r +h Cheryl.txt`.

Why Learn Commands?

With many Windows Vista and 7 problems, some solutions involve working from a command prompt until a Windows update fixes the problem or simply always involves using a command from a prompt. Commands can also be used in a script. A script is a group of commands in one file that automate a particular task. For example, say that you want to write a script to stop a computer print spooler and delete all spooled files that are in the queue to be printed. The following commands could be written in Notepad and saved to a file called *DeletePrint.cmd*:

```
net stop spooler
del %systemroot%\system32\spool\printers\*.shd
del %systemroot%\system32\spool\printers\*.spl
net start spooler
```

Once the file is saved, you could copy this file to a hard drive and just type `DeletePrint` and press [Enter], and the four commands execute.

In today's computing environment, a technician frequently has to do things to hundreds, or even thousands, of computers. Scripts and Windows PowerShell can help. Windows PowerShell is an automation technology to help technicians and network administrators automate support functions. Windows 7 ships with PowerShell as an accessory. Every command that you can type from a command window (and a lot more) can be executed from within PowerShell.

Command Format

When Windows does not boot, a technician must work from a command prompt. Some of the most frequently used commands are outlined on the following pages. Items enclosed by brackets are optional. Items in italics are command specific values that you must enter. When the items are separated by a `|` (bar), one of the items must be typed. The / (forward slash) is used with a **command switch** to modify or control how a command executes. For example, with the `dir` command, you could simply type `dir` and press [Enter]. You could also type `dir /p` and display things one page at a time or `dir /w` and display the output in a wide format. Note that not all options shown may be available when using Recovery Console. Most commands have more options than what is shown. Use the Internet or `help` to see more options.

The section that follows contains a command reference. Some of these commands are used in the labs of this chapter or within chapter text and labs for the chapters that follow. Some commands are operating system–dependent. This list is by no means comprehensive. Visit the microsoft.com website for a complete listing.

How to get help when working from a prompt

To get help while working from a prompt, type `help` *`command_name`* or type *`command_name`* `/?`. For example, to get help for the `attrib` command, type `help attrib` or `attrib /?`.

Tech Tip

ATTRIB

The `attrib` command is used to control the attribute for a file or folder.

Syntax: `attrib [+|-h] [+|-r] [+|-a] [+|-s][drive:][path]filename [/S][/D]`

Explanation:
`+` adds an attribute.
`-` takes away an attribute.
`h` is the hidden attribute.
`r` is the read-only attribute.
`a` is the archive file attribute.
`s` is the system attribute.
`[drive:]` is the drive where the file is located.
`[path]` is the directory/subdirectory where the file is located.
`filename` is the name of the file.
`[/S]` includes subfolders.
`[/D]` includes folders

Example: `attrib +h c:\cheryl.bat` sets the hidden attribute for a file called *Cheryl.bat* located on the hard drive.

Notes: The `dir` command (typed without any switches) is used to see what attributes are currently set. You may set more than one attribute at a time.

BCDEDIT

The `bcdedit` command is used at the command prompt or System Recovery environment in Windows Vista and Windows 7 to modify and control settings contained in the BCD (boot configuration data) store, which controls how the operating system boots. The BCD store is similar to the *Boot.ini* file in previous editions of Windows.

Syntax: `bcdedit [/createstore] [/copy] [/create] [/delete] [/deletevalue] [/set] [/enum] [/bootsequence] [/default] [/displayorder] [/timeout]`

Explanation:
`[/createstore]` creates a new empty BCD store that is not a system store.
`[/copy]` is used to make a copy of a specific boot entry contained in the BCD store.
`[/create]` is used to create a new entry in the BCD store.
`[/delete]` is used to delete an element from a specific entry in the BCD store.
`[/deletevalue]` is used to delete a specific element from a boot entry.
`[/set]` is used to set a specific entry's option value.
`[/enum]` is used to list entries in a store.
`[/bootsequence]` is used to specify a display order that is used one time only. The next time the computer boots, the original display order is shown.
`[/default]` selects the entry used by the boot manager when the timeout expires.
`[/displayorder]` is used to specify a display order that is used each time the computer boots.
`[/timeout]` is used to specify, in seconds, the amount of time before the boot manager boots using the default entry.

Example: `bcdedit / set Default debug on`
This command troubleshoots a new operating system installation for the operating system that is the default option that appears in the Boot Manager menu.

Notes: Use the `bcdedit /? types` command to see a list of data types. Use the `bcd /? formats` command to see a list of valid data formats. To get detailed information on any of the options, type `bcdedit /?` followed by the option. For example, to see information on how to export the BCD, type `bcd /? export`.

BOOTCFG

The `bootcfg` command is used to change, delete, configure, or query entries set in the *Boot.ini* file for Windows XP and earlier.

Syntax: When used from a command prompt within the operating system:
`bootcfg [/copy |/delete |/query |/timeout | /default] [arguments]`

Explanation: `[/copy]` creates a copy of the current boot entry [operating systems] section of *Boot.ini* and this can be used to add options.
`[/delete]` is used to delete the existing boot entry [operating systems] section of *Boot.ini*. An argument must be used to specify which boot entry is to be deleted.
`[/query]` displays the current boot entries.
`[/timeout]` is used to change the timeout value for the *Boot.ini* file.
`[/default]` is used to change the default operating system defined in the *Boot.ini* file.
`[arguments]` are options normally available with a specific command. To see what arguments are available for a specific parameter type `bootcfg`, press the Spacebar once, then a forward slash (/), then the specific parameter such as `copy` or `delete`, press the Spacebar once, and type `/?`. An example is `bootcfg /copy /?`.

Example: `bootcfg /delete /id 1` deletes the second boot entry from the *Boot.ini* file.

BOOTREC

The **`bootrec`** command is used from Recovery Console (XP) or the System Recovery environment (Vista/Windows 7) to repair and recover from hard drive problems.

Syntax: `bootrec [/FixMbr] [/FixBoot] [/ScanOs] [/RebuildBcd]`

Explanation: `[/FixMbr]` repairs the hard drive MBR (master boot record) by copying a new MBR to the system partition. The existing partition table is not altered.
`[FixBoot]` repairs the hard drive boot sector if it has been corrupted and replaces it with a non-Windows Vista/Windows 7 boot sector or, if an earlier version of Windows has been installed, *after* Windows Vista or Windows 7.
`[/ScanOs]` looks for compatible operating system installations that do not currently appear on the Boot Manager list.
`[/RebuildBcd]` scans all disks for operating systems compatible with Windows Vista or Windows 7 and optionally rebuilds the BCD (boot configuration data). The BCD store provides structured storage for boot settings that is especially helpful in multiple operating system environments. Discovered operating systems can be added to the BCD store.

Example: `bootrec /fixmbr`
This command could be used if a virus has destroyed the master boot record.

Notes: If you receive an "Element not Found" error when using the `bootrec` command, the hard drive partition might not be active. Use the Vista/Windows 7 recovery environment command prompt and the `diskpart` command to select the drive disk number (if you only have one and it has one partition, it will be the command `select disk 0`, as an example), and then type the command `active`. Exit the `diskpart` utility and reboot the computer. Re-access the System Recovery environment and rerun the `bootrec` command.

If the system needs new BCD and rebuilding it did not help, you can export the existing BCD and then delete the current BCD. To export the BCD, type `bcdedit /export x:\folder` (where `x:\folder` is the location to where you want the BCD store exported). Then type `c:`, `cd boot`, `attrib bcd -s -h -r`, `ren c:\boot\bcd bcd.old`, `bootrec /RebuildBcd` to create a backup copy of the BCD store, make it so it is not hidden and can be deleted, and then rebuild it.

CD

The **`cd`** command is used to navigate through the directory structure.

Syntax: `cd [drive:][path][..]`

Explanation: `[drive:]` specifies the drive (if a different one than the current drive) to which you want to change.

[path] is the directory/subdirectory to reach the folder.
[..] is used to change to the parent directory (moves you back one directory in the tree structure).

Example: C:\Windows>cd..
C:\>
This command moves you from the *Windows* directory (folder) to the parent directory, which is the root directory (C:\).
C:\>cd \Windows
This command moves you from the root directory to the *Windows* directory on the C: drive.

CHKDSK

The **chkdsk** command checks a disk for physical problems, lost clusters, cross-linked files, and directory errors. If necessary, the chkdsk command repairs the disk, marks bad sectors, recovers information, and displays the status of the disk.

Syntax: chkdsk [*drive*:] [/r] [/f] [/i] [/b]
Explanation: [*drive*:] specifies the drive to check.
[/r] locates bad sectors and attempts recovery of the sector's information.
[/f] fixes drive errors.
[/i] checks only index entries on NTFS volumes.
[/b] With NTFS, the switch re-evaluates bad clusters.
Example: chkdsk d: This command checks the disk structure on the D: drive.
Notes: This command can be used without switches. In order for the chkdsk command to work, the file *Autochk.exe* must be loaded in the *System32* folder or used with the correct path and run from the Windows disc. If one or more files are open on the drive being checked, chkdsk will prompt you to schedule the disk to be checked the next time the computer is restarted.

CHKNTFS

The chkntfs command can display whether a particular disk volume is scheduled for automatic disk checking the next time the computer is started, or the command can be used to modify automatic disk checking.

Syntax: chkntfs *volume*: [/D] [/X] [/C]
Explanation: *volume*: specifies the drive volume to display or modify.
[/D] places the computer back to default behavior (all drives are checked at boot time and chkdsk is run on those that are dirty).
[/X] excludes a particular volume from the default boot-time check.
[/C] schedules a drive to be checked at boot time. The chkdsk command will be run if the drive is dirty.
Example: chkntfs c: Displays whether the drive is dirty or scheduled to be checked on the next computer reboot.

CIPHER

The cipher command displays or alters file or folder encryption.

Syntax: cipher [/e |/d] [/f] [/q] [/k] [/u [/n]] [*path*|
Explanation: [/e] encrypts the specified folder, including files that are added in the future.
[/d] decrypts the specified folder.
[/f] forces encryption or decryption because, by default, files that have already been encrypted or decrypted are skipped.
[/q] reports essential information about the encryption or decryption.
[/k] creates a new file encryption key.
[/u] updates the encryption key to the current one for all encrypted files if the keys have been changed. /u works only with the /n option.
[/n] finds all encrypted files. It prevents keys from being updated. It is used only with /u.
[*path*] is a pattern, file, or folder.

Example: `cipher /e Book\Chap1`
This command encrypts a subfolder called *Chap1* that is located in a folder called *Book*.
`cipher /e /s:Book`
This command encrypts all subfolders in the folder called *Book*.
`cipher Book`
This command displays whether the *Book* folder is encrypted.
`cipher Book\Chap 1\*`
This command display whether any files in the *Chap1* subfolder of the *Book* folder are encrypted.

Notes: Multiple parameters are separated with spaces. Read-only files and folders cannot be encrypted.

CLS

The `cls` command clears the screen of any previously typed commands.

Example: `C:\Windows>cls`

CMD

The **`cmd`** command is executed from the *Run/Search programs and files* text box. (*Start* > *Run* (XP)/*Search programs and files* (Vista/7) > type `cmd.exe` > press Enter.) A command prompt window appears. Type `exit` to close the window.

Syntax: `cmd [/c string]`

Explanation: `[/c string]` specifies that the command interpreter is to perform the command specified by the *`string`* option and then stop.

Example: `cmd /c chkdsk d:` This command runs the `chkdsk` program on the `D:` hard drive volume using the command line.

COPY

The `copy` command is used to copy one or more files to the specified destination.

Syntax: `copy [/a] [/y] [/-y] source [target]`

Explanation: `[/a]` indicates an ASCII text file.
`[/y]` suppresses the prompt to overwrite an existing file.
`[/-y]` prompts to overwrite an existing file.
`source` is the file that you want to copy and it includes the drive letter and the path if it is different from your current location.
`[target]` is the location you want to put the file and it includes the drive letter and path if it is different from your current location.

Example: `copy c:\cheryl.bat a:\`
This command takes a file called *Cheryl.bat* that is located in the root directory of the hard drive and copies it to the floppy drive.

Notes: You do not have to put a target if the file is going to the current location specified by the command prompt. If a file already exists, you will be prompted whether or not to overwrite the file. Compressed files that are copied from the Windows disc are automatically uncompressed to the hard drive as they are copied.

DEFRAG

The `defrag` command is used to locate and reorder files so they are contiguous (not fragmented) and improve system performance.

Syntax: `defrag [drive:] [/a] [/c] [/x]`

Explanation: `[drive:]` is the drive letter where the files are located.
`[/a]` is used to analyze the drive volume specified.
`[/c]` includes all volumes.
`[/x]` consolidates free space on the specified volume.

Example: `defrag c: d: /a`
This command defragments the `C:` and `D:` drives and analyzes them.

Notes: Multiple switches can be used as long as spaces appear between them. Multiple drive letters (volumes) can be used with a single command.

DEL

The **`del`** command is used to delete a file.

Syntax: `del name [/p][/f][/s]`

Explanation: `name` is the file or directory (folder) that you want to delete and it includes the drive letter and the path if it is different from your current location.
`[/p]` is used to prompt for confirmation before deleting.
`[/f]` is used to force read-only files to be deleted.
`[/s]` is used to delete files from all subdirectories.

Example: `C:\Windows>del c:\cheryl.bat`
This command deletes a file called *Cheryl.bat* that is located in the *Windows* directory on the hard drive.

DIR

The **`dir`** command is used to list files and folders and their attributes.

Syntax: `dir [drive:] [path] [filename] [/a:attribute] [/o] [/p] [/s] [/w]`

Explanation: `[drive:]` is the drive letter where the files are located.
`[path]` is the directory/subdirectory to reach the folder.
`[filename]` is the name of a specific file.
`[/a:attribute]` is used to display files that have specific attributes where the attributes are `D`, `R`, `H`, `A`, and `S`. `D` is for directories; `R` is for read-only; `H` is for hidden; `A` is for archive; and `S` is for system files.
`[/o]` displays the listing in sorted order. Options you can use after the `o` are `E`, `D`, `G`, `N`, and `S`. `E` is by alphabetic file extension; `D` is by date and time, with the oldest listing shown first; `G` shows the directories listed first; `N` displays by alphabetic name; and `S` displays by size from smallest to largest.
`[/p]` displays the information one page at a time.
`[/s]` includes subdirectories in the listing.
`[/w]` shows the listing in wide format.

Example: `dir c:\windows`
This command shows all of the files and folders (and their associated attributes) for the *Windows* folder that is located on the `C:` drive.

DISABLE

The `disable` command is used to disable a system service or hardware driver.

Syntax: `disable name`

Explanation: `name` is the name of the service or driver that you want to disable.

Notes: You can use the `listsvc` command to show all services and drivers that are available for you to disable. Make sure that you write down the previous *START_TYPE* before you disable the service in case you need to restart the service.

DISKPART

The **`diskpart`** command is used to manage and manipulate the hard drive partitions.

Syntax: `diskpart [/add|/delete] [devicename] [drivename | partitionname] [size]`

Explanation: `[/add |/delete]` is used to create a new partition or delete an existing partition.
`[devicename]` is the name given to the device when creating a new partition, such as \Device\HardDisk0.

`[drivename]` is the drive letter used when deleting an existing partition such as `E:`.
`[partitionname]` is the name used when deleting an existing partition and can be used instead of the *drivename* option. An example of a *partitionname* is `Device\HardDisk0\Partition2`.
`[size]` is used when creating a new partition and is the size of the partition in megabytes.

Notes: You can just type the `diskpart` command without any options and a user interface appears that helps when managing hard drive partitions. Labs 7.4 and 7.5 demonstrate this command.

DXDIAG

The `dxdiag` command is used to perform DirectX diagnostics.

Syntax: `dxdiag [/dontskip] [whql:on|/whql:off] [/64bit target] [/x filename] [/t filename]`

Explanation: `[/dontskip]` causes all diagnostics to be performed even if a previous crash in `dxdiag` has occurred.
`[/whql:on]` checks for WHQL digital signatures.
`[/whql:off]` prevents checking for WHQL digital signatures.
`[/64bit target]` uses 64-bit DirectX diagnostics.
`[/x filename]` saves XML information to the specified filename and quits.
`[/t filename]` saves TXT information to the specified filename and quits.

Notes: When DirectX diagnostics checks for WHQL digital signatures, the Internet may be used.

ENABLE

The `enable` command is used to enable a system service or hardware driver.

Syntax: `enable name [start-type]`

Explanation: *name* is the name of the service or driver that you want to disable.
`[start-type]` is when you want the service or driver scheduled to begin. Valid options are as follows:
SERVICE_BOOT_START
SERVICE_SYSTEM_START
SERVICE_AUTO_START
SERVICE_DEMAND_START

Example: `enable DHCP client service_auto_start`

Notes: You can use the `listsvc` command to show all services and drivers that are available for you to enable. Make sure that you write down the previous value before you enable the service in case you need to restart the old service or driver.

EXIT

The `exit` command closes the command prompt environment window. If in Recovery Console mode, this command closes Recovery Console and restarts the computer.

Example: `C:\Windows>exit`

EXPAND

The `expand` command is used to uncompress a file from a Windows XP CD or a CAB file. A CAB file is a shortened name for a cabinet file. A CAB file holds multiple Windows XP files or drivers that are compressed into a single file. Cabinet files are normally located in the i386 folder on the Windows XP CD. Technicians frequently copy the CAB files onto the local hard drive, so that when hardware and/or software is installed, removed, or re-installed, the Windows CD does not have to be inserted.

Syntax: `expand [-i] source [destination]`

Explanation: `[-i]` renames files but ignores the directory structure.
source is the name of the file, including the path that you want to uncompress.
`[destination]` is the path to where you want to place the uncompressed file.

Example: `expand d:\i386\access.cp_ c:\windows\system32\access.cpl` expands (uncompresses) the compressed file *Access.cp_* and puts it into the *C:\Windows\Sysytem32* folder with the name *Access.cpl*.

Notes: You may not use wildcard characters with the *source* parameter.

EXPLORER

The `explorer` command is used to start Windows Explorer from a command prompt.

Syntax: `explorer`

FDISK

The `fdisk` command was used to create and manage FAT16 and FAT32 disk partitions.

Example: `FDISK`

Notes: `FDISK` was replaced with the `diskpart` command in Windows XP and higher.

FIXBOOT

The **`fixboot`** command is used to rewrite the hard drive's boot sector.

Syntax: `fixboot [driveletter:]`

Explanation: `[driveletter:]` is the drive letter (and a colon) of the hard drive volume that you want to place in a new boot sector.

Example: `fixboot c:`

Notes: If you do not specify the `driveletter:` parameter, the boot sector that is repaired is the system boot volume's boot sector.

FIXMBR

The **`fixmbr`** command rewrites the startup partition's Master Boot Record.

Syntax: `fixmbr [name]`

Explanation: `[name]` is the name of the device that you want to repair its Master Boot Record.

Example: `fixmbr \Device\HardDisk0`

Notes: If you do not type the `name` parameter, Disk 0 is the default. Use the `map` command to see valid device names. Run an antivirus scan before using this command.

FORMAT

The **`format`** command is used to format a disk and can be used to format it for a particular file system.

Syntax: `format [driveletter:] [/q] [/fs:filesystem] [/v:label] [/x]`

Explanation: `[driveletter:]` is the drive letter for the disk or hard drive volume that you want to format.

`[/q]` is the parameter used if you want to perform a quick format.

`[/fs:filesystem]` is the parameter used if you want to specify a file system. Valid values are as follows: FAT, FAT32, exFAT, and NTFS.

`[/v:label]` The `/v:` must be part of the command followed by the name of the volume assigned.

`[/x]` is used to dismount the volume first, if necessary.

Example: `format c: /fs:ntfs`

Notes: If no `/fs:filesystem` parameter is specified, the NTFS file system is used. FAT is FAT16. FAT16 hard drive volumes cannot be more than 4GB in size

GPRESULT

The `gpresult` command is used to display group policy settings. A group policy determines how a computer is configured for both system and user (or a group of users) settings.

Syntax: `gpresult [/s computer] [/u domain\user] [/p password] [/user target_user] [ /r] [/v] [/z]`

Explanation: `[/s computer]` is an optional parameter used to specify a specific remote computer using the computer name or IP address; otherwise, the local computer is selected by default.

`[/u domain\user]` specifies authentication for the remote computer.

`[/p password]` specifies a password for the remote computer user ID.

`[/user target_user]` specifies to display a specific user's group policy settings.

`[/v]` outputs data in verbose mode.

`[/z]` displays all available data about the group policy.

Examples: `gpresult /r`
`gpresult /s 10.3.207.15 /u pearson\cschmidt /p G#t0Ut0fH3R3`

HELP

The **`help`** command displays information about specific commands.

Syntax: `help [command]`
Explanation: `[command]` is the name of the command for which you want help.
Example: `help expand`
Notes: If you do not specify the *`command`* parameter when using the `help` command, all commands are listed.

IPCONFIG

The `ipconfig` command is used to view and control information related to the network adapter.

Syntax: `ipconfig [/allcompartments] [/all|/renew [adapter] | /release [adapter]|/renew6 [adapter]|/release6 [adapter]|/flushdns|displaydns|/registerdns|/showclassid [adapter]|/setclassid adapter [classid]|/showclassid6 [adapter]|/setclassid6 adapter [classid]]`
Explanation: `[/allcompartments]` displays information regarding all compartments and, when used with the `/all` option, shows detailed information about all compartments.
`[/all]` displays all configuration information, including IP and MAC addresses.
`[/renew]` renews the IPv4 address optionally for a specific adapter.
`[/release]` releases the IPv4 address optionally for a specific adapter.
`[/renew6]` renews the IPv6 address optionally for a specific adapter.
`[/release6]` releases the IPv6 address optionally for a specific adapter.
`[/flushdns]` removes all entries from the DNS resolver cache.
`[/displaydns]` shows the contents of the DNS resolver cache.
`[/registerdns]` refreshes DHCP leases and re-registers recently used DNS names.
`[/show classid]` displays all configured IPv4 DHCP class IDs allowed optionally for a specific adapter.
`[/setclassid adapter]` configures an adapter for a specific IPv4 DHCP class ID. A class ID is used to have two or more user classes that are configured as different DHCP scopes on a server. One class could be for laptops, while a different class could be for desktop computers in an organization.
`[/showclassid6 adapter]` displays all configured IPv6 DHCP class IDs allowed optionally for a specific adapter.
`[/setclassid6 adapter]` configures an adapter for a specific IPv6 DHCP class ID.
Examples: `ipconfig /all`
`ipconfig /release`
`ipconfig /renew`
Notes: The three commands above are essential to a technician. `ipconfig /all` verifies whether an IP address has been configured or received from a DHCP server. `ipconfig /release` releases a DHCP-sent IP address. `ipconfig /renew` starts the DHCP request process.

LISTSVC

The `listsvc` command lists all of the services, hardware drivers, and their start-types available. The `listsvc` command is useful to use before using the `disable` or `enable` command.

Syntax: `listsvc`
Example: `C:\Windows>listsvc`

LOGON

The `logon` command is used to list all Windows installations and prompts for the local Administrator password.
Syntax: `logon`

MAP

The **map** command is used to list the computer's drive letters, types of file systems, volume sizes, and physical device mappings.

Syntax: `map [arc]`

Explanation: `[arc]` is the Advanced RISC Computing path instead of the Windows device paths. This parameter is used when you are repairing or re-creating the *Boot.ini* file.

MD

The **md** command is used to create a directory (folder).

Syntax: `md [driveletter:][dirname]`

Explanation: `[driveletter:]` is the drive letter for the disk or volume on which you want to create a directory (folder). It can also include the path.
`[dirname]` is the parameter used to name the directory (folder).

Example: `md c:\test`

Notes: You may not use wildcard characters with this command. The `mkdir` command can also be used to create a directory.

MORE

The `more` command is used to display a text file.

Syntax: `more filename`

Explanation: `filename` is the path and name of the text file you want to display on the screen.

Example: `more c:\boot.ini`

Notes: The Spacebar allows you to view the next page of a text file. The Enter key allows you to scroll through the text file one line at a time. The Esc key allows you to quit viewing the text file.

MSCONFIG

The `msconfig` command is used to start the System Configuration utility from a command prompt instead of a control panel. The System Configuration utility is commonly used to troubleshoot boot issues specifically related to software and services. The Startup tab lists software loaded when the computer boots, and a checkbox allows you to disable and enable the particular application. The same concept is used with the Services tab, which contains checkboxes beside services started when the computer boots.

Syntax: `msconfig`

MSINFO32

The `msinfo32` command is used to bring up the System Information window from a command prompt. The System Information window contains details about hardware and hardware configurations as well as software and software drivers.

Syntax: `msinfo32 [/computer computer_name]`

Explanation: `[/computer computer_name]` starts the System Information utility for a remote computer.

Examples:
```
msinfo
msinfo /computer Cheryl_Dell
```

MSTSC

The `mstsc` command starts the Remote Desktop utility.

Syntax: `mstsc [/v:computer[:port]]`

Explanation: `[/v:computer[:port]]` specifies the specific remote computer by name or IP address and port number to which you want to connect.

Example: `mstsc /v:Cheryl-PC`

Notes: The default port number for Remote Desktop is 3389, but if a different port has been specified, then you can specify a port using this command.

NBTSTAT

The `nbtstat` command is used to display statistics relevant to current TCP/IP connections on the local computer or a remote computer using NBT (NetBIOS over TCP/IP).

Syntax: `nbtstat [-a remotename] [-A IPaddress] [-c] [-S]`

Explanation: `[-a remotename]` shows the NetBIOS name table for a remote computer designated by *remotename*.

`[-A IPaddress]` shows the NetBIOS name table for a remote computer designated by *IPaddress*.

`[-c]` shows the NetBIOS name cache, names, and resolved IP addresses.

`[-S]` shows NetBIOS client and server sessions.

Examples:

```
nbtstat -S
nbtstat -A 10.5.8.133
```

NET USE

The `net use` command is used to attach to a remote network device.

Syntax: `net use [drive_letter] [\\server_name\share_name /user:domain_name\user_name [password]]`

Explanation: `drive_letter` is the letter (followed by a colon) that `net use` assigns to the network device connection.

`\\server_name` is the name of the network device to which to connect.

`share_name` is the name of the share.

`domain_name` is the domain used to validate the user.

`user_name` is the user to be validated.

`[password]` is an optional entry so the system does not prompt for a password. If this option is not entered, a password prompt appears and the system automatically assigns a drive letter once a connection is made.

Example: `net use \\ATC227-01\cisco /user:cisco\student`

NETSTAT

The `netstat` command is used to attach to a remote network device.

Syntax: `netstat [-a] [-e] [-n] [-o] [-p protocol] [-r] [-s]`

Explanation: `[-a]` shows all connections and listening port numbers.

`[-e]` shows Ethernet statistics and can be used with the `-s` option.

`[-n]` shows addresses and port numbers.

`[-o]` shows active TCP connections.

`[-p protocol]` shows specific connections that are using a specific protocol. The protocol parameter can be one of the following: IP, IPv6, ICMP, ICMPv6, TCP, TCPv6, UDP, UDPv6.

`[-r]` shows the routing table.

`[-s]` shows statistics for a particular protocol.

Examples:

```
netstat
netstat -a
netstat -p TCP
```

Note: The parameters used with this command must be preceded by a dash rather than the / (slash) used by most commands.

NOTEPAD

The `notepad` command starts the Windows Notepad accessory.

Syntax: `notepad`

NSLOOKUP

The `nslookup` command is used for troubleshooting DNS issues.

Syntax: `nslookup [-option] [hostname] [server]`

Explanation: [-*option*] is a variety of options that can be used, such as exit, finger, help, ls, lserver, root, server, and set. See Microsoft TechNet for a complete listing.
[*hostname*] is a name of a host, such as the computer name for a specific computer in the organization.
[*server*] is the URL of a specific server, such as www.pearsoned.com.

Examples: nslookup www.pearsoned.com
nslookup -querytype=hinfo -timeout=10

Notes: The second example changes the default query type to a host and the timeout to 10 seconds. You must have at least one DNS server IP address configured on a network adapter (which you can view with the ipconfig /all command) in order to use the nslookup command. There are two modes of operation: non-interactive and interactive. The non-interactive has more commands than shown in the examples given. The interactive mode is started by simply typing nslookup and pressing Enter.

NTBACKUP

The ntbackup command is used in Windows XP and lower to perform backup operations. In Windows Vista or 7 the command is wbadmin.

Syntax: ntbackup backup [systemstate] "@*bks_file_name*" [/a] [/v:{yes | no}] [/m {*backup_type*}]

Explanation: [systemstate] sets the backup type to normal (or copy) because the System State data is backed up.
"@bks_*file_name*" specifies the name of the backup selection file (.bks file) to be used for the backup. The @ symbol must precede the name of the file.
[/a] appends data to a backup. The /g or /t options must be used with this option, but the /p option cannot be used with it.
[/v:{yes|no}] determines whether data is verified.
[/m {*backup_type*}] determines the type of backup done (normal, copy, differential, incremental, or daily).

Example: ntbackup backup \\cheryl-Dell\c$ /j "CSchmidt Backup 1" /f "d:\backup1.bkf"

PING

The ping command is used to test connectivity to a remote network device.

Syntax: ping [-t] [-a] [-n *count*] [-l *size*] [-i *ttl*] [-S *source_addr*] [-4] [-6] *target*

Explanation: [-t] pings the destination until stopped with Ctrl+C keystrokes. To see the statistics and continue, use the Ctrl+[Break] keys.
[-a] resolves IP addresses to hostnames.
[-n *count*] defines how many pings (echo requests) are sent to the destination.
[-l *size*] defines the buffer size (length of packet).
[-i *ttl*] defines a time to live value from 0 through 255.
[-S *source_addr*] defines the source IP address to use.
[-4] forces the use of IPv4.
[-6] forces the use of IPv6.
target is the destination IP address.

Examples: ping -t www.pearsoned.com
ping -n 2 -l 1450 165.193.130.107

Notes: The first example pings the Pearson Technology Education website indefinitely until the Ctrl+C keys are used. The second example sends two echo requests (pings) that are 1450 bytes to the Pearson Technology Education website.

RD

The rd command is used to remove a directory (folder).

Syntax: rd [*driveletter*:][*path*] *name*

Explanation: `[driveletter:]` is the drive letter for the disk or hard drive volume from which you want to remove a directory (folder).
`[path]` is the optional path and name of the directory (folder) you want to remove.
`name` is the name of the folder/directory to remove.

Example: `rd c:\Test\Junkdata` removes a directory (folder) called *Junkdata* that is a subdirectory under a directory (folder) called *Test*. This directory is located on the hard drive (`c:`).

Notes: You do not have to use the `driveletter:` parameter if the default drive letter is the same as the one that contains the directory to be deleted.

REGSVR32

The **regsvr32** command is used to register `.dll` files in the Windows registry.

Syntax: `regsvr32 [/u] name`

Explanation: `name` is the name of the `.dll` file that will be registered.
`[/u]` is an optional switch used to unregister a `.dll` file.

Example: `Regsvr32 wuapi.dll` registers a Windows update DLL file.

Notes: There is a 64-bit version of this file found in the *SysWow64* folder.

REN

The `ren` command is used to rename a file or directory (folder).

Syntax: `ren [driveletter:][path] name1 name2`

Explanation: `[driveletter:]` is the drive letter for the disk or hard drive volume in which you want to rename a file or a directory (folder).
`[path]` is the optional path telling the operating system where to find the file or directory (folder) you want to rename.
`name1` is the old name of the file or directory (folder) that you want to rename.
`name2` is the new name of the file or directory (folder).

Example: `ren c:\cheryl.bat c:\newcheryl.bat`

Notes: The renamed file cannot be placed in a new location with this command. Move or copy the file after you rename it if that is what you want to do. The `*` and `?` wildcard characters are not supported.

ROBOCOPY

The **robocopy** command is used to copy files, but has a lot more parameters than COPY or XCOPY.

Syntax: `robocopy [source] [destination] [file [file]...] [options]`

Explanation: `[source]` specifies the source directory in the drive:| path format or the \\server\share path format.
`[destination]` specifies the destination directory in the drive:| path format or the \\server\share path format.
`[file]` is the files to copy, including wildcards. The default is `*.*`.
`[options]` includes various options, such as `/s` to copy subdirectories (but not empty ones), `/e` to copy subdirectories (including empty ones), `/mov` to move files and delete the source, `/move` to move files and directories and delete the source, `/a` to copy files with the archive attribute set, and `/m` to copy files with the archive attribute set and to reset the archive bit.

Examples: `robocopy c:\users\cschmidt\My Documents\Book d:\ /e`
`robocopy \\CSchmidt\Book \\RLD\SchmidtBook`

Notes: The first command copies the contents of the *Book* subfolder to the D: drive and includes any empty directories.
The second command copies all files from the *CSchmidt* computer share called *Book* to the *RLD* computer network share called SchmidtBook.

SET

The set command is used to display and view different variables.

Syntax: set [*variable* = *value*]

Explanation: *variable* is one of the following:

AllowWildCards, which is the variable used to enable wildcard support for the commands that normally do not support wildcards.

AllowAllPaths, which is the variable that allows access to all of the computer's files and folders.

AllowRemovableMedia, which is the variable that allows files to be copied to removable media.

NoCopyPrompt, which is the variable that disables prompting when overwriting a file.

value is the setting associated with the specific variable.

Example: set allowallpaths = true allows access to all files and folders on all drives.

set allowremovablemedia = true allows you to use a flash (thumb) drive or floppy.

set allowwildcards = true allows you to use wildcards at the command prompt.

Notes: To see all of the current settings, type set without a variable and the current settings display. The set command can be used only if it is enabled using the Group Policy snap-in.

SFC

The **sfc** command is used to start the System File Checker utility from a command prompt. The System File Checker verifies operating system files.

Syntax: sfc [/scannow] [/verifyonly] [/scanfile=*file_name*] [/verifyfile=*file_name*] [/offwindir=*windows_directory*] [/offbootdir=*boot_directory*]

Explanation: [/scannow] is used to scan all protected system files and repair those that are damaged, if possible.

[/verifyonly] scans all protected system files but does not repair any detected problems.

[/scanfile=*file_name*] scans the specified file and repairs it if necessary. *file_name* should contain the full path.

[/verifyfile=*file_name*] verifies the specified file but does not repair it. *file_name* should contain the full path.

[/offwindir=*windows_directory*] is used for offline repairs for the specified Windows directory.

[/offbootdir=*boot_directory*] is used for offline repairs for the specified boot directory.

Examples:

```
sfc /scannow
sfc /scannow /offwindir=c:\Windows
```

SHUTDOWN

The **shutdown** command is used to restart or shut down a local or remote computer.

Syntax: shutdown [-l] [-s] [-r] [-a] [-f] [-m [*computer_name*]] [-t *xx*] [-c "*message*"]

Notes: If this command is used without any parameters, the command logs off the current user. You cannot use the -a parameter except during the timeout period.

Explanation: [/l] logs off the current user.

[-s] shuts down the computer.

[-r] reboots the computer.

[-a] aborts the shutdown process.

[-f] forces active applications to close.

[-m [*computer_name*] specifies a specific computer to shut down.

[/t *xx*] specifies the number of seconds waited before shutting down the computer.

[-c "*message*"] specifies a 127 maximum character message shown in the System Shutdown window.

Examples:

```
shutdown -f -m \\Raina-PC -t 30 -c "Going down in 30 seconds, daughter"
```

SYSTEMINFO

The `systeminfo` command is used to display detailed configuration information about a specific computer.

Syntax: `systeminfo [/s computer] [/u domain\user] [/p password] [/fo [table | list | csv]]`

Explanation: `[/s computer]` is an optional parameter used to specify a specific remote computer using the computer name or IP address; otherwise, the local computer is selected by default.

`[/u domain\user]` specifies authentication for the remote computer.

`[/p password]` specifies a password for the remote computer user ID.

`[/fo [table | list | csv]]` defines whether the output displays in table format, list format, or csv (comma separated values) format. The default is to display in table format.

Examples:

```
systeminfo
systeminfo /s CSchmidt /u pearson\cschmidt /p G#TOUTOFH3R#
```

SYSTEMROOT

The `systemroot` command sets the current directory as the system root.

Syntax: `systemroot`

Notes: The `systemroot` command is only available through Recovery Console.

TASKKILL

The **`taskkill`** command is used to halt a process or task.

Syntax: `taskkill [/s computer] [/u domain\user] [/p password] [/pid process_id] [/im name] [/f] [/t]`

Explanation: `[/s computer]` is an optional parameter used to specify a specific remote computer using the computer name or IP address; otherwise, the local computer is selected by default.

`[/u domain\user]` specifies authentication for the remote computer.

`[/p password]` specifies a password for the remote computer user ID.

`[/pid process_id]` specifies a specific process ID to halt.

`[/im name]` specifies a specific image or application name to halt.

`[/f]` forcefully terminates the process.

`[/t]` a "tree kill" that kills all child processes associated with the process ID.

Examples:

```
taskkill /pid 1230 /pid 1231 /pid 1242
taskkill /im iexplore.exe
```

TASKLIST

The **`tasklist`** command is used to list process IDs for active applications and services.

Syntax: `tasklist [/s computer] [/u domain\user] [/p password] [/fo {table|list|csv}] [/v]`

Notes: This command should be used before the `taskkill` command.

If no computer is specified, the default is the local computer.

Explanation: `[/s computer]` is an optional parameter used to specify a specific remote computer using the computer name or IP address; otherwise, the local computer is selected by default.

`[/u domain\user]` specifies authentication for the remote computer.

`[/p password]` specifies a password for the remote computer user ID.

`[/fo {table|list|csv]` specifies the output format (table, which is the default, list, or CSV).

`[/v]` displays output in a verbose format.

Examples:

```
tasklist /fo csv
```

TELNET

The `telnet` command is used in Windows XP and earlier operating systems to access a remote network device. A better tool to use would be SSH.

Syntax: `telnet [destination]`

Explanation: `[destination]` is the name or IP address of the remote network device.

TRACERT

The `tracert` command is used to verify the path taken by a packet from source device to destination.

Syntax: `tracert [-d] [destination]`

Explanation: `[-d]` does not attempt to resolve intermediate router IP addresses to names and speeds up the tracert process.

`[destination]` is the targeted end device, listed by IP address or name.

Example: `tracert -d www.pearsoned.com`

TYPE

The `type` command is used to display a text file.

Syntax: `type filename`

Explanation: `filename` is the path and name of the text file you want to display on the screen.

Example: `type c:\boot.ini`

Notes: The Spacebar allows you to view the next page of a text file. The Enter key allows you to scroll through the text file one line at a time. The Esc key allows you to quit viewing the text file.

WBADMIN

The `wbadmin` command replaced the `ntbackup` command and is used in Windows Vista/7 to perform backups and restores.

Syntax: `wbadmin [start backup] [stop job] [get versions] [get items]`

Notes: Each parameter listed for `wbadmin` has options (settings) that follow. Use the `/?` after each parameter to see these options—for example, `wbadmin start backup /?`.

Explanation: `[start backup]` begins the backup process.

`[stop job]` halts the currently running backup.

`[get versions]` provides a list of available backups from the local computer or from a remote computer.

`[get items]` provides a list of items included in a particular backup.

Examples: `wbadmin start backup`

Notes: You cannot recover backups that were made with `ntbackup` using the `wbadmin` command, but you can download the `ntbackup` command/application from Microsoft.

If no parameters are specified after `wbadmin start backup`, the settings within the daily backup schedule are used.

WSCRIPT

`wscript.exe` is the command used to bring up a Windows-based script property sheet. This property sheet is used to set script properties. The command line version is `cscript.exe`.

XCOPY

The **`xcopy`** command is used to copy and backup files and directories.

Syntax: `xcopy source [destination] [/e] [/h]`

Explanation: `source` is the full path from where the file(s) are copied.

`[destination]` is the optional destination path. If the destination is not given, the current directory is used.

`[/e]` copies all directories and subdirectories including empty ones.

`[/h]` copies hidden and system files.

Example: `xcopy c:\users\cheryl\Documents\Chap1\Chap1.docx e:\Book\Chap1`

This command copies a file called *Chap1.docx* (which is located in folder called *Chap1* that is a subfolder of the *Documents* folder, which is a subfolder of the *cheryl* folder, which is a subfolder of the *users* folder) to the E: drive and places it in the *Chap1* subfolder that is contained in the *Book* folder.

Notes: The `xcopy` command normally resets read-only attributes when copying.

Tech Tip

Operation requires elevation

If a message appears from within the command prompt window that the requested operation requires elevation, close the command prompt window. Re-locate the *Command Prompt* Windows Accessory and right-click on the option. Select *Run as administrator* and re-execute the command from the prompt.

Soft Skills—Staying Current

Technicians must stay current in the rapidly changing field of computers. Benefits of staying current include (1) being able to understand and troubleshoot the latest technologies, (2) being able to recommend upgrades or solutions to customers, (3) saving time troubleshooting (and time is money), and (4) being someone considered for promotion. A variety of methods are used by technicians to stay current, including the following:

- Subscribe to a magazine or an online magazine
- Subscribe to a news list that gives you an update in your email
- Join or attend association meetings or seminars
- Take a class
- Read books
- Talk to your department peers and supervisor

Staying current in technology in the past ten years has been a challenge for all, but the rapidly changing environment is what draws many of us to the field.

Chapter Summary

- An operating system can use a GUI or a command line environment.
- Important Windows components include icons, the taskbar, the notification area, the Start button, desktop shortcuts, and the Recycle Bin.
- Right-click on a shortcut and select *Properties* to see the path to the original file.
- Control panels modify the Windows registry. Technicians commonly use control panels to modify how the hardware, software, and operating system environment functions and appears.
- Windows Explorer is commonly used to manipulate files and folders. Windows My Documents or the various Windows Vista/7 libraries (Documents, Music, Pictures, and Videos) are commonly part of the path to stored documents and subfolders.
- Deleted files are stored on the hard drive in a folder called Recycle Bin. The Recycle Bin must be emptied to release hard drive space. This is relevant only to original files stored on hard drives.
- Windows supports encryption and compression. Encrypted files that are moved or copied on NTFS volumes remain encrypted. If an encrypted file or folder is moved to a FAT16 or FAT32 volume, the file/folder is decrypted and the person doing the copying must have authorization to perform encryption.
- The Windows registry is a database of everything within the Windows environment. Configuring Control Panel settings modifies the registry. Use `regedit` or `regedt32` to manually modify the registry.
- You can recover the operating system by using a Windows or manufacturer-provided recovery disc, a recovery partition, a previously created image, a reload of the operating system and service packs, and using the System Restore tool.
- Commands are used in two environments: (1) a command prompt environment used when the GUI tools do not or cannot correct a problem and (2) when using a scripting environment to deploy the operating system and/or updates to multiple computers. Command switches that alter the way the command performs or outputs information. Use the `command /?` or `help` to receive help on any particular command.
- Technicians must stay current in the IT field to move up or maintain their current job status. Methods used to stay current include associations, magazines, classes, books, and peers.

Key Terms

notification area (Windows)....................478
notification area (mobile).......................481
OK button....................479
operating system..........472
path..............................475
radio button.................480
rd.................................511
Recovery Console.........494
recovery disc................492
Recycle Bin...................475
regedit........................491
regedt32......................491
regsvr32......................512
registry.........................490
robocopy......................512
root directory...............496
service pack..................490
sfc...............................513
shortcut........................475
shutdown......................513
snapshot.......................494
Start button..................476
subdirectory..................497
system bar....................481
system image................492
taskbar..........................476
taskkill.......................514
tasklist.......................514
user profile....................490
virtual machine............494
virtualization................493
wildcard........................499
Windows Explorer........472
WinRE..........................494
xcopy...........................515

Review Questions

1. [T | F] Deleted files can be recovered from the Recycle Bin.
2. What *Start* menu option is used to access various icons or links that can be used to configure the computer?
3. Describe the most common mistake made when working with dialog boxes.
4. In the filename *Opsys_Quiz 4.docx*, what characters represent the extension?
5. Describe the process to set Windows Explorer so that file extensions are shown.
6. A user is working in Microsoft Word. He saves the document called *Ltr1.docx* to a folder called *Homedocs*. The *Homedocs* folder is a subfolder of the *Work* folder located on the D: hard drive volume. Write the complete path for the *Ltr1.docx* file.
7. [T | F] File and folder compression can degrade computer performance.
8. What Windows 7 versions do not support encrypting a file with software provided in the operating system?
9. What should you create before making changes to the registry?
   [boot disk | backup tape | boot CD | registry backup]
10. What command is used to create a directory from a command prompt?
    [CD | MD | DIR | MAD]
11. What Windows Control Panel category is used to adjust how and when Windows updates are installed?
    [System and Security | Network and Internet | Hardware and Sound | Programs]
12. List three recovery methods used to recover an operating system.
13. List one method of accessing a command prompt when Windows 7 is operational.

14. Consider the following directory structure from the `c:` drive root directory.

    2014_Term (directory)

    CompRepair (subdirectory)

    Opsys (subdirectory)

    Cisco8 (subdirectory)

    VOIP (subdirectory)

    If the prompt is `C:\2014_Term>` and you wanted to move into the *VOIP* subdirectory, what command do you type?

    a. `CD VOIP`

    b. `CD..`

    c. `CD C:\`

    d. `CD C:\VOIP`

15. The __________ and __________ file extensions are used with executable files.
16. The Windows database that stores hardware and software configuration information is called the ______________.
17. List one registry editor. ______________
18. What technology would allow having Windows XP, Windows 7, and CentOS on a host computer where each of these operating systems are in a separate "machine."
    [compression | encryption | virtualization | defragmentation]
19. What command would be used on a computer where a specific application has stopped?
    [`taskkill` | `net stop` | `quit` | `stop`]
20. What are two of the most popular mobile operating systems for tablets and smartphones? (Select two.) [Android | Red Hat | Windows 7 Express | Mobile Ops | Mobile Pocket | Fedora | Apple iOS]

Exercises

Lab 11.1 XP Basic Usage

Objective: To be able to work effectively with the Windows XP desktop including working with the *Start* button, managing the display through the *Control Panel*, changing *Start* button properties, obtaining help, performing file, folder, and computer searches, and accessing programs

Parts: Computer with Windows XP and Notepad installed

Procedure: Complete the following procedure and answer the accompanying questions.

1. Power on the computer and log on to Windows XP if necessary.

Working with the *Start* Menu

2. Click the *Start* button located in the bottom-left corner. The top of the *Start* menu shows who is currently logged on to the computer. Users are created so that the system can be individualized when multiple people use the same computer.

   Is your computer loaded with the classic *Start* button menu or the simple *Start* menu? Note that the classic *Start* button looks like previous Windows versions (a single column of words).

3. To see a dialog box and make changes to the *Start* button menu, right-click the *Start* button > *Properties* > *Start Menu* tab > *Customize* button.

   Take note of the *General* tab, which has three sections: *Icon size*, *Programs*, and *Show on Start menu*. The *Icon size* section controls the size of *Start* menu program icons.

The *Programs* section has an option for setting the number of frequently used software shown on the left side of the *Start* menu. The *Clear List* button is used to clear the most frequently used software list being tracked by the operating system. It does not clear the software listed under the *Programs Start* button option. The *Show on Start* section allows you to select the software used to access the Internet and email software.

4. Click the *Advanced* tab. The *Advanced* tab contains three sections: *Start menu settings*, *Start menu items*, and *Recent documents*. The *Start menu items* section controls which items display on the *Start* menu.

   Using the scroll bar in the Start menu items section, determine if the *Network Connections* option displays by default on the Start menu. Document your findings.

5. The *Clear List* button in the *Recent documents* section is used to clear the current list of recently accessed documents. Click the *Cancel* button.
6. Click the *Cancel* button and then click the *Start* button. Shortcuts for this step include pressing Ctrl+Esc or pressing ⊞, if available.

   What are the top four options in the right column of the Start menu?

7. The *My Documents* option represents a folder that is the default storage location for saved files. *My Pictures*, *My Videos*, and *My Music* are subfolders (a folder within a folder) of the *My Documents* folder. A file is a document. A folder is a storage unit for files. Click the *My Computer* Start button option. The *My Computer* option contains access to drives installed or connected to the computer. Floppy drives, hard drives, optical drives, tape drives, and so on are given drive letters such as `A:` or `C:`.

   What drives are available through the *My Computer* option?

Working with Control Panels

8. Close the *My Computer* window by clicking the *Close* button (the red X button) in the upper-right corner. Click *Start > Control Panel*. The *Control Panel* option allows access to Control Panel icons that are used to configure the computer. There are two ways to view control panels: *Classic Control Panel* and *Category Control Panel*. The default XP view is by category. If the words "Pick a category" *do not* appear at the top of the screen, click the *Switch to the Category View* option located in the left pane.

   List two Control Panel categories shown on the screen.

9. Table 11.8 shows common XP control panels and functions of each one.

   Click the *Switch to the Classic View* option located in the left window.

   List three Control Panel categories shown on the screen.

Table 11.8 Common Windows XP control panels

Control panel	Function
Accessibility Options	Used to change the way the keyboard, sounds, display, and mouse function within Windows; used for people with disabilities
Add/Remove Hardware	Used to install and remove hardware devices
Add/Remove Programs	Used to install and remove software applications
Administrative Tools	Used to monitor and configure Windows
Date/Time	Used to change the date and time
Display	Used to control monitor functions such as desktop appearance, screen saver, and size of objects
Folder Options	Used to change file associations and how folder contents are displayed
Fonts	Used to add or remove system fonts
Internet Options	Used to change settings related to an Internet connection
Keyboard	Used to change the keyboard driver, repeat rate, and cursor blink rate
Mouse	Used to change the mouse driver, click speed, and pointer shape
Network and Dial-up	Used to add, remove, and configure network connections
Phone and Modem Options	Used to install a modem and control modem and dialing properties
Power Options	Used to reduce electrical power use in devices such as a monitor or hard drive
Printers	Used to add, remove, or change the properties of a printer
Regional Options	Used to set the time zone and to set the format for numbers and currency
Scheduled Tasks	Used to schedule things such as backups and disk defragmentation utilities
Sounds and Multimedia	Used to add/remove multimedia device drivers, set system event sounds, and change audio/video settings for multimedia devices
System	Used to view system configuration information, configure the computer for multiple hardware configurations, and change system settings
User and Passwords	Used to add/remove user accounts, set passwords, and set/view various security settings

In Table 11.9, fill in the correct control panel for each function. Use a computer that has XP installed to discover the correct control panel.

Table 11.9 Selecting a Windows XP control panel

Control panel	Function
	Used to configure the mouse buttons for a left-handed person
	Used to mute the computer speaker sound
	Used to configure the date to be April 15, 201X
	Used to define how fast a character repeats when a specific key is held down
	Used to define what page (home page) appears every time Internet Explorer starts
	Used to configure the computer network (IP) address
	Used to install a printer
	Used to access Device Manager

Working with the *Display* Control Panel

10. Double-click the *Display* control panel.

    What five tabs are listed across the top of the window?

11. Click the *Screen Saver* tab. Click the *Screen Saver* down arrow to see a list of pre-installed screen savers and click one of the options. Click the *Preview* button. The screen saver appears. Move the mouse to regain control.
12. Click the *Power* button. The *Power Options Properties* window appears.

    Table 11.10 shows the various power options available in Windows XP.

    What power option would your teacher use if he or she was using the computer to teach class and document why you think this?

Table 11.10 Windows XP power schemes

Power option	Purpose
Home/Office Desk	Monitor turns off after 15 minutes of inactivity, hard drive(s) turns off after 30 minutes, and computer turns off after 20 minutes
Portable/Laptop	Same times as *Home/Office Desk* settings
Presentation	Standby options for hard drive, monitor, and computer system are disabled
Always On	Monitor turns off after 30 minutes of inactivity, hard drive(s) turn off after 1 hour, and the computer system never goes into standby

Power option	Purpose
Minimal Power Management	Monitor turns off after 15 minutes of inactivity
Max Battery	Same as *Minimal Power Management* standby options

13. Click the *Cancel* button. You return to the *Display Properties* window. Click the *Cancel* button.
14. In the *Control Panel* window, click *Switch to Category View* to return to the default view. Close all Control Panel windows. Click the *Start* button.

Obtaining Help

15. Click *Help and Support*. The *Help and Support* window contains links to online and locally stored help topics.
16. The most commonly used help topics are listed on the left. On the right are the custom manufacturer options and a *Did you know?* category. Across the top are *Index, Favorites, History, Support,* and *Options*. Click the *Index* icon.

    What is the first item listed on the left?
17. Locate the Performance and Maintenance link. Select the *Advanced Performance and Maintenance Tools* option on the left.

    What is the first problem listed?
18. Note that instead of scrolling through topics, you can type a subject in the *Search* textbox and topics appear for you to select. To see a list of Windows XP troubleshooting topics, type `troubleshooting` in the *Type in the keyword to find:* textbox. A list of troubleshooting topics immediately displays.

    Is sound listed as one of the troubleshooting topics?
19. Close the *Help and Support Center* window.

Searching for Files, Folders, and Computers

20. Click the *Start* button and select *Search*. The *Search* option is used to hunt for files, other computers on the network, people listed in your address book, and information located on the Internet.
21. Click the *All files and folders* option. In the *All or part of the file name* box, type `*.hlp`. The `*` means the entire first part of any filename. The `.` (period) separates the filename from the file extension. The extension is automatically added by software applications. Windows help files all have the `.hlp` extension. So, the search criteria specified is for all Windows help files. Click the *Search* button.

    How many help files did the system find?
22. Locate and click the *Show Desktop* taskbar button. The button looks like a desk blotter with a pencil in the center and is normally located to the immediate right of the *Start* button.
23. Right-click the *My Computer* icon and select *Properties*. Click the *Computer Name* tab.

    Write the computer name.

    Find another computer or ask a classmate for the name of a different computer. Write the other computer name.

Tech Tip

What to do if *My Computer* is not on the desktop

If the *My Computer* icon does not show on the desktop, click the *Start* button and point to the *Control Panel* option. If the Control Panel window shows the Classic Control Panels, click the *Switch to Category View* option in the left panel. Select the *Appearance and Themes* Control Panel category. Click the *Change the computer's theme task*, click the *Desktop* tab, click the *Customize Desktop* button, and in the *Desktop icons* section, select the desktop icons to be added. Click the *OK* button twice and close the Control Panel window.

24. Click the *Cancel* button and then click the *Search Results* taskbar button, which brings you back to the same search window used before. Click the *Start a new search* option in the left window.
25. Click the *Computers or people search* option. At the *What are you looking for?* window, click *A computer on the network*. At the *Computer Name:* prompt, type the name of your classmate's computer and click *Search*. The computer should appear in the right window pane.

Instructor initials: ______________

26. Close the search results window.

Starting Applications

27. Software applications are accessed through the *Start* button. Click the *Start* button. The left column contains the most recently used applications. If a program is not listed there, you can access it through the *All Programs* option. Point to *All Programs*. Point to *Accessories* and click *Notepad*. The Notepad application opens.
28. Type `This is a test.` Click the *File* menu bar option, *Save*, then type `text` in the *File name* textbox, and click the *Save* button. Click the *Close* button in the upper-right corner. Re-access the *Start* button menu.

    Does the Notepad application now appear in the left column of the Start menu?
29. Click the *Start* button and click *Run*. Run is used to type a command or search for a particular executable file. An executable file is one that has `.exe`, `.com`, or `.bat` as a file extension. In the *Open* textbox, type `notepad` and click *OK*. The Notepad application opens. Close the Notepad application using the *Close* button.

Using the *Run* Option

30. Click *Start* and click *Run* again. Click the *Browse* button. The *Browse* option allows you to search for a particular executable file. Most people keep their documents in the *My Documents* folder. Click the *My Documents* icon in the *Browse* window left panel. Click the *Cancel* button and return to the *Run* window. Click the *Cancel* button.

Recycle Bin

31. Use the *Search* option previously covered to locate the test file created in Notepad. Click once on the file icon and press the [Del] key. A *Confirm file delete* window appears. Click *Yes*. The file is sent to the Recycle Bin, which is a desktop icon that represents a folder on the hard drive.

    The Recycle Bin holds deleted files and folders. When a file or folder is deleted, it is not immediately discarded; instead, it goes into the *Recycle Bin* folder. Once a file or folder is in the Recycle Bin, it can be removed. This is similar to a piece of trash being retrieved from an office trash can. A technician must remember that the files and folders in the Recycle Bin take up hard drive space and that users frequently forget to empty the files and folders. Click the *Show Desktop* taskbar icon.
32. Double-click the *Recycle Bin* desktop icon. The document should be listed in the window.

    Does the *text.txt* file appear in the *Recycle Bin* window?___ If not, redo the steps to create and delete the file.

Instructor initials: ____________

33. Click the *File* menu option and click *Empty Recycle Bin*. A *Confirm file delete* window appears. Click *Yes*. The name disappears from the *Recycle Bin* window (as well as any other files that were located in the Recycle Bin). Close the *Recycle Bin* window.

Creating a Shortcut

34. Click *Start* > *All Programs* > *Accessories* > *Windows Explorer* > *Search* icon. The search icon is used the same way the search *Start* menu option works. Click the *All files and folders* option. In the *All or part of the filename* textbox, type `notepad.exe`. Click the *Look in* down arrow and select *Local hard drives*. Click the *Search* button.
35. More than one Notepad file may exist. Pick one and right-click the file icon. Click the *Create shortcut* option. A window appears stating that a shortcut cannot be created here and prompts if the shortcut is to be created on the desktop. Click *Yes*. Close the *Search* window.
36. Access the desktop and verify that the Notepad shortcut is on the desktop.

Instructor initials: ______________

37. Delete the shortcut and empty the Recycle Bin using the previous steps.

Instructor initials: ______________

38. When finished working on the computer for the day, the computer needs to be turned off or shut down properly. All applications and windows should be closed and then special steps need to be taken for shutting down. Click *Start* and select *Turn off computer*. The *Turn off computer* dialog box appears, as shown in Figure 11.24.

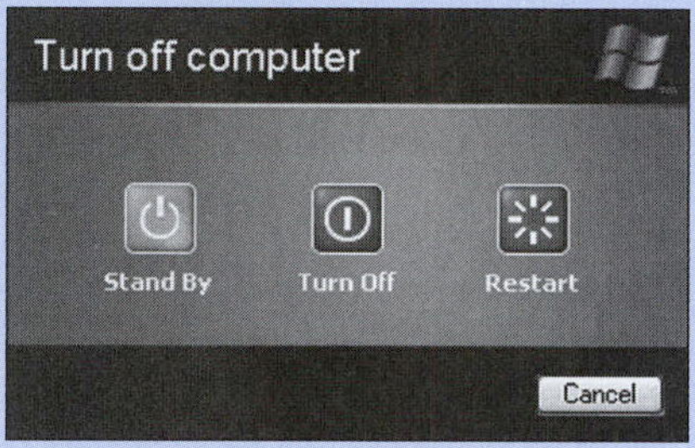

Figure 11.24 Windows XP Turn off computer dialog box

If the computer has ACPI (Advanced Configuration and Power Interface) enabled, the computer shows a *Stand By* option. If ACPI is not enabled, the computer shows a *Hibernate* button instead of a *Stand By* button on the left side of the window. The *Cancel* button can be used to return to the Windows work environment. The four turn off options that can be shown in the dialog box and their purposes are listed in Table 11.11.

Table 11.11 Windows XP Turn off computer options

Option	Purpose
Hibernate	Saves the current work to disk and powers the computer down. When power is restored, the programs currently being used are available. The *Power Options* control panel must be enabled.
StandBy	Keeps the current work, but puts the computer in low power mode. The *Power Options* control panel must be enabled.
Turn Off	Used to shut the computer off
Restart	Used when new software or hardware has been installed or when the computer locks

39. Click the *Turn off* option to turn off the computer properly.

Lab 11.2 Windows Vista/7 Basic Usage

Objective: To be able to work effectively with the Windows Vista/7 desktop, including working with the Start button; managing the display through the Control Panel; changing Start button properties; obtaining help; performing file, folder, and computer searches; and accessing programs

Parts: Computer with Windows Vista or 7 and the Windows Notepad application installed

Procedure: Complete the following procedure and answer the accompanying questions.

1. Power on the computer and log on to Windows if necessary.

Working with the *Start* Menu

2. Click the *Start* button. The top right of the Start menu on some systems shows who is currently logged on to the computer. Users are created so that the system can be individualized when multiple people use the same computer.

   What do you think is the difference between the applications listed on the left and those listed on the right side of the Start button menu?

3. You can make changes to the Start button menu by right-clicking the *Start* button > *Properties* > *Start Menu* tab > *Customize* button.

   What is the current setting for the Control Panel option?
   [Display as a link | Display as a menu | Don't display this item]

   What is the current setting for Games?
   [Display as a link | Display as a menu | Don't display this item]

   How many recent programs are currently set to display?

4. Click *Cancel*. Select the *Taskbar* tab.

   List three options that can be customized through this tab.

5. Select the *How do I customize the taskbar* link. Using the information available, answer the questions that follow.

   How can you tell if the taskbar is locked or unlocked without moving it?

   What toolbars can be added to the taskbar?

   How can a taskbar that is hidden be reactivated?

6. Close the Windows Help and Support window.
7. Click on the *Notification Area* tab (Vista) or the *Customize* button in the Notification area (7).

   List three system icons.

8. Click the *Toolbars* tab.

   List any enabled toolbars.

9. Click *Cancel*. Press Ctrl+Esc or press ⊞ to re-access the Start button.

   What are the top four options in the right column of the *Start* menu?

10. The *Documents* option represents a folder that is the default storage location for saved files. *Pictures*, *Music*, and *Games* also represent folders. A folder can contain another folder, and this folder is commonly called a subfolder. A file is a document created by an application. Files are stored and organized in folders. Click the *Computer* Start button option. The *Computer* option contains access to drives installed or connected to the computer. Floppy drives, hard drives, optical drives, tape drives, and so on are given drive letters such as A: or C:.

    What drive letters are available through the *Computer* option?

Working with Control Panels

11. Select the *Control Panel* Start button option. *Control Panel* allows access to Control Panel icons or links used to configure the computer. There are two ways to view control panels: *Classic* and *Category*. The default view is by category. In Vista, if the words "System and Maintenance" *do not* appear in the right pane, select the *Control Panel Home* link in the left pane. In Windows 7, select *Category* in the View by: drop-down menu.

    List two Control Panel categories shown on the screen.

12. In Vista, click the *Classic View* option located in the left window. In Windows 7, select *Large icons* or *Small icons* in the View by: drop-down menu. The classic view/large or small icons is the older method for accessing any particular control panel. Return to the *Category* control panel view.

    Table 11.12 shows common Vista/7 Control Panel categories and types of functions performed within each one. Some systems have special control panels due to the hardware installed or type of computer such as a netbook or tablet. Notice how some of the options are found in multiple categories.

Table 11.12 Common Windows Vista or 7 Control Panel categories*

Control Panel category	Subcategory	Function
System and Maintenance (Vista)/System and Security (7)	Welcome Center (Vista)	Used to access basic computer information, information on how to use Windows Vista, and Vista help videos
	Backup and Restore	Used to save or restore files and folders to or from a different location
	System	Used to view basic computer properties, such as RAM, processor type, and computer name
	Windows Update	Used to customize how Vista/7 updates are received and installed
	Power Options	Used to configure power saving modes
	Indexing Options*	Used to configure how Vista searches for files and folders more efficiently
	Problem Reports and Solutions (Vista)	Used to receive help with or view a history of computer problems

Control Panel category	Subcategory	Function
	Performance Information and Tools (Vista)	Used to obtain information about the computer speed and possible solutions related to speed
	Device Manager (Vista)	Used to view and update hardware settings
	Administrative Tools	Used for such tasks as freeing up hard disk space, managing hard drive partitions, scheduling tasks, and viewing event logs
	Action Center (7)	Used to view personal information, view a history of computer problems, view performance information, configure backup, troubleshoot problems, and restore the computer to a previous time
Security (Vista)	Security Center (Vista)	Used to view and modify computer firewall and update settings
	Windows Firewall	Used to enable and customize security firewall features
	Windows Update	Used to customize how updates are received and installed
	Windows Defender*	Used to scan the computer for unwanted software
	Internet Options (Vista)	Used to customize Internet Explorer
	Parental Controls (Vista)	Used for changing, enabling, and disabling settings related to family member access
	BitLocker Drive Encryption (7)	Change or use encryption options
Network and Internet	Network and Sharing Center	Used to check the status and modify network-related settings as well as share files, folders, and devices on the network
	Internet Options	Used to customize Internet Explorer
	People Near Me*	Used to configure the computer for software such as Windows Meeting Place
	Sync Center*	Used to synchronize mobile devices or network shares
	HomeGroup (7)	Used to view and change sharing and password options
Hardware and Sound	Printers (Vista)	Used to add, delete, or customize printer settings
	Devices and Printers (7)	Used to add/remove a device, scanner, camera, printer, and mouse as well as access Device Manager
	AutoPlay	Used to change how media is automatically handled when a disc or type of file is added or inserted

Control Panel category	Subcategory	Function
	Sound	Used to manage audio devices and change sound schemes
	Mouse (Vista)	Used to customize mouse and mouse button settings
	Power Options	Same as found in the System and Maintenance (Vista)/System and Security (7) category
	Personalization (Vista)	Used to customize the desktop, adjust monitor settings, select a theme, or change the mouse pointer
	Scanners and Cameras (Vista)	Used to add, delete, or customize settings related to scanners or cameras
	Keyboard*	Used to customize keyboard settings
	Device Manager (Vista)	Same as found in the System and Maintenance category
	Phone and Modem Options*	Used to install a modem and control modem and phone dialing properties
	Game Controllers*	Used to add, remove, and customize USB joysticks, gamepads, and other gaming devices
	Windows SideShow (Vista)	Used to customize SideShow settings
	Pen and Input Devices	Used to configure pen options for a tablet PC
	Color Management*	Used for advanced color settings on disc plays, scanners, and printers
	Tablet PC Settings	Used to configure tablet and screen settings on a tablet PC
	Display (7)	Used to adjust resolution, configure an external display, or make text larger/smaller
	Bluetooth Devices	Used to install, configure, and adjust Bluetooth wireless devices.
Programs	Programs and Features	Used to uninstall and change programs as well as enable/disable Windows features such as games, telnet server, telnet client, TFTP client, and print services
	Windows Defender*	Same as found in the Security category
	Default Programs	Used to remove a startup program, associate a file extension with a particular application, or select the program used with a particular type of file
	Windows SideShow (Vista)	Same as found in the Hardware and Sound category
	Windows Sidebar Properties (Vista)	Used to add gadgets to the sidebar as well as customize the gadgets displayed on the desktop

Control Panel category	Subcategory	Function
	Desktop Gadgets (7)	Used to add/remove/restore desktop interactive objects
Mobile PC	Windows Mobility Center	Used on laptops to adjust screen brightness, audio volume, wireless enabling and strength status, presentation settings, and external display control
	Power Options	Used on laptops and has the same function as found in the System and Maintenance category
	Personalization	Used on laptops and has the same function as found in the Hardware and Sound category
	Tablet PC Settings	Used on laptops and has the same function as found in the Programs category
	Pen and Input Devices	Used on laptops and has the same function as found in the Hardware and Sound category
	Sync Center	Used on laptops and has the same function as found in the Network and Internet category
User Accounts and Family Safety	User Accounts	Used to add, remove, or modify accounts allowed access to the computer
	Parental Controls	Same as found in the Security (Vista)/System and Security (7)
	Windows CardSpace	Used to manage relationships and information such as a user ID and password for websites and online services. The personal card information is kept encrypted on the local hard drive.
	Credential Manager (7)	Used to store username/password in a vault for easy logon to sites and/or computers
Appearance and Personalization	Personalization	Same as found in the Hardware and Sound category
	Taskbar and Start menu	Used to customize the Start menu and taskbar by adding or removing icons
	Fonts	Used to customize available fonts
	Folder Options	Used to configure how folders are viewed and acted upon, including what files are seen
Clock, Language, and Region	Date and Time	Used to configure time, date, time zone, clocks for different time zones
	Region and Language Options	Used to configure the format for date, time, currency, etc. that are region specific. Also used to customize keyboard settings
Additional Options		Holds special control panels that are system specific, such as a NVIDIA video display or Java control panel

*Note that in Windows 7, particular options can be found by typing in the subcategory in the *Search Control Panel* textbox.

Fill in Table 11.13 with the correct Control Panel category and subcategory.

Table 11.13 Determine the correct control panel

Control Panel category	Control Panel subcategory	Task
		Used to configure the mouse buttons for a left-handed person
		Used to mute the computer speaker sound
		Used to configure the date to be in the format April 15, 201X
		Use to define how fast a character repeats when a specific key is held down
		Use to define what page (home page) appears every time Internet Explorer starts
		Used to configure an IP address on a wireless network adapter
		Used to set a printer as the default printer
		Used to see if Windows recognizes a particular piece of hardware

Working with the Display

13. Select the *Hardware and Sound* control panel category. In Vista, select the *Personalization* link; select *Display Settings* (Vista). In Windows 7, select *Display*. Note that you may be required to search throughout this area to answer the questions.

    What is the current resolution?

    How many bits are used for color?

14. Continuing with the *Display* link, locate and select the *Advanced Settings* button or link.

    What adapter is being used?

    How much video memory does the adapter have?

    How much total video memory is available?

15. Click the *Monitor* tab.

    What refresh rate is used?

16. Click *Cancel* on this window and the next window. In Vista, click the *Screen Saver* link. In Windows 7, select the *Personalization* link in the bottom left; select the *Screen Saver* link in the bottom right. Use the *Screen Saver* down arrow to see a list of pre-installed screen savers and click one of the options. Click the *Preview* button. The screen saver appears. Move the mouse to regain control.

17. Click the *Change power settings* link. The Power Options Properties window appears. Table 11.14 shows the various power options available in Windows Vista and 7.

    What power option would a teacher use when using a laptop to teach a four-hour class?

Table 11.14 Windows Vista/7 default power schemes*

Power scheme	Purpose
Balanced (Vista/7)	Default mode; processor adapts to activity being performed; performance provided when the computer is in use; power savings when the computer is inactive. Display powers down after 15 minutes; hard drive powers down after 20 minutes and goes to sleep after 20 minutes.
Power saver (Vista/7)	Provides maximum battery life for laptops. Display and hard drive power down after 20 minutes, and the system goes to sleep after one hour.
High performance (Vista/7)	Maximum system performance and responsiveness. Display and hard drive power down after 20 minutes, but the system never sleeps.
Customized (Vista/7)	A scheme created by the user that has different settings than the default three schemes

*Note that a computer manufacturer may provide additional power schemes.

18. Close all Control Panel windows.

Obtaining Help

19. Click *Help and Support* from the Start button menu. The Help and Support window contains links to online and locally stored help documents.
20. In Vista the standard help links are Windows Basics, Table of Contents, Security and Maintenance, Troubleshooting, Windows Online Help, and What's New. In Windows 7 the standard three links are How to get started with your computer, Learn about Windows Basics, and Browse Help topics. In both Vista and 7 the Search Help textbox is used by typing a word or series of words on a specific topic. Note that the Help and Support window may vary depending on the computer manufacturer.

    What is the first link listed in the help window?

21. In either Vista or 7, type `monitor quality` and press Enter.

    List three settings used to improve display quality.

22. To see a list of troubleshooting topics, type troubleshooting in the *Search help* textbox. A list of troubleshooting topics immediately displays. Select the *Offline Help* menu arrow.

    What menu options appear?
23. Select *Settings*. Notice how you can customize the type of help you receive by enabling or disabling the online help checkbox.
24. Close the *Windows Help and Support Center* window.

Searching for Files, Folders, and Computers

25. Click the *Start* button and find the *Start Search* (Vista)/*Search programs and files* (7) textbox, located directly above the Start button. This option is used to hunt for files, other computers on the network, people listed in your address book, and information located on the Internet.

26. In the textbox, type `system configuration`, but do not press Enter. Notice how the program shows in the panel. Always keep in mind that applications are simply a type of file that brings up the specific software. Also, any files that contain the words "System Configuration" appear under the files list. Select the *System Configuration* program from the list. Close the window once the question has been answered.

    List five tabs found in the System Configuration window.

Tech Tip

Changing UAC (User Access Control) settings

Windows Vista/7 has a UAC dialog box that frequently appears, asking for permission to do something. To change UAC settings, use the *User Accounts* control panel > select an account > *Change User Account Control settings*. The UAC settings can also be disabled through the System configuration utility (`msconfig` command) > *Tools* tab > *Disable UAC* (Vista)/*Change UAC Settings* (7) option > *Launch* button > select the desired level.

27. Bring up the search list for system configuration, but don't press Enter again.

    In Vista, click the *Search the Internet* option at the bottom of the list.

    In Windows 7, click on the *See more results* link and scroll to the bottom of the list; locate and select the *Internet* icon.

    List one URL that the system found.

28. Locate the name of the computer, using a control panel previously explored. Exchange computer names with a classmate.

    Your computer name ______________________________

    Classmate's computer name _________________________

29. Return to the computer *Start Search* (Vista)/*Search programs and files* (7) textbox and type in your classmate's computer name and press Enter. In the resulting window in the Folders panel on the left, select the *Network* option.

    Does the remote computer name appear? [Yes | No]

Instructor initials: ____________

30. Close the window.

Starting Applications

31. Software applications are accessed through the Start button. Click the *Start* button. The left column contains the most recently used applications. If a program is not listed there and the application is installed, you can access it through the All Programs option. Point to *All Programs*; locate and click the *Accessories* option. Locate and click *Notepad*. The Notepad application opens.
32. Type `Whatever you are be a good one. -Abraham Lincoln`. Click the *File* menu option, *Save*, then type `quote` in the *File name* textbox. Notice the path for where the document is saved located at the top of the window. The folder and subfolders are separated by arrows.

    Write the path for where the document will be saved.

33. Click the *Save* button. Click the *Close* button (the button with the X) in the right corner. Re-access the *Start* button menu.

    Does the Notepad application now appear in the left column of the Start menu? [Yes | No]

34. In the *Start Search* (Vista)/*Search programs and files* (7) textbox, type `notepad`, but do not press the Enter key. The Notepad application is listed under the Programs section. In the *Start Search* (Vista)/*Search programs and files* (7) textbox, delete the word *notepad* and type `quote`, but do not press Enter. Your file (and any others that have the word "quote" in the filename or document) will appear under the Files section of the list. Notice the icon beside the filename. Click on the *Quote* document. The document opens. Close the document and application.

Recycle Bin

35. Right-click the *Start* button and select the *Explore* (Vista)/*Open Windows Explorer* (7) option. Using the information you wrote down for Step 32, click on the first folder you wrote down. It should be located under the Folders (Vista), Desktop (7), or Documents section of the left panel. Double-click on the second (and any subsequent) folder you wrote down. Locate the file called *quote*. Do not open the file, just browse until the filename appears in the major window.
36. Right-click on the *quote* filename. Notice that there is a Delete option. Do not click on this option. Click away from the filename on an empty part of the window and then click once on the *quote* filename to select it. The name is highlighted when it is selected. Press the *Delete* key. The *Are you sure you want to move this file to the Recycle Bin?* dialog box appears. Click *Yes*. The file is sent to the Recycle Bin, which is just a folder on the hard drive.

    The Recycle Bin holds deleted files and folders. When a file or folder is deleted, it is not immediately discarded; instead, it goes into the Recycle Bin folder. Once a file or folder is in the Recycle Bin, it can be removed. This is similar to a piece of trash being retrieved from an office trash can. A technician must remember that the files and folders in the Recycle Bin take up hard drive space and that users frequently forget to empty these deleted files and folders.

Tech Tip

Files deleted from Recycle Bin cannot be retrieved

Once the Recycle Bin has been emptied, the deleted files cannot be recovered without the use of special software.

37. From the window where you located the now-deleted *quote* document, locate the *Recycle Bin* icon in the Folders panel (Vista); for Windows 7, the Recycle Bin icon is commonly located on the desktop—select *Desktop* from the Favorites section. Double-click on this icon.

    Does the *quote* text document appear in the Recycle Bin window? If not, redo the steps in this section to create and delete the file.

Instructor initials: ____________

38. Select the *Empty the Recycle Bin* option from the top menu. A confirmation window appears, asking if you are sure you want to permanently delete the file. Click *Yes*. The name disappears from the Recycle Bin window (as do those of any other files that were located in the Recycle Bin). Close the window.

Pinning an Application to the Start Menu

39. Click *Start* > *All Programs* > *Accessories* and locate the *Notepad* application. Right-click the *Notepad* application and select the *Pin to Start Menu* option.
40. Click the *Start* button. Notice how the Notepad application appears at the top of the Start menu. Once the application is pinned, it always appears in that top list.

Instructor initials: ____________

41. Right-click the *Notepad* Start button option and select *Unpin from Start Menu*. The application is removed immediately but still resides in All Programs.

Other Windows Vista/7 Differences

42. One of the things that is different in Windows Vista and 7 from Windows XP is the gadgets. Gadgets are mini applications that stay on the desktop. By default, they load to the right, but you can customize where they go. Right-click on the desktop and select *Gadgets*.

    List three gadgets you would find useful to have on the desktop. Student's choice, but common answers are Calendar, Clock, CPU Meter, Currency, Easy Audio Capture, Feed Headlines, Picture Puzzle, Slide Show, Weather, and Windows Media Center.

Windows Vista/7 Shutdown Options

43. When finished working on the computer for the day, the computer needs to be turned off or shut down properly. All applications and windows should be closed, and then special steps need to be taken for shutting down. Click *Start* and locate the *Start Search* (Vista)/ *Search programs and files* (7) textbox you have been using. Immediately to the right of that textbox are two symbols and a right arrow in Windows Vista or a Shut down button in Windows 7. See Figure 11.25.

    The shutdown options that commonly appear are listed in Table 11.15, along with the purpose of each one.

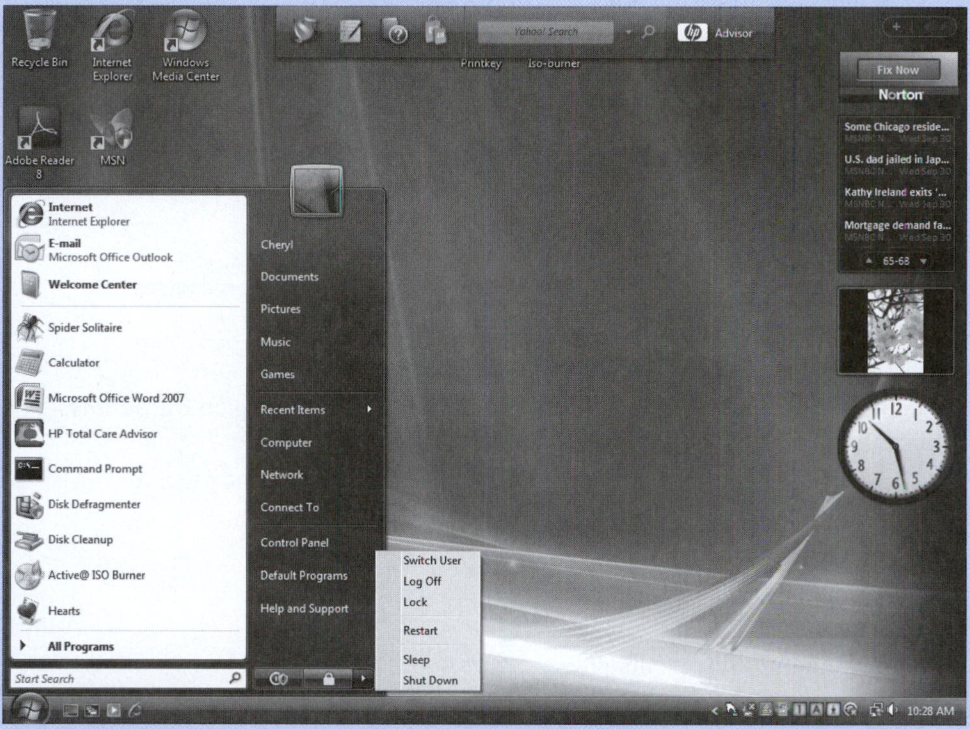

Figure 11.25 Windows Vista log off and power options

Table 11.15 Windows Vista/7 shutdown options

Option	Purpose
Switch User	Allows another user to switch to his or her own environment (desktop, files, etc.).
Log Off	Keeps the computer powered on but logs off the current user.
Lock	Locks the computer, such as when someone goes to lunch. All settings and current applications are left untouched.
Restart	Used when new software or hardware has been installed or when the computer locks.
Sleep	Reduces power consumption but keeps the applications and settings that are currently on the screen.
Shut Down	Powers off the computer.

44. Select the *Shut down* option unless directed otherwise by the instructor or lab assistant.

Lab 11.3 Introduction to Mobile Operating Systems

Objective: To be able to interact with and customize a mobile device

Parts: Android or Apple iOS device

Procedure: Complete the following procedure and answer the accompanying questions.

1. Turn on the mobile device and enter the required swipe pattern, PIN, or password. If you do not know how to turn on the device, look for a power button on the side of the device.
2. Press the home button (Apple iOS) or home icon (Android). If the home icon is not showing, touch the screen where it normally appears (bottom left, center icon).

   List three apps found on the home page.

3. Take your finger to swipe left or right to see if there are additional home pages.

   Were there additional home pages? [Yes | No]

   If so, how many additional home pages were present?
4. On the home page, locate the *Settings* application. Open it by tapping on the *Settings* icon.

   What setting would be used to change the graphic shown on the home page?

   What setting would be used to configure 802.11 wireless settings?

   What setting would be used to configure the device for Bluetooth ear buds?

   What setting would be used to configure a password on the device?

   What setting would be used to change how long the device is inactive before going into a low power mode?

5. Frequently, to solve a problem for a mobile device or to obtain a new feature, an operating system upgrade is required. Before installing a new operating system, the current version is needed.

   If you are on an Apple iOS device, select the *General* settings option. Select *About*.

   If you are on an Android device, the Settings option used may vary due to the open source nature of Android. Common methods used to obtain the OS version are to tap *About phone* or *About tablet*.

   Record the current version of operating system.

6. Return to the home page by pushing the home button (Apple device) or touching the home icon (normally bottom left corner center icon on an Android device). Note that to answer the questions that follow, you may need to swipe your finger to see other home screens or to touch the *Applications*.

   What app is used to view photos on the device?

   What app is used to surf the Internet?

   What app is used to check email?

   What app is used to purchase an application?

   How much battery life is left on the device?

   How did you determine how much battery time is left?

7. Power off the device. Return the device to the proper location.

Instructor initials: ____________

Lab 11.4 Windows XP/Vista/7 Taskbar Options

Objective: To be able to interact with and customize the Windows taskbar

Parts: Computer with Windows XP/Vista/7 installed

Procedure: Complete the following procedure and answer the accompanying questions.

1. Turn on the computer and verify that the operating system loads. Log on if necessary.

Taskbar Options

2. Locate the taskbar on the bottom of the screen. If it is not showing, move the mouse to the bottom of the screen and the taskbar will pop up.
3. To modify or view the Taskbar settings, right-click a blank area of the taskbar. A menu appears. *Note*: In XP, you can also use the *Start* > *Control Panel* > if categories are shown, select *Appearance and Themes* > *Taskbar and Start Menu*. If the *Control Panel* classic view is used, the *Taskbar and Start Menu* control panel is used. In Vista or 7 control panels, select the *Appearance and Personalization* link followed by the *Taskbar* and *Start Menu* link.
4. Click the *Properties* option. The *Taskbar and Start Menu Properties* window appears.
5. Click the *Taskbar* tab. The options available on this screen relate to how things are shown on the taskbar. The items with a check in the checkbox to the left are active. To remove a check mark, click in the checkbox that already contains a check in it. To put a check mark in a box, click once in an empty box. Table 11.16 shows the functions of the options.

   Which of the five options are currently enabled, if any?

   What is the current taskbar location? [bottom | right | left | top]

Table 11.16 Windows taskbar options and functions

Option	Function
Lock the taskbar	Prevents the taskbar from being moved
Auto hide the taskbar	Hides the taskbar until the pointer is moved to the taskbar area; use the *Keep the taskbar on top of other windows* option in conjunction with this option to ensure the taskbar is visible when selected
Keep the taskbar on top of other windows (XP/Vista)	Ensures that the taskbar is visible even when a maximized window displays of other windows
Group similar taskbar buttons (XP/Vista)	Collapses multiple windows used by the same application buttons into one button
Show Quick Launch (XP/Vista)	Displays the Quick Launch bar on the taskbar
Show window properties (thumbnail) (Vista)	Available on Vista Home Premium and higher; shows a miniature version of open windows
Taskbar location on screen (7)	Sets whether the taskbar appears at the bottom (default), or to the left, right, or top.
Taskbar buttons (7)	Optionally combines similar labels

6. Ensure the *Auto-hide the taskbar* option is enabled and all other taskbar options are disabled. Click the *Apply* button and click *OK*. The taskbar disappears from view.
7. Point to the screen where the taskbar is normally located. The taskbar appears. Click *Start* > *All Programs* > *Accessories* > *WordPad*. Maximize the screen by clicking the maximize button, which is the center button at the top right side of the window.

   What happened to the taskbar?
8. Move the pointer to the screen area where the taskbar is normally located.

   Did the taskbar appear? [Yes | No]
9. Close the *WordPad* window. Bring the taskbar options back up and reset them to their original configuration. Refer to the answer to Question 5 for enabled options.

Instructor initials: ______________

10. Right-click an empty taskbar space and select *Properties*. At the bottom of the *Taskbar* tab is the *Notification area* section (XP/7) or click on the *Notification Area* tab (Vista). The notification area is also called the systray. A sign (<, <<, or ▲) marks the beginning of the area. Two common options are *Show the clock* and *Hide inactive icons*. The *Show the clock* option displays the time in the notification area. The *Hide inactive icons* option hides taskbar icons that are not currently in use. On the taskbar, click the notification area sign to view hidden inactive icons. The *Customize* button is used to change the settings in Windows 7.

    Did the computer have any inactive icons that displayed once the < was clicked? [Yes | No]
11. Back in the Taskbar and Start Menu properties window, click the *Start Menu* tab.

    The two XP or Vista options shown are *Start menu* and *Classic Start menu*. These are used to determine how the *Start* menu displays. The *Classic Start* menu option displays the *Start* menu like older Windows versions.

Windows 7 has a privacy section that determines whether recently opened programs or items display.

Which *Start* menu option is currently selected on this machine?

12. Click the *Customize* button.

    List three things that can be changed through this option.

    In XP, the *General* tab controls the *Start* menu icon size, the number of programs shown in the Start menu's left pane, and what options (if any) are displayed for Internet and email applications. The *Clear List* button is used to clear the most frequently accessed programs displayed in the left pane.

    In Vista/7, the options can be customized using radio buttons and checkboxes. Scroll through the options to see the selections. Even the size of the Start menu icons can be set in this window. In Vista, stay in this window to answer the next question.

    Using the information shown, how many applications currently can display in the *Start* menu's left pane?

13. In XP, click the *Advanced* tab. The Advanced tab contains Start menu settings and controls how items appear as well as the Recent Documents setting.

    In Vista/7, use the scroll bar to determine how documents appear on the Start menu.

    Using the vertical scroll bar, determine whether Help or Help and Support is enabled, meaning that it displays as a Start menu item.

    Is Help enabled? [Yes | No]

14. Click the *Cancel* button (twice in Vista or 7).

Quick Launch Toolbar (XP/Vista) or Taskbar (7)

15. Quick Launch is the taskbar area located to the immediate right of the Start button in XP or Vista. In Windows 7, buttons are simply attached to the taskbar. There are several ways to add an item to the Quick Launch bar. The easiest way is demonstrated here. Use the *Start* menu > *Search* (XP), *Start Search* textbox (Vista), or *Search programs and files* (7) > *All files and folders link* (XP only). In XP, Vista, or 7, type `wordpad` in the textbox and in XP press Enter. In Vista/7 do not press Enter.
16. In the Search results window, right-click the *WORDPAD.EXE* filename and drag the file to the Quick Launch or taskbar area. Release the right mouse button and *Copy Here*, *Move Here*, *Create Shortcuts Here*, and *Cancel* options (XP), *Move to Quick Launch* (Vista), or *Pin to taskbar* (7) display.
17. Select the *Copy Here* option (XP), *Move to Quick Launch* (Vista), or *Pin to taskbar* (7). To access the *WordPad* Quick Launch icon, click the double arrows in the *Quick Launch* window or just click on the WordPad icon. Any items that have been added to the Quick Launch or taskbar area appear and can be selected. If the *WordPad* option is not available, redo Steps 15 and 16.
18. Click the *WordPad Quick Launch* option. The WordPad application displays. Close WordPad. Close the *Search results* window (XP).

Instructor initials: ____________

Tech Tip

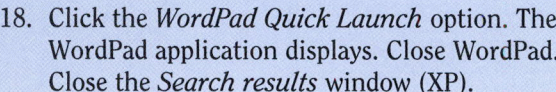

What to do if the Quick Launch toolbar is missing

If the Quick Launch toolbar is missing from the taskbar, right-click an empty taskbar space, select *Toolbars* and click the *Quick Launch* option. The Quick Launch toolbar then displays on the taskbar.

19. To remove the *WordPad* icon from the Quick Launch toolbar or taskbar, right-click the Quick Launch area or taskbar *WordPad* option. Select the *Delete* (XP/Vista) or *Unpin this program from taskbar* (7) option. A warning message appears that states that the WordPad option will not be available if it is deleted. Click *Yes* and the WORDPAD.EXE file used in the Quick Launch bar is sent to the Recycle Bin. Note that as long as the *Copy Here* option (XP) was selected, the WordPad application is still available.
20. Use the *Accessories* Start menu option to access the WordPad application.

    Is the WordPad application still available?

    If so, show the window to the instructor or lab assistant. If WordPad does not start, you did not select the *Copy Here* option in Step 17. If this is the case, the WordPad application must be removed from the Recycle Bin and placed in its proper folder. The default folder is Program Files\Windows NT\Accessories.

Instructor initials: ______________

21. Power off the computer properly.

Lab 11.5 Windows XP/Vista/7 File and Folder Management

Objective: To be able to create folders, move files, and copy files to new locations

Parts: Computer with Windows XP/Vista/7 installed

Formatted 3.5-inch disk or flash drive

Procedure: Complete the following procedure and answer the accompanying questions.

Note: There are multiple ways to do some of the steps in this exercise. Some steps have an alternate method for doing the same procedure. For these steps, you may use either method.

1. Click *Start* > *All Programs* > *Accessories* > *Notepad*. Type the following:

```
Develop a passion for learning. If you do, you will never cease to grow. -Anthony J.
D'Angelo
```

2. Click the *File* menu option and click *Save*.
3. Insert a formatted disk into the floppy (`A:`) drive or attach a flash drive. Click the down arrow in the *Save in* textbox (XP) or the down arrow next to the left of the user name in the top pane (Vista), or down arrow (7), as shown in Figure 11.26. Select *Computer*, then the appropriate drive option for the media you are using. In the *File name* textbox, type `Quote 1` and select the *Save* button.

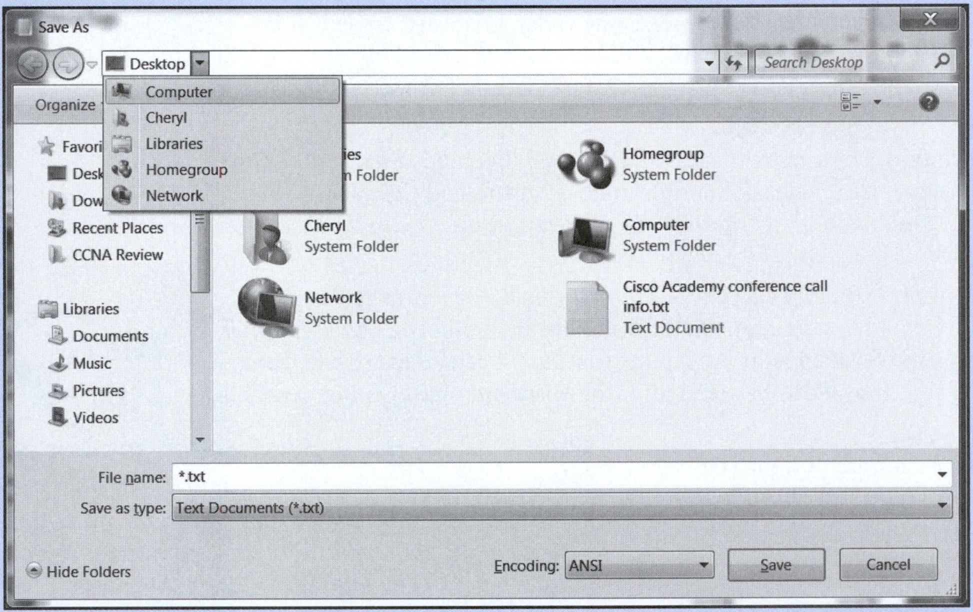

Figure 11.26 Windows 7 path selection arrow

4. In Notepad, click *File* > *New*. Type the following:

```
The man who graduates today and stops learning tomorrow is uneducated the day after.
-Newton D. Baker
```

5. Click *File* > *Save* from the menu options. The *Save in* textbox (XP) or the top line (Vista/7) should show the drive option you selected previously. If it does not, select the appropriate drive media. In the *File name* textbox, type `Quote 2` and select *Save*.
6. Click *File* > *New*. Type the following:

```
Don't just learn the tricks of the trade. Learn the trade. -James Bennis
```

7. Click *File* > *Save*. The *Save in* textbox (XP) or the top line (Vista/7) should show the drive option selected previously. If it does not, select the appropriate drive media. In the *File name* textbox, type `Quote 3` and select *Save*.
8. Click *File* > *New*. Type the following:

```
Nine-tenths of education is encouragement. -Anatole France
```

9. Click *File* > *Save*. The *Save in* textbox (XP) or the top line (Vista/7) should show the drive option selected previously. If it does not, select the appropriate drive media. In the *File name* textbox, type `Quote 4` and select *Save*.
10. Click *File* > *New*. Type the following:

```
Technology is dominated by two types of people--Those who understand what they do not
manage, and those who manage what they do not understand. -Source Unknown
```

11. Click *File* > *Save*. The *Save in* textbox (XP) or the top line (Vista/7) should show the drive option selected previously. If it does not, select the appropriate drive media. In the *File name* textbox, type `Quote 5` and select *Save*.
12. Close the Notepad application by clicking the *Close* button (which is the button in the upper-right corner with an X).
13. Right-click the *Start* button and select *Explore* (XP/Vista)/*Open Windows Explorer* (7). In the left window, use the vertical scroll bar to locate and select the drive media you are using.
14. In the right window, locate the five files you just created, called *Quote 1*, *Quote 2*, *Quote 3*, *Quote 4*, and *Quote 5*. If the files are not there, redo the steps used to create them.

Instructor initials: ______________

Create a Folder

Note: The method shown below that is preceded by the label *Alternative* is an alternate way to perform the same steps. For these steps, you may use either method.

15. In the right *Explorer* window, right-click an empty space. Point to the *New* option and click the *Folder* option. A folder appears in the right window with the words *New Folder* highlighted. Type `Learning Quotes` and press [Enter].

    XP alternative: Click the *File* menu option.

    Vista alternative: Click the *Organize* down arrow and select *New Folder*. Point to the *New* option and click the *Folder* option.

    7 alternative: Click the *New folder* option from the top line.

    In all versions, a folder appears in the right window with the words *New Folder* highlighted. Type `Learning Quotes` and press [Enter].
16. Create another new folder called *General Quotes* using the steps outlined in Step 15.

Instructor initials: ______________

Copy a File

17. In the right Explorer window, right-click the file named *Quote 1*. A submenu appears. Select the *Copy* option.

Alternative: In the right Explorer window, click the file named *Quote 1*. Click the *Edit* menu option. In Vista/7, click the *Organize* down arrow.

Then in all operating system versions, click the *Copy* option from the drop-down menu.

18. In the right window, double-click the *Learning Quotes* folder.

    In XP, notice how the *Windows Explorer Address* textbox changes to `X:\Learning Quotes` (where `X:` is the drive letter you are using).

    In Vista/7, the path appears across the top of the window. The right window is empty because the folder does not have any files or subfolders in it yet.

19. In the right window, right-click and a submenu appears. Click *Paste* and the Quote 1 file appears in the right window.

    XP alternative: Click the *Edit* menu option.

    Vista/7 alternative: Click the *Organize* down arrow.

    In both XP and Vista, select *Paste*. The *Quote 1* file appears in the right window.

20. In the left window, click the drive option for the media you are using.

    In XP, notice how the *Window Explorer Address* textbox changes to a different drive letter.

    In Vista/7, the path across the top of the window changes.

21. Copy the files named *Quote 2* and *Quote 3* into the *Learning Quotes* folder using the methods outlined in previous steps.

Copy Multiple Files

22. In the left window, click the drive option for the media you are using.
23. Locate the files called *Quote 4* and *Quote 5* in the right window.
24. In the right window, click once on the *Quote 4* filename. The name is highlighted.
25. Hold the Shift key down and click once on the *Quote 5* filename. Both the *Quote 4* and *Quote 5* filenames are highlighted. *Note*: The Shift key is used to select files that are consecutive in a list (one right after the other). If you wanted to select files that are not consecutive, use the Ctrl key to select the files.
26. Right-click the files named *Quote 4* and *Quote 5*. A submenu appears. Click the *Copy* option.

    XP alternative: Click the *Edit* menu option and select *Copy*.

    Vista/7 alternative: Click the *Organize* down arrow and select *Copy*.

27. Double-click the *General Quotes* folder.

    In XP, notice the *Windows Explorer Address* textbox.

    In Vista/7, the path across the top changes to `X:\General Quotes` (where `X:` is the drive media you are using) and the right window is empty because the folder does not have any files or subfolders in it yet.

28. In the right window, right-click an empty space and a submenu appears. Select *Paste*. The *Quote 4* and *Quote 5* files appear in the right window.

    XP alternative: Select the *Edit* menu option.

    Vista/7 alternative: Click the *Organize* down arrow and select *Paste*.

    The *Quote 4* and *Quote 5* files appear in the right window.

    How many folders are located in the root directory?

    How many files are located in the root directory?

    How many files are located in the *Learning Quotes* folder?

    How many files are located in the *General Quotes* folder?

Instructor initials: ______________

Copying a File from One Folder to Another

29. In the left window, click the drive option for the media you are using.
30. Open the *Learning Quotes* folder located under the drive option that you are using. The files *Quote 1*, *Quote 2*, and *Quote 3* appear in the right window.
31. In the right window, right-click the *Quote 3* file. From the submenu that appears, select *Copy*.

    XP alternative: In the right window, click the *Quote 3* file. Click *Edit* from the menu and select *Copy*.

    Vista/7 alternative: In the right window, click the *Quote 3* filename. Click *Organize* from the menu and select *Copy*.
32. Open the *General Quotes* folder located under the drive media option you are using. The *Quote 4* and *Quote 5* files appear in the right window and the Address textbox shows General Quotes.
33. In the right window, right-click an empty space and a submenu appears. Select *Paste* and the *Quote 3*, *Quote 4*, and *Quote 5* files appear.

    XP alternative: Click the *Edit* menu option. Select *Paste* and the *Quote 3*, *Quote 4*, and *Quote 5* files appear.

    Vista/7 alternative: Click the *Organize* down arrow and select *Paste*. The *Quote 3*, *Quote 4*, and *Quote 5* files appear.
34. Using the same procedures previously described, copy the *Quote 1* and *Quote 2* files from the *Learning Quotes* folder into the *General Quotes* folder. At the end of this step you should have three files (*Quote 1*, *Quote 2*, and *Quote 3*) in the *Learning Quotes* folder and five files (*Quote 1*, *Quote 2*, *Quote 3*, *Quote 4*, and *Quote 5*) in the *General Quotes* folder.

Moving a File

35. Create a folder on the disk you are using called *My Stuff*. Refer to the steps earlier in the exercise if you need assistance.
36. Open the folder called *General Quotes*. In the right window, all five files appear.
37. In the right window, click once on the *Quote 1* file to highlight it. Hold down the Ctrl key and click the *Quote 3* file. Both the *Quote 1* and *Quote 3* filenames are highlighted. *Note*: The Ctrl key is used to select nonconsecutive files, whereas the Shift key is used to select files that are listed consecutively (one right after another).

> **Tech Tip**
>
> **The purpose of Cut and Paste**
>
> The *Cut* and *Paste* options are used to move a file from one folder to another.

38. Right-click either the *Quote 1* or *Quote 3* filename. Select the *Cut* option.

    XP alternative: Select the *Edit* menu option. Click *Cut*. The *Cut* option is used to move a file from one folder to another.

    Vista/7 alternative: Click the *Organize* down arrow and select *Cut*. The *Cut* option is used to move a file from one folder to another.
39. Open the *My Stuff* folder. The right window is empty because no files have been copied or moved into the *My Stuff* folder yet. In the right window, right-click and select *Paste*. The *Quote 1* and *Quote 3* files appear in the right window.

    XP alternative: Select the *Edit* menu option and click *Paste*. The *Quote 1* and *Quote 3* files appear in the right window.

    Vista/7 alternative: Click the *Organize* down arrow and select *Paste*. The *Quote 1* and *Quote 3* files appear in the right window.

40. Using the procedures just learned, move the *Quote 1* file from the *Learning Quotes* folder into the *General Quotes* folder.

    How many files are located in the *Learning Quotes* folder?

    How many files are located in the *General Quotes* folder?

    How many files are located in the *My Stuff* folder?

Instructor initials: ______________

Deleting Files and Folders

41. Open the *My Stuff* folder. The *Quote 1* and *Quote 3* files appear in the right window.
42. In the right window, select the *Quote 1* and the *Quote 3* files. Both the *Quote 1* and *Quote 3* filenames are highlighted.
43. Press the Del key on the keyboard. A message appears on the screen asking, *Are you sure you want to delete these 2 items?* Click *Yes*.

    XP alternative: Select the *File* menu option and choose *Delete*. A *Confirm Multiple File Delete* message appears on the screen asking, "Are you sure you want to delete these 2 items?" Select *Yes*.

    Vista/7 alternative: Click on the *Organize* down arrow and select *Delete*. A confirmation message appears. Select *Yes*.

> **Tech Tip**
>
> **Deleted files on external media are not put in Recycle Bin**
>
> When deleting files from a floppy disk, an optical disc, a thumb drive, or other external media, the files are not placed in the Recycle Bin—they are deleted. When deleting files from a hard drive, the files get placed in the Recycle Bin.

44. Select the *My Stuff* folder. The *My Stuff* folder is highlighted. Press the Del key on the keyboard. A *Confirm Folder Delete* message appears on the screen asking, "Are you sure you want to remove the folder "My Stuff" and all its contents?" Click the *Yes* button.

    XP alternative: Select the *File* menu option and choose *Delete*. A *Confirm Multiple File Delete* message appears on the screen asking, "Are you sure you want to remove the folder "My Stuff" and all its contents?" Click the *Yes* button.

    Vista/7 alternative: Click the *Organize* down arrow and select *Delete*. A confirmation message appears. Select *Yes*.

> **Tech Tip**
>
> **Skipping the Recycle Bin for deleted hard drive files**
>
> If you want to permanently delete a file from a hard drive (the file will not get placed in the Recycle Bin), hold the [Shift] key down while pressing the Del key.

Instructor initials: ______________

45. Using the previously demonstrated procedures, delete the *Learning Quotes* folder and the *General Quotes* folders and all files contained within each folder as well as the original *Quote* files.
46. Close the *Windows Explorer* window.

Challenge

47. Using Notepad, create three text files and save them to the external media in a folder called *My Files*.
48. On the hard drive or on external media, create a folder called *Computer Text*.
49. Copy the two of the three text files from the *My Files* folder into the folder called *Computer Text*.
50. Move the third text file from the *My Files* folder into the folder called *Computer Text*.

Instructor initials: ______________

> **Tech Tip**
>
> **Retrieving a deleted file**
>
> To restore a file that has been accidentally placed in the Recycle Bin, open the Recycle Bin, right-click the file, and click the *Restore* option or click *Restore this item*.

51. Permanently delete the folder called *Computer Text* and all files within this folder.

Instructor initials: ______________

52. Delete the folder called *My Files* and all files within this folder.

Instructor initials: ______________

Lab 11.6 Managing Files on a Mobile Device

Objective: To be able to copy files or send files using an Android or Apple iOS-based device

Parts: Android device or Apple iPad

Procedure: Complete the following procedure and answer the accompanying questions.

Android

1. If working on an Apple device, please go to Step 16. Power on the Android device.
2. Access the Camera app by touching the *Camera* icon on the home page.
3. Normally within the Camera app, there is an icon of a camera or a circle that you touch to take the picture. Frequently, there is a sound effect of a camera shutter. Take a picture.
4. Return to the home page by touching the home icon. If the home icon is not showing, touch the screen where it normally appears (bottom left, center icon).
5. Locate and access (touch) the *File Manager* app.
6. Unless the settings have been changed, most photos are stored by default on internal storage. Touch the *internal storage* option. The internal storage folders list to the right.
7. Locate and open (touch) the *DCIM* folder.
8. Locate and open the *Camera* folder.
9. To open a picture, touch the filename. Frequently there are options such as rotating or cropping the photo found by touching just outside the photograph.

   What photo options are available?

10. Return to the file listing by using the *return* button. The return button is the button on the screen that is a return arrow such as the one shown here: ⮌ If the return button is not shown, you can touch the bottom left of the screen and the return arrow normally shows.
11. Enable the checkbox by the name of the photograph by touching the checkbox.
12. Options either appear or you can touch an icon normally located in the upper right or left corner that allow options to appear. Locate the options that include the copy function.
13. Go to another folder located on your internal storage. Select the *Paste* option.

Instructor initials: ______________

14. Delete the original and copied photograph.

Instructor initials: ______________

15. Power off the device and return it to the original location.

Apple

16. Power on the Apple device.
17. Access the Camera app by touching the *Camera* icon on the home page.
18. Tap the icon of the camera to take the picture. Frequently, there is a sound effect of a camera shutter. Take a picture.
19. Notice how a small image of the photograph is available in the lower-left corner. Tap the graphic of the photo. Note that you can also access the photograph using the *Photos* home page icon.

20. Options are available in the top right corner. If these options have disappeared, just tap the photo.

    Describe three options available at the top of a photograph.

21. Select the option that has a box with an arrow in it. Select *Email Photo*.
22. In the *To:* textbox, type a valid email address such as your own by tapping inside the blank space to the right of To:. See the instructor if you don't know of an email address to use.

    What email address did you use?
23. In the *Subject* textbox, type `Class photo`. Notice how the photo is already attached to the email.
24. Tap the *Send* button in the top right corner of the email.
25. Take another photograph.
26. Either using the *Camera* app or the *Photos* app, relocate the original photograph.
27. Tap the photo to bring up the options in the right corner if they are not showing. Select the *Slideshow* icon.
28. Select a type of transition by tapping the *Transitions* option.

    What transition did you choose? Student dependent
29. Select *Start Slideshow*. Stop the slideshow by tapping on the screen.

Instructor initials: ____________

30. Delete the two photographs.

Instructor initials: ____________

31. Power off the device and return it to the original location.

Lab 11.7 Windows XP/Vista/7 File Extension

Objective: To be able to associate a file extension with a file type

Parts: Computer with Windows XP/Vista/7 installed

Formatted 3.5-inch disk or flash drive

Procedure: Complete the following procedure and answer the accompanying questions.

1. Select *Start* > *All Programs* > *Accessories* option and click the *Notepad* menu selection. Type the following:

   `I hear and I forget. I see and I remember. I do and I understand. -Confucius`
2. Select the *File* menu option and choose *Save*.
3. Insert a formatted disk into the floppy (`A:`) drive or attach a flash drive. Select the appropriate drive option for the media you are using. In the *File name* textbox, type `Junk`. Click the *Save* button.
4. Close the Notepad application.
5. Right-click the *Start* button and select *Explore* (XP/Vista)/*Open Windows Explorer* (7).
6. In XP, select the *Tools* menu option and choose *Folder Options*.

   In Vista/7, select the *Organize* menu option and select *Folder and Search Options*.

   In all operating systems, click the *View* tab. If the *Hide (file) extensions for known file Types* checkbox contains a check mark, click inside the checkbox to remove the check mark. If the checkbox is empty, ignore this step. Click *OK*.
7. In the left Explorer window, use the vertical scroll bar to locate and select the disk media you used to save the file. Locate the *Junk.txt* file in the right window and double-click the icon.

   What happened?

Did the Notepad application open with the *Junk* file open?

8. Close the Notepad application.
9. In the Explorer window, right-click the file called *Junk*. Click the *Rename* option. Ensure the entire filename, *Junk.txt*, is highlighted. Type `junk.abc` and press Enter. *Junk.txt* is renamed to *junk.abc*. A rename warning box appears stating that, "If you change a filename extension, the file may become unusable." It also asks, "Are you sure you want to change it?" Click *Yes*.

   What does the *junk.abc* file icon look like now?

10. Double-click the *junk.abc* file icon.

    What happened when you double-clicked on the *junk.abc* file icon?

11. Click the *Select the program from a list of installed programs* radio button and click *OK*. Scroll until you reach the *Notepad* icon. Click the *Notepad* icon and then click *OK*.

    What happened when you clicked the *OK* button?

12. In the Notepad application, select the *File* menu option and choose *New*.
13. Type the following:

    `The only real mistake is the one from which we learn nothing. -John Powell`

14. Select the *File* menu option and click *Save as*. Ensure the disk media option that you are using is the destination. In the *File name* textbox, type `Junk2` and click *Save*.
15. Close the Notepad application.
16. Using Explorer, rename the *Junk2.txt* file to *Junk2.abc*. A rename warning box appears stating that, "If you change a filename extension, the file may become unusable." It also asks, "Are you sure you want to change it?" Select *Yes*. Notice the file icon after the change.

    How is the icon different from before?

17. Double-click the *Junk2.abc* icon.

    What happened when you double-clicked the *Junk2.abc* icon?

Instructor initials: ______________

Lab 11.8 Windows XP/Vista/7 Attributes, Compression, and Encryption

Objective: To be able to identify and set file and folder attributes, compression, and encryption

Parts: Computer with Windows XP/Vista/7 installed

Formatted 3.5-inch disk, or flash drive

Procedure: Complete the following procedure and answer the accompanying questions.

Note: The compression and encryption portions of this exercise require an NTFS partition.

Managing File Attributes

1. Click *Start* > *All Programs* > *Accessories* > *Notepad*. Type the following:

   `Aim for success, not perfection. -Dr. David M. Burns`

2. Select the *File* menu option and choose *Save*. Insert a formatted disk into the floppy (`A:`) drive, or attach a flash drive. Select the appropriate drive option for the media you are using. In the *File name* textbox, type `Attribute File` and click *Save*.

3. Close the Notepad application.
4. Right-click the *Start* button and select the *Explore* (XP/Vista)/*Open Windows Explorer* (7) option.
5. In the left pane, click the option for the disk media you are using. The *Attribute File* file should be listed in the right panel. If not, redo the previous steps to create the file.
6. Select the *Attribute File* file in the right pane. In XP, select the *File* menu option and select *Properties*. In Vista/7, select the *Organize* menu option and select *Properties*. The same results can be obtained by right-clicking the file and selecting *Properties*. The file attributes are listed at the bottom and by clicking the *Advanced* button in Windows Vista/7.

   What file attributes are listed for the *ATTRIBUTE FILE* file?

   What file attribute is enabled by default?
7. The Archive attribute is enabled so that the file is selected for backup by default. Backup applications use this attribute when backing up data. Click the *Read-only attribute* checkbox and click *OK*.
8. Double-click the *Attribute File* filename. The application opens with the typed text shown. Add the following to the quote:

   ```
   Never give up your right to be wrong, because then you will lose the ability
   to learn new things and move forward with your life. -David M. Burns
   ```
9. Click the *File* menu option and select *Save*. Click the *Save* button.

   What happens when the Save option is chosen?
10. Click the *OK* (XP) or *Yes* > *OK* (Vista/7) button and then click *Cancel*.
11. Click the *Close* button in the Notepad window. When asked if you want to save the changes, click *No* (XP) or *Don't Save* (Vista/7). The read-only attribute prevented the file from being changed.
12. In the *Windows Explorer* window, right-click the *Attribute File* file and select *Properties*. Select the *Hidden* file attribute checkbox and click *OK*.
13. In the XP *Windows Explorer* window, select the *View* menu option and click *Refresh*. This step is not needed in Vista/7.

    What happened to the *Attribute File filename*?
14. In the Windows Explorer window, select the *Tools* (XP)/*Organize* (Vista/7) > *Folder Options* (XP) or *Folder and Search Options* (Vista/7) > *View* tab > *Hidden files and folders* > *Show hidden files and folder* (XP/Vista)/*Show hidden files, folders, and drives* (7) radio button. This option is used to see files or folders that have the hidden attribute set or enabled. To make this change applicable to all folders, click the Apply to all folders (XP) or Apply to Folders (Vista/7) button. A Folder views dialog box appears stating that the change will occur the next time the folder is opened. Click *Yes* and then click *OK*.

    Does the *ATTRIBUTE FILE* file appear in the Windows Explorer right pane? If not, press the F5 key to refresh the window or select the *Refresh* option from the *View* menu (XP).

    How does the file icon differ from before?

15. Click the *Windows Explorer View* (XP)/*Views* (Vista) menu option and select *Thumbnails* (XP)/*Small Icons* (Vista). In Windows Explorer for Windows 7, click the *Change your view* icon that contains a down arrow on the right side of the menu bar; select *Small icons*.

    How do the icon(s) now appear in the Windows Explorer right pane?

16. Under the *View* (XP)/*Views* (Vista)/*Change your view* (7) menu option, select the *List* option.

    How does the *ATTRIBUTE FILE* filename now appear in the right pane?

17. From the Windows Explorer menu, select *View* (XP)/*Views* (Vista)/*Change your view* (7) and then select *Details*.

    Why do you think that a technician would prefer the Details view option over any other option?

18. Delete the *Attribute File* file from the external media.

    Did either the hidden or read-only attribute stop the *ATTRIBUTE FILE* file from being deleted? [Yes | No]

19. To reset all folder options back to the default attributes, select the *Tools* (XP)/*Organize* (Vista/7) option from the Windows Explorer menu > *Folder Options* (XP) *Folder and Search Options* (Vista/7) > *View* tab > *Restore defaults* > *Apply to all folders* (XP) or *Apply to folders* button (Vista/7). A folder views dialog box appears. Click *Yes* followed by *OK*.

Instructor initials: ______________

Using Compression

Note: The disk volume must have an NTFS file system on it in order to do this section. To check the file system, open *My Computer* (XP)/*Computer* (Vista/7). Right-click the hard drive volume that contains Windows and select *Properties*. In the Properties window near the top, the type of file system is listed.

20. Create a file called *Compression File* using Notepad and save it in the *My Documents* (XP)/*Documents* (Vista/7) folder on the hard drive. If necessary, refer to a previous exercise for steps. The text to be placed in the file follows. Copy this text repeatedly in the document until you have four pages of text.

    ```
    The most successful career must show a waste of strength that might have
    removed mountains, and the most unsuccessful is not that of the man who is
    taken unprepared, but of him who has prepared and is never taken. On a tragedy
    of that kind, our national morality is duly silent. -Edward M. Forster
    ```

21. Close the *Notepad* application window. Using Windows Explorer, locate *Compression File*.

    What is the current *Compression File* file size?

22. Right-click the filename and select *Properties*. Click the *Advanced* button. In the Advanced Attributes dialog box, locate the *Compress or Encrypt attributes* section. Click the *Compress contents to save disk space* checkbox. This option is used to compress a file or folder. Click the *OK* button. Again, click the *OK* button to finish the process. Keep in mind that in order to save disk space efficiently, the file needs to be at least 4K of disk space.

    Using Windows Explorer, locate the file called *Compression File* and determine the file size.

    Document the file size.

Instructor initials: ______________

23. Permanently delete the *Compression File*. Have a classmate verify the file deletion by printing his/her name.

    Is the file *completely* deleted? [Yes | No]

Enabling Encryption

Note: The disk volume must have an NTFS file system on it in order to do this section.

24. Create a file called *Encryption File* using Notepad and save it to *My Documents* (XP)/ *Documents* (Vista/7). If necessary, refer to a previous exercise for steps. The text to be placed in the file follows:

```
I do not fear computers. I fear the lack of them. -Isaac Asimov
```

25. Close the *Notepad* application window. Using Windows Explorer, locate the file named *Encryption File*.

    What is the current *Encryption File* file size?

26. Right-click the filename and select *Properties*. Click the *Advanced* button. In the Advanced Attributes dialog box, locate the *Compress or Encrypt attributes* section. Click the *Encrypt contents to secure data* checkbox, the option used to encrypt a file or folder. Note that the checkbox may not be available on some Vista/7 versions. See the Tech Tip. Click the *OK* button twice. A dialog box appears asking if you want to encrypt the file and the parent file or encrypt only the file. Click the *Encrypt the file only* radio button and click *OK*.

    What is the current *Encryption File* file size after encryption?

Tech Tip

Limited encryption support on Vista/7 Home

Vista/7 Starter, Home Basic, and Home Premium versions do not fully support encrypting files. In these versions, the `cipher` command can be used at the command prompt to decrypt files, an encrypted file can be modified, and an encrypted file can be copied to the computer.

Instructor initials: ______________

27. Permanently delete the *Encryption File* file.

    Have a classmate verify the file deletion by printing his or her name. Is the file *completely* deleted? [Yes | No]

28. Properly power off the computer.

Lab 11.9 Using REGEDIT in Windows XP/Vista/7

Objective: To become familiar with the REGEDIT registry-editing utility

Parts: Computer with Windows XP/Vista/7 installed and administrator rights

Formatted 3.5-inch disk or flash drive

Procedure: Complete the following procedure and answer the accompanying questions.

Notes: `REGEDIT` is a utility used for editing the Windows registry. With `regedit`, you can view existing registry settings, modify registry settings values, or create new registry entries to change or enhance the way Windows operates. In this lab, you will use `regedit` to view the system BIOS and video BIOS information on your computer.

Caution: Editing the registry can cause your computer to run erratically, or not run at all! When performing any registry editing, follow *all* directions carefully, including spelling, syntax use, and so on. Failure to do so may cause your computer to fail!

Viewing Registry Information

1. In XP, from the *Start* menu > *Run* > type **`regedit`** > *OK*.

   In Vista/7, from the *Start Search* (Vista)/*Search programs and files* (7) textbox, type **`regedit`** > in the *Programs* section, click on *Regedit* > *Continue* (Vista)/*Yes* (7) button, if necessary. The `regedit` utility opens.

2. In the left window, expand *Hkey_Local_Machine*, *Hardware*, and *Description* by clicking the + (plus) symbol (XP) or arrow (Vista/7) located to the left of the name. Click the *System* option located under *Description*. In the right window, the system BIOS and video BIOS information display.

   What is the system BIOS date?

   Who is the manufacturer of the system BIOS?

   When was the video BIOS manufactured?

Instructor initials: ____________

Exporting and Importing a Registry Section

3. `Regedit` can be used to backup and restore part or all of the registry. To illustrate this point, a portion of the registry will be exported to disk and then imported into the registry. Ensure the following option is still selected in the Registry Editor window:

   Hkey_Local_Machine\Hardware\Description\System

4. Select the *File* menu option and choose *Export*. The Export Registry File window opens.
5. Insert a formatted disk into the floppy (`A:`) drive or attach a flash drive. Click the down arrow in the *Save in* textbox and select the appropriate drive option for the media you are using. In the *File name* textbox, type **`Registry System Section`** and click the *Save* button. The specific registry key is saved to disk.
6. To restore the registry (or a portion of it as in this exercise), click the *File* menu option and select *Import*. The screen should list the file located on the external disk media, but if it does not, select the appropriate drive letter option for the disk media you are using.
7. Click the *Registry System Section* filename and click the *Open* button. A message appears when the section is successfully inserted into the registry. Show this message to the instructor or lab assistant.
8. Close the `regedit` utility.

Instructor initials: ____________

Lab 11.10 Modifying the Windows XP Start Button

Objective: To be able to modify the *Start* button menu

Parts: A computer with a Windows XP operating system loaded

Procedure: Complete the following procedure and answer the accompanying questions.

Start Menu Icon Size

1. Once Windows boots, right-click the *Start* button > *Properties* > *Customize* button. The *General* tab contains two radio buttons that control the size of the icons found on the start menu.

   What start menu icon size radio button is currently selected?

2. Select the opposite radio button. Click *OK* > *Apply* > *OK*.
3. Select the *Start* button to test the icon size change.
4. Return the icon size to the original setting.

Customizing the Number of Start Menu Programs Shown

5. Right-click the *Start* button > *Properties* > *Customize* button. Locate the *Programs* section. The number of programs shown on the left side (bottom portion) of the *Start* button menu can be modified in this section.

   How many programs are currently set to appear on the *Start* button?

6. Click the *Cancel* button and when returned to the previous menu, click *Cancel* again. Click the *Start* button and verify that the number of programs shown is correct. Windows automatically adds the most often utilized programs to the list, but the maximum is set through the *General* tab from which you just returned.
7. Right-click the *Start* button > *Properties* > *Customize* button.

   What is the maximum number of programs that you can have on the *Start* button?
8. Increase the number of programs shown on the *Start* button menu. When finished click *OK* > *Apply* > *OK*.
9. Click the *Start* button. The number of programs shown on the bottom of the Start menu should be the number specified on the *General* tab. If not, access an application not listed on the menu, close the application, and click the *Start* button again.
10. Return the number of *Start* button menu programs to the original setting.

Modifying Default Icon Settings

11. By default, Windows XP displays web browser and email client icons in the upper section, left column of the *Start* menu. To change this behavior, right-click *Start* button > *Properties* > *Customize* button. Locate the *Show on Start menu* section.

    Is Internet enabled (checked)?

    Is Email enabled (checked)?
12. Change the two settings in the *Show on Start menu* section to something different. Click *OK* > *Apply* > *OK*.
13. Select the *Start* button.

    Have the changes been implemented? [Yes | No]
14. Return the *Show on Start menu* section to the original settings. Verify by selecting the *Start* button.

Customizing the Start Menu Programs

15. By default, the Windows XP *Start* menu has links to My Computer, My Documents, My Pictures, My Music, Help and Support, Run, and so on in the right column. Click the *Start* button.

    Write three items found in the Start button menu right column.
16. Right-click the *Start* button > *Properties* > *Customize* button > *Advanced* tab. Locate the *Start menu items* section. Some of the options located there have three possible selections: (1) *Display as a link*; (2) *Display as a menu*; and (3) *Don't display this item*.

    Display as a link means that when the menu option is selected, it opens in a new window. With *Display as a menu*, the option will have an arrow to the side allowing you to access all options that windows would normally contain.

    What is the current setting for Control Panel?
17. Click the *Cancel* button and when returned to the previous menu, click *Cancel* again. Click the *Start* button and observe the current *Control Panel* option on the menu.

    Does the *Control Panel* option appear as described? [Yes | No]
18. Right-click the *Start* button > *Properties* > *Customize* button > *Advanced* tab. Locate the *Start menu items* section. Change the *Control Panel* menu option to one of the other menu settings. Click *OK* > *Apply* > *OK*.

19. Select the *Start* button and select the *Control Panel* menu option.

    How is the *Control Panel* option different?

20. Return the *Control Panel Start* menu item to its original setting.

Adding a Program to the Start Menu

21. Click *Start* button > *Search* > *All Files and Folders* link > type `charmap` in the *All or part of the file name* textbox > *Search* button. *Charmap* is the file used to execute the Character Map program. It is commonly found in the *C:\Windows\System32* folder if you do not want to wait on the Search program.

Note: If the *charmap* file is not installed, any program file can be used for this part of the exercise.

22. Right-click the *charmap* file. Select the *Pin to Start Menu* option. Click the *Start* button.

    Where on the *Start* button menu is the Character Map application added?

23. To remove a customized application, click the *Start* button, right-click the unwanted item (*charmap* in this case), and select *Unpin from Start Menu*.

Instructor initials: ______________

Lab 11.11 Modifying the Windows Vista/7 Start Button

Objective: To be able to modify the *Start* button menu

Parts: A computer with the Windows Vista or 7 operating system loaded

Procedure: Complete the following procedure and answer the accompanying questions.

Start Menu Icon Size

1. Once Windows boots, right-click the *Start* button > *Properties* > *Customize* button. The radio buttons and checkboxes are used to configure the look of the Start menu. Icon size is controlled by a checkbox at the end of the list.

   What Start menu icon size radio button is currently selected? [Normal | Large]

2. Set the setting to the opposite (that is, if the box is already checked, uncheck it, and if the box is unchecked, then check it). Click *OK* > *Apply* > *OK*.
3. Click the *Start* button to test the icon size change.
4. Return the icon size to the original setting.

Customizing the Number of Start Menu Programs Shown

5. Right-click the *Start* button > *Properties* > *Start menu* tab > *Customize* button. Locate the *Number of recent programs to display* selectable number option. The number of programs shown on the left side (bottom portion) of the *Start* button menu can be modified using the up and down arrows that control the number.

   How many programs are currently set to appear on the *Start* button?

6. Click the *Cancel* button and, when returned to the previous menu, click *Cancel* again. Click the *Start* button and verify that the number of programs shown is correct. Windows automatically adds the most often utilized programs to the list, but the maximum is set through the window from which you just returned.

7. Right-click the *Start* button > *Properties* > *Customize* button.

   What is the maximum number of programs that you can have on the *Start* button?
8. Increase the number of programs shown on the *Start* button menu. When finished, click *OK* > *Apply* > *OK*.
9. Click the *Start* button. The number of programs shown on the bottom left of the Start menu should be the number specified. If it is not, access an application not listed on the menu, close the application, and click the *Start* button again.
10. Return the number of *Start* button menu programs to the original setting.

Modifying Default Icon Settings

If Windows 7 is installed, proceed to Step 15.

11. By default, Windows Vista displays web browser and email client icons in the upper section of the left column of the *Start* menu. To change this behavior, right-click *Start* button > *Properties* > *Customize* button. Locate the *Show on Start menu* section.

    Is the Internet link enabled (checked)?

    Is the E-mail link enabled (checked)?
12. In Vista, change the two settings in the *Shown on Start menu* section to something different. Click *OK* > *Apply* > *OK*.
13. Select the *Start* button.

    Have the changes been implemented? [Yes | No]
14. Return the Start menu to the original settings. Verify by selecting the *Start* button.

Customizing the Start Menu Programs

15. By default, the Start menu has links to Documents, Pictures, Music, Help and Support, and so on in the right column. Click the *Start* button.

    What are three items found in the Start button menu right column?
16. Right-click the *Start* button > *Properties* > *Customize* button. Locate the *Computer* section. Some of the options located in this window have three possible selections, similar to the Computer section: (1) Display as a link, (2) Display as a menu, and (3) Don't display this item.

    Display as a link means that when the menu option is selected, it opens in a new window. With *Display as a menu*, the option will have an arrow to the side allowing you to access all options that windows would normally contain.

    What is the current setting for Control Panel?
17. Click the *Cancel* button and, when returned to the previous menu, click *Cancel* again. Click the *Start* button and observe the current *Control Panel* option on the menu.

    Does the Control Panel option appear or not appear as configured? [Yes | No]
18. Right-click the *Start* button > *Properties* > *Customize* button. Locate the *Control Panel* section. Change the *Control Panel* menu option to one of the other menu settings. Click *OK* > *Apply* > *OK*.
19. Select the *Start* button and select the *Control Panel* menu option.

    How is the Control Panel option different?
20. Return the *Control Panel* item to its original setting.

Adding a Program to the Start Menu

21. Click *Start* button > type **charmap** in the *Start Search* (Vista)/*Search programs and files* (7) textbox. `Charmap` is the file used to execute the Character Map program. It is commonly found in the C:\Windows\System32 folder.

    Note: If the *Charmap* file is not installed, any program file can be used for this part of the exercise.

22. Locate *charmap* in the resulting *Programs* list. Right-click the *charmap* file and select the *Pin to Start Menu* option. Click the *Start* button.

    Where on the Start button menu is the Character Map application added?

23. To remove a customized application, click the *Start* button, right-click the unwanted item (*charmap* in this case), and select *Unpin from Start Menu*.

Instructor initials: ______________

Lab 11.12 Basic Commands at a Command Prompt

Objective: To execute basic commands at a command prompt

Parts: A Windows-based computer with command prompt access

The ability to save a file to the hard drive *or* access to a floppy drive/flash drive

Procedure: Complete the following procedure and answer the accompanying questions.

Note: For each step requiring a typed command the Enter key must be pressed to execute the command. This instruction will *not* be given with each step.

1. Power on the computer and log on if necessary. When Windows loads, exit to a command prompt.

   Windows XP: (1) *Start* > *Run* > type **CMD** > *OK*; (2) *Start* > *All Programs* > *Accessories* > *Command Prompt*.

   Windows Vista/7: (1) *Start Search* (Vista)/*Search programs and files* (7) textbox > type **CMD** > press Enter.

   Does a prompt display? If not and you followed every step correctly, contact your instructor.

   What prompt displays on the screen? This is the folder (directory) from which you are starting.

2. At the command prompt, type **cd**.

   The prompt changes to `C:\>`. If a message appears stating invalid command or invalid directory, you made a typing error. If you suspect an error, verify the backslash is after `cd` and that there are no extra spaces. The backslash starts from the left side and goes to the right (\). Other commands use a forward slash, which would be in the opposite direction `/`.

   `cd` is the command for change directory, which tells the operating system to go to a different directory in the tree structure. The `\` after the `cd` command tells the operating system to go to the root directory. An alternative way of typing this command is `cd \`. Notice the space between the `cd` command and the backslash. There are usually different ways to do every command from a prompt. Note that the `cd\` command allows you to return to the root directory at any time.

3. At the command prompt, type **dir**.

   A list of files and directories appears. Files are the items that show an extension to the right of the filename, file size, and file creation date. File extensions frequently give clues as to which application created the file. Directories have a `<DIR>` entry to the right of the name.

List one file including its extension and one directory shown on the screen. Using Table 11.4 or the Internet, try to determine the application that created the file and write that application (if found) beside the filename.

4. When the number of files shown exceeds what can be displayed on the screen, the files quickly scroll off the screen until all files finish displaying. The DIR command has a switch that controls this scrolling. A command switch begins with a forward slash and enhances or changes the way a command performs. At the command prompt, type **dir /p**.

   After looking at the data on the screen, press Enter again. Continue pressing Enter until the prompt reappears. The /p switch (when used with the dir command, of course) tells the operating system to display the files one page at a time.

5. At the prompt, type **dir /2**.

   What is the function of the /w switch?

6. Multiple switches can be used with a DOS command. At the prompt, type the following command:

   dir /w/p

   Using the dir command /w and /p switches cause files to display in a wide format, one page at a time.

7. Different versions of Windows have documentation with online help. To find out the operating system version loaded on the computer, type **ver**.

   Who is the operating system manufacturer and what version is being used on the computer?

8. At the prompt, type **dir /? | more**. To create the vertical bar used in the command, hold down the Shift key and, while keeping it held down, press the key directly above the Enter key. It is the same key as a backslash. A short explanation of the command appears followed by the command syntax (instructions or rules for how the command is to be typed). A technician needs to be able to understand command syntax to determine what commands to type when unfamiliar with a command. The | symbol is called the pipe symbol. The | more command tells the operating system to display the output one page at a time. Perform the following activities and then press any key to continue until you return to a prompt.

   Write one switch that can be used with the DIR command along with a short explanation of its purpose.

9. Type **cd*xxxxx***, where the *xxxxx* is replaced by the name of the directory you wrote as the answer to Question 3. For example in Question 3, if I wrote the directory name *Casino*, I would type cd\Casino at the prompt. The prompt changes to the name of the directory (folder) that I just typed.

10. Type the following command: **dir a*.***

    The a*.* is not a switch. This command is directing the operating system to list all files or subdirectories that start with the letter A. The *.* part means all files. The directory you chose may not have any files or subdirectories that start with the letter A. If this occurs, the operating system displays the message "File not found." The * is known as a wildcard. A wildcard substitutes for one or more characters. The first asterisk (*) is the wildcard for any name of a file. The second asterisk is the wildcard for any extension.

Does the operating system list any files or subdirectories that start with the letter A? If so, write one of them in the following space. If not, did the operating system let you know this? If so, write the message displayed.

11. Type the following command: `cd..`

    The `..` tells the operating system to move back (or up if you think about the structure in Windows Explorer) one directory in the directory structure. Since you are one level down (because of typing the `cd\`*xxxxx* command), this command returns you to the root directory.

    If you wanted to display a list of all files in the root directory that start with the letter C, what command would you type? Try the command you think is right on the computer to see if it works.

    Do any commands start with the letter C? If so, write at least one of them down.

    Does the *COMMAND.COM* file appear in the list of commands that start with the letter C?

On Your Own

a. Change to the directory that contains Windows. The directory name is normally *Windows* or *WINNT*. If you cannot determine what directory contains Windows, use the `dir` command again or contact your instructor or lab assistant.

   Write the command you used to do this.

   List two Windows files that begin with the letter D.

b. Return to the root directory.

   Write the command you used.

12. *Note*: If you are not allowed to create and save a file on the hard drive, you can do this part from the root directory of another drive such as the floppy drive or a flash drive.

    From the root directory of whatever drive you are using (designated as `X:\`), you are going to create a file using the `copy con:` command that will later be read using a different command. The name of the file will be *LadyVOLS.txt*. You are going to type the commands below exactly as they appear and at the end of each line press [Enter]. Note that no message appears. For example, if your flash drive is the E: drive, your first line will be `copy con: E:\LadyVOLS.txt` and you will press the [Enter] key. Continue typing as directed.

```
copy con: X:\LadyVOLS.txt [Enter]
This is a fine mess you've gotten me into Ollie. [Enter]
This computer is about to EXPLODE if you press Enter one more time. [Enter]
Go get that Earth creature and bring back the Uranium Pew36 Space Modulator. [Enter]
Can you sing Rocky Top? [Enter]
```

    Press [F6]. `^z` (caret Z) appears on the screen. Press [Enter]. A message appears stating that one file copied. If this did not occur, repeat this step.

13. From the root directory, use the `TYPE` command to view the text file you just created by using the following command: `type ladyvols.txt`

    What is the result of using the `type` command?

    Can you edit and change the file using this command? [Yes | No]

    Have a classmate verify your file displays and sign his or her name beside your answer.

Classmate's printed name ____________________________

Classmate's signature ____________________________

14. The DEL command is used to delete files. From the root directory, delete the file you just created using the following command: **del ladyvols.txt**

    Why do you think you did not have to type del x:\ladyvols.txt (the full path) in the last step?

Lab 11.13 The COPY, MD, DEL, and RD Commands

Objective: To correctly use the COPY, MD, DEL, and RD commands

Parts: A Windows computer with command prompt access

The ability to save a file to the hard drive *or* access to a floppy drive/flash drive

Procedure: Complete the following procedure and answer the accompanying questions.

Note: For each step requiring a typed command, the Enter key must be pressed to execute the command. This instruction will *not* be given with each step.

1. Power on the computer and log on if necessary. When Windows loads, access a command prompt. There are multiple methods that can be used. Use a previous lab for instructions.

   Note: This next section requires the ability to create folders and files. If this is not permitted on the hard drive, do this section from a floppy disk or flash drive.

2. At the command prompt type the command to go to the drive you will be using. For example, if you are using the floppy drive, type **A:** and press Enter. If you are using a flash drive that uses the drive letter G, you would type **G:** and press Enter. The command is as follows: *x:* (where *x* is the drive letter where you are allowed to create files). The prompt changes to the appropriate drive. At the command prompt, type **cd**.

   What is the purpose of the cd command?

   What is the purpose of the cd\ command?

3. Create a directory (folder) called *Class*: **md class**
4. Use the dir command to verify the directory creation. If it is not created, redo Step 3.
5. When the directory is created, move into the *Class* directory using the cd command: **cd class**

   If you use the dir command at this point, what two entries are automatically created in a directory?

6. Within the *Class* directory, create a subdirectory (subfolder) called *SubFolder1*: **md subfolder1**
7. Move from the *CLASS* folder into the subfolder just created: **cd subfolder1**

   In Step 7, would the cd *x*:\Class\SubFolder1 (or whatever media you are using) command have worked as well? Why or why not?

8. From the *SubFolder1* directory, move back one directory: **cd..**

   What does the prompt look like at this point?

9. Make another subdirectory called *SubFolder2*.

   Have another student verify that both subdirectories have been created by using the dir command. Have them sign their name on your answer sheet if the *Class* directory has two subdirectories that have the correct title.

Classmate's printed name ______________________

Classmate's signature ______________________

10. Return to the root directory.

On Your Own

a. Using the `copy con:` command as described in a previous lab, create two text files within the *SubFolder1* directory. Name the files with your first initial and last name, plus 1-1 and 1-2. The file extension will be *txt*. For example, the filenames of *cschmidt1-1.txt* and *cschmidt1-2.txt* would be in *SubFolder1*.

b. Within *SubFolder2*, create two files. Name the files with your first initial and last name, plus 2-1 and 2-2. The file extension will be *.txt*. For example, the filenames of *cschmidt2-1.txt* and *cschmidt2-2.txt* would be located in *SubFolder2*.

c. Use the `dir` command to verify the two files exist in the two subdirectories.

Have another student verify that two files are created in the two subdirectories. Ensure that the two names are correct and are readable. Have him/her sign his/her name and write the command he/she used to verify what you typed inside each file.

Classmate's printed name ______________________

Classmate's signature ______________________

d. Return to the root directory of the `x:` drive (the media where you are allowed to create files).

Draw an image of your directory structure that you have created.

Since you are sitting at the root directory of the drive, what do you think would be the results of the following command:

```
COPY C:\WINDOWS\SYSTEM32\ATTRIB.EXE
```

11. *Note*: This step assumes that Windows has been loaded in a directory (folder) called *Windows*. If it is loaded in a different directory, substitute the name of that directory for *Windows* in the commands. You have to substitute `x:\Class` with a drive letter different from `x:` for the drive letter you are using to create these files.

From the root directory, type the following command:

```
copy C:\windows\sysstem32\attrib.exe x:\class
```

To what location do you think the file was copied?

12. From the root directory verify that the command has been copied by typing the following command: **`dir \class`**

What is the size of the *attrib.exe* file?

13. To copy the `attrib.exe` command from the *Class* folder into *SubFolder2* (from the root directory), use the following command:

```
copy \class\attrib.exe \class\subfolder2
```

14. Verify that the file copied correctly using the following command:

    `dir \class\subfolder2`

    The *attrib.exe* file should be listed. If it is not, redo Step 13.

    What is the size of the *attrib.exe* file in the *SUBFOLDER2*?

15. Copy your first text file from your second subdirectory into your first subdirectory using the following command. *FLAST2-1.TXT* is your first initial and last name followed by *2-1.txt*.

    `copy \class\subfolder2\flast2-1.txt \class\subfolder1`

16. Verify that the file copied: `dir \class\subfolder1`

    Write the exact command you would use to copy the first text file from *SubFolder1* into *SubFolder2* from the root directory. Have the instructor or lab assistant verify your command.

17. Execute the command to copy the first text file from *SubFolder1* into *SubFolder2* from the root directory command prompt. Verify the copy.

    What command was used to verify the copy in Step 16?

    Write the exact command to copy the first text file from *SubFolder2* into the *Class* directory.

18. A directory can be created within a subdirectory from the root directory. To create a subdirectory called *Fun* within the *SubFolder2* directory, use the following command from the root directory. Notice how you must insert the backslashes when you have multiple directories to go through to create the subdirectory. We just used a space before.

    `md \class\subfolder2\fun`

19. Verify the subdirectory creation: `dir \class\subfolder2`

    A directory called *Fun* should be listed in the output.

    What is the total amount of space the three files located within *SubFolder2* occupy?

20. To copy all the files located in *SubFolder2* into the newly created *Fun* subdirectory, the following command is used:

    `copy \class\subfolder2 \class\subfolder2\fun`

21. Use the `DIR` command as follows to verify the copy:

    `dir \class\subfolder2`

22. Wildcards can be used with the `copy` command. To copy all the files that start with the letter A from the *Fun* subdirectory into the *SubFolder1* subdirectory, the following command is used:

    `copy \class\subfolder2\fun\a*.* \class\subfolder1`

    How many files were copied?

Instructor initials: ______________

23. The `del` command is used to delete files. Wildcards can also be used with this command. Delete all the files located in the *Fun* subdirectory using the following command. The `*.*` is the wildcard representing all files with any extension.

    `del \class\subfolder2\fun\*.*`

    When prompted if you are sure, type `Y` and press Enter. Verify the files are deleted with the `dir` command:

    `dir \class\subfolder2\fun`

24. The `rd` command is used to remove directories and subdirectories. Remove the *Fun* subdirectory:

    `rd \class\subfolder2`

25. Type the command used to remove the *SubFolder2* subdirectory:

    `rd \class\subfolder2`

    What was the operating system response and what do you think has to be done as a result?

26. Delete the files in the *SubFolder2* subdirectory:

    `del \class\subfolder2\*.*`

    When prompted if you are sure, type `Y` and press Enter. Verify the files are deleted with the `dir` command:

    `dir \class\subfolder2`

27. Remove the *SubFolder2* subdirectory:

    `rd \class\subfolder2`

    Verify the results:

    `dir \class`

On Your Own

a. Using the `del`, `rd`, and `dir` commands, delete all files, subdirectories, and directories that you have created and verify the deletions.

   Write each command you are going to use *before* attempting this part.

   Write each command used to delete the files, subdirectories, and directories that have been created as part of this exercise.

   Have another student verify your work. Have them sign as well as print their name verifying that all of the files created during this lab have been deleted.

Classmate's printed name ______________________

Classmate's signature ______________________

Lab 11.14 The ATTRIB Command and Moving Around in the Directory Structure

Objective: To use the ATTRIB command and to work correctly from a prompt when dealing with directories and subdirectories

Parts: A computer with a Windows operating system loaded

Access to modify files on the hard drive or a disk such as a floppy disk or flash drive

Procedure: Complete the following procedure and answer the accompanying questions.

Note: For each step requiring a typed command the Enter key must be pressed to execute the command. This instruction will *not* be given with each step.

1. Power on the computer and log on if necessary. Access a command prompt.
2. From the root directory of a disk that can have files and directories created, type the following command to create a directory called *Junk*: `md junk`
3. Under the *Junk* directory, make subdirectories called *Sub1*, *Sub2*, and *Sub3*. Use the following commands:

   ```
   cd junk
   md sub1
   md sub2
   md sub3
   ```

4. Return to the root directory. Verify by looking at the command prompt after returning to the root directory.

   What command makes the root directory the current directory?

   Write the command prompt as it appears on your screen.

5. Make a new directory called *Trash* from the root directory. Within the *Trash* directory, make subdirectories called *Sub1*, *Sub2*, and *Sub3*. Use the following commands:

   ```
   md trash
   cd trash
   md sub1
   md sub2
   md sub3
   ```

6. Return to the root directory.

On Your Own

a. Make a new directory called *Garbage* from the root directory. Within the *Garbage* directory, make subdirectories called *Sub1*, *Sub2*, and *Sub3*. Verify the directory and subdirectories were created.

   Write the commands to create a directory called *Garbage* and the three subdirectories.

b. Using previously described commands and exercises, create three files called *Special1.txt*, *Special2.txt*, and *Tickle.txt*. Place them in the *Garbage\Sub1* subdirectory.

   Write the commands to create the files for the *SUB1* subdirectory.

c. From the root directory, copy all files that begin with the letter *S* from the *Garbage\Sub1* subdirectory and place them in the *Trash\Sub3* subdirectory.

   Write the commands to copy *S* files from the *Garbage\Sub1* subdirectory to the *Trash\Sub3* subdirectory.

How many files copied?

d. Copy any file that begins with *T* from the *Garbage\Sub1* subdirectory and place them in the *Sub2* subdirectory of the *Junk* directory.

Write the commands to copy *T* files from one subdirectory to another subdirectory.

How many files copied?

Draw a diagram of how your directory structure that you have created in this exercise including all directories, subdirectories, and files.

7. To make all files in the *Sub3* subdirectory of the *Trash* directory read-only, use the `attrib` command with the `+r` switch. From the root directory, type the following command:

   `attrib +r \trash\sub3\*.*`

8. To verify the read-only attribute is set, type the following command:

   `attrib \trash\sub3\*.*`

   The *Sub3* subdirectory should list two files. Both have an R beside them indicating that the read-only attribute is set. If the two files do *not* have the read-only attribute set, perform the previous step again.

9. The best way to prove that the files are read-only is to try to delete them. Type the following command:

   `del \trash\sub3\*.*`

   When asked if you are sure, type `Y` and press Enter. A message appears on the screen stating, “Access is denied.” Then, the command prompt appears. If the access denied message does not appear, the files were deleted which means the read-only attribute was not set. If this is the case, redo this exercise starting with *On Your Own* Step c above.

10. Hide the *Junk\Sub2* subdirectory using the following command:

    `attrib +h \junk\sub2`

    No message appears on the screen. The command prompt appears again.

11. To verify that the directory is hidden, type the following command:

    `dir \junk`

    The *Sub2* subdirectory should not appear in the list.

12. Use the `attrib` command to verify that the directory is hidden by typing the following command:

    `attrib \junk\sub2`

    The directory listing appears with an H beside the name.

13. Some operating system files are automatically marked as system files when the operating system is installed. From the root directory of the C: drive, type the following command to see what files are marked already as system files:

    `attrib`

    List any files that have the system attribute.

On Your Own

a. Hide the *Special1.txt* file located in the *Sub1* subdirectory of the *Garbage* directory.

   Write the command you used for this step.

b. Verify that the Special1.txt file is hidden by using the `dir` and `attrib` commands.

   Write the command you used for this step.

   Have a classmate print his/her name and his/her signature as well as a statement describing how the person verified that you were in the correct directory.

Classmate's printed name ________________________

Classmate's signature ___________________________

Instructor initials: _____________

c. Remove the hidden attribute from the *Special1.txt* file in the *SUB1* subdirectory of the *Garbage* directory. If necessary, use `Help` to find the switch to remove an attribute.

   Write the command used in this step.

d. Have a classmate verify that the *Special1.txt* file is no longer hidden.

   Have the classmate write the command he/she used, his/her printed name, and his/her signature.

Classmate's printed name ________________________

Classmate's signature ___________________________

14. Ensure that you are at the root directory.
15. Moving around within subdirectories can be challenging when you are first learning commands. Move to the *Sub3* subdirectory of the *Trash* directory.

    What command did you use to perform Step 15?
16. To move to the *Sub1* subdirectory from within the *Sub3* subdirectory, type **`cd..`**; then type **`cd sub1`** to move into the correct subdirectory.

    What does the command prompt look like now?
17. A shortcut to move up one directory is to type `cd..` from within the *Sub1* subdirectory. The prompt immediately changes to one level up (the *Trash* directory). Type **`cd..`**

    The command prompt changes to `X:\Trash>`.

18. Using the `cd..` command again returns one level back in the directory structure to the root directory. Type **`cd..`** and the command prompt changes appropriately.

On Your Own

a. From the root directory change to the *Sub2* subdirectory of the *Garbage* directory.

   Write the command used in this step.

   How can one verify that the current directory is *Garbage\Sub2*?

b. From the *Garbage\Sib2* subdirectory, change the current directory to the *Sub3* subdirectory of the *Trash* directory.

   Write the command you used in this step.

   Have a classmate print his/her name and his/her signature as well as a statement describing how the person verified that you were in the correct directory.

Classmate's printed name ________________________

Classmate's signature ___________________________

19. Using the `cd..` command, move from *Trash\Sub3* to *Trash*.
20. Using the `cd..` command, move from *Trash* to the root directory.

On Your Own

a. Using the `attrib`, `del`, and `rd` commands, delete the *Trash* and *Garbage* directories including all subdirectories underneath them. Write all commands before you attempt this step.

   Write all commands used in this step.

b. Using the `attrib`, `del`, and `rd` commands, delete the *Junk* directory and all subdirectories. Write all commands before attempting this step.

   Write all commands used in this step.

Instructor initials: _____________

Lab 11.15 Backup Software and the Archive Bit

Objective: To explore backup options and how they affect the archive attribute using Windows 7

Parts: A computer with Windows 7 installed

External drive, flash drive with over 1GB of free space, or optical media

Procedure: Complete the following procedure and answer the accompanying questions.

Note: This lab requires both command prompt and Windows skills.

1. Power on the computer and log into Windows 7.
2. Create or select a folder that contains at least three files. This will be the folder you will be using to back up the data.

   What folder did you select?

3. From the *Start* menu, access *All Programs* > *Accessories* > right-click *Command Prompt* > *Run as administrator* > *Yes*.
4. Use the `CD` command to move into the directory (folder) chosen in Step 2. A hint for you is that you must change directory into users and the username used to log into the computer before you can located the Documents folder. You may want to use Windows Explorer to get the full path. The prompt should be the folder name. For example, if the folder is in *Documents* and is called *2012 Book leftover stuff*, then the prompt will be as follows (with Cheryl being the username used to log into the computer):

   ```
   C:\Users\Cheryl\Documents\2012 Book leftover stuff>
   ```

   Document the command(s) used to accomplish this step.

5. Use the `DIR` command to verify that at least three files are in the folder.

   Document three files found in the folder chosen in Step 2.

6. Depending on the folder chosen in Step 2, the command prompt window may need to be changed by clicking on the command prompt icon in the upper left corner > *Properties* > *Layout* tab > *Window Size/Width* change to a larger number.
7. Use the `attrib` command to determine the attributes set by default on a file saved on a Windows computer. The attribute(s) list to the far left, there is a space, and then the full path to the filename. Leave the command prompt window open.

   Document the attribute(s) found for the three files. The A is for the archive attribute. The R is for the read-only attribute. The H is for the hidden attribute.

8. Access the *System and Security* Control Panel. Select *Backup and Restore*.
9. If a backup has been done before, select the *Change settings* link; otherwise, select the *Set up backup* link.
10. Ensure the optical media or external drive is attached to the computer and recognized as a drive letter. Insert the optical media if necessary.
11. Select the appropriate backup destination (optical drive or external drive letter) > *Next*.
12. Select the *Let me choose* button > *Next*.

13. Expand folders as necessary by clicking on the arrows and locate the folder chosen in Step 2 > *Next*.
14. Click the *Save settings and run backup* button.
15. Once the backup has finished, return to the command prompt window and reissue the `attrib` command.

    Did the archive attribute change for the three files? [Yes | No]

    Describe the backup file on the external drive, optical media, or flash drive. In other words, how does the Windows Backup software save the file?

16. Windows backup does not have the ability to do incremental or differential backups, but purchased backup software and some freeware backup software can.
17. Using Windows Explorer copy one of the files from the folder selected in Step 2 to the desktop.
18. Using the command prompt window, type `cd \` to return to the root directory.
19. Use the `cd` command to access the Desktop directory. A sample command would be `cd\users\Cheryl\desktop` if the person who signed onto the computer used the "Cheryl" account.

    Document the exact command you used to access the desktop director.

20. Use the `attrib` command to determine whether a copied file changes the archive bit.

    Document your findings.

Optional Challenge

21. Locate a backup tool freeware application and install it on the computer. Make a backup of the same files in the folder selected in Step 2. Then modify one of the files and fun the backup again.

    Document your findings.

Cleanup

22. Permanently delete the file copied to the desktop.
23. Close all windows.

Instructor initials: ______________

Lab 11.16 Creating a Boot Floppy Disk in Windows XP

Objective: To create a bootable floppy disk in the Windows XP environment

Parts: A Windows XP–based computer that has a floppy drive installed

1 blank formatted disk

Procedure: Complete the following procedure and answer the accompanying questions.

1. Boot the computer and log on if necessary.
2. Insert the floppy disk into the drive.
3. Open Explorer. Right-click the *3 1/2 Floppy (A:)* option. Select *Format . . .*
4. Select the *Create an MS-DOS startup disk* checkbox to enable it.

5. Click the *Start* button followed by *OK*. When the format is finished, click *OK*.
6. Ensure the computer BIOS is set to boot from floppy disk and the disk is inserted into the drive. Reboot the computer to a command prompt using the disk.

Instructor initials: ____________

Can you use any of the commands you have learned? If so, which ones?

7. Remove the disk and reboot the computer normally.

Lab 11.17 Installing and Exploring Windows XP Recovery Console

Objective: To install Recovery Console on a computer hard drive and have it available as a boot option

Parts: Windows XP computer with permissions to install software

Windows XP installation CD, XP service pack CD, or access to the folder where the service pack is installed

Procedure: Complete the following procedure and answer the accompanying questions.

Note: In order to access Recovery Console, the Administrator password is required.

1. Insert the Windows XP installation CD into the optical drive. If the welcome screen appears, close it.
2. Click the *Start* button > *Run* > type `x:\I386\Winnt32 /cmdcoms` (where `x:` is the drive letter for the optical drive) > Enter. This starts the Recovery Console installation process.

   Note that if you receive an error message stating that you have a service pack installed that is higher than the CD version, you have two choices: (1) use a Windows XP service pack CD or (2) install Recovery Console using the XP service pack installation file. If you choose the latter, you must know or locate the folder that holds the service pack. This is commonly in the root directory of `c:` and called I386.
3. When asked if you want to install Recovery Console, click *Yes*, and follow the prompts on the screen.
4. Once Recovery Console is installed, restart the computer. When the computer restarts, a menu appears with both Windows XP or Recovery Console listed. Select the *Recovery Console* option.
5. After the Recovery Console loads a list of numbered partitions that contains Windows lists. A prompt asks which Windows installation you would like to log onto. Most machines only have 1. Type `1` and press Enter.
6. When prompted for the Administrator password, type it and press Enter.
7. Type **`dir`**. A listing of the files in the *Windows* folder appears one page at a time. Press the Spacebar to see another page. Press Esc to exit the listing. The letters to the side designate attributes for the files.

`a` = archive	`h` = hidden
`d` = directory	`r` = read-only
`e` = encrypted	`s` = system

   From the output shown, list three entries that are directories and three entries that are system files.

8. Type **`map`**. Drive letters that are available through Recovery Console display.

   What drive letters do you have available?

   Are you allowed access to an optical drive through Recovery Console? [Yes | No]
9. Type **`help`**. Commands that are available in this mode list on the screen.

Based on the output displayed, determine whether a command is available or not through Recovery Console. Document your findings in Table 11.17.

Table 11.17 Recovery Console commands

Command	Available	Not Available
`attrib`	_____	_____
`cipher`	_____	_____
`copy`	_____	_____
`disable`	_____	_____
`enable`	_____	_____
`expand`	_____	_____
`fdisk`	_____	_____
`fixboot`	_____	_____
`prompt`	_____	_____
`rd`	_____	_____
`set`	_____	_____
`tree`	_____	_____
`type`	_____	_____

10. Type **`listsvc`** to see a listing of services that are available. The `enable` and `disable` commands are used to start and stop a service that might be causing problems.
    List three services that are automatically started in Recovery Console mode.

11. From the prompt, type **`cd\`**.
    What happened? Why do you think this behaves this way?

12. Type **`exit`** to leave Recovery Console and boot normally.

Lab 11.18 Creating a Windows 7 System Repair Disc

Objective: To create a system repair disc in the Windows 7 environment

Parts: A Windows 7-based computer that has an optical drive installed
1 blank DVD

Procedure: Complete the following procedure and answer the accompanying questions.

1. Boot the computer and access the system BIOS. Ensure the system is set to boot from the optical drive first.
2. Save the settings and exit BIOS. Boot into Windows 7.
3. Click the *Start* button > *Control Panel* > *System and Security* link > *Backup and Restore* > *Create a system repair disc* link.
4. Select the appropriate optical drive and insert a blank DVD into the drive.
5. Select the *Create disc* button.
   How often do you think a home user should create a system repair disc?

When the system repair disc is complete, what is the recommended label for the repair disc?

What is the difference between a system repair disc and a system image disc?

6. Once the disc has been created, click the *Close* button followed by *OK*.

Using the System Repair Disc

7. After labeling the system repair disc, re-insert it into the drive.
8. Power down the computer.
9. Power on the computer using the power button. A prompt may appear that tells you to press any key to start the computer from a CD or DVD. Press any key to boot from the system repair disc.
10. Select the appropriate language and keyboard settings. Click *Next*.
11. From this screen, you can either use Windows recovery tools or restore the system from a previously created system image. For this exercise, select the radio button that begins *Use recovery tools*, ensure the correct operating system is highlighted, and click *Next*.

    List three options from the resulting menu.

Instructor initials: ____________

12 Select *Shutdown*.

Lab 11.19 Creating a Windows 7 System Image Disc

Objective: To create a system repair disc in the Windows 7 environment

Parts: A Windows 7-based computer that has an optical drive installed

1 blank DVD

Procedure: Complete the following procedure and answer the accompanying questions.

1. Boot the computer and access the system BIOS. Ensure the system is set to boot from the optical drive first.
2. Save the settings and exit BIOS. Boot into Windows 7.
3. Click the *Start* button > *Control Panel* > *System and Security* link > *Backup and Restore* > *Create a system image* link.

   What three options are available?

4. Determine from the instructor or lab assistant the appropriate storage medium and select the appropriate radio button. Click *Next*.
5. Select at least the operating system to back up.

   What is the amount of space required to do the system image?

6. Click *Next*. Optionally insert media as directed and select *Start backup*.

   While the image is being created, what option(s) do you have on the screen?

Instructor initials: ____________

(Optional) Using the System Image Disc

7. In order to use the system image disc, you can (1) use the Recovery Control Panel, or (2) you can restore starting from a Windows 7 installation disc or system repair disk using the following steps once you boot from the disc: A prompt may appear that tells you to press any key to start the computer from a CD or DVD. Press any key to boot from the system repair disc or Windows 7 installation disc. Select the appropriate language and keyboard settings. Click *Next*. If you booted from a system recovery disc, select the radio button for a system repair disc and click *Next*. If you booted from the Windows installation disc, select *Repair your computer*. (3) Finally, you can do the following if you don't have a Windows 7 installation disc or a system repair disc. Reboot the computer and as the computer is booting press F8 to access the Windows Advanced Boot Options screen. Select *Repair your computer*, select the appropriate keyboard, and click *Next*. Select a user name, type a password, and click *OK*. Select *Image Recovery* and follow the instructions.

   For this lab, use the Recovery control panel since the computer is working. Click the *Start* button and type `recovery` in the *Search programs and files* textbox.

8. Select *Recovery* from the resulting list.

   Document the path through control panels to reach this option.

9. Select the *Advanced recovery methods* link. Select the *Use a system image you created earlier to recover your computer* option. Follow the instructions on the screen to recovery your computer.

Instructor initials: ______________

Activities

Internet Discovery

Objective: Access the Internet to obtain specific information regarding a computer or its associated parts

Parts: Access to the Internet

Procedure: Complete the following procedure and answer the accompanying questions.

1. Locate an Internet site that has a tutorial for Windows 7 troubleshooting or usage.

2. What is the latest service pack for Windows 7 Professional? Write the service pack number and the URL of the location where you found this information.

3. List three things that you think would be useful from the Customizing the Out-of-Box Experience for IT Pros website and explain why you think they would help the technician.

4. Find a web-based article on the differences between Windows 7 Home and Professional editions. Write the name of the article and the URL.

5. The Windows registry can be edited to allow users to automatically be logged into the Windows environment. Locate a website that demonstrates how to edit the Windows registry for any version of the Windows Vista operating system.

   Write the URL and one tip you discovered.

6. Locate a website that describes three things to do if Windows 7 (any version) will not boot. Write the URL.

Soft Skills

Objective: To enhance and fine-tune a technician's ability to listen, communicate in both written and oral form, and support people who use computers in a professional manner

Activities:

1. On a piece of paper or an index card, list two topics you would like to hear about if you were to attend a local association PC users' group meeting. Share this information with your group. Consolidate ideas and present five of the best ideas to the class.

2. In a team environment, select one of the five ideas presented in Activity 1 to research. Every team member presents something about a latest technology to the rest of the class. The class votes on the best presented topic and the most interesting topic.

3. On an index card, document a question that several students have asked the teacher about how to do a particular task. Exchange cards with one classmate. Correct each other's grammar, punctuation, and capitalization. When you have your original card, exchange your card with a different classmate and perform the same task. Rewrite your index card based on the recommendations of your classmates. Keep in mind that all their suggestions are just that, suggestions. You do not have to accept their suggestions. A complaint of industry is that technicians do not write well. Practice helps with this issue.

Critical Thinking Skills

Objective: To analyze and evaluate information and to apply learned information to new or different situations

Activities:

1. Windows Vista will not boot. What will be the first thing, second thing, and third thing you try? Explain your reasoning.

2. In a paragraph, explain why or why you would not use the Command Prompt repair option as a first attempt in a Windows boot failure.

3. Explain a situation of when you would use a Windows boot disc or find one on the Internet. Detail the drawbacks to using it. Student's own opinion, but some drawbacks include the system you are working on has service packs and updates installed, whereas the optical disc does not.
4. Find a specific problem on the Internet and what the person did to repair the problem using the command prompt. Share your findings with the class.

A+ Certification Exam Tips

- ✓ This chapter and the next chapter cover concepts related to the 802 exam, the second exam to obtain the A+ certification. CompTIA recommends that you have one year of experience before taking the exam. Students *have* been able to pass this exam right after taking the course, however. You will have to be good in troubleshooting, the Windows environment, commands, networking, and security in order to pass the exam.
- ✓ Go into every Windows control panel and ensure that you know what configuration items are controlled by the different control panels.
- ✓ Be familiar with the commands and how to work in the command prompt environment. The following commands are on the certification exam: `ping`, `tracert`, `netstat`, `ipconfig`, `net`, `nslookup`, `nbtstat`, `taskkill`, `bootrec`, `shutdown`, `tasklist`, `md`, `rd`, `cd`, `del`, `fdisk`, `format`, `copy`, `xcopy`, `robocopy`, `diskpart`, `sfc`, `chkdsk`, `command /?`, `fixboot`, `fixmbr`, `msconfig`, `regedit`, `cmd`, `services.msc`, `mmc`, `mstsc`, `notepad`, `explorer`, `msinfo32`, `regsvr32`, `defrag`, and `dxdiag`. Practice these commands (and the various switches used with them) the week before taking the 802 exam. Know when to use them. Ask yourself what would be wrong that would force you to use a particular command.

chapter 12

Windows XP, Vista, and 7

Chapter Objectives:

In this chapter you will learn:

- To distinguish between the Windows XP, Vista, and 7 operating systems
- To install, configure, and troubleshoot Windows XP, Vista, and 7
- To install hardware and software
- About various tools and features, such as System Restore, driver roll back, and WinRE
- What Windows goes through to boot the system and how to troubleshoot boot problems
- About the Computer Management console, Task Manager, and Event Viewer
- How to avoid burnout in the IT field

CompTIA Exam Objectives:

What CompTIA exam objectives are covered in this chapter?

- ✓ 802-1.1 Compare and contrast the features and requirements of various Microsoft operating systems.
- ✓ 802-1.2 Given a scenario, install, and configure the operating system using the most appropriate method.
- ✓ 802-1.3 Given a scenario, use appropriate command line tools.
- ✓ 802-1.4 Given a scenario, use appropriate operating system features and tools.
- ✓ 802-1.5 Given a scenario, use Control Panel utilities.
- ✓ 802-1.7 Perform preventive maintenance procedures using appropriate tools.
- ✓ 802-1.9 Explain the basics of client-side virtualization.
- ✓ 802-2.1 Apply and use common security prevention methods.
- ✓ 802-2.2 Compare and contrast common security threats.
- ✓ 802-4.6 Given a scenario, troubleshoot operating system problems with appropriate tools.
- ✓ 802-4.7 Given a scenario, troubleshoot common security issues with appropriate tools and best practices.

Windows XP Overview

As with other Windows versions that are available now, Windows XP is either a 32- or 64-bit OS (operating system). You might sometimes see the 32-bit version referred to as an x86 version. Microsoft created several different editions of Windows XP, and Table 12.1 summarizes the differences.

Table 12.1 Windows XP editions

XP edition	Description
Windows XP Professional	A version still used by a few businesses; many home users use as well. Supports encryption, network domains, a large range of support tools, remote access, and security.
Windows XP Professional x64	A 64-bit operating system that can run 64-bit applications as well as the older 32-bit applications designed for XP Professional. Virtual memory is expanded to 16 terabytes. Requires a 64-bit processor, 256MB of RAM, and 1.5GB of hard disk space as a minimum.
Windows XP Home	A 32-bit-only version that is similar to XP Professional but not as robust; does not allow connecting to a network domain and does not support encryption.
Windows XP Tablet PC	Specifically designed for notebook and laptop computers. Has more pen and speech capabilities, such as converting handwriting to text or using the input panel, designed for people on the go.
Windows XP Media Center	A 32-bit-only version designed for home multimedia (video, music, pictures) computers as well as tools for online entertainment; has higher hardware requirements than the other 32-bit XP versions because of the entertainment focus: 1.6GHz or higher CPU and 256MB RAM.

32-bit Windows XP supports 32-bit Windows applications, 16-bit applications, and some DOS applications (only those that do not access hardware directly); every 32-bit application runs in its own 2GB memory space; all 16-bit Windows applications run in a single virtual machine; a virtual machine simulates a single computer with its own memory, hardware devices, and software configuration. 64-bit Windows can do all of this in addition to supporting 64-bit applications.

DOS and 16-bit Windows applications run in a single 2GB memory space. The Windows XP VMM (virtual machine manager) handles allocating memory to applications. A single block called a page is 4KB. A **page file** is used to store files and may also retrieve a file located on a disk. This file is called a paging file.

Windows XP supports **WFP** (Windows file protection). WFP protects system files (files critical to the operating system) and some TrueType fonts. WFP runs in the background. When WFP detects that a file has been altered or deleted, it copies a replacement file from the Windows\System32\Dllcache folder, the Windows XP CD, or a network share (a shared folder that contains a copy of the XP CD).

Windows Vista/7 Overview

Like Windows XP, Vista, and 7 come in 32- and 64-bit versions: Starter (32-bit only), Home Basic, Home Premium, Business (Vista only), Professional (7 only), Enterprise, and Ultimate. Depending on the version, enhanced features include improved security; a graphical environment called **Windows Aero** that includes a Windows sidebar that contains gadgets such as a clock, live thumbnails (hold your mouse over an application icon and all open documents are shown in a separate thumbnail), transparent icons (icons that you can see through), animations, and themes; quick access to tools and files; the Narrator (text-to-speech that reads the screen); an onscreen keyboard; the **UAC** (User Account Control) to notify you of potential security issues before anything is added to or removed from the system; disk partitions that can be resized without loss of data; WinRE (Windows Recovery Environment) when things go wrong; and full support of IP version 6 (IPv6), the latest protocol for Internet communication. Figure 12.1 shows an example of the thumbnails and a Windows Aero desktop.

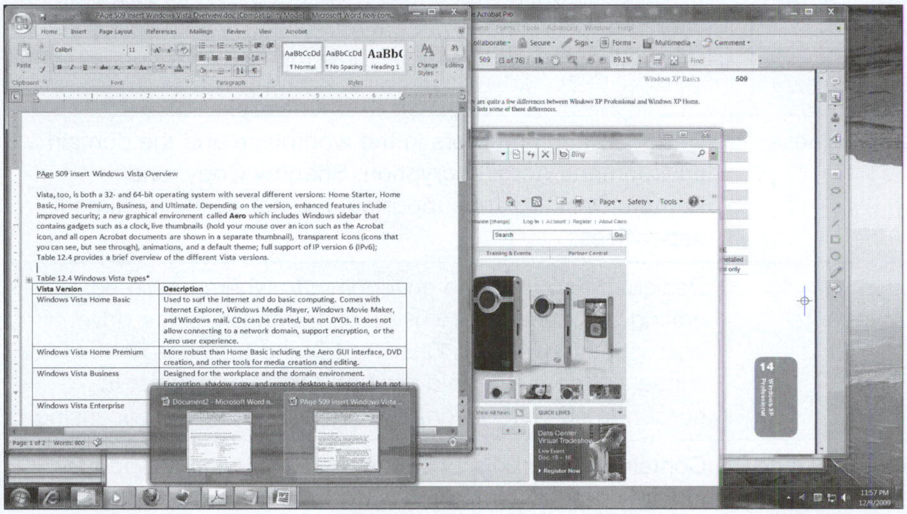

Figure 12.1 **Windows Aero desktop with thumbnails**

In order to use Windows Aero, the following minimum requirements must be met:

- Vista/7 Home Premium or higher
- 1GHz 32-bit processor or higher
- 1GB of RAM or higher
- 128MB graphics memory
- Graphics card set to 32-bit color or higher
- Monitor refresh rate 10Hz or higher
- Windows theme set to Windows Vista or 7
- Display color scheme set to Windows Aero
- *Appearance and Personalization* control panel > *Personalization* link > *Windows* color option > *Enable transparency* option enabled (checked)

Table 12.2 provides a brief overview of the different Windows Vista and 7 versions.

Table 12.2 Windows Vista/7 editions*

Vista/7 edition	Description
Vista/7 Starter	A 32-bit-only version used with low-cost computers and with tablets.
Vista/7 Home Basic	Used to surf the Internet and do basic computing. Comes with Internet Explorer, Windows Media Player, Windows Movie Maker, and Windows Mail. CDs can be created, but not DVDs. It does not allow connecting to a network domain (but can join a homegroup home network created from a Windows 7 computer), support EFS encryption, or provide the full Aero user experience. Windows 7 Home Basic is only sold in certain areas.
Windows Vista/7 Home Premium	More robust than Home Basic, includes the Aero GUI interface, DVD creation, creating /joining a homegroup (7) home network, and other tools for media creation and editing.
Windows Vista Business	Designed for computers in the workplace and the domain environment. Aero, encryption, Shadow Copy, and Remote Desktop are supported, but not all the multimedia capabilities.
Windows Vista/7 Enterprise	Designed for corporate environments where multimedia editing and creation are used; supports BitLocker drive encryption (covered in Chapter 15) and provides multi-lingual support. Not sold through retail centers but to corporate and educational institutions, using bulk licensing.
Windows Vista/7 Ultimate	Contains all the Enterprise features, including support for multiple processors, but includes some extras that are downloadable from Microsoft. These include fun utilities and work-related tools, such as the Windows BitLocker Drive Preparation Tool, AppLocker to prevent unwanted corporate applications, and DirectAccess for connecting to the corporate network without a VPN (virtual private network; VPNs are covered in Chapter 15).

*Each of these editions comes in a 32- and 64-bit version.

Besides having to choose a Windows version, deciding on a 32-bit or 64-bit version is also required. This decision is based on the type of processor that is installed. Through Windows Explorer, right-click the computer and select *Properties* to see the current version. 64-bit processors have been available for some time, but a 64-bit operating system is a big step. It took over 12 years for a 32-bit operating system to become the norm in business and home computing environments. Even though Windows XP had a 64-bit version, many consumers have not considered using a 64-bit operating system until Windows Vista or 7. Many books and advertisements refer to a 32-bit processor as an x86 chip, so 32-bit editions might be seen or referred to as an x86 version. 64-bit processors are frequently shown as x64. Table 12.3 lists the differences between 32-bit and 64-bit Windows.

Table 12.3 32-bit and 64-bit Windows

32-bit Windows	64-bit Windows
32-bit or 64-bit processor	64-bit processor
4GB RAM limitation	1 to 192+GB RAM supported (Home Basic 8GB; Home Premium 16GB; Business, Professional, Enterprise, and Ultimate 192GB+ maximum)
32 bits processed at a time	64 bits processed at a time
32-bit drivers required	64-bit device drivers required, and they must be digitally signed
32-bit applications and some support for older 16-bit applications	32- or 64-bit application support; 16-bit application support using the Program Compatibility Wizard or downloading and using Windows XP Mode (covered later in this chapter)
	Protection for the operating system kernel (the core of the operating system) Better support for multiple processors
DEP (Data Execution Prevention) prevents a specific type of security attack by using both hardware and software technology	"Always-on" DEP support for 64-bit processes

Windows Vista and 7 improve upon WFP with **WRP** (Windows Resource Protection) that protects operating system files, folders, and important registry keys using ACLs (access control lists). Changes made to a monitored file or folder cannot be changed even by an administrator unless he or she takes ownership and adds the appropriate ACEs (access control entities). Any file that cannot be repaired by `SFC.EXE` (System File Checker), can be identified with the following administrator command:

```
findstr /C:"[SR] Cannot repair member file" %windir%\logs\cbs\cbs. log>sfcdetails.txt
```

Use Notepad or the `edit` command to open the file (normally located in C:\Windows\System32 folder). From an elevated command prompt, the following commands are used to grant administrators access to the protected files, so they can be replaced:

```
takeown /f filename_including_path
```

where *`filename_including_path`* is the full path and file name to the problem file.

```
icacls filename_including_path/GRANT ADMINISTRATORS:F
```

Then use the `COPY` command to replace the file with a known good one.

```
copy source_filename destination_filename
```

where the source and destination are the full path and file.

Use `SFC` to solve system file problems

Use the `sfc /scannow` command as an administrator to replace any protected system files that have problems.

Tech Tip

Logging on to Windows

With Windows installed, the first screen to appear when you boot the computer is the welcome screen, which allows users to log into the computer. A user can log in to the local computer, a workgroup (small network used in Windows XP/Vista/7), a homegroup (Windows 7 network), or a domain (a network with a server). See Chapter 14 for more information on network types. To log in, click a user account icon and enter a password (if necessary) or press Ctrl+Alt+Del to go to the Log On to Windows screen.

> **Tech Tip**
>
> **XP local Administrator login**
>
> Note that the local Administrator account (the master account that is allowed to change everything on the local machine) is not a user icon. You must press Ctrl+Alt+Del twice in Windows XP and enter the correct user ID and password to use the Administrator account.

`Winlogon.exe` controls the user login process on a Windows computer, and this file is located in the \Windows\System32 folder. This file also controls how the desktop looks for individual users through the Hkey_Current_User registry key. Starting with Vista and continuing on with 7, the `winlogon` process can work with credential providers such as a password or smartcard that can be user selected or event driven.

Pre-Installation of Windows

Windows XP, Vista, or 7 can be installed from a central location using a network or locally using discs. The pre-installation of any operating system is more important than the installation. Technicians who grab a disc and load a new operating system without going through a preparation process are asking for trouble. It is important to follow these steps before installing Windows:

1. Decide whether the installation will be an upgrade or a clean install and which version of the operating system is to be loaded. Take into account software application compatibility.
2. Decide whether the computer will have more than one operating system installed.
3. Plan the partition/volume size and select the file system.
4. Determine whether the hardware is compatible.
5. Obtain any drivers, upgrades, or hardware replacements.
6. Back up any data files.
7. Scan for viruses, and then disable the virus protection during the installation process.
8. Temporarily disable any power management or disk management tools.

The first decision to make when planning to install an operating system is whether to upgrade from another operating system or to perform a clean install. An **upgrade** or in place upgrade is when a computer already has an older operating system on it and a newer operating system is being installed. A **clean install** puts an operating system on a computer that does not have one, or removes the existing operating system and installs a new operating system. There are three reasons to perform a clean install:

- The computer does not have an operating system already installed.
- The current operating system is not upgradable to the desired Windows version.
- The current operating system is upgradable to a specific Windows version, but the existing files and applications are going to be reloaded.

When you decide to upgrade, you must take into account what operating system is already installed, what hardware is installed, what applications are being used, and whether they are compatible with the new operating system. When Windows is installed as an upgrade, the user's applications and data are preserved if the operating system is installed in the same folder (directory) as the original operating system. If Windows is installed in a different folder, then all applications must be reloaded.

Windows XP Professional supports upgrading from the following operating systems:

- Windows 98
- Windows Me
- NT Workstation 4
- 2000 Professional
- XP Home

Note that Windows XP Home edition only supports upgrades from Windows 98 and Windows ME.

Microsoft describes an in-place installation as an installation that requires no movement of files. Table 12.4 shows the Windows XP versions and corresponding Vista versions that can be used for in-place upgrade. Table 12.5 shows the possible Windows 7 upgrades. All the "in-place" upgrade scenarios in Tables 12.4 and 12.5 that have "No" as an in-place option may have a clean Windows installation performed on a separate hard drive partition.

Table 12.4 Windows Vista in-place upgrade scenarios

	Vista Home Basic	Vista Home Premium	Vista Business	Vista Ultimate
XP Professional	No	No	Yes	Yes
XP Professional x64	No	No	No	No
XP Home	Yes	Yes	Yes	Yes
XP Media Center	No	Yes	No	Yes
XP Tablet PC	No	No	Yes	Yes

Table 12.5 Windows 7 in-place upgrade scenarios

	7 Home Basic	7 Home Premium	7 Professional	7 Enterprise	7 Ultimate
XP	No	No	No	No	No
Vista Home Basic	Yes	Yes	No	No	Yes
Vista Home Premium	No	Yes	No	No	Yes
Vista Business	No	No	Yes	Yes	Yes
Vista Enterprise	No	No	No	Yes	No
Vista Ultimate	No	No	No	No	Yes

The Microsoft **Upgrade Advisor** application should always be used before upgrading Windows. Upgrade Advisor can be downloaded, installed, and executed to see if a Windows XP, Vista, or 7 computer can function well with a higher version of Windows Vista or 7. Upgrade advisor checks hardware, connected devices, and existing applications, and makes recommendations before an upgrade. It might seem unusual to think you would run it on a Vista- or 7-based computer, but with the different versions of Vista and 7, the Upgrade Advisor is commonly used to see if a more powerful version is an option.

Tech Tip

Attach every device for Upgrade Advisor

Be advised that any devices normally used with a computer, especially USB devices, should be connected to the computer before starting Upgrade Advisor.

In order to take advantage of Windows reliability, enhancements, and security features, sometimes a clean installation is the best choice. Because a clean installation involves formatting the hard drive, the user's data must be backed up and all applications re-installed once the Windows installation is complete. Also, all user-defined settings are lost.

Upgrading from a version of Windows XP to Vista (upgrading XP to 7 is not allowed) and keeping operating system settings and files is not always possible for an in-place upgrade. Even when Microsoft states that it *can* be done, there is no guarantee that all applications and settings will work after the upgrade. In a corporate environment, if custom software is involved, contact the software developer for any known issues or test the software in a test environment before deploying corporate-wide. The information may be posted on the software developer website. Also, Microsoft has a list of compatible software for many of the popular applications and games on their website.

The Easy Transfer program or the USMT (User State Migration Tool) can be used to migrate data when replacing XP with Windows 7. Windows Easy Transfer (`migwiz.exe`) is free from Microsoft to copy files and operating system settings to another drive, to removable media, over a network, or to another storage location. Once the operating system is installed, the files and settings are re-applied to the upgraded computer. This tool can also be used when a computer is being replaced and a data migration is required, such as when Windows 7 is replacing XP.

IT staff use the **USMT** to perform large deployments of Windows. This tool is used from a command line for more control and customized settings, including registry changes. The `scanstate.exe` and `loadstate.exe` commands are used to transfer file and user settings. Not all 16- or 32-bit applications can be used in the 64-bit Windows environment, but try the **compatibility mode** available using the Program Compatibility Wizard after Windows is installed: *Start > Control Panel > Programs > Run programs made for previous versions of Windows*.

Tech Tip

Use Windows Help and Support for software compatibility verification

Windows has a help function that can check for software compatibility. To access this tool, *Start > Help and Support* (XP)/*Search programs and files* (7) > type **`Program Compatibility Wizard`**.

If the Program Compatibility Wizard does not work, the Windows XP Mode is an option. **Windows XP Mode** is an optional program that can be downloaded and used in Windows Vista and 7 Professional, Ultimate, and Enterprise editions. Once it is downloaded and installed, access the software by clicking on the *Start* button > *All Programs > Windows Virtual PC > Virtual Windows XP*. Hardware including optical and USB drives are normally accessible through Windows XP Mode, but not all hardware may work in this environment. Also, Windows XP Mode is not suited for graphic-intensive games or applications.

Windows XP Mode can be customized for a specific Windows version. Right-click the *Windows XP mode* Start button option and select *Properties > Compatibility* tab. A drop-down compatibility mode menu allows the choice of Windows versions starting with Windows 95. Note that an application installed in Windows XP Mode appears in both the Windows XP Mode application list (within the Windows Virtual PC folder) and in the Windows 7 application list.

Another option is to manually assign a particular application to be compatible with an older (selectable) Windows version. Locate the application in the Start button menu. Right-click the application and select *Properties > Compatibility* tab > enable (check) the *Run this program in compatibility mode for* checkbox > use the drop down menu to select the specific operating system > use the specific video and administrator options available in the *Settings* and *Privilege Level* sections > click *Apply* > click *OK*.

Once you have determined whether the software is compatible with Windows, you may have to obtain software patches, upgrades, or buy a new version of the application. This is best done before installing Windows. Be proactive, not reactive—solve any problems you can *before* upgrading or installing any operating system. Such preparation is usually more work than the actual installation process, but any omitted steps will cost you more time in the long run.

OEM OS cannot go to another computer

An OEM (original equipment manufacturer) version of Windows that is sold as part of a computer sale is not transferable to another computer.

Tech Tip

Can't put one copy of an OS on two machines

The retail version of one copy of Windows cannot be installed on two computers at once. However, a retail version of Windows (as opposed to OEM versions) can be uninstalled on one computer and put on a different computer.

Tech Tip

The second pre-installation step is to determine whether to install more than one operating system. This situation is often called a dual-boot or multi-boot scenario. Both operating systems are best installed onto separate drive partitions. Otherwise, you could use virtualization to install and use multiple operating systems. Virtualization is covered later in this chapter.

The third step is to determine how large to make the drive partition (called volumes in Vista/7) and select the file system to be used. One option is to place the operating system in one partition and data in a separate partition to make it easier to back up the data. Drives can be partitioned during the Windows installation process, Otherwise, the entire drive is used.

During the installation process, when the partition is created, you are asked whether you want to do a full format or a quick format. A **full format** identifies and marks bad sectors so they will not be used for data storage. A **quick format** skips this analysis. Microsoft recommends doing a quick format if the hard disk has been formatted before and you are sure there are no damaged sectors. A best practice is that if the drive is an older drive, do a full format (but remember this is time intensive); otherwise, do a quick format. A full format would also be done any time you want to ensure that data is erased, such as installing a hard drive that was removed from another computer.

The file system should be NTFS for the following reasons:

- Security (individual files can be protected)
- More efficient use of cluster space
- Supports file compression
- Supports larger hard drive partition sizes
- Includes journaling, which helps to rebuild the file system after a crash or power failure. FAT is non-journaling—it does not track changes made to the file system.

An issue that is relevant only when upgrading is whether to convert an old FAT16 or FAT32 hard drive partition to NTFS. Once a partition is converted to NTFS, the partition cannot be changed. If you are unsure whether to convert a partition, leave it unchanged and later use the `convert` command to upgrade (without losing any data).

Using the `convert` command

The `convert` command can be used to change a FAT(16) or FAT32 partition to NTFS and keep the data from the old partition. Use `convert x: /fs:ntfs` (where `x:` is the drive to be converted to NTFS). Remember, once you go to a higher file system, you cannot go back.

Tech Tip

The fourth step when installing Windows is to determine what computer hardware is installed. Table 12.6 lists the minimum and preferred hardware requirements for installing Windows XP Professional. Table 12.7 lists the requirements for most Vista versions. One of the things that might influence your choice of Windows version is the amount of memory supported by the different flavors. Table 12.8 lists those maximums, and Table 12.9 shows the requirements to install Windows 7.

Table 12.6 Windows XP Professional hardware requirements

Component	Minimum requirements	Recommended requirements
CPU	Intel Pentium or AMD K6/Athlon/Duron 233MHz	300MHz or higher
RAM	64MB	128MB or higher
Hard disk space	1.5GB	>1.5GB
Video	VGA or higher	SVGA with plug and play monitor
Optical drive	CD or DVD drive	CD or DVD drive (12x or higher)
Input device	Keyboard and mouse or pointing device	Keyboard and mouse or pointing device

Table 12.7 Vista Home Premium, Business, and Ultimate recommended hardware requirements*

Component	Minimum	Recommended
Processor	800MHz 32-bit or 64-bit multiple core	1GHz 32-bit or 64-bit multiple core and dual processors
RAM	512MB	1GB
Hard drive space	20GB drive with a minimum of 15GB of available space	40GB drive with a minimum of 15GB of available space
Graphics	SVGA	128MB of video memory and support for DirectX9 or higher with WDDM driver, Pixel Shader 2.0 in hardware, 32-bit color
Optical drive	CD-ROM	DVD-ROM
Sound		Audio output
Network		Internet connectivity

*Note that a tablet PC or touch screen monitor is required to use Windows Tablet and Touch Technology that is available in these versions. The Windows BitLocker encryption tool requires a USB 2.0 flash drive or a TPM version 1.2 or higher motherboard chip.

Table 12.8 Windows Vista memory maximum

Windows Vista/7 version	32-bit maximum memory	64-bit maximum memory
Starter	1GB (Vista) 2GB (7)	N/A
Home Basic	4GB	8GB
Home Premium	4GB	16GB
Business(Vista only), Professional (7 only) Enterprise, and Ultimate	4GB	128GB (Vista) 192GB (7)*

*As of press time.

Table 12.9 Windows 7 hardware requirements

Component	Minimum
Processor	1GHz
RAM	1GB (32-bit)/2GB (64-bit)
Graphics	Support for DirectX9 or higher with 1.0 WDDM driver
Hard drive space	16GB (32-bit)/32GB (64-bit)

Once hardware has been verified, you have to obtain hardware device drivers specific to the operating system from the hardware manufacturer's website as the fifth step. The hardware device may have to be upgraded or replaced. Sometimes, older operating system drivers do work, but many times the older drivers do not work or they do not work properly. This is the cost of going to a more powerful operating system. The customer may also decide at this point not to upgrade, but to buy a computer with the desired version of Windows already installed instead.

Tech Tip

Ensure that the BIOS update is the right one

Do *not* download a BIOS update unless you are sure it is compatible with your computer. Installing an invalid update can damage your computer system and cause it not to operate.

The Microsoft Upgrade Advisor tool may have recommended getting updated drivers for specific piece of hardware. Drivers related to hard drives are especially critical to the installation process: hardware RAID, motherboard AHCI mode, SATA hard drive (especially when installing or re-installing Windows XP), and hard drives over 2TB. Obtain any of these hard drive-related drivers *before* the installation or you will not be able to install the operating system to that hard drive.

The sixth step is one of the most important: In any upgrade, hardware change, or software change, you must back up the user data. Whether you do a clean install or an upgrade, if the user has data on the computer, it must be backed up before starting the installation process. Also, before backing up the data, remove any unwanted files and/or applications that are no longer needed in order to free up hard drive space.

Tech Tip

Antivirus software causes issues

Whether doing a clean install or upgrade, disable the antivirus protection until after the installation. If possible, disconnect the computer from the network before disabling the software.

The seventh step in planning for a Windows installation is to scan the system for viruses. Viruses can cause havoc on an upgrade or clean install. The next section provides more information about the most common types of viruses.

The last step in the pre-installation checklist is to remove any power- or disk-management tools that are loaded. They can interfere with the new tools provided with Windows and can prevent an operating system from installing.

Viruses

Before installing a new operating system on a computer that already has an operating system loaded, you should run a virus scan with the latest virus scanning software version. A **virus** is a computer program that is designed to do something to your computer that changes the way the computer originally operated. Examples include infecting the computer so it does not boot, infecting a particular application so it does not operate or performs differently, and erasing files. Some viruses are not written to cause harm but simply to cause mischief, such as a program that puts a picture on the screen.

Viruses can cause many unusual and frustrating problems during an operating system installation. Some technicians think that by high-level formatting the hard drive no virus can exist. This is a mistake. Do not take that chance. Take a few moments to scan the hard drive for viruses. Table 12.10 shows common virus types and their descriptions.

Table 12.10 Virus types

Virus	Description
BIOS virus	Designed to attack computers with flash BIOS. Rewrites the BIOS code so the computer does not boot.
Boot sector (MBR) virus	Replaces or alters information in boot sectors or in the Master Boot Record. These viruses spread whenever you boot off a disk. Examples include Michelangelo, Junkie, and Ohio.
File virus	Replaces or attaches itself to a file that has a `COM` or `EXE` extension (an executable file). By attaching itself to this type of file, a virus can prevent the program from starting or operating properly. It can also be triggered for a particular event such as a date as well as loaded into RAM and affect other `COM` or `EXE` files. Examples include Friday the 13th, Enigma, Loki, and Nemesis.
Hijack virus or browser hijacker	Forces a web browser page to a particular website that is not the URL typed by the user. This can also just be malware, which is covered in detail in Chapter 15.
Macro virus	Written in a specific language and attaches itself to a document created in a specific application such as Excel or Word. Once the document (along with the virus) is opened and loaded into memory, the virus can attach itself to other documents.
Trojan (horse) program	Does not replicate as a virus does but does destroy data. Frequently hides a virus problem because it appears as a legitimate program to a virus checker. When the virus executes, the computer does something the user does not expect such as put a message or picture on the screen. The virus does not replicate (copy itself somewhere else), but it can be used to gather information such as user IDs and passwords that can later be used to hack into the computer. Trojan examples include Aids Info Disk, Twelve Tricks A and B, and Darth Vader.
Stealth virus	Written to avoid antivirus software detection. When the antivirus program executes, the stealth virus provided the antivirus software with a fake image.
Polymorphic virus	Constantly changes in order to avoid detection by an antivirus program.
Worm virus	Makes a copy of itself from one drive to another and can use a network to replicate itself. The most common types of worm viruses today are in the form of email messages.
Phage virus	Rewrites an executable file with its own code and then destroys other programs and files.

The following are common symptoms of a virus:

- Computer does not boot.
- Computer hard drive space is reduced.
- Applications will not load.
- An application takes longer to load or function than it used to.
- Hard drive activity increases (especially when no work is being done by the user and the antivirus scan is not running).
- An antivirus software message appears.
- The number of hard drive sectors marked as bad steadily increases.
- Unusual graphics or messages appear on the screen.
- Files are missing (deleted).
- A message appears that the hard drive cannot be detected or recognized.
- Strange sounds come from the computer.

Be responsible

A technician is responsible for ensuring that any computer deployed has an antivirus application installed and that the application is configured to receive virus signature updates. Educate users about viruses and what to do if a computer gets one.

Tech Tip

If a virus is detected or even suspected, run an antivirus program. Note that the computer may have to be booted into Safe Mode, Recovery Console (XP), or WinRE (Vista/7). If the computer can reach the Internet, download and install the Microsoft Safety Scanner. If Internet connectivity is too slow or not an option, restart the computer and press the F8 key before Windows loads. Access the *Safe Mode with Networking* and use the Internet to download and install the Microsoft Safety Scanner application.

Antivirus applications can be configured to run in manual mode (on demand) or as scheduled scans. Also quarantine the infected computer(s). This means you should disconnect the computer from the network until the computer is virus free. Some antivirus programs can quarantine a computer automatically if the computer has a virus. Many antivirus software programs have the ability to quarantine files—files that appear to the antivirus program as possible virus-infected or suspicious files that might be dangerous. A message normally appears with a list of files that have been quarantined, and each one must be identified as a valid file or to be left in the quarantine (unusable) until a new version of the antivirus signature files has been updated and can identify the file.

The time to get an antivirus program is *before* a virus infects the computer because the damage may be irreversible, especially if backups are not performed. Always back up data files before upgrading to a new operating system. Backups are an important part of any computer support plan.

Free antivirus applications do exist, including **Microsoft Security Essentials**, which is available for download from Microsoft.com. This product can be used on Windows XP, Vista, and 7, but not Windows 8. Windows 8 has antivirus protection and other security features integrated as part of the operating system.

An operating system upgrade or installation can be affected by other software. For example, some antivirus software can be set to load into memory when the computer boots and runs continuously. The antivirus software can prevent the upgrade or patch (service pack) from installing. Other types of software that can prevent an operating system from being upgraded are power management and disk management software/tools. Disable these utilities and applications before attempting an operating system installation or upgrade.

Installation/Upgrade of Windows

After completing all the pre-installation steps, you are ready to install Windows. The installation process is easy if you performed the pre-installation steps. Hands-on exercises follow that guides you through a clean installation (one where no other operating system is on the machine), an upgrade of XP, an installation of Vista, and an installation of Windows 7. The number-one piece of advice to heed is to do your installation/upgrade research first. The number of possible problems will be greatly reduced.

During the Windows XP installation process, the computer must be restarted three times. This has been improved upon by the Windows Vista and 7 installation process. In the XP first phase, a selection must be made whether to upgrade or perform a clean installation, the product key must be entered, and a basic hardware check including available disk space must be accomplished. The computer restarts. After the restart, the second phase begins and setup runs in text mode. During this process, a partition to install Windows can be chosen and setup files are copied to the partition. The computer restarts and the third phase begins. During this portion, devices are installed, the Administrator password is entered, and the operating system is created. The system restarts a final time and the logon screen is presented. Windows Vista and 7 have a similar process in that you can partition the drive, select a preconfigured partition, and select a password.

Part of the installation process is to select the type of network: home, work, or public. Computers on a home network could be a part of a homegroup or workgroup. Computers on a work network can see and share information with other work computers but cannot create or join a homegroup by default. With a public network, a computer attaches to an unsecure network, as in a restaurant or book store. Your computer is not visible to other computers by default when the public network option is chosen. (Table 12.11 shows these types.) Note that you can bypass the network configuration and configure it later. Networking is covered in more depth in Chapter 14.

Tech Tip

Windows XP/Vista/7 mandatory activation

Microsoft requires activation of Windows within 30 days. Activate by phone or the Internet. No name or personal information is required.

Table 12.11 Network types

Network type	Description
Workgroup	Normally found in a Windows XP home network or small business. You can configure Vista/7 for this type, but file and print sharing are not automatically enabled as they are with a homegroup.
Homegroup	Normally created in a Windows 7 home or small business environment that automatically turns on file and print sharing. Note that computers with Windows Vista7 Starter or Home Basic can join a homegroup, but not start one. All Windows 7 operating systems can join the Homegroup.
Domain	A corporate environment where users authenticate with a centralized user ID and password. Whatever machine the user goes to, the user ID and password would be the same if the computer has been configured to be on the domain.

Corporate Windows Deployment

Corporate computer installations are much more involved than any other type of deployment. Computers are installed in bulk instead of one at a time, as in a home or small business. The computers are frequently the same model and have the same software installed (see Figure 12.2).

Figure 12.2 Corporate computer deployment

Disk imaging is common in the corporate environment. Disk imaging software makes an exact copy (a binary copy) of the files loaded on the hard drive. The copy is then pressed to an optical disc, an external drive, or put on a network drive to be copied and deployed onto other computers.

Companies need automated installation tools to help with this process. Tools that can help with this are Windows XP's Sysprep tool, imaging software such as Symantec Corporation's Ghost program, Microsoft's Setup Manager, Windows SIM (System Image Manager), and MDT (Microsoft Deployment Toolkit). An image can be created and deployed to multiple computers. Table 12.12 describes some of these tools.

Table 12.12 Corporate computer deployment tools

Tool	Description
Sysprep	When a prototype computer has Windows, Windows updates, all drivers, and applications installed, Sysprep is used with XP to remove the SID (security identifier—a unique number assigned to a computer by a network domain controller) and with XP/Vista/7 to remove other unique information such as computer name, network domain, etc. The computer is then imaged and the image is deployed to other computers. A third-party utility such as Symantec Ghost Walker or Microsoft's `newsid.exe` can be used to reassign the SIDs once the drive image has been deployed.
SIM (System Image Manager)	Used in Windows Vista/7 to create and configure answer files, install applications, apply service packs and updates to an image, and to add device drivers. Once the Windows Vista/7 `unattend.xml` answer file is created, you can use the file to answer the installation questions as the files are downloaded from a share or server on the network. SIM is part of the Windows AIK (Automated Installation Kit).
WDS (Windows Deployment Services)	Uses the corporate network(s) to deploy Windows-based operating systems, drivers, updates, and applications.
Microsoft Setup Manager	Generates a text file (`unattend.txt`) that contains all the answers to questions asked during the Windows XP installation process.
MDT (Microsoft Deployment Toolkit)	A GUI shell to make Windows deployment easier. Tools such as USMT, ACT (Application Compatibility Toolkit), MAP (Microsoft Assessment and Planning Toolkit), and the volume licensing application are inside the MDT shell.

When making a Windows 7 image, you have to remove the unique identifiers from the computer before deploying the image to the other computers. This would include a computer name, SID (security identifier—a unique number used in XP), a network domain, etc. You must also reset or re-arm the Windows activation clock if a single activation key is used. Without doing this, you are prompted for the Windows 7 product key as soon as the computer boots. By re-arming the activation clock, you have a 30-day grace period before having to re-enter the product key.

To get corporate computer images across a network, a variety of methods can be used, as shown in Table 12.13.

Tech Tip

Three re-arms with Windows 7

There is no limit to the number of times a computer can be re-imaged, but there is a limit to how many times a computer can be re-armed or have the Windows activation clock reset. You can use the Sysprep tool to reset the re-arm count. To see how many times the computer has been re-armed, use the `slmgr /dlv` command.

Table 12.13 Corporate computer deployment methods

Method	Description
PXE boot (preboot execution environment)	Many computers have a PXE boot option which can modified to search for the network device that has the computer image. Other programs can be manually configured with the network device information. In either case, the computer finds this network device and obtains an image.
LTI (lite touch installation)	An image can be deployed with little interaction using the MDT. Windows 7, software, drivers, and updates are added to a network share and configuration files are created. Burn the boot images to optical media. Boot the destination computer with the boot image and the installation files are pulled across the network and installed without further intervention.
Unattended installation or **ZTI** (zero-touch installation)	The MDT is used in conjunction with Microsoft's Configuration Manager to image a computer without having to touch the remote computer. Other software can also be used.
Remote network installation	A server or network share has the created image that is accessed and deployed to a computer on a remote network. Network bandwidth is affected and this may interfere with normal business operations. For this reason, remote installations are commonly done during light network usage time or during off hours.

When deploying Windows Vista or 7, licensing is handled a bit differently. Larger businesses buy a VLK (volume license key). Two other choices are MAK or KMS. With **MAK** (Multiple Activation Key), the Internet or a phone call must be used to register one or more computers. This method has a limited number of activations, but more licenses can be purchased. The **KMS** (Key Management Service) method is used in companies with 25 or more computers to deploy. Technical support staff can also use a deployment tool that allows automating product key entry and customizing disc installation images so the computer users are not prompted for a key the first time they use a software package. KMS is a software application installed on a computer. All newly installed Vista- or 7-based computers register with the computer that has KMS installed. Every 180 days, the computers are re-activated for the Windows license. Each KMS key can be used on two computers up to 10 times.

Any existing data can be backed up to another hard drive, a network drive, or pressed to one or more optical discs. Remember to restore the data once the upgrade has been completed or the new computer installed.

Verifying the Installation

In any upgrade or installation, verification that the upgrade is successful is critical in both home and business environments. After an upgrade has been done, verify that all applications still function. After a new installation has been completed, ensure that all installed hardware is detected by Device Manager.

Tech Tip

Reinitialize antivirus software

If the antivirus software was disabled through BIOS and/or through an application, re-enable it after the operating system installation is complete. Verify that all settings are in accordance with the user requirements and/or departmental/organizational standards.

Troubleshooting a Windows Installation

Installation problems can be caused by a number of factors. The following list shows the most common causes of problems and their solutions:

- Incompatible BIOS—Obtain compatible BIOS, replace the motherboard with one that has compatible BIOS, or do not upgrade or install the higher Windows version.
- BIOS needs to be upgraded—Upgrade (flash) the BIOS.
- Incompatible hardware drivers—Obtain the appropriate Windows version drivers from the hardware manufacturer (not Microsoft).
- Incompatible applications—Obtain upgrades from the software manufacturer, use Windows XP Mode, use the Program Compatibility Wizard, use a dual-boot environment, use virtualization (covered later in this chapter).
- Minimum hardware requirements have not been met—Upgrade the hardware. The most likely things to check are the CPU and RAM.
- A virus is present—Run an antivirus program and remove the virus.
- Antivirus software is installed and active. It is halting the installation/upgrade—Disable through BIOS and/or through the application. Restart the Windows installation and re-enable once the operating system installation is complete.
- Pre-installation steps have not been completed—Go back through the list.
- The installation disc is corrupted (not as likely as the other causes)—Try the disc in another machine and see if you can see the contents. Check if a scratch or dirt is on the disc surface. Clean the disc as necessary.
- Incorrect registration key—Type in the correct key to complete the installation. The key is located on the disc, disc case, or in an email.
- If the Windows XP installation cannot find a hard drive, it is most likely due to a SATA drive being used and a driver is not available for the controller. Download the driver, put on a floppy/flash drive or use a software program such as nLite to create a custom XP installation CD that includes the downloaded driver.
- A STOP message occurs when installing a dual-boot system—Boot from the Windows XP, Vista, or 7 installation disc rather than the other operating system.
- The computer locks up during setup and shows a **BSOD** (blue screen of death)—Check the BIOS and hardware compatibility. Also, if an error message appears, research the error on the Internet.
- A message appears during setup that a device driver was unable to load—Obtain the latest device drivers that are compatible and restart the setup program.
- After upgrading to Windows 7, the computer freezes. Boot to Safe Mode and check Device Manager for errors. If no errors are present, disable the following devices if present: video adapter, sound card, network card, USB devices and controller (unless keyboard/mouse is USB), optical drive, modem, unused ports. Enable each disabled device one at a time until the blue screen appears. Once the problem device is known, obtain the appropriate replacement driver.
- The Windows 7 0xC004F061 activation error is caused by a product key being used for an upgrade Windows 7 version and a previous Windows version was not on the computer when the installation was performed. If the drive was formatted *before* starting the installation, the upgrade product key cannot be used. Install 7 with the current Windows running or if you want to format the hard drive and an upgrade version is being used, do so through the Windows 7 installation process: boot with upgrade DVD, click *Custom (advanced)*, and select *Drive options (advanced)*.

Tech Tip

Installation halts

Try removing any nonessential hardware, such as network cards, modems, and USB devices, and start the installation again. Re-install the hardware after Windows is properly installed.

Two text files located in the folder in which Windows XP was loaded can be helpful in determining the installation problem—Setuplog.txt and Setupapi.log. These files can be opened with any word processor including Notepad. Vista has two similar files called Setupapi.dev.log and Setupapi.app.log. Table 12.14 lists important log files that are created during Windows 7 setup. Note that *X:* is the drive where Windows is loaded (normally C:).

Table 12.14 Windows 7 Setup log files

Log file location	Description
X:\Windows\setupapi.log	Device and driver changes, service pack and hotfix installations
X:\$Windows.~BT\Sources\ Panther\setupact.log	Setup actions performed during the install
X:\$Windows.~BT\Sources\Panther\setuperr.log	Setup installation errors
X:\$Windows.~BT\Sources\ Panther\PreGatherPnPList.log	Initial capture of devices information
X:\$Windows.~BT\Sources\Panther\miglog.xml	User directory structure and SID information
X:\Windows\Inf\setupapi.dev.log	Plug and play devices and driver information
X:\Windows\Inf\setupapi.app.log	Application installation information
X:\Windows\Panther\PostGatherPnPList.log	Device information after the online configuration

Dual-Booting Windows

Sometimes users like to try a new operating system while keeping the old operating system loaded. A computer that has two operating systems loaded is known as a dual-boot computer. If Windows is installed on an NTFS partition, only a Windows version that supports NTFS (Windows NT and higher) can access files in the partition, if required.

Tech Tip

When dual-booting, do the oldest operating system first

When multiple operating systems are installed, use a separate partition/volume for each operating system and install the oldest operating system first.

Once installed, the Windows Boot Manager window appears, showing the older version of Windows as "Earlier Version of Windows" and the newly added "Microsoft Windows Vista", "Windows 7" or both. From this screen, you can choose the older operating system with the "Earlier Version of Windows" option or accept the default option. In Windows XP, these settings can be changed using the following process: open *Windows Explorer* > right-click *Computer* > *Properties* > *Advanced system settings* link > from the Startup and Recovery section, select *Settings* button. The default operating system can be selected from the drop-down menu in the System startup section. The time to display the options in the Windows Boot menu is selectable in seconds as well as via an enable/disable checkbox.

In Windows Vista or 7, the boot settings are changed using the **`bcedit`** command: *Start* > *All Programs* > *Accessories* > right-click *Command Prompt* and select *Run as administrator* > type `bcdedit /?` to see a list of switches.

Table 12.15 lists tips for working with the `bcdedit` command.

Table 12.15 `bcdedit` **tips**

`bcdedit` command	Description
`bcdedit /export` *`filename`*	Used to export the current BCD registry in case of mistake.
`bcdedit /import` *`filename`*	Used to restore the BCD from a backup file.
`bcdedit /enum`	Used to view the existing boot menu entries.
`bcdedit /default` *`id`*	Used to configure the default entry. *`id`* is the identifier for the specific Windows version; for example, if the older version of Windows XP is shown as `{ntldr}`, the command would be `bcdedit /default {ntldr}`.
`bcdedit /timeout seconds`	Used to change the time the menu displays.

Virtualization

As introduced in Chapter 11, PC or client virtualization is the process of running multiple operating systems on a single host machine. PC virtualization allows older software to be executed in a protected environment, new software to be tested in an environment that won't affect the normal operating system, and two operating systems (or more) to be installed that cannot see or interfere with one another (refer to Figures 2.13 and 11.21).

Tech Tip

You have to buy the OS license

A common misconception about virtualization is that you don't have to buy both operating systems when two operating systems are installed. This is not always true. Depending on the virtual software used, if you wanted to install Windows XP in one virtual machine and Windows 7 in another virtual machine, and Windows Server 2008 in a third virtual machine, you would have to purchase all three operating systems.

The hypervisor, as mentioned in Chapter 11, is like an orchestra conductor for virtualization. The hypervisor is responsible for managing and overseeing the operation of the VMs (virtual machines). The hypervisor oversees RAM, hard drive space, and processor(s) that are shared between the VMs. There are two types of hypervisors: Type 1 and Type 2. A **Type 1 hypervisor** is also known as a native hypervisor because the operating system runs on top of the hypervisor. Examples of Type 1 hypervisors include VMware's ESXI and Microsoft's Hyper-V. A **Type 2 hypervisor**, also known as a hosted hypervisor, runs on top of a host operating system such as Windows 7 . VMware Workstation, Oracle VirtualBox, and Windows Virtual PC are examples of Type 2 hypervisors.

Tech Tip

Enable virtualization in the BIOS

You may have to enable virtualization in the BIOS before you can install any type of virtualization software (including Virtual PC/Windows XP Mode) on the computer.

Most Windows 7 Professional, Enterprise, and Ultimate computers can use the Windows XP Mode or Microsoft's Windows Virtual PC. Windows XP Mode is a program downloaded from Microsoft that uses virtualization to run Windows XP applications in a virtualized, protected environment. Windows Virtual PC allows other Windows operating systems (none older than XP) to run inside Virtual PC as well as one click access to Windows XP Mode, which is integrated into Virtual PC. Table 12.16 lists the requirements for Virtual PC, which is Microsoft's emulator.

Table 12.16 Microsoft Virtual PC requirements

Component	Requirement
Processor	1GHz
RAM	2GB
Available hard disk space	15GB per virtual machine

Microsoft provides the Hardware-Assisted Virtualization Detection Tool to quickly determine if your computer will support Windows XP Mode or Virtual PC:

- If the message "There is no hardware-assisted virtualization support in the system" appears, then virtualization is not supported.
- If the message "Hardware-assisted virtualization is disabled" appears, then virtualization has not been enabled in the BIOS.

Tech Tip

You can still get a virus

A common misconception about virtualization is that you don't have to worry about security because you are in a "protected" environment. This is not true. The protection is that one operating system is protected from the other operating system, but all virtual machines are susceptible to viruses and security attacks. Install the appropriate protection and see Chapter 15 for more information on security.

Each virtual machine can connect to a network using one of two basic options:

- Internal network—The internal network option allows a particular VM access to other virtual machines that (may be on a different computer or another VM on the same computer) connect to the same network.
- External network—The external network option allows a particular VM access to a different (external) network from within the VM. In a college environment, for example, if the student computer can access the Internet and that same computer is configured for virtualization, a VM on that student computer can be configured for the external network and have access to the Internet.

Labs 12.4 through 12.6 show basic virtualization configuration. More networking information is available in Chapter 13 and 14. Virtualization has been very popular with servers but now applies to desktop operating systems as well. Technicians are expected to be familiar with virtualization because it is found in both home and corporate environments.

Reloading Windows

Sometimes it's necessary to do a **repair installation** (sometimes called an in-place upgrade or a re-installation) of Windows XP, Vista, or 7, such as when Windows will not start normally or in Safe Mode, or when it has a registry corruption that cannot be solved with System Restore. Before you reload Windows, back up any existing data. The installation process should not disturb the data, but there is always a chance that it could.

Tech Tip

All existing system restore points are removed when Windows is re-installed

Once Windows has been installed, no preexisting restore points are kept. You should ensure that the System Restore utility is enabled and back up your data after Windows is installed. You should also apply any service packs and patches after the re-installation is complete.

There are two ways to reload Windows XP from the XP CD: (1) from within a booted XP environment or (2) by booting from the XP CD. If you boot XP and insert the CD, select the *Install Windows XP option* > *Upgrade (Recommended)* in the *Installation Type* menu > *Next* > accept the license > *Next* > enter the product key > *Next* > select *I accept this agreement* > *Next* > follow the instructions on the screen. If you boot from the CD, press [Enter] to setup Windows XP now > press [F8] on the license agreement > select your current Windows XP installation > press [R] to repair XP > follow the directions on the screen.

Windows Vista and 7 do not normally have to be reloaded as much as Windows XP did. Windows Vista and 7 computers are more likely to have a computer that allows booting from a flash drive. The operating system image can be copied or downloaded and placed on the flash drive. Change the BIOS settings to boot from the flash drive, and the installation process starts. Windows Vista and 7 have great tools that help with startup problems, a corrupt registry, and missing or corrupt boot configuration files. These tools are covered later in this chapter.

Updating Windows

Almost daily, new vulnerabilities are found in every operating system. Windows has a method called Windows Update or Automatic Updates for upgrading the operating system. To configure Windows XP for automatic updates, click the *Start* button > *Control Panel* > *Classic* view > *System* Control Panel > *Automatic Updates* tab. Figure 12.3 shows this screen, and Table 12.17 details the options.

Tech Tip

What is the difference between a patch, a service pack, and a hotfix?

A **patch** is an update to an operating system. Microsoft releases patches when they are needed for emergency fixes to vulnerabilities and routinely about once a month. A **service pack** is a group of patches; it makes it easier to install one update rather that a large number of separate patches. A **hotfix** has one or more files that fix a particular software problem. Use the `systeminfo` command to see what hotfixes have been applied.

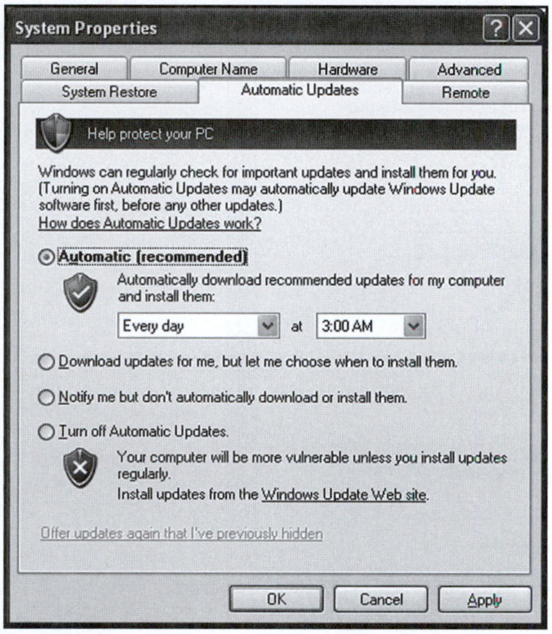

Figure 12.3 Windows XP Automatic Updates window

Table 12.17 Windows XP Automatic Updates options

Automatic Update Option	Description
Automatic (recommended)	The computer automatically downloads an update from Microsoft across the Internet and installs the update(s). You can do it daily or weekly and choose the time. The computer must be on.
Download updates for me, but let me choose when to install them	Once the updates are downloaded an icon appears in the notification area. You can point to the icon to get a message about the status. You can double-click the icon to install the updates.

Automatic Update Option	Description
Notify me but don't automatically download or install them	Windows recognizes when you connect to the Internet and searches for updates, but does not download them. A message appears telling you when an update is available and asks if you want to download or install it.
Turn off automatic updates	Automatic updates are disabled. Sometimes this option is required when installing some software, but it is not an option that you would normally choose.

One way to access Windows Update settings in Vista or 7 is from the *Start* button > *All Programs* > *Windows Update* > *Change Settings*. (See Figure 12.4.) From this window in Vista, only two options are available: (1) Use recommended settings, and (2) install important updates only. The recommended settings option automatically updates and installs updates classified as "Important" and "Recommended." The second setting automatically downloads and installs only updates that are classified as "Important" by Microsoft. For better fine tuning, technicians should always use the *Windows Update* control panel link in Vista and 7, which offers more options. Figure 12.4 shows the options available from Windows 7.

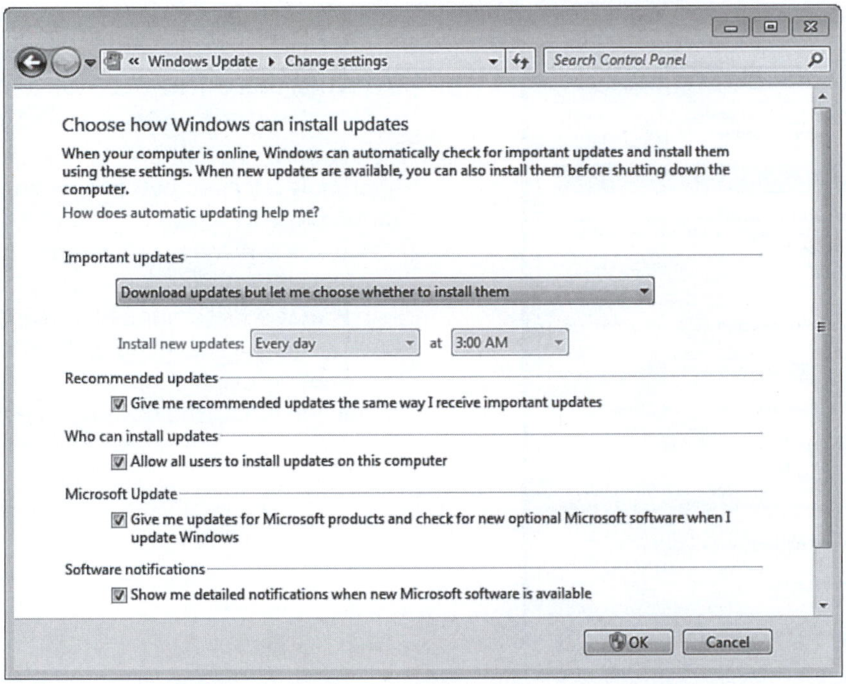

Figure 12.4 Windows Update

Tech Tip

Windows notification update icon

In the taskbar notification area, an icon appears when an update has been downloaded and is ready to be installed in XP and if a member of the Administrator group in Vista/7. The icon on the left is for XP and the right icon is for Windows 7.

The Windows Vista and 7, the *Windows Update* link is available from the *System and Maintenance* (Vista)/*System and Security* (7) control panel link > *Windows Update* (Vista/7) > *Change Settings*. The Important Updates section has the following options:

- Install updates automatically (recommended)
- Download updates but let me choose whether to install them
- Check for updates but let me choose whether to download and install them
- Never check for updates (not recommended)

You can see Table 12.17 for the descriptions; Windows Vista and 7 options are worded similarly to Windows XP options.

Tech Tip

Updates must be installed

Depending on which option is chosen from the System control panel, updates may be downloaded, but you may have to manually install them. A system is not protected unless the updates are installed. This is also true for installed applications.

There are also some options such as how to handle recommended options, whether or not all users on the computer can install updates, and whether or not to receive updates for other Microsoft products such as Internet Explorer at the same time as receiving operating system updates. If a newly installed service pack causes problems and must be removed, use the `spuninst.exe` command.

Tech Tip

You must be an administrator to change Automatic Update settings

You must be logged in as the Administrator or a user that is a member of the Administrators group in order to modify Automatic Updates settings.

To customize how the notifications appear in Vista, right-click the *Start* button > *Properties* > *Notification Area* tab > *Customize* button. In Windows 7, right-click the *Start* button > *Properties* > *Taskbar* tab > locate the *Notification area* section > *Customize* button > locate *Windows Update* option under *Icons* column > select the appropriate behavior.

Backing Up/Restoring the Windows Registry

The registry is a database that contains information about the Windows environment including installed hardware, installed software, and users. The registry should be backed up whenever the computer is fully functional and when any software or hardware changes are made.

Back up the registry

The registry should be backed up and restored on a working computer *before* disaster hits. The time to learn how to restore the registry is not when the computer is down.

Tech Tip

The registry can be backed up and restored several different ways:

- Using the `regedit` program
- Using the Backup utility
- Using the System Restore tool (covered later in this chapter)

The `regedit` program allows you to export the registry to a file that has the extension `.reg`. The file can be imported back into the computer if the computer fails. The `regedit` program and the Backup utility both back up the entire registry.

The Backup utility in XP is accessed through *Start* button > *All Programs* > *Accessories* > *System Tools* > *Backup*. In Windows 7 from the *Start* menu > *Control Panel* > *System and Security* > *Backup and Restore*. The Backup utility is the preferred method for backing up the Windows registry, but in Vista/7 the full version of the Backup tool (the part that can back up the registry) is only available in Windows Vista/7 Business, Professional, Enterprise, or Ultimate versions. (See Figure 12.5.) The backup option to look for specifically in Windows XP is the System State, which is discussed in the next section.

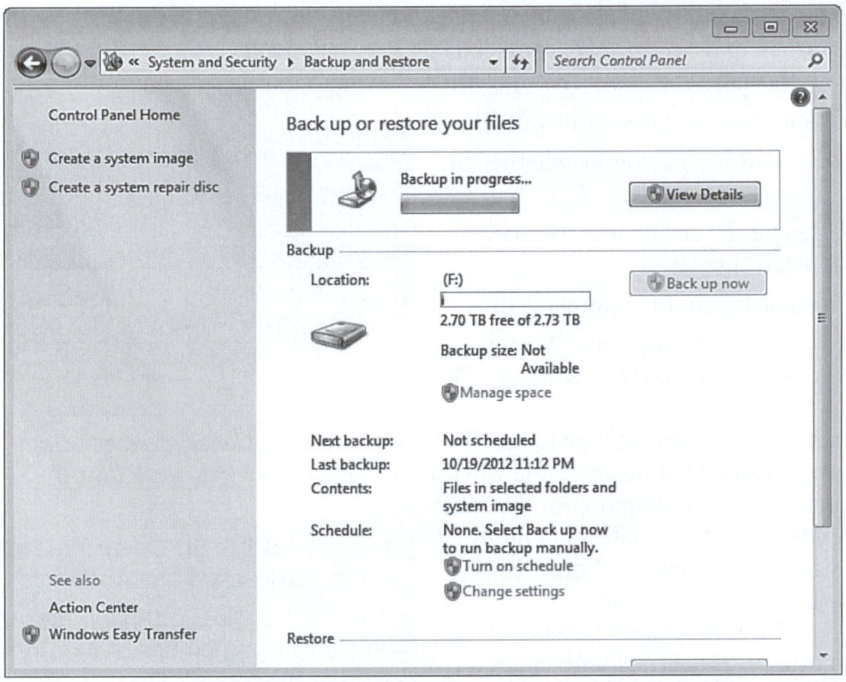

Figure 12.5 Windows Backup and Restore window

Backing Up and Restoring the Windows System State

One option available in the Windows XP Backup utility is the System State. The System State is a group of important Windows XP files including the registry, the system files, the boot files, and the COM+ Class Registration database. With the Backup utility, you cannot back up or restore these items individually. They are all needed because they depend on one another to operate properly. The registry files are located in a folder normally labeled *%systemroot%*\Repair\Regbackup (which is normally C:\Winnt\Repair\Backup or C:\Windows\Repair\Backup, depending on the type of installation). The registry can be restored without having to restore the other System State files.

Tech Tip

Who can use the Backup program?

In order to use the Backup program, you must be an administrator (XP, Vista, or 7) or in XP, a member of the Backup Operators group.

In order to correct a problem with the system files, registry, or Windows XP boot failure, you must restore the registry. You may also have to restore the System State files (which includes the registry) to make the system operational again. To start the restoration process, install Windows XP to the same folder that it was installed in originally. When you are prompted to format the hard drive volume or leave it, select the *Leave the current file system intact* option. Use the Backup utility to restore the System State and/or the registry. Click the *Restore* tab and select the device that holds the backed-up files.

The Windows Vista and 7 Backup and Restore link can also be used to back up the system state (even though that option is not shown like it is in XP). This link can also be used to back up files and an entire disk image. To access this link, click on the *Start* button > *Control Panel* > *System and Maintenance* (Vista)/*System and Security* (7) > *Backup and Restore* > *Create a system repair disc*. Refer to Figure 12.5 to see the link in the left pane. Labs at the end of this chapter demonstrate how to do this.

Configuring Windows Overview

One of the most common windows used by technicians is the *Control Panel* window. A control panel is a method for configuring various components. Each control panel icon represents a Windows utility that allows you to customize a particular part of the Windows environment. The number of control panels displayed depends on the type of computer and the components contained within the computer. Windows has two control panel views—*Classic* and *Category*. Figure 12.6 shows the Windows 7 control panels, in Category view.

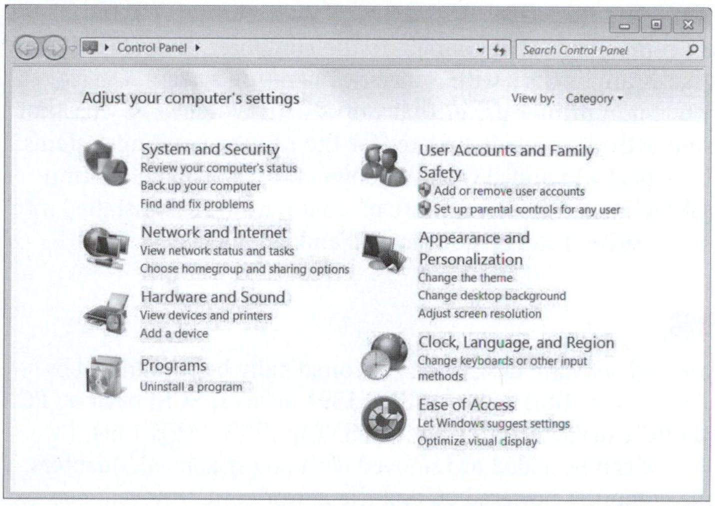

Figure 12.6 Windows 7 Control Panel categories

Technicians must know which control panel category to use for changing a computer's configuration. Review the control panels from Chapter 11. Windows XP, Vista, and 7 have some configuration options that are unique to that particular operating systems. A technician should be familiar with these differences. More labs at the end of this chapter help familiarize you with several control panel categories. Table 12.18 shows the unique control panels by operating system.

Table 12.18 Windows unique control panels

Windows XP	Windows Vista	Windows 7
Add/remove programs	Tablet PC settings	HomeGroup
Network connections	Pen and input devices	Action Center
Printers and faxes	Offline files	RemoteApp and Desktop Connections
Automatic updates	Problem ports and solutions	Troubleshooting
Network setup Wizard	Printers	Devices and Printers

Note that the RemoteApp and Desktop Connections Control Panel link is used to access a computer such as a workplace computer from a remote place. The configuration requires a URL from the network administrator to make this connection.

12 Windows XP, Vista, and 7

Configuring Windows

Technicians must frequently add new hardware and software using the operating system. Windows has specific tools for these functions. Using the correct procedure is essential for success. The following sections highlight many of the tasks a technician must perform:

- Adding devices
- Removing hardware components
- Adding a printer
- Installing/removing software

Hardware devices are physical components that connect to the computer. A **device driver** is a piece of software that allows hardware to work with a specific operating system. Device drivers are operating system dependent. A printer driver that works with Windows XP may not work with Windows 7. Not all manufacturers provide updates for the newer operating systems. Also, some device drivers are automatically included with Windows and are updated continuously through Windows updates. A technician must be aware of what hardware is installed into a system so that the latest compatible drivers can be downloaded and installed.

Adding Devices

Plug and play devices are hardware and software designed to automatically be recognized by the operating system. These devices include USB devices; IEEE 1394 devices; SCSI devices; PC Card and ExpressCard devices; PCI/PCIe devices; and printers. eSATAp, USB, IEEE 1394, PC Card devices, and ExpressCard devices can be added or removed with power applied. Adapters are installed and removed with the computer powered off and the power cord removed. See Figure 12.7.

Figure 12.7 Adding hardware to a Windows PC

The keys to a successful device installation are as follows:

- Possessing the most up-to-date device driver for the specific installed operating system
- Following the directions provided by the device manufacturer

Once a device is installed, power on the computer. The Windows *Found New Hardware* Wizard appears. Windows XP attempts to find a driver for the new device. Plug and play devices make use of a special `.CAB` (cabinet) file called `driver.cab` located in *%winroot%*\Driver Cache\i386 folder (where *%winroot%* is normally `C:\Winnt` or `C:\Windows`). If Windows XP detects new hardware, it will automatically search `driver.cab` for a driver. If a driver cannot be found, a dialog box appears. The best policy with any operating system is to use the latest driver even if the operating system detects the device. Labs 12.16 and 12.17 outline how to install a new hardware driver.

Windows Vista and 7 do not use the `driver.cab` system. Instead, they use driver packages that are stored in an indexed database. The drivers are stored in the *Windows\System32\DriverStore\FileRepository* folder. All driver files that are not part of the operating system must be imported into this folder before the driver package can be installed. Drivers created for earlier Windows versions may need to be updated.

Some Windows device drivers use digital signatures, which is sometimes called driver signing or a signed driver. The digital signature confirms that the device driver for a particular piece of hardware has met certain criteria for WHQL (Windows hardware quality lab) tests and is compatible with Windows. Digital signatures are required for 64-bit kernel mode drivers in Windows Vista and 7. Figure 12.8 shows this concept.

Tech Tip

Installing a device driver requires Administrator rights

Remember that if the operating system cannot configure a device and prompts for a device driver, you must have Administrator rights to install the driver.

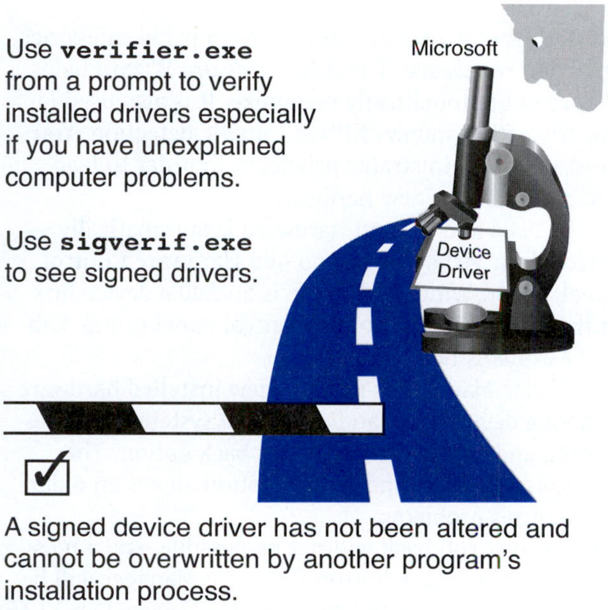
Use **verifier.exe** from a prompt to verify installed drivers especially if you have unexplained computer problems.
Use **sigverif.exe** to see signed drivers.
Microsoft
Device Driver
A signed device driver has not been altered and cannot be overwritten by another program's installation process.

Figure 12.8 Signed drivers

From Vista/7's Advanced Boot Options menu (press F8 on startup), select the *Disable Driver Signature Enforcement* option if you suspect that Windows is not booting because of an unsigned driver. The computer boots normally and not in Safe Mode (which is covered later in this chapter).

In Windows XP, there are three file signature verification options—*Ignore*, *Warn*, and *Block*. Table 12.19 shows what these three options do.

Table 12.19 Windows XP file signature verification options

Option	Description
Ignore	Allows all device drivers to be installed regardless if a digital signature is present or not
Warn	Displays a warning message whenever a driver that does not have a digital signature is attempted
Block	Prevents any device drivers that do not have a digital signature from being installed

To modify how drivers are handled in Windows Vista, access the *System and Maintenance* control panel > *System* > *Advanced system settings* link > *Continue* button > *Hardware* tab > *Windows Update Driver Settings* button. The three options available are as follows:

- Check for drivers automatically (recommended)
- Ask me each time I connect a new device before checking for drivers
- Never check for drivers when I connect a device

For Windows 7, use the *System and Security* control panel > *System* > *Advanced system settings* link > *Hardware* tab > *Device Installation Settings* button. The options available in Windows 7 are as follows:

- Yes, do this automatically (recommended)
- No, let me choose what to do
  - Always install the best driver software from Windows Update
  - Install driver software from Windows Update if it is not found on my computer
  - Never install driver software from Windows Update

Windows XP has a control panel called *Add Hardware* or, if using control panel categories, the *Printers and Other Hardware* category > *Add Hardware*. The *Add Hardware* Wizard helps you configure hardware that Windows XP does not automatically recognize. It is also used for plug and play devices that don't install properly with Windows XP's automatic detection. You must have Administrator privileges in order to load device drivers for new hardware.

Tech Tip

Driver roll back requires administrator rights

You must have administrator rights to access or use the *driver roll* back option in Device Manager.

In Vista and 7, most hardware is automatically detected. In Vista, there is no Add Hardware Control Panel, but in Windows 7 there is an Add a device link in the Hardware and Sound Control Panel group. Lab 12.17 explains how to do this.

Device Manager is used to view installed hardware devices, enable or disable devices, troubleshoot a device, view and/or change system resources such as IRQs and I/O addresses, update drivers, and access the driver roll back option. The **driver roll back** option is available in Windows XP, Vista, and 7. This option allows an older driver to be re-installed when the new driver causes problems.

If the device driver has not been updated, driver roll back will not be possible, and a message screen displays stating this fact and the driver roll back button in Device Manager will be disabled. The troubleshooting tool should be used instead to troubleshoot the device. Lab 12.15 details how to use the driver roll back feature.

Tech Tip

Put oldest adapters closest to the power supply

Place older adapters in motherboard expansion slots closest to the power supply because Windows checks expansion slots in order, starting with the closest to the power supply.

Sometimes, Windows installs the wrong driver for an older device or adapter. To uninstall or disable such a driver, in Device Manager, right-click the device and choose the appropriate option. Sometimes, the computer must reboot, and Windows will re-install the wrong driver (again). The solution to this is to disable the device and then manually install it. Lab 12.16 illustrates how to disable a device. To manually install new hardware in Windows XP, follow these steps:

1. Click the *Start* button and select the *Control Panel* option.
2. From *Category* view > *Printers and Other Hardware* > *Add Hardware* from the left pane.
3. Make sure the new hardware is physically connected. Select *Yes, I have already connected the hardware* > *Next*.
4. Use the Installed hardware scroll bar to find and select the *Add a new hardware device* checkbox > *Next*.

5. Select the manual option and select the type of hardware being installed. Scroll through the manufacturer list or have an XP-compatible driver ready and click the *Have Disk* button to install the appropriate driver. Click the *Next* button to finish the device driver installation.

To manually install a driver in Windows Vista or 7, follow these steps:

1. Open the *Device Manager* link by using the *System and Maintenance* (Vista)/*System and Security* (7) Control Panel.
2. Expand categories as needed to locate the device for which the driver is to be installed. Note that to display hidden devices in Device Manager, select *Show hidden devices* from the *View* menu option.
3. Right-click the device name and select *Update Driver Software*.
4. Select *Browse my computer for driver software*, click *Let me pick from a list of device drivers on my computer*, and select *Have Disk*. Click the *Browse* button to locate the extracted files. Click the *.inf* file designed to work with Vista/7.
5. Follow the dialogs that continue to update the driver. If you are prompted with a warning about driver compatibility, you can click *No* and continue installing the driver. You can always remove it or roll back the driver if it does not install correctly or if it does not work.

Tech Tip

Too many tray icons

Many programs and some drivers place icons in the system tray (the area to the right of the taskbar). Vista and 7 do a better job of consolidating them, but if they are not used, remove them. Right-click *Start* button > *Properties* > *Notification Area* tab > *Customize* button.

If an `.inf` file cannot be found in a folder from your driver download, look in subfolders or other folders that might hold the file. You could always download the driver again and pay attention to the folder name in which the driver is stored. If there are multiple `.inf` files in the folder, you may have to try them one at a time until you find the one that works with your hardware. Always reboot Windows after a driver installation, even if the system does not prompt for a reboot.

In Vista or 7, if you cannot install a device driver by its installation program, you can try running the installation program in compatibility mode, try using administrative credentials, or try manually installing it using Device Manager.

To run the driver installation program in compatibility mode, locate and right-click the executable file for the driver installation program. Select *Properties* > *Compatibility* tab > enable the *Run this program in compatibility mode for* checkbox > select a version of Windows XP > click *OK*. Double-click the executable file to start the installation process.

To use administrative credentials in Windows Vista or 7, locate the executable file used to start the driver installation process. Right-click the filename and select *Run as administrator* as shown in Figure 12.9. Provide the Administrator password if required. Click *Continue*. Follow the installation instructions as normal.

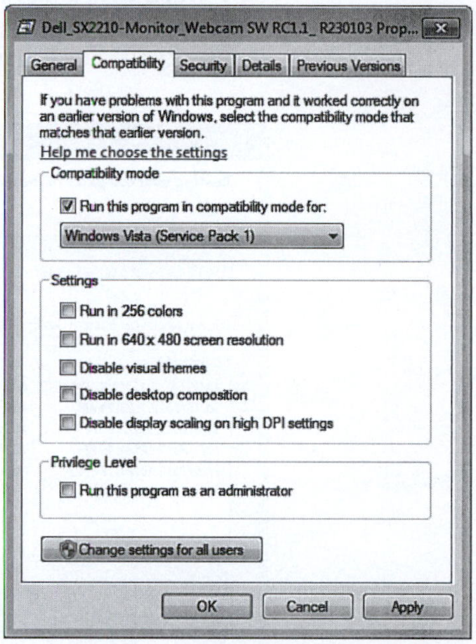

Figure 12.9 Installing a driver in compatibility mode

System Restore

Any kind of hardware or software installation can cause a system not to boot or operate correctly. The **System Restore** utility can be used to return the system to an operable state so you can try the installation again or determine a better method. The System Restore program that makes a snapshot image of the registry and backs up certain dynamic system files.

The program does not affect your email or personal data files. This program is similar to the *Last Known Good Configuration* Advanced Boot Options menu item, but more powerful. Each snapshot is called a **restore point**, and multiple restore points are created on the computer; you can select which one to use.

Tech Tip

BSOD after a Windows update

Windows updates include device driver updates. If the computer fails to boot after a Windows update, reboot the computer to WinRE Safe Mode and use the System Restore tool to restore the registry to an earlier time so the problem can be researched. If multiple updates were installed, try loading the updates one at a time.

Restore points are created weekly and whenever a system update occurs in Windows Vista/7. However, you can do a restore point at any time especially before doing an important upgrade or installation. A particular amount of disk space is used for restore points. When new restore points are created, the older ones are removed automatically. System Restore is your number-one tool for solving problems within the operating system and registry.

System Restore can also be used if you suspect that the registry is corrupt. For example, if an application that worked fine yesterday, but today displays a message that the application cannot be found, you may have a virus, a corrupt application executable file, or a corrupt registry. Run an antivirus check first with updated virus definitions. If free of viruses, use the System Restore utility to roll back the system to yesterday or the day before this problem occurred. Sometimes System Restore works best if executed from Safe Mode (covered later in this chapter). If System Restore does not fix the problem, re-install the application.

System Restore requires a file system of NTFS. Windows Vista and 7 use a different type of System Restore technology than Windows XP used; Vista and 7 use **Shadow Copy** technology, which uses a block-level image instead of monitoring certain files for file changes. Backup media can be optical discs, flash devices, other hard drives, and server storage, but not tape. Figure 12.10 shows how you can select a specific date during the System Restore process.

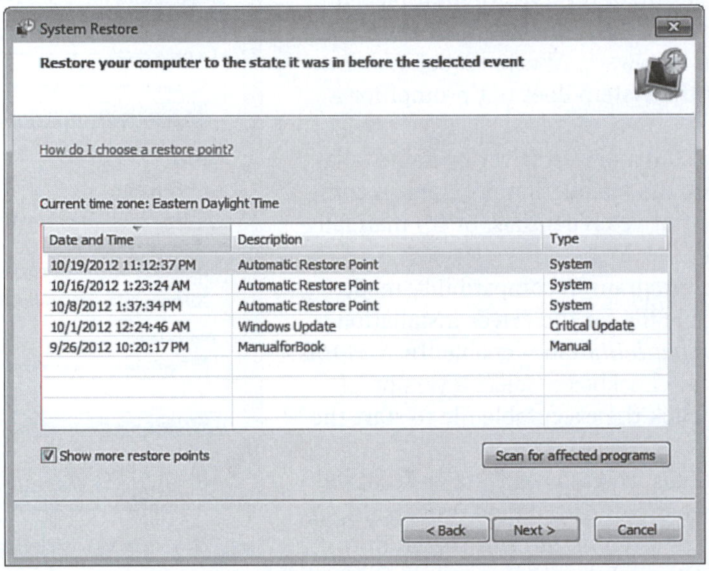

Figure 12.10 Windows System Restore

Tech Tip

You can run System Restore from a command prompt

If Windows does not load properly, you can execute it from a command prompt with the command `%systemroot%\system32\restore\rstrui.exe`. In Windows Vista/7, the `rstrui.exe` command can be found in the Windows\System32 folder.

Installing/Removing Software

No computer is fully functional without software. One thing you should know about the newer Windows versions is that they may not support some of the older 16-bit software. Use the Program Compatibility wizard or download and use the Windows XP Mode virtual environment for older applications loaded in Windows Vista and 7.

Most software today is 32- or 64-bit, comes on an optical disc or is downloaded, and includes an autorun feature. If the disc has the autorun feature, an installation wizard steps you through installing the software when the disc is inserted into the drive (Figure 12.11). If there is not an autorun feature on the disc, then the XP *Add or Remove Programs* Control Panel is used to install or remove the software. Table 12.20 shows common locations for the 32- and 64-bit applications.

Figure 12.11 Installing software

Table 12.20 Default locations for 32- and 64-bit files

Folder	Description
System32	Used for 64-bit Windows system files
Program Files	Used for 64-bit application files
SysWOW64	Used for 32-bit Windows system files (Note that the WOW in the folder name stands for Windows 32-bit on Windows 64-bit.)
Program Files (x86)	Used for 32-bit application files

In Windows Vista and 7, the Programs Control Panel is used to add and remove applications. This link is also used to configure which programs are the default programs such as for email or a web browser. Desktop gadgets in the Aero environment can be customized from here as well.

To access the Add or Remove Programs Control Panel in Windows XP: *Start > Control Panel > Add or Remove Programs > Add New Programs > CD or Floppy* button and ensure that the software disc is inserted in the appropriate drive. If a `setup.exe` file cannot be found on the designated disc, the system prompts with a dialog

Tech Tip

Launch an application

Once an application is installed in Windows XP, Vista, or 7, launch the application by clicking the *Start* button > *All Programs* >, locate the application name, and click it.

box. Use the *Browse* button to locate the installation file. Click the *Finish* button to complete the process. To remove a software application in Windows XP, use the same *Add or Remove Programs* Control Panel. The *Add or Remove Programs* Control Panel can also be used to update operating system components. Labs 12.19 and 12.20 illustrate these concepts.

DLLs (dynamic link libraries) are reusable code that can be used by multiple applications. A DLL must be registered with the Windows registry in order to function. Sometimes, DLL registry links are broken and the DLLs must be re-registered using the `regsvr32.exe` command. Refer to Chapter 11 to see the syntax. You might also have to remove and then re-install a particular application in order to fix a particular DLL. Microsoft has a database of DLLs to help with DLL version conflicts.

Microsoft Management Console

The **Microsoft Management console**, often called **Computer Management console**, holds snap-ins, which are tools used to maintain a computer. To access the console, click the *Start* button > *Control Panel*. In XP, select the *Performance and Maintenance* category > *Administrative Tools* > *Computer Management*. In Vista, select the *System and Maintenance* Control Panel; in Windows 7, select the *System and Security* Control Panel link. Then in both Vista and 7, select *Administrative Tools* > double-click *Computer Management*. You can start the Microsoft Management console and open a saved console using the `mmc` *`path\filename`*`.msc` command.

Tech Tip

Adding administrative tools to the Start button

To add the administrative tools to the *Start* button's *All Programs* option, right-click an empty space on the *Taskbar* > *Properties* > *Start Menu* tab > *Customize*. In XP, select the *Advanced* tab > use the *Start* menu items section's vertical scroll bars to locate the *System Administrative Tools* section > *Display on the All Programs menu* radio button > *OK*. In Vista/7, scroll to the *System Administrative Tools* section > select a radio button to put the tools either on *All Programs* or on the Start button menu.

Figure 12.12 shows the Microsoft Computer Management console screen. The Computer Management console allows a technician to manage shared folders and drives, start and stop services, look at performance logs and system alerts, and access Device Manager to troubleshoot hardware problems.

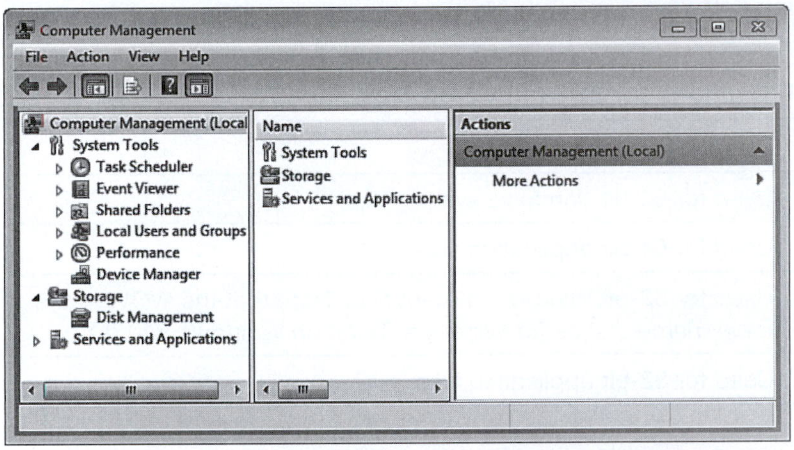

Figure 12.12 Microsoft Computer Management console

Tech Tip

Using Component Services

One particular snap-in called *Component Services* can be used to configure and administer COM (Component Object Model) components, COM+ applications, and the DTC (Distributed Transaction Coordinator). In Windows 7, type `component services` in the *Search programs and files* textbox and press Enter to access.

The three major tool categories found in the Computer Management console are *System Tools*, *Storage*, and *Services and Applications*. The System Tools include Task Scheduler (Vista/7), Event Viewer, Shared Folders, Local Users and Groups, Device Manager, Performance (7), Reliability and Performance (Vista),and Performance Logs and Alerts (XP).

The Shared Folders tool is used to view shares, sessions, and open files. Shares can be folders that have been shared on the computer, printers, or a network resource such as a scanner. Sessions list network users who are currently connected to the computer as well as the network users' computer names, the network connection type (Windows, NetWare, or Macintosh), how many resources have been opened by the network user, how long the user has been connected, and whether or not this user is connected using the Guest user account. Open files are files that are currently opened by network users. In order to use the Shared Folders tool, you must be a member of the Administrators or Power Users group (XP only).

In the left Computer Management window pane, expand the *Shared Folders* option and click the *Shares* option. The network shares appear in the right pane. Double-click any of the shares to view the Properties window. From this window, using the *Share Permissions* or *Security* tabs, permissions can be set for shared resources. Permissions are covered later in this chapter. Figure 12.13 shows the Properties window for a shared folder called *Sharp* on an XP computer.

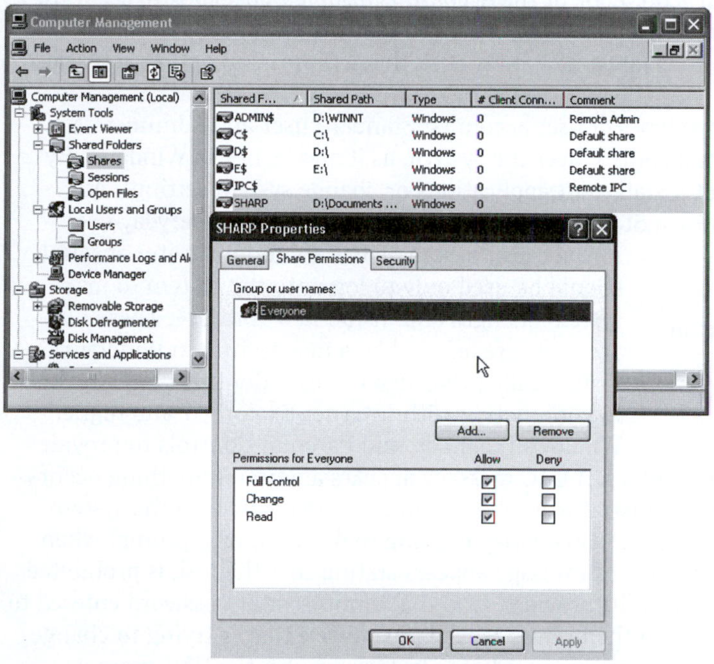

Figure 12.13 Shares window

The Local Users and Groups tool is used to create and manage accounts for those who use the computer or computer resources from a remote network computer. These accounts are considered local users or local groups and are managed from the computer being worked on. In contrast, domain or global users and groups are administered by a network administrator on a network server. Permissions are granted or denied to files, folders, and network resources such as a shared printer or scanner. Rights can also be assigned. Rights are computer actions such as performing a backup or shutting down the computer. Open the *Local Users and Groups* option by expanding the *Local Users and Groups* selection in the *Computer Management* window. Double-click the *Users* option and a list of current users displays in the right pane. Figure 12.14 shows an example of local users that have been created for a Windows 7 computer.

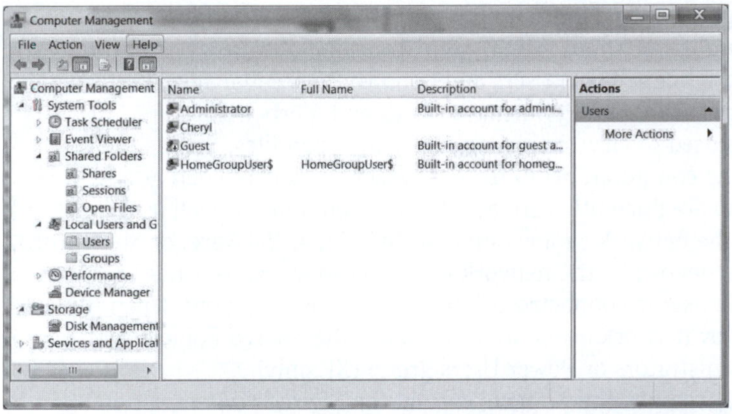

Figure 12.14 **Computer Management console Local Users and Groups—Users window**

Notice in Figure 12.14 that the Guest account has a small down arrow in the lower-right corner of its icon. (In Windows XP, it is a red X.) This means the account has been disabled. In Vista or 7, double-click the *Guest* icon. Look at the *Account is disabled* checkbox to see if the account is disabled. The box is checked by default, meaning that the Guest account is not available for use. In XP, Vista, and 7, to create a new user, click the *Action* menu option and select *New User*.

Windows Vista and 7 have two types of user accounts: Standard user and Administrator. The Administrator account has full control over the system, as it always has in Windows. By default, the Standard user cannot install most applications or change system settings. All users on the computer should have a Standard user account that is used for everyday use. Any account designated as an Administrator account should be used only to log onto the system to make system changes and install new software. These two accounts are affected by a new feature in Windows Vista/7 called UAC (User Access Control). UAC works in conjunction with Internet Explorer 7 and higher, Windows Defender, and Parental Controls to provide a heightened awareness to security issues. A UAC message appears anytime something occurs that normally would require an administrator-level decision to make changes to the system. An application that has a security shield icon overlay is going to display a UAC prompt when executed. If a Standard user is logged in, a message appears stating that the task is prohibited or that Administrator credentials must be provided (and the Administrator password entered to proceed). This is to protect users from themselves as well as software that is trying to change the system. Even if a person is logged in with an Administrator account, the UAC prompt appears to confirm the action that is about to be performed.

Tech Tip

Where are the local user settings?

Windows Vista/7 local user settings are found in the following folder: *%userprofile%*\AppData\Local (for example, C:\Users\Cheryl\AppData\Local).

The following configurations help with UAC:

- To configure a specific application to run in an elevated mode—meaning it has the administrator access token given to it or permission given to it to run—right-click the application and select *Properties* > *Compatibility* tab > under the Privilege level select *Run this program as administrator* > *OK*.
- If a user demands that the UAC be disabled, use the System Configuration window (`msconfig`) *Tools* tab. Select the *Disable UAC* option (Vista) or *Change UAC Settings* (7). Also, an individual account can be changed through the *Change security settings* (Vista)/*Change User Account Control settings* (7) link from within the User Accounts Control Panel.

Device Manager is used after installing a new hardware device and seeing if Windows recognizes the device. It is also used to change or view hardware configuration settings, view and install device drivers, return (roll back) to a previous device driver version, disable/enable/uninstall devices, and print a summary of all hardware installed. Expand a section.

Double click any device and the Properties window appears. The General tab can contain a *Troubleshoot* button that can help diagnose hardware problems. Click the *Device Manager* option in the Computer Management window's left pane, and the Device Manager hardware categories appear in the right pane. Expand any category to view the individual hardware devices. Double-click any hardware device to open the device's Properties window. Figure 12.15 shows the Device Manager window.

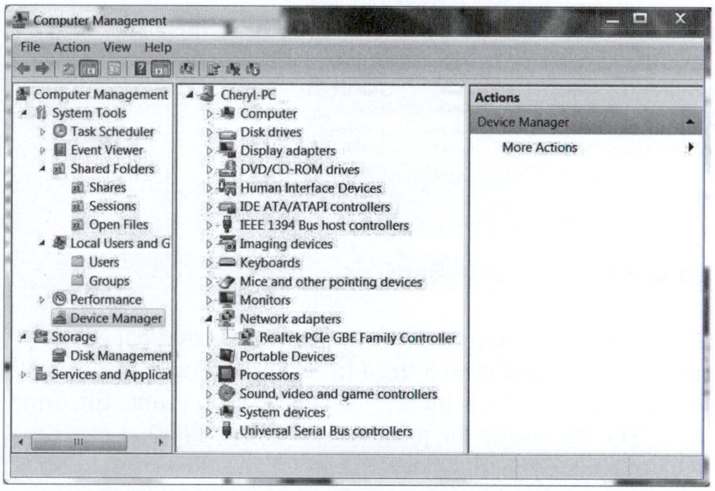

Figure 12.15 Computer Management console—Device Manager window

The *Storage* Computer Management category includes Removable Storage, Disk Defragmenter, and Disk Management tools in Windows XP and just the Disk Management tool in Windows Vista/7. The *Disk Management* tool is used to manage hard drives including volumes or partitions. Drives can be initialized; volumes created; volumes formatted for FAT, FAT32, and NTFS; RAID configured; and remote drives managed.

Tech Tip

Defragmentation requires Administrator rights

Note that only a member of the Administrators group can defragment a hard drive.

The XP *Windows Disk Defragmenter* tool analyzes hard drive volumes and consolidates files and folders into contiguous (one right after another) space. Files and folders become fragmented due to file creation and deletion over a period of time. A defragmented volume has better performance than a volume that has files and folders located throughout the drive. In Vista/7, this tool is accessed by right-clicking a drive letter from Windows Explorer and selecting *Properties* > *Tools* tab > *Defragment Now*.

Tech Tip

All Windows disk management tools require Administrator rights

You must be a member of the Administrators group to perform any disk management tasks.

The *Services and Applications* section can contain a multitude of options, depending on the computer and what is loaded on it. Common options include Telephony, WMI Control, Services, and Indexing Service. A frequently used option is *Services*. A service is an application that can be started using this window or configured so it starts when the computer boots. By clicking the *Services* option, a list of services installed on the computer is displayed in the right window. Double-click any service, and the service *Properties* window appears. From this window on the *General* tab, a service can be started, stopped, paused, resumed, or disabled on the local computer and on remote computers, but you must be logged on as a member of the Administrators group to change a service. Figure 12.16 shows the Computer Management console Services window and some examples of installed services.

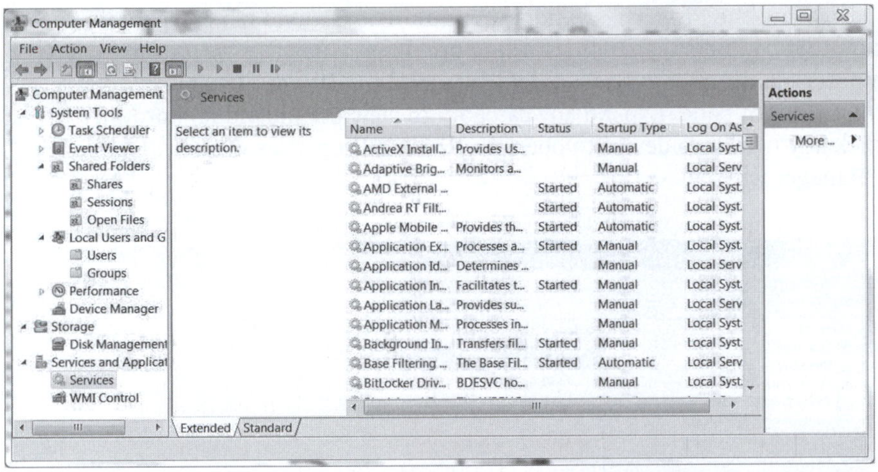

Figure 12.16 Computer Management console—Services window

If you double-click a service, you can use the *Recovery* tab to determine what happened when a service fails a first time, a second time, and even a third time. For example, if the print service fails the first time, a restart occurs. Once the print service fails a second time, the print server can be restarted automatically. The third time the print service fails, a file that pages a technician can be executed.

Advanced Boot Options Menu

When Windows does not boot properly, the Windows **Advanced Boot Options** menu can be used. Tools that can be used to troubleshoot Windows boot problems include Last Known Good Configuration, Safe Mode, Recovery Console (XP) or Windows Recovery Environment (Vista or higher), and Automated System Restore Wizard (XP) or Startup Repair Tool (Vista or 7). Table 12.21 gives a brief description of these options.

Tech Tip

Press F8 during startup

When Windows is booting, press the F8 key to access the Windows Advanced Boot Options menu.

Table 12.21 Windows Advanced Boot Options window

Boot option	Description
Safe Mode	Uses a minimum set of drivers and services to start Windows. A commonly used option.
Safe Mode with Networking	Same as Safe Mode, but includes a NIC driver.
Safe Mode with Command Prompt	Same as Safe Mode except Windows Explorer (GUI mode) is not used, but a command prompt appears instead. This option is not used very often.
Enable VGA Mode (XP only)	Used when Safe Mode does not work and you suspect the default video driver is not working.
Enable low resolution video (640[ts]480) (Vista or 7)	Used when Safe Mode does not work and you suspect the default video driver is not working.
Last Known Good Configuration	A very popular option used when a change that was just implemented caused the system to not boot properly.

Boot option	Description
Debugging Mode	Debugging information can be sent through the serial port to another computer running a debugger program. This option is not used very often.
Enable Boot Logging	Enables logging for startup options except for the *Last Known Good Configuration* option. The logging file is called ntbtlog.txt.
Disable automatic restart on system failure (Vista or 7)	Prevents Windows from automatically rebooting after a system crash.
Disable driver signature enforcement (Vista or 7)	Allows drivers that are not properly signed to load during startup.
Start Windows Normally	Restarts Windows and attempts to boot normally.
Repair Your Computer (Vista or 7)	Used if system recovery tools are installed on the hard disk. Otherwise, these tools are available when booting from the Windows installation DVD.
Reboot	Restarts Windows.

When to use the Last Known Good Configuration boot option

Tech Tip

Whenever the *Last Known Good Configuration* option is used, all configuration changes made since the last successful boot are lost. However, since the changes are the most likely cause of Windows not booting correctly, Last Known Good Configuration is a useful tool when installing new devices and drivers that do not work properly.

If Last Known Good Configuration does not work properly, boot the computer into Safe Mode, which is covered in the next section. If Windows works, but a hardware device does not work and a new driver has been recently loaded, use the *driver roll back* option for the device.

Safe Mode is used when the computer stalls, slows down, or does not work right, or problems are caused by improper video, intermittent errors, or new hardware/software installation. Safe Mode is used to start Windows with minimum device drivers and services. Software that automatically loads during startup is disabled in Safe Mode and user profiles are not loaded.

What loads when booting into Safe Mode?

Tech Tip

When the computer boots in Safe Mode, the mouse, keyboard, CD/DVD, and 640×480 default video device drivers are the only items loaded.

Safe Mode allows you to access configuration files and make necessary changes, troubleshoot installed software and hardware, disable software and services, and adjust hardware and software settings that may be causing Windows to not start correctly. The bottom line is that Safe Mode puts the computer in a "barebones" mode so you can troubleshoot problems.

Overview of the Windows Boot Process

Windows can be booted using a variety of methods as shown in Table 12.22. Some of these methods may require additional BIOS configuration especially the order in which the computer looks to devices for an operating system (boot order). Some of these options may not be supported.

Table 12.22 Windows boot options

Boot option	Description
Hard drive	Most common method used to boot Windows on a computer.
Optical drive	Requires the Windows disc to be inserted into the drive. Used in troubleshooting scenarios if F8 cannot be pressed to reach the Advanced Boot Options menu.
USB	An operating system must be installed on the USB device and the computer must support booting from USB; USB is available as a BIOS option in the boot order.
PXE (preboot execution environment)	Boots from a computer image housed on a network device. Commonly used for booting a computer over a network.

With Windows there are two types of partitions that are important during the boot process—the system partition/volume and the boot partition/volume. The **system partition** (XP and lower) or **system volume** (Vista and higher) is the active drive partition that has the files needed to load the operating system. The system partition is normally the `c:` drive (the active partition). The **boot partition** (XP and lower) or **boot volume** (Vista and higher) is the partition or logical drive where the operating system files are located. One thing that people sometimes forget is that the system partition and the boot partition can be on the same partition. These partitions are where certain boot files are located.

Every operating system needs specific files that allow the computer to boot. These files are known as **system files** or startup files. Table 12.23 shows the system files and their specific location on the hard drive.

Table 12.23 Windows system files

Startup filename	File location
`boot.ini` (XP)	Root directory of system partition
`bootmgr.exe` (Vista and higher)	Root directory of system partition
`bootsect.dos` (needed with XP if the computer is a dual- or multi-boot system)	Root directory of system partition
`hal.dll`	*%systemroot%*\System32*
`ntbootdd` (used on XP with SCSI drives that have the SCSI BIOS disabled)	Root directory of system partition
`ntdetect.com` (Windows XP)	Root directory of system partition
`ntldr` (Windows XP)	Root directory of system partition
`ntoskrnl.exe`	*%systemroot%*\System32*
`winload.exe`	*%systemroot%*\System32*
`winresume.exe`	Root directory of system partition
`bcd` (Vista and higher)	*%systemroot%*\Boot
`system` (registry file)	*%systemroot%*\System32\Config\System
`winlogon.exe`	*%systemroot%*\System32

*%systemroot% is the boot partition and the name of the folder under the folder where Windows is installed (normally `C:\Winnt` or `C:\Windows`)

Reading about Windows files can be confusing because the file locations frequently have the entries %*systemroot*% and %*systemdrive*%. This is because computers can be partitioned differently. If you install Windows onto a drive letter (a partition or logical drive) other than the active partition (normally `c:`), the startup files can be on two different drive letters. Also, you do not have to take the default folder name of *Winnt* or *Windows* (depending on the type of installation) to install Windows. To account for these different scenarios, Microsoft uses the %*systemroot*% to represent the boot partition, the partition and folder that contains the majority of the Windows files. %*systemdrive*% represents the root directory. On a computer with a single operating system, this would be `c:\`.

Tech Tip

Example of %systemdrive% and %systemroot%

If Windows XP is installed onto the `c:` drive and the `c:` drive is the active partition, then the `boot.ini`, `bootsect.dos`, `hyperfil.sys`, `ntbootdd.sys`, `ntdetect.com`, and `ntldr` files would all be in the root directory of `c:`. The `hal.dll` and `ntoskrnl.exe` files would be located in the *System32* folder (located in either the *Winnt* or *Windows* folder) on the `c:` drive.

The boot process for any Windows version is actually quite involved, but the major steps for Windows XP are as follows:

1. Power on the computer.
2. POST executes.
3. BIOS searches BIOS saved configuration for the boot device order and checks for a boot sector. If the boot device is a hard drive, BIOS reads the Master Boot Record, and locates and loads the information into sector 0 of the system partition. The contents of sector 0 define the type of file system, the location of the bootstrap loader file, and start the bootstrap loader. With Windows XP, this file is `ntldr`.
4. `ntldr` starts in real mode so that old software can be loaded. Then XP is switched to 32-bit mode and the file system begins to load.
5. `ntldr` reads the `boot.ini` file and displays the various operating system choices contained within the `boot.ini` file. If something other than Windows XP is chosen, the `bootsect.dos` file takes over. If Windows XP is chosen, the `ntdetect.com` file executes.
6. `ntdetect.com` detects the computer's hardware and ACPI tables are read so that XP can detect power management features.
7. `ntldr` passes the hardware information to the `Ntoskrnl.exe` file.
8. The operating system kernel, `ntoskrnl.exe`, executes and the `hal.dll` file loads. **HAL** (hardware abstraction layer) is a layer between the operating system and the hardware devices. The HAL allows Windows XP to run with different hardware configurations and components without affecting (or crashing) the operating system.
9. The Hkey_Local_Machine\System registry key loads. This registry key is located in the %*systemroot*%\System32\Config\System file. This key has information found during the hardware detection process and is used to determine which device drivers to load.
10. The operating system kernel initializes and `NTLDR` passes control to it. The Starting Up process bar displays. During this time, a hardware key is created, device drivers load, and services start.
11. The `winlogon.exe` file executes and the logon screen appears. While the logon process is occurring, XP detects plug and play devices.

The Windows Vista/7 boot process has changed to the following:

1. Power on the computer.
2. POST executes.

Tech Tip

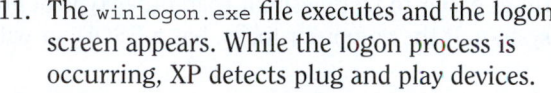

Installing Vista/7 with older operating systems

Be careful installing Vista or 7 with an older operating system. Windows Vista or 7 overwrites the MBR, boot sector, and boot files. That is why very few Windows versions are upgradable to Vista or 7.

3. BIOS searches the BIOS saved configuration for the boot device order and checks for a boot sector. If the boot device is a hard drive, BIOS reads the MBR and locates and loads the information into sector 0 of the system partition. The contents of sector 0 define the type of file system and the location of the bootstrap loader file and start the bootstrap loader. With Windows Vista/7, this file is `bootmgr.exe`.
4. The Windows Boot Manager (`bootmgr.exe`) reads boot configuration data from the BCD (Boot Configuration Data) database file. Boot Manager replaces the older `boot.ini` file, can be edited with `bcdedit.exe`, and allows better support for non-Windows operating systems to coexist with Vista/7. On multi-boot systems, a menu appears. Note that Boot Manager can be accessed by pressing the Spacebar during startup.
5. If Vista/7 is chosen or the only choice, `winload.exe` takes control as the operating system boot loader. This file takes the place of `ntldr` and is responsible for loading the operating system kernel (`ntoskrnl.exe`) and device drivers.

Note that if a UEFI/EFI BIOS is installed, the boot order could be modified. UEFI supports a fast boot and booting from a pre-operating system environment that could include Internet connectivity and access to applications such as an antivirus application.

Speeding Up the Windows Boot Process

The following tips can help reduce the time Windows takes to become operational:

- Configure BIOS boot options so that the drive used to boot Windows is listed as the first option.
- Configure BIOS for the fast boot option or disable hardware checks.
- If multiple operating systems are installed, use the `msconfig` utility *Boot* tab to reduce the boot menu timeout value.
- Remove unnecessary startup applications using the `msconfig` utility.
- Have available hard disk space and keep the drive defragmented. Note that Vista and 7 are automatically configured to defragment the hard drive at 1:00 a.m. on Wednesday. If the computer is powered off, defragmentation occurs when the computer next boots.
- Disable unused or unnecessary hardware using Device Manager.
- Use Windows **ReadyBoost** to cache some startup files to a 256MB+ flash drive, SD card, or CF card. Right-click the device to access the *Properties* option and select the *ReadyBoost* tab. Note that ReadyBoost does not increase performance on a system that boots from a SSD, so Windows 7 (not Vista) disables ReadyBoost as an option when an SSD is in use.
- In Windows 7, use the *System and Security* Control Panel > *Administrative Tools* > *Services*. In XP, use *Control Panel* > *Administrative Tools* > *Services*. Change services that are not needed the moment Windows boots to use the *Automatic (Delayed Start)* option instead of Automatic.

Troubleshooting the Windows Boot Process

Troubleshooting the boot process is sometimes easier to troubleshoot than other type of problems that can occur within the operating system. If the computer locks, has a BSOD, or will not start, try the following:

- Remove the power cord, re-insert the power cord and power the computer on again. Make note of any beeps or error codes. Use these to troubleshoot.
- Determine the last thing that was done before the computer refused to boot. Boot the computer to Safe Mode. Use the System Restore utility to bring the computer back to a date before the issue occurred.

- Boot to Safe Mode and run the SFC (System File Checker) to replace missing or corrupt operating system files or load an appropriate graphics driver.
- Use the Last Known Good Configuration option from the Advanced Boot Options menu.
- For information on recovering the Windows OS, see Chapter 11.
- For information on troubleshooting storage devices, see Chapter 7.

Quite a few things can cause Windows to not boot properly. For example, a non-bootable disk inserted into the floppy drive or media inserted into an optical drive can cause Windows not to boot. If none of the hard drives contain an active partition or if the hard drive's boot sector information is missing or corrupt (see Chapter 7), any of the following messages or events could appear:

- "Invalid partition table"
- "Error loading operating system"
- "Missing operating system"
- "`Boot:` Couldn't find `NTLDR`" (XP)
- "`NTLDR` is missing" (Windows XP)
- "`BOOTMGR` is missing" (Windows Vista and higher)
- "Windows has blocked some startup programs"
- "The Windows boot configuration data file is missing required information" (Windows Vista and higher)
- "Windows could not start because the following file is missing or corrupt"

Also note that if you receive a message that you have an invalid boot disk, a disk read error, or an inaccessible boot device, troubleshoot your hard drive and/or BIOS settings.

If the computer shows "Invalid boot disk," ensure that the BIOS boot order settings are correct, no virus is installed, and that the first boot device has a valid operating system installed or on disc. Depending on the installed OS, you can also use the `fdisk /mbr`, `bootrec /fixmbr`, `bootrec /fixboot`. Use other `bootrec` command options if multiple operating systems are installed.

Tech Tip

How to stop programs that automatically load at startup from running

To disable startup programs, hold down the Shift key during the logon process and keep it held down until the desktop icons appear.

Windows has a wealth of tools and start modes that can be used to troubleshoot the system. If Windows boots, but still has a problem, try to solve the problem without booting into one of these special modes. For example, if one piece of hardware is not working properly and the system boots properly, use Device Manager and the troubleshooting wizards to troubleshoot the problem. Another problem can be caused by an application that loads during startup.

For a permanent change to an application starting automatically, move or delete the startup shortcuts from the one of the following places:

- %*systemdrive*%\Documents and Settings\Username\Start Menu\Programs\Startup
- %*systemdrive*%\Documents and Settings\All Users\Start Menu\Programs\Startup
- %*systemdrive*%\Users\All Users\Microsoft\Windows\Start Menu\Programs\Startup
- %*windir*%\Profiles\Username\Start Menu\Programs\Startup
- %*windir*%\Profiles\All Users\Start Menu\Programs\Startup
- %*windrive*%\Profiles\All Users\Microsoft\Windows\Start Menu\Programs\Startup

If a startup problem appears to occur before the "Starting Windows" logo appears, the causes are typically missing startup files, corrupt files, or hardware problems . The Windows Vista and 7 `bootsect /nt60 all` (or a drive letter instead of `all` if multiple operating systems are installed) can be used to manually repair the boot sector. The `bootsect.exe` file is available from the *Boot* folder of the Windows Vista/7 DVD and can be executed from within Windows Recovery Environment (WinRE) covered later in this chapter or from within Windows. If the

Windows logo appears, but there is a problem before the logon prompt appears, the problem is usually with misconfigured drivers and/or services. If problems occur after the logon window appears, then (1) look to startup applications (hold down the Shift key during startup) or (2) see if the `userinit.exe` file has issues. Use the *Advanced Boot Options* startup menu (press F8 during startup), and from a command prompt, use the `sfc /scannow` command to fix the userinit file.

Windows XP ASR (Automated System Recovery)

ASR (Automated System Recovery) replaced the Emergency Repair Disk used by NT and 2000 Professional and it uses the Windows Backup tool to back up important system files used to start Windows XP. Automated System Recovery does not back up data files (although the Backup program can be used to back up data, too).

To create an Automated System Recovery disk, you will need a 1.44MB floppy disk and media such as a CD or tape (for a tape drive). The floppy is used to boot the system and then you can restore the files if the hard drive crashes or the operating system is inoperable.

To use the disk and media created with Automated System Recovery, you will need the floppy disk created when the system was backed up, the backup media written to when the system was backed up, and the original Windows XP CD. Start the computer using the Windows XP CD. During the Setup process, press the F2 key. A prompt appears to insert the Automated System Recovery floppy disk into the floppy drive. Insert the disk and follow the screen directions to restore the system.

WinRE

In Windows Vista and 7, Microsoft replaced the Recovery Console and ASR with the **WinRE** (Windows Recovery Environment), which is accessed by booting from a Windows Vista or 7 installation DVD > select the language parameters > click *Repair your computer* > select an operating system > click *Next*. Some computers have a recovery partition that would contain these tools or it is available through the Advanced Boot Options F8 menu. See the computer documentation for details. The tools are shown in Figure 12.17 and explained in Table 12.24.

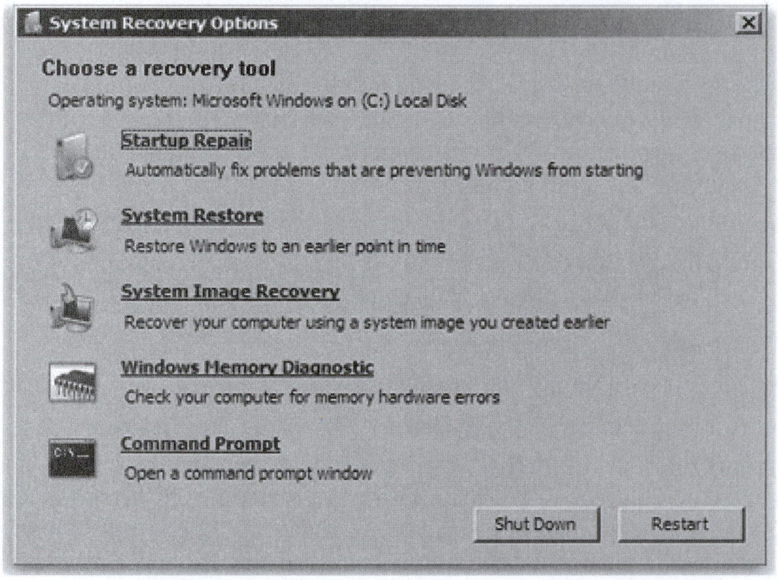

Figure 12.17 Windows 7 WinRE menu

Table 12.24 WinRE tools

Tool	Description
Startup Repair	Analyzes a computer and tries to fix any missing or damaged system files or BCD (Boot Configuration Data) files. This tool can be run multiple times. After a single repair and system reboot, try the tool again (and again). The system could have multiple problems.
System Restore	Works like the System Restore utility in Windows but is used to return the system to an earlier time, such as before a service pack was installed and the system stopped booting.
Complete PC Restore (Vista)/ System Image Recovery (7)	Available in Vista Business, Enterprise, and Ultimate and all versions of Windows 7 to restore the contents of the hard drive from some type of backup media, such as another hard drive or DVDs.
Windows Memory Diagnostic Tool	Used to heavily test RAM modules to see if they are causing the system to not boot. The tool runs tests repeatedly until it is manually stopped. Microsoft states that it is unlikely that repeating the test will result in a newly detected error. An extended test is available from the diagnostic menu.
Command Prompt	Unlike the Windows XP Recovery Console, which has a limited number of executable commands, the Command Prompt option allows execution of any command-line program.

Windows Vista and 7 have a great command-line utility, `bootrec.exe`, which you can use when the Startup Repair option does not work after multiple attempts:

- `bootrec /fixmbr`—Used to resolve MBR issues; writes a Windows Vista or 7 compatible MBR to the system partition.
- `bootrec /fixboot`—Used if the boot sector has been replaced with a non-Windows Vista or 7 boot sector, if the boot sector has become corrupt, or if an earlier Windows version has been installed *after* Windows Vista or 7 was installed and the computer was started with the `ntldr` instead of `bootmgr.exe`.
- `bootrec /scanos`—Used when any Windows Vista or 7 operating system has been installed and is not listed on the Boot Manager menu; scans all disks for any and all versions of Windows Vista or 7.
- `bootrec /rebuildbcd`—Used when the BCD file needs to be rebuilt; gives the option to select the installation to add to the BCD store. If rebuilding the BCD file does not fix the startup issue, the current BCD can be exported, deleted, and then rebuilt. The following commands can be used:

```
bcd edit /export x:\bcd_backup
c:
cd boot
attrib bcd -s -h -r
ren c:\boot\bcd bcd.old
bootrec /rebuildbcd
```

System Configuration Utility

The **System Configuration utility** (`msconfig` command) is used to disable startup programs and services one at a time or several at once. This graphical utility reduces the chances of making typing errors, deleting files, and other misfortunes that occur when technicians work from a command prompt. Only an administrator or a member of the Administrators group can use the System Configuration utility.

To start the System Configuration utility in Windows XP, click *Start > Run >* type `msconfig` and press Enter. In Windows Vista's *Start Search* or 7's *Search programs and files* textbox, type `msconfig`, and press Enter. Figure 12.18 shows the System Configuration utility *General* tab.

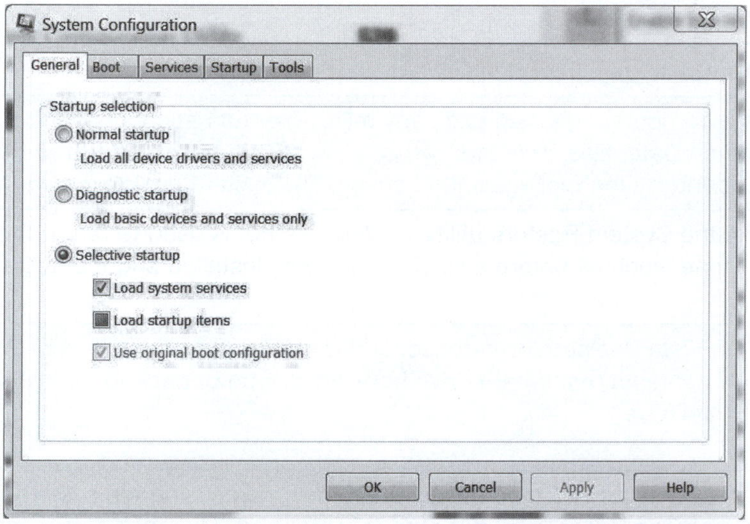

Figure 12.18 Windows 7 System Configuration utility—General tab

In Windows Vista and 7, the SYSTEM.INI, WIN.INI, and BOOT.INI tabs are not available as they are in XP. The first tab is *General*. The *General* tab has three radio buttons: Normal startup, Diagnostic startup, and Selective startup. *Normal startup* is the default option and all device drivers and services load normally when this radio button is selected.

The *Diagnostic startup* radio button is selected when you want to create a clean environment for troubleshooting. When *Diagnostic startup* is chosen and Windows is restarted, the system boots to Safe Mode and only the most basic device drivers and services are active.

The *Selective startup* radio button is the most common troubleshooting tab on the General tab. When *Selective startup* is chosen, you can pick which startup options load. Using the divide-and-conquer method of troubleshooting, find the startup file that is causing boot problems. Start with the first checkbox, *Load system services*, and deselect the checkbox > *OK* and restart the computer. When you determine which file is causing the problem (the problem reappears), click the System Configuration tab that corresponds to the problem file and deselect files until the exact problem file is located.

The *Boot* tab allows you to control and modify the Windows boot environment similarly to the BOOT.INI tab in XP. The *Boot* tab functions include selecting the default operating system and the time allotted to wait for the default operating system to load if no other operating system is chosen from the boot menu in a multiple operating system situation. Advanced options on this tab include defining the number of processors and maximum memory as well as whether *PCI Lock and Detect HAL* are enabled.

The *Services* and *Startup* tabs in the System Configuration window are also quite useful when troubleshooting boot problems. Certain applications, such as an antivirus program or the printer, run as services. Many of these services are started during the boot process. The *Services* tab can be used to disable and enable these boot services. Enable the *Hide all Microsoft Services* option to view and manipulate third-party (non-Microsoft) services. The *Startup* tab allows you to enable and disable Windows-based startup programs. Figure 12.19 shows a sample Startup tab screen.

Tech Tip

The *Tools* tab is useful

The Vista/7 System Configuration Tools tab allows launching such options as Task Manager, Performance Monitor, and Internet Options from Internet Explorer—items that might need to be changed as a result of a startup issue.

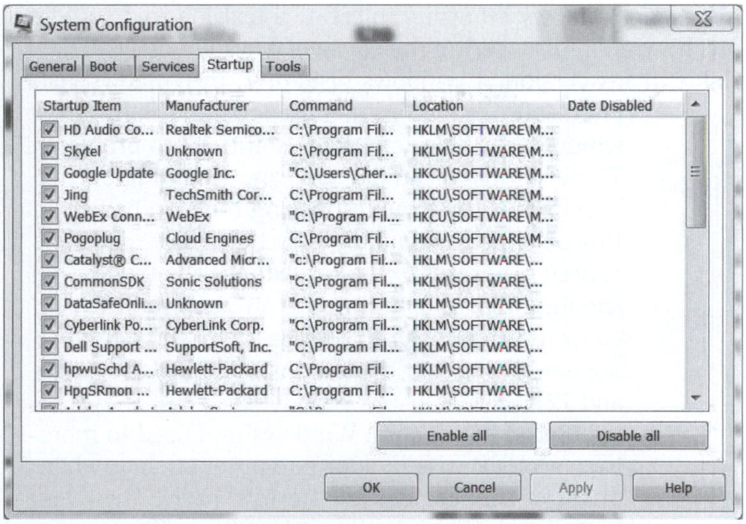

Figure 12.19 System Configuration utility—Startup tab

Task Manager and Event Viewer

Task Manager is a Windows-based utility that displays applications currently loaded into memory, processes that are currently running, processor usage, and memory details. To activate Task Manager, press Ctrl+Alt+Del. Another way of accessing Task Manager is to right-click the taskbar and select *Task Manager* (XP/Vista) or *Start Task Manager* (7). Task Manager is commonly used to kill (stop) programs that have quit responding. Task Manager is also a great way to get a graphical overview of how the system is performing or which programs are using a lot of memory. Labs 12.27 and 12.30 at the end of this chapter demonstrate these concepts. Figure 12.20 shows the Task Manager *Applications* tab that has the list of applications currently running on a computer.

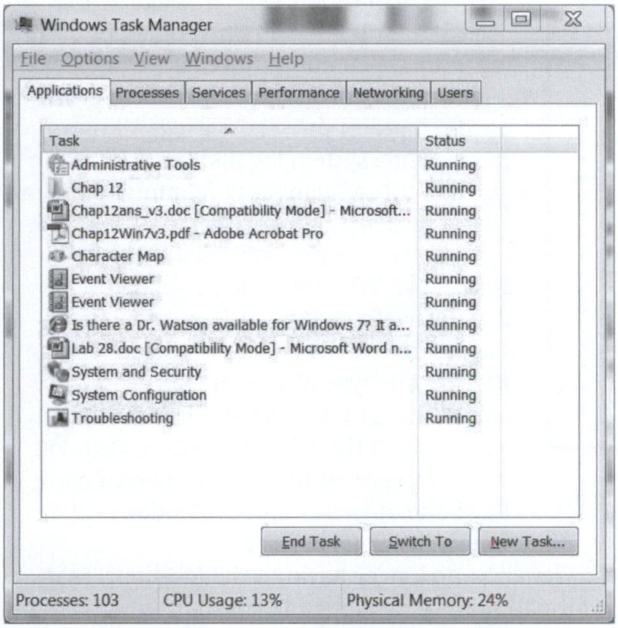

Figure 12.20 Task Manager—Applications tab

Microsoft created the **Dr. Watson** Windows XP utility to create a text log that could be used to help Microsoft and a technician in discovering the cause of a system crash. The Dr. Watson utility is not available in any version of Windows Vista or 7. In Windows Vista, Microsoft has the Problem Reports and Solutions window that helps check for solutions to problems. These solutions can be saved and viewed later. In Windows 7, the troubleshooting tool can be used. From the Start menu, type `troubleshooting` in the *Search programs and files* textbox. The troubleshooting tool lists first in the output list. These control panel links can also be accessed through `msconfig` *Tools* tab, as demonstrated in Labs 12.25 and 12.26.

Tech Tip

What to do if a system is not responding

Once inside the Task Manager window > *Applications* tab > locate and click the troublesome application > *End Task* button. Normally, if an application is causing a problem, the status shows the application as "not responding."

Tech Tip

What to do with a BSOD

Sometimes when Windows crashes, a blue screen with an error code and numbers appears on the screen. Check Event Viewer for a system event. Try to reboot with the power button, but it may require you to remove the computer's power cord, reinsert the power cord, and re-power on the computer. Once restarted, you can research the error message and problem on the Internet.

Event Viewer is a Windows tool used to monitor various events in your computer such as when a driver or service does not start properly. The Event Log (XP) or Windows Event Log (Vista/7) service starts automatically every time a computer boots to Windows. This service is what allows the events to be logged and then Event Viewer is used to see the log.

Access Event Viewer in Windows XP by clicking the *Start* button > *Control Panel* > *Performance and Maintenance* > *Administrative Tools* > *Event Viewer*. In Vista, select the *System and Maintenance* Control Panel or in Windows 7, select the *System and Security* Control Panel > *Administrative Tools* > *Event Viewer*. The left window contains the Event Viewer logs. In Windows XP, these include the application log, the security log, and the system log. The application log displays events associated with a specific program. The programmers who design software decide which events to display in the Event Viewer's application log. The security log displays events such as when different users log in to the computer (both valid and invalid logins). A technician can pick which events are displayed in the security log. All users can view the system log and the application log, but only a member of Administrators can enable security log information.

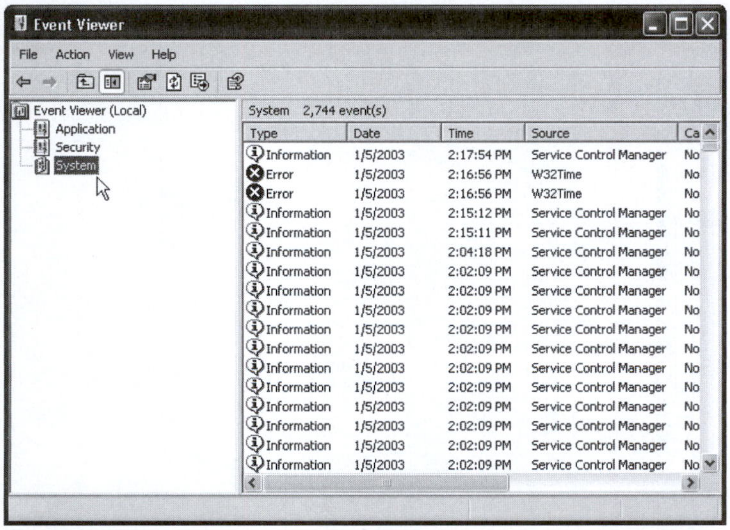

Figure 12.21 Windows XP Event Viewer—System log

The most commonly used log is the system log. The system log displays events that deal with various system components such as a driver or service that loads during startup. The type of system log events cannot be changed or deleted. Click the system log option in the left panel. The system log events displays in the right window. Figure 12.21 shows an example of Windows XP Event Viewer system log.

Windows Vista and 7 improve on Event Viewer by no longer having a 300MB limit, as in prior versions, by allowing Event Viewer information to be forwarded to a remote computer, and by allowing the collection of events from multiple remote computers. Windows Vista/7 Event Viewer has two types of logs: Windows logs and Applications and Services logs (see Figure 12.22).

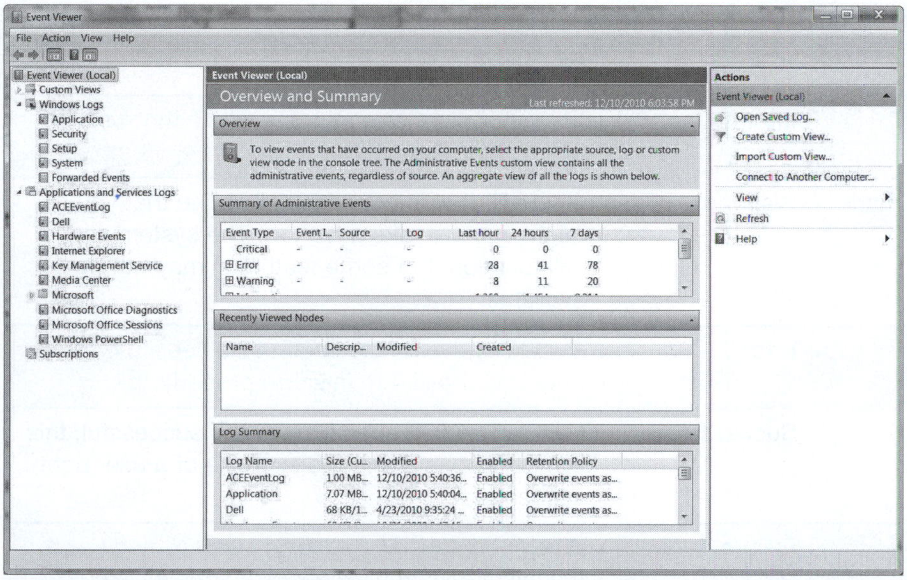

Figure 12.22 Windows 7 Event Viewer

Within the Windows Logs section, there are the traditional application, security, and system logs, along with two new ones: setup and forwarded events. Also, there is a new Applications and Services Logs section. Table 12.25 summarizes the types of things you might see in these logs. Event Viewer can display five different types of events. The events and related symbols are shown in Table 12.26.

Table 12.25 Windows Vista/7 Event Viewer logs

Major log category	Log	Description
Windows Logs	Application	Contains events logged by software applications. The company who writes the software applications decide what to log.
	Security	Contains events specified by administrators such as valid and invalid logon attempts, and network share usage.
	Setup	Contains setup events logged by software applications.
	System	Contains Windows system events such as when a driver or service fails to load or start.
	Forwarded Events	Contains events from remote computers.
Applications and Services Logs	Vendor-specific	Contains logs from a specific application or Windows component. The logs can be one of four types: admin, operational, analytic, and debug. The admin log is for normal users and technical support staff. The operational event is used by technical staff to analyze a problem. The analytic and debug events would more likely be used by the application developer. Both create a large amount of entries and should be used for a short period of time only.

Table 12.26 **Event Viewer symbols**

Symbol	Type of event	Description
Lowercase "i"	Information	Normal system operations such as the system being initialized or shut down.
Exclamation mark	Warning	An event that is not critical, but one that you might want to take a look at. The system can still function, but some feature(s) may not be available.
X	Error	A specific event failed such as a service or device that failed to initialize properly.
Yellow key	Success Audit	You can audit a specific event. If successful, this symbol appears and the exercise of a user right succeeded.
Yellow lock	Failure Audit	When you specify a specific event to audit and the event fails, the yellow lock appears. An example is when you are auditing a system login and someone tries to log in that does not have a valid username or password, then the system creates a Failure Audit event.

Double-click an Event Viewer event to see more information about it. Figure 12.23 shows a System log warning event window. Event viewer logs can be saved as files and viewed later. This is especially useful with intermittent problems. Use the *Action* menu item (XP) or *Actions* section (Vista/7) to save and retrieve saved event viewer log files.

Tech Tip

What to do if the Event Viewer log is full

Start Event Viewer > *Action* menu option > *Properties* > *General* tab > *Clear log* button. The *Log Size* option may need to be changed: *Overwrite events older than 0 days, Maximum log size, or Overwrite events as needed.*

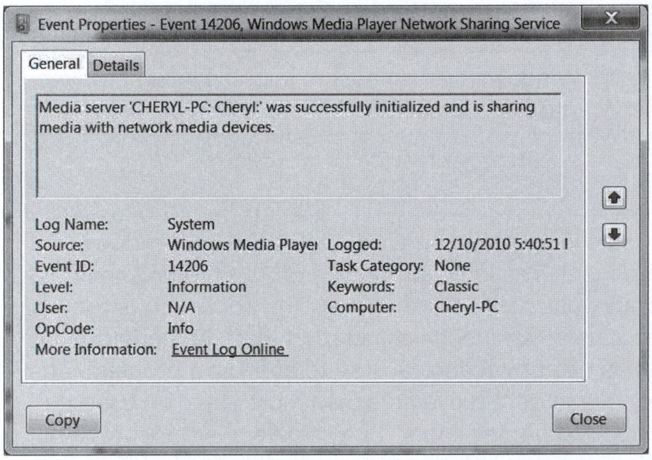

Figure 12.23 **Event Viewer—System log event**

Troubleshooting a Service That Does Not Start

Some Windows services start automatically each time the computer boots. If one of these services has a problem, there is normally an error message that appears during the boot sequence. You can use the System Configuration utility (`msconfig`) previously discussed to enable and disable startup services. You can also use Event Viewer to see if the service loaded properly. Another program that you can use is the Services snap-in used from the Computer Management tool. Or, from a command prompt type **`services.msc`**, and press Enter. The *Services* tool allows you to view what services have been started and stopped and, if desired, allows you to stop a service. Open the Services snap-in and double-click any service.

The Service window opens and on the General tab are the *Stop* and *Start* buttons that can be used to control the service. Figure 12.24 shows the iPod service. The service loads every time the computer starts. Notice in Figure 12.24 that because the iPod service is already started, the only action that can be performed is to stop the service by clicking the *Stop* button.

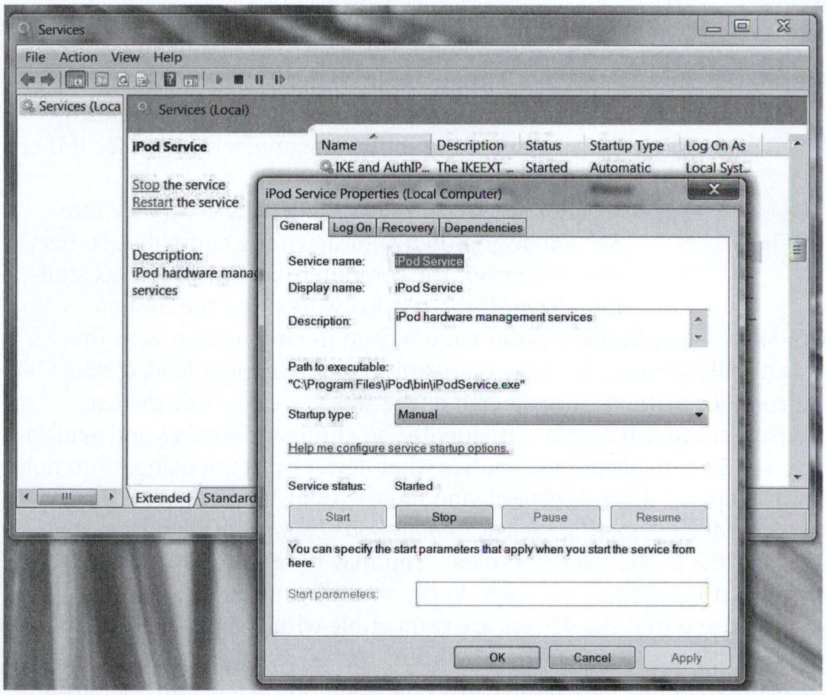

Figure 12.24 Services snap-in—General tab window

Windows Reboots

One of the hardest problems to solve is an intermittent problem and when Windows reboots spontaneously or shuts down spontaneously, a lot of different things could be the issue. Spontaneous reboots could be caused by a newly installed Windows update, a newly installed application, or a newly updated driver. A corrupt device driver could also be the culprit, but that is a hard one to find. An Internet search on your specific hardware devices might speed up the troubleshooting process. A spontaneous reboot can also be caused by a virus or malware. See Chapter 15 for more on those security issues. Other hardware issues could be RAM, processor, video card, and hard drive. You can quickly see why spontaneous reboots would be one of the hardest ones to narrow the field.

A spontaneous reboot however, is different from a spontaneous shut down. A spontaneous shut down tends to be a heat related problem. Check CPU and case fans. Some BIOS menus have options that display internal temperatures. Start taking readings on that. A failing CPU, overloaded power supply, or failing power supply could also cause a spontaneous shut down.

Shutdown Problems

Windows should be shut down properly when all work is finished. Before Windows can shut down, the operating system sends a message to all devices, services, and applications. Each device or system service that is running sends a message back saying it is okay to shut down now. Any active application saves data that has not been previously saved and sends a message back to the operating system that it is okay to shut down.

If the system has trouble shutting down, it is due to devices, services, or applications. The most common problem is an application that does not respond. When this happens, press Ctrl+Alt+Del to access Task Manager. Manually stop any applications that show a status of not responding. You can also click any other applications and stop them to see if they are causing the problem. Sometimes a program will not show a status of not responding until you try to manually stop the application from within Task Manager. If a single application continually prevents Windows from shutting down, contact the software manufacturer to see if there is a fix or check online.

Tech Tip

Try the restart option instead of the shutdown option

If you cannot stop the problem application or determine whether the problem is a service or hardware, try restarting the computer instead of shutting down. Once the computer restarts, try shutting down again. As a last resort, use the computer power button to power the computer off.

For services problems, boot the computer into Safe Mode and then shut down the computer. Notice whether or not the computer had any problems shutting down. If the process works, use the System Configuration window *General* tab *Selective startup* radio button in conjunction with the *Services* tab to selectively disable services. Because there are so many services loaded, you might try the divide and conquer method—disable half of the services to narrow the list.

A device does not cause a shutdown problem frequently, so eliminate services and applications first. Then, while working on the computer, notice what devices you are using. Common devices are video, hard drive, optical drive, keyboard, and mouse. Boot to the Advanced Boot Options menu by pressing F8 during booting. Select *Enable Boot Logging*. Once the system boots, locate the `ntbtlog.txt` file in the *Windows* folder. You may have to set folder options within Windows Explorer to list the file and access it. Verify that all your devices have the most up-to-date drivers loaded and that the drivers are compatible with the installed version of Windows.

Sometimes, USB or IEEE 1394 FireWire ports can stop a computer from shutting down or powering off. Check the event logs to see if any device did not enter a suspend state. A feature called USB selective suspend allows the Windows hub driver to suspend a particular USB port and not affect the other USB ports. This is particularly important to laptops, netbooks, and ultrabooks because of power consumption. Suspending USB devices when the device is not in use conserves power. If this is causing the problem, this default behavior can be modified using the *Power options* Control Panel link and accessing the *Advanced power settings*.

Monitoring System Performance

It is important for a technician to understand how a computer is performing and to be able to analyze why a computer might be running slow. In order to do that, a technician must know what applications are being run on the computer and their effects on the computer resources. A technician must also be able to monitor the computer's resource usage when problems occur, change the configuration as needed, and observe the results of the configuration change.

Utilities commonly used to monitor system performance include Task Manager, Windows XP's System Monitor and Performance Logs and Alerts, and Windows Vista/7's Reliability Monitor and Performance Monitor. Task Manager is used to monitor your current system's performance. **System Monitor** is used to monitor real-time data about specific computer components. **Performance Logs and Alerts** allows creating logs about the computer performance and creating alerts that notify you when a specific instance being monitored reaches a defined threshold. It includes a summary graph of processor and memory usage.

Windows Vista/7 **Reliability Monitor** provides a visual graph of system stability and details on events that might have affected the computer's reliability. **Performance Monitor** is a visual graph in real time or from a saved log file providing data on specific computer components.

Although Task Manager has been discussed in a previous section, how to use it to monitor computer performance was not discussed. Access Task Manager and click the *Make Performance* tab. Task Manager immediately starts gathering CPU and memory usage statistics and displays them in graph form in the window as shown in Figure 12.25.

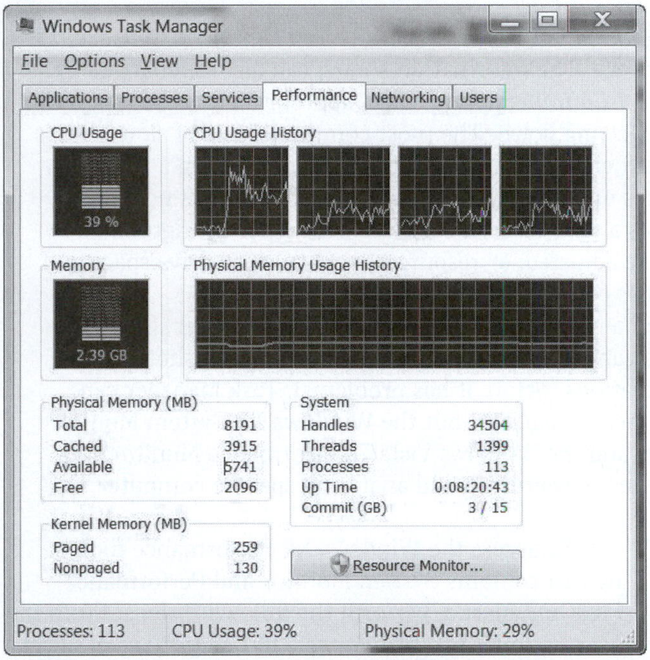

Figure 12.25 Task Manager—Performance tab

What to do if you think memory is the problem

Tech Tip

You can add RAM; create multiple paging files when multiple hard drives are installed in the system; manually set the paging file size; run one application at a time; don't use Aero (Vista/7); close unnecessary windows; upgrade or add another hard drive; delete unused files; defragment the hard drive.

The first window on the left, CPU Usage, shows the processor usage percentage, or what percentage of time the processor is working. Actually, the percentage of time the processor is running a thread is a more accurate statement. A thread is a type of Windows object that runs application instructions. The window on the right, CPU Usage History, is a graph of how busy the processor is over a period of time.

The second window on the left for Windows XP is PF Usage, and it shows the amount of virtual memory (the paging file) being used. If the display shows that the paging file is near the maximum, you can adjust the page file size with the following steps:

1. Click the *Start* button and select *Control Panel*.
2. Use the *Performance and Maintenance Control Panel* > *System* > *Advanced* tab > *Performance* section *Settings* button.
3. Click the *Advanced* tab, locate the *Virtual Memory* section, and click the *Change* button.

In Vista or 7, the second window on the left displays memory usage for the current moment. The graphic on the right is memory usage over time. To see how much memory an individual process is using, use the *Processes* tab and locate the program executable file. The CPU and memory usage show in separate columns on the *Processes* tab.

Memory is a frequent bottleneck for computer performance issues. Task Manager can also be used to see the total amount of RAM installed and how much RAM is available. Look in the *Physical Memory* information section of the Task Manager *Performance* tab to see this information.

Task Manager also has the *Networking* tab that is useful to technicians. The *Networking* tab shows a graph of network performance. The information shown can also be changed by selecting the *View* menu option > *Select Columns* option select appropriate checkboxes > *OK*.

Sometimes a computer can start slowing down. The most common cause of slowdown is that the computer's resources are insufficient or an application is monopolizing a particular resource such as memory. Other causes of slowdowns include a resource that is not functioning properly or is outdated, such as a hard drive; a resource that is not configured for maximum performance and needs to be adjusted; or resources, such as hard drive space and memory, that are not sharing workloads properly and need to be adjusted.

Viewing system performance when a problem occurs is good, but it is easier if the normal performance is known. A baseline can help with this. A **baseline** is a snapshot of computer performance during normal operations (before it has problems). Task Manager can be used to get an idea of what normal performance is, but the Windows XP System Monitor and Performance Logs and Alerts tools and the Windows Vista/7 Performance Monitor and Reliability Monitor tools are better suited to capturing and analyzing specific computer resource data.

Tech Tip

When do I need to do a baseline?

A baseline report is needed before a computer slowdown occurs.

To access the Windows XP Performance tool (which contains System Monitor and Performance Logs and Alerts), perform the following steps: From the *Start* menu > *Control Panel* > in *Category view* select *Performance and Maintenance* > *Administrative Tools* > double-click *Performance*.

Another way to access the Performance tool is from a command prompt by typing `perfmon.msc` and pressing Enter. In Windows XP, click the *System Monitor* option and the tool starts collecting and displaying real-time data about the local computer or, if configured, from remote computers. A previously captured log file can also be loaded. Data can be displayed in Graph, Histogram, and Report views.

In Windows Vista and 7, select the *Performance Monitor* option from the left pane in the *Reliability and Performance* tool. In Windows 7, use the *System and Security* Control Panel > *Administrative Tools* > double-click *Performance Monitor*. Inside Performance Monitor, counters are used. A **counter** is a specific measurement for an object. Common objects include cache, memory, paging file, physical disk, processor, network interface, system, and thread. Select the + (plus sign) in Performance Monitor to select various counters. At the bottom of the window is a legend for interpreting the graph including what color is used for each of the performance measures and what counter is being used. Table 12.27 shows common counters used while within Performance Monitor. Figure 12.26 shows an example of the Performance Monitor within Windows 7.

Table 12.27 Performance Monitor counters

Computer component	Object name	Counters
Memory	Memory	Available Bytes and Cache Bytes
Hard Disk	Physical Disk	Disk Reads/sec and Disk Writes/sec
Hard Disk	Logical Disk	% Free Space
Processor	Processor	% Processor Time (All instances)

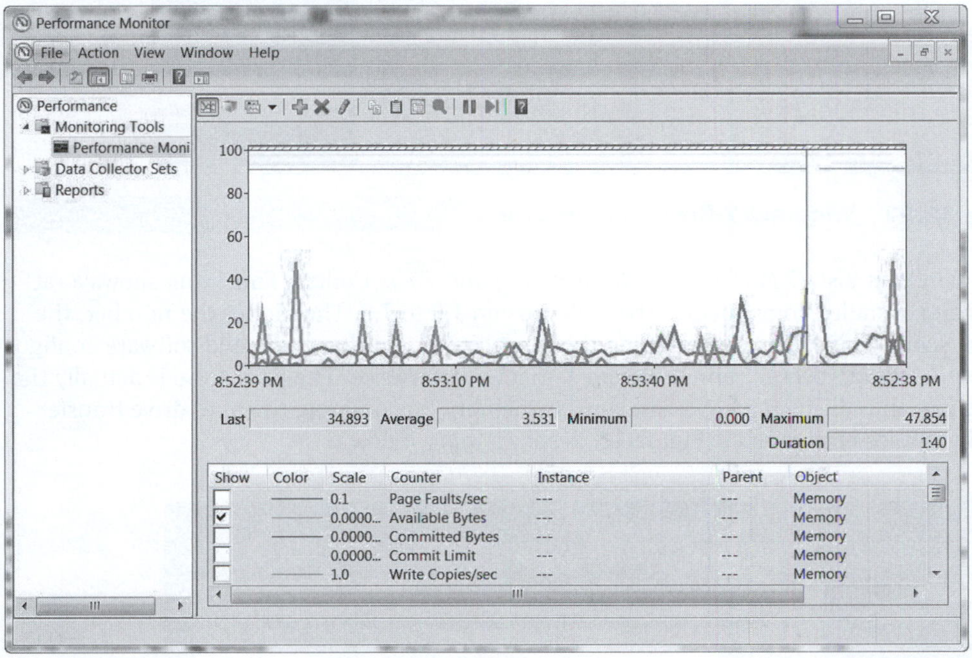

Figure 12.26 Windows 7 Performance Monitor

The Windows 7 **Resource Monitor** (previously found on the main page of Windows Vista's *Performance Monitor* option) is a nice graphical tool that requires little work, but shows the main components of a system. Access the tool by selecting the *Open Resource Monitor* link from within the Performance Monitor window or access the *System and Security* Control Panel > *System* > *Performance Information and Tools* link at the bottom of the left panel > *Advanced tools* > *Open Resource Monitor*. Figure 12.27 shows the Resource Monitor in Windows 7.

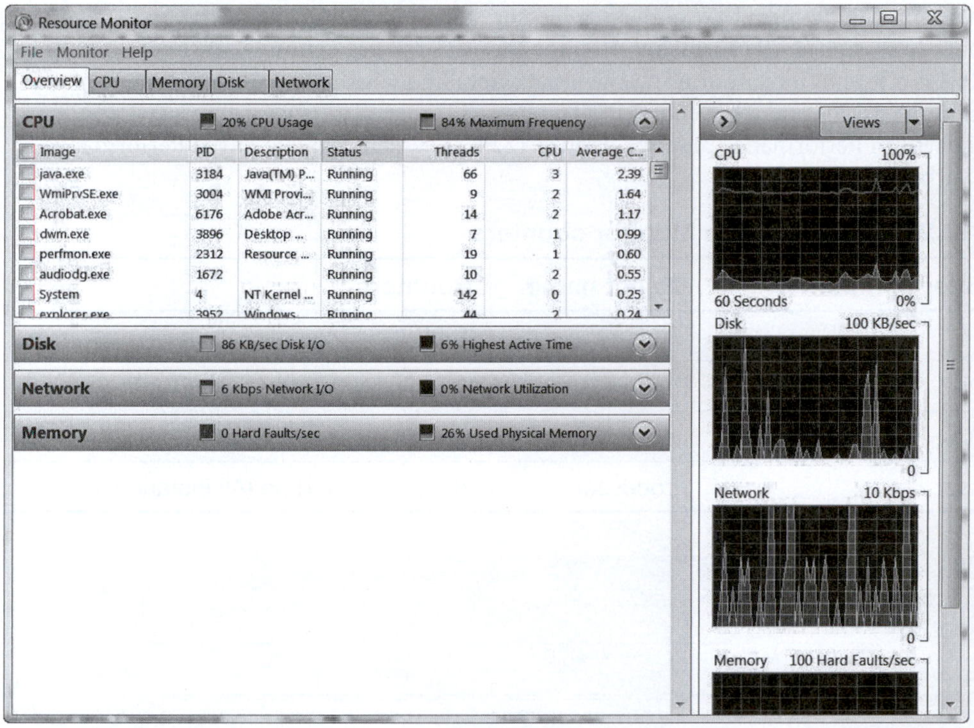

Figure 12.27 Windows 7 Resource Monitor

The Windows Vista/7 *Performance Information and Tools* Control Panel link shows a rating for major installed components. The scale is from 1.0 to 7.9. The higher the number, the better the score. This rating is measuring the capability of your hardware and software configuration to give you an overall rating for your Windows experience. The base score is actually the lowest rate of an individual component such as memory, the desktop, the hard drive transfer rate, and graphics performance. Figure 12.28 shows this window.

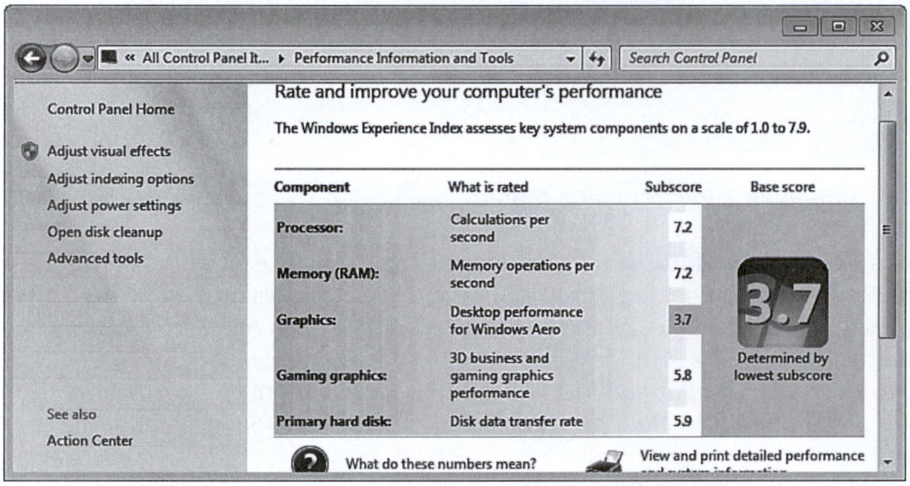

Figure 12.28 Windows 7 Performance Information and Tools

Running any performance monitor tool affects the computer performance, especially when using the Graph view and sampling large amounts of data. The following steps help when running any performance monitoring tool:

1. Turn off any screen saver.
2. Use *Report* view instead of Graph view to save on resources.

3. Keep the number of counters being monitored to a minimum.
4. Sample at longer intervals such as 10 to 15 minutes rather than just a few seconds or minutes apart.

A tool that is only available in XP is Dr. Watson. Dr. Watson is a utility that automatically loads when an application starts. Dr. Watson can detect and display troubleshooting information as well as create a text log file (`drwtsn32.log`) when a system or application error occurs. A technician might need this information when communicating with Microsoft or the application developer's technical support. Make notes of any messages that appear on the screen when any type of problem occurs.

To start Dr. Watson in Windows XP, click the *Start* button > *Run* > type `drwtsn32` and press Enter. Click the application error and click the *View* button. The default location for the log file is C:\Documents and Settings\All Users\Application Data\Microsoft\DrWatson. When an error occurs, Dr. Watson appends information to the end of this log file.

Microsoft Vista and 7 do not include the Dr. Watson tool but has the Problem Reports and Solutions window instead. The settings allow Windows Vista/7 to automatically report problems and check for solutions, to check for solutions only when a problem occurs, or to report problems and check for solutions at any time. In Vista, access the *System and Maintenance* Control Panel > *Problem Reports and Solutions* link. In Windows 7, access the *System and Security* Control Panel > *Action Center* > *Maintenance* section. See Figure 12.29 and notice the *Check for solutions* link.

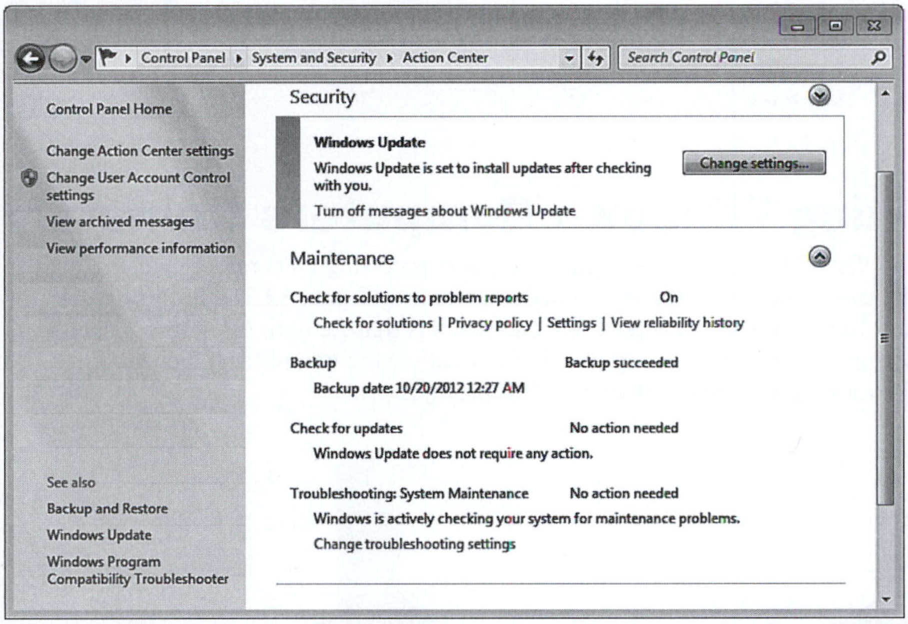

Figure 12.29 Action Center > Maintenance section

Windows Vista and 7 handle the logs and reports differently than Windows XP. A **data collector set**, which organizes data to be viewed, logged, and reviewed later, can contain performance counters, event trace data and system information such as registry key values. To create a data collector set, use the Performance Monitor tool to create counters to monitor. From the *Action* menu item, select *New* > *Data Collector Set*. Type a name for the set and click *Next*. The default directory for the saved set is the *%systemdrive%/PerfLogs/Admin/* folder. Click *Finish*.

Expand the *Data Collector Sets* item in the left pane and expand the *User Defined* section. Right-click the saved performance monitor and select *Start*. The data gathering starts. Right-click the data collector set name again and select *Stop*. Expand the *Reports* section and the *User Defined* area. Expand the named data collector set and double-click the saved file.

The Vista/7 Reliability Monitor is also new, and it is used to give a visual and detailed report on the reliability of the computer by category. The details are to help technicians troubleshoot the cause of something that causes the system to become unreliable. In Vista, the Reliability Monitor is found as an option within the Reliability and Performance Monitor. In Windows 7 it is a separate tool found by typing `reliability monitor` in the *Search programs and files* textbox from the *Start* menu. Figure 12.30 shows this tool.

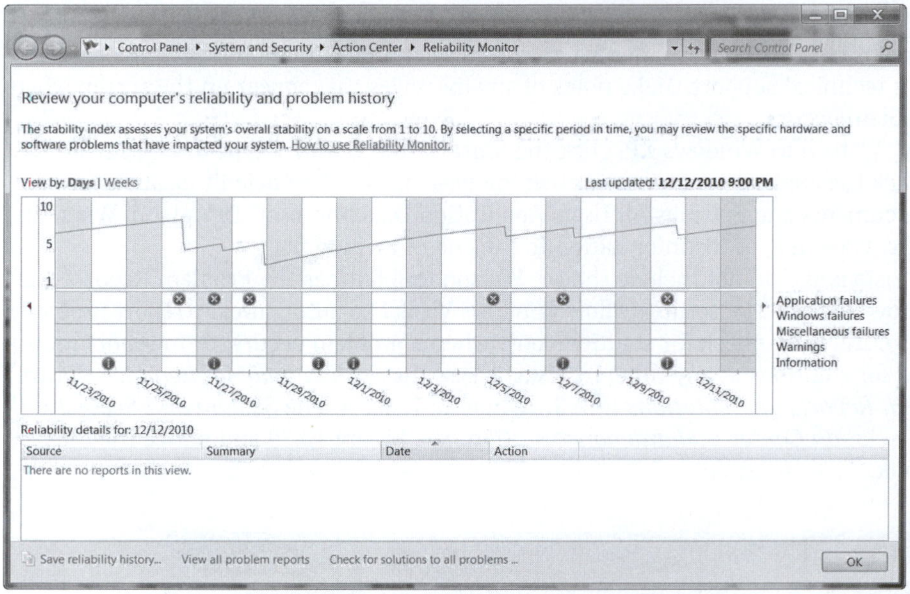

Figure 12.30 Windows 7 Reliability Monitor

Supporting Windows Computers Remotely

Windows XP and Vista/7 Professional and higher support accessing a PC remotely using two Microsoft products—Remote Desktop and Remote Assistance (Figure 12.31). Both products allow a computer to be accessed remotely. The difference is that Remote Assistance displays a prompt at the remote computer asking permission to allow the computer to be viewed remotely and Remote Desktop does not display this prompt.

Figure 12.31 Remote service

Using Remote Desktop (the **mstsc** command) requires the following elements:

- The remote desktop must have some type of network connectivity.
- The computer used to access the remote desktop must run Windows XP Professional, Windows Vista/7 Professional or higher, Windows Server, or must have some type of terminal services running.
- Any firewalls between the two computers must allow ports 3389 and 80 to be open.
- The remote PC must have the Remote Desktop application installed.
- You need to know the computer name of the remote PC.
- You need to have a user account with a password on the remote PC.

When you are on a computer that is remotely accessing another computer, there is a bar across the top of the screen that contains the remote computer name. This is how you know that you are on another computer. The user on the remote computer is logged off.

Both Remote Desktop and Remote Assistance are useful for those working a help desk and for technicians who must support computers located in other locations. With Remote Assistance, one computer user (the Expert) views another computer user's (the Novice) desktop using a secure connection.

Remote Assistance (`msra` command) can be initiated using any of the following methods:

- Windows Messenger service
- Email an invitation
- Send an invitation as an email attachment
- Use Easy Connect (Windows 7 only)

Remote Desktop is disabled by default in Windows Vista and 7. Open *Windows Explorer* and right-click *Computer* > *Properties* > *Remote Settings* link from left panel. In the Windows Vista and 7 environment, Remote Assistance now supports computers that use NAT (network address translation); however, you may have to go into the Windows Firewall application and in the left panel select *Allow a program through Windows Firewall*. Select the *Exceptions* tab and locate *Remote Assistance*. You must also set up a password for the guest user and manually send the password to the person being invited to take over the computer. In Windows 7, to use Windows Remote Assistance, type `remote assistance` in the *Search files and folders* textbox. Click the *Windows Remote Assistance* option. See Figure 12.32 to see the available options.

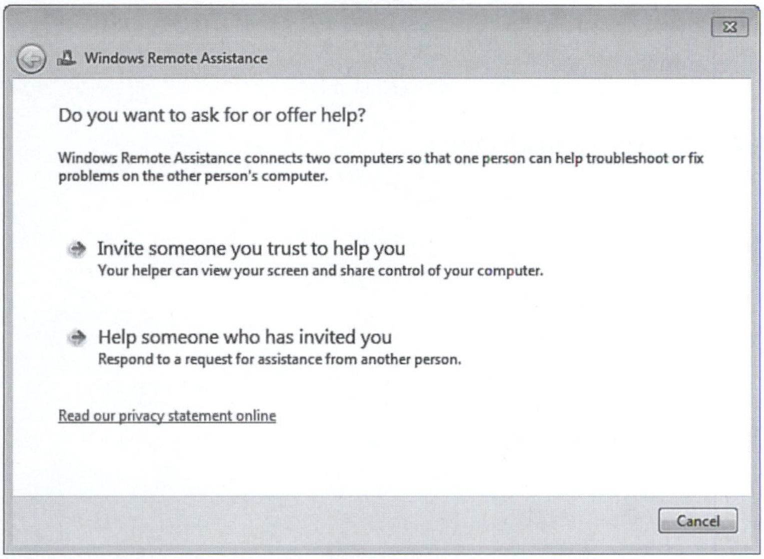

Figure 12.32 Windows Remote Assistance

Preventive Maintenance for Your Operating System

Your operating system is a key component of a working system. Preventive maintenance can help avoid issues and reduce downtime when properly applied. No application or hardware can work without an operating system. It is important that you keep your operating system healthy. The following suggestions can help:

- Always have an antivirus software program that has current virus definitions.
- Make frequent data backups.
- Have a backup of your operating system. Many external hard drives include backup software. Remember that Windows XP Home and Vista Home Basic/Premium do not include a backup utility.
- Ensure that the System Restore utility is enabled.
- Update the operating system with service packs and patches.
- Use the Task Scheduler tool to automate some of the preventive maintenance tasks. You can use the `at` command (type `at /?` to see the options) to create a script file or have an application run at a specific time.

Soft Skills—Avoiding Burnout

Many technicians get tired of the fast pace of technology (see Figure 12.33). As a person matures, it seems to takes more effort to stay current in the skills required for business. One of the attractions to technology for many students is how technology is always changing; however, it is this speed of change that provides such a challenge even to seasoned veterans. Sometimes, a technician is in the same job for more than three years, and burnout is evident. Burnout—commonly caused by too much work and stress—is a mental state that can also affect emotional and physical capabilities. Technicians should monitor their own attitude and mental state constantly and watch for warning signs associated with burnout:

- Overreaction to common situations
- Constant tiredness
- Reduced productivity
- Poor attitude
- Lack of patience with customers or peers
- Feeling of a loss of control
- Use of food, drink, or drugs as coping mechanisms

Figure 12.33 Burnout

Burnout can be prevented and dealt with if it is recognized. Working too much, having too many responsibilities, and expecting too much of yourself can all lead to burnout. The following list can help you recognize and cope with burnout:

- Take vacations during which you do not stay in contact with work.
- Set reachable goals, even on a daily basis.
- Take a couple breaks during the day and do something nontechnical.
- Learn something new that is not related to technology.
- Have good eating, sleeping, and exercising routines.
- Subscribe to a positive saying or joke of the day.

Chapter Summary

- Windows operating systems can be 32-bit or 64-bit. The 32-bit versions are limited to a maximum of 4GB of RAM. 32-bit operating systems or applications are sometimes referred to as x86 instead of 32-bit.
- Windows operating systems come in different editions that have various features and tools. For example, the Home versions cannot join corporate network domains or encrypt files/folders.
- Windows XP has WFP and Windows Vista/7 have WRP to protect the key operating system files. `sfc /scannow` checks system files.
- There are specific operating system in-place upgrade paths that are permitted. Otherwise, a clean install must be performed. You must activate the Windows license by phone or Internet. A repair installation is performed when Windows has to be reloaded. Use the Upgrade Advisor before upgrading Windows.
- Multiple operating systems can be installed. (Install the oldest one first, and install the operating systems on separate partitions.) Virtualization can also be used to have multiple operating systems installed.
- Compatibility mode, Windows XP Mode, or virtualization can be used to allow older applications to operate properly.
- No machine should be deployed without antivirus software installed. Symptoms of a virus include the computer not booting, computer running slowly, hard drive activity increases, files are missing, applications do not work or do not work properly, unusual messages or graphics appear, etc.
- Corporate Windows deployment involves creating a master image and deploying that image across a network. Deployment methods include PXE boot, unattended installations. LTI, and remote network installation. Network bandwidth is affected by imaging.
- Operating system installation failures are often caused by lack of planning for the installation: insufficient or incompatible hardware, incompatible software, and lack of operating-specific drivers.
- A computer that uses virtualization must have more hardware than a single operating system environment.
- To back up the Windows registry, use regedit, the Backup utility, or the System Restore tool.
- Windows updates include device driver updates. Use the driver roll back feature or System Restore when an update causes the system to not work.
- The Computer Management console is used to access System tools (Task Scheduler, Event Viewer, Shared Folders, Local Users and Groups, Performance, and Device Manager), Storage, and Services and Applications.
- The Advanced Boot Options menu is commonly used when the tools within Windows cannot be used in the normal boot environment. The most commonly used options are Safe Mode, Safe Mode with Networking, Enable low resolution (Vista/7), Last Known Good Configuration, Disable automatic restart on system failure (Vista/7), Disable driver signature enforcement (Vista/7), and Repair Your Computer (Vista/7).
- The `bootrec` command can be used to detect and repair master boot issues, operating system files, or the boot sector.
- The System Configuration utility (`msconfig`) can be used to control what applications load during the boot process.
- Task Manager can be used to display system performance, stop applications that are not working properly, and to view which applications and processes are taking up memory.
- Event Viewer logs issues with applications and the operating system to provide a historical record and timeline of when things occur.

- Remote Assistance (the `msra` command) and Remote Desktop (the `mstsc` command) are used to control and use a remote computer. Remote Assistance displays a prompt requesting permission.
- Task Scheduler can be used to perform preventive maintenance on a regular basis. Preventive maintenance can reduce downtime and includes keeping the operating system and applications patched, keeping the antivirus definitions current, and keeping the hard drive defragmented and with ample space.
- Technicians can do positive things to avoid burnout including getting good rest, avoiding drugs and alcohol, do non-technical things, and have good time-management skills.

Key Terms

Review Questions

1. What is the maximum amount of RAM that can be recognized by any version of 32-bit Windows 7?
2. A customer has an older 16-bit game as well as some newer 32-bit games. The customer is considering upgrading to 64-bit Windows 7. Will there be any issues with this? If so, what are they and how might they be resolved?

3. What `sfc` switch is used to replace a corrupt system file in Windows 7?
4. List three steps to be taken *before* installing Windows XP, Vista, or 7.

5. [Yes | No] Is the Upgrade Advisor tool available from the Windows Vista or 7 installation disc?
6. What Microsoft tool checks software applications to see if they will run after Windows 7 upgrade is installed?
7. [T | F] Microsoft requires Windows 7 activation within 10 days of installation.
8. A large college would most likely use [MAK | KMS] for activating Windows 7 licenses.
9. How is network bandwidth affected when computer cloning is being performed?
10. List two solutions for having both Windows 7 and one other operating system?
11. [T | F] Existing restore points are deleted if Windows is re-installed.
12. [T | F] Device drivers are specific for a particular Windows operating system version.
13. In what way does a Windows update affect device drivers?
14. What user group is allowed to perform the driver roll back?
15. If a device has to be manually installed in Windows 7, what utility is used and what file extension is required for the driver?
16. What is the purpose of the System Restore utility?
17. You just installed a new sound card and loaded the driver, but when Windows boots, the computer locks. What boot option should you use to help with this problem?
18. When would a technician use Event Viewer?
19. Detail specifically how Task Manager can be used to monitor computer performance?
20. List three things a student can do to avoid burnout in school.

Exercises

Lab 12.1 Windows XP Clean Installation

Objective: To be able to install Windows XP on a hard drive that does not have an operating system installed or any partitions

Parts: Computer with a hard drive that does not have partitions or an operating system installed and that has a CD drive installed

Windows XP CD

Note: If partitions currently exist on the hard drive, see Chapter 7 for information on removing partitions.

Procedure: Complete the following procedure and answer the accompanying questions.

1. Insert the Windows XP CD into the optical drive and turn on the computer. Some computers require you to press a key or require special BIOS settings to boot from the CD. Perform the appropriate steps to allow the computer to boot from the CD. The setup screen displays. If the CD is an evaluation copy of XP, press Enter to display the licensing agreement.
2. Press F8 to accept the licensing agreement. The hard drive partitioning screen appears.

3. Check with the instructor on how much space is desired for the partition. The partition must be a minimum of 2GB.

   What size partition did you choose for the Windows XP installation?

4. Select a hard drive area that is unpartitioned and press C to create a partition. A prompt appears asking for the partition size. Use the answer obtained in Step 3 and enter this information. Note that Enter can be pressed to use all available space for the partition. Press Enter to install Windows XP on the partition just created.

5. A screen appears prompting you to format the newly created partition. Select *NTFS* as the type of file system used. The drive is formatted, and setup files are copied to the drive.

6. When prompted to restart the computer, remove the CD from the drive and press Enter.

7. When prompted to insert the CD into the drive, re-insert the Windows XP CD into the drive and click the *OK* button.

8. Accept the default path for the Windows XP installation by clicking the *OK* button. After copying more files, you are prompted for regional settings. Set the appropriate language and click *Next*.

9. The Personalize Your Software page appears. This is what applications use for product registration and document identification. Leave this information blank and click the *Next* button. The Product Key page appears.

10. Enter the product key located on the back of the Windows XP case, written on the CD, or provided by the student assistant or instructor. Click the *Next* button.

    Check with the lab assistant or instructor for the name that will be given to the computer as well as the Administrator password.

    Document this information.

    Computer name: ______________________

    Administrator password: ____________________________

11. The setup program prompts for the computer name and Administrator password. Type the computer name and Administrator password. Click the *Next* button.

12. If a modem is installed, the modem dialing information is displayed. The correct country, area code, number to access an outside line, and so on, are required. Contact the lab assistant or instructor for this information, enter it, and click the *Next* button. If a modem is not installed (or after this information is entered), the date and time page appears. Set the date and time as appropriate and click the *Next* button.

13. If a network card is installed in the computer, the network settings page displays. Enter the appropriate networking information provided by the instructor and click *Next*. The setup process continues copying files and installing the operating system and then restarts the computer. After the restart, the Welcome to Microsoft Windows screen appears.

    Does the welcome screen appear? Show this screen to the instructor.

Instructor initials: ____________

14. Click the *Next* button and the *Internet Connection* screen appears. Select *skip this step*.

15. When asked if you want to activate Windows, select the *wait until later* option.

16. When prompted, do not select to set up user accounts. This process is covered in another lab.

17. Click the *Finish* button.

    Does Windows boot properly after the installation process?

Instructor initials: ____________

Lab 12.2 Windows XP Upgrade Installation

Objective: To be able to install Windows XP on a hard drive that already has an operating system installed

Parts: Computer with a hard drive that has Windows 98, Windows Me, NT Workstation 4.0, or Windows 2000 installed and that has an optical drive installed

Windows XP CD

Procedure: Complete the following procedure and answer the accompanying questions.

1. Power on the computer and log on as necessary. Contact the instructor or lab assistant for the user ID and password, if necessary. Insert the Windows XP CD into the CD-ROM drive. The Welcome to Microsoft Windows XP screen should appear. Click *Install Windows XP*. The setup process collects information about the computer to ensure it is upgradable.
2. When asked what type of installation to use, select *Upgrade* and click the *Next* button.
3. Click the radio button to accept the licensing agreement and click the *Next* button.
4. Enter the product key located on the back of the CD case, written on the CD, or provided by the instructor or lab assistant and click the *Next* button.
5. The dynamic update is optional and can be used only if an Internet connection is available. The dynamic update updates installation files. Contact the instructor or lab assistant to determine if the dynamic update is necessary.

   Was the dynamic update performed?
6. The setup process copies installation files and restarts. When prompted to choose a Windows installation, *do not select anything*. Windows automatically selects the correct version. The XP logo appears, more files are copied, and the computer reboots again.
7. You may be asked to enter a computer name if the old computer name is not appropriate. If necessary, type an appropriate computer name and click the *Next* button. The Tour Windows screen appears.
8. When asked to activate the product, select the option to bypass this step. Click the *Finish* button.
9. When asked to setup user accounts, contact the instructor or lab assistant to verify if any should be created.

   Were any user accounts created? If so, list them.
10. Click the *Next* button and the XP desktop appears.

Lab 12.3 Windows 7 Installation

Objective: To be able to install Windows 7 on a hard drive that does not have an existing operating system

Parts: Computer with the minimum hardware requirements for Windows 7 and a DVD drive, Windows 7 DVD or virtual image of the installation disc

Note: The screens may appear a little differently with different service packs and Windows 7 versions.

Procedure: Complete the following procedure and answer the accompanying questions.

1. Configure the BIOS to boot from the CD/DVD drive.
2. Insert the Windows 7 installation DVD into an optical drive and turn on the computer. The Windows 7 Setup program starts automatically if the BIOS was configured correctly.
3. Select the appropriate regional options and click *Next*.
4. Select *Install Now* to start the Windows 7 installation.
5. Read the EULA (end user licensing agreement). Select the *I accept the License Terms* option and click *Next*.

6. The two options that appear for Windows 7 is to upgrade or to perform a custom installation. To install Windows 7 as a clean install, click the *Custom (Advanced)* option.
7. When prompted for where to install Windows 7, select the *Drive options (advanced)* option.
8. Delete a partition, create a partition, and format a partition as needed. When finished selecting the partition, click Next. If a RAID or SCSI driver is needed, install it at this point.
9. The computer restarts and Windows 7 loads and completes the installation. A username and a computer name are required. The computer name must be unique. Contact the instructor or lab assistant for a unique name if necessary.
10. Contact the instructor for a password for the user account.

    Print the exact password to be used using appropriate upper and lowercase letters.

11. Enter the password, hint, and click *Next*.
12. Enter the product key provided. Check with the instructor or lab assistant if you do not have one. Note that you can leave this blank to experiment with the different versions of Windows 7. They all come on the same DVD. You must eventually install a version for which you have a license. Do not experiment with different Windows 7 versions if upgrading from a prior version of Windows as this is not allowed once the old version is upgraded.
13. In the Help Protect Your Computer and Improve Windows Automatically dialog box, select the *Use Recommended Settings* option.
14. In the Review Your Time and Date Settings dialog box, select the appropriate time zone and date options. Click *Finish*.
15. Contact your instructor or lab assistant for the appropriate computer location. If the instructor or assistant is not available, select the *Work* option.
16. Click *Start* and the Windows logon appears.

Instructor initials: ______________

Lab 12.4 Installing VMware Workstation

Objective: To be able to install VMware Workstation 9 in preparation for future VMware Workstation labs

Parts: Windows computer with administrator rights to install software
Internet access to download 30-day trial of VMware Workstation

Procedure: Complete the following procedure and answer the accompanying questions.

1. If VMware Workstation 9 is not already downloaded on the computer, go to http://www.vmware.com and download this software.

   Is VMware Workstation already installed on the computer. [Yes | No]

   Is the same version of VMware Workstation downloaded for 32-bit Windows as 64-bit Windows? If you do not know, research this on the Internet. [Yes | No]
2. Start the VMware installer. When the Setup Type window appears, select *Typical*.
3. Leave the default location and click *Next*.
4. Leave the *Check for product updates* option enabled and click *Next*.
5. Either enable or disable the *Help improve VMware Workstation* checkbox.

   What option did you choose? [Enable | Disable]
6. Leave the shortcut checkboxes enabled and click *Next*. Click *Continue*.
7. Either enter a license key provided by the instructor or lab assistant or select the *Skip* option. Note that no key is needed for the 30-day trial.

8. Once the installation is complete, the VMware Workstation icon appears on the desktop. Note that you may be prompted to restart the computer before using the software.

Instructor initials: ______________

Lab 12.5 Installing Windows into a VMware Workstation Virtual Machine

Objective: To be able to install a version of Windows into a VMware Workstation virtual machine

Parts: Windows computer with administrator rights that has VMware Workstation installed

Windows installation disc or ISO image

Procedure: Complete the following procedure and answer the accompanying questions.

1. Double click the VMware Workstation icon from the desktop or access the software from the Start button menu. VMware Workstation begins. Figure 12.34 shows the VMware Workstation area.

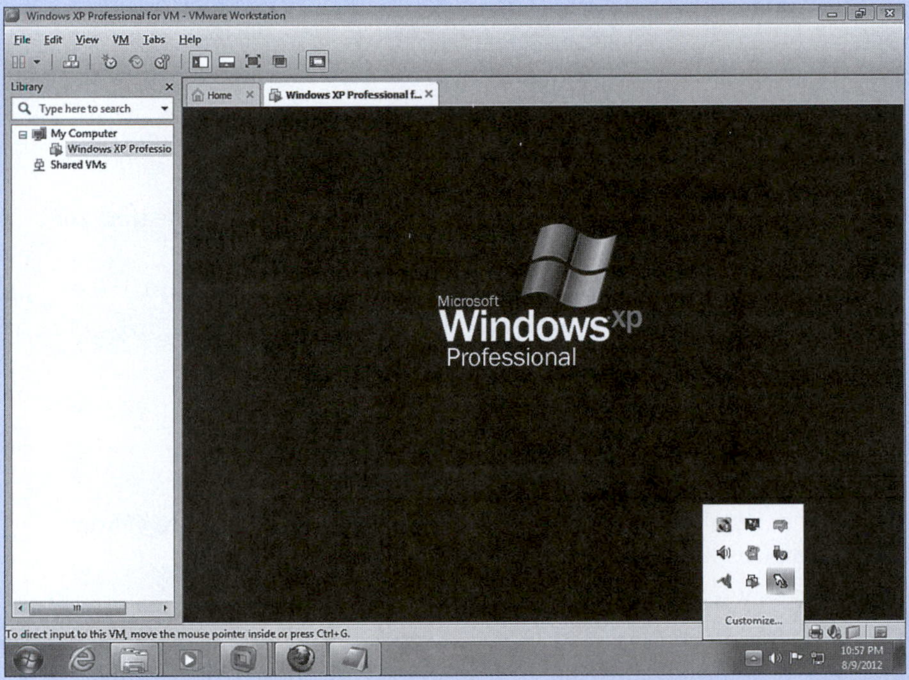

Figure 12.34 **VMware Workstation**

2. Click the *Create a New Virtual Machine option*. If this is the first time the VMware Workstation software has been accessed, select the *Yes, I accept the terms in the license agreement* radio button and click *OK*.
3. Select the *Typical (recommended)* radio button and click *Next*.
4. If you have a Windows installation disc, insert it now and select the *Installer disc* option. Otherwise, select the *Installer disc image file (iso)* radio button and browse to the location of the Windows installer ISO file. Click *Next*.
5. Enter the Windows product key as provided by the instructor or lab assistant. Note that the installation can proceed without a key. If Windows 7 or higher is being installed, select the Windows version from the drop down menu. Optionally, enter a username and password as directed by the instructor or lab assistant. Click *Next*. If a license key was not entered, you will be reminded of that and must click Yes to continue.

Was a username and password selected as part of this installation process? If so, document the username and password. [Yes | No]

6. Enter a name for the machine (or leave the default) and select a hard drive location to store the virtual machine file. Click *Next*.

   What name did you install to the virtual machine?

   Document the path to the folder that contains the virtual machine file.

7. Keep the default disk size unless instructed to change by the instructor or student assistant and select the *Store virtual disk as a single file* radio button. Click *Next*.
8. Look over the virtual machine settings.

   What is the default amount of RAM?

   What type of network adapter is installed?

   What other devices are automatically installed?

9. Notice that the *Power on this virtual machine after creation* checkbox is automatically enabled. Click *Finish*. Note that if you have removable devices attached, you may receive a message. Also, you will need a licensed version of VMware Workstation to power on any virtual machines. The Windows setup installation process begins if a proper ISO file was found. Answer the installation prompts just as you would a normal Windows installation process.
10. Notice how the virtual machine is within its own tab. Right-click the tab that contains your new virtual machine.

    Document at least four available options that are available from the menu.

11. Click away from the tab.

    What message appears at the bottom of the screen that relates to controlling the virtual machine?

12. Locate the VM in the Library window panel on the left. Right-click the virtual machine you just created.

    Are the options the same as the ones you saw when you right-clicked the virtual machine tab? [Yes | No]

13. Select the *View* > *Full Screen* menu options. The virtual machine displays in the full window, looking exactly like a typical Windows screen.
14. Locate and click the VM icon in the top left corner. Select *Restore* to close full screen mode and return to the VMware Workstation area.

Instructor initials: ______________

15. Log in to the Windows environment and continue the installation process if necessary.
16. Shut down the version of Windows being used within the virtual environment. It is very important to shut down the Windows version inside the virtual machine as it is to shut down Windows properly on an unvirtualized computer.
17. Power off the virtual machine.

Lab 12.6 Working with a VMware Workstation Virtual Machine

Objective: To be able to customize a VMware Workstation virtual machine, create a snapshot, add an icon or software, and revert to a saved snapshot.

Parts: Windows computer with administrator rights that has VMware Workstation installed and a saved virtual machine

Procedure: Complete the following procedure and answer the accompanying questions.

1. Using whatever method you would like including physical examination, examine the host computer hardware and document the findings.

   How many physical processors are installed in the computer?

   What method did you use to determine this fact?

   How many processors are shown within Device Manager?

   Is this how many processors are installed or is this how many cores are within the processor?

   How did you determine this fact?

   If Hyper-Threading is enabled, is the number of Intel processors seen within Task Manager Performance tab affected? [Yes | No]

   Why or why not?

   How much RAM is present in the computer?

   How many network ports are present in the computer?

   How many floppy drives are installed in the computer?

2. Launch VMware Workstation. From the Home tab, select the *Open a Virtual Machine* link. Browse to the location of a previously created virtual machine and double-click the file name, or click the file name and select *Open*.

   How many processors are detected?

   Is a printer detected? [Yes | No]

3. Select the *Edit virtual machine settings* link.

   What is the maximum amount of memory that can be allocated to this VM?

   Is this more than the physical RAM on the host computer? [Yes | No]

   Is this what you expected? [Yes | No] Why or why not?

   List one instance of where you might want to use the maximum.

4. Click *Processors* in the Device column.

   How many processors are currently allocated?

   What is the maximum number of processors?

   How many cores per processor are currently allocated?

   What is the maximum number of cores per processor?

   How does this compare to the information you documented about the host computer in Step 1?

5. Select the *Network adapter* option from the Device column.

   How many network adapters are shown?

   Does this match the number of network ports on the physical host computer? [Yes | No]

6. Select the *Floppy* option.

   How many floppy drives were installed on the physical host computer?

   Why do you think this would be included in a virtual machine?

7. Select the *Sound Card* option.

What is the device status?

8. Select the *Options* tab. Select the *General* settings option. From this screen, you can rename the virtual machine and see the guest operating system. You can also set the default directory where snapshots are stored.

   What is the working directory where VMs are stored?

9. Select the *Power* option.

   What power options, if any, are enabled?

10. Select the *Snapshots* option. Notice how you can take a snapshot every time the computer is powered off. Click *Cancel*.
11. From the main VMware Workstation window, right-click the tab that contains the virtual machine that has already been created.
12. Select *Power > Power on to BIOS*.

    What type of virtual BIOS is used?

    Is the virtual system time the same as the host machine? [Yes | No]

    Does the mouse work in the virtual BIOS window? [Yes | No]
13. Using the directions on the screen, select the *Boot* BIOS menu option.
14. Using the directions on the screen, change the boot order so the hard drive is first and the CD-ROM drive is last.
15. Select the *Main* menu option and access *Keyboard Features*.
16. Change the Num Lock key to be *On* by default.
17. Press F10 to save and exit the BIOS.

    When do you think a technician would ever enter the virtual BIOS instead of the host computer BIOS?

    Do you think that changes within the virtual BIOS affect the host computer BIOS? Why or why not?

18. Press Enter to save the changes and boot the virtual machine.

    What message, if any appeared?

19. Hold the mouse pointer inside the VMware Workstation window. Do not click. Notice the mouse directions at the bottom of the window.

    What keystroke(s) will allow you to move outside the VM?
20. Now hold the mouse pointer outside the VMware Workstation window. Notice the mouse directions have changed at the bottom of the VMware Workstation window.

    What keystroke(s) will allow you to direct input to the VM?
21. From the VM menu option, select *Snapshot > Take Snapshot*. A snapshot is the virtual machine at this point and time. Another way of looking at the snapshot is that it is the operating system as it stands right now. You could make changes to the operating system and then if the changes didn't work well, then you could revert back to the virtual machine that was the snapshot.

22. Name the snapshot something meaningful such as Windows *X* base load. Click *Take Snapshot*.

    What did you name the snapshot?

23. Create a shortcut icon to any application on the virtual machine desktop.

    What shortcut did you create?

24. Shut down Windows within the virtual machine.
25. Power off the virtual machine.
26. Open the same virtual machine again, but do not power on the virtual machine.
27. Right-click the virtual machine tab and point to *Snapshot*.
28. Click the name of the snapshot you took in Step 22. Refer to the answer in Step 22 if necessary.
29. Click *Yes* to retain the snapshot.

    Is the shortcut icon you created in Step 23 there? [Yes | No]

    Explain why you think this happened.

Instructor initials: ______________

30. Shut down Windows in the virtual environment.
31. Power down the virtual machine.

Lab 12.7 Windows XP/Vista/7 Registry Modification

Objective: To be able to modify the Windows XP, Vista, or 7 registry when given directions to do so

Parts: Computer with Windows XP, Vista, or 7 loaded

Notes: You must be an administrator or a member of the Administrators group to change registry settings. Sometimes you are given directions by Microsoft to edit the registry in order to fix a problem. It is very important that you follow the directions exactly as shown.

Procedure: Complete the following procedure and answer the accompanying questions.

1. Power on the computer and verify that Windows loads. Log on to the computer using the user ID and password provided by the instructor or lab assistant.
2. Open *Windows Explorer* and right-click any folder.

   Which editing options are available for a folder? Select all that apply. [*Cut* | *Copy* | *Paste* | *Copy To Folder* | *Move To Folder* | *Delete* | *Rename* | *Send To*]

3. In XP, select the *Start* button > *Run* > type **`regedit`** and press Enter.

   In Vista/7, locate the *Start* button *Search* (Vista)/*Search programs and files* (7) textbox, type **`regedit`**, and press Enter.

4. Expand the *Hkey_Classes_Root* option by clicking the + in XP or the ▷ in Vista/7.
5. Scroll down to locate and expand *AllFileSystemObjects*. Note that items beginning with character such as . (period), are before the alphabetized list of other objects.
6. Expand the *shellex* object and locate *ContextMenuHandlers*. Shellex is a shell extension key that lets you customize the Windows interface.
7. Right-click *ContextMenuHandlers* > *New* > *Key*. When the new folder (key) appears, type **`Copy To`** because this registry modification adds a new option to the right-click menu called *Copy To*.
8. The Copy To object should still be selected in the left window. Double-click the *(Default)* name in the right panel. The Edit String window appears.
9. In the *Value data* textbox, type the following value exactly as shown (the 0s are zeroes): **`{C2FBB630-2971-11D1-A18C-00C04FD75D13}`**

Click *OK*.

10. Verify the change has occurred. Open *Windows Explorer* and right-click any folder.

    Does the *Copy To Folder* option appear as an option? If not, redo the lab.

Instructor initials: ______________

11. Using the same process, create another new key under *ContextMenuHandlers* and name the key *Move To*. The value data for the Move To key is as follows:

    `{C2FBB631-2971-11D1-A18C-00C04FD75D13}`

12. Use Windows Explorer to create two new folders. Copy a couple of files into each folder. Use the new *Copy To* and *Move To* options you just created.
13. Delete any folders that you have created.
14. To delete keys in Registry Editor, select the *Copy To* key in the left panel. From the *Edit* menu option, select *Delete* and select *Yes* when asked to verify. Delete the *Move To* key using the same process.

Instructor initials: ______________

15. Close the *Registry Editor* window.

    Using the Internet or magazines, locate a registry edit that you think would improve Windows.

    Write the URL or magazine title and date as well as a brief description of the edit.

Lab 12.8 Windows XP System State Backup

Objective: To be able to back up the Windows XP System State using the Backup utility

Parts: Computer with Windows XP installed

Note: In order to do this exercise, the student must have local Administrator privileges. The System State can be quite large (a common size is 400MB), so adequate hard drive or flash drive space must be available.

Procedure: Complete the following procedure and answer the accompanying questions.

1. Turn on the computer and verify that the operating system loads.
2. Log on to Windows XP using the user ID and password provided by the instructor or lab assistant.
3. Click the *Start* button and point to the *All Programs* selection. Point to the *Accessories* option, point to *System Tools*, and click the *Backup* menu selection. The *Backup* Wizard starts.
4. Click the *Advanced Mode* option (which is an underlined option in the words appearing in the window).
5. Click the *Backup* tab and select the *System State* checkbox to enable it.
6. Select where the backup is to be stored by clicking the *Browse* button.

   What drive and folder is being used to store the System State backup?

7. Click the *Start Backup* button. The *Backup Job information* dialog box appears. Click the *Start* button located in the window to start the backup.
8. When the backup finishes, the *Backup Progress* window shows that the backup is complete. Show this to your instructor.

Instructor initials: ______________

9. Click the *Close* button. Close the *Backup Utility* window.
10. Use Windows Explorer to locate the BACKUP.BKF file and permanently delete it.

    Have a classmate verify the BACKUP.BKF file is *permanently* deleted.

Lab 12.9 Windows 7 Backup

Objective: To be able to back up files including the operating system if necessary using the Backup and Restore utility

Parts: Computer with Windows 7 installed and administrator rights

Procedure: Complete the following procedure and answer the accompanying questions.

Note: Even though only three files are backed up using this process, the same process can be used to back up the computer.

1. Create a new folder called *Stuff* under *Documents*.
2. Create three text files of any name and place them in the new *Stuff* folder.
3. Access the *System and Security* control panel link > *Backup and Restore* > *Set up backup* link (Note that if the Backup and Restore link has already been accessed, then the *Change settings* link can be used to complete the lab.) > select a backup destination designated by the instructor or lab assistant > *Next* > select the *Let me choose* radio button.

   Note: The *Let Windows choose* radio button could be used to back up the entire operating system and files.
4. Deselect all enabled checkboxes > expand *OS (C:)* by clicking on the arrow beside it > expand *Users* > expand the user name used to log into the computer > expand *Documents* > select the *Stuff* folder to enable it for backup > *Next* > *Save settings and run backup* button.
5. The backup executes. Show the instructor the completed backup.

Instructor initials: ______________

6. Delete the *Stuff* folder and the three files contained within it.

Lab 12.10 Windows Automatic Update Utility

Objective: To be able to configure a computer for automatic updates to the Windows operating system.

Parts: Computer with Windows XP, Vista, or 7 loaded

Internet access

Note: You must be an administrator or a member of the Administrators group to change Automatic Updates settings.

Procedure: Complete the following procedure and answer the accompanying questions.

1. Power on the computer and verify that Windows loads. Log on to the computer using the user ID and password provided by the instructor or lab assistant.
2. In XP, select the *Start* button > *Control Panel* > *Classic* view > *System* > *Automatic Updates* tab.

   In Vista, select the *System and Maintenance* Control Panel > *Windows Update* link. Click the *Change settings* link.

   In Windows 7, click the *Start* button > *Control Panel* > *System and Security* link > *Windows Update* link.

   What option is currently selected?

   Which option do you think most large corporations would want as standard and why do you think this?

3. Close the Windows Update window.
4. Click the *Cancel* button to close the Automatic Updates window.

Lab 12.11 Windows XP Mouse, Keyboard, Accessibility, and Sound Options

Objective: To be able to use the appropriate control panels to configure a mouse and keyboard, and enable disabilities options

Parts: Computer with Windows XP installed

Procedure: Complete the following procedure and answer the accompanying questions.

1. Turn on the computer and verify that the operating system loads.
2. Log on to Windows XP using the user ID and password provided by the instructor or lab assistant.
3. Click the *Start* button and select the *Control Panel* option. Pick a Category should display in the right window. If it does not, click the *Switch to Category View* option in the left pane.

Keyboard Configuration

4. Click the *Printers and Other Hardware* Control Panel category. Click the *Keyboard* icon. The Keyboard Properties window appears.
5. Click the *Speed* tab. The *Keyboard Properties* window contains two tabs—*Speed* and *Hardware*. The *Speed* tab has three settings: repeat delay, repeat rate, and cursor blink rate.

   List the current keyboard settings for each of the three options.

6. The *repeat delay* option configures the duration of wait time before a key starts repeating. This is especially important for people who do not type well or who have to use a device such as a pencil to press keys. The *repeat rate* is an adjustment for how fast characters repeat across the screen. The *cursor blink rate* controls how many times the cursor blinks per second. Adjust each of these settings and test them using the *Click here and hold down a key to test repeat rate* area.
7. Configure the keyboard settings back to their original configuration. Refer to the settings determined after Step 5.
8. Click the *Hardware* tab. The Hardware tab is used to access the keyboard troubleshooting wizard and the keyboard driver. Click the *Properties* button.

   What is the current device status as shown in the window?

9. Click the *Driver* tab. The Update driver button is used to load a new keyboard driver. Click the *Cancel* button twice and return to the *Printers and Other Hardware* control category window.

Mouse Configuration

10. Click the *Mouse* icon. The Mouse Properties window appears. Some of the settings are standard, but others depend on the mouse manufacturer.

    List the tabs that are available in the Mouse Properties window.

11. On the Buttons tab, there are three standard options—*Button configuration*, *Doubleclick speed*, and *ClickLock*. The *Button configuration* section is where the mouse buttons can be reversed for left-handed people.

    Is the *Switch primary and secondary buttons* option enabled for left-handed people?

    What is the current setting for *Doubleclick speed*?

12. Adjust the Doubleclick speed and test it using the test folder located in the right window of this section.
13. Reset the Doubleclick speed setting to its original configuration. Refer to the answer determined after Step 11.
14. The ClickLock setting is so you can select an option and drag the mouse without holding down the left mouse button. Once a click is made for more than a second, the button locks and the icon can be dragged. When a second click is made, the mouse unlocks.

    Is the *Turn on ClickLock* option enabled or disabled?

15. The mouse troubleshooter and driver is accessed through the Hardware tab. Click the *Hardware* tab. Click the *Troubleshoot* button. The Mouse Troubleshooter window appears. Close the *Mouse Troubleshooter*.
16. Re-access the Mouse Control Panel *Hardware* tab. Click the *Properties* button.

    In the Mouse Properties window, what is the mouse's device status?

Instructor initials: ____________

17. Click the *Driver* tab. Just like with the keyboard, the Update Driver button is used to load a new mouse driver.
18. Click the *Cancel* button twice to return to the Printers and Other Hardware Control Panel category. Click the *Back* button to return to the Control Panel categories.

Accessibility Options

19. Accessibility options are not just for people with disabilities. The settings can be adjusted by any computer user to make his or her computer environment more comfortable. Click the *Accessibility Options* category. Click the first task, *Adjust the contrast for text and colors on your screen*. The Accessibility Options window opens with the Display tab active.
20. The two configuration sections are High Contrast and Cursor Options. Click the *Use High Contrast* checkbox to enable it and click the *Apply* button. A "Please wait" message appears and then the screen changes.

    What is different about the display when the high contrast option is enabled?

Instructor initials: ____________

21. Click the *Use High Contrast* checkbox to disable it and click *Apply*. The screen returns to normal. Click the *Cancel* button and the Accessibility Options Control Panel category window reappears.
22. Click the second task, *Configure Windows to work for your hearing, vision, and mobility needs*. The *Accessibility* Wizard appears. This wizard steps through visual, auditory, and motor skills settings. Click the *Next* button. The Text Size window appears.

    What is the default text size setting?
23. Click the *Next* button and the Display Settings window appears.

    What options are currently enabled?
24. Click the *Next* button and the Set Wizard Options window appears.

    What four options are available?

25. The option that is probably the most vague is the Administrative option. This option is used to turn certain accessibility features off if the computer sits idle and make the accessibility features available to one user or all users. Click the *Cancel* button. A Save Changes message box appears. Click the *No* button so that the configuration changes are not kept.

Instructor initials: ______________

Table 12.28 lists available XP accessibility features and their functions.

Table 12.28 Windows XP accessibility options

Option	Description
StickyKeys	Used for one finger or mouth stick typing and permits one keystroke at a time; used with key combinations such as Ctrl+A
FilterKeys	Adjusts the keyboard so inadvertent adjacent keystrokes are ignored
ToggleKeys	Emits a beep when Num Lock, Caps Lock, or Scroll Lock keys are pressed (on)
Microsoft Magnifier	Enlarges a small portion of the screen
The Narrator	Reads information displayed on the screen
MouseKeys	Allows pointer manipulation with one finger, mouth stick, or the numeric keypad
ShowSounds	Applications that have closed-caption ability can provide visual feedback
SoundSentry	Sends a visual cue when a computer sound is generated
NetMeeting	Allows Internet conferencing for hearing impaired users

Controlling Sound

26. Access the *Sounds, Speech, and Audio Devices* Control Panel category. Select the *Adjust the system volume* task.

    What are the five tabs in the *Sounds and Audio Devices Properties* window?

27. The Volume tab is used to control the volume for the entire computer system and speaker configuration. The Mute checkbox is used to mute all of the computer's sound. The Place volume icon in the taskbar is used to add a volume control icon in the taskbar in the notification area. The Device Volume slide bar sets the computer's value settings. Click the *Advanced* button located in the Device Volume section. The Play Control window opens.

    What is the current status of the mute buttons displayed in the Play Control window? Use Table 12.29 to document the findings.

Table 12.29 Windows XP current accessibility options configuration

Play control setting	Enabled or disabled
Play Control Mute all	
Wave Mute	
MIDI Mute	
CD Audio Mute	
Line-In Mute	

28. Click the *Play Control Mute all* checkbox to enable it. If it is already enabled, leave the setting turned on (enabled). Close the *Play Control* window. Return to the *Sounds and Audio Devices Properties* window. You will have to re-access the Control Panel category.

    What is the current status of the Mute checkbox located in the Device Volume section? [Enabled | Disabled]

29. Return all Play Control settings back to their original settings and return to the *Sounds and Audio Devices Properties* window.

Instructor initials: ____________

30. Click the *Speaker volume* button. The Speaker volume screen has a left and right speaker volume. This setting does not affect speakers that simply plug into the Line out connection on the sound adapter or built into the motherboard. Click the *Cancel* button.
31. The *Advanced* button in the Speakers settings section is used to configure speakers for such things as headphone usage and surround sound. Click the *Advanced* button in the Speakers settings section and click the *Speakers* tab. The Speakers setup list is used to specify external speakers. Computers such as ones in a business environment or a lab can be configured for no speakers.

    What speaker, if any, lists in the *Speakers setup* drop-down list?

32. To disable speakers, click the *Speakers setup* down arrow and select the *No Speakers* option. Click the *Cancel* button twice and close the Control Panel window.
33. Power off the computer properly.

Lab 12.12 Configuring Windows 7 Ease of Access

Objective: To be able to configure Windows 7 for customers who need customized environment for visual, auditory, and physical reasons

Parts: Computer with Windows 7 installed

Procedure: Complete the following procedure and answer the accompanying questions. Note that not all steps are shown and you are to click some settings to explore based on the question asked.

1. To access the Ease of Access Center, click the *Start* button > *Control Panel* > *Ease of Access* link.
2. Select the *Let Windows suggest settings* link.

   What recommendations does Microsoft make available to someone at the workplace who has trouble seeing images on the screen because of the office lighting? Note that you have to make selections based on the scenario given to obtain this information.

3. You should be at the *Recommended settings* window after answering the last question. If not, redo Steps 1 and 2 and read the accompanying note. Ensure that the computer has speakers attached and, on the recommendation screen, select the *Turn on Narrator* checkbox and leave the automatically enabled recommendations enabled. Click *Apply*.
4. In the Microsoft Narrator window, ensure that the *Echo User's Keystrokes* and *Announce System Messages* options are enabled. They are normally enabled by default.
5. Enable the *Announce Scroll Notifications* checkbox and select the *Voice Settings* button.

   What are the default voice, speed, volume, and pitch settings?

6. Click the *Cancel* button; select the *Exit* button. Click *Yes*. From the Recommend settings window, click *OK*.
7. Select the *Start Narrator* link from the Ease of Access Center.

   How do you think this setting would be beneficial in a work environment?

   List at least one disadvantage of this setting.

8. Click *Exit* from within the Microsoft Narrator window. Click *Yes*.
9. Select the *Get recommendations to make your computer easier to use* link. Disable the *Lighting conditions make it difficult to see images on my monitor* checkbox.
10. Select the *Images and text on TV are difficult to see (even when I'm wearing glasses)* check-box. Click *Next* four times and then click *Done* to view Microsoft's recommendations.

    What three options are recommended (checked) by Microsoft for this situation?

11. In the *Change the color and size of mouse pointers* section, select the *Large Inverting* radio button. Select *Apply*.
12. Move the mouse and open *Windows Explorer*.

    Describe your experience.

    Do you think office workers who do not have a visual impairment would enjoy this feature?

13. Change the mouse pointer back to *Regular white*. Disable the *Turn on Narrator* checkbox. Ensure that the *High contrast color scheme* is selected, with all associated checkboxes enabled. Select *Apply*.
14. Hold down the left Alt key and while keeping the key held down, press and hold the left Shift key. While holding down both of these keys, press the PrtScn key (Alt+left Shift+PrtScn). Release all three keys.

    What audio signal do you hear?

    From information in the message, document how to disable the keyboard shortcut if these specific keys are used for another application.

15. Click *Yes*.

    Describe the difference in screen appearance.

    Do you like the high contrast?
16. Use the same keys again to disable the high-contrast setting. Click *Cancel* in the Recommended settings window.
17. Re-select the *Get recommendations to make your computer easier to use link*. Remove the enabled option checkbox from the *Eyesight* window and click *Next*.
18. In the *Dexterity* window, select the *Pens and pencils are difficult to use* checkbox. Click *Next* or *Done* until you reach Microsoft's recommendations.

What option(s) are recommended by Microsoft?

What are Toggle Keys?

19. Open *Notepad.* Notice the blinking cursor in the top left corner.
20. Back in the *Recommended settings* window, notice the setting for *Set the thickness of the blinking cursor*. Change the thickness of the blinking cursor to 5. Click *Apply*.
21. Return to Notepad and notice the difference in the blinking cursor.
22. Return to the *Recommended Settings* window and return the thickness to the default setting of *1*. Close *Notepad*.
23. Return to the *Recommended Settings* window.

    What are Sticky Keys?

    Who might benefit from Sticky Keys?

24. Click on the *Set up Filter Keys* link.

    What are Filter Keys?

    What is the default amount of time the Shift key has to stay depressed to toggle on Filter Keys?

    By default, do you see a warning message, do you hear a tone, or do you get both a message and a tone when Filter Keys is active? [warning message | tone | both]

    What are Bounce Keys?

    What is the default time between keystrokes if the Bounce Keys feature is enabled?

    Is this setting adjustable? [Yes | No]

25. Click in the *Type text here to test settings* textbox. Type `hello`.

    What happened?

26. Click the *Set up Repeat Keys and Slow Keys* link.
27. Click in the *Type text here to test settings* textbox. Click and hold the `h` key down until it appears in the textbox. Finish typing the word `hello` as a message.

    What indication did you get, besides seeing it appear in the textbox, that the letter "took"?

Instructor initials: ______________

28. Click *Cancel* to return to the *Set up Filter Keys* screen.

    What are the other settings this window offers?

29. Click *Cancel* to return to the *Ease of Access Center*.
30. Re-access the *Get recommendations to make your computer easier to use* link. Return to the *Dexterity* window and clear the checkbox for *Pens and pencils are difficult to use*. Click *Next*.
31. On the *Hearing* window, select the *Conversations can be difficult to hear (even with a hearing aid)* checkbox. Click *Next* or *Done* until you reach the Microsoft recommendations.

    What options are available?

32. Enable the *Turn on visual notifications for sounds (Sound Sentry)*. Select the visual warning of *Flash active window*. Click *Apply*. Leave that window open and access the *Hardware and Sound* Control Panel. In the *Sound* section, select the *Change system sounds* link. On the *Sounds* tab, select a Windows notification that has a speaker beside it. Click the *Test* button.

    Even if your computer does not have speakers, what visual clue do you get that a sound is being made?

33. Click *Cancel* and return to the *Recommended Settings* window. Remove the check from the *Turn on visual notifications for sounds (Sound Sentry)*. Click *Apply*. Click *Cancel* to return to the Ease of Access Center.
34. Re-access the *Get recommendations to make your computer easier to use* link. Return to the *Hearing* window and disable the *Conversations can be difficult to hear (even with a hearing aid)* option. Click *Next* to advance to the *Speech* options screen. Enable the *Other people have difficulty understanding me in a conversation (but not due to an accent)* option. Click *Next* or *Done* until you reach Microsoft's recommendations.

    What is Microsoft's recommendation?

35. Click the *Completing the questionnaire again* link. Return to the *Speech* page and enable the *I have a speech impairment* checkbox.

    Did this change Microsoft's recommendations? If so, what is the recommendation(s)?

36. Return to the questionnaire and disable all options from the *Speech* page and click *Next* to advance to the Reasoning window. Select the *I have a learning disability, such as dyslexia* option. Click *Done*.

    What does Microsoft recommend for this type of person?

Instructor initials: ____________

37. Click *Cancel*. Close the *Ease of Access Center* window.

Lab 12.13 Windows XP System Restore Utility

Objective: To be able to configure and use the System Restore utility

Parts: Computer with Windows XP loaded

Notes: You must be an administrator or a member of the Administrators group to perform System Restore. If the system has System Restore disabled, this lab may need to be done in two different class periods.

Procedure: Complete the following procedure and answer the accompanying questions.

1. Power on the computer and verify that XP loads. Log on to XP using the user ID and password provided by the instructor or lab assistant.
2. Select the *Start* button > *All Programs* > *Accessories* > *System Tools* > *System Restore* > *System Restore Settings* link.
3. If System Restore is turned off, uncheck the *Turn off System Restore* checkbox and complete this lab later.

    On the System Restore tab, is System Restore turned on or off?

    How much disk space is being used for System Restore?

4. Click the *Apply* button if changes have been made and click *OK* to close the System Restore window.
5. Back on the Welcome to System Restore window, ensure that the *Restore my computer to an earlier time* radio button is enabled and click *Next*.

6. A calendar appears where you can select a day when System Restore has created a restore point. Only the bolded days are valid. Select a valid system restore point and click *Next*. Click *Next* again. The system restarts.
7. A status bar appears showing the System Restore progress. The computer restarts and a message appears that the system has successfully been restored. Show the instructor this screen.

Instructor initials: ______________

8. Click *OK*.

Lab 12.14 Windows 7 System Restore Utility

Objective: To be able to configure and use the System Restore utility

Parts: Computer with Windows 7 installed and administrator rights

Notes: You must be an administrator to perform System Restore. If System Restore has been disabled, this lab may have to be done over two class periods. One class period would be used to enable it and schedule a restore point and the next class period to perform the system restore. Also note that an antivirus update or a Windows update might have to be re-installed as a result of the system restore.

Procedure: Complete the following procedure and answer the accompanying questions.

1. Power on the computer and verify that Windows 7 loads. Log on to Windows using the user ID and password provided by the instructor or lab assistant.
2. Select the *System and Security* Control Panel link. Select the *Backup and Restore* Control Panel link.
3. Select the *Recover system settings on your computer* link at the bottom of the window.
4. Select the *Open System Restore* button.

   What are two reasons that system restore might be used?

   [T | F] System restore does not affect personal data documents.

   [Yes | No] Can a recently installed application be affected by using the System Restore utility?

   [Yes | No] Is the System Restore process reversible?
5. Click the *Next* button.

   Are any restore points available? If so, list the latest one.
6. Select the *Show more restore points* checkbox.

   What is the oldest restore point available?
7. Select the newest (one at the top of the list) restore point and click *Next*.

   What does Windows recommend creating if you have recently changed your Windows password?
8. Click *Finish* to confirm rolling back your system to an earlier time.

   Under what conditions can the System Restore changes not be undone?
9. Click *Yes* to the dialog message. The system restarts as part of the System Restore process.

Instructor initials: ______________

10. Log into Windows 7 and ensure that the system works.
11. Once the system has been restored to an earlier time, install any antivirus or Windows updates that have been affected by this system restore.

Lab 12.15 Upgrading a Hardware Driver and Using Driver Roll Back Using Windows XP/Vista/7

Objective: To install an updated driver under the Windows XP, Vista, or 7 operating system

Parts: Computer with Windows XP, Vista, or 7 installed
Internet access

Note: In this lab a new driver is loaded, but then the old driver is re-installed with the driver roll back feature. The student must be logged in as a user with local Administrator rights to perform this lab.

Procedure: Complete the following procedure and answer the accompanying questions.

1. Turn on the computer and verify that the operating system loads. Log in to Windows using the user ID and password provided by the instructor or lab assistant.
2. Select an installed hardware device and locate an updated driver using the Internet. Download the driver to the hard drive. Note that some drivers may come in a compressed file and must be uncompressed before continuing the procedure.

   What device did you select to upgrade?

   What location (path, folder, desktop, etc.) was used to download the driver?

Instructor initials: ______________

Installing the Driver

3. Open *Device Manager*.
4. Click the + (plus sign) beside the hardware category that contains the device being upgraded.
5. Right-click the device name and click the *Properties* selection.
6. Click the *Driver* tab.
7. In Windows XP, click the *Update Driver* button. The *Update Hardware* Wizard screen appears. Select the *Install from a list or specific location (Advanced)* radio button and click *Next*. Click the *Don't search. I will select the driver to install* radio button and click *Next*. Click the *Have Disk* button, use the *Browse* button to locate the downloaded file, and click *OK*. A list of models might appear. If so, select the correct model and click *Next*. Finish the driver update.

   In Windows Vista/7, click the *Update Driver* and select *Search automatically for updated driver software* to not only look on the computer for an updated driver but also search the Internet. Note that if a driver has been downloaded, use the *Browse my computer for driver software* link to locate the downloaded driver.

Instructor initials: ______________

Using Driver Roll Back

8. Use *Device Manager*, right-click the device name again, and select *Properties*.
9. Click the *Driver* tab and click the *Roll Back Driver* button. Click the *Yes* button to roll back the driver. If the device driver has not been updated, driver roll back will not be possible and a message screen will display this fact.

Instructor initials: ______________

10. Close all windows and power off the computer properly.

Lab 12.16 Disabling a Hardware Driver Using Windows XP, Vista, or 7

Objective: To disable a driver under the Windows XP, Vista, or 7 operating system

Parts: Computer with Windows XP, Vista, or 7 and a network adapter installed

Note: The student must be logged in as a user with local Administrator rights to perform this lab. In this lab, a driver is disabled and then re-enabled. Sometimes Windows can install the wrong driver, in which case the driver must be disabled and then manually re-installed.

Procedure: Complete the following procedure and answer the accompanying questions.

1. Turn on the computer and verify that the operating system loads. Log in to Windows using the user ID and password provided by the instructor or lab assistant.
2. Using *Device Manager*, expand the *Network adapters* category.

   What network adapter is installed in the computer?
3. Right-click a network adapter and click the *Disable* selection.

   What message displays on the screen?
4. Click the *Yes* button.

   In Device Manager, how is a device that has its driver disabled displayed differently from any other device?
5. In *Device Manager*, right-click the same network adapter and click the *Enable* option. The device is re-enabled and appears normally in the window.

Instructor initials: ______________

6. Close the *Device Manager* window and all other windows.

Lab 12.17 Installing Hardware Using Windows XP/Vista/7

Objective: To install a new hardware component under the Windows XP, Vista, or 7 operating system

Parts: Computer with Windows XP, Vista, or 7 installed

New device to install

Access to the Internet

Note: The student must be logged in as a user with local Administrator rights to perform this lab. In this lab, the Internet is used to obtain the device's installation instructions and latest device driver, and then the new hardware device is installed.

Procedure: Complete the following procedure and answer the accompanying questions.

1. Log in using the user ID and password provided by your instructor or lab assistant.
2. Using the Internet, locate the manufacturer's instructions for installing the device.

   Who is the device manufacturer?
3. Using the Internet, locate the latest device driver that is compatible with the version of Windows being used.

   Does the device have an appropriate driver for the version of Windows being used? [Yes | No]

   What is the device driver version being downloaded?
4. Connect the device to the computer using the proper installation procedures.

5. Boot the computer. Usually Windows automatically detects the new hardware and begins the *Found New Hardware* Wizard. If it does not present this wizard, look to see if the hardware device vendor supplied an installation program. If so, use this program to install the device. If no vendor-supplied installation program is available, use the *Add Hardware* Control Panel (XP), *Device Manager* (Vista), or *Devices and Printers/Add a device* link (7) as described in the chapter, to install the device. Install the device driver based on the device type and manufacturer's instructions.

   Did the Found New Hardware Wizard begin?

6. Test the device installation.

Instructor initials: ______________

Lab 12.18 Installing Administrative Tools in Windows XP

Objective: To be able to install Administrative Tools in Windows XP

Parts: Computer with Windows XP installed user ID that has Administrator rights
Windows XP CD

Note: In this lab, if Administrative Tools is already loaded, it will be removed and re-installed.

Procedure: Complete the following procedure and answer the accompanying questions.

1. Turn on the computer and verify that the operating system loads. Log in to Windows XP using the user ID and password provided by the instructor or lab assistant. Ensure that the user ID is one that has Administrator rights.

Verifying if Administrative Tools Is Already Loaded

2. Click the *Start* button, point to *All Programs*, and look for an *Administrative Tools* item.

   Does the *Administrative Tools* item appear in the All Programs list?

Removing Administrative Tools from the Start Menu

Note: The steps in this section are performed because the Administrative Tools item is already installed in the system. If Administrative Tools is not already installed, skip to the *Installing Administrative Tools to the Start Menu* section.

3. Right-click the *Start* button and select the *Properties* option. Click the *Start Menu* tab.
4. Click the *Customize* button. The Customize Start Menu window opens. In the Start Menu items section, locate the System Administrative tools section and click the *Don't display this item* radio button. Click the *OK* button. Click the *OK* button again. Verify that the Administrative Tools no longer displays in the All Programs list.

Instructor initials: ______________

Installing Administrative Tools to the Start Menu

5. Right-click the *Start* button and select the *Properties* option. Click the *Start Menu* tab.
6. Click the *Customize* button. The Customize Start Menu window opens. In the Start Menu items section, click the *Advanced* tab, locate the *System Administrative tools* section, and click in the *Display on the All Programs menu* radio button. Click the *OK* button. Click the *OK* button again. Verify that the Administrative Tools displays in the All Programs list.

   Note: An alternate way of accessing Administrator Tools is *Start* > *Control Panel* > *Classic* view > *Administrative Tools*.

Instructor initials: ______________

Does the All Programs menu contain Administrative Tools? If not, redo the Installing Administrative Tools section.

List two Administrative Tools provided with XP.

Lab 12.19 Installing and Removing Windows XP Components

Objective: To be able to install and remove Windows XP components

Parts: Computer with Windows XP installed

User ID that has Administrator rights

Approximately 18MB of free hard disk space

Note: In this lab if Windows XP's Accessories and Utilities component is already installed, it is removed and re-installed. If the Accessories and Utilities component is not already installed, it will be installed, removed, and re-installed. The Accessories and Utilities component requires about 17.5MB of hard disk space. The final objective of this lab is to have Accessories and Utilities installed.

Procedure: Complete the following procedure and answer the accompanying questions.

1. Turn on the computer and verify that the operating system loads. Log in to Windows XP using the user ID and password provided by the instructor or lab assistant. Ensure that the user ID is one that has Administrator rights.

Verifying if Accessories and Utilities Are Already Loaded

2. Click the *Start* button and click the *Control Panel* option. Access the *Add or Remove Programs* Control Panel by clicking the *Category* view or double-clicking the *Classic view* control panel icon.
3. Click the *Add/Remove Windows Components* icon located on the left portion of the Add or Remove Programs window. The Windows Components window opens.

   Is the Accessories and Utilities option enabled (checked)? [Yes | No]

   If so, proceed to the *Removing Accessories and Utilities* section below. Remove the components and then proceed to the *Installing Accessories and Utilities* section to re-install the components. If the Accessories and Utilities option is not installed (unchecked), proceed to the *Installing Accessories and Utilities* section, install the components, then go to the *Removing Accessories and Utilities* section and uninstall the components, then, finally, re-install the components. When this lab is complete, the Accessories and Utilities component should be installed.
4. You can double-click any component to view the subcomponents. Try this procedure on your own. Close all windows and proceed to the appropriate section based on the answer to the question in Step 3.

Removing Accessories and Utilities

5. Click the *Start* button and click the *Control Panel* option. Access the *Add or Remove Programs* Control Panel by clicking the *Category* view or double-clicking the *Classic* view control panel icon.
6. Click the *Add/Remove Windows Components* icon located on the left portion of the Add or Remove Programs window. The Windows Components window opens.
7. Click the *Accessories and Utilities* checkbox to deselect (uncheck) it and click the *Next* button. The files are deleted.

8. Click the *Finish* button and verify that accessories and utilities are uninstalled using the previously described procedures.

   Has the Accessories and Utilities component been removed? Have a classmate verify.

Classmate's printed name: ______________________________

Classmate's signature: ______________________________

Installing Accessories and Utilities

9. Click the *Start* button and click the *Control Panel* option. Access the *Add or Remove Programs* Control Panel by clicking the *Category* view or double-clicking the *Classic view* control panel icon.
10. Click the *Add/Remove Windows Components* icon located on the left portion of the Add or Remove Programs window. The Windows Components window opens.
11. Click the *Accessories and Utilities* checkbox to select (enable) it. If the box is already checked, go to the *Removing Accessories and Utilities* section. Click the *Next* button. A prompt appears to insert the Windows XP CD. Insert the CD and the files copy.
12. Click the *Finish* button, close all Add/Remove Components Control Panel windows, and verify that Accessories and Utilities are installed using the previously described procedures.

    Is the Accessories and Utilities Windows XP component installed? Show this component to your instructor.

Instructor initials: ______________

Lab 12.20 Installing and Removing Windows Vista/7 Components

Objective: To be able to install and remove Windows Vista/7 components

Parts: Computer with Windows Vista/7 installed and administrator rights

Procedure: Complete the following procedure and answer the accompanying questions.

1. Turn on the computer and verify that the operating system loads. Log in to Windows using the user ID and password provided by your instructor or lab assistant. Ensure that the user ID is one that has Administrator rights.

Verifying and Installing Windows Features

2. Open *Windows Explorer*, right-click *Computer*, and select *Properties*. Select the *System Protection* link.
3. Create a system restore point by clicking the *Create* button. In the description textbox type `class` followed by the current date. Click *Create*. A dialog box appears when the restore point has been successfully created. Click *OK*.

   According to the chapter text, what makes Windows Vista/7's System Restore utility different from the one used in Windows XP?

4. Click *OK* in the System Properties window.
5. Access the *Programs* Control Panel to select the *Turn Windows features on or off* link from the Programs and features section.

   List three enabled Windows features.

List three Windows features that are turned off.

6. Notice how the Games option is controlled through this section. Expand the *Games* option.

   List three available games.

7. Check with your instructor or lab assistant for a specific feature to turn on. One option would be to turn on the TFTP client if it is not enabled.

   List the program to be enabled.

8. Select the checkbox for the feature to be enabled and click *OK*. Note that enabling the feature might take a few minutes.
9. Re-access the *Turn Windows features on or off* link to verify that the feature now shows as enabled.

Instructor initials: ____________

10. Remove the check from the feature you just enabled and verify that the feature is removed successfully.
11. Select the *Default Programs* link (from the *Programs and Features* (Vista)/*Programs* (7) control panel link). Select the *Set your default programs* link.

    List the options available from this window.

12. Select *Internet Explorer* from the Programs list. Select the *Choose defaults for this program* link.

    List the extensions that are automatically opened by Internet Explorer.

    List protocols that are automatically recognized from the address line in Internet Explorer.

13. Click *Cancel* and *OK* to return to the Default Programs window.
14. Select the *Associate a file type or protocol with a program* link.

    List one program that does not have a program extension or protocol associated with it.

15. Leave this window open and create and save a Notepad document called `Superdog.txt`.

    Document the location where this document is saved.

16. Open *Windows Explorer* and locate the *Superdog.txt* file. In Vista, select the *Views* menu option. In Windows 7, select the *Views* drop-down arrow as shown in Figure 12.35.

    What is the current view?

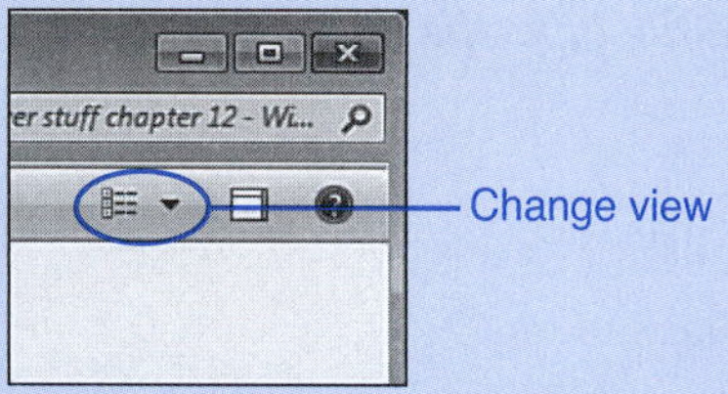

Figure 12.35 **Windows 7 Explorer—Views menu access**

17. Select the *List* view. Select the *Organize* menu option and select *Folder and Search Options*. Select the *View* tab.

    What is the current setting for Hide extensions for known file types? [Enabled | Disabled]

18. Ensure that the *Hide extensions for known file types* option is disabled (unchecked). Click *OK*.
19. Return to Windows Explorer and ensure that the `.txt` extension is visible on the `Superdog.txt` filename. Right-click the *`Superdog.txt`* file and select *Rename*. Rename the `.txt` extension to *`.cas`* (or your own initials, if they are not a common file extension). When the message window appears, click *Yes*.

    How did the appearance of the file change?

20. Right-click the *Superdog* file and select *Properties*.

    What application does Windows assign to open the document?

21. Click the *Change* button. Notice that the *Always use the selected program to open this kind of file* checkbox at the bottom of the window is enabled. Select *Notepad* and *OK*. Click *Apply* and *OK*.
22. Locate the *Superdog* file in Windows Explorer and double-click the icon.

    Does the file open? If so, in what application?

23. Close the *Superdog* file. Return to the *Set Associations* window. Scroll down until you see the extension you used when you renamed the *Superdog* filename. Show your instructor or lab assistant the file extension.

Instructor initials: ______________

24. Select the file extension in the list and click the *Change program* button. Use the *Browse* button to find the WordPad application. Use the Search feature inside Browse, if necessary. Once you find WordPad, select it and click *Open*. Click *OK*.
25. Close the *Set Associations* window. Return to *Windows Explorer*. Locate the *Superdog* file and double-click the icon.

    Does the file open? If so, in what application?

26. Close the file. Permanently delete the file by holding down the *Shift* key while pressing *Delete*. Click *Yes* to permanently delete the file.
27. On your own, create another file that ends in the same file extension. Try to open it.

    What happens?

28. Close the file and permanently delete the file.
29. Re-open the *System Restore utility*.
30. Select the *Choose a different restore point* radio button and click *Next*.
31. Select the *class+date* restore point and click *Next*. Click *Finish*. Read the message that appears and click *Yes*. The system restores the system to the time before this lab was started. The system reboots, and a dialog box appears, telling you whether the restore point was successful. Click *Close*.

32. Reopen the *Programs* Control Panel and select the *Make a file type always open in a specific program* link.
33. Scroll through the list.

    Is the unique file extension used in this lab located in the list?
34. Show the instructor or lab assistant the file extension (or lack of one).

Instructor initials: ____________

35. Close the *Set Associations* window.

Lab 12.21 Windows XP Microsoft Management Console

Objective: To be able to access Microsoft Management Console, see what folders are being shared, view and add a user, access Device Manager, access disk management tools, and view current services

Parts: Computer with Windows XP and Administrative Tools installed

Note: If Administrative Tools is not already installed, use Lab 12 to install it.

Procedure: Complete the following procedure and answer the accompanying questions.

1. Turn on the computer and verify that the operating system loads. Log in to Windows XP using the user ID and password provided by the instructor or lab assistant. Ensure that the user ID is one that has Administrator rights.
2. To access Microsoft Management Console, click the *Start* button, point to the *Control Panel* option, point to *Administrative Tools*, and click the *Computer Management* option.

   Using the Help menu item, determine what each of the three major Computer Management sections are used for and complete Table 12.30. Write the description found in Help.

Table 12.30 **Windows XP help on Computer Management options**

Computer Management section	Description
System Tools	
Storage	
Services and Applications	

3. Return to the Computer Management window and, if necessary, click the plus sign beside System Tools to expand it. If necessary, click the + (plus sign) beside Shared Folders to expand it and click the *Shares* folder. Shares are used when the computer is in a network environment. Other users on different computers can access resources on this computer. When networking is enabled, default administrative shares are created for each hard drive partition. Administrative shares can be easily identified by the $ (dollar sign) after the share name.

   List two default shares located on this machine. If none are available, document this fact.

4. If necessary, click the + (plus sign) by *Local Users and Groups* to expand it and click the *Users* folder.

   List two users shown in the Computer Management window.

5. To add a new user who will have access to this computer, click the *Action* menu option and select *New User*. The New User window opens. Click the *Question mark* icon located in the upper-right corner of the window. An arrow with an attached question mark appears as the pointer. Move the pointer to inside the *User name* textbox and click. A *Help* box appears.

   Based on the information in the help balloon, what is the maximum number of characters the user name can contain?

   Can spaces be used within the user name?

6. In the *User name* textbox, type **`Jeff Cansler`**. In the *Full name* textbox, type **`Jeffrey Wayne Cansler`**. In the *Description* textbox, type **`Brother`**. In the *Password* and the *Confirm password* textboxes, type **`test`**. Click in the *User must change password at next logon* checkbox to disable it. Click in the *User cannot change password* textbox to enable this option. Click the *Create* button. Click the *Close* button. The Jeff Cansler user icon appears in the Computer Management console window.

   Have a classmate verify the Jeff Cansler user icon. Have him/her double-click the icon to verify your settings. Are the settings correct? If not, redo the previous step.

Classmate's printed name: ______________________________

Classmate's signature: ______________________________

7. Log off the computer and log back on using the Jeff Cansler user name with a password of test.

   Did the logon work correctly? If not, log back on using the user ID and password given to you in the beginning of the lab by the lab assistant or instructor and redo Step 6.

8. Log off the computer and log back on using the user ID and password given to you by the lab assistant or instructor. Access the *Computer Management* window and double-click the *Jeff Cansler* user icon. Click the *Member of* tab.

   To what group does the Jeff Cansler user automatically belong?

9. Click the *Add* button. The Select Groups window opens. In the *Enter the object names to select* textbox, type **`Administrators`** and click the *Check Names* button. Click the *OK* button. The display changes to `Jeff Cansler` belonging to both the Users and Administrator groups. Click the *Apply* button and then the *OK* button.

Instructor initials: ____________

10. Return to the Jeff Cansler user window and click the *Profile* tab. The Profile tab is used to specify a home directory for the user, run a logon script that sets specific parameters for the user, input a path that specifies where the user stores files by default, or input a shared network directory where the user's data is placed. The *Profile path* textbox is where you type the location of the profile using a UNC (Universal Naming Convention). An example is `\\ocsic\profiles\jcansler`. The *Logon script* textbox is where you type the name of the logon script file, for example, `startup.bat`. The *Home folder Local path* textbox is where you type the full path for where the user's data is stored by default. An example is `d:\users\jcansler`. The *Connect* radio button is used to assign a network drive letter and specify the location of a network directory where the user's data is stored. An example is `\\ocsic\users\jcandata`. Click the *Cancel* button to return to the Computer Management window. Notice that users that are disabled have a red *X* on their icon.

    Are any users disabled? If so, list them.

11. In the Computer Management window, click the *Groups* folder.

    List two default groups.

12. Double-click the *Administrators* group icon. The Administrators group has total control of the local machine.

    Are any users listed as part of the Administrators group?
    If so, list them.

    Fill in Table 12.31 with the purpose of each user group type. Use the *Help* menu item for more information than what is shown in the window.

Table 12.31 Windows XP user group types

Group	Description
Administrators	
Backup Operators	
Guests	
Power Users	
Users	

13. Click the *Cancel* button and then click the *Users* folder located in the Computer Management window. Click the *Jeff Cansler* user icon. Click the red *X* button or click the *Action* menu item and select *Delete*. A message appears asking if you are sure that you want to delete this user. Click the *Yes* button.
14. Go into the Administrators group and verify that Jeff Cansler no longer appears there.

    Have a classmate verify that the Jeff Cansler user icon is deleted. Is the Jeff Cansler user icon deleted? If not, redo the previous step.

Classmate's printed name: ______________________________

Classmate's signature: ______________________________

15. Click the *Device Manager* option located in the Computer Management window. Device Manager is used to access and manage hardware devices installed in the computer. It is also used to load new drivers and roll back to old drivers.

16. Click the + (plus sign) by the computer's name if the list is not already expanded. Click the + (plus sign) by the *Computer* category.

    Does the computer have ACPI enabled?

17. If the computer has ACPI enabled, double-click the *ACPI* option. The window that opens is similar to all individual device windows although the tabs may vary depending on the device.

    The *General* tab has a device status window where you can see whether Windows believes the device is working properly.

    The *Driver* tab contains information about the driver version, a button to update the driver, and a button to roll the driver back to a previous version.

Tech Tip

Don't always believe the message that the device is working properly

Just because Windows states that a device is working does not make it so. There is also a Troubleshooter button on the General tab that can be used to troubleshoot the individual device.

18. Click the *Cancel* button and, if necessary, click the + (plus sign) beside the *Storage* category to expand it. Click the *Disk Management* subcategory. The right Computer Management window displays information about each type of hard disk partition created on the drive.

    The top window shows information about each disk partition including total capacity, file system, free space percentage, and so forth. The bottom windows show the partitions in graphical form.

19. Right-click the first disk partition (Disk 0) graph in the lower window and select the *Properties* option. An alternate method for getting to this screen is to click the *Action* menu item and select *Properties*. The Disk Properties window opens.

20. On an NTFS partition, the General tab contains a Disk Cleanup button that can be used to clean up temporary files and delete applications not used, Windows components not used, log files, and old system restores. Click the *Tools* tab.

    What tools are listed on the Tools tab?

    Match the following tool to its associated task.

____Backup	a. Scans the disk for damage
____Error-checking	b. Used to restore system files that have been saved
____Defragmentation	c. Locates file clusters that are not consecutive (contiguous) and places the files in order

21. The Disk Management tool can be used to create disk partitions, delete partitions, convert partitions to NTFS, create logical drives, and convert basic disks to dynamic disks. Click the *Cancel* button.

22. If necessary, click the + (plus sign) by the *Services and Applications Computer Management* category to expand it. Click the *Services* subcategory. A service is an application that runs in the background (you do not see it on the taskbar). The Services window is used to start, stop, pause, resume, or disable a service. You must be a member of the Administrators group to use this tool.

    List two services that start automatically when the computer starts and two services that require manual starting.

23. Double-click the *Computer Browser* service. The General tab is used to start, stop, pause, or resume a service (depending on its current state). The buttons in the Service status section are used to control these actions. The General tab is also used to set whether or not the service starts when the computer boots. Click the *Startup type* down arrow to see a menu of startup options.
24. Close the *Service* window without making any changes to the service and close the *Computer Management* window.

Instructor initials: ____________

Lab 12.22 Windows 7 Microsoft Management Console

Objective: To be able to access and use the major utilities found in the Microsoft Management Console

Parts: Computer with Windows 7 installed and administrator rights

Notes: You must be an administrator to utilize the Microsoft Management Console utilities.

Procedure: Complete the following procedure and answer the accompanying questions.

1. Power on the computer and verify that Windows 7 loads. Log on to Windows using the user ID and password provided by the instructor or lab assistant.
2. To access Microsoft Management Console, click the *Start* button > *Control Panel* > *System and Security* link > *Administrative Tools* > double-click the *Computer Management* option.

   Determine the subcategories for each of the major Computer Management sections. Write the subcategories using Table 12.32.

Table 12.32 Windows 7 Computer Management console

Computer Management section	Subcategories
System Tools	
Storage	
Services and Applications	

3. Return to the *Computer Management* window and, if necessary, click the arrow beside *System Tools* to expand the section. If necessary, click the arrow beside *Shared Folders* to expand that section. Click the *Shares* folder. Shares are used when the computer is in a network environment. Other users on different computers can access resources on this computer. When networking is enabled, default administrative shares are created for each hard drive partition. Administrative shares can be easily identified by the $ (dollar sign) after the share name.

   List two default shares located on this machine. If none are available, document the fact.

4. If necessary, expand *Local Users* and *Groups* and click the *Users* folder.

   List the users shown in the Computer Management window.

5. To add a new user who will have access to this computer, click the *Action* menu option and select *New User*. The New User window opens. Click the *Question mark* icon located in the upper-right corner of the window. An arrow with an attached question mark appears as a pointer. Move the pointer to inside the *User name* textbox and click. A Help box appears.

Based on the information in the help balloon, what is the maximum number of characters the user name can contain?

Can a plus sign (+) be used within the user name?

6. In the *User name* textbox, type **`Jeff Cansler`**. In the *Full name* textbox, type **`Jeffrey Wayne Cansler`**. In the *Description* textbox, type **`Brother`**. In the *Password* and the *Confirm password* textboxes, type **`test`**. Ensure that the *User must change password at next logon* checkbox is disabled (not checked). Click in the *User cannot change password* checkbox to enable this option. Click the *Create* button. Click the *Close* button. The Jeff Cansler user icon appears in the Computer Management window.

   Have a classmate verify the Jeff Cansler user icon. Have the classmate double-click the icon to verify your settings. Are the settings correct? If not, redo the previous step.

Classmate's printed name: ______________________

Classmate's signature: ______________________

7. Log off the computer and log back on using the Jeff Cansler username with a password of *test*.

   Did the log on process work correctly? If not, log back on using the user ID and password given to you by the lab assistant or instructor for the beginning of the lab and redo Step 6.

8. Log off the computer and log back on using the user ID and password given to you by the lab assistant or instructor (the original user ID and password). Access the *Computer Management* window and double-click the *Jeff Cansler* user icon. Click the *Member of* tab.

   To what group does the Jeff Cansler user automatically belong?

9. Click the *Add* button. The Select Groups window opens. In the *Enter the object names to select* textbox, type **`Administrators`** and click the *Check Names* button. Click the *OK* button. The information shown changes to the user, Jeff Cansler, belonging to both the Users and Administrator groups. Click the *Apply* button and then the *OK* button.

Instructor initials: ____________

10. Re-open the Jeff Cansler user window and click the *Profile* tab. The *Profile* tab is used to specify a home directory for the user, run a logon script that sets specific parameters for the user, input a path that specifies where the user stores files by default, or input a shared network directory where the user's data is placed. The *Profile path* textbox is where you type the location of the profile using a UNC. An example is `\\ocsic\profiles\jcansler`. The *Logon script* textbox is where you type the name of the logon script file, for example `startup.bat`. The *Home folder Local path* textbox is where you type the full path for where the user's data is stored by default. An example is `D:\users\jcansler`. The *Connect*radio button is used to assign a network drive letter and specify the location of a network directory where the user's data is stored. An example is `\\ocsic\users\jcandata`. Click the *Cancel* button to return to the Computer Management window. Notice that users that are disabled have a small down arrow on their icon.

    Are any users disabled? [Yes | No]

11. In the Computer Management window, click the *Groups* folder.

    List two default groups.

12. Double-click the *Administrators* group icon. The Administrators group has total control of the local machine.

    Are any users listed as part of the Administrators group? If so, list them.

    Fill in Table 12.33 with the purpose of each group type. Use the *Help* menu item for more information than what is shown in the window.

Table 12.33 Windows 7 User Groups

Group	Description
Administrators	
Backup Operators	
Guests	
Users	

13. Click the *Cancel* button and then click the *Users* folder located in the Computer Management window. Click the *Jeff Cansler* user icon. Click the red *X* button or click the *Action* menu item and select *Delete*. A message appears asking if you are sure that you want to delete this user. Click the *Yes* button.
14. Go into the *Administrators* group and verify that Jeff Cansler no longer appears there.

    Have a classmate verify that the Jeff Cansler user icon is deleted. Is the Jeff Cansler user icon deleted? If not, redo the previous step.

Classmate's printed name: ____

Classmate's signature: ____

15. Click the *Device Manager* option located in the Computer Management window. This utility can also be accessed by typing `devmgmt.msc`. Device Manager is used to access and manage hardware devices installed in the computer. It is also used to load new drivers and roll back to an older driver.
16. In the right panel, click the arrow by the computer name if the list is not already expanded. Expand the *Computer* category.

    Does the computer have ACPI enabled? This would be evidenced by a computer subcategory. [Yes | No]
17. If the computer has ACPI enabled, double-click the *ACPI* option. The window that opens is similar to all individual device windows although the tabs may vary depending on the device. The *General* tab has a device status window where you can see whether Windows believes the device is working.

    The *Driver* tab contains information about the driver version, a button to update the driver, and a button to roll the driver back to a previous version. The *Details* tab shows additional information about the specific device.

Tech Tip

Don't always believe Windows when it says the device is working properly

Just because Device Manager states a device is working properly does not make it so. Some devices have a Troubleshooter button on the General tab that can be used to troubleshoot a problem with the device.

18. Click the *Cancel* button and, if necessary, expand the *Storage* category in the left pane. Click the *Disk Management* subcategory. The right pane displays information about each type of hard disk partition created on the drive. The top window shows information about each disk partition including total capacity, file system, free space percentage, and so forth. The bottom windows show the drives and partitions in graphical form.
19. Right-click the first disk partition (Disk 0) graph in the lower window and select the *Properties* option. An alternate method is to click the *Action* menu item and select *Properties*. The Disk Properties window opens.
20. On an NTFS partition, the General tab contains a *Disk Cleanup* button that can be used to clean up temporary files and delete applications not used, Windows components not used, log files, and old system restores. Click the *Tools* tab.

    What tools are listed on the Tools tab?

    Match the following tool to its associated task.

____Backup	a. Scans the disk for damage
____Error-checking	b. Used to restore system files that have been saved
____Defragmentation	c. Locates file clusters that are not consecutive contiguous) and places the files in order

21. The Disk Management tool can be used to create disk partitions, delete partitions, convert partitions to NTFS, create logical drives, and convert basic disks to dynamic disks. Click the *Cancel* button.
22. If necessary, expand the *Services and Applications* Computer Management category. Click the *Services* subcategory. A service is an application that runs in the background (you do not see it on the taskbar). The Services window is used to start, stop, pause, resume, or disable a service. You must be a member of the Administrators group to use this tool.

    List two services that start automatically and two services that require manual starting.

23. Double-click the *Computer Browser* service. The General tab is used to start, stop, pause, or resume a service (depending on its current state). The buttons in the Service status section are used to control these actions. The General tab is also used to set whether or not the service starts when the computer boots. Click the *Startup type* down arrow to see a menu of startup options.
24. Close the *Service* window without making any changes to the service and close the *Computer Management* window.

Instructor initials: ____________

Lab 12.23 Exploring Windows XP Boot Options

Objective: To explore Windows XP boot options that are used to troubleshoot startup problems

Parts: Computer with Windows XP installed that has the ability to boot from a CD

User ID that has Administrator rights

Windows XP CD

Note: In this lab, you will boot without startup programs loaded, boot to Safe Mode, boot to Safe Mode with Command Prompt, boot to Enable Boot Logging and examine the NTBTLOG.TXT file, and boot to Recovery Console and examine commands using the command prompt.

Procedure: Complete the following procedure and answer the accompanying questions.

1. Turn on the computer and verify that the operating system loads. Log in to Windows XP using the user ID and password provided by the instructor or lab assistant. Ensure that the user ID is one that has Administrator rights.

Verifying Startup Folder Contents

2. Right-click the *Start* button and click the *Explore* option.
3. Locate the *Documents and Settings* folder and expand it if necessary. Locate the *All Users* folder (located under *Documents and Settings*) and expand it if necessary. Locate the *Start Menu* subfolder (located under *All Users*) and expand it if necessary. Locate the *Programs* subfolder (located under the *Start Menu* folder) and expand it if necessary. Click the *Startup* folder located under the *Programs* folder.

   Are there any program shortcuts listed in the Startup folder? If so, list at least one of the programs.

Classmate's printed name: ______________________________

Classmate's signature: ________________________________

   If there is no program shortcut, create a shortcut to the Notepad application and place it in the *Startup* folder.

4. Restart the computer and verify that the program listed in the Startup folder starts automatically when the computer boots. If it does not, redo the lab.

Instructor initials: ____________

Preventing Startup Programs from Loading

5. Restart the computer and while the computer boots and the login process occurs, press the Shift key until the desktop icons appear. Pressing the Shift key stops startup programs from loading automatically. This technique works when any program that starts automatically is causing problems. If this does not work for you, shut down the computer properly, power off, power back on, log in, and press the Shift key during the login process.

   What indication do you have that holding down the Shift key while booting stopped the application from loading?

6. Using Windows Explorer, delete the shortcut located in the *Startup* folder.

   Have a classmate verify that you only deleted the shortcut and not the application. Has the shortcut been deleted? [Yes | No]

Classmate's printed name: ________________________________

Classmate's signature: ________________________________

Using Boot Options

7. Restart the computer and press the F8 key as the computer boots. The Windows Advanced Boot Options menu appears. If it does not, repeat this procedure until it does. Select the *Safe Mode* option and press Enter.

   What is different about the Windows XP login screen?

   Why do you think the Administrator user icon appears in Safe Mode and not during the regular boot sequence?

8. Log in as Administrator.

   How do you know that the computer is running in Safe Mode?

9. Click the *Yes* button.

   Did your program in the *Startup* folder automatically start?

   Are Administrative Tools available through the *Start* button's *All Programs* list?

   To what Control Panel view does the system default?

10. Double-click the *Administrative Tools* control panel. Double-click the *Computer Management* icon. Access the *Services* folder.

    List two automatic services that have a status of *started*.

11. Notice how there are quite a few services that are automatic services that did not start in Safe Mode. Close the *Computer Management* screen and the *Administrative Tools* window.

12. Restart the computer and press the F8 key to see the Windows Advanced Boot Options menu.

    List the boot options available.

    Match the following definitions to the appropriate boot option:

    ___ Safe Mode

    ___ Safe Mode with Command Prompt

    ___ Enable Boot Logging

    ___ Last Known Good Configuration

    a. Starts the system with minimum files and drivers and only typed commands can be used

    b. Records the boot process into a text file that can later be viewed and used for troubleshooting

    c. Starts the system with minimum file and drivers including VGA video drivers

    d. Used when a newly installed piece of hardware or software causes the system not to boot properly

13. Select the *Safe Mode with Command Prompt* option and log in as Administrator.

    What is different about the desktop appearance?

14. Click the *minimize* button, which is the left-most button in the upper-right corner of the `cmd.exe` window.

    What does the screen look like now?

15. The *Safe Mode with Command Prompt* option is used to start the system with minimum files and drivers and a command prompt where you must type commands instead of working through a graphical interface. Type **`exit`** at the command prompt.

    What happened to the screen?

Instructor initials: ____________

16. Press Ctrl+Alt+Del and the Task Manager window appears. Click the *Shut Down* menu option and select *Restart*. Restart the computer, press the F8 key to see the Windows *Advanced Boot Options* menu. Select the *Enable Boot Logging* option.

    Does the Administrator user ID appear as a login choice?

17. Log in to Windows XP.

    How does the desktop appear when using the Enable Boot Logging option?

18. Using Windows Explorer, locate the file `ntbtlog.txt` and double-click the file icon to open the file.

    List two drivers that loaded properly.

    List two drivers that did not load.

Instructor initials: ______________

19. Close the `ntbtlog.txt` window and close all Windows Explorer windows.

Recovery Console

20. Shut the computer down and power off. Insert the Windows XP CD into the drive and power on the computer. The Welcome to Setup screen appears. If the computer does not boot from the Windows XP CD, the BIOS settings probably need to be adjusted. Press R at the Welcome to Setup screen. The Recovery screen appears.
21. Press the number that corresponds to the partition that contains XP.
22. Type the Administrator password. Contact a lab assistant or the instructor if the password is unknown. The Recovery Console loads.

    Write down what the prompt looks like.

23. The Recovery Console is used as a last resort—when other boot options do not solve the problem. At the prompt, type **`copy`** and press Enter. An error message appears. Command prompt usage must be very precise and exact commands with proper switches must be used.
24. Type **`help copy`** and press Enter. Help information on the copy command appears.
25. Type **`copy /?`** and press Enter. Again, help information appears.
26. Type **`help`** and press Enter. A list of Recovery Console commands appears. Press the Spacebar to see the rest of the command list.

Instructor initials: ______________

27. Remove the XP CD and type **`exit`**. The system boots normally.

Lab 12.24 Exploring Windows 7 Boot Options

Objective: To explore Windows 7 boot options that are used to troubleshoot startup problems

Parts: Computer with Windows 7 installed that has the ability to boot from a CD/DVD

User ID that has Administrator rights

Windows 7 DVD or virtual image of the DVD

Note: In this lab, you will boot without startup programs loaded, boot to Safe Mode, boot to Safe Mode with Command Prompt, boot to Enable Boot Logging and examine the `ntbtlog.txt` file, and boot to Recovery Console and examine commands using the command prompt. If the Windows 7 DVD or image of the installation disc is not available, then that one section could be skipped.

Procedure: Complete the following procedure and answer the accompanying questions.

1. Turn on the computer and verify that the operating system loads. Log in to Windows using the user ID and password provided by your instructor or lab assistant.

Using Boot Options

2. Restart the computer and press the F8 key as the computer boots. If the *Advanced Boot Options* window does not appear, shut down the computer and restart. Press F8 as the computer boots. The *Advanced Boot Options* menu appears. Select the *Safe Mode* option and press Enter. Log in as Administrator, as necessary.

   When would a technician use the Safe Mode option as opposed to the Safe Mode with Command Prompt option?

   How does the look of the screen in Safe Mode differ from the look of the normal Windows desktop?

   What Windows Help and Support topic automatically displays?

   According to the information presented, how can you easily tell you are running in Safe Mode?

   According to the information displayed, if Windows successfully boots into Safe Mode, what suspect problems are eliminated?

   What information is displayed as a suggestions for what to try next if the Safe Mode boot process is successful?

3. Access the *Administrative Tools* control panel link. Open *Computer Management*. Expand the *Services and Applications* category. Access the *Services* option.
4. Notice that there are quite a few services that are automatic services that did not start in Safe Mode.

   List two services that did not automatically start because Safe Mode with Networking was used.

5. Close the *Computer Management* and any control panel windows.
6. Restart the computer and press the F8 key to access the *Advanced Boot Options* menu.

   List the boot options available.

Match each of the following definitions to the appropriate boot option:

___ Safe Mode

___ Safe Mode with Command Prompt

___ Enable Boot Logging

___ Last Known Good Configuration (advanced)

a. Starts the system with minimum files and drivers, and only typed commands can be used

b. Records the boot process into a text file that can later be viewed and used for troubleshooting

c. Starts the system with minimum files and drivers, including the default video drivers

d. Used when a newly installed piece of hardware or software causes the system not to boot properly

7. Select the *Safe Mode with Command Prompt* option. Log in using the same user name and password.

   What is different about the desktop appearance compared to the desktop before the reboot?

8. Click the *minimize* button, which is the left-most button in the upper-right corner of the `cmd.exe` window.

   What does the screen look like now?

9. The *Safe Mode with Command Prompt* option is used to start the system with minimum files and drivers and a command prompt where you must type commands instead of working through a graphical interface. Re-access the `cmd.exe` window. Type **`dir`** at the command prompt.

   How many files are available?

   How many directories are available?

Instructor initials: ____________

10. Type **`dir r*.*`** at the command prompt.

    List three files that are executables that start with the letter R.

11. Type **`rstrui`** at the command prompt.

    What happened as a result of typing this command?

12. Close the window that appeared.

13. From the command prompt window, type **`exit`**.

    What happened as a result of typing this command?

14. Press Ctrl+Alt+Del. Select the *red power* button menu in the lower-right corner and select *Restart*. Restart the computer and press the F8 key to see the *Advanced Boot Options* menu. Select the *Enable Boot Logging* option.

    How does the desktop appear when using the Enable Boot Logging option?

15. Using the *Start* button *Search programs and files* textbox, locate and access the `ntbtlog.txt` file.

List two drivers that loaded properly.

List two drivers that did not load.

Instructor initials: ______________

16. Close all windows.

Recovery Environment

17. Shut the computer down and power off. Insert the Windows 7 installation disc into the drive and power on the computer. If prompted, press a key to start Windows from the disc. A menu appears with a default option selected. Press Enter. If the computer does not boot from the Windows disc, the BIOS settings probably need to be adjusted.
18. Choose the appropriate language settings and click *Next*.
19. Select *Repair your computer*. In the System Recovery Options window, select the *Use recovery tools that can help fix problems starting Windows*. Enable the *Select an operating system to repair* radio button.
20. Ensure that the operating system is selected and click *Next*.

    List the recovery tool options.

    Which option would be used to repair a system file?

    Which option would be used to check RAM?

    Which option would be for advanced technicians?

    Which option configures the system to an earlier time such as before a Windows update?

Instructor initials: ______________

21. Select the *Memory Diagnostic* link. Select the *Restart now and check for problems (recommended)* link. Do not press a key when the system reboots and asks "Press a key to boot from CD or DVD."

    List one status message.

22. Once the test executes and the computer reboots, again, do not press any key even when the message prompts to press a key to boot from CD or DVD. Once Windows reboots, log in again. Open Event Viewer by accessing the following control panel links: *System and Security > Administrative tools*. Double-click *Event Viewer* to open the tool.
23. Expand *Windows Logs*. Click the *System* Windows log. Right-click *System* and select *Find*.
24. In the *Find what* textbox, type the following:

    `MemoryDiagnostics-Results`

    Be very careful that you type exactly as shown and click *Find Next*. The corresponding line highlights.
25. Close the *Find* window. Double-click the highlighted line to see the results of the memory diagnostic check. Select the *Details* tab.

    What are the results shown in the friendly view?

    What Event ID did Windows assign?
26. Close all windows. Remove the Windows disc and return to the instructor or lab assistant.

Lab 12.25 Windows XP System Configuration Utility

Objective: To be able to use the System Configuration utility to troubleshoot boot problems

Parts: Computer with Windows XP installed

User ID that has Administrator rights

Note: In this lab, create a shortcut to an application and then use the System Configuration utility to prevent it from loading. Explore various options that can be used within the System Configuration utility.

Procedure: Complete the following procedure and answer the accompanying questions.

1. Turn on the computer and verify that the operating system loads. Log in to Windows XP using the user ID and password provided by the instructor or lab assistant. Ensure that the user ID is one that has Administrator rights.

Creating an Application Shortcut in the Startup Folder

2. Right-click the *Start* button and click the *Explore* option.
3. Locate the *Documents and Settings* folder and expand it if necessary. Locate the *All Users* folder (located under *Documents and Settings*) and expand it if necessary. Locate the *Start Menu* subfolder (located under *All Users*) and expand it if necessary. Locate the *Programs* subfolder (located under the *Start Menu* folder) and expand it if necessary. Click the *Startup* folder located under the *Programs* folder.
4. Use the *Search* Start button option to locate the original Notepad application (`notepad.exe`). Create a shortcut to the Notepad application and place it in the *Startup* folder located under the *Programs* folder (see Step 3). Lab 11.1 in Chapter 11 explains how to create a shortcut.

   Have a classmate verify your shortcut (especially that it is a shortcut and not a copy of the application or the application itself). Is the icon in the Startup folder a shortcut icon?

Classmate's printed name: ____________________________

Classmate's signature: ____________________________

5. Restart the computer and verify that the Notepad program starts automatically when the computer boots. If it does not, redo.

Instructor initials: ____________

System Configuration Utility

6. Click the *Start* button, click the *Run* option, type **msconfig** and press Enter. The System Configuration utility window opens.

   What is the purpose of the System Configuration utility?

   What five tabs are available through the System Configuration utility?

7. Click the *Diagnostic Startup—load basic devices and services only* radio button. Click the *Apply* button and then click the *Close* button. A System Configuration message box appears. Click the *Restart* button. When the computer restarts, log in with the same user ID used previously.

   What is different about the way Windows XP loads?

   Did the Notepad application automatically start?

8. Click the *OK* button. Click the *Selective Startup* radio button found on the *General* tab. Checkboxes are now available so that you can select the startup files that are to be loaded the next time the computer boots. Click the *Load Startup Items* checkbox. Click the *Apply*

button and then click *Close*. Click the *Restart* button and the system restarts. Log in using the same user ID and password.

Did the Notepad application automatically start? Why or why not?

9. Click the *OK* button. Click the *Normal Startup—load all device drivers and services* option located on the *General* tab.
10. Click the *Startup* tab. Click the *Shortcut to notepad* checkbox to disable it.

Instructor initials: ______________

11. Click the *Apply* button and then click *Close*. Click the *Restart* button. When the computer restarts, log in using the same user ID and click *OK*.

    Did the Notepad application automatically start? Why or why not?

    What is different about the System Configuration utility's General tab?

    Match the correct System Configuration utility tab to its characteristic.

    ____ General ____ `BOOT.INI`

    ____ `SYSTEM.INI` ____ Services

    ____ `WIN.INI` ____ Startup

    a. Contains the [386enh] section

    b. Contains applications that begin every time the computer boots

    c. Contains a section called [boot loader] that details operating system boot options

    d. Has an option to choose which boot files are processed

    e. Contains an option called Application Management

    f. Used with old Windows 3.x applications and contains a section called [fonts]

12. Click the *General* tab and select the *Normal Startup* radio button. Click the *Apply* button and then click *Close*. Click the *Restart* button. Log in using the same user ID.
13. Once the computer reboots, remove the shortcut to the Notepad application from the *Startup* folder.

    Is the Notepad shortcut (and not the original application) deleted?

Instructor initials: ______________

Lab 12.26 Windows 7 Startup Configuration

Objective: To be able to use the System Configuration tool to troubleshoot startup problems

Parts: Access to Windows 7 with a user ID that has administrator rights

Procedure: Complete the following procedure and answer the accompanying questions.

1. Turn on the computer and verify that the operating system loads. Log in to Windows 7 using the user ID and password that has full administrator rights and that is provided by your instructor or lab assistant.
2. Open *Windows Explorer* > locate and select the *Organize* menu option > *Folder and Search Options* > *View* tab.

    What is the current setting for the Hidden files and folders option?
    [Don't show hidden files, folders, or drivers | Show hidden files, folders, and drives]

    What is the current setting for the Hide extensions for known file types?
    [Enabled | Disabled]

What is the current setting for Hide protected operating system files (Recommended)? [Enabled | Disabled]

3. Configure the following settings:

   Show hidden files, folders, and drives—enabled

   Hide extensions for known file types—enabled

   Hide protected operating system files (Recommended)—enabled

   Click *Yes* (if prompted) > *Apply* > *OK*. Close *Windows Explorer*.

4. Re-open *Windows Explorer* and locate the *Start* folder using the path that follows:

   x:\ProgramData\Microsoft\Windows\Start Menu\Programs\Startup (where *x*: is the drive where Windows is installed, such as C:)

   Leave the Windows Explorer window open once the Startup folder has been found. Place a shortcut to the *WordPad* application in the Startup folder. Refer to a previous lab if you cannot do this task. Click *Continue* if prompted.

5. Restart the computer and ensure that the WordPad application automatically opens. Do not immediately suspect something is amiss if WordPad does not open quickly. Windows services and drivers load first. If WordPad does not open eventually, redo the lab until the WordPad application opens automatically as part of the startup process.

Instructor initials: ______________

6. From the *Start* menu, type **`msconfig`** in the *Search programs and files* textbox and press Enter. The System Configuration window opens.

   What is the purpose of the System Configuration utility?

   What five tabs are available in the System Configuration utility window?

7. On the *General* tab, select *Selective Startup*. Ensure that the *Load startup items* checkbox is disabled (unchecked). This setting is used when a problem occurs and you suspect a startup application is the culprit. Leaving system services enabled allows services configured through the Administrative Tools/Services Control Panel link to load (even though these services may be the problem). By doing this, you can divide the problem in half by proving that one of the startup applications is the problem or that none of the startup applications are causing the problem. If the computer starts and the problem does not appear, one of the services may be the problem. Click the *Startup* tab.

   What options, if any, are automatically checked now?

8. Click the *Enable all* button. Scroll through the list to locate the *Microsoft Windows Operating System* item. (Note that it is frequently the last item. You can expand the *Startup Item* column temporarily to see the full words by holding the mouse over the line that separates the *Startup Item* column from the *Manufacturer* column until the mouse cursor turns into a double arrow symbol. Click on the separating line and drag it slowly to the right to increase the *Startup Item* column width. When finished return the column to the original size.)

9. Select the *Microsoft Windows Operating System* option to deselect it. Expand the *Command* column temporarily to ensure that the path is correct for the `wordpad.exe` file. If this is not the correct option, select another option with the words *Microsoft Windows Operating System* that has the path for the `wordpad.exe` file. Ensure that the check mark is removed from this item. This prevents the WordPad application from opening as part of the boot process, but all other services and startup files/applications execute.

10. Click *Apply* > *OK*. A System Configuration Manager application message box appears. Select the *Restart* button. When the computer restarts, log in using the same user ID and password.

    What is different about how the system boots now?

11. Open the *System Configuration* utility again.

    How does the *Load startup items* checkbox appear and what do you think this means based on what you have done?

12. The Selective startup (and associated options) as well as the Startup tab are some of the best tools you can use for a startup problem. Normally you would disable all applications and then re-enable an application one application at a time until you find the problem. Also, the reverse can be tried—enable all applications and then disable them one by one until you find the problem.

    Click the *Diagnostic Startup—Load basic devices and services only* radio button. Click the *Apply* button > *OK* > *Restart*.

    What is different about the way Windows loads now?

    Did the WordPad application automatically start?

13. Open the *System Configuration* utility again. Click the *Normal Startup—Load all device drivers and services* option located on the *General* tab.
14. Select the *Boot* tab.

    List three boot options that can be customized.

    What is the default timeout value for the boot menu?

15. Click *Apply* > *OK* > *Restart*.
16. Once the system restarts, reopen the *System Configuration* utility. Select the *Services* tab.

    List three services currently enabled.

17. Select the *Tools* tab that is new to Windows Vista and 7.

    List all utilities that can be started from the *Tools* tab.

18. Select the *Registry Editor* option and click *Launch*. The Registry Editor opens.
19. Close the Registry Editor window. Close the System configuration utility window.
20. Re-access the *Startup* folder and delete the *WordPad* shortcut.
21. Reopen *Windows Explorer* and configure the *View* tab as it was originally set in Step 2.

    Show the instructor or lab assistant the correct Windows Explorer settings.

Instructor initials: __________ (See Step 2 answers for Windows Explorer settings.)

Lab 12.27 Halting an Application Using Task Manager in Windows XP/Vista/7

Objective: To use Task Manager to halt an application

Parts: Computer with Windows XP, Vista, or 7 installed

Note: At times, it may become necessary to halt an application that is hung or stalled. Windows provides a method to accomplish this through the Task Manager utility.

Procedure: Complete the following procedure and answer the accompanying questions.

1. Turn on the computer and verify that the operating system loads. Log in to Windows using the user ID and password provided by the instructor or lab assistant. Ensure that the user ID is one that has Administrator rights.
2. From the *Start* menu, choose *All Programs*, *Accessories*, and then select *Notepad*. The Notepad utility opens.
3. To access Task Manager, simultaneously press Ctrl, Alt, and Del. In Vista/7, select the *Start Task Manager* link. The *Task Manager* window opens.

   What type of things can you view from Task Manager?

4. Select the *Applications* tab.

   What applications, if any, are listed as open?

5. Click the *Untitled—Notepad* option and click the *End Task* button. Notepad closes.

   Were you able to close the Notepad application from within Task Manager?

6. Close the *Task Manager* window.

Instructor initials: ______________

Lab 12.28 Using Windows XP Event Viewer

Objective: To be able to use the Event Viewer program to troubleshoot problems

Parts: Computer with Windows XP installed and a user ID that has Administrator rights

Note: In this lab, evaluate a computer event to see how to gather information using Event Viewer.

Procedure: Complete the following procedure and answer the accompanying questions.

1. Turn on the computer and verify that the operating system loads. Log in to Windows XP using the user ID and password provided by the instructor or lab assistant. Ensure that the user ID is one that has Administrator rights.
2. Event Viewer is used to monitor various events such as when drivers and services load (or fail to load and have problems). Click the *Start* button and click the *Control Panel* option. If in Control Panel *Category* view, click the *Performance and Maintenance* category and click *Administrative Tools*. If in *Classic* view, double-click the *Administrative Tools* Control Panel icon and then double-click the *Event Viewer* icon. The *Event Viewer* window opens.
3. Click the *Application* log located in the left pane. Application events are listed in the right pane.

   Are there any warning events listed? If so, list one of them.

   Are there any information events listed? If so, list one of them.

4. Double-click any application event.

   Do you have any way of copying the event's information to the clipboard where it can later be copied into a text file? If so, list the details of how to do this.

5. Close the *Event Properties* window. Click the *System* log located in the left pane. System events are listed in the right pane.

   What is the most common type of system event?

6. Double-click any of the individual events. Click the button that looks like two pieces of paper directly under the *Up* and *Down* arrow buttons.

7. Click the *Start* button. Click the *Run* option. Type **`clipbrd`** and press Enter. The event is copied to the Clipboard and the `clipbrd` command opens the Clipboard Viewer.
8. Open Notepad by clicking the *Start* button, pointing to *All Programs*, pointing to *Accessories*, and clicking the *Notepad* option.
9. Click the *Edit* menu option and select *Paste*.

   What appeared in Notepad?

Instructor initials: ____________

10. The event information can be saved as a text file and referenced later especially when there is a problem. Close *Notepad* without saving the document. Close *Event Viewer*.

Lab 12.29 Using Windows Vista/7 Event Viewer

Objective: To be able to use the Event Viewer program to troubleshoot problems

Parts: Computer with Windows Vista or 7 installed and a user ID that has Administrator rights

Note: In this lab, evaluate a computer event to see how to gather information using Event Viewer.

Procedure: Complete the following procedure and answer the accompanying questions.

1. Turn on the computer and verify that the operating system loads. Log in to Windows using the user ID and password provided by your instructor or lab assistant. Ensure that the user ID is one that has Administrator rights.
2. Event Viewer is used to monitor various events such as when drivers and services load (or fail to load and have problems). From the *Start* menu > *Control Panel* > *System and Maintenance* (Vista)/*System and Security* (7) > *Administrative Tools* > double-click *Event Viewer*. The Event Viewer window opens to the Overview and Summary window.

   How many total warning administrative events occurred on this computer?
3. Scroll down in *Summary of Administrative Events* and expand the *Audit Success* category. Select and double-click the line with the highest audit success event ID.

   From the General tab, what was the account name?
4. In the right panel, select the *Attach Task to This Event*. Type your first initial and last name as the name of the basic task, for example cschmidt. Click *Next* on the following two windows.

   What three actions can be taken from this screen?
5. Click *Cancel*.
6. Expand the *Windows Logs* category in the left panel. Select the *Application* subcategory.

   List the application that caused the first event.
7. Select the *Security* subcategory from the left panel. Double-click the first *Audit Success* event.

   What account name was used?
8. Close the *Event Properties* window. Select the *System* subcategory from the left panel. Double-click the first event listed.

   List the source of the first event.
9. Select the *Copy* button.
10. From the *Start* menu > *All Programs* > *Notepad* > *Edit* menu item > *Paste*.

    What appeared in Notepad?

Instructor initials: ____________

11. The event information can be saved as a text file and referenced later, especially when there is a problem. Close Notepad without saving the document. Close the *Event Properties* window.
12. In Event Viewer, expand *Applications and Services Logs*. Expand the *Microsoft* folder and the *Windows* folder. Expand the *TaskScheduler* to locate and click the *Operational* event log.

    What is the first informational TaskScheduler event logged?
13. Close *Event Viewer*.

Lab 12.30 Using Task Manager to View Performance

Objective: To be able to use the Task Manager program to evaluate basic computer performance

Parts: Computer with Windows XP, Vista, or 7 installed

User ID that has Administrator rights

Note: In this lab, evaluate a computer event to see how to gather information using Event Viewer.

Procedure: Complete the following procedure and answer the accompanying questions.

1. Turn on the computer and verify that the operating system loads. Log in to Windows using the user ID and password provided by the instructor or lab assistant. Ensure that the user ID is one that has Administrator rights.
2. Press the Ctrl+Alt+Del keys to bring up Task Manager. In Vista/7, select *Start Task Manager*. Click the *Performance* tab. The Performance tab is used to view CPU and page file usage (Vista)/memory usage (7).
3. Open *Notepad*, access the Internet if possible, open a game if possible, and start other applications.

    What happens to the CPU usage as displayed in Task Manager?

    What is the page file usage (PF Usage) in XP or the Memory usage in Vista/7?

    What is the total physical memory?

    How much memory is available?

Instructor initials: ______________

4. Task Manager is a great way to see a snapshot of the status of two of the most important pieces of hardware, the CPU and RAM (even though the Task Manager application increases both the CPU and memory usage). Close all windows.

Lab 12.31 Using the System Monitor Utility in Windows XP

Objective: To use the System Monitor utility to track individual computer components

Parts: Computer with Windows XP installed and Administrative Tools loaded

Procedure: Complete the following procedure and answer the accompanying questions.

1. Turn on the computer and verify that the operating system loads. Log in to Windows XP using the user ID and password provided by the instructor or lab assistant. Ensure that the user ID is one that has Administrator rights.
2. Click the *Start* button and click the *Control Panel* option. If in Category view, click the *Performance and Maintenance* category and click *Administrative Tools*. If in Classic view, double-click the *Administrative Tools* Control Panel icon and then double-click the *Performance* icon. The Performance window opens. The Performance utility allows you to track individual computer component's performance. This is done through individual counters.
3. In the left window, click the *System Monitor* item.

4. Click the *Add* button (the button that has a plus sign on it) or right-click in the right window and click the *Add Counters* option. The Add Counters dialog box opens.
5. Click the *Performance object* down arrow. A list of system components appears such as processor, physical disk, paging file memory, etc. Select the *Memory performance* object.
6. Once a system component has been selected, individual counters for that component can be selected and monitored. In the Select counters from list window, click the *Available Bytes* counter. Click the *Add* button.
7. Click the *Performance* object down arrow. Select the *Paging File performance* object.
8. In the Select counters from list window, click the *%Usage* counter. Click the *Add* button.

   Using the Explain button, find out for what the *%Usage* counter is used. Document the purpose of the *%Usage* counter.
9. Close the *Explain text* message box. Using the method outlined in Steps 5 through 8, select two more counters to be monitored.

   What two counters did you add?
10. Click the *Close* button. The right window in the Performance window displays a graph of the various counters. You may need to start some applications, do some cutting and pasting, or surf the Internet to see some of the counter activity. When finished, close the *Performance* window.

Instructor initials: ______________

Lab 12.32 Using the Performance Monitor Utility in Windows XP

Objective: To use the System Monitor utility to track individual computer components

Parts: Computer with Windows XP installed and Administrative Tools loaded

Procedure: Complete the following procedure and answer the accompanying questions.

1. Turn on the computer and verify that the operating system loads. Log in to Windows XP using the user ID and password provided by the instructor or lab assistant. Ensure that the user ID is one that has Administrator rights.
2. Click the *Start* button and click the *Control Panel* option. If in Control Panel Category view, click the *Performance and Maintenance* category and then click *Administrative Tools*. If in Classic view, double-click the *Administrative Tools* Control Panel icon and then double-click the *Performance* icon. The Performance window opens. The Performance utility allows you to track individual computer component's performance. This is done through individual counters.
3. Click the *Performance Logs and Alerts* option in the left panel. Click the + (plus sign) if necessary to expand the *Performance Logs and Alerts* category.

   What are the three types of logs tracked by this utility?
4. Counter logs are used to create a log file using objects and counters you select. Click the *Counter logs* option in the left panel.
5. Click the *Action* menu item and select *New Log Settings*.
6. In the *Name* textbox, type `Memory Usage` and click the *OK* button.
7. Click the *Add Counters* button. Click the *Performance* object down arrow and select *Memory*. In the *Select counters from list* window, click the *Available bytes* counter, and click the *Add* button. In the *Select counters from list* window, click the *Cache bytes* counter, and click the *Add* button. Click the *Close* button. The counters appear in the Counters window.
8. Click the *Log Files* tab. The Log Files tab is used to select what type of file is created. The default type of file is a binary file, but a text file can be selected. Click the *Log file type* down arrow and select the *Text File (Comma delimited)* option.

9. The Configure button is used to specify the location of the log file. Click the *Configure* button.

   What is the default location (folder) for the log file?

10. Click the *Cancel* button. Click the *Schedule* tab. The Schedule tab is used to define the start and stop time for the log file. The default is to start the log and keep going until it is manually stopped. In the Stop log section, click the *At* radio button. Change the time to two minutes after the current time. Make sure the date is today's date. (The default is one day later.) In other words, you will only be logging for two minutes. Click the *Apply* button and click the *OK* button. The Memory Usage log file appears in the right panel.
11. After two minutes, access the *WordPad* accessory. Click the *File* menu option and select *Open*. Click the *Files of type* down arrow and select *All Documents*. Use the *Look in* drop-down box or the icons on the left to locate the Memory Usage file. Reference your answer following Step 9 for the name of the folder and drive letter. Click the file name and click the *Open* button. The Memory Usage log file appears. The first set of numbers is the date followed by the time. The next two numbers are the counters that were requested: Available bytes and Cache bytes.

    On the first logged event line, what is the number of available bytes and cache bytes?

Instructor initials: ____________

12. Return to the Performance window and click the *Memory Usage* counter log that you created earlier. Click the red *X* (delete) icon. An alternative method for doing the same thing is to click the *Action* menu item and click the *Delete* option.
13. Click the *Alerts* log in the left panel. Click the *Action* menu item and select *New Alert Settings*. In the *Name* textbox, type **`Memory Alert`** and click the *OK* button. The *Alerts* option is used to set a counter that triggers an alert event to be sent to Event Viewer.
14. Click the *Add* button. In the *Performance* object drop-down menu, select *Memory*. In the *Select counters from list* window, use the scroll bars to locate the *Available Bytes* counter. Click the *Explain* button.

    What does the Available Bytes counter log measure?

15. Close the *Explain Text* window. Click the *Add* button. Click the *Close* button. On the *General* tab, type **`1`** in the *Limit* textbox. (Note that this is not a value you would normally pick, but is used for illustration purposes.) Click the *Action* tab. The Action tab is used to specify what happens when an alert is generated. The default is to send an alert into the application event log.
16. Click the *Schedule* tab. The Schedule tab is used to define the start and stop time for the log file. The default is to start the log and keep going until it is manually stopped. In the *Stop log* section, click the *At* radio button. Change the time to two minutes after the current time. Make sure the date is today's date. In other words, you will only be logging for two minutes. Click the *Apply* button and click the *OK* button. The Memory Alert log file appears in the right panel.
17. Open Event Viewer and open the Application event log by clicking *Application* in the left panel. Look in the right panel. The first few application events should have event code 2031. Double-click one of these events.

Instructor initials: ____________

Write down the event description.

18. Close Event Viewer and return to the Performance window. Click the *Alerts Performance Logs and Alerts* category. Click the *Memory Alert* log. Click the red *X* (delete) icon. An alternative method for doing the same thing is to click the *Action* menu item and click the *Delete* option.
19. Close the Performance window.

Lab 12.33 Performance and Reliability in Windows 7

Objective: To be able to use Windows 7 tools to verify performance, measure reliability, and troubleshoot startup problems

Parts: Access to Windows 7 with a user ID that has administrator rights

Procedure: Complete the following procedure and answer the accompanying questions.

1. Turn on the computer and verify that the operating system loads. Log in to Windows 7 using the user ID and password that has full administrator rights and that is provided by your instructor or lab assistant.
2. From the *Start* menu > *Control Panel* > *System and Security* > *Administrative Tools* > double-click *Performance Monitor* > select the *Open Resource Monitor* link. The information shown on the overview tab is known as the key table. It always contains a complete list of running (active) processes for the system. You can filter the data and look at the information more granularly by using the specific tabs.
3. Select the *CPU* tab. Notice the individual processes in the Processes section. Select a particular process by clicking in the checkbox by the process name. The top graph shows that particular process in relation to the total CPU usage.

   How many CPU threads are used by the Performance Monitor application?

4. Deselect the individual process(es) you selected in the Processes section. Expand the *Services* section. Notice the last column—Average CPU. This column shows the average percentage of CPU consumption by a particular service.

   What service is taking the most CPU power?
5. Select the *Memory* tab. Notice the Commit (KB) column. This column shows the amount of virtual memory reserved by Windows for a particular process.

   List two processes and the amount of virtual memory being used by the system for each process.

6. The Working Set column shows the amount of physical memory used by a particular process.

   Which process is using the most motherboard RAM?
7. Select the *Disk* tab. Open any file and save it to a different location on the hard drive if possible. Return to the *Disk* tab and notice the disk activity.
8. Select the *Network* tab. Connect to the Internet and return to this tab.

   How many TCP connections are active?
9. Close the *Resource Monitor* window and return to the *Performance Monitor* window.
10. Ensure that the top object, *Performance*, is selected in the left panel. Notice the *System Summary* section in the center of the right panel.

    What is the available memory in megabytes?

    Scroll down to see the *PhysicalDisk* component. What is the percentage of idle time?

    Locate the *Processor Information* section. What is the total percent of processor time?

12 Windows XP, Vista, and 7

11. Expand the *Monitoring Tools* object in the left panel. Select the *Performance Monitor* tool.

    What is the default counter shown?

12. Select the plus symbol (+) from the graphical menu at the top of the chart. Scroll through the counters list until you locate and click the *PhysicalDisk* counter down arrow (▼). Click once on the *Disk Reads/sec* counter. In the *Instances of selected object* window, select the number that corresponds to your primary hard drive partition. Click *Add*. Continue by using the same process to add the following counters.

PhysicalDisk	Disk Writes/sec
LogicalDisk	% Free Space
Memory	Available Bytes
Memory	Cache Bytes
Processor	% Processor Time (All instances)

13. Click *OK*. If a message appears saying that one of the counters is already enabled, click *OK*.

14. Allow the system to run at least two minutes. Do things on the computer during this time. Afterward, click the *Freeze Display* menu icon that looks like a pause button on a CD/DVD player or press Ctrl+F.

15. Select the *Change Graph Type* drop-down menu item to *Histogram bar*. Note that this is the third icon from the left on the graphic menu at the top of the graph. Select the *Available bytes* counter.

    What is the average number of available bytes of memory?

16. Click the *Cache Bytes* counter row.

    What is the maximum number of bytes in cache memory?

    Look at the bar graph. Which is higher, the number of disk reads per second or the disk writes per second?

Instructor initials: ______________

17. Change the graph type to the *Report* view.

    Which one of these views do you think will be most used by a technician?

18. Click the *Start* button. Type **`reliability monitor`** in the *Search programs and files* textbox. Select the *View reliability history* link from the resulting list.

    Describe any event that the system considered important enough to potentially affect the computer reliability.

19. Close all windows.

20. Click the *Start* button > *Control Panel* > *System and Security* > locate (but don't click) the *System* section > locate and click the *Check the Windows Experience Index* link.

    What is the base score?

    What component(s) rate the highest subscore?

21. Close all windows.

Lab 12.34 Installing and Using Remote Desktop in Windows XP

Objective: To be able to configure a computer for remote accessing using the Remote Desktop tool as well as access and administer the computer remotely

Parts: Two computers with Windows XP loaded

Windows XP CD

Note: You must have the ability to create users on the remote computer or have a user ID already created that has a password assigned.

Procedure: Complete the following procedure and answer the accompanying questions.

Remote Computer

1. On the computer that is to be accessed remotely, power it on and verify that XP loads. Log on to XP using the user ID and password provided by the instructor or lab assistant.
2. If the computer has a user ID that has a password, this step can be skipped. Otherwise, access the *User* Control Panel by selecting the *Start* button > *Control Panel* > *Classic* view > *User Accounts* > *Create a new account* > type **`tester`** in the *Name* textbox > select *Next* > *Limited* radio button > *Create Account* button. Add a password by clicking the *Change an account link* > *tester* > *Create a password link* > in the *Type a new password* textbox, type **`tester`** > in the *Type the password again to confirm* textbox, type **`tester`** > *Create password*. Close the User Accounts window.
3. Install the Remote Desktop application by clicking the *Start* button > *Control Panel* > *Add or Remove Programs* > *Add/Remove Windows Components* > *Internet Information Services* > *Details* button > *World Wide Web Service* > *Details* button > *Remote Desktop Web Connection* checkbox > *OK* > *OK* > *Next* > you may be prompted to insert the XP CD > *Finish* button. Close the Add or Remove Programs window. Close the Control Panel window.
4. Ensure that the computer has all the latest security updates by temporarily disabling the World Wide Web publishing service and obtaining/installing the updates. Click the *Start* button > *Run* > type **`net stop w3svc`** and press Enter. A message appears stating the World Wide Web publishing service has been stopped. Install Microsoft Windows updates by clicking the *Start* button > *All Programs* > *Windows Update* and follow the directions on the screen. Once updated, re-enable the World Wide Web publishing service by clicking the *Start* button > *Run* > type **`net start w3svc`** and press Enter. The `net` command is used by networking and PC support staff. Table 12.34 lists some of the most commonly used commands.

Table 12.34 `net` commands

Command	Description
`net start`	Can start services within Windows when enclosed within quotation marks. Examples include alert, browser, DHCP client, event log, plug and play, server, workstation, schedule, and spooler. It can also be sued to start non-Windows services.
`net stop`	Can stop services. See `net start` explanation.
`net use`	Used to connect or disconnect a computer from a network resource as well as view information about network connections.
`net view`	Lists computers in a workgroup or a specific computer's shared network resources.

5. Start the Remote Desktop configuration by obtaining the computer name—click the *Start* button > *Control Panel* > *Classic* view > *System* > *Remote* tab.

   Write the name of the computer exactly as it is shown.
6. Configure Remote Desktop for the particular user by ensuring the *Allow users to connect remotely to this computer* checkbox is enabled > *Apply* button > *Remote Users* button > *Add* button > in the *Enter object names to select* textbox, type **`tester`** > *OK*.
7. Click *OK* and close the System Properties window.

Firewall Configuration

8. Ensure that any firewalls enabled between the remote system and the PC used to connect to the remote allow Remote Desktop to be used. If using Windows Firewall on the PC being accessed remotely, click the *Start* button > *Control Panel* > *Classic* view > *Security Center* > *Windows Firewall* link > *Exceptions* tab > enable the *Remote Desktop* checkbox (and ensure a group policy does not override this setting). If using a third-party firewall software application, ensure that ports 3389 and 80 are open.

Second Computer Configuration

9. On the computer used to access the first computer, access the Remote Desktop application by clicking the *Start* button > *All Programs* > *Accessories* > *Communications* > *Remote Desktop Connection*. In the *Computer* textbox, type in the computer name previously recorded (the computer name of the remote desktop) and click *Connect*.
10. In the *User name* textbox, type **`tester`** > in the *Password* textbox, type **`tester`** > *OK*. Add a shortcut desktop icon to any application not already shown. Show the new shortcut icon to the instructor.

Instructor initials: ____________

11. Experiment with the controls at the top of the *Remote Desktop* window. Notice how you can minimize the window and be back on your own desktop. Notice the push pin icon on the far left. This keeps the Control Panel window active at the top of a full screen. If you click the push pin to turn the icon sideways, the Control Panel window recedes. To get the window to reappear, move your mouse pointer to the top of the window for a moment. Click the push pin again to make the *Control Panel* stay.
12. Close the Remote Desktop connection by clicking the *Close* button at the top of the screen.

Removing the User and Shortcut

13. On the original computer, remove the shortcut that was just created.
14. On the original computer, remove the *tester* user using the User Accounts Control Panel. Show the changes to the instructor.

Instructor initials: ____________

Lab 12.35 Windows 7 Remote Desktop

Objective: To be able to configure a computer for remote access using the Remote Desktop tool

Parts: Two computers with Windows 7 loaded

Notes: The Remote Desktop tool is disabled by default and you can only connect to (take over) computers running Windows 7 Professional, Enterprise, or Ultimate, but all Windows 7 versions can initiate the Remote Desktop connection.

You must have the ability to create users on the remote computer or have a user ID already created that has a password assigned.

Procedure: Complete the following procedure and answer the accompanying questions.

1. On the computer that is to be accessed remotely, power it on and verify that Windows 7 loads. Log in using the user ID and password provided by the instructor or lab assistant.
2. If both computers have a user ID with full administrator rights and a password, this step can be skipped. Otherwise, access the *Start* button > *Control Panel* > *User Accounts and Family Safety* > *User Accounts* > *Manage another account* > *Create a new account* link > type **`tester`** in the *New account name* textbox > select the *Administrator* radio button > select the *Create Account* button. Add a password by clicking the *tester* icon > *create a password* link > in the *New password* textbox, type **`tester`** > in the *Confirm new*

password textbox, type `tester` > click the *Create password* button. Close the User Accounts window. Login using the "tester" account on both computers.

3. On both computers, open *Windows Explorer*. Locate and right-click the *Computer* item. Select *Properties*.

   Document the full computer name for both computers

   Computer 1

   Computer 2

4. On both computers, select the *Remote settings* link. The *Remote* tab should be active.

   What is the current setting? [Don't allow connections to this computer | Allow connections from computers running any version of Remote Desktop (less secure) | Allow connections only from computers running Remote Desktop with Network Level Authentication (more secure)]

5. In the Remote Desktop section, select the *Allow connections from computers running any version of Remote Desktop (less secure)* radio button.

   What warning appears, if any?

6. If necessary, click *OK* on the message. Click *OK*.
7. On computer 1, select the *Start* button > *All Programs* > *Accessories* > *Remote Desktop Connection*.
8. In the Remote Desktop Connection window, type the other computer's full computer name in the *Computer* textbox. Click *Connect*.
9. Enter a password. Click *Yes* on the request for a certification or if a certificate warning appears.

   What happened to the remote computer?

10. On the computer that is doing the controlling, add a new shortcut to the desktop of the remote computer. When finished, click the close button in the blue control panel located in the top center of the screen. Click *OK*.
11. On the remote computer, login. Notice the new desktop shortcut.

Instructor Initials: ____________ (Check for new desktop shortcut.)

12. Delete the newly installed desktop shortcut on the remote computer.
13. Return all settings back to the original configuration. See Step 4 answer.
14. Remove the *tester* user account from any computer if it was created.

Lab 12.36 Windows 7 Task Scheduler

Objective: To become familiar with the Task Scheduler tool and the AT command

Parts: Computer with Windows 7 installed and administrator rights

Procedure: Complete the following procedure and answer the accompanying questions.

Using Task Scheduler

1. From the *Start* menu, type `task` in the *Search programs and files* textbox and select *Task Scheduler* from the resulting list. Task Scheduler opens, as shown in Figure 12.36.

   Based on the information shown in the Overview of Task Scheduler pane, where are tasks stored?

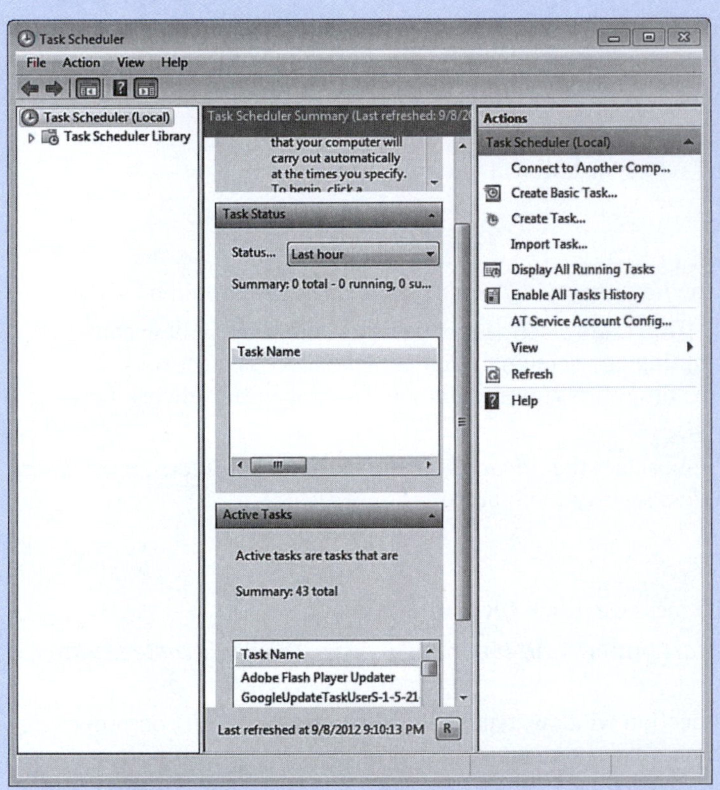

Figure 12.36 Task Scheduler

2. In the *Actions* pane, select *Create Basic Task...* In the *Name* textbox, type your last name > *Next*. Notice the Trigger action is highlighted and Daily is the default task time > *One time* radio button > *Next* > select *5 minutes* from the current date and time > *Next*.

   What three actions can you take using this wizard?

3. Select the *Display a message* radio button and select *Next*. In the Title textbox, give a brief description of this message such as `Scheduled downtime`. In the Message textbox, type a respectable message that a technician might send. An example might be as follows: `Attention students, faculty, and staff. Our scheduled maintenance window will begin in 15 minutes. The server will be down for approximately 2 hours. Thanks for your patience.` Click *Next*.
4. Enable the *Open the Properties dialog for this task when I click Finish* checkbox > *Finish* button.

   What three security options are available?

5. Select the *Run whether user is logged on or not* radio button and click *OK*. Enter the proper credentials with a username and password. Contact the instructor or lab assistant if unsure.

   What three actions can you take using this wizard?

6. Create another scheduled task that runs one time, runs a specific program at a specific time. Show the instructor this task credentials through the Task Scheduler Library and the task working.

   Document the scheduled task and start time.

Instructor initials: ____________

Activities

Internet Discovery

Objective: To access the Internet to obtain specific information regarding a computer or its associated parts

Parts: Access to the Internet

Procedure: Use the Internet to answer the following questions.

1. Find a website that offers Windows 7 freeware tools. Write the name of the website and the URL where this information was found.

2. What is the latest service pack available from Microsoft for Windows 7? Write the answer and the URL where you found the answer.

3. Find a website that details how to set up DualView. Write the web address as well as the questions to configure DualView.

4. Microsoft always has minimum requirements for any of its operating systems. Find a website that tells you what your system should have to run Windows 7 Ultimate efficiently.

   Write the name of the company that posts the recommendation, the minimum requirements cited, as well as the URL.

5. You get the error code 0x80072F8F on a Windows Vista computer when trying to get a Windows update.

   Find a website that describes this error and write the cause and URL.

6. Find a certification related to a Microsoft operating system. List the certification and the average salary associated with the certification.

   List any and all URLs used to find this information.

Soft Skills

Objective: To enhance and fine tune a future technician's ability to listen, communicate in both written and oral form, and support people who use computers in a professional manner

Activities:

1. In groups of two or three students, one student inserts a problem related to Windows XP, Vista, or 7 on the computer. The other two students use the Remote Desktop utility to find the problem and then repair it. Document each problem, along with the solution provided. Exchange roles so that each student practices the repair and documentation.
2. Divide into five groups. The following are five questions about operating systems: (1) What should you do *before* installing an operating system? (2) What are alternatives to XP, Vista, or 7 as an operating system, and what are pros and cons of these alternatives? (3) What is the difference between an active partition, a system partition, and a boot partition in regard to XP, Vista, or 7? (4) What operating systems can be upgraded to Windows XP, Vista, or 7? What is the difference between a clean install and an upgrade, and what determines which one you do? (5) What differences can be seen for a Windows hard drive that has a FAT32 partition and one that has an NTFS partition? Each group is assigned one of these five areas or another set of five questions related to Windows XP, Vista, and/or 7. Each group is allowed 20 minutes (and some whiteboard space or poster-sized paper) to write their ideas. Each group member helps to present his/her ideas to the class.
3. Find a magazine article related to a Windows solution or feature. Share your findings with the class.

Critical Thinking Skills

Objective: To analyze and evaluate information as well as apply learned information to new or different situations

Activities:

1. Based on the information given in the chapter about Remote Assistance, along with any directions found on the Internet or through Windows help, configure two computers for Remote Assistance and allow a person to take over a computer remotely.

   Write the steps needed to do this process. Share the steps with other groups and refine the steps until non-technical people could use the steps provided as a class to configure a computer for Remote Assistance.
2. Find a Windows registry hack online, in a book, or from a magazine. Analyze the hack for whether or not it is beneficial to normal users, whether it is beneficial to technicians, whether or not you would recommend it to a fellow student, and whether or not you would recommend it to your parents. Write a brief description of your findings including the implications of installing the registry modification.
3. Using any research method and resource, determine the pros and cons of upgrading to Windows 7 from Windows Vista. Make a list of things to check before upgrading.

A+ Certification Exam Tips

- ✓ This chapter and the next chapter cover concepts relating to the 220-802 exam, the second exam to obtain the A+ certification. CompTIA recommends that you have one year of experience before taking the exam. Students *have* been able to pass this exam right after the course, however.
- ✓ Redo all the labs. Ensure that you pay attention to the purpose of the tool and consider why (or in what situation) you would use each Windows tool.
- ✓ When your own computer momentarily slows down, use some of the tools to examine the cause.
- ✓ Ensure that you know how to control the boot process and use the Advanced Boot Options menu effectively. Go into each of those menus before the exam and be confident that you know when to use each one.
- ✓ Know the difference between Remote Assistance and Remote Desktop and the port number that must be opened through a firewall.
- ✓ Know the upgrade paths for Windows 7.
- ✓ Be able to articulate the difference between the Windows XP, Vista, and 7 control panels.
- ✓ Be able to control, upgrade, and roll back a device driver.
- ✓ Know the different user groups and what they can do.
- ✓ Know virtualization emulator requirements and the purpose of the hypervisor.

chapter 13

Internet Connectivity

Chapter Objectives

In this chapter you will learn:

- To configure an internal external modem
- To explain basic handshaking between a DTE device and a DCE device
- To use Windows tools when working with modems
- To cable and configure a DSL modem and a cable modem
- Other Internet connectivity options such as satellite, broadband wireless, WiMax, and wireless modems
- Why VoIP is important to technicians
- To perform basic modem troubleshooting
- The benefits of mentoring in the IT field

CompTIA Exam Objectives:

What CompTIA A+ exam objectives are covered in this chapter?

- ✓ 801-1.4 Install and configure expansion cards.
- ✓ 801-1.7 Compare and contrast various connection interfaces and explain their purpose.
- ✓ 801-1.11 Identify connector types and associated cables.
- ✓ 801-2.7 Compare and contrast Internet connection types and features.
- ✓ 801-2.9 Compare and contrast network devices, their functions, and features.
- ✓ 802-1.6 Setup and configure Windows networking on a client/desktop.
- ✓ 802-4.5 Given a scenario, troubleshoot wired and wireless networks with appropriate tools.

Internet Connectivity Overview

Connecting to the Internet can be done in a variety of ways: via analog modem, ISDN, cable modem, DSL modem, satellite modem, fiber, wirelessly, power line, or cellular network. Each of these technologies has a unique installation method and configuration, but they all have in common the ability to connect a computer to an outside network. Each technology is a viable option for connectivity in a specific situation. By examining the technologies and understanding them, you can offer customers connectivity options. More information about troubleshooting network connectivity is provided in Chapter 14. Let's start with the oldest method: analog modems.

Modems Overview

One of the few serial devices still in operation is the modem. Traditionally, there were other serial devices, including mice, trackballs, printers, digitizers, plotters, and scanners. Serial printers might still be found today, if a printer needs to be located 50 feet or less from the computer.

A modem (modulator/demodulator) connects a computer with the outside world through a phone line. This type of technology is frequently called a **dial-up network** because the modem uses the traditional phone line to "dial up," or call, another modem. Modems can be internal or external peripheral devices. An internal modem is an adapter installed in an expansion slot. An external modem attaches to a serial port. A modem converts a signal transmitted over the phone line to digital 1s and 0s to be read by the computer. It also converts the digital 1s and 0s from the computer and modulates them onto the carrier signal and sends the data over the phone line. Modems normally connect to a remote modem through the phone line. Figure 13.1 shows two modems connecting two computers.

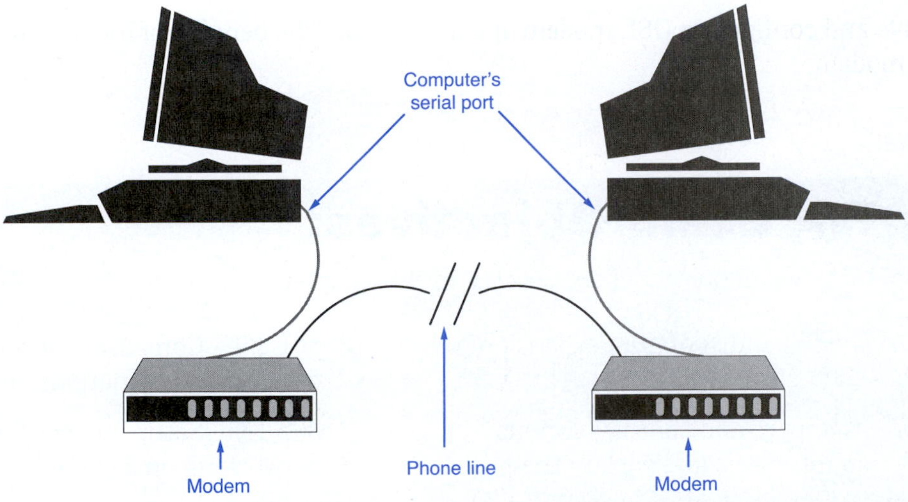

Figure 13.1 Sample modem connection

Tech Tip

When connecting a modem to a phone line, be careful with the cabling

Some modems have two jacks on the back. The labeling varies, but one jack is usually labeled PHONE and the other labeled LINE. The LINE jack is for the cable that goes from the modem to the phone wall jack. The modem's PHONE jack is an optional jack to connect a telephone to the modem. Figure 13.2 shows the ports on an internal modem.

Figure 13.2 Internal modem ports

Serial Communication Overview

A serial device such as a modem transmits or receives information 1 bit at a time and is traditionally connected to a serial port. With modern computers, a USB-to-serial converter (see Figure 13.3) is used to attach an external serial device such as a modem. Serial cables should be no more than 50 feet long. The possibility for data loss is more likely with distances greater than 50 feet.

Figure 13.3 USB-to-DB-9 converter

Serial devices are frequently external and connect to a serial port. A device such as an internal modem may be on an adapter. Serial ports are also known as asynchronous ports, COM ports, or RS232 ports. **Asynchronous** transmissions add extra bits to the data to track when each byte starts and ends. Synchronous transmissions rely on an external clock to time the data reception or transmission. Basic terminology associated with asynchronous transmissions is found in Table 13.1.

Tech Tip

Configuring transmission speeds

When configuring a serial port or using an application, the configured speed is the rate at which the serial port transmits. This is not the speed for an external serial device that connects to the port (such as a modem).

Table 13.1 Serial asynchronous transmission terminology

Term	Description
start bit	Used in asynchronous transmissions to signal the start of the data.
stop bit	Used in asynchronous transmissions to signal the end of the data.
RS232C	Standard approved by the EIA (Electronics Industries Alliance) for the serial port used in a computer. Because serial devices use the 9- or 25-pin connector defined by this standard, they are commonly called RS232 serial devices.
bps (bits per second)	A measurement used to describe the transmission speed of serial devices and ports. Settings include 110, 300, 1200, 2400, 4800, 9600, 19200, 38400, 57600, and 115200. The application software must match the serial device or serial port's bits per second rate.
baud	The number of times an analog signal changes in 1 second. Some use this term to speak of the modem speed. With today's modulation techniques, modems can send several bits in one cycle, so it is more accurate to specify modem speed in bits per second (bps).
UART (Universal Asynchronous Receiver/ Transmitter)	A chip on the motherboard for an integrated serial port or on the adapter of an internal modem. It converts a data byte into a serial data stream of single 1s and 0s for transmission. It also receives the bit stream and stores data in its own buffers until the processor can accept the data.

How to Configure Serial Ports and Devices

Serial ports and devices such as internal modems have three important configuration parameters (and others as well, as discussed later): interrupt, I/O (input/output) address, and COM port number. An internal modem has all these parameters; an external modem uses these same parameters, but they are assigned to the serial port to which the external modem connects. Use Device Manager to identify these system resources. Exercises at the end of this chapter show how to view serial device resources.

Tech Tip

Application settings and hardware settings must match

Applications that communicate or control serial devices must have the application settings match the hardware settings, or communication will not occur.

An understanding of how serial devices operate is essential to a technician's knowledge base if analog modems are in the geographic area. Before installing a serial device and configuring its associated software, a technician must be familiar with the terminology associated with serial device installation. Table 13.2 lists the various serial port settings.

Table 13.2 Serial port settings

Setting	Explanation
Data bits	Determines how many bits make up a data word. It is usually 8 bits per data word but can be 7 or lower.
Parity	A simple method of checking data accuracy. When parity is used, both computers must be set to the same setting. The choices for parity include none, odd, even, space, and mark. With a space parity setting, both computers always set the parity bit to 0. With the mark parity setting, both computers always set the parity bit to 1. The most common setting is none for modems.
Stop bits	The number of bits sent to indicate the end of the data word. The number of stop bits can be 1, 1.5, or 2. One stop bit is the common choice.
FIFO setting	Used to enable or disable the UART chip's FIFO buffer. This setting gives the processor time to handle other tasks without the serial device losing data. If data is lost, it will have to be retransmitted later, when the microprocessor turns its attention back to the serial device.
Flow control	Determines how two serial devices communicate. Can be set using software or physical pins on the serial port (hardware). Also called handshaking, which allows a serial device to tell the sending serial device, "Wait, I need a second before you send any more data."
Handshaking	The order in which things happen to allow two serial devices to communicate. Knowing this order helps with troubleshooting.

How does parity work?

Tech Tip

Parity can be either even or odd. Take the example of a computer that uses even parity. If the data sent is 10101010, a total of four 1s is sent, plus a 0 for the parity bit. Four is an even number; therefore, the parity bit is set to 0 because the total number of 1s must be an even number when even parity is used. If the data sent is 10101011, a total of five 1s is sent, plus an extra 1 for the parity bit. Because five is an odd number and the system uses even parity, the extra parity bit is set to 1 to make the total number of 1s an even number.

The two common methods for flow control are XON/XOFF (software method) and RTS/CTS (hardware method). **XON/XOFF** handshaking sends special control characters when a serial device needs more time to process data or is ready to receive more data. If one modem needs the remote modem to wait, it will send a certain character (usually Ctrl + S). Then, when the modem is ready to accept more data, a different control character (usually Ctrl + Q) is sent.

RTS/CTS (hardware handshaking) uses specific wires on the serial connector to send a signal to the other device to stop or start sending data. The CTS (clear to send) and the RTS (request to send) signals indicate when it is okay to send data. Modem communication normally uses hardware flow control (RTS/CTS) instead of software flow control. Table 13.3 delineates hardware flow control.

Table 13.3 Hardware handshaking

Order of execution	Explanation
Both devices (the DTE and the DCE) power on and are functional.	
The DTE sends a signal over the DTR (data terminal ready) line.	The DTE says, "I'm ready."
The DCE sends a signal over the DSR (data set ready) line.	The DCE says, "I'm ready, too."
The DTE sends a signal over the RTS (request to send) connector pin.	The DTE (such as the computer) says, "I would like some data."
The DCE sends a signal on the CTS (clear to send) connector pin.	The DCE (such as the modem) says, "Okay, here comes some data."
Data transmits 1 bit at a time over a single line.	

The RS232 serial communication standard was developed during a time when mainframes were the norm. A mainframe terminal known as a DTE connected to a modem known as a DCE. In today's world, **DTE** (data terminal equipment) includes computers and printers. On a DTE serial connector, certain pins initiate communication with a DCE device, such as a modem. Table 13.4 shows the common signal names as well as the common abbreviations for the signals used with DTE devices.

Table 13.4 DTE signal connections

Signal abbreviations	Signal name
TD	Transmit data
DTR	Data terminal ready
RTS	Request to send

DCE (data circuit-terminating equipment) includes devices such as modems, mice, and digitizers. On the DCE side, the signal names relate more to receiving data. Table 13.5 lists the common signal names used with DCE devices.

Table 13.5 DCE signal connections

Signal abbreviation	Signal name
RD	Receive data
DSR	Data set ready
CTS	Clear to send
CD	Carrier detect
RI	Ring indicator

To avoid problems, install the internal modem or attach the serial device and determine what COM port, IRQ, and I/O settings have been assigned to the device.

56Kbps Modems

Analog modems are the slowest type of Internet connectivity. Modems transmit and receive at different speeds. A faster modem means less time on the phone line and less time for processor interaction. However, because modems connect to other modems, the slowest modem determines the fastest connection speed. A slow modem can only operate at the speed for which it was designed. Connecting to a faster modem will not make the slower modem operate any faster. Fortunately, speedy modems can transmit at lower speeds. As a general rule, a modem's speed setting should be set to its maximum throughput.

The phone line limit was once thought to be 28.8Kbps, then 33.6Kbps, and finally 56Kbps. The 56Kbps data transfer rate is possible only if the transmitted (analog) signal converts to digital one time during the data transmission. Digital phone lines are quieter than their analog counterparts, have less noise on the line, and allow faster data transmissions. For example, consider the scenario of a person dialing into an office network from home that is shown in Figure 13.4.

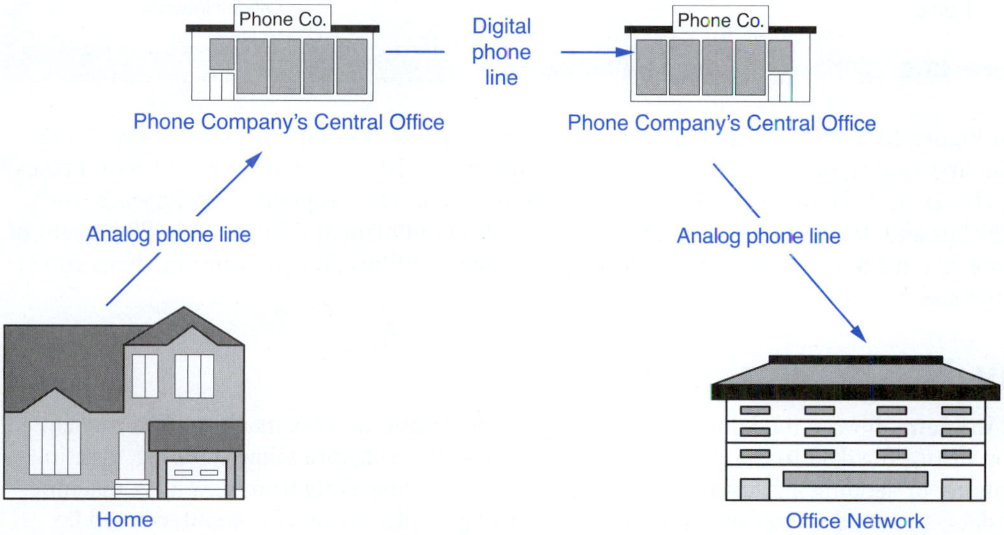

Figure 13.4 **Normal modem usage**

Notice in Figure 13.4 that the signal converts twice. The first time is when the analog signal enters the phone company's central office. Between central offices, the signal stays digital. Then, when the signal leaves the central office to travel to the work building, the signal converts from a digital signal to an analog signal. 56Kbps transmission speeds do not support two conversions.

If the workplace has a digital line from the phone company or if a person dials into an Internet provider that has a digital phone connection, 56Kbps throughput on a 56Kbps modem is achievable. Figure 13.5 shows the difference.

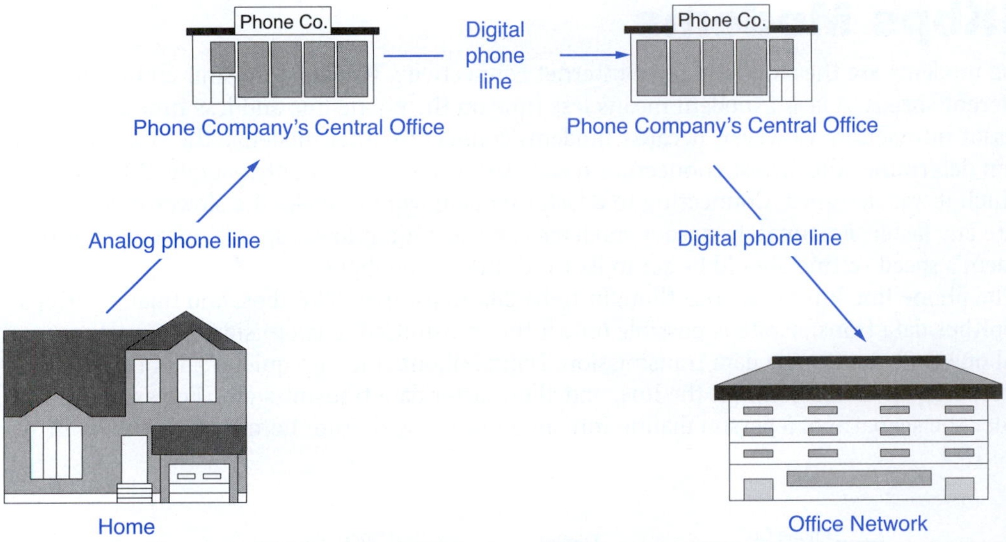

Figure 13.5 56Kbps modem connection

In Figure 13.5, only one analog-to-digital conversion exists—the one between the home and the first central office. 56Kbps speeds, in theory, can exist when only one conversion takes place. However, if the modem cannot run at 56Kbps, the modem supports lower speeds, such as 33.6Kbps and 28.8Kbps. Studies estimate that 56Kbps will run at 56Kbps 10 to 20 percent of the time, about the same estimated percentage of time 33.6Kbps and 28.8Kbps modems run at their top speed.

Fax Modems

A **fax modem** allows a modem to use a computer and printer as a fax machine. The modem portion brings the data to the computer. The facsimile (fax) software allows viewing, printing, replying to, or sending a fax. A regular modem sends data differently from how a fax machine sends data, so a modem can send faxes only if it is a fax modem. Not all computer-based fax machines can handle modem data transfers, but a fax modem can do both modem and fax transfers.

Fax standards handled by CCITT (ITU now) are in groups. Group I through Group IV concern fax machines. Group I and Group II are slow. A Group III bis fax modem transfers data up to 14,400bps. Group IV fax modems transmit over a digital ISDN line at speeds up to 64Kbps. ISDN technology is discussed next.

The Internet has changed fax capabilities. Fax machines can now be used to send a fax that is received in an email account at the final destination. The fax machine can connect to a phone line that connects to a fax gateway. The fax gateway connects to a network and sends the message in email format to the final destination. A fax machine that adheres to the ITU T.37 iFax standard allows a fax machine to be connected to the data network. The fax machine formats the fax into email format for distribution to a person's email account or to the destination fax machine that has its own email address account and connects to a network.

Digital Modems and ISDN

A digital modem connects a computer directly to a digital phone line rather than to a traditional analog phone line. One type of digital phone line available from the phone company is an ISDN line. An **ISDN** (Integrated Services Digital Network) line has three separate channels: two B channels and a D channel. The B channels handle data at 64Kbps transmission speeds. The D channel is for network routing information and transmits at a lower 16Kbps. The two B channels can combine into a single channel for video conferencing, thus allowing speeds up to 128Kbps. They are available in large metropolitan areas for reasonable rates making it an affordable option for home office use. But due to recent technologies, such as cable modems and xDSL modems (covered later in this chapter), ISDN is not a popular option today.

VoIP

VoIP (Voice over IP), shown in Figure 13.6, uses a corporate data network or the Internet for phone traffic rather than using the traditional **PSTN** (public switched telephone network). Traditionally, companies used a separate network structure for the data network (the network where computers and printers connect), for the phone network, and for the video network. **Convergence** is a term used to describe how these data, voice, and video technologies are now using one network structure instead of multiple ones.

Figure 13.6 VoIP

Products are available that allow a user to use an Internet connection to make phone calls rather than the traditional phone network. There are also free software applications and email accounts that allow voice and video connections using the Internet. Through these applications, the quality may not be as good as with the traditional PSTN. There is no guaranteed **QoS** (quality of service) provided. However, in the corporate network, QoS is often implemented in conjunction with VoIP.

Technicians must be aware of VoIP for two reasons: (1) A digital phone installed in a corporate office must be connected to the network in a similar fashion to the PC (see Figure 13.7); and (2) a digital phone may be a software application (a soft phone) that has to be installed and configured on a computer.

Figure 13.7 VoIP phone

VoIP has also affected fax capabilities. A fax machine can have a VoIP adapter installed and connect to a VoIP gateway. The VoIP gateway connects to a phone line that has a destination fax machine attached. One must realize that once something is converted into 1s and 0s, if that device can be networked, then it is just data to the network and can be transmitted.

One last thing to remember about VoIP in the corporate environment is that no corporate network can do away with the PSTN connection to the traditional phone network. A corporate environment will always need to be able to communicate with the outside world and especially be able to contact emergency services such as the police, fire, and emergency responders.

Cable Modems

One of the most popular items in the modem industry is the **cable modem**, which connects a computer to a cable TV network. Cable modems can be internal or external devices. If a cable modem is external, two methods commonly exist for connectivity to a PC—a NIC (network interface card) is installed in the computer and a cable attaches between the NIC and the cable modem or the cable modem connects to a USB port. Figures 13.8 and 13.9 show these two types of connections.

Tech Tip

Cable TV and cable modems

Some cable Internet providers will not provide Internet access through their network unless you have the cable TV service as well.

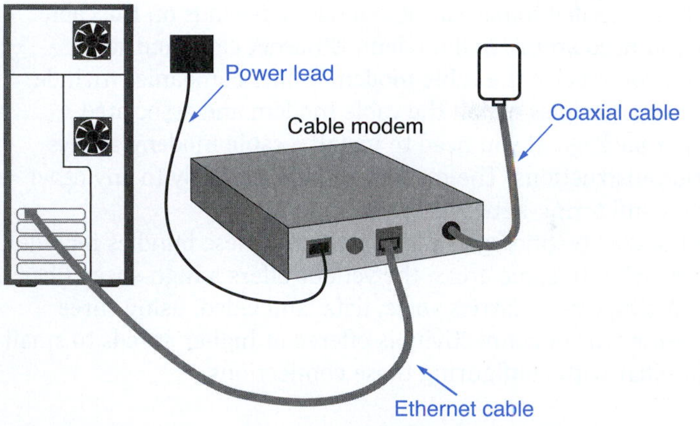

Figure 13.8 **Cable modem and NIC connectivity**

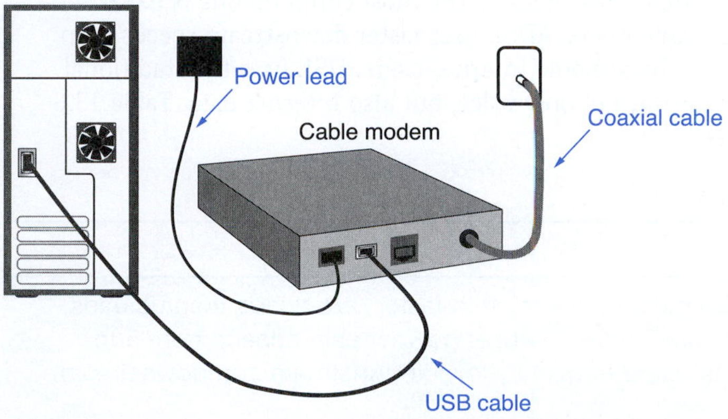

Figure 13.9 **Cable modem and USB connectivity**

Cable modem operation is not hard to understand. Internet data comes in through cable TV coax cable. The coax cable plugs into the cable modem. The cable modem then sends the information out its built-in Ethernet port. A network cable connects from the cable modem's Ethernet port into an Ethernet port on the computer. To send data to the Internet, the reverse happens: The computer sends the data out its Ethernet port into the cable modem. The cable modem sends the data out the coax cable onto the cable TV company's network, which is a high-speed fiber network. Fiber networks are covered in Chapter 14.

Two terms that are often associated with cable modems are upstream and downstream. **Upstream** refers to data that are sent from your home to the Internet. **Downstream** refers to the data pulled from the Internet into your computer, as when you download a file or view a web page. With cable modems, downstream transfer rates are faster than upstream transfers. Downstream speeds can be as high as 100+Mbps for consumers and even higher for businesses. Upstream speeds vary; with an external cable modem, they tend to be between 384Kbps and 20Mbps. Even though upstream speeds are slower, cable modems are a huge improvement over analog (dial-up) modems.

The speed of a cable modem connection depends on two things: (1) the cable company and (2) how many people in the area share the same cable TV provider. Each cable channel uses 6MHz of the cable's bandwidth. **Bandwidth** is the capacity of the communications channel. Bandwidth is also known as *throughput* or *line speed*. The cable company designates one of the 6MHz channels as Internet access. Several homes can use the same channel, which reduces the amount of bandwidth each house has available. If you have three neighbors who all use the same cable vendor and they all are Internet warriors, you will have slower access than if you were the only person in the neighborhood connected.

The minimum amount of hardware needed to have a cable modem depends on the cable company's specifications. Whether you need an internal modem, Ethernet card, and so on depends on the company from which you receive the cable modem. Some companies include them as part of their rate. Some cable companies install the cable modem and associated software and hardware as part of their package. If you need to install a cable modem, always follow the manufacturer's installation instructions. The modem installs similarly to any other adapter. Chapter 14 includes tips on configuring network adapters.

Cable vendors frequently offer bundled technologies to subscribers. These bundles include phone, Internet, and cable TV connectivity. In some areas, the vendor offers a high-speed fiber network connection to each house. A single fiber carries voice, data, and video, using three different optical wavelengths. This same type of connectivity is offered at higher speeds to small businesses. A technician must be familiar with configuring these connections.

xDSL Modems

xDSL is another modem technology. The *x* in the term xDSL refers to the various types of **DSL** (digital subscriber line) that are on the market. The most common one is **ADSL** (Asymmetrical DSL), but there are many others. ADSL uses faster downstream speeds than upstream. This performance is fine for most home Internet users. DSL uses the traditional phone line to be able to send and transmit not only voice, but also Internet data. Table 13.6 shows the most common DSL types.

Table 13.6 DSL technologies

DSL type	Comments
ADSL	Asymmetrical DSL—most common, with faster downloads than uploads; upstream speeds from 0.5 to 3.5Mbps; downstream speeds from 5 to 150Mbps; uses a different frequency level for upstream and downstream communications
G.SHDSL	Symmetric High-speed DSL—upgrade to SDSL that supports symmetric data rates up to 4.6Mbps
HDSL	High bit-rate DSL—symmetrical transmission (equal speed for downloads/uploads); speeds up to 1.5Mbps
PDSL	Power line DSL—modulates data speeds from 256K to 2.7Mbps onto electrical lines and sometimes called Broadband over Power line (BPL)
RADSL	Rate-Adaptive DSL—developed by Westell and allows a modem to adapt to phone line conditions; speeds up to 2.2Mbps
SDSL	Symmetric DSL—same speed, up to 1.5Mbps, in both directions
UDSL	Also known as Uni-DSL or Ultra-high-speed DSL, with speeds up to 200Mbps and backward compatible with ADSL, ADSL2+, VDSL, and VDSL2
VDSL2	Upgrade of VDSL that supports voice, video, data, and HDTV, with speeds from 1 to 150Mbps downstream

With DSL modems, bandwidth is not shared between people in the same geographic area. The bandwidth paid for is exclusive to the user. DSL is not available in all areas. The DSL Reports website (http://www.dslreports.com) lists major DSL vendors, other Internet technology vendors, and geographic areas, plus a rating on the service.

An internal or external DSL modem can be used and connected to a regular phone line. The phone line can be used for calls, faxes, and so on at the same time as the modem. An external modem can connect to a USB port or an Ethernet network card. Figure 13.10 shows DSL modem ports, including the DSL connector, which connects to the wall outlet and is labeled DSL; the optional USB port, which could have a USB cable connected to a computer; and the four Ethernet LAN connections, which could have connections to one or more computers, printers, external network storage, and so on.

Figure 13.10 DSL modem ports

If a DSL implementation uses an internal modem, it occupies an expansion slot (usually PCI) and is configured the same way as an internal modem. Always follow the manufacturer's installation instructions. Some vendors install a DSL modem and configure the computer as part of their package. Also note that a PC views a DSL connection as a network connection.

A drawback to DSL is that the DSL signal needs to be separated from the normal phone traffic. DSL providers normally ship **phone filters** that must connect to each phone outlet, and a phone, fax machine, or voice recorder attaches to the filter. The connection from the DSL modem to the phone outlet does not have a filter on it.

Tech Tip

Corporate DSL, cable, or fiber

Corporate Internet connectivity can use DSL, cable, or fiber connections. Chapter 14 provides more information on fiber cabling.

This chapter does not go into firewalls and network security; they are discussed in later chapters. It is very important when installing cable modems and DSL modems to look at information on proxy servers, firewalls, disabling file sharing, and so on. When using these technologies, a computer is more prone to attacks, viruses, theft of computer files, and computer takeover. Figure 13.11 shows three different ways to connect a cable or DSL modem. The example on the left is the least secure. File sharing should not be enabled on computers connected in this manner.

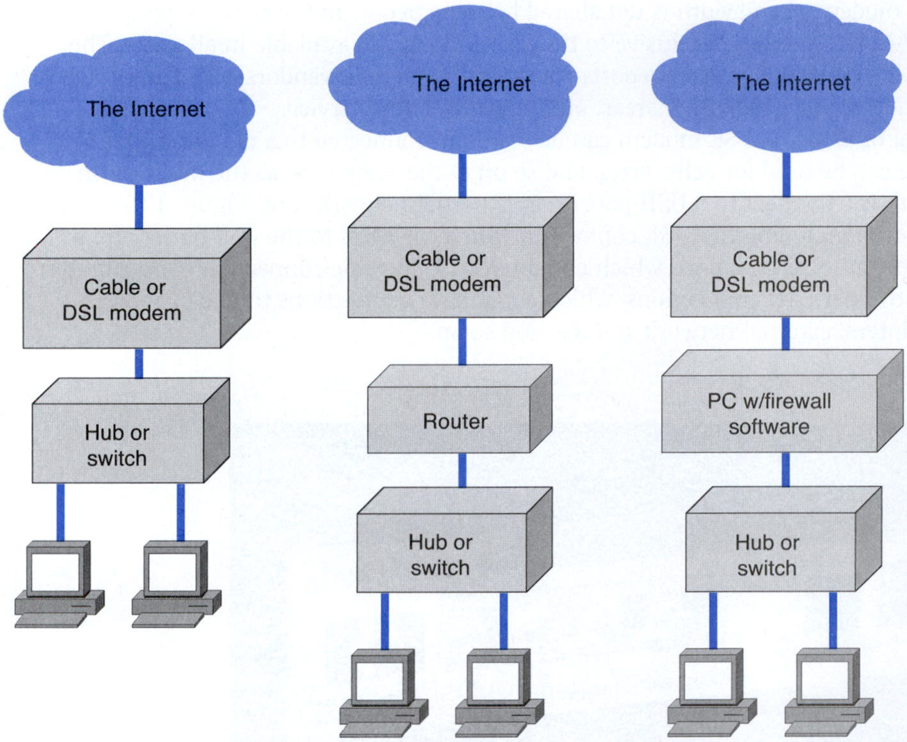

Figure 13.11 Cable/DSL modem connectivity

Troubleshooting Cable and DSL Modems

Since most cable and DSL modems are external, the best tool for troubleshooting connectivity problems is the lights on the front of the modem. The lights will vary between vendors, but common ones are listed in Table 13.7.

Table 13.7 Cable/DSL modem lights and troubleshooting*

Light	Explanation
Power	Indicates power to the modem
ENET, E, or Ethernet	Usually indicates connectivity between the PC and the modem; if unlit, ensure that you are using Ethernet (if using USB, this will be unlit), check cabling, and check PC network card settings
USB or U	Usually indicates connectivity between the PC and the modem; if unlit, ensure that you are using USB (if using a NIC, this light will be unlit), check cabling, and check *Device Manager* to see if the modem is recognized
Internet, Ready, or Rdy	Stays lit when the modem has established an Internet connection
PC	Used instead of Ethernet or USB lights to show the status of the connection between the modem and the PC
Cable, data, or D/S	Usually blinks to indicate connectivity with Internet provider
Link status	Usually flashes when acquiring a connection with a provider and is on steady when a link is established

*Note that you should refer to the modem documentation for the exact status of the lights.

Once you have checked lights and possibly checked cables, if you still have a problem, power off the modem, power it back on, and reboot the computer. Give the modem a couple minutes to initialize. Most modems have a reset button that can also be used, but powering off and powering back on works without having to wipe all the configuration information. If a modem is still not working after you take these steps, contact the service provider.

Satellite Modems

An option available to areas that do not have cable or DSL service is satellite connectivity. The satellite relays communication back to receivers on Earth. Satellite connectivity requires a satellite dish and a **satellite modem** at a minimum. It may also require an analog modem and other equipment, depending on the satellite provider. If connected via satellite, the data goes from the computer to the satellite dish mounted outside the home to another satellite dish (and maybe more), up to the satellite orbiting Earth, down to the **ISP** (Internet service provider), and from the ISP to the website requested; the web page returns via the same path it took. Satellite connectivity is not as fast as cable or DSL connectivity, but it can be five to seven times faster than dial-up. The downstream speeds can be from 9Kbps to 24Mbps but typically are around 500Kbps. Some providers offer the same upstream speeds.

With a satellite modem, TV programs accessed via the satellite can be watched at the same time that web pages are downloaded from the Internet. However, drawbacks to satellite modems are important to mention:

- The initial cost of installing a satellite modem can be high.
- If other people in the area subscribe to the same satellite service, speed is decreased during peak periods.
- Initial connections have a lag time associated with them, so playing multiplayer games is not very practical.
- VPNs (virtual private networks) are normally not supported.
- Weather elements, such as high winds, rain, and snow, affect performance and connectivity.

Modem Preventive Maintenance

The old adage "an ounce of prevention is worth a pound of cure" is especially true in the case of modems. A power surge can come across a phone line just as it can travel over an electrical power line. Most people think and worry about the computer problems that could result from power surges, but they do not stop to think about surges through the phone line. To provide protection for a modem and a computer, purchase a special protection device called a phone line isolator or a modem isolator at a computer or phone store. A power surge through the phone line or cable can take out many components inside a computer, including the motherboard.

Some surge protectors also have modem protection. A cable from the computer plugs into the surge protector. A separate cable connects to another jack on the surge protector, and the other end plugs into the phone or cable company wall jack. The surge protector must, of course, be plugged into a grounded outlet.

Mobile Connectivity

A portable computer may have a modem PC Card or ExpressCard installed in the portable computer. Modem PC Cards are Type II cards that fit into a Type II or a Type III slot. Some modem cards are combo cards—both a modem and a NIC. Modem PC Cards have a special connector called a dongle that attaches to them and allows an RJ-11 cable to be plugged into the card. Dongles can also be used with laptop network PC Cards. Analog modems are not very common today in the U.S., but Figure 13.12 shows a NIC modem PC Card with a dongle attached.

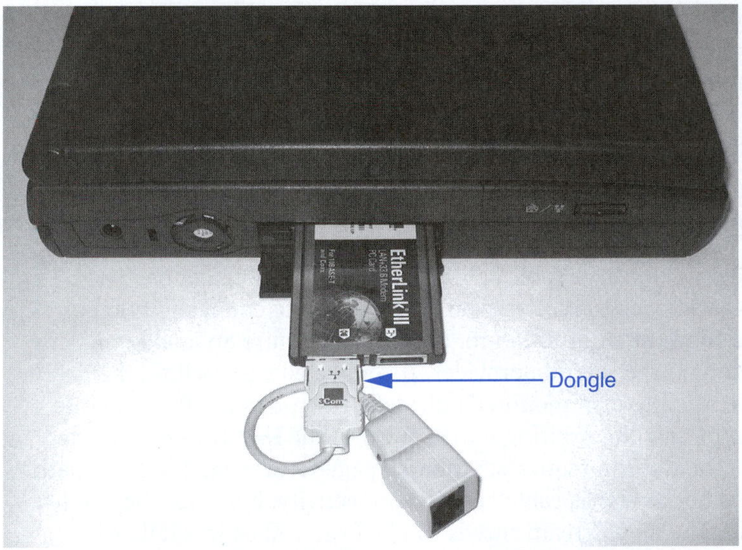

Figure 13.12 3Com NIC/modem combo PC Card with a dongle

Figure 13.13 Wireless hot spot

An increasingly popular feature with laptops is connectivity called **wireless broadband**, with download speeds up to 45Mbps. This technology is sometimes referred to as wireless or cellular WAN. Cell phone companies and Internet providers offer PC Cards, ExpressCards, USB modems, mobile data cards, or integrated laptop connectivity to have the ability to receive, create, and communicate Internet information within a coverage area. For people who travel a lot, this option gives connectivity in places where data connectivity has not previously been feasible.

Some smartphones, computers, and tablets can become **wireless hot spots**. Using their wireless connection, a USB port, Bluetooth wireless connectivity, or the cellular network, such a device can provide wireless Internet connectivity to others in the immediate vicinity (see Figure 13.13). Some cell service providers offer this option as part of the cellular plan. The term *wireless hot spot* is also used to refer to an area of wireless connectivity (normally free) such as in a park, coffee shop, or museum. More information on wireless connectivity is provided in Chapters 14 and 15.

Another wireless technology that can be used to connect to the Internet is **WiMAX**. WiMAX is similar to your home or corporate wireless network, but on a much larger scale for a larger coverage area. WiMAX is defined in the IEEE 802.16 standard and can provide Internet access at speeds up to 1Gbps. WiMAX can also be used for connectivity as part of a cellular network.

A home or portable device can have a WiMAX receiver similar to the wireless broadband receivers. Such a device communicates with a tower that has a WiMAX antenna. This is known as a non-line-of-sight connection. The WiMAX antenna mounted on a tower connects wirelessly with another WiMAX antenna mounted on a tower, which might connect to a third WiMAX tower. These between-tower connections are known as **line-of-sight networks** or line-of-sight backhauls. Eventually, the last WiMAX tower connects via cable to the ISP. Figure 13.14 summarizes the wireless concepts.

Laptop wireless WAN connectivity

Tech Tip

A laptop that ships with integrated wireless WAN capabilities does not need an additional adapter or antenna. However, the BIOS must have the option enabled. Some laptops might have a key combination or a switch to enable the connection. The wireless application software is available through the Start button.

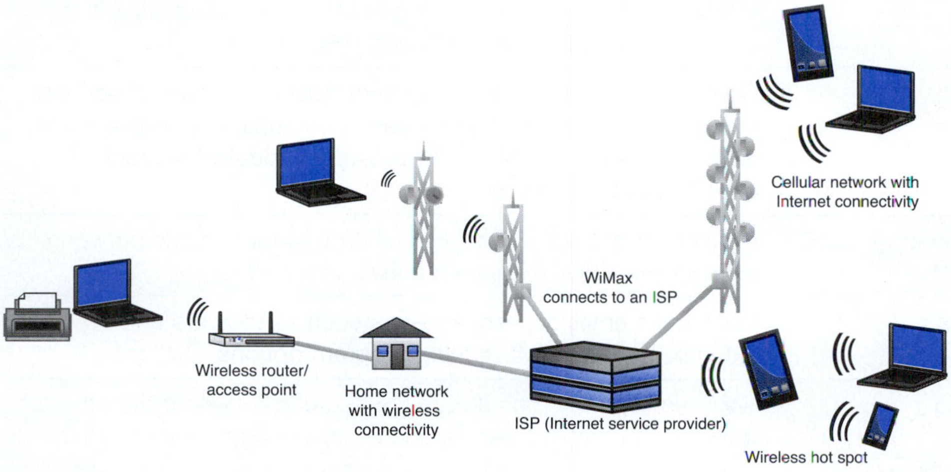

Figure 13.14 Wireless Internet connectivity

Web Browsers

A web browser is a graphical interface between a user and the Internet. Common web browsers include Microsoft's Internet Explorer (commonly called IE), Mozilla's Firefox, and Google's Chrome (not to be confused with Google's Chrome OS, which is a Linux-based operating system). Because Internet Explorer ships with Windows, most textbooks use this browser to explain concepts instead of all three.

Most browsers are customizable, and many of the settings relate to security, so they are covered in Chapter 15. To get to those settings, click on *Tools* or the Tools icon that looks like a gear in the top-right corner of Internet Explorer. Internet Explorer version 9 has seven main Internet Options tabs (see Figure 13.15). A user uses these tabs to configure the browser experience. Note that these options can also be reached using the Internet Options Control Panel in all versions of Windows. Table 13.8 explains the main purposes of the main tabs.

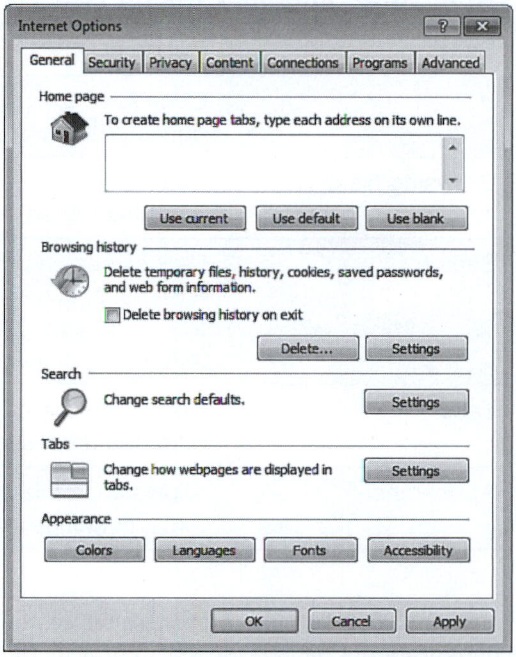

Figure 13.15 Internet Options tabs

Table 13.8 Purposes of the Internet Options tabs

Tab	Purpose
General	Configures the home page (the page that opens every time Internet Explorer opens or the home icon is clicked), deletes or configures how long the browsing history (the websites visited) are kept, configures how tabs are organized and behave, and enables customization of the font, language, and color scheme.
Security	Customizes security options for sites that you trust and ones that you want blocked (see Chapter 15).
Privacy	Configures how your private information is handled, including cookies and pop-ups (see Chapter 15).
Content	Contains Parental Controls, Content Advisor, control of security certificates, AutoComplete for ease of completing on-line forms, and Feeds and Web Slices for providing updated content directly into the browser.
Connections	Configures dial-up (phone line) or VPN (virtual private network) information. VPNs are covered in Chapter 15.
Programs	Configures email access, add-ons such as toolbars and extensions, and HTML-editing program options.
Advanced	Shows a list of options that might be set throughout the other tabs, also presented here in one easily configured list of check-boxes.

The General tab is one of the most common used tabs. Table 13.9 explains the purpose of its main sections.

Table 13.9 Internet Explorer General tab sections

Section	Purpose
Home page	Configures the page that opens every time Internet Explorer opens or the home icon is clicked
Browsing history	Deletes or configures how long the browsing history (the websites visited) is kept
Search	Defines search providers, such as Bing or Google, what toolbars are visible, accelerators (allows information to be automatically filled in or a map appear based on a searched for address), and InPrivate options
Tabs	Configures the browsing tabs (not the configuration tabs) and other features, such as warnings and pop-ups
Appearance	Allows customization of the browser environment, including the fonts, language, and color scheme

Lab 13.5 at the end of this chapter demonstrates the basics of Internet Explorer configuration. Chapters 14 and 15 provide more information and labs on networking, network security, and Internet security.

Soft Skills—Mentoring

Every great technician can tell you that he or she had at least one mentor along the way. When you hear the word *mentor*, it probably conjures up other words and phrases in your head—coach, guidance, teacher, adviser, positive influence, leadership, setting an example, and so on. No technician can attain his or her ultimate level without being mentored and mentoring someone else along his or her career path. Also, no technician can learn everything from a book or from experience. Others helping us along the way enable us to learn faster and more efficiently.

When you enter your first (second, third, or fourth) job in the IT field, you should take a few days to look around the company. Find someone who appears to be very professional and knowledgeable—someone who you want to emulate. Talk to that person and explain your goals. Ask if he or she will mentor you and detail what you would like—whether it is help you with problems you cannot solve or advice about office politics.

Mentoring is an important part of life. Not only should you consider being mentored, but you should consider mentoring others. Many technicians hoard information from other technicians and computer users. Knowledge is power, and by sharing information with others and helping them along the way, you cement and expand your own knowledge.

Chapter Summary

- Serial ports are also called asynchronous ports, COM ports, and RS232 ports.
- Serial ports use either XON/XOFF (software method) or RTS/CTS (hardware method) for flow control.
- Serial ports must be configured for the number of bits, parity, stop bits, FIFO setting, flow control, and handshaking. The two sides of the connection must match.
- The speed at which a 56K modem can transmit is limited by the number of analog-to-digital conversions.
- Internet connectivity can be provided by an analog modem, satellite modem, ISDN, cable modem, fiber, DSL modem, or wirelessly through the cell phone network, a wireless hot spot, WiMAX, or a wireless network.
- Cable modem bandwidth is shared by the number of subscribers in an area. A direct fiber connection might be an option.
- A DSL modem uses a phone line. ADSL has a faster downstream than upstream speed.
- WiMax networks are line-of-sight networks.
- VoIP uses a corporate network and/or the Internet for voice connectivity. Internet-based VoIP does not offer QoS.
- Technicians frequently have to configure Internet browsers. In Internet Explorer, you use the Internet Options tabs for configuration.
- Mentoring is important when you get started as a technician and as you gain experience.

Key Terms

ADSL 706
asynchronous 697
bandwidth 705
baud 698
bps 698
cable modem 704
convergence 703
data bits 699
DCE 700
dial-up network 696
downstream 705
DSL 706
DTE 700
fax modem 702
FIFO setting 699
flow control 699
handshaking 699
ISDN 702
ISP 709
line-of-sight network ... 711
parity 699
phone filter 707
PSTN 703
QoS 703
RS232C 698
RTS/CTS 699
satellite modem 709
start bit 698
stop bit 698
upstream 705
VoIP 703
WiMAX 710
wireless broadband 710
wireless hot spot 710
xDSL 706
XON/XOFF 699

Review Questions

1. Which of the following are names for a computer's serial port? (Select all that apply.) [COM port | asynchronous port | synchronous port | LPT port | RS232 port]
2. What setting determines how two serial devices establish communication? [data bits | stop bits | parity | flow control]
3. What port would be used to connect an external modem if the motherboard did not have a serial port? [IEEE 1394 | eSATA | DVI | USB]
4. What is the biggest limitation to a 56Kbps modem transmitting at 56Kbps?

5. What is VoIP?
   a. a cable modem technology
   b. a method used to wirelessly connect to the Internet
   c. using a network to carry voice traffic
   d. communicating faster on the network on downloads than on uploads
6. What component is added to phone jacks that have a phone or answering machine attached when DSL technology is used to connect to the Internet so that both data and voice and be transmitted over the same circuitry?
   [modem surge protector | phone filter | ISP | RJ-11 connector]
7. [T | F] A cable modem is a good investment for a home modem. Explain your answer.
8. Explain how a NIC is used with a cable modem.
9. List one drawback to a cable modem.
10. What does asymmetrical mean in relation to an ADSL modem?
11. Can a phone be used at the same time as a DSL modem? Explain why or why not.
12. What is the first thing you should check if your Internet connectivity is down and you have a DSL modem installed?
13. What is wireless broadband?
14. Would WiMAX be a good technology for a country that does not have a very strong wired Internet connectivity infrastructure? Why or why not?
15. A new laptop has an integrated wireless WAN. The customer thinks there is a missing wireless antenna. What should you advise the customer?
16. [T | F] A hot spot provides wired network connectivity.
17. What would be the purpose of an Ethernet connection on a cable modem or a DSL modem?
    a. connect the PC to the phone jack on the wall
    b. connect the PC to the jack provided by the Internet provider
    c. connect the PC to the modem
    d. connect the modem to the jack provided by the Internet provider
18. A customer has a new laptop with wireless WAN capabilities; however, the software does not connect to the Internet. What would you suggest to the customer?
19. What is a phone line isolator?
20. List two ways mentoring can help in the IT field.

Exercises

Lab 13.1 Exploring Serial Devices in Windows XP

Objective: To explore serial devices and their properties using Windows XP

Parts: A computer with Windows XP installed and, optionally, a modem

Procedure: Complete the following procedure and answer the accompanying questions.

1. Power on the computer and log on using the user ID and password provided by the instructor or lab assistant.
2. Click the *Start* button and click *Control Panel*.
3. If in Category View, click *Performance and Maintenance*. In both views, open *Administrative Tools* and double-click the *Computer Management* icon.
4. In the left window, click *Device Manager*. In the right window, expand the *Ports* option.
5. Right-click *Communications Port (Com1)* and select *Properties*.

   What options are available under the Device Usage drop-down menu?

   What is the status of the serial port?
6. Click the *Troubleshoot* button. When the generic hardware device troubleshooter opens, click the *Next* button.
7. Click the *Yes, my hardware is on the HCL* or *I have already contacted the manufacturer and installed updated drivers, but I still have a problem* radio button and then click *Next*.

   What is the next question the troubleshooter poses?

   If a new driver was just installed, what Windows XP feature can be used?
8. Close the *Help and Support Center* window and click the *Port Settings* tab.

   What is the default serial port speed setting?
9. Click the *Driver* tab and click the *Driver Details* button.

   List any drivers, including the complete path associated with the serial port.
10. Click the *OK* button.

    What is the purpose of the Roll Back Driver button?
11. Click the *Resources* tab.

    What IRQ and I/O addresses are assigned?

Instructor initials: ____________

12. Click the *OK* button.

Modems

Note: Skip this section if a modem is not installed. If unsure, perform the tasks to see if the steps work.

13. Expand the *Modems* Device Manager category. Right-click a specific modem and select *Properties*. Click the *Modem* tab.

    What COM port does the modem use?

    What is the maximum port speed?

    Is 115,200bps the speed at which the modem transmits over the phone line? Explain your answer.

14. Click the *Diagnostics* tab and click the *Query Modem* button.

    What was the first *AT* command that was sent to the modem?

15. Click the *View log* button.

    Scroll to the bottom of the log. What communications standard(s) does the modem use? Modem dependent, but a common answer is V.90

16. Close the Notepad log. Click the *Resources* tab.

    What IRQ and I/O addresses does the modem use?

Instructor initials: ______________

17. Close the *Modem Properties* window. Close the *Computer Management* window.

Lab 13.2 Exploring Serial Devices in Windows Vista/7

Objective: To explore serial devices and their properties using Windows Vista and Windows 7

Parts: A computer with Windows Vista or Windows 7 installed

Either a serial port with an external modem attached or an internal modem

Procedure: Complete the following procedure and answer the accompanying questions.

1. Power on the computer and log on using the user ID and password provided by the instructor or lab assistant.
2. Click the *Start* button and click *Control Panel*.
3. Click the *System and Maintenance* (Vista) or *System and Security* (7) Control Panel.
4. Click the *Device Manager* link. Note that you may have to scroll down to see this option.
5. Expand the *Ports* option.
6. If *Communications Port (Com1)* is available, right-click and select *Properties*.

   What tabs are available?

   What is the status of the serial port?

7. Click the *Port Settings* tab.

   What is the maximum number of bits per second?

8. Click the *Advanced* button.

   What UART is being used?

   What COM port is assigned? Machine dependent, but a common answer will be COM1.

9. Click *Cancel*.
10. Click the *Driver* tab and click the *Driver Details* button.

    List any drivers, including the complete path associated with the serial port.

11. Click the *OK* button.

    What is the purpose of the *Roll Back Driver* button?

12. Click the *Resources* tab.

    What IRQ and I/O addresses are assigned?

Instructor initials: ____________

13. Click the *OK* button.

Modems

Note: Skip this section if an internal modem is not installed. If unsure, perform the tasks to see if the steps work.

14. Expand the *Modems* Device Manager category. Right-click a specific modem and select *Properties*. Click the *Modem* tab.

    What COM port does the modem use?

    What is the maximum port speed?

    Is the setting for the maximum bits per second on a serial port the speed at which the external modem transmits over the phone line? Explain your answer.

    Why would you want the speaker volume enabled when first installing a modem?

15. Click the *Diagnostics* tab and click the *Query Modem* button.

    What was the first AT command that was sent to the modem?

16. Click the *View log* button. Scroll to the bottom of the log.

    What communications standard(s) does the modem use?

17. Close the Notepad log. Click the *Resources* tab.

    What IRQ and I/O addresses does the modem use?

Instructor initials: ____________

18. Close the *Modem Properties* window. Close the *Device Manager* window.
19. Close the *Control Panel* window.

Lab 13.3 Windows XP Direct Cable Connection

Objective: To connect two computers, using either a null serial or null parallel cable so that one computer can access files or resources on the other computer

Parts: Two Windows XP computers

A null serial or parallel cable

Note: Networking must previously be installed or installed during the Direct Cable Connection installation. The steps of this process are beyond the scope of this chapter.

Procedure: Complete the following procedure and answer the accompanying questions.

1. Connect the null serial or parallel cable between the two computers.
2. Power on the computer and logon as an administrator or with a user ID that has administrator permissions. See the instructor or lab assistant for more details.

3. Before installing Windows XP's Direct Cable Connection, check to see if a null serial cable is being used. Look to see if the cable attaches to the serial port or parallel port. If it is a serial connection, the cable must first be installed as a modem. If a null serial cable is being used, go to the Serial Connection Pre-installation section. If a serial connection is not being used, skip this section.

Serial Connection Pre-installation

4. Access the *Phone and Modem Options* Control Panel and select the *Modems* tab. Click the *Add* button.
5. Enable the *Don't detect my modem, I will select it from a list* checkbox and click *Next*.
6. Locate the *Standard Modem Types Manufacturer* option and click it. In the right pane, select *Communications cable between two computers* and click *Next*.
7. Select the port that has the null serial cable attached. Click *Finish* and click *OK*.

Direct Cable Connection Installation

8. Click the *Start* button and click *Control Panel*. Double-click *Network Connections*.
9. Under Network Tasks, click the *Create a new connection* icon and click *Next*. Under Network Connection Type, select *Set up an advanced connection* and click *Next*. If configuring the first computer (the host), select *Accept incoming connections* in the *Type of Connection You Want* window and click *Next*. If configuring the second computer (the guest), select *Connect directly to another computer* and click *Next*. The host computer is the one sharing resources. The guest computer is the one that is accessing the shared resources. Click the *Next* button.
10. Select the type of cable being used checkbox and click *Next*.
11. Select the *Do not allow virtual private connections* radio button and click *Next*.
12. Select the users who will be allowed to connect and click *Next*.
13. In the *Networking software* window, ensure that a networking protocol such as TCP/IP and File and Printer Sharing are enabled. Note that the *Properties* button can be used, if necessary, to configure the networking protocol parameters. See Chapter 14 for more details on TCP/IP addressing. Click *Next* and click the *Finish* button.
14. Go to the second computer and perform exactly the same procedure except select *Connect directly to another computer* in Step 2.

Instructor initials: ______________

Lab 13.4 Internal and External Modem Installation

Objective: To be able to install an internal modem and an external modem and establish communication between two computers

Parts: Internal modem
External modem with serial cable
Two Windows XP computers
Windows XP HyperTerminal communication software
Two RJ-11 phone cables
Two analog phone ports or a phone line simulator

Note: Two internal modems or two external modems could also be used to perform this lab, with very few adjustments.

Procedure: Complete the following procedure and answer the accompanying questions.

1. Power on the computer and ensure that it boots properly.
2. Shut down the computer properly and remove the power cord from the back of the computer.

Internal Modem Installation

3. Install the internal modem into an available slot.
4. Re-install the computer cover, re-install the computer power cord, and power on the computer. The *Found New Hardware* Wizard appears if this is the first time the computer has had this adapter installed.
5. Install the correct modem driver, using either the one from Microsoft or the one provided with the modem.
6. Access the Device Manager through the *System* Control Panel (or the *Performance and Maintenance* category and then the *System* Control Panel). Click the *Hardware* tab and click *Device Manager*. Expand the *Modems* category. Right-click the internal modem that was just installed and select *Properties*.

   Under the General tab, what is the device status? It should be that the modem is working properly. If it is not, perform appropriate troubleshooting until it does display that message.
7. Click the *Diagnostics* tab. Click the *Query modem* button.

   List at least two AT commands and the response that is shown in the information window.
8. Click the *View log* button.

   What do you think a technician could do with this information?
9. Close the *Notepad log* window.
10. Click the *Resources* tab.

    What memory range does the adapter use?

    What IRQ is the adapter using?
11. Click the *Advanced* tab.

    When do you think you would use the Extra initialization commands textbox?
12. Click the *Advanced Port Settings* button.

    What COM port is used with this adapter?

    Are FIFO buffers used by default?
13. Click the *Cancel* button on the next two screens to exit the *Properties* window.
14. Connect an RJ-11 phone cable from the internal modem port (the one that is *not* labeled phone) to the analog phone line or to a port on the simulator.

External Modem Installation

15. On the second computer, attach the power cord to the external modem and attach the other end to power outlet. Connect the serial modem cable between the modem and the PC.

    What COM port are you attaching the modem?

    If you do not know, research this until you do. Do not proceed until you determine the COM number assigned to the serial port being used.
16. Turn on the external modem. A *Found New Hardware* balloon normally appears. If Windows detects the modem, after a short period, a message appears, saying that the hardware is ready to use.
17. Access the *Phone and Modem Options* Control Panel. Click the *Modems* tab.

    Does the modem appear in the list? If not, troubleshoot until it does.

    What COM port is listed in the *Attached to* column of the display?

18. Ensure that the correct modem is selected and click the *Properties* button.

    On the *General* tab, what is the device status?

19. Click the *Modem* tab. This tab is where you can control the speaker volume, maximum port speed, and dial control option. Click the *Diagnostics* tab and click the *Query Modem* button. Watch the lights on top of the modem as the PC communicates with the external modem. This ability to watch the connectivity is an advantage of having an external modem.

    List the first command and response listed in the dialog window as a result of the modem query.

    Click the *Advanced* tab. What can you do from this tab?

20. Click the *Driver* tab.

    What is the purpose of the *Roll Back Driver* option?

21. Click the *Cancel* button on the next two screens to exit the *Properties* window.

22. Notice the documented markings for the external modem's phone ports. The port that has the symbol for an RJ-11 connection is used to connect to a phone outlet. The port that has the symbol for a phone is where you can optionally attach an analog phone to the modem. Connect an RJ-11 phone cable from the external modem port to another phone outlet or to a phone network simulator.

    What phone number is assigned to the wall outlet or port used for the internal modem?

    What phone number is assigned to the wall outlet or port used for the external modem?

Communication Between the Two Modems

23. The HyperTerminal program is a communications program that has shipped with Windows products since the first version of Windows. On the computer that has an external modem attached, access the HyperTerminal application (normally available through the *Accessories* option). The *New Connection* window appears. Figure 13.16 shows this window.

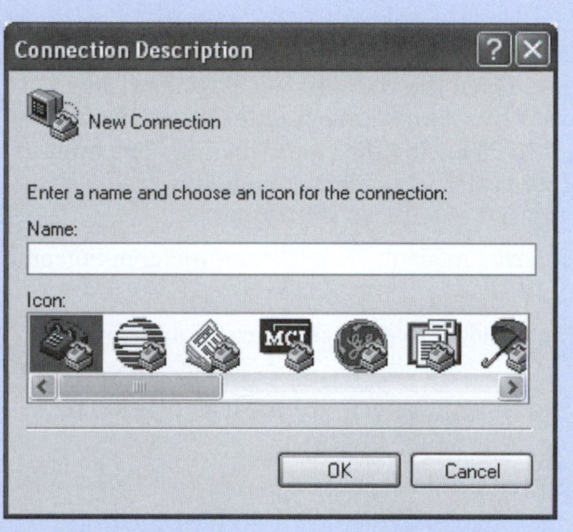

Figure 13.16 HyperTerminal window

24. Click the *Cancel* button. From the *File* menu option, select *Properties*. In the *Connect using* drop-down list, select the modem. Figure 13.17 shows how the modem appears in the drop-down list.

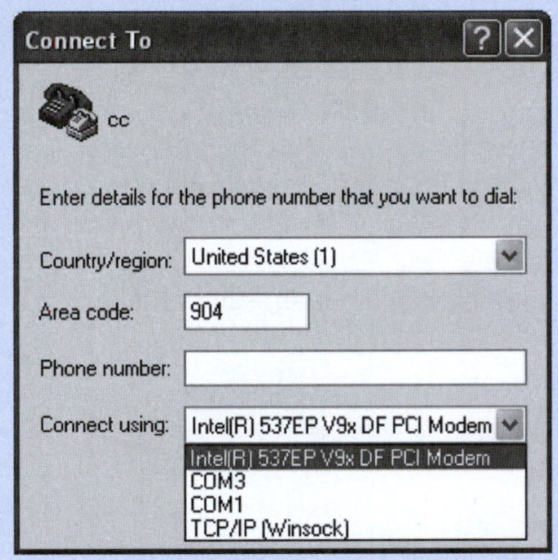

Figure 13.17 **HyperTerminal modem selection**

25. Click the *Configure* button.

    What is the default flow control used by this external modem?

    Is error compression enabled or disabled by default?

26. Click the *Advanced* tab.

    What is the default setting for the number of data bits, whether parity is used, the number of stop bits, and the type of modulation used?

27. Click the *Cancel* button. In the *Properties* window, click the *OK* button. In the HyperTerminal window, type `AT` and press Enter. The modem responds with the message *OK* when the modem is working properly. The `AT` command tells the modem that you want its "ATtention."

28. On the computer that has the internal modem, access HyperTerminal. In the *Name* textbox, type your name and click *OK*. Enter the area code in the *area code* textbox and ensure that the *Connect using drop-down* option is set to the internal modem. Click *OK* and *Cancel*.

29. From the HyperTerminal window for the external modem, type **`ATE1`** so that the commands you type will show in the window. From the HyperTerminal window, type **`atdt_`***`xxxxxxx`* (where the *x*s are replaced with the phone number of the other modem). `atdt` gets the modem's attention and tells it to dial using the "tone" method. The number that follows is the phone number to dial. If the external modem volume is turned up, you will hear a phone ringing.

30. From the HyperTerminal window for the internal modem, click the *Call* menu option and select *Wait for call*.

    What message appears in the HyperTerminal window that is used to control the external modem?

31. In the HyperTerminal window that is used to control the external modem, type **`Hello to you`**. Look at the HyperTerminal window for the internal modem.

    What indication, if any, do you see in the HyperTerminal window?

32. Show the HyperTerminal message to the teacher.

33. From the HyperTerminal window that controls the external modem, select the *Call* menu option and select *Disconnect*.

    What indication do you have in the HyperTerminal window that controls the internal modem that the modem connection is no longer active?

34. Power off the external modem. Disconnect the phone cable. Remove the power connector. Remove the serial modem cable from the back of the PC and the back of the external modem. Replace all parts to their storage location.
35. Disconnect the analog phone cable from the internal modem.
36. On the computer that has the internal modem, power off the computer, remove the power cord, and remove the internal modem. Place the modem inside the antistatic bag. Return the modem, phone cable, and software to the proper storage location.

Lab 13.5 Introduction to Internet Explorer Configuration

Objective: To become familiar with basic Internet Explorer configuration options

Parts: Windows computer

Note: This lab has been tested on Internet Explorer versions 8 and 9, but many parts will also be applicable to earlier versions.

Procedure: Complete the following procedure and answer the accompanying questions.

1. Power on the computer and ensure that it boots properly.
2. Open Internet Explorer.

   From either the *Tools* link or the *Help (?)* link, select *About Internet Explorer* to determine the Internet Explorer version.
3. In the upper-right corner of the Internet Explorer window, select the *Tools* link. Note that this may be an icon that looks like a gear.
4. Select *Internet Options*.

   What URL is listed as the home page?

   Is the *Delete browsing history on exit* option enabled or disabled? [enabled | disabled]

   List one corporate scenario where you think the business security policy would require that this option be enabled.
5. Select the *Settings* button in the *Search* section.

   List any search providers listed and whether the site can provide search suggestions (whether search suggestions are enabled, disabled, or not available).

   How do you think the *Prevent programs from suggesting changes to my default search provider* checkbox at the bottom of the window might help users?
6. Click the *Close* button. Select the *Settings* button in the *Tabs* section.

   [T | F] To enable tabbed browsing when it has been disabled, you must close all Internet Explorer windows and then reopening Internet Explorer to activate the change.

   Based on the configured options, what currently happens when a new tab is opened?

   What do you think the most secure pop-up setting would be for a corporate environment, and why do you think this?

From the choices provided, what is your favorite way of handling program links provided in a website?

7. Click *Cancel*. Click the *Colors* button.

   Is the *Use Windows colors* option selected (enabled)? [enabled | disabled]

8. Disable the *Use Windows colors* option. Select the *Use hover color* option.

   Based on what you see as the default settings, which option might you change for a red/green colorblind person in a corporate environment?

   What color is the default hover color?

9. Click *Cancel*. Click the *Languages* button.

   What two prefix and suffix options are available?

13. Click *Cancel*. Select the *Fonts* button.

    What is the current font setting for web pages?

14. Click *Cancel*. Select the *Accessibility* button.

    List one example of when you might use the formatting options presented in a home computer environment.

15. Click *Cancel* twice and close *Internet Explorer*.

Activities

Internet Discovery

Objective: To obtain specific information regarding a computer or its associated parts on the Internet

Parts: Computer with Internet access

Questions: Use the Internet to answer the following questions.

1. Locate a cable modem website that explains how to increase speed on a cable modem. Write the URL where you found the answer as well as the recommendation.

2. Determine whether cable or DSL modems are supported in your area. If so, determine as many vendors as you can for these products.

3. Find one vendor of VDSL in the United States and write down the name of the vendor and the URL where you found the answer.

4. Find a website that describes how modem chat scripts are done and that provides an example of one. Write the URL and your own explanation of chat scripts.

5. Determine how much a vendor charges to enable the mobile hot spot option or a phone that supports it. Document the amount or phone model number and the URL where you found this information.

6. Find a vendor in your state that sells wireless broadband for a laptop. What type of technology does it use (USB, PC Card, ExpressCard, integrated, etc.)? Write the URL, the vendor name and model number, and the cost.

Soft Skills

Objective: To enhance and fine-tune a future technician's ability to listen, communicate in both written and oral forms, and support people who use computers in a professional manner

Afsctivities:

1. The class is divided into three groups—two groups that will be debating against one another and a third group of judges. The judges have 45 minutes to determine the rules and consequences of how the debate is to be conducted. During the same 45 minutes, the two debating groups will be researching material and planning a strategy for either cable modems or DSL modems. At the end of 45 minutes, the debate will start, and the judges will mediate with the rules they establish and present to the two teams before the debate begins. The judges, along with the instructor, determine which group proved its point the best.
2. Using whatever resources are available, research one of the following that has been assigned to you. Share the results individually with the class.
   - What is the largest number of IRQs supported by an analog modem that you could find?
   - What is the fastest DSL, cable, or analog connection within a 60-mile radius of your school?
   - What is the most common type of Internet connectivity for home users in your area?
   - What is the most common type of Internet connectivity among businesses in your area?
   - What is the type and speed of Internet connectivity at your school?
   - What is the type and speed of Internet connectivity at a college in your state?
   - Which types of DSL services are available in your state?
   - Which types of cable modem services are available in your state?

Critical Thinking Skills

Objective: To analyze and evaluate information as well as apply learned information to new or different situations

Activities:

1. In groups of three, research one of the following issues, as designated by the instructor. Share your findings with the other groups.
   - The pros and cons of changing the operating system on a smartphone so that it can be a hot spot. Be prepared to share the group findings.

- What wireless broadband options are available from one of the most popular mobile phone providers in the area? Detail one option, rate plan, and cost. Be prepared to share your findings.
- Determine the best small business class Internet connectivity rates in the area where your school is located. Share at least two competitors' rates if possible. Detail the connectivity speeds and costs per vendor and be prepared to share your findings.
- Find at least three VoIP solutions for home users. Prepare a chart that shows vendors, options, pros and cons of each option, costs, and customer ratings (and comments, if possible). Be prepared to share your findings.

2. In groups of two, write two analog/cable/DSL modem problems on two separate index cards. Give one problem to another class group and the other problem to a different class group. Your group will receive two index cards from two different groups as well. Solve the problems given to you, using any resource available. Share your group findings with the class.

A+ Certification Exam Tips

✓ The Internet connection types that are on the 220-801 exam are as follows: cable, DSL, dial-up, fiber, satellite, ISDN, cellular (mobile hot spot), line of sight wireless, and WiMax. Be able to describe these technologies.

✓ Know pros and cons of each Internet connection type.

✓ Know when each Internet connection type would be used.

✓ Know the purpose of a VoIP phone.

✓ The 220-802 exam includes the *Internet Options* Control Panel, which includes the tabs that can also be accessed from within Internet Explorer. Be familiar with each tab and why a technician would use the tab. Before the exam, re-examine those options.

chapter 14

Introduction to Networking

Chapter Objectives:

In this chapter you will learn:

- How networks can be wired (or wireless)
- How to identify common network cables
- How Ethernet works
- About the OSI and TCP/IP models and different protocols
- To identify MAC, IPv4, and IPv6 addresses
- To set up wired and wireless networks
- Common network troubleshooting tools
- To configure and access a network printer
- How to configure apps on a mobile device
- How to be a proactive technician

CompTIA Exam Objectives:

What CompTIA A+ exam objectives are covered in this chapter?

- ✓ 801-1.2 Differentiate between motherboard components, their purposes, and properties.
- ✓ 801-1.7 Compare and contrast various connection interfaces and explain their purpose.
- ✓ 801-2.1 Identify types of network cables and connectors.
- ✓ 801-2.2 Categorize characteristics of connectors and cabling.
- ✓ 801-2.3 Explain properties and characteristics of TCP/IP.
- ✓ 801-2.4 Explain common TCP and UDP ports, protocols, and their purpose.
- ✓ 801-2.5 Compare and contrast wireless networking standards and encryption types.
- ✓ 801-2.6 Install, configure, and deploy a SOHO wireless/wired router using appropriate settings.
- ✓ 801-2.7 Compare and contrast Internet connection types and features.
- ✓ 801-2.8 Identify various types of networks.
- ✓ 801-2.9 Compare and contrast network devices, their functions, and features.
- ✓ 801-2.10 Given a scenario, use appropriate networking tools.
- ✓ 801-3.1 Install and configure laptop hardware and components.
- ✓ 801-3.2 Compare and contrast the components within the display of a laptop.
- ✓ 801-3.3 Compare and contrast laptop features.
- ✓ 801-4.2 Given a scenario, install, and configure printers.
- ✓ 801-5.1 Given a scenario, use appropriate safety procedures.
- ✓ 802-1.2 Given a scenario, install and configure the operating system using the most appropriate method.
- ✓ 802-1.3 Given a scenario, use appropriate command line tools.
- ✓ 802-1.4 Given a scenario, use appropriate operating system features and tools.
- ✓ 802-1.5 Given a scenario, use Control Panel utilities.
- ✓ 802-1.6 Setup and configure Windows networking on a client/desktop.
- ✓ 802-1.8 Explain the differences among basic OS security settings.
- ✓ 802-1.9 Explain the basics of client-side virtualization.
- ✓ 802-3.2 Establish basic network connectivity and configure email.
- ✓ 802-3.5 Execute and configure mobile device synchronization.
- ✓ 802-4.5 Given a scenario, troubleshoot wired and wireless networks with appropriate tools.

Networking Overview

Many networks are found all around us. The following are a few examples:

- The network of roads and interstate highways
- The telephone network
- The electrical network that provides electricity to our homes
- The cellular network that allows cell phones/smartphones to connect to one another as well as connectivity between cell phones/smartphones and the wired telephone network and the Internet
- The air traffic control network
- Your network of friends and family

A network as it relates to computers is two or more devices that have the ability to communicate with one another and share resources. A network allows computer users to share files; communicate via email; browse the Internet; share a printer, modem, or scanner; and access applications and files. Networks can be divided into four major categories based on the size of the network—PAN, LAN, MAN, and WAN. Table 14.1 describes these different networks.

Table 14.1 Types of networks

Network type	Description
PAN (personal area network)	Personal devices such as PDAs, cell phones, laptop computers, and pocket video games that can communicate in close proximity through a wired network or wirelessly. Playing a game between two laptop computers wirelessly is an example of a PAN.
LAN (local area network)	A group of devices that can share resources in a single area such as a room, home, or building. The most common type of LAN is Ethernet. A LAN can be wired or wireless. The computers in a networked classroom is an example of a LAN.
MAN (metropolitan area network)	Connectivity between sites within the same city. A MAN connects multiple LANs. MANs can be wireless or use fiber-optic cable. Multiple college campuses connected together is an example of a MAN.
WAN (wide area network)	Communication between LANs on a larger geographic scale. The Internet is an example of a WAN just as two networks located in two cities is a WAN.
WLAN (wireless LAN)	A wireless network that consists of an access point and some wireless devices including laptops, netbooks, ultrabooks, tablets, and smartphones. A wireless network can be short range such as when Bluetooth is used or a wider coverage such as a wireless network for a home or business. Wireless bridges might be used connect devices between two buildings.
WWAN (wireless WAN)	Wireless connectivity for a larger geographic area using a mix of technologies such as cellular or WiMAX (covered later in this chapter).

Today, networks are vital to businesses. They can also be found in many homes. A technician must have a basic understanding of the devices that make up networks and learn how to connect them to existing networks.

Types of Local Area Networks

There are two basic types of LANs, a server-based network and a peer-to-peer network. With a server-based network, computer users log in to a main computer called a server where they are authenticated (authorized to use the network). The server is a more powerful computer than a normal workstation. The server contains information about who is allowed to connect to the network, and to what network resources (files, printer, and applications) the network user is allowed access. Another name for a server-based network is **client/server network**. Windows computers in a server-based network are commonly called a **domain**, or a Microsoft Active Directory domain. One or more dedicated servers log and track users and resources. Domains are commonly found in the business environment.

When working in a corporate environment, technicians commonly have to put new computers, replacement computers, or repaired computers on the domain. This requires special rights to be assigned to the technician; end users are not normally allowed to add computers to the domain. If a computer ever displays a message that the trust relationship is broken, the computer must be reconnected to the domain.

A peer-to-peer network does not have a centralized server. Instead, each computer is its own server and resources are shared between the workstation computers. The computer user sets up passwords to allow others access to the resources on or directly connected to that computer. A person uses the network to access remote files, printers, applications, and so forth from his/her own workstation. Server-based networks are more common in businesses, whereas peer-to-peer networks are more common in homes and very small businesses. A server-based network can consist of 10 or more computers; in contrast, a peer-to-peer network usually has fewer (2 to 9) computers.

Windows computers in a peer-to-peer network are known as a **workgroup** or a homegroup. Two or more computers configured with the same workgroup name can share devices such as printers as well as files and folders. No central server or domain controller is used. Many homes and small businesses use a workgroup environment. Figure 14.1 shows the basic difference between the corporate domain environment (where there would be servers and lots of networking equipment) and the type of devices that would be in a home network or a workgroup.

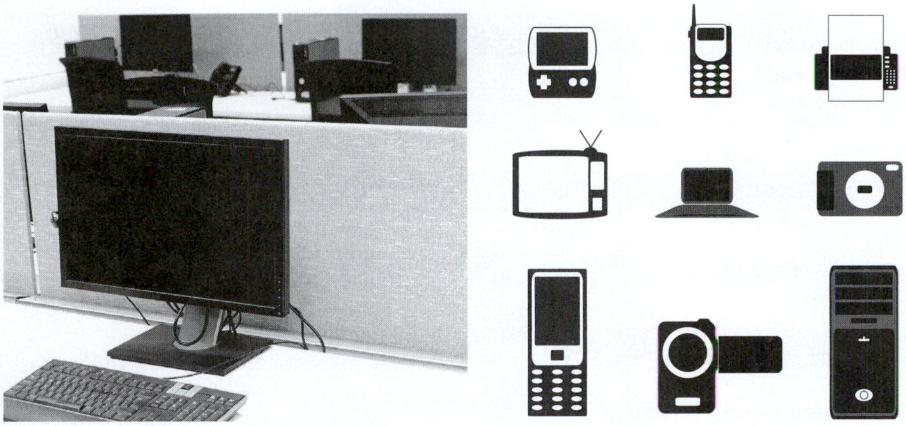

Corporate domain environment

Home network devices

Figure 14.1 Client/server environment versus workgroup environment

A server-based network is more secure than a peer-to-peer network. This is because the server is normally in a locked network room or wiring closet. Servers have a special operating system loaded on them called a NOS (network operating system), such as Microsoft Windows Server 2008 or Server 2012, Red Hat Enterprise Linux, and Sun Solaris. A network operating system has utilities that allow computer user management (who is allowed onto the network), resource management (what network applications, files, printers, and so on a user can use), and security management (what a user is allowed to do with a resource such as read, write, and read and write). One user ID and password is all a remote user needs to access many network resources located throughout the business organization.

Figure 14.2 shows how a server-based network can be configured. The network has one server in the center, four workstations, and two laser printers. The server has a database of users—CSchmidt, RDevoid, and MElkins—and their associated passwords. The server also has three applications loaded—Microsoft Excel, Microsoft Project, and Microsoft Word. These applications and associated documents are stored on the server. Whether or not the users can access these applications and documents and what they can do within each document is also stored on the server. In the Permission column of the table located in Figure 14.2 is either R for Read or R/W for Read/Write. This is an indication of what the user can do in a particular application. For example, user CSchmidt has read and write access to Excel, Project, and Word. This means that she can open, look at, and modify documents in any of these three applications. MElkins can only read Excel and Word documents, but she can read and write Microsoft Project documents. CSchmidt can print to either of the laser printers, but RDevoid prints only to the LP1 laser printer.

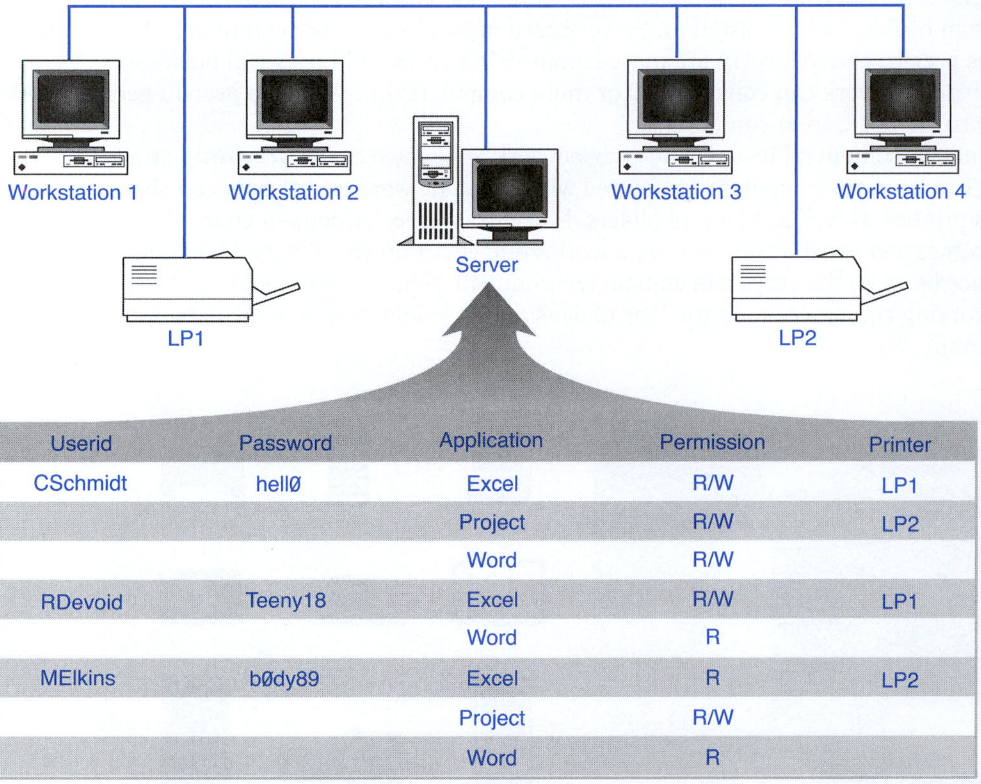

Userid	Password	Application	Permission	Printer
CSchmidt	hellØ	Excel	R/W	LP1
		Project	R/W	LP2
		Word	R/W	
RDevoid	Teeny18	Excel	R/W	LP1
		Word	R	
MElkins	bØdy89	Excel	R	LP2
		Project	R/W	
		Word	R	

Figure 14.2 Server-based network

A peer-to-peer network is not as expensive or as secure as a server-based network. A server is more expensive than a regular workstation, and it requires a network operating system. Since peer-to-peer networks do not use a dedicated server, costs are reduced. Instead of a network operating system, each workstation uses an operating system such as Windows XP, Windows Vista, or Windows 7. A peer-to-peer network is not as secure as a server-based network because each computer must be configured with individual user IDs and passwords. Figure 14.3 shows how a peer-to-peer network is configured.

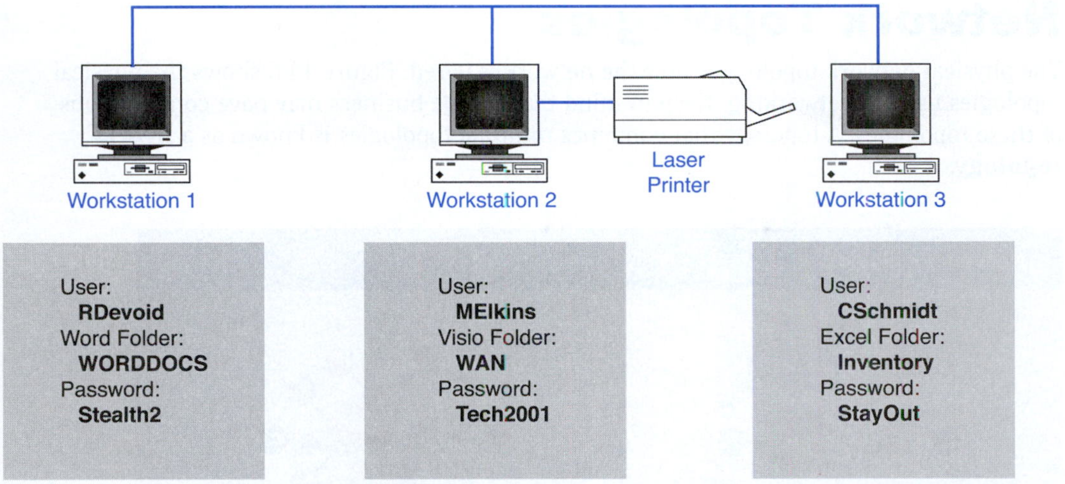

Figure 14.3 Workgroup (peer-to-peer) network

Figure 14.3 shows three workstations, labeled Workstation 1, Workstation 2, and Workstation 3. Workstation 2 has a shared printer for everyone to use. There are three people in this company: Raina Devoid, Cheryl Schmidt, and Melodie Elkins. RDevoid normally works at Workstation 1 and she has shared a folder on the hard drive called *WORDDOCS* that has a password of Stealth2. CSchmidt and MElkins can access the documents located in *WORDDOCS* from their own workstations as long as they know the password is Stealth2. If RDevoid wants to access MElkins' *WAN* folder, RDevoid must know and remember that the password is Tech2001. If MElkins' changes the password on the *WAN* folder, MElkins must remember to tell the new password to anyone who needs access. The password is only used when accessing the *WAN* folder documents.

Tech Tip

Peer-to-peer networks are for small networks

You can see that the more resources that are shared on a peer-to-peer network, the more passwords and the more cumbersome password management will be. That is the reason peer-to-peer networks are used in very small network environments.

A peer-to-peer network password is only effective across the network. The password is not effective if someone sits down at the workstation. For example, if a summer intern, Ken Tinker, sits down at Workstation 3, Ken has full access to the *Inventory* folder and documents. Even though the folder is password protected for the peer-to-peer network, Ken is not using the network to access the folder so the password is useless. Ken could be prevented from accessing the folder if user IDs and passwords are implemented for individual machines. The problem of having access to a workstation and all its resources simply by sitting down at a computer is not as much of a threat today because of the newer operating systems' features.

Management of network resources is much harder to control on a peer-to-peer network than on a server-based network. Each user is required to manage the network resources on one computer and password management can become a nightmare. Remember with peer-to-peer networks that anyone who knows the password can access the folder across the network. Server-based networks are normally more secure because (1) passwords are managed centrally at the server and (2) the server is normally locked in a wiring closet or server room.

When configuring Windows for a network, you are presented with three choices: home network, work network, or public network. Depending on what you choose, will be the type of network you select as shown in Figure 14.4. In order to have a network, the following are required: network adapters (NICs), network media (cable or air), and an operating system with network options enabled. The following sections explore these concepts.

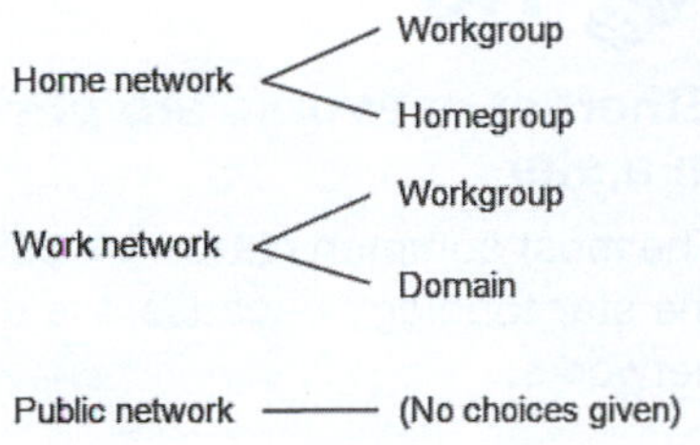

Figure 14.4 Windows and homegroup/workgroup/domain

Network Topologies

The physical network topology is how the network is wired. Figure 14.5 shows the physical topologies used in networking. Keep in mind that a large business may have combinations of these topologies. A topology that combines multiple topologies is known as a **hybrid topology**.

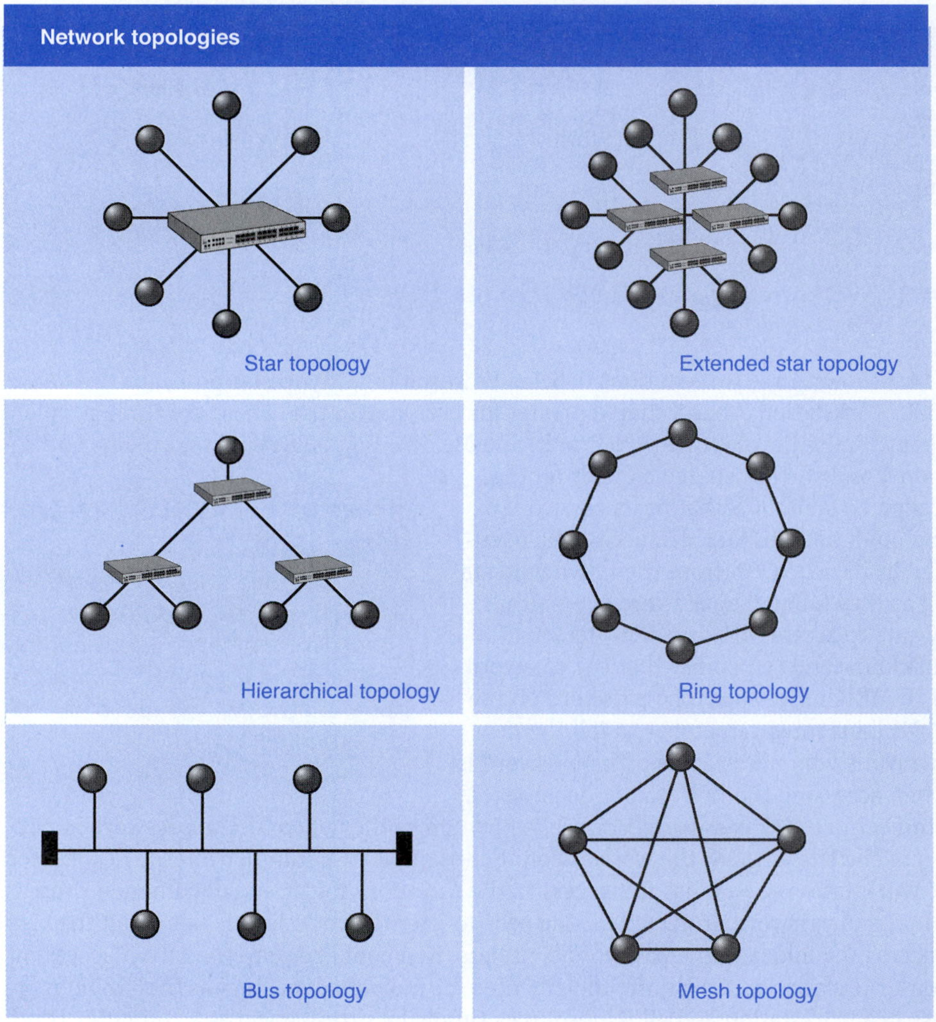

Figure 14.5 **Network topologies**

Ethernet networks are the most common type of LAN. Each network device connects to a central device, normally a hub or a switch. Both the **hub** and the **switch** contain two or more RJ-45 network jacks. The hub is not as intelligent as a switch. The switch takes a look at each data frame as it comes through the switch. The hub is not able to do this. Figure 14.6 illustrates a hub or switch. You sometimes have to look at the model number to tell the difference because they are similar in appearance.

Tech Tip

Ethernet networks are physically wired in a star

The most common network topology used today is the star topology because it is used with Ethernet networks.

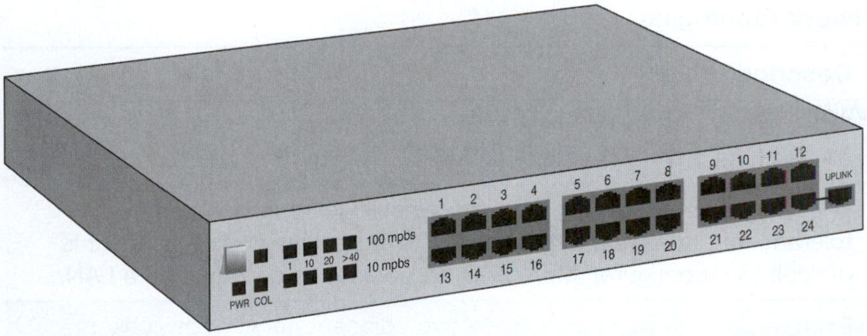

Figure 14.6 Switch

In a star topology, each network device has a cable that connects between the device and the hub or switch. If one computer or cable fails, all other devices continue to function. However, if the hub or switch fails, the network goes down. The hub or switch is normally located in a central location, such as a network wiring closet. Figure 14.7 shows how a star topology is cabled. By looking at how each device connects to a central location, you can easily see why it is called a star.

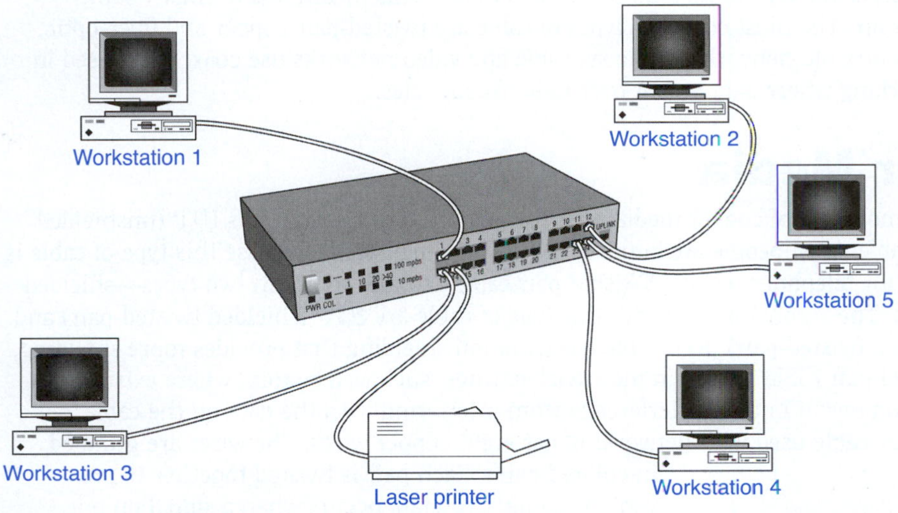

Figure 14.7 Star topology

More cable is used in wiring a star topology than with the old bus topology, but the type of cable used is comparatively cheap. Star topologies are easy to troubleshoot. If one network device goes down, the problem is in the device, cable, or port on the hub/switch. If a group of network devices goes down, the problem is most likely in the device that connects them together (hub or switch). When looking at Figure 14.7, you can tell that if Workstations 1, 2, 3, 4, and 5 cannot communicate with one another, the problem is the switch in the middle. If only Workstation 3 cannot communicate with the other network devices, the problem is in Workstation 3, the cable that connects Workstation 3, or port 13 on the switch. Table 14.2 summarizes various network topologies.

Table 14.2 Network topologies

Topology	Description
Bus	Not common anymore. Takes less cable (cheaper), but if there is a break in the bus, the network is down.
Mesh	With a break in the cable, the network still works (it is very fault tolerant), but it takes a lot of cable. It is expensive and complex (it is difficult to reconfigure). More likely to be used in a WAN than a LAN.
Ring	Each network device connects to two adjacent network devices. Is easy to install but requires expensive parts. FDDI (Fiber Distributed Data Interface) networks use ring topology.
Star	Is the easiest to install and is the most common, and a break in a workstation cable does not affect the rest of the network.

Network Media Overview

Networks require some type of medium to transmit data. This medium is normally some type of cable or air. The most common types of cable are twisted-pair copper and fiber-optic, although some very old networks used coax cable and video networks use coax. Air is used in wireless networking where data is sent over radio frequencies.

Copper Media

The most common type of copper media used with computer networking is UTP (unshielded twisted-pair) cable. Most people are familiar with twisted-pair cable because this type of cable is used in homes for telephone wiring. Twisted-pair cable actually comes in two types—shielded and unshielded. The acronyms used with this type of cable are **STP** (shielded twisted-pair) and **UTP** (unshielded twisted-pair). STP cable has extra foil shielding that provides more shielding. Shielded twisted-pair cable is used in industrial settings, such as a factory, where extra shielding is needed to prevent outside interference from interfering with the data on the cable.

Twisted-pair cable used with networking has eight copper wires. The wires are grouped in colored pairs. Each pair is twisted together to prevent crosstalk. Crosstalk occurs when a signal on one wire interferes with the signal on an adjacent wire. The wires are wrapped in a vinyl insulator. Figure 14.8 shows unshielded twisted-pair cable.

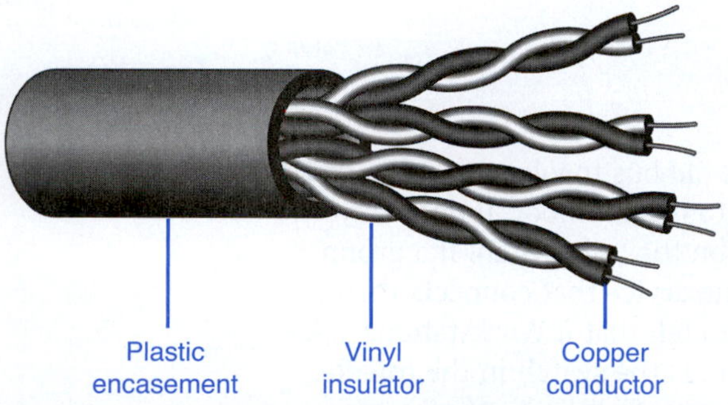

Figure 14.8 UTP cable

UTP cable is measured in gauges. The most common sizes of UTP cable are 22-, 23-, 24-, or 26-gauge unshielded twisted-pair cables. UTP cables come in different specifications called categories. The most common are categories 5e (which is an enhanced version of 5) and 6. People usually shorten the name Category 5 to CAT 5, CAT 5e, CAT 6, and so on. The categories determine, in part, how fast the network can run. Table 14.3 shows some of the categories of UTP cable.

Tech Tip

Label both cable ends

When installing any type of network cable, you should label both ends with a unique identifier that normally includes the building and/or room number.

Table 14.3 UTP cable categories

Category	Description
3	Mainly installed for telephone systems in many office buildings. Commonly called voice grade cable, but has the ability to run up to the older 10Mbps Ethernet or 16Mbps Token Ring topologies.
5	No longer a recognized standard as it was replaced by CAT 5e.
5e	Known as CAT 5 enhanced. Can be used with 10BaseT, 100BaseT, and 1000BaseT (Gigabit) Ethernet networks. Cables are rated to a max of 328 feet (100 meters). However, Ethernet cabling from the end device to the network device normally consists of three runs: (1) the cable from a patch panel to the wall at a maximum of 295 feet (90 meters), (2) the 16-foot (5 meter) maximum patch cable from the wall to a network device, and (3) a 16-foot (5 meter) patch cable from a patch panel to a switch. The total length of cable from device to patch panel is 328 feet (100 meters). Supports frequencies up to 100MHz per pair.
6	Supports Gigabit Ethernet better than CAT 5e but uses larger-gauge (thicker) cable. Supports frequencies up to 250MHz per pair. More stringent specifications to prevent crosstalk (signals from one wire going over into another wire).
6a	Supports 10GbaseT Ethernet and frequencies up to 500MHz.

A special type of UTP or STP cable is plenum cable. a Plenum is a building's air circulation space for heating and air conditioning systems. **Plenum cable** is treated with Teflon or alternative fire retardant materials so it is less of a fire risk. Plenum cable is less smoke producing and less toxic when burning than regular networking cable.

The alternative to plenum cable is **PVC** (polyvinyl chloride) cable that has a plastic cable insulation or jacket. PVC is cheaper than plenum cable, but it can have flame-retardant added to make it flame-retardant if necessary to become compliant with building codes. PVC is usually easier to install than plenum cable.

In order to avoid extra troubleshooting time, most businesses install their network cable according to the ANSI/TIA/EIA-568-A or 568-B standard. This standard specifies how far the cable can extend, how to label it, what type of jack to use, and so forth. Figure 14.9 illustrates the common RJ-45 cable standards used in industry.

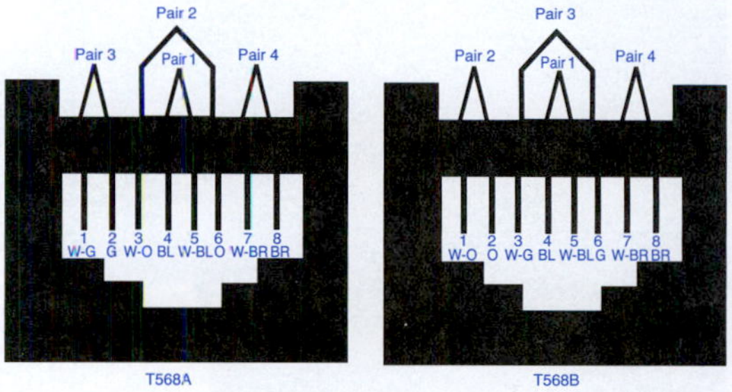

Figure 14.9 UTP wiring standards

To connect a computer to a switch or network wall outlet a **straight-through cable** is used. This is also known as a patch cable. Both ends of the cable would be wired to the T568A standard or both ends of the cable would be wired to the T568B standard (more popular method). This is commonly called a patch cable. When connecting two computers together (or two switches), a **crossover cable** is used. Labs 14.2 and 14.3 at the end of this chapter demonstrate how to create these cables.

Tech Tip

Network two PCs without a switch or hub

If you have two PCs with Ethernet NICs installed, you can connect them with a crossover cable attached to the RJ-45 jack on each NIC.

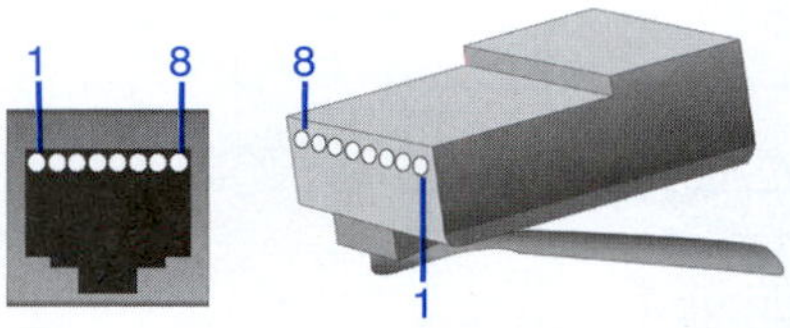

Figure 14.10 RJ-45 pin 1 assignments

Figure 14.10 shows the location of pin 1 on an RJ-45 connector.

A common mistake when making a cable is not pushing the wires to the end of the RJ-45 connector. Before crimping (securing using a tool called a crimper) the wires into the connector, look at the end of the RJ-45 connector. You should see each wire jammed against the end of the RJ-45 connector. With twisted-pair cable, all network devices connect to one central location such as a patch panel, hub, or switch. Look back to Figure 14.7 to see how straight-through cables are used to connect each network device to a switch.

Tech Tip

Push the cable firmly into the jack

When installing network cable, it is important to insert the UTP cable fully into the RJ-45 jack and to insert the colored wires in the standardized order. One of the most common mistakes that new technicians make when putting an RJ-45 connector on UTP cable is putting on the RJ-45 connector upside down.

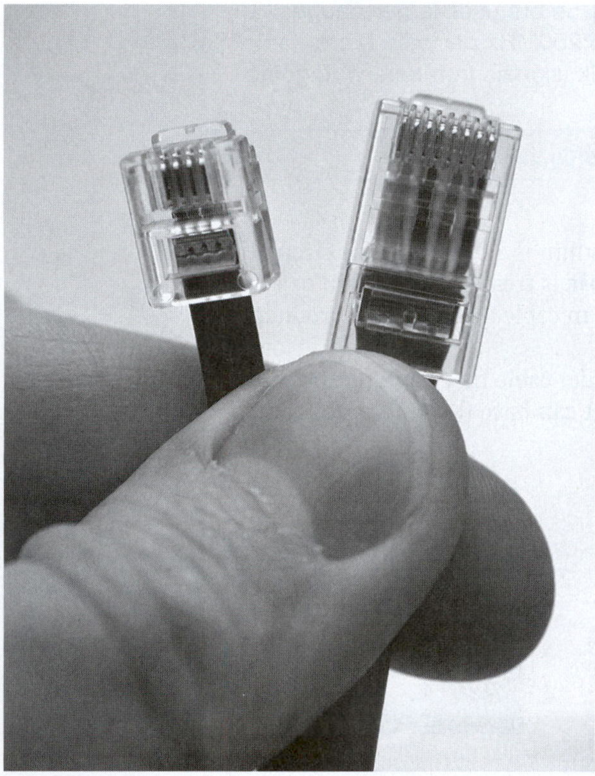

Figure 14.11 RJ-11 and RJ-45 connectors

New technicians commonly mistake an RJ-11 phone jack or connector with an RJ-45 network jack or connector. An RJ-11 connector has four conductors (wires), and an RJ-45 connector has eight conductors, as shown in Figure 14.11, where the RJ-11 connector is on the left.

Another type of copper cable is **coaxial cable** (usually shortened to *coax*). Coax cable is used in star and bus topologies and is most popularly found in video networks such as those that connect TVs in a school. Most people have seen coax cable in their homes. The cable used for cable TV is coax cable, but is a different type than the cable used with network cabling. Coax cable has a center copper conductor surrounded by insulation. Outside the insulation is a shield of copper braid, a metallic foil, or both, that protects the center conductor from EMI. Figures 14.12 and 14.13 show coax cable and the BNC connector as well as the F connector.

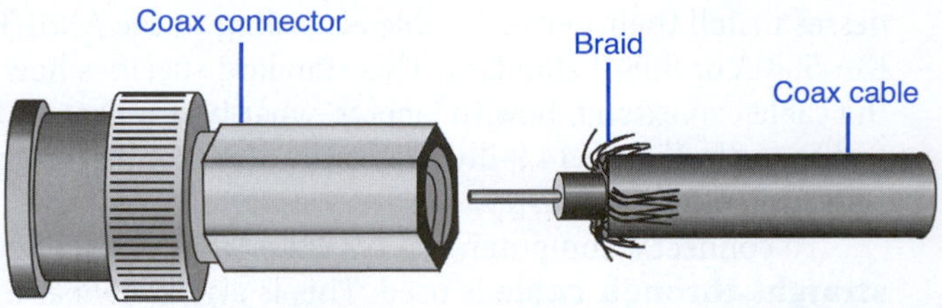

Figure 14.12 Coax cable with a BNC connector

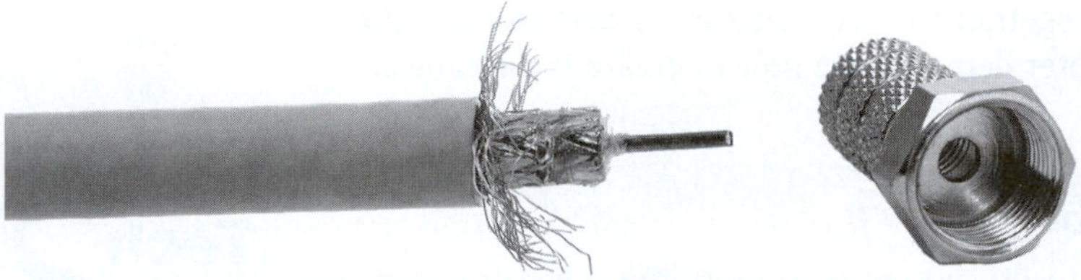

Figure 14.13 Coax cable with an F connector

Table 14.4 lists types of coax cables.

Table 14.4 Coax cable types

Coax cable type	Description
RG*-58 A/U	Used in old 10Base2 (Thinnet) networks and allows distances up to ~607 feet (185 meters).
RG-6	This is the type of cable least likely to be used in a network. It is suitable for distributing signals for cable TV, satellite dish, or rooftop antenna. It has better shielding than RG-59.
RG-59	This type of cable is not used in LANs. It is used in video installations.

*RG stands for radio grade.

Fiber Media

Fiber-optic cable is made of glass or a type of plastic fiber and is used to carry light pulses. Fiber-optic cable can be used to connect a workstation to another device, but in industry, the most common use of fiber-optic cable is to connect networks together forming the network backbone. Copper cable is used to connect workstations together. Then fiber cable is used to interconnect the networks, especially when the network is located on multiple floors or multiple buildings.

There are many different types of fiber connectors and some of them are proprietary. Four of the most common types of connectors used with fiber-optic cable are MT-RJ (common in home installations), ST, SC, and LC. Figure 14.14 shows two of these connectors.

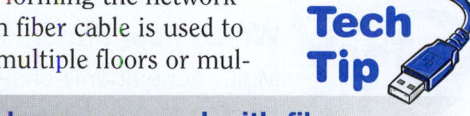

Tech Tip

Two cables are normal with fiber

Each fiber-optic cable can carry signals in one direction, so an installation normally has two strands of fiber-optic cable in separate jackets. Fiber is used in the ring and star topologies.

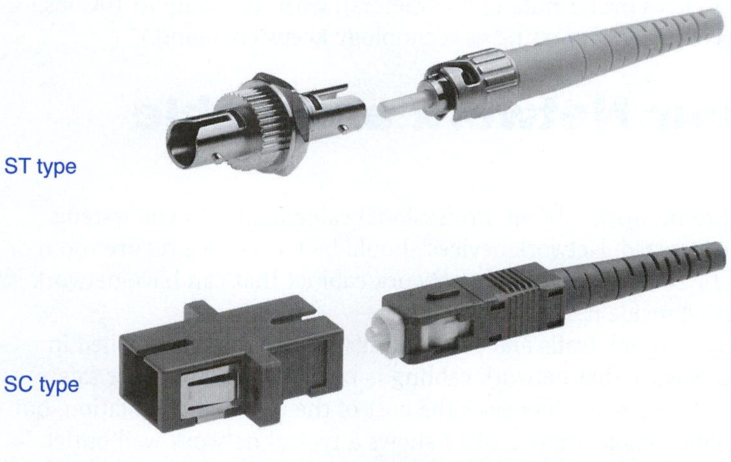

Figure 14.14 Fiber-optic connector types

Fiber-optic cable has many advantages, including security, long-distance transmission, and bandwidth. Many government agencies use fiber-optic cable because of the high security it offers. Unlike signals from other cable media, light signals that travel down fiber are impossible to detect remotely. Also, because light is used instead of electrical signals, fiber-optic cable is not susceptible to interference from EMI- or RFI-producing devices. Fiber-optic cable is the most expensive cable type, but it also handles the most data with the least amount of data loss. Figure 14.15 shows fiber-optic cable.

The two major classifications of fiber are single-mode and multi-mode. **Single-mode** fiber-optic cable has only one light beam sent down the cable. **Multi-mode** fiber-optic cable allows multiple light signals to be sent along the same cable.

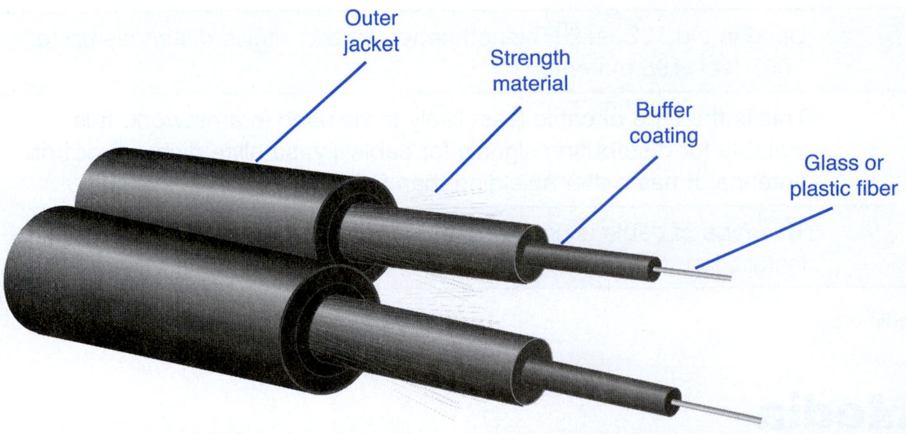

Figure 14.15 Fiber-optic cable

Which fiber should I use?

Multi-mode fiber is cheaper and more commonly used than single-mode fiber and is good for shorter-distance applications; however, single-mode fiber can transmit a signal farther than multi-mode and supports the highest bandwidth.

Single-mode cable is classified by the size of the fiber core and the cladding. Common sizes include 8/125 to 10/125 microns. The first number represents the size of the core; the second number is the size of the cladding. Single-mode cable allows for distances over 50 miles (80,000 meters) at speeds over 100Gbps. Multi-mode cable (50/125 and 62.5/125 microns), on the other hand, can support distances over 1 mile (2,000 meters), with speeds up to 10Gbps. (Note that fiber's maximum speeds keep increasing as technology keeps changing.)

Protecting Your Network and Cable Investment

Quite a bit of money is applied to network cabling. Professional cable management systems can help keep network cables organized. Network devices should be locked in a secure room or cabinet when possible. Figure 14.16 shows a lockable network cabinet that can have network devices as well as cabling installed inside it.

Network cable can be pulled through walls and over ceilings, but should be installed in conduit or raceways if possible. Ensure that network cabling is not a tripping or other safety hazard in any location. Of course, this really increases the cost of the network installation, but it protects the network cable—and people. Figure 14.17 shows a typical network wall outlet.

Figure 14.16 Network lockable cabinet

Figure 14.17 Network wall outlet

Ladder racks are also a popular network cable accessory, installed to hold multiple cables going across a room or from one side of the room to a network rack that is located away from the wall. Figure 14.18 shows a network cable ladder rack that has tubes through which cable is pulled.

Figure 14.18 Network cable ladder rack

Figure 14.19 and Table 14.5 show and describe tools used in making cable and troubleshooting cable issues.

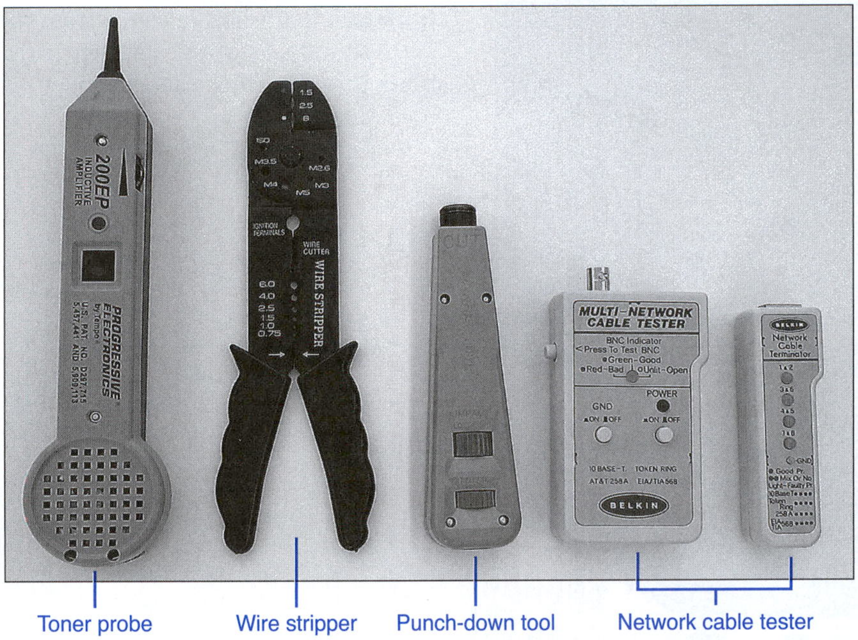

Figure 14.19 Network tools

Table 14.5 Network cabling tools

Tool	Description
Toner probe	A tone generator (not shown in Figure 14.19) is connected to a cable or inserted into a network jack. The tone generator injects a tone down the cable. The toner probe is touched to the other end of a cable to identify it. The tone generator/toner probe combination is used to identify cables when they are not labeled or are labeled incorrectly.

Tool	Description
Wire stripper	Used in creating straight-through UTP patch cables or crossover cables.
Punch down tool	Used to connect network cables to a patch panel or phone cable to a punch down block.
Network cable tester	Used to check coaxial and UTP cable (depending on the model).
Crimper (see Figures 14.59, 60, and 61)	Used to permanently attach an RJ-45 or RJ-11 connector to cable.

Ethernet Issues and Concepts

Ethernet is the most common type of LAN, and more time must be spent on understanding it because technicians constantly add and remove devices from an Ethernet network. Some issues related to Ethernet include full-duplex and half-duplex transmissions, network slowdowns, and increasing bandwidth.

Ethernet networks were originally designed for **half-duplex** (both directions, but only one direction at a time) transmission on a 10Mbps bus topology. The more workstations on the same network, the more collisions occur and the more the network slows down. In addition, with half-duplex Ethernet, less than 50 percent of the 10Mbps available bandwidth could be used because of collisions and the time it takes for a network frame to transmit across the wire.

Tech Tip

What does CSMA/CD mean to a network?

CSMA/CD is the access method used with Ethernet networks—the rules for how data gets on the network. The CS stands for "Carrier Sense," which means that the PC checks the network cable for other traffic. MA, for "Multiple Access," means that multiple computers can access the network cable simultaneously. CD, for "Collision Detection," provides rules for what happens when computers access the network at the same time.

Today's Ethernet networks support speeds of 10Mbps, 100Mbps, 1,000Mbps (1Gbps), and 10,000Mbps (10Gbps). Most Ethernet NICs are 10/100/1000, which means they can run at either 10, 100, or 1000Mbps using **full-duplex** (transmit/receive simultaneously). Table 14.6 lists the different types of Ethernet networks.

Table 14.6 Ethernet standards

Ethernet type	Description
10BaseT	10Mbps over CAT 3 or 5 UTP cable
100BaseT	100Mbps over CAT 5 or higher UTP cable
1000BaseT	Also known as Gigabit Ethernet. 1000Mbps or 1Gbps over CAT 5 or higher UTP cable
1000BaseSX	1Gbps using multi-mode fiber
1000BaseLX	1Gbps using single-mode fiber
10GBaseSR	10Gbps over multi-mode fiber
10GBaseLX4	10Gbps over multi-mode and single-mode fiber
10GBaseLR	10Gbps up to 6.2 miles (10 km) using single-mode fiber

Ethernet type	Description
10GBaseER	10Gbps up to 24.85 miles (40 km) using single-mode fiber
10GBaseT	10Gbps over UTP (CAT 5e or higher) or STP cable

In the term 100BaseT, the 100 means that the network runs at 100Mbps. The T at the end of 100BaseT means that the computer uses twisted-pair cable. The 1000 in 1000BaseT means that 1000Mbps is supported. Base means that the network uses baseband technology. Baseband describes data that is sent over a single channel on a single wire. In contrast, broadband is used in cable TV systems and it allows multiple channels using different frequencies to be covered over a single wire.

Tech Tip

Why full-duplex is better than half-duplex

With full-duplex, collisions are not a problem because full-duplex takes advantage of the two cable pairs (one for receiving and one for transmitting). Full-duplex Ethernet creates a direct connection between the transmitting station at one end and the receiving circuits at the other end and allows 100 percent of the available bandwidth to be used in each direction.

Full-duplex more than doubles the amount of throughput on a network because of the lack of collisions and transmitting both directions simultaneously. Full-duplex is used when a switch is used to connect network devices together. Full-duplex connectivity uses four wires (two pairs). Two of the wires are used for sending data and the other two wires are used for receiving data. This creates a collision-free environment. Using a switch instead of a hub as a central connectivity device speeds up Ethernet transactions because a switch has more intelligence than a hub and creates a collision-free, full-duplex environment. Switches are very common devices in today's business network environment.

Tech Tip

Why a switch is better than a hub

When a workstation sends data to a hub, the hub broadcasts the data out all ports except for the port that originally transmits the data. A switch, on the other hand, keeps a table of addresses. When a switch receives data, the switch looks up the destination MAC address (an address burned into a NIC) in the switch table and forwards the data out the port for which it is destined.

Network Standards

IEEE (Institute for Electrical and Electronics Engineers) committees create network standards called the 802 standards. Each standard is given an 802.x number and represents an area of networking. Standardization is good for the network industry because different manufacturers' network components work with other manufacturers' devices. Table 14.7 lists the various 802 standards.

Table 14.7 IEEE 802 standards

802 standard	Description
802.1	Bridging and Management
802.2	Logical Link Control
802.3	CSMA/CD Access Method
802.4	Token-Passing Bus Access Method
802.5	Token Ring Access Method

802 standard	Description
802.6	DQDB (Distributed Queue Dual Bus) Access Method
802.7	Broadband LAN
802.8	Fiber-Optic
802.9	Isochronous LANs
802.10	Security
802.11	Wireless
802.12	Demand Priority Access
802.14	Cable modems
802.15	WPANs (wireless personal area networks), including Bluetooth
802.16	Broadband Wireless Access (WiMAX)
802.17	Resilient Packet Ring
802.20	Mobile Broadband Wireless Access
802.22	Super-Wi-Fi or WRAN (wireless regional area network)

For more information about the 802 standards, access the IEEE website, at http://standards.ieee.org/about/get/802/802.html.

The OSI Model

The International Organization for Standardization (ISO) has developed a model for network communications known as the OSI (Open Systems Interconnect) model. The **OSI model** is a standard for information transfer across the network. The model sets several guidelines, including (1) how the different transmission media are arranged and interconnected, (2) how network devices that use different languages communicate with one another, (3) how a network device goes about contacting another network device, (4) how and when data gets transmitted across the network, (5) how data is sent to the correct device, and (6) how it is known if the network data was received properly. All these tasks must be handled by a set of rules, and the OSI model provides a structure into which these rules fit.

Can you imagine a generic model for building a car? This model would state that you need some means of steering, a type of fuel to power the car, a place for the driver to sit, safety standards, and so forth. The model would not say what type of steering wheel to put in the car or what type of fuel the car must use, but is just a blueprint for making the car. The OSI model is a similar model in networking.

The OSI model divides networking into different layers so that it is easier to understand (and teach). Dividing the network into distinct layers also helps manufacturers. If a particular manufacturer wants to make a network device that works on Layer 3, the manufacturer only has to be concerned with Layer 3. This division helps networking technologies emerge much faster. Having a layered model also helps to teach network concepts. Each layer can be taught as a separate network function.

The layers of the OSI model (starting from the top and working down) are application, presentation, session, transport, network, data link, and physical. Figure 14.20 shows this concept.

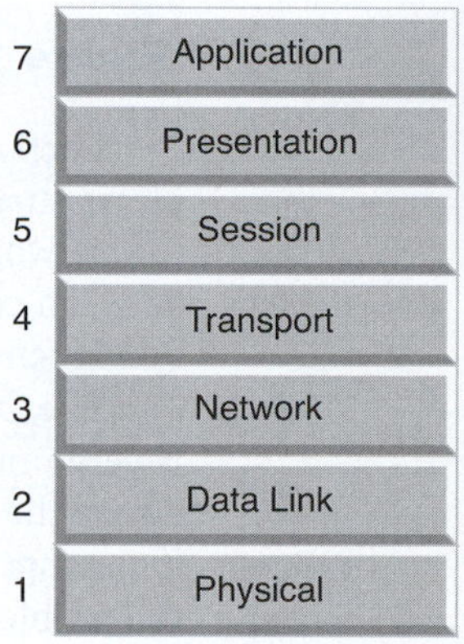

Figure 14.20 OSI model layers

Each layer of the OSI model uses the layer below it (except for the physical layer, which is on the bottom). Each layer provides some function to the layer above it. For example, the data link layer cannot be accessed without first going through the physical layer. If communication needs to be performed at Layer 3 (the network layer), then the physical and data link layers must be used first.

Tech Tip

OSI mnemonic

A mnemonic to help remember the OSI layers is: A Person Seldom Takes Naps During Parties. For example, *A* in the phrase is to remind you of the application layer. P in Person is to remind you of the presentation layer, and so on.

Each layer of the OSI model from the top down (except for the physical layer) adds information to the data being sent across the network. Sometimes this information is called a *header*. Figure 14.21 shows how a header is added as the packet travels down the OSI model. When the receiving computer receives the data, each layer removes the header information. Information at the physical layer is normally called *bits*. When referring to information at the data link layer, use the term *frame*. When referring to information at the network layer, use the term *packet*.

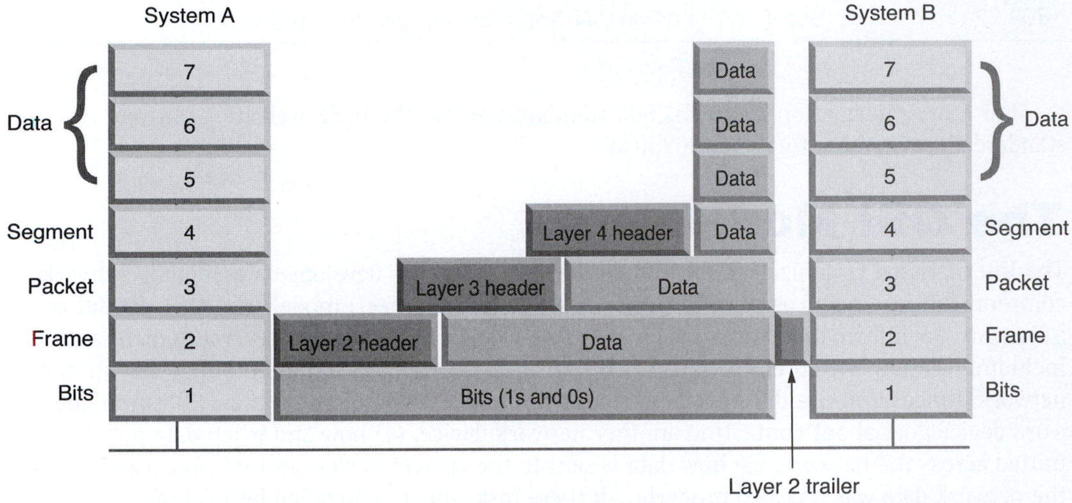

Figure 14.21 OSI peer communication

Each of the seven OSI model layers performs a unique function and interacts with the layers surrounding it. The bottom three layers handle the physical delivery of data across the network. The top four layers handle the ins and outs of providing accurate data delivery between computers and their individual processes, especially in a multitasking operating system environment.

The OSI model is very confusing when you are first learning about networking, but it is very important. Understanding the model helps when troubleshooting a network. Knowing where the problem is occurring narrows the field of what the solution may be. For example, if a computer has problems communicating with a computer on the same network, then the problem is most likely a Layer 1 or a Layer 2 problem because Layer 3 takes care of communication between two networks. Therefore, a technician would check the cabling and NIC settings because they are Layer 1and 2 things that could be the issue. Table 14.8 summarizes the OSI model.

Table 14.8 OSI model

OSI model layer	Description
Application	Provides network services (file, print, and messaging services) to any software application running on the network.
Presentation	Translates data from one character set to another.
Session	Manages the communication and synchronization between network devices.
Transport	Provides the mechanisms for how data is sent, such as reliability and error correction.
Network	Provides path selection between two networks. **Routers** reside at the network layer and send data toward the destination network. Encapsulated data at this layer is called a packet.
Data link	Encapsulates bits into frames. Can provide error control. MAC address is at this layer. Switches reside at data link layer.
Physical	Defines how bits are transferred and received. Defines the network media, connectors, and voltage levels. Data at this level is called bits.

The TCP/IP Model

A **network protocol** is a data communication language. A protocol suite is a group of protocols that are designed to work together. **TCP/IP** (Transmission Control Protocol/Internet Protocol) is the protocol suite used in networks today. It is the most common network protocol and is required when accessing the Internet. Most companies (and homes) use TCP/IP as their standard protocol. The TCP/IP protocol suite consists of many protocols, including TCP (Transmission Control Protocol), IP (Internet Protocol), DHCP (Dynamic Host Configuration Protocol), FTP (File Transfer Protocol), and HTTP (Hypertext Transfer Protocol), to name a few. The TCP/IP model describes how information flows through the computer when TCP/IP-based protocols are being used. The TCP/IP model has only four layers, in contrast to the seven layers in the theoretical OSI model. Because there are fewer layers and because the TCP/IP model is made up of protocols that are in production, it makes it easier to study and understand networking from a TCP/IP model prospective. Figure 14.22 shows the TCP/IP model, and Table 14.9 describes the layers.

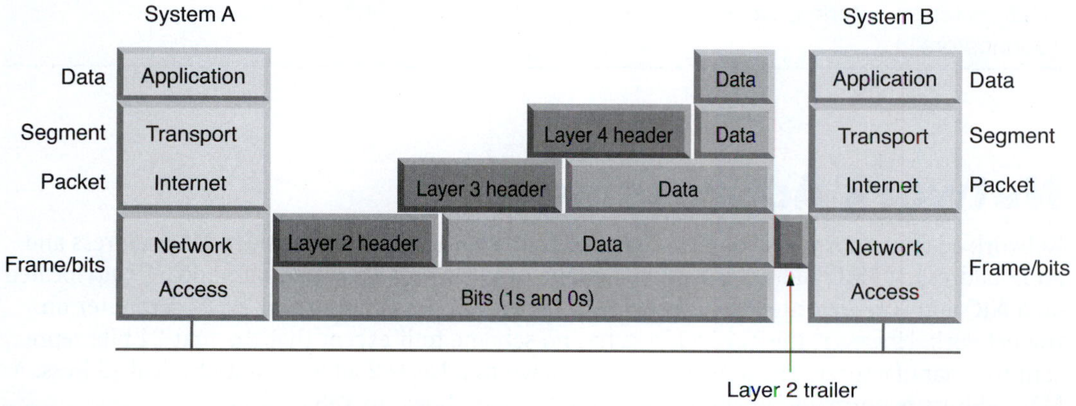

Figure 14.22 TCP/IP message formatting

Table 14.9 TCP/IP model layers

TCP/IP model layer	Description
Application	TCP/IP-based application-layer protocols format data specific for the purpose. Is equivalent to the application, presentation, and session layers of the OSI model. Protocols include HTTP, Telnet, DNS, HTTPS, FTP, TFTP, TLS, SSL, POP, SNMP, IMAP, NNTP, and SMTP.
Transport	Transport-layer protocols add port numbers in the header so the computer can identify which application is sending the data. When data returns, this port number allows the computer to determine into which window on the screen to place the data. Protocols include TCP and UDP.
Internet	Sometimes called the internetwork layer. IP is the most common Internet layer protocol. IP adds a source and destination **IP address** to uniquely identify the source and destination network devices. An IP address is a unique 32- or 128-bit number assigned to a NIC.
Network access	Called link layer in the original RFC (Request for Comment). Defines how to format the data for the type of network being used. For example, if Ethernet is being used, an Ethernet header, including unique source and destination MAC addresses, will be added here. A **MAC address** is a unique 48-bit hexadecimal number burned into a chip on the NIC. The network access layer would define the type of connector used and put the data onto the network, whether it be voltage levels for 1s and 0s on the copper cable or pulses of light for fiber.

Table 14.10 shows what devices operate at the OSI and TCP/IP model layers.

Table 14.10 Devices and the OSI and TCP/IP models

Network device	OSI layer	TCP/IP layer
Router, wireless router	Network	Internet (internetwork)
Switch, wireless access point, wireless bridge	Data link	Network access
Hub, wireless antenna, cable, connectors	Physical	Network access

Network Addressing

Network adapters normally have two types of addresses assigned to them—a MAC address and an IP address. A MAC address is a 48-bit unique number that is burned into a ROM chip located on a NIC and is represented in hexadecimal. A MAC address is unique for every computer on the network. However, the MAC address has no scheme to it except that the first 24 bits represent the manufacturer. The MAC address is known as a Layer 2 address or a physical address. A MAC address is normally shown in one of the formats shown in Table 14.11.

Table 14.11 MAC address formats

Address format	Description
00-11-11-71-41-10	Groups of two hexadecimal digits each are separated by hyphens.
01:11:11:71:41:10	Groups of two hexadecimal digits are separated by colons.
0111.1171.4110	Groups of four hexadecimal digits are separated by periods.

The IP address is a much more organized way of addressing a computer and it is sometimes known as a Layer 3 address, in reference to the OSI network layer. There are two types of IP addresses: IPv4 (IP version 4) and IPv6 (IP version 6). **IPv4** is the most common IP addressing used on LANs. The IPv4 address is a 32-bit number that is entered into a NIC's configuration parameters. This address is used when multiple networks are connected and when accessing the Internet. The IPv4 address is shown using dotted decimal notation, such as 192.168.10.4.

Tech Tip

What is in an IPv4 address?

An IPv4 address is separated into four sections called *octets*. Each number is separated by periods and represents 8 bits. The numbers that can be represented by 8 bits are 0 to 255.

IPv6 addresses are 128 bits in length and shown in hexadecimal format. IPv6 addresses are used by corporate devices and by some Internet service providers, and more conversions of IPv4 to IPv6 coming soon. An example of an IPv6 address is fe80::13e:4586:5807:95f7. Each set of four digits represents 16 bits. Anywhere there are just three digits, such as 13e, there is a zero in front that has been left off (013e). Anywhere there are double colons (::), a string of zeros has been omitted. Only one set of double colons is allowed in an IPv6 address. Many network cards are assigned IPv6 addresses, even if IPv6 is not being used.

One IPv6 address assigned to a NIC is a link-local address. An IPv6 link-local address is used to communicate on a particular network. This address cannot be used to communicate with devices on a different network. A link-local address can be manually assigned or more commonly, automatically assigned. Figure 14.23 shows a home computer that has an IPv6 link-local address that has been automatically assigned.

```
Ethernet adapter Local Area Connection:

   Connection-specific DNS Suffix  . : gateway.2wire.net
   Link-local IPv6 Address . . . . . : fe80::13e:4586:5807:95f7%10
   IPv4 Address. . . . . . . . . . . : 192.168.1.64
   Subnet Mask . . . . . . . . . . . : 255.255.255.0
   Default Gateway . . . . . . . . . : 192.168.1.254
```

Figure 14.23 IPv6 link-local address

IPv4 addresses are grouped into five classes: Class A, B, C, D, and E. Class A, B, and C addresses are used by network devices. Class D addresses are used for multicasting (sending traffic to a group of devices such as in a distributed video or a web conference session), and Class E addresses are used for experimentation. It is easy to tell which type of IP address is being used by a device: All you have to look at is the first number shown in the dotted-decimal notation. Table 14.12 shows the classes of addresses.

Table 14.12 Classes of IPv4 addresses

Class	First octet (number) of the IP address
Class A	0 to 127
Class B	128 to 191
Class C	192 to 223

If a computer has the IP address 12.150.172.39, the IP address is a Class A address because the first number is 12. If a computer has the IP address 176.10.100.2, it is a Class B IP address because the first number is 176. A computer with an IP address of 200.1.1.1 uses a Class C address. Addresses are also classified as public addresses and private addresses. A private address is used inside a home or business. This address is not allowed to be transmitted across the Internet. The service provider or company translates the address to a public address that is seen on Internet. Table 14.13 shows the private IP address ranges for each of the IPv4 classes.

Table 14.13 IPv4 private IP addresses

Class	First octet (number) of an IP address
Class A	10.x.x.x (where the x represents any number from 0 to 255)
Class B	172.16.x.x through 172.16.31.x.x
Class C	192.x.x.x

IP Addressing

An IP address is broken into two major parts—the network number and the host number. The **network number** is the portion of an IP address that represents which network the computer is on. All computers on the same network have the same network number. The **host** portion of an IP address represents the specific computer on the network. All computers on the same network have unique host numbers or they will not be able to communicate.

The number of bits that are used to represent the network number and the host number depends on which class of IP address is being used. With Class A IP addresses, the first 8 bits (the first number) represent the network portion, and the remaining 24 bits (the last three numbers) represent the host number. With Class B IP addresses, the first 16 bits (the first two numbers) represent the network portion, and the remaining 16 bits (the last two numbers) represent the host number. With Class C IP addresses, the first 24 bits (the first three numbers) represent the network portion, and the remaining 8 bits (the last number) represent the host number. Figure 14.24 illustrates this point.

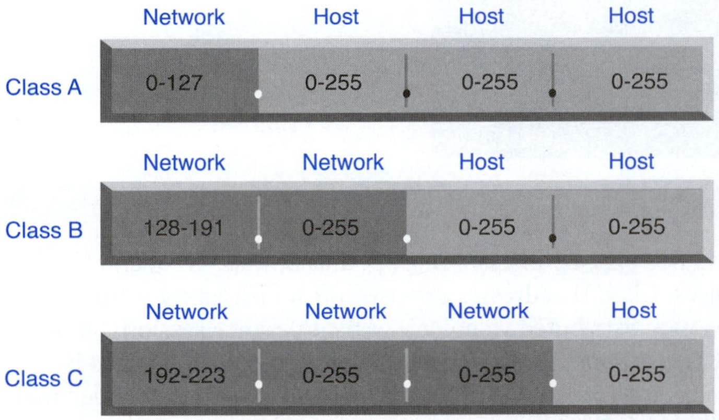

Figure 14.24 IP addressing (network and host portions)

In order to see how IP addressing works, it is best to use an example. Say that a business has two networks connected with a router. On each network, there are computers and printers. Each of the two networks must have a unique network number. For this example, one network has the network number of 193.14.150.0, and the other network has the network number of 193.14.151.0. Notice how these numbers represent a Class C IP address because the first number is 193.

With a Class C IP address, the first three numbers represent the network number. The first network uses the numbers 193.14.150 to represent the network part of the IP address. The second network uses the numbers 193.14.151 in the network part of the address. Remember that each network has to have a different network part of the IP address than any other network in the organization. The last part of the IP address (the host portion) will be used to assign to each network device. On the first network, each device will have a number that starts with 193.14.150 because that is the network part of the number and it stays the same for all devices on that network. Each device will then have a different number in the last portion of the IP address—for example, 193.14.150.3, 193.14.150.4, and 193.14.150.5.

On the second network, each device will have a number that starts with 193.14.151 because that is the network part of the IP address. The last number in the IP address changes for each network device—for example, 193.14.151.3, 193.14.151.4, 193.14.151.5, and so on. No device can have a host number of 0 because that number represents the network and no device can have a host number of 255 because that represents something called the broadcast address. A **broadcast address** is the IP address used to communicate with all devices on a particular network.

In this example, no network device can be assigned the IP addresses 193.14.150.0 or 193.14.151.0 because these numbers represent the two networks. Furthermore, no network device can be assigned the IP addresses 193.14.150.255 or 193.14.151.255 because these numbers represent the broadcast address used with each network. An example of a Class B broadcast is 150.10.255.255. An example of a Class A broadcast is 11.255.255.255. Figure 14.25 shows this configuration.

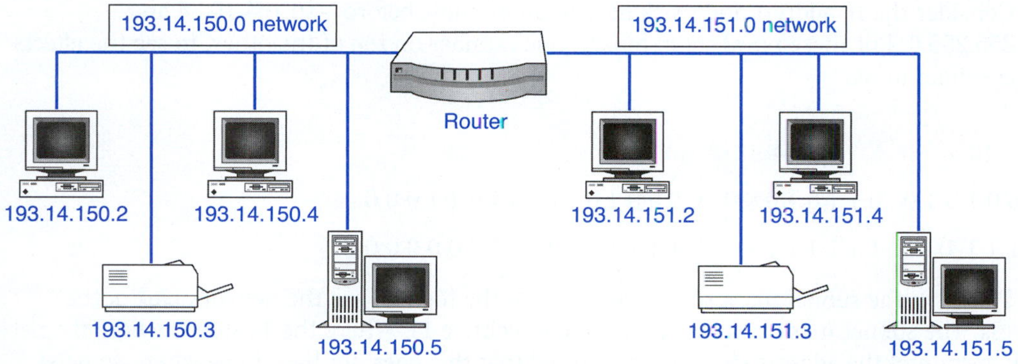

Figure 14.25 IP addressing (two-network example)

Notice in Figure 14.25 that each device to the left of the router has an IP address that starts with 193.14.150 (the network number), and each device has a unique last number. The same is true for the devices to the right of the router, except that they are on the 193.14.151.0 network.

In addition to assigning a computer an IP address, you must also assign a subnet mask. The **subnet mask** (sometimes shortened to *mask*) is a number that a computer uses to determine which part of the IP address represents the network and which portion represents the host. The default subnet mask for a Class A IP address is 255.0.0.0; the default subnet mask for a Class B IP address is 255.255.0.0; the default subnet mask for a Class C IP address is 255.255.255.0. Table 14.14 recaps this important information.

Table 14.14 IP address information

Class	First number	Network/host number	Subnet mask
A	0–127	N.H.H.H*	255.0.0.0
B	128–191	N.N.H.H*	255.255.0.0
C	192–223	N.N.N.H*	255.255.255.0

*N = network number; H = host number

Subnetting Basics

In business, a subnet mask used does not usually correspond to the class of IP address being used. For example, at a college, the IP address 10.104.10.88 and subnet mask 255.255.255.0 are assigned to a computer. The 10 in the first octet shows that this is a class A IP address with a default mask of 255.0.0.0. The 255 in the subnet mask is made up of eight 1s in binary in the first octet (11111111) followed by all 0s in the remaining octets (00000000.00000000.00000000).

The purpose of the subnet mask is to tell you (and the network devices) what portion of the IP address is the network part. The rest of the address is the host portion of the address. The network part of any IP address is the same 1s and 0s for all computers on the network. The rest of the 1s and 0s can change and be unique addresses for the network devices on the same network.

The following important rules relate to subnetting:

- The network number *cannot* be assigned to any device on the network.
- The network number contains all 0s in the host portion of the address. Note that this does not mean that the number will be 0 in decimal. This is explained next.
- The broadcast address (the number used to send a message to all devices on the network) *cannot* be assigned to any device on the network.
- The broadcast address contains all 1s in the host portion of the address. Note that this does not mean that the number will be 255 in decimal.

Consider the IP address and mask used as an example before—10.104.10.88 and 255.255.255.0. Put these numbers in binary, one number on top of the other, to see the effects of the subnet mask:

```
     10              104              10               88
0 0 0 0 1 0 1 0 . 0 1 1 0 1 0 0 0 . 0 0 0 0 1 0 1 0 . 0 1 0 1 1 0 0 0
1 1 1 1 1 1 1 1 . 1 1 1 1 1 1 1 1 . 1 1 1 1 1 1 1 1 . 0 0 0 0 0 0 0 0
```

The 1s in the subnet mask show which bits in the top row are the network part of the address. The subnet mask is always a row of consecutive 1s. Where the 1s stop is where the network portion of the address stops. Keep in mind that this does not have to be where an octet stops, as in this example. A good technique is to draw a line where the 1s in the subnet mask stop, as shown in the example that follows:

```
     10              104              10          |     88
0 0 0 0 1 0 1 0 . 0 1 1 0 1 0 0 0 . 0 0 0 0 1 0 1 0 | 0 1 0 1 1 0 0 0
1 1 1 1 1 1 1 1 . 1 1 1 1 1 1 1 1 . 1 1 1 1 1 1 1 1 | 0 0 0 0 0 0 0 0
                                                  |
```

Tech Tip

Subnet mask in prefix notation

Subnet masks in network documentation are commonly shown in prefix notation, using a slash with the number of consecutive 1s found in the subnet mask. For example, 10.104.10.88 255.255.255.0 is shown as 10.104.10.88/24, and 192.168.10.213/27 is the same as a 255.255.255.224 subnet mask.

At this point, there is no other purpose for the subnet mask. You can get rid of it, as shown in the example that follows:

```
10          104         10       |  88
00001010.01101000.00001010|01011000
```

All 1s and 0s to the left of the drawn line are the network portion of the IP address. All devices on the same network will have this same combination of 1s and 0s up to the line. All 1s and 0s to the right of the drawn line are in the host portion of the IP address:

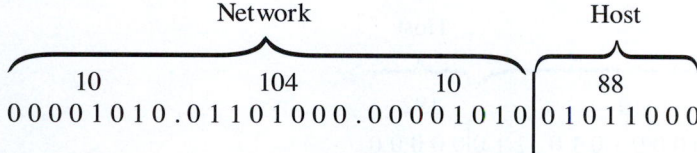

```
              Network                  Host
10          104         10       |  88
00001010.01101000.00001010|01011000
```

The network number, the IP address used to represent an entire single network, is found by setting all host bits to 0. The resulting number is the network number:

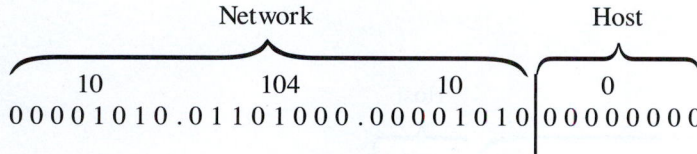

```
              Network                  Host
10          104         10       |  0
00001010.01101000.00001010|00000000
```

The network number for the network device that has the IP address 10.104.10.88 is 10.104.10.0. To find the broadcast address, the IP address used to send a message to all devices on the 10.104.10.0 network, set all the host bits to 1:

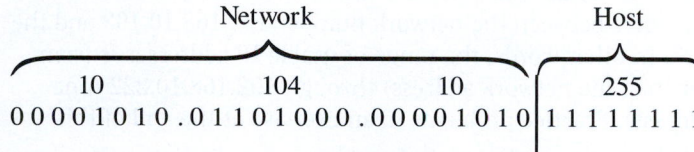

```
              Network                  Host
10          104         10       |  255
00001010.01101000.00001010|11111111
```

The broadcast IP address is 10.104.10.255 for the 10.104.10.0 network. This means that hosts can be assigned any addresses between the network number 10.104.10.0 and the broadcast address 10.104.10.255. Another way of stating this is that IP addresses 10.104.10.1 through 10.104.10.254 are usable IP addresses on the 10.104.10.0 network.

Consider the IP address 192.168.10.213 and the subnet mask 255.255.255.224 assigned to a computer in a college. What would be the network number and broadcast address for this computer? To find the answer, write 192.168.10.213 in binary octets. Write the subnet mask in binary under the IP address:

```
192         168         10          213
11000000.10101000.00001010.11010101
11111111.11111111.11111111.11100000
```

Now draw a line where the 1s in the subnet mask stop:

```
192         168         10          213
11000000.10101000.00001010.110|10101
11111111.11111111.11111111.111|00000
```

Remove the subnet mask because it is not needed anymore:

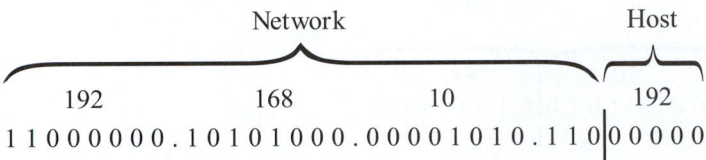

```
192        168        10         213
11000000.10101000.00001010.110|10101
```

Set all host bits to 0 to find the network number:

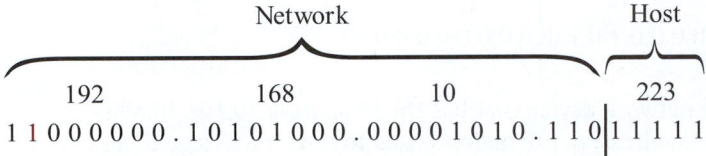

```
          Network                 Host
192        168        10         192
11000000.10101000.00001010.110|00000
```

The network number for the network device that has IP address 192.168.10.213 is 192.168.10.192. To find the broadcast address, set all host bits to 1. Set all host bits to 1 to find the broadcast address:

```
          Network                 Host
192        168        10         223
11000000.10101000.00001010.110|11111
```

The broadcast address for the network device that has the IP address 192.168.10.213 is 192.168.10.223. Notice how all eight bits are used to calculate the number 223 in the last octet. Valid IP addresses are any numbers between the network number 192.168.10.192 and the broadcast IP address 192.168.10.223. In other words, the range of usable IP addresses is from 192.168.10.193 (one number larger than the network address) through 192.168.10.222 (one number less than the broadcast address). Practice problems in an exercise at the end of this chapter help you explore this concept.

Wireless Networks Overview

Wireless networks are networks that transmit data over air using either infrared (1 to 400THz range) or radio frequencies (2.4GHz or 5GHz range). Most wireless networks in homes and businesses use radio frequencies. Wireless networks operate at Layers 1 and 2 of the OSI model.

Wireless networks are very popular in home and business computer environments and are great in places that are not conducive to having cabling, such as outdoor centers, convention centers, bookstores, coffee shops, and hotels, as well as between buildings and in between non-wired rooms in homes or businesses. Wireless networks can be installed indoors or outdoors.

Laptops and portable devices are frequently used to connect to wireless networks and have wireless capabilities integrated into them. Laptops also normally have wired network connections. A technician must be familiar with installation, configuration, and troubleshooting of both wired and wireless technologies.

Tech Tip

What if I want wireless connectivity for my desktop computer?

Desktop workstations usually have integrated RJ-45 Ethernet connections, but if wireless networking is desired, then a wireless NIC usually has to be added.

Bluetooth

Bluetooth is a wireless technology for PANs. Bluetooth devices include PDAs (personal digital assistants), audio/visual products, automotive accessories, keyboards, mice, phones, printer adapters, cameras, wireless cell phone headsets, sunglasses with radios and wireless speakers, and other small wireless devices. Bluetooth works in the 2.4GHz range, similarly to business wireless networks, has three classes of devices (1, 2, and 3) that have a range of approximately 20 feet (6 meters), 72 feet (22 meters), and 328 feet (100 meters), respectively, and a maximum transfer rate of 24Mbps. Bluetooth supports both data and voice transmissions. Up to eight Bluetooth devices can be connected in a piconet (a small network). Bluetooth has always had security features integrated into it, including 128-bit encryption (scrambling of data, as discussed later in this chapter) that uses a modified form of SAFER+ (Secure and Fast Encryption Routine). Bluetooth is a very viable network solution for short-range wireless solutions. Figure 14.26 shows a Bluetooth cell phone headset.

Figure 14.26 **Bluetooth cell phone headset**

Windows Vista and 7 support Bluetooth better than Windows XP. With Windows XP, when you connect a Bluetooth adapter to the computer, it should work if Windows XP Service Pack 2 or higher has been installed. If the Bluetooth adapter is one that Windows XP does not recognize, Windows XP may provide generic software support.

A Bluetooth PAN provides computer-to-computer connectivity between Bluetooth devices. Each computer must support a PAN in order to join the network. Once a Bluetooth device is added, you can use the Bluetooth systray option to select *Join a Personal Area Network*. A dialog box will appear, showing devices to which the computer can connect. Select a device and click *Connect*. Chapter 1 provides more information on how to configure and troubleshoot Bluetooth connectivity.

Tech Tip

Missing Bluetooth Control Panel

If the Bluetooth Devices control panel does not display or if the Bluetooth icon is not in the notification area (systray) on the task bar, type `bthprops.cpl` at a command prompt.

Wireless Networks

The most common components of a wireless network are wireless NICs, an access point, a wireless bridge, and a wireless router. Table 14.15 describes the purposes of these parts.

Table 14.15 Common wireless devices

Wireless device	Description
AP (access point)	The central connecting point for a wireless network. Coordinates wireless access for wireless devices. Commonly connects to a wired network.
Wireless NIC	Integrated into a wireless devices such as a laptop, netbook, or tablet.
Wireless router	An AP/router device that normally has both wireless devices and a few wired Ethernet ports
Wireless bridge	A physical device or software that connects two or more networks. Could connect a wireless network to a wired network. An example of a wireless bridge is a building where all devices connect wirelessly to the bridge. The bridge connects to the wired network, which eventually connects to the Internet. Many access points or wireless routers can be placed in bridged mode.

Major types of wireless NICs include integrated ports, PC Card/ExpressCard, USB, PCI, and PCIe. Figure 14.27 shows a wireless NIC that could be attached to a laptop or desktop USB port.

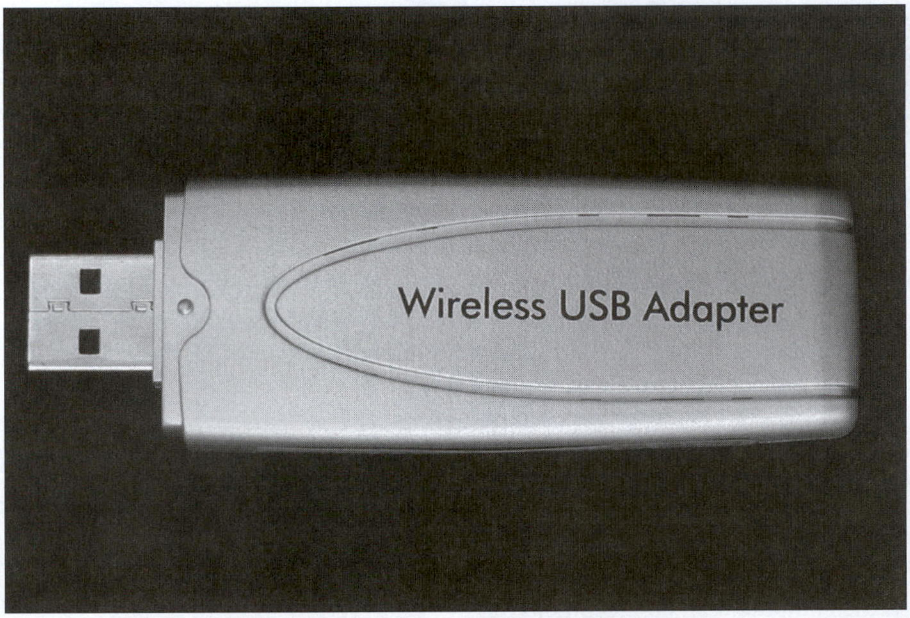

Figure 14.27 Netgear USB wireless NIC

An AP (access point) is a device that receives and transmits data from multiple computers that have wireless NICs installed. Figure 14.28 shows a D-Link access point. The AP has two connectors on the side—an Ethernet connector and a power connector. The Ethernet connector allows the access point to be accessed through the wired network.

Tech Tip

PoE (power over Ethernet) can power devices

Some APs can be powered through the attached Ethernet cable using a standard called PoE.

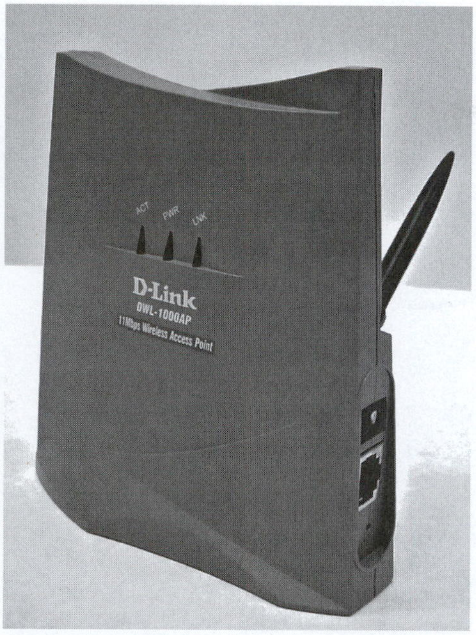

Figure 14.28 A D-Link access point

The easiest way to describe an access point is to think of it as a network hub, but instead of connecting wired devices and sharing bandwidth, the AP connects wireless devices that share bandwidth. Figure 14.29 shows a wireless network with an access point and multiple wireless devices.

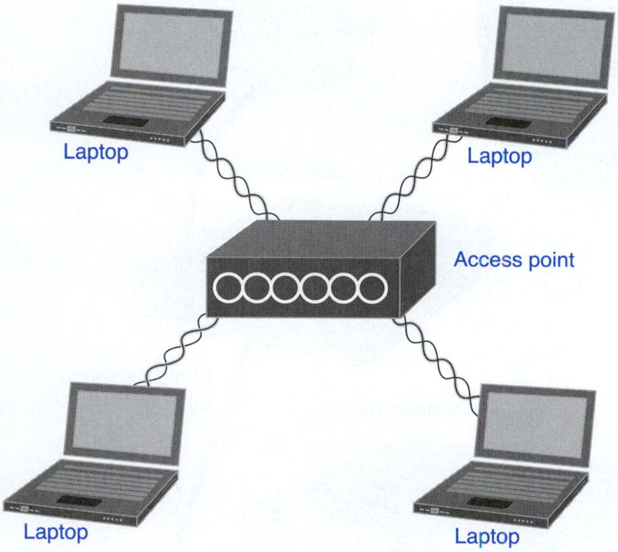

Figure 14.29 Infrastructure mode wireless network

The access point can also be wired or connect wirelessly to another AP, have a wired or wireless connection to a wireless repeater (extender), or connect to a wired network. The access point can then relay the transmission from a wireless device to another network or to the Internet through the wired network. Figure 14.30 shows a D-Link access point connected to a NETGEAR switch. This switch could also be further connected to other network infrastructure devices such as another switch or a router.

Figure 14.30 D-Link access point connected to NETGEAR switch

When multiple devices connect to an access point (whether that access point is wired to a LAN or not). Home networks frequently use an integrated services router that allows wireless and wired connectivity. Figure 14.31 shows how a wireless access point connects in this type of environment. Notice how the access point connects to a wired network and gives the wireless devices access to the Internet.

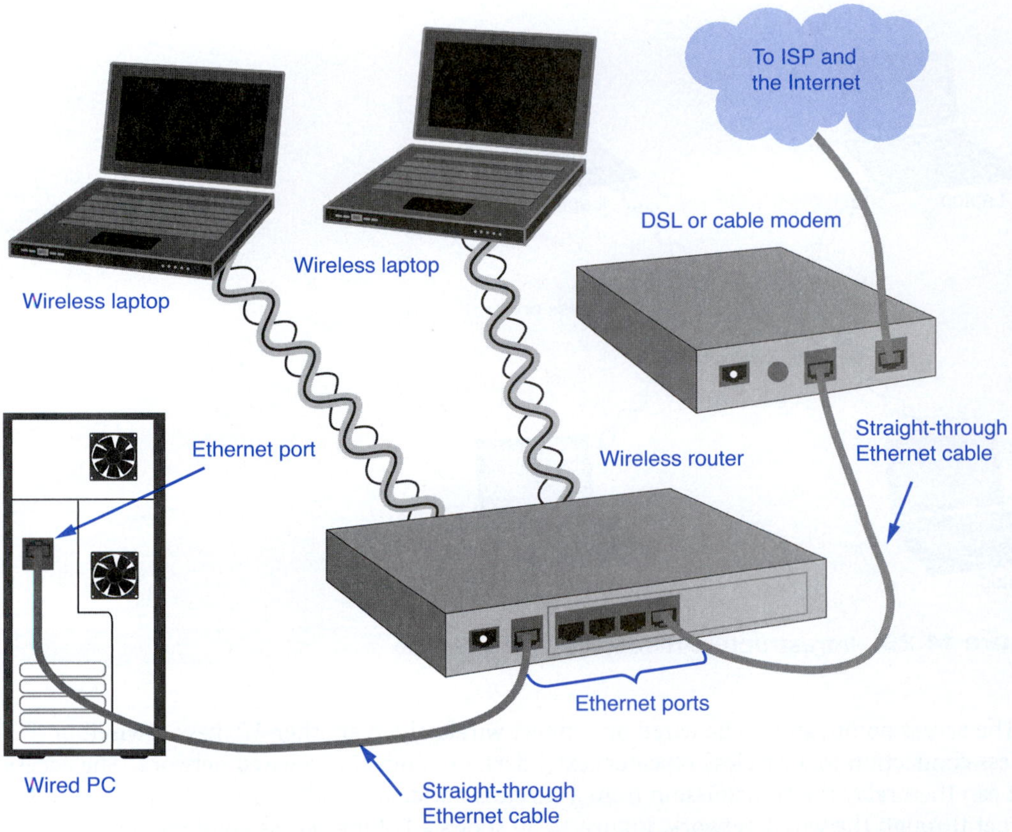

Figure 14.31 Wireless and wired network connectivity

Each access point can handle 30 to 200 network devices depending on vendor, wireless network environment, amount of usage, and the type of data being sent. Each AP is assigned an **SSID** (service set identifier). An SSID is a set of 32 alphanumeric characters used to differentiate between different wireless networks. Wireless NICs can automatically detect a wireless network or the SSID can be manually configured.

If two access points are used and they connect two different wireless networks, two different SSIDs would be used. Figure 14.32 shows this concept. If two access points connect to the same wireless network, the same SSID is used. Figure 14.33 shows this concept.

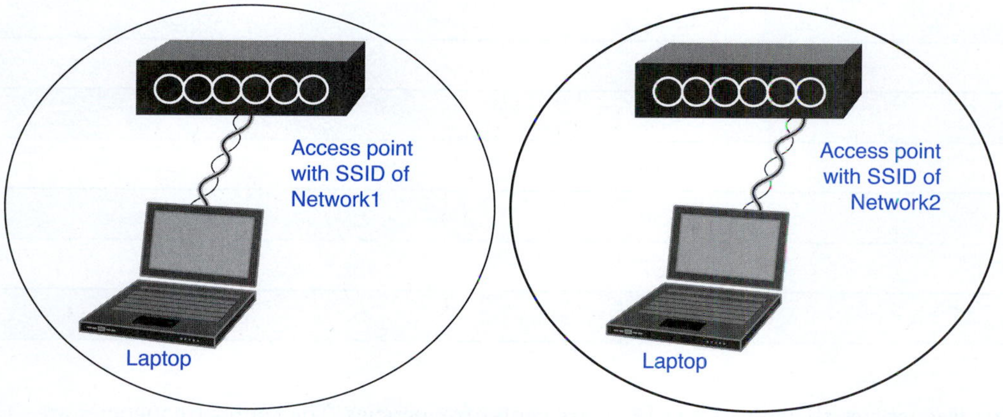

Figure 14.32 Two separate wireless networks with two SSIDs

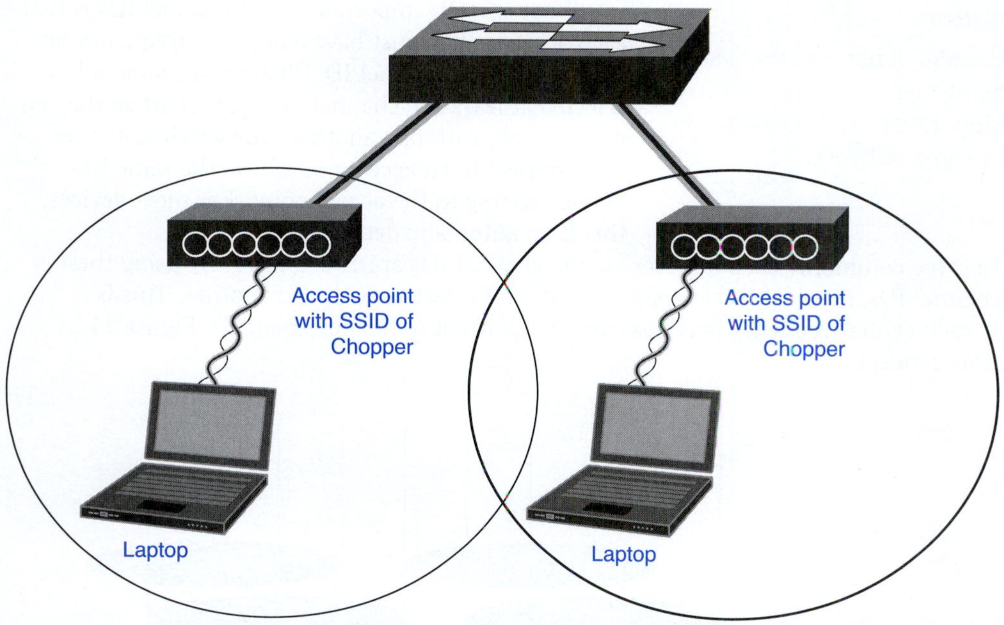

Figure 14.33 One extended wireless network with the same SSID on both access points

In addition to SSIDs, an access point can be configured with a password and a channel ID. When an access point is purchased, a default password is assigned. Because default passwords are available on the Internet, the password needs to be changed immediately so that unauthorized access is not permitted. The **channel ID** defines at what frequency the access point operates. With APs that have a 2.4GHz antenna, up to 14 channels are available depending on what part of the world the wireless network is being deployed. In the United States, only 11 channels are used, and they are listed in Table 14.16.

Table 14.16 Wireless frequency channels

Channel ID number	Frequency (in GHz)
1	2.412
2	2.417
3	2.422
4	2.427
5	2.432
6	2.437
7	2.442
8	2.447
9	2.452
10	2.457
11	2.462

Tech Tip

Channel ID must match

The channel ID (frequency) must be the same between an access point and a wireless NIC in order for communication to occur between any wireless devices on the same network.

The frequencies shown in Table 14.16 are center frequencies. The center frequencies are spaced 5MHz apart. Each channel is actually a range of frequencies. For example, the channel 1 range is 2.401 to 2.423 with the center frequency being 2.412. The channel 2 range is 2.406 to 2.428 with the center frequency being 2.417.

What is really important about channel IDs is that each access point must have a different frequency or nonoverlapping channel ID. Channel IDs should be selected at least five channel numbers apart so they do not interfere with one another. The wireless devices that connect to an access point have the same frequency setting as the access point. For most devices, this is an automatic detection feature.

The three commonly used nonoverlapping channel IDs are 1, 6, and 11. By using these three channel IDs, the three access points would not interfere with one another. This is because each center frequency overlaps with the adjacent frequency channels. Figure 14.34 shows this concept.

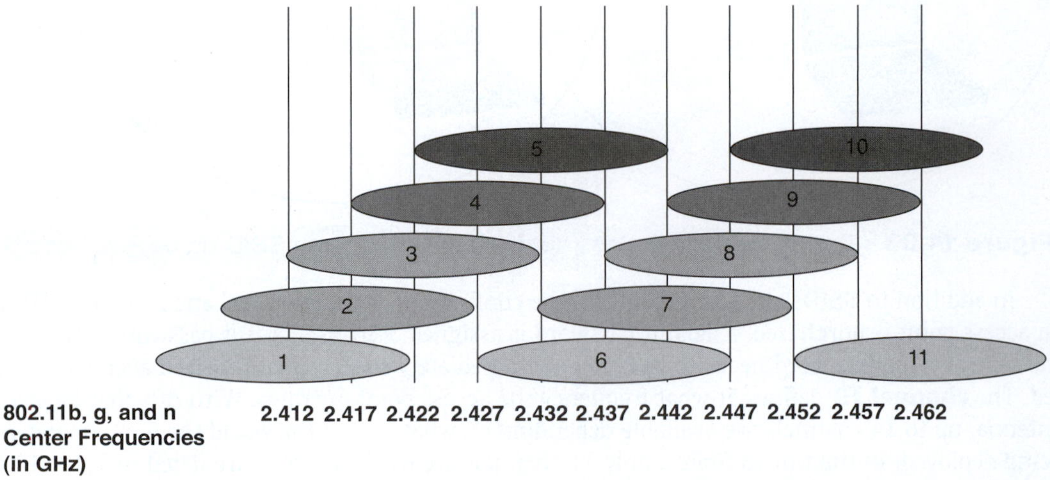

Figure 14.34 802.11b/g/n 2.4GHz nonoverlapping channels

Notice in Figure 14.34 that each center frequency is 5MHz from the next center frequency. Also notice that each channel is actually a range of frequencies, shown by the shaded ovals. Channels 1, 6, and 11 clearly do not overlap and do not interfere with each other. Other nonoverlapping channel combinations could be Channels 2 and 7, Channels 3 and 8, Channels 4 and 9, and Channels 5 and 10. The combination of Channels 1, 6, and 11 is preferred because it gives you three channels with which to work. Figure 14.35 shows a different way of looking at how Channels 1, 6, and 11 do not overlap.

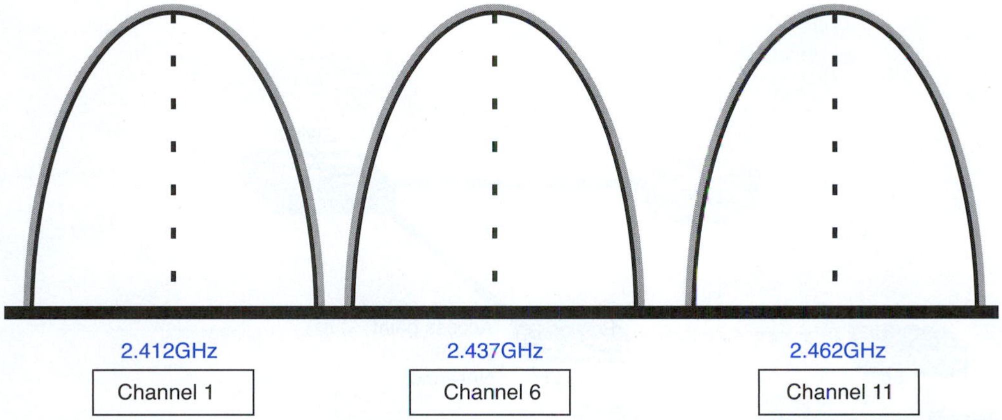

Figure 14.35 **Channel IDs 1, 6, and 11**

Figure 14.36 shows how the three nonoverlapping channels can be used to have extended coverage even with multiple access points.

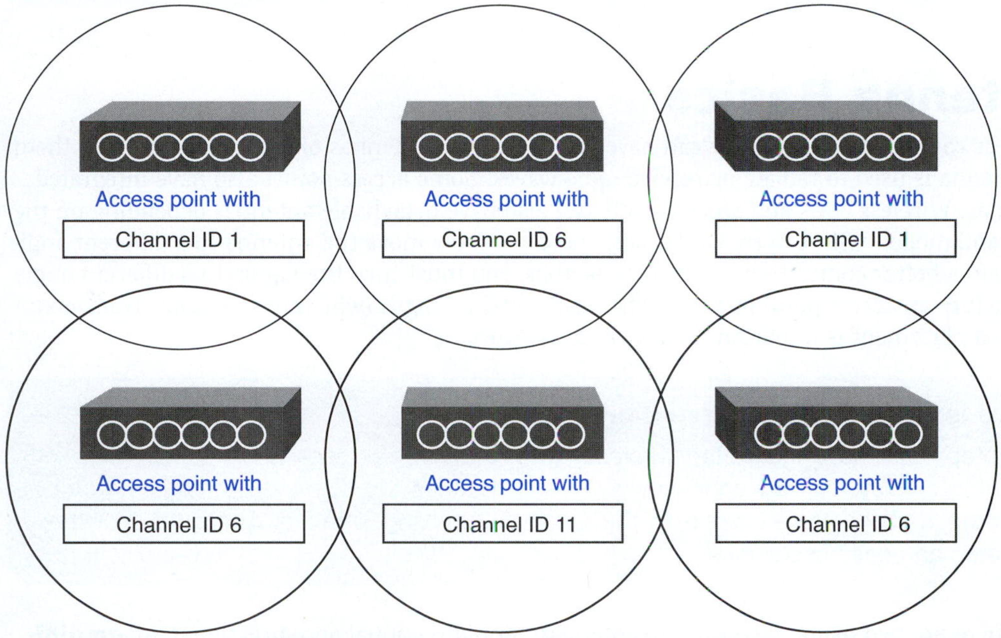

Figure 14.36 **802.11b/g/n nonoverlapping channel IDs**

With 802.11a, 12 20MHz channels are available in the 5GHz range. Out of these 12 channels, 8 can be nonoverlapping. The 802.11a standard breaks the 5GHz range into three subranges called UNII1 (UNII stands for Unlicensed National Information Infrastructure), UNII2, and UNII3. UNII1 is for indoor use only, UNII2 is for both indoor and outdoor use, and UNII3 is for outdoor use only. In the United States, most chipsets support only UNII1 and UNII2, so four channels can be chosen from the UNII1 range and four channels from the UNII2 range.

Some access points can be configured as a repeater to extend the coverage area of the wireless network. In this instance, the access point cannot normally be connected to the wired LAN. Instead, the repeater access point attaches to a "root" access point. The repeater access point allows wireless devices to communicate with it and relays the data to the other access point. Both access points will have the same SSID. Figure 14.37 shows this concept.

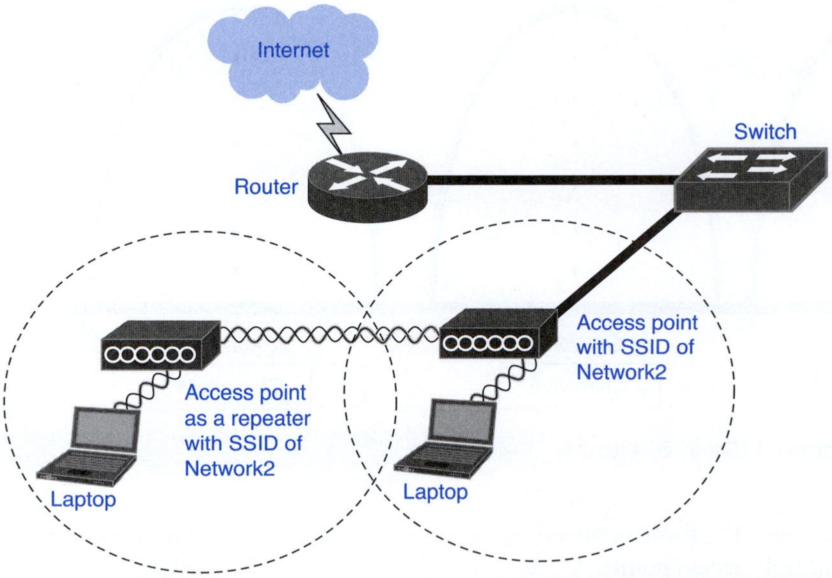

Figure 14.37 Access point as a repeater

Antenna Basics

Wireless cards and access points can have either external antennas or antennas built into them. An antenna is used to radiate or receive radio waves. Some access points also have integrated antennas. Wireless NICs and access points can also have detachable antennas depending on the make and model. With external antennas, you can simply move the antenna to a different angle to obtain a better connection. With some laptops, you must turn the laptop to a different angle to attach to an access point or have a stronger signal strength (which means faster transfers). Antenna placement is important in a wireless network.

Tech Tip

Where is the wireless antenna on a laptop?

For laptops that have integrated wireless NICs, the wireless antenna is usually built into the laptop display for best connectivity. This is because the display is the tallest point of the laptop and therefore closest to the wireless receiving antenna. The quality of these integrated antennas is diverse.

There are two major categories of antennas: omnidirectional and directional. An **omnidirectional antenna** radiates energy in all directions. Integrated wireless NICs use omnidirectional antennas. Figure 14.38 shows an integrated wireless NIC in a laptop computer. Notice in Figure 14.38 that the wires attach to two posts on the wireless NIC. These wires are what connect the antenna to the wireless NIC. If a laptop always has low signal strength, ensure these two wires are attached.

Figure 14.38 Laptop wireless NIC

A **directional antenna** radiates energy in a specific direction. Each antenna has a specific radiation pattern. A radiation pattern (sometimes called a propagation pattern) is the direction(s) the radio frequency is sent or received. It is the coverage area for the antenna that is normally shown in a graphical representation in the antenna manufacturer's specifications. Figure 14.39 shows the difference in radiation patterns between omnidirectional and directional antennas.

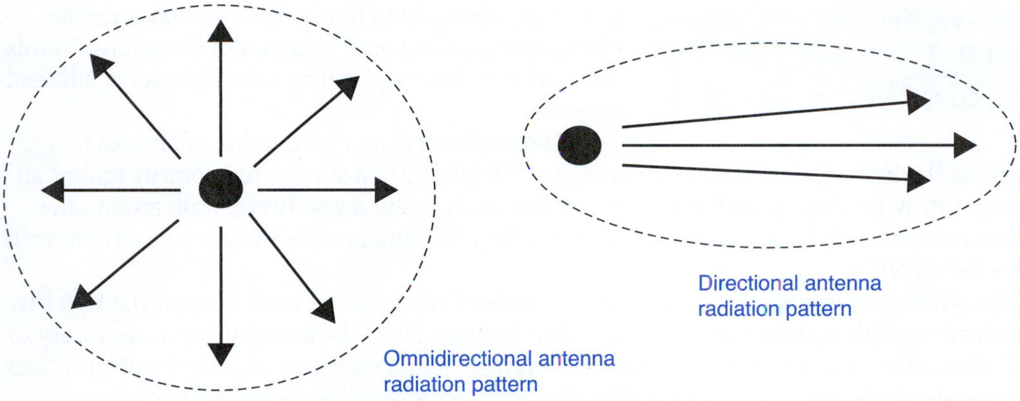

Figure 14.39 Basic antenna radiation patterns

A wireless network installer must be familiar with an antenna's radiation pattern so that the appropriate type of antenna can be chosen for the installation. As a signal is radiated from an antenna, some of the signal is lost. Attenuation is the amount of signal loss of a radio wave as it travels (is propagated) through air. Attenuation is sometimes called path loss. Attenuation is measured in decibels. The decibel is a value that represents a measure of the ratio between two signal levels.

Things that affect an antenna's path loss are the distance between the transmitting antenna and the receiving antenna, what obstructions are between the two antennas, and how high the antenna is mounted. Another factor that affects wireless transmission is interference, including radio frequencies being transmitted using the same frequency range and external noises. Other wireless devices, wireless networks, cordless phones, and microwave ovens are common sources of interference.

An important concept in relationship to antennas is gain, and in order to understand gain, an isotropic antenna must be discussed. An isotropic antenna is not real; it is an imaginary antenna that is perfect in that it theoretically transmits an equal amount of power in all directions. The omnidirectional radiation pattern shown in Figure 14.39 would be the pattern of an isotropic antenna.

Antenna gain is measured in dBi, which is a measurement of decibels in relationship to an isotropic antenna. (The *i* is for isotropic.) Some antennas are shown with a measurement of dBd instead of dBi. This measurement is referenced to a dipole antenna. (The *d* at the end is for dipole.) 0 dBd equals 2.14 dBi. More gain means more coverage in a particular direction. Gain is actually logarithmic in nature.

Imagine a round balloon that is blown up. The balloon represents an isotropic radiation pattern—it extends in all directions. Push down on the top of the balloon, and the balloon extends out more horizontally than it does vertically. Push on the side of the balloon, and the balloon extends more in one horizontal directional than the side being pushed. Now think of the balloon's shape as an antenna's radiation pattern. Antenna designers can change the radiation pattern of an antenna by changing the antenna's length and shape, similarly to how a balloon's looks can be changed by pushing on it in different directions. In this way, different antennas can be created to serve different purposes.

A **site survey** is an examination of an area to determine the best wireless hardware placement. To take such a survey, temporarily mount an access point. With a laptop that has a wireless NIC and site survey software, walk around the wireless network area to see the coverage range. Most vendors provide site survey software with their wireless NICs.

The site survey can also be conducted by double-clicking the network icon on the task bar. The signal strength is shown in the window that appears. Move the access point as necessary to avoid attenuation and obtain the largest area coverage. Radio waves are affected by obstructions such as walls, trees, rain, snow, fog, and buildings, so for a larger project the site survey may need to be done over a period of time. You can see the wireless antenna signal strength in the systray part of the task bar. You can also see it from within the wireless NIC properties window. Figure 14.40 shows a laptop wireless antenna signal strength display.

Tech Tip

The higher the decibel rating, the better the signal

As a wireless device is moved farther away from an access point or another wireless device, the more attenuation occurs. Walls, trees, obstacles, or other radio waves can cause attenuation. The type of radio antenna and the antenna gain also affect the signal strength.

Tech Tip

What is gain?

Antenna gain is the antenna's output power in a particular direction compared to the output power produced in any direction by an isotropic or dipole antenna.

Tech Tip

Understanding gain

A 3dB gain is twice the output power. 10dB is 10 times the power, 13dB is about 20 times the power, and 20dB is 100 times the power. Gain that is shown with a negative value means there is a power loss. For example, a –3dB gain means the power is halved.

A wireless locator can be used to determine whether there are wireless networks or hot spots in the area. There are also wireless devices that can be attached to pets, people, keys, remotes, and so on. A wireless locator device is used to locate these devices. A phone or mobile device app can also be used to locate a powered mobile device or locate a person who has a mobile device with this enabled.

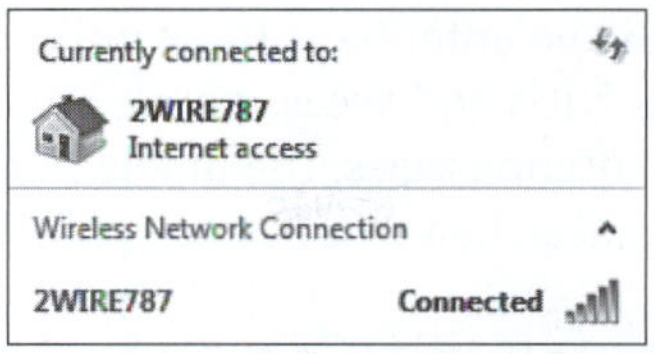

Figure 14.40 Signal strength

There are many different types of antennas, but four common ones are parabolic, Yagi, patch, and dipole. Parabolic antennas can come in either grid or dish type models, and they are usually used in outdoor environments. Parabolic dishes are used to provide the greatest distances in a wireless network. Parabolic dish antennas may not come with mounting hardware, so you should research whether additional hardware is needed before purchasing one. Figure 14.41 shows a parabolic dish antenna.

Other antennas include Yagi, patch, MIMO, and dipole antennas. A Yagi antenna can be used indoors or outdoors, depending on the manufacturer. It is used for long-distance communication and normally is not very large or difficult to mount. A patch antenna can also be used indoors and outdoors. Patch antennas can be mounted to a variety of surfaces including room columns or walls.

MIMO (multiple input/multiple output) uses multiple 2.4GHz and 5GHz antennas. These antennas may be external or built into the wireless device. By using multiple antennas greater wireless speeds can be achieved. Figure 14.42 shows a wireless router that uses MIMO.

Figure 14.41 Parabolic dish antenna

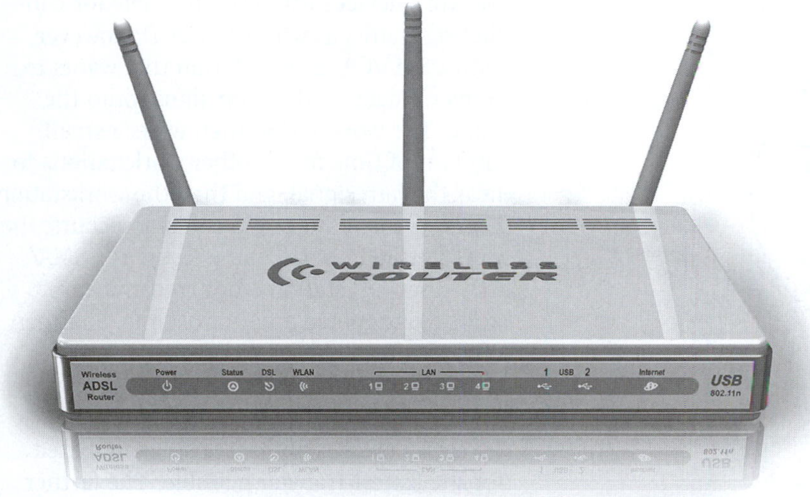

Figure 14.42 Wireless router that uses MIMO

A dipole antenna is frequently referred to as a *rubber ducky*. A dipole antenna attaches to wireless NICs and access points and is used in indoor applications. Of all the previously mentioned antenna types, the dipole has the lowest range. Refer to Figure 14.30 to see a dipole antenna attached to an access point from D-Link Systems, Inc.

Wireless Network Standards

The IEEE 802.11 committees define standards for wireless networks, and they can be quite confusing. Table 14.17 shows the current and proposed wireless network standards.

Table 14.17 IEEE 802.11 standards

Standard	Purpose
802.11a	Came after the 802.11b standard. Has speeds up to 54 Mbps but is incompatible with 802.11b. Operates in the 5GHz range.
802.11b	Operates in the 2.4000 and 2.4835GHz radio frequency ranges, with speeds up to 11Mbps.
802.11e	Provides standards related to quality of service.
802.11g	Operates in the 2.4GHz range, with speeds up to 54Mbps, and is backward compatible with 802.11b.
802.11i	Relates to wireless network security and includes AES (Advanced Encryption Standard) for protecting data.
802.11n	Operates in the 2.4 and 5GHz ranges and is backward compatible with the older 802.11a, b, and g equipment. Speeds up to 600Mbps using MIMO antennas.

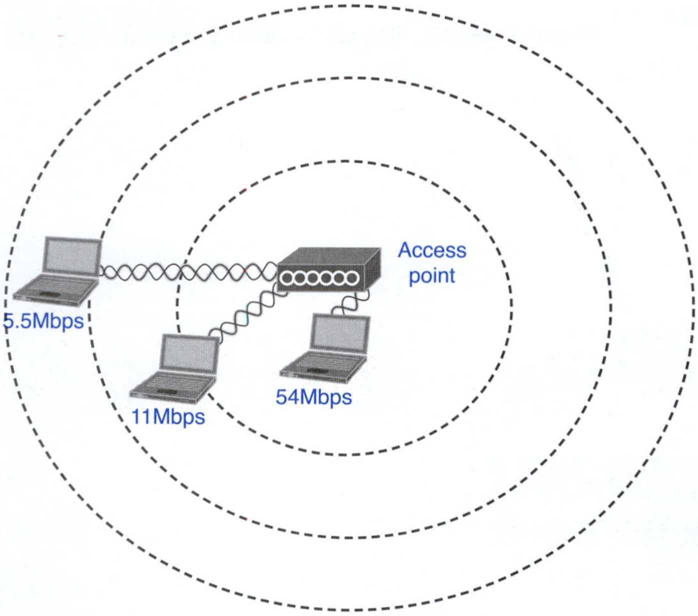

Figure 14.43 Access point speed ranges

802.11-based wireless networks use CSMA/CA (Carrier Sense Multiple Access/Collision Avoidance) as an access method. Network devices listen on the cable for conflicting traffic, as with CSMA/CD; however, with CSMA/CA, a workstation that wants to transmit data sends a jam signal onto the cable. The workstation then waits a small amount of time for all other workstations to hear the jam signal, and then the workstation begins transmission. If a collision occurs, the workstation does the same thing as CSMA/CD—the workstation stops transmitting, waits a designated amount of time, and then retransmits.

Data transfer speed between the wireless NIC and an access point or another wireless device is automatically negotiated for the fastest transfer possible. The farther away from an access point a wireless device is located, the lower the speed. Figure 14.43 shows this concept.

Wired or Wireless NIC Installation

When you install a NIC in a computer, you must take four or more configuration steps before connecting to the network:

1. Determine that an appropriate slot, port, or integrated wireless NIC is available. For example, a NIC can be integrated into the motherboard, require a PCI/PCIe slot, a mini-PCI/PCIe slot, connect to a USB port, or insert into a laptop slot (ExpressCard or CF NIC—a CompactFlash card that has an RJ-45 NIC port).
2. Obtain and install the appropriate NIC driver.
3. Give the computer a unique name and optionally join a workgroup or domain.
4. Configure TCP/IP.

Other things could be required, depending on the network environment. For example, if the system is a peer-to-peer network, file and print sharing must be enabled. If a wireless network is being configured, the SSID and possibly the security parameters need to be entered. If TCP/IP is configured, some other configuration parameters may be necessary. Labs 14.1, 14.2, and 14.8 at the end of the chapter demonstrate these concepts.

Tech Tip

How to name a computer

Name a computer using the *Network Connections* (XP) or *System* (Vista/7) control panel. Each device on the same network must be given a unique name.

When configuring TCP/IP, an IP address and subnet mask must be assigned to the network device. The IP address is what makes the network device unique and what allows it to be reached by other network devices. There are two ways to get an IP address: (1) statically define the IP address and mask or (2) dynamically use DHCP.

Tech Tip

What happens if you assign the same IP address?

Entering an IP address that is a duplicate of another network device renders the new network device inoperable on the network.

When an IP address is statically defined, someone manually enters an IP address and mask into the computer through the *Network Connections* (XP) or *Network and Sharing Center* (Vista/7) Control Panel. Lab 14.4 at the end of this chapter demonstrates this. Most support staff do not statically define IP addresses unless the device is an important network device such as a web server, database server, network server, router, or switch. Instead, DHCP is used. Figure 14.44 shows the window that appears once you select *TCP/IPv4* and click the *Properties* button.

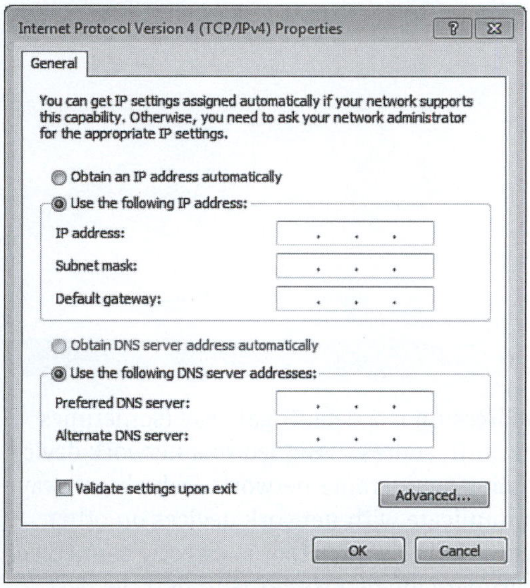

Figure 14.44 IP address configuration

DHCP (Dynamic Host Configuration Protocol) is a protocol used to assign IP addresses to network devices. A DHCP server (software configured on a network server or router) contains a pool of IP addresses. When a network device has been configured for DHCP and it boots, the device sends out a request for an IP address. A DHCP server responds to this request and issues an IP address to the network device. DHCP makes IP addressing easier and keeps network devices from being assigned duplicate IP addresses.

> **Tech Tip**
>
> **My computer's IP address changes**
>
> The IP address can change each time the computer boots because with DHCP, you can configure the DHCP server to issue an IP address for a specific amount of time.

Windows computers support **APIPA** (Automatic Private IP Addressing), which assigns an IP address and mask to the computer when a DHCP server is not available. The addresses assigned are 169.254.0.1 to 169.254.255.254. No two computers get the same IP address. APIPA will continue to request an IP address from the DHCP server at five minute intervals. If you can connect to other computers on your local network, but you cannot reach the Internet or other networks, it is likely the DHCP server is down and Windows has automatically assigned an APIPA address. To determine if APIPA is configured, open a command prompt window and type `ipconfig /all`. If you see the words *Autoconfiguration Enabled Yes*, APIPA is turned on. If the last word is *No*, APIPA is disabled.

> **Tech Tip**
>
> **One DHCP server can provide addresses to multiple networks**
>
> A DHCP server can give out IP addresses to network devices on remote networks as well as the network to which the DHCP server is directly connected.

An **alternative configuration** can also be used. An alternative configuration is used when a DHCP could not assign an IP address such as when there are network problems or the DHCP server is down. An **alternative address** could also be used on a laptop where at work, DHCP is used, but at home, the addresses are statically assigned. Figure 14.45 shows the *Alternate Configuration* tab settings.

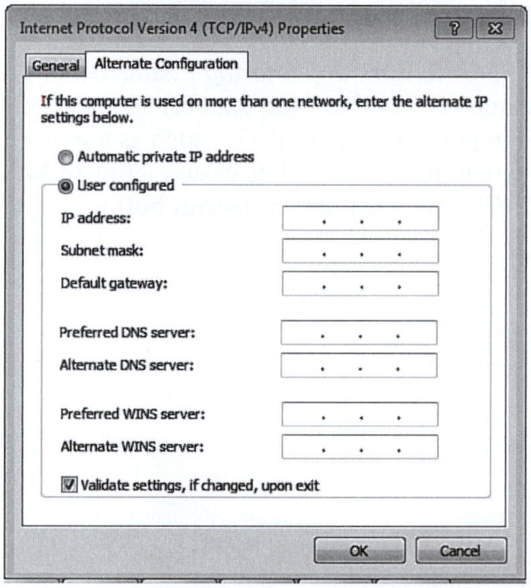

Figure 14.45 Alternate Configuration tab

Another important concept that relates to IP addressing is a default gateway (sometimes called gateway of last resort). A **default gateway** is an IP address assigned to a network device that tells the device where to send a packet that is going to a remote network. Default gateway addresses are important for network devices to communicate with network devices on other networks. The default gateway address is the IP address of the router that is directly connected to that immediate network. Keep in mind that the primary job of a router is to find the best path to another network. Consider Figure 14.46.

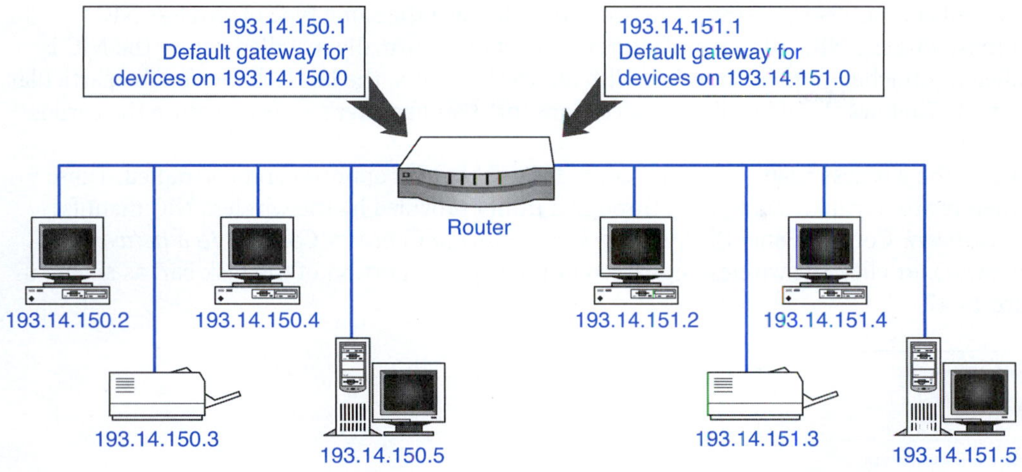

Figure 14.46 Default gateway

Network devices on the 193.14.150.0 network use the router IP address 193.14.150.1 as a default gateway address. When a network device on the 193.14.150.0 network wants to send a packet to the other network, the device sends the packet to the default gateway, the router. The router, in turn, looks up the destination address in its routing table and sends the packet out of the other router interface (193.14.151.1) to the device on the 193.14.151.0 network.

The default gateway address for all network devices on the 193.14.151.0 network is 193.14.151.1, the router's IP address on the same network. Any network device on 193.14.151.0 sending information to another network sends the packet to the default gateway address. For network devices on the 193.14.151.0 network, the gateway address is 193.14.151.1.

Tech Tip

How do I assign a default gateway?

If you are statically assigning an IP address, the default gateway address is configured using the *Network Connections* (XP) or *Network and Sharing Center* (Vista/7) Control Panel. Your computer can automatically receive a default gateway through DHCP just like receiving an IP address and mask.

Other elements of TCP/IP information that may need to be configured or provided through DHCP include DNS server IP addresses. A **DNS** (Domain Name System) **server** (sometimes called a domain name server) is an application that runs on a network server that provides translation of Internet names into IP addresses. DNS is used on the Internet, so you do not have to remember the IP address of each site to which you connect. For example, DNS would be used to connect to Pearson Education, Inc. by translating the URL (uniform resource locator) of http://www.pearsoned.com into the IP address 159.182.16.65. **Client-side DNS** is configuring a computer to use one or more DNS servers. A computer can be programmed for one or more DNS server IP addresses using DHCP. The DHCP server must be configured for this. Otherwise, a technician can manually configure the system for one or more DNS server IP addresses through the *Network* (XP) or *Network and Sharing Center* (Vista/7) Control Panel.

Tech Tip

DNS servers provide name resolution

If a Windows computer is on an Active Directory domain, Active Directory automatically uses DNS to locate other hosts and services using assigned domain names.

If a DNS server does not know a domain name (it does not have the name in its database), the DNS server can contact another DNS server to get the translation information. Common three letter codes used with DNS (three letters used at the end of a domain name) are com (commercial sites), edu (educational sites), gov (government sites), net (network-related sites), and org (miscellaneous sites). Wired and wireless adapters require IP addresses, default gateways, and DNS configuration, but before any wired or wireless adapters are installed or configured, the basic configuration parameters should be determined.

Not all computers in a wireless network have to have the same type of wireless NIC. With most wireless NICs, the manufacturer's software is normally installed before the NIC is installed or attached to the computer. With all wireless NICs, the latest driver for the particular version of Windows should be downloaded from the manufacturer's website before the card is installed.

Once the wireless adapter is installed, SSID and security options can be installed. These parameters are normally configured through a utility provided by the wireless NIC manufacturer, *Network* Control Panel (XP), *Network and Sharing Center > Connect to a network* link (Windows7), or click the wireless signal icon in the systray portion of the task bar, as shown in Figure 14.47.

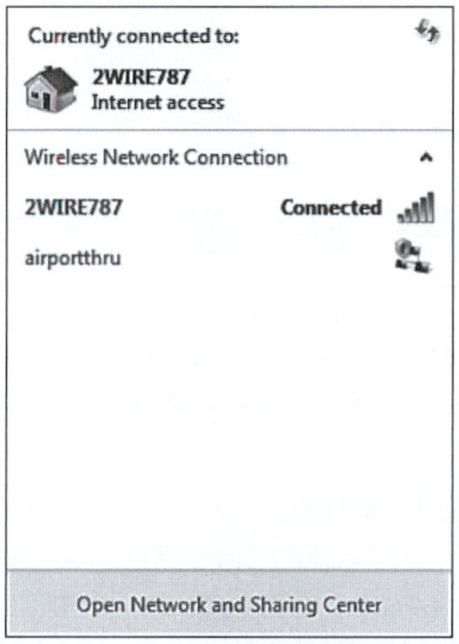

Figure 14.47 Wireless networks

Tech Tip

Disable Windows control of the wireless NIC if other utilities are used

If a vendor provides a method of controlling the wireless NIC with utilities associated with the NIC, use those and *not* Windows. Otherwise, uninstall the wireless NIC software provided by the vendor.

To manually configure a wireless NIC, you can use the Windows Vista/7 *Network and Sharing Center* Control Panel link. Use the *Set up a new connection or network* link to access the *Manually connect to a wireless network* option. Figure 14.48 shows the options.

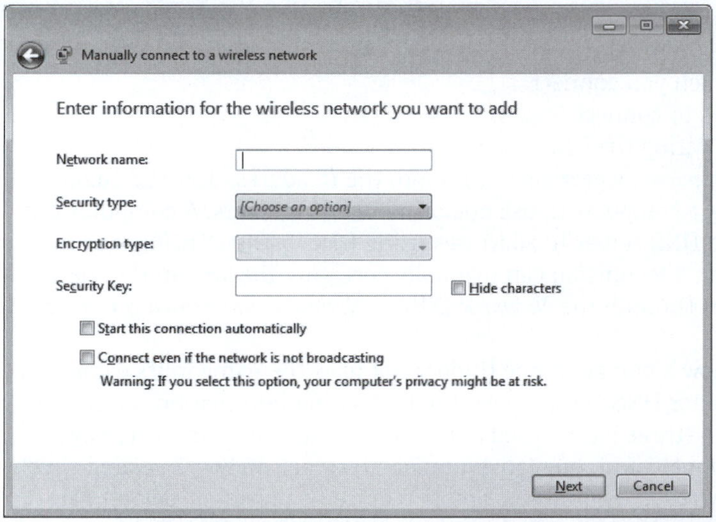

Figure 14.48 Windows 7 wireless network configuration window

Wireless NICs are very easy to install. The utilities that are provided with the NICs are quite sophisticated, but easy to use. Always follow the manufacturer's instructions. All the screens and configuration utilities have the same type of information. Understanding what the configuration parameters means is important. The hardest part about configuring wireless NICs is obtaining the correct parameters before installation begins. Incorrectly inputting any one of the parameters will cause the wireless NIC not to associate with the access point or remote wireless device and not transmit. Planning is critical for these types of cards.

Both wired and wireless NICs have some optional parameters that can be manually configured. These options are presented in Table 14.18 and shown in Figure 14.49. Access these parameters by right-clicking on the NIC from within the *Network* or *Networking and Sharing Center* Control Panel and selecting *Properties* > *Configure* button > *Advanced* tab.

Table 14.18 **Network card properties**

Configuration property	Description
Half-duplex/full-duplex/auto	The default is auto, to automatically negotiate whether transmission occurs in full duplex mode (both directions simultaneously) or half duplex mode (both directions, but only one at a time). This might be combined with the Speed configuration option.
Speed	Normally automatically configured, but manual options include 1Gbps, 100Mbps, and 10Mbps.
Wake-on-LAN	Wake-on-LAN allows the computer to be brought out of a low power mode to have configuration changes or updates made. Usually enabled through the BIOS, but through the NIC properties *Advanced* tab. Other options might include Wake on magic packet or WOL.
QoS (quality of service)	Some NICs have the ability to have QoS features enabled. This allows tagging certain packets for priority transmission. Other similar options might be Priority and VLAN or Tagging.

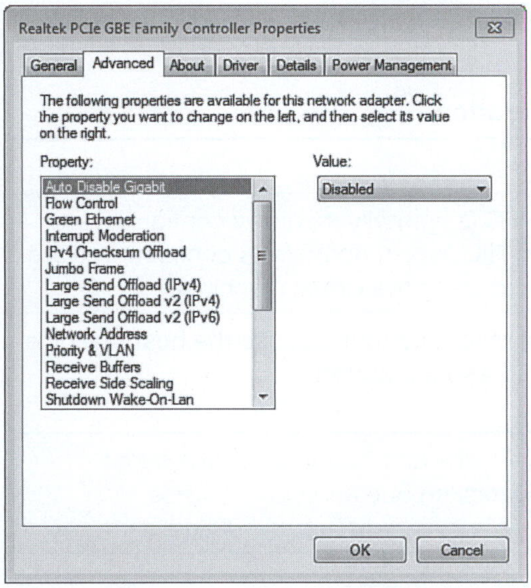

Figure 14.49 **NIC advanced properties**

Wireless Broadband

Another type of wireless device that you might configure is a wireless broadband device. A wireless broadband device is normally a USB device, but some mobile devices have integrated broadband access. Software is normally installed by either a disc or from the device itself. The device commonly has a phone number/account number associated with the broadband card. Figure 14.50 shows the type of information provided for a wireless broadband USB device.

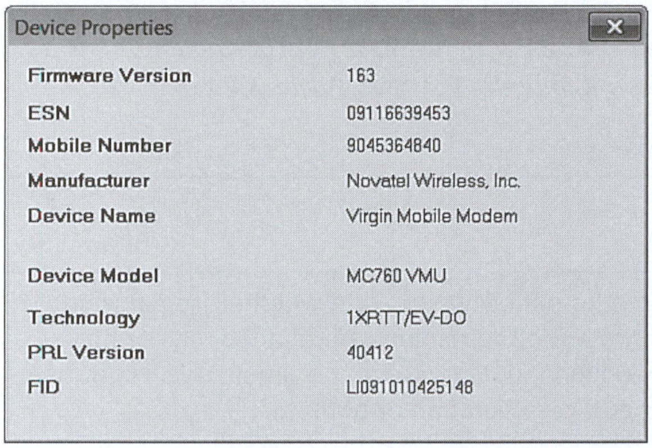

Figure 14.50 Wireless broadband properties

Virtualization Network Issues

When you configure a computer for virtualization, part of that virtualization is a virtual NIC. One virtual NIC is normally standard in a virtual machine. More virtual NICs can be assigned. Each virtual NIC has its own MAC address and can have an IP address assigned. If more than one virtual machine is installed, each can communicate with the other machine based on the NIC settings configured. Furthermore, the virtual NIC can go through the real NIC and have Internet access in the virtual environment.

Rather than go into all of different virtualization vendors' products, let's examine VMware Workstation's NIC settings. Other vendors have similar configurations. In VMware workstation, a NIC can be configured for bridged, NAT (network address translation), or host-only mode. Table 14.19 describes these modes.

Table 14.19 Virtualized NIC modes of operation

Mode	Description
Bridged	Usually the default mode. The NIC is normally manually configured and has access to the host machine NIC (which normally is connected to the Internet and provides Internet access to the virtual machine).
NAT (network address translation)	Cannot be seen by other virtual machines, but can use the host machine NIC for Internet access. DHCP is also supported.
Host-only	Other virtual machines configured with an IP address on the same network can see and communicate with one another. DHCP is supported.

Access Point/Router Installation

Many wireless access points have the ability to route. The router connects the wired network and the wireless network together. A router is also good to have so that DHCP can be provided for both the wired and the wireless networks and provide a firewall for network security. Firewalls are covered in Chapter 15.

Many of the parameters needed for wireless NIC configuration are also needed for access point installation. However, installing an access point is more involved because it is the central device of the wireless network. The following list helps with access point installation. The questions should be answered *before* the access point is installed. Some of the security options that follow are discussed in Chapter 15:

- What SSID is to be used?
- What static IP address will be assigned to the device?
- Is WEP, WPA, WPA-PSK, WPA2-PSK, TKIP, AES, or any other security option enabled?*
- What security key lengths, security keys, or passphrases are used?*
- Is MAC address filtering enabled?*
- Is there power available for the access point? Note that some access points can receive power through an in-line switch.
- How will the access point be mounted? Is mounting hardware provided with the access point, or does extra equipment have to be purchased?
- Where should the access point be mounted for best coverage of the wireless network area? Where should the antenna be placed or how should it be angled? Perform a site survey to see best performance. Temporarily mount the access point. With a laptop that has a wireless NIC and site survey software, walk around the wireless network area to see the coverage range. The site survey can also be conducted by double clicking the network icon on the task bar; the signal strength is shown in the window that appears. Move the access point as necessary to avoid attenuation and obtain the largest area coverage.
- What channel ID will be used?
- Will the access point connect to the wired network and, if so, is there connectivity available where the access point will be mounted?

*Note that these security options are discussed in Chapter 15.

Wireless networking is an important and popular technology. Technicians today must be familiar with this technology as corporations and home users install these types of products. Because the technology is reasonably priced, many new technicians install their own wireless network for the experience. Enjoy this technology because more wireless technologies are evolving.

Configuring a Networked Printer

There are three ways to network a printer:

1. Connect a printer to a port on a computer that is connected to the network and share the printer.
2. Set up a computer or device that is designated as a print server. Connect the print server to the network.
3. Connect a printer with a network connector installed directly on the network. Printers can also be password protected on the network. A networked printer is very common in today's home and business computing environments. Networking expensive printers such as laser printers and color printers is cost-effective.

Tech Tip

Do your wireless homework

Whether installing a wired or wireless network printer, obtain IP address, subnet mask, default gateway, SSID, and security information before starting the installation.

A printer that is connected to a workstation can be shared across the network by enabling File and Print Sharing. An exercise at the end of this chapter explains how to do this.

With Microsoft operating systems, networked printers are much easier to configure than they used to be. To connect and use a networked printer, use the *Add Printer* Wizard. A prompt is available that asks whether the printer is local or networked. A local printer is one that is directly attached to the computer and a networked printer is one attached to another workstation, a print server, or directly connected to the network.

The steps for installing a wireless printer are similar to installing a wired network printer once the printer is attached to the wireless network. Before installing a wireless printer, you need to ensure a functional wireless network is in the area. You need to know the SSID and any security settings configured on the wireless network. Normally, wireless printers are configured using one of the following methods:

- Install software that comes with the printer *before* connecting the printer. Then use the software to enter the wireless network SSID and optional security parameters.
- Use the controls on the front panel of the printer to configure the wireless settings.
- Use a USB connection to the printer until the wireless network configuration options are entered.

Gathering the wireless configuration information is mandatory before you configure any device, including printers for a wireless network.

Network Troubleshooting

Tech Tip

What does `ping` do?

The `ping` command can be used to determine if the network path is available, if there are delays along the path, and whether the remote network device is reachable. `ping` sends a packet to an IP destination (that you determine) and a reply is sent back from the destination device (when everything is working fine).

One way to troubleshoot a network is to determine how many devices are affected. For example, if only one computer cannot communicate across a network, it will be handled differently than if several (or all) computers on a network cannot communicate. If a network port is suspect, try another cable or use a loopback plug to test the port. The easiest way to determine how many devices are having trouble is by using a simple test. Since most computers use TCP/IP, one tool that can be used for testing is the **`ping`** command.

Tech Tip

How can I check the TCP/IP stack on my own NIC?

The `ping` utility can be used to test a NIC as well as the TCP/IP protocol running on the NIC, with the command `ping 127.0.0.1` (IPv4), `ping ::1` (IPv6), or `ping localhost`. `localhost` is a hostname that is translated to an IP address known as a private IP address, or a loopback address, which means it cannot be used by the outside world.

Tech Tip

What the `ping localhost` results mean

If a `ping` is successful (that is, you get a message that a reply was received from 127.0.0.1 or ::1), then the TCP/IP protocol stack is working correctly on the NIC. If the `ping` responds with a No or a 100% packet loss error, TCP/IP is not properly installed or functioning correctly on that one workstation.

The `ping` command can be used to check connectivity all around the network. Figure 14.51 shows a sample network that is used to explain how `ping` is used to check various network points.

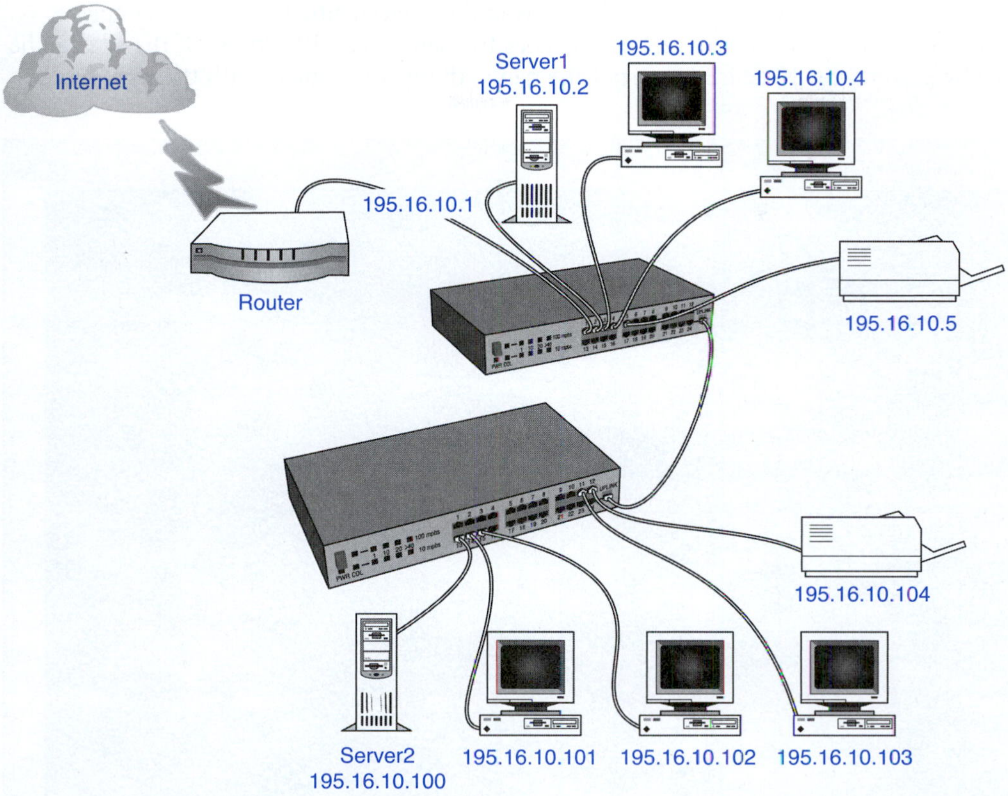

Figure 14.51 **Sample network troubleshooting scenario**

The network consists of various network devices, including two servers and two laser printers. The devices connect to one of two switches that are connected using the uplink port. This port allows two similar devices to be connected with a standard Ethernet cable or fiber cable. A router connects to the top switch and the router connects to the Internet.

The 195.16.10.3 workstation cannot access a file on Server2 (195.16.10.100). The first step in troubleshooting is to `ping` Server2. If this is successful, the problem is in Server2 or the file located on the server.

If the `ping` is unsuccessful, there is a problem somewhere between the workstation and the server or on the server. Ping another device that connects to the same switch—from workstation 195.16.10.3, `ping` Server1 (195.16.10.2). A successful `ping` tells you the connection between the 195.16.10.3 workstation and the switch is good, the switch is working, the cable connecting to Server1 is fine, and Server1 is functioning.

Now `ping` workstation 195.16.10.101 (a device other than the server on the remote switch). If the `ping` is successful, (1) the uplink cable is operational; (2) the second switch is operational; (3) the cable that connects workstation 195.16.10.101 to the switch is good; and (4) the 195.16.10.101 workstation has been successfully configured for TCP/IP. If the `ping` is unsuccessful, one of these four items is faulty. If the `ping` is successful, the problems could be the (1) Server2 cable, (2) switch port to which the server connects, (3) server NIC, (4) server configuration, or (5) file on Server2.

Tech Tip

Use `ping -t`

`ping x.x.x.x -t` (replace the `x.x.x.x` with an IP address or a URL) issues a continuous `ping` to a remote location. The `ping` will not stop until the Ctrl + C keys are pressed.

To see the current IP configuration, use the **`ipconfig`** command from a command prompt. The `ipconfig /all` command can be used to see both wired and wireless NICs if both are installed as shown in Figure 14.52. Access the *Start* button > *All Programs* > *Accessories* > *Command Prompt*. Labs 14.1, 14.4, 14.5, and 14.8 at the end of this chapter guide you through the processes of configuring a NIC, TCP/IP, and sharing network resources.

Use the `ping` command followed by the name of the device being tested, for example, `ping www.pearsoned.com`. A DNS server translates the name to an IP address. If the site can be reached by `ping`ing the IP address, but not the name, there is a problem with the DNS server.

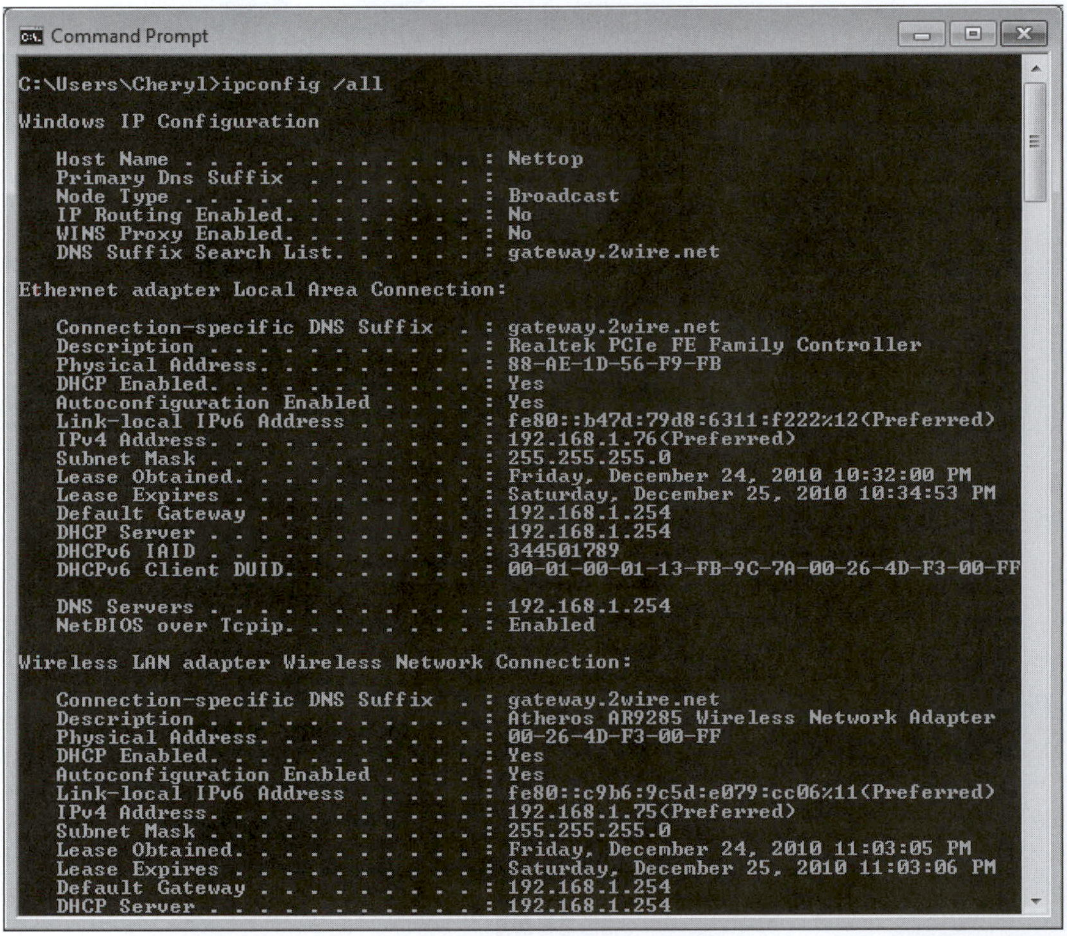

Command Prompt
C:\Users\Cheryl>ipconfig /all
Windows IP Configuration
Host Name . . . . : Nettop
Primary Dns Suffix . . . . :
Node Type . . . . : Broadcast
IP Routing Enabled. . . . . : No
WINS Proxy Enabled. . . . . : No
DNS Suffix Search List. . . . . . : gateway.2wire.net
Ethernet adapter Local Area Connection:
Connection-specific DNS Suffix . : gateway.2wire.net
Description . . . . : Realtek PCIe FE Family Controller
Physical Address. . . . . : 88-AE-1D-56-F9-FB
DHCP Enabled. . . . . : Yes
Autoconfiguration Enabled . . . . : Yes
Link-local IPv6 Address . . . . . : fe80::b47d:79d8:6311:f222%12(Preferred)
IPv4 Address. . . . . : 192.168.1.76(Preferred)
Subnet Mask . . . . : 255.255.255.0
Lease Obtained. . . . . : Friday, December 24, 2010 10:32:00 PM
Lease Expires . . . . : Saturday, December 25, 2010 10:34:53 PM
Default Gateway . . . . : 192.168.1.254
DHCP Server . . . . : 192.168.1.254
DHCPv6 IAID . . . . : 344501789
DHCPv6 Client DUID. . . . . : 00-01-00-01-13-FB-9C-7A-00-26-4D-F3-00-FF
DNS Servers . . . . : 192.168.1.254
NetBIOS over Tcpip. . . . . : Enabled
Wireless LAN adapter Wireless Network Connection:
Connection-specific DNS Suffix . : gateway.2wire.net
Description . . . . : Atheros AR9285 Wireless Network Adapter
Physical Address. . . . . : 00-26-4D-F3-00-FF
DHCP Enabled. . . . . : Yes
Autoconfiguration Enabled . . . . : Yes
Link-local IPv6 Address . . . . . : fe80::c9b6:9c5d:e079:cc06%11(Preferred)
IPv4 Address. . . . . : 192.168.1.75(Preferred)
Subnet Mask . . . . : 255.255.255.0
Lease Obtained. . . . . : Friday, December 24, 2010 11:03:05 PM
Lease Expires . . . . : Saturday, December 25, 2010 11:03:06 PM
Default Gateway . . . . : 192.168.1.254
DHCP Server . . . . : 192.168.1.254

Figure 14.52 `ipconfig /all`

`nslookup` is a program tool that helps with DNS server troubleshooting. `nslookup` allows you to see domain names and their associated IP addresses. When an Internet site (server) cannot be contacted by its name but can be contacted using its IP address, there is a DNS problem. `nslookup` can make troubleshooting these types of problems easier. To see this tool in action, bring up a command prompt and type `nslookup http://www.pearsonhighered.com` and press [Enter]. The IP address of the Pearson web server appears. Type `quit` to return to the command prompt.

The **`tracert`** command is also a commonly used tool. The `tracert` command is used to display the path a packet takes through the network. The benefit of using the `tracert` command is that you can see where a fault is occurring in a larger network. You can also see the network latency. Network latency is the delay measured from source to destination.

The following list contains methods that can help with NIC troubleshooting:

- From a command prompt window, use `ping localhost` to test the NIC.
- `ping` another device on the same network.
- `ping` the default gateway.
- `ping` a device on a remote network.

- Use the `tracert` command to see if the fault is inside or outside the company.
- Check the status light on the NIC to see if the physical connection is good. Different NICs have different colored lights, but the two most common colors used with status lights to indicate a good connection are green and orange. Some status lights indicate the speed at which the NIC is operating (10Mbps, 100Mbps, or 1Gbps).
- Check the status light on the hub or switch that is used to connect the workstation NIC to the network. Green is a common color for a good connection on these devices.
- Check cabling. Even though the status lights may indicate that the connection is good, the cabling can still be faulty.
- Update the device driver by obtaining a newer one from the NIC manufacturer website.
- Check the IP addressing used. Use the `ipconfig` command from a prompt to ensure the NIC has an IP address assigned. If you get a duplicate IP address error message, change the IP addressing to DHCP or another statically assigned (not used already) address.
- If on laptop, ensure that the wireless NIC is enabled. Look for a button or a keystroke combination that re-enables the wireless antenna, as well as ensuring the NIC is not disabled in the *Network Connections* (XP) or *Network and Sharing Center* (Vista/7) *Control Panel* link > *Change adapter settings* link.
- If your network connection shows limited connectivity or you cannot reach the Internet at all, try rebooting the PC (because of a 169.254.x.x address) or the router (if in a home or small business network). If this is a wireless connection, check security settings, the wireless button that controls the wireless antenna, or a wireless Fn key that toggles the wireless NIC. If wired, the cable could be an issue.
- If the network connection is intermittent or slow on a wireless connection, move closer to the AP, change position of the wireless device, or add another AP in the area to extend the wireless network. If on a wired connection, check cabling and duplex settings. Replace a hub with a switch.

Network Printer Troubleshooting

To begin troubleshooting a network printer, do all the things that are normally done when troubleshooting a local printer. Check the obvious things first. Does the printer have power? Is the printer online? Does the printer have paper? Are the printer's connector(s) secured tightly? Is the correct printer driver loaded? If all of these normal troubleshooting steps check out correctly, the following list can help with networked printers:

- Print a test page and see if the printer's IP address outputs or see if the printer is labeled with its IP address. If so, `ping` the printer's IP address to see if there is network connectivity between the computer and the printer. Use the `tracert` command to see if there is a complete network path to the printer.
- Check the printer's *Properties* page to see if the printer has been paused.
- Cancel any print jobs in the print queue and resubmit the print job.
- Reset the printer by powering it off and back on. If it connects to a print server device, reset it too.
- If the printer has never worked, try a different version of the print driver.

Network Terminology

In the networking field, there are a great many acronyms and terms with which you must be familiar. Table 14.20 shows a few of the most common terms.

Table 14.20 Common network terms

Term	Description
ARP (Address Resolution Protocol)	In order to send a message using the TCP/IP protocol stack, a computer needs four key addresses: source IP, source MAC, destination IP, and destination MAC. Of course the computer sending the message knows the source IP and MAC addresses. When the computer does not know the destination MAC address, but knows the destination IP address, ARP (Layer 2 protocol) is used to discover that MAC address.
Backbone	The part of the network that connects multiple buildings, floors, networks, and so on together.
Bandwidth	The width of a communications channel that defines its capacity for data. Examples include up to 56Kbps for analog modems, 64 to 128Kbps for ISDN and up to 100Gbps for an Ethernet network.
Baseband	The entire cable bandwidth is used to transmit a digital signal. Because LANs use baseband, there must be an access method used to determine when a network device is allowed to transmit (token passing or CSMA/CD).
Broadband	Cable bandwidth is divided into multiple channels. On these channels, simultaneous voice, video, and data can be sent.
CDMA (Code Division Multiple Access)	A protocol used in cellular networks as an alternative to GSM.
FastEthernet	An extension of the original Ethernet standard that permits data transmission of 100Mbps. FastEthernet uses CSMA/CD just like the original Ethernet standard.
FDDI (Fiber Distributed Data Interface)	A high-speed fiber network that uses the ring topology and the token passing method of access.
GSM (Global System Mobile)	The most widely used digital technology for cellular networks.
HTML (Hypertext Markup Language)	The programming language used on the Internet for creating web pages.
ICMP (Internet Control Message Protocol)	A Layer 3 protocol used when troubleshooting or evaluating networks. The `ping`, `pathping`, and `tracert` commands use ICMP.
Infrared	Infrared is used with wireless keyboards, mice, presentation pointers, and other input devices. A few laptop computers have infrared ports that allow them to communicate with other devices (such as another computer or printer) across a wireless network. The common term used with this is IrDA (Infrared Serial Data Link).
NAT/PAT (Network Address Translation/ Port Address Translation)	A method of conserving IP addresses. NAT uses private IP addresses that become translated to public IP addresses. PAT does the same thing except uses fewer public IP addresses by "overloading" one or more public IP addresses by tracking port numbers.
POP (Point of Presence)	A POP is an Internet access point. Note that POP also means Post Office Protocol) which is covered in the next section.
SSL (Secure Sockets Layer)	A protocol used to transmit Internet messages securely. This protocol is used with HTTPS and online shopping websites to secure credit card information.

Term	Description
TCP (Transmission Control Protocol)	A connection-oriented protocol that ensures reliable communication between two devices. TCP and UDP are the two most common transport-layer protocols. TCP is used when a connection needs to be made, and if the data is not received, the data is resent. Website connections and some file transfer protocols use TCP.
Telnet	An unsecure application that allows connection to a remote network device. Use SSH instead.
UDP (User Datagram Protocol)	A Layer 4 connectionless protocol that applications use to communicate with a remote device. TCP and UDP are the two most common transport-layer protocols. UDP is used when a connection is not that important, low overhead is needed (the UDP header is a lot smaller than a TCP header) or when speed is of the essence. VoIP and DHCP use UDP at Layer 4.
VoIP (Voice over IP)	A method of sending a phone conversation using network connectivity instead of traditional telephone circuits and wiring. This can include connectivity through the Internet. VoIP can be implemented by installing software on your computer and using speakers or headphones and an integrated or external microphone. Another method can use special network-enabled phones that connect to an RJ-45 jack on your DSL or cable modem the same way your computer connects. In businesses, VoIP phones connect to an RJ-45 data jack that is wired to a network switch. Figure 14.53 shows a Cisco IP phone.

Figure 14.53 Cisco IP phone

The TCP/IP Model in Action

To see the TCP/IP model in action, imagine opening a web browser with two separate windows: http://www.pearsoned.com and http://www.google.com. Two separate packages of data would be formed. For example, since HTTP data is being sent, HTTP will specify how the data is to be formatted at the application layer. So, web page 1 gets HTTP data at the application layer and moves down to the transport layer (inside the computer). At the transport layer, TCP is used for HTTP traffic, and TCP adds a source port number 51116 and a destination port number 80 as part of building the transport-layer header. All this HTTP and TCP information moves down to the Internet layer, where IP adds a source and destination IP address. Because Pearson Education's web server has the IP address 74.125.47.99, that is the destination IP address. The packet continues moving down the model to the network access layer, and because the LAN is an Ethernet LAN, a source MAC address and destination MAC address are added. The data and all the headers are placed onto the Ethernet cable and sent on their way. The same thing happens with the second web page, except that at the transport layer, TCP adds port number 51117 and destination port number 80.

Tech Tip

Use `netstat` to view current connections

To see current connections and associated port numbers, bring up a command prompt and type `netstat`.

When the Pearson Education web server delivers the web page to the computer, the data is, of course, from the web server, but the TCP port numbers are reversed. The web server places port number 80 as the source port number and port number 51116 as the destination port number. The source and destination IP addresses and MAC addresses are reversed as well. When the original computer gets the message, it knows which browser window generated port number 51116, and it places the Pearson Education information from the web server into the correct browser window. The same is true when the Google request comes back from the Google web server. TCP/IP-based protocols are required to send and receive data through the Internet. Table 14.21 shows some of the most popular protocols, a description, and the TCP/IP port number commonly used. Table 14.22 has some of the common protocols or network standards and the TCP/IP model layer at which they operate.

Table 14.21 TCP/IP protocols and port numbers

Protocol	Common port number	Description
DNS (Domain Name System)	53	Translation of Internet names and URLs into IP addresses
FTP (File Transfer Protocol)	20/21	Sending/receiving of files from one computer to another network device
HTTP (Hypertext Transfer Protocol)	80	Browser-based Internet communication standard
HTTPS (HTTP over SSL (Secure Sockets Layer))	443	Encrypted HTTP communication through an SSL session
IMAP (Internet Message Access Protocol)	143	Email retrieval
LDAP (Lightweight Directory Access Protocol)	389	Used to access, maintain, and distribute directory/database-type information

Protocol	Common port number	Description
MAPI (Messaging Application Programming Interface)	N/A	Microsoft-proprietary protocol normally used with MAPI/RPC (Remote Procedure Call) for Microsoft Outlook to communicate with a Microsoft Exchange server. RPC uses a dynamically assigned port number.
NTP (Network Time Protocol)	123	Used to synchronize time between network devices
POP3 (Post Office Protocol version 3)	110	Email retrieval
RDP (Remote Desktop Protocol)	3389	Microsoft protocol used to connect to a remote computer
SFTP (Secure File Transfer Protocol)	22	File transfer, using the SSH protocol suite
SMB (Server Message Block)	445	A means of providing access to shared network devices and files
SMTP (Simple Mail Transfer Protocol)	25	Used to transmit email and commonly uses in conjunction with MIME (Multipurpose Internet Mail Extensions) to include non-ASCII character sets and other rich media content within the email.
SNMP (Simple Network Management Protocol)	161/162 or 10161/10162	Used to monitor, communicate with, and manage network devices
SSH (Secure Shell)	22	A means of secure data communication including remote connectivity of devices and file transfer
Telnet	23	Used to connect to a remote network device; is not secure

Table 14.22 TCP/IP layers and associated protocols/standards

Layer	Protocols
Application	HTTP, HTTPS, Telnet, SSH, FTP, SFTP, DNS
Transport	TCP, UDP
Internet (Internetwork)	IP, DHCP, ICMP
Network access	ARP, 802.3 (Ethernet), 802.11 a, b, g, and n (wireless)

Sharing

When you double-click the *My Network Places/Network* desktop icon, you can view other network devices by their assigned names. You can also view them by typing `nbtstat -n` at a command prompt. Knowing a network device name is important when accessing a network share across the network. A **network share** is a folder or device that has been shared and is accessible from a remote computer.

The command prompt can also be used to access network shares by typing the computer name and the share name using the UNC (Universal Naming Convention). For example, a computer called *CSchmidt* has a network share called *TESTS*. By typing `\\CSchmidt\TESTS` at the command prompt, you can access the network share. Figure 14.54 shows the *Sharing* tab.

Tech Tip

How to share a folder

To share a folder, use *Computer* or *Explorer*. Locate the folder to be shared and right-click it > *Properties* > *Sharing* tab > *Share* or *Advanced Sharing* button. In the *Advanced Sharing* > *Share Name* text box, type a name for the network share. This name appears in Windows Explorer—My Network Places (XP) or *Network* (Vista/7)—on other computers when accessed across the network.

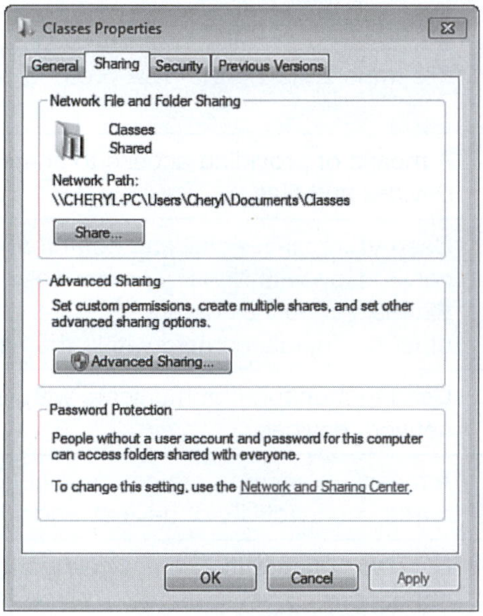

In a network, it is common to map a drive letter to a frequently used network share. To map a drive letter to a network share, click the *Start* button > *Computer* (Vista/7) > *Map Network Drive* > select a drive letter in the *Drive* box > in the *Folder* text box, type the UNC for the network share or use the *Browse* button to select the network share. The *Reconnect at Logon* check box allows you to connect to the mapped drive every time you log on. Figure 14.55 shows the windows to map drive letter `z:` to the shared folder called *Book*.

Figure 14.54 Windows 7 Sharing tab

Tech Tip

Mapping from a prompt

A drive can be mapped from a command prompt. Use the `net /?` command for more help. For example, a computer with the name *TECH01* has a share called *Cheryl*. The following command can be used to attach to it using the drive letter `M:`

```
net use m: /persistent:yes \\TECH01\Cheryl
```

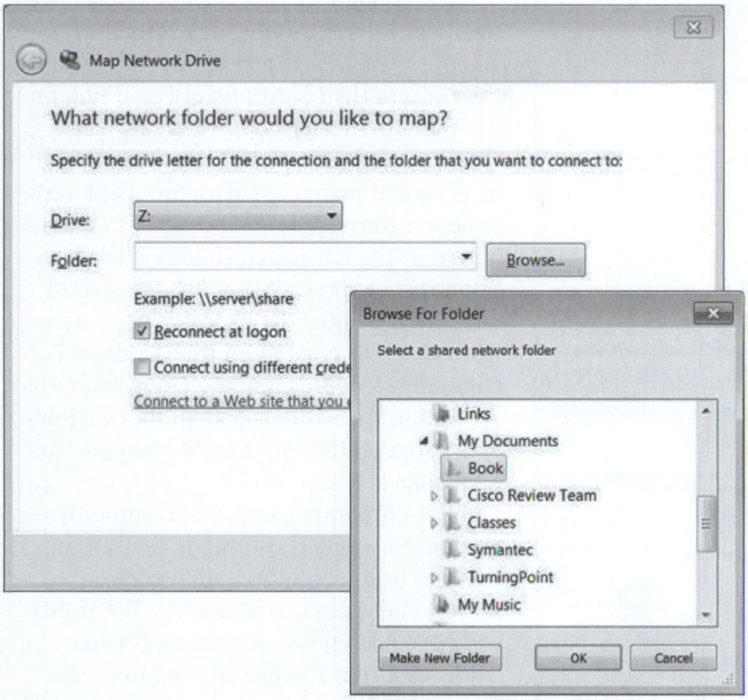

Figure 14.55 Windows 7 Map Network Drive window

Computer users commonly have network shares mapped to a drive letter for frequently used network shares. It is faster to access a network share by drive letter than by searching around for the share through *My Network Places* (XP) or *Network* (Vista/7).

Windows 7 makes it easier to create a network at home with the HomeGroup option. Be aware, though, that Windows 7 Starter and Home Basic versions can join but not create a homegroup. To access the HomeGroup Wizard to create or join a network, click the *Start* button > *Control Panel* > *Network and Internet* link > *HomeGroup*. Part of the process is to create a password that is used to add other computers to the homegroup. Another part of the configuration process is to determine what to share such as pictures, music, videos, documents, and printers. These particular libraries are then made available to other computers on the same network. Figure 14.56 shows the process for a computer to join a homegroup.

If Windows XP or Vista computers need to access information from a Windows 7 computer that is on a HomeGroup network, then access the *User* Control Panel link on the Windows 7 computer to create a new *Standard user* account. Then, from the XP or Vista computer, use Windows Explorer to access the *Network/My Network Places* option in the left panel. Double-click the Windows 7 computer that has the shared documents. Enter the username and password that was created on the Windows 7 computer. Double-click the *Users* share that appears in the window and all file and folders shared on the Windows 7 computer are accessible.

For corporate users, you commonly must use a domain username (a username that has been configured on a centralized server) and a domain password. The rights you have been given determine the network resources you are allowed to access. A common parameter that must be entered when logging into a domain or a corporate resources is a username and password. Commonly, the domain name must also be specified. If a company domain called GoBig had a user with the username JTech (who had the password 5tay-ouT), Joe Tech might be prompted for a username and password and have to type GoBig\JTech for the username because the DOMAIN\Username format specifies the domain and then the appropriate user ID, followed by the appropriate password in the password textbox.

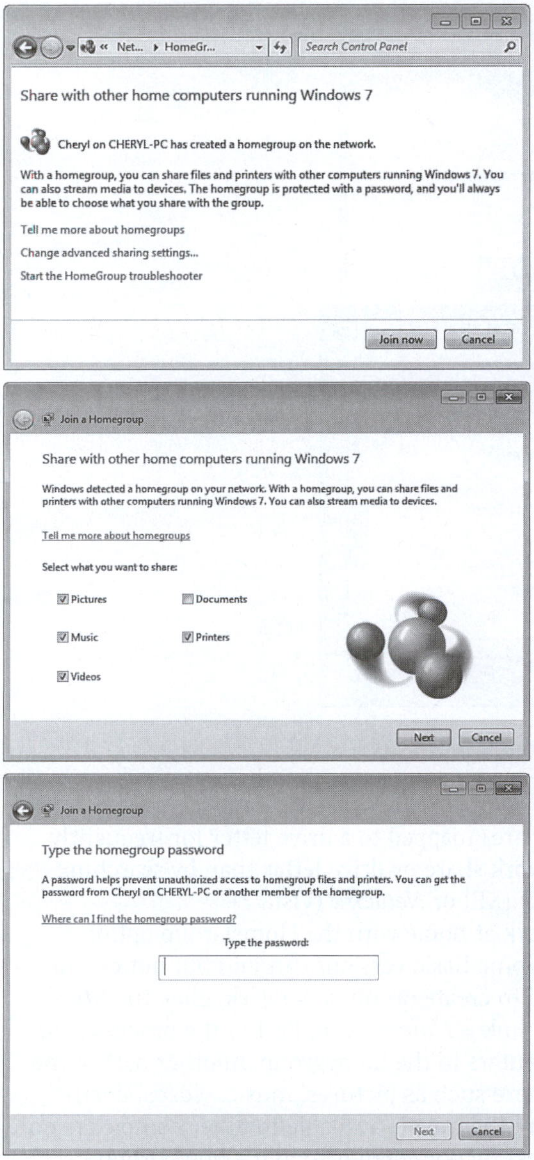

Figure 14.56 Homegroup configuration

Email

Another common Internet software application is an email (electronic mail) application to send messages across the Internet. Microsoft Live Mail and Outlook are two examples. Another popular freeware email software program is Eudora Light. Many Internet providers also have their own email package.

When you send an email message to someone, your email client software formats the message and sends it to an email server. The email server has the following functions:

- Has a database of email accounts
- Stores messages (email) sent and received
- Communicates with other email servers
- Uses the DNS protocol to locate the other servers

Remember that a DNS server keeps a database of locations and can contact a higher-level DNS server if a location is unknown.

A technician must be familiar with troubleshooting browser and email applications. A good place to start is with the user ID and password, POP3, and SMTP settings. To configure a mobile device for email, see the "Mobile Apps" section later in the chapter.

Forwarding email

To configure a particular application such as Google Gmail to be forwarded to another application such as Outlook, key information must be gathered: (1) a list of protocols used to send and receive email such as IMAP, SMTP, POP3, and SSL; and (2) associated protocol port numbers. The technician must then go into the email application and configure an incoming mail server and an outgoing mail server settings, based on the gathered information.

Tech Tip

Network Connectivity

Most people are familiar with wired and wireless network, but there are many methods used to create a network, especially a network that gets you into a building. The type of connection, protocol, and settings that you configure on the remote computer depends on the company to which you are connecting. A connection protocol used with dial-up networking is PPP. PPP (Point-to-Point Protocol) is a connection-oriented Layer 2 protocol that encapsulates data for transmission over various connection types.

Before creating a remote connection, you should always determine what parameters are to be entered *before* starting the configuration. Contact the network administrator for exact details on how to configure the remote connection. If the connection is to the Internet via an ISP, detailed instructions are available on the ISP's website and/or with the materials that come with the Internet package from the ISP.

There are many types of network connections. Businesses use various types of network connections leased from the local phone company or a provider. Table 14.23 shows the types of network connections and bandwidth.

Table 14.23 Network connection types

Connection type	Speed
POTS (Plain Old Telephone Service)	2400bps to 115Kbps analog phone line to perform dial-up networking
ISDN (Integrated Services Digital Network)	Another method for dial-up networking—64Kbps to 1.544Mbps digital line
Frame Relay	56K to 1.544Mbps
56K point to point	56K guaranteed bandwidth between two points
T1	1.544Mbps guaranteed bandwidth between two points
T3	44Mbps guaranteed bandwidth between two points
DSL (Digital Subscriber Line)	256Kbps and higher; shares data line with voice line
Broadband cable or satellite	56Kbps (broadband satellite) to 30Mbps and higher
ATM (Asynchronous Transfer Mode)	Up to 2Gbps
MetroE (MetroEthernet)	Speeds of 1, 10, 40, or 100Gbps, using Ethernet technology to connect to the Internet or connect multiple sites/buildings

Mobile Device Network Connectivity

Mobile devices would be useless if they could not connect to a network. This section explores common network connectivity options, including 802.11-based wireless networks, cellular network, and GPS connectivity. Also, since a network is commonly used to get apps (applications) downloaded and installed on mobile devices, we explore network apps, device synchronization, and app configuration.

Note that because Android devices are created using an open source operating system, configuration options can be different from one device to another. By default, when most mobile devices are configured for wireless networks, the device will connect. If you walk out of range of that wireless network and another one is configured, the device will switch over to the second wireless network. If no wireless networks are within range, the mobile device will swap over to the cellular network if you are connected to the network. Table 14.24 has the basic connectivity configuration options for Android and Apple iOS devices. Note that Airplane mode disables all types of connectivity. In this mode, you could still view a movie or play a game without Internet, cellular, or wireless connectivity.

Table 14.24 Mobile device network configuration options

Connectivity method and device	Path
802.11 wireless—Android	Settings > Wireless and network(s)
802.11 wireless—Apple iOS	Settings > Wi-Fi
Bluetooth network—Android	Settings > Wireless and network(s) > Bluetooth settings
Bluetooth network—Apple iOS	Settings > Bluetooth
Cellular network—Android	Settings > Wireless and network(s) > Mobile networks
Cellular network—Apple iOS	Settings > General > Cellular Data
GPS—Android	Settings > Location services or Location and security > Use GPS satellites
GPS—Apple iOS	Settings > Location
Airplane mode—Android	Settings > Wireless and network(s) > Flight mode or Airplane mode
Airplane mode—Apple iOS	Settings > Airplane Mode

Mobile Apps

Mobile devices most commonly use a wireless, cellular, or Bluetooth network to install apps from Google Play or Market, Apple's App Store or iTunes, Amazon's App Store, and a host of other content sources, but there are other ways to get an app: manually install (side load), use a USB cable (commonly requires a file management app), use your storage media and a media reader, use an app such as Bump to transfer an application (or photos), or through a QR (Quick Response) code between two devices (see Figure 14.57). Note that whatever method you use to install an app, you must ensure that the app is from a trusted source or a trusted app developer. Be sure to see what permissions are given when an app is installing. Table 14.25 shows tasks that are commonly done with apps.

Figure 14.57 QR code

Table 14.25 Mobile device tasks*

Task	Platform	Description
Delete an app	Android	Press and hold the app icon and drag it to the trash can
Delete an app	iOS	Press and hold the app icon until it jiggles and press the X that appears beside the icon. Press the menu key to stop the jiggling.
Stop an app	Android	Settings > Applications > Manage applications > tap the specific application name > tap Force stop
Force an app to close	iOS	Touch and hold the app icon until it jiggles. Tap the circle icon that has a bar across it.
Move an app icon	Android/iOS	Press and hold the app icon until it jiggles and drag the icon to another location. If the location is another home screen, hold the icon on the edge of the screen until the new location appears.
Create a folder to hold apps	Android	Press an empty part of the home screen and select folder. To move an item to the folder, press and drag the icon into the folder.
Create a folder to hold apps	iOS	Press and hold the app icon until it jiggles. Drag the icon onto another app icon. A folder is created that contains both icons. Other icons can now be added.

*Because Android is open source, the exact steps may vary. Also, Apple iOS is constantly being updated/upgraded.

Some apps have data that can be synchronized with other devices. Examples include the following:

- Contacts
- Programs
- Email
- Photos
- Music
- Videos
- Files

iTunes is used to synchronize data between Apple iOS devices and Windows computers. You can connect to iTunes using a wireless network or the cellular network. A USB cable can also be used to connect two devices and synchronize them.

iTunes can also be used to manage and restore iOS devices when they are registered (activated) with Apple. The version of iTunes requires the following hardware and software requirements (as of press date):

- 1GHz processor
- 512MB RAM
- Windows XP (SP2) or higher

iTunes has a 64-bit version for 64-bit Windows operating systems. There is no such application for Android devices. The individual app may support synchronization with Google. You can view and add apps by using the *Settings* > *Personal* (which is not used on some Android devices) > *Accounts and sync* or whatever method used by the particular application.

Because mobile devices have limited storage capacity compared to other computing devices, remote backup of data is important. Apple provides 5GB of free storage (at press time) with iCloud. You can use iCloud to back up things like your contacts, calendar, ringtones, photos/videos, and data. Google provides backup of the calendar, mail, and contacts. Other cloud storage vendors, such as Google, DropBox, and SugarSync, provide free cloud storage. There are apps provided to manage your backup. Some apps support cloud storage. With cloud storage, you can store your photos, images, files, app data, and so on, and your app will look to that storage (if you have configured it so) for the data.

Email configuration for a mobile device includes knowing quite a bit of technical information (as it does when you forward email from one application to another). An Android device comes with Gmail. If you have a Gmail account, you can use it to begin configuration of the phone or tablet. Otherwise, a Gmail account will be created. To configure an Android device for an email account, perform the following generic steps (keeping in mind the open source nature of Android):

1. At the home screen, tap the *Email* icon.
2. Enter an email address and password > *Next*.
3. Select the type of account and enter the account specifics such as domain and server name > *Next*.

Tech Tip

Email no current on your smartphone?

Check Internet connectivity. If you have Internet access, power off the phone then power the phone back on again.

For Apple iOS devices, the Apple iCloud option can be used to provide email and store iOS and content. iCloud is normally configured as part of the initial configuration of an Apple iOS device. If not, use the *Settings* > *iCloud* option to do so. Other email accounts can be configured on an iOS device, using the following steps:

1. At the home screen, tap the *Settings* icon.
2. Select *Mail, Contacts, Calendars*.
3. Select *Add Account*.
4. Select the type of service (Exchange, Gmail, iCloud, Yahoo, AOL, Microsoft Hotmail, or Other).
5. Provide the necessary connection information for the selected service.
6. Tap *Save*.

A technician may be required to configure mobile devices for corporate users. Part of the email configuration might include protocols such as IMAP, SMTP, POP3, and SSL, as well as the associated protocol port numbers used on the company's servers. A technician would have to obtain this information from the network staff.

Soft Skills—Being Proactive

A good technician is proactive, which means that the technician thinks of ways to improve a situation and anticipates problems and fixes them before being told to. A proactive technician follows up after a service call to ensure that a repair fixed the problem rather than waiting for another help desk ticket that states that the problem is unresolved. When something like a theft or a problem with a customer occurs, a proactive technician provides a list of recommended solutions or procedural changes to the supervisor rather than waits for the supervisor to delineate what changes must occur.

For example, consider a technician at a college. The technician is responsible for any problems logged by computer users through the help desk. The technician is also responsible for maintaining the computer classrooms used by various departments. Each term, the technician reloads the computers with software updates and changes requested by the teachers. A proactive technician checks each machine and ensures that the computer boots properly and that the load is successful. The technician does not wait for the first day of the term or for a teacher to report a problem to the help desk.

Another example involves checking new software. When the computers are reloaded each term, a faculty member is asked to check the load. A proactive technician has a list of "standard" software loaded on the computer such as the operating system, service pack level, and any applications that are standard throughout the college. A separate list would include the changes that were applied to the computer. Then the faculty member can simply look at the list and verify the load. Being proactive actually saves the technician and the faculty member time each term.

The opposite of being proactive is being reactive. A reactive technician responds to situations only when there is a problem. The technician is not looking for ways to avoid problems. For example, a proactive technician ensures a computer is configured for automatic updates of virus scanning software. A reactive technician waits until a help desk ticket is created for a computer that exhibits unusual behavior (it has a virus).

As a student, practice being proactive with your life. Start an assignment a day before you would normally start it. Talk to your teacher about your grade in advance (before the day preceding the final). Bring a pencil and paper to school (don't wait until you arrive at school to realize that you don't have them and have to borrow from someone).

Chapter Summary

- Networks are created to share data and devices and connect to the Internet. Types of networks include PANs, LANs, MANs, and WANs.
- Networks can be wired or wireless. Wired networks use copper (UTP, STP, and coaxial) or fiber-optic media.
- A peer-to-peer network is composed of a small number of computers, whereas the client/server type of network is used in companies in a domain environment. A domain environment has a server that provides authentication to resources with a centralized user ID and password. A peer-to-peer network manages the usernames on a computer-by-computer basis, which is grows less secure and more difficult to manage as the network grows.
- Ethernet is the most common type of LAN, and it is wired in a star or extended star topology. A hub or switch is used to connect the devices. Each network connects to a router for communication with other networks. The router's IP address is the default gateway for all network devices on a particular LAN.
- Computers must have IP addresses to participate in a TCP/IP-based network (and gain access to the Internet). IPv4 is the most common addressing used on computers today, but IPv6 addresses are slowly being assigned and used by corporate devices and Internet providers.
- IP addresses are grouped by classes, with a particular subnet mask for each class. Each default mask can be changed to further subdivide a network for more efficient and manageable addressing. DHCP can be used to provide addresses to network devices or a static address can be assigned. Public addresses are routable on the Internet. Private addresses are used within homes and companies. These addresses can be translated using NAT/PAT to public addresses.
- TCP/IP is a suite of protocols that includes the following important ones: FTP, Telnet, SMTP, DNS, HTTP, HTTPS, POP3, IMAP, RDP, DNS, LDAP, SNMP, SSH, SFTP, TCP, UDP, IP, and ICMP.
- The OSI model is a theoretical model with seven layers: application, presentation, session, transport, network, data link, and physical. The TCP/IP model is a working model and contains four layers: application, transport, internet (internetwork), and network access. Common application protocols include TFTP, FTP, SFTP, Telnet, SMTP, DNS, HTTP, HTTPS, POP3, LDAP, DNS, SNMP, and SSH. The device and applications that work at Layer 3 (network or internet layers) include a router, IP, and ICMP. The devices and applications that work at Layer 2 (data link or network access) include a switch, access point, and ARP. Keep in mind that Ethernet has Layer 2 specifications. That is why a MAC address is a Layer 2 address. The devices that work at Layer 1 (physical or network access) are cable, connectors, hubs, and wireless antennas.
- 802.11 and Bluetooth are types of wireless networks. Bluetooth is used in PANs, and 802.11 is used in wireless LANs. 802.11 wireless NICs include 802.11a, b, g, and n. 802.11a and n work in the 5GHz range; 802.11b, g, and n work in the 2.4GHz range. 802.11 antennas are either directional or omnidirectional.
- The key tools for troubleshooting a networked computer are the `ipconfig`, `ping`, `nslookup`, `tracert` commands, and a cable tester.
- To configure email on any device, you need to know certain parameters, such as the protocol used, the application used, the username, the password, the domain, SSL settings, and port numbers.
- Mobile devices are commonly configured for Bluetooth, cellular, and 802.11-based networks, and apps are installed using the networks. Some items are automatically backed up by Google for Android devices and Apple iCloud for iOS devices. iTunes is used to synchronize and update Apple iOS photos, music, movies, and operating systems.
- A technician should be proactive as opposed to reactive and should prevent problems and situations whenever possible.

Key Terms

Review Questions

1. Match the network type on the left with the scenario on the right.

____ MAN	a. Home network of four PCs
____ LAN	b. City of Schmidtville networks
____ PAN	c. Hewlett-Packard corporate networks
____ WAN	d. Bluetooth network of two devices

2. Match the following:

a. CAT 3 UTP	____ Common type of LAN cable
b. CAT 5e UTP	____ Delivers TV stations inside a home
c. Coax	____ Voice-grade phone network cable
d. Fiber	____ Backbone cable

3. When installing UTP, what is the most common mistake technicians make?

4. Match the TCP/IP model layer to the description. Note that a layer can be used more than once.

a. Application	____ HTTP	____ a straight-through cable	____ a NIC
b. Transport	____ a router	____ UDP	____ DNS
c. Internet	____ a switch	____ IP	____ TCP
d. Network access	____ ICMP	____ MAC address	____ a wireless antenna

5. Explain the difference between half-duplex and full-duplex transmissions.

6. What does the *100* mean in the term 100BaseT?
7. Which network device works at Layer 1 and sends received data out all its ports (except the port that received the data)?
8. What is the most common network protocol suite and the protocol suite required to communicate on the Internet?
9. Which type of address is 48 bits long?
10. Which type of address is called a Layer 3 address?
11. Which type of IP address uses 128 bits? [IPv4 | IPv32 | IPv6 | IPv64]
12. Draw a vertical line between the network number and the host number for each of the following IP addresses (assuming the default subnet mask):

    141.2.195.177

    193.162.183.5

    100.50.70.80
13. What protocol could be used to issue an IP address to network devices? [DNS | DHCP | ICMP | ARP]
14. What protocol is used to convert URLs to IP addresses? [HTTP | SSH | SSL | UDP | DNS]
15. Two access points connect and extend *the same* wireless network. List the SSIDs for each access point in the following chart:

Access point	SSID
Access Point 1	
Access Point 2	

16. Two access points (AP1 and AP2) operating in the 2.4GHz range have overlapping coverage areas. List the two channel IDs to assign to each access point by filling in the following chart:

Access point	Channel ID
AP1	
AP2	

17. [T | F] When communicating with an access point, a wireless NIC and an access point must be configured to the same frequency.

18. Match the following definitions. Note that not all options on the right are used.

____ 802.11a	a. Operates in the 2.4GHz range, with speeds up to 54Mbps
____ 802.11b	b. Operates in the 2.4GHz range, with speeds up to 2Mbps
____ 802.11g	c. Operates in the 2.4GHz range, with speeds up to 11Mbps
____ 802.11i	d. Security specification
____ 802.11n	e. Operates in the 5GHz range, with speeds up to 54Mbps
	f. Specifies interoperability between access points
	g. Standard for quality of service
	h. Standard for wireless interference
	i. Backward compatible with 802.11a, b, and g

19. Reference Figure 14.58. What IP address is the default gateway for host 203.145.15.2?

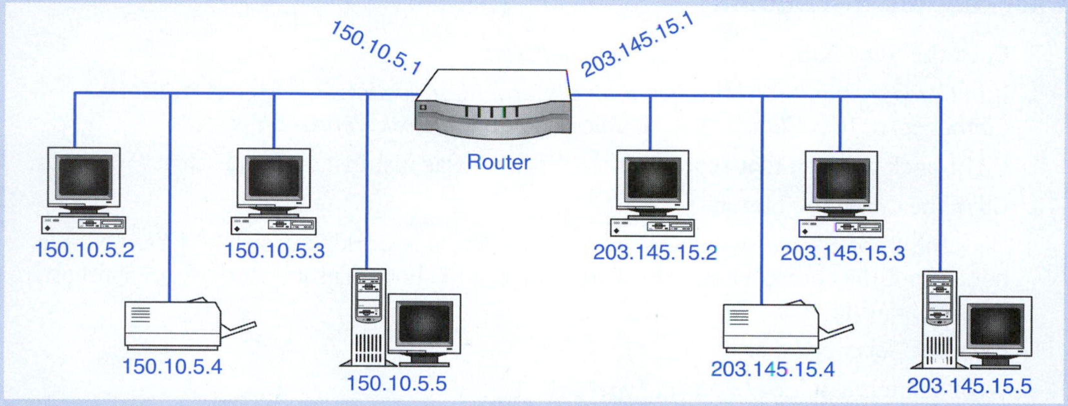

Figure 14.58 Network scenario

20. What command is used to determine whether another network device is reachable?

Exercises

Lab 14.1 Installing and Configuring a NIC Using Windows XP

Objective: To be able to configure a NIC using Windows XP

Parts: Computer with Windows XP installed
NIC adapter
Optional NIC driver disk or CD

Note: The method used to install a NIC in Windows XP is vendor specific. Follow the NIC manufacturer's instructions when installing a NIC. The directions given below are generic for most adapters. Also, you must have rights to install hardware on the computer. Check with the lab assistant or instructor if the computer will not allow hardware to be installed.

Procedure: Complete the following procedure and answer the accompanying questions.

Installing a NIC

1. If possible, download the latest driver for the NIC to be installed later in the exercise.
2. Power off the computer and remove the computer's power cord.
3. Remove the computer cover and install the NIC into an available expansion slot. Use proper ESD precautions when installing an adapter.
4. Re-install the computer's power cord and power on the computer. If necessary, log on to Windows XP using the appropriate user ID and password.
5. Windows XP recognizes that new hardware has been installed and starts the *Found New Hardware* Wizard.
6. Insert any CD or disk that came with the NIC, if available. Follow the prompts on the screen. Windows XP may have a driver for the NIC if one is not available. If not, use the downloaded driver. A NIC cannot operate without a driver. Once the wizard completes, click the *Finish* button. The computer may have to be reloaded.

Checking the Installation

7. Click the *Start* button and select *Control Panel*.
8. If in *Category* view, select *Network and Internet Connections*, and select *Network Connections*. If in *Classic* view, double-click the *Network Connections* icon.
9. Right-click the icon that represents the NIC that was just installed and select *Properties*.
10. Click the *Configure* button.

    Does the *Device Status* window show that the device is working properly? [Yes | No] If not, reboot the computer and check again. If it still shows a problem, perform appropriate troubleshooting.
11. Click the *Advanced* tab.

    What value is assigned to Media Type?
12. Click the *Driver* tab.

    What is the driver version?

    Can the driver be updated from this tab? [Yes | No]

    What is the purpose of the *Roll Back Driver* button?

Lab 14.2 Creating a Straight-Through CAT 5, 5e, or 6 Network Patch Cable

Objective: To create a functional CAT 5, 5e, or 6 UTP network cable

Parts: UTP cable
RJ-45 connectors
Stripper/crimper tool
UTP cable tester

Note: Standard Ethernet networks are cabled with either UTP cable or RG-58 coaxial cable. In this exercise, you create a standard cable for use with Ethernet networks connected through a central hub or switch.

Procedure: Complete the following procedure and answer the accompanying questions.

1. Category 5 UTP cable consists of four twisted pairs of wires, color coded for easy identification. The color-coded wires are colored as follows:

   Pair 1: White/orange and orange

   Pair 2: White/blue and blue

   Pair 3: White/green and green

   Pair 4: White/brown and brown

2. Using the stripper/crimper tool, strip approximately 1/2 inch (1 centimeter) of the protective outer sheath to expose the four twisted pairs of wires. Most strippers have a strip gauge to ensure stripping the proper length. See Figure 14.59.

   Note: In order to make it easier to sort the wire pairs, the sheathing can be stripped farther than 1/2 inch (1 centimeter), and the wires can be sorted properly and trimmed to the proper length.

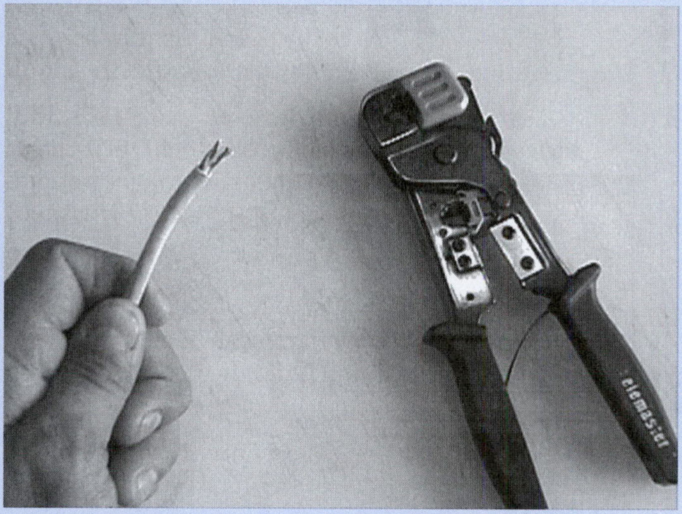

Figure 14.59 **Strip the cable sheathing**

3. Untwist the exposed wire pairs. Be careful that you do not remove more twist than necessary. Sort the wires according to the following:

   Wire 1: White/orange

   Wire 2: Orange

   Wire 3: White/green

   Wire 4: Blue

   Wire 5: White/blue

   Wire 6: Green

   Wire 7: White/brown

   Wire 8: Brown

   Ethernet cable utilizes wires 1, 2, 3, and 6. Using the above wiring scheme means that the cable will use the white/orange-orange and white/green-green wire pairs.

   Will both ends of the cable need to follow the same wiring schematic?

4. Insert the sorted and trimmed cable into an RJ-45 connector. The RJ-45 connector key (tang) should face downward with the open end toward you while you insert the wires. Verify that all eight wires fully insert into the RJ-45 connector and that they are inserted in the proper order. See Figure 14.60.

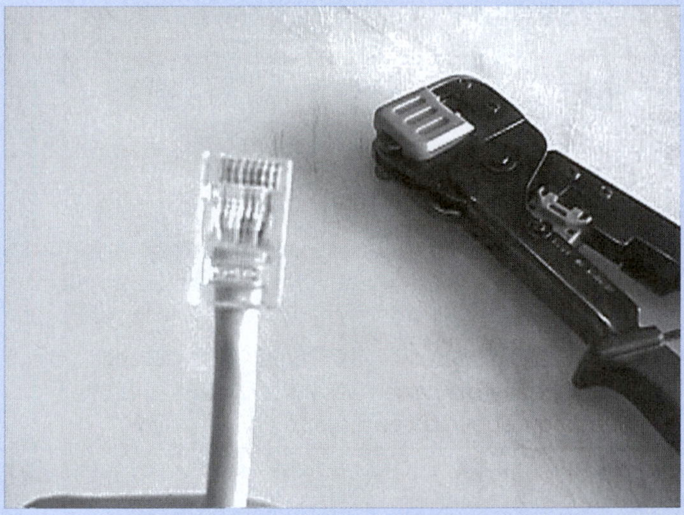

Figure 14.60 **Push wires firmly into the RJ-45 connector in the correct order**

5. Insert the cable-connector assembly into the stripper/crimper tool and crimp the connector firmly. See Figure 14.61.

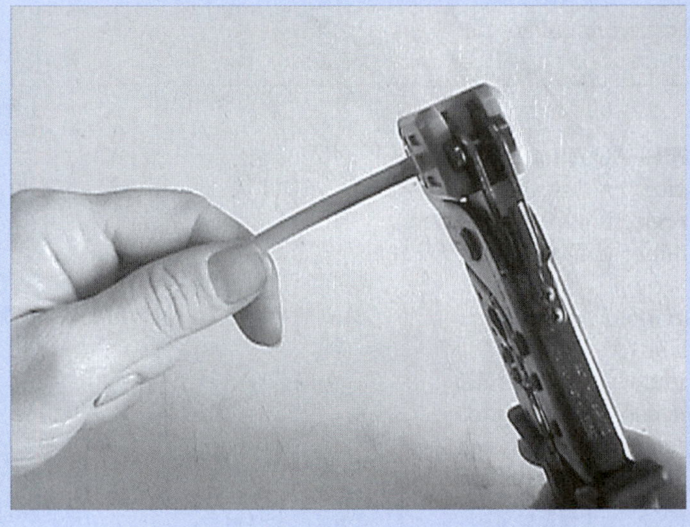

Figure 14.61 **Crimp the RJ-45 connector firmly**

6. Remove the cable/connector assembly from the stripper/crimper tool and verify that the wires fully insert into the connector and that they are in the proper order.
7. Repeat Steps 2 through 6 for the other end of the CAT 5 UTP cable.

   Can the cable be used at this point? [Yes | No]

8. Before using the cable, it should be tested with a cable tester to verify that you have end-to-end continuity on individual wires and proper continuity between wire pairs. Insert the RJ-45 connector into the proper cable tester receptacle and verify that the cable is functional. See Figure 14.62.

Instructor initials: ____________

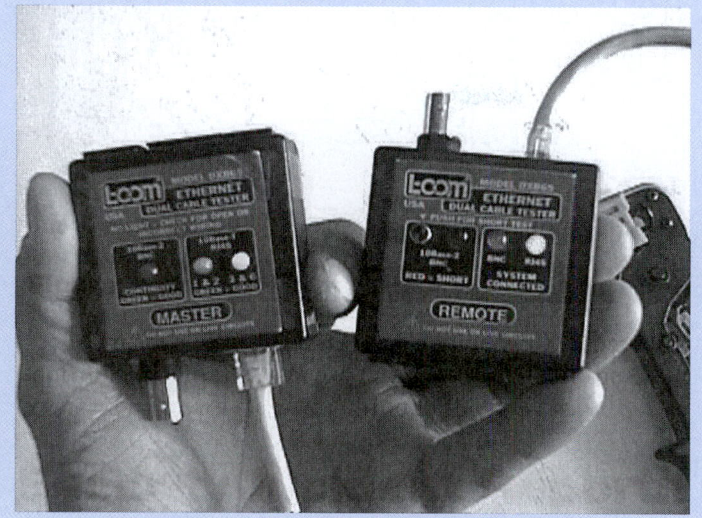

Figure 14.62 Network cable testers

Lab 14.3 Creating a CAT 5, 5e, or 6 Crossover Network Cable

Objective: To create a functional UTP crossover cable

Parts: UTP cable
RJ-45 connectors
Stripper/crimper tool
UTP cable tester

Note: In normal situations, straight-through UTP cable is used to connect to a central hub or switch. In this exercise, you create a crossover cable for use when directly connecting two network devices (computers *without* using a central hub or switch).

Procedure: Complete the following procedure and answer the accompanying questions.

1. Category 5 UTP cable consists of four twisted pairs of wires that are color coded for easy identification. The color-coded wires are as follows:

   Pair 1: White/orange and orange

   Pair 2: White/blue and blue

   Pair 3: White/green and green

   Pair 4: White/brown and brown

2. Using the stripper/crimper tool, strip approximately 1/2 inch (1 centimeter) of the protective outer sheath to expose the four twisted pairs of wires. Most tools have a strip gauge to ensure stripping the proper length.

   Note: In order to make it easier to sort the wire pairs, the sheathing can be stripped farther than 1/2 inch (1 centimeter). The wires can then be sorted properly and trimmed to the proper length.

3. Untwist the exposed wire pairs. Be careful that you do not remove more twist than necessary. Sort the wires as follows:

   Wire 1: White/orange

   Wire 2: Orange

   Wire 3: White/green

Wire 4: Blue

Wire 5: White/blue

Wire 6: Green

Wire 7: White/brown

Wire 8: Brown

Ethernet networks utilize wires 1, 2, 3, and 6. Using the above wiring scheme means the cable will use the white/orange-orange and white/green-green wire pairs.

When making a crossover cable, will both ends of the cable need to follow the same wiring schematic? [Yes | No]

4. Insert the sorted and trimmed cable into an RJ-45 connector. The RJ-45 connector key (tang) should face downward with the open end toward you while you insert the wires. Verify that all eight wires fully insert into the RJ-45 connector, and that they are inserted in the proper order.
5. Insert the cable-connector assembly into the stripper/crimper tool and crimp the connector firmly.
6. Remove the cable/connector assembly from the stripper/crimper tool and verify that the wires are fully inserted into the connector and that they are in the proper order.
7. To create the crossover cable, the wire pairs must be put in a different order. To accomplish this, repeat Steps 2 through 6 on the *opposite* end of the cable, but when sorting the wire pairs, use the following color codes.

Wire 1: White/green	Wire 5: White/blue
Wire 2: Green	Wire 6: Orange
Wire 3: White/orange	Wire 7: White/brown
Wire 4: Blue	Wire 8: Brown

8. Verify both ends of the cables, ensuring that the tang is downward and the colored wires are in the correct order. You can also check the very ends of the connectors to see if you see the tip of the copper wire pushed against the end. See Figure 14.63.

Can the crossover cable be used at this point? [Yes | No]

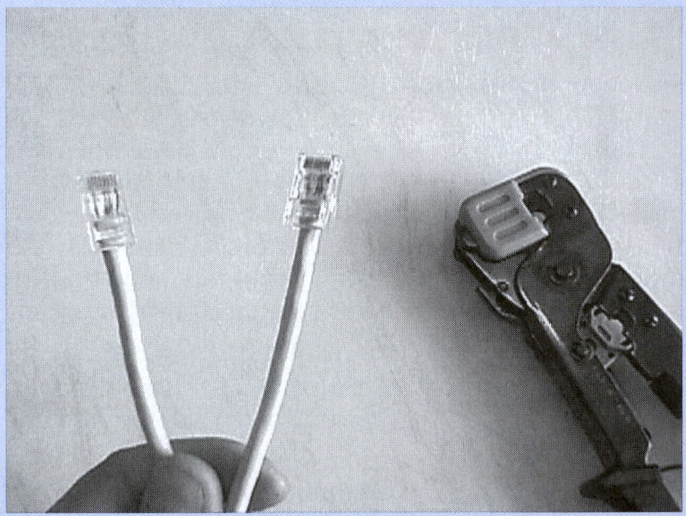

Figure 14.63 Verify the color codes on both connectors

9. Before using the crossover cable, it should be tested with a cable tester. This verifies that you have end-to-end continuity on individual wires and proper continuity between wire pairs. Insert the RJ-45 connector into the proper cable tester receptacle and verify that the cable is functional.

   Note: Your cable tester must have the capability to test crossover cables.

Instructor initials: ____________

Lab 14.4 Networking with Windows 7

Objective: To be able to put two Windows 7 computers into a network workgroup

Parts: Two computers with Windows 7 installed

One crossover cable *or* two straight-through cables and a hub or switch

Procedure: Complete the following procedure and answer the accompanying questions.

1. Power on the first computer and log on to Windows 7, if necessary. Do one of the following: (1) connect a crossover between the two computers NICs or (2) connect a straight-through cable from each computer to the hub or switch and power on the switch.
2. Right-click the *Start* button and select *Open Windows Explorer* (7). Right-click *Computer* in the left pane and select *Properties*. Locate the *Computer name, domain, and workgroup settings* section.

   Document the current settings:

   Original Computer 1 name: ____

   Original Full computer 1 name: ____

   Original Computer 1 description, if entered:______________________________

   Is Computer 1 on a workgroup or domain? [Workgroup | Domain]

   Original workgroup/domain name for Computer 1: ____________________________
3. Select the *Change settings* link to the right of the computer name section. Click *Continue*, if necessary.
4. Select the *Computer Name* tab. Click the *Change* button. Select the *Workgroup* radio button. Name the Workgroup something unique.

   Changed workgroup/domain name: ______________________________
5. Click the *OK* button, and a Computer Name/Domain Changes window appears. Click *OK*. Click the *OK* button when prompted, click *Close*, and click *Restart now*.
6. Power on the second computer and log on to Windows, if necessary.
7. Right-click the *Start* button and select *Explore*. Right-click *Computer* in the left pane and select *Properties*. Locate the *Computer name, domain, and workgroup settings* section.

   Document the current settings:

   Original Computer 2 name: ____

   Original Full computer 2 name: ____

   Original Computer 2 description if entered: ______________________________

   Is Computer 2 on a workgroup or domain? [Workgroup | Domain]

   Original workgroup/domain name for Computer 2: __________________________
8. On the second computer, select the *Change settings* link to the right of the computer name section. Click *Continue*, if necessary.
9. Select the *Computer Name* tab. Click the *Change* button. Select the *Workgroup* radio button.

   Name the Workgroup something unique.

   Changed workgroup/domain name : ________________________________

10. Click the *OK* button, and a Computer Name/Domain Changes window appears. Click *OK*. Click the *OK* button when prompted, click *Close*, and click *Restart now*.
11. When both computers have rebooted, the IP addresses need to be configured manually. On both computers, click the *Start* button > *All Programs* > *Accessories* > *Command prompt*. In the new window type `ipconfig /all`.

    On Computer 1, what is the IPv4 address on the Ethernet adapter?

    On Computer 1, what is the IPv6 address on the Ethernet adapter?

    On Computer 1, what is the subnet mask?

    On Computer 1, what is the default gateway?

    On Computer 1, what is the MAC address?

    On Computer 2, what is the IPv4 address on the Ethernet adapter?

    On Computer 2, what is the IPv6 address on the Ethernet adapter?

    On Computer 2, what is the subnet mask?

    On Computer 2, what is the default gateway?

    On Computer 2, what is the MAC address?

    Who is the network adapter manufacturer for Computer 2?

    How many hexadecimal characters are shown in the Computer 1 IPv6 address?

    How many bits does this represent?
12. Complete this step on both computers. Close the Command Prompt window. Select the *Start* button > *Control Panel* > *Network and Internet* link > *Network and Sharing Center* > *Change advanced sharing settings*.

    Document the current Sharing and Discovery settings for both computers:

	Computer 1	Computer 2
Network discovery	________	________
File sharing	________	________
Public folder sharing	________	________
Printer sharing	________	________
Password protected sharing	________	________
Media sharing/streaming	________	________

13. On both computers from the Network and Sharing Center, select the *Change adapter settings* link from the left menu. Right-click the *Local Area Connection* adapter and select *Properties*. Click *Continue*, if prompted. Locate and select the *Internet Protocol Version 4 (TCP/IPv4)* option. Click *Properties*.

    Document the settings for Computer 1 and Computer 2:

    Computer 1 IP address, mask and default gateway OR obtains an IP address automatically?

    Computer 1 Preferred and alternate DNS server(s) IP addresses OR obtains DNS server address automatically?

    Computer 2 IP address, mask and default gateway OR obtains an IP address automatically?

    Computer 2 Preferred and alternate DNS server(s) IP addresses OR obtains DNS server address automatically?
14. On Computer 1, select the *Use the following IP address* radio button and type in the following information:

    IP address: `192.168.1.1`

    Subnet mask: `255.255.255.0`

    Default gateway: `192.168.1.254`

Click the *OK* button. Click the *Close* button at the bottom of the *Local Area Connection Properties* screen.

15. On Computer 2, select the *Use the following IP address* radio button and type in the following information:

    IP address: `192.168.1.2`

    Subnet mask: `255.255.255.0`

    Default gateway: `192.168.1.254`

    Click the *OK* button. Click the *Close* button at the bottom of the *Local Area Connection Properties* screen.

16. On both computers, using previously described procedures, open a command prompt and verify that the IPv4 address has been applied.

    From a Computer 1 command prompt, type **`ping 192.168.1.2`**.

    What was the response?

17. Access the *Network and Sharing Center* control panel link > *Change advanced sharing settings* link. Configure the following settings:

    - Network discovery > *Turn on network discovery*
    - File and print sharing > *Turn on file and print sharing*
    - Public folder sharing > *Turn on sharing so anyone with network access can read and write files in the public folder*

    Use the *Save changes* button.

18. On Computer 1, using Windows Explorer locate the *Public* folder. Create a text file in the folder called *Surprise.txt* with the following message typed in it:

    `Technology makes it possible for people to gain control over everything, except over technology. -John Tudor`

19. On Computer 2, use Windows Explorer to access the *Network* option from the left pane. In the right pane, double-click the Computer 1 name. Note that if no passwords are assigned to the existing user account, a password will have to be applied to the account on both machines.

20. Double-click the *Public* folder. Double-click the *Public Documents* folder. Open the *Surprise.txt* document. Try modifying the text inside and saving it on Computer 1.

    Were you successful? [Yes | No]

21. Close the *Surprise.txt* document on both computers. From Computer 1, try `ping`ing Computer 2 now.

    Was the **`ping`** successful? [Yes | No]

    Which Network and Sharing Center option that was enabled do you think allowed the **`ping`** through?

    What is a disadvantage to sharing files through the Public folder?

Instructor initials: ____________

22. On both computers, access the *System and Security* (7) *Control Panel* > *Administrative Tools* > *Windows Firewall with Advanced Security* in the right pane. Click *Continue*, if necessary. Select the *Inbound rules* option from the left pane. Expand the *Name* column section by placing the cursor over the dividing line between the *Name* column and the *Group* column. When the cursor turns to a crosshairs symbol, click and drag the line to the right to widen the *Name* column.

    Is the domain profile for *Connect to a Network Projector (TCP-in)* inbound rule enabled? [Yes | No]

    Is *Core Networking—Destination Unreachable (ICMPv6-In)* enabled for any profile? [Yes | No]

What do the green and gray checkmarks on the left indicate?

How many types of network discovery rules are available for selection? [Fewer than 10 | Between 10 and 20 | More than 20]

Is *Remote Assistance* allowed on this computer? [Yes | No] If so, for what profile?

Is *Remote Desktop* allowed on this computer? [Yes | No] If so, for what profile?

Locate the name of the rule that affects the echo request and echo reply ICMP messages for IPv4. Document the name of the rule.

23. Close all windows.
24. Place both computers back in the original workgroup/domain. Refer to Step 7 for the original settings.
25. Configure both computers to the original Sharing and Discovery settings. Refer to Step 12 for the original settings.
26. Place both computers to the original IPv4 IP address, mask, default gateway, and DNS settings. Refer to Step 13 for the original settings. Have a classmate verify the original workgroup/domain settings from Step 7, the Sharing and Discovery settings from Step 12, and the original IPv4 IP address, mask, default gateway, and DNS settings from Step 13.

Classmate printed name ______________________________

Classmate signature ______________________________

27. Remove the cable and put the computers back to the original cabling configuration. Ensure that the computer works and has the same access as it had before you began this lab.

Instructor initials: __________

Lab 14.5 Connecting to a Windows XP/Vista/7 Shared or Networked Printer

Objective: To be able to properly share a printer and use a shared or networked printer using Windows XP/Vista/7

Parts: Two networked computers with a printer attached to one and either Windows XP, Vista, or 7 installed

Procedure: Complete the following procedure and answer the accompanying questions.

1. Power on the computer that has the printer attached. If necessary, log on to Windows, using the appropriate user ID and password.
2. Click the *Start* button and select *Control Panel*.
3. In Windows XP, if in *Category* view, select the *Printers and Other Hardware* option and then select *Printers and Faxes*. If in XP *Classic* view, double-click the *Printers and Faxes* option.

   In Windows Vista/7, access the *Network and Sharing Center* Control Panel. Ensure that *Printer sharing* is enabled. Lab 14.4 details how to do this. Then in Vista/7, access the *Printers* Control Panel.
4. Right-click the printer to be shared and select the *Properties* option.
5. Click the *Sharing* tab and select the *Share this printer* radio button/checkbox. If the option is grayed out, select the *Change sharing options* button (Vista)/*Network and Sharing Center* link (7). Make changes as necessary. Back in the original printer properties window, ensure the *Share this printer* and *Render print jobs on client computers* checkboxes are enabled. Click *OK* if necessary.
6. In the *Share* name textbox, type in a unique printer name and limit it to eight characters if possible. It is very important that this name is unique.

What name was assigned to the printer? ______________________

7. Click the *OK* button.

Printing to a Shared or Networked Printer

8. On the second computer, open the *Printers and Faxes* (XP)/*Devices and Printers* (7)/*Printers* (Vista/7) Control Panel, using the previously described steps.
9. On Windows XP, in the *Printer Tasks* window on the left side, click the *Add a printer* option.

   In Vista/7, click the *Add a Printer* menu option. The *Add Printer* Wizard opens. Click the *Next* button.
10. In XP, click the *A network printer*, or *A printer attached to another computer* radio button.

    In Vista/7, click the *Add a network, wireless, or Bluetooth printer* option.
11. In Windows XP, there are two methods to finding a shared or networked printer:
    - Select the *Find a printer in the directory* radio button, click *Next*, click the *Browse* button, select the printer location, and click the *OK* button. Click the *Find Now* button, select the printer, and click the *OK* button.
    - Select the *Connect to this printer* (or, to browse for a printer, select this option and click *Next*) radio button. Either type the name of the printer using the format `\\computer_name\printer_share_name` or browse the network for the printer name, click the *Next* button, select the printer in the *Shared printers* window, and click the *Next* button.

    In Vista/7, the printer link should be listed in the window. Click *Next* if the printer is there and then click the *Install driver* button. If the printer is missing, click *The printer that I want isn't listed*. Three methods can be used to find a shared or networked printer:
    - Click the *Browse for a printer* radio button and click *Next*. Double-click the computer icon that has the printer attached. Select the printer and click the *Select* button and click *Next*.
    - Select the *Shared printer by name* radio button. Either type the name of the printer using the format `\\computer_name\printer_share_name` or browse the network for the printer name, click the *Next* button, select the printer, and click *Next*.
    - Select the *Add a printer using a TCP/IP address or hostname* radio button and click *Next*. Type the hostname or IP address. Click *Next*.
12. For all versions of Windows, select one of these options and locate the shared printer. Print a test page to the shared printer.

    Does the test page print properly? If not, perform appropriate printer troubleshooting.

Lab 14.6 Installing a Dial-Up Connection Using Windows XP

Objective: To understand how to create a dial-up connection when using Windows XP

Parts: Windows XP computer with a modem and Dial-up Network installed correctly

Phone number of a dial-up server

Optionally a username and password to the access server

Note: The Windows Dial-up Network (DUN) utility allows you to create and configure dial-up connections that allow connectivity to access servers. In this exercise, you create a dial-up connection using Windows XP.

Procedure: Complete the following procedure and answer the accompanying questions.

1. Power on the computer. If necessary, log on to Windows XP using the appropriate user ID and password.
2. Click the *Start* button and select the *Control Panel* option.

3. If in *Category* view, select the *Network and Internet Connections* option and select *Network Connections*. If in *Classic* view, double-click the *Network Connections* icon.
4. In the *Network Tasks* window on the left, select the *Create a new connection* option. The *New Connection* Wizard opens. Click the *Next* button.
5. Select the *Connect to the Internet* radio button and click *Next*.
6. Select the *Set up my connection manually* radio button and click *Next*.
7. Select the *Connect using a dial-up modem* radio button and click *Next*.
8. In the ISP Name, type a name that refers to the dial-up connection you are creating.

   What name was chosen for the dial-up connection?
9. Click the *Next* button. In the *Phone number* textbox, type in the phone number given to you by your instructor or lab assistant. This is the phone number to the dial-in access server. Once typed, click the *Next* button.
10. Some servers require a username and password to access the server. Type the username, password, and retype the password in the *Confirm password* textbox. Click the *Next* button. Click the *Finish* button.
11. Return to the *Network Connections* window and an icon with the dial-up connection name chosen in Step 8 lists in the window. Double-click the icon and test the connection.

    Did the dial-up connection work? If not, perform appropriate troubleshooting.

Lab 14.7 Identifying Basic Wireless Network Parts

Objective: To be able to identify basic parts of a wireless network and determine the type of wireless network being used

Using Figure 14.64, identify the major parts of a wireless network. For the number 5 blank, document whether this network would most likely be for a home or a corporate network and explain why.

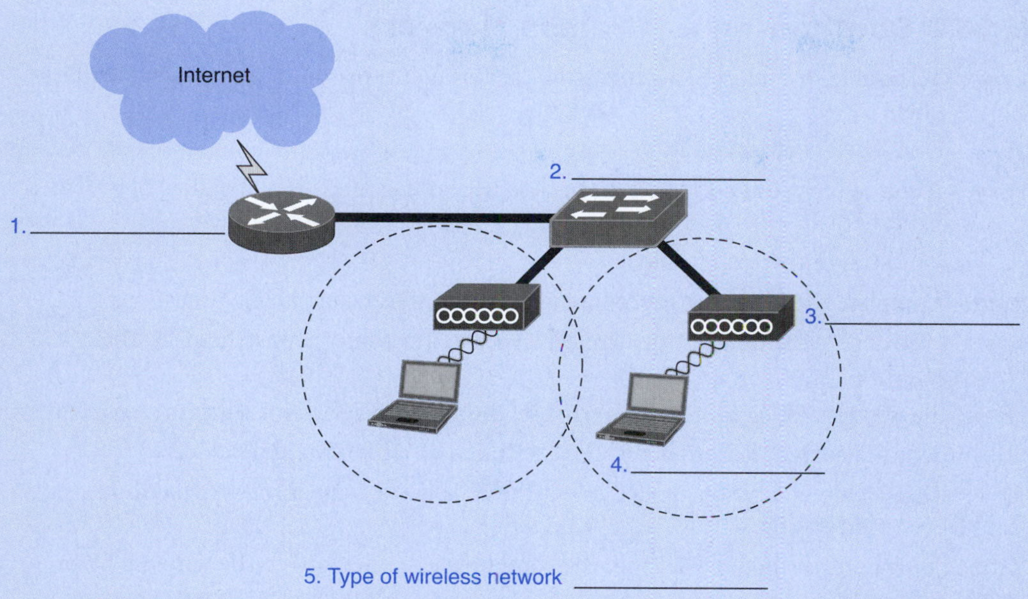

Figure 14.64 Wireless network components

Lab 14.8 Installing a Wireless NIC

Objective: To install a wireless NIC into a computer and have it attach to an access point

Parts: A computer with access to the Internet and permission to download files

A wireless NIC

An access point that has already been configured by the instructor or lab assistant

Note: In order to verify that a wireless NIC works once installed, it must have another wireless device such as another computer with a wireless NIC installed or an access point. This lab assumes that an access point is available and allows attachment of wireless devices. The students will need any security information such as WEP key before they begin. Each student will download the installation instructions and driver for the wireless NIC. Frequently these files may be in zipped or PDF format. The computer they are using may need to have Adobe's Acrobat Reader and/or a decompression software package loaded.

Procedure: Complete the following procedure and answer the accompanying questions.

1. Determine what type of wireless NIC is being installed.

   What type of wireless NIC is being installed? [PCI | USB | PC Card | ExpressCard | PCIe]

   Who is the manufacturer of the wireless NIC?

   What operating system is being used on the computer in which the wireless NIC will be installed?

2. Using the Internet, determine the latest version of wireless NIC driver for the operating system being used and download the driver.

   What is the latest driver version?

3. Using the Internet, download the installation instructions for the wireless NIC being used.

   What is the name of the installation document?

4. Open the document that details how to install the wireless NIC.
5. Follow the directions and install the wireless NIC.

   Does the wireless NIC automatically detect a wireless network? If not, contact the lab assistant or instructor for any settings that must be configured on the wireless NIC.

   List any specifications given to you by the instructor/lab assistant.

Lab 14.9 Configuring a Wireless Network

Objective: To be able to configure a wireless AP (access point) or router and attach a wireless client

Parts: One wireless access point or router

A computer with an integrated wireless NIC or a wireless NIC installed as well as an Ethernet NIC

One straight-through cable

Procedure: Complete the following procedure and answer the accompanying questions.

1. Obtain the documentation for the wireless AP or router from the instructor or the Internet.
2. Reset the wireless AP or router as directed by the wireless device manufacturer.

   Document the current Ethernet NIC IPv4 settings. [DHCP | Static IP address]

   If a static IP address is assigned, document the IP address, subnet mask, default gateway, and DNS configuration settings.
3. Attach a straight-through cable from the computer Ethernet NIC to the wireless AP or router.
4. Power on the computer and log on, if necessary.
5. Configure the computer NIC with a static IP address or DHCP, as directed by the wireless device manufacturer.
6. Open a web browser and configure the wireless AP or router with the following parameters:
   - Change the default SSID.
   - Leave SSID broadcasting enabled for this lab.
   - Do not configure wireless security at this time.
   - Change the default password used to access the wireless AP/router.

   Document the current settings:

   SSID: ___________

   Password for wireless device access: ___________
7. Save the wireless AP or router configuration.
8. Disconnect the Ethernet cable.
9. Enable the wireless NIC and configure it for the appropriate SSID.
10. Configure the wireless NIC for a static IP address or DHCP as directed by the wireless AP or router manufacturer.
11. Open a web browser and access the wireless AP or router. If access cannot be obtained, troubleshoot as necessary or reset the wireless AP or router to default configurations and restart the lab.

    What frequency (channel) is being used by the wireless AP or router and the wireless NIC for connectivity?
12. Show the instructor the connectivity.

Instructor initials: _____________

13. Reset the wireless AP or router to the default configuration settings.
14. Reset the computer(s) to the original configuration settings.

Lab 14.10 Wireless Network Case Study

Objective: To design and price a wireless network, based on the parameters given

Parts: Computer with Internet access

Note: The instructor or lab assistant can speak on behalf of the faculty members if any design questions arise.

Scenario: A building has just been renovated to include faculty offices and two new classrooms, as shown in Figure 14.65. The only wired networks are in the computer classroom (not shown) and the administrator's office (not shown). The wired network allows access to the Internet. The wired network connections are in the wiring closet shown in the diagram at the intersection of the two hallways. Five faculty members are being issued laptop computers. The laptops do not include wireless NICs. The faculty members want to be able to use their laptops in their classrooms and offices. There are also comfortable chairs in the hallways and faculty would like to be able to use their laptops in the hallways as well. The faculty would like (1) access to the Internet and (2) access to a printer. Currently, there are no printers in the classrooms or the faculty area that they can use.

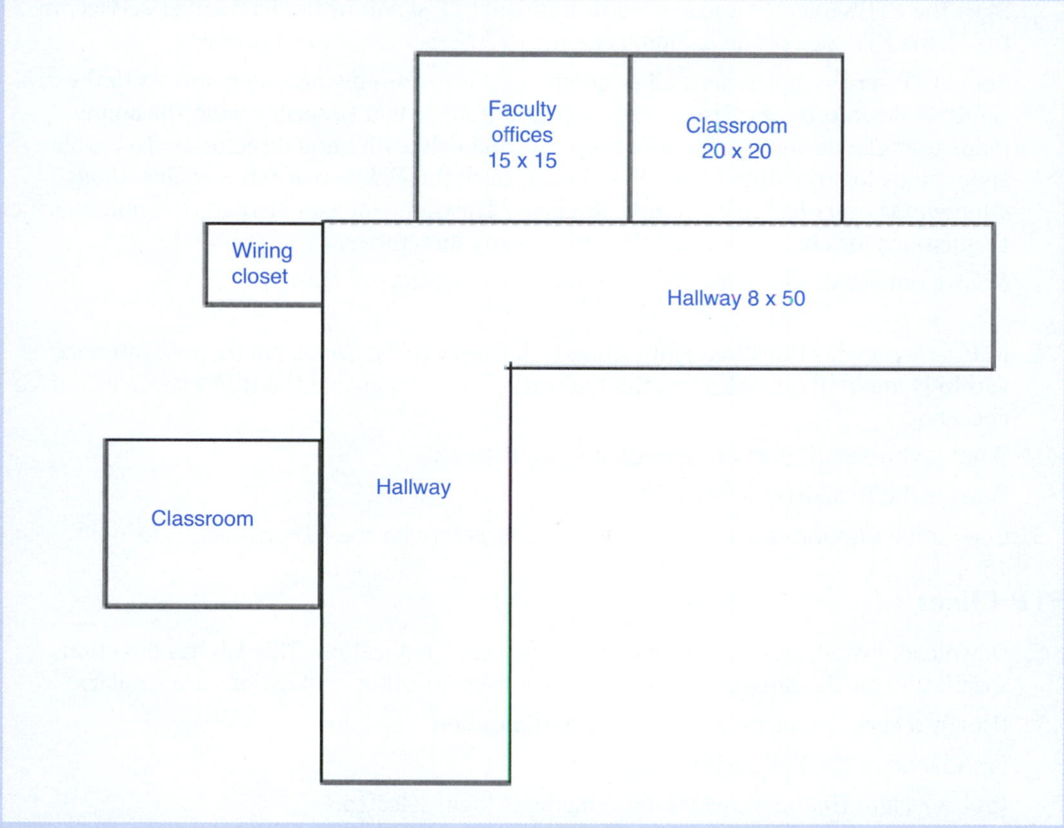

Figure 14.65 Building floor plan

Tasks:

- Design a wireless network to allow faculty to use their laptops and gain access to the Internet. Provide this drawing in electronic form to the instructor. This can be done in Word or in Visio or some other drawing program.

- Provide a detailed list of wireless network parts, part numbers, prices, and a web link where the prices were obtained. This will include antenna type, a printout of the wireless antenna radiation pattern, and antenna coverage range.
- Provide the instructor with a typewritten list of policies and configuration settings for the wireless network. You are the designer and implementer and what you decide goes.

Lab 14.11 FTP Server and Client

Objective: To transfer files from one network device to another, using FTP server and client software

Parts: An application or freeware application that provides the FTP server service

An application or freeware application that provides the FTP client service

Procedure: Complete the following procedure and answer the accompanying questions.

FTP Server

1. Download, install, and open an FTP server freeware application. This lab has directions specifically for Home FTP Server, but the steps for other applications are similar.
2. Start the FTP server. You may need to start the FTP server or the FTP server service. In the Home FTP Server application, click the *FTP Server* tab > *Start Server*.
3. Some FTP server applications allow anonymous users or anyone who connects to the server to download files. Also, some applications allow you to specify what the anonymous user can do such as download, upload, and delete files and directories. To enable anonymous logins within Home FTP Server, click the *FTP Server* tab > enable *Allow anonymous users (allow all active)* checkbox. This same tab can be used to enable specific permissions for creation and deletion of files and directories.

   Make a note as to where the default anonymous directory is located.

4. FTP server applications frequently allow web connectivity. To enable the web interface within Home FTP Server, select the *Web interface* tab > enable the *Web interface enabled* checkbox.

   What is the default port number used for FTP server?

   What is the IP address of the FTP server?

5. Copy some files into the default anonymous directory on the FTP server.

FTP Client

6. Download, install, and open an FTP client freeware application. This lab has directions specifically for the SmartFTP client, but the steps for other applications are similar.
7. Usually a client requires the following configuration:

   (a) Address of the FTP server

   (b) User login ID and password *or* anonymous login selected.

   In the SmartFTP client, type in the FTP server IP address in the *address* textbox > click the *Anonymous* button (option) > click the green arrow to connect. The FTP client displays the files that were copied into the anonymous directory.

Instructor initials: ____________

Tightening Security

8. Create a user on the FTP server. In the Home FTP Server, click the *New Member* button > *General* tab > type a name in the *User Name* textbox > type `class999` in the *Password* textbox.

Make a note of the home directory and permissions for this user.

9. Click *Apply*. Test the user account from the FTP client application by creating a new entry with the appropriate user ID and password. In SmartFTP, click the *File* menu option > select *disconnect* to disconnect the previous login session. Click the *File* menu option > *New Remote Browser* > in the *Host* textbox, type the FTP server IP address > in the *User Name* textbox, type the *exact* username that was typed in the FTP server application > In the *Password* textbox, type **`class999`** > in the *Name* textbox, type **`FTP with login`** > *OK*. The client connects to the FTP server.

Instructor initials: ______________

10. Within the client application, close the FTP session. For the SmartFTP client, use the *Close* button in the upper-right corner of the *FTP with login* tab. Close all tabs and sessions.
11. Delete FTP client entries. From within SmartFTP client, click the *Favorites* menu option > *Edit Favorites Quick Connect* option in the left pane > click once on the FTP server IP address in the right pane > *Edit* menu option > *Delete* > *Yes*. Delete the FTP with login option using the same technique.

Instructor initials: ______________

Lab 14.12 Subnet Practice Lab

Objective: To be able to determine the subnet number, broadcast address, and IP addresses that can be assigned to network devices

Parts: None needed

Procedure: Complete the following procedure and answer the accompanying questions.

1. Determine the network address for the following IP address and subnet mask combinations.

   210.141.254.122 255.255.255.192

   206.240.195.38 255.255.255.224

   104.130.188.213 255.255.192.0

   69.89.5.224 255.240.0.0

   10.113.71.66 255.128.0.0
2. Determine the broadcast address for the following IP address and subnet mask combinations.

   166.215.207.182 255.255.255.240

   198.94.140.121 255.255.255.224

   97.57.210.192 255.255.224.0

   133.98.227.36 255.255.192.0

   14.89.203.133 255.128.0.0
3. Determine the valid IP addresses on the networks that contain the following IP address and subnet mask combinations.

   131.107.200.34 255.255.248.0

   146.197.221.238 255.255.255.192

   52.15.111.33 255.255.248.0

   192.168.10.245/30

   209.218.235.117 255.255.255.128

Activities

Internet Discovery

Objective: To access the Internet to obtain specific information regarding a computer or its associated parts

Parts: Access to the Internet

Procedure: Complete the following procedure and answer the accompanying questions.

1. On an HP Pavilion dm3z laptop, you cannot get the wireless NIC to attach to the wireless network. What are some steps you can take, as recommended by HP, to help in this situation?

   Write at least three solutions as well as the URL where you found the solution.

2. What does the term Wake on Wireless mean and at what URL did you locate the answer?

3. A computer with a Linksys (Cisco) LNE 100TX 10/100 Ethernet NIC on a Windows Vista computer cannot access the Internet. What are four things Linksys recommends you do? Write the answers and the URL where you found the answer.

4. Find an Internet forum that discusses Bluetooth and Windows 7 on Lenovo laptops. Write the URL where you found the information.

5. Find an Internet site that explains the differences between CAT 5e and CAT 6 UTP cable. Write one difference between the two standards, the name of the article or site, and the URL where you found the information.

Soft Skills

Objective: To enhance and fine-tune a technician's ability to listen, communicate in both written and oral form, and support people who use computers in a professional manner

Activities:

1. Using the Internet, find and access a utility that tests your soft skills. Compare your scores with others in the class and determine how you might improve in specific weak areas.
2. In groups of two, one person puts a network problem in a computer, while the other person is out of the room. When the other person comes back, they troubleshoot the problem by asking questions of the user (as if they were on the phone helping them). The person performing the troubleshooting cannot touch the computer. Discuss strategies for doing this better before swapping roles.
3. In groups of two or three, brainstorm three examples of a technician being reactive rather than proactive. List ways the technician could have been more proactive for each example. Share your findings with other teams.

Critical Thinking Skills

Objective: To analyze and evaluate information as well as apply learned information to new or different situations

Activities:

1. A home user connects to the Internet. The ISP provides hard drive space for the user's web page. Is this a network? Why or why not? Write your answer in a well-written paragraph using good grammar, capitalization, and punctuation.
2. Use the Internet, magazines, newspapers, or books to find a network installation case study. Make a table of terms they use that were introduced in this chapter. On the left side, list the term and, on the right side, define or describe how the term relates to the network installation. Analyze the installation and discuss with a team. Make a checklist of approved processes and of recommended changes to implemented processes. Share your team findings with the class.
3. In a team environment, design a wired and wireless network for a small business with 10 computers. Name the business, provide a design and implementation plan, provide a list of items for which you should do more research. Share your plan with the class.

A+ Certification Exam Tips

- ✓ This chapter provides information related to both the 220-801 and 220-802 exams. The mobile device section and the configuration of email on a mobile device as well as network troubleshooting relate to the 220-802 exam (the second exam to obtain the A+ certification). CompTIA recommends that you have one year of experience before taking the exam.
- ✓ Know the purpose of the network devices hub, router, AP, and switch and at what layer(s) they operate.
- ✓ Know the OSI and TCP/IP models, protocols that work at each layer, the purposes of the protocols, and port numbers used by the protocols. Know the difference between TCP and UDP.
- ✓ Know when to use the appropriate networking tool, whether a physical tool or a command.
- ✓ Know what to do when one or more computers cannot connect to the Internet or when they have an IP address conflict.
- ✓ Know how to manually configure an IP address on a computer, an AP, a printer, or any other network device. Know how to configure an alternative configuration on a computer.
- ✓ Know how to effectively use the `ipconfig` and `ping` commands.
- ✓ Know how to configure Internet Explorer using the various tabs.
- ✓ Know the different types of wireless networks and their compatibility with each other.
- ✓ Know how to manually assign 2.4GHz channels so multiple wireless APs can coexist.
- ✓ Know the purpose of an IP address, a default gateway, and a subnet mask.
- ✓ Know the difference between an IPv4 address and an IPv6 address.
- ✓ Recognize when an address is a private IP address and understand the difference between a public IP address and a private IP address.
- ✓ Know the different types of network connectors.

chapter 15

Computer and Network Security

Chapter Objectives

In this chapter you will learn:

- What is in a security policy
- Mobile device security methods and devices
- How to perform operating system and data protection
- How to optimize security for Windows
- How to configure wireless security options
- Common techniques used when dealing with irate customers

CompTIA Exam Objectives

What CompTIA exam objectives are covered in this chapter?

- ✓ 801-1.1 Configure and apply BIOS settings.
- ✓ 801-2.5 Compare and contrast wireless networking standards and encryption types.
- ✓ 801-2.6 Install, configure, and deploy a SOHO wireless/wired router using appropriate settings.
- ✓ 801-2.9 Compare and contrast network devices, their functions, and features.
- ✓ 801-3.3 Compare and contrast laptop features.
- ✓ 801-5.3 Given a scenario, demonstrate proper communication and professionalism.
- ✓ 801-5.4 Explain the fundamentals of dealing with prohibited content/activity.
- ✓ 802-1.1 Compare and contrast the features and requirements of various Microsoft Operating Systems.
- ✓ 802-1.4 Given a scenario, use appropriate operating system features and tools.
- ✓ 802-1.5 Given a scenario, use Control Panel utilities.
- ✓ 802-1.6 Setup and configure Windows networking on a client/desktop.
- ✓ 802-1.8 Explain the differences among basic OS security settings.
- ✓ 802-1.9 Explain the basics of client-side virtualization.
- ✓ 802-2.1 Apply and use common prevention methods.
- ✓ 802-2.2 Compare and contrast common security threats.
- ✓ 802-2.3 Implement security best practices to secure a workstation.
- ✓ 802-2.4 Given a scenario, use the appropriate data destruction/disposal method.
- ✓ 802-2.5 Given a scenario, secure a SOHO wireless network.
- ✓ 802-2.6 Given a scenario, secure a SOHO wired network.
- ✓ 802-3.3 Compare and contrast methods for securing mobile devices.
- ✓ 802-4.7 Given a scenario, troubleshoot common security issues with appropriate tools and best practices.

Security Overview

Computer and network security relates to the hardware, software, and data protection of PCs and mobile devices. Large books are devoted to the topic of computer and network security. This chapter focuses on issues related to a PC technician job and the processes and terminology with which the technician should be familiar. Security needs to be a concern of everyone in a business or a home. And this, of course, also includes the people who repair and support PCs—the technicians. A technician must be able to implement and explain security concepts. Every technician has the responsibility of promoting security consciousness and training users to be good stewards of equipment and data is essential.

Security Policy

A **security policy** is one or more documents that provide rules and guidelines related to computer and network security. Every company, no matter what size or how many employees, should have a security policy. Small businesses tend to have general operating procedures that are passed verbally from one employee to another, but it is best to have these processes documented in detail.

Common elements of a security policy are shown in Table 15.1.

Table 15.1 Security policy elements

Security policy component	Description
Physical access	Describes who is allowed into a building, to what part of the building they have access, and badge/key control. Defines who has keys to the wiring closets and server rooms as well as who is allowed in such places. Delineates what type of security log is kept when a person is allowed access to a space.
Antivirus	States whether antivirus software is required on every system, possibly what product is used, how updates are obtained, and steps taken when a machine is not compliant or if a person refuses to be compliant.
Acceptable use	Defines who has access to and what level of usage is appropriate for the company-provided information resources such as email and Internet. Sometimes it defines what data can be taken from the company and data storage limitations such as no personal data is to be stored on a server or workstation PC. This section normally includes statements about gaming and web surfing during work hours as well as consequences for violations. The details might include defining what web browser and hardware platforms are supported. It might include the process for assigning folder and file rights and what to do if an account has been disabled.
Password	Guidelines for protecting passwords such as not writing them down, a timeline for changing passwords, the number and type of characters required, and processes for forgotten passwords such as whether or not the new password can be given by phone or by email only.
Email usage	Defines who owns the email because it resides on a company server, how long email is stored, proper usage of email, and when it is backed up. Lawsuits related to this area continue to find for the company regarding email rights since the data is stored on company-owned and provided servers.
Remote access	Contains statements relevant to who is allowed, type(s) of remote access permitted, company resources that can be accessed remotely, the process to obtain desired rights and access, and what type of security level is required.
Emergency procedures	Details what to do when something is missing and the steps to take if a natural disaster such as a hurricane occurs. Stipulates who overrides a security policy and authorizes access to someone.

Even though not every company has a security policy, specific points relating to the security policy are referenced throughout this chapter. Whether written or just accepted company guidelines, many implementations are based on a particular company's rules for computer and network security.

Physical Security

Typical physical security includes door locks, cipher locks, keys, guards, and fences, but physical security regarding computers can mean much more. For several years, companies have been using electronic key cards for physical access to rooms instead of keys. Electronic key cards are part of an access control system which includes the key cards, door readers, and software to control and monitor the system. Electronic key cards have many benefits, including the following:

- They are easy to program and issue/revoke compared to issuing a key and getting it back from a dismissed employee or one who quits.
- Data is stored in a database instead of in a checkout form.
- Access to information, such as who entered a room and at what time, can be logged and monitored more easily than with a checkout sheet.
- More layers of control can be exercised with key cards. With metal keys, the usual process is to give a key for each room, issue a submaster key for an entire wing, or issue a master key for the entire building.
- When keys are issued and one is lost, the lock must be rekeyed and new keys issued. When an electronic key card is lost, the old card is deactivated, and a new one is issued.

Tech Tip

Watch out for tailgating

Tailgating is the practice of an unauthorized person entering behind an authorized person. Prevention of tailgating requires training and diligence by all employees.

Other electronic devices and technologies also provide access to computers and rooms. Table 15.2 lists and describes security devices that help with the physical security of computers.

Table 15.2 Physical security devices

Device/ technology	Description
Smart card	A small ID-sized card that can store data, be encrypted, require authorization for changing, and wiped through a card reader or interact wirelessly with a card reader. Used in government IDs (with such info as medical/dental records) mobile phones as a subscriber ID module, driver's licenses, and employee badges.
Key fob	Used for keyless entry to cars and buildings and interior doors such as a fitness room in an apartment complex.
RFID (radio frequency ID)	A technology that allows automatic identification of people, objects, or animals. Uses an RFID tag that is read by wirelessly by an RFID reader. Used in libraries, inventory systems, computers, hospital equipment, and in locating lost pets or people.
RSA (Rivest Shamir Adleman) security token	RSA is a security algorithm method used with a security token, hardware token, DES card, **authentication*** token or card. May be in a form of a smart token, key fob, small calculator-sized, or USB-attached device. A PIN is frequently required, and a security token (think of it like a password) is generated. Enter the token for network access.

Device/ technology	Description
TPM (Trusted Platform Module)	A microcontroller chip on a motherboard used for hardware/ software authentication. Stores info such as security certificates, passwords, and encryption keys. It can authenticate hardware devices. Applications can use for file and folder encryption, local passwords, email, VPN/PKI authentication, and wireless authentication.
Computer cage	Physical protection for a computer or laptop in a public location.
Tracking module	Located inside mobile devices and commonly requires a vendor contract. Used to track assets and provide recovery options if the device is lost or stolen. Might include a remote data wiping service.
Privacy filter	Prevents shoulder surfing; only allows viewing the screen clearly if you are sitting directly in front of the monitor to prevent shoulder surfing.
Mantrap	A method of separating a non-secure area from a secured area. This could be two doors with a guard, keypad, or some other security means on the second door.

**Authentication* is a term used when describing the process of proving who you are before being allowed onto the computer, to remotely access into a network, or to be allowed access to a network resource such as a printer or shared document.

Smart cards or security tokens are often described as using two-factor authentication. This type of authentication is familiar to most people—you need something you have, such as your ATM card or your security token device, and something you know, such as a PIN number. This is more secure than a password, which is only one factor. Figure 15.1 shows a smart card, Figure 15.2 illustrates a key fob, and Figure 15.3 shows a photo of a security token.

Figure 15.1 Smart card

Figure 15.2 Electronic key fob

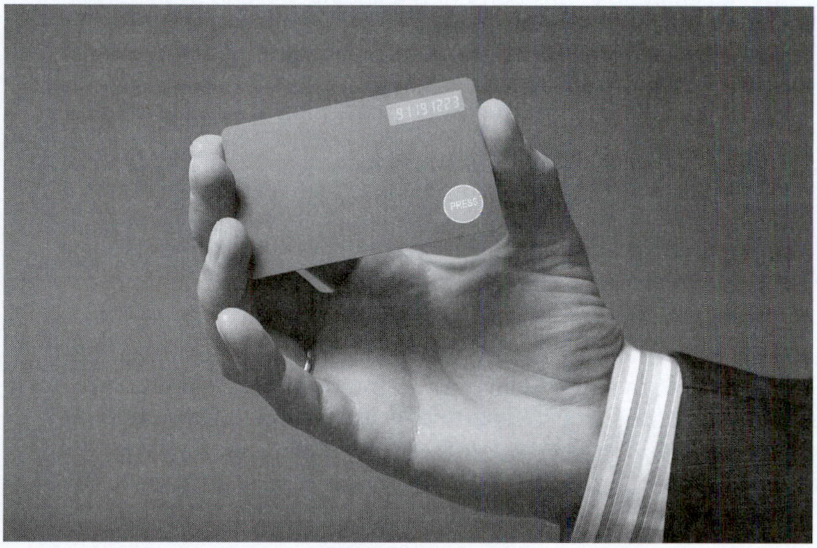

Figure 15.3 Security token

An expanding field related to this is **biometrics**, which is authenticating (proving who someone is) based on one or more physical traits such as a fingerprint, eyeball (retina), or hand. Behavioral traits, such as voice and signature, can also be used. Voice can actually be both physical and behavioral. A less complex system could just compare voice with a stored voice print. The more complex systems compare tone and inflection too, which is more in the behavioral realm.

Multifactor authentication is when two or more methods are required to gain access to a computer, network room, or other shared media. Using a bank ATM requires multifactor authentication: (1) the ATM card and (2) a PIN code. With computers, one of the two things could be something the users know such as a password or PIN and the second security measure could be a token, smart card, USB security key device, or a biometric device such as a fingerprint reader or face recognition through a webcam. Biometrics add one more security layer to authentication.

Biometrics are more secure because a biometric system is more difficult to bypass than are a user ID and password. The trait is less likely to be lost than a password. Also, biometrics requires that the person being authenticated is present when gaining access. Biometrics is more expensive to implement than a user ID/password scheme. Examples of biometric devices used to allow someone to gain access to a room, locker, or device are listed in Table 15.3.

Table 15.3 Biometric devices

Device	Description
Fingerprint reader	Requires a finger to be placed against a reader and compared against a stored image. Used in the notebook market, with some vendors having these devices already installed. Can be attached to an existing computer easily via a PC Card, ExpressCard, or USB.
Facial recognition	Integrated laptop webcams can be used. Another system, takes a photo and compares it with an image database (resource intensive).
Hand scanner	Requires a palm of the hand to be placed against a reader and is more secure than a fingerprint reader. Higher-end systems can analyze veins in the palm.
Retinal scanner	Sometimes called an eye scanner or an iris scanner. According to LG Electronics, the human iris is the most distinguishable characteristic.
Voice recognition	A person speaks into a microphone before gaining access to a computer or physical space. Also called speech recognition, but not the same as the software used to input data instead of typing.

Applications for biometric devices are not limited to computer/network security. Disney World uses biometrics to ensure that the same person uses a multiday pass. Airports use biometrics for employee-only area access. Police departments use biometrics to gain access to evidence and gun lockers. These devices will need to be installed and maintained by the computer and network support staff. Figures 15.4 and 15.5 show a fingerprint scanner and a retinal scanner.

Tech Tip

Use the *Lock Computer* option

When away from your desk, use the *Lock Computer* option by pressing Ctrl + Alt + Del and selecting *Lock Computer*.

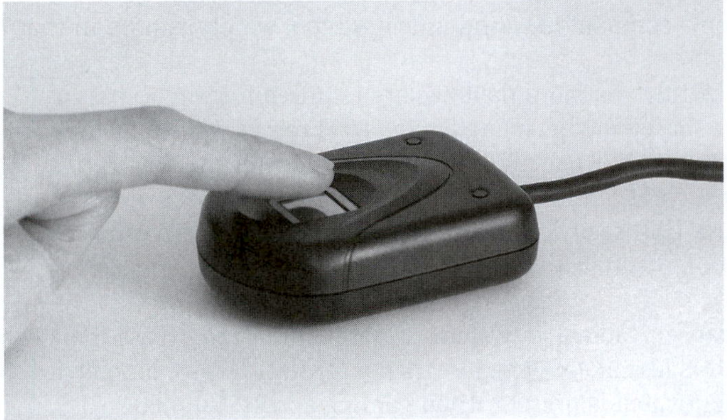

Figure 15.4 Fingerprint scanner

Figure 15.5 Iris scanner

You might be required to use the system BIOS Setup program to activate an integrated biometric device. To use the biometric device, optionally download a driver, and install and use a specific application that is available for download, comes with the device or computer, or an application pre-installed on the computer.

Most computers have BIOS options that prevent others from altering the settings. Table 15.4 shows some BIOS options related to security.

Table 15.4 BIOS security options

BIOS option	Description
Supervisor	Unrestricted access to all BIOS options
User	Allows a limited number of configuration changes such as time and boot sequence.
Boot or Power-on password	Required before BIOS looks for an operating system. This is not the Windows user password.

In a corporate environment, the supervisor password is commonly configured. Other options that may affect the corporate environment include the following:

- Enabling/disabling device options
- Enabling/disabling ports
- Viewing/changing security levels
- Restoring security settings to the default values

Laptop computers have special security needs, and locking and tracking devices are available for them. Use a nondescript bag to carry a laptop to reduce the chance of it being stolen. Have an engraved permanent asset tag attached. Most laptops have a USS (universal security slot) that allows a cable lock or laptop alarm to be attached. Special software packages exist that have the laptop automatically contact a tracking center in case of theft. Figure 15.6 shows a USS on a notebook computer.

Figure 15.6 Universal security slot

Protecting the Operating System and Data

Several chapters have contained important security-related tips, steps, and information related to protecting the operating system and data. Some of the most important ones follow:

- Use the NTFS file system.
- Ensure that operating system and application service packs and updates are applied regularly (good patch management). If a Windows update fails, a message usually appears when the machine reboots. Try the update again; sometimes an update might fail when being installed with other updates. Successfully install as many as you can and then reinstall the failed updates one by one.
- Install antivirus software with the latest virus definitions.
- Encrypt data that needs to be protected.
- Use BitLocker, BitLocker To Go, and TPM (Trusted Platform Module). **BitLocker** encrypts an entire disk volume and requires two NTFS disk partitions. **BitLocker To Go** is used to encrypt and password protect external drives and removable media that are 128MB are larger. Use BitLocker To Go Reader on a Windows XP or Vista machine to use a drive that has been encrypted with BitLocker To Go.
- Optionally place operating system files and data files on separate hard drive partitions.
- Some firmware or driver versions may cause security issues. Keep the versions updated.
- If using virtualization, don't forget that each virtual machine needs the same protection as an individual computer. All concepts in this chapter apply not just to the host machine, but to each virtual machine as well.
- If donating an older computer or replacing a hard drive, the data needs to be removed and partition(s) deleted and re-created; some hard drive manufacturers have utilities that rewrite a hard drive with all 1s or all 0s to prevent data remnants from being recovered. A company that has extremely sensitive data stored on a hard drive should destroy the hard drive by (1) secure erasing, which requires special software, (2) degaussing (using electromagnets to change the drives magnetic fields or 1s and 0s; can be expensive and requires drive disassembly), or (3) drilling through drive platters (see Figure 15.7) and then destroying the pieces with a hammer.

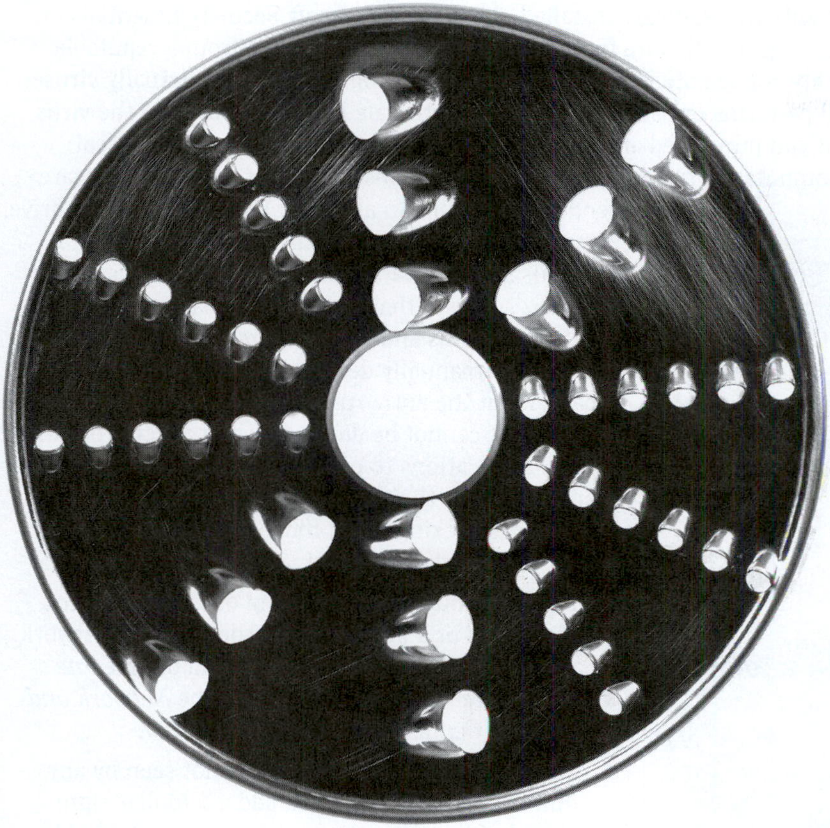

Figure 15.7 **Drilled hard drive platter**

- Use the System Protection program to control restore points. Use the *System* Control Panel > *System Protection* link or in Explorer, right-click *Computer* > *Properties* > *System Protection* link > *System Protection* tab > *Configure*. See Lab 15.2 for details.
- Disable USB ports through the BIOS and password protect the BIOS to prevent using external USB drives that might have a virus.
- Disable AutoRun to prevent software or programs from automatically starting from an optical disc, flash drive, or external drive. Note that AutoPlay is when you insert a disc such as a music CD and the music automatically starts playing or the user is prompted for the default action. Use the following steps to disable AutoPlay and AutoRun so the action will not occur and the user will not be prompted. Note that specific Windows security updates are also required (see http://support.microsoft.com for more details):
    1. From a command prompt or the Start textbox, type `gpedit.msc` and press Enter
    2. Expand *Administrative Templates* > click *System* (XP) or expand *Windows Components* (Vista/7).
    3. On an XP computer, right-click *Turn off Autoplay* > *Properties* > *Enabled* > *All drives* > *Turn off Autoplay* > *OK*.
    4. On a Vista/7 computer, click *Autoplay Policies* > double-click *Turn off Autoplay* > click *Enabled* > select *All drives* > restart the computer.

If you suspect that a system has a virus because the computer is running slow, crashes, or locks; applications are behaving abnormally or not at all; files are missing; file attributes have changed; the hard drive is constantly active; the network is constantly active; email is hijacked; you get access denied messages; or system files are renamed or removed, check for updated virus signatures from the antivirus software vendor. Disconnect the computer from the network or disable the wireless NIC to prevent the virus from spreading to other computers. Run an antivirus program. You might be required to use the `SFC /scannow` command after removing a virus.

If you don't have antivirus software installed, download Microsoft Security Essentials or another free antivirus program. Ensure that the free antivirus program is from a reputable download site. There are rogue antivirus websites that post programs that are actually viruses.

If the system still performs unusually, try booting into Safe Mode and running the virus checker from there. If you purchased an antivirus disc, run the software from the optical disc. Go to another computer to research your support options from your antivirus software vendor. Boot from an alternate boot source (flash drive, external hard drive, operating system disc). Some antivirus software vendors have bootable discs with antivirus software that can be downloaded.

Tech Tip

Manually delete files, if necessary

If the antivirus software or other preventive software applications state that a particular file cannot be deleted, make a note of the file and its location. Explorer view options may have to be adjusted before viewing/deletion can occur.

Some worms and Trojan Horse viruses require that files be manually deleted because they cannot be repaired, but the antivirus software will "quarantine" the file so it cannot be dangerous and affect other files. Test all applications to ensure that they operate. Then manually delete the file that is quarantined.

Besides backing it up, the following are several things you can do to protect your locally stored data:

Tech Tip

All subfolders are shared when a folder is shared

When you share a folder, all subfolders are automatically shared unless you make the subfolders private.

- If the computer you are using does not need to share files or a printer with others on the network, use the *Network* Control Panel and disable *File and Printer Sharing* (XP) or use the *Network and Sharing Center* (Vista/7) *Control Panel*.
- To create a shared folder that is not seen by any others across the network, add a $ (dollar sign) to end of the share name. An example of a hidden shared folder is Book$.
- In XP, make any folder in your user profile private such as *My Documents*, *Desktop*, *Start Menu*, *Cookies*, and *Favorites* (or any subfolder of these). Note that Vista/7 does not support private folders. Lab 15.3 at the end of this chapter demonstrates these techniques.
- Encrypt (scramble so they cannot be read) files or folders.

Because of quarantined files or the need to check system files, a technician is required to be very familiar with Windows Explorer display options. In Windows XP, use the Windows Explorer *Tools* > *Folder Options* > *View* tab. In Windows Vista and 7, use the *Organize* > *Folder and search options* > *View* tab. Also in Vista/7 Windows Explorer, you can use the use the *Organize* > *Layout* option or the *Folder Options* Control Panel to configure how folders/files are displayed and what information is included with that display. Table 15.5 summarizes the security-related *View* tab options.

Table 15.5 Folder Options > View tab

Function	Description
View hidden files	XP: *Hidden files and folders* section > enable *Show hidden files and folders* Vista/7: *Organize* > *Folder and search options* > *Hidden files and folders* section > enable *Show hidden files, folders, and drives*
View file extensions	XP: *Files and folders* section > uncheck *Hide extensions for known file types* Vista/7: *Organize* > *Folder and search options* > *Files and folders* section > uncheck *Hide extensions for known file types*

Function	Description
View system files	XP: *Files and folders* section > uncheck *Hide protected operating system files (Recommended)* Vista/7: *Organize* > *Folder and search options* > *Files and folders* section > uncheck *Hide protected operating system files (Recommended)*
Sharing menu/ options	XP: *Files and folders* section > enable *Use simple file sharing (Recommended)* Vista/7: *Organize* > *Folder and search options* > *Files and folders* section > enable *Use Sharing Wizard (Recommended)*

Tech Tip

What is the maximum number of concurrent users?

A maximum of 10 users (XP) or 20 users (Vista/7) can simultaneously use the same shared folder.

NTFS volumes can have files, folders, and subfolders encrypted using **EFS** (Encrypting File System). The EFS algorithm originally used DES (Data Encryption standard), which uses 56- or 128-bit encryption, but now the EFS algorithm uses AES (Advanced Encryption Standard), SHA (Secure Hash Algorithm), smart-card–based encryption, and in Windows 7, ECC (elliptical curve cryptography).

When a folder or subfolder is encrypted, all newly created files within the folder or subfolder are automatically encrypted. If any files are copied or moved into an encrypted folder or subfolder, those files are automatically encrypted. System files cannot be encrypted. EFS can use a CA (certificate authority) such as one issued from a server or use a self-signed certificate as demonstrated in Lab 15.1 at the end of this chapter.

Tech Tip

Can you encrypt someone else's files?

The answer is yes if you have the write attribute, create files/write data, and list folder/read data permissions for the file.

Some data from computers must be printed as part of normal business operations. Some printed material must be kept in a locked environment (such as a safe, cabinet, or file cabinet). When the material is no longer needed, it can be shredded by a shredding service or using a shredder in the office (see Figure 15.8). Shredders are available for reasonable prices, but they are not the best option in a corporate environment because reconstruction can be done with most models. For day-to-day business and personal documents, shredding is still a good practice to keep other people from taking documents out of the trash bin (dumpster diving) and using the information for mal gain.

Figure 15.8 Shredding

DEP (Data Execution Prevention)

DEP is a security measure implemented in both hardware and software to prevent malicious software from running on a Windows-based computer. DEP is always on and enabled for 64-bit versions of Windows, but the policy can be managed. With DEP that is hardware-based, the CPU supports enforcing no execute (AMD processors) or execute disable (Intel processors). The processor marks memory with an attribute indicating that data inside that memory location should not be executable (it should just be another type of data or code). Different processors have different capabilities, but at a minimum, the processor can display a message if code tries to execute from those memory locations marked as no execute or execute disable.

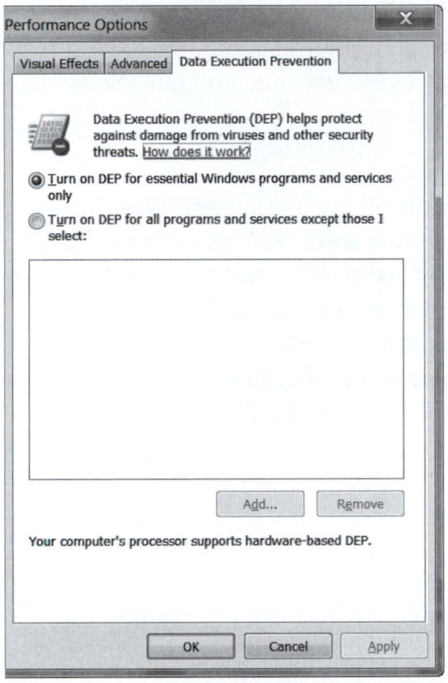

Figure 15.9 DEP on Windows 7

With software-enforced DEP, if a program tries to run from a memory location that should not have executable code, the application is closed and a message appears. Software-enforced DEP is available in Windows XP Service Pack 2 and higher and all versions of Vista and 7. To see this feature in Vista or 7, *System* (Vista) or *System and Security* (7) Control Panel > *System* (7) > *Advanced System Settings* link > *Settings* button in the *Performance* area > *Data Execution Prevention* tab. Figure 15.9 shows the two options. The Data Execution Prevention tab also shows at the bottom of the window whether the processor is capable of DEP.

Protecting Access to Local and Network Resources

Several techniques exist to protect computer access, and some of them have been considered as part of physical access. Authentication is used to determine what network resources can be used. **Authorization** is the part of the operating system or network controls in place to determine what resources such as files, folders, printers, video conferencing equipment, scanners, and so on, can be accessed and used.

A great analogy for authentication is the clubhouse that many of us made as children. A secret tap at the door or a special password was the only way to gain access to the private domain. Most people are familiar with the user ID and password method of authentication. Other means could be used including the previously discussed biometric devices. All of these provide an additional layer of security beyond the user ID and password method. Windows and other operating systems and applications use the Kerberos protocol to provide authentication. Kerberos uses a KDC (key distribution center) to authenticate users, applications, and services. Password protection is a common method used though, and some password guidelines are listed in Table 15.6.

Table 15.6 Computer/network password guidelines

Device/ technology	Description
Reminders	Do not write down your password. Many computer users write down their password and keep it close to the computer. Do not put your password in a document stored on the same computer.
Number of characters	Use eight or more characters with uppercase and lowercase letters interspersed with numerals and special characters.
Format	Do not use consecutive letters or numbers on the keyboard, such as *asd* or *123*, because they are easy for someone who is watching to use to guess the password. Do not use passwords that are words such as *children* or *happiness* because there are password dictionaries that are used to hack passwords. These dictionaries even include foreign words and names.
Social	People's eyes tend to stray toward movement. If someone is standing near you, "shoulder surfing" when you are logging in, ensure that their eyes are averted or wait until they move to type your password into the system. Obtain a privacy filter.
Screen saver/lock computer	Use a screen saver or lock the computer with the ⊞+ L option. Configure the screen saver using the *Display* (XP)/*Personalize* (7) control panel link to configure the screen saver and require the login credentials to re-access the computer.

Prevent a computer from being seen through the network

Tech Tip

In XP, *Start* > *Control Panel* > *Classic* view and *Administrative Tools*.

In Vista/7, *System* Control Panel > *Administrative Tools*.

Then, in all Windows versions *Services* > double-click *Computer Browser* > *Startup type* drop-down menu, select *Disabled* > *Apply* > *OK* > restart the computer.

Windows allows several user ID and password options, including the following:

- Local user ID and password created and maintained on the local PC
- Computer that is part of the workgroup where the user ID and password are created, stored, and maintained on the local computer (similar to the local PC)
- Computer that is part of a domain and the user ID and password are created, stored, and maintained on a centralized network server

A workgroup or peer-to-peer environment is a LAN where each computer maintains its own networked resources, such as whether a file or printer is shared with others. Workgroup networks are more common in home and small business environments. A domain environment is more common in the business world where network servers are used to authenticate logins, provide for file storage, and provide services such as email and web access. Another name for a domain environment is a server-based network. Figure 15.10 illustrates a workgroup environment; Figure 15.11 shows how a domain environment is different.

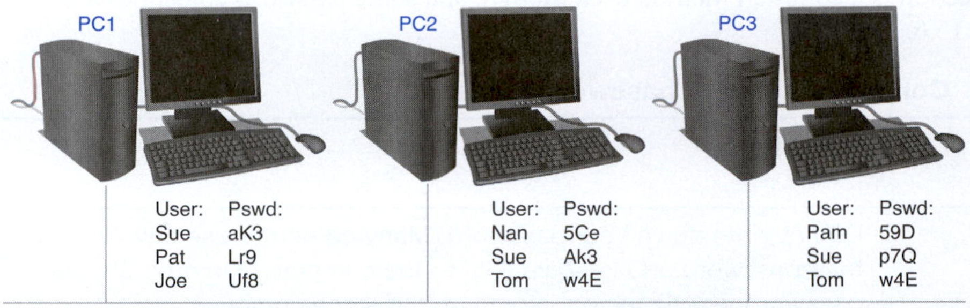

Figure 15.10 Windows workgroup model

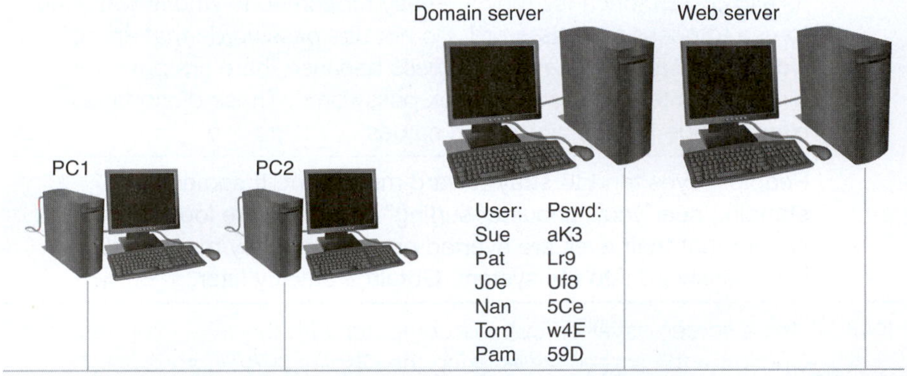

Figure 15.11 Windows domain model

Some companies use single sign-on for user authentication. Single sign-on allows a user to authenticate with a minimum of a user ID and password. With that authentication, the user is allowed access to multiple systems/servers, devices such as printers, copiers, and even networked based applications. The alternative is that the users are prompted to authenticate or log in each time they access such network connections as the work computer, email, or the shared files server.

Whether in a local- or domain-based network, users can be added and placed into groups for ease of management. Table 15.7 shows the default local users/groups for Windows XP and 7. Note that in Windows Vista/7 home versions local groups are not supported.

Table 15.7 Windows default users/groups

Windows version	User or group	Description
XP/Vista/7	Administrator (user)	Has total control of the computer; best practice is to rename the account and password protect it;create another user account that belongs to the administrator group and has a complex password
XP/Vista/7	Administrator (group)	A user account that has been created and placed in this group that has total control of the computer
XP/Vista/7	Guest (user)	Used by those that do not have an account on the computer; normally does not require a password; best practice is to disable
Vista/7	Standard user (user)	The default type of account created when you create a user; the user is required to get an administrator to make changes to software, hardware, or security settings
XP/Vista/7	Backup operators (group)	Can back up and restore files and folders regardless of permissions assigned; cannot change security settings; can access the computer from a remote location
XP	Power users (group)	Cannot change administrator or backup operator group settings; can create user accounts and modify/delete only those accounts they created; cannot take ownership of files, modify device drivers, or manage the security logs
Vista/7	Power users (group)	Same as a Standard user account (change things like time zone or date/time)
XP/Vista/7	Users (group)	Can perform common tasks and create local groups, but cannot share folders or printers
Vista/7	Remote desktop users (group)	Can log on to the computer from a remote location
Vista/7	Offer Remote Assistance Helper (group)	Can use the Remote Assistance program to help the computer user
Vista/7	Network Configuration Operators (group)	Can make TCP/IP changes and release/renew IP addresses
Vista/7	Performance Log Users (group)	Can manage local or remote performance logs and alerts

Another method of controlling login passwords is through a local- or domain-based account policy. Policies can define the desktop, what applications are available to users, what options are available through the *Start* menu, whether users are allowed to save files to external media, and so on. A domain or group policy can be created and applied to every computer on the domain.

A local policy is created on a computer, and it could be used to disable auto-playing of optical discs, prevent users from shutting down or restarting a computer, turn off personalized menus, or keep someone from changing the Internet Explorer home page. A local policy might be implemented in a workgroup setting. A group policy is more common in a corporate environment, and a group policy can overwrite a local policy. The local policy is accessed by typing `gpedit.msc` from a command prompt or in the *Search* textbox in Windows Vista/7. The `secedit` command is used to configure or analyze the security policy.

Passwords continue to be an issue today for everyone. Different requirements, user IDs, and passwords, cause stress for many folks. A password manager is an application that is on one computer or a USB drive, mobile app, or web browser plug-in that locally or remotely stores passwords used to access an account. When stored remotely, the passwords and associated data (site, device, etc.) should be encrypted.

Through the defined policy, criteria for auditing can also be set. **Auditing**, sometimes called event logging or just logging, is the process of tracking events that occur on the network such as someone logging into the network. In the business environment, a server with special auditing software is sometimes devoted to this task because it is so important to security. Lab 15.6 at the end of this chapter details how to configure a local security policy, log events, and view those audited items. Figure 15.12 shows the Local Group Policy Editor window.

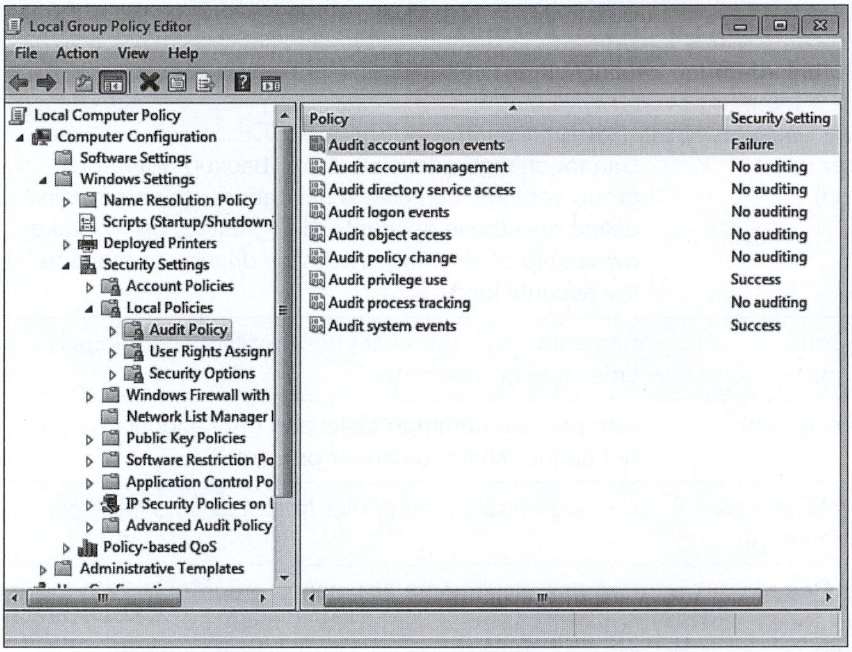

Figure 15.12 Local Group Policy Editor window

File and folder security protection is also a concern. A subfolder and any files created within that subfolder all inherit security permissions from the parent folder or the folder that contains the subfolder. This feature can be disabled when necessary.

Files and folders can be shared in a network workgroup, a homegroup, or a domain. A **local share** is something—a printer, folder, or media device—that is shared on a specific computer. **Administrative shares** are shares created by Microsoft for drive volumes and the folder that contains the majority of Window files. An example of an administrative share is a drive volume letter (such as C) followed by the dollar sign ($) symbol (C$). The admin$ administrative share is used to access to the folder that contains the Windows operating system files.

Windows automatically creates these administrative shares, but by default Windows Vista and 7 prevent local accounts from accessing administrative shares through the network. If this feature is desired in Windows Vista or 7, a registry edit must be made. In Windows XP, the `net share` *`share_name$`* `/delete` command can be used to disable a particular administrative share. However, this is reset when the computer is restarted. A batch file could be created and put in the startup folder to make this a more permanent solution.

Any local share can be made a **hidden share**, which is a share that is not seen by default through the network. To make a share a hidden share, add the dollar sign ($) symbol to the share name. This might be beneficial to a computer user who wants to access something from his or her remote computer without making it visible to other network users.

Permissions

Monitoring the users and groups and the devices, data, and applications they have access to is important. Permissions control what can or cannot be done to files, folders, and devices from a remote connection. User-assigned permissions can cause havoc. Network administrators and end users can set permissions on folders, and these permissions can affect another user's access to files and folders. Technicians need to be familiar with permissions.

There are two types of permissions that can be assigned in Windows: shared folder permissions and NTFS file/folder permissions. Shared folder permissions provide access to data across a network. Shared folder permissions are the only way to secure network resources on FAT16 or FAT32 drives. NTFS file/folder permissions provide tighter control than shared folder permissions. NTFS permissions can be used only on NTFS drives.

In XP, to share a folder using shared folder permissions, locate the folder using *Explorer* > right-click the folder > *Sharing and Security* > *Sharing* tab > *Share this folder*. Permissions are set by clicking the *Permissions* button. Besides sharing this folder and allowing access to another user across the network, you can limit the number of users who can access this folder. Figure 15.13 shows this window.

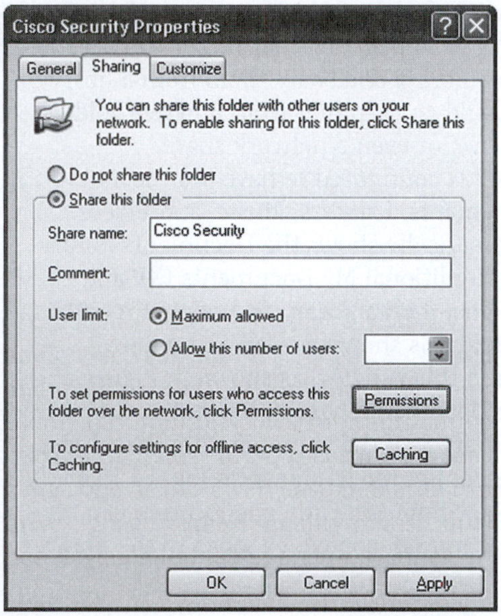

Figure 15.13 **Folder permissions—Sharing tab**

Windows Vista and 7 support sharing a folder in a similar fashion as XP, but they use a new folder called the Public folder. The default path for the Public folder is C:\Users\Public. You can copy or move any files to the Public folder. This makes it easier to share files with someone, but files that are copied into it take twice as much hard drive space because they are in two folders.

> **Tech Tip**
>
> **Vista/7 password protection**
>
> You can enable or disable password protection through the Network and Sharing Center on a workgroup/homegroup computer. If password protection is enabled, the person accessing the folder from a remote location must have a user account and password on the computer with the share.

If sharing is enabled for the Public folder, anyone with a user account and password on the computer that contains the data, in addition to any user on the network, can see all files and folders in the Public folder. You can set permissions so that the folder is inaccessible or restrict anyone from changing files or creating new files. However, you cannot pick and choose what files can be seen by individuals.

In Vista/7, to share a folder other than the Public folder, use *Windows Explorer* > right-click the folder > *Share* (Vista)/*Share with* (7). You can do one of the following at this point:

- Type the name of the person and click Add.
- If the computer is attached to a network domain, click the arrow to the right of the textbox > *Find* > type the name of the person with whom you want to share the folder > *Check Names* > *OK*.
- If the computer is on a workgroup, click the arrow to the right of the textbox, click the appropriate name, and click *Add*. If the name does not appear, click the arrow to the right of the textbox and click *Create a new user* to create the user account.
- If the computer is part of a homegroup, you can select *Homegroup (Read)* or *Homegroup (Read/Write)* and the folder will be shared with the appropriate permissions.

> **Tech Tip**
>
> **Principle of least privilege**
>
> When sharing access to a folder or to a server room, you should give access to what is needed and no more. Giving someone access to an entire drive or building when they just need access to a particular folder or room puts the entire hard drive or company at risk.

Windows 7 uses libraries. A library is similar to a folder, but a library contains files that are automatically indexed for faster searching, viewing, and access. For example, a teacher might store training video clips in a library and share them from a library. This library could contain files from different folders, an external drive, or even a network share.

Windows 7 is configured to have four default libraries: Documents, Printers, Music, and Videos. Explorer automatically shows the Documents library instead of the traditional My Documents (XP and below) or Documents (Vista/7). If you right-click the Documents library and select Properties, you can see that both a particular user's Documents folder is shown as well as a public Documents folder. Notice the *Include a folder* button in this window, as shown in Figure 15.14. This button allows more folders to be included in the Documents library. No matter the source of the files, they are all controlled through a single library as if the contents were stored in a single location. Each default library has two locations configured as shown in Figure 15.14. The public location is used by any user logged onto the computer. Only one location can be configured as the default save location for files that are moved, copied, or saved to the library.

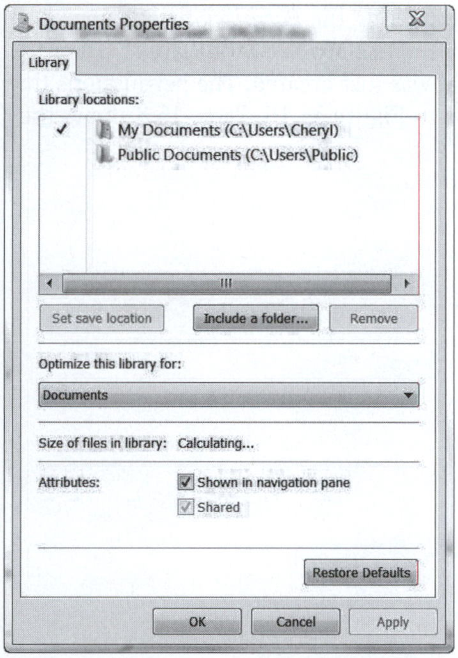

Figure 15.14 **Windows 7 libraries**

Some people find Windows Vista/7 folder sharing more difficult than sharing in Windows XP. The Windows XP method can be used in Vista/7 by right-clicking a folder and selecting *Properties* > *Sharing* tab > *Advanced Sharing* button > enable the *Share this folder* checkbox > *Permissions* button. To share files on a home network, create a homegroup. In Windows 7 Home Basic and Starter, you can only join a homegroup, not create one. Right-click a folder and use the *Share with* menu option.

You can also share files and folders by using the Public folder. In Windows Explorer, expand any of the libraries and notice the Public folder, as shown in Figure 15.15. Drop a file or folder into one of these Public folders, and others have access. Note that "Public" file sharing is turned off by default, and you cannot restrict individual files within any of the Public folders.

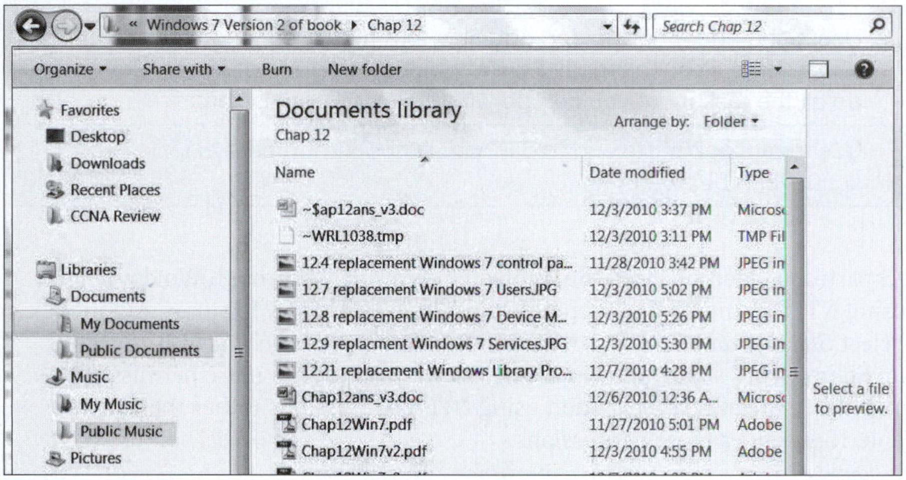

Figure 15.15 **Windows 7 Public Documents folder**

Once you share a folder, you set the permissions by clicking the *Permissions* button. To test a shared folder permission, go to another computer and use My Network Places (XP) or Network (Vista/7) to locate the computer and share what was just created. The permissions that can be set are Full Control, Change, and Read, as shown in Figure 15.16. Table 15.8 shows the effects of setting one of these permissions.

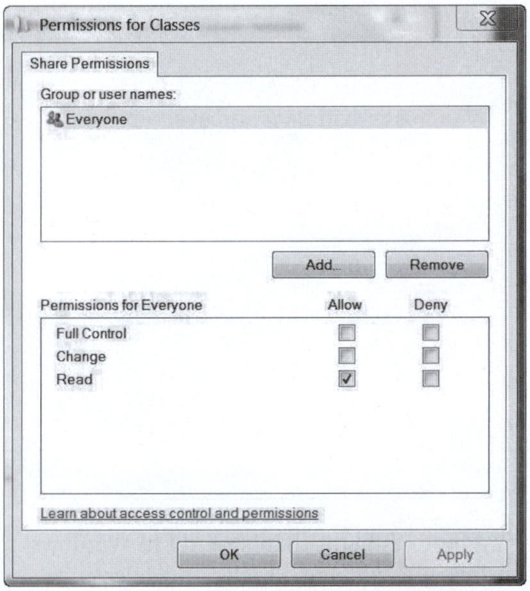

Figure 15.16 Folder permissions—share permissions

Table 15.8 Share permissions

Permission	Description
Full Control	Users can do everything, such as change the file permissions, take ownership of files, and perform everything that can be done with the *Change* permission.
Change	Users can add a new folder, add files to a folder, change the data in file, add data to files, change the file attributes, delete folders and files, and do all the tasks that you can do with the *Read* permission.
Read	Users can look at file and folder names and attributes. Also, files and scripts can be executed.

On an NTFS partition, additional security protection is available through Windows. To share a folder using NTFS permissions, locate the folder using Windows Explorer. Right-click the folder and select *Sharing and Security* (XP), *Sharing* (Vista), or *Properties* (7), and click the *Security* tab. Figure 15.17 shows this window. Notice how there are more permissions that can be administered on an NTFS partition using NTFS permissions rather than share permissions. Table 15.9 defines these permissions.

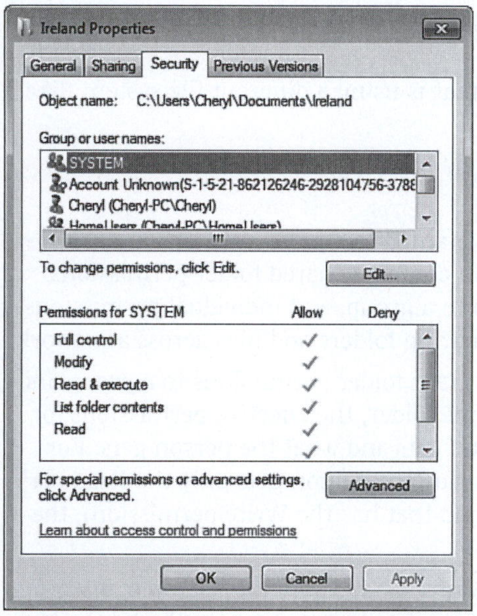

Figure 15.17 Windows 7 NTFS permissions—Security tab

Tech Tip

Share permissions are only applicable across a network

Notice that shared folder permissions are applicable only across a network. This type of share does not prevent someone sitting at the computer from accessing files and folders. For the best protection across a network and at the computer, use NTFS file and folder permissions.

Table 15.9 NTFS permissions

Permission	Description
Full Control	Users can do anything in the files and folder, including delete, add, modify, and create.
Modify	Users can list items in a folder, read data, and write data, but they cannot delete subfolders and files and cannot take ownership.
Read & Execute	Users can list items in a folder and read a file, but they cannot change or delete the file or create new files. Users can execute applications contained within the folder.
List Folder Contents	Users can only look inside a folder.
Read	Users can display folder and subfolder attributes and permissions as well as look at a particular file.
Write	Users can add files or folders, change attributes for the folder and add or append to data in a file.

Inherited permissions are permissions that are propagated from what Microsoft calls a parent object. For example, if a folder is given the Read permission, then all files within that folder cannot be changed (they are read-only). If a subfolder is created, it inherits that permission. If the allow/deny checkboxes for any object are selected, the current permissions have been inherited.

There can also be issues when copying or moving is performed on objects that have NTFS permissions set. Here are some guidelines for copying and moving:

- When you copy a file/folder on the same or different NTFS drive letter, the copy inherits the destination folder permissions.
- When you move a file/folder on the same NTFS drive letter, the original permissions of the object are retained.

- When you move a file/folder to a different NTFS drive letter, the moved object inherits the destination folder permissions.
- When you copy or move a file/folder to a drive that is using a different file system (like FAT), the object loses all of its permissions.
- If you change permissions on a folder that already has content, only the new content inherits the changed permissions.

Effective permissions are the final permissions granted to a person for a particular resource. Effective permissions are important when you combine shared folder permissions given to an individual, shared folder permissions given to a group, and individual permissions. The list that follows outlines some helpful tips when sharing folders and files across a network:

- Folder permissions are cumulative—when you grant folder permissions to a group and then grant an individual permissions to that same folder, the effective permissions for that person is the combination of what the group gets and what the person gets. For example, if the group gets the Write permission and the person gets only the Read permission (and the person is a member of the group that has the Write permission), the person can both read and write files to the folder.
- Deny overrides any allowed permission set for a user or a group. For example, if a group is denied access to a folder, but a person is specifically allowed access to the folder, the person is not allowed to access the folder.
- When NTFS and shared folder permissions are both used, the most restrictive of the two is the effective permissions.

Windows Vista and 7 provide help in determining effective permissions. In Windows 7, right-click a file or folder > *Properties* > *Security* tab > *Advanced* button > *Effective Permissions* tab (see Figure 15.18). Note that what is shown is only in regard to NTFS permissions. Share permissions are not part of the Windows calculation for this window. Permissions are a common problem, and a computer technician must be familiar with the effects of misconfiguring them.

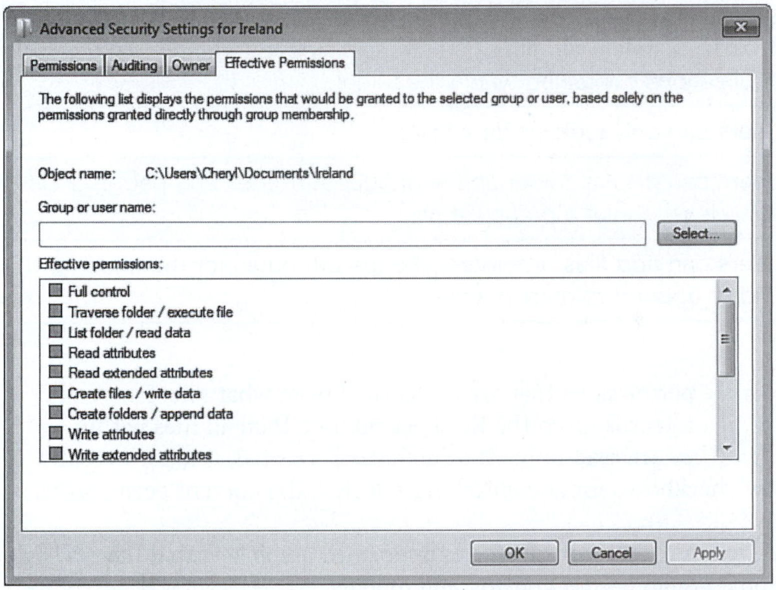

Figure 15.18 Windows 7 effective permissions

Internet Security

The Internet is commonly accessed through a browser, and configuring the browser is one of the first steps to configuring security. Browsers are commonly upgraded to provide improved security options. Before upgrading an Internet browser, you must determine the current web browser version. With many Windows-based applications, the version is determined by starting the application, clicking *Help > About x* (where *x* is the name of the application), or selecting the question mark menu item. With Internet Explorer (IE), the first two numbers listed are the software version numbers. There is another value called cipher strength that is a bit value for encryption; **encryption** is a protection method used to change data so it cannot be recognized. Encryptions algorithms include DES, 3DES, and AES.

Tech Tip

Why keep your Windows and web browser current?

Internet hackers frequently target browsers, and constant updates are provided to counter these attacks.

When people connect to the Internet, they normally do so through a web browser. Any web browser can usually be configured for various security options. Since Microsoft operating systems ship with Internet Explorer, it is covered here. But similar options are available in most browsers.

One issue with browsers is that they can be hijacked (see Figure 15.19). A hijacked browser either replaces the home page with another one or directs whatever web page is being used to a different one. This is called a browser redirect. Besides sending you to another web page, a browser redirect can also be used to install a rootkit or install more malware (bad software) that includes keystroke loggers (to record your keystrokes including your ID and password), DNS hijack, or a rogue HOSTS file. A **rootkit** can be used to act as a backdoor to your operating system and may be used to do things that require administrator access. Rootkits can also be downloaded and installed to a flash drive. The HOSTS file is a text file used to manually map a hostname to a particular IP address. The following recommendations can help with a hijacked browser issue:

Figure 15.19 Hijacking

- Change the home page URL to your normal home page and not the hijacked page. In Internet Explorer, browse to the web page you want to be the home page. In Internet Explorer 9, right-click the Home icon. In Internet Explorer 7 or 8, click the down arrow next to the Home icon. > *Add or Change Home Page > Use this webpage as your only home page > Yes.*

- If pop-ups appear continuously, use Task Manager to stop the `iexplore.exe` process. Re-open Internet Explorer and ensure the pop-up blocker is turned on: *Internet Options* > *Privacy* tab > enable *Turn on Pop-up Blocker*. Otherwise, use an alternative browser, such as Google Chrome or Mozilla Firefox.
- If necessary, start the computer in Safe Mode with Networking. If the web browser works properly, a DLL file has been added to the computer. Run a scan with your antivirus or antispyware application. Otherwise, you can download and install Microsoft Security Essentials for free.
- Start the browser with no add-ons to see if one of them is causing the problem. How you do this depends on the browser. In Internet Explorer, perform the following: *Start* > *All Programs* > *Accessories* > *System tools* > *Internet Explorer (No Add-ons)*. If the browser starts working, turn on the add-ons one by one to determine which one caused the problem.
- Determine whether the HOSTS file has been modified and includes some rogue entries. The HOSTS file can be found in the folder C:\Windows\system32\drivers\etc folder.

Spam is another problem. **Spam** comes in unsolicited email from a company or person previously unknown. People who send this type of email are known as spammers. Most email applications have spam filters, but they cannot catch all of them. Most email applications also allow you to create a rule to block messages from a particular source or subject line. Figure 15.20 demonstrates the concept of a spam filter.

Figure 15.20 Spam

Other issues related to email include email messages being sent in clear text. If such an email is intercepted, the message is easy to read. PGP (Pretty Good Privacy) and S/MIME (Secure Multipurpose Internet Mail Extension) are frequently used to provide encryption and authentication for email messages.

Avoid checking email on a public computer or an unsecure network. If an email account gets hijacked (the user cannot log in using normal procedures, contacts in response to constant emails or spam from the hijacked account, or the account has a lot of undeliverable emails), then perform the following steps:

1. Contact the email account company to report the problem.
2. Ensure that Windows, antivirus, and antimalware software updates have been applied.
3. Ensure that you have an alternate email account available when you have to register with a site, such as for online shopping.
4. Try logging in to the account from a different computer to see if email settings have been changed. If you can get to the account, change the password.
5. Create rules in your email account to delete files from specific nontrusted sources.

Most web browsers allow some method of deleting cookies. A **cookie** is a special program written to collect information and store it on the hard drive. A cookie could be used for a variety of things, but some examples include your preferences when you visit a website, rotating banner ads at the top of a website so you do not see the same ones repeatedly, and tracking what Internet sites you visit. Internet Explorer stores cookies as a separate file.

You can configure a web browser to accept all cookies, block all cookies, or notify you every time a cookie is offered by a web server. In Internet Explorer, access the *Tools* menu option > *Internet Options* > *General* tab > *Browsing History* section > *Delete*. The *Delete* button gets rid of cookies, passwords, form data, history, and temporary Internet files. See Figure 15.21.

Cookies can also be controlled through the *Internet* zone settings located on the *Security* tab in Internet Explorer. The zones are the four categories shown with icons at the top of the page in Figure 15.22.

Click the *Internet* zone (the world icon) to adjust the settings. The *Internet* zone is the default zone that all websites fall into unless a website is specifically added to another zone such as the *Trusted sites* zone. Use the slider bar to adjust the security levels. These settings help against rogue spyware installations and advertisement pop-ups.

Active scripting is an important security setting in a web browser. Active scripts are programs written for the Internet and are used on news sites, online shopping sites, and web-based email sites to make a web page more dynamic and one that constantly changes. However, some active scripting can be harmful because it can be used as a mechanism to transmit a worm virus into the computer. For this reason, a technician should define what Internet sites are often used that might be programmed with scripting. If active scripting is used on a site not listed, a message appears on the screen and you can either view the page or refuse it.

To configure Internet Explorer to handle active scripting this way, open Internet Explorer > *Tools* menu > *Internet Options* > *Security* tab > *Trusted Sites* > *Sites* button. In the *Add this website to the zone* textbox, type the web address for a site you visit often that might use active scripting > *Add*. Continue adding as many sites as you need.

From the *Security* tab, select the *Internet* icon. Click the *Custom Level* button. Figure 15.23 shows the window that appears. Each of the security settings can be manually configured, and Table 15.10 explains the options.

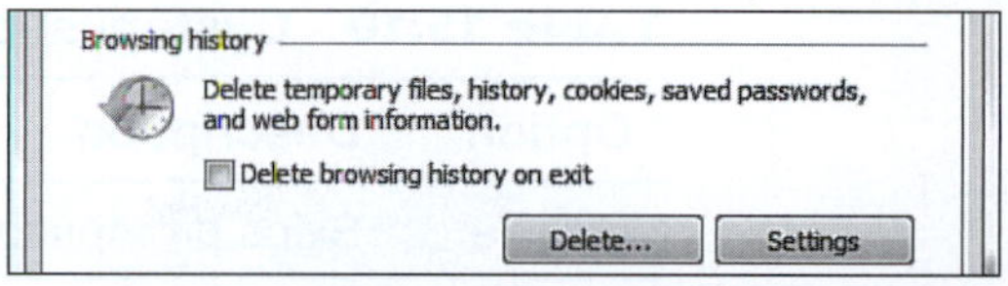

Figure 15.21 Internet Explorer General tab—Browsing history

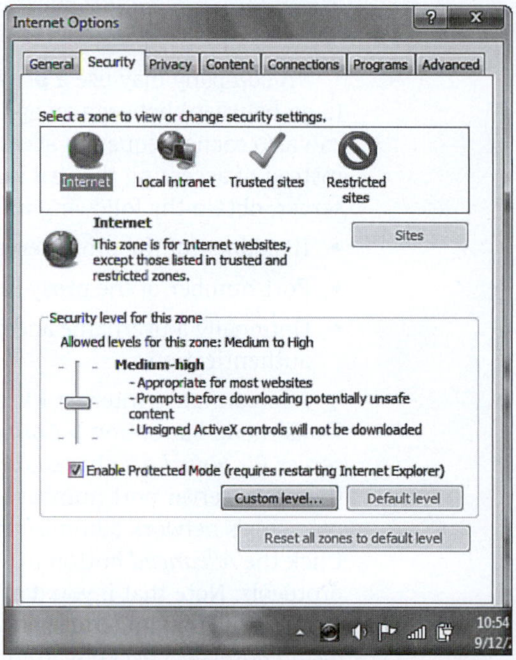

Figure 15.22 Internet Explorer Security tab

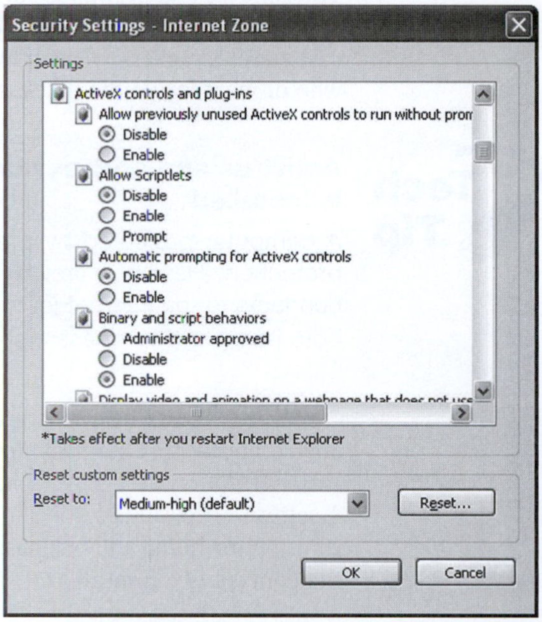

Figure 15.23 Custom security settings

Table 15.10 Custom security options

Option	Description
Disable	Skips prompting and automatically refuses the action or download.
Enable	Automatically proceeds with the option.
Prompt	Prompts for approval before proceeding with the option. Note that not all options have a Prompt choice.

A company may use a **proxy server** to protect its network. This server acts as an agent (a go-between) between an application such as a web browser and a real server. A proxy server can also cache frequently accessed web pages and provide them when requested from a client instead of accessing the real web server. To configure any device or application for a proxy server, obtain the following information:

- IP address of the proxy server
- Port number of the proxy server
- Optionally a username and password, but some organizations use server-based authentication

To configure Internet Explorer to use a proxy server, use the *Internet Options* from the *Tools* menu bar option > *Connections* tab > *LAN Settings* button > select the *Use a proxy server for your LAN* checkbox > in the *Address* textbox, type the proxy server IP address > type the proxy server port number in the *Port* textbox. This information can be obtained from the company's network administrator or through **WPAD** (Web Proxy AutoDiscovery) protocol. Click the *Advanced* button to set individual IP addresses and port numbers for different protocols. Note that if you don't want the proxy server to be used when accessing resources in the local domain (and speed up this type of access), select the *Bypass proxy server for local addresses* checkbox. Improperly configured proxy settings can cause the computer to be redirected to an invalid website and have no Internet connectivity.

Computer security is a huge concern. If a computer connects to the Internet, it should be connected behind a firewall. A **firewall** protects one or more computers from outside attacks. The concept of a firewall is similar to building a moat with a drawbridge around a castle. The castle is the inside network, the moat with the drawbridge is the firewall, and all outside the castle are "attackers." The drawbridge can control who or what has access to the castle and who or what leaves the castle.

Tech Tip

Antivirus and antispyware applications are needed even when a firewall is installed

A computer protected by a firewall still needs antivirus and antispyware applications for protection. Having a firewall on each computer as well as on a router or modem that connects to the Internet (or a device dedicated to providing firewall services) is common in both home and business environments.

A firewall can be a software application or hardware and should be implemented for any computer that connects to another network, especially a computer that connects to the Internet. A firewall keeps hackers from accessing a computer that connects to the Internet. A software firewall is a good solution for individual computers. A hardware firewall is a good solution for home and business networks. Both can be used concurrently. Figure 15.24 shows the concept of a firewall.

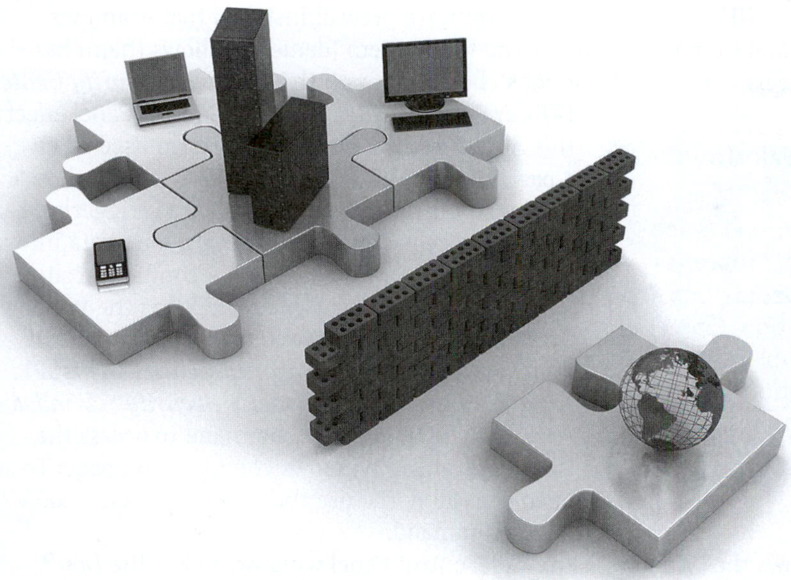

Figure 15.24 Firewall

In a corporate environment, a firewall can create an area called the **DMZ** (demilitarized zone). Servers such as web servers can reside in the DMZ, and customers can use that server without having to be let into the part of the network where the sensitive corporate data resides. Figure 15.25 shows this concept.

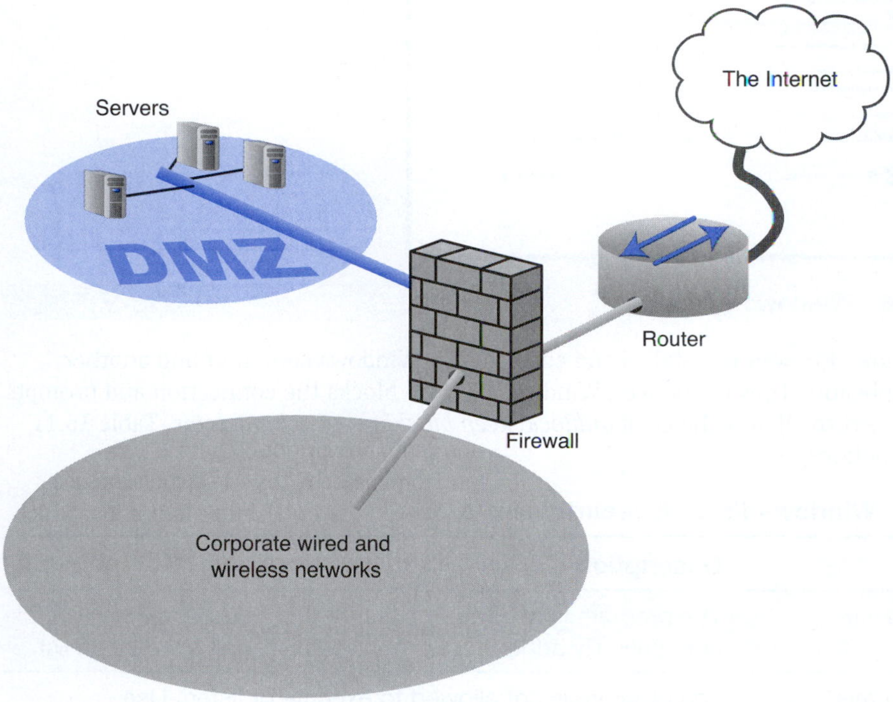

Figure 15.25 DMZ

A DMZ could also be created by having two firewalls, with one firewall connected to the router as shown before and the DMZ connected to that firewall and to a second firewall. The second firewall also connects to the internal corporate network, so the setup looks like this:

Internet | Firewall | DMZ | Firewall | Internal corporate network

Tech Tip

Allowing a program through Windows Firewall

Locate and right-click the program you want to allow Internet connectivity. Select *Properties* > *Shortcut* tab > right-click in the *Target* textbox (the path highlights) > *Copy* > *Cancel* button. Open the Security Center and Windows Firewall. Select the *Exceptions* tab > *Add Program* button > *Browse* button > right-click in the *File name* textbox and select *Paste* > *OK* > OK.

Microsoft Windows XP, Vista, and 7 have a software firewall installed that examines packets travelling to and from the computer and filters them (denies or allows them) based on a configured ACL (access control list). Options chosen through the *Windows Security Center* (XP) or *Action Center* (Vista/7) Control Panel affect this ACL. **Port forwarding** is a term used when a packet is allowed through the firewall based on a particular port number/protocol. Port triggering is a similar concept. **Port triggering** allows data into a computer temporarily based on a configured situation.

To verify whether Windows XP has the Windows firewall enabled, click the *Start* button > *Control Panel* > *Classic* view > *Security Center*. In Vista/7, *Start* button > *Control Panel* > *Security* > *Windows Firewall*. Use the `wf.msc` command to access the Vista/7 Advanced Windows configuration page. To see open firewall ports, use the `netsh firewall show state` command.

Figure 15.26 shows the Windows 7 Firewall Control Panel window. In XP, the *Don't Allow Exceptions* checkbox is used to block all incoming traffic when a computer is used in a restaurant or public place. In Vista/7, the *Block all incoming connections* checkbox provides the same security option.

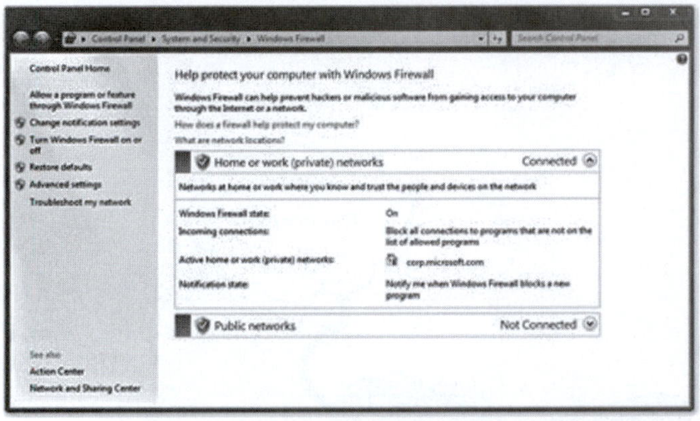

Figure 15.26 Windows 7 firewall

When Windows Firewall is installed and enabled on a Windows computer and another computer or application tries to connect, Windows Firewall blocks the connection and prompts with a security alert to allow a choice of *unblock*, *keep blocking*, or *ask me later*. Table 15.11 describes these options.

Table 15.11 Windows firewall security alerts

Alert	Description
Unblock this program	The program is allowed to execute and the program is automatically added to the Windows Firewall exceptions list.
Keep blocking this program	The program is not allowed to execute or listen. Use whenever you do not know the source of the alert.
Keep blocking this program, but ask me again later	Does not allow the program to execute or listen, but the next time you access the site, the security alert will prompt you again.

Windows Vista and 7 have up to three possible network location settings (depending on the Windows version) that configure the firewall differently:

- The *Private (Home or Work)* network location setting turns file sharing and network discovery on through the firewall so communication will be easier at work or in a private home network.
- The *Public* setting configures these settings to be off through the firewall to help protect your computer when you are on a public network such as when you are in an airport.
- The *Domain* setting is when the computer participates in a Windows Active Directory domain environment.

Table 15.12 shows Windows firewall issues and solutions to help with troubleshooting.

Table 15.12 Windows firewall troubleshooting

Windows firewall issue	Resolutions
The firewall is blocking all connections	Access Windows Firewall and disable the *Don't allow exceptions* (XP) or *Block all incoming connections* (Vista/7) checkbox.
The firewall is blocking a specific application	If a dialog box appears, select the *Unblock* option to allow it through. If the dialog box does not appear, access Windows Firewall and use the *Exceptions* tab to create a rule that will allow the application through the firewall.
No one can ping a Vista/7 computer	Ensure that *File and Print Sharing* is enabled through the *Network and Sharing Center* Control Panel. Access the *Administrative Tools* link and select *Windows Firewall with Advanced Security*. Select *Inbound rules* in the left pane. Select *New Rule* in the *Actions* column. Select the *Custom* radio button and *Next*. Select the *All programs* radio button and *Next*. Select *ICMPv4* from the *Protocol Type* drop-down box. Select the IP addresses to which this rule will apply and name the rule.
Windows Firewall is turned off every time the computer restarts	Another security firewall is installed.
No one can access local files and/or a shared printer	File and Print Sharing has not been enabled.

Many Internet sites send unwanted code to the computer via the web browser. This unwanted code can be offered as a special utility to speed up Internet access or is included as part of a downloaded song or application. Table 15.13 lists some of these malicious types.

Table 15.13 Unsolicited Internet message types

Type	Description
spyware	Collects personal information without consent through logging keystrokes, accessing saved documents, and recording Internet browsing. Results in unsolicited pop-ups and identify theft.
adware	A program that automatically displays marketing advertisements as an integrated part of a website or as a pop-up.
malware	Also known as badware. Includes software code that is designed to damage a computer system (lockups, slowness, applications won't run or run incorrectly, etc.).
grayware	A generic term for applications or files that are not viruses, but that affects computer performance and/or cause unexpected and unsolicited events to occur. Can come from downloading shareware or freeware, infected emails, selecting an advertisement shown in a pop-up window, or through a Trojan virus. Spyware, adware, and malware are all types of grayware.

There are freeware programs available as well as full security suites such as the ones from McAfee or Symantec that include software firewalls and components to prevent these types of malicious software applications from executing. Microsoft Vista and 7 come with **Windows Defender**, which works with Internet Explorer to warn for spyware. The MBSA (Microsoft Security Baseline Analyzer) can be used to identify security misconfigurations on computers. Configure your browser so that a security warning appears or you are asked or warned of potential security threats. Antivirus, antimalware, antispyware software is available for free or can be purchased. Common ones include Ad-aware, Spybot, and MalwareBytes.

Windows Defender is available in all versions of Windows Vista and higher and is available for download for computers that have Windows XP SP2 and higher. Windows Defender works in the background looking for spyware. Windows Defender can be customized in terms of when updates are downloaded and how often it scans the computer, and it shows detailed information about software that is installed on the computer. Lab 15.7 explores some of the Windows Defender options.

If you suspect that a computer is affected by malware or a virus, perform the following steps:

1. Disconnect the computer from any wired or wireless network to quarantine the infected system.
2. Disable the System Restore tool. If the virus or malware is part of a system restore point and the antivirus or antimalware software cannot remove it.
3. Repair the infected system by running antivirus/antimalware software. If the software is not successful removing the virus, use a good machine to check the antivirus/antimalware software website for possible updates or software that can be downloaded for such a situation. Use Safe Mode or the original operating system discs, if necessary.
4. Once the system is repaired, ensure that the system is configured for operating system and anti-everything updates. Re-enable the System Restore tool.
5. Educate the user on security best practices.

All technicians (and employees) should be aware of social engineering. **Social engineering** is a technique used to trick people into divulging information, including their own personal information or corporate knowledge. Social engineering does not just relate to computers but can be done over the phone, through online surveys, or through mail surveys. No auditing or network security applications and devices can help with such deviousness.

A related concept is phishing. **Phishing** (pronounced "fishing") is a type of social engineering that attempts to get personal information, and it comes through email from a company that appears legitimate. Phishing emails target ATM/debit or credit card numbers and PINs, Social Security numbers, bank account numbers, Internet banking login IDs and passwords, email addresses, security information such as a mother's maiden name, full name, home address, or phone number. Internet Explorer 7 and higher includes a phishing filter, which proactively warns the computer user when he or she goes to a site that is a known phishing site or when a site contains characteristics common to phishing sites. See Figure 15.27.

Figure 15.27 Phishing

Attacks can come from outside or from within a corporate network. Table 15.14 lists various types of network attacks.

Table 15.14 Types of network attacks

Type of attack	Description
Access	Frequently uses multiple dictionaries, including foreign ones to gain access to accounts, databases, servers, and/or network devices. Types of attacks include man-in-the-middle, port redirection, buffer overflow, and password.
ARP spoofing	Sending of an Ethernet frame with a fake source MAC address to trick other devices to sending traffic to a rogue device.
Backdoor	Also known as trapdoor, a planted program that executes to bypass security and/or authentication.
Brute force	Repeated attempts to check all possible key combinations to gain access to a network device or stored material.

Type of attack	Description
DoS (denial of service)	A string of data/messages sent to overload a particular firewall, router, switch, server, access point, computer, etc., in an attempt to deny service to other network devices.
DDoS (distributed denial of service)	A group of infected computers attack a single network device by flooding the network with traffic.
Reconnaissance	Attempts to gather information about the network before launching another type of attack. Tools used include port scanners, pings, and packet-sniffing programs.
Replay	A valid network message or certificate is re-sent, usually in an attempt to gain logon procedures.
Smurf	Uses the ICMP protocol to ping a large amount of network traffic at a specific device to deny that device network access, ping a nonexistent device to generate a lot of network traffic, or ping all network devices to generate a lot of traffic in ICMP replies.
TCP/IP hijacking	A stolen IP address is used to gain access and/or authorization information from the network.
Vulnerability scanner	A software program used to assess network devices to identify weaknesses such as unpatched operating systems, open ports, or missing/outdated virus scanning software.

Tech Tip

Both sides of the VPN tunnel must match

The two devices used to create a VPN tunnel must have identical VPN settings, or the VPN tunnel will not be formed.

A popular business solution for security is a VPN. A **VPN** (virtual private network) is a special type of secure network created over the Internet from one network device to another. One example is a home PC that connects to a corporate server and has access to company resources that cannot be accessed any other way except by being on a computer on the inside network. The VPN connection makes it appear as if the home computer is on the inside corporate network. Another example is when a branch office network device connects to a corporate server, VPN concentrator, firewall, or other network device. Once connected, the branch office network device connects as if it were directly connected to the network.

To configure a VPN in Windows XP, Use the *Network Connections* Control Panel > *Create a new connection* > *Next* > *Connect to the network at my workplace* > *Virtual Private Network Connection* > *Next* > enter a name for the connection > *Next* > enter the IP address or fully qualified domain name of the network device on the other end of the VPN connection > *Next* > select the users allowed to use this connection > *Next* > *Finish*.

To configure a VPN in Windows Vista/7, open the *Network and Sharing Center* Control Panel. Select the *Set up a new connection or network link* > *Connect to a workplace* > *Next* > *Use my Internet connection (VPN)* > enter the IP address or fully qualified domain name of the network device on the other end of the VPN connection > *Next* > enter the required credentials > click *Connect*. Figure 15.28 illustrates these concepts.

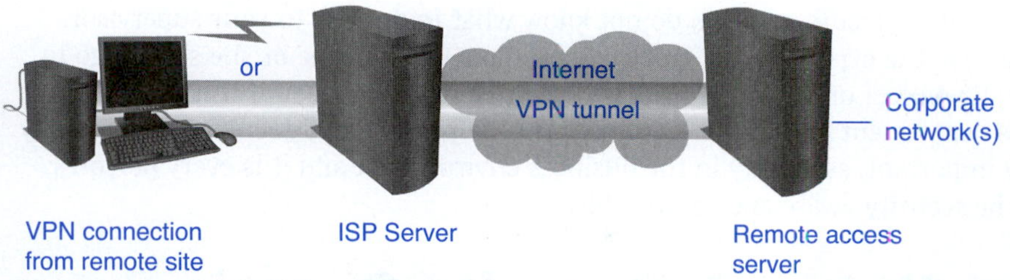

Figure 15.28 VPN connectivity

To create a VPN connection on a Windows XP computer, open the *Network Connections* Control Panel. In the *Network tasks* section, select the *Create a new connection* link. The *New Connection* Wizard steps you through the process.

Security Incident Reporting

Many companies define what to do when a security incident has occurred. However, in some businesses or in an incident that occurs on a home network, people are not always sure what to do. These are the steps to take:

1. Identify the issue. (See Table 15.15 for issues and best practices.)
2. Report the issue through the proper channels.
3. Preserve the data/device by documenting the incident and creating a chain–of-custody form that travels with the data/device as more people get involved. Chain-of-custody forms commonly have the following information.
   - What is the issue (data/device/etc.)?
   - How did you get involved with the evidence?
   - When did you see the issue?
   - What did you do to handle the issue?
   - To what person did you turn over the issue, data, device, etc.?

Table 15.15 Incident reporting and actions

Type of event	Description
Virus	Disconnect the computer from the Internet and run a full scan. Once virus-free, most antivirus software companies have a process for connecting to them automatically to receive a report of the virus scan. You can also notify your Internet provider and file a complaint with the FBI Internet Crime Complaint Center.
Spyware or grayware	Use a freeware or other software application to remove the application. Many of the security suites have a method of reporting found incidents. Submit a report using the FTC Consumer Complaint Form.
Phishing	Notify the agency from which the contact was received. Report the incident to CERT (the U.S. computer emergency readiness team) at http://www.us-cert.gov/nav/report_phishing.html.
Child exploitation	Use parental control software, log off immediately, and notify your local police department and/or the nearest FBI field office. You can also report the event to the National Center for Exploited and Missing Children.
Software piracy	Report incidents of organized software piracy to the SIIA (Software and Information Industry Association) and the BSA (Business Software Alliance).

If a security incident occurs, and you do not know what to do, talk to your supervisor. He or she should have the experience to guide you or know to whom he or she should go to resolve the issue. If you feel uncomfortable talking to your supervisor about this, consider the human resources department or a higher administrator. Reporting and documenting security violations is very important, especially in the business environment and it is every person's responsibility to be security-aware and responsible.

Wireless Network Security Overview

Security has been a big concern with wireless network installers because most people are not familiar with network or wireless security. A Bluetooth wireless PAN is secure because it uses a modified version of SAFER+ (Secure and Fast Encryption Routine). However, wireless LANs tend to not be secure. Wireless access points (APs) are an integral part of a wireless LAN and normally mounted in the ceiling or on the wall where they are conspicuous. Normal networking equipment such as hubs, switches, routers, and servers are locked in a cabinet or behind a locked door in a wiring closet. Customized cabinets can be purchased to secure APs indoors and outdoors.

Data transmitted over air can be in clear text, which means that with special frame capturing software on a computer with a wireless NIC installed, the data can be captured and viewed. Negotiation between the wireless devices and the AP can be in clear text and that information can be captured. All frames include a source MAC address and someone with a computer with a wireless NIC installed can capture the frame, use the MAC address to gain access to other resources. (This is known as session hijacking or MAC spoofing.) By default, most APs transmit their SSIDs in clear text. All of these issues must be considered when installing a wireless network.

Tech Tip

How a firewall helps a wireless computer

A firewall can protect a computer connected to a wireless network; however, the firewall cannot prevent the data being sent wirelessly from being hijacked. The firewall simply protects a hacker from accessing the computer.

Wireless Authentication and Encryption

The original 802.11 standards define two mechanisms for wireless security: authentication and data confidentiality. The two types of authentication are open and shared key. **Open authentication** allows a wireless network device to send a frame to the access point with the sender's identity (MAC address). Open authentication is used when no authentication is required. **Shared key authentication** requires the use of a shared key, which is a group of characters that the wireless network device and access point must have in common. Shared key authentication does not scale well with larger wireless networks because each device must be configured with the shared key authentication (very time-consuming), the users must be told of the shared key and their individual stations configured for this, or a server is used to provide the shared key automatically. Also, when manually input shared keys are used, the key is not changed very often which leads to security issues. (See Figure 15.29.)

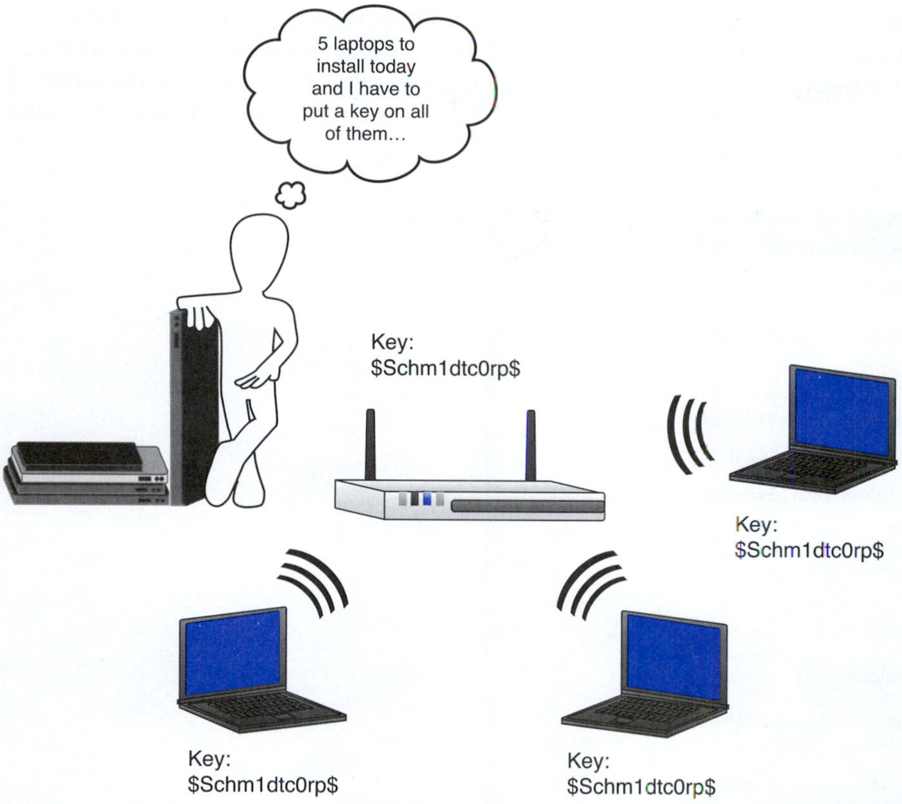

Figure 15.29 Wireless security keys

APs that support 802.1x authentication use some form of EAP (Extensible Authentication Protocol). When any type of EAP is used, the user or client to be authenticated is called a *supplicant*. An authentication server holds valid usernames and passwords. The device that is in the middle that takes the client request and passes it on to the server is known as the authenticator. An AP can be an authenticator.

When shared key authentication is being used, WEP must be enabled. **WEP** (Wired Equivalent Privacy) encrypts data being transmitted. Encryption is the process of converting data into an unreadable format. WEP commonly has two versions: 64-bit and 128-bit. Some vendors may have 256-bit. 64- and 128-bit WEP may also be seen as 40- and 104-bit. This is because each of the two versions uses a 24-bit initialization vector: 40 plus 24 equals 64 and 104 plus 24 equals 128. Sometimes you might even see that in documentation or website wording, the author mixes the two types of numbers, such as 40-bit and 128-bit, so it can be confusing.

Tech Tip

How many characters do you type with WEP?

If 64-bit WEP is being used, five 5 characters are entered (5 times 8 bits—1 for each ASCII character—equals 40 bits) or 10 hexadecimal characters (10 times four bits—1 for each hexadecimal character—equals 40 bits). If 128-bit WEP is being used and entering the key in ASCII, 13 characters are entered. And if hexadecimal is being used with 128-bit WEP, 26 characters are typed.

With WEP enabled, the shared "secret" key is normally entered into the wireless NIC configuration window. Vendors have a variety of ways of inputting this alphanumeric key, but normally it is input in either hexadecimal or ASCII characters.

Some wireless NIC manufacturers allow entering multiple WEP keys; however, only one key is used at a time. The multiple WEP keys are for multiple environments such as a WEP key for the business environment and a WEP key for the home wireless network using the same wireless NIC. Figure 15.30 shows the configuration dialog box for a wireless NIC and where the WEP is enabled.

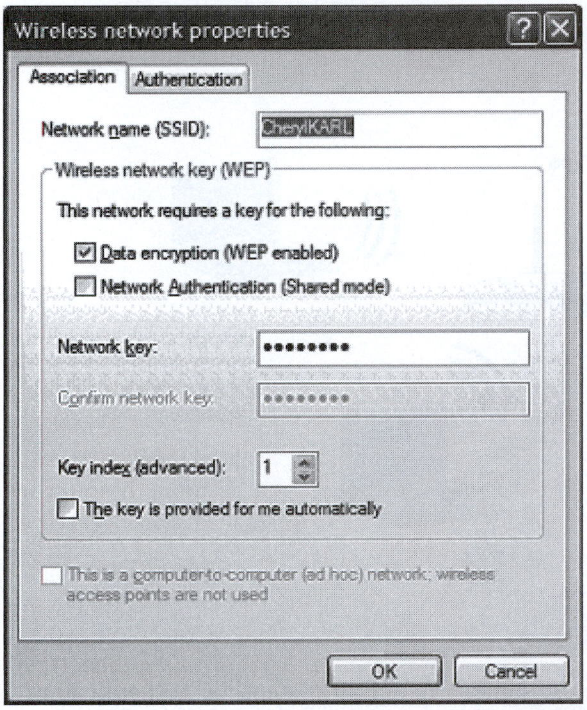

Figure 15.30 Wireless NIC properties with WEP enabled

Notice in Figure 15.30 that there is a checkbox for enabling WEP. Most installations require that the WEP key be entered manually. Notice that this adapter does not allow you to specify the length of the WEP key, so it is the 64-bit version. Note that some vendors have configuration utilities that allow wireless NIC configuration instead of the normal right-clicking the wireless NIC and selecting *Properties*.

Tech Tip

Use vendor software

When a vendor provides software for controlling a wireless NIC, use it! Do not have Windows and the vendor software compete to control the wireless NIC. In XP, use the *Wireless Networks* tab to disable Windows from controlling the NIC. In Vista/7, use the *Administrative Tools* Control Panel to select *Services*. Locate *WLAN AutoConfig* to disable from controlling the NIC.

WEP can be hacked. With special software on a laptop that has a wireless NIC installed, WEP can be compromised. Enabling WEP is better than using no encryption whatsoever. However, an improvement on WEP is **WPA** (Wi-Fi Protected Access). WPA uses **TKIP** (Temporal Key Integrity Protocol) or **AES** (Advanced Encryption Standard) to improve security. TKIP is an improvement on WEP in that the encryption keys change. Even better than TKIP is AES, which is an encryption standard with key sizes of 128-, 192-, or 256-bits. AES has been used in wireless government networks for some time. The 802.11i wireless standard specifically deals with wireless security.

WPA2 is an improvement that includes dynamic negotiation between the AP and the client for authentication and encryption algorithms. WPA2 is a common choice for securing wireless networks. The 802.11i standard includes RSN (Robust Security Network), which includes some features of WPA2. Third-party products can be used with some vendors' wireless solutions and some vendors provide extra security of their own with their NIC cards and access points. The drawback to this is that other vendors' products are normally incompatible.

To manually configure wireless settings in Windows Vista/7, use the *Network and Internet* control panel link > *Manage Wireless Networks* > *Add* link > *Manually create a network profile* link. The *Security type* drop-down menu has the following options: No authentication (open), WEP, WPA2-Personal, WPA-Personal, WPA2-Enterprise, WPA-Enterprise, and 802.1x. If you select WPA/WPA2, then *TKIP* or *AES* are available from the *Encryption type* drop-down menu. Figure 15.31 shows this window for Windows 7.

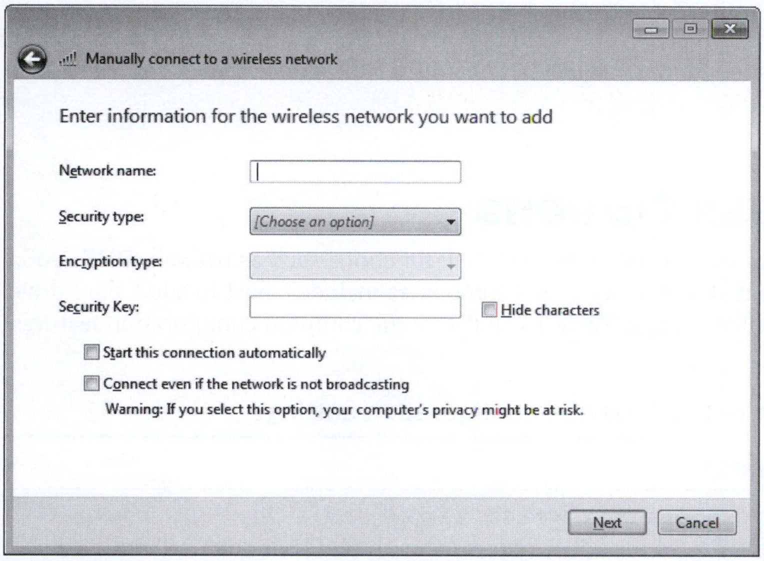

Figure 15.31 Windows 7 wireless security window

WPS (Wi-Fi Protected Setup) configures the SSID and WPA2 wireless security key for an AP or client devices. It supports 802.11a, b, g, and n devices, including computers, access points, consumer electronics, and phones. The standard allows four ways to configure a wireless network:

- A PIN (personal identification number) is entered. This PIN is sometimes found on a sticker or display on the wireless product.
- A USB device attaches to the AP or wireless device to provide configuration information.
- A button is pushed or clicked. This method is known as PBC (push button configuration).
- The NFC (near field communication) where the wireless device is brought close to the AP (or a device known as the Registrar) and the configuration is applied. RFID tags are suited for this method.

Tech Tip

Avoid WPS

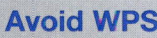

Because of security issues with WPS, disable this mode if possible and do not use it.

Default Settings

All wireless networks have security features. An access point is likely to come with a default password and SSID. Change both of these settings as soon as the access point is powered on. Default passwords are posted on the Internet, and a hacker could lock out access from the access point.

Change the access point's default password during installation. Do not leave it set to the default. The default passwords are well known by many others who could attempt to hack or penetrate the wireless network. Make the password a strong one. Use as many characters as feasible. Use uppercase and lowercase letters. Include non-alphanumeric characters, such as #, %, &, or @.

Tech Tip

Never leave an access point password set to the default

One of the first things to do after powering on an access point and connecting to it is change the default password.

As mentioned previously, the SSID (service set identifier) is used to allow wireless devices to attach to the access point or to another wireless device. Almost all access points are configured for SSID broadcasting. **SSID broadcasting** is where the access point periodically sends out a beacon frame that includes the SSID. Wireless NICs can detect this SSID automatically and attach to the access point. This can be a security issue.

Tech Tip

Disable SSID broadcasting

If possible, disable SSID broadcasting and manually enter the SSID into any wireless NIC's configuration. Even though this requires more effort, it protects the wireless network to some extent.

More Wireless Options

Wireless access points sometimes include other network functions such as firewall, DMZ, QoS, DHCP server, router, integrated switch ports, and sometimes include a port to add a hard drive and support network-accessible storage. Table 15.16 lists some common configuration features included in such devices.

Table 15.16 Common network device configuration settings

Option	Description
Wireless	Used to configure basic wireless settings such as the SSID. Also includes a link to security options such as MAC filtering, authentication, and encryption.
Security	Used to enable/disable a firewall and configure firewall features such as VPN or allow particular network ports to be opened to allow certain types of traffic through.
Storage	Allows monitoring and control of an attached storage device or even support an FTP (File Transfer Protocol) server.
Administration	Allows configuration of the device such as password, IP address assignment, and event logging. Could also include configuration of features such as VoIP or QoS (quality of service), which allows one type of traffic such as voice which cannot tolerate delay take priority over another type of traffic.
Maintenance	Allows viewing the current status of the various components as well as access to any logging that is enabled.

Wireless Security Conclusion

Wireless security is an important issue. The following list recaps some of the important issues and provides recommendations along with a few suggestions for a more secure wireless network:

- Change the default SSID and password. Make the password as long as possible and include non-alphanumeric characters.
- Enable encryption on the access point to the highest level possible and still allow wireless NIC access. Use authentication when possible.
- Put the wireless network on its own subnetwork and place it behind a firewall if possible.

- If provided, enable MAC authentication (MAC filtering) on the access point. MAC authentication allows you to input valid MAC addresses that are allowed to associate to the access point. Even though time consuming, it is a good feature for small wireless networks.
- If supported, authenticate using an authentication server.
- If the SSID is manually configured, periodically change the SSID.
- Assign a static IP address to the access point rather than using DHCP for it.
- Disable remote management of the access point.
- Place the access point in the center of the wireless network and not next to an outside window.
- Use wireless network scanning software to test the network security.
- Require that wireless clients use a VPN (virtual private network) tunnel to access the access point.
- If a rogue access point (an unauthorized AP) is found on the network, disconnect the device and confiscate it. Try and determine who owns the device and report them.

Wireless networks have a strong presence today and will continue to do so in the future. The 802.1x and 802.11 standards are constantly being improved to tighten security for wireless networks so that they rival wired solutions.

Wireless Network Troubleshooting

Troubleshooting wireless networks is sometimes easier than troubleshooting wired networks because of the mobility factor. A laptop with a wireless NIC installed can be used to troubleshoot connectivity, configuration, security, and so on. Most wireless network problems stem from inconsistent configuration. The standards deployed must be for the lowest common denominator. For example, if a wireless NIC supports only 64-bit WEP encryption, then that must be what is used even if 128-bit WEP, WPA, or WPA2 is available on some of the cards.

The list that follows are some general wireless networking tips designed to get a technician going in the right direction. Most of these tips have been discussed in previous sections, but it is nice to have the following troubleshooting list in one spot:

- Is the SSID correct?
- Is the wireless NIC seen by the operating system? (Use *Device Manager* to check.) Check the mobile device for a wireless disable button or use a Fn key to disable/enable the wireless NIC.
- Is the correct security level enabled? If WEP, is the WEP key correctly configured? Is the WEP key length correct?
- Is the correct security key being used? Check the configuration.
- Can any devices attach to the access point? If not, check the access point.
- Is anything causing interference or attenuation? Check antenna placement.
- Is there a channel ID overlap problem?
- If a manufacturer's utility is being used and Windows XP is installed, does the *Network Properties* window have the *Use Windows to configure my wireless network settings* checkbox unchecked? If not, uncheck this checkbox to allow the utility to configure the wireless NIC. For Vista or 7, automatic wireless network configuration is enabled by default. A program from the wireless NIC manufacturer can be installed and used instead. If the customer wants to use Windows Vista or 7 instead of the software provided, click *Start > All Programs > Accessories* locate and right-click on *Command Prompt > Run as administrator.* At the prompt, type `netsh wlan show` settings. From the output, determine whether the Windows automatic wireless configuration is disabled. You may have to disable the wireless NIC and uninstall the vendor software in order to use Windows to control the NIC.

Mobile Security

Many of the issues for wireless connectivity for laptops also apply to smartphones and tablets. But smartphones and tablets have issues of their own (see Figure 15.32).

Figure 15.32 Mobile security

- Many think that because the devices do not have hard drives, they do not need antivirus software. This is a misconception. Install antivirus software on mobile devices where possible. Depending on the device, the antivirus software may not be able to automatically scan for viruses or even have a set scheduled scan time.
- Mobile devices can run each app in a sandbox—a separated space from other apps. This behavior provides a natural security mechanism for applications.
- Mobile device OS upgrades and updates are just as important as updates on a full-sized computer.
- Many mobile devices have GPS tracking capability that can be used to locate a lost or stolen phone. This may be a paid service.
- A paid service or an app on the phone can provide the ability to perform a remote lock or a remote wipe. The remote lock disables the phone so it cannot be accessed. The remote wipe deletes all data from the device.

Most mobile devices have the ability to have a PIN, security pattern, face recognition unlock, or password enabled that activates when the device is inactive. If forgotten on an iOS device, you must recover the iOS using iTunes. For an Android device, some devices support entering the Gmail account information; check the Web for recovery procedures. To configure basic mobile security, perform the following:

- For an Android device, select Settings > *Location & Security* > *Set* up screen lock.
- On an iOS device, use the *Settings* > *General* > *Passcode lock On* option. You can also configure the *Auto-Lock* time. On an iPad, you can use the *iPad Cover Lock/Unlock On* option.

Some mobile devices have configuration settings for what happens if the security method fails, such as an incorrectly entered password. Some devices have a default value. For an extra security precaution, some devices can be configured for what happens to the device after a set number of failed attempts, such as disabling the device or even erasing the data. Most mobile device users that have this ability enabled have the data backed up to the cloud.

A Final Word About Security

Whether wired or wireless, standalone PC or networked PC, or full desktop computer or smartphone, data and device security are important. Security measures must always be taken. Technicians must be aware of the latest threats, take proactive measures to implement security, and must share their knowledge with users so the users can take proactive steps. Security risks and threats cause technicians a lot of work and time. These threats and attacks cost billions in lost data and time to businesses. Because most technicians do not see themselves as a dollar figure on a spreadsheet, they don't realize that if the business loses money as a result of security threats, that the business has to cut costs, and one of those costs could be the technical position. Think about it and be proactive in guarding against security threats.

Soft Skills—Building Customer Trust

It is fitting in the security chapter to discuss building a trust relationship with the customer. Trust begins with professionalism. Be professional in your attire, attitude, written communication, and oral communication. Trust also includes being honest with the customer. If you are going to be late, let the customer know that. If you need to do more research, explain the situation. No one can be expected to know all technical information.

Trust also involves being honest if you find confidential material. Do not use or discuss any material you see while in a customer area. If you see confidential material, let the customer know you have seen the material. If the material is a password, let them know and recommend that they change the password immediately.

Do not touch or move things or papers in a customer area. Always ask the customer to move or put things away to clear the area you need. Do not try to work around a mess. Simply explain that you will need space in order to determine and/or repair the problem.

Trust involves giving customers documentation related to the product just installed or replaced. Trust involves doing what you say you will do. If you say you will call back to check on the situation in the next 24 hours, do so. If you say you will drop off the documentation the following week, do that. Be true to your word.

Trust also involves being honest about billing. Do not overcharge customers. When presenting the customer with the invoice or work order, explain any details with patience. Do not allow them to argue with you over facts or time. Your time is valuable too.

You never know where you are going to meet your next boss. Every time you step into a customer area or talk to a customer, it might lead to a professional reference, a job recommendation, a job lead, or a promotion. Part of building that customer relationship is building trust. Be professional in all that you do.

Chapter Summary

- A security policy guides a company in security matters. The policy defines such things as physical access, antivirus, acceptable usage of devices and data, password policies, email usage guidelines, remote access strategies, and emergency procedures.
- Physical security can include door access, key control, authentication methods including the use of smart cards, key fobs, RFID, biometric devices, physical protection of network devices such as servers, APs, switches, and routers, as well as privacy filters.
- BIOS security options include configuring a supervisor/user password, disabling unused ports, disabling USB ports, and disabling device options.
- To protect the operating system, use NTFS, and have a plan for updating the operating system, web browser, antivirus, antimalware, and antispyware. Encrypt files and folders as necessary. Use BitLocker and TPM technologies, implement a firewall, and disable AutoRun.
- If a computer with sensitive data on the hard drive is to be donated, moved, or sold, perform the following: (1) secure erasing, (2) degaussing, and (3) drilling through drive platters and then destroying the pieces with a hammer.
- If virtualization is used, ensure that each virtual machine has adequate protection (firewall, antivirus, antimalware, and antispyware).
- ome virus or malware files are quarantined and must be manually deleted.
- The Windows guest account should be disabled; the administrator account should have be renamed and have a strong password. User accounts provide the amount of administration dictated by what the person needs (principle of least privilege).
- Permissions should be assigned appropriately to remotely accessed files and folders. Use either share permissions or NTFS permissions (for more control), but not both on the same network share. If a file is placed in a folder that has permissions, the file inherits the folder permissions. Effective permissions are the bottom line permissions someone has when group permissions and individual permissions have been granted.
- A hijacked browser can cause a different home page to appear, a particular web page to be displayed, a rootkit or other malware to be installed, different DNS settings to be applied, or a new or updated HOSTS file applied.
- Email applications now protect against spam, but you can also create rules to block messages from a particular source or subject line.
- Cookies store typed information including sign-ons, sites visited, passwords, and data entered through the web browser.
- Internet Explorer can be customized to various levels of alerts and protection.
- When a security incident occurs, identify the issue, report it through the proper channels and to the appropriate authorities, and preserve the data by using a chain-of-custody form.
- On a wireless network, implement encryption and authentication. Change default SSIDs and passwords.
- Secure a mobile device with a PIN, facial recognition, a password, or a passcode/pattern. Secure important data using remote backups to the cloud. Remote data wiping can be configured if the device is compromised or stolen.
- When dealing with a customer, a co-worker, or your boss, maintain your professionalism and do everything you can to build trust.

Key Terms

Review Questions

1. Match the security policy component below with a definition from the list that follows.

    ____ physical access

    ____ acceptable use

    ____ remote access

    ____ password

    a. The specific web browser that is allowed to be installed

    b. Defines if the code used to access an account such as shared network storage is allowed to be sent using email

    c. The type of security required for a remote VPN connection

    d. The time, day, and year someone entered a network server room

2. Describe two-factor authentication.

3. List two BIOS options associated with PC access.

4. List three recommendations for laptop security.

5. List five recommendations for protecting the operating system.

6. What is BitLocker?

7. [T | F] A new file is created and stored in an encrypted folder. The file must be manually encrypted since it was added after the folder was encrypted.

8. Describe the security rights for a subfolder when the parent folder is shared.

9. List three password guidelines you would recommend that a company use.

10. Where are domain user passwords stored? [local database | registry | network server | in the cloud]

12. Describe the difference between a local policy and a domain policy.

13. What two things are needed in order to configure a computer for a proxy server?

    [IP address of the proxy server | MAC address of the proxy server | administrator name on the proxy server | IP address of the local computer | MAC address of the local computer | port number on the proxy server | Administrator password on the local computer]

14. What is the purpose of a DMZ?

15. [T | F] A virtual machine should have antispyware installed.

16. What Internet Explorer *Tools* menu option allows active scripting sites to be added for sites you trust? [General | Security | Privacy | Content | Connections | Programs]

17. No one can ping a specific Windows 7 computer. What administrative tool can be used to change this default behavior? [Windows Firewall | Local Security Policy | Internet Explorer > Internet options | Windows Defender]

18. What type of unsolicited Internet message records the URLs visited and keystrokes used? [virus | grayware | spam | spyware]

19. An unofficial email is sent from your bank, asking you to click a link to verify your account information. What type of social engineering is this? [phishing | grayware | spyware | VPN]

20. Match the incident on the left with the action on the right. Even though some of the answers might have multiple answers, the final answers will be such that each answer is used only once.

____ virus	a. BSA
____ child exploitation	b. police department
____ software piracy	c. CERT
____ phishing	d. FBI Internet crime center

Exercises

Lab 15.1 Encrypting a File and Folder

Objective: To provide security for a particular file and folder, enable encryption using Windows XP, Vista, or 7

Parts: A computer with Windows XP/Vista/7 loaded with at least one NTFS partition

Note: Two user accounts are needed and possibly created for this exercise—one that encrypts a file and the other account to test the encryption. If two user accounts are not available, most of the lab can still be performed or a second user account can be added. This lab is best demonstrated with two accounts that have local administrator rights.

Procedure: Complete the following procedure and answer the accompanying questions.

1. Power on the computer and log on using the user ID and password provided by the instructor or lab assistant.
2. Access the Computer Management Console: In XP, *Start* > *Control Panel* > *Classic* view > *Administrative Tools* > *Computer Management*. In Vista/7, click on the *Start* button > *Control Panel* > *System and Maintenance* (Vista)/*System and Security* (7) > *Administrative Tools* > double-click *Computer Management*.
3. Expand the *Storage* option and open *Disk Management*.

   How many disk partitions are available? Do any drive partitions use NTFS? If so, how many?

   Note that if no drive partitions use NTFS, this exercise cannot be completed.
4. Close the *Computer Management* window. Open *Windows Explorer*. Create a text file called *Security Test.txt* and save in the *My Documents* (XP) or *Documents* (Vista/7) folder.
5. Right-click the *Security text.txt* file and select *Properties*. From the *General* tab, select the *Advanced* button.
6. Enable the *Encrypt contents to secure data* and click *OK*. Click the *Apply* button and the warning message shown in Figure 15.33 appears.

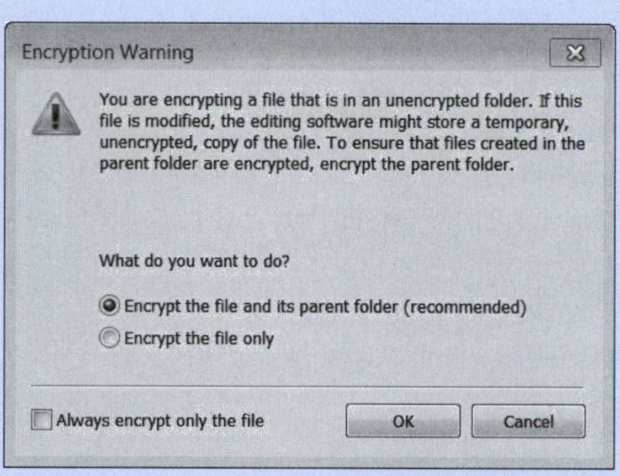

Figure 15.33 **Windows 7 encryption warning message**

7. The default would be to encrypt the Security text.txt file and to encrypt the *My Documents/Documents* folder. This may not be what you want to do. Select the *Encrypt the file only* radio button and the *OK* button on the screen and the one that follows.
8. In Windows Explorer, click on an empty spot in the right pane.

   Is there any indication the file is encrypted? If so, what is it?
   You might need to create an unencrypted file to be able to answer this question.
9. In Windows Explorer, access the *Properties* window of the *Security text.txt* file again and select the *Advanced* button. From the *Advanced Attributes* window, select the *Details* button. If this is not available, ensure you are on a file (and not a folder).

   What user(s) can access the encrypted file?
10. Notice the certificate thumbprint number to the right of the user. EFS can request a digital certificate from a CA (certificate authority) such as a server or if one is not available, EFS can use a self-signed certificate.

    What are the first 16 hexadecimal digits used for the digital certificate?
    Compare these digits with a fellow classmate. Are the digital certificates the same?
    If so, why do you think they are the same?

If they are different, why do you think they are different?

11. Notice the data recovery agent section at the bottom of the window. One or more users (such as the administrator) can be designated as a data recovery agent. A data recovery agent is issued a recovery certificate used for EFS data recovery on encrypted files. Click *Cancel* on three different windows to exit the *Properties* window.
12. From Windows Explorer, open the *Security Test.txt* file, modify it, and save it.

    From Windows Explorer, does the file appear to still be encrypted?
13. Log off the computer and log back on as a different user. If a different user does not exist, create one by using the *User Accounts* Control Panel if possible.
14. Use Windows Explorer, to locate and open the *Security Test.txt* file located under the other username. Modify the file and save it, if possible.

    Were there any problems opening, modifying, or saving the file?

    In one or more complete sentences, explain what happened and why you think it occurred this way.
15. Log off the computer and log back on as the original user.
16. Access the *My Documents/Documents* folder and create a new folder called *Test*. Copy the *Security Test.txt* file into the new *Test* folder.

    Is the copied file encrypted in the *Test* folder?
17. Within the *Test* folder, create a new text file called *Security Test2.txt*.

    Is the newly created file encrypted?
18. Encrypt the *Test* folder using the default encryption setting.

    Does it change anything within the folder? If so, what does it change?
19. Within the *Test* folder, create and save a new file called *Security Test3.txt*.

    Is the newly created file encrypted?
20. Delete the *Security Test.txt*, *Security Test2.txt*, and *Security Test3.txt* files.

    Was there any indication that the files were encrypted when they were deleted?
21. Permanently delete the *Test* folder and any files created in the *My Documents/Documents* folder.

Lab 15.2 Using Windows Vista/7 System Protection

Objective: To manually control the settings involved with system restore points using System Protection

Parts: A computer with Windows Vista/7 loaded with at least one NTFS partition

Note: This lab requires local administrator rights.

Procedure: Complete the following procedure and answer the accompanying questions.

1. Power on the computer and log on using the user ID and password provided by the instructor or lab assistant.
2. Access Windows Explorer and right-click *Computer* > *Properties* > *System Protection* tab.

   In the *Protection Settings* section, document the available drives.

   Document whether protection is currently on or off for each of the available drives.

3. Click *Configure*.

   What three options are available for *Restore Settings*?

   Microsoft says, "System Protection can keep copies of system settings and previous versions of files." Do you think that this means system files, user data files, or both? Explain your reasoning.

   Thinking as a technician, which setting is optimum for most users?

   Give one situation where you think that a technician would select the *Only restore previous versions of files* option.

   Give one situation where a technician would recommend the *Turn off system protection* option.

4. Ensure that the *Restore system settings and previous versions of files* radio button is enabled. By default, Windows uses a maximum of 10 percent of the hard drive for System Protection. However, the system allows you to adjust this amount in the Disk Space Usage section. Note that if you turn off system protection, you cannot use System Restore.

   What is the current *Max Usage*?

   Describe a situation where a technician would want to configure the machine for more than 10 percent of the hard disk space reserved for system protection.

5. Click *Cancel*.

   Can a restore point be manually created from the System Properties window? [Yes | No]

6. Click *Cancel*.

Instructor initials: ______________

Lab 15.3 Making a Folder Private in XP

Objective: To provide security for a particular folder by making it private within Windows XP

Parts: A computer with Windows XP loaded with at least one NTFS partition

Note: Two user accounts are needed for this exercise—one that makes a folder private and the other account to test process. If two user accounts are not available, most of the lab can still be performed or a second user account can be added. This lab is best demonstrated with two accounts that have local administrator rights.

Procedure: Complete the following procedure and answer the accompanying questions.

1. Power on the computer and log on using the user ID and password provided by the instructor or lab assistant.
2. Access the Computer Management Console: *Start* > *Control Panel* > *Classic* view > *Administrative Tools* > *Computer Management*.
3. Expand the *Storage* option and select *Disk Management*.

   How many disk partitions are available?

   Do any drive partitions use NTFS?

   If so, how many?

   Note that if no drive partitions use NTFS, this exercise cannot be completed.

4. Close the *Computer Management* window. Open Windows Explorer. Within the *My Documents* folder, create a subfolder called *Private1*. Create a text file called *Private Text1.txt* and save it to the *Private1* folder. Also create a subfolder called *Private2* within *My Documents* and create a text file within the *Private2* folder called *Private Text2.txt*.
5. Using Windows Explorer, right-click the *Private1* subfolder and select *Sharing and Security*.

   What are the three tabs available?

   What is the purpose of the *Customize* tab?
6. Click the *Sharing* tab. Enable the *Make this folder private* checkbox. Click *Apply* and *OK*.
7. Return to Windows Explorer.

   Is there any visual indication that the folder is a private folder?
8. Log off and log on with another user account (preferably one with administrator rights).
9. Access *Windows Explorer* and browse to the other user account's *My Documents* area. Note that for the second account, *My Documents* is called the first user account name followed by the word documents. For example, if my login is CSchmidt, the folder will be called *CSchmidt's Documents*.

   Is the private folder (*Private1*) viewable? Is the private folder accessible?

   If the private folder is accessible, can you change the document stored there?

   If the private folder is inaccessible, what message is displayed?
10. Try accessing the *Private2* folder.

    Is the *Private2* folder accessible?

    Can you modify and save the Private2.txt document located in Private2?
11. Log off as the second user account. Log back on with the first user account.
12. Open Windows Explorer and delete the *Private1* and *Private2* folders.

    Was there any messages that related to the Private1 folder being private during the deletion?

    If so, what message(s) appeared?

Lab 15.4 Sharing a Folder in Windows XP

Objective: To create a folder and share its contents with another computer on the same network as well as explore security options

Parts: Two networked computers with Windows XP loaded

Procedure: Complete the following procedure and answer the accompanying questions.

1. Power on the computer and log on using the user ID and password provided by the instructor or lab assistant.
2. On the first computer, use Windows Explorer to create two folders under *My Documents*. Name the folders *READ* and *WRITE*.
3. Within the *READ* folder, create a text document called *readme.txt*. Within the *WRITE* folder, create a text document called *changeme.txt*.
4. Using Windows Explorer, right-click the *READ* folder and select *Sharing and Security*. Select the *Sharing* tab and the *Share this folder on the network* checkbox to enable it. Leave the share name as *READ*. Click *Apply* followed by *OK*.

   How can you tell this folder is shared in Windows Explorer?

5. Using Windows Explorer, right-click the *WRITE* folder and select *Sharing and Security*. Select the *Sharing* tab and the *Share this folder on the network* checkbox to enable it. Also select the *Allow network users to change my files* checkbox to enable it. Leave the share name as *WRITE*. Click *Apply* followed by *OK*.
6. Using Windows Explorer, right-click *My Computer* and select *Properties*. Select the *Computer Name* tab.

   What is the full computer name as shown in the window?
7. Close the window. On the second computer, click the *Start* button and *Run*. In the textbox type the UNC (universal naming convention) of `\\computer_name\READ` (where `computer_name` is the name you wrote down) and press [Enter]. Note that if you get an error message, you did not type the command correctly, you mistyped the name of the computer, you did not name the share `READ` correctly, or you mistyped `READ`.

   What appears on the screen?
8. Double-click the *readme.txt* file.

   Did the file open?
9. Add a few words to the file. Click the *File* menu option and *Save*. Leave the file name the same and click the *Save* button.

   Did the file save?
10. Click *OK* and *Cancel*. Close the file and do not save. Close the *READ* window.
11. Sometimes users would like a drive letter permanently assigned in Windows Explorer to a shared folder on another computer. To do this, open Windows Explorer and select the *Tools* menu option followed by *Map Network Drive*. Accept the drive letter assigned. In the folder name, type `\\computer_name\WRITE` (where `computer_name` is the name you wrote down) and press [Enter]. Note that if you get an error message, you did not type the command correctly, you mistyped the name of the computer, you did not name the share `WRITE` correctly, or you mistyped `WRITE`.

    What appears in the address line?

    Does this correspond to the letter that was assigned?
12. Double-click to open the *changeme.txt* file. Add a few words to the file. Click the *File* menu option and *Save*. Leave the file name the same and click the *Save* button.

    Did the file save?
13. Close the file and close the window that contains the file.
14. From Windows Explorer, scroll down until you see `WRITE on 'computer_name' (X:)`, where `X:` is the drive letter assigned. You may need to use the horizontal scrollbar to see the entire name. Double-click this option. You are instantly reconnected to the network share. If you want this share to always be there, you have to enable the *Reconnect at logon* checkbox when you map the network share.

Instructor initials: ______________

15. Close Windows Explorer. On the original computer, use Windows Explorer to delete the *READ* folder.

    Did any messages appear? If so, what did they say?
16. Use Windows Explorer to delete the *WRITE* folder.

    Have a classmate print and sign his or her name on your answer sheet proving that they verified the deletion of the *READ* and *WRITE* folders.

Classmate printed name ________________________________

Classmate signature ________________________________

Lab 15.5 Sharing a Folder in Windows 7

Objective: To be able to share a folder and understand the permissions associated with a network share

Parts: Access to two Windows 7 computers with a user ID that has administrator rights

Procedure: Complete the following procedure and answer the accompanying questions.

1. Turn on both computers and verify that the operating system loads. Log in to Windows 7 using the user ID and password that has full administrator rights and that is provided by your instructor or lab assistant.
2. On the first computer, use Windows Explorer to created two folders under *Documents*. Name the folders *READ* and *WRITE*.
3. Within the *READ* folder, create a text document called *readme.txt*. Within the *WRITE* folder, create a text file called *changeme.txt*.
4. On both computers, determine the computer name by accessing the *System* Control Panel link. Determine the IP addresses of both computers using the `ipconfig` command.

   Document your findings.

Computer	Computer name	IP address
Computer 1		
Computer 2		

5. On both computers, access the *Network and Sharing Center* Control Panel link to document the current *Advanced Sharing Settings*.

Computer 1	Computer 2
Network discovery [On | Off]	Network discovery [On | Off]
Media streaming [On | Off]	Media streaming [On | Off]
Public folder sharing [On (read only, password required) | On (password required) | Off]	Public folder sharing [On (read only, password required) | On (password required) | Off]
Printer sharing [On | Off]	Printer sharing [On | Off]
File sharing connections [Use 128-bit encryption to help… | Enable file sharing…]	File sharing connections [Use 128-bit encryption to help… | Enable file sharing…]

6. On both computers, enable the following settings.
   - File and Printer Sharing
   - Public folder sharing
   - Network discovery

7. On both computers, ensure that the Windows 7 *Use Sharing Wizard* is enabled by typing **`folder options`** in the *Search programs and files* Start button option. Select the *Folder Options* item from the resulting list > *View* tab > locate the *Advanced Settings* section > locate the *Use Sharing Wizard (Recommended)* option and ensure it is enabled. Apply changes as necessary.

   What is the current setting for the *Use Sharing Wizard* option? [Enabled | Disabled]

8. In Windows Explorer on the first computer, right-click the *READ* folder > *Properties* > *Sharing* tab.

   Document the share network path that appears in the window.

   ____

9. Select the *Advanced sharing* button > enable the *Share this folder* checkbox > select the *Caching* button.
10. Select the *Configure Offline Availability for a Shared Folder help* link.

    What is the purpose of caching?

    [Y | N] Is offline availability enabled by default for a shared folder?

    What command can be used from a command prompt to configure caching options for a shared folder?
11. Close the help window.
12. In the Offline Settings window, leave the option to the default.

    What is the default setting for offline access?

13. Click *OK*. In the Advanced Sharing window, select the *Permissions* button. Notice how the Everyone group is listed by default.

Notes: If you want to share with someone who is not listed, use the *User Accounts* Control Panel to create the account, then select that account name in the Permissions window.

If the local or domain policy requires a password, one should be put on the user account. Best practice is to require passwords on all user accounts.

If the Everyone user account is selected and password protection is being used, a user account is still needed to gain access.

   What permissions are enabled by default for the Everyone group? [Full control | Change | Read]

14. Click *OK* on the two windows and then click the *Close* button.
15. Open the *Computer Management* console. Expand *System Tools* and *Shared Folders*. Click *Shares* in the left pane. The READ share lists in the right pane. If the share is missing, redo this lab from the beginning. Close the *Computer Management* window.
16. On the second computer, log on as the user given access in Step 13 or use the user ID and password provided by the instructor or lab assistant.
17. On the second computer, open *Windows Explorer*. Select *Network* in the left pane. In the right pane, locate and double-click the name of the first computer.

Notes: If the computer does not list, click the *Start* button and in the *Search programs and files* textbox, type `\\computer_name` (where `computer_name` is the name of the first computer). Press Enter.

18. On the second computer, locate the *READ* share and the *readme.txt* document. Double-click the *readme.txt* file.

    [Y | N] Did the file open?

19. Add a few words to the file. Click the *File* > *Save* menu option. Leave the filename the same and click the *Save* button. When asked if you want to replace the file, click *Yes*.

    [Y | N] Did the file save?

20. Close the file and close the window that contains the file.
21. On the second computer inside the *Search programs and files* Start button option, type the share path documented in Step 8 and press Enter. If an error occurs, check your typing or redo the steps to get a correct share path documents in Step 8.

    What happened?

22. Close the window. On the second computer, open *Windows Explorer*. Right-click *Computer* in the left pane and select *Map Network Drive*. Use the *Drive* drop-down menu to select a drive letter. In the *Folder* textbox, type the share path for the READ share documented in Step 8. Click *Finish*. The share opens with the drive letter documented in the path at the top of the window. Note that you may have to expand the left pane to see the drive letter.

Instructor initials: _____________

23. On the second computer, again access *Windows Explorer* and locate the drive letter that was just mapped to a network drive. Because Windows share paths can be lengthy, a common practice is to use a mapped network drive for the share.

    How can you easily identify mapped drive letters in Windows Explorer (besides a quite high drive letter in some cases)?

24. Close all windows on the second computer.
25. In Windows Explorer on the first computer, right-click the *WRITE* folder > *Properties* > *Sharing* tab.

    Document the share network path that appears in the window.

26. Select the *Advanced Sharing* button > enable the *Share this folder* checkbox.
27. Select the *Permissions* button.
28. Select the correct username or group and enable the *Change Allow* checkbox. Click *OK* on two windows and then click the *Close* button.
29. On the second computer, locate the *changeme.txt* document.
30. Modify and save the *changeme.txt* file.
31. On the first computer, open the *changeme.txt* file.

    [Y | N] Was the file changed?

Instructor initials: _____________

32. On the second computer, try changing the name of the *changeme.txt* file.

    [Y | N] Could you change the name of the *changeme.txt* file?

33. Verify whether the filename changed on the first computer.

    [Y | N] Did the filename change on the first computer? If so, what is the new name?

34. On the second computer, right-click the *WRITE* folder and select *Always available offline*.

    What indication is given that a folder is available offline?

    [Y | N] Can a particular file be given this same attribute?

35. Disconnect the second computer from the network by removing the network cable from the network adapter.
36. From a command prompt on the second computer, ping the first computer using the IP address documented in Step 4.

    [Y | N] Did the ping succeed?

37. So with no network access, open the *WRITE* folder and access the *changeme.txt* file. Modify the file and save it.
38. Reconnect the second computer to the network.
39. From the first computer, access the *WRITE* folder.

    [Y | N] Were the document changes made when computer two was disconnected from the network saved on the first computer?
40. On the second computer, again access the *changeme.txt* file and try to permanently delete the file.

    [Y | N] Could you permanently delete the *changeme.txt* file?
41. On the first computer, create a subfolder under the *READ* folder. Name the folder *SUB_READ*. Create a text file in the *SUB_READ* folder called *sub_file.txt*.
42. On the second computer, locate and right-click the *SUB_READ* shared folder. Select *Properties*.

    What attributes does this folder have? [Read-only | Hidden | None]
43. On the second computer in *Windows Explorer*, locate the *sub_file.txt* file. Select *Properties*.

    What attributes, if any, are shown as enabled by default? [Read-only | Hidden | None]
44. Click *Cancel*. Try to modify the *sub_file.txt* file.

    [Y | N] Could you change the *sub_file.txt* file?

Instructor initials: ____________

45. On the second computer, remove the mapped drive (and any drive that you created on your own) by using *Windows Explorer* to locate the mapped drive letter under *Computer* in the left pane. Right-click the mapped drive and select *Disconnect*.
46. On the first computer, permanently delete the *READ* and *WRITE* folders and all files and subfolders contained within them.
47. On the first computer, put the *Advanced sharing settings* options back to the original configuration. Refer to the documentation in Step 5. Put the *Use Sharing Wizard* back to the original setting as documented in Step 7. Show your lab partner the documented settings and the current configuration. Have your lab partner use the table that follows to document that the computer has been put back to the original configuration.

Computer 1 (permanently deleted folders/sharing settings)
Printed name of lab partner
Signature of lab partner

48. On the second computer, put the *Advanced sharing settings* options back to the original configuration. Refer to the documentation in Step 5. Put the *Use Sharing Wizard* back to the original setting as documented in Step 7. Show your lab partner the documented settings and the current configuration. Have your lab partner use the table that follows to document that the computer has been put back to the original configuration.

Computer 2 (permanently deleted folders/sharing settings)
Printed name of lab partner
Signature of lab partner

49. On both computers, delete any user accounts that have been created. Note that you must be logged in as an administrator in order to delete user accounts.

Lab 15.6 Creating a Local Security Policy for Passwords

Objective: To provide additional security by requiring certain password parameters as a local computer security policy

Parts: A computer with Windows XP Professional/Vista/7 loaded

Procedure: Complete the following procedure and answer the accompanying questions.

Notes: Local administrator rights are required for this lab. The computer should be part of a workgroup, not a domain. However, even though domain policy requirements override local policy, the lab may still work as written.

1. Power on the computer and log on using the user ID and password provided by the instructor or lab assistant.
2. Access the *Local Security Policy Console: Start* > *Administrative Tools* Control Panel > double-click *Local Security Policy*.
3. Expand the *Account Policies* option.

   What two options are available?
4. Click the *Password Policy* subcategory. Table 15.17 details these options.

Table 15.17 Windows password policy option descriptions

Option	Description
Enforce password history	The number of unique and new passwords must be used before an old password can be reused.
Maximum password age	The number of days a password has to be used before it has to be changed.
Option	**Description**
Minimum password age	The fewest number of days a user has to use the same password.
Minimum password length	The fewest number of characters required for the password. The least the password can be is zero. The more characters required, the better the security. A common setting is seven or eight. Fourteen characters is the most you can require in this setting.
Passwords must meet complexity requirements	Sets higher standards for the password such as the password cannot be the username, must be six characters or more, requires uppercase and lowercase letters, numerals, and symbols such as # or !.
Store password using reversible encryption for all users in the domain	If enabled, passwords are stored using reversible encryption. Used only if an application uses a protocol that requires knowledge of a user password for authentication purposes.

Use Table 15.18 to document the current settings.

Table 15.18 Current password policy settings

Option	Current setting
Enforce password history	
Maximum password age	
Minimum password age	
Minimum password length	
Passwords must meet complexity requirements	
Store password using reversible encryption for all users in the domain	

5. Change the password policy settings to the options shown in Table 15.19.

Table 15.19 New password policy settings

Option	New setting
Enforce password history	One password remembered
Minimum password length	Seven characters
Passwords must meet complexity requirements	Enabled

6. Create a new user account by clicking the *Start* button > *User Accounts* Control Panel > *Manage another account* (7)/*Create a new account* (XP/Vista/7) link > type `Teststudent` for the new account name > *Next* and *Limited* radio button (XP)/*Standard user* (Vista/7) > *Create Account* button. The Teststudent icon appears in the window.

   What indication is given that a policy is in place?

7. Log off as the current user. Log in as *Teststudent*.

   What message appeared upon logon?

8. In the *New Password* and *Confirm New Password* textboxes, type `test` followed by clicking the *OK* button (XP) or right arrow (Vista/7).

   What requirements display?

9. Click *OK*. In the *New Password* and *Confirm New Password* textboxes, type `Tester9#` and click *OK*.

   What message displays?

10. Log off as *Teststudent* and log back in using the original user account.
11. Return to the *Security Policy* console. Expand *Local Policies* and select *Audit Policy*.

    What is the current setting for audit account logon events? [No auditing | Success | Failure | Success and Failure]

List three other items that can be audited.

12. Double-click the *Audit account logon events* option. The two options are success and failure and both options can be enabled. Success logs every time someone logs into the computer. Failure logs every failed logon attempt. Enable both the *Success* and *Failure* checkboxes > *Apply* button > *OK* button.
13. Log off as the current user and log in as *Teststudent* using the password of *Tester?1*.

    What message appeared?

14. Click *OK* and this time type the correct password of *Tester9#*. Log off as Teststudent. Log back on as the original computer user.
15. To see events that have been enabled and logged, click the *Start* button > *Administrative Tools* Control Panel > *Event Viewer* > *Security* option in the left pane (XP). The top three events show the current successful login and the failure/successful login of *Teststudent* user.

    In Vista/7, expand the *Windows Logs* category on the left and select *Security*. Scroll down to select a line that shows as an *Audit Failure*, as shown in Figure 15.34.

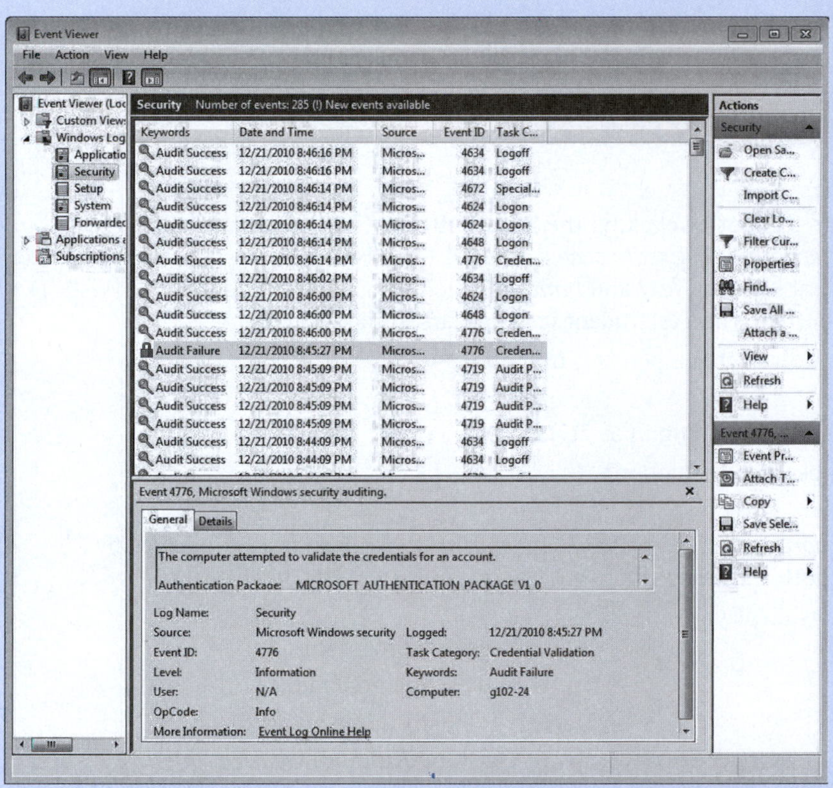

Figure 15.34 **Windows 7 Event Viewer Security log window**

16. Close *Event Viewer*. Return to the *Security Policy* console. Set the *Audit account logon events* setting back to the original setting. Refer to Step 11 for the original settings.

    Have a classmate verify your setting and print and sign his or her name on your answer sheet.

Classmate printed name ______________________ ____________________

Classmate signature ____

17. Configure the *Password Policy* settings back to their original configuration. Refer to Step 4 for the original settings.

    Have a classmate verify your setting and print and sign his or her name on your answer sheet.

Classmate printed name ______________________ ____________________

Classmate signature ____

18. Expand *Local Policies*. Select the *User Rights Assignment* option. Use Table 15.20 to document the current settings for various options.

Table 15.20 Windows user rights assignment settings

Option	Current setting
Access this computer from the network	
Allow log on through Remote Desktop Services	
Deny log on locally	
Force shutdown from a remote system	
Generate security audits	
Load and unload device drivers	
Restore files and directories	
Shut down the system	
Take ownership of files or other objects	

19. Select the *Security* option in the left pane. Use Table 15.21 to document the current settings for various options.

Table 15.21 Windows security settings

Option	Current setting
Accounts: Administrator account status	
Accounts: Guest account status	
Accounts: Rename administrator account	
Devices: Allow to format and eject removable media	
Devices: Prevent users from installing printer drivers	
Interactive logon: Message text for users attempting to log on	
Interactive logon: Prompt user to change password before expiration	
Interactive logon: Require smart card	
Network access: Let Everyone permissions apply to anonymous users	
Network access: Shares that can be accessed anonymously	
Network security: Force logoff when logon hours expire	
Shutdown: Allow system to be shut down without having to log on	

20. Close the Security Policy console. Access *User Accounts* and remove the *Teststudent* user account.

    Have a classmate verify your setting and print and sign his or her name on your answer sheet.

Classmate printed name ________________ ________________

Classmate signature ________________________________

21. Close the *User Accounts* window and reboot the computer.

Lab 15.7 Windows Defender in Windows 7

Objective: To be able to use System Configuration and Windows Defender to troubleshoot boot and spyware problems

Parts: Computer with Windows 7 installed

User logon that has administrator rights

Note: In this lab, you will explore various options that can be used within the System Configuration and Windows Defender windows.

If the computer has a third-party security suite such as Norton or McAfee that has antispyware or antimalware, the Windows Defender application may not be enabled.

Procedure: Complete the following procedure and answer the accompanying questions.

1. Turn on the computer and verify that the operating system loads. Log in to Windows 7 using the user ID and password provided by your instructor or lab assistant.
2. Open *Windows Explorer*. From the *Organize* menu option > *Folder and Search Options* > *View* tab.

   What is the current setting for the Hidden files and folders section? [Do not show hidden files and folders enabled | Show hidden files and folders enabled]

   What is the current setting for the *Hide extensions for known file types* option? [Enabled | Disabled]

   What is the current setting for the *Hide protected operating system files (Recommended)* option? [Enabled | Disabled]
3. Configure the following Windows Explorer settings:
   - *Show hidden files, folders, and drives radio button*—enabled (checked)
   - *Hide extensions for known file types*—disabled (unchecked)
   - *Hide protected operating system files (Recommended)*—disabled (unchecked)

   Click *Yes* (if prompted) > *Apply* > *OK*. Close *Windows Explorer*.
4. Open the *Start* menu and in the *Search Programs and Files* textbox, type `defender` > click *Windows Defender*. Note that if a note appears that Windows Defender is turned off, select the *click here to turn it on* option. You might have to obtain updates before continuing.

   Was Windows Defender disabled? [yes | no]
5. Select the *Tools* menu option > *Options*.

   What actions are defined from this window?
6. Select the *Tools* menu option > *Quarantined items*.

   List any software that Windows Defender has prevented from executing.
7. Select the *Tools* menu option > *Allowed items*.

   List any software that is not be monitored by Windows Defender.

What happens if an item is removed from the list and how did you find this information?

8. Select the *Tools* menu option > *Options* > *Real-time protection* from the left pane.

   Is real-time protection enabled? [yes | no]

   What options are available besides enabling real-time protection?

9. Select *Excluded file types* from the left pane.

   What file extension is given as an example of a file type to exclude?

10. Select the *Advanced* option from the left pane.

    What type of scanning is enabled? [scan archive files | scan email | scan removable drives | use heuristics | create restore point]

    What will a machine do if it uses heuristics?

11. Select *Advanced* from the left pane.

    What two options are configured from here?

12. If Windows Defender was disabled when you started this lab. See the answers found in Steps 6 and 8. Deselect the *Use this program* checkbox. If Windows Defender was disabled when you started this lab, click *Automatic scanning* from the left pane. Ensure the *Automatically scan my computer (recommended)* option is disabled (unchecked). Click *Save*. You receive a message that Windows Defender is turned off.
13. Return Windows Explorer to the original settings. See the settings as the answers found in Step 2.
14. Show the instructor that the settings are re-configured to the original settings.

Instructor initials: ______________

16. Close the *Windows Defender* window.

Lab 15.8 Configuring a Secure Wireless Network

Objective: To be able to configure a secure wireless AP (access point) or router and attach a wireless client

Parts: One wireless access point or router

A computer with an integrated wireless NIC or a wireless NIC installed as well as an Ethernet NIC

One straight-through cable

Procedure: Complete the following procedure and answer the accompanying questions.

1. Obtain the documentation for the wireless AP or router from the instructor or Internet.
2. Reset the wireless AP or router as directed by the wireless device manufacturer.

   Document the current Ethernet NIC IPv4 settings. [DHCP | static IP address]

   If a static IP address is assigned, document the IP address, subnet mask, default gateway, and DNS configuration settings.

3. Attach a straight-through cable from the computer's Ethernet NIC to the wireless AP or router.
4. Power on the computer and log on, if necessary.

5. Configure the computer with a static IP address or DHCP, as directed by the wireless device manufacturer.
6. Open a web browser and configure the wireless AP or router with the following parameters:
   - Change the default SSID
   - Disable SSID broadcasting enabled for this lab
   - Configure the most secure encryption and authentication supported by both the wireless NIC client and the wireless AP or router
   - Change the default password used to access the wireless AP or router

   Document the settings after you have configured them:

   SSID:

   SSID broadcasting disabled? [yes | no]

   Password for wireless device access:

   Type of security used:
7. Save the wireless AP or router configuration.
8. Disconnect the Ethernet cable.
9. Enable the wireless NIC and configure it for the appropriate SSID.
10. Configure the wireless NIC for a static IP address or DHCP, as directed by the wireless AP/router manufacturer.
11. Open a web browser and access the wireless AP or router. If access cannot be obtained, troubleshoot as necessary or reset the wireless AP or router to default configurations and restart the lab.

    What frequency (channel) is being used by the wireless AP or router and the wireless NIC for connectivity?
12. Show the instructor the connectivity.

Instructor initials: ____________

13. Open a command prompt and type **`netsh wlan show settings`** to see the wireless network settings.
14. If Windows XP is being used, use the **`sc query w2csvc`** command. (Vista/7 do not have the Wireless Zero Control service.)
15. Reset the wireless AP or router to the default configuration settings.
16. Reset the computer(s) to the original configuration settings.

Instructor initials: ____________

Activities

Internet Discovery

Objective: To become familiar with researching computer security concepts using the Internet

Parts: A computer with Internet access

Questions: Use the Internet to answer the following questions.

1. Access the Internet Crime Complaint Center to answer the questions that follow. At the time of writing, the URL is http://www.ic3.gov.

What are three recommendations from the site list in regard to spam?

What is Internet crime, according to this website? Write the answer and the URL at which you found the answer.

2. Access the U.S. Computer Emergency Readiness Team website and access the technical user link to answer the questions that follow. At this writing, the URL is http://www.us-cert.gov.

   What are the top three high-rated vulnerabilities for the past week?

   List three recommendations made by this site for a new computer being connected to a network.

3. Access the National Institute of Standards and Technology Computer Security Resource Center website to answer the questions that follow.

   Access the glossary of security terms. Windows allows programming of ACLs (access control lists).

   What are they and how do they relate to computer security?

   Select the CSRC site map link. List one security section that you find interesting and define one term from that section that is not in this chapter.

4. Access the Business Software Alliance website to answer the questions that follow.

   According to the website, what percentage of software installed is pirated?

   Access the *Anti-Piracy* link.

   What is the current maximum fine for each software pirated? Additionally, what is the penalty for copyright infringement?

Soft Skills

Objective: To enhance and fine-tune a future technician's ability to listen, communicate in both written and oral form, and support people who use computers in a professional manner

Activities:

1. Prepare a presentation on any topic related to network security. The topic can relate to wired or wireless security. Share your presentation with the class.
2. In small groups, find a security policy on the Internet or use any of your school's computer policies. Critique the policy and make recommendations for how the policy can provide for stronger security.

Critical Thinking Skills

Objective: To analyze and evaluate information as well as apply learned information to new or different situations

Activities:

1. Create a wired workgroup network. Before users are created, determine what security policies will be enforced. Document the security policy. Also determine what activities are logged. Share folders between the computers with security implemented. Document the shares and policies. View and capture activities logged and include with the documentation. Present your design, implementation, and monitoring to the class.
2. In teams, build a wired and wireless network with security in place. Document the security as if you were presenting it to a home network customer who hired you to build and implement it.

A+ Certification Exam Tips

- ✓ This chapter has information relating to both the 801 and 802 exams and is the most complex chapter because so many security issues need to be experienced in order to know exactly what things to try. As a starting point, be very familiar with the Internet Explorer *Internet Options* tabs. Review them right before the 802 exam.
- ✓ Be very familiar with wireless security techniques: default usernames, SSID, encryption, SSID broadcasting, MAC filtering, radio power levels, and static IP addressing.
- ✓ Know what to do if you happen across prohibited content/data.
- ✓ Review what to do with security problems such as computer slowdowns, lockups, pop-ups, viruses, malware, and spam.
- ✓ Know the symptoms of a virus and malware.
- ✓ For mobile devices, be able to compare and contrast passcode locks, remote wipes, remote backup applications, failed login attempts restrictions, locator apps, antivirus, and patching/OS updates.

Glossary

Numerals

56Kbps modem A modem that produces higher transmission speeds and uses traditional phone lines. Actual modem speed is determined by the number of analog to digital conversions that occur through the phone system.

A

A/V (audio/video) A technology that involve manipulating sound as well as graphics. People who work in A/V editing might need specialized audio and video adapters, a large fast hard drive, and dual (or more) monitors.

AAC (Advanced Audio Compression) A sound file format that provides file compression.

AC (alternating current) The type of electrical power from a wall outlet.

AC circuit tester A device used to check a wall outlet's wiring.

accelerometer A technology used in mobile devices to detect screen orientation and adapt what is shown on the screen for that viewing mode. A gyroscope measures and maintains that orientation.

access point A component of a wireless network that accepts associations from wireless network cards.

access time The amount of time it takes to retrieve data from memory or a device.

ACL (access control list) A means of providing a security filter where traffic is allowed or denied based on configured parameters.

ACPI (Advanced Configuration and Power Interface) Technology that allows the motherboard and operating system to control the power needs and operation modes of various devices.

ACR (advanced communications riser) Technology developed by a group of companies including AMD, VIA Technologies, Motorola, and 3Com (now owned by Hewlett Packard). ACR not only supports audio, modem, and networking but also DSL modems. It is found on motherboards and supports AMD processors.

active listening An effective communication technique used to ensure what the speaker says is accurately received.

active matrix A technology used in LCD monitors where displays have a transistor for each pixel. Contrast with passive matrix.

active terminator A type of end to a SCSI chain that allows for longer cable distance and provides correct voltage for SCSI signals.

actuator arm Holds the read/write heads over hard disk platters.

adapter An electronic circuit card that connects into an expansion slot. Also called a controller, card, controller card, circuit card, circuit board, and adapter board.

Add Printer Wizard A Windows utility used to install a local or network printer.

administrative share A share created by Microsoft for drive volumes and the folder that contains the majority of Windows files. An administrative share has a dollar sign at the end of its name.

ADSL (Asymmetrical DSL) A type of digital subscriber line (DSL) that provides speeds up to 150Mbps; it provides faster downloads than uploads.

Advanced Boot Options A Windows boot menu used to access tools used for troubleshooting. Press F8 when the computer is booting (and before Windows load) in order to access the Advanced Boot Options menu.

Aero See *Windows Aero*.

AES (Advanced Encryption Standard) Used in wireless networks and offers encryption with 128-, 192-, and 256-bit encryption keys.

AGP (accelerated graphics port) An extension of the PCI bus (a port) that provides a dedicated communication path between the expansion slot and the processor. AGP is used for video adapters.

AHCI (Advance Host Controller Interface) One mode of operation for SATA drives, which allows SATA devices to be inserted or removed when power is applied and communication between the host controller and attached SATA devices.

air filter Traps air dust and dirt particles on air flow intake openings (not exhaust). Can be either removable or built into a case.

Alerts An option used to select object and counters, set when tracking is to begin, set how often the system is monitored, and set how alerts are to be handled. By default, alerts are sent to *Event Viewer's* application event log.

alternative address A method of assigning an IP address used when the DHCP server is down or the server could not assign an IP address such as when there are network problems.

alternative configuration A method of configuring IPv4 parameters that will be used if the main IPv4 parameters (such as DHCP) cannot be used or are impractical to use. A good use of an alternative configuration is when a laptop is used both at work and at home. At work, DHCP could be configured, but at home, the alternative configuration might contain a statically assigned IP address.

ALU (arithmetic logic unit) The part of a processor that does mathematical manipulations.

AMD (Advanced Micro Devices) A company that makes processors, graphics processors, and chipsets. AMD is the largest rival of Intel.

amp Short for ampere, a measurement of current.

amplification Increasing the strength of a sound. Amplification output is measured in watts. Sound cards usually have built-in amplification to drive the speakers. Many speakers have built-in amplifiers to boost the audio signal for a fuller sound.

AMR (audio/modem riser) A motherboard connector used for a combination audio and modem adapter. Motherboard manufacturers use AMR as an option to offer a different version of the same motherboard.

antenna A component that attaches to wireless devices or is integrated into them. An antenna is used to radiate or receive radio waves.

antenna gain A measure of an antenna's output power in a particular direction compared to output power produced in any direction by an isotropic antenna.

antistatic wrist strap A strap that connects a technician to a computer that equalizes the voltage potential between the two to prevent ESD.

AP (access point) The central connecting point for a wireless network. Coordinates wireless access for mobile wireless devices.

APIC (Advanced Programmable Interrupt Controller) A type of controller that supports more interrupts than the traditional 16 (24 is one example) and allows interrupt sharing between devices. There are two common types: LAPIC and I/O APIC. LAPIC is normally integrated into each CPU and has its own timer, whereas the I/O APIC is used throughout any of the peripheral buses and is integrated into the chipset.

APIPA (Automatic Private IP Addressing) A Microsoft Windows option that allows a computer to automatically receive an IP address from the range 169.254.0.1 to 169.254.255.254.

application layer (OSI) Layer 7 of the OSI model, which defines how applications and the computer interact with a network.

application layer (TCP/IP) The top layer of the TCP/IP model. It formats data specific for a particular application. It is equivalent to the OSI model's application, presentation, and session layers. Common application layer protocols include Telnet, HTTP, HTML, DNS, POP, IMAP, and FTP.

application log An *Event Viewer* log that displays events associated with a specific program. Programmers who design software decide which events to display in the *Event Viewer's* application log.

Apply button A button located in the bottom-right corner of a dialog box; clicking the Apply button saves any changes the user has applied to the window.

APU (accelerated processing unit) A processor that combines the CPU (central processing unit) with a GPU (graphics processor unit).

architecture A set of rules governing the physical structure of a computer. It regulates bit transfer rate, adapter configuration, and so on.

archive attribute A designation that can be attached to a file that marks whether the file has changed since it was last backed up by a software program. The `RESTORE`, `XCOPY`, and `MSBACKUP` commands use the archive attribute as well as third-party backup software applications.

ARP (Address Resolution Protocol) A protocol used to discover the destination MAC address when the destination IP address is known.

artifact An unusual pattern or distortion that appears on a screen, such as green dotted or vertical lines, colored lines on one side of the screen, or tiny glitters, which could indicate problems like overheated GPU, insufficient air flow, or video driver.

aspect ratio An LCD characteristic that describes a ratio of monitor width compared to height. An LCD with an aspect ratio of 16:9 is a wide screen monitor in that it is wider than it is high.

ASR (automated system recovery) A means of creating a bootable disk with Windows XP using the Windows *Backup* tool.

asynchronous Transmissions that do not require a clock signal but instead use extra bits to track the beginning and end of the data.

ATA standard (AT Attachment standard) The original IDE interface that supported two drives. Now in two types—PATA and SATA.

ATAPI (AT Attachment Packet Interface) The hardware side of the IDE specification that supports devices such as optical drives and tape drives.

ATM (Asynchronous Transfer Mode) A wide area network telecommunications technology that uses 53-byte cells to carry voice, video, and data.

attenuation The amount of signal loss for a radio wave at it travels through air or as the signal travels down a cable.

`ATTRIB` A command used to designate a file as hidden, archived, read-only, or as a system file.

ATX (Advanced Technology Extended) A form factor for motherboards, cases, and power supplies.

audio/video editing PC A computer used to create and modify sound or video files. The computer commonly has multiple powerful multi-core processors, maximum system RAM, specialized video and audio cards, one or more very fast and large-capacity hard drives, good speakers, quality mouse, dual displays, and possibly a digital tablet and/or scanner.

auditing Tracking network events such as logging onto the network domain. Auditing is sometimes called event logging or simply logging.

authentication The process of determining whether a network device or person has permission to access a network.

authorization Controls what network resources such as file, folders, printers, video conferencing equipment, fax machines, scanners, and so on can be accessed and used by a legitimate network user or device.

auto-switching A type of power supply that monitors the incoming voltage from the wall outlet and automatically switches itself accordingly. Auto-switching power supplies accept voltages from 100 to 240VAC at 50 to 60Hz. They are popular in netbooks and laptops.

AV hard drive (audio/video hard drive) A special hardware component associated with home theater configuration. This drive is quiet.

average access time The time required to find and retrieve data on a disk or in memory.

average seek time The time required for a drive to move from one location to another.

B

backbone A network part that connects multiple buildings, floors, networks, and so on.

backlight A fluorescent lamp or LEDs that are always on for an LCD.

back side bus Connections between a CPU and the L2 cache.

bandwidth The communications channel width that defines its capacity for carrying data.

baseband A networking technology where the entire cable bandwidth is used to transmit a digital signal.

baseline A snapshot of a computer's performance (memory, CPU usage, etc.) during normal operations (before a problem or slowdown is apparent).

basic disk A Windows term for a drive that has been partitioned and formatted.

basic storage A Windows term for a partition. Contrast with *dynamic storage*.

batch file A file that has the extension of *BAT* that executes multiple commands when a single command is entered at a prompt.

baud The number of times an analog signal changes in 1 second. If a signal is sent that changes 600 times in 1 second, the device communicates at 600 baud. Today's signaling methods (modulation techniques, to be technically accurate) allow modems to send several bits in one cycle, so it is more accurate to talk in bits per second rather than baud.

`bcdedit` A command used to modify the Windows Vista or 7 boot settings.

BD (Blu-ray disc) An optical media with a higher data capacity than a CD or DVD.

Berg A type of power connector that extends from the computer's power supply to a floppy drive.

bi-directional printing Printing that occurs from left to right and right to left to provide higher printing speeds.

biometrics A device used to authenticate someone based on one or more physical traits such as a fingerprint, eyeball (retina), or hand, or a behavioral trait such as voice or signature.

BIOS (basic input/output system) A chip that contains computer software that locates the operating system, POST, and important hardware configuration parameters. Also called ROM BIOS, Flash BIOS, or system BIOS.

bit An electrically charged 1 or 0.

BitLocker A Microsoft utility that encrypts an entire disk volume, including operating system files, user files, and swap files. The utility requires two disk partitions at a minimum.

BitLocker To Go A Microsoft application used to encrypt and password protect external drives and removable media that are 128MB are larger.

blackout A total loss of AC power.

Bluetooth A wireless technology for personal area networks.

Blu-ray A type of optical disk technology that uses a blue laser instead of a red laser (like the kind used in CD/DVD drives) to achieve the higher disc capacities.

BNC (Bayonet Neill–Concelman) A connector used on coaxial cable.

boot A term used to describe the process of a computer coming to a usable condition.

boot partition A type of partition found in Windows that contains the operating system. The boot partition can be in the same partition as the system partition, which is the part of the hard drive that holds hardware-specific files.

boot sector Previously called DBR or DOS boot record, this section of a disk contains information about the system files (the files used to boot the operating system).

boot sector virus A virus program placed in a computer's boot sector code, which can then load into memory. Once in RAM, the virus takes control of computer operations. The virus can spread to installed drives and drives located on a network.

boot volume A storage unit that contains the majority of the operating system files. Can be the same volume as the system volume, which contains the boot files.

`BOOTREC` Windows command used to repair and recover from hard drive problems.

bps (bits per second) The number of 1s and 0s transmitted per second.

broadband A networking technology where the cable bandwidth is divided into multiple channels; thus, the cable can carry simultaneous voice, video, and data.

broadcast See *broadcast address*.

broadcast address IP address used to communicate with all devices on a particular network.

brownout A loss of AC power due to electrical circuits being overloaded.

browser A program that views web pages across the Internet. Common web browsers are Internet Explorer, Firefox, Chrome, Safari, Opera, and NeoPlanet.

BSOD (blue screen of death) The monitor screen displays all blue and the computer locks or is nonfunctional.

BTX (balanced technology extended) A form factor for motherboards.

buffer memory Memory installed in optical drives and hard drives used to reduce transfer time when writing data to the drive by securing more data than requested and placing the data in the buffer. It holds the extra data in the drive and constantly sends data to the processor instead of waiting on the drive.

bus Electronic lines that allow 1s and 0s to move from one place to another.

bus frequency multiple A motherboard setting for the internal microprocessor speed.

busmaster DMA Another name for UDMA (Ultra DMA); allows the IDE interface to control the PCI bus for faster transfers.

bus-mastering A feature that allows an adapter to take over the external data bus from the processor to execute operations with another bus-mastering adapter.

bus-powered hub A device with no external power supply that allows other USB devices to be connected and powered by the bus. Contrast with a self-powered hub.

bus speed The rate at which a computer pathway used for transmitting 1s and 0s operates.

bus topology A network wherein all devices connect to a single cable. If the cable fails, the network is down.

byte 8 bits grouped together as a basic unit.

C

C-RIMM (Continuity RIMM) A blank module used for empty memory slots when RIMM technology is used.

CAB file A shortened name for a cabinet file. The file holds multiple files or drivers that are compressed into a single file. CAB files are normally located in the i386 folder on the Windows XP CD.

cable modem A modem that connects to the cable TV network.

cable select A setting used on PATA IDE devices when a special cable determines which device is the master and which one is the slave.

cache memory Designed to increase microprocessor operations.

Cancel button Located in bottom right corner of the window; clicking it ignores any changes the user has made and restores parameters to their original state.

capacitive keyboard A reliable, but more expensive, keyboard.

capacitor An electronic component that can hold a charge.

CAPTCHA A type of test found on websites to ensure that a human is filling out a form, for example, and not a computer or script. A group of random letters and numbers are shown. The human must type the exact characters in order for the form or information to be submitted.

CardBay A PC Card standard that allows laptop computers to be compatible with USB and IEEE 1394 serial interfaces. It is backward compatible and does not require a driver or support by the operating system.

CardBus An upgraded standard from the 16-bit local bus standard to the PCMCIA that allows 32-bit transfers at up to 33MHz speeds.

CAS (column address strobe) In a memory module, the time (in clock cycles) for the processor to move on to the next memory address. Therefore, the smaller the number, the better (i.e., faster). Also known as CAS latency, or CASL.

CCFL (cold cathode fluorescent lamp) The older flat-panel backlight technology used before LED backlights were used.

CD (compact disc) A storage medium that holds up to 700MB of data, such as audio, video, and software applications.

`CD` Also known as `CHDIR` command. Used from a command prompt to change into a different directory.

CD-R (compact disc-recordable) A CD drive that can create a compact disc by writing once to the disc. See also *WORM*.

CD-RW (compact disc rewritable) A CD drive that can write data multiple times to a particular disc.

CDFS (Compact Disc File System) A file system for optical media.

Certified W-USB A type of USB that supports high-speed, secure wireless connectivity between a USB device and a PC at speeds of 480Mbps (~10 feet) or 110Mbps (~30 feet). Wireless USB uses ultra-wideband, low-power radio over a range of 3.1 to 10.5GHz.

CFS (Compact File Set) A file format used for archiving and distributing applications.

channel ID Used in wireless networks to define the frequency used to transmit and receive.

charging A laser printing process that can also be known as conditioning. This process gets the drum read for use by applying a uniform voltage on the drum surface using a primary/main corona or a conditioning roller.

charging USB port A port that is able to provide power to charge and run an unpowered attached device such as a flash drive.

checkbox Provides the user the ability to enable an option or not. Clicking in the checkbox places a check mark that enables the option. Clicking again removes the check mark and disables the option.

chipset One or more motherboard chips that work in conjunction with the processor to allow certain computer features, such as motherboard memory and capacity.

`CHKDSK` A program that locates clusters that are disassociated from the appropriate data file.

CHS addressing (cylinders heads sectors addressing) The method the BIOS uses to talk to the hard drive, based on the number of cylinders, heads, and sectors of the drive.

CL rating (column address strobe [CAS] latency) The amount of time (clock cycles) that passes before the processor moves on to the next memory address. Chips with lower access times (CL rating) are faster than those with higher access times (larger numbers).

clamping speed The time that elapses from an overvoltage condition to when surge protection begins.

clamping voltage The voltage level at which a surge protector begins to protect a computer.

cleaning A laser printing process that describes removing residual toner from the drum by using a wiper blade or brush.

clean install Loading of an operating system on a computer that does not already have one installed.

client/server network A network environment where a computer (the server) has something (a file, a printed document, or an application, for example) that is given to another network device (the client).

clock An electronic component that provides timing signals to all motherboard components. A PC's clock is normally measured in MHz.

clock speed The rate at which timing signals are sent to motherboard components (normally measured in MHz).

Close button Located in the upper-right corner of a dialog box with an X, a button that is used to close the dialog box.

cluster The minimum amount of space that one saved file occupies.

`CMD` A command issued from the Run utility in Windows to bring up a command prompt window.

CMOS (complementary metal oxide semiconductor) A special type of memory on a motherboard in which Setup configuration is saved.

CNR (Communications Network Riser) Intel's design that allows integration of network, sound, and modem functions. It shares space with, is located right beside, or is located between other motherboard expansion slots.

coaxial cable A type of cabling used in video connections. Has a copper core, surrounded by insulation and shielding from EMI.

cold boot Executes when the computer is turned on with the power switch. Executes POST.

COM*x* Designation for a communications port, where the *x* represents a COM port number, such as COM1 or COM2.

command prompt Otherwise known as a prompt, a text-based environment where commands are entered.

command switch An option used when working from a command prompt that allows a command to be controlled or operated on differently.

CompactFlash (CF) A type of removable flash memory storage that can be inserted into many devices, such as disk drives, cameras, PDAs, mobile phones, and tablet PCs.

Compatibility mode A Microsoft Windows tool used to emulate older operating systems so older applications or hardware can be used on a newer operating system.

component/RGB video Three RCA jacks commonly found on TVs, DVD players, and projectors. The three connections are for luminescence or brightness and two jacks for color difference signals.

Component Services A Microsoft Management Console snap-in that can be used to configure and administer COM (Component Object Model) components, COM+ applications, and the DTC (Distributed Transaction Coordinator).

composite video A yellow RCA port normally found on projectors, TVs, gaming consoles, stereos, and optical disc players.

compression Compaction of a file or folder to take up less disk space.

Computer A section within Windows Explorer.

Computer Management console A Windows tool that displays a large group of tools on one screen.

conditioning roller Used in a laser printer to generate a large uniform negative voltage to be applied to the drum.

`CONFIG.SYS` A file that contains multiple lines used to control or configure the computer environment, such as memory, CD-ROM, screen display, and so on. The file is no longer required in today's operating systems.

context menu A menu of options usually available from the main menu that is brought up by right-clicking on an item.

continuity An electrical resistance measurement to see if a wire is good or broken.

contrast ratio An LCD characteristic that describes the difference in light intensity between the brightest white and the darkest black. A higher contrast ratio is a better characteristic.

Control Panel A Windows icon that allows computer configuration such as adding or removing software, adding or removing hardware, configuring a screen saver, adjusting a monitor, configuring a mouse, installing networking components, and so on.

convergence A term used to describe how data, voice, and video technologies are now using one network structure instead of separate ones.

CONVERT A command issued from a command prompt that changes an older file system into NTFS.

cookie A program that collects information that is stored on a hard drive. This information could include your preferences when visiting a website, banner ads that change, or what websites you have visited lately.

COPY A command used from a command prompt to transfer one or more files from one place to another.

COPY CON: A command used to copy the characters entered from a keyboard (the console). An archaic way to create batch files.

counter A specific measurement for an object in the Windows System Monitor tool.

counter log A Performance Tool option used to create a log file using selectable objects and counters.

cpi (characters per inch) A printing measurement that defines how many characters are printed within an inch. The larger the CPI, the smaller the font size.

cps (characters per second) The number of characters a printer prints in 1 second.

CPU See *processor*.

CPU bus frequency A motherboard setting for external microprocessor speed.

CPU speed The rate at which the CPU operates. It is the speed of the front side bus multiplied by the multiplier. Normally measured in MHz or GHz.

CPU throttling Reducing the clock frequency in order to reduce power consumption.

CRC (cyclic redundancy check) An advanced method of data error checking.

C-RIMM (continuity RIMM) A blank module used to fill empty memory slots on the motherboard when using RIMMs, because the memory banks must be tied together. RIMMs are packaged RDRAMs (Rambus DRAM).

CRIMM See *C-RIMM*.

crossover cable Cabling used to connect two like devices (for example, two computers, two switches, or two routers).

crosstalk A type of EMI where signals from one wire interfere with the data on an adjacent wire.

CRT (cathode ray tube) The main part of a monitor, the picture tube.

CSMA/CA (Carrier Sense Multiple Access/Collision Avoidance) A common access method (set of communication rules governing networked devices) used in wireless and older Apple networks.

CSMA/CD (Carrier Sense Multiple Access/Collision Detection) A common access method (set of communication rules governing all network devices) used by Ethernet.

CTS (clear to send) Part of the RTS/CTS hardware handshaking communication method. Specific wires on the serial connector are used to send a signal to the other device to stop or start sending data. The CTS and RTS (request to send) signals indicate when it is okay to send data.

current A term that describes how many electrons are going through a circuit.

cylinder On a stack of hard drive platters, the same numbered concentric tracks of all platters.

D

DAC (discretionary access control) A method of controlling access based on someone's identity or the group to which the user belongs.

daisy chaining Connecting multiple devices together by using cabling; commonly used with parallel SCSI devices.

data bits A serial device setting for how many bits make up a data word.

data collector set Data collected through Performance Monitor in Windows Vista and higher operating systems.

data link layer Layer 2 of the OSI model, which accurately transfers bits across the network by encapsulating (grouping) them into frames (usable sections).

DB-25 A 25-pin D-shell male (serial) or female (parallel) port.

DB-9 A 9-pin D-shell male serial port.

dBd A measurement of antenna gain as referenced to a dipole antenna.

dBi A measurement of antenna gain as referenced to an isotropic antenna.

DBR (DOS boot record) An area of a disk that contains system files.

DC (direct current) The type of power a computer needs to operate.

DCE (data circuit terminating equipment) A term that refers to serial devices such as modems, mice, and digitizers.

DDoS (Distributed Denial of Service) A type of security attack in which several computer systems are used to attack a network or device with the intent of preventing access such as to a web server.

DDR (double data rate) Data is transmitted on both sides of the clock signal and uses 184 pins. Sometimes called DDR SDRAM or DDR RAM.

DDR2 (double data rate 2) An upgrade to the DDR SDRAM standard and sometimes is called DDR2 RAM. It includes the following modules—DDR2-400, DDR2-533, DDR2-667, DDR2-800, and DDR2-1000. DDR2 uses 240-pin DIMMs and is not compatible with DDR; however, the higher-end (faster) DDR2 modules are backward compatible with the slower DDR2 modules.

DDR3 (double data rate 3) An upgrade from DDR2 for speeds up to 1600MHz that better supports dual- and quad-core processor-based systems.

DDR3L A DDR3 module that runs at a lower voltage (1.35V) than the 1.5V or higher DDR/DDR2/DDR3 modules. Less voltages means less heat and less power consumed.

DDR DIMM A type of dual in-line memory module used in AMD and Intel-based computers and higher-end servers.

DDR RAM (double data rate RAM) A memory module that can send data on both the rising and falling sides of a clock signal, unlike SDRAM that sends data only on the rising clock cycle. Therefore, DDR RAM can send twice as much data as SDRAM.

DDR SDRAM (double data rate synchronous dynamic RAM) A memory technology where new memory addresses are placed on the address bus before the prior memory address retrieval and execution are complete. SDRAM synchronizes its operation with the CPU clock signal to speed up memory access.

decoder In DVD drives, hardware or software that converts the MPEG-2 video.

default gateway The IP address of a Layer 3 device, such as a router, that is directly connected to its immediate network. It tells a device on its network where to send a packet destined for a remote network.

default printer When a computer can use multiple printers, the one printer that all applications use by default. A computer user can change the printer to a different one though the Print dialog window. To mark a printer as default, right-click the printer icon and click the Set as default option.

defragmentation A process of reordering and placing files in contiguous sectors.

degausser A device that demagnetizes monitors. Also called a degaussing coil.

`DEL` A command issued from a command prompt that is used to delete a file or folder.

density control blade A part inside a laser printer's toner cartridge that controls the amount of toner released to the drum.

DEP (data execution prevention) Software- and hardware-based security measures to prevent malicious software from executing in specific memory locations.

desktop The interface between the user and the applications, files, and hardware, and is part of the graphical user interface environment. It is the area where all work is performed.

developing A term used to describe a laser printer process in which toner is attracted to the laser printer drum.

developing cylinder A component inside a laser printer's toner cartridge that applies a static charge to the toner so it will be attracted to the drum. Sometimes called a developing roller.

device driver Special software that allows an operating system to access a piece of hardware.

Device Manager A Windows program that is used to view and configure hardware.

DFS (Distributed File System) A Microsoft-provided set of network services that allow easy access to network shares.

DHCP (Dynamic Host Configuration Protocol) A method to automatically assign IP addresses to network devices from a pool of IP addresses.

dial-up network A network formed by using a modem that connects to the traditional phone network. The modem is used to connect to a remote network device.

dialog box A window used by the operating system that allows user interaction to set preferences on various software parameters.

DIB (dual independent bus) Using two buses (a back side and front side bus) to relieve the bottleneck when the CPU communicates with RAM, L2 cache, chipset, PCI bus, and so on.

differential backup Backs up files that have changed since the last full backup (files that have the archive bit set to on), but the backup software does not reset the archive bit like the incremental backup does.

digital modem A modem that transmits directly on digital phone lines.

digital signature Confirms that the hardware or updated driver being installed is compatible with Windows; sometimes called driver signing.

DIMM (dual in-line memory module) A style of 168-, 184-, or 240-pin memory chip normally used for RAM chips on Pentium and higher motherboards.

DIN connector A round connector with small holes, normally keyed with a metal piece or notch so that the cable inserts only one way. Examples include keyboard and mouse connectors.

DIP (dual in-line package) A style of memory chip that has a row of pins down each side and is used for older ROM chips.

DIR A command used from a command prompt that displays the contents of a directory.

directional antenna A type of antenna that radiates energy in a specific direction.

directory In older operating systems, an electronic container that holds files and even other directories. Today's operating systems use the term *folder*.

DirectX A Microsoft technology that integrates multimedia drivers, application code, and 3D support for audio and video.

disc A term used to describe CDs, DVDs, and BDs.

Disc-at-Once (DAO) A type of drive that allows a disk to be made rather than the alternative of Track-at-Once, in which the laser stops writing normal data after a track is finished.

disk Media used to store data.

Disk Administrator A Windows program that allows testing, configuration, and preventive maintenance on hard disks.

disk cache A portion of RAM set aside for hard drive data that speeds up hard drive operations. A cache on a hard drive controller is also known as a data buffer.

Disk Cleanup A Windows utility that helps free up hard drive space by emptying the Recycle Bin, removing temporary files, removing temporary Internet files, removing offline files, and so on.

disk duplexing A technique that uses two disk controllers and allows the system to continue functioning if one hard drive fails. Data is written to both sets of hard drive systems through the two controllers. Disk duplexing is considered to be RAID level 1.

Disk Management A Windows tool used to partition and manage hard drives.

disk mirroring A process that protects against hard drive failure by using two or more hard drives and one disk controller. The same data is written to both drives. If one hard drive fails, the other hard drive continues to function. Disk mirroring is considered to be RAID level 1.

DISKPART A command-based utility used in preparing hard disk partitions and volumes for use.

DisplayPort A port, developed by VESA (Video Electronics Standards Association), that can send and receive audio and video signals. Used primarily for display devices and can connect to a single link DVI or HDMI port with the use of a converter.

DLP (Digital Light Processing) A technology used in projectors and rear projection TVs that is an array of miniature mirrors used to create pixels on a projection surface.

DLT (digital linear tape) A type of magnetic tape used when backing up computer data to a tape drive.

DMA channel (direct memory access channel) A number assigned to an adapter that allows the adapter to bypass the microprocessor to communicate directly with the RAM chips. DMA mode allows data transfer between the hard drive and RAM without going through the CPU.

DMA mode (direct memory access mode) Allows data transfer between a hard drive and RAM without going through the CPU.

DMZ (demilitarized zone) A network area that is separate from the corporate network but contains servers that are accessible to outside devices.

DNS server (Domain Name System server) Application on network server that translates Internet names into IP addresses.

docking station A part that has connections for a monitor, printer, keyboard, and mouse that allows a laptop computer to be more like a desktop system.

Documents The default library grouping used by Window 7 applications when saving files.

domain A term used in Windows server-based networks where users are required to have logins and file storage, email, and Web-based services are commonly provided.

DoS (Denial of Service) A type of security attack in which the intent is to make a machine or a network unusable.

dot matrix printer See *impact printer*.

dot pitch The distance between like-colored phosphorous dots on adjacent dot triads.

dot triad A grouping of three phosphorous color dots combined to make a single image on the monitor.

double-sided memory A single memory module that contains two memory modules in one container (two banks). Data is still sent to the CPU 64 bits at a time. Some use the terms single-sided and double-sided to describe memory modules that have chips on one side (single-sided) or both sides (double-sided). Another name is double-ranked memory.

downstream A term used to describe information pulled from the Internet such as when viewing web pages or downloading a file.

downstream port A USB port used to connect a USB hub or USB device.

dpi (dots per inch) A printer measurement used with ink jet and laser printers that refers to how many dots are produced in an inch.

Dr. Watson A Windows XP utility that detects and displays troubleshooting information when a system or program error occurs.

DRAM (dynamic random-access memory) One of two major RAM types that is less expensive but also slower than SRAM. DRAM requires periodic refreshing of the electrical charges holding the 1s and 0s.

driver See *device driver*.

driver rollback A feature in Windows that allows an older driver to be re-installed when a new driver causes problems.

driver signing A technology that verifies whether a driver has been digitally signed and approved to work with the specific Windows operating system environment.

drive type A number that corresponds to a drive's geometry assigned during SETUP configuration.

drive wiping A technique used to eradicate personal or corporate data from a hard drive before donating or re-using a computer.

drop-down menu An option box with a down arrow; clicking the arrow reveals additional choices for the option.

D-shell connector A connector with more pins or holes on the top side than the bottom so that a cable inserts in only one direction. Examples include parallel, serial, and video ports.

DSL (digital subscriber line) A type of Internet connection that uses the traditional phone line. A filter is needed on each phone outlet that has a normal analog device attached to separate the analog sound from the Internet data.

DTE (data terminating equipment) A term that refers to computers and printers.

dual-boot Ability to boot from one of two installed operating systems.

dual-channel A system in which the motherboard memory controller chip handles processing of memory requests more efficiently by handling two memory paths simultaneously.

dual-core A type of processor that combines two CPUs in a single unit. Note there are now tri-core, quad-core, hexa-core, and even octa-core processors.

dual-ported memory A type of memory used on video adapters that allows data to be read from and written to simultaneously.

dual-rail power supply A term used to describe two +12 volt lines available in a power supply.

dual-voltage memory Motherboard memory modules that operate at the 1.35V level that use less power and produce less heat. All memory modules must be 1.35V modules to operate at 1.35 volts.

DUN (dial-up networking) A remote computer that dials into the Internet or a corporation using a modem.

DVD (digital versatile disc or digital video disc) A newer media technology than CDs but having less capacity than a Blu-ray disc.

DVD drive A drive that supports CDs as well as music and video DVDs.

DVD-R WORM technology used with DVD drives that is similar to CD-R drives. DVD-R discs can use one or two sides and are available in 3.95GB, 4.7GB, and 9.4GB. DVD-R discs are sometimes shown as two different types, DVD-R(A) and DVD-R(G). DVD-R(A) targets the "authoring" business for professional development of DVDs. DVD-R(G) is more for home users and lay people. Both can be read by most DVD players and drives, but DVD-R(G) drives usually cannot write to DVD-R(A) media.

DVD+R A type of read/write DVD supported by the DVD+RW Alliance that can record (one time per disc) up to 4.7GB on single-sided DVD+R discs.

DVD-RAM A type of drive that uses a laser to heat the disc and to magnetically charge it. Data can be written to the disc.

DVD-R DL (DVD-R dual layer) Similar to DVD-R in that it can record one time. Uses double-layered discs to store up to 8.5GB and supported by the DVD Forum.

DVD+R DL (DVD+R dual layer) Similar to DVD+R in that it can record one time. Uses double-layered discs to store up to 8.5GB and supported by the DVD+RW Alliance.

DVD-ROM A technology that produces discs with superior audio and video performance and increased storage capacity.

DVD-RW (DVD-rewritable) A type of read/write DVD format supported by the DVD Forum. Similar to DVD-R except you can erase and rewrite data. Uses 4.7GB discs and most DVD-ROM drives and DVD-Video players support this format. Sometimes known as DVD-R/W or DVD-ER.

DVD+RW (DVD read and write) A drive that can be read from and written to and that holds 3GB.

DVD±RW (DVD-rewritable) A type of read/write DVD format that is supported by both the DVD Forum and the DVD+RW Alliance. These drives reads most CD, DVD, and DVD+R DL discs and writes to CD-R, CD-RW, DVD+R, DVD-R, DVD-RW, and DVD+RW discs.

DVI (Digital Visual Interface) A port on a digital video adapter that is used to connect flat panel monitors to the computer.

DVI-A A type of dual-link connector that is less common than DVI-D or DVI-I. It is used to carry a DVI signal to an analog display, most commonly a CRT monitor.

DVI-D A type of video connector used with digital monitors.

DVI-I The most common type of DVI video connector that is used with both analog and digital monitors.

DVI port (digital video/visual interface) A port on a video adapter that is used to connect flat panel monitors to the computer.

DVR (digital video recorder) A special hardware component to a home theater configuration to record TV shows, transfer data from a camcorder or camera, or store movies or media for playback.

`DXDIAG` A Windows command to access DirectX software that helps resolve DirectX display and sound driver problems.

dynamic disk A Windows term for volumes that can be resized and managed without rebooting.

dynamic storage A disk that has been configured for the Windows operating system. The unit can be resized and managed without rebooting and contains primary partitions, extended partitions, logical drives, and dynamic volumes.

E

ECC (error correcting code) Uses a mathematical algorithm to verify data accuracy. ECC is more expensive than parity and the motherboard or memory controllers must also have additional circuitry to process ECC.

`ECHO OFF` A command used from a command prompt that prevents characters from being displayed on the screen.

ECP (extended capabilities port) An old 25-pin female parallel port that had full-duplex bi-directional capabilities.

`EDIT` A command used to bring up a text editor. A text editor allows file creation and modification.

EEPROM (electrically erasable programmable read-only memory) A nonvolatile memory technology used to store a small amount of data. EEPROMs used to be used for the computer BIOS. Flash memory is used today.

effective permissions The final permissions granted for a particular resource. Folder permissions are cumulative—the combination of the group and the person's permissions. The deny permission overrides any allowed permission set for a user or a group. When NTFS and shared folder permissions are both used, the more restrictive of the two becomes the effective permissions.

EFS (Encrypting File System) A Windows encryption feature that only the authorized user may view or change a file encrypted with EFS.

EIDE (Enhanced Integrated Drive Electronics) A term that signifies two IDE connectors (four devices) and support of the ATAPI standard.

electronic key card An alternative to a key for room or building access.

EMF (enhanced metafile) A spooled print data format that defines how data is stored on the hard drive (spooled) before being sent to the printer. EMF is the default setting and is a non-printer dependent format that performs faster than RAW. If you are having printing problems, and the documentation or your research directs you to change the spooling data format, this is the setting referenced. In contrast, the RAW data format is printer-specific and requires extra time to convert the printing data before it is saved to the hard drive.

EMI (electromagnetic interference) Electronic noise generated by electrical devices. Also called EMR (electromagnetic radiation).

EMP (electromagnetic pulse) A burst of energy that could cause an electronic surge that could be damaging to equipment.

encoding The way in which binary 1s and 0s are placed on a hard drive.

encryption A method of securing data from unauthorized users. Data is converted into an unreadable format.

energy absorption/dissipation A surge protector feature which describes that the greater number of joules that can be dissipated, the more effective and durable a surge protector is.

ENERGY STAR A set of energy efficiency standards including those relating to total energy requirements, low power mode(s), and an efficient power supply that a product must meet to meet this standard.

EPEAT rating system A rating system that works in conjunction with the EPA (Environmental Protection Agency) to identify products that have a green (and clean) design.

EPP (enhanced parallel port) An old 25-pin parallel port that allowed half-duplex bi-directional communication.

EPROM (erasable programmable read-only memory) Nonvolatile memory that is programmed with a small amount of data.

erase lamp A component inside a laser printer that neutralizes any charges left on the drum so that the next printed page receives no residuals from the previous page.

ERD (emergency repair disk) An older disk used to repair Windows NT Workstation and Professional.

eSATA (external serial ATA) A port used to connect external SATA devices to a computer.

eSATA port A nonpowered port used to connect external storage devices at a maximum of two meters.

ESCD (extended system configuration data) Data that provides the BIOS and operating system a means for communicating with plug and play devices. As the computer boots, the BIOS records legacy device configuration information. Plug and play devices use this information to configure themselves and avoid conflicts. Once an adapter has resources assigned and the resources are saved in ESCD, the resources do not have to be recalculated unless a new device is added to the computer.

ESD (electrostatic discharge) Occurs when stored up static electricity is discharged in an instantaneous surge of voltage. Cumulative effects of ESD weaken or destroy electronic components.

Ethernet A network system that carries computer data along with audio and video information. Ethernet adapters are the most common network cards.

Ethernet port An RJ-45 port used to connect a device to the wired network.

EVDO (Evolution-Data Optimized or Evolution-Data Only) A standard typically used to provide wireless broadband Internet connectivity.

Event Viewer A Windows tool used to monitor various events in the computer.

EVGA (Extended Video Graphics Array) A video standard that represented a 1024×768 resolution.

exabyte (EB) 1 billion times 1 billion bytes, or 2^{60}(1,152,921,504,606,800 bytes).

executable file A file with a *BAT*, *EXE*, or *COM* extension that starts an application, a utility, or a command. A file on which the operating system can take action.

exFAT A file system type that improves upon FAT32 by having a theoretical maximum file size of 16EB, maximum volume size of 64ZB (but 512TB is current limit), smaller cluster sizes than FAT32, and an increased number of files allowed in a directory. Created for external storage media such as Flash drives and hard drives for saving images/video.

expansion slot A motherboard socket into which adapters are connected.

Explorer A Windows-based application that details certain information for all folders and files on each drive. It is used most commonly to copy or move files and folders. Sometimes called Windows Explorer.

exposing A laser printer process that has also been called the writing phase. Light is directed toward the drum to put 1s and 0s on the drum surface. Everywhere the light hits the drum changes the drum surface voltage.

ExpressCard A replacement for PC Card technology that supports advanced serial technologies PCI-Express or USB connectivity through the ExpressCard slot and is used in laptop computers.

Extended Graphics Array See *XGA*.

extended partition A hard drive division.

extension In operating systems, the three or more characters following the filename and a period (.). The extension associates the file with a particular application that executes the file.

external command A command located on a disk that the operating system must locate before the command can execute.

external data bus The electronic lines that allow the microprocessor to communicate with external devices. Also known as external data path or external data lines. See also *bus*.

external data lines See *external data bus*.

F

FAT (file allocation table) A method of organizing a computer's file system.

FAT (file system type) A file system type also known as FAT16.

FAT12 A very old file system that was originally designed for floppy disks.

FAT16 A file system supported by DOS and all Windows versions since DOS. DOS and Windows 9x have a 2GB limit. Newer Windows operating systems have a 4GB limit.

FAT32 A file system that supports hard drives up to 2TB in size.

fault tolerance The ability to continue functioning after a hardware or software failure. An example of fault tolerance with hard drives is RAID configurations.

fax modem A device that functions as a modem and uses the printer and computer as a fax machine.

FDD (floppy disk drive) A drive that accepts floppy disks.

FDDI (Fiber Distributed Data Interface) A high-speed fiber network that uses ring topology and token passing access method.

`FDISK` A command used to partition a FAT16 or FAT32 partition on a hard drive.

feed assembly The part of a computer responsible for taking the paper through the printer.

female port A type of connector on a motherboard or a separate adapter with recessed portions (or holes) that accept a male cable's pins.

fiber-optic cable An expensive network cabling made of plastic or glass fibers that carry data in the form of light pulses. Handles the greatest amount of data with least amount of data loss. Comes in single-mode and multi-mode.

FIFO setting A serial device setting that enables or disables the UART's buffer.

file An electronic container holding data or computer code that serves as a basic unit of storage.

file system Defines how data is stored on a drive. Examples of file systems include FAT16, FAT32, exFAT, and NTFS.

file virus A program that replaces or attaches to executable files (those with .com or .exe extensions). The virus can cause the application to not start or operate properly. It can also load into RAM and affect other executable files.

filename A term used to describe the name of a file. In older operating systems, the filename was limited to eight characters plus a three-character extension. Today's operating systems allow filenames up to 255 characters long.

firewall Software or a hardware device that protects one or more computers from being electronically attacked.

FireWire See *IEEE 1394*.

FireWire port A serial technology developed by Apple. See also *IEEE 1394*.

firmware Combines hardware and software attributes. An example is a BIOS chip that has instructions (software) written into it.

`FIXBOOT` A Windows command to repair the hard drive boot sector if it has been corrupted and replaces it with a non-Windows Vista/Windows 7 boot sector or, if an earlier version of Windows has been installed after Windows Vista or Windows 7.

`FIXMBR` A Windows command to repair the hard drive MBR (master boot record) by copying a new MBR to the system partition. The existing partition table is not altered.

flash memory A type of nonvolatile memory that holds data when the power is off.

flash BIOS A type of motherboard memory that allows updates by disk or by downloading Internet files.

flat When recording a CD, the CD has pits and flats. The pits are indentations along the track. Flats (also called lands) separate the pits.

floppy disk A flexible disk (or diskette) made of oxide-coated Mylar used in 3.5-inch drive sizes.

floppy drive An older storage device that accepts floppy disks.

flow control A serial device setting that determines the communication method.

flyback transformer A CRT part used to boost voltage to the high level needed by the CRT.

Fn A function key that, when used in conjunction with another key, provides a specific function such as turning up speakers, connecting to an external monitor, or turning on the wireless adapter. This key is commonly found in laptops.

FPM (fast page mode) An older memory technology used to speed up memory access.

folder In Windows-based operating systems, an electronic container that holds files as well as other folders. Folders were previously called directories in older operating systems.

form factor The shape and size (height, width, and depth) of motherboards, adapters, memory chips, power supplies, and so on. Before building or upgrading, make sure the device's form factor fits the computer case.

FORMAT A command used to prepare a disk for use.

formatted (disk) A disk that has been prepared to accept data.

fragmentation Occurs over time as files are saved on the hard drive in clusters not adjacent to each other, which slows hard disk access time.

frame The encapsulated data found at Layer 2 of the OSI model.

frequency response The number of samples taken by a sound card.

frequency response range The range of sounds a speaker can reproduce.

FRU (field replaceable unit) A term used to describe a computer part that can be replaced without having to send the entire computer to the manufacturer.

FSB (front side bus) Part of the dual independent bus that connects the CPU to the motherboard components.

FTP (File Transfer Protocol) A standard used when transferring files from one computer to another across a network.

full backup A method of backing up a hard drive where the archive attribute is used. The backup software backs up all selected files and sets the archive bit to off.

full-duplex A serial device setting that allows the sending and receiving device to send data simultaneously. On a cable, the ability to transmit data in both directions simultaneously.

full format During an installation process to partition a hard drive, this command identifies and marks bad sectors on the drive so they will not be used for data storage.

fully buffered memory A technology used in network server memory that requires a special memory controller sometimes advertised as FBDIMMs.

fuser cleaning pad The pad located above the laser printer's fuser roller that lightly coats it with silicon to prevent the paper sticking to the roller.

fusing A laser printing process where toner is melted into paper.

fusing roller A laser printer part responsible for heating the toner and melting it into the paper.

G

game port An old 15-pin female D-shell input port that was used to connect a joystick to the computer.

gaming PC A computer design that includes a powerful processor, high-end video or specialized GPU, a good sound card, and high-end cooling due to the demands placed on hardware when playing computer-based games.

Gb An abbreviation for gigabit

GB See *gigabyte*.

GDDR4 SDRAM (graphics double data rate SDRAM) A power-efficient video memory upgrade to GDDR3 that has speeds up to 3.2GHz.

GDI (Graphics Device Interface) The part of Windows that handles representing and transmitting graphical objects to output devices such as printers, monitors, and overhead projectors. In Windows XP, GDI+ is the improved-upon model and it handles graphical images better as well as support for file formats such as JPEG and PNG. Windows Vista further upgraded GDI with XPS (XML paper specification). Windows 7 includes GDI hardware acceleration and improves GDI performance using the Windows Display Driver Model v1.1.

geo-tracking The ability to track where a GPS capable mobile device, such as a cell phone, is located. Companies can also use it to locate lost or stolen mobile devices.

gigabyte Approximately 1 billion bytes of information (exactly 1,073,741,824 bytes); abbreviated GB.

gigahertz 1 billion cycles per second (1GHz). Expresses the speed of a microprocessor.

GPS (Global Positioning System) A satellite-based navigation system that transmits location information to receivers in mobile devices. Most mobile devices have GPS capability.

GPT (GUID, or globally unique identifier, partition table) A type of partition table available in 64-bit Windows editions. GPTs can have up to 128 partitions and volumes up to 18EB.

GPU (graphics processing unit) A video adapter processor that assists in video communication between the video adapter and the system processor. Also known as video processor, video coprocessor, or video accelerator.

grayware A generic term for applications or files that affect computer performance and/or cause unexpected and unsolicited events to occur. Can come from downloading shareware or freeware, infected emails, selecting an advertisement shown in a pop-up window, or through a Trojan virus. Spyware, adware, and malware are all types of grayware.

grounding Occurs when the motherboard or adapter is not installed properly and has a trace touching the computer's frame.

GSM (Global System for Mobile Communications) A telecommunications standard known as second generation or 2G for protocols used on cellular networks.

GUI (graphical user interface) In operating systems, an interface in which the user selects files, programs, and commands by clicking pictorial representations (icons) rather than typing commands at a command prompt.

gyroscope A technology used in mobile devices that measures and maintains screen orientation. Used in conjunction with an accelerometer so that a mobile device can be turned and the screen orientation also turns.

H

HAL (hardware abstraction layer) The layer between the operating system and hardware devices that allows Windows to run different hardware configurations and components without crashing the operating system.

half-duplex A serial device setting that allows either the sending or the receiving device to send data, one device at a time. On a cable, the ability to transmit in both directions but not at the same time.

handshaking The method by which two serial devices negotiate communications.

hard drive A sealed data storage medium on which information is stored. Also called a hard disk.

hardware A tangible, physical item, such as the keyboard or monitor.

hardware decoder Sometimes called an MPEG-2 decoder used when converting an MPEG DVD file into a format that can be displayed. A software decoder puts the burden on the CPU to decode and uncompress the video data from the DVD. Video card manufacturers have added MPEG-2 video decoding support to decrease the CPU load.

HAV (hardware assisted virtualization) A required feature of Microsoft's Windows Virtual PC. This feature is available on some computers and it can be enabled or disabled through the system BIOS.

HCL (hardware compatibility list) A Microsoft list of hardware that is known to work when used with a particular operating system.

HDD (hard disk drive) A mechanical drive with metal platters used to store data.

HDMI (High-Definition Multimedia Interface) An upgraded digital interface that carries audio and video over the same cable.

`hdwwiz.exe` The command used to open the Add Hardware wizard.

head crash Occurs when a read/write head touches a platter, causing damage to the heads or the platter.

heap Memory allocated to Windows core files that records every Windows action, such as each mouse click, each resizing of a window, and so on.

Help button A question mark button located in the upper-right corner of a dialog box. Clicking it allows access to information on various topics.

hertz A measurement of electrical frequency equal to one cycle per second. Abbreviated Hz.

hexa-core A six-core processor.

hidden attribute A designation that keeps a file from being seen in directory listings. However, with today's operating systems, this attribute does not help because the operating system makes it very easy to see hidden files.

hidden share A share that has a dollar sign ($) added to the share name so that the share is not shown to a remote networked computer.

high-level format A process that sets up the file system for use by the computer. It is the third and last step in preparing a hard drive for use.

home screen The starting place for any mobile device running either iOS or Android and is where application icons are found. This is also the GUI interface for input to the operating system.

home server A server commonly used to be a Web server, print server, control home devices, manage backups, and/or be access from outside the home. A home server commonly includes the ability to stream sound or video, share files, have a Gigabit NIC, or have a RAID hard drive array.

HomeGroup A Windows 7 feature to make home networking easier to configure and join.

horizontal scanning frequency The rate at which a monitor's beam moves across the screen.

host Another name for a network device. It also represents a part of an IP address. An IP address has a network portion and a host portion.

host address A portion of an IP address that represents the specific network device.

host machine In a virtualization environment, the real computer.

hot fix Software that has one or more files that fix a particular software problem. Contrast this to a patch or a service pack.

hot swapping Allows adapters to be inserted into a slot or devices to be attached/unattached while the computer is powered.

hot spot See *wireless hot spot*.

HPA (Host Protected Area) A hidden part of the hard drive that is used to reinstall the operating system. It sometimes contains applications that are installed when the computer was sold. Using an HPA reduces the amount of hard drive space available to the operating system.

HPFS (High-Performance File System) A file system used with the OS/2 operating system.

HPPCL (Hewlett-Packard printer control language) A popular print software that translates between the printer and the computer.

HT (Hyper-Threading Technology) A technology created by Intel that is an alternative to using two processors. HT allows a single processor to handle two separate sets of instructions simultaneously.

HTML (Hypertext Markup Language) A programming language used to create Internet web pages.

HTPC (home theater PC) A special hardware component to a home theater configuration, which has a compact form factor case and motherboard with quiet fans and quiet power supply fan.

HTTP (Hypertext Transfer Protocol) A standard for Internet data communication.

HTTPS (HTTP over SSL) Encrypted HTTP communication through an SSL session. Web pages are encrypted and decrypted.

hub A device used with the universal serial bus or in a star network topology that allows multiple device connections. A network hub cannot look at each data frame coming through its ports like a switch does.

HVD (high voltage differential) A SCSI-2 standard that allowed longer SCSI bus lengths and required a differential terminator. HVD was removed from the SCSI-3 standards.

hybrid topology A physical network that shows how a network is wired combining multiple topology types.

Hyper-Threading Technology See *HT*.

HyperTransport AMD's I/O architecture in which a serial-link design allows devices to communicate in daisy chain fashion without interfering with any other communication. Thus, I/O bottleneck is mitigated.

hypervisor In a virtualization environment, the software that is used to create the virtual machine and allocate resources to the virtual machine. Also called virtual machine monitor or virtual machine manager.

I

I/O address (input/output address) A port address that allows an external device to communicate with the microprocessor. It is analogous to a mailbox number.

I/O APIC A type of controller that supports more interrupts than the traditional 16 that used throughout the peripheral buses and is integrated into the chipset. Compare with LAPIC which is normally integrated into each CPU and has its own timer.

I/O shield A part that allows for optimum air flow and grounding for the motherboard ports.

ICH (I/O controller hub) A part of the chipset that controls such motherboard components as SATA ports, PCI and PCIe slots, USB ports, audio ports, and integrated network cards. Also known as the south bridge.

ICMP (Internet Control Message Protocol) A Layer 3 protocol used for troubleshooting network connectivity. Commands that use ICMP include `ping`, `pathping`, and `tracert`.

icon An operating system graphic that represents a file, application, hardware, and shared network resources.

ICR (intelligent character recognition) An OCR-like (optical character recognition) technology that allows fonts and handwriting to be learned by the computer.

IDE (Integrated Drive Electronics) An interface that evolved into the ATA (now PATA) standard that supports internal storage devices.

IDS (intrusion detection system) Software or hardware that is designed to detect potential security issues that could be or allow an illegal entry to the computer or network. The IDS could log the incident, contact someone, and/or perform security measures to prevent invasion.

IEEE (Institute of Electrical and Electronics Engineers) An organization that provides a framework for defining standards relating to computers and networks.

IEEE 1284 A standard that defines what connections are used with printers and how data is transferred through the parallel port.

IEEE 1394 port A port that uses the IEEE 1394 standard for high-speed audio and video device data transfers known as FireWire. A single port supports the connectivity of up to 63 devices.

IIS (Internet Information Services) A Microsoft Web server application.

IMAP (Internet Mail Access Protocol) A protocol used to receive email through the Internet.

impact printer Sometimes called a dot matrix printer. A type of printer that physically impacts a ribbon which places an image on the paper.

incremental backup A method used in conjunction with a full backup. The incremental backup goes faster because it only backs up files that have changed since the last backup.

indexing A Microsoft Windows configurable feature that allows quick searches for files and folders.

infrared A technology utilizing infrared light that allows devices to communicate across a wireless network. Examples are laptop computers, printers, and handheld computing devices.

infrared port A wireless port found on laptop computers and small portable printers used for close wireless connectivity.

infrastructure mode A type of wireless network that contains an access point for wireless devices to be connected together.

inherited permissions Windows NTFS permission type that is propagated from what Microsoft calls a parent object. For example, if a folder is given the permission of Read, then all files within that folder inherit the read only attribute.

inkjet printer A type of printer that squirts ink through tiny nozzles to produce print. Ink jet printers produce high-quality, high-resolution, color output.

input device Used to enter data into a computer. Some examples are keyboard, mouse, joystick, touch screen, trackball, camera, game console, scanner, and digital pen.

INT 13 interface (Interrupt 13 interface) A standard that allows a system BIOS to locate data on the hard drive.

integrated motherboard A motherboard that contains ports such as mouse, keyboard, video, NIC, and USB ports.

Intel Corporation The largest processor manufacturer in the world. Intel also makes chipsets, motherboards, network cards, microcontrollers, and other electronic chips and components.

interlacing A scanning method used with monitors in which only the odd numbered pixel rows are scanned, followed by the even numbered pixel rows.

internal command A command that is part of the command interpreter that the operating system does not have to locate in order to execute. An example of an internal command is `DIR`.

internal data bus The electronic lines inside a microprocessor. See also *bus*.

Internet appliance An older term used to describe any device that can connect to the Internet through a wired or wireless network.

Internet Explorer An application used to access the Internet through a network or dial-up access.

interrupt See *IRQ*.

IOPS (input/output operations per second) A measurement of hard drive speed for both magnetic drives and SSDs that takes into account sequential reads/writes as well as random reads/writes.

IP (Internet Protocol) A Layer 3 protocol that is part of the TCP/IP protocol suite.

IP address A type of network adapter address used when multiple networks are linked. Known as a Layer 3 address, in IPv4 it is a 32-bit binary number with groups of eight bits separated by a dot. This numbering scheme is also known as dotted-decimal notation. Each eight-bit group represents numbers from 0 to 255. An IPv4 IP address example is 113.19.12.102. Also see IPv4 and IPv6.

`ipconfig` A command used from a command prompt in Windows to view the current IP settings.

IPP (Internet Printing Protocol) A protocol used for network-connected printers that can include remote print job management and print configuration such as media size or print resolution.

IPsec (Internet Protocol Security) A suite of protocols for securing a communication session such as a VPN tunnel.

IPv4 (Internet Protocol version 4) A type of IP address that uses 32 bits (four groups of 8 bits each) shown as decimal numbers in dotted-decimal format. An example of an IPv4 address is 192.168.10.1.

IPv6 (Internet Protocol version 6) A type of IP address that uses 128 bits represented by hexadecimal numbers. An example of an IPv6 IP address is fe80::13e:4586:5807:95f7. Each set of four digits represents 16 bits.

IrDA (Infrared Data Association) A term used to describe the association or the protocols developed by the association. The protocols relate to wireless infrared standards.

IRQ (interrupt request) A microprocessor priority system that assigns a number to each expansion adapter or port to facilitate orderly communication.

IRQ steering A PCI bus property that allows many PCI devices to share the limited and fixed number of IRQs, thus preventing competing devices from slowing or stopping CPU processing.

ISA (Industry Standard Architecture) The oldest of the three types of computer architectures. Allows 16-bit data transfers.

ISDN (Integrated Services Digital Network) A digital phone line that has three separate channels, two B channels, and a D channel. The B channel allows 64Kbps transmission speeds. The D channel allows 16Kbps transmissions.

ISO (Industry Standards Organization or International Organization for Standardization) An international group that provides technical specifications related to computers, networks, and telecommunication.

isotropic antenna A type of antenna used as a reference for other antennas. It is not a real antenna. An isotropic antenna theoretically transmits an equal amount of power in all directions.

ISP (Internet service provider) A vendor that provides connection to the Internet.

J

JBOD (just a bunch of disks or just a bunch of drives) A term given to combining more than one drive that is recognized as a single drive letter or a single virtual disk. This is similar in concept to RAID, but is not one of the RAID levels.

joule dissipation capacity A measure of a surge protector's ability to absorb overvoltage power surges. The higher the capacity, the better the protection.

jumper A plastic cover for two metal pins on a jumper block.

K

kb Abbreviation for kilobit.

kB See *kilobyte*.

keyboard Allows users to communicate and input data to the computer.

keyboard port DIN connector on the motherboard into which only the keyboard cable must connect.

keyed A connector or cable that has an extra metal piece that allows correct connections.

kibibyte A binary prefix term that is used to describe 2^{10} or 1,024 and is abbreviated KiB. Instead of saying that it is 1 kilobyte, which people tend to think of as approximately 1,000 bytes, the term kibibyte is used.

kilobyte Approximately 1,000 bytes of information (exactly 1,024 bytes).

KMS (Key Management Service) A service used in companies that have 25 or more Windows Vista or 7 computers to deploy. KMS is a software application installed on a computer. All newly installed Windows Vista- or 7-based computers register with the computer that has KMS installed. Every 180 days, the computer is re-activated for the license. Each KMS key can be used on two computers up to 10 times. Contrast with *MAK*.

KVM switch (keyboard, video, mouse switch) A component that allows multiple computers to be connected to a single keyboard, monitor, and mouse.

L

L1 cache Fast memory located inside the microprocessor.

L2 cache Fast memory located inside the processor.

L3 cache Any fast cache memory installed on the motherboard when both L1 and L2 cache are on the processor.

LAN (local area network) A group of devices sharing resources in a single area such as a room or a building.

LAPIC (local APIC) A type of interrupt controller that supports more interrupts than the traditional 16. LAPIC is normally integrated into each CPU and has its own timer. Compare to I/O APIC which is used throughout any of the peripheral buses and is integrated into the chipset.

laptop A computer model that is portable.

laser lens A component of the optical drive that reads the data from the optical disc; susceptible to dust accumulation. Also known as an objective lens.

laser printer A type of printer that produces output using a process similar to a copier. Laser printers are the most expensive type of printer.

Last Known Good Configuration Used when the Windows configuration has been changed by adding hardware or software that is incompatible with the operating system or when an important service has been accidentally disabled.

latency In networking, the amount of delay experienced as a packet travels from source to destination.

LC (Lucent connector) A connector used with fiber-optic cable.

LCD (liquid crystal display) A video technology used with laptops and flat screen monitors. The two basic types of LCD are passive matrix and active matrix.

LED (light-emitting diode) A video output technology which is a low power, low heat, long lasting electronic device utilizing liquid crystals.

library Windows 7 storage that is similar to a folder but that is automatically indexed for faster searching.

Li-ion battery A lithium battery, which is very light and can hold a charge for a long period of time; found in cell phones and portable devices such as cameras.

line conditioner A device that protects a computer from overvoltage and undervoltage conditions as well as adverse noise conditions. Also known as a power conditioner.

line-of-sight network In WiMAX wireless networks, the between-towers connection that travels from WiMAX tower to WiMAX tower. Also called line of sight backhauls.

liquid cooling system An alternative to a fan or sink for processor cooling. Liquid is circulated through the system. Heat from the processor is transferred to the cooler liquid.

local administrator A user account that has full power over a Windows-based computer. A local administrator can install hardware and software; use all of the administrative tools; create and delete hard drive partitions or volumes; and create, delete, and manage local user accounts.

local share Something such as a printer, folder, or disc that has been made available across a network.

logical drive A division of an extended partition into separate units, which appear as separate drive letters.

long filename An extended filename in Windows that can be up to 255 characters in length instead of the DOS filename format of eight characters with a three-character extension.

loopback address A private IP address of 127.0.0.1 or ::1 that is used to test a NIC's basic network setup and the TCP/IP stack.

loopback plug A device used in troubleshooting that allows port testing.

lost cluster A sector on a disk that the file allocation table cannot associate with any file or directory.

LPD/LPR (Line Printer Daemon/Line Printer Remote) A protocol used for controlling and managing network printers.

LPT (line printer terminal) The name assigned to the parallel printer port. LPT*x* was used where *x* was the port number such as LPT1 or LPT2.

lumen A measure of light output or brightness—how much visible light is coming out of equipment such as lamps, lighting equipment, or projectors.

LVD (low voltage differential) A parallel SCSI signaling type that is required for all SCSI devices that adhere to the Ultra SCSI standards. LVD uses a lower voltage than HVD and is backward compatible with SE.

M

MAC address (Media Access Control address) One of two types of addresses assigned to network adapters, used when two devices on the same network communicate. Known as a Layer 2 address.

macro virus A program that attaches to a document written by a specific application, such as Microsoft PowerPoint. Once the document is opened into RAM, the virus attaches to other documents.

MAK (Multiple Activation Key) A method in which the Internet or a phone call must be made to register one or more Windows Vista or 7 computers. This method has a limited number of activations.

male port A connector on a motherboard or adapter with protruding pins that accepts a cable with a female connector.

MAN (metropolitan area network) Describes networks that span a city or town.

MAP (Microsoft Assessment and Planning Toolkit) Used for planning a Windows deployment in a corporate environment.

MAPI (Messaging Application Programming Interface) A Microsoft-proprietary protocol used with email.

marking The part of the printer that places the image on the paper. Also called the marking engine or marking subsystem.

master A jumper setting used to configure a PATA IDE device; the controlling device on the interface.

Mb An abbreviation for megabit.

MB See *megabyte*.

MBR (master boot record) A program that reads the partition table to find the primary partition used to boot the system.

MBSA (Microsoft Baseline Security Analyzer) A tool used to identify security misconfigurations.

MCBF (mean cycles between failures) A performance comparison measurement which is found by dividing the MTBF (mean time between failures) by the duration time of a cycle (operations per hour). The lower the number, the better the performance.

MCH (memory controller hub) A part of a chipset that connects directly to the processor. The MCH controls RAM and video expansion slots. It is also called the north bridge.

MD A command issued from a command prompt that is used to create a directory (folder) or subdirectory.

mebibyte A binary prefix value used to describe a value of 2^{20} or 1,048,576 and abbreviated MiB.

mechanical keyboard A keyboard that is less expensive than capacitive keyboards and more prone to failure.

mechanical mouse A mouse that uses a rubber ball to move the pointer.

media player A special hardware component to a home theater configuration that allows streaming entertainment, watch your own videos and photos, or listen to your own music and possible wireless connectivity.

megabyte Approximately 1 million bytes of data (exactly 1,048,576 bytes). Abbreviated as MB.

megahertz The speed at which microprocessors and coprocessors are measured. Equal to 1 million cycles per second; abbreviated MHz. See also *hertz*.

memory The part of a computer that temporarily stores applications, user documents, and system operating information.

memory address A unique address for memory chips.

Memory Diagnostic Tool A tool accessed by booting from Advanced Boot Options menu in Windows Visa/7 to thoroughly test RAM.

mesh topology A network in which all devices connect to each other by cabling to provide link redundancy for the maximum fault tolerance.

MFD (multi-function device) A device such as an all-in-one printer that includes a printer, scanner, copier, and fax machine. The term might also be used to describe a network device that commonly includes a router, access point, and switch.

MFP (multi-function product, printer, or peripheral) Also known as an all-in-one printer. See also *MFD*.

MHz (megahertz) A measurement of speed for processors (older ones), motherboards, and memory.

microDIMM A type of DIMM used in portable computers such as a laptop.

microprocessor See *processor*.

microSD A storage device with nonvolatile flash memory used for mobile devices.

Microsoft Management Console Holds snap-ins or tools used to maintain the computer. Also known as the Computer Management console.

Microsoft Security Essentials A free anti-virus program for Windows XP, Vista, and 7 (but not Windows 8).

MIDI (Musical Instrument Digital Interface) An interface built into a sound card to create synthesized music.

MIME (Multipurpose Internet Mail Extension) When used with SNMP, allows non-ASCII character sets and other rich media content to be included with email.

MIMO (multiple input/multiple output) A term used to describe 802.11n wireless technology where multiple antennas operate cooperatively to increase throughput on a wireless network.

miniSD A storage device with nonvolatile flash memory used for mobile devices.

mini PCI A 32-bit 33MHz standard used in laptops, docking stations, and printers.

mini PCIe A 52-bit expansion slot or card used in mobile devices.

mini-DIN A motherboard connector sometimes called a PS/2 connector that is used to connect keyboards and mice.

MLC (multi-level cell) A cell that stores more than 1 bit in a memory cell that is used in a SSD (solid state drive). Contrast with *SLC*.

MMC (Microsoft Management Console) Also known as the Computer Management Console. Holds tools such as Device Manager, Disk Management, Local Users and Groups, Event Viewer, Task Scheduler, Performance, Shared Folders, and Services.

MMX Microprocessors that have 57 more multimedia instructions that speed up multimedia applications such as sound and video.

modem (modulator/demodulator) A device that connects a computer to a phone line, or connects computers and mobile devices to broadband, wireless, Wi-Fi, Bluetooth, or satellite networks.

modem isolator See *phone line isolator*.

modulation The process of adding data to a carrier signal. Examples include frequency modulation and amplitude modulation.

Molex A type of power connector that extends from the computer's power supply to various devices.

monitor Displays information from the computer to the user.

motherboard The main circuit board of a computer. Also known as the mainboard, planar, or systemboard.

mount To make a drive available and recognizable to the operating system.

mouse A data input device that moves the cursor or selects menus and options.

mouse port A DIN connector on the motherboard that should only accept the mouse cable.

MOV (metal oxide varistor) An electronic component built into some surge protectors to absorb overvoltage spikes or surges.

MP3 (Moving Picture Experts Group Layer 3) A sound format that compresses an audio file and has the extension of MP3.

MP4 (Moving Picture Experts Group Layer 4) A sound format that compresses an audio file and has the extension of MP4.

MPEG (Moving Picture Experts Group) An organization of professionals who create audio and video compression and transmission standards.

MRW (also called Mount Ranier or EasyWrite) A Phillips, Sony, Microsoft, and HP improvement on the UDF file format used on CDs and DVDs that saves files to read/write discs as if they were hard drives. It also supports defect management and works on different hardware platforms. MRW is natively supported in Windows Vista and greater.

`MSCDEX.EXE` A DOS-based program that assigns a drive letter to the CD-ROM drive.

`MSCONFIG` A system configuration utility command that allows an Administrator to enable or disable services, access control panel links, and control applications.

MSDS (material safety data sheet) A document that contains information about a product, its toxicity, storage, and disposal.

MSI (message signaled interrupt) A type of interrupt method that delivers up to 32 interrupts to the CPU using software and memory space on behalf of a single device. A PCIe card is required to support MSI.

MSI-X (message signaled interrupt) A type of interrupt method that allows a device to allocate up to 2,048 interrupts. Note that most devices do not use this many. A PCIe card is required to support MSI-X.

`MSTSC` A command used to control and use a remote computer; brings up the Remote Desktop utility.

MTBF (mean time between failures) The average number of hours before a device fails.

MUI (multilingual user interface) A Microsoft Windows and Office feature that allows for multiple languages to be installed on a single computer.

multi-boot A situation in which a computer can boot from two or more operating systems.

multi-mode A type of fiber-optic cabling that allows multiple light signals to be sent along the same cable.

multiplier A motherboard setting used to determine CPU speed (multiplier times bus speed equals CPU speed).

multisession A type of optical drive that has the ability to store data on a disc and then add to it later.

multitouch A technology used on mobile devices to use a finger or knuckle to interface with the operating system by pinching, spreading, rotating, or swiping.

My Computer The desktop icon that allows access to files, applications, software, and hardware located in or on the Windows XP or older computer.

My Documents The default folder (directory) location on the Windows XP or older hard drive for files the user saves. Also, the icon that quickly accesses the default directory.

My Network Places The Windows XP and older option used to access network resources.

N

NAC (network access control) A term used to describe a method of controlling access or authenticating a device or user onto the network.

nanometer A measurement of processor technology length equal to .000000001 meter (1 time 10-9). For example, chipsets created using 22nm technology have more transistors in the same amount of space as chipsets created using 32nm or 45nm technology.

nanosecond One-billionth of a second.

NAS (network-attached storage) A special hardware component of virtualization to increase storage space that can be shared with other devices.

NAT/PAT (Network Address Translation/Port Address Translation) Terms sometimes used interchangeably or globally to mean conserving IP addresses. A method of conserving IP addresses. NAT uses private IP addresses that become translated to public IP addresses. PAT does the same thing except uses fewer public IP addresses by "overloading" one or more public IP addresses by tracking port numbers.

native resolution The number of pixels going across and down a flat panel monitor. This resolution is the specification for which the monitor was made and is the optimum resolution.

`NBTSTAT` (NetBIOS over TCP/IP) A command used to display statistics relevant to current TCP/IP connections on the local computer or a remote computer using NBT.

`NET USE` The `net` command is used to control and monitor network devices. Many subcommands are used with the `net` command; for example, the `net use` command is used to attach to a remote network device.

`NETSTAT` A command used to view current network connections and the local routing table for a PC.

NetBEUI A nonroutable network protocol commonly found on peer-to-peer networks. Can work only on simple networks, not on linked networks.

NetBIOS (Network Basic Input/Output System) An older method of providing name resolution and connectivity methods for both connectionless and connection-oriented communication sessions.

network Two or more devices capable of communicating and sharing resources between them.

network layer Layer 3 of the OSI model that coordinates data movement between two devices on separate networks.

network number The portion of an IP address that represents which network the computer is on.

network port A port used to connect a computer to other computers, including a network server.

network share A folder or network device that has been shared and is accessible from a remote computer.

network topology A map of how the physical or logical paths of network devices connect.

NFS (Network File System) An open standard protocol used for sharing files across a network.

NIC (network interface card) An adapter used to connect a device to a network.

NiCd (nickel cadmium) An older type of battery used in laptops.

NiMH (nickel-metal hydride) A battery that has been replaced by Li-ion batteries.

NLX (New Low Profile Extended) A motherboard form factor.

NNTP (Network News Transfer Protocol) A protocol used to deliver news to network clients. Uses TCP port 119. If TLS (Transport Layer Security) is used, then the port number is commonly 563.

non-parity A type of memory chip that is cheaper and does not do error checking.

nonvolatile memory Memory that remains even when the computer is powered off. ROM and flash memory are examples of nonvolatile memory.

north bridge Describes the connection from the CPU to RAM, the video expansion slot, and to the PCI/PCIe bus.

notification area (mobile) A place on mobile devices that contains information such as battery life, wireless signal strength, time, or external media connectivity. Usually in the lower-right corner on a tablet and at the top of the display on a smartphone.

notification area (Windows) The far right area of the taskbar, which contains information about an application or tool, such as security, network access, speaker control, or date and time.

`nslookup` A Windows troubleshooting tool that displays network domain names and their associated IP addresses.

NTFS (New Technology File System) File system used with operating systems today (starting with Windows NT).

NTLDR (new technology loader) A file used during the Windows XP boot process. In Windows Vista and 7, this function is performed by the Windows Boot Manager that calls the `winload.exe` executable file to handle the boot process.

NTP (Network Time Protocol) A protocol that synchronizes time between network devices.

null modem cable A cable that connects two computers together without the use of a modem.

O

OCR (optical character recognition) A technology used to convert an image into text. Commonly used application in conjunction with scanners.

octa-core An eight-core processor.

ODD (optical disk drive) A collective term for CD, DVD, and BD because they use optical discs that are read from, written to, or both.

OEM (original equipment manufacturer) The original producer of a product. That product is bought by a company that rebrands or sells the part or computer under its own name.

ohm A measurement of electrical resistance.

OK button A button located in bottom-right side of a dialog box that can be clicked to save any changes applied and close the window.

OLED (organic LED) Does not require a backlight like LCDs, but has a film of organic compounds placed in rows and columns that can emit light. Is light weight and has a fast response time, low power usage, and a wide viewing angle.

omnidirectional antenna A type of antenna that has a radiation pattern in all directions.

on-die cache L2 cache when housed in the processor packaging.

open authentication Used in wireless networks; allows a wireless device to send a frame to the access point with the sender's identity (MAC address).

operating system A piece of software used to load a computer and make it operational.

optical drive A storage device that accepts optical discs such as CDs, DVDs, or BDs that have data, music, video or software applications.

optical mouse A mouse that has optical sensors used to move the pointer.

OS See *operating system*.

OSI model (Open Systems Interconnect Model) A standard for information transfer across a network that was developed by the International Standards Organization. The model has seven layers; each layer uses the layer below it, and each layer provides some function to the one above it.

outline font Fonts computed from a mathematical formula, also known as vector fonts.

output device A piece of computer hardware that receives (not sends to) data from a computer. An example of an output device is a monitor.

overclocking Manually changing the front side bus speed and/or multiplier to increase CPU and system speed, but at a cost of increasing the CPU operating temperature.

overvoltage A condition when the AC voltage is over the rated amount of voltage.

ozone filter A part of a laser printer that filters out the ozone produced by the printer.

P

packet Encapsulated data found at Layer 3 of the OSI model.

PAE (physical address extension) A feature provided by Intel that allows up to 64GB of physical memory to be used for motherboards that support it.

page In Windows disk caching, a 4KB block of memory space. The operating system swaps or pages the application to and from the temporary swap file as needed if RAM is not large enough to handle the application.

page file A single block of memory space, 4KB in size, used to store files and may also retrieve a file located on a disk.

PAN (personal area network) A network of personal devices such as PDAs, cell phones, laptop computers, and pocket video games that can communicate in close proximity through a wired network or wirelessly. A Bluetooth wireless keyboard and mouse is a PAN.

paper transport The part of a printer that moves paper through the printer.

Parallel ATA See *PATA*.

parallel port A old 25-pin female D-shell connector used to connect an older printer to a motherboard.

parity A method of checking data accuracy.

partition A process used to divide a hard drive so that the computer sees more than one drive.

partition table A table that holds information about the types and locations of partitions created. Occupies the outermost track on the platter (Cylinder 0, Head 0, Sector 1), and is part of the Master Boot Record.

pass-through terminator Used with SCSI devices; has an extra connector on it and allows a device that does not have terminators to be terminated through the connector that attaches to the cable.

passive terminator One type of SCSI chain end that is susceptible to noise interference over long cable distances. Used with SCSI-1 devices.

PAT See *NAT/PAT*.

PATA (Parallel ATA) A technology used with IDE devices that allows two devices per channel.

patch A piece of software that fixes a specific problem in an application or operating system.

path A reference that tells where a file is located among drives and folders (directories).

PC (personal computer) A common name for a computer, taken from the IBM PC brand.

PC Card A common local bus architecture used in laptops. Also known as PCMCIA.

PCI (Peripheral Component Interconnect) A common 64-bit, 66MHz local bus standard found in today's computers.

PCIe A point-to-point serial bus used for motherboard adapters. Each bit can travel over a lane and each lane allows transfers up to 250MBps with a maximum of 32 lanes (which gives a total of 8GBps transfer rate).

PCI-X A parallel PCI bus that can operate at 66, 133, 266, 533, and 1066MHz and is backward compatible with the previous versions of the bus but allows for faster speeds.

PCL (Printer Command Language) A type of printer PDL (Page Description Language) such as HPPCL that is used on HP printers; handles the overall page look and has commands that treat the entire document as a single graphic.

PCMCIA (Personal Computer Memory Card Industry Association) See *PC Card*.

PDL (Page Description Language) Software inside a printer that translates between the printer and the computer. Examples are HPPCL and PostScript.

Performance Logs and Alerts A Windows XP utility that allows the creation of graphs, bar charts, and text reports.

Performance Monitor A Windows tool that monitors resources such as memory and CPU usage, and allows creation of graphs, bar charts, and text reports.

Performance utility A utility that monitors memory and other hardware parameters usage aspects.

petabyte (PB) 1 thousand terabytes, or 2^{50} (1,125,899,906,842,600 bytes).

PGA (pin grid array) A type of processor housing.

PGA2 (pin grid array 2) A type of processor housing used in mobile devices.

phishing (pronounced "fishing") A type of social engineering that attempts to get personal information through email from a company that appears legitimate. Targets obtaining ATM/debit or credit card numbers and PINs, Social Security numbers, bank account numbers, an Internet banking login ID and password, an email address, security information such as a mother's maiden name, full name, home address, or phone number.

phone filter A part used with DSL Internet connectivity that must be attached to every phone outlet. The traditional analog device connects to this part. The filter allows the DSL signal to be separated from the normal analog traffic.

phone line isolator A surge protector for the modem, protecting against power fluctuations in a phone line. Also known as a modem isolator.

physical layer Layer 1 of the OSI model, which defines how bits are sent and received across the network without regard to their structure.

physical network topology A term that describes how a network is wired.

picosecond One-trillionth of a second.

picture cell The smallest image shown on the front of a monitor made up of three color phosphorous dots.

PII (personally identifiable information) A method of identifying, locating, or contacting a particular person.

PIN (personal identification number) A unique identifier used to access an account or device such as a mobile tablet.

pin 1 A designated pin on every cable and connector that must be mated when attaching the two. Usually designated by a stenciled or etched number, a color stripe, and so on.

pin firing The act of a printwire coming out of a dot matrix printer's print head and impacting the paper.

`ping` A network troubleshooting command used to test TCP/IP communications and determine whether a network path is available, whether any delays exist along the path, and if a remote network device is reachable. Use `ping` with the private IP address 127.0.0.1 or ::1 to test a NIC's basic network setup.

pipeline Separate internal data buses that operate simultaneously inside the microprocessor.

pipe symbol A character (|) used at the command prompt that allows control of where or how the output of the command is processed. For example, a command can be "piped" to display only one screen at a time.

pit Area along the track of a compact disc.

pixel Short for picture element, the smallest displayable unit on a monitor.

PKI (Public Key Infrastructure) A method of managing digital security certificates.

plasma A display that has little chambers containing plasma gas. When electricity is applied inside the chambers, excited electrons hit red, green, and blue phosphorous dots that glow.

platter A metal disk of a hard drive on which binary data is recorded.

plenum cable A type of cable that is treated with fire retardant materials so it is less of a fire risk.

PnP (plug and play) A bus specification that allows automatic configuration of an adapter.

polymorphic virus A program that changes constantly to avoid detection by antivirus scanning.

POP (Point of Presence) An Internet access point.

POP3 (Post Office Protocol) Used to retrieve email from a mail server.

port A connector located on the motherboard or on a separate adapter.

port forwarding The process of sending data through a firewall based on a particular port number or protocol.

port replicator A part that is similar to a docking station. It attaches to the laptop computer and allows more devices such as a monitor, keyboard, and mouse to be connected.

port triggering Temporarily sending data through a firewall based on a preconfigured condition.

PoS (point of sale) A terminal, computer, or printer used in retail.

POST (power-on self-test) Startup software contained in the BIOS chip that tests individual hardware components.

POST card PCI/PCIe adapter or USB attached card that performs hardware diagnostics and displays the results as a series of codes on a LED display or LED lights.

PostScript A type of printer software that translates between the printer and the computer.

POTS (plain old telephone service) The traditional analog phone network used to connect homes and small businesses.

power A measurement expressed in watts that represents how much work is being done.

power good signal A signal sent to the motherboard from the power supply during POST that signifies that power is acceptable.

power rating A measurement expressed in watts-per-channel that represents how loud the speaker volume can go up without distorting the sound.

power supply A device that converts AC voltage into DC voltage that the computer can use to power all internal and some external devices.

power supply tester A tool used to check DC voltages sourced from the power supply.

PPP (Point-to-Point Protocol) A connection-oriented Layer 2 protocol that encapsulates data for transmission over remote networks.

PPTP (Point-to-Point Tunneling Protocol) A method/protocol used to create a VPN.

preemptive multitasking A type of multitasking in Windows that allows the operating system to determine which application gets the processor's attention and for how long.

prefix notation A method used to describe a subnet mask. It includes a forward slash followed by a number such as /24. The number is how many consecutive bits are set in the subnet mask.

presentation layer Layer 6 of the OSI model that defines how data is formatted, encoded, converted, and presented from the sender to the receiver, even though a different computer language is used.

preventive maintenance Something that is done to prolong the life of a device.

PRI (Primary Rate Interface) 24 64K channels used with ISDN.

primary corona A wire in the laser printer responsible for generating a large negative voltage to be applied uniformly to the laser's drum.

primary partition The first detected drive on a hard drive.

print cartridge A container that holds the ink and the nozzles for the ink jet printer. Also known as an ink cartridge.

print driver A piece of software that coordinates between the operating system and the printer.

print engine The part of a printer that translates commands from the computer and provides feedback when necessary. The print engine is the brains of the printer operation.

print head The part of the dot matrix printer that holds the printwires and impacts the ribbon.

print server A device (computer or separate device) that connects to a printer used by multiple people through a network.

print spooler Also known as a print manager, a software program that intercepts the request to print and sends print information to the hard drive where it is sent to the printer whenever the microprocessor is not busy with other tasks. A print spooler allows multiple print jobs to be queued inside the computer so other work can be performed.

printwire A component of a dot matrix printer's print head that is a single wire that connects to a spring and impacts a ribbon to make a single dot on the paper.

privacy filter A physical filter added to a monitor to distort the display output for anyone except for the person looking directly at the screen. Also known as a privacy screen.

processing A laser printing process where the data is converted from the printer language into a bitmap image. This process is also known as raster image processing.

processor The central 32- or 64-bit electronic chip that determines the processing power of a computer. Also known as microprocessor or CPU (central processing unit).

Program Compatibility Wizard A program that is used to check for software application compatibility with a newer Windows version.

PROM (programmable read-only memory) Nonvolatile memory that is programmed once with a small amount of data.

`PROMPT` A command used to change how the command prompt appears. See also *command prompt*.

proxy server A server that acts as a go-between for an application and another server.

PS/2 mouse A mouse that connects to a 6-pin DIN port.

PSTN (Public Switched Telephone Network) A term that describes the traditional phone network including satellite, cellular, wired and wireless worldwide connectivity.

PSU (power supply unit) See *power supply*.

PVC (polyvinyl chloride) Cable that has a plastic insulation or jacket that is cheaper and easier to install than plenum cable. It can have flame-retardant added.

PXE boot (preboot execution environment) An option some computers have that can be modified to search for the network device that holds the computer image.

Q

QoS (quality of service) A collection of techniques used to ensure that the most important corporate data, voice, and/or video is sent before other noncritical data that may get dropped as a result.

QPI (Quick Path Interconnect) An Intel technology used as an alternative to the FSB (front side bus) in which a point-to-point connection is made between the processor and a motherboard component.

quad-core Four processors on a single motherboard by having either two dual-core CPUs installed on the same motherboard or two dual-core CPUs installed in a single socket.

quadruple-channel A memory type in which a motherboard can access four memory modules simultaneously.

quick format During an installation process, a function used to prepare a hard drive partition, but does not identify and mark bad sectors so that they will not be used for data storage. A full format, in contrast, does evaluate the drive for bad sectors, but takes quite a bit longer to prepare the partition for use.

Quick Launch bar Located immediately to the right of the *Start* button in the taskbar, a section of the taskbar that contains icons used for opening applications.

R

radiation pattern Sometimes called a propagation pattern, the direction(s) a radio frequency is sent or received.

radio button Similar to a checkbox, a round space on a dialog box that allows the user to enable a single option by clicking it. A solid dot in the button means the option is enabled; an absence of the dot means a disabled option.

RAID (redundant array of independent disks) Allows writing to multiple hard drives for larger storage areas, better performance, and fault tolerance.

RAID 0 Also called disk striping without parity, enables data to be alternatively written on two or more hard drives but be seen by the system as one logical drive. RAID level 0 does not protect data if a hard drive fails; it only increases system performance.

RAID 1 Also called disk mirroring or disk duplexing, it protects against hard drive failure. See also *disk mirroring* and *disk duplexing*. Requires two drives at a minimum.

RAID 5 A term that describes putting data on three or more hard drives, with one of the three drives used for parity. See also *RAID*.

RAM (random-access memory) A volatile type of memory that loses its data when power to the computer is shut off.

RAM drive A virtual hard disk created from RAM.

random-access time A performance comparison measurement, it is the amount of time a drive requires to find the appropriate place on the disc and retrieve information.

RAS (remote access service) The collection of hardware and software that allows remote connectivity and control of network devices.

RAS (row address strobe) A signal that selects a specific memory row.

raster A monitor's brightness pattern.

RAW volume A part of a hard drive that has been set aside as a volume but has never been high-level formatted and does not contain a specific type of file system.

`RD` A Windows command used to remove a directory (folder).

RDRAM Proprietary memory developed by Rambus, Inc.

RDP (Remote Desktop Protocol) A Microsoft protocol used for accessing and controlling networked computers and mobile devices.

read/write head The part of a floppy or hard drive that electronically writes binary data on disks.

read-ahead caching A type of disk caching that attempts to guess what the next data requested will be and loads that data into RAM.

read-only attribute A designation that can be applied to a file so the file is not accidentally erased.

ReadyBoost A utility that can speed up the Windows boot process by caching some startup files to a 256MB+ Flash drive, SD card, or CF card.

Recovery Console A Windows XP tool that allows the administrator to boot the computer to a command prompt and access the hard drive.

recovery disc A disc used to boot a system when you don't have an original operating system disc and then restore the computer from a previously saved system image. Sometimes called a system repair disc.

Recycle Bin A location in Windows-based operating systems where user-deleted files and folders are held. This data is not discarded from the computer. The user must empty the Recycle Bin to erase the data completely.

refresh (process) A rewrite of the information inside memory chips.

refresh rate The maximum time a monitor's screen is scanned in 1 second.

`REGEDIT` A Windows utility used to modify and back up the registry.

`REGEDT32` One of two Windows registry editors. See also *registry* and *REGEDIT*.

region code A setting on a DVD or Blu-ray drive or disc that specifies a geographic region. The drive's region code must match the disc's region code in order to play.

registered memory Memory modules that have extra chips (registers) near the bottom of the module that delay all data transfers by one clock tick to ensure accuracy.

registry A central Windows database file that holds hardware and software configuration information.

`REGSVR32` A command used to register .dll files in the Windows registry.

Reliability Monitor A tool that provides a visual graph in Windows Vista or 7 of how stable the system is and details on events that might have affected the system reliability.

repair installation Used when you have to reload the Windows operating system. Sometimes called an in-place upgrade or a re-installation.

resistance A measurement in ohms of how much opposition is applied to an electrical circuit.

resolution The number of pixels shown on a monitor or the output of a printer.

Resource Monitor A graphic tool that shows performance for the main system components.

restore point A snapshot image of the registry and some of the dynamic system files that have been saved previously by the System Restore utility. This is used when the Windows computer has a problem.

return The center (round) AC outlet plug. Other terms used are common or neutral.

RFI (radio frequency interference) A specific type of EMI noise that occurs in the radio frequency range. Often results from operation of nearby electrical appliances or devices.

RGB/component video Red, green and blue RCA jacks for connecting a scanner or camera.

RIMM A trademark of Rambus, Inc., that is a type of memory module used on video adapters and that may be used on future motherboards.

ring topology A network that is physically wired like a star network but, logically, passes control from one device to the next in a continuous fashion using a token.

RIP (Routing Information Protocol) A basic protocol used to route data from one network to another using hop count (how many routers the packet goes through) as a metric for determining the best path through the network.

RIS (remote installation service) A service that allows PXE-enabled devices to execute specific variables used to remotely control and even reload a remote device.

RISC (reduced instruction set computer) A type of computing device that uses a small set of instructions to operate. Contrast with CISC devices. Common RISC devices include smartphones and tablets.

riser board A board that connects to the motherboard that holds adapters.

RJ (registered jack) A connector used in phone and wired networking. The most popular types are RJ-11 and RJ-45.

RJ-11 A type of connector used with analog modems and traditional phone jacks.

RJ-45 A type of connector used on Ethernet network cards and ports. Used to connect a device to the wired network.

RMA (return materials authorization) A number used to track and return defective parts (normally under warranty).

`ROBOCOPY` A command used to copy files. It has more parameters than `COPY` or `XCOPY`.

ROM (read-only memory) A nonvolatile type of memory that keeps data in chips even when the computer is shut off.

ROM BIOS (ROM basic input/output system) See *BIOS*.

root directory The starting place for all files on a disk. A floppy is limited to 127 entries and a hard drive to 512 entries. The designation for a floppy drive's root directory is A:\ and for the hard drive it is C:\.

rootkit Malicious software that hackers install to gain administrator access to an operating system. It can also be downloaded and installed to a flash drive.

router A network device that determines the best path to send a packet. Works at OSI model Layer 3.

RS232C A serial interface standard.

RTC (real-time clock) The computer clock that keeps track of the current time.

RTS (request to send) Part of the RTS/CTS hardware handshaking communication method. Specific wires on the serial connector are used to send a signal to the other device to stop or start sending data. The CTS (clear to send) and RTS signals indicate when it is okay to send data.

RTS/CTS (request to send/clear to send) A method of serial device handshaking that uses signals on specific pins of the connector to signal the other device when to stop or send data.

S

S/PDIF (Sony/Phillips digital interface format) Defines how audio signals are carried between audio devices and stereo components. It can also be used to connect the output of a DVD player in a PC to a home theater or some other external device.

S-Video port A composite video port, coded yellow, that uses a 7-pin mini-DIN connector.

Safe Mode A Windows option used when the computer stalls, slows down, does not work properly, has improper video settings or intermittent errors, or when a new hardware/software installation causes problems. In Safe Mode, Windows starts with minimum device drivers and services.

sag A momentary undervoltage condition that occurs when the wall outlet AC voltage drops.

SAN (storage area network) A collection of storage media that is centrally managed and available to a multitude of network devices such as servers, network-based applications, virtual machines, and users.

SAS (serial-attached SCSI) SAS devices connect in a point-to-point bus. Used in the enterprise environment where high reliability and high mean time between failures is important.

SATA (Serial ATA) A point-to-point architecture for IDE devices that provides faster access for attached devices.

SATA 1 (Serial ATA 1) A SATA device that has a maximum transfer rate of 1.5Gbps.

SATA 2 (serial ATA 2) A SATA device that has a maximum transfer rate of 3Gbps.

SATA 3 (serial ATA 3) A SATA device that has a maximum transfer rate of 6Gbps.

SATA-PM (Serial ATA Port Multiplier) A device used to connect multiple eSATA devices to a single eSATA port.

satellite modem A type of modem that can provide Internet access at speeds faster than an analog modem, but slower than cable or DSL access.

SC (subscriber connector) An older fiber connector.

SC (subscription channel) A video channel that normally costs extra.

scalable font A font that can be created at any size. An outline font is an example of a scalable font.

SCANDISK An older software program used to detect and repair lost clusters.

scanner An input device that allows printed documents to be brought into the computer and, from there, digitally displayed, printed, saved, or emailed.

SCP (Secure Copy Protocol) A means of using SSH to securely transfer one or more files across a network.

scribe A plastic tool that helps with prying plastics parts or covers off laptop and mobile devices.

SCSI (Small Computer System Interface) An interface standard that connects multiple small devices to the same adapter via a SCSI bus.

SCSI ID The priority number assigned to each device connected by a SCSI chain.

SD (Secure Digital) A storage device with nonvolatile flash memory used for mobile devices.

SDRAM (synchronous DRAM) Provides very fast burst memory access by placing new memory addresses on the address bus before prior memory address retrieval and execution completes. SDRAM synchronizes its operation with the CPU clock signal to speed up memory access.

SE (single ended) A type of SCSI electrical signal and terminator used with most SCSI devices. Both active and passive terminators can be used with this signaling method.

SEC (single-edge connector) A type of connector used with older slot-based processors.

sector The smallest amount of storage space on a disk or platter, holding 512 bytes of data.

Secure Sockets Layer See *SSL*.

security log A type of *Event Viewer* log that displays information such as when different users login, including both valid and invalid users.

security policy One or more documents that provide rules and guidelines related to computer and network security.

self-powered hub A type of hub power mode in which an external power supply is attached.

Serial ATA See *SATA*.

serial port Either a 9-pin male D-shell connector or a 25-pin male D-shell connector. Transmits 1 bit at a time and is used for input devices such as mice, modems, digitizers, trackballs, and so on.

server-based network A basic type of LAN in which users log in to a controlling computer, called a server, that knows who is authorized to connect to the LAN and what resources the user is authorized to access. Usually found in businesses that have 10 or more computers.

service A Windows process that provides a specific function to the computer.

`services.msc` A command that allows you to view what services have been started and stopped and, if desired, allows you to stop a service.

service pack An upgrade or a patch provided by a manufacturer for an operating system.

service release Software available from a manufacturer to fix a known problem (bug) in its applications program.

Session-at-Once A type of CD drive that allows multiples sessions to be recorded on a single disc. These discs can normally be read by computer-based CD drives, but not audio CD drives such as ones found in a vehicle. Compare with Disc-at-Once and Track-at-Once.

session layer Layer 5 of the OSI model, which manages communication and administrative functions between two network devices.

Setup Software that tells a computer about itself and the hardware it supports, such as how much RAM memory, type of hard drive installed, current date and time, and so on.

`SFC` A command used to start the System File Checker utility. The System File Checker verifies operating system files.

`SFC /scannow` The most common `SFC` option used that checks and replaces any Windows files and .dll files that might have issues. This is especially important after removing some viruses.

SFF (small form factor) A smaller motherboard form factor that is likened to storage boxes such as a shoe box or a small storage bin.

SFX12V A type of power supply used with MicroAtx and FlexATX motherboards.

SGRAM (synchronous graphics RAM) Memory chips used on video adapters and graphics accelerators to speed up graphics-intensive functions.

Shadow Copy A Windows Vista and 7 technology used with the System Restore program that uses a block-level image instead of monitoring certain files for file changes.

shadow mask A screen used in monitors that direct the electron beams to the front of the monitor.

shared key authentication A method of authentication used in wireless networks that uses a group of characters that both the wireless device and the access point have in common.

shared system memory The amount of motherboard RAM used for video because the amount of video memory on the video adapter or built into the motherboard is not enough for the application(s) being used.

shielding Cancels out and keeps magnetic interference from devices.

shortcut An icon with a bent arrow in lower-left corner. It is a link to a file, a folder, or a program on a disk. If the file is a document, it opens the application used to create the document.

Show Desktop An icon you can click to reduce all open windows on the screen and show the desktop. Click it again, and the original document reappears.

`SHUTDOWN` A command used to restart or shut down a local or remote computer.

SID (security identifier) A unique number assigned to a Microsoft-based computer.

sidebar A feature in Windows Vista and 7 that is a collection of customizable desktop gadgets.

sigverif.exe A command used to view signed device drivers.

SIM (System Image Manager) Used in Windows Vista/7 to deploy an image of one computer to multiple computers.

SIMM (single in-line memory modules) An older type of motherboard memory chip/module using either 30-pin and 72-pin connectors.

simple volume A Windows term for the storage 0-pin or 72-pin unit that contains the files needed to load the operating system. The system volume and the boot volume can be the same unit.

single (IDE setting) An IDE setting used when only one device connects to the interface and cable.

single link A type of DVI video connection that allows resolutions up to 1920×1080.

single-mode A type of fiber-optic cabling that sends one light beam down the cable.

single-ported memory Memory that can be written to or read from, but not simultaneously.

single-sided memory A memory module that the CPU accesses at one time. The module has one "bank" of memory and 64 bits are transferred out of the memory module to the CPU. More appropriately called single-banked memory. Note that the memory module may or may not have all of its "chips" on one side.

site survey Used in wireless network design to determine the best wireless hardware placement for the optimum coverage area.

slave An IDE setting for the second device added to the cable. The device should be a slower device than the master.

SLC (single-level memory cell) A cell that stores 1 bit in a memory cell and is more expensive and longer lasting than an MLC.

sleep-and-charge USB port A computer port that provides power to an attached device (power to charge the device) even when the computer is powered off.

SLI (Scalable Link Interface) An NVIDIA technology that connects two or more video cards so that they may share resources from each card to provide better computer graphics.

S.M.A.R.T. (Self-Monitoring, Analysis, and Reporting Technology) A feature that started with PATA drives that allowed the device to send messages about possible failures or data loss.

SmartMedia A card, smaller than a credit card, that is used to hold audio and video files.

SMB (server message block) A means of providing access to shared network devices and files.

SMP (symmetric multiprocessing) The ability for an operating system to support two CPUs simultaneously.

SMTP (Simple Mail Transfer Protocol) A standard used for email or for transferring messages across a network from one device to another.

snapshot In a virtualization environment, a copy or backup of the VM at a particular point in time that can be used to revert the VM to that point in time. It is similar in concept to a restore point.

SNMP (Simple Network Management Protocol) A standard that supports network monitoring and management.

social engineering A technique used to trick people into divulging information including their own personal information or corporate knowledge.

SO-DIMM (small-outline DIMM) A special small DIMM used in laptop computers.

software An application consisting of a set of instructions that makes the hardware work.

software decoder A type of DVD decoder that puts the burden on the CPU to decode and uncompress the MPEG-2 video data from the DVD. Video card manufacturers have added MPEG-2 video decoding support to decrease the CPU's load. Contrast with hardware decoder.

SOHO (small office/home office) A description given to a small network that might consist of wired and wireless devices, Internet connectivity, VoIP, and even a VPN connection into the corporate network.

solder joint A solder connection on the back of a motherboard or an adapters.

SO-RIMM (small-outline RIMM) A small RIMM used in laptop computers.

sound card An adapter card (also known as an audio card) that has several ports that converts digital signals to audible sound, and also the reverse. Common devices that connect to the ports include microphones, speakers, and joysticks.

south bridge A connection from the processor to parts of the motherboard including the PCI/PCIe (non-video) slots, ports, and other motherboard components. Also called the front side bus.

SP*x* (Service Pack *x*) A particular service pack level, such as Service Pack 1 or Service Pack 2. See also *service pack*.

spam Email that is unsolicited and comes from unknown people or businesses.

spanned volume A Windows term used to describe hard drive space created from multiple hard drives.

SPD (serial presence detect) An extra EEPROM feature that allows the system BIOS to read the EEPROM (which contains memory information such as capacity, voltage, error detection, refresh rates, data width, etc.) and adjust motherboard timings for best CPU to RAM performance.

SPDIF See *S/PDIF*.

SPGA (staggered pin grid array) A processor package type used by Intel.

spike An overvoltage condition of short duration and intensity.

SPS (standby power supply) A device that provides power to the computer only after it first detects an AC voltage power out condition.

SRAM (static random-access memory) Memory that is faster but more expensive than DRAM. SRAM is also known as cache memory, or L2 cache.

SSD (solid state drive) A drive that uses nonvolatile Flash memory and no moving parts to store data. It is faster but more expensive than a hard drive.

SSH (secure shell) A means of secure data communication including remote connectivity of devices and file transfers.

SSID (service set identifier) A set of up to 32 alphanumeric characters used in wireless networks to differentiate between different networks.

SSID broadcasting Used with wireless network access points to periodically send out a beacon frame that includes the SSID. Wireless devices can automatically detect the SSID from this beacon.

SSL (Secure Sockets Layer) A protocol used to transmit Internet messages securely.

ST (straight tip) A type of fiber connector.

standby power Power that is always provided, even when a computer is powered off. It is why you have to unplug a computer when working inside it.

standoff A plastic connector on the bottom side of a motherboard.

star topology The most common Ethernet network topology, in which each device connects to a central hub or switch. If an individual device or cable fails, the rest of the network keeps working. But, if the hub or switch fails, the entire network goes down.

start bit A bit used in asynchronous communications that signals the beginning of each data byte.

Start button Located in the lower-left hand corner of the Windows desktop, a button that is used to access and launch applications, files, utilities, and help, as well as to add/remove hardware and software.

stealth virus A virus program that presents a fake image to antivirus scanning to make itself invisible to scanning.

stop bit A bit used in asynchronous communications that signals the end of each data byte.

STP (shielded twisted pair) Network cable with extra foil to prevent outside noise from interfering with data on the cable.

straight-through cable A network cable that uses twisted pair copper wires and RJ-45 connectors at each end. The cable uses the same pinout and is also known as a patch cable.

striped volume A Windows term describing how data is written across two to 32 hard drives. It is different from a spanned volume in that each drive is used alternately instead of filling the first hard drive before going to the second hard drive. Other names include striping or RAID 0.

subdirectory A directory contained within another directory. Today's subdirectories are called subfolders.

subnet A portion of a network number that has been subdivided so that multiple networks can use separate parts of a single network number. Subnets allow more efficient use of IP addresses. Also called subnetwork or subnetwork number.

subnet mask A number the computer uses to determine which part of an IP address represents the network and which portion represents the host.

surge An overvoltage condition that is like a spike but with a longer duration.

surge protector A device that helps protect power supplies from overvoltage conditions. Also known as surge strip or surge suppressor.

SVGA (super VGA) A type of monitor that displays at least an 800×600 resolution and connects to a 15-pin D-shell connector.

swap file A temporary file in hard disk space used by Windows that varies in size depending on the amount of RAM installed, available hard drive space, and the amount of memory needed to run the application.

switch In star networks, a Layer 2 central controlling device. Looks at each data frame as it comes through each port.

SXGA+ (Super Extended Graphics Array) An improvement over SXGA to support resolutions up to 1400×1050.

synchronous Describing transmissions that require the use of a clock signal.

system attribute A file designation to mark a file as a system file. By default, files with this attribute set do not show in directory listings.

system bar On a mobile tablet, the bottom area, containing a back button, home button, recent applications opened, and the notification area.

System Configuration utility A Windows utility that allows boot files and settings to be enabled/disabled for troubleshooting purposes. The command that brings this utility up is `msconfig.exe`.

system file A file that is needed to allow a computer to boot. A file type that is also known as a startup file.

system image Contains a saved copy of the operating system and all user files that can be used to restore a damaged or corrupted computer.

System Monitor A Windows utility that monitors specific computer components and allows creation of graphs, bar charts, and text reports.

system partition A type of active hard drive partition that contains the hardware-specific files needed to load the operating system.

system resources The collective set of interrupt, I/O address, and DMA configuration parameters.

System Restore A utility that makes a snapshot of the registry and backs up certain dynamic system files. When a problem occurs, this utility can be used to take your system back to a time before the error started.

System State Contains a group of interrelated files including the registry, system files, boot files, and COM+ Class Registration database. One cannot back up or restore these files individually.

system volume A Windows term describing the storage space that holds Windows operating system files used to boot the computer.

T

tab Often found along the top of dialog boxes. Clicking a tab displays a group of related standard options that users may change to their personal preferences.

tailgating A breach of physical security that occurs when an unauthorized person enters a secure space behind an authorized person. Training and diligence by all employees is the only way to stop tailgating.

Task Manager A Windows-based utility that displays memory and processor usage data, and displays currently loaded applications as well as currently running processes.

taskbar On a Windows program, the bar that runs across the bottom of the desktop. It holds buttons that represent files and applications currently loaded into RAM. It also holds icons representing direct access to system tools.

`TASKKILL` A command used to halt a process or task.

`TASKLIST` A command used to list process IDs for active applications and services. Note this command should be used before the `TASKKILL` command.

TCP (Transmission Control Protocol) An OSI model Layer 4 standard that ensures reliable communication between two devices.

TCP/IP (Transmission Control Protocol/Internet Protocol) The most widely used network protocol stack for connecting to the Internet. Developed by the Defense Advanced Research Projects Agency in the 1970s, it is the basis of the Internet.

TDR (time domain reflectometer) A device used to check fiber connectivity.

Telnet An application that allows connection to a remote network device.

terabyte (TB) Approximately 1 trillion bytes of information, or 2^{40} (1,099,511,627,776 bytes).

textbox An area with a dialog box where the user may type preferred parameters applied to the software in use.

TFT (thin film transistor) A type of array used in LCDs to direct the liquid crystal to block the light from the backlight.

TFTP (Trivial File Transfer Protocol) An non-secure means of quickly transferring files from one device to another device.

TFX12V A type of power supply used with MicroATX and FlexATX motherboards.

thermal printer A printer commonly used in retail that uses heat and special thermal paper to create the printed image.

thermal wax transfer A type of printer that uses wax-based inks similar to the solid ink printer, but it prints in lower resolutions.

thick client A business computer that has applications loaded on the local hard drive. Contrast with thin client.

thin client A type of computer that does not have all the ports and components (such as a hard drive) of a traditional PC.

thread A unit of programming code that receives a slice of time from Windows so it can run concurrently with other units of code or threads.

throttle management The ability to control processor speed by slowing the processor down when it is not being used heavily or is running too hot.

Thunderbolt A type of video port on PCIe adapters or on Apple computers.

TKIP (Temporal Key Integrity Protocol) A method of encryption that is an improvement over WEP because the encryption keys periodically change.

token passing The common access method (set of communication rules governing network devices) used by fiber and Token Ring networks.

touch screen An alternative way to input device into a computer. Used in kiosks.

TouchFlo A multitouch technology for mobile devices developed by HTC Corporation which distinguishes between a finger and a stylus and responds appropriately.

tower A computer model with a motherboard that mounts perpendicular to the floor.

TPM (Trusted Platform Module) A motherboard chip used for hardware and software authentication. The TPM can authenticate hardware devices. Applications can use the TPM for file and folder encryption, local passwords, email, VPN/PKI authentication, and wireless authentication.

Trace log A *Performance Tool* option used to trigger data recording once a threshold has been reached.

`tracert` A network troubleshooting command that displays the path a data packet takes through a network, thus allowing one to see where a fault occurs in larger networks.

track A concentric circle on a formatted floppy disk or a hard drive platter.

Track-at-Once Sometimes called TAO, a technology in which a laser stops writing normal data after a track is finished. This type of drive supports the disc having both audio and data. Compare with Disc-at-Once.

transfer corona A wire inside the laser printer that applies a positive charge to the back of the paper so the toner is attracted to the paper as it moves through the printer.

transfer roller A roller inside the laser printer that replaces the transfer corona. The roller applies a positive charge to the back of the paper so the toner is attracted to the paper as it moves through the printer.

transferring A laser printer process where the toner (image) moves from the drum to the paper.

transport layer Layer 4 of the OSI model, which determines details on how the data is sent, supervises the validity of the transmission, and defines protocol for structuring messages.

triple-channel A type of memory execution in which motherboards access three memory modules simultaneously.

tri-core CPU A single unit that contains three processors.

Trojan horse virus A virus program that appears to be a normal application but, when executed, changes something. It does not replicate but could gather information that can later be used to hack into one's computer.

TrueType font A type of outline font that can be scaled and rotated.

TV tuner card An adapter that allows a computer to receive and display television-based video on a computer monitor.

TVS rating (transient voltage suppressor) A measure of a surge protector's ability to guard against overvoltage conditions. The lower the TVS rating, the better.

twisted cable A type of floppy or hard drive cable having crossed wires and that physically moves the drive selection jumper from the second to the first position.

twisted-pair cable Network cable made of eight copper wires twisted into four pairs. Can be shielded or unshielded.

`TYPE` A command used to display a file's contents on the screen.

Type 1 hypervisor Hypervisors manage and oversee the operation of virtual machines. A Type 1 hypervisor has the operating system running on top of the hypervisor. Also known as a native hypervisor.

Type 2 hypervisor In a virtualization environment, a hypervisor that runs on top of a host operating system to manage and oversee the virtual machine. Also known as a hosted hypervisor.

Type A-B-C fire extinguisher A fire extinguisher that can be used on either Type A, Type B, or Type C fires.

Type C fire extinguisher A fire extinguisher that can be used only on electrical fires.

U

UAC (User Access Control) A Windows Vista/7 dialog box that appears and asks permission to do something that might be harmful or change the operating system environment. Some changes require an administrator password to continue.

UART (universal asynchronous receiver/transmitter) A chip that coordinates the serial port or device activity.

UDF (universal disk format) A file system commonly used in optical media.

UDMA (Ultra DMA) Allows the IDE interface to control the PCI bus for faster transfers.

UDP (User Datagram Protocol) A Layer 4 connectionless standard that applications use to communicate with a remote device.

UEFI (Unified Extensible Firmware Interface) The interface between the operating system and firmware. It is used today in configuring device such as kiosks and touch screen technologies.

UL 1449 VPR A voltage protection rating standard developed by Underwriters Laboratories to measure the maximum amount of voltage a surge protector will allow through to attached devices.

unattended installation A method of installing Windows where the remote computer does not have to be touched. Use Microsoft Deployment Toolkit in conjunction with Configuration Manager.

unbuffered memory Memory that does not delay all data transfers by one clock tick to ensure accuracy as registered memory does. Used in low- to medium-powered computers.

unbuffered SDRAM A type of memory used frequently in low- to medium-priced home computers.

UNC (universal naming convention) Used at the command prompt to obtain network shares.

undervoltage A condition that occurs when AC power drops below 100 volts, which may cause the computer's power supply to draw too much current and overheat.

upgrade Installing a newer or more powerful operating system where one already exists. An upgrade can also be installing newer hardware.

Upgrade Advisor A Microsoft tool that can be downloaded and executed to determine if a Windows XP, Vista, or 7 computer can function well with a higher version of Windows installed.

UPS (uninterruptible power supply) A device that provides power for a limited time to a computer or device during a power outage.

upstream A term used to describe information that is sent to the Internet, such as transmitting email or uploading a file to a server.

upstream port A USB port used to connect a computer to another computer or another hub.

URL (uniform resource locator) A method of accessing Internet resources.

usable host numbers The number of host bits (and associated IP addresses) that can be used by network devices residing in a subnetwork.

usable subnets The number of subnetworks that can be used when an IP network number is subdivided to allow more efficient use of IP addresses.

USB (universal serial bus) A bus that allows 127 devices to be connected to a single computer port.

USB flash drive Sometimes called a flash drive or a memory stick, a drive that allows storage via a USB port.

USB OTG (USB on the go) Allows two USB devices to communicate without the use of a PC or a hub that is backward compatible with the USB 2.0 standard.

USB port A port on a motherboard or on an adapter that allows the connection of up to 127 devices.

user profile All settings associated with a specific user, including desktop settings, network configurations, and applications that the user has access to. It is part of the registry.

USMT (User State Migration Tool) A tool used to perform large deployments of Windows XP Professional.

UTP (unshielded twisted pair) The most common network cable. Comes in different categories for different uses. See also *twisted-pair cable*.

UXGA (Ultra Extended Graphics Array) Describes resolutions up to 1600×1200 and over 16 million colors. Sometimes used on powerful laptops and when using applications in which more of the screen needs to be seen (such as spreadsheets).

V

vector font A font derived from a mathematical formula. Plotters frequently use vector fonts.

`verifier.exe` A command used to verify installed drivers.

vertical scan rate The rate at which the monitor's electron beam draws the entire screen.

VGA (video graphics array) A type of monitor that displays at least a 640×480 resolution or greater and connects to a 15-pin D-shell connector.

VGA port A type of 15-pin three-row video port that normally has a CRT monitor attached.

video capture card An adapter that allows video to be taken from a camera, DVD, recorder, or live video, edited if necessary, and saved.

video port A connector on a motherboard or a separate adapter for hooking up the monitor. Two variations are the VGA and DVI. VGA connects CRT monitors. DVI is commonly used with flat panel monitors.

video processor Sometimes known as a video coprocessor or video accelerator, the processor on a video adapter that coordinates communication between the adapter and the main microprocessor.

viewable size The diagonal length of an LCD screen.

virtualization A process that allows a computer to run multiple operating systems without affecting each other, share hardware, and provide a test environment for software that may not be compatible on a specific platform.

virtual machine A way for an operating system to appear as a separate computer to each application. One computer that has two or more operating systems installed that are unaware of each other due to virtualization software.

virtual memory A method of simulating extra memory by using the hard disk space as if it were RAM.

virtualization PC A computer that has multiple operating systems in a virtual environment where one operating system has no interaction with the other operating system—they are independent of one another. A virtualization PC has multiple powerful multi-core processors, maximum RAM, mutliple fast large capacity hard drives, 1Gbps network connection, virtualization software, and a possible NAS.

virus A program designed to change the way a computer originally operated.

VIS (viewable image size) The actual area of a monitor seen by a user.

VMM (Virtual Memory Manager) A Windows component that uses hard disk space as if it were RAM.

VoIP (Voice over IP) A way of sending phone calls over the Internet or over networks that traditionally transmitted only data.

volatile memory Memory that does not remain when power is removed.

volt The measurement for voltage.

voltage An electronic measurement of the pressure pushing electrons through a circuit. Voltage is measured in volts.

volume A hard drive term used to describe all of a hard drive or hard drive portions that have been combined into one unit. In Windows Vista and 7, all hard drive divisions are called volumes.

VPN (virtual private network) A remote computer connecting to a remote network by "tunneling" over an intermediate network, such as the Internet or a LAN.

VRAM (video RAM) Dual-ported memory found on video adapters.

W

Wake on LAN A BIOS and adapter feature that allows a network administrator to remotely control power to a workstation, and allows a computer to come out of the sleep mode.

Wake on Ring A BIOS and adapter feature that allows a computer to come out of sleep mode when the telephone rings, so the computer can accept fax, email, and so on, when the user is absent.

WAN (wide area network) Two or more LANs communicating, often across large distances. The most famous WAN is the Internet.

warm boot Restarting a computer by pressing Ctrl+Alt+Del or by clicking the Windows Restart option. Puts less strain on a computer than a cold boot.

watt The electrical measure in which computer power supplies are rated.

WDT (Windows Deployment Toolkit) A GUI shell used to deploy Windows in a corporate environment.

wear leveling The process of writing and erasing data in different memory blocks of SSDs (solid state drives) to prolong the life of the drive.

Web cam Short for Web camera, a small camera used for communicating via video across the Internet.

WEP (Wired Equivalent Privacy) A type of encryption that is sometimes used in wireless networks.

WFP (Windows File Protection) A Windows 2000 and XP feature that protects system files. If WFP detects a file that is altered, deleted, or overwritten, it obtains a copy of the original file and places the copied file in the proper folder. Windows Vista and 7 use WRP (Windows Resource Protection)

Wide XGA See *WXGA*.

wildcard A special character used at the command prompt when typing commands. The ? character is used to designate "any" for a single character place, whereas the * character denotes any characters from that place forward.

WiMAX A wireless technology that could be used to connect the Internet with a large scale coverage area and access speeds up to 1Gbps. Also used for connectivity as part of a cellular network.

Windows Aero A look and feel for the computing environment in Windows Vista and higher that includes transparent icons, animations, and customized desktop gadgets.

Windows Defender A Windows application in Windows Vista and 7 that is used to detect spyware.

Windows Explorer See *Explorer*.

Windows XP mode A downloadable program for Vista/7 to provide a virtual Windows XP mode for applications that will not work in the normal operating system environment.

WinRE (Windows Recovery Environment) An alternative to Console Recovery found on the Windows Vista and 7 installation disc that includes multiple tools used to troubleshoot Windows when it does not work properly.

WINS server (Windows Internet Naming Service server) A server that keeps track of IP addresses assigned to a specific computer name.

wireless broadband A feature available from service providers that allows PC Cards, USB modems, mobile data cards, or integrated laptop connectivity to have the ability to receive, create, and communicate Internet information within a specific coverage area.

wireless hot spot A place where wireless Internet connectivity is available.

wireless network A type of network that uses air as the media to connect devices.

workgroup A term given to a peer-to-peer Windows network. A workgroup does not use a server to authenticate users during the login process.

WORM (write-once, read-many) A technology that writes data once to a disk. Often used to make backups or to distribute software.

worm virus A virus program that replicates from one drive to another. The most common worm virus today is an email message that, once opened, sends the virus to every address in the user's address book.

WPA (Wi-Fi Protected Access) A data encryption program that uses TKIP (Temporal Key Integrity Protocol) or AES (Advanced Encryption Standard) to improve security.

WPA2 An improvement over WPA that includes dynamic negotiation between the AP and the client for authentication and encryption algorithms. It is a common choice for securing wireless networks.

WPAD (Web Proxy Autodiscovery) A method of discovering the proxy server IP address and port number.

WPS (Wi-Fi Protected Settings) A method used to easily configure a wireless device for the SSID and WPA2 security.

write amplification The minimum amount of storage space affected by a request to write data on a solid state drive. For example, if the SSD has 128KB erase block with a 4KB file to be saved, 128KB of memory is erased before the 4KB file is written.

write-behind caching A type of disk caching that stores data on the RAM and later records it to the disk.

WRP (Windows Resource Protection) A tool that protects system files and registry keys in Windows Vista and Windows 7. Replaces WFP, which Windows 2000 and XP use.

WUXGA (Wide Ultra Extended Graphics Array) Describes resolutions of 1920×1200.

WXGA (Wide XGA) Resolutions up to 1366×768, using over 16 million colors are supported. This is usually used by those who like to view a DVD on a computer monitor. Other variations include WSXGA and WUXGA.

X

`xcopy` An external command used to transfer files from one place to another in the command prompt environment.

xD (extreme digital) A storage device with nonvolatile Flash memory used for mobile devices.

xDSL Used to describe the various types of digital subscriber lines (DSLs) available for connecting to the Internet. Examples include ADSL, CDSL, DSL Lite, HDSL, RADSL, SDSL, VDSL, and x2/DSL.

XGA (Extended Graphics Array) Developed by IBM to describe resolutions of 1024×768 and 64K of colors.

XON/XOFF A method of handshaking that uses special control characters to coordinate data transmissions.

XPS (XML Paper Specification) The Windows Vista graphics language for print drivers. XPS handles representing and transmitting graphical objects to output devices such as printers, monitors, and overhead projectors. Documents sent to printers that support XPS will not have to be converted to a printer-specific language. XPS not only affects printing but also document viewing.

Z

ZIF socket (zero insertion force socket) A common CPU socket that has a lever that provides easy access for CPU removal.

ZIP (zigzag inline package) A type of chip packaging that had offset pins. Similar to DIP but not as wide.

ZTI (zero-touch installation) A method of imaging a computer without having to physically touch the computer. Commonly used in a corporate environment.

Index

Symbols

A

Index

C

Index

D

E

Index

F

G

H

I

Index

M

Index

O

P

Index

Index

S

T

V

W

X

Y

Z

Index

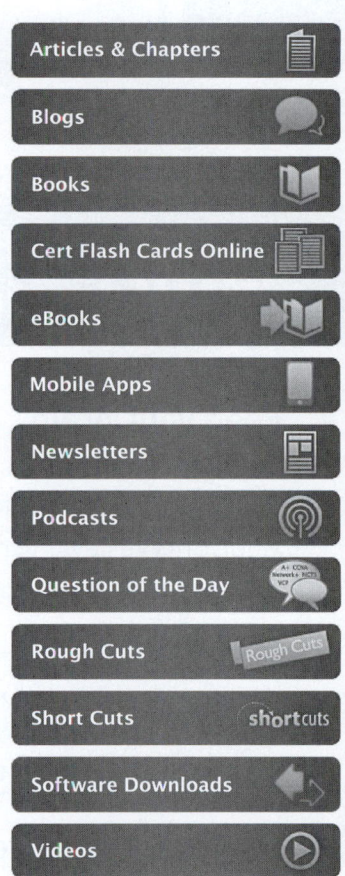